SECOND EDITION

MINNESOTA FLORA

An Illustrated Guide to the Vascular Plants of Minnesota

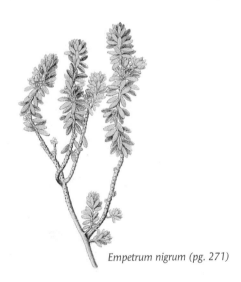

Empetrum nigrum (pg. 271)

STEVE W. CHADDE

"Heaven is under our feet as well as over our heads."
— Henry David Thoreau, Walden

MINNESOTA FLORA

An Illustrated Guide to the Vascular Plants of Minnesota

Second Edition

Steve W. Chadde

ISBN: 978-1-951682-07-1

Grateful acknowledgment is given to the BIOTA OF NORTH AMERICA PROGRAM (www.bonap.org) for permission to use their species distribution data to generate the distribution maps.

The author can be reached via email: steve@chadde.net

VERSION 2.1 10/14/2019

CONTENTS

PREFACE

Growing up in the Midwest, I was fortunate to spend many holidays with relatives in the Grand Marais area of northeastern Minnesota. We would explore the Lake Superior shoreline, swim in the many inland lakes, and hike the forest trails. I owned a set of the pocket-sized nature guides published by Golden Press, including those for trees, wild flowers, mushrooms, aquatic life, butterflies, mammals, and rocks. So equipped, I tried to collect, identify, and name many of the natural features around me. From that humble beginning, and with the passing of many years, I am pleased to present the first modern, comprehensive treatment of the vascular flora of the state of Minnesota, comprising over 1,900 plant species in 141 families.

Of course, as in any work of this type, I owe a debt of gratitude to the legion of botanists who have gone before; their collections, research papers, and floristic treatments were invaluable in the preparation of this Flora. Of special note is the comprehensive checklist of the state's flora prepared by Anita Cholewa of the Bell Museum of Natural History (2011). In some cases, I have adapted keys prepared by others, especially those prepared for Michigan's flora and available online (Reznicek et al., 2011). Omissions and errors, however, are mine, and corrections and additions will be incorporated as needed to keep the Flora as up-to-date as possible. My fond wish is that the Flora will be a useful reference to Minnesota's plant life and will be of value to those working to conserve and protect the state's native plants and plant communities.

— Steve Chadde
October 2013

SPECIES DESCRIPTIONS

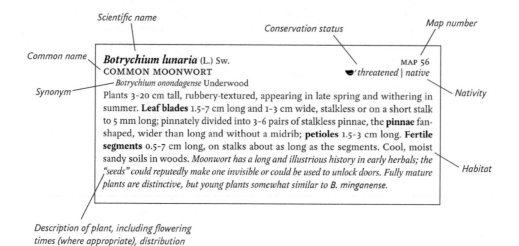

Scientific name

Conservation status

Map number

Common name

Synonym

Nativity

Habitat

Botrychium lunaria (L.) Sw.
COMMON MOONWORT   MAP 56
— *Botrychium onondagense* Underwood   ❧ *threatened | native*
Plants 3-20 cm tall, rubbery-textured, appearing in late spring and withering in summer. **Leaf blades** 1.5-7 cm long and 1-3 cm wide, stalkless or on a short stalk to 5 mm long; pinnately divided into 3-6 pairs of stalkless pinnae, the **pinnae** fan-shaped, wider than long and without a midrib; **petioles** 1.5-3 cm long. **Fertile segments** 0.5-7 cm long, on stalks about as long as the segments. Cool, moist sandy soils in woods. *Moonwort has a long and illustrious history in early herbals; the "seeds" could reputedly make one invisible or could be used to unlock doors. Fully mature plants are distinctive, but young plants somewhat similar to B. minganense.*

Description of plant, including flowering times (where appropriate), distribution notes, identification tips, etc.

ABBREVIATIONS

BOTANICAL

❧ endangered or threatened in Minnesota

spp. species (plural)

ssp., subsp. subspecies

var. variety

× hybrid (or times)

* An asterisk following a species name in the key means that the species is listed under ADDITIONAL SPECIES and is not fully described (usually introduced or adventive species of limited occurrence in Minnesota)

MEASUREMENT

cm centimeter

dm decimeter

m meter

mm millimeter

GEOGRAPHICAL

c central

n northern

ne northeastern

nw northwestern

s southern

se southeastern

sw southwestern

w western

Minn Minnesota

INTRODUCTION

MINNESOTA FLORA is a field-oriented guide to essentially all of the vascular plants—ferns and fern relatives, conifers, and flowering plants—considered native to the state of Minnesota, plus nearly all of the vascular plant species considered as introduced or adventive to the state. Not treated are a number of ornamental and cultivated plants that do not typically spread from their planting sites, and a handful of species known from the state by a single, usually old collection. The focus of the Flora is on the identification of every vascular plant species in the state that is reproducing without human assistance, using a combination of keys, descriptions, habitat information, illustrations, and distribution maps. Included are members of 141 plant families, over 700 genera, and more than 1,900 plant species.

Vascular plants are characterized by the presence of water- and nutrient-conducting vascular tissue (xylem and phloem) in their roots, stems, and leaves. Nonvascular plants (green algae, mosses, liverworts, and hornworts) are excluded from the Flora, but several common examples which may resemble vascular plants are illustrated on page 82.

Although there have been local floras, treatments of certain plant groups, and plant checklists, there has never been a comprehensive flora published for Minnesota. The first published list of the vascular plants of Minnesota is that by Lapham (1875); he included 896 plants for the state, based chiefly on his own collections and observations. In 1884, Upham published a catalogue of the state's flora, listing 1,540 species. Moore and Tryon (1946) cited 1,874 species of vascular plants. In 1965, Lakela described the plants of St. Louis and Lake counties and included 1,179 species. In 1991, Ownbey and Morley published a modern checklist and atlas of the state's flora. There have also been publications for portions of the state's flora such as the ferns (Tyron 1980), and orchids (Smith 2012). The most recent checklist (and of great help in the preparation of this flora) was prepared by Anita F. Cholewa in 2011.

ARRANGEMENT OF THE TAXA

The terms **taxa** (plural) or **taxon** (singular) refer to any category of classification, from kingdom down to species and varieties. All plants treated in this text belong to three informal groups, presented in order: (1) **ferns and fern relatives,** (2) **gymnosperms (conifers)**, and, by far the largest group, (3) **angiosperms**. The angiosperms are subdivided into two classes, the **dicotyledons** or "dicots" (sometimes termed Magnoliopsida) and the **monocotyledons** or "monocots" (sometimes termed Liliopsida). These subdivision names derive from the observation that the dicots most often have two cotyledons, or embryonic leaves, within each seed. The monocots usually have only one, but the rule is not absolute either way. From a diagnostic point of view, the number of cotyledons is neither a particularly handy nor a reliable character, but provides a simple way to organize plant families into smaller groups. Dicots include many familiar trees, shrubs, and "wildflowers," such as those of the Aster Family; the monocots include the large grass and sedge families, and also smaller famiIes such as Juncaceae, Orchidaceae, and Typhaceae.

Within each of the divisions, families are listed alphabetically. Under each family, genera and species are also listed alphabetically. If there is more than one genus in a family, a key is provided to the genera. Likewise, if there is more than one species in a genus, a key to the species is provided. For each species treated in the text, the following information is provided: scientific name, common name, synonyms (other formerly accepted scientific names), whether native or introduced in the state or of conservation concern (endangered or threatened), a description of the plant's vegetative, floral and fruiting characters, flowering period, and habitat. In addition, a map generated from the BONAP database (Biota of North America Program, www.bonap.org), shows verified county distribution patterns within the state. Finally, most descriptions are accompanied by a line drawing.

Placement of monocots and dicots genera within families, with several exceptions, follows that of the **Angiosperm Phylogeny Group IV system** (APG IV) of 2016. The APG was formed in the late 1990s, when researchers from major institutions around the world gathered with the goal of providing a modern, widely accepted classification of angiosperms. Their first attempt at a new system was published in 1998 (the APG system). To date, three revisions have been published, in 2003 (APG II), 2009 (APG III), and in 2016 (APG IV), each superseding the previous system.

The major exception to APG IV is the retention of the traditional Liliaceae (Lily Family) to facilitate field use of the Flora; however the APG IV families segregated from the traditional Liliaceae are noted for each genera and presented in tabular form on page 596. Another exception is the retention of the Dipsacaceae (Teasel Family), and not including Minnesota's two genera within Caprifoliaceae (Honeysuckle Family). Other deviations from APG IV regarding generic placement are noted in the text.

Similarly, fern families have been updated to reflect recent realignment of some families and genera. In the past, ferns had been loosely grouped with other spore-bearing vascular plants, these often called "fern allies" or "lycophytes." However, recent studies suggest an important dichotomy within vascular plants, separating the fern relatives or lycophytes (less than 1% of all vascular plant species) from a group termed the euphyllophytes. Euphyllophytes comprise two major groups: the spermatophytes (seed plants), which number more than 260,000 species, and the monilophytes (ferns), with over 9,200 species, including horsetails, whisk ferns, and all "true ferns." Genetic studies also reveal surprises about the relationships among true ferns and fern allies. True ferns appear to be closely related to horsetails, and in fact these plants are now grouped within the true ferns. Also, plants commonly called fern relatives (clubmosses, spike-mosses and quillworts) are, in fact, not closely related to the true ferns.

Nomenclature of genera and species is not based on a single source, but in general, conforms to that of the published volumes of The Flora of North America series (*www.efloras.org*), the BONAP database (Biota of North America Program, *www.bonap.org*), and The Plant List, a collaboration between the Royal Botanic Gardens (Kew), and the Missouri Botanical Garden (*www.theplantlist.org*). Common names largely reflect those of the BONAP database, or sometimes are names in popular use locally.

NATIVITY

Native Species

Native plants are those assumed to have been present in some part of Minnesota prior to European settlement. Also included are plants believed to have arrived in the state more recently via natural migration from areas adjoining Minnesota and in which they are clearly native.

Introduced Species

Several different terms can be used to indicate the status of **introduced** (or non-native) species in Minnesota's flora. Each introduced plant is different in terms of its origin, persistence, rate of spread, etc. Introduced species include those that were deliberately planted and which may escape and reproduce locally. **Waifs** are species normally found in cultivation, such as tomatoes or watermelons, that are occasionally found sprouted from seeds in waste areas and yards; these usually persist for only a single season. Some ornamental species such as lilacs and day-lilies are planted and usually remain in place but continue to live indefinitely, often growing at old home sites. **Adventive species** are those that appear here and there, usually from accidental introductions or as escapes from cultivation, but are apparently not firmly established nor spreading in the state. **Naturalized species** are those non-native species, such as timothy (*Phleum pratense*) that have arrived deliberately or accidentally in Minnesota, and have become firmly established as part of the flora; populations may be large or cover extensive areas. Most introduced species in the Flora are of Asian or European origin. These species from other continents are also referred to as **exotic species**.

Invasive Species

The Minnesota Department of Agriculture maintains a list of species considered "noxious"; see their website *www.mda.state.mn.us* for details). There are other invasive or potentially invasive taxa present in the state, which are or could become ecologically important pests in natural habitats; these plants are noted in the species descriptions. "Most invasive species are ecological pioneers and colonizers which, once introduced, quickly establish themselves in ecologically disturbed communities. Invasive species typically displace native flora due to faster growth rates, efficient dispersal mechanisms, and tolerance of a wider range of conditions. Invasive species often lack natural predators and diseases which control populations in their native environments" (Wisconsin DNR).

Examples of invasive species in Minnesota include common buckthorn (*Rhamnus cathartica*) and introduced honeysuckles such as *Lonicera morrowii, L. tatarica* and *L. × bella* which have replaced native understory shrubs in many woods and thickets in the southern half of the state. Other species are more recent introductions but are already spreading into relatively undisturbed places; notable examples include glossy buckthorn (*Frangula alnus*) and garlic mustard (*Alliaria petiolata*).

WETLAND STATUS CATEGORIES

The National Wetland Plant List (NWPL) is a list of wetland plants and their assigned indicator statuses. An indicator status reflects the likelihood that a particular plant occurs in a wetland or upland. The five indicator statuses are:

- **OBL Obligate Wetland** - Plants that almost always occur in wetlands (i.e. almost always in standing water or seasonally saturated soils.

- **FACW Facultative Wetland** - Plants that usually occur in wetlands, but may occur in non-wetlands.

- **FAC Facultative** - Plants that occur in wetland and non-wetland habitats.

- **FACU Facultative Upland** - Plants that usually occur in non-wetlands but may occur in wetlands.

- **UPL Obligate Upland** - Plants that almost never occur in wetlands (or in standing water or saturated soils).

A list of Minnesota's plants on the NWPL begins on page 727. Plants with no indicator rating are species rarely if ever found in wetlands, or species of limited occurrence in the state, or otherwise without an indicator assignment. The indicator status ratings are based on the 2012 definitions prepared for the National Wetland Plant List (Lichvar and Kartesz 2012). The indicators are routinely used in wetlands research and delineation studies, and also provide insight into each species' habitat preferences.

A species' indicator status may vary based on the region of its occurrence. Minnesota lies within two delineation regions (see map, page 742):

- **GP Great Plains Region**

- **NCNE Northcentral-Northeast Region** (Northcentral Subregion)

- **MW Midwest Region**

Most of the state lies within the Midwest and Northcentral-Northeast regions. A portion of western Minnesota lies within the Great Plains region. For current listings of Minnesota's plants on the National Wetland Plant List and their indicator status ratings, see the NWPL website: *wetland_plants.usace.army.mil*.

CONSERVATION STATUS

Because of their rarity, primarily as a result of habitat loss, 86 plant species are listed as endangered by the state of Minnesota; a further 93 species are listed as threatened (based on list effective August 19, 2013). These species are noted in the Flora by the ❧ symbol, followed by their status:

- **Endangered** - A species is considered endangered if the species is threatened with extinction throughout all or a significant portion of its range within Minnesota.

- **Threatened** - A species is considered threatened if the species is likely to become endangered within the foreseeable future throughout all or a significant portion of its range within Minnesota.

The website of the Minnesota Dept. of Natural Resources (*http://dnr.state.mn.us*) maintains a list of species listed as endangered, threatened, or of special concern (an additional category for plants but not afforded legal protection). Sightings of uncommon taxa should be reported to the state's Natural Heritage Information System (NHIS); see website (*www.dnr.state.mn.us/eco/nhnrp/nhis.html*) for details.

VEGETATION OF MINNESOTA

Minnesota may be divided into four broad vegetation zones:

- **Northern coniferous forest**
- **Eastern deciduous forest**
- **Aspen parkland**
- **Prairie**

- **Northern coniferous forest**
Coniferous forest covers about one-third of the state, primarily in the northeast. Dominant trees include balsam fir, white spruce, black spruce, paper birch and quaking aspen. Drier sites had a larger component of pines (white pine, red pine) and on the driest or most fire-prone sites, jack pine is common.

Wetlands occupy large portions of the coniferous forest zone. Notable are the extensive Red Lake peatlands of north-central Minnesota, supporting wet forests of black spruce and tamarack, smaller areas of northern white cedar, balsam-poplar, paper birch, and quaking aspen, and open bogs, patterned peatlands, and other types of shrub and herbaceous wetlands.

- **Eastern deciduous forest** The original deciduous forest of Minnesota has been largely altered by agriculture and urban development. This forest was the westernmost extension of the deciduous forest formation of eastern North America. Typical components of the forest are sugar maple, basswood, oak and elm. Northward, yellow birch becomes important. Along major rivers, floodplain forests of silver maple, green ash, black willow, American elm, and cottonwood occur; poison ivy and stinging nettle are common. In the south, swamp white oak and buttonbush reach their northern limit.

- **Aspen parkland** Located in northwestern Minnesota, aspen parkland forms an ecotone between the coniferous forest to the east and north and prairie to the west and south. The parkland occupies a flat, sometimes poorly drained landscape left by Glacial Lake Agassiz. Low-lying areas feature sedge meadow and low prairie wetlands; uplands may be dominated by extensive groves of quaking aspen mixed with other trees such as bur oak and northern pin oak, and various shrubs.

- **Prairie** Southern and western Minnesota once supported tallgrass prairie which covered about one-third of the state. Dominant grasses included big bluestem (*Andropogon gerardii*) and Indian grass (*Sorghastrum nutans*). Due to conversion to agriculture, less than one percent of undisturbed prairie remains. Also lost have been many of the small, scattered low-lying depressions called "prairie pothole wetlands", with less than 10 percent of these wetlands remaining. Various sedges and grasses such as bluejoint (*Calamagrostis canadensis*) and prairie cordgrass (*Spartina pectinata*) were common.

More detailed descriptions of the state's natural communities have been prepared by the Minnesota Dept. of Natural Resources: *www.dnr.state.mn.us/npc/classification.html*

In addition, a myriad of lakes, ponds, bogs, marshes, and other aquatic and wetland features are present, especially in nothern Minnesota. Some important **wetland types** are listed below (based on Chadde, 2013):

- **Open water communities** These plant communities occur in shallow to deep water of lakes, ponds, rivers and streams. Plants are free-floating, or submergent (anchored to the bottom and with underwater and/or floating leaves). A controlling factor of these communities is that water levels remain deep enough so that emergent vegetation typical of marshes is unable to establish.

- **Marshes** Marshes are dominated by emergent plants growing in permanent or nearly permanent shallow to deep water. Shallow water marshes are covered with up to about 15 cm of water for all or most of the growing season, but water levels may sometimes drop to the soil surface. Deep marshes have standing water between 15 and 100 cm or more deep during most of the growing season. A mix of emergent species and aquatic species of the adjoining open water are present.

■ **Sedge meadows** Sedge meadows are dominated by members of the Sedge Family (Cyperaceae), with grasses (Poaceae) and rushes (*Juncus*) often present. Other herbaceous species are usually present only as scattered individuals. Because of differences in their species composition, sedge meadows can be subdivided into those occurring in northern portions of the region and those occurring southward. Soils are typically organic deposits (peat or muck), and saturated throughout the growing season. Common tussock sedge (*Carex stricta*) is a major component of sedge meadows, forming large hummocks composed of a mass of roots and rhizomes. Periodic fires may help maintain the dominance of the sedges by killing invading shrubs and trees.

■ **Wet meadows** Wet meadows occur on saturated soils, and are dominated by grasses (especially *Calamagrostis canadensis*) and other types of perennial herbaceous plants. Soils may be inundated for brief periods (1-2 weeks) in the spring following snowmelt or during floods. Shrubs occur only as scattered plants.

■ **Low prairie** Low prairies are dominated by grasses and grasslike plants. These communities are similar to wet meadows but are dominated by native grasses and other herbaceous species characteristic of the prairie. Low prairie communities primarily occur in southern and western Minnesota, but are occasional in the north on sandy plains or in wet swales.

■ **Calcareous fens** Calcareous fens are an uncommon wetland type, both in Minnesota and worldwide. They typically develop on sites that are sloping and with a steady flow of groundwater rich in calcium and magnesium bicarbonates (Curtis 1971). The calcium and magnesium bicarbonates precipitate out at the ground surface, leading to a highly alkaline soil. Such conditions are tolerated by a fairly small group of plants termed "calciphiles." Sphagnum mosses are absent or sparse. Due to their uniqueness, calcareous fens support a large number of rare plant species such as these members of the Sedge Family (Cyperaceae): *Carex sterilis, Eleocharis rostellata, Rhynchospora capillacea*, and *Scleria verticillata*.

■ **Open bogs** Open bogs are found most commonly in northern portions of Minnesota, but also occur as small relict features to the south. Technically, true bogs are extremely nutrient-poor, receiving nutrients only from precipitation. Many of the region's bogs may better be termed "poor fens," but given the widespread use of the term among scientists and general public alike, "bog" is used throughout this book. Bogs have a characteristic, nearly continuous carpet of sphagnum moss, and are dominated by shrubs of the Heath Family (Ericaceae), especially leatherleaf (*Chamaedaphne calyculata*), members of the Sedge Family (Cyperaceae), and scattered herbs such as pitcher plant (*Sarracenia purpurea*) and sundew (*Drosera*). Stunted trees of black spruce (*Picea mariana*) and tamarack (*Larix laricina*) may be present; this type of bog is sometimes termed "muskeg." Soils are composed entirely of saturated organic peat.

■ **Conifer bogs** Conifer bogs are similar to open bogs except that trees of black spruce and/or tamarack are predominant. Sphagnum moss carpets the ground surface. Shrubs of the Heath Family (Ericaceae), sedges, and a small number of other species occur. Soils are organic, saturated peats.

■ **Shrub-carrs** Shrub-carrs are dominated by tall shrubs. Soils are organic peat or muck, or alluvial soils of floodplains, and are often saturated throughout the growing season, and sometimes inundated during floods. Willows (*Salix*) and dogwoods (*Cornus*) are especially characteristic.

■ **Alder thickets** Alder thickets are a tall, deciduous shrub community similar to shrub-carrs except that speckled or tag alder (*Alnus incana*) is dominant, and often forming dense colonies. Alder thickets are common in northern Minnesota along rivers and streams, or along the wet margins of marshes, sedge meadows and bogs.

■ **Hardwood swamps** Hardwood swamps are dominated by deciduous trees such as black ash (*Fraxinus nigra*), red maple (*Acer rubrum*), and yellow birch (*Betula alleghaniensis*). Southward, silver maple (*Acer saccharinum*) increases in importance; northward, northern white cedar (*Thuja occidentalis*) may be present. American elm (*Ulmus americana*) may be present, but in greatly reduced numbers than formerly due to losses from Dutch elm disease. Soils are saturated during much of the growing season, and may be covered with shallow water in spring.

■ **Conifer swamps** Conifer swamps are forested wetlands dominated primarily by tamarack (*Larix laricina*) and black *spruce (Picea mariana)*. In areas where the water is not as stagnant and in areas underlain by limestone, northern white cedar (*Thuja occidentalis*) may form dense stands. Conifer swamps occur almost entirely in northern Minnesota. Soils are usually peat or muck, and vary in reaction from acidic and nutrient-poor, to neutral or alkaline and relatively fertile. Tamarack is most abundant on acid soils, while northern white cedar is most common on neutral or alkaline soils. Soils are typically saturated much of the growing season, and sometimes covered with shallow water. Sphagnum moss may be present, but does not usually form a continuous mat.

■ **Floodplain forests** Floodplain forests are dominated by deciduous hardwood trees growing on alluvial soils along rivers. These forests often have standing water during the spring, with water levels dropping to the surface (or below) in summer and fall. Typical trees include silver maple (*Acer saccharinum*), green ash (*Fraxinus pennsylvanica*), black willow (*Salix nigra*), eastern cottonwood (*Populus deltoides*), and river birch (*Betula nigra*). The diversity of the undergrowth is high, as flood waters remove and deposit alluvium, creating microhabitats suitable for many species.

■ **Seasonally flooded basins** Seasonally flooded basins are poorly drained, shallow depressions in glacial deposits (kettles), low spots in outwash plains, or depressions in floodplains. The basins may have standing water for a few weeks in the spring or for short periods following heavy rains. Soils are typically dry, however, for much of the growing season. In western and southern Minnesota, attempts are made to cultivate the basins, and in combination with the fluctuating water level, these areas are often dominated by a wide array of annual or weedy plant species.

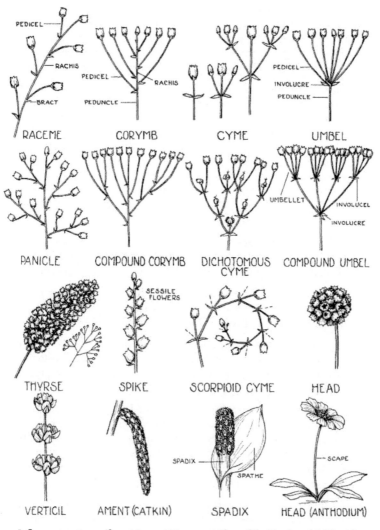

Inflorescence types (from Mason, H.L. 1957. *A Flora of the Marshes of California*).

SUMMARY OF GROUP KEYS

FERNS AND FERN RELATIVES

SEED PLANTS

FERNS & FERN RELATIVES

FERN GROUPS
Includes true ferns and fern relatives

1   Plants aquatic, either floating and unattached, or rooting and often completely submersed . . . . **GROUP 1**
1   Plants of various wetland, upland, and rock habitats 2
   2   Leaves not "fern-like;" unlobed, variously awl-shaped, scale-like, or grass-like (the fern relatives will key here plus one species of *Asplenium*) . . . . **GROUP 2**
   2   Leaves "fern-like," variously lobed or divided (true ferns will key here; the following groups are based on size of frond and habitat, either soil or rock) 3
      3   Plants small, leaf blades (not including the stipe) small, less than 30 cm long or wide (some species will key both here and in the next lead no. 3) 4
         4   Plants growing on rock, rock walls, or over rock in thin soil . . . . **GROUP 3**
         4   Plants terrestrial, growing in soil, not associated with rock outcrops . . . . . **GROUP 4**
      3   Plants larger, leaf blades medium to large, more than 30 cm long or wide 5
         5   Plants growing on rock, or over rock in thin soil mats or pockets of soil . . **GROUP 5**
         5   Plants growing in soil, not associated with rock outcrops . . . . **GROUP 6**

FERNS, GROUP 1
Aquatic ferns; plants floating, or rooted and submersed

1   Plants aquatic, floating (***Azolla***). . . . . **SALVINIACEAE**
1   Plants aquatic, rooted, sometimes exposed on shores as water levels drop 2
   2   Plants resemble a clover, with 4 terminal leaf segments . . . . **MARSILEACEAE**
   2   Leaves linear, from a swollen, corm-like base (***Isoetes***). . . . . **ISOETACEAE**

FERNS, GROUP 2
Fern relatives; leaves unlobed, awl-shaped, scalelike, or grasslike, and not "fern-like"

1   Stems obviously jointed; leaves small and scalelike, in a whorl from the joints or nodes, or sometimes absent; spores borne in a terminal conelike strobilus covered with peltate scales (i.e., scales more or less round and attached at middle like an umbrella **EQUISETACEAE**
1   Stems not jointed; leaves scalelike or larger, but if scalelike not in whorls from the nodes; spores borne variously, but if in a terminal strobilus the scales not peltate. . . 2
   2   Leaves linear, grasslike, 1-50 cm long (***Isoetes***) . . . . **ISOETACEAE**
   2   Leaves various (scalelike, awl-like, moss-like, or flat), but not linear and grasslike   3
      3   Leaves very numerous and overlapping along creeping, ascending, or erect stems; the leaves usually scalelike or awl-like, 0.5-2 (-3) mm wide, typically sharp- or hair-tipped; sporangia borne in strobili. 4
         4   Sporangia borne in flattened or 4-sided strobili sessile at tips of leafy branches; spores and sporangia of two sizes, the megasporangia larger and borne at base strobili . . . . **SELAGINELLACEAE**
         4   Sporangia borne either in axils of normal foliage leaves, or in strobili sessile at tips of leafy branches, or stalked on specialized branches with fewer and smaller leaves; spores and sporangia of one size. 5
            5   Leafy stems erect, simple or dichotomously branched, the ultimate branches upright; sporophylls like the sterile leaves or only slightly smaller, in annual bands along the stem; vegetative reproduction by leafy gemmae near tip of stem (***Huperzia***). . . . . **LYCOPODIACEAE**
            5   Leafy stems prostrate or erect, if erect then generally branched, the ultimate branches spreading (horizontal) or ascending; sporophylls differing from sterile leaves, either broader and shorter, or more spreading, grouped into terminal cones; lacking vegetative reproduction by gemmae 6
               6   Plants of wetlands, mostly on moist or wet sand or peat; leaves herbaceous, pale or yellow-green, dull, deciduous; leafy stems

creeping; rhizome dying back annually to an underground vegetative
tuber at tip (***Lycopodiella***). . . . . **LYCOPODIACEAE**

  6 Plants of uplands, mostly in moist to dry soils; leaves stiff, bright to
dark green, shiny, evergreen; leafy stems mainly erect, treelike,
fanlike, or creeping (if creeping, then the leaves with a hairlike tip);
rhizome trailing, perennial 7

    7 Shoots flat-branched, 1-5 mm wide (including the leaves); leaves
scalelike, dimorphic, overlapping and appressed to stem, in 4
ranks; strobili on long, branched stalks (***Diphasiastrum***). . . . . . . **LYCOPODIACEAE**

    7 Shoots round-branched, usually 5-8 mm wide (including the
leaves), leaves awl-shaped, monomorphic (though sometimes
differing in size), separate, spreading or ascending, in 6 ranks;
strobili sessile at stem tips (***Lycopodium***) . . . . **LYCOPODIACEAE**

  3 Leaves not as above 8

    8 Plants with 1 (-several) leaves, the sterile leaf blade ovate, entire-margined,
obtuse, the longer fertile portion with 2 rows of sporangia somewhat
embedded in it (***Ophioglossum***). . . . . **OPHIOGLOSSACEAE**

    8 Plant with many leaves, generally 5 or more, not divided into separate sterile
and fertile segments, the leaves lance-shaped with a long-tapering tip (often
with a plantlet which can root to form new plants) (***Asplenium rhizophyllum***) **ASPLENIACEAE**

FERNS, GROUP 3
Small ferns, growing on rock or on rock in thin soil

1 Fronds pinnatifid or 2-pinnatifid, most of the pinnae not fully divided from one
another (the rachis winged by leaf tissue for most or all its length). 2

  2 Fronds 2-pinnatifid, at least the lowermost pinnae deeply lobed (***Phegopteris***) . . . **THELYPTERIDACEAE**

  2 Fronds 1-pinnatifid. 3

    3 Blades with long, narrow tapering tip, upper portion of blade unlobed or only
slightly lobed; sori elongate (***Asplenium***). . . . . **ASPLENIACEAE**

    3 Fronds without a long, narrow tapering tip; blade lobed for most of its length;
sori round (***Polypodium***). . . . . **POLYPODIACEAE**

1 Fronds pinnate, pinnate-pinnatifid, 2-pinnate, or even more divided (rachis naked for
most of its length, but often winged in upper portion). 4

  4 Fronds 1-pinnate or 1-pinnate-pinnatifid. 5

    5 Sori on the undersurface of the leaf, away from the margins (***Asplenium***). . . . . **ASPLENIACEAE**

    5 Sori on the undersurface of the leaf, along margins and more-or-less hidden
beneath either the unmodified inrolled leaf margin or under a modified,
reflexed false indusium 6

      6 Stipes green to straw-colored for at least the upper 1/3, rachis green; fronds
dimorphic, the fertile longer than the sterile and with narrower segments
(***Cryptogramma***). . . . . **PTERIDACEAE**

      6 Stipes and rachis dark brown to almost black throughout; fronds similar or
somewhat different (***Pellaea***) . . . . **PTERIDACEAE**

  4 Fronds 2-pinnate or more divided 7

    7 Blade broadly triangular in outline (***Gymnocarpium***). **CYSTOPTERIDACEAE**

    7 Blade elongate, mostly lance-shaped, generally 4x or more as long as wide, not
notably triangular in outline 8

      8 Sori on margins, usually more-or-less hidden under the inrolled margin of
the pinnule 9

        9 Sori round or oblong, distinct and separate along the pinnule margins;
fronds bright-green, smooth, herbaceous, delicate, and flexible
(***Adiantum pedatum***). . . . . **PTERIDACEAE**

        9 Sori continuous along the pinnule margins; fronds mostly dark-green,
often hairy, leathery, tough, and stiff. 10

          10 Fronds 2-3-pinnate, more or less densely hairy (***Cheilanthes***) . . . . . . **PTERIDACEAE**

          10 Fronds 1-2-pinnate, smooth or sparsely and inconspicuously hairy
(***Pellaea***) . . . . **PTERIDACEAE**

    8 Sori not on margins, either naked, or slightly to strongly hidden by indus . 11

11 Blades 3-12 cm long; sori elongate, covered by a flap-like, entire indusium
(*Asplenium*) .... ASPLENIACEAE

11 Blades 4-30 (-50) cm long; sori round, surrounded or covered by an
entire, fringed, or divided indusium............................. 12

   12 Veins reaching margin; indusium attached under one side of sorus,
hoodlike or pocketlike, arching over sorus; stipes smooth or
sparsely covered with scales, stipe bases not persistent (*Cystopteris*) CYSTOPTERIDACEAE

   12 Veins ending short of margin; indusium attached under sorus, cuplike
(divided into 3-6 lobes which surround the sorus from below) or of
numerous tiny hairs, which extend out from under sorus on all sides;
stipes often densely covered with scales, stipe bases persistent
(*Woodsia*) .... WOODSIACEAE

FERNS, GROUP 4
Small ferns, terrestrial, growing in soil, not associated with rock outcrops

1 Stipe branched once dichotomously, each branch with 3-7 pinnae in one direction
only, the outline of the blade fan-shaped, often wider than long (*Adiantum pedatum*) PTERIDACEAE

1 Stipe not branched dichotomously, the outline of the blade either longer than wide
or triangular and about as wide as long 2

  2 Fronds pinnatifid or 2-pinnatifid, most of the pinnae not fully divided from one
another (the rachis winged by leaf tissue for most or all of its length).......... 3

    3 Sporangia borne on an erect stalk that arises at or above ground level from stipe
of sterile leaf blade (joining stipe of sterile leaf above the rhizome) (*Botrychium,
Botrypus*)...................................... OPHIOGLOSSACEAE

    3 Sporangia either borne on normal leaf blades or on specialized (fertile) frond. 4

      4 Fronds all alike, sori on normal leaf blades (*Phegopteris*) .... THELYPTERIDACEAE

      4 Fronds of two types; sori on fronds significantly different than normal
fronds (*Onoclea sensibilis*) .... ONOCLEACEAE

  2 Fronds 1-pinnate, 1-pinnate-pinnatifid, 2-pinnate, or even more divided (the rachis
naked for most of its length, or often winged in the upper portion) 5

    5 Fronds broadly triangular in outline, about as broad as long; sporangia borne
on an erect stalk that arises at or above ground level from the stipe of the sterile
leaf blade (joining the stipe of the sterile leaf above the rhizome) 6

      6 Sporangia borne on normal leaf blades (*Gymnocarpium*) .... CYSTOPTERIDACEAE

      6 Sporangia borne on an erect stalk that arises at or above ground level from
the stipe of the sterile leaf blade (joining the stipe of the sterile leaf above
the rhizome) (*Sceptridium*) .... OPHIOGLOSSACEAE

    5 Fronds lance-shaped in outline, much longer than broad; sporangia either borne
on normal leaf blades, on slightly dimorphic blades, or on an erect stalk that
arises at or above ground level from the stipe of the sterile leaf blade (joining
the stipe of the sterile leaf above the rhizome) 7

      7 Blades 1-8 cm long; sporangia borne on an erect stalk that arises at or above
ground level from the stipe of the sterile leaf blade (joining the stipe of the
sterile leaf above the rhizome) (*Botrychium*) .... OPHIOGLOSSACEAE

      7 Blades 10-30 (-100) cm long; sporangia either on normal leaf blades or on
slightly modified blades 8

        8 Fronds evergreen, dark green, somewhat leathery (*Polystichum*)...... DRYOPTERIDACEAE

        8 Fronds light to medium green, herbaceous, deciduous to semi-evergreen 9

          9 Sori elongate; leaf blades somewhat dimorphic, the fertile larger and
erect, the sterile smaller and prostrate, the larger leaf blades 2-4 (-
6.5) cm wide (*Asplenium platyneuron*) .... ASPLENIACEAE

          9 Sori round; leaf blades monomorphic; the larger leaf blades 5-15 cm
wide (*Thelypteris*) .... THELYPTERIDACEAE

FERNS, GROUP 5
Medium to large ferns, growing on rock, or over rock in thin soil

1 Fronds 1-pinnate-pinnatifid or less divided, the pinnae entire, toothed, lobed or pinnatifid 2
    2 Sori elongate, the indusium flap-like, attached along the side; leaf blades (if more than 30 cm long) less than 7 cm wide (*Asplenium platyneuron*) . . . . **ASPLENIACEAE**
    2 Sori circular or globular, the indusium peltate, kidney-shaped, or cuplike; leaf blades (if more than 30 cm long) more than 5 cm wide. 3
        3 Fronds 1-pinnate, the pinnae toothed and each with a slight to prominent lobe near the base on the side towards the leaf tip, dark green, somewhat leathery; indusia peltate (*Polystichum*) . . . . **DRYOPTERIDACEAE**
        3 Fronds 1-pinnate-pinnatifid, the pinnae pinnatifid, generally lacking a prominent basal lobe, light green to dark green, herbaceous to slightly leathery; indusium either kidney-shaped or cuplike 4
            4 Vascular bundles in the stipe 3-7 (*Dryopteris*) . . . . **DRYOPTERIDACEAE**
            4 Vascular bundles in the stipe 2, uniting above 5
                5 Indusium kidney-shaped, arching over the sorus (*Thelypteris*) . . . . **THELYPTERIDACEAE**
                5 Indusium cuplike, attached beneath sorus and consisting of 3-6 lance-shaped to ovate segments (*Woodsia*) . . . . **WOODSIACEAE**
1 Fronds 2-pinnate or more divided, the pinnae divided to their midribs. 6
    6 Sori marginal and borne on underside of the false indusium; stipes and rachis shiny black or reddish-black, glabrous except at the very base of the stipe; pinnules fan-shaped or obliquely elongate (*Adiantum*) . . . . **PTERIDACEAE**
    6 Sori not marginal, borne on undersurface of leaf blade (or if marginal, as in *Pteridium*, borne on undersurface of the leaf); stipes darkened only near base (if at all), rachis green, tan, or reddish; pinnules not notably fan-shaped or obliquely elongate 7
        7 Blades broadly triangular in outline, about as long as wide (*Pteridium aquilinum*) **DENNSTAEDIACEAE**
        7 Blades elongate, mostly lanceolate, generally 4x or more longer than wide. . . 8
            8 Vascular bundles (3-) 5 (-7) in the stipe; mostly larger woodland ferns (*Dryopteris*) . . . . **DRYOPTERIDACEAE**
            8 Vascular bundles 2 in the stipe (or joining near the leaf blade into 1); ferns of woodlands and rocky places 9
                9 Fronds 1-pinnate-pinnatifid; indusium cuplike, attached beneath the sorus and consisting of 3-6 lanceolate to ovate segments; mostly smaller ferns on rock (*Woodsia*) . . . . **WOODSIACEAE**
                9 Fronds 2-pinnate-pinnatifid; indusium flaplike or pocketlike, attached at one side of the sorus and arching over it 10
                    10 Fronds 10-30 cm wide, the tip acute to acuminate; indusium flaplike (*Athyrium filix-femina*) . . . . **ATHYRIACEAE**
                    10 Fronds 4-9 cm wide, the tip long-attenuate; indusium pocketlike or hoodlike (*Cystopteris bulbifera*) . . . . **CYSTOPTERIDACEAE**

FERNS, GROUP 6
Medium to large ferns, growing in soil (not on rock outcrops)

1 Blades broadly (about equilaterally) triangular, pentagonal, or flabellate in outline, 0.7-1.3x as long as wide. 2
    2 Blades fan-shaped in outline, the stipe branched once dichotomously, each branch bearing 3-7 pinnae (*Adiantum pedatum*) . . . . **PTERIDACEAE**
    2 Blades broadly triangular in outline, the stipe not branched dichotomously. 3
        3 Sporangia in a stalked, specialized, fertile portion of the blade; texture of mature blades somewhat fleshy; plants solitary from a short underground rhizome with thick, mycorrhizal roots; plants of moist woods (*Botrypus virginianus*) . . . . **OPHIOGLOSSACEAE**
        3 Sporangia in marginal, linear sori, indusium absent, protected by the revolute leaf margin and a minute false indusium; texture of mature leaf blades hard and

stiff; plants colonial from deep rhizomes; plants of moist to dry woods and openings (*Pteridium aquilinum*) . . . . **DENNSTAEDIACEAE**

1 Fronds elongate in outline, mostly ovate, lanceolate, oblanceolate, or narrowly triangular, 1.5-10x or more as long as wide. 4

   4 Fronds 2-pinnate or more divided, the pinnae divided to their midribs 5

      5 Blade divided into sterile and fertile portions; sterile pinnae located below terminal fertile pinnae, the sterile pinnules 30-70 mm long and 8-23 mm wide, finely toothed, tip rounded to somewhat pointed; fertile pinnae greatly reduced in size, the fertile pinnules 7-11 mm long and 2-3 mm wide (*Osmunda regalis*) . **OSMUNDACEAE**

      5 Blade not divided into sterile and fertile portions, the pinnules bearing sporangia only slightly if at all reduced in size, both fertile and sterile pinnules mostly 4-20 mm long and 2-10 mm wide. 6

         6 Vascular bundles (3-) 5 (-7) in the stipe (*Dryopteris*) . . . . **DRYOPTERIDACEAE**

         6 Vascular bundles 2 in the stipe (or joining upwards near leaf blade into 1) . 7

            7 Fronds more than 10 cm wide, the tip acute to acuminate; indusium flaplike; pealike bulblets absent (*Athyrium filix-femina*) . . . . **ATHYRIACEAE**

            7 Fronds 4-9 cm wide, the tip long-tapering; indusium pocketlike or hoodlike; bulblets often present on upper portion of blade (*Cystopteris bulbifera*) . . . . **CYSTOPTERIDACEAE**

   4 Fronds 1-pinnate-pinnatifid or less divided; the pinnae entire, toothed, lobed or pinnatifid 8

      8 Fronds 1-pinnate or 1-pinnate-pinnatifid, the pinnae fully divided from one another (rachis naked for most of its length, but often winged in upper portion); fronds dimorphic or not (*Onoclea sensibilis*) . . . . **ONOCLEACEAE**

      8 Fronds 1-pinnatifid, most of the pinnae not fully divided from one another (rachis winged by leaf tissue for most or all of its length); fronds dimorphic, the fertile much modified, stiff and/or woody 9

         9 Rhizomes long-creeping, fronds scattered, forming patches (*Thelypteris*) . **THELYPTERIDACEAE**

         9 Rhizomes short-creeping, the fronds clustered, not forming patches (or rhizomes of both long and short, but fronds borne only in clusters on the short erect rhizomes in *Matteucia*). 10

           10 Plants medium to large, fronds typically 60-300 cm tall; fronds either strongly dimorphic, the fertile fronds very unlike the sterile, brown at maturity (*Matteucia* and *Osmunda cinnamomea*) or fertile pinnae very unlike the sterile, brown at maturity, borne as an interruption in the blade, with normal green pinnae above and below (*Osmunda claytoniana*); rachises scaleless, stipes scaleless (except at the base in *Matteucia*) 11

              11 Fronds strongly tapering to the base from the broadest point (well beyond the midpoint of the blade), lowermost pinnae much less than 1/2 as long as the largest pinnae (*Matteucia struthiopteris*) . . . . **ONOCLEACEAE**

              11 Fronds slightly if at all tapering to the base, about equally broad through much of their length, lowermost pinnae much more than 1/2 as long as the largest pinnae (*Osmunda*) . . . . **OSMUNDACEAE**

          10 Plants mostly smaller, the fronds 30-100 cm tall (except *Dryopteris goldiana* to 15 dm); fronds not at all or only slightly dimorphic, the fertile differing in various ways, such as having narrower pinnae (as in *Polystichum acrostichoides*, *Diplazium*, and *Thelypteris palustris*) or fertile fronds taller and more deciduous (as in *Asplenium platyneuron* and *Dryopteris cristata*), but not as described in the first lead; rachises and stipes variously scaly or scaleless, but at least the stipe and often also the rachis scaly if the plants over 1 m tall. 12

            12 Sori elongate, the indusium elongate, attached along one side as a flap 13

               13 Stipe and rachis lustrous brownish black; fertile fronds 2-8 (-12) cm wide (*Asplenium platyneuron*). . . . . **ASPLENIACEAE**

               13 Stipe and rachis green; fertile fronds 10-20 (-30) cm wide 14

                  14 Fronds 1-pinnate-pinnatifid (the pinnae pinnatifid) (*Deparia acrostichoides*). . . . . **ATHYRIACEAE**

                  14 Fronds 1-pinnate (the pinnae entire) (*Diplazium pycnocarpon*) **ATHYRIACEAE**

            12 Sori roundish; the indusium kidney-shaped or nearly round, attached by a central stalk, or sometimes absent 15

15 Fronds 1-pinnate, the pinnae toothed and each with a slight to prominent lobe near the base on the side towards the leaf tip, dark green, subcoriaceous to coriaceous; indusia peltate (round, stalk attached to the center) (*Polystichum acrostichoides*) . . . . **DRYOPTERIDACEAE**
15 Fronds 1-pinnate-pinnatifid, the pinnae pinnatifid, generally without prominent basal lobe, light green to dark green, herbaceous to somewhat leathery; indusium kidney-shaped. 16
    16 Vascular bundles in the stipe 4-7 (*Dryopteris*) . . . . **DRYOPTERIDACEAE**
    16 Vascular bundles in the stipe 2, uniting upwards (*Thelypteris*) . . . . **THELYPTERIDACEAE**

SEED PLANTS

SEED PLANT GROUPS
Includes leads to 15 Group Keys and to several families with specialized features

1 Plants aquatic, the leaves or plant body entirely submersed or floating on the surface of the water (at most, the inflorescence and bracts, not leaves, held above the surface **GROUP 7**
1 Plants with at least some leaves or stems above the water, or plants terrestrial 2
    2 Plants woody (trees, shrubs, and woody vines), with erect, trailing, or viny above-ground stems living through the winter and continuing to grow the next season (leaves may be evergreen or deciduous). . . . . **GROUP 8**
    2 Plants herbaceous, the perennial parts, if any, below or on the surface of the ground (to which the stems die back each year), not producing woody stems which survive the winter well above ground [hence, without aerial evergreen leaves (although there may be basal winter-green leaves) 3
        3 Plant lacking green color (often wholly parasitic or saprophytic) and the leaves none at flowering time or reduced to tiny scales) . . . . **GROUP 9**
        3 Plant with green color and the leaves usually developed (occasionally the stems photosynthetic, as in cacti) 4
            4 Inflorescences producing only small bulblets or tufts of little leaves (or modified floral parts), but no flowers or fruit. . . . . **GROUP 10**
            4 Inflorescences normal 5
                5 Perianth parts (2), 3, (4), or 6 (never 5) and leaves (or other green photosynthetic parts when leaves are absent or reduced) parallel-veined (the 3 or more main veins running from base of blade to apex and ± parallel, with or without minute cross-veins), entire, simple . . . . **GROUP 11**
                5 Perianth parts various (often 5) but leaves netted-veined (or with only the midvein conspicuous), entire or toothed, simple or compound (the main veins, if more than 1, branching and ± reticulate). 6
                    6 Inflorescence a dense "head" (either a true head or a spadix), consisting of few to many small sessile flowers on a common receptacle (not merely an elongate spike), subtended by 1 or more small or large bracts . . . . **GROUP 12**
                    6 Inflorescence not an involucrate head, or if head-like the individual flowers short-pediceled and/or the "head" not immediately subtended by 1 or more bracts 7
                        7 Plants leafless but with thick, fleshy, green stem segments often bearing strong spines . . . . **CACTACEAE**
                        7 Plants not both leafless and with spiny fleshy stems 8
                            8 Inflorescence of "false flowers" consisting of small cup-like structures (uniform in texture and not composed of separate parts like bracts or scales) each bearing 1-5 glands on its rim (sometimes with additional petaloid appendages) and including 2 or more stamens and 1 central stalked 3-lobed pistil (which ripens into an exserted, 3-lobed capsule); sap milky (*Euphorbia*) . . . . **EUPHORBIACEAE**
                            8 Inflorescence various, but not composed of such structures; pistil only rarely stalked (and if so, not 3-lobed); sap various . 9

9   Anthers and stigma fused into a central structure obscuring the individual reproductive parts; ovaries 2, ripening into follicles, the seeds each with a tuft of hairs (except *Vinca*); sap milky .... **APOCYNACEAE**

9   Anthers and stigmas not fused to each other, of diverse but recognizable structure; ovaries, seeds, and sap various but not combined as above........................... 10

  10 Flowers unisexual, containing one or more stamens or pistils, but not both .... **GROUP 13**

  10 Flowers all or mostly bisexual, containing both stamen(s) and pistil(s) (although these may not all be equally mature at the same time) 11

    11 Perianth none.............................. 12

      12 Leaves deeply lobed or compound .... **RANUNCULACEAE**

      12 Leaves unlobed, entire (*Callitriche, Hippuris*)... **PLANTAGINACEAE**

    11 Perianth present (but not always conspicuous) ... 13

      13 Perianth of only one series (calyx or corolla)... 14

        14 Ovary inferior .... **GROUP 14**

        14 Ovary (or ovaries) superior.............. **GROUP 15**

      13 Perianth of two series (both calyx and corolla). 15

        15 Ovaries 2 or more in each flower .... **GROUP 16**

        15 Ovary 1 in each flower (styles or stigmas may be separate) 16

          16 Ovary inferior .... **GROUP 17**

          16 Ovary superior..................... 17

            17 Stamens more numerous than the petals........................ **GROUP 18**

            17 Stamens the same number as the petals or lobes (not lips) of the corolla, or fewer....................... 18

              18 Petals separate .... **GROUP 19**

              18 Petals connate at least at the base 19

                19 Corolla regular and the stamens the same number as its lobes . **GROUP 20**

                19 Corolla either bilaterally symmetrical or the stamens fewer than its lobes (not lips), or both conditions present ..... **GROUP 21**

SEED PLANTS, GROUP 7
Aquatic plants, with all leaves underwater or floating on water surface

---

1 Plants without distinct stem and leaves, free-floating at or below surface of water (except where stranded by drop in water level), the segments (internodes) small (to 15 mm long, but in most species much smaller), often remaining attached where budded from parent plant... 2

  2 Plant body once to several times equally 2-lobed or 2-forked .... **RICCIACEAE** (a family of liverworts, see page 82)

  2 Plant body not consistently 2-lobed or 2-forked .... **ARACEAE**

1 Plants with distinct stem and/or leaves, usually anchored in substrate, mostly larger. 3

  3 Plants with floating leaves present (blades, or at least their terminal portions, floating on the surface of the water, usually ± smooth and firm in texture, especially compared with submersed leaves, or submersed leaves none)................. 4

    4 Blades of some or all floating leaves on a plant sagittate or deeply lobed at base, or compound, or peltate (± circular, with the stalk attached on the underside) 5

      5 Floating blades compound (4-foliolate) (*Marsilea*, a fern).............. **MARSILEACEAE**

      5 Floating blades simple 6

        6 Floating blades (at least some of them) sagittate, the tip and lobes acute (Note that plants with sagittate leaves extending above the water surface will not key here) (*Sagittaria*) .... **ALISMATACEAE**

      6 Floating (and any other) blades circular to ± elliptic in outline, peltate or rounded at tip with deep sinus at base. 7

         7 Leaves rounded at tip with deep sinus at base . . . . **NYMPHAEACEAE**

         7 Leaves peltate   8

            8 Leaves circular, large (1 dm or more in diameter); flowers yellow **NELUMBONACEAE**

            8 Leaves elliptic, less than 1 dm in their longest dimension, flowers reddish   . . . . **CABOMBACEAE**

  4 Blades of floating leaves all unlobed (at most subcordate at base), simple, the petiole small or absent in ribbon-like leaves. 9

      9 Floating leaves small (less than 1 cm long), crowded in a terminal rosette; submersed leaves distinctly opposite; flowers solitary, axillary (***Callitriche***) . **PLANTAGINACEAE**

      9 Floating leaves larger, not in a rosette; submersed leaves alternate, basal, or absent; flowers mostly in a terminal inflorescence. 10

        10 Leaves narrow and ribbon-like, the blades many times longer than wide, without distinct petiole (though in some species a sheath surrounds the stem) 11

          11 Leaves ± rounded at tip (even if tapered), the floating portion smooth and shiny, somewhat yellow-green to bright green when fresh, occasionally keeled but midvein scarcely if at all more prominent than others; leaf not differentiated into blade and sheath, the submersed portion similar to the floating but more evidently with a fine closely checkered pattern; flowers and fruit in spherical heads (***Sparganium***) **TYPHACEAE**

          11 Leaves sharply acute at tip, the floating portion rather dull, ± blue-green when fresh, with midrib; leaf including a sheath around stem and a membranous ligule at junction of sheath and blade; flowers and fruit in paniculate spikelets . . . . **POACEAE**

        10 Leaves (at least floating ones) with ± elliptic blades and distinct petiole 12

          12 Leaves all basal; petals 3, white . . . . **ALISMATACEAE**

          12 Leaves cauline (along the stem), alternate or opposite; petals 4-6, pink or dull and inconspicuous (white in *Caltha natans*) 13

            13 Flowers individually peduncled in a few-flowered, open inflorescence; rare in ne Minn (***Caltha natans***) . . . . **RANUNCULACEAE**

            13 Flowers sessile in spikes, pink or dull and inconspicuous; mostly common species   14

              14 Veins netted; flowers bright pink, in dense ovoid to cylindrical spikes (***Persicaria amphibia***). . . . . **POLYGONACEAE**

              14 Venation parallel; flowers dull, in narrow cylindrical spikes. . **POTAMOGETONACEAE**

3 Plants without any floating leaves, entirely submersed (except sometimes for inflorescences and associated bracts). 15

  15 Leaves (or leaf-like structures) all basal and simple. 16

      16 Leaves flat, widest about the middle or parallel-sided 17

        17 Leaf blades not over twice as long as wide juvenile . . . . **NYMPHAEACEAE**

        17 Leaf blades more than twice as long as broad 18

          18 Leaves stiff and erect or somewhat outcurved, less than 20 cm long 19

            19 Base of leaf somewhat sheathing, with a membranous ligule (as in a grass) at base of spreading blade (***Pontederia***) . . . . **PONTEDERIACEAE**

            19 Base of leaf not sheathing and with no ligule (***Sagittaria***) . . . . . . **ALISMATACEAE**

          18 Leaves limp, more than 20 cm long, ribbon-like 20

            20 Midvein not evident, all veins of essentially equal prominence, with the tiny cross-veins giving a checkered appearance to the leaf, which is thus uniformly marked with minute rectangular cells ca. 1-2 mm long or smaller (***Sparganium***). . . . . **TYPHACEAE**

            20 Midvein (and usually some additional longitudinal veins) evident, the veins not all of equal prominence, not dividing the leaf into minute rectangular cells. 21

              21 Leaves with the central third (or more) of distinctly different pattern (more densely reticulate) than the two marginal zones; plants dioecious, the staminate flowers eventually liberated from a dense inflorescence submersed at base of plant, the pistillate solitary on a long ± spiraled stalk which reaches the surface of the water; plants without milky juice (***Vallisneria***) . **HYDROCHARITACEAE**

21 Leaves ± uniform in venation, not 3-zoned; plants monoecious, with emergent inflorescence of white-petaled flowers (but these scarce on plants with submersed tape-like leaves); plants often with milky juice (*Sagittaria*) . . . . **ALISMATACEAE**

16 Leaves (or similar vegetative stems) filiform or terete or only slightly flattened (especially basally), elongate and limp to short and quill-like, less than twice as broad as thick 22

22 Major erect structures solitary, spaced along a simple or branched delicate rhizome, consisting either of rather yellowish stems bearing minute alternate bumps as leaves or of filiform leaves mostly buried in the substrate and with a few minute bladder-like organs 23

23 Leaves merely minute alternate bumps on stem; bladders not present; flowers sessile, inconspicuous, regular (*Myriophyllum tenellum*) . . . . **HALORAGACEAE**

23 Leaves filiform, mostly buried in substrate (only the green tips, incurled when young, protruding); bladders (minute) usually present on the delicate branching rhizomes and buried leaf bases; flowers short-pediceled, showy (yellow or purple), bilaterally symmetrical (*Utricularia*) . . . . **LENTIBULARIACEAE**

22 Major erect structures solitary to densely tufted, consisting of filiform or quill-like leaves or stems, with neither alternate bumps or bladders . 24

24 Leaves very limp (retaining no stiffness when removed from water and hence irregularly sinuate, bent, or matted on herbarium specimens) though a stiffer straight stem may also be present, mostly more than 20 cm long, ca. 0.2-1 mm wide 25

25 Leaves slightly expanded basally for ca. (0.7-) 2-10 cm, sheathing the next inner leaf at least dorsally (usually the sheath continued ventrally as an almost invisible membrane), with tiny ligule or pair of auricles at the summit; rhizome various; inflorescence a lateral spikelet or terminal cyme (*Schoenoplectus subterminalis*) . . . . **CYPERACEAE**

25 Leaves (actually vegetative stems) terete their entire length, not expanded basally nor sheathing each other, but each separate and closely surrounded at base for ca. (0.6-) 1 cm or more by a very delicate membranous tubular sheath (this sometimes requiring careful dissection to distinguish); rhizome less than 2 mm in diameter; inflorescence (rare on plants otherwise entirely submersed) a single strictly terminal spikelet 26

26 Rhizome reddish, at least on older portions; leaves (vegetative culms) mostly over 20 cm long, very limp; fertile culm triangular in cross-section on emersed portion, much larger in diameter than the hair-like vegetative culms, but spikelet no thicker than culm (*Eleocharis robbinsii*) . . . . **CYPERACEAE**

26 Rhizome whitish throughout; leaves often shorter, usually stiffer; fertile culms terete, no larger than the vegetative culms, but spikelet distinctly thicker than culm (*Eleocharis acicularis*) **CYPERACEAE**

24 Leaves usually firm (retaining stiffness when removed from water and hence straight or with an even curve in herbarium specimens), less (in most species much less) than 20 cm long, of various widths 27

27 Leaves filiform throughout, not broader basally nor sheathing each other, solitary (rarely) or in small tufts along a filiform whitish rhizome, each leaf (actually a vegetative stem) closely surrounded at its base for ca. 6 mm or more by a very delicate membranous tubular sheath (this sometimes requiring careful dissection to distinguish); inflorescence (rare on completely submersed plants) a single terminal spikelet (*Eleocharis acicularis*) **CYPERACEAE**

27 Leaves linear or tapered from base to apex, or if otherwise uniformly filiform then expanded at base or sheathing each other, without individual tubular sheaths as described above; inflorescence various 28

28 Leaf in cross-section appearing composed of 2 hollow tubes, linear (± parallel-sided), broadly rounded at tip; flowers bilaterally symmetrical, in a few-flowered raceme (***Lobelia dortmanna***)................................... **CAMPANULACEAE**

28 Leaf not (or rarely) of 2 hollow tubes, tapered and ± acute (or filiform); flowers regular and racemose, or solitary, or in a dense head or spike, or plant producing spores at base 29

    29 Roots with prominent cross-septate appearance (checkered with fine transverse lines); inflorescence a small whitish or gray head (flowering in shallow or rarely deep water and on wet shores)................................... **ERIOCAULACEAE**

    29 Roots not distinctly septate or cross-lined; inflorescence not as above 30

        30 Leaves rather abruptly expanded at base to enclose sporangia, often dark green, composed of 4 hollow tubes (in cross-section), surrounding a hard corm-like stem; plant submersed (unless stranded), non-flowering (***Isoetes***, a fern relative) .... **ISOETACEAE**

        30 Leaves gradually and slightly expanded or grooved on one side at a somewhat sheathing base but not composed of 4 tubes nor enclosing sporangia and no corm-like stem present; plants (except *Subularia*) not flowering when submersed but only on wet shores .. 31

            31 Leaves somewhat flattened at least basally, widest at the base, gradually tapered to sharp apex; plants with buried rhizome (***Juncus pelocarpus***)........ **JUNCACEAE**

            31 Leaves ± terete, scarcely or no wider at base than at middle, of ± uniform width at least to the middle (or even slightly thicker there before tapering to apex); plants with rhizomes or stolons at, near, or above surface of substrate 32

                32 Plants with green stolons strongly arching above substrate; leaves filiform, ± uniform in diameter, ca. 0.5-1 mm thick, truncate at tip (***Ranunculus flammula***)..................... **RANUNCULACEAE**

                32 Plants producing delicate horizontal white to green stolons at or near (above or below) surface of substrate (in addition to stouter short rhizome); leaves ca. 0.7-3 mm thick at middle, whence tapered to apex (***Littorella***) .... **PLANTAGINACEAE**

15 Leaves cauline, simple or compound (basal and dissected in one species) 33

33 Leaves compound, dissected, forked, or deeply lobed................. 34

    34 Leaves apparently in a basal rosette, few (***Sium suave***) .... **APIACEAE**

    34 Leaves definitely cauline: opposite, whorled, or alternate 35

        35 Leaves all or mostly opposite or whorled................... 36

            36 Leaves (or whorled branches) rolled inward at tip when young, bearing tiny stalked bladders; flowers emersed, bilaterally symmetrical, purple or yellow (***Utricularia***)................. **LENTIBULARIACEAE**

            36 Leaves not inrolled at tip, without bladders; flowers various but not as above 37

                37 Leaves once or twice dichotomously forked, the segments usually sparsely toothed along one edge; flowers inconspicuous, axillary, submersed .... **CERATOPHYLLACEAE**

                37 Leaves not dichotomously forked, the segments entire; flowers emersed or (rarely) submersed................... 39

                    38 Leaves pectinate; flowers inconspicuous, in all but the rarest species emersed in terminal spike (***Myriophyllum***).. **HALORAGACEAE**

                    38 Leaves with no definite central axis, much dissected; flowers emersed in a showy yellow head (usually with at least one pair of merely serrate opposite leaves below it) (***Bidens beckii***) .... **ASTERACEAE**

        35 Leaves definitely all alternate 39

39 Leaves with a definite central axis (following midvein); flowers various 40

  40 Leaves pectinate (the lateral segments not again branched); flowers inconspicuous, axillary; fruit a nutlet (**Proserpinaca**) . **HALORAGACEAE**

  40 Leaves with lateral segments further narrowly divided; flowers with white corollas, in emersed raceme; fruit a silique (**Rorippa aquatica**) .... **BRASSICACEAE**

39 Leaves with no definite central axis (except sometimes after initially forking at the stem); flowers emersed, with conspicuous corolla 41

  41 Petiole present (sometimes very short), ± adnate to a stipular sheath; plants without bladders; flowers regular, white or yellow, with numerous separate carpels forming achenes (**Ranunculus**) .... **RANUNCULACEAE**

  41 Petioles and stipular sheaths absent; plants with small stalked bladders on leaves or on separate branches; flowers bilaterally symmetrical, yellow or purplish, with a single pistil producing a capsule (**Utricularia**) .... **LENTIBULARIACEAE**

33 Leaves simple, unlobed, usually entire (toothed in a few species)........ 42

42 Leaves much reduced, ± scale-like, not over 7 mm long, never distinctly opposite or whorled 43

  43 Leaves minute, yellowish, merely widely spaced bumps or scales on stem (**Myriophyllum tenellum**) .... **HALORAGACEAE**

  43 Leaves to 7 mm long, green or brownish, loosely overlapping (page 82) .... *liverworts, aquatic mosses*

42 Leaves much longer or distinctly opposite or whorled (or both conditions) 44

  44 Leaves alternate, with ligule-like stipules (these wholly adnate to leaves in *Ruppia*) 45

    45 Leaf blades ± filiform, terete or at least half as thick as broad, and the stipule adnate to leaf base for 10-30 mm or more, forming a sheath around the stem .... **POTAMOGETONACEAE**

    45 Leaf blades definitely flattened and several times as broad as thick (even if narrow), or stipule little if at all adnate to blade (or both conditions) 46

      46 Blades flattened, ribbon-like (up to 5 or even 7.5 mm wide), with no definite midrib (no central vein more prominent than others except rarely toward base); flowers solitary, rare, cleistogamous in axils of submersed leaves or (these almost never on submersed plants) with 6 bright yellow tepals (**Heteranthera**) .... **PONTEDERIACEAE**

      46 Blades flattened with a definite midrib or filiform; flowers in spherical or cylindrical spikes, neither cleistogamous nor with showy yellow perianth .... **POTAMOGETONACEAE**

  44 Leaves opposite or whorled, without stipules 47

    47 Leaves nearly filiform, not over 0.5 mm wide, very gradually tapered from base to apex but not abruptly expanded basally, perfectly smooth; plants perennial by slender rhizomes; flowers axillary, 1 staminate flower (a single stamen) and (1) 2-several carpels at a node; fruit slightly curved and minutely toothed on convex side (**Zannichellia**)................................ **POTAMOGETONACEAE**

    47 Leaves broader; or if filiform then abruptly expanded basally and with apiculate or toothed margins, the plants annual, and the fruit solitary and ellipsoid 48

    48 Leaves definitely whorled............................ 49

      49 Whorled structures ("branches") cylindrical, elongate, usually stiff with calcium deposits; plants with distinctive musky odor (**Chara**, a macro-algae, see page 82) .... **CHARACEAE**

      49 Whorled structures (true leaves) flattened, short (not over 20 mm long) or elongate and very limp; plants without 50 odor 51

51 Leaves 6-12 (usually 9) in a whorl, not over 2.5 mm wide, ca. 12-25 times as long as wide; flowers bisexual, apetalous, sessile in axils of emersed leaves or bracts (*Hippuris*) .... **PLANTAGINACEAE**

51 Leaves mostly 3-4 (rarely 6) in a whorl, 0.8-5 mm wide, at most 10-13 times as long; flowers bisexual or unisexual, but with petals 52

52 Leaves mostly 3 (rarely 6) in a whorl, very thin (2 cell layers) and delicate; stem round (not angled), smooth; flowers unisexual, with 3 often pink petals, at least the pistillate long-stalked from entirely submersed stem (*Elodea*) .... **HYDROCHARITACEAE**

52 Leaves mostly 4 in a whorl, stiff and firm; stem 4-sided, often with minutely retrorse-scabrous angles; flowers bisexual, with 3-4 white petals (usually not developed on wholly submersed plants) (*Galium*) . **RUBIACEAE**

48 Leaves opposite (in some species, with bushy axillary tufts of leaves which may give a falsely whorled appearance)....... 53

53 Largest leaves at least 1-4 cm long, with distinct petiole and expanded, entire blade 54

54 Leaf blades ± orbicular, with orange to black glandular dots on underside; flowers 5-merous with showy yellow petals and superior ovary (*Lysimachia nummularia*) .... **PRIMULACEAE**

54 Leaf blades ± diamond-shaped, without glandular dots; flowers 4-merous, inconspicuous, with inferior ovary (*Ludwigia palustris*)........................... **ONAGRACEAE**

53 Largest leaves smaller, or sessile, or toothed (or all of these) 55

55 Leaves large, 3-13 cm long, 5-20 mm wide.......... 56

56 Leaves sessile and clasping, limp, at most obscurely and remotely toothed; flowers (rarely present on plants with all foliage submersed) in axillary racemes (*Veronica anagallis-aquatica*).................. **PLANTAGINACEAE**

56 Leaves sessile, clasping, tapered, or petioled, stiff, often regularly crenate or toothed; flowers various; includes submersed plants of normally terrestrial or emergent plants, often members of LAMIACEAE . **(see description at left)**

55 Leaves small (shorter or narrower than the above, or usually both) 57

57 Leaves linear and bidentate at apex when well submersed, often becoming obovate, ± weakly 3-nerved, and not necessarily bidentate toward summit of stem (or in floating rosettes); fruit solitary in axils, somewhat heart-shaped, of two 2-seeded segments (*Callitriche*) .... **PLANTAGINACEAE**

57 Leaves filiform to orbicular or tapered from base to apex, but essentially uniform on a plant and if linear not bidentate at apex; fruit various 58

58 Leaves at least 6 times longer than wide, wider at base than at middle; fruit absent or solitary in axils of leaves and ± ellipsoid (*Najas*) .... **HYDROCHARITACEAE**

58 Leaves less than 3 times as long as wide, often nearly round 59

59 Stems forming moss-like mats but the erect or ascending tips (above rooted nodes) less than 3 cm long; leaves with at most 1 weak nerve; stipules minute but usually evident with some leaves; flowers axillary, inconspicuous .... **ELATINACEAE**

59 Stems greatly elongate (generally 10-30 cm); leaves more evidently veined; stipules none; flowers terminal, yellow (but usually absent

on plants with all leaves submersed) 60
- 60 Stems stiffly erect; leaves weakly pinnately veined (with evident midvein), with reddish to blackish shiny dots (these often also on stem) (*Lysimachia terrestris*) **PRIMULACEAE**
- 60 Stems ± lax; leaves 3-nerved, without dark dots or flecks (though emersed leaves have translucent dots) (*Hypericum boreale*) **HYPERICACEAE**

SEED PLANTS, GROUP 8

Woody plants (trees, shrubs, woody vines, and small evergreen creeping plants such as *Vinca*, *Linnaea*, and *Mitchella*)

---

1 Leaves scalelike (ca. 4 mm or less long and often appressed/imbricate) or needle-like, evergreen (except in *Larix* in Pinaceae) 2
- 2 Plant with leaves scale-like (or less than 3 mm long) 3
  - 3 Leaves alternate (*Hudsonia*) . . . . **CISTACEAE**
  - 3 Leaves opposite or whorled 4
    - 4 Plants fragrant when crushed, producing small dry or berry-like female cones but never flowers or true fruit . . . . **CUPRESSACEAE**
    - 4 Plants not fragrant, parasitic, less than 1.5 cm high, on branches of conifers, blooming in very early spring without showy perianth (*Arceuthobium*) . . . **VISCACEAE**
- 2 Plant with leaves needle-like or narrowly linear (over 3 mm long) 5
  - 5 Leaves opposite or whorled . . . . **CUPRESSACEAE**
  - 5 Leaves alternate or in clusters 6
    - 6 Seed solitary in a red, fleshy, cup-like aril; leaves flattened, with strongly decurrent base, persistent, appearing 2-ranked, all green on both sides (may be yellowish beneath) . . . . **TAXACEAE**
    - 6 Seeds borne on scales of a dry woody cone; leaves flattened or not (but if so, not strongly decurrent, readily falling when dry, not 2-ranked, and/or with white lines beneath) 7
      - 7 Leaves evergreen (except *Larix* with leaves spirally arranged), arranged in clusters, spiraled around the stem, or in flattened 2-ranked sprays; cones slightly to very much longer than wide, the cone scales flattened **PINACEAE**
      - 7 Leaves deciduous, arranged in flattened 2-ranked sprays; cones globular, with peltate cone scales . . . . **CUPRESSACEAE**
1 Leaves with expanded (or dissected) blades, neither scale-like nor needle-like, if linear, then herbaceous, not stiff; deciduous or occasionally evergreen; occasionally absent at flowering time 8
- 8 Leaves opposite or whorled or nearly so (evident from scars if leaves not expanded at anthesis) 9
  - 9 Flowers appearing before leaves are expanded 10
    - 10 Perianth of both calyx and corolla 11
      - 11 Ovary superior; petals separate; flowers often unisexual (*Acer*) . . . . **SAPINDACEAE**
      - 11 Ovary inferior; petals united; flowers bisexual 12
        - 12 Flowers numerous in terminal cymes (*Sambucus*) . . . . **ADOXACEAE**
        - 12 Flowers in pairs on axillary peduncles (*Lonicera*) . . . . **CAPRIFOLIACEAE**
    - 10 Perianth of only one cycle of parts, or none 13
      - 13 Inflorescence an ament (catkin); bud scale 1 (*Salix purpurea*) . . . . **SALICACEAE**
      - 13 Inflorescence otherwise, of clustered or pediceled flowers but not an elongate ament; bud scales more than 1 14
        - 14 Flowers staminate or bisexual 15
          - 15 Stamens 2 (-4) (*Fraxinus*) . . . . **OLEACEAE**
          - 15 Stamens 5 or more 16
            - 16 Calyx lobes 4; stamens 8; buds scurfy-pubescent (*Shepherdia*) **ELAEAGNACEAE**
            - 16 Calyx lobes 5; stamens ca. 5-10; buds not scurfy-pubescent (*Acer*) . . . . **SAPINDACEAE**
        - 14 Flowers pistillate 17
          - 17 Ovary with 2 divergent lobes (*Acer*) . . . . **SAPINDACEAE**
          - 17 Ovary unlobed 18
            - 18 Floral tube with a prominent disk at its summit; buds scurfy-pubescent; young fruit rotund (*Shepherdia*) . . . . **ELAEAGNACEAE**

18 Floral tube without a prominent disk; buds not scurfy; young fruit strongly flattened (*Fraxinus*)........................ **OLEACEAE**

9 Flowers appearing after the leaves have expanded (i.e., leaves present)...... 19

19 Leaves compound.. 20

20 Plant a climbing or trailing vine 21

21 Leaves pinnately compound; corolla well developed, showy, bilaterally symmetrical; flowers bisexual; stamens 4; pistil 1 (*Campsis*) **BIGNONIACEAE**

21 Leaves all or mostly trifoliolate; corolla none (though calyx may be showy and regular); flowers unisexual; stamens and pistils numerous (*Clematis*) .... **RANUNCULACEAE**

20 Plant erect, not a vine 22

22 Petals none; fruit a samara (winged)......................... 23

23 Ovary 2-lobed; fruit united in pairs; stamens ca. 5-10; leaflets usually 3-5 (*Acer negundo*) .... **SAPINDACEAE**

23 Ovary not lobed; fruits not paired; stamens 2 (-4); leaflets 5-11 (*Fraxinus*) .... **OLEACEAE**

22 Petals well developed and conspicuous; fruit various but not a samara 24

24 Petals united; leaves pinnately compound with 5 or more leaflets; fruit fleshy (*Sambucus*).................................. **ADOXACEAE**

24 Petals separate; leaves trifoliolate or palmately or pinnately compound; fruit dryish 25

25 Leaflets 3; flowers in drooping panicles; petals and stamens 5; fruit an inflated, indehiscent, inflated capsule .... **STAPHYLEACEAE**

25 Leaflets mostly 5-7; flowers in erect panicles; petals 4-5, stamens 6-8; fruit a firm, leathery, usually 1-2-seeded capsule (*Aesculus*) .... **SAPINDACEAE**

19 Leaves simple 26

26 Stamens more numerous than the petals or lobes of the corolla (or of the calyx if corolla is absent), or flowers strictly pistillate 27

27 Petals united .... **ERICACEAE**

27 Petals separate or none 28

28 Stamens usually more than 10; corolla yellow or white 29

29 Leaves scale-like; style 1; ± prostrate shrub less than 2 dm tall (*Hudsonia*) .... **CISTACEAE**

29 Leaves well developed; styles 3-5 (sometimes ± coherent); shrubs to 2-3 m tall.................................. 30

30 Flowers yellow; petals usually 5; leaves entire (*Hypericum*) **HYPERICACEAE**

30 Flowers white; petals usually 4 (-5); leaves ± entire (but ciliate) or dentate with irregularly spaced, often inconspicuous teeth (*Philadelphus*)................... **HYDRANGEACEAE**

28 Stamens 10 or fewer, or flowers strictly pistillate; corolla pink, green, greenish-yellow, or white 31

31 Leaves palmately lobed, toothed; fruit a samara, united in pairs (*Acer*) .... **SAPINDACEAE**

31 Leaves unlobed, entire or toothed; fruit a berry or capsule, not paired 32

32 Plant a bushy shrub, with scurfy or stellate pubescence (*Shepherdia*) .... **ELAEAGNACEAE**

32 Plant barely woody at base, glabrous to somewhat tomentose but not scurfy or stellate pubescent; flowers bisexual with showy pink (to white) petals; fruit a capsule 33

33 Leaves evergreen, very shiny, toothed; stigma nearly sessile (*Chimaphila*) .... **ERICACEAE**

33 Leaves deciduous, ± dull, entire; stigma on an elongate style .... **LYTHRACEAE**

26 Stamens the same number as the lobes or petals of the corolla or fewer 34

34 Petals separate 35

35 Flowers in terminal inflorescences .... **CORNACEAE**

35 Flowers axillary 36

36 Fruit a red to purple capsule, the seeds enclosed in a red or orange aril; styles unlobed; stamens alternating with the petals (*Euonymus*) .... **CELASTRACEAE**

36 Fruit a dry inconspicuous capsule or fleshy and indehiscent, the seeds not arillate; styles often lobed; stamens opposite the petals .... **RHAMNACEAE**

34 Petals united 37

37 Ovary inferior 38

38 Flowers and fruits in dense spherical peduncled heads or paired at the ends of trailing branches; leaves entire, with broad stipules between the petiole bases .... **RUBIACEAE**

38 Flowers and fruits pediceled in small clusters or ± branched inflorescences; leaves entire or toothed, with stipules none or slender and partly adnate to petioles..................... 39

39 Leaves of flowering shoots or flowering portions of shoots entire or somewhat undulate or sinuous, not sharply or regularly toothed.................................. **CAPRIFOLIACEAE**

39 Leaves with margins lobed, ± regularly toothed, crenate, or finely crenulate, or at least with regular minute gland-like teeth 40

40 Calyx lobes up to 1.5 mm long and broadly triangular to broadly rounded or virtually absent; corolla rotate (flat with very short tube); style very short or essentially absent; fruit fleshy with one pit (*Viburnum*)......... **ADOXACEAE**

40 Calyx lobes (1.6-) 2-6.5 (-7.5) mm long, linear or narrowly lanceolate; corolla tubular; style elongate, conspicuous; fruit dry 41

41 Corolla yellow, turning orange or even flushed with red; ovary and fruit glabrous (occasionally pubescent) .... **DIERVILLACEAE**

41 Corolla pink (sometimes pale); ovary and fruit densely glandular-bristly or bristly .... **CAPRIFOLIACEAE**

37 Ovary superior 42

42 Corolla bilaterally symmetrical......................... 43

43 Tree with large cordate ± whorled leaves (*Catalpa*)...... **BIGNONIACEAE**

43 Herbs with opposite leaves, scarcely woody at the base (*Hyssopus, Thymus*) .... **LAMIACEAE**

42 Corolla regular 44

44 Ovaries 2 (but styles and stigmas united); plant an evergreen creeper with blue flowers solitary in the leaf axils (*Vinca*) .... **APOCYNACEAE**

44 Ovary 1; plant erect, with flowers in inflorescences .... **OLEACEAE**

8 Leaves alternate 45

45 Leaves deeply dissected into linear-filiform segments, aromatic (*Artemisia*) .. **ASTERACEAE**

45 Leaves simple, compound (then leaflets broader than linear-filiform), or absent at anthesis, aromatic or not 46

46 Plants dioecious 47

47 Plant a climbing vine (or trailing in absence of support for tendrils or twining stem) 48

48 Stems with tendrils 49

49 Leaves entire; stems prickly (at least below); perianth of 6 tepals **SMILACACEAE**

49 Leaves toothed; stems unarmed; perianth of 5 petals and 5 (sometimes vestigial) sepals.............................. **VITACEAE**

48 Stems without tendrils (aerial roots may be present along stem) ... 50

50 Leaves trifoliolate; plants climbing by adventitious roots (*Toxicodendron*) .... **ANACARDIACEAE**

50 Leaves simple or with more than 3 leaflets; plants climbing by twining stems 51

51 Leaves pinnately veined, simple (*Celastrus*).............. **CELASTRACEAE**

51 Leaves palmately veined or compound 52

52 Sepals and petals each 6; leaves ± peltate (petiole attached in from margin of the blade), at most somewhat lobed but not toothed .... **MENISPERMACEAE**

52 Sepals (often vestigial) and petals each 5; leaves with marginal petiole, toothed .... **VITACEAE**

73 Twigs and leaves with milky sap; calyx minute, 4-parted; leaves palmately veined (or fruit in a large spherical fleshy structure) . . . . **MORACEAE**

73 Twigs and leaves with watery sap; calyx usually none or 2-parted; leaves pinnately veined (fruit in aments or small clusters) . . . . **BETULACEAE**

70 Flowers not in aments or heads (often bisexual and/or conspicuous) 74

  74 Perianth none or apparently of a single series of parts 75

    75 Stamens more numerous than the segments or lobes (if any) of the perianth (or perianth none)   76

      76 Stamens 8; perianth lobes 4 (or essentially none) (*Dirca palustris*) . . . . . **THYMELAEACEAE**

      76 Stamens 5-7 or 9; perianth lobes or segments 5 or 6 77

        77 Leaves densely tomentose beneath, margins revolute; perianth segments 5 (*Rhododendron*) . . . . **ERICACEAE**

        77 Leaves slightly if at all pubescent, not revolute; perianth segments 6 **LAURACEAE**

    75 Stamens the same number as the lobes or segments of the perianth 78

      78 Styles 2, 3, or 5   79

        79 Leaves with prominent, straight ± parallel lateral veins running into the principal teeth; flowers bisexual, the perianth shallowly lobed; ovary flattened and winged; fruit a samara . . . . **ULMACEAE**

        79 Leaves with lateral veins curved and ascending, weaker and the branches anastomosing near the margins; flowers usually unisexual, the perianth lobed nearly or quite to the base; ovary not flattened, fruit a drupe (*Celtis*)   . . . . **CANNABACEAE**

      78 Style 1 (may be branched above) 80

        80 Plant a vine, climbing or trailing by tendrils . . . . **VITACEAE**

        80 Plant an erect shrub or tree 81

          81 Inflorescences terminal . . . . **CORNACEAE**

          81 Inflorescences lateral 82

            82 Leaves beneath and branchlets silvery-scurfy; stamens 4 (*Elaeagnus*)   . . . . **ELAEAGNACEAE**

            82 Leaves and branchlets glabrous or nearly so, not scurfy; stamens 4-6   83

              83 Stamens alternating with the sepals . . . . **RHAMNACEAE**

              83 Stamens opposite the sepals . . . . **AQUIFOLIACEAE**

  74 Perianth clearly differentiated into calyx and corolla 84

    84 Ovaries at least 3, distinct   . . . . **ROSACEAE**

    84 Ovary 1 85

      85 Corolla bilaterally symmetrical (or petal only 1); stamens 10 (usually with some of the filaments connate) . . . . **FABACEAE**

      85 Corolla essentially regular; stamens various 86

        86 Petals united   87

          87 Stamens more numerous than the corolla lobes . . . . **ERICACEAE**

          87 Stamens the same number as the corolla lobes 88

            88 Stamens adnate to the corolla (and falling with it if the corolla is deciduous); plants vining to shrubby; fruit a red berry or drupe   89

              89 Flowers white, on short (< 5 mm) pedicels; leaves toothed **AQUIFOLIACEAE**

              89 Flowers purple (except in rare albinos), pedicels > 7 mm; leaves entire-margined (though sometimes lobed) . . . . **SOLANACEAE**

            88 Stamens free from the corolla; plant an erect or trailing shrub (not climbing); fruit various 90

              90 Stigma on a well developed style; fruit a capsule . . . . **ERICACEAE**

              90 Stigma nearly sessile; fruit a red drupe . . . . **AQUIFOLIACEAE**

        86 Petals separate   91

          91 Ovary at least partly inferior 92

            92 Stamens more than the number of petals 93

              93 Style 1   94

                94 Petals united; unarmed shrubs (*Vaccinium*) . . . . **ERICACEAE**

                94 Petals free; thorny tree or large shrub (*Crataegus*) . . . . **ROSACEAE**

              93 Styles 2-5   . . . . **ROSACEAE**

            92 Stamens the same number as the petals 95

              95 Petals 4   96

    96 Flowers white, in terminal cymes, blooming in early to
      mid-summer; fruit fleshy; leaves entire. . . . . **CORNACEAE**

    96 Flowers yellow, in small axillary clusters, blooming in
      late fall; fruit a capsule; leaves with rounded teeth . . . **HAMAMELIDACEAE**

  95 Petals 5 97

    97 Flowers in umbels, umbels either solitary or arranged
      in larger inflorescences . . . . **ARALIACEAE**

    97 Flowers in racemes, small axillary clusters, or domes or
      flat-topped corymbs. 98

      98 Flowers in racemes or small axillary clusters; small
        shrubs less than 2 m tall . . . . **GROSSULARIACEAE**

      98 Flowers in terminal, domed or flat-topped corymbs;
        large shrubs or small trees more than 2 m tall
        (*Crataegus*). . . . . **ROSACEAE**

  91 Ovary entirely superior. 99

    99 Stamens more than twice as many as the petals. 100

      100 Corolla yellow; fruit a capsule . . . . **CISTACEAE**

      100 Corolla white to pink; fruit indehiscent. 101

        101 Inflorescence apparently borne at the middle of
          a tongue-shaped bract; leaves palmately veined
          (*Tilia*). . . . . **MALVACEAE**

        101 Inflorescence borne normally; leaves pinnately
          veined . . . . **ROSACEAE**

    99 Stamens twice as many as the petals or fewer 102

102 Leaves compound 103

  103 Leaves even-pinnate or even-bipinnate; fruit a large woody legume (pod splitting
    on 2 sutures) . . . . **FABACEAE**

  103 Leaves odd-pinnate, trifoliolate, or palmate; fruit a samara, drupe, berry, or 4-5-
    lobed capsule 104

    104 Inflorescences terminal. 105

      105 Fruit a samara, in loose open cymes; leaves trifoliolate, punctate with
        translucent oil glands (*Ptelea*) . . . . **RUTACEAE**

      105 Fruit a glandular-pubescent drupe, in dense panicles; leaves pinnately
        compound, without translucent glands. . . . . **ANACARDIACEAE**

    104 Inflorescences lateral or axillary 106

      106 Leaflets strongly spiny-toothed; flowers yellow (*Berberis*). . . . . **BERBERIDACEAE**

      106 Leaflets without spines; flowers greenish yellow. 107

        107 Leaves palmately compound with mostly 5-7 leaflets, if trifoliolate
          then leaflets sharply toothed or pinnately lobed; plant a vine with
          tendrils; stamens opposite the petals (i.e., alternate with the sepals)
          (*Parthenocissus*) . . . . **VITACEAE**

        107 Leaves trifoliolate or pinnately compound with entire or nearly
          entire leaflets; plant a shrub or vine with adventitious roots (not
          tendrils); stamens alternating with the petals (i.e., opposite the
          sepals) (*Toxicodendron*). . . . . **ANACARDIACEAE**

102 Leaves simple 108

  108 Styles 2, separate to the base; petals 4, yellow, linear. . . . . **HAMAMELIDACEAE**

  108 Style 1 or 3 (may be lobed or cleft at summit); petals various 109

    109 Stems spiny; flowers yellow, 6-merous (*Berberis*) . . . . **BERBERIDACEAE**

    109 Stems unarmed; flowers white, pink, or greenish, 4-5-merous 110

      110 Stamens more numerous than the petals; inflorescence an umbel or raceme;
        plant a low evergreen subshrub. . . . . **ERICACEAE**

      110 Stamens the same number as the petals; inflorescence various; plant a
        bushy shrub, deciduous except in *Rhododendron* 111

        111 Leaves evergreen, densely white- or brown-tomentose beneath, revolute
          (*Rhododendron*) . . . . **ERICACEAE**

        111 Leaves deciduous, glabrous or nearly so, with flat margins 112

          112 Stamens alternating with the sepals (i.e., opposite the petals); style
            3-lobed. . . . . **RHAMNACEAE**

          112 Stamens opposite the sepals (i.e., alternating with the petals); style
            nearly or quite absent . . . . **AQUIFOLIACEAE**

SEED PLANTS, GROUP 9
Herbaceous plants lacking both green color and developed leaves at flowering time

1 Plants not anchored in the ground, solely parasitic on and attached to stems of other plants at maturity 2
  2 Stem up to 15 mm long, with minute opposite leaves (scale-like); flowers in May, unisexual (plants dioecious), the staminate with stamens adnate to calyx lobes, the pistillate with inferior ovary; parasites on conifers (**Arceuthobium**) . . . . **SANTALACEAE**
  2 Stem elongate, with minute alternate leaves; flowers in late summer, bisexual, the stamens partly adnate to corolla and the ovary superior; parasites on flowering plants (**Cuscuta**) . . . . **CONVOLVULACEAE**
1 Plants clearly anchored in the ground, not attached to other above-ground plants . . 3
  3 Stem buried in ground; flowers in late winter or earliest spring, crowded in a spadix with a nearly or partly buried hood-like brownish or mottled spathe (green leaves from rhizome appearing after flowering); stamens 4; plant with skunk-like odor (**Symplocarpus**) . . . . **ARACEAE**
  3 Stem or flower stalk above ground; flowers later, solitary or in a few- to many-flowered raceme, umbel, or head; stamens various; plant with odor, if any, not skunk-like 4
    4 Flowers completely 3-merous and regular, in an umbel on a naked peduncle arising from an underground, onion-smelling bulb . . . . **LILIACEAE**
    4 Flowers not completely 3-merous, regular or bilaterally symmetrical, not in an umbel, on aerial stems 5
      5 Scale-like leaves (and branches if any) opposite; flowers less than 5 mm long 6
        6 Stem thick and fleshy, appearing jointed, the flowers deeply embedded in it (**Salicornia**) . . . . **AMARANTHACEAE**
        6 Stem normal, slender and wiry, the flowers not at all embedded in it . . 7
          7 Sepals and petals each 5, separate; stamens 5-10; styles 3 (**Hypericum gentianoides**) . . . . **HYPERICACEAE**
          7 Sepals and petals each 4 and each series connate basally; stamens 4; style 1 (**Bartonia**) . . . . **GENTIANACEAE**
      5 Scale-like leaves alternate (or apparently none); flowers of various size . . . 8
        8 Inflorescence a single dense, short spike with spirally arranged scales; flowers lacking petals and sepals; stem with tubular sheaths at base (**Eleocharis**) . . . . **CYPERACEAE**
        8 Inflorescence of normal flowers not aggregated into a single dense spike, flowers with at least tiny petals, often showy; stem without tubular sheaths at base (except some Orchidaceae) 9
          9 Petals 5, mostly united in a tube, the flower slightly to distinctly bilaterally symmetrical, not spurred; stamens 4 . . . . **OROBANCHACEAE**
          9 Petals 3-5 but not united in a tubular corolla, the flower regular or strongly bilaterally symmetrical (sometimes spurred); stamens various 10
          10 Perianth strongly bilaterally symmetrical; stamens 1-2 11
            11 Sepals and petals 3, the lower petal a definite lip, the others little modified; ovary inferior; plants of various habitats but not aquatic; perianth of various colors . . . . **ORCHIDACEAE**
            11 Sepals apparently 2 and petals 5, but corolla basically 2-lipped; ovary superior; plants of wet shores, ponds, and bog pools, with perianth yellow or purple (**Utricularia**) . . . . **LENTIBULARIACEAE**
          10 Perianth regular; stamens 4-10 12
            12 Corolla at least 5 mm long; stamens 8-10 . . . . **ERICACEAE**
            12 Corolla less than 5.5 mm long; stamens 4 13
              13 Flowers sessile; plant of wet lake shores, nearly or quite aquatic; stigmas 4, conspicuously exposed (corolla barely 2 mm long); fruit an indehiscent nutlet (**Myriophyllum tenellum**) . . . . **HALORAGACEAE**
              13 Flowers long-pediceled; plant of peaty habitats but not aquatic; stigma inconspicuous (corolla longer); fruit a capsule (**Bartonia**) . . . . **GENTIANACEAE**

SEED PLANTS, GROUP 10
Inflorescence apparently converted to bulblets, tufts of leaves, etc.

1   Leaves with flat, net-veined (or dissected) blades............................ 2
    2   Leaves with narrow, sparsely toothed leaflets or further dissected; stem hollow; bulblets produced in the axils of broad-based acuminate bracts or leaves, not transversely segmented (*Cicuta bulbifera*) .... **APIACEAE**
    2   Leaves simple and entire; stem solid; bulblets otherwise (*Lysimachia terrestris*) .. **PRIMULACEAE**
1   Leaves terete or slender and parallel-veined 3
    3   Bulblets in a ± spherical head or umbel; plants with odor of onion or garlic (*Allium*) **LILIACEAE**
    3   Bulblets not in a distinct umbel or spherical head; plants without strong odor... 4
       4   Leaves terete, septate (with hard cross-partitions, easily seen on dry specimens or felt by gently pinching a leaf and drawing it between the fingers) (*Juncus*) . **JUNCACEAE**
       4   Leaves flat, neither terete nor septate.................................. 5
          5   Stem ± triangular and solid (*Scirpus*) .... **CYPERACEAE**
          5   Stem terete, with hollow internodes .... **POACEAE**

SEED PLANTS, GROUP 11
Monocots; leaves with parallel veins

1   Plant a climbing or twining vine, in most species with tendrils; flowers unisexual; leaves net-veined.. 2
    2   Inflorescence an umbel; plants with tendrils; ovary superior; fruit a berry ...... **LILIACEAE**
    2   Inflorescence spicate to paniculate; plant without tendrils; ovary inferior; fruit a capsule .... **DIOSCOREACEAE**
1   Plant not a vine and without tendrils; flowers bisexual or unisexual; leaves parallel-or net-veined... 3
    3   Inflorescence a spadix, subtended by a spathe which may be broad and hood-like or elongate; leaves in some species compound or net-veined 4
       4   Leaves narrow, sword-like, with ± parallel sides; spathe appearing like a continuation of the leaf-like peduncle (the spadix thus apparently lateral).... **ACORACEAE**
       4   Leaves expanded; spathe clearly differentiated from peduncle............. **ARACEAE**
    3   Inflorescence not a spadix (if flowers in a head, this with neither an elongate fleshy axis nor a conspicuous subtending spathe); leaves simple, rarely net-veined (in *Smilax ecirrata, Trillium,* and some *Alismataceae*) 5
       5   Perianth much reduced: absent, or composed solely of bristles (these small and stiff or elongate and cottony), or of chaffy or scale-like parts, never conspicuously petaloid.. 6
          6   Individual flowers subtended by 1 or 2 scales; leaves ± elongate, grass-like, usually with a sheath at the base surrounding the stem; fruit a 1-seeded grain or nutlet (achene)   7
             7   Each fertile flower subtended by a single scale (others may be at base of spikelet); sheaths of leaves closed (margins connate); stems frequently triangular (but 4-several-angled or terete in many species), usually solid; leaves usually 3-ranked (especially in a species with terete hollow stem); stamens with filament attached to end of anther; fruit a definitely 2- or 3-sided (rarely nearly terete) nutlet .... **CYPERACEAE**
             7   Each flower subtended by 2 scales (almost opposite each other, one rarely absent); sheaths often open; stems ± terete (sometimes flattened), never triangular; leaves not clearly 3-ranked (basically 2-ranked); stamens with filament attached near middle of anther (or apparently so because of sagittate anthers); fruit usually a grain neither flattened (2-sided) nor triangular   .... **POACEAE**
          6   Individual flowers subtended by no scales or only by bristles, or with a regular perianth of chaffy scales (or tepals); leaves and fruit various...... 8
             8   Inflorescence a single, very compact, almost spherical head (terminating an erect scape), less than 12 mm across......................... 9
                9   Surface of head (tips of receptacular bracts) white-woolly; flowers chaffy, not concealed by involucral bracts; roots with abundant conspicuous transverse markings........................ **ERIOCAULACEAE**

    9 Surface of head (bracts) glabrous; flowers yellow or largely concealed
by bracts; roots without transverse markings . . . . **XYRIDACEAE**

  8 Inflorescence not a single terminal head and/or exceeding 12 mm. 10

    10 Inflorescence composed of separate staminate and pistillate portions,
the former consisting of conspicuous stamens, sooner or later
withering, leaving only the pistillate portion conspicuous . . . . **TYPHACEAE**

    10 Inflorescence composed of bisexual flowers, without conspicuously
separate staminate and pistillate portions 11

      11 Flowers in a branched or umbellate inflorescence, solitary or,
more often, clustered into small heads of 2 or more; fruit a 3- to
many-seeded capsule . . . . **JUNCACEAE**

      11 Flowers in a single elongate spike or zigzag raceme; fruit
indehiscent or a 1-2-seeded follicle. 12

        12 Spike (truly a spadix) apparently lateral; fruit of each flower
indehiscent . . . . **ACORACEAE**

        12 Spike or raceme terminal; fruit of each flower consisting of 3
or 6 1-2-seeded follicles 13

          13 Pedicels bractless; carpels 3 or 6, erect and ± adherent to
a central axis at maturity; leaves all basal or nearly so,
without a terminal pore . . . . **JUNCAGINACEAE**

          13 Pedicels bracted; carpels 3, widely divergent in fruit; leaves
mostly cauline, each with a terminal pore . . . . **SCHEUCHZERIACEAE**

5 Perianth at least in part of ± conspicuous white or colored petals 14

14 Flowers bilaterally symmetrical 15

    15 Ovary inferior; fertile stamens 1 or 2, united with the pistil; flowers not
blue (almost any other color) . . . . **ORCHIDACEAE**

    15 Ovary superior; fertile stamens 3 or 6, free; flowers blue (except albinos),
at least in part 16

      16 Sepals colored like the petals; stamens 6, all fertile; flowers in a dense
elongate inflorescence (***Pontederia***) . . . . **PONTEDERIACEAE**

      16 Sepals greenish, unlike the petals; stamens 6, 3 with imperfect
anthers; flowers few (***Commelina***). . . . . **COMMELINACEAE**

14 Flowers regular (radially symmetrical). 17

    17 Sepals and petals of quite different color and/or texture, the former
green or brownish 18

      18 Leaves in a single whorl of 3 on the stem . . . . **LILIACEAE**

      18 Leaves all basal or, if cauline, not in a single whorl of 3. 19

        19 Petals yellow; flowers in a single compact head less than 12 mm
across . . . . **XYRIDACEAE**

        19 Petals blue, purple, white, or pink; flowers in a more open or
larger inflorescence 20

          20 Pistils several in each flower, each developing into an achene;
stamens 6-many; flowers unisexual or bisexual; petals white
or pinkish; leaves often broadly elliptic or sagittate, usually ±
net-veined, all basal . . . . **ALISMATACEAE**

          20 Pistil 1 in each flower, developing into a capsule; stamens 6;
flowers bisexual; petals blue, purple, or deep pink (except in
occasional albinos); leaves elongate, clearly parallel-veined,
basal and cauline (***Tradescantia***) . . . . **COMMELINACEAE**

    17 Sepals and petals both colored and petaloid, usually similar in shape
(tepals) or the sepals (in Iris) of different size and shape. 21

      21 Ovary inferior (flowers bisexual). 22

        22 Stamens 3; leaves equitant . . . . **IRIDACEAE**

        22 Stamens 6; leaves not equitant 23

          23 Ovary only half-inferior, part of it adnate to the perianth,
glabrous (at most granular-roughened) (***Aletris, Anticlea***) . . . . **LILIACEAE**

          23 Ovary clearly inferior 24

            24 Foliage and ovary hairy (***Hypoxis***) . . . . **HYPOXIDACEAE**

            24 Foliage and ovary glabrous . . . . **LILIACEAE**

      21 Ovary superior (or flowers unisexual). 25

        25 Pistils 6, united only at the very base, ripening into follicles;
stamens 9; flowers pink, in an umbel terminating a long scape . **BUTOMACEAE**

25 Pistil 1, sometimes the carpels slightly separate near the summit;
stamens 3-6; flowers and inflorescence various. 26

  26 Stamens 3; tepals 6, yellow; plants creeping on wet shores
(*Heteranthera*) . . . . **PONTEDERIACEAE**

  26 Stamens and tepals 4 or 6, the latter yellow or not; plants
erect, of various habitats 27

    27 Flowers or inflorescences lateral, arising from the axils of
alternate cauline leaves or scales 28

      28 Leaves scale-like, mostly brownish or yellowish, those
on the much-branched upper portion of the plant
subtending short green filiform branches (often
mistaken for leaves) . . . . **LILIACEAE**

      28 Leaves broad, flat, green (scale-like leaves or bracts may
be present in addition to normal leaves). 29

        29 Leaves net-veined with long or short (but distinct)
petioles; flowers unisexual, in umbels of several to
many . . . . **SMILACACEAE**

        29 Leaves parallel-veined, sessile, clasping, or perfoliate
at base; flowers bisexual, 1-5 at a node . . . . **LILIACEAE**

    27 Flowers or inflorescences terminal on scapes or leafy
(simple or branched) stems. . . . . **LILIACEAE**

SEED PLANTS, GROUP 12

Flowers in an involucrate head (i.e., the flowers clustered in a head above a whorl of bracts)

1 Flowers on a thick fleshy axis (inflorescence a spadix) subtended by a single large
overtopping or enveloping bract (spathe); perianth none or of 4 tepals 2

  2 Leaves narrow, sword-like, with ± parallel sides; spathe appearing like a
continuation of the leaf-like peduncle (the spadix thus apparently lateral) . . . . . . **ACORACEAE**

  2 Leaves expanded; spathe clearly differentiated from peduncle and terminal. . . . . **ARACEAE**

1 Flowers not in a spadix overtopped by a spathe; perianth various. 3

  3 Leaves parallel-veined, all basal, and less than 5 mm broad 4

    4 Flowers yellow, mostly concealed by bracts; roots without transverse markings;
surface of head (bracts) glabrous   **XYRIDACEAE**

    4 Flowers chaffy, not concealed by involucral bracts; roots with abundant
conspicuous transverse markings; surface of head white-woolly (tips of
receptacular bracts)   . . . . **ERIOCAULACEAE**

  3 Leaves net-veined or if parallel-veined then cauline and more than 5 mm broad . 5

    5 Ovary inferior. 6

      6 Leaves opposite (very rarely whorled), toothed or pinnatifid; corolla 4-
lobed, lilac-purple (sometimes pale); stamens 4, separate . . . . **DIPSACACEAE**

      6 Leaves and corolla not combined as above, e.g., leaves alternate and/or
entire or corolla 5-lobed and/or not lilac-purple. 7

        7 Margins of cauline leaves and inflorescence bracts with stiff spines;
corolla of separate petals; calyx present (no pappus); stamens separate
(*Eryngium*) . . . . **APIACEAE**

        7 Margins of cauline leaves and bracts various (spiny in a few species);
corolla of united petals; calyx none (but a pappus of scales, awns, or
bristles often present); stamens almost always fused in a ring around the
style . . . . **ASTERACEAE**

    5 Ovary superior 8

      8 Leaves alternate, compound; involucral bract 3-foliolate; flowers strongly
bilaterally symmetrical, papilionaceous (as in other legumes) (*Trifolium*) . . **FABACEAE**

      8 Leaves opposite, simple; flowers often nearly or quite regular 9

        9 Plant with minty odor; ovary deeply 4-lobed, with 1 style; petals united **LAMIACEAE**

        9 Plant without minty odor; ovary not lobed, with 2 styles; petals separate
(*Petrorhagia, Dianthus*)   . . . . **CARYOPHYLLACEAE**

SEED PLANTS, GROUP 13
Herbaceous plants with single-sex flowers

---

1 Leaves compound 2
  2 Leaves palmately compound (or 3-foliolate). 3
    3 Flowers in umbels 4
      4 Leaves cauline, in a single whorl (***Panax***). . . . . **ARALIACEAE**
      4 Leaves alternate and basal (***Sanicula***) . . . . **APIACEAE**
    3 Flowers in spikes or panicles 5
      5 Margins of leaflets entire; flowers at the base of a prolonged fleshy spadix subtended by a single large bract (spathe) (***Arisaema***). . . . . **ARACEAE**
      5 Margins of leaflets toothed; flowers on normal herbaceous (but not fleshy) pedicels or axes. 6
        6 Leaves all opposite; plant a vine; perianth showy (***Clematis***) . . . . **RANUNCULACEAE**
        6 Leaves alternate on upper part of stem; plant erect; perianth minute and inconspicuous (***Cannabis***) . . . . **CANNABACEAE**
  2 Leaves pinnately compound or more than once compound 7
    7 Flowers in panicles (***Thalictrum***) . . . . **RANUNCULACEAE**
    7 Flowers in tight ovoid heads or umbels 8
      8 Leaves once pinnately compound; flowers in tight heads; perianth 4-merous (***Sanguisorba***). . . . . **ROSACEAE**
      8 Leaves 2-3 times compound; flowers pediceled, in umbels; perianth 5-merous (***Aralia***) . . . . **ARALIACEAE**
1 Leaves simple 9
  9 Plant with leaves all basal 10
    10 Flowers in dense spikes (or 1-3 at base in *Littorella*) . . . . **PLANTAGINACEAE**
    10 Flowers pediceled in panicles (***Rumex***) . . . . **POLYGONACEAE**
  9 Plant with leaves all or mostly cauline 11
    11 Leaves peltate or pubescent with forked/stellate hairs . . . . **EUPHORBIACEAE**
    11 Leaves neither peltate nor with forked/stellate hairs 12
      12 Leaves opposite or whorled 13
        13 Flowers solitary in axils of leaves; perianth none; stamen 1 . . . . **PLANTAGINACEAE**
        13 Flowers in axillary or terminal inflorescences 14
          14 Leaves hastate, otherwise unlobed but entire to coarsely or irregularly toothed; pistillate flowers and fruit mostly concealed by a pair of bracts with margins ± united at base (***Atriplex***) . . . . **AMARANTHACEAE**
          14 Leaves not hastate, in some species deeply lobed, in some closely toothed; pistillate flowers without 2 basal bracts 15
            15 Inflorescence terminal; corolla white or colored 16
              16 Stem leaves deeply pinnately lobed; style 1; stamens 3-4 (***Valeriana***) . . . . **CAPRIFOLIACEAE**
              16 Stem leaves unlobed; styles 3-7; stamens 10 (***Silene***). . . . . **CARYOPHYLLACEAE**
            15 Inflorescence axillary; corolla none or of reduced scales. 17
              17 Leaves entire; inflorescence (spike) shorter than the peduncle (***Plantago***) . . . . **PLANTAGINACEAE**
              17 Leaves toothed; inflorescence longer than the peduncle. . . . 18
                18 Plant a vine; leaves deeply 3-7-lobed (***Humulus***) . . . . **CANNABACEAE**
                18 Plant erect, not a vine; leaves unlobed . . . . **URTICACEAE**
      12 Leaves alternate (at least at upper nodes) 19
        19 Evergreen subshrubs with leathery leaves (***Pachysandra,*** cultivated and reported to occasionally escape) . . . . **BUXACEAE**
        19 Herbaceous plants with thin, non-persistent leaves 20
          20 Flowers with 6 petaloid tepals and 6 stamens or 3 carpels (dioecious); inflorescences on long peduncles from the nodes (not terminal); leaves with several prominent longitudinal veins (including midrib). 21
            21 Plant a vine with twining stems (no tendrils); inflorescence a spike, raceme, or panicle; ovary inferior, ripening into a winged capsule . . . . **DIOSCOREACEAE**
            21 Plant erect or a vine with tendrils; inflorescence an umbel; ovary superior, ripening into a berry . . . . **SMILACACEAE**

20 Flowers either with other numbers of tepals, stamens, and carpels or the inflorescence terminal (on main stem or branches); leaves various but without several prominent long veins 22
    22 Perianth with both calyx and corolla (sometimes very inconspicuous); plants climbing or trailing, with tendrils . . . . . . **CUCURBITACEAE**
    22 Perianth absent or of 1 series of parts (tepals); plants erect or prostrate, without tendrils 23
        23 Flowers very small, in axillary clusters [plants monoecious; look for pistillate flowers for keying] 24
            24 Style 1; stamens 4 or 5 25
                25 Flowers in long-peduncled, loose, spreading branched axillary clusters or, if smaller and fewer-flowered, then clusters sessile and leaves entire; mostly widespread species . . . . **URTICACEAE**
                25 Flowers in short-peduncled, dense, ± spherical clusters in the axils of the crenate-dentate leaves; uncommon introduced species (*Fatoua*) . . . . **MORACEAE**
            24 Styles (or sessile stigmas) 2–3; stamens various 26
                26 Styles 3, branched; bracts in inflorescence well developed and at least 5–10-lobed (*Acalypha*) . . . . **EUPHORBIACEAE**
                26 Styles 2–3, unbranched; bracts in inflorescence unlobed (may be toothed) (*Amaranthus, Atriplex*) . . . . **AMARANTHACEAE**
        23 Flowers small or not, in chiefly terminal inflorescences (spikes, panicles, or racemes on main stem and/or branches) 27
            27 Flowers consistently 3-merous (tepals 6, stamens 6, carpels 3); stipules united into a sheath (ocrea) surrounding the stem above each node (*Rumex*) . . . . **POLYGONACEAE**
            27 Flowers not consistently 3-merous (tepals 5 or fewer, stamens usually 5, styles often 2); stipules none . . . . **AMARANTHACEAE**

SEED PLANTS, GROUP 14

Herbaceous dicots with bisexual flowers, perianth in 1 series, ovary inferior

1 Stamens more numerous than the 1–4 perianth lobes or parts 2
    2 Perianth with 1–3 (rarely 4) lobes; stamens 6 or 12 . . . . **ARISTOLOCHIACEAE**
    2 Perianth 4-parted; stamens 8 or numerous 3
        3 Leaves pinnately compound; stamens numerous (*Poterium*) . . . . **ROSACEAE**
        3 Leaves simple; stamens normally 8 (*Chrysosplenium*) . . . . **SAXIFRAGACEAE**
1 Stamens the same number as or fewer than the perianth lobes or parts, or perianth 5-merous (or both conditions)   4
    4 Leaves all or mostly opposite or whorled 5
        5 Inflorescence a dense terminal cluster of flowers (sessile or nearly so) 6
            6 Leaves apparently whorled; bracts below the inflorescence large and white (*Cornus canadensis*)   **CORNACEAE**
            6 Leaves clearly opposite; bracts below the inflorescence greenish or inconspicuous 7
                7 Heads subtended by several involucral bracts below a receptacle with sessile flowers . . . . **DIPSACACEAE**
                7 Heads not subtended by a distinct involucre, with visible branching structure; flowers sessile but not on a common receptacle (*Valeriana, Valerianella*) . . . . **CAPRIFOLIACEAE**
        5 Inflorescence of solitary, axillary, or clearly pediceled flowers 8
            8 Leaves compound, in a single whorl (*Panax*) . . . . **ARALIACEAE**
            8 Leaves simple or deeply lobed, opposite or in several whorls (rarely the lower alternate in *Valeriana*)   9
                9 Leaves in whorls (*Galium*)   . . . . **RUBIACEAE**
                9 Leaves opposite 10
                    10 Plant low and densely matted, with linear leaves; perianth 5-merous (*Scleranthus*)   . . . . **CARYOPHYLLACEAE**

10 Plant prostrate or erect, but with broader leaves; perianth 5- or 4-merous 11

  11 Flowers in rather dense terminal inflorescences (at ends of stem and branches); stamens 3 (occasionally 4) (*Valeriana, Valerianella*) **CAPRIFOLIACEAE**

  11 Flowers 1-few in axils or solitary at ends of branches; stamens various 12

    12 Styles 2; flowers solitary at ends of branches; plant flowering in May (*Chrysosplenium*) .... **SAXIFRAGACEAE**

    12 Style 1; flowers sessile, axillary; plant flowering in summer (*Ludwigia palustris*) .... **ONAGRACEAE**

4 Leaves alternate or basal 13

  13 Leaves entire, simple and unlobed; flowers in cymes or few-flowered cymules; style 1 .... **SANTALACEAE**

  13 Leaves (at least the cauline ones) toothed or crenulate, often deeply lobed or compound; flowers in umbels, axillary, or ovoid to cylindric heads; styles 2, 3, or 5 (1 in *Sanguisorba*) 14

    14 Tepals and stamens each 5 15

      15 Styles 5; fruit fleshy, berry-like (*Aralia*) .... **ARALIACEAE**

      15 Styles 2; fruit dry, splitting into 2 achene-like indehiscent parts (mericarps)................................ 16

        16 Leaves simple, with crenate margins (*Hydrocotyle*) .... **ARALIACEAE**

        16 Leaves, at least the cauline, compound, dissected, or deeply lobed **APIACEAE**

    14 Tepals and stamens each 3 or 4 17

      17 Stamens and tepals 3 (*Proserpinaca*) .... **HALORAGACEAE**

      17 Stamens and tepals 4 18

        18 Leaves with conspicuous stipules, pinnately compound and strongly toothed (*Sanguisorba minor*) .... **ROSACEAE**

        18 Leaves without stipules .... *GO TO COUPLET 11*

SEED PLANTS, GROUP 15

Herbaceous dicots with bisexual flowers, perianth in 1 series, superior ovary

---

1 Ovaries more than 1 in each flower, the carpels separate at least above the middle of the ovaries 2

  2 Stipules conspicuous; leaves pinnately compound (*Sanguisorba minor*) .... **ROSACEAE**

  2 Stipules none or leaves simple 3

    3 Ovaries united for most of lower half; leaves simple, unlobed (*Penthorum*) .. **PENTHORACEAE**

    3 Ovaries distinct; leaves of most species lobed or compound .... **RANUNCULACEAE**

1 Ovary 1 in each flower (bearing 1 or more styles), the carpels united at least below the styles 4

  4 Leaves bipinnately compound, fruit a legume .... **FABACEAE**

  4 Leaves simple or compound (but not bipinnate); fruit not a legume......... 5

    5 Plants with a solitary large (ca 3-5 cm wide) white flower between a single usually opposite or subopposite pair of long-petioled cauline eccentrically peltate and deeply lobed leaves (*Podophyllum*)...................... **BERBERIDACEAE**

    5 Plants with more flowers per stem or, if only one, then leaves not as above 6

      6 Stamens more than twice as many as the perianth lobes or parts 7

        7 Leaves tubular, open at apex and hence pitcher-like .... **SARRACENIACEAE**

        7 Leaves flat, of normal structure, simple or compound but not hollow 8

          8 Perianth small and inconspicuous (stamens more showy); leaves compound with definite flat broad leaflets .... **RANUNCULACEAE**

          8 Perianth well developed, showy; leaves simple or dissected into very narrowly linear segments........................... 9

            9 Leaf blades entire, unlobed except for deeply cordate base; plants aquatic (*Nuphar*)............................. **NYMPHAEACEAE**

            9 Leaf blades deeply lobed or dissected; plants terrestrial .... **PAPAVERACEAE**

      6 Stamens only twice as many as the perianth lobes or parts, or fewer .. 10

        10 Style 1 or none (stigmas may be 2 or more) 11

          11 Stamens more numerous than the perianth divisions 12

    12 Flowers bilaterally symmetrical; perianth colorful (white, yellow, or pink) .... **PAPAVERACEAE**

    12 Flowers regular; perianth dull, greenish 13

        13 Leaves opposite; flowers mostly axillary (*Ammannia*) **LYTHRACEAE**

        13 Leaves alternate or basal; flowers mostly terminal ...... **BRASSICACEAE**

  11 Stamens the same number as or fewer than the perianth lobes or parts   14

    14 Leaves alternate or basal............................ 15

        15 Perianth parts (and stamens) 6, 8, or 9............... **BERBERIDACEAE**

        15 Perianth parts (and usually stamens) 4............... 16

            16 Leaves simple, entire (*Parietaria*) .... **URTICACEAE**

            16 Leaves pinnately compound with toothed leaflets (*Sanguisorba minor*) .... **ROSACEAE**

    14 Leaves opposite 17

        17 Flowers solitary or few in axils of leaves, sessile or nearly so   .... **LYTHRACEAE**

        17 Flowers in terminal inflorescences (on stems and branches). 18

            18 Perianth showy, pink to purple; inflorescences each subtended by a conspicuous petaloid or papery 5-lobed involucre which enlarges as fruit matures .... **NYCTAGINACEAE**

            18 Perianth reduced, inconspicuous, whitish or scarious; inflorescences subtended at most by very small bracts (*Froelichia*) .... **AMARANTHACEAE**

  10 Styles 2 or more   19

    19 Flowers embedded in a succulent segmented stem; leaves reduced to tiny opposite scales (*Salicornia*)................. **AMARANTHACEAE**

    19 Flowers not embedded in a succulent stem; leaves not scalelike 20

        20 Leaves opposite or whorled......................... 21

            21 Margins of leaves crenate; stamens normally 8 (*Chrysosplenium*) .... **SAXIFRAGACEAE**

            21 Margins of leaves entire; stamens various, but usually not numbering 8 22

            22 Leaves opposite .... **CARYOPHYLLACEAE**

            22 Leaves whorled .... **MOLLUGINACEAE**

    20 Leaves alternate 23

        23 Plant with a ± membranous stipular sheath (ocrea) surrounding the stem above each node .... **POLYGONACEAE**

        23 Plant lacking stipules of any kind .... **AMARANTHACEAE**

SEED PLANTS, GROUP 16

Herbaceous dicots with bisexual flowers, perianth of 2 series, ovaries 2 or more in each flower

1 Style and/or stigmas united (i.e., 1 in each flower, but style may be branched)...... 2

  2 Ovaries 2; corolla regular, of united petals; stamens 5; sap in most species milky **APOCYNACEAE**

  2 Ovaries 4 or more; corolla regular or bilaterally symmetrical, of united or separate petals; stamens 2, 4, 5, or numerous; sap not milky 3

    3 Petals separate; ovaries apparently 5 or more; stamens numerous, their filaments connate, at least for much of their length, into a tube around the style; leaves palmately veined (may be deeply lobed) .... **MALVACEAE**

    3 Petals united; ovaries apparently 4; stamens 2, 4, or 5, their filaments not connate (but ± adnate to corolla); leaves mostly pinnately veined 4

      4 Leaves alternate (except at lower nodes in the rare *Plagiobothrys*); stamens 5; corolla regular (bilaterally symmetrical only in the very bristly *Echium*); stems not angled (rarely winged) and foliage not aromatic .... **BORAGINACEAE**

      4 Leaves opposite; stamens 2 or 4; corolla bilaterally symmetrical or in a few genera essentially regular; stems usually 4-angled ("square") and foliage often aromatic when bruised (minty or citrus-like) .... **LAMIACEAE**

1 Style and stigmas separate (1 on each ovary, or scarcely developed) 5

  5 Perianth bilaterally symmetrical   6

    6 Leaves deeply cleft; stamens numerous; perianth with spurs; fruit a follicle (3 per flower) (***Aconitum, Delphinium***) . . . . **RANUNCULACEAE**

    6 Leaves shallowly lobed; stamens 5; perianth without spurs; fruit a capsule (***Heuchera***) . . . . **SAXIFRAGACEAE**

 5 Perianth regular 7

    7 Sepals (or sepal-like bracts) 3   8

       8 Plant aquatic, with peltate (often floating) round or shield-shaped alternate floating leaf blades or palmately dissected opposite submersed leaves. . . . **CABOMBACEAE**

       8 Plant terrestrial, with leaves neither peltate nor palmately dissected 9

          9 Petals and usually carpels 3; stamens 3 or 6; leaves cauline, deeply and narrowly pinnate-lobed   . . . . **LIMNANTHACEAE**

          9 Petals 5 or more, carpels and stamens numerous; leaves basal, with 3 (-7) broad lobes (***Hepatica***) . . . . **RANUNCULACEAE**

    7 Sepals 4 or more. 10

     10 Leaves peltate, the blades round, often floating, and mostly more than 15 cm broad; flowers mostly over 10 cm broad, with carpels embedded in a top-shaped receptacle   . . . . **NELUMBONACEAE**

     10 Leaves not peltate, the blades (of leaflets, if leaves compound) neither round nor as broad as 15 cm; flowers smaller and carpels not embedded in receptacle 11

       11 Sepals separate to the base; stamens and petals individually falling from the receptacle after anthesis. . . . . **RANUNCULACEAE**

       11 Sepals, petals, and stamens united to form a saucer- or cup-like floral tube ("hypanthium") at the margin of which the stamens and petals are borne. 12

         12 Carpels as many as, or more than, the petals. 13

           13 Leaves succulent, simple, entire, estipulate . . . . **CRASSULACEAE**

           13 Leaves not succulent, deeply lobed or compound, toothed, stipulate   . . . . **ROSACEAE**

         12 Carpels fewer than the petals 14

           14 Leaves simple, at most shallowly lobed. . . . . **SAXIFRAGACEAE**

           14 Leaves clearly compound. . . . . **ROSACEAE**

SEED PLANTS, GROUP 17

Herbaceous dicots with bisexual flowers, perianth of 2 series, ovary inferior

1 Stamens twice as many as the petals (or nearly so). 2

  2 Style 1 (sometimes very short)   3

    3 Petals spreading; herbaceous plants; fruit a capsule or dry and indehiscent . . **ONAGRACEAE**

    3 Petals strongly reflexed; creeping evergreen wetland subshrubs; fruit a berry (***Vaccinium oxycoccos*** and *V. macrocarpon*). . . . . **ERICACEAE**

  2 Styles 2 or more. 4

    4 Sepals 2; leaves succulent; styles 3 . . . . **PORTULACACEAE**

    4 Sepals (4-) 5; leaves not succulent; styles 2 . . . . **SAXIFRAGACEAE**

1 Stamens the same number as the petals or corolla lobes, or fewer 5

  5 Petals united 6

    6 Cauline leaves alternate   7

       7 Corolla bilaterally symmetrical (***Lobelia***) . . . . **CAMPANULACEAE**

       7 Corolla regular   . . . . **CAMPANULACEAE**

    6 Cauline leaves opposite or whorled (rarely the lower alternate in *Valeriana* with pinnate leaves) 8

       8 Leaves whorled. . . . . **RUBIACEAE**

       8 Leaves opposite 9

         9 Stipules present (connate around the stem). . . . . **RUBIACEAE**

         9 Stipules absent. 10

          10 Flowers sessile in terminal heads 11

            11 Heads subtended by several involucral bracts below a receptacle with sessile flowers . . . . **DIPSACACEAE**

            11 Heads not subtended by a distinct involucre, with visible branching structure; flowers sessile but not on a common receptacle (***Valeriana, Valerianella***) . . . . **CAPRIFOLIACEAE**

   10 Flowers visibly pediceled (even if crowded) or axillary 12
     12 Flowers numerous, in rather dense terminal inflorescences (at
       ends of stem and branches) (*Valeriana, Valerianella*) . . . . **CAPRIFOLIACEAE**
     12 Flowers axillary or on paired pedicels on a peduncle 13
       13 Leaves strictly entire, stems erect (*Triosteum*) . . . . **CAPRIFOLIACEAE**
       13 Leaves shallowly toothed on apical half; stems trailing; flowers
         on paired pedicels on a peduncle (*Linnaea*) . . . . **CAPRIFOLIACEAE**
 5 Petals separate 14
  14 Stamens and petals each 2 (*Circaea*) . . . . **ONAGRACEAE**
  14 Stamens (fertile) and petals each 4 or 5 (stamens sometimes alternating with
   staminodia, which may have gland-tipped divisions) 15
   15 Petals 4 16
    16 Principal leaves apparently whorled; flowers in a dense head like
     terminal cluster subtended by 4 large white bracts (*Cornus canadensis*) **CORNACEAE**
    16 Principal leaves alternate; flowers neither in a head-like terminal cluster
     nor subtended by 4 large white bracts (*Ludwigia*) . . . . **ONAGRACEAE**
   15 Petals 5 17
    17 Leaves simple; styles 2 or stigmas 4 and sessile; inflorescence various . 18
     18 Flowers in panicles, in cymes, or solitary . . . . **SAXIFRAGACEAE**
     18 Flowers in umbels . . . . **APIACEAE**
    17 Leaves compound; inflorescence an umbel 19
     19 Styles 5; fruit berry-like (*Aralia*) . . . . **ARALIACEAE**
     19 Styles 2–3; fruit various 20
      20 Leaves alternate or basal; fruit dry, splitting into 2 achene-like
       indehiscent parts (mericarps). . . . . **APIACEAE**
      20 Leaves in a single whorl; fruit berry-like (*Panax*) . . . . **ARALIACEAE**

SEED PLANTS, GROUP 18

Herbaceous dicots with bisexual flowers, perianth of 2 series, ovary 1 and superior, stamens more numerous than the petals

---

1 Corolla bilaterally symmetrical 2
 2 Sepals all or partly petal-like in appearance or prolonged into a spur 3
  3 Spur none; stamens 6, 7, or 8; leaves entire . . . . **POLYGALACEAE**
  3 Spur present on one of the sepals 4
   4 Leaves merely crenate or toothed; stamens 5 . . . . **BALSAMINACEAE**
   4 Leaves palmately cleft; stamens numerous (*Consolida*) . . . . **RANUNCULACEAE**
 2 Sepals not petal-like in form or appearance, usually green 5
  5 Sepals 2, separate, usually deciduous early in anthesis; leaves dissected or twice-
   compound . . . . **PAPAVERACEAE**
  5 Sepals 4 or more, usually ± connate 6
   6 Lower 2 petals forming a laterally compressed "keel" that encloses the
    stamens; leaves once-compound (simple only in *Crotalaria*) . . . . **FABACEAE**
   6 Lower petals not forming a keel nor enclosing the stamens 7
    7 Flowers completely 5-merous (sepals and petals 5, stamens 5 or usually
     10); pistil long-beaked; corolla pink or purple; leaves deeply lobed or
     cleft or compound (the main stem leaves opposite and toothed or cleft) **GERANIACEAE**
    7 Flowers with at least the carpels fewer than 5; corolla and leaves various 8
     8 Leaves simple, deeply lobed to entire 9
      9 Styles 3 (or more); upper petal larger than the others . . . . **RESEDACEAE**
      9 Style 1; upper petal(s) no larger than the others 10
       10 Sepals and petals each 4; stamens 6 . . . . **BRASSICACEAE**
       10 Sepals and petals each (4) 5–7; stamens 2x as many . . . . **LYTHRACEAE**
     8 Leaves compound 11
      11 Flowers small, in dense terminal spikes, with 5 anthers, one large
       and 4 smaller petals arising from a column of stamens (*Dalea*) . . . **FABACEAE**
      11 Flowers not in dense spikes and not so modified 12
       12 Petals and sepals each 4; fruit a capsule (*Polanisia*) . . . . **CLEOMACEAE**
       12 Petals and sepals each 5; fruit a legume . . . . **FABACEAE**
1 Corolla regular (radially symmetrical) 13

13 Leaves tubular, open at apex and hence pitcher-like; style greatly expanded, large and umbrella-shaped . . . . **SARRACENIACEAE**

13 Leaves flat or at most succulent, of usual shapes; style not unusually expanded. . 14

  14 Plants with a solitary large (ca 3-5 cm wide) white flower between a single, usually opposite, long-petioled pair of deeply lobed leaves (*Podophyllum*). . . . **BERBERIDACEAE**

  14 Plants with more flowers per stem or, if only one, then leaves not as above . . 15

    15 Sepals 2 16

      16 Leaves lobed, compound, or coarsely toothed, not succulent; sap in most species colored (yellow to orange) . . . . **PAPAVERACEAE**

      16 Leaves unlobed, entire, succulent; sap watery . . . . **PORTULACACEAE**

    15 Sepals 3 or more 17

      17 Stamens more than 2x as many as the petals. 18

        18 Leaves compound 19

          19 Plant clammy-pubescent; leaves palmately compound with 3 entire leaflets (*Polanisia*) . . . . **CAPPARACEAE**

          19 Plant glabrous or with a little non-glandular pubescence; leaves twice-compound with numerous sharply toothed leaflets . . . . . **RANUNCULACEAE**

        18 Leaves simple 20

          20 Plant truly aquatic, with all leaves basal, the petioles all arising from a rhizome buried under water (except when stranded). . . . 21

            21 Leaves rounded at tip with deep sinus at base . . . . **NYMPHAEACEAE**

            21 Leaves peltate 22

              22 Leaves circular, large (1 dm or more in diameter); flowers yellow . . . . **NELUMBONACEAE**

              22 Leaves elliptic, less than 1 dm in their longest dimension, flowers reddish . . . . **CABOMBACEAE**

          20 Plant terrestrial, with at least some leaves on the stem 23

            23 Style 1 (or none, with 3 sessile stigmas). . . . . **CISTACEAE**

            23 Styles 2 or more, evident 24

              24 Leaves opposite, with translucent dots; petals yellow (*Hypericum*) . . . . **HYPERICACEAE**

              24 Leaves alternate, without translucent dots; petals of various colors. . . . . **MALVACEAE**

      17 Stamens twice as many as the petals or fewer. 25

        25 Stamens fewer than twice as many as the petals 26

          26 Styles 2-5; leaves opposite or whorled, simple and entire. 27

            27 Petals yellow (*Hypericum*). . . . . **HYPERICACEAE**

            27 Petals white, pink, or red 28

              28 Stamens 9, in 3 distinct groups of 3 each, with 3 conspicuous glands alternating with the groups (*Triadenum*) **HYPERICACEAE**

              28 Stamens various but neither 9 nor in groups . . . . **CARYOPHYLLACEAE**

          26 Style 1 or none; leaves usually alternate, simple or compound, entire or toothed 29

            29 Sepals 5 (of which the 2 outer ones may be much reduced); petals 3, minute (shorter than the calyx), reddish (*Lechea*). . . **CISTACEAE**

            29 Sepals and petals each 4; petals usually ± showy, colors various 30

              30 Leaves palmately compound, with entire leaflets; stamens 6 or more, but not with 2 distinctly shorter; pedicels subtended by bracts (*Cleome*). . . . . **CAPPARACEAE**

              30 Leaves simple or if palmately compound the leaflets coarsely toothed; stamens 6, of which 2 are distinctly shorter; pedicels usually bractless . . . . **BRASSICACEAE**

        25 Stamens exactly twice as many as the petals 31

          31 Petals 3 32

            32 Leaves alternate, compound or deeply pinnately lobed (*Floerkea*) . . . . **LIMNANTHACEAE**

            32 Leaves in a single whorl, simple and unlobed (*Trillium*) . . . . . **TRILLIACEAE**

          31 Petals 4 or more 33

            33 Sepals and petals each 6 or more (*Lythrum*). . . . . **LYTHRACEAE**

            33 Sepals and petals each 4 or 5 34

34 Leaves compound or deeply divided nearly to base of blade . 35
   35 Leaves opposite. 36
      36 Leaves uniformly trifoliolate . . . . **OXALIDACEAE**
      36 Leaves pinnate, or variously palmately compound or
      lobed 37
         37 Petals yellow; leaves pinnately compound; plant
         prostrate and hairy. . . . . **ZYGOPHYLLACEAE**
         37 Petals pink to purple or red; leaves palmately
         compound or lobed; plant ± erect, hairy or not
         (*Geranium*). . . . . **GERANIACEAE**
   35 Leaves alternate. 38
      38 Styles 5; leaves with 3 obcordate leaflets . . . . **OXALIDACEAE**
      38 Style 1; leaves various, but if 3-foliolate, the leaflets not
      obcordate. 39
         39 Leaves palmately compound (*Cleome*). . . . . **CAPPARACEAE**
         39 Leaves pinnately compound . . . . **FABACEAE**
34 Leaves simple and entire, toothed, or shallowly lobed. 40
   40 Style 1   41
      41 Floral tube ("hypanthium") present, with petals and
      sepals borne at its margin; petals white to (usually) pink-
      purple   42
         42 Anthers opening by terminal pores, very showy
         (curved, yellow, appearing set at 90° on the filament)
         and stamens becoming skewed toward one side of
         the flower. . . . . **MELASTOMATACEAE**
         42 Anthers opening by longitudinal slits, not especially
         showy; stamens not skewed . . . . **LYTHRACEAE**
      41 Floral tube none, all parts arising directly from the
      receptacle; petal color various 43
         43 Sepals of 2 sizes, the 2 outer ones very much
         narrower and often shorter than the 3 inner ones
         (appearing as mere appendages on them); petals
         yellow . . . . **CISTACEAE**
         43 Sepals all of nearly the same size and shape; petals
         white, greenish, or pink. . . . . **ERICACEAE**
   40 Styles 2 or more. 44
      44 Ovary lobed, with a style on each lobe. 45
         45 Leaves not succulent, all or mostly basal, (cauline
         leaves, if any, few and small or a single pair); lobes
         of ovary 2 . . . . **SAXIFRAGACEAE**
         45 Leaves succulent, all or mostly cauline; lobes of
         ovary 4 or 5 . . . . **CRASSULACEAE**
      44 Ovary unlobed, the styles all arising together 46
         46 Petals yellow; leaves with translucent dots
         (*Hypericum*). . . . . **HYPERICACEAE**
         46 Petals white to pink or red (never yellow); leaves
         without translucent dots . . . . **CARYOPHYLLACEAE**

SEED PLANTS, GROUP 19

Herbaceous dicots with bisexual flowers, perianth of 2 series, ovary 1 and superior, stamens the same number as the petals or fewer, and petals separate

1 Leaves compound or dissected 2
  2 Flowers solitary on leafless peduncles arising from the ground 3
    3 Corolla bilaterally symmetrical, spurred; petals 5 .... **VIOLACEAE**
    3 Corolla regular, without spur; petals mostly 8 (*Jeffersonia*) .... **BERBERIDACEAE**
  2 Flowers on leafy stems 4
    4 Leaves dissected or 2-3-times compound; inflorescence open, peduncled ... 5
      5 Petals and stamens each 6; leaves 2-3-times compound, with flat, broad
        leaflets (*Caulophyllum*) .... **BERBERIDACEAE**
      5 Petals and stamens each 5; leaves dissected .... **GERANIACEAE**
    4 Leaves pinnately compound; flowers in a dense terminal spike (*Dalea*) ...... **FABACEAE**
1 Leaves entire or toothed to deeply lobed 6
  6 Leaves opposite or whorled 7
    7 Sepals 2 or 3; petals 2-6.. 8
      8 Plant aquatic or stranded on wet shores; sepals and petals each 2 or 3.... **ELATINACEAE**
      8 Plant terrestrial; sepals 2; petals 5 or 6 9
        9 Stem leaves 2; flowers pedunculate .... **MONTIACEAE**
        9 Stem leaves numerous; flowers essentially sessile.................. **PORTULACACEAE**
    7 Sepals and petals each 4-6 (or more)................................ 10
    10 Leaves deeply palmately lobed.................................... **GERANIACEAE**
    10 Leaves entire or merely toothed 11
      11 Style 1, sometimes very short or the stigma ± sessile 12
        12 Floral tube or disk well developed, with sepals and petals borne at
        its margin .... **LYTHRACEAE**
        12 Floral tube or disk none.................................... **PRIMULACEAE**
      11 Styles 2-5 13
        13 Flowers completely 5-merous, including 5 styles; stamens with
        filaments connate at the base around the ovary; ovary 5- (or 10-)
        locular .... **LINACEAE**
        13 Flowers with styles usually fewer than 5 (and petals sometimes 4);
        stamens not connate; ovary with 1 locule 14
          14 Petals yellow; leaves with translucent dots (*Hypericum*) .... **HYPERICACEAE**
          14 Petals white to pink or red; leaves without translucent dots **CARYOPHYLLACEAE**
  6 Leaves alternate or basal 15
    15 Leaves shallowly to deeply palmately lobed........................... 16
      16 Corolla bilaterally symmetrical, spurred; style 1..................... **VIOLACEAE**
      16 Corolla regular or nearly so, not spurred; styles 2 (*Heuchera*) .... **SAXIFRAGACEAE**
    15 Leaves unlobed or pinnately lobed 17
      17 Styles 2 or more 18
        18 Leaves essentially all basal; flowers white .... **DROSERACEAE**
        18 Leaves cauline; flowers yellow .... **LINACEAE**
      17 Style 1 or none 19
        19 Floral tube well developed and prolonged, with sepals and petals borne
        at its margin... **LYTHRACEAE**
        19 Floral tube none or very little developed.......................... 20
        20 Corolla bilaterally symmetrical, saccate or spurred at the base..... **VIOLACEAE**
        20 Corolla regular, without a spur 21
          21 Petals and sepals each 4................................. **BRASSICACEAE**
          21 Petals and sepals each 5................................. 22
            22 Leaves pinnately lobed or dissected (*Erodium*) .... **GERANIACEAE**
            22 Leaves entire or merely toothed 23
              23 Flowers solitary, terminal; styles essentially none (stigmas
              4, nearly sessile); stamens alternating with cleft, gland-
              tipped staminodia (*Parnassia*)..................... **CELASTRACEAE**
              23 Flowers in a terminal umbel or raceme; style present;
              staminodia none 24
                24 Principal leaves all basal; inflorescence a stalked umbel **PRIMULACEAE**
                24 Principal leaves all or partly cauline; inflorescence a
                terminal raceme (*Lysimachia*).................... **PRIMULACEAE**

SEED PLANTS, GROUP 20

Herbaceous dicots with bisexual flowers, perianth of 2 series, ovary 1 and superior, corolla regular and stamens the same number as its lobes, and petals united

1 Leaves all basal 2
  2 Leaves covered with conspicuous stalked glands......................... **DROSERACEAE**
  2 Leaves without stalked glands... 3
    3 Perianth 4-merous; flowers in spikes or heads; corolla scarious .... **PLANTAGINACEAE**
    3 Perianth 5-merous; flowers in umbels; corolla petaloid................... **PRIMULACEAE**
1 Leaves all or mostly cauline 4
  4 Ovary deeply 4-lobed, appearing like 4 separate ovaries [and also keyed as such] but with one style arising deep in the midst of the lobes 5
    5 Leaves opposite; stamens 2 or 4; stems 4-angled ("square") and foliage aromatic (minty or citrus-like) .... **LAMIACEAE**
    5 Leaves alternate (except at lower nodes in the adventive *Plagiobothrys*); stamens 5; stem not angled (rarely winged) and foliage not aromatic .... **BORAGINACEAE**
  4 Ovary not conspicuously lobed (may be slightly 4- or 2-lobed or notched at apex, where style arises)... 6
    6 Leaves opposite (or whorled), at least below the inflorescence 7
      7 Flowers in dense heads or short spikes; corolla 4-lobed................ 8
        8 Corolla scarious; leaves linear, entire (***Plantago***) .... **PLANTAGINACEAE**
        8 Corolla petaloid; leaves lance-elliptic, toothed (***Phyla***) .... **VERBENACEAE**
      7 Flowers in crowded or more open racemes or other inflorescences; corolla lobes 4-7 9
        9 Stamens opposite the corolla lobes (i.e., each stamen arising and oriented above the middle of a lobe) and readily visible .... **PRIMULACEAE**
        9 Stamens alternating with the corolla lobes (sometimes hidden in a corolla tube or closed corolla) 10
          10 Lobes of corolla 4 .... **GENTIANACEAE**
          10 Lobes of corolla 5 11
            11 Stigmas 3; ovary with 3 locules .... **POLEMONIACEAE**
            11 Stigma 1 (may be 2-lobed); ovary with 2 (or 4 or 5) locules 12
              12 Leaves glabrous; ovary 1-locular; fruit a 2-valved capsule.... **GENTIANACEAE**
              12 Leaves strongly clammy-pubescent; ovary 2-locular; fruit a berry or a 2-valved capsule (***Leucophysalis***, in part) .... **SOLANACEAE**
      6 Leaves alternate, at least below the inflorescence 13
        13 Blades of leaves deeply lobed, dissected, or compound................ 14
          14 Plant a twining or trailing vine 15
            15 Corolla deeply funnel-shaped (or even trumpet-shaped) .... **CONVOLVULACEAE**
            15 Corolla ± flat (rotate) (***Solanum***) .... **SOLANACEAE**
          14 Plant, whether erect or prostrate, not a vine....................... 16
            16 Anthers forming a cone around the pistil...................... **SOLANACEAE**
            16 Anthers clearly separate 17
              17 Leaves 3-foliolate .... **MENYANTHACEAE**
              17 Leaves otherwise lobed, compound, or dissected 18
                18 Leaves pinnately compound or pinnately dissected into entire filiform lobes; ovary 3-locular; stigmas or style branches 3; capsule 3-valved .... **POLEMONIACEAE**
                18 Leaves not compound: pinnatifid or bipinnatifid, the segments not both entire and filiform; ovary 1-locular; stigmas or style branches 2; capsule 2-valved .... **BORAGINACEAE**
        13 Blades of leaves entire, toothed, or at most shallowly lobed (or merely cordate)... 19
          19 Leaves reduced to small scales; flowers 4-merous (***Bartonia***) .... **GENTIANACEAE**
          19 Leaves developed; flowers mostly 5-merous...................... 20
            20 Flowers or inflorescences axillary........................... 21
              21 Fruit a 4-seeded capsule; corolla large, funnel-shaped; stigmas clearly 2, separate (except in *Ipomoea*, where at most 2-3-lobed) **CONVOLVULACEAE**
              21 Fruit a many-seeded berry or capsule; corolla large and funnel-shaped (*Datura*) or ± flat (rotate) or bell-shaped; stigma 1 ...... **SOLANACEAE**
            20 Flowers or inflorescences terminal........................... 22

  22 Flowers solitary; corolla over 7 cm long (*Datura*). . . . . **SOLANACEAE**
  22 Flowers in clusters; corolla smaller. 23
    23 Inflorescence branched (panicle or cyme). 24
      24 Leaves linear to narrowly lanceolate, less than 8 cm long
        (*Collomia*) . . . . **POLEMONIACEAE**
      24 Leaves broad and at least 10 cm long (*Nicotiana*). . . . . **SOLANACEAE**
    23 Inflorescence simple (spike, raceme, or umbel) 25
      25 Anthers separate, at least some of them on hairy filaments;
        fruit a capsule (*Verbascum*) . . . . **SCROPHULARIACEAE**
      25 Anthers forming a cone around the pistil, on glabrous
        filaments; fruit a berry (*Solanum*). . . . . **SOLANACEAE**

SEED PLANTS, GROUP 21

Herbaceous dicots with bisexual flowers, perianth of 2 series, ovary 1 and superior, corolla either bilaterally symmetrical or stamens fewer than its lobes, or both and petals united

---

1 Fertile (anther-bearing) stamens 5 2
 2 Ovary deeply 4-lobed; plant strongly bristly-hairy; fruit (1-) 4 nutlets (*Echium*). . . **BORAGINACEAE**
 2 Ovary not lobed; plants glabrous or with dense clammy pubescence; fruit a capsule
 (*Verbascum*). . . . . **SCROPHULARIACEAE**
1 Fertile stamens 2 or 4 3
 3 Corolla with a spur or sac at the base. 4
  4 Calyx 2-parted (*Utricularia*) . . . . **LENTIBULARIACEAE**
  4 Calyx 5-parted 5
   5 Leaves all basal, glandular-sticky above; flowers solitary on scapes
   (*Pinguicula*) . . . . **LENTIBULARIACEAE**
   5 Leaves all or mostly cauline and not sticky (glandular in *Chaenorrhinum*);
   flowers not solitary. . . . . **PLANTAGINACEAE**
 3 Corolla not prolonged into a spur or sac at the base 6
  6 Stem leaves all alternate. 7
   7 Corolla nearly regular, the lobes equaling or exceeding the tube (*Veronica*) **PLANTAGINACEAE**
   7 Corolla bilaterally symmetrical, ± 2-lipped, the lobes (not lips) distinctly
   shorter than the tube 8
    8 Bracts of inflorescence contrasting with the leaves, cream, yellow, or red
    at least apically (*Castilleja*) . . . . **OROBANCHACEAE**
    8 Bracts of inflorescence the same color as the leaves, green or purplish-
    green 9
     9 Cauline leaves deeply pinnately lobed (*Pedicularis*) . . . . **OROBANCHACEAE**
     9 Cauline leaves unlobed (at most shallowly toothed) . . . . **PLANTAGINACEAE**
  6 Stem leaves all or mostly opposite or whorled. 10
   10 Ovary deeply 4-lobed, appearing like 4 separate ovaries around the base of
   the single style [and also keyed as such], the fruit (1-) 4 nutlets; plants usually
   with a 4-angled ("square") stem and often a minty or citrus-like aroma when
   bruised. . . . . **LAMIACEAE**
   10 Ovary not 4-lobed (at most, somewhat 2-lobed), the fruit a capsule; stem in
   only a few species 4-angled or with aroma when bruised 11
    11 Fertile stamens 2 12
     12 Flowers in axillary racemes or spikes . . . . **SCROPHULARIACEAE**
     12 Flowers in terminal racemes or spikes, or solitary or paired in the
     axils of the leaves 13
      13 Corolla almost regular, with a 4-5-lobed limb. . . . . **PLANTAGINACEAE**
      13 Corolla clearly two lipped 14
       14 Pedicels minutely glandular-pubescent, with a pair of sepal-
       like bractlets at their summit, subtending the calyx; capsules
       ovoid or spherical (*Gratiola*). . . . . **PLANTAGINACEAE**
       14 Pedicels smooth and glabrous, without bractlets; leaves not
       gland-dotted; corolla whitish to purple; capsule distinctly
       ellipsoid . . . . **LINDERNIACEAE**
    11 Fertile stamens 4 15
     15 Corolla nearly regular, the lobes about equal. 16

16 Corolla salverform (trumpet-shaped, with a slender tube of almost uniform diameter) (**Verbena**) . . . . **VERBENACEAE**

16 Corolla funnel-shaped or bell-shaped, with a tube broad toward its summit   17

  17 Calyx lobes 4, or short and relatively broad and 0-4; or corolla yellow   18

    18 Corolla pink to purple (white in albinos); calyx and other parts glabrous (at most scabrous) or with hairs of distinctly different lengths (**Agalinis**) . . . . **OROBANCHACEAE**

    18 Corolla bright yellow; calyx tube, pedicels, and/or stems with hairs of uniform or mixed lengths (not of 2 distinct lengths and only rarely completely glabrous) 19

      19 Capsule (like the calyx tube, pedicels, and stem) ± densely pubescent with short uniform eglandular hairs (**Aureolaria**) . . . . **OROBANCHACEAE**

      19 Capsule glabrous; calyx tube, pedicels, and/or stems with viscid or minute gland-tipped hairs (**Mimulus**) . . . **PHRYMACEAE**

  17 Calyx lobes 5, lanceolate to bristle-like, longer than the calyx tube; corolla pink to purple (**Ruellia**, unverified report for Minnesota)   . . . . **ACANTHACEAE**

15 Corolla strongly bilaterally symmetrical 20

  20 Mature flowers and fruit strongly reflexed, nearly sessile and in remote pairs on opposite sides of a spike-like terminal raceme; calyx with 3 upper teeth bristle-like and 2 lower teeth broadly triangular (**Phryma**) . . . . **PHRYMACEAE**

  20 Mature flowers and fruit not strongly reflexed, and otherwise not as above (long-pediceled, alternate, and/or crowded); calyx with teeth equal or subequal (never bristle-like). 21

    21 Upper lip of corolla apparently absent (the corolla split lengthwise above) or much shorter than the lower lip and (except in *Phyla*) 4-lobed 22

      22 Flowers in dense short spikes or heads on long axillary peduncles (**Phyla**). . . . . **VERBENACEAE**

      22 Flowers not in dense heads or spikes . . . . **LAMIACEAE**

    21 Upper lip of corolla well developed, of 2 lobes (or these ± fused into one), often nearly or quite as long as the lower lip   23

      23 Inflorescence terminal and branched (± paniculate); stamens 4 fertile plus 1 staminodium 24

        24 Leaves below the inflorescence distinctly petioled; corolla brownish, less than 12 mm long; staminodium broad (ca. 1-2 mm) and flat at the free apex (mostly adnate to the upper lip), glabrous (**Scrophularia**) . . . **SCROPHULARIACEAE**

        24 Leaves below the inflorescence sessile; corolla white to purple-violet, ca. 15-30 (-45) mm long; staminodium slender, elongate (of similar diameter and length as the style), close to lower lip of corolla, bearded at the apex (**Penstemon**) . . . . **PLANTAGINACEAE**

      23 Inflorescence a spike or raceme (no branched stalks), or flowers all axillary; stamens 4 fertile, in most genera with no staminodium (or only a very rudimentary one) 25

        25 Leaves (especially middle and lower ones) deeply pinnately toothed or lobed ca. one-third or more the distance to the midrib 26

          26 Flowers (and fruit) less than 6 mm long (**Leucospora**) . . . . **PLANTAGINACEAE**

          26 Flowers (and usually fruit) over 10 mm long . . . **OROBANCHACEAE**

        25 Leaves of main stem toothed or entire but not so deeply pinnately toothed or lobed (uppermost leaves or bracts may have small basal lobes). 27

27 Sepals separate nearly or quite to the base; flowers in a compact terminal inflorescence (**Chelone**)   . . . . **PLANTAGINACEAE**

27 Sepals (at least at anthesis) fused ca. 1/3 or more the length of the calyx; flowers
   solitary in the leaf axils or in a loose terminal inflorescence. 28
   28 Flowers (all or many of them, especially lower ones) in the axils of alternate bracts
      in a distinct terminal or racemose inflorescence . . . . **OROBANCHACEAE**
   28 Flowers all solitary in the axils of opposite (or whorled) leaves or bracts 29
      29 Lobes less than 1/3 the total length of the calyx, or corolla bright yellow (or
         both conditions) (*Mimulus*) . . . . **PHRYMACEAE**
      29 Lobes ca. 1/2 or more the total length of the calyx; corolla blue, purple, white,
         or cream (rarely yellow). . . . . **OROBANCHACEAE**

PARTS OF A FERN

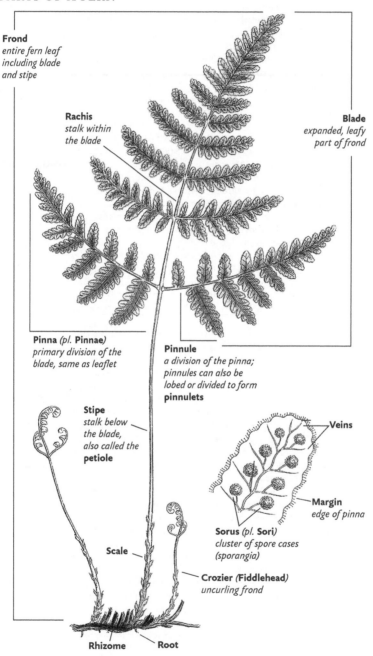

Frond
*entire fern leaf
including blade
and stipe*

Rachis
*stalk within
the blade*

Blade
*expanded, leafy
part of frond*

Pinna (pl. Pinnae)
*primary division of the
blade, same as leaflet*

Pinnule
*a division of the pinna;
pinnules can also be
lobed or divided to form*
pinnulets

Stipe
*stalk below
the blade,
also called the*
petiole

Veins

Margin
edge of pinna

Sorus (pl. Sori)
*cluster of spore cases
(sporangia)*

Scale

Crozier (Fiddlehead)
uncurling frond

Rhizome   **Root**

FERNS & FERN RELATIVES

Aspleniaceae SPLEENWORT FAMILY

ASPLENIUM *Spleenwort*

Mostly small ferns, with short rootstocks covered by old petiole-bases, and a tuft of small to medium-sized leaves ("fronds"); the blades firm, simple, pinnate, or 2-pinnate, and often evergreen. Veins free or forking. Sori (clusters of spore containers) elongate, occurring along the veinlets. Indusium (covering over sori) usually membranous, attached lengthwise along one side of the sorus. Species usually of rock crevices and where shaded and mossy.

1 Blades simple. . . . . *A. rhizophyllum*
1 Blades once-pinnate 2
    2 Leaves of two types, the fertile long and upright, the sterile shorter and spreading, pinnae with conspicuous basal lobes overlapping rachis . . . . *A. platyneuron*
    2 Leaves all alike; pinnae bases not overlapping rachis . . . . *A. trichomanes*

Asplenium platyneuron (L.) B.S.P.
MAP 1
EBONY-SPLEENWORT
native

Tufted fern with 2 types of leaves; the **fertile leaves** stiff and upright, 20-40 cm long and 2.5-4 cm wide, gradually tapered to the base; **pinnae** linear-oblong or basal pinnae triangular, widely separated; **rachis** satiny chestnut purple; **sterile leaves** shorter and widely spreading; **sori** linear-oblong and on the veins. —Crevices of shady sandstone cliffs, in moss or in shallow soil over rocks, also in partial shade in open woods. *The stiff, upright fertile blades are distinctive.*

Asplenium rhizophyllum L.
MAP 2
WALKING FERN
native
    Camptosorus rhizophyllus (L.) Link

Tufted fern with fronds 5-30 cm long or longer, clustered at the end of an erect or ascending scaly rhizome. **Leaves** evergreen, entire, 1-3 cm wide at the cordate or auriculate base, usually tapering to a long caudate tip; veins reticulate; **sori** elongate, scattered along the veins; **indusium** attached on one side of the sorus. —Shaded rocks, usually of limestone, less commonly on sandstone or rarely quartzite. *The tips of the arching blades often root to form new plants, hence the name walking fern.*

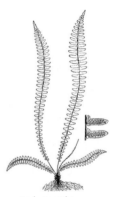

Asplenium platyneuron

Asplenium trichomanes L.
MAP 3
MAIDENHAIR-SPLEENWORT
native

Fern with **leaves** 6-20 cm long or longer, forming a dense tuft from a compact rhizome. **Petiole** and **rachis** purple brown; old rachises persistent; **blades** linear, pinnate; **pinnae** usually opposite or subopposite, oval, rounded to cuneate at the inequilateral base and slightly toothed on the sides and at the blunt apex; **sori** linear, situated on the veins between the midrib and the margin.—Crevices on sandstone, limestone or quartzite, where moist or dry.

Asplenium rhizophyllum

Asplenium trichomanes

1. Asplenium platyneuron   *2. Asplenium rhizophyllum*   *3. Asplenium trichomanes*

Athyriaceae LADY FERN FAMILY

Medium to large ferns. *Deparia* and *Diplazium*, formerly considered as part of *Athyrium*, are now treated as separate species. The degree of blade division helps separate our 3 species (see key), and in contrast to *Deparia*, *Athyrium* has a more deeply grooved rachis, which is continuous from rachis to costa (vs. discontinuous in *Deparia*).

1 Pinnae margins finely toothed, but otherwise undivided . . . . *Diplazium pycnocarpon*
1 Pinnae deeply lobed or divided, margins sometimes finely toothed 2
    2 Blades 2-pinnate (the pinnae again divided), the pinnules also sometimes deeply lobed . *Athyrium filix-femina*
    2 Blades with deeply lobed pinnae (1-pinnate-pinnatifid) . . . . *Deparia acrostichoides*

ATHYRIUM *Lady Fern*

Athyrium filix-femina L.   MAP 4
LADY FERN   *native*
   Athyrium angustum (Willd.) K. Presl

Clumped fern, rhizomes short and ascending. **Leaves** deciduous, sterile and fertile leaves similar; **petioles** with brown, linear scales; **blades** elliptic, 2-pinnate, broadest at middle or slightly below middle; pinnae short-stalked or stalkless; **sori** generally somewhat curved to hook-shaped, less often straight; **indusia** elongate, laterally attached.—Common; moist deciduous woods, streambanks, wetland margins, shaded rock outcrops.

Athyrium filix-femina

DEPARIA *Silvery Glade Fern*

Deparia acrostichoides (Swartz) M. Kato   MAP 5
SILVERY GLADE FERN; SILVERY SPLEENWORT   *native*
   Athyrium thelypterioides (Michx.) Desv.

Large fern from creeping rhizomes. **Leaves** deciduous, 50-100 cm long, sterile and fertile leaves alike; petioles straw-colored (but dark red-brown at base), with brown lance-shaped scales; **blades** lance-shaped to oblong in outline, tapered at tip and distinctly narrowed toward base; deeply lobed, the segments blunt to somewhat tapered at their tip, margins entire to slightly lobed. **Sori** crowded, elongate, straight or sometimes curved, the **indusia** silvery and shiny when young.—Moist, rich deciduous or mixed woods, especially in swales, ravines, depressions; streambanks.

Deparia acrostichoides

DIPLAZIUM *Glade Fern*

Diplazium pycnocarpon (Spreng.) Broun   MAP 6
GLADE FERN   ❧*threatened* | *native*
   Athyrium pycnocarpon (Spreng.) Tidestrom

Tufted ferns with **leaves** to 80 cm long or longer, forming a crown at the end of a stout rhizome. **Sterile blades** lance-shaped, to 15 cm wide, pinnate; **pinnae** long-tapered to a tip, rounded to truncate at the base; **fertile pinnae** lance-linear. **Sori** linear, located on the veins in rows between the midrib and the margin; **indusium** opening along one side.—Rich moist woods and ravines. *The sterile blades of glade fern somewhat resemble those of* **Christmas fern** *(Polystichum acrostichoides), but are deciduous rather than evergreen; both species are rare in Minnesota.*

4. *Athyrium filix-femina*   5. *Deparia acrostichoides*   6. *Diplazium pycnocarpon*   *Diplazium pycnocarpon*

Cystopteridaceae BLADDER FERN FAMILY

Small to medium ferns; 2 genera in Minnesota: *Cystopteris* and *Gymnocarpium*.

1 Blades ternate (divided into 3 more or less equal parts); indusium absent . . . . ***Gymnocarpium***
1 Blades 1-pinnate; indusium present . . . . ***Cystopteris***

CYSTOPTERIS *Bladder fern*

Delicate, medium-sized ferns, with 2-3-pinnate blades arising from short creeping rhizomes. Veins free. Indusium hood-shaped, thin, withering, attached at one side and arching over the rounded sori.

HYBRIDS

Cystopteris* × *illinoensis R.C. Moran (Illinois bladder fern), sterile hybrid between *C. bulbifera* and *C. tenuis*; reported from Rice County.

1 Blades elliptic to lance-shaped, typically widest at or slightly below middle of blade; rachis and pinnule midribs without glandular hairs 2
  2 Stems covered with yellow hairs; leaves clustered 1-4 cm below protruding apex of stem . . . . ***C. protrusa***
  2 Stems without hairs; leaves clustered at apex of stem 3
    3 Pinnae usually at acute angle to rachis and often curving toward apex of blade; pinnae margins rounded-toothed . . . . ***C. tenuis***
    3 Pinnae usually perpendicular to rachis and not curving toward apex of blade; pinnae margins sharp-toothed . . . . ***C. fragilis***
1 Blades elliptic to triangle-shaped, usually widest at base; rachis and pinnule midribs sparsely to densely covered with glandular hairs 4
  4 Rachis often with bulblets, rachis and midribs usually densely glandular-hairy; blades narrowly to broadly triangle-shaped, apex of blade long-tapered . . . . ***C. bulbifera***
  4 Rachis occasionally with bulblets, rachis and midribs usually only sparsely glandular-hairy; blades narrowly triangle-shaped to ovate lance-shaped, apex of blade short-tapered 5
    5 Blades ovate to lance-shaped, widest above base . . . . ***C. laurentiana***
    5 Blades triangle-shaped, widest at or near base . . . . ***C. tennesseensis***

Cystopteris bulbifera (L.) Bernh.   MAP 7

BULBLET FERN; BLADDER FERN   *native*

Clumped fern, **rhizomes** short and thick. **Leaves** deciduous, 30-100 cm long, sterile and fertile leaves similar but sterile blades usually shorter than fertile; **petioles** much shorter than blades; **blades** lance-shaped, 6-15 cm wide at base, long tapered to tip, with 20-30 pairs of pinnae; the veins ending in a notch (sinus). **Sori** round, on a small vein; **indusia** hoodlike and attached at its base, covered with scattered, short-stalked glands. Green **bulblets**, 4-5 mm wide, are produced on lower side of rachis (main stem of leaf) toward upper end of blade, these falling and forming new plants.—Rocky streambanks, ravines, seepy slopes, cedar swamps, and moist, shaded, often calcium-rich rocks and cliffs. *Distinguished from Cystopteris fragilis, a common fern of moist woods, by the blade broadest at base, most veins ending in a notch, and the small bulblets on underside of rachis. In fragile fern, blade broadest above its base, most veins end in a tooth, and bulblets are absent.*

Cystopteris bulbifera
pinna (l), sorus, (c), bulblet (r)

Cystopteris fragilis (L.) Bernh.   MAP 8

BRITTLE BLADDER FERN   *native*

Fern with **leaves** 10-35 cm long or longer, tufted from short creeping rhizomes. **Blades** lance-shaped, 3-8 cm wide or wider near the base, bipinnate; **pinnae** pinnatifid to lobed, and at least the basal pinnules varying from orbicular to triangular and rounded to the base; veins mostly ending in a tooth or on the unnotched margin. **Indusium** up to 1 mm long and more or less cleft at the apex. —Sheltered crevices in cliffs, moist banks, and wooded talus slopes. *Petioles translucent (when held to a light), with veins of the blade extending to the very tips of the teeth, and a smooth rachis.*

Cystopteris fragilis

Cystopteris laurentiana (Weatherby) Blasdell
ST. LAWRENCE BLADDER FERN
MAP 9
native

Cystopteris fragilis (L.) Bernh. var. *laurentiana* Weath.

Fern with tufted **leaves** from a short creeping rhizome, to about 60 cm long. **Petioles** light brown to red-tinged. **Blades** ovate, to about 30 cm long and 12 cm wide; sterile blades usually shorter than the fertile. **Indusium** to 1 mm wide, very finely glandular.—Calcareous rock or slopes. *This species combines the attributes of its presumed parents, C. fragilis var. fragilis and C. bulbifera. It is usually an upright, vigorous plant larger than typical C. fragilis. The veins extend both to the teeth-tips and to the sinuses.*

Cystopteris protrusa (Weatherby) Blasdell
LOWLAND BLADDER FERN
MAP 10
native

Cystopteris fragilis (L.) Bernh. var. *protrusa* Weatherby

Fern with **leaves** 20-50 cm long, scattered along a creeping rhizome. **Petioles** greenish, straw-colored, or pale brown. **Blades** lance-shaped, to 25 cm long, 5-10 cm wide; sterile blades usually shorter, bipinnate; pinnules sharply toothed, ovate-lance-shaped; lower pinnules tapered to a stalk-like base; veins mostly ending in a tooth or on the unnotched margin. **Indusium** to 0.5 mm long, shallowly toothed or entire at its tip.—Under deciduous trees on riverbottom benches. *Distinguished from Cystopteris fragilis by the long internodes on the rhizome, the greenish or straw-colored petioles, the softer, larger blades, and the lower pinnules, which taper to a stalk-like base.*

Cystopteris protrusa

Cystopteris tennesseensis Shaver
TENNESSEE BLADDER FERN
MAP 11
native

Cystopteris fragilis (L.) Bernh. var. *tennesseensis* (Shaver) McGregor

Fern with creeping stems. **Leaves** all alike, crowded near the tip of the stem, to 40 cm long; nearly all blades with sori. **Petioles** usually dark brown at base, becoming straw-colored above, shorter than the blade, and sparsely scaly at its base. **Blades** triangular in outline, twice pinnate-pinnatifid, usually widest at or near base, apex short-tapered to a tip; rachis and costae sometimes with bulblets (these often deformed); pinnae usually perpendicular to the rachis, not curved toward blade-tip.—Moist, rocky woods.

Cystopteris tenuis (Michx.) Desv.
UPLAND BRITTLE BLADDER FERN
MAP 12
native

Cystopteris fragilis (L.) Bernh. var. *mackayi* Lawson

Similar to *C. fragilis*, but the **pinnules** oblong to lance-shaped and evenly wedge-shaped at the base; the **indusium** about 0.5 mm long and shallowly toothed or entire at its tip.—In habitats similar to *Cystopteris fragilis*, but more often on streambanks, rotted logs, and in moist openings.

Cystopteris tenuis

GYMNOCARPIUM *Oak Fern*

Small ferns with 3-parted delicate blades, the blades glabrous or glandular, arising singly from slender rootstocks. Sori round. Indusium absent. Veins free, simple, or forking. Northern oak fern (*G. dryopteris*) is common; our other two species are much less frequent.

7. Cystopteris bulbifera

8. Cystopteris fragilis

9. Cystopteris laurentiana

10. Cystopteris protrusa

1 The two lower divisions of the blade nearly as long as the terminal division; blades membranous and thin; rachis glabrous . . . . ***G. dryopteris***

1 The two lower divisions of the blade about half the length of terminal division; blades firm and somewhat stiff; rachis in part densely glandular 2

   2 Innermost pinnules of lowest pair of pinnae only slightly longer than opposite upper pinnules; upper blade surface glabrous; acidic or neutral rock . . . . ***G. jessoense***

   2 Innermost pinnules of lowest pair of pinnae much longer than opposite upper pinnules; upper blade surface moderately glandular; limestone and calcareous rock . . . . ***G. robertianum***

Gymnocarpium dryopteris (L.) Newman
NORTHERN OAK FERN
MAP 13
native

Small, delicate fern with **leaves** to 30 cm long or longer, arising singly from a slender blackish rhizome. **Blades** glabrous or nearly so, triangular in outline, 3-parted; the **pinnae** pinnate-pinnatifid. **Sori** small, located near the margin. Cool rocky woods, swamp margins, and shaded slopes.—Cool, moist coniferous and mixed woods; swamp margins, base of talus slopes. *The small, delicate, triangular blades oriented parallel to the ground and yellow-green in color are distinctive.*

Gymnocarpium jessoense (Koidzumi) Koidzumi
NAHANNI OAK FERN
MAP 14
native

Small fern with **leaves** to 30 cm long, arising singly from a slender blackish rhizome. **Blades** narrowly triangular in outline, 3-parted, bipinnate-pinnatifid, glandular; the innermost **lower pinnules** usually only slightly longer than the corresponding **upper pinnules**. **Sori** small, located near the margin.—Shaded cliffs and talus. *The blade and rachis are glandular, as in **limestone oak fern** (G. robertianum); Nahanni oak fern, however, is smaller and more slender, the pinnae usually curve upwards, and the pinnules curve outwards.*

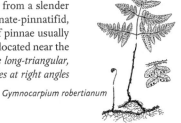

Gymnocarpium dryopteris

Gymnocarpium robertianum (Hoffmann) Newman
LIMESTONE OAK FERN
MAP 15
native

Small to medium fern with **leaves** to 40 cm long, arising singly from a slender blackish rhizome. **Blades** triangular in outline, 3-parted, bipinnate-pinnatifid, glandular, the innermost basal pinnules of the lowermost pair of pinnae usually much longer than the corresponding upper pinnules. **Sori** small, located near the margin.—Limestone cliffs, outcrops and pavements (alvars). *The long-triangular, glandular blades (including glands on the upper surface), with pinnules at right angles are distinctive.*

Gymnocarpium robertianum

Dennstaedtiaceae BRACKEN FERN FAMILY

PTERIDIUM *Bracken Fern*

Pteridium aquilinum (L.) Kuhn
BRACKEN FERN
MAP 16
native

Coarse fern with **leaves** 30-70 cm or more long, often forming large colonies from the long-creeping rhizomes. **Blades** triangular in outline, usually 3-parted, 30-50 cm wide; **lower pinnules** more or less pinnatifid; **upper pinnules** entire, glabrous or slightly hairy on underside, with revolute margins. **Sporangia** borne in marginal sori on the underside of the pinnules; sporangia covered by a nearly

11. Cystopteris tennesseensis   *12. Cystopteris tenuis*   *13. Gymnocarpium dryopteris*   *14. Gymnocarpium jessoense*

continuous **false outer indusium** formed by the revolute pinnae margin. Plants growing in shade tend to have more or less horizontal blades; blades of plants growing in sun tend to be upright and stiff.—Ubiquitous in open drier woods, pine plantations, old fields, and sandy openings.

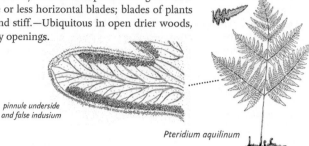

pinnule underside
and false indusium

Pteridium aquilinum

Dryopteridaceae WOOD FERN FAMILY

Medium to large ferns; rhizomes short, stout and scaly. Leaves dark green, sometimes evergreen; petioles shorter than blades, straw-colored or green, with chaffy scales near base. Sterile and fertile leaves alike or slightly different; sterile leaves sometimes persisting over winter; blades 1-3 pinnate, the smallest segments commonly toothed or lobed, veins simple to 1- or 2-branched. Sori round, on underside veins of pinnae; indusia round to kidney-shaped.

1 Fronds 1-pinnate-pinnatifid to more divided, the pinnae pinnatifid or themselves fully divided, lacking a prominent basal lobe, light green to dark green, herbaceous to nearly leathery; indusia kidney-shaped . . . . ***Dryopteris***
1 Fronds 1-pinnate, the pinnae toothed and each with a slight to prominent lobe near the base on the side towards the leaf tip, dark green, leathery or nearly so; indusia peltate (umbrella-like) . . . . ***Polystichum***

DRYOPTERIS *Wood-Fern*

Medium to large ferns; rhizomes short, stout and scaly, often covered with old petiole bases. Leaves dark green, sometimes evergreen; petioles shorter than blades, straw-colored or green, with chaffy scales near base. Sterile and fertile leaves alike or slightly different; sterile leaves sometimes persisting over winter; blades 1-3 pinnate, the smallest segments commonly toothed or lobed, veins simple to 1- or 2-branched. Sori round, on underside veins of pinnae; indusia round to kidney-shaped.

HYBRIDS
Hybrids may be recognized by an appearance intermediate between the parent species, and the presence of abortive spores. Three *Dryopteris* hybrids are reported for Minnesota:
• *Dryopteris* × *boottii* (Tuckerman) Underwood: *D. cristata* × *D. intermedia;* leaves more dissected than *D. cristata;* Becker and Winona counties.
• *Dryopteris* × *triploidea* Wherry: *D. carthusiana* × *D. intermedia*; leaves similar to parents but often somewhat larger; mostly n and e Minn.
• *Dryopteris* × *uliginosa* (A. Braun ex Dowell) Druce: *D. carthusiana* × *D. cristata*; usually in swamps and wet woods; n and e Minn.

1 Blades small, very scaly on underside; old leaves conspicuous and persistent curled tufts at base of plant . . . . .
. . . . ***D. fragrans***
1 Blades large, scales few or absent 2
  2 Sori on margins of blade segments; blades leathery gray-green and paler on underside . . . . ***D. marginalis***
  2 Sori near middle of smallest blade segments; blades various 3
    3 Lowest pinnules on lowest pinnae stalkless 4
      4 Leaves of 2 types; the sterile leaves shorter than fertile; the pinnae of fertile leaves usually turned to a nearly horizontal position . . . . ***D. cristata***
      4 Sterile and fertile leaves similar; pinnae of fertile leaves in same plane as blade . . . . ***D. goldiana***
    3 Lowest pinnules on lowest pinnae stalked 5
      5 Lowermost inner pinnule shorter than adjacent lower pinnule . . . . ***D. intermedia***
      5 Lowermost inner pinnule longer than next outer one 6
        6 Lower basal pinnule on basal pinna closer to the second upper pinnule than to the inner or first upper pinnule . . . . ***D. expansa***
        6 Lower basal pinnule on basal pinna closer to the inner upper pinnule than to the second upper pinnule . . . . ***D. carthusiana***

Dryopteris carthusiana (Villars) H. P. Fuchs
SPINULOSE WOOD-FERN

MAP 17
native

> *Dryopteris austriaca* var. *spinulosa* (O.F. Müll.) Fisch.
> *Dryopteris spinulosa* (O.F. Müll.) Watt

Clumped fern, **rhizomes** short-creeping. **Leaves** all alike, deciduous, smooth except for chaffy, pale brown scales near base of petioles; **blades** 2- to nearly 3-pinnate, 2-6 dm long and 1-4 dm wide, tapered to tip, slightly narrowed at base; **pinnae** usually 10-15 pairs, alternate to nearly opposite, narrowly lance-shaped; **pinnules** toothed to deeply lobed, mostly 5-40 mm long and 3-10 mm wide, the teeth tipped with a small spine; innermost lower pinnule longer than next outer one and 2-3x longer than opposite upper pinnule. **Sori** halfway between midvein and margin; **indusia** 1 mm wide, without stalked glands.—Moist to wet woods, hummocks in swamps, thickets; also drier sand dunes and ridges.

Dryopteris cristata (L.) A. Gray
CRESTED WOOD-FERN

MAP 18
native

Clumped fern, **rhizomes** short-creeping with ascending tips. Sterile and fertile leaves somewhat different, the outer **sterile leaves** waxy, persistent and smaller than inner fertile leaves; **fertile leaves** deciduous, 3-8 dm long. **Blades** 1-pinnate to nearly 2-pinnate, narrowly lance-shaped, 2-6 dm long and 7-15 cm wide, tapered to tip, narrowed at base; **pinnae** 5-9 cm long and to 4 cm wide, typically twisted to a nearly horizontal position, giving a "venetian blind" appearance to blades; pinnae segments to 20 mm long and 8 mm wide, with small spine-tipped teeth; petioles with sparse, pale brown, long-tapered scales. **Sori** round, midway between midvein and margin; **indusia** smooth, 1 mm wide.—Swamps, thickets, open bogs, fens and seeps.

Dryopteris carthusiana

Dryopteris expansa (K. Presl) Fraser-Jenkins & Jermy
SPREADING WOOD FERN

MAP 19
native

> *Dryopteris assimilis* S. Walker

Fern with **leaves** to 1 m long, forming a large, more or less upright crown at the end of the upright, chaffy rhizome. **Petioles** usually shorter than the blades, with brown-tinged, often dark-centered, ovate scales. **Blades** broadly triangular to ovate, abruptly tapering to the tip, twice pinnate to tripinnate; **pinnae** short-stalked; **basal pinnae** triangular, inequilateral; the inner, lowermost pinnule on each lowermost pinna closer to the second upper pinnule than to the first upper pinnule. **Indusia** glabrous, or rarely finely glandular.—Cool moist woods.

Dryopteris fragrans (L.) Schott
FRAGRANT WOOD FERN

MAP 20
native

Fern of rocky habitats with **leaves** to 30-40 cm long, forming a spreading or ascending crown from the rhizome; **old leaves** curled, shriveled, and persistent at the plant base. **Petioles** to 15 cm long, glandular and chaffy. **Blades** leathery, tapered from the middle to the base and tip; pinnae overlapping and often inrolled, densely chaffy with brownish scales; pinnae lance-shaped, pinnately cleft or crenate; rachises and pinnae glandular. **Indusia** large and often overlapping, whitish, becoming tan, often ragged on their margins.—Cliffs and talus slopes (often somewhat calcareous). *Dryopteris fragrans somewhat resembles the smaller **rusty cliff fern** (Woodsia ilvensis) found in similar habitats, but the curled, persistent old leaves drooping below plants of fragrant wood fern are distinctive.*

Dryopteris cristata

Dryopteris fragrans

15. Gymnocarpium robertianum   *16. Pteridium aquilinum*   *17. Dryopteris carthusiana*   *18. Dryopteris cristata*

Dryopteris goldiana (Hook.) A. Gray

GOLDIE'S WOOD-FERN

MAP 21
native

Clumped fern; **rhizomes** short-creeping, to 1 cm thick, densely scaly. **Leaves** to 1 m long; **blades** 30-60 cm long and 20-40 cm wide, deciduous late in season, the upper part abruptly narrowed to a small, tapered tip, the tip often mottled with white; pinnae with small, often rounded teeth; **petioles** brown, slightly shorter than blades, with narrow, pale brown scales 1-2 cm long, lower scales with a dark midstripe. **Sori** close to midveins, with a smooth **indusia** 1-2 mm across.—Moist hardwood forests, shaded streambanks, talus slopes; soils rich in humus and usually neutral.

Dryopteris intermedia (Muhl.) A. Gray

FANCY WOOD-FERN

MAP 22
native

Dryopteris spinulosa var. *intermedia* (Muhl. ex Willd.) Underw.

Clumped fern, **rhizomes** ascending. **Leaves** in an open vaselike cluster of evergreen leaves; **blades** broadest just above base and abruptly tapered near tip, 2-5 dm long and 1-2 dm wide, 2-pinnate; **pinnae** at right angles to stem, lowermost inner pinnule usually shorter than next outer pinnule, pinnules toothed and tipped with small spines; **petioles** 1/3 as long as blade, with pale brown scales with a darker center, petioles and stems with small, gland-tipped hairs. **Sori** midway between midvein and margin, the **indusia** 1 mm wide, covered with stalked glands.—Moist hardwood and mixed hardwood-conifer forests, hummocks in swamps; soils rich in humus, slightly acid to neutral.

Dryopteris goldiana

Dryopteris marginalis (L.) A. Gray

MARGINAL WOOD FERN

MAP 23
❥ *endangered | native*

Fern with **leaves** mostly 25-60 cm long, crowded to form a crown; lower part of the petiole covered with light brown lance-shaped scales. **Blades** 10-20 cm wide, dark green above, gray-green below, leathery, lance-shaped to ovate, 2-pinnate; pinnae lance-shaped; **pinnules** oblong, entire to deeply lobed. **Sori** located near the margins; **indusia** smooth, whitish, becoming light brown.—Rocky woods. *The leathery or spongy character of the nearly evergreen blades and the nearly marginal sori are characteristic.*

Dryopteris intermedia

pinna underside

Dryopteris marginalis

POLYSTICHUM *Holly Fern*

Large, tufted ferns with mostly evergreen, leathery blades; the petioles usually scaly, arising from short, stout, chaffy rhizomes. Sori round; indusia round, attached at the center.

1 Sori located on reduced upper pinnae . . . . *P. acrostichoides*
1 Sori on underside of typical pinnae . . . . *P. braunii*

19. *Dryopteris expansa*   20. *Dryopteris fragrans*   21. *Dryopteris goldiana*   22. *Dryopteris intermedia*

Polystichum acrostichoides (Michx.) Schott
MAP 24
CHRISTMAS FERN ✎*endangered | native*
Fern with dark green, nearly evergreen **leaves** 40-70 cm long. **Petiole** and **rachis** chaffy. **Blades** lance-shaped, 7-12 cm wide or wider, pinnate; **pinnae** oblong to lance-shaped, auricled at the base on the upper side; margins finely toothed. **Sori** borne on smaller upper pinnae.—Rich woods and shaded rocky slopes.

Polystichum braunii (Spenner) Fée
MAP 25
BRAUN'S HOLLY FERN ✎*threatened | native*
Medium to large fern with **leaves** to 1 m long, forming a crown at the end of a short ascending rhizome. **Petiole** about one-sixth the length of the blade, chaffy. **Blades** dark green, broadly lance-shaped, narrowed at the base; rachis with persistent chaff; **pinnae** lance-shaped; pinnae generally once-pinnate, the margins with incurved bristle-tipped teeth. **Sori** in two rows near the midrib; **indusia** often erose.—Rocky woods, along rocky streams, and on shaded cliffs within moist northern forests. *A large tufted fern, with dark green blades, the pinnae with bristle-tipped teeth.*

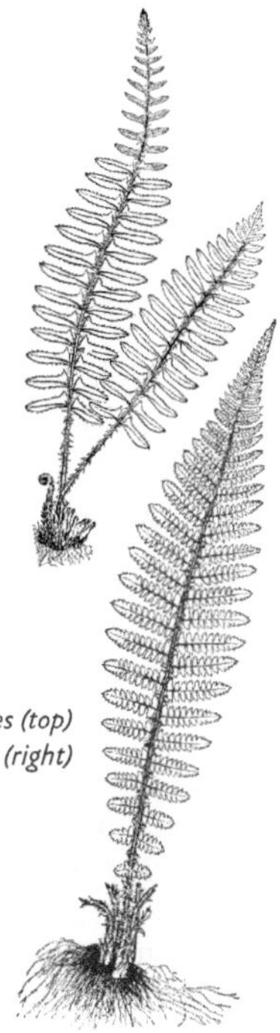

Polystichum acrostichoides (top)
Polystichum braunii (right)

Equisetaceae HORSETAIL FAMILY

EQUISETUM *Horsetail; Scouring-Rush*

Rushlike herbs with dark rhizomes. Stems annual or perennial, grooved, usually with large central cavity and smaller outer cavities, unbranched or with whorls of branches at nodes. Leaves reduced to scales, united into a sheath at each node; top of sheath divided into dark-colored teeth. Spores in cones at tips of green or brown fertile stems.

HYBRIDS
· *Equisetum* × *ferrissii* Clute: *E. hyemale* × *E. laevigatum*, common nearly statewide.
· *Equisetum* × *litorale* Kuehl ex Rupr.: *E. arvense* × *E. fluviatile*, se Minn.
· *Equisetum* × *mackaii* (Newman) Brichan: *E. hyemale* × *E. variegatum*, n Minn.
· *Equisetum* × *nelsonii* (A.A. Eat) Schaffn.: *E. laevigatum* × *E. variegatum*, mostly nw Minn.

1 Stems evergreen (annual in *E. laevigatum*); unbranched or with a few scattered branches, branches not in regular whorls (scouring rushes) 2
  2 Stems solid (central cavity absent); stems small, slender and sprawling . . . . *E. scirpoides*
  2 Stems hollow (central cavity present); stems larger, usually upright. 3
    3 Stems 1-3 dm tall, with 5-12 ridges, central cavity to 1/3 diameter of stem . . . . *E. variegatum*
    3 Stems usually taller, with 16-50 ridges, central cavity more than half diameter of stem 4
      4 Cones with a distinct, small sharp tip; stem sheaths with a black band at tip and base . . . . . *E. hyemale*
      4 Cones blunt-tipped, sheaths with black band at tip only . . . . *E. laevigatum*
1 Stems annual; usually with regular whorls of branches, sometimes unbranched (horsetails) 5
  5 Stems unbranched 6
    6 Stems green 7
      7 Stems with 9-25 shallow ridges; central cavity more than half diameter of stem; sheath teeth entirely black or with narrow white margins . . . . *E. fluviatile*
      7 Stems with 5-10 strongly angled ridges; central cavity less than 1/3 diameter of stem; sheath teeth with white margins and dark centers . . . . *E. palustre*
    6 Stems brown or flesh-colored 8
      8 Sheath teeth papery and red-brown, teeth joined and forming several broad lobes . . . . . *E. sylvaticum*
      8 Sheath teeth black or brown, not papery, separate or joined in more than 4 small groups 9
        9 Stems withering after spores mature, remaining unbranched. . . . . *E. arvense*
        9 Stems persistent, becoming branched and green . . . . *E. pratense*

5 Stems with regular whorls of branches 10

  10 First internode of each branch shorter than the subtending sheath of the main stem 11

    11 Stems with 9-25 shallow ridges; central cavity more than half diameter of stem; sheath teeth more than 12, entirely black or with narrow white margins . . . . ***E. fluviatile***

    11 Stems with 5-10 strongly angled ridges; central cavity about same size as outer cavities; sheath teeth 5-6, with white margins and dark centers . . . . ***E. palustre***

  10 First internode of each branch equal or longer than the subtending sheath of the main stem 12

    12 Stem branches themselves branched; sheath teeth papery and red-brown, teeth joined and forming several broad lobes . . . . ***E. sylvaticum***

    12 Stem branches unbranched; sheath teeth black or brown, not papery, separate or joined in more than 4 small groups 13

      13 Stem branches ascending; teeth of branch sheaths gradually tapering to a slender tip . . . ***E. arvense***

      13 Stem branches spreading; teeth of branch sheaths broadly triangular . . . . ***E. pratense***

Equisetum arvense L.

COMMON OR FIELD HORSETAIL

MAP 26

native

Stems annual, upright from creeping, branched, tuber-bearing **rhizomes** covered with dark hairs. Sterile and fertile stems unalike; **sterile stems** appearing in spring as fertile wither, green, regularly branched, 1-6 dm tall and 2-5 mm wide, with 10-14 shallow ridges, the ridges usually rough-to-touch; **central cavity** 1/3-2/3 stem diameter; **sheaths** with 6-14 persistent, black-brown teeth 1-2 mm long; branches numerous in dense whorls, usually without branchlets, upright or spreading, 3-5-angled, solid. **Fertile stems** flesh-colored, shorter than sterile stems and with larger sheaths, maturing in early spring and soon withering, unbranched, to 3 dm tall and 8 mm wide; sheaths with 8-12 dark brown teeth. **Cones** blunt-tipped, long-stalked at end of stem, 0.5-3 cm long.—Common; streambanks, meadows, moist woods, ditches, roadsides and along railroads; calcareous fens.

Equisetum arvense

Equisetum fluviatile L.

WATER-HORSETAIL

MAP 27

native

Stems annual, fertile and sterile stems alike, to 1 m or more tall, from smooth, shiny, light brown, creeping **rhizomes**; **stems** with 9-25 shallow, smooth ridges; **central cavity** large, about 4/5 stem diameter; **stem sheaths** green, 6-10 mm long; teeth 12-24, persistent, 2-3 mm long, dark brown to black, sometimes with narrow white margins; **branches** none or few, to many and regularly whorled from middle nodes, spreading, without branchlets, 4-6-angled, hollow. **Cones** 1-2 cm long at tips of stems, long-stalked, blunt-tipped, deciduous, maturing in summer.—In standing water of marshes, ponds, peatlands, ditches.

Equisetum hyemale L.

COMMON SCOURING-RUSH

MAP 28

native

Equisetum affine Engelm.

Stems evergreen, persisting for more than 1 year, fertile and sterile stems alike, from black, slender rhizomes; **stems** mostly unbranched or with few, short, upright branches from upper nodes, to 15 dm tall but usually shorter, 4-14 mm wide, with 14-50 rounded, very rough ridges; **central cavity** at least 3/4 stem diameter; **stem sheaths** 5-15 mm long, with a dark band at tip and usually also at base, the teeth dark brown to black with chaffy margin, 2-4 mm long, deciduous or persistent. **Cones** stalkless or short-stalked at tips of stems, sharp-pointed, eventually

Equisetum fluviatile

23. *Dryopteris marginalis*

24. *Polystichum acrostichoides*

25. *Polystichum braunii*

26. *Equisetum arvense*

deciduous, 1-2.5 cm long, maturing in summer, or old stems sometimes developing branches with cones in the following spring.—Often forming dense colonies in seeps, wet to moist meadows, shores, streambanks, ditches, roadsides and along railroads; usually where sandy or gravelly.

Equisetum laevigatum A. Braun
SMOOTH SCOURING-RUSH   MAP 29   *native*

Stems mostly annual, fertile and sterile stems alike, from brown or black rhizomes; **stems** mostly unbranched or with a few upright branches, 3-10 dm tall and 3-8 mm wide, smooth and rather soft, with 10-32 ridges; **central cavity** 2/3-3/4 stem diameter; **stem sheaths** with a single dark band at tip, or rarely lowest sheaths with a dark band at base or entirely black; teeth dark brown or black with chaffy margins, free or partly joined in pairs, 1-4 mm long, soon deciduous. **Cones** short-stalked at tips of stems, rounded with a small sharp point, maturing in early summer and eventually deciduous.—Wet meadows, low prairie, streambanks, floodplains, seeps, and ditches, often where sandy or gravelly.

Equisetum hyemale

Equisetum palustre L.
MARSH-HORSETAIL   MAP 30   *native*

Stems annual, erect, fertile and sterile stems alike, from creeping, branched, shiny black rhizomes; **stems** 2-8 dm tall, with 5-10 pronounced ridges, the ridges mostly smooth; **central cavity** small, 1/6-1/3 stem diameter; **sheaths** green, loose and flared upward; teeth 5-6, free or partly joined, persistent, 3-7 mm long, brown to black, with pale, translucent margins; branches few and irregular, to many and whorled at upper nodes, upright, without branchlets, 5-6-angled, hollow. **Cones** long-stalked at tips of stems, 1-3 cm long, blunt-tipped, maturing in summer, deciduous.—Wetland margins, streambanks, alder thickets, fens; often in shallow water.

Equisetum laevigatum

Equisetum pratense Ehrh.
MEADOW-HORSETAIL   MAP 31   *native*

Stems annual and erect, sterile and fertile stems unalike, from creeping, dull black rhizomes. **Sterile stems** regularly branched, 2-5 dm tall and 1-3 mm wide; 8-18-ridged, the ridges roughened by silica on middle and upper stem; **central cavity** 1/3-1/2 stem diameter; main **stem sheaths** 2-6 mm long, the teeth persistent, 1-2 mm long, free or partly joined in pairs, brown with white margins and a dark midstripe; branches slender, many in regular whorls from middle and upper nodes, without branchlets, horizontal or drooping, mostly 3-angled, solid. **Fertile stems** uncommon, appearing in early spring before sterile stems and persisting, at first unbranched, fleshy and brown (without chlorophyll), later becoming green at nodes and producing many small green branches, mostly 1-3 dm tall; sheaths and teeth about twice as long as on sterile stems. **Cones** long-stalked at tips of stems, to 2.5 cm long, blunt-tipped, deciduous.—Moist woods, streambanks and meadows.

Equisetum scirpoides Michx.
DWARF SCOURING-RUSH   MAP 32   *native*

Stems evergreen, very slender, fertile and sterile stems alike, from widely branching rhizomes; **stems** 5-30 cm long and only 0.5-1 mm wide, in dense clusters, usually unbranched and zigzagged, upright or trailing; **central cavity** absent, 3 small outer cavities present; **sheaths** green with broad black band at tip,

Equisetum palustre

27. *Equisetum fluviatile*   28. *Equisetum hyemale*   29. *Equisetum laevigatum*   30. *Equisetum palustre*

loose and flared above, with 3-4 teeth; teeth with white, chaffy margin, ±
persistent, but tips usually soon deciduous. **Cones** black, small, 3-5 mm long,
sharp-tipped.—Mossy places and moist, shaded woods, the stems often partly
buried in humus.

Equisetum sylvaticum L.
WOODLAND-HORSETAIL

MAP 33
native

Stems annual, erect, sterile and fertile stems unalike, from creeping, shiny light
brown **rhizomes**, tubers occasionally present. **Sterile stems** green, 3-7 dm tall
and 1.5-3 mm wide, with 10-18 ridges, rough-to-touch with sharp, hooked silica
spines; **central cavity** 1/2-2/3 stem diameter; **sheaths** green at base, red-brown
and flaring at tip; teeth brown, 3-5 mm long, joined in 3-5 broad lobes. Stems
densely branched in regular whorls from the nodes, the branches themselves
branched, often curving downward, 4-5-angled, solid. **Fertile stems** at first pink-
brown (without chlorophyll), fleshy, unbranched, becoming green and branched
as in sterile stems; sheaths and teeth larger than in sterile stems. **Cones** 1.5-3 cm
long, stalked, blunt-tipped, deciduous.—Wet or swampy woods, thickets, usually
in partial shade.

Equisetum sylvaticum

Equisetum variegatum Schleicher
VARIEGATED SCOURING-RUSH

MAP 34
native

Stems evergreen, fertile and sterile stems alike, from creeping, much-branched,
smooth **rhizomes**; may form thick colonies; **stems** 1-3 dm tall and 1-2.5 mm wide,
with 5-12 shallow, rough ridges, branched near base and otherwise usually
unbranched; **central cavity** 1/4-1/3 stem diameter, smaller outer cavities present;
sheaths green at base with a broad black band above; teeth persistent, with a dark
brown or black midstripe and wide white margins, abruptly narrowed to a
hairlike, deciduous tip 0.5-1 mm long. **Cones** to 1 cm long, strongly sharp-tipped,
maturing in summer or persisting unopened until following spring.—Wet
calcareous open areas such as shores, low places in dunes, borrow pits and
ditches. *Equisetum variegatum may form hybrids with E. hyemale and E. laevigatum,
sometimes making identification of this species difficult.*

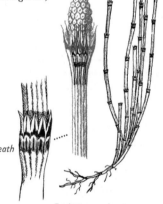
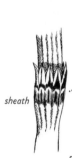

sheath

Equisetum variegatum

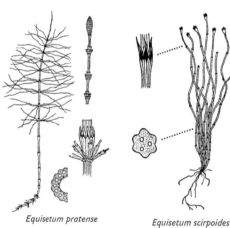
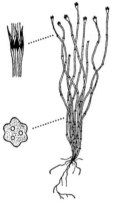

Equisetum pratense

Equisetum scirpoides

31. *Equisetum pratense*   32. *Equisetum scirpoides*   33. *Equisetum sylvaticum*   34. *Equisetum variegatum*

Isoetaceae QUILLWORT FAMILY

ISOETES *Quillwort*

Perennial aquatic or emergent herbs. Leaves simple, entire, linear, from a 2-3 lobed rhizome (corm). Outermost and innermost leaves typically sterile. Outer fertile leaves have a pocketlike structure (sporangia) bearing whitish spores (megaspores; about 0.5 mm in diameter, magnification needed to see features); inner fertile leaves have numerous small microspores.

1　Megaspores conspicuously covered with small spines . . . . *I. echinospora*
1　Megaspores not spiny 2
　　2　Plants normally underwater; leaves without outer fibrous strands . . . . *I. lacustris*
　　2　Plants underwater or on exposed, drying shores; leaves with 4 or more fibrous . . . . *I. melanopoda*

Isoetes echinospora Durieu
SPINY-SPORED QUILLWORT
Isoetes braunii Durieu
Isoetes muricata Durieu

MAP 35
native

Leaves linear, 7-25 or more, 5-15 cm long and 0.5-1.5 mm wide, usually erect, soft, bright green to yellow-green, tapered from base to a very long, slender tip, without peripheral strands from base; **corm** 2-lobed. **Sporangium** 4-8 mm long, usually brown-spotted when mature, half or more covered by a membranous flap (velum). **Megaspores** round, white, 0.3-0.6 mm wide, covered with short, sharp to blunt spines.—Shallow water (to 1 m deep) of lakes, ponds and slow-moving rivers; plants rooted in mud, sand, or gravel.

Isoetes lacustris L.
LAKE QUILLWORT
Isoetes hieroglyphica A.A. Eaton
Isoetes macrospora Durieu

MAP 36
native

Leaves several to many, 5-20 cm long and 1-2 mm wide, stiff and erect or with leaf tips curved downward, dark green, fleshy and twisted, peripheral strands from base usually absent; **corm** 2-lobed. **Sporangium** to 5 mm long, usually not spotted; membranous flap (velum) covering up to half of sporangium. **Megaspores** round, white, 0.6-0.8 mm wide, with ridges forming an irregular netlike pattern.—Underwater in shallow to deep water of cold lakes, ponds and streams.

Isoetes melanopoda Gay & Durieu
BLACK-FOOT QUILLWORT

MAP 37
❤*endangered* | *native*

Leaves 10-50 cm long and 0.5-2 mm wide, black at base with a pale line running down middle of inner side, 4 peripheral strands from base usually present. **Sporangium** 5-20 mm long, brown-spotted when mature, up to 2/3 covered by membranous flap (velum). **Megaspores** 0.3-0.5 mm wide, covered with short, low ridges.—Underwater to emergent in temporary ponds, wet streambanks, ditches and swales.

Isoetes echinospora

Isoetes lacustris
megaspore

Isoetes melanopoda
megaspore

35. *Isoetes echinospora*　　　36. *Isoetes lacustris*　　　37. *Isoetes melanopoda*　　　38. *Diphasiastrum complanatum*

Lycopodiaceae CLUBMOSS FAMILY

Low, trailing evergreen herbs resembling large mosses. Leaves needlelike or scalelike, alternate or opposite on stem. Spore-bearing leaves (sporophylls) similar to vegetative leaves or in conelike clusters at tips of upright stems.

1 Horizontal stems absent; sporangia in axils of unmodified leaves . . . . ***Huperzia***
1 Horizontal stems present; sporangia in axils of modified, reduced sporophylls, the sporophylls grouped into upright or nodding strobili 2
  2 Strobili upright on leafy peduncles, the peduncle leaves not reduced in size; wetland species . . . .
   . . . . ***Lycopodiella inundata***
  2 Strobili sessile or on peduncles, the peduncles if present with scattered, small leaves; species mostly of upland habitats 3
    3 Ultimate shoots and their leaves 5-12 mm wide, rounded in cross-section; leaves not strongly overlapping . . . . ***Lycopodium***
    3 Ultimate shoots and their leaves to 6 mm wide, 4-angled or flattened in cross-section; leaves overlapping . . . . ***Diphasiastrum***

DIPHASIASTRUM *Ground-Pine*

Small plants of drier habitats resembling miniature trees; branches flattened or 4-angled in cross-section; leaves 4-ranked, neither spine- nor hair-tipped. Strobili (cones) stalked, the stalks branched into segments of equal length.

HYBRIDS
· *Diphasiastrum* × *habereri* (House) Holub, hybrid between *D. digitatum* × *D. tristachyum*.
· *Diphasiastrum* × *zeilleri* (Rouy) Holub, hybrid between *D. complanatum* × *D. tristachyum*.

1 Stem branchlets cordlike, nearly square in cross-section, usually waxy blue-green color . . . . ***D. tristachyum***
1 Stem branchlets flat in cross-section, usually green 2
  2 Branchlets regularly fan-shaped and arching, without conspicuous constrictions between seasonal growth; most strobili with sterile tips . . . . ***D. digitatum***
  2 Branchlets irregular, with conspicuous constrictions; most strobili without sterile tips . . . . . . ***D. complanatum***

Diphasiastrum complanatum (L.) Rothm.

NORTHERN RUNNING-PINE
  Lycopodium complanatum L.

MAP 38
native

Horizontal stems mostly below the surface of the ground; leaves scale-like. **Upright stems** to about 30 cm tall, with forking branchlets. **Branchlets** flattened, often strongly constricted between yearly growths, 2-4 mm wide. **Leaves** 4-ranked. **Strobili** 1 or 2 on peduncles.—Woodlands and clearings. *Conspicuous annual constrictions present, giving plants a somewhat irregular appearance, in contrast to the regularity of fan ground-pine (D. digitatum). The strobili are also irregular in number per peduncle (varying from 1-4), and the naked peduncles are very slender.*

Diphasiastrum digitatum (Dill.) Holub

FAN GROUND-PINE
  Lycopodium digitatum Dill.

MAP 39
native

Horizontal stems mostly on or near the surface of the ground; leaves distant, scale-like. **Upright stems** to about 30 cm high, the branchlets of the branches arched and fan-like; constrictions between yearly growth absent or only slightly

Diphasiastrum complanatum

39. Diphasiastrum digitatum   *40. Diphasiastrum tristachyum*   *41. Huperzia appressa*   *42. Huperzia lucidula*

evident. **Branchlets** 2-3 mm wide. **Leaves** 4-ranked. **Strobili** mostly 3 or 4 on peduncles; peduncle branched at one point.—Dry woods and clearings. *The branchlets are very regular and fan-like, annual constrictions are lacking, and the strobili are usually in groups of 4 on long, naked peduncles.*

Diphasiastrum tristachyum (Pursh) Holub

MAP 40

DEEP-ROOT GROUND-PINE

native

Lycopodium tristachyum Pursh

Horizontal stems usually deeply buried; leaves scalelike. **Upright stems** to 30 cm tall. **Sterile branches** ascending to loosely divergent, flattened, 1-1.5 cm wide. **Leaves** 4-ranked, blue-green, lance-shaped. **Strobili** 2-6 on leafy-bracted peduncles.—Dry, sometimes sandy woods and clearings. *The clusters of branches are vase-shaped and crowded, bluish green and white waxy on their underside; annual constrictions are present along the branches; the peduncles often branch and then branch again, resulting in 4 strobili.*

Diphasiastrum digitatum

HUPERZIA *Fir-Moss*

Low evergreen perennials with erect shoots; leaves spreading or appressed and upright. Spores borne at base of upper leaves.

HYBRIDS

• *Huperzia* × *bartleyi* (Cusick) Kartesz & Gandhi, hybrid between *H. lucidula* × *H. porophila;* Lake County.

• *Huperzia* × *buttersii* (Abbe) Kartesz & Gandhi, hybrid between H. *lucidula* × *H. selago;* resembles a slender *H. lucidula,* but distinguished by presence of abortive spores and scattered stomata on upper leaf surface; ne Minn (Cook, Lake and St. Louis counties).

1 Leaves obovate, widest above the middle, spreading to ± reflexed, the upper portion of at least the larger leaves with distinct teeth; shoots "shaggy" with conspicuous annual constrictions; usually growing on soil . . . . ***Huperzia lucidula***

1 Leaves lance-shaped, widest below the middle, leaves (at least those on the upper stem) often ascending, entire or with a few small teeth; annual constrictions absent or faint. 2

    2 Leaves lance-shaped with sides nearly parallel; stomates on upper surface of each leaf number 2-50 (view fresh leaves under 20x lens to see the light-colored, dot-like stomates). ***Huperzia porophila***

    2 Leaves lance-shaped (as above) or ovate or triangular; if leaf shape is inconclusive, then number of stomates on upper leaf surface is greater than 60. 3

        3 Leaves near base of plant essentially same size as those on upper portion; gemmae formed in a single whorl at end of the annual growth . . . . ***Huperzia selago***

        3 Leaves near base of plant conspicuously longer than those on upper portion; gemmae formed throughout upper portions of shoot. . . . . ***Huperzia appressa***

Huperzia appressa (Desv.) Á. & D. Löve

MAP 41

MOUNTAIN FIR-MOSS

native

Huperzia appalachiana Beitel & Mickel

Stems short, to only 10 cm long; clustered; annual constrictions absent. **Leaves** ascending, narrowly lance-shaped or with the sides parallel; stomates on both surfaces; margins entire; upper stem leaves smaller than those of lower stem. **Sporangia** in distinct zones on upper stems.—Cliffs, talus slopes, where open and exposed, on moss or thin soil; ne Minn.

Huperzia lucidula (Michaux) Trev.

MAP 42

SHINING FIR-MOSS

native

Lycopodium lucidulum Michx.

Stems light green, creeping and rooting, upcurving stems forked several times, to 25 cm high, crowded with shiny dark green leaves which persist for more than one season. **Leaves** in mostly 6 rows, spreading or curved downward, in alternating groups of longer sterile and shorter fertile leaves, giving shoots a ragged look. **Sterile leaves** 6-12 mm long, toothed and broadest above middle; sporophylls barely widened and with small teeth or entire at tip.—Moist to wet conifer and hardwood forests. *Small two-lobed buds (gemmae) produced in some upper leaf-axils; these may sprout into new plants after falling onto moist humus.*

Huperzia lucidula

Huperzia porophila (Lloyd & Underwood) Holub
ROCK CLUBMOSS

MAP 43
❧ *threatened* | native

Lycopodium porophilum Lloyd & Underwood
Lycopodium selago L. var. *porophilum* (Lloyd & Underwood)

Shoots erect, 12-15 cm long, leaves of mature portion slightly smaller than leaves of juvenile portion; annual constrictions distinct to indistinct. **Leaves** reflexed at base, ascending at stem apex (forming cluster) and spreading for most of stem length, sparse, yellow-green to green, lustrous; largest leaves lance-shaped with roughly parallel sides, 5-8 mm long; smallest leaves triangular, widest at base, 3-6 mm long; margins almost entire or a few large teeth. Gemmiferous branchlets produced in 1-3 pseudowhorls at end of annual growth; **gemmae** 4-5 mm long; lateral leaves 1-1.5 mm wide, acute, widest above middle.—Shaded sandstone ledges.

Huperzia porophila

Huperzia selago L.
NORTHERN FIR-MOSS

MAP 44
native

Lycopodium selago L.

Horizontal stems short; upright stems forked from base, 6-20 cm long and 2-3 mm wide (stem only). **Leaves** persistent, yellow-green, in 8-10 rows, 3-6 mm long and to 1 mm wide, swollen and concave at base, gradually tapered to tip, mostly without teeth, uniform in length; leaves appressed to stem, giving stems a smooth, cylindric outline. **Sporophylls** similar to vegetative leaves; sporangia produced early in season in leaf axils, followed later by sterile leaves. Upper axils with small, 2-lobed reproductive buds (gemmae).—Cedar swamps, streambanks, sandy lake shores, usually where mossy; also in wet, sandy borrow pits.

Huperzia selago

LYCOPODIELLA *Bog Clubmoss*

Lycopodiella inundata (L.) Holub
NORTHERN BOG CLUBMOSS

MAP 45
native

Lycopodium inundatum L.

Low, creeping perennial of wet habitats. **Stems** elongate and trailing, deciduous but with evergreen buds at tips, rooting throughout. **Upright shoots** fertile, unbranched, leafy, scattered along horizontal stems. **Leaves** in 8-10 rows, those on underside of trailing stems twisted upward, narrowly lance-shaped, margins ± entire. **Fertile shoots** few, erect, to 1 dm high, with spreading leaves. **Spores** borne in terminal, leafy cones; the cones 1.5-5 cm long and 6-12 mm wide; sporophylls green, base widened and with a pair of teeth.—Acidic, open sphagnum bogs, wet sandy shores and streambanks; disturbed wetlands, sandy borrow pits.

Lycopodiella inundata

LYCOPODIUM *Ground-Pine*

Plants mainly trailing on ground. Roots emerging from point of origin on underside of main stems. Horizontal stems on substrate surface or subterranean, long-creeping. Upright shoots scattered along horizontal stem, 5-16 mm diameter, round or flat in cross section, unbranched or with 1-4 lateral branchlets. Leaves not imbricate, linear to linear lance-shaped; leaves on horizontal stems scattered, appressed; leaves on lateral branchlets mostly 6-ranked or more, monomorphic with few exceptions, appressed, ascending to spreading, margins entire to dentate. Gemmae absent. Strobili single and sessile, or multiple and pedunculate; peduncle, when present, conspicuously leafy; sporophylls extremely reduced, much shorter than peduncle or stem leaves. Sporangia kidney-shaped.

43. Huperzia porophila

44. Huperzia selago

45. Lycopodiella inundata

46. Lycopodium annotinum

1 Stroboli stalked; upright stems with 2-5 branches, not forming small tree-like shapes; leaves tipped with hairs . 2

  2 Stroboli mostly single on stalk (rarely in pairs and then nearly stalkless); leaves apppressed or ascending on stem . . . . *L. lagopus*

  2 Stroboli 2-5; leaves spreading or somewhat ascending . . . . *L. clavatum*

1 Stroboli not stalked 3

  3 Stems creeping and horizontal; stroboli single at end of upright, mostly unbranched shoot . . . *L. annotinum*

  3 Stems upright, much-branched and tree-like; stroboli 1-7 at end of shoot 4

    4 Branches flat in cross-section; leaves of unequal sizes . . . . *L. obscurum*

    4 Branches round in cross-section; leaves of equal sizes 5

      5 Leaves on main stem below branches dark green and appressed to stem, soft to touch . . . . . *L. hickeyi*

      5 Leaves on stem below branches pale green and spreading, prickly . . . . *L. dendroideum*

Lycopodium annotinum L.

STIFF GROUND-PINE

   Spinulum annotinum (L.) Haines

MAP 46
native

Lycopodium annotinum

Stems elongated, prostrate, mostly unbranched, rooting at intervals; leaves uniform but the lower leaves turned upward. **Erect stems** simple to forked several times, increasing annually to 20 cm or more in height. **Leaves** 8-ranked, more or less stiff and hard, linear-subulate to linear-oblance-shaped, with a sharp spinule. **Strobili** sessile at the ends of leafy stems.—Moist woods and clearings, exposed rocky and peaty habitats.

Lycopodium clavatum L.

RUNNING GROUND-PINE

MAP 47
native

Stems elongated, horizontal on the surface of the ground, forking, rooting at intervals; leaves uniform, but lower leaves turned upward. **Erect branches** at first simple, becoming dichotomous; **fertile branches** with a leafy-bracted peduncle bearing 2 to several sessile or short-stalked strobiles. **Leaves** linear-subulate, incurved-spreading, usually tipped with a soft white hair-like bristle. Bracts of strobili yellow, fimbriate-erose, at least the lower with white filiform tips.—Dry woods and clearings. *Mature fruiting plants present no problems in identification; young or sterile plants sometimes confused with* **Lycopodium annotinum**. *The extended, soft, hair-like bristles on the leaf tips are useful for identification.*

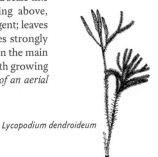

Lycopodium clavatum

Lycopodium dendroideum Michx.

TREE GROUND-PINE

   Dendrolycopodium dendroideum (Michx.) Haines

   Lycopodium obscurum L. var. *dendroideum* (Michx.) D.C. Eat.

MAP 48
native

Subterranean stems creeping, branching, and rhizome-like, with broad scale-like leaves; **aerial stems** upright, 10-30 cm high, simple below, forking above, constricted between the seasonal growth. **Lower leaves** strongly divergent; leaves of lateral branchlets in 2 dorsal, 2 ventral, and 2 lateral ranks; leaves strongly decurrent, the free part linear-attenuate. **Strobili** sessile and terminal on the main axis, or dominant branches and produced in the second, third, or fourth growing season.—Woods and clearings. *Quickly identified by grasping the base of an aerial stem; this will feel distinctly prickly because of the stiff divergent leaves.*

Lycopodium dendroideum

47. *Lycopodium clavatum* 48. *Lycopodium dendroideum* 49. *Lycopodium hickeyi* 50. *Lycopodium lagopus*

Lycopodium hickeyi W.H. Wagner, Beitel & Moran MAP 49
PENNSYLVANIA GROUND-PINE *native*
  Dendrolycopodium hickeyi (W.H. Wagner, Beitel & R.C. Moran) A. Haines
  Lycopodium obscurum L. var. *isophyllum* Hickey
Similar to *L. obscurum* in that leaves of lower portion of stem are strongly appressed to slightly divergent; **leaves** of branchlets are all of equal size and linear-attenuate; all leaves lie in planes tangential to the branchlet axis.—Woods.

Lycopodium lagopus (Laestad.) Zinserl. MAP 50
ONE-CONE GROUND-PINE *native*
  Lycopodium clavatum L. var. *lagopus* Laestad.
Horizontal stems on substrate surface. **Upright shoots** clustered, dominant main shoot branches 2-3, mostly in lower half; **lateral branchlets** few and like the upright shoots; annual bud constrictions abrupt and conspicuous, branches mostly erect. **Leaves** ascending to appressed, medium green, 3-5 mm long, margins entire; apex with narrow hairlike tip 1-3 mm long. **Peduncles** 3.5-12.5 cm long, unbranched, with remote pseudowhorls of appressed leaves. **Strobili** solitary (if double, usually nearly sessile).—Fields and openings in woods.

Lycopodium obscurum L. MAP 51
PRINCESS-PINE *native*
  Dendrolycopodium obscurum (L.) Haines
Similar to *L. dendroideum*, from which it may be distinguished by the strongly appressed to slightly divergent leaves on the lower portion of the aerial shoot. **Leaves** of the lateral branchlets arranged in 1 dorsal, 1 ventral, and 4 lateral ranks; leaves of ventral rank linear-attenuate to long triangular, smaller than leaves of other ranks; leaves of other ranks linear-acute.—Woods.

Lycopodium obscurum

Marsileaceae WATER-CLOVER FAMILY

MARSILEA *Water-Clover*

Marsilea vestita Hook. & Grev. MAP 52
HAIRY WATER-CLOVER ❧ *endangered | native*
Aquatic, creeping, perennial fern. **Stem** a slender rhizome, rooting in mud and only at nodes; **petioles** 2-20 cm long, sparsely hairy; **blades** floating or emergent, divided into 4 pinnae resembling a 4-leaf clover, 5-20 mm long and 5-15 mm wide, usually hairy on both sides. **Sporangia** in a single oval sporocarp borne on a short stalk at or near base of petiole, the **sporocarp** brown, 4-7 mm long, covered with stiff, flat hairs; **sori** in 2 rows inside the sporocarp.—Margins of shallow prairie pools, rainwater pools on rock outcrops. *Minnesota at eastern edge of species' range; more common in Great Plains and western USA.*

Marsilea vestita

Onocleaceae SENSITIVE FERN FAMILY

Large coarse ferns with creeping hairy rhizomes (*Onoclea*) or with stolons on ground surface (*Matteuccia*); sterile and fertile fronds strongly different, the sterile fronds deciduous, pinnatifid to 1-pinnate-pinnatifid; fertile fronds persistent. Sori enclosed under recurved margin of pinna segment (outer false indusium) and a tiny true inner indusium (membranous or of hairs).

51. *Lycopodium obscurum*   52. *Marsilea vestitaa*   53. *Matteuccia struthiopteris*   53A. *Onoclea sensibilis*

1　Sterile blades solitary from creeping rhizomes, deeply divided into lobes (or the lowermost divisions pinnae) . .
　. . . . . *Onoclea sensibilis*

1　Sterile blades in a circle from a thick crown; pinnate with lobed pinnules . . . . *Matteuccia struthiopteris*

MATTEUCCIA　*Ostrich Fern*

Matteuccia struthiopteris (L.) Todaro
OSTRICH FERN

MAP 53
native

Large, colony-forming fern; **rhizomes** deep and long-creeping, black, scaly, producing erect leafy crowns. **Sterile leaves** upright, 1-pinnate, to 2 m tall and 15-50 cm wide; blades much longer than petioles, abruptly narrowed to tip, gradually tapered to base, stems ± hairy; each pinnae deeply divided into 20 or more pairs of pinnules, these 3-6 mm wide at base and rounded at tip; veins not netlike. **Fertile leaves** stiff and erect within a circle of sterile leaves, green at first, turning brown or black, much shorter than sterile leaves (to 6 dm tall), produced in mid to late summer and often persisting into following year; fertile blades 1-pinnate, pinnae upright or appressed, 2-6 cm long and 2-4 mm wide, the margins inrolled and covering the **sori**; **indusia** with a jagged margin.—Wet and swampy woods, streambanks, seeps, and ditches.

ONOCLEA　*Sensitive Fern*

Onoclea sensibilis L.
SENSITIVE FERN

MAP 53A
native

Medium fern, in clumps of several leaves, spreading by branching **rhizomes** and forming large patches. **Leaves** upright, with petioles about as long as blades. **Sterile leaves** deciduous, 1-pinnate at base, deeply cleft upward; the stem broader-winged toward the tip; blades 15-40 cm long and 15-35 cm wide, with 8-12 pairs of opposite pinnae, these deeply wavy-margined or coarsely toothed, 1-5 cm wide, with scattered white hairs on underside veins, the veins joined and netlike. **Fertile leaves** produced in late summer and persisting over winter, shorter than sterile leaves; fertile blades 1-pinnate, pinnae upright, divided into beadlike pinnules with inrolled margins covering the sori; veins not joined. **Sori** round and covered by a hoodlike **indusia**, becoming dry and hard.—Swampy woods and low places in forests, wet meadows, calcareous fens, roadside ditches, wet or moist wheel ruts; sometimes weedy. *Leaves of* **Onoclea** *susceptible to damage from even light frosts, hence the common name of sensitive fern.*

Onoclea sensibilis

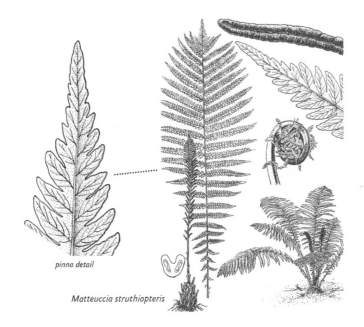

pinna detail

Matteuccia struthiopteris

Ophioglossaceae ADDER'S-TONGUE FAMILY

Perennial herbs from short, erect rhizomes having several fleshy roots. Plants produce one leaf each year on a single stalk (stipe), with bud for next year's leaf at base of stipe. Leaves divided into a fertile segment (sporophyll) and a sterile expanded blade. Sterile blades entire (*Ophioglossum*), or lobed or 1–3x pinnately divided (*Botrychium, Botrypus, Sceptridium*). Spores in numerous round sporangia borne on simple or branched fertile blades.

1   Sterile blades simple, entire; veins netlike; sporangia embedded in rachis of spike . . . . . . *Ophioglossum pusillum*
1   Sterile blades pinnately lobed or dissected; veins forked; sporangia exposed, often on a branched structure . . 2
  2   Sterile blades somewhat leathery, persisting over winter; blades with distinct stalk, usually 5-25 cm long in fertile plants; fertile portion of frond joining sterile portion at or near ground level. . . . . *Sceptridium*
  2   Plants deciduous, withering in fall; blades usually ± unstalked, large (more than 5 cm long) or much smaller (in some species of *Botrychium*), herbaceous or sometimes fleshy; fertile portion of frond joining sterile portion well above ground level 3
    3   Sterile blades triangular, 3–4x pinnate, stalkless and mostly 5-25 cm wide; fertile portion erect, appearing to be a continuation of stipe . . . . *Botrypus virginianus*
    3   Sterile blades short-triangular, oblong, or linear; lobed (simple) to 3-pinnate (usually 1-pinnate to 2-pinnate-pinnatifid), mostly 1-5 cm wide; fertile portion of blade upright or spreading . . . . *Botrychium*

BOTRYCHIUM *Grape-Fern; Moonwort*

Mostly small plants with one leaf, the blade divided into sterile and fetile segments. Sterile portion of blade pinnately divided or lobed, fertile portion branched to form a panicle bearing the sporangia.

ADDITIONAL SPECIES

• *Botrychium acuminatum* W.H. Wagner (Tailed moonwort) similar to *B. matricariifolium*, and previously considered a form of that species, but the pinnae much more separated, and have much narrower lobes (or lobes none). Known from ne Minn (Cook, Lake and St. Louis counties), Michigan, and Lake Superior region of Ontario; typical habitats are vegetated Great Lakes shoreline dunes and sandy places inland from dunes.

• *Botrychium ascendens* W.H. Wagner (Triangle-lobe moonwort, ☛*endangered*), St. Louis and Crow Wing counties. Pinnae of sterile blade wedge- shaped, angled upward, outer margins toothed, lower pinnae sometimes divided into 2 lobes and also bearing sporangia; found in open, grassy fields.

• *Botrychium gallicomontanum* Farrar & Johnson-Groh (Frenchman's Bluff moonwort, ☛*endangered*), known from nw Minn on Frenchman's Bluff in Norman County and several locations in Kittson County, and from Glacier National Park in Montana. Habitats are dry, sandy to gravelly, mid to tall grass prairie. Found growing with *B. campestre* and *B. simplex* and intermediate in form and possibly a hybrid between these 2 species. Distinguishing features include the large space between the lowest pinnae pair and the next pinnae pair, the strongly ascending pinnae, and the distinctly stalked sterile blade.

• *Botrychium lineare* W.H. Wagner (Narrow-leaf moonwort, ☛*endangered*), St. Louis County. Plants small, leathery, pale green; sterile blade with 4-6 widely spaced pinnae pairs, the pinnae very narrowly spoon-shaped, sometimes divided into 2 spreading lobes; somewhat similar to *B. campestre* but pinnae in that species wider and less deeply lobed. Reports from other regions suggest an affinity for gravelly or limestone habitats.

• *Botrychium pseudopinnatum* W.H. Wagner (False daisy-leaf moonwort), known from St. Louis County, plus reported from Douglas County in nw Wisconsin. May be more widespread in northern parts of our region as often confused with the more common daisy-leaf moonwort (*B. matricariifolium*). The sporophore of *B. pseudopinnatum* tends to be more branched, and plants are a lustrous deep green vs. the dull paler green of *B. matricariifolium*.

1   Sterile blade (trophophore) simple to lobed, lobes rounded to square and angular, stalks usually 1/2 to 2/3 length of sterile blade; rare plant of shaded woods (*Botrychium mormo*), or more common and often in open grassy fields (*Botrychium simplex*) 2
  2   Segments of sterile leaves rounded, margins mostly entire; plants herbaceous in texture, green; habitats various, in forests or open ground . . . . *B. simplex*
  2   Segments of sterile leaves angular, outer margins often coarsely dentate; plants ± succulent; shiny yellow-green; rare in shady forest understories, often concealed by leaf litter; . . . . *B. mormo*
1   Sterile blade pinnately lobed (either if actual pinnae or simply lobed), lobes of varying shapes, stalk usually less than 1/4 length of sterile blade; plants often in open sunny places; dunes, streambanks, roadsides, on trails and openings in forests, etc. 3
    3   Basal pinnae or segments of sterile blade with venation like the ribs of a fan; midrib absent 4

    4   Basal pinnae broadly fan-shaped (almost perfect half moons) with narrow stalks . . . . ***B. lunaria***

    4   Basal pinnae narrowly fan- or wedge-shaped to nearly linear. 5

        5   Sterile blade at least partially folded longitudinally when alive (conduplicate), usually not more than 4 cm long by 1 cm wide; pinnae up to 5 pairs; basal pinnae usually 2-parted 6

           6   Sterile blade very fleshy; fertile portion of blade usually less than 1.5 times length of sterile blade; pinnae mostly linear; basal pinna lobes ± equal; plants appearing in late spring . . . . . . ***B. campestre***

           6   Sterile blade herbaceous; fertile portion of blades usually 1.5–4 times the length of vegetative blades; pinnae asymmetrically fan-shaped; basal pinna lobes unequal; plants appearing in summer . . . . . .
. . . . ***B. pallidum***

        5   Sterile blade flat or folded only at base when alive, usually up to 10 long by 2.5 cm wide; pinnae up to 10 pairs; basal pinnae unlobed, or if lobed, not usually 2-parted 7

           7   Sterile blade narrowly oblong (sterile blade widest above base), firm to herbaceous; pinnae fan-shaped, margins shallowly crenate; proximal fertile portion of blade branches 1-pinnate . . . .
. . . . ***B. minganense***

           7   Sterile blade narrowly deltate (sterile blade widest at lowest pinna pair); pinnae spatulate to linear spatulate, margins entire to very coarsely and irregularly dentate; most proximal fertile portion of blade branches usually 2-pinnate . . . . ***B. spathulatum***

  3   Basal pinnae or segments of sterile blade with pinnate venation; midrib present. 8

    8   Fertile portion of blade 3-parted, with 3 major branches from near base of stalk at sterile blade . . . .
. . . . ***B. lanceolatum***

    8   Fertile portion of blade unbranched or with loosely pinnate branches smaller than the single main stem . 9

        9   Pinnae of small to medium sterile blades at least wavy-margined; larger blades with long narrow "teeth" especially on basal pinnae; sand dunes, occasional inland; ne Minn . . . . ***B. acuminatum****

        9   Pinnae of small sterile blades mostly smooth margined but appearing unevenly branched; large blades regularly multi-pinnate . . . . ***B. matricariifolium***

Botrychium campestre W.H. Wagner & Farrar

IOWA MOONWORT

                                  MAP 54

                                   native

Small plants, sometimes less than 5 cm tall and hard to see if surrounded by taller vegetation. Plants succulent, developing early in growing season, with aboveground portion drying by mid-summer. **Sterile blade** fleshy, once pinnate, sessile to the common stalk, oblong in outline, longitudinally folded; to about 4 cm long and 1.3 cm wide; usually divided into 5 pairs of linear or linear-spatulate segments; margins crenate or dentate and also usually notched into 2 or several smaller segments. **Common stalk** short, less than 3 cm long. **Sporophore** often

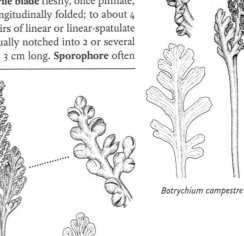

Botrychium campestre

tropophore

Botrychium gallicomontanum

sporophore

Botrychium lineare

Botrychium pseudopinnatum

large relative to size of sterile blade.—Inconspicuous in prairies, dunes, grassy railroad sidings, and fields over limestone. *Leaves appear in early spring and wither in late spring and early summer, long before those of other moonworts.*

Botrychium lanceolatum (Gmel.) Angstr.   MAP 55
TRIANGLE MOONWORT   ❧*threatened* | *native*

Plants 6-30 cm tall, dark green, smooth, appearing in early summer and persisting to fall. **Stems** about 5x longer than blades; blades triangular in outline, 1-8 cm long and 1-5 cm wide, stalkless or on a short stalk to 6 mm long, divided into 2-5 pairs of sharp-pointed, toothed pinnae, lowermost pair the largest. **Fertile segment** 2-9 cm long, mostly twice pinnate, on a stalk 1-3 cm long.—Moist, humus-rich woods, hummocks in swamps, streambanks. *Ours are var. angustisegmentum, found from Nfld and Ontario to Minn, becoming increasingly rare southward to NJ and Ohio.*

Botrychium lanceolatum

Botrychium lunaria (L.) Sw.   MAP 56
COMMON MOONWORT   ❧*threatened* | *native*

   Botrychium neolunaria Stensvold & Farrar sp. nov. ined., *B. onondagense* Underwood

Plants 3-20 cm tall, rubbery-textured, appearing in late spring and withering in summer. **Leaf blades** 1.5-7 cm long and 1-3 cm wide, stalkless or on a short stalk to 5 mm long; pinnately divided into 3-6 pairs of stalkless pinnae, the **pinnae** fan-shaped, wider than long and without a midrib; **petioles** 1.5-3 cm long. **Fertile segments** 0.5-7 cm long, on stalks about as long as the segments.—Cool, moist sandy soils in woods. *Stensvold and Farrar (2016) stated that our plants represent a genetically distinct, North American species which they termed **Botrychium neolunaria**. They treated plants traditionally named as B. lunaria as a circumpolar species occuring in North America only at high latitudes in Canada.*

Botrychium lunaria

Botrychium matricariifolium (A. Braun ex Dowell) A. Braun ex Koch   MAP 57
DAISY-LEAF MOONWORT   *native*

Plants to about 30 cm tall, membranous to fleshy. **Leaf blades** narrowly deltoid to ovate, short-stalked, inserted above the middle, pinnatifid to bipinnate-pinnatifid; segments of blade blunt and usually toothed. **Fertile segment** paniculate. **Spores** mature in June and July.—Acidic soil in old sandy and sterile fields, dry wooded slopes, rocky woods, moist cedar woods, and rich swamps. *This species is somewhat larger than **Botrychium simplex**. The shape of the blade is variable (deltoid to ovate) but it is stalked, and the toothed segments are distinctive (compare B. lanceolatum).*

Botrychium minganense Victorin   MAP 58
MINGAN MOONWORT   *native*

Plants to 30 cm long, somewhat membranous. **Leaf blades** narrowly oblong, sessile or nearly so, inserted below the middle, pinnate or occasionally pinnate-pinnatifid at the base; segments of blades opposite, obovate, rhomboidal or oblong, frequently incised, remote. **Fertile segment** paniculate. **Spores** mature in July and August.—Moist hardwood forests, aspen-balsam fir woods, and old clearings; soils mostly circumneutral. *Botrychium minganense can be distinguished from B. lunaria by its yellowish green hue and by its trough-shaped sterile segments, which are ascending rather than at right angles to the stalk and which rarely overlap with each other.*

Botrychium matricariifolium (l)
Botrychium minganense (r)

54. *Botrychium campestre*

55. *Botrychium lanceolatum*

56. *Botrychium lunaria*

57. *Botrychium matricariifolium*

Botrychium mormo W.H. Wagner
LITTLE GOBLIN MOONWORT   MAP 59
                              ❧ *threatened | native*

Our tiniest moonwort, uncommon; **leaves** appearing in late spring to fall or sometimes not appearing above the leaf litter. Plants to about 8-10 cm high but often smaller; yellow-green, somewhat shiny. **Sterile blade** variable; blade of well-developed plants with 2-3 pairs of small blunt lobes; blade in smaller plants may be nearly absent. **Sporophore** to about 3 cm long, with several sporangia embedded in the fleshy stalk.—Extremely sporadic in mature deciduous forests, typically dominated by sugar maple or basswood, and sometimes with eastern hemlock or northern white cedar. Sites shaded and moist; soils loamy, with a rich litter layer.

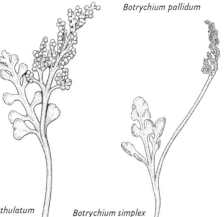

Botrychium pallidum W.H. Wagner
PALE MOONWORT   MAP 60
                                         native

Plants 2.5-7 cm tall, waxy pale green to whitish. **Sterile blade** to 4 cm long by 1 cm wide, 1-pinnate, with up to 5 pairs of fan-shaped pinnae, each pair of pinnae often folded towards each other; basal pinnae usually divided into 2 unequal lobes, the upper lobe larger; margins entire to irregularly toothed. **Sporangia** sometimes present on lobes of lower pinnae. **Sporophore** longer than sterile blade, the sporangia on short branches from main stalk.—Open fields, dry sand and gravel ridges, roadsides, wet depressions, marshy lakeshores, tailings basins, second-growth forests; soils sandy.

Botrychium mormo

Botrychium simplex E. Hitchc.
LEAST MOONWORT   MAP 61
                                         native

Plants to ca. 15 cm tall, rather fleshy. **Blades** simple, lobed or pinnately divided, inserted at the base or towards the middle; segments of blade oblong, rhomboid or kidney-shaped, and usually overlapping, with the basal segments occasionally pinnatifid. **Fertile segment** simple or compound. **Spores** mature in late May and June.—Pastures, meadows, lakeshores, and gravelly slopes. *Easily overlooked in the field due to its small size and presence below surrounding taller grasses.*

Botrychium spathulatum W.H. Wagner
SPOON-LEAF MOONWORT   MAP 62
                              ❧ *endangered | native*

Leaf single, erect, to 12 cm long; shiny yellowish-green, leathery. **Sterile blade** sessile or short-stalked (less than 1 mm long); pinna pairs mostly 4-5 (7), spoon- or fan-shaped, widest at tip; **lowest pinnae** largest, commonly folded over rachis; **pinnae** mostly widely spaced and not overlapping, outer pinna margins entire or lobed. **Sporophore** 1-2x length of the trophophore; 1-2 times pinnately divided into segments bearing the sporangia. Leaves appearing late spring through summer.—Sand dunes, old fields, grassy railways, often where underlain by limestone. *Botrychium spathulatum has long been confused with the more common **B. minganense**, with which it often grows in the Lake Superior region; leaves appear later in B. spathulatum than in B. minganense.*

Botrychium pallidum

Botrychium spathulatum

Botrychium simplex

58. *Botrychium minganense*

59. *Botrychium mormo*

60. *Botrychium pallidum*

61. *Botrychium simplex*

BOTRYPUS *Rattlesnake Fern*

Botrypus virginianus (L.) Holub
RATTLESNAKE FERN
Botrychium virginianum (L.) Sw.

MAP 63
native

Plants 40-75 cm tall, appearing in spring, withering in autumn, not overwintering. **Blade** (trophophore) broadly triangular, sessile, to 25 cm long and to 1.5x as wide, 3-4x pinnate, thin and herbaceous. **Pinnae** to 12 pairs, usually somewhat overlapping and slightly ascending; pinnules lance-shaped and deeply lobed, the lobes linear, sharply toothed and pointed at tip. **Spore-bearing portion** (sporophore) 2-pinnate, 0.5-1.5x length of trophophore.—Occasional in swamps of cedar and black spruce; more common in moist to fairly deciduous woods. *Rattlesnake fern is widespread in North America, occurring across Canada and all of the USA apart from Utah.*

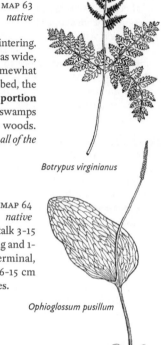

Botrypus virginianus

OPHIOGLOSSUM *Adder's-Tongue*

Ophioglossum pusillum Raf.
NORTHERN ADDER'S-TONGUE

MAP 64
native

Plants erect, 7-30 cm tall, from slender rhizomes. **Leaves** 1, entire, on a stalk 3-15 cm long; blades upright, oval to ovate, rounded to acute at tip, 3-8 cm long and 1-4 cm wide, conspicuously net-veined. **Sporangia** in 2 rows in a terminal, unbranched fertile segment, 1-5 cm long and 2-4 mm wide, on a stalk 6-15 cm long.—Wet sandy meadows and prairies, wetland margins, sandy beaches.

Ophioglossum pusillum

SCEPTRIDIUM *Grape Fern*

Small to medium leathery ferns found in a variety of moist to dry, open to shaded habitats, often where sandy. Sterile blades dissected, winter-green; sporophore short-lived, withering by late summer. Sterile blade and sporophore joined near or below ground level.

1　Sterile blade segments deeply cut more than half way to the midvein, the entire blade lacerate . . . . **S. dissectum**
1　Sterile blade segments finely to coarsely toothed 2
　　2　Ultimate segments of blade ± uniform in size; sterile blade segments finely toothed to ± entire; dissection of blade into segments extending to within 1 cm of apex at tips of blades 3
　　　　3　Segments of sterile blade rounded at base; symmetrically tapered to an often ± blunt tip; larger segments mostly 9-17 mm long; margins nearly entire or finely and inconspicuously toothed . . . . **S. multifidum**
　　　　3　Segments of sterile blade usually (obliquely) asymmetrical and angular, cuneate to the apex; larger segments mostly 4-9 mm long; margins clearly finely dentate, especially visible in immature leaves . . . **S. rugulosum**
　　2　Ultimate segments of blades variable in size, the apical segments much longer than the laterals; sterile blade segments coarsely and ± irregularly toothed or cut; dissection of blade into segments stopping at ca. 1-2.5 cm from apex at tips of blades 4
　　　　4　Overwintering leaves green, not bronze; larger (terminal) segments of vegetative blades narrowly to broadly ovate, obtuse to rounded at apex, ± symmetrical at base; margins toothed but never lacerate **S. oneidense**
　　　　4　Overwintering leaves bronze-colored (or green if covered by leaves); larger (terminal) segments of sterile blades lance-shaped, acute, and strongly asymmetric at base; margins toothed to irregularly cut . . . .
　　　　　　. . . . . **S. dissectum**

62. Botrychium spathulatum　　*63. Botrypus virginianus*　　*64. Ophioglossum pusillum*　　*65. Sceptridium dissectum*

Sceptridium dissectum (Spreng.) Lyon
CUT-LEAF GRAPE FERN
MAP 65
native

Botrychium dissectum Spreng.
Botrychium obliquum Muhl.

Leaves to 30 cm long; stem and blade less leathery than *S. multifidum*; **blades** long-petioled, triangular, 3-parted, attached at or near the base; ultimate divisions of blade cut in linear segments; segments more or less notched at the apex. **Fertile segment** paniculate. **Spores** mature Sept.-Nov.—Sterile hilltops, dry pastures, dry woodlands, and grassy banks. *Blades often turn bronze or reddish in late fall.*

Sceptridium multifidum (Gmel.) Nishida ex Tagawa
LEATHERY GRAPE FERN
MAP 66
native

Botrychium multifidum (Gmel.) Trev.

Leaves to 20 cm long; stem and blade coriaceous; **blades** evergreen, long-petioled, 3-parted, attached near the base of the plant; ultimate segments of blade crowded, sometimes imbricate, ovate, more or less the same size, obtuse or somewhat acute. **Fertile segment** paniculate. **Spores** mature in Aug and Sept.—Grassy hillsides, sterile fields, exposed meadows, and sandy open places.

Sceptridium dissectum

Sceptridium oneidense (Gilbert) Holub
BLUNT-LOBE GRAPE FERN
MAP 67
❦*threatened* | *native*

Botrychium oneidense (Gilbert) House

Leaves 40 cm long or longer; stem and blade somewhat leathery; blades triangular, 3-partedly decompound, little divided, attached at or near the base; chief terminal segments of blade broadly ovate and obtuse. **Fertile segment** paniculate. **Spores** mature in Sept-Oct.—Rich moist woodland. *The broad, rounded divisions and the preference for shaded habitats are characteristic.*

Sceptridium rugulosum (W..H. Wagner) Skoda & Holub
TERNATE GRAPE FERN
MAP 68
native

Botrychium rugulosum W.H. Wagner

Leaves 25 cm long or longer, thin and membranous; **blades** inserted at the base, 3-parted, with the three major divisions stalked; ultimate segments of blade all about the same size, ovate to oblong, acutish, serrate or entire, and concave. **Fertile segment** paniculate. **Spores** mature Aug-Oct.—Swampy woods, brushy fields, and wooded streambanks.

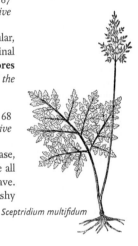

Sceptridium multifidum

Osmundaceae ROYAL FERN FAMILY

OSMUNDA *Royal Fern*

Perennial ferns with large rootstocks and exposed crowns covered with old roots and stalks, sending up tufts of coarse leaves. Leaves 1-2-pinnate, differentiated into sterile and fertile segments. Sporangia in round clusters, spores green. *The fibrous roots (osmunda fibre) were formerly used as a medium for growing orchids and bromeliads.*

1 Leaves 2-pinnate, pinnae ± entire; sporangia on upper half of fertile leaves . . . . ***O. regalis***
1 Leaves 1-pinnate, sterile pinnae deeply cleft; sporangia only near middle of fertile leaves, or fertile and sterile leaves separate 2
   2 Fertile and sterile leaves separate, fertile leaves cinnamon-colored, sterile leaves with a tuft of wool in axil of pinnae . . . . ***O. cinnamomea***

66. *Sceptridium multifidum*   67. *Sceptridium oneidense*   68. *Sceptridium rugulosum*

2 Fertile pinnae near middle of vegetative leaves, with sterile pinnae above and below fertile portion, fertile portion green-black, pinnae mostly without tuft of wool in axil. . . . . ***O. claytoniana***

Osmunda cinnamomea L.

CINNAMON-FERN

Osmundastrum cinnamomeum (L.) K. Presl

MAP 69
native

Large clumped fern, to 1 m or more tall. **Blades** of sterile leaves to 30 cm wide, gradually tapered to tip, 1-pinnate, with conspicuous tuft of white or brown woolly hairs at base of each pinna, **pinnae** stalkless and deeply cleft into segments, with fringe of short hairs on margins; **petioles** densely hairy when young. **Fertile leaves** at center of crown, surrounded by taller sterile leaves, without leafy tissue, arising in spring or early summer and turning cinnamon brown, withering and inconspicuous by midsummer.—Swamps, bog-margins, wooded streambanks, and low wet places; soils acid.

Osmunda cinnamomea

Osmunda claytoniana L.

INTERRUPTED FERN

MAP 70
native

Clumped fern to 1 m or more tall; often forming large colonies. **Outer leaves** usually sterile, **inner leaves** larger and with 2-5 pairs of fertile pinnae in middle of blade; fertile segments to 6 cm long and 2 cm wide and much smaller than vegetative segments above and below them; **sporangia clusters** at first green-black, turning dark brown and withering. **Blades** 4-10 dm long and 15-30 cm wide; pinnae stalkless and deeply cut into segments, with smooth or slightly hairy margins. **Petioles** covered with tufts of woolly hairs when young, becoming smooth or sparsely hairy with age, the hairs not forming tufts at pinna-bases (as in *O. cinnamomea*).—Moist or seasonally wet depressions in forests, hummocks in swamps, low prairie, wet roadsides; often in drier places than *Osmunda cinnamomea* or *O. regalis*.

Osmunda regalis L.

ROYAL FERN

MAP 71
native

Large fern to 1 m or more tall. **Blades** broadly ovate in outline, 4-8 dm long and to 3-5 dm wide, 2-pinnate into ± opposite divisions (pinnules), these well-spaced, oblong, rounded at tips, with entire or finely toothed margins. **Fertile leaves** with uppermost several pinnae replaced by sporangia clusters. **Petioles** smooth, green or red-green, to 3/4 length of blade.—Bogs, swamps, alder thickets and shallow pools; soils usually acidic.

Osmunda claytoniana

69. *Osmunda cinnamomea*   70. *Osmunda claytoniana*   71. *Osmunda regalis*

Osmunda regalis

Polypodiaceae POLYPODY FERN FAMILY

POLYPODIUM *Polypody*

Polypodium virginianum L.

ROCK POLYPODY

Polypodium vulgare auct. non L. p.p.

MAP 72
native

Evergreen, colony-forming fern. **Leaf blades** to 50 cm long from a creeping rhizome; oblong lance-shaped; pinnatifid, leathery; veins free. **Sori** round, midway between the midvein and margin, and occurring on the upper segments; **indusia** absent.—In shallow humus on rocks, in crevices, on woodland banks, and rarely on mossy stumps and in crotches of trees. *Easily identified by the small evergreen blades and its colony-forming habit on rocky slopes, talus, boulders, and ledges.*

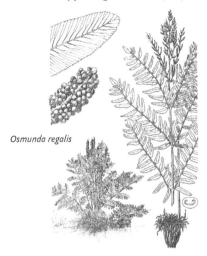

Polypodium virginianum

Osmunda regalis

Pteridaceae MAIDENHAIR FERN FAMILY

Delicate to coarse ferns, deciduous, or evergreen. Blades pinnate to decompound. Sori marginal, protected by the indusium, which opens toward the margin, or by the reflexed margins of the pinnae, or borne along the veins and lacking an indusium.

1　Blade segments separate from one another . . . . *Adiantum pedatum*
1　Blade segments not separate and distinct 2
　　2　Leaves of two types, the fertile much longer than the sterile; petioles dark brown near base, green above . .
　　　　. . . . . *Cryptogramma stelleri*
　　2　Fertile and sterile leaves mostly similar; petioles dark brown to black 3
　　　　3　Smallest blade segments more than 4 mm wide . . . . *Pellaea*
　　　　3　Smallest segments less than 4 mm wide　. . . . . *Cheilanthes feei*

ADIANTUM *Maidenhair Fern*

Adiantum pedatum L.
NORTHERN MAIDENHAIR FERN

MAP 73
native

Leaves 30-60 cm tall, in colonies arising from horizontal rhizomes. **Petioles** lustrous purple-brown, forking at the summit into two arching rachises, each of which is divided several times, thus forming a semicircular blade 15-35 cm wide or wider. **Pinnules** short-stalked, obliquely triangular oblong; terminal pinnule fan-shaped; main vein along the lower margin; upper margin cleft, with lobes thus formed blunt. **Sori** elongate, borne on the upper margins of the lobes of the pinnules; **indusium** formed by the inrolled margin.—Wooded, sometimes rocky slopes in humus-rich soil. *The arching and palmately divided lustrous purple-brown rachises and fan-shaped pinnules are distinctive.*

Adiantum pedatum

CHEILANTHES *Lip Fern*

Cheilanthes feei T. Moore
SLENDER LIP FERN

MAP 74
native

Small evergreen ferns of dry rocky places; **rhizome** short and much branched, bearing numerous brown to blackish, hyaline-margined scales. **Leaves** 5-20 cm long, tufted. **Leaf blades** 2-10 cm long, oblong to ovate, tripinnate; **pinnae** deltoid to ovate-oblong; rachis and lower side densely tomentose with pale brown hairs; upper surface with soft whitish hairs; ultimate segments small and rounded. **Petioles** 3-10 cm long, dark purplish brown, with a few scarious-margined scales at the base and tawny hairs above. Margins of segments somewhat inrolled but

Cheilanthes feei

not covering the mature sporangia, which cover the entire lower surface.—Crevices of limestone or calcareous cliffs. *Distinguished from other ferns by the small, bead-like segments of the pinnae.*

CRYPTOGRAMMA *Rockbrake*

Cryptogramma stelleri (Gmel.) Prantl
MAP 75
FRAGILE ROCKBRAKE
native

Small ferns of rocky places with dimorphic leaves, from branched or elongate rhizomes. **Leaves** glabrous, deciduous, dimorphic, scattered along the horizontal rhizome. **Sterile leaves** almost flaccid, 3-10 cm long; **blades** ovate to ovate-deltoid, bipinnate; pinnules oblong or ovate; **petioles** purplish. **Fertile leaves** stiffer than sterile blades, 9-21 cm long; **pinnules** lance-shaped to oblong. **Sori** marginal, covered by a continuous indusium formed by the reflexed margin.—Moist, shaded, usually calcareous crevices and cliffs. *Plants may be easily overlooked later in the season as they turn brown and wither.*

Cryptogramma stelleri

PELLAEA *Cliffbrake*

Small tufted plants from compact rootstocks. Blades firm; petioles and rachises wiry; pinnae gray green; veins free. Sori marginal and confluent under the inrolled and altered margin of the fertile pinnules. Plants gray-green in color that blends well with their habitat of limestone rock crevices.

1 Petiole and rachis scurfy and with incurved hairs . . . . *P. atropurpurea*
1 Petiole and rachis glabrous or with a few spreading hairs . . . . *P. glabella*

Pellaea atropurpurea (L.) Link
MAP 76
PURPLE-STEM CLIFFBRAKE
native

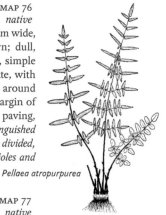

Leaves similar to somewhat dimorphic; **fertile frond** 10-35 cm long, 3.5-8 cm wide, longer than the sterile frond. **Petioles** and **rachis** dark purple brown; dull, pubescent, with incurved hairs. **Pinnae** rigid, evergreen, bluish green, simple above, bipinnate below; **fertile pinnae** linear to oblong or narrowly ovate, with the lower pinnules stalked; **sterile pinnules** ovate-oblong. **Sori** situated around the margins of the fertile pinnules; **indusium** formed by the inrolled margin of pinnule.—Dry, steep, exposed, limestone rock slopes or cliffs, limestone paving, and tops of large talus boulders. *Similar to Pellaea glabella but may be distinguished from it by the usually taller, more upright habit, with fertile blades that are more divided, that are darker blue green to olive green, and that have markedly hairy petioles and rachis.*

Pellaea atropurpurea

Pellaea glabella Mett.
MAP 77
SMOOTH CLIFFBRAKE
native

Leaves all similar, 10-25 cm long or longer, usually shorter than those of *P. atropurpurea*, open and spreading out beyond the rock face. **Petioles** and **rachis** dark reddish brown, smooth, and lustrous. **Pinnae** rigid, evergreen, bluish green, simple above, pinnate below; **basal pinnae** persistent; **pinnules** sessile or nearly so, oblong lance-shaped. **Sori** situated around the margins of the fertile pinnules; **indusium** formed by the inrolled margin of pinnule.—Crevices of dry, sometimes partly shaded, limestone cliffs. *A distinctive species of high, steep limestone cliffs and blending well with the background rock.*

72. *Polypodium virginianum*

73. *Adiantum pedatum*

74. *Cheilanthes feei*

Pellaea glabella

Salviniaceae WATER FERN FAMILY

AZOLLA *Mosquito-Fern*

Azolla cristata Kaulfuss
CRESTED MOSQUITO-FERN
    Azolla caroliniana Willd.
    Azolla mexicana Schltdl. & Cham. ex K. Presl
    Azolla microphylla Kaulfuss

MAP 78
native

Small annual aquatic fern; plants free-floating or forming floating mats several cm thick, sometimes stranded on mud; roots few and unbranched. **Stems** lying flat, 1-1.5 cm long, green or red, covered with small, alternate, overlapping leaves in 2 rows; **leaves** 2-lobed, the upper lobe to 1 mm long, emergent; lower lobe underwater and larger than the upper. **Sporangia** of 2 kinds; larger female megaspores (to 0.6 mm long) and tiny male spores (microsporangia), and borne in separate sporocarps. **Sporocarps** usually in pairs on underwater lobes of some leaves.—Local in quiet water of river backwaters and ponds.

Azolla cristata

Selaginellaceae SELAGINELLA FAMILY

SELAGINELLA *Spikemoss*

Trailing, evergreen herbs with branched, leafy stems, rooting at branching points. Leaves small and overlapping. Spore-bearing leaves similar to vegetative leaves and clustered in cones at ends of branches. Megaspores 4 in each sporangium, yellow or white; microspores numerous and very small, red or yellow, covered with small spines.

1   Leaves and stems firm and evergreen, the plants forming small tufts 2.5-5 cm high; leaves crowded, very narrow, tipped by a bristle; cones four-angled . . . . **S. rupestris**

1   Leaves and stems lax and subevergreen or deciduous; plants forming small mats; cones nearly round in cross-section . . . . **S. selaginoides**

Selaginella rupestris (L.) Spring
LEDGE SPIKE-MOSS
    Lycopodium rupestre L.

MAP 79
native

Stems prostrate, forming open mats. **Leaves** decurrent on the sides of the stem; leaves linear-lance-shaped, about 2.8 mm long (including the approximately 0.7 mm long scabrous seta), grooved on the back, ciliate. **Sporophylls** narrowly ovate, apiculate, ciliate, about as long as the leaves.—Sand dunes and open or shaded, dry, often igneous rocky bluffs.

Selaginella selaginoides (L.) Link
NORTHERN SPIKEMOSS

(NO MAP)
🖤*endangered | native*

Trailing, evergreen plants forming small mats. **Stems** branched, leafy, rooting at branching points. **Sterile stems** prostrate, 2-5 cm long; **fertile stems** upright, deciduous, 5-10 cm high and 0.5 mm wide (stem only), changing upward into broader sporophylls. **Leaves** overlapping in multiple spiral rows, all alike, 2-4 mm long and l mm wide, with sharp tips and sparsely hairy margins; spore-bearing leaves similar to vegetative leaves and clustered in cones at ends of branches; **cones** ± cylindric but with 4 rounded angles, 1.5-3 cm long and to 5 mm wide. **Megaspores** 4 in each sporangium, yellow-white, with low rounded projections on the 3 flat surfaces.—Mossy hummocks in cedar swamps and fens; Cook Co.

Selaginella selaginoides

75. Cryptogramma stelleri   *76. Pellaea atropurpurea*   *77. Pellaea glabella*   *78. Azolla cristata*

Thelypteridaceae MARSH FERN FAMILY

Medium-sized deciduous ferns, spreading by rhizomes to form colonies; sterile and fertile fronds usually alike, 1-pinnate to pinnate-pinnatifid, with transparent needle-like hairs; sori usually on veins (but not marginal) on pinna underside; indusia present and often soon withering, or absent (*Phegopteris*).

1   Leaf blades broadly triangular in outline, broadest at base, lowermost pinnae directed downward; indusia absent
     . . . . *Phegopteris*

1   Blades lance-shaped in outline, broadest above base; indusia present . . . . *Thelypteris*

PHEGOPTERIS *Beech-Fern*

Deciduous ferns with creeping rhizomes. Leaf blades triangular in outline, 1-pinnate-pinnatifid (the pinnae deeply lobed); rachis winged, with spreading, ovate-lance-shaped scales; veins free, simple or often forked, veins of segment reaching margin or nearly so; underside hairs unbranched, unicellular. Sori round to oblong, indusia absent.

1   Rachis winged to base; underside of blade sparsely hairy . . . . *P. hexagonoptera*
1   Rachis not winged at base; underside of blade usually densely hairy and scaly . . . . *P. connectilis*

Phegopteris connectilis (Michaux) Watt

NORTHERN BEECH-FERN   MAP 80

     Dryopteris phegopteris (L.) C.Chr.   *native*
     Thelypteris phegopteris (L.) Slosson

Fern with long, slender, scaly and densely hairy **rhizomes**. **Leaves** triangular, 15–25 cm long and 6-15 cm wide; **blades** 1-pinnate, the pinnalike divisions joined by a wing along rachis, except for lowermost pair which are free and angled downward; **pinnules** oblong, rounded at tip, and usually hairy; **petioles** longer than blades, hairy, with narrow, brown scales.—Cool moist woods, thickets, streambanks, sphagnum moss hummocks, shaded rock crevices.

Phegopteris hexagonoptera (Michx.) Fée

BROAD BEECH-FERN   MAP 81

     Thelypteris hexagonoptera (Michx.) Weatherby   ❧ *endangered | native*

Leaves 30-60 cm long or longer. **Leaf blades** broadly triangular, 15-30 cm wide or wider, about as broad as long, tapering to the top, pinnate-pinnatifid; middle and upper pinna-like divisions lance-shaped; lower pinna-like divisions unequally ovate to lance-shaped, not projected forward; all divisions connected by a wing; the segments, especially of the lower pinnae, often deeply pinnatifid. **Petiole** naked except at the base; **rachis** not chaffy or with almost colorless scales; rachis and veins minutely glandular puberulent. **Sori** small, near the margin.—Rare in rich, often rocky woods and on wooded slopes. *Phegopteris hexagonoptera has all the divisions of the blade connected to the rachis, including the basal pair. In shape, the blade is more broadly triangular in broad beech fern than in northern beech fern. The shape of the basal segments is unlike that in P. connectilis, being widest in the middle and lobed again rather than entire.*

Phegopteris connectilis

Phegopteris hexagonoptera

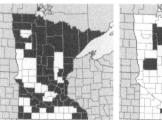

79. Selaginella rupestris   *80. Phegopteris connectilis*   *81. Phegopteris hexagonoptera*

THELYPTERIS *Marsh-Fern*

Thelypteris palustris Schott
MARSH-FERN

MAP 82
native

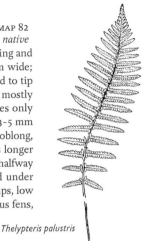

Small to medium ferns from slender rhizomes; **rhizomes** slender, spreading and branching. **Leaves** deciduous, ± hairy, erect, 20-60 cm long and to 15 cm wide; blades broadly lance-shaped, short-hairy on rachis and midveins, tapered to tip and only slightly narrowed at base; 1-pinnate, pinnae in 10-25 pairs, mostly alternate, narrowly lance-shaped, to 2 cm wide. Sterile and fertile leaves only slightly different; **sterile leaves** thin and delicate, pinnules blunt-tipped, 3-5 mm wide, veins once-forked. **Fertile leaves** longer than sterile leaves; pinnules oblong, 2-4 mm wide, the margins rolled under, veins mostly 1-forked; petioles longer than blades, black at base, hairless and without scales. **Sori** round, located halfway between midvein and margin, sometimes partly covered by the rolled under margin; **indusia** irregular in shape, usually with a fringe of hairs.—Swamps, low areas in forests, sedge meadows, forest depressions, open bogs, calcareous fens, marshes.

Thelypteris palustris

Woodsiaceae CLIFF FERN FAMILY

WOODSIA *Cliff Fern*

Small tufted ferns arising from compact rootstocks. Indusium of thread-like or plate-like segments, more or less arched over the round sori. Sometimes confused with *Cystopteris*, distinguishing features include:in *Woodsia* petioles scaly nearly to base of blade (in *Cystopteris*, scales absent except near base of petioles); petioles opaque in *Woodsia* and translucent in *Cystopteris* (visible when held up to the light in the field); veins in *Woodsia* less distinct and appear to stop short of the margin; in *Cystopteris*, veins clearly extend to the margin; in *Woodsia*, old petiole bases persist as either an even or uneven stubble (see key).

HYBRIDS
Woodsia × abbeae Butters is a hybrid between *W. ilvensis* and *W. oregana*, known from mostly ne Minn.

1 Stipe jointed above base, the old stubble more or less uniform height. 2
   2 Fronds delicate, smooth; stipe green; blade to only 1.5 cm wide, lower pinnae reduced to wings; indusium splitting into short hairs; rare in ne Minn . . . . *W. glabella*
   2 Fronds firm; stipe and lower rachis brown; indusium splitting into many long hairs. 3
      3 Blade narrow, nearly smooth; rare in Minn . . . . *W. alpina*
      3 Blade wider, densely hairy; widespread species . . . . *W. ilvensis*
1 Stipe not jointed, the stubble irregular 4
   4 Indusium shallowly split into wide segments . . . . *W. obtusa*
   4 Indusium deeply split into narrow segments 5
      5 Pubescence a mix of gland-tipped and long white hairs; pinnae crowded; rare in ne Minn . . *W. scopulina*
      5 Pubescence of gland-tipped hairs only, or hairs absent; pinnae spaced. . . . . *W. oregana*

Woodsia alpina (Bolton) S.F. Gray
ALPINE WOODSIA

MAP 83
🗨*threatened* | *native*

Small deciduous fern; **leaves** in dense clusters; sterile and fertile leaves alike; 10-20 cm long. **Blades** lance-shaped, broadest below middle; 1-pinnate-pinnatifid (barely so), bright green; **pinnae** 8 to 15 pairs, largest pinnae with 1-3 pairs of pinnules, the shorter ones merely fan-shaped; margins nearly entire, merely lobed; veins free, simple or forked. **Petioles** red-brown or dark purple when mature, jointed above base at swollen node halfway up petiole, red-brown lance-shaped scales at base, fewer upwards. **Rootstock** erect,with numerous persistent stipe bases of nearly equal length. **Sori** round, near the margin; **indusium** dissected into hairlike segments enveloping sorus, unravelling with maturity; sporangia brownish. —Crevices and ledges of moist, partially shaded cliffs of acidic rock.

Woodsia alpina

Woodsia glabella R. Br. ex Richardson (NO MAP)
SMOOTH WOODSIA ✅*threatened | native*
Small deciduous fern; **leaves** in small clusters; sterile and fertile leaves alike; 5-15
cm long. **Blades** linear to linear lance-shaped, 1-pinnate-pinnatifid; pale green,
without hairs; **pinnae** 7 to 9 pairs, sessile, largest pinnae with 1-3 pairs of
pinnules, lower pinnae sometimes fan-shaped; margins entire or crenate, often
folding downwards. **Petioles** green or straw-colored throughout, jointed above
base at swollen node, to only ca. 3 cm long; scales broadly lance-shaped, to 4 mm,
yellow-brown at base, smooth above the joint. **Rootstock** with abundant
persistent petiole bases of nearly equal length. **Sori** small, near margin; **indusium**
a saucer-shaped disk underneath sori, dissected into hairlike segments, these
visible only while sori young; sporangia brownish.—Crevices in moist, north-
facing cliffs, the rock basic to acidic. Cook and Lake counties.

Woodsia glabella

Woodsia ilvensis (L.) R. Br. MAP 84
RUSTY CLIFF FERN *native*
Small fern with **leaves** 10-30 cm long, 2-3 cm wide, oblong lance-shaped, pinnate
to bipinnate; **pinnae** oblong lance-shaped; margins of the segments crenate and
usually somewhat inrolled. **Petioles** jointed, with the old petiole-bases persistent
and about the same length; **rachis** and undersurface of the blade usually brown-
chaffy. **Sori** round and close together on the underside; **indusia** of many long
ciliate segments.—Dry, often exposed, rocks and crevices of cliff faces and talus,
the rock usually acidic. *Plants are both scaly and glandular.*

Woodsia obtusa (Spreng.) Torr. MAP 85
BLUNT-LOBED WOODSIA *native*
Small fern with **leaves** 10-30 cm long, 2-10 cm wide. **Blades** broadly lance-shaped,
pinnate; **pinnae** mostly separate from one another; lower pinnae triangular;
middle and upper pinnae ovate lance-shaped, pinnatifid, or pinnate at the base.
Petioles not jointed; **rachis** straw-colored, glandular-hairy. **Sori** round, located
near the margins; **indusia** covering the sori, splitting into several jagged lobes
later in the season.—Usually on talus, occasionally on shaded ledges and rocky
slopes. *Woodsia obtusa is an erect, rather robust species resembling* **Cystopteris fragilis***,
with which it often grows; W. obtusa is stiffer, with glands and scales on the axes and
veins.*

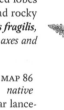

*Woodsia ilvensis
pinnae detail (upper)
habit (lower)*

Woodsia oregana D.C. Eat. MAP 86
OREGON WOODSIA *native*
Small fern with **leaves** mostly 10-30 cm long, 1-3 cm wide. **Blades** linear lance-
shaped; **pinnae** opposite, mostly separate from one another, triangular-oblong;
pinnules oblong, blunt, with marginal crenulate-serrate teeth often inrolled.
Petioles not jointed; rachis dark brown at base, becoming straw-colored above,
glabrous or finely glandular, usually without scales. **Sori** round; **indusia** of narrow
and threadlike segments.—Crevices of calcareous ledges and cliffs. *Somewhat
similar to* **Woodsia ilvensis** *but usually without scales and on calcareous rather than acid
rock; the stubble is uneven rather than even as in W. ilvensis.*

Woodsia scopulina D.C. Eaton Windham MAP 87
ROCKY MOUNTAIN WOODSIA ✅*threatened | native*
Small deciduous fern; rootstock erect, with few to many old stipe bases of unequal
length. **Leaves** clumped, sterile and fertile leaves alike, to 30 cm long. **Blades**

Woodsia oregana

82. Thelypteris palustris

83. Woodsia alpina

84. Woodsia ilvensis

tapering to both ends, truncated at base, mostly 2-pinnate but variable, gray-green, glandular and sparsely hairy on both surfaces; **pinnae** 10 to 15 pairs, lowest distinctly reduced, sessile or nearly so, pairs further apart the closer to the base; margins dentate or lobed. **Petioles** shiny, chestnut-brown, with persistent bases of unequal lengths; scales tan; **rachis** with glandular hairs and scattered, white, hairlike scales. **Sori** round, near the margin; **indusium** of strap-like lobes encircling sorus, frayed at tips; sporangia brown, maturing to black.—North-facing cliffs of slate rock; sites cool, moist and shaded.

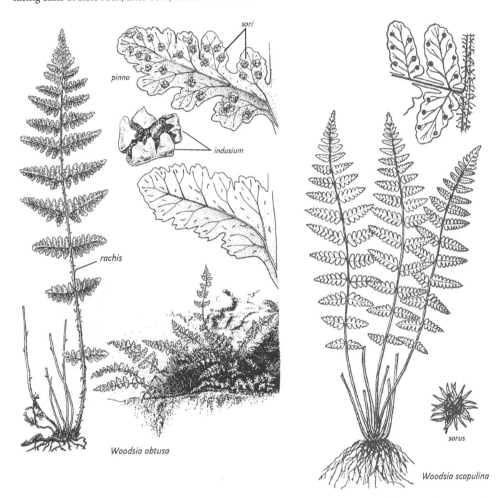

Woodsia obtusa

Woodsia scopulina

85. Woodsia obtusa   *86. Woodsia oregana*   *87. Woodsia scopulina*

CONIFERS

Cupressaceae CYPRESS FAMILY

Trees or shrubs; leaves opposite or whorled, sometimes dimorphic, separated by short internodes or overlapping. Flowers monoecious or dioecious, solitary, axillary or terminal. Staminate flowers of several stamens with short filaments. Pistillate flowers with opposite or whorled carpels or with 1-3 terminal ovules. Fruit a cone, or becoming fleshy and berry-like.

1   Trees or shrubs; cones berry-like and fleshy . . . .*Juniperus*
1   Trees; cones woody or leathery . . . . *Thuja*

JUNIPERUS *Juniper*

Trees or shrubs; leaves evergreen, scale-like or subulate, opposite or in whorls of 3. Flowers monoecious or dioecious, axillary and short-stalked, or terminal. Staminate flowers catkin-like; stamens numerous, opposite or whorled. Pistillate flowers of several scales, the lower sterile, the terminal sometimes fertile, or sometimes sterile and the ovules terminal. Cone-scales at maturity becoming fleshy and coalescent, forming an indehiscent, usually colored, berry-like fruit with 1-10 seeds; seeds plump, wingless.

1   Leaves in clusters of three, linear and sharp-pointed, jointed at base; cones in leaf axils . . . .*J. communis*
1   Leaves scale-like, not jointed; cones at end of branches 2
  2   Tree or upright shrub . . . .*J. virginiana*
  2   Prostrate shrub . . . .*J. horizontalis*

Juniperus communis L.   MAP 88
COMMON JUNIPER   *native*
Evergreen shrub. **Leaves** in whorls of 3, crowded, linear, sharp-pointed, 6-15 mm long, marked with a median white stripe above. **Fruit** bluish or black, 6-13 mm in diameter, normally 3-seeded.—Dry woods, old fields, dried bogs, rocky bluffs. *Ours* **var. depressa** *Pursh., with branches soon becoming decumbent and forming large circular patches eventually several meters in diameter, usually flat-topped and 0.5-2 m tall; leaves spreading or ascending.*

Juniperus communis

Juniperus horizontalis Moench   MAP 89
CREEPING JUNIPER   *native*
Evergreen shrub; **branches** prostrate, often greatly elongate, bearing numerous erect **branchlets** 1-3 dm tall. **Leaves** mostly scale-like and appressed, varying from ovate, 1-2 mm long, to oblong and to 4 mm long. **Fruit** blue, 5-8 mm in diameter, on short recurved pedicels; seeds 3-5 mm long, not pitted.—On rocks, sandy openings, sandy or gravelly shores, sand dunes and beach ridges.

Juniperus virginiana L.   MAP 90
EASTERN RED CEDAR   *native*
Shrub or tree with dense crown, to 20 m tall. **Leaves** of two forms, often on the same plant; **scale-like leaves** appressed, ovate to ovate-lance-shaped, 2-4 mm long, obtuse or subacute, convex on the back; **subulate leaves** spreading or ascending, sharp-pointed, 5-7 mm long; intermediate types occur. **Fruit** subglobose, blue, glaucous, 5-7 mm in diameter; seeds ovoid, 3-4 mm long, with deep or shallow pits near the base.—Old fields, open hillsides, dry woods, stabilized sand dunes.

Juniperus horizontalis

Juniperus virginiana

THUJA *Arbor-Vitae*

Thuja occidentalis L.
NORTHERN WHITE CEDAR; ARBOR-VITAE

MAP 91
native

Shade-tolerant tree to 20 m tall, cone-shaped with widely spreading branches, sometimes layered at base, trunk to 1 m wide or more, **bark** reddish or gray-brown, in long shreddy strips; **twigs** flattened, in fanlike sprays. **Leaves** scale-like and overlapping, 3-6 mm long and 1-2 mm wide, yellow-green, aromatic, persisting for 1-2 years. **Seed cones** small, brown, 1 cm long, maturing in fall and persisting over winter.—Cold, poorly drained swamps where *Thuja* may form dense stands; soils neutral or basic, usually highly organic, water not stagnant; also along streams, on gravelly and sandy shores, and dry soils over limestone.

Thuja occidentalis

Pinaceae PINE FAMILY

Resinous trees with evergreen or deciduous, needlelike leaves. Male and female cones separate but borne on same tree. Male cones small and soft, falling after pollen is shed. Female cones larger, with woody scales arranged in a spiral. Seeds on upper surface of scales.

ADDITIONAL SPECIES
Pseudotsuga menziesii (Mirbel) Franco (Douglas-fir), native to nw USA and w Canada; known from Winona County, where likely an escape from a planting.

1 Leaves grouped into clusters 2
  2 Leaves evergreen, in clusters of 2-5 needles . . . . *Pinus*
  2 Leaves deciduous, with many leaves in each cluster . . . . *Larix laricina*
1 Leaves not in clusters, alternate on branches 3
  3 Cones upright; leaves attached directly to branch, not leaving a bump when shed . . . . *Abies balsamea*
  3 Cones drooping; leaves attached to a persistent short stalk 4
    4 Leaves flat in cross-section, soft . . . . *Tsuga canadensis*
    4 Leaves four-sided in cross-section, stiff . . . . *Picea*

ABIES *Fir*

Abies balsamea (L.) Miller
BALSAM FIR

MAP 92
native

Shade-tolerant tree to 25 m tall, crown spirelike, trunk to 6 dm wide; **bark** thin, smooth and gray, becoming brown and scaly with age; lower branches often drooping; **twigs** sparsely short-hairy. **Leaves** evergreen, linear, 12-25 mm long and 1-2 mm wide, blunt or with a small notch at tip, flat in cross-section, twisted at base and arranged in 1 plane (especially on lower branches), or spiraled on twigs. **Seed cones** 5-10 cm long and 1.5-3 cm wide, with broadly rounded scales. —Cold boreal forests, swamps, and moist forests in northern Minn; southward, mostly restricted to fens.

Abies balsamea

ADDITIONAL SPECIES
Abies fraseri (Pursh) Poir. (Fraser fir), native to se USA; in Minn known from Kanabec County where likely a plantation escape.

88. *Juniperus communis*   89. *Juniperus horizontalis*   90. *Juniperus virginiana*   91. *Thuja occidentalis*

LARIX *Larch*

Larix laricina (Duroi) K. Koch
TAMARACK; EASTERN LARCH

MAP 93
native

Shade-intolerant tree to 20 m tall, crown narrow, trunk to 6 dm wide; **bark** smooth and gray when young, becoming scaly and red-brown; **twigs** yellow-brown, ± horizontal or with upright tips. **Leaves** deciduous, in clusters of 10-20, linear, 1-2.5 cm long and less than 1 mm wide, soft, blunt-tipped, bright green, turning yellow in fall. **Seed cones** 1-2 cm long and 0.5-1 cm wide, ripening in fall and persisting on trees for 1 year.—Cold, poorly drained swamps, bogs and wet lakeshores.

ADDITIONAL SPECIES
Larix decidua Mill. (European larch), native to Eurasia; reported from Dakota and St. Louis counties.

Larix laricina

PICEA *Spruce*

Evergreen trees; bark thin and scaly, resin blisters common in white spruce (*Picea glauca*). Leaves linear, square in cross-section, stiff, spreading in all directions around twig, jointed at the base to a short projecting sterigma which persists on the leafless branches. Cones borne on last year's branches, drooping, with persistent scales much exceeding the bracts. Seeds wing-margined. *Several species are commonly cultivated, especially* **Norway spruce** *(Picea abies)*.

ADDITIONAL SPECIES
Picea pungens Engelm. (Blue spruce), native to w USA; in Minn known from Lake of the Woods County where a probable plantation escape.

1   Leaves mostly 0.5-1.2 cm long, blunt-tipped; twigs with rust-colored hairs; cones ovoid, less than twice as long as wide when open . . . . *P. mariana*
1   Leaves mostly 1-2 cm long, sharp-tipped; twigs glabrous; cones more than twice as long as wide 2
    2   Cones 2.5-5 cm long; native species . . . . *P. glauca*
    2   Cones larger, 12-15 cm long; introduced species . . . . *P. abies*

Picea abies (L.) Karst.
NORWAY SPRUCE

MAP 94
introduced

Trees to 30 m; crown cone-shaped; **bark** gray-brown, scaly; **branches** short and stout, the upper ascending, the lower drooping; **twigs** stout, reddish brown, usually glabrous. **Leaves** 1-2.5 cm, 4-angled in cross section, rigid, light to dark green, bearing stomates on all surfaces, apex blunt-tipped. **Seed cones** (10-)12-16 cm long; scales diamond-shaped, widest near middle, 18-30 x 15-20 mm, thin and flexuous, margin at apex erose to toothed, apex extending 6-10 mm beyond seed-wing impression.—Introduced from Europe, *P. abies* is the most widely cultivated spruce in North America, widely planted as a shade tree, sometimes used for reforestation, and now locally naturalized in woods.

Picea abies

Picea glauca (Moench) Voss
WHITE SPRUCE

MAP 95
native

Moderately shade-tolerant tree to 30 m tall (often smaller), crown conelike, trunk to 60 cm or more wide; **bark** thin, gray-brown; **branches** slightly drooping, hairless. **Leaves** evergreen, linear, 1.5-2 cm long, 4-angled in cross-section, stiff,

Picea glauca

92. *Abies balsamea*   93. *Larix laricina*   94. *Picea abies*

waxy blue-green, sharp-tipped. **Cones** 2.5-6 cm long, scales fan-shaped, rounded at tip, the tip entire.—Moist to sometimes wet forests; absent from wetlands where water is stagnant.

Picea mariana (Miller) BSP.
BLACK SPRUCE   MAP 96

native

Moderately shade-tolerant tree to 25 m tall (often smaller), crown narrow, often clublike at top, trunk to 25 cm wide; **bark** thin, scaly, gray-brown; **branches** short and drooping, often layered at base. **Leaves** evergreen, linear, 6-18 mm long, 4-angled in cross-section, stiff, waxy blue-green, mostly blunt-tipped. **Seed cones** 1.5-3 cm long, scales irregularly toothed, persisting for many years.—Cold, acid, sphagnum bogs, swamps, and lakeshores; often where water is slow-moving and low in oxygen; less common in calcium-rich, well-aerated swamps dominated by northern white cedar (*Thuja occidentalis*). *Black spruce can be distinguished from white spruce (Picea glauca) by its shorter needles, the branches with fine, white to red-brown hairs, the smaller, rounded seed cones with toothed scale margins, and its occurrence in generally wetter (and sometimes stagnant) habitats.*

Picea mariana

PINUS *Pine*

Trees (ours) with dimorphic branches and leaves, the foliage leaves borne on dwarf branches only, solitary or in clusters of 2-5. Staminate flowers catkin-like, in fascicles at the base of the current year's growth, each composed of numerous spirally imbricate stamens. Pistillate flowers forming a cone consisting of numerous spirally imbricate cone-scales, each subtended by a bract and bearing 2 inverted ovules at the base. Fruit a hard woody cone, maturing at the end of the second or third season and often long persistent on the tree; seeds winged.

ADDITIONAL SPECIES
Pinus rigida Mill. (Pitch pine), native to e USA and Canada; in Minn known from Washington County where a plantation escape.

1 Leaves in clusters of 5; cones 10-25 cm long	*P. strobus*
1 Leaves in clusters of 2; cones less than 10 cm long	2
2 Leaves 10-15 cm long	*P. resinosa*
2 Leaves 2.5-10 cm long	3
3 Cones persistent on branches; bark dark gray	*P. banksiana*
3 Cones not persistent on branches; bark of upper trunk becoming orange-brown	*P. sylvestris*

Pinus banksiana Lamb.
JACK PINE   MAP 97

native

Usually a small tree, but occasionally to 20 m or more tall, with spreading branches. **Leaves** in pairs, usually somewhat curved, 2-3.5 cm long, 1-1.5 mm wide. **Cones** erect or strongly ascending, usually somewhat curved or unsymmetrical, conic, yellowish-brown, 3-5 cm long; seeds about 1.5 cm long. —Dry or sterile, sandy or rocky soil.

Pinus resinosa Soland.
RED PINE   MAP 98

native

Tree, occasionally 40 m tall. **Leaves** in clusters of 2, slender, soft and flexible, 10-15 cm long, dark green. **Cones** spreading, conic-ovoid, 4-8 cm long; seeds 1.5-2 cm long.—Dry sandy or rocky soil; often used in plantations.

Pinus banksiana

95. Picea glauca   *96. Picea mariana*   *97. Pinus banksiana*   *98. Pinus resinosa*

Pinus strobus L.

MAP 99

EASTERN WHITE PINE
native

Tall tree, occasionally as much as 70 m tall, with thick furrowed bark. **Leaves** in clusters of 5, very slender, pale green and glaucous, 8-13 cm long. **Cones** cylindric, 10-15 cm long; seeds, including the wing, 2-3 cm long.—In many different habitats, but preferring fertile or well-drained, sandy soil.

Pinus sylvestris L.

MAP 100

SCOTCH PINE
introduced (naturalized)

Tree to 30 m tall, the larger branches conspicuously orange-brown. **Leaves** in pairs, bluish-green, stiff, usually twisted, 3-7 cm long, about 1.5 mm wide. **Cones** soon reflexed, short-ovoid to oblong, often bent, 3-6 cm long.—Native of Europe, where it is an important source of lumber; planted and persisting, and occasionally escaped in Minnesota.

Pinus strobus

TSUGA *Hemlock*

Tsuga canadensis (L.) Carr.

MAP 101

EASTERN HEMLOCK
endangered | *native*

Tree to 30 m tall, the bark often purple-brown; twigs pubescent. **Leaves** linear, 8-15 mm long, blunt, marked beneath with two white strips of stomata, usually minutely spinulose on the margin (best detected by touch), on short (about 1 mm) petioles, spirally disposed on the twigs but forming a flat spray by twisting of the petioles. **Cones** at maturity pendulous on short peduncles, their scales much larger than the minute bracts; thickly ellipsoid, 12-20 mm long; seeds winged. —Moist soil, especially on rocky ridges and hillsides. *An important component of our northern forests, useful for lumber and tanbark; often cultivated in a number of horticultural forms.*

Tsuga canadensis

Taxaceae YEW FAMILY

TAXUS *Yew*

Taxus canadensis Marsh.

MAP 102

CANADA YEW; GROUND HEMLOCK
native

Straggling evergreen shrub; **stems** ascending, to 2 m tall. **Leaves** spirally arranged on the stem, linear, 1-2 cm long, 1-2 mm wide, abruptly narrowed to a sharp point, tapering at base to a poorly defined petiole. **Staminate flowers** solitary in the axils; **pistillate flowers** in pairs, each subtended by its pair of scales. **Fruit** a fleshy red aril, about 5 mm long, open at the top.—Coniferous and mixed woods. *A favored winter browse for deer.*

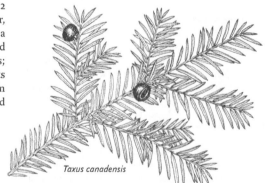

Taxus canadensis

99. *Pinus strobus*

100. *Pinus sylvestris*

101. *Tsuga canadensis*

102. *Taxus canadensis*

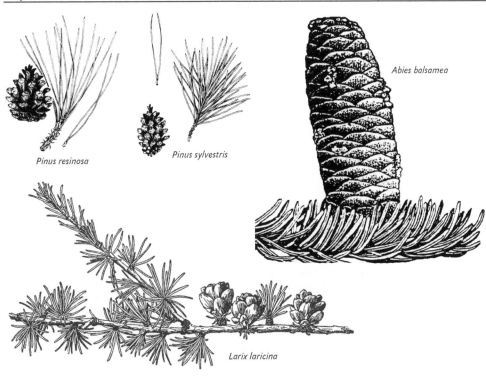

Pinus resinosa

Pinus sylvestris

Abies balsamea

Larix laricina

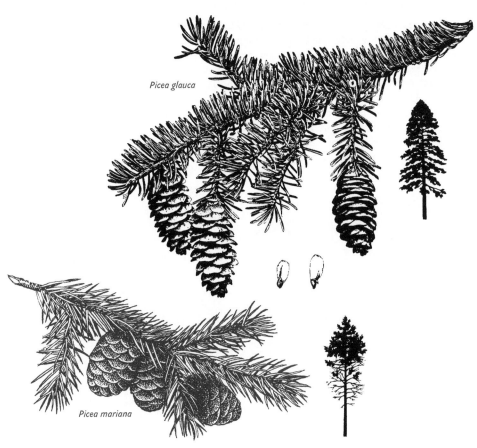

Picea glauca

Picea mariana

Nonvascular Species

Many species of plants traditionally termed 'nonvascular' are present in Minnesota. This group includes mosses, liverworts, hornworts, and algae. Due to their form and size, some of these plants may appear to be vascular species. Several genera found in aquatic and wetland habitats are typical examples:

Muskgrass or Stonewort (*Chara* spp., Characeae) is a macro-algae easily confused with vascular aquatic plants. Plants of *Chara* are gray-green, and have a gritty texture and strong musky odor when rubbed. When dried, *Chara* will turn whitish due to calcium deposits. Although not having true roots, *Chara* will loosely attach itself to the bottom of lakes and ponds via rhizoids (thread-like structures), and will sometimes form extensive colonies in shallow water, especially where calcium-rich. More than 30 species of *Chara* have been identified in the United States.

Another stonewort, **Nitella**, is similar but plants have no skunky odor, and stems and branches are typically bright green and smooth to the touch.

The **aquatic liverworts**, *Riccia* and *Ricciocarpus* are occasionally encountered in quiet waters of Minnesota. These nonvascular plants resemble the duckweeds in size and growth habit. *Riccia fluitans* appears as a very narrow (ca. 1 mm wide), bifurcating, ribbonlike thallus, free- floating and lacking rhizoids. *Ricciocarpus natans* is larger, has a broadly lobed rosette form with numerous rhizoids on the underside. When stranded on mud, the thallus is nearly radially symmetric with the rhizoids anchored in the substrate. The free-floating form is more bilaterally symmetric with conspicuous reddish rhizoids trailing beneath the thallus.

Sphagnum mosses (*Sphagnum* spp.), while not likely to be confused with vascular plants, are mentioned here due to their importance in creating and maintaining water-logged conditions, especially in low-lying areas of northern Minnesota. The resultant acidic, saturated environment supports vascular species typical of conifer swamps, bogs, and poor fens. Sphagnum mosses are absent from calcareous fens. *Sphagnum* are characterized by the presence of a capitulum or head-like structure composed of a tight whorl of young branches. This is one of many adaptations of the rootless *Sphagnum* to help maintain a wet environment favorable to its growth.

Chara spp.

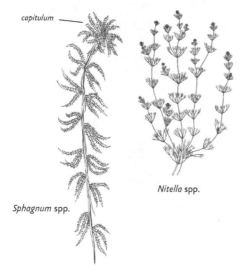

capitulum

Sphagnum spp.

Nitella spp.

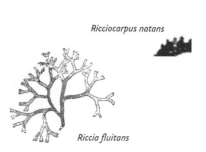

Ricciocarpus natans

Riccia fluitans

DICOTS

Adoxaceae MUSKROOT FAMILY

Our 2 shrubby genera, *Sambucus* and *Viburnum*, were previously included in Caprifoliaceae.

1   Plants small herbs . . . . *Adoxa moschatellina*
1   Plants woody shrubs or small trees. 2
     2   Leaves pinnately compound; fruit with 3 (or more) seed-like pits . . . . *Sambucus*
     2   Leaves simple; fruit with only 1 pit. . . . . *Viburnum*

ADOXA *Moschatel*

Adoxa moschatellina L.
MUSKROOT

MAP 103
native

Delicate, musk-scented herb, 10-20 cm tall, from a scaly rhizome. **Basal leaves** long-petioled, 2-3 times divided, the divisions oblong to obovate; **stem leaves** 1-pair, similar but smaller. **Head** with usually 5 greenish or yellowish flowers 8 mm wide, on a peduncle to 10 cm long. **Flowers** perfect, dimorphic; lateral flowers with 3 sepals and a 5-lobed corolla; terminal flower usually with 2 sepals and a 4-lobed corolla; stamens 8 or 10. **Fruit** a dry drupe, with 4 or 5 nutlets. May-July. —Shaded, damp cliffs and slopes. *An inconspicuous circumpolar species apart from the shiny quality of the pale green leaves.*

Adoxa moschatellina

SAMBUCUS *Elder*

Shrubs or small trees. Stems pithy, the bark with wartlike lenticels. Leaves pinnately divided. Flowers in large, rounded terminal clusters; small, perfect; calyx lobes tiny or none; corolla spreading, united at base, 5-lobed, white; stamens 5; stigmas 3. Fruit a red or dark purple, berrylike drupe with 3 nutlets.

1   Flowers opening in summer after leaves developed, in broad, nearly flat clusters; fruit purple-black, edible;
    leaflets usually 7 . . . . *S. canadensis*
1   Flowers opening in late spring with unfolding leaves, in pyramid-shaped or rounded clusters; fruit red, inedible;
    leaflets usually 5 . . . . *S. racemosa*

Sambucus canadensis L.
COMMON ELDER

MAP 104
native

   Sambucus nigra subsp. *canadensis* (L.) R. Bolli

Shrub to 3 m tall; spreading underground and forming thickets. Young stems soft or barely woody, smooth; older stems with warty gray-brown bark; inner pith white. **Leaves** large, opposite, pinnately divided into 5-11 (usually 7) leaflets, the lower pair of leaflets sometimes divided into 2-3 segments; leaflets lance-shaped to oval, tapered to a long sharp tip, base often asymmetrical, smooth or hairy on underside, especially along veins; margins with sharp, forward-pointing teeth. **Flowers** small, white, 5-parted, 3-5 mm wide, numerous, in flat or slightly rounded clusters 10-15 cm wide at ends of stems. **Fruit** a round, purple-black, berrylike drupe; edible. July-Aug (blooming when fruit of *Sambucus racemosa* is about ripe).—Floodplain forests, swamps, wet forest depressions, thickets, shores, meadows, roadsides, fencerows.

Sambucus canadensis

Sambucus racemosa L.
RED-BERRIED ELDER

MAP 105
native

   Sambucus pubens Michx.

Shrub to 3 m tall. **Stems** soft or barely woody; twigs yellow-brown and hairy, branches with warty gray-brown bark; inner pith red-brown. **Leaves** large, opposite, pinnately divided into 5-7 (usually 5) leaflets, the leaflets lance-shaped to ovate, tapered to a long sharp tip, smooth or hairy on underside; margins with small, sharp, forward-pointing teeth. **Flowers** small, white, 5-parted, 3-4 mm wide, many, in elongate, pyramidal or rounded clusters at ends of stems, the clusters 5-12 cm long and usually longer than wide. **Fruit** a round, red, berrylike drupe, inedible. May-June (flowers opening with developing leaves).—Occasional in swamps and thickets; more common in moist deciduous forests, roadsides and fencerows.

Sambucus racemosa

VIBURNUM *Squashberry; Arrow-Wood*

Shrubs or small trees. Leaves simple, entire, toothed, often palmately lobed. Flowers white or pink, in rounded clusters at ends of stems, sometimes outer florets larger and sterile. Calyx lobes and corolla lobes each 5; stamens 5; style 1; stigmas 1-3. Fruit a fleshy drupe with a single large seed; white, yellow, pink, or orange at first, maturing to orange, red, or blue-black.

ADDITIONAL SPECIES

· *Viburnum dentatum* L. (Southern arrow-wood) native to se USA; known from Lake and St. Louis counties where probably planted.

1 Leaves not lobed; pinnately veined 2
   2 Leaves entire, wavy-margined or finely sharp-toothed; lateral veins not terminating in the teeth 3
   2 Leaves with large spreading teeth; lateral veins terminating in the teeth . . . . *V. rafinesquianum*
      3 Leaf underside with branched hairs . . . . *V. lantana*
      3 Leaf underside glabrous or scurfy, without branched hairs . . . . *V. lentago*
1 Leaves 3-lobed; palmately veined from base of leaf 4
   4 Outer flowers large and sterile, much larger than inner flowers . . . . *V. opulus*
   4 Flowers all similar . . . . *V. edule*

Viburnum edule (Michx.) Raf.

SQUASHBERRY

Viburnum pauciflorum Bach. Pyl. ex Torr. & A. Gray

MAP 106
native

Shrub 1-2 m tall. **Stems** upright or spreading; twigs brown-purple, smooth, often angled or ridged. **Leaves** opposite, mostly shallowly 3-lobed and palmately veined (leaves at ends of stems often unlobed), 5-12 cm long and 3-12 cm wide, tapered to a sharp tip; underside veins hairy; margins coarsely toothed; petioles 1-3 cm long, **Flowers** creamy-white, small, in few-flowered, stalked clusters 1-3 cm wide, on short, 2-leaved branches from lateral buds on last year's shoots. **Fruit** a round, berrylike drupe 6-10 mm long, yellow at first, becoming orange or red. June-July; fruit ripening in late-summer.—Moist, shaded talus slopes.

Viburnum edule

Viburnum lantana L.

WAYFARING-TREE

MAP 107
introduced

Tall shrub. Young **stems**, naked winter buds, petioles, and lower leaf-surface gray-pubescent with stellate hairs. **Leaf blades** oblong to ovate, 5-10 cm long, acute or obtuse, finely serrate, rounded or cordate at base, pinnately veined; petioles 1-3 cm long. **Flowers** in short-stalked cymes, about 7-rayed; flowers all alike, about 4 mm wide. **Fruit** a red drupe, 8-10 mm long; seed a stone, furrowed on both sides. June.—Native of Eurasia; cultivated and occasionally escaped.

103. Adoxa moschatellina   *104. Sambucus canadensis*   *105. Sambucus racemosa*   *106. Viburnum edule*

Viburnum lentago L.
NANNY-BERRY

MAP 108
native

Tall shrub or small tree, glabrous throughout or minutely scurfy on the inflorescence or petiole. **Leaf blades** ovate, varying to oblong or orbicular, 5-8 cm long, all or the uppermost abruptly and sharply acuminate, sharply and finely serrate, the teeth often incurved and callous-tipped. **Flowers** in sessile cymes, 5-10 cm wide, with 3-5 (rarely 7) rays; flowers 4-8 mm wide. **Fruit** a drupe blue-black with a whitish bloom, ellipsoid to subglobose, 8-14 mm long; seed a flat, oval stone, scarcely grooved. May-June.—Woods and roadsides.

Viburnum opulus L.
HIGH-BUSH CRANBERRY

MAP 109
native-introduced

Viburnum lentago

Shrub, 3-4 m tall. Young **stems** smooth. **Leaves** opposite, maple-like, sharply 3-lobed and palmately veined, 5-10 cm long and about as wide, the lobes tapered to sharp tips; smooth or hairy beneath, especially on the veins; margins entire or coarsely toothed, petioles grooved, 1-3 cm long, with several club-shaped glands present near base of blade. **Flowers** white, in large, flat-topped clusters 5-15 cm wide at ends of stems; outer flowers sterile with large petals, surrounding the inner, smaller fertile flowers. **Fruit** an orange to red, round or oval drupe, 10-15 mm long. June.—Swamps, fens, streambanks, shores, ditches.

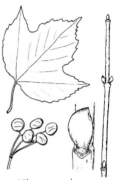

Our native plants are var. *americanum*:

1   Larger petiolar glands less than 1 mm long (rarely absent), usually stalked and flat topped . . . . **var. americanum**
1   Larger petiolar glands (0.8-) 0.9-1.5 (-2) mm long, usually sessile and with the apex indented . . . . **var. opulus**

Viburnum opulus

Viburnum rafinesquianum J.A. Schultes
DOWNY ARROW-WOOD

MAP 110
native

Viburnum affine Bush ex C.K. Schneid.

Shrub to 1.5 m tall, the younger **stems** glabrous or very sparsely stellate. **Leaf blades** ovate lance-shaped to ovate, or even subrotund, 3-7 cm long, acuminate or acute, at base obtuse, truncate or subcordate; petioles short, pubescent, most with a pair of linear stipules near their base. **Flowers** in cymes, these sessile or on peduncles to 6 cm long, 4-7-rayed; hypanthium glandular. **Fruit** a blue-black, flat-ellipsoid drupe, 6-8 mm long; seed a flattened stone, shallowly grooved on both sides. May-June.—Moist woods, thickets.

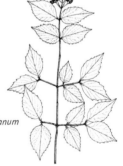

Viburnum rafinesquianum

Amaranthaceae   AMARANTH FAMILY

Our species annual or perennial herbs. Leaves simple, alternate, or occasionally opposite (*Salicornia*). Flowers small, often aggregated into large spikes, panicles, or heads, in some species with conspicuous colored bracts. Flowers perfect or unisexual; sepals usually 5; petals absent; ovary superior, 1-chambered. Fruit a 1-seeded utricle; seeds lenticular. The Amaranthaceae now includes former members of the Chenopodiaceae.

ADDITIONAL SPECIES
· *Axyris amaranthoides* L. (Russian pigweed), native to Siberia; ne Minn (Kittson, Red Lake, Roseau counties).
· *Monolepis nuttalliana* (Schultes) Greene (Nuttall's povertyweed), native; Clay and Renville counties.

107. Viburnum lantana   *108. Viburnum lentago*   *109. Viburnum opulus*   *110. Viburnum rafinesquianum*

1 Leaves opposite; either much reduced and scale like or with white silky-woolly hairs on both surfaces 2

  2 Leaves linear-lanceolate; stem and leaves (both surfaces) with white silky-woolly hairs . . . . ***Froelichia***

  2 Leaves much reduced and scale-like, scarious, glabrous, connate; stem branches succulent, glabrous, appearing jointed, the flowers entirely sunk in the fleshy internodes. . . . . ***Salicornia***

1 Leaves alternate (or the lower sometimes opposite), well developed, white silky-woolly pubescence absent 3

  3 Leaf tips with a sharp spine over 0.5 mm (usually ca. 1 mm, even longer on bracts subtending flowers); leaves filiform, ± terete; fruit horizontal, ca. 1-1.3 mm long, slightly broader, covered by the perianth; tepals with transverse keel or wing sometimes longer than body of tepal . . . . ***Salsola***

  3 Leaf tips at most with mucro less than 0.5 mm long; leaves various in width, flat; fruit and perianth various 4

    4 Flowers unisexual (plants monoecious or dioecious); tepals and bracts acute, scarious or fruit in most if not all flowers enveloped by a pair of bracteoles (perianth absent) 5

      5 Bracts and tepals all acute, scarious. . . . . ***Amaranthus***

      5 Bracts beneath pistillate flowers broad and usually tuberculate and toothed with margins partly fused, obtuse to acute but herbaceous in texture (or even hardened in one species), tepals herbaceous. . . . . .
      . . . . ***Atriplex***

    4 Flowers mostly bisexual; fruit not enveloped by bracts but perianth may cover it; bracts herbaceous or firm and hardened, not scarious. 6

      6 Leaves linear to narrowly lanceolate, less than 4 (-6) mm broad, entire, 1 (-3)-nerved 7

        7 Inflorescence and leaves beneath farinose; flowers crowded on short branches that exceed their subtending bracts . . . . ***Chenopodium pratericola***

        7 Inflorescence and leaves not farinose; flowers 1-3 in the axils of longer bracts 8

          8 Leaves and bracts green to the tips, not mucronate; bracts long-ciliate, especially basally; fruit horizontal, round, less than 1 mm long, enclosed by the perianth (each tepal with a transverse wing) . . . . ***Bassia scoparia***

          8 Leaves tipped with a non-green sharp mucro less than 0.5 mm long (no longer, or even absent, on bracts subtending flowers); bracts glabrous to pubescent but not long-ciliate; fruit various. 9

            9 Fruit vertical, flattened, usually narrowly wing-margined, ca. (2-) 3-4.5 mm long, greatly exceeding the tiny scarious perianth; sandy (not saline) habitats . . . . ***Corispermum***

            9 Fruit horizontal (or mostly so), less than 1 mm long and 1.5 mm broad, enclosed by the perianth; saline habitats . . . . ***Suaeda***

      6 Leaves usually at least 4 mm broad, toothed to sinuate or crenulate on the margin (if entire, then pinnate- or 3-nerved and not linear) 10

      10 Fruit horizontal, completely encircled by the connate wing of the perianth; styles 3 . . . . ***Cycloloma***

      10 Fruit horizontal or vertical, but the perianth without connate wing; styles usually 2. 11

        11 Tepals with transverse (but separate) wings; leaves entire, not over 5 mm wide; fruit horizontal; bracts long-ciliate, especially basally . . . . ***Bassia scoparia***

        11 Tepals not transversely winged (may be keeled); leaves and fruit various; bracts not ciliate . . 12

          12 Leaves (and rest of plant) neither glandular nor pubescent, but farinose in some species . . .
          . . . . ***Chenopodium***

          12 Leaves with yellow to orange resinous glands or gland-tipped hairs at least beneath, not farinose; bruised plant strongly aromatic . . . . ***Dysphania***

AMARANTHUS *Amaranth*

Annual herbs; stems erect, ascending, or prostrate, usually much branched. Leaves alternate, petiolate, entire or sinuate, stipules absent. Flowers in small clusters in the axils, or aggregated into axillary or terminal, simple or panicled spikes; flowers small, each subtended by bracts, the bracts sometimes colored and showy; stamens and pistils in different flowers on the same or different plants; calyx of 3-5 scarious or membranous sepals separate to the base; stamens 2-5; ovary short and broad, compressed; style short or none; stigmas 2 or commonly 3, pubescent. Fruit a thin-walled or leathery utricle, indehiscent or commonly opening at the middle, crowned by the persistent stigmas; seed flattened or lenticular.

ADDITIONAL SPECIES

• *Amaranthus hypochondriacus* L. (Prince's-feather); native to sw USA; adventive mostly near cultivated fields but unlikely persistent in the state's flora.

1 Plants dioecious (with staminate and pistillate flowers on separate plants) . . . . ***A. tuberculatus***

1 Plants monoecious (with staminate and pistillate flowers separate but on same plants); the flowers intermixed or in separate inflorescences 2

  2 Flowers all or nearly all in small clusters from the leaf axils (a small terminal panicle may also be present) 3

Amaranthus albus L.

MAP 111

TUMBLEWEED   *native*

Plants bushy-branched, to 1 m high and wide; **stems** whitish. **Leaves** of the flowering branches elliptic to oblong or obovate, 5-30 mm long, pale green, obtuse or rounded, attenuate at base to a long petiole; early leaves often up to 8 cm long. **Flowers** in short dense axillary clusters; bracts rigid, subulate, about twice as long as the flowers; sepals of the pistillate flowers commonly 3, uneven, the longest about equaling the utricle. **Fruit** a lenticular utricle, 1-2 mm long, opening at the middle, wrinkled when dry; seeds lenticular, to 1 mm wide. —Disturbed areas such as roadsides and railways; also sandy lakeshores and streambanks.

Amaranthus albus

Amaranthus blitoides S. Wats.

MAP 112

MAT AMARANTH   *introduced (naturalized)*

Stems prostrate, much branched, 2-6 dm long. **Leaves** numerous, often crowded, pale green, oblong to obovate, 14 cm long, obtuse or rounded, attenuate into a long petiole. **Flowers** in short dense axillary clusters; **bracts** about equaling the sepals, acuminate, scarcely aristate; sepals of the pistillate flowers normally 5, occasionally 4, ovate to oblong, unequal in length. **Utricle** thick-lenticular, 2-2.5 mm long, about equaling the longest sepal, smooth or nearly so, circumscissile at the middle; seed nearly circular, 1.4-1.7 mm wide.—Disturbed areas such as yards and along roads and railways; native of the western states, weedy throughout much of Minnesota.

Amaranthus hybridus L.

MAP 113

SMOOTH AMARANTH   *introduced*

Stems stout, erect, usually freely branched, up to 2 in. tall. **Leaves** ovate or rhombic-ovate, up to 15 cm long. **Inflorescence** of numerous, slender, cylindric, green or red spikes about 1 cm thick, the lateral 1-8 cm, the terminal up to 15 cm long, aggregated into a long, erect, decompound terminal panicle, usually also with numerous smaller panicles or solitary spikes in the upper axils; **bracts** equaling or up to twice as long as the sepals; sepals of the pistillate flowers equaling or slightly longer than the utricle, oblong, acute, minutely aristate. **Utricle** 1.5-2 mm long, circumscissile at the middle; seed about 1 mm wide. —Weedy, especially in corn and soybean fields.

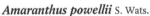

Amaranthus blitoides

Amaranthus powellii S. Wats.

MAP 114

GREEN AMARANTH   *introduced (naturalized)*

Stems to 2 m tall, freely branched, glabrous or finely hairy. **Leaves** long-petioled, lance-ovate, mostly to 10 cm long in well developed plants. **Inflorescence** terminal, stiff, dense and spike-like, unbranched or with a few widely spaced long branches, dull greenish, not showy; **bracts** about 5 mm long, much longer than

111. Amaranthus albus

112. Amaranthus blitoides

113. Amaranthus hybridus

114. Amaranthus powellii

the sepals and fruits, with a very thick, excurrent midrib; sepals 3–5, with simple midvein, those of the pistillate flowers sharply acute, unequal, 2–3 mm long, the longer (outer) ones generally surpassing the fruit; stamens as many as the sepals; **Fruit** slightly rugose; seeds dark brown, 1–1.3 mm wide.—Weedy in cultivated fields and on roadsides.

Amaranthus retroflexus L.

RED-ROOT AMARANTH

MAP 115

introduced

Stems stout, erect, usually branched, finely villous, up to 2 in. tall. **Leaves** long-petioled, ovate or rhombic-ovate, up to 1 dm long. **Terminal panicle** of several or many, short, densely crowded, ovoid, obtuse spikes, the whole 5–20 cm long; similar but smaller panicles produced from the upper axils; **bracts** rigid, subulate, much longer than the calyx, 4–8 mm long; sepals of the pistillate flowers 5, oblong lance-shaped, rounded or truncate, mucronate, 3–4 mm long, much exceeding the utricle. **Utricle** compressed, 1.5–2 mm long, circumscissile at the middle, the upper part rugulose; seeds round-obovate, dark red-brown, 1–1.2 mm long. —Weedy along roadsides and in fields and gardens, rarely along sandy lakeshores. *A. powellii resembles A. retroflexus in general habit but is nearly glabrous, with sharp acute sepals.*

Amaranthus retroflexus

Amaranthus tuberculatus (Moq.) Sauer

ROUGH-FRUIT AMARANTH

MAP 116

native

Acnida altissima (Riddell) Moq. ex Standl.

Annual herb. **Stems** erect to spreading, usually much-branched, 2–15 dm tall, usually hairless. **Leaves** alternate, ovate to lance-shaped, variable in size, larger leaves 4–10 cm long, smaller leaves 1–4 cm long. **Flowers** either staminate or pistillate flowers and on different plants, in spikes from leaf axils and at ends of stems; staminate flowers with 5 sepals, 2–3 mm long and 5 stamens; pistillate flowers without sepals or petals (rarely with 1–2 small sepals). **Fruit** a utricle 1–2 mm long; seeds red-brown, 1 mm wide. July-Sept.—Exposed sandy or muddy shores, streambanks, wet meadows and ditches.

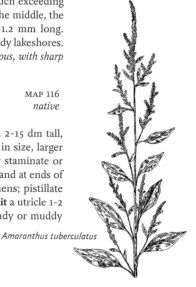

Amaranthus tuberculatus

ATRIPLEX *Spearscale; Orache*

Annual or perennial herbs or shrubs, usually mealy or with bran-like scales; flowers minute, sessile or short-pediceled in glomerules at the nodes, in the upper axils, or in terminal spikes; stamens and pistil in separate flowers on the same or different plants; sepals 3–5; stamens 3–5. Pistillate flowers all or mostly enclosed by 2 broad bracteoles, perianth absent; styles 2. Fruit an utricle.

ADDITIONAL SPECIES

• *Atriplex micrantha* Ledeb (Two-scale saltbush), introduced; reported (but not verified) from far w Minn near North Dakota border.

1 Plants weedy; bracteoles not spongy-thickened near base . . . . ***A. patula***
1 Plants of saline habitats, not especially weedy; bracteoles spongy-thickened near base . . . . ***A. prostrata***

Atriplex patula L.

HALBERD-LEAF ORACHE

MAP 117

introduced (naturalized)

Taprooted annual herb. **Stems** erect to sprawling, usually branched, 2–10 dm long. **Leaves** alternate (or the lowest opposite), lance-shaped or triangular, 2–8 cm long and 1–6 cm wide, with outward pointing basal lobes, gray and mealy when young, becoming dull green and smooth with age; petioles present, or absent on upper leaves. **Flowers** tiny, green; either staminate or pistillate but on same plant, usually intermixed in crowded spikes from leaf axils and at ends of stems, the spikes without bracts or with a few small bracts near base of spikes; **staminate flowers** with a 5-lobed calyx and 5, stamens; **pistillate flowers** without sepals or petals, surrounded by 2 sepal-like, small bracts, these expanding and enclosing fruit when mature. **Fruit** lens-shaped, dark brown to black, 1–3 mm wide. Aug-Sept. —Shores, streambanks and mud flats, usually where brackish; disturbed places.

Atriplex patula

Atriplex prostrata Bouchér
HASTATE ORACHE
 Atriplex hastata L.
 Atriplex triangularis Willd.

Plants erect and to 1 m tall, or prostrate. **Leaves** green, the principal ones 2–10 cm long by 2–9 cm wide, hastate to triangular or rhomboidal, with sharp basal angles or lobes. **Inflorescence** leafless except at base; fruiting bracteoles foliaceous and spongy-thickened toward the base, obscurely to more or less evidently veined, 3–10 mm long, triangular-ovate, the lateral angles rounded, entire or toothed. Seeds dimorphic, brown or black. 1-3 mm wide.—Saline soil.

MAP 118
introduced

BASSIA *Smotherweed*

Bassia scoparia (L.) A.J. Scott
MEXICAN-FIREWEED
 Kochia scoparia (L.) Schrad.

MAP 119
introduced (naturalized)

Atriplex prostrata

Annual hairy herb. **Stems** erect, bushy-branched, to 1 m tall, usually villous above. **Leaves** linear to narrowly lance-shaped, sessile. **Flowers** solitary or paired, perfect or pistillate, sessile in the axils of bracts, forming dense, axillary or terminal spikes; calyx 5-lobed, at maturity 2.5 mm wide, each sepal incurved over the fruit and bearing a short dorsal wing; stamens 5; styles 2 or 3,exserted, villous, to 2 mm long; pericarp thin, free; seed 1.5 mm wide. Late summer.—Native of Asia; occasionally escaped from cultivation, especially along railroads and highways where salt applied in winter. *Plants turn bright red in fall.*

Bassia scoparia

CHENOPODIUM *Goosefoot*

Taprooted annual herbs. Stems erect to spreading. Leaves alternate, mostly lance-shaped to broadly triangular, somewhat fleshy and often mealy on lower surface. Flowers perfect, small and numerous, green or red-tinged, in dense spike-like clusters from leaf axils or at ends of stems, the spikes with small leafy bracts; sepals often curved over the fruit; petals absent; stamens 1-5; styles 2-3. Fruit a 1-seeded utricle; seeds with edge vertical or horizontal.

ADDITIONAL SPECIES
• *Chenopodium desiccatum* A. Nels. (Narrow-leaf goosefoot), native to w USA; Scott and Wabasha counties.
• *Chenopodium strictum* Roth, native to n Great Plains; reported from several c Minn counties.

1 Fruit (achene) erect; sepals mostly 3 2
  2 Leaves white-mealy on underside, dull green above .... *C. glaucum*
  2 Leaves not white-mealy when mature, green on upper and lower sides 3
    3 Flower clusters few, 5–15 mm wide when mature, becoming fleshy .... *C. capitatum*
    3 Flower clusters numerous, up to 5 mm wide, not fleshy .... *C. rubrum*
1 Fruit (achene) horizontal; sepals 5 4
  4 Mature sepals rounded to conform with fruit, the midvein not much raised .... *C. simplex*
  4 Mature sepals raised, folded, or hood-like, the calyx appearing somewhat star-shaped 5
    5 Leaves narrow, linear to lance-shaped, mostly entire .... *C. pratericola*
    5 Leaves wider, lance-shaped to ovate or triangular 6
      6 Seed loosely enclosed by dry, brittle pericarp .... *C. standleyanum*
      6 Seed tightly enclosed by thin, membranous pericarp 7
        7 Pericarp smooth (check with a hand lens) .... *C. album*
        7 Pericarp roughened (check with hand lens) .... *C. berlandieri*

115. Amaranthus retroflexus   *116. Amaranthus tuberculatus*   *117. Atriplex patula*   *118. Atriplex prostrata*

Chenopodium album L.
LAMB'S QUARTERS; PIGWEED

MAP 120
native

Annual; leaves and inflorescence often red or reddish late in the season. **Stems** stout, erect, usually much branched, to 1 m or more tall. **Leaves** green or more or less white-mealy, broadly rhombic-ovate to lance-shaped, 3-10 cm long, broadly cuneate at base, the larger almost always toothed. **Flowers** in dense glomerules, these forming interrupted or continuous spikes grouped into a terminal panicle; calyx more or less white-mealy, its segments covering the fruit. Pericarp thin and delicate, when dry minutely rugulose-reticulate; seeds black, shining, usually 1-1.5 mm wide, smooth or sculptured. Highly variable.—Fields, gardens, roadsides, waste ground, dry woods, and barrens.

Chenopodium berlandieri Moq.
PITSEED GOOSEFOOT

MAP 121
native

Much like *C. album*, but the pericarp evidently roughened and cellular-reticulate when viewed at 10-20x; a minute (0.1 mm) undivided style-base persistent on the fruit.—Native but weedy.

Chenopodium album

Chenopodium capitatum (L.) Ambrosi
STRAWBERRY-BLITE

MAP 122
native

Annual herb. **Stems** erect or ascending, 2-6 dm tall, branched from the base. Lower petioles often exceeding the blades, the upper much shorter. **Leaves** triangular or triangular-hastate, up to 10 cm long, acute, broadly truncate to an acute base, above the lateral angles entire to coarsely sinuate-dentate. **Flowers** in globose clusters 5-10 mm wide at anthesis, in the upper axils or in a terminal leafless spike; **calyx** deeply 5-parted, the segments oblong to obovate, concave, at maturity commonly enlarged, fleshy, confluent, bright red; seeds vertical, dull black, about 1.5 mm wide, flattened, narrowly margined.—Woodland clearings, often following a fire, roadsides, and waste places.

Chenopodium glaucum L.
OAK-LEAF GOOSEFOOT

MAP 123
introduced

Annual herb. **Stems** upright to sprawling, 1-6 dm long, usually branched from base, sometimes red-tinged. **Leaves** lance-shaped to ovate, 1-4 cm long and to 2 cm wide, dull green above, densely white-mealy on underside (especially when young); margins entire, wavy, or with few rounded teeth; petioles slender, shorter on upper leaves. **Flowers** in small, often branched, spike-like clusters from leaf axils, the spikes often shorter than leaves; sepals mostly 3; petals absent; seeds dark brown, shiny, 1 mm wide. Aug-Oct.—Shores, streambanks, and disturbed areas such as railroad ballast and barnyards; soils often brackish. Introduced from Eurasia.

Chenopodium berlandieri

Chenopodium pratericola Rydb.
DESERT GOOSEFOOT

MAP 124
native (adventive)

Annual herb. **Stems** erect, to 8 dm tall, commonly with many ascending branches. **Leaves** erect or ascending, linear to narrowly lance-shaped, cuspidate, entire, 1-3-nerved without apparent secondary veins, cuneate to a short petiole, glabrous or glabrescent above, densely and usually completely white-mealy beneath, the principal ones commonly 2-4 cm long, 2-5 mm wide. **Inflorescence** white-mealy throughout, of numerous small glomerules disposed in short, terminal or subterminal, erect or ascending spikes, forming a slender panicle; sepals carinate

Chenopodium pratericola

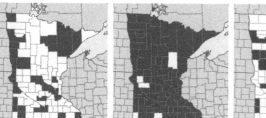

119. Bassia scoparia   *120. Chenopodium album* 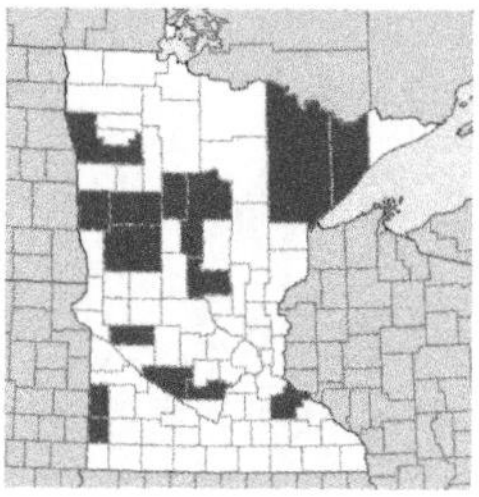   *121. Chenopodium berlandieri*   *122. Chenopodium capitatum*

at maturity. Pericarp easily separable; seeds black, shining, about 1 mm wide. Occasional on lakeshores, prairies, barrens, and waste ground.—Native of w USA, considered adventive in Minnesota.

Chenopodium rubrum L.
MAP 125
RED GOOSEFOOT　　　　　　　　　　　　　　　　　　*native*

Annual herb. **Stems** usually erect, sometimes sprawling, 1-8 dm long, often branched from base. **Leaves** lance-shaped to broadly triangular, 2-10 cm long and 1-8 cm wide, green and often red-tinged on both surfaces, smooth, not mealy; margins wavy-toothed or lobed; petioles present. **Flowers** small, in upright, branched spikes from leaf axils and at ends of stems, the spikes often longer than leaves; sepals 3, red; petals absent; seeds dark brown, shiny, to 1 mm wide. Aug-Oct.—Lakeshores, streambanks, disturbed areas.

Chenopodium simplex (Torr.) Raf.
MAP 126
MAPLE-LEAF GOOSEFOOT　　　　　　　　　　　　　　*native*

Annual herb. **Stems** erect, bright green, to 1.5 m tall. **Leaves** long-petioled, broadly ovate to deltoid, 5-20 cm long, truncate to rounded or cordate at base, bearing on each side 1-4 large teeth separated by broadly rounded sinuses. **Inflorescence** a loose, sparsely flowered, terminal panicle of short, interrupted spikes, the branches often white-mealy; **calyx** sparsely or not at all mealy; seeds horizontal, loosely or tightly enclosed in the readily separable pericarp, shiny black, 1.5-2.5 mm wide, with a bluntly keeled margin.—Disturbed ground and moist woods.

Chenopodium rubrum

Chenopodium standleyanum Aellen
MAP 127
WOODLAND GOOSEFOOT　　　　　　　　　　　　　　*native*

Annual herb. **Stems** slender, erect or arched, to 1 m tall. **Leaves** green or sparsely white-mealy, lance-shaped or rarely ovate, to 8 cm long, entire or the larger with a few low teeth, acute or cuneate at base. **Flowers** single to few in small glomerules, these forming short interrupted spikes, the latter grouped into a loose, open, slender, often nodding, terminal panicle; **calyx** more or less white-mealy, scarcely covering the fruit. Pericarp smooth, papery, fragile, easily separable; seed black, shining, about 1 mm wide, smooth to faintly striolate.—Dry open woods.

CORISPERMUM *Bugseed*

Chenopodium simplex

Corispermum americanum (Nutt.) Nutt.
MAP 128
BUGSEED　　　　　　　　　　　　　　　　　　　　*native*
　　Corispermum orientale Lam.

Annual herb. **Stems** slender, much branched, 16 dm tall, often pubescent when young, especially about the inflorescence. **Leaves** often deciduous early, linear, 1-6 cm long, 1-3 mm wide, glabrous or sparsely pubescent. **Spikes** densely to loosely flowered, 2-10 cm long, 3-8 mm wide; bracts ovate, 4-10 mm long, long-acuminate, concealing the fruits, the lowest often approximating the leaves in shape and size. **Fruit** obovate, 2-4 mm long, with a pale firm wing to 0.5 mm wide.—Sandy shores and soils, occasionally adventive along railways and waste places.

Chenopodium standleyanum

ADDITIONAL SPECIES

• *Corispermum pallasii* Steven (Siberian bugseed, MAP 129), introduced.

• *Corispermum villosum* Rydb. (Hairy bugseed), native; Clay County, and perhaps n and c Minn (unverified).

123. *Chenopodium glaucum*　　124. *Chenopodium pratericola*　　125. *Chenopodium rubrum*　　126. *Chenopodium simplex*

CYCLOLOMA *Winged-Pigweed*

Cycloloma atriplicifolium (Spreng.) Coult.   MAP 129
WINGED-PIGWEED   *native*

Annual branched herb. **Stems** 1-8 dm tall, pubescent when young, soon
glabrescent. **Leaves** pale green, early deciduous, lance-shaped in outline, coarsely
and irregularly sinuate-toothed, the lower up to 8 cm long, the upper
progressively reduced. All terminal branchlets bearing flowers, forming spikes
2-6 cm long. **Flowers** closely sessile, subtended by tiny bracts, perfect or pistillate;
calyx persistent, 5-lobed to about the middle, the segments usually keeled,
incurved over the ovary; stamens 5, flattened; styles 2 or commonly 3. **Fruit**
plano-convex, purple-black, puberulent; seeds about 1.5 mm wide.—Dry or sandy
ground, weedy.

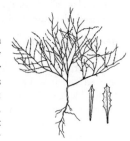

Cycloloma atriplicifolium

DYSPHANIA *Wormseed*

Previously included in genus *Chenopodium.*

1   Leaf blades ± copiously covered with short spreading gland-tipped hairs; stem with abundant stalked glands;
    flowers in branched axillary cyme . . . . ***D. botrys***
1   Leaf blades with mostly sessile glands on the underside; stem glabrous or pubescent, but not or only sparsely
    glandular; flowers in axillary and terminal spike-like inflorescences . . . . ***D. ambrosioides***

Dysphania ambrosioides (L.) Mosyakin & Clemants   (NO MAP)
MEXICAN TEA; WORMSEED   *introduced*
   Chenopodium ambrosioides L.

Annual or perennial, unpleasantly aromatic. **Stems** erect, to 1 m tall, with
numerous ascending branches. **Leaves** beset with minute yellow glands, the lower
leaf blades lance-shaped to ovate, to 12 cm long, deeply sinuate-pinnatifid to
merely serrate, cuneate at base, the upper progressively reduced, less toothed or
entire. **Flowers** sessile in small glomerules which are disposed in slender,
elongate, bracted or bractless spikes, these in turn forming large or small, open
or compact, terminal panicles; **calyx** glabrous to minutely pubescent, not
obviously glandular. Seeds horizontal or vertical, thick-lenticular, 0.7-1 mm wide,
dark brown, shining. Highly variable.—Native of tropical Amer; naturalized in
gardens, roadsides, and waste places. *To be expected in extreme southeastern Minn
on drying river beds and lake bottoms (known from adjacent Iowa and Wisc).*

Dysphania botrys (L.) Mosyakin & Clemants   MAP 130
JERUSALEM-OAK   *introduced*
   Chenopodium botrys L.

Annual, pubescent with short glandular hairs, strongly but not unpleasantly
aromatic. **Stems** 2-6 dm tall, simple or branched from near the base. **Leaves**
oblong to ovate in outline, the lower up to 8 cm long, sinuate-pinnatifid, the upper
much smaller, pinnately lobed to coarsely toothed, or those of the flowering
branches entire. **Panicles** numerous, axillary, forming large, more or less
cylindric, terminal inflorescences; calyx glandular-pubescent, its segments
rounded on the back. Seeds all or mostly horizontal, thick-lenticular, dull, dark
brown, to 0.8 mm wide.—Native of Europe; a weed in waste places.

Dysphania botrys

127. Chenopodium standleyanum   *128. Corispermum americanum*   *129. Corispermum pallasii*   *130. Cycloloma atriplicifolium*

FROELICHIA *Cottonweed*

Froelichia floridana (Nutt.) Moq.   MAP 131
COMMON COTTONWEED   *native*
Annual herb. **Stems** 5-15 dm tall, erect, finely pubescent to thinly lanate. **Leaves** opposite, narrowly spatulate, canescent above, thinly tomentose beneath, the principal leaves 5-10 cm long, 1-2 cm wide; upper internodes progressively longer. **Flowers** perfect, each subtended by a scarious bract and 2 bractlets, in elongate, woolly, terminal spikes; the flowers and fruits early deciduous, and the attached fruits, flowers, and buds forming a conic spike 2-3 cm long; **bractlets** rotund, scarious, much shorter than the calyx. Mature **calyx** tubular, becoming conic and hard in fruit, densely woolly, 6 mm long, bearing 2 lateral, entire, dentate, or erose wings; one face often with 2 tubercles or short ridges, the other often with one. **Fruit** a membranous utricle.—Dry places, especially where open and sandy.

Froelichia floridana

SALICORNIA *Glasswort*

Salicornia rubra A. Nels.   MAP 132
WESTERN GLASSWORT   ✎ *threatened | native*
Taprooted annual herb; plants succulent, green to bright red. **Stems** 0.5-2 dm long; branches opposite, fleshy, jointed at nodes, breaking apart when plants are trampled. **Leaves** opposite, small and scalelike, 1-2 mm long. **Flowers** in spikes 1-5 cm long at ends of stems; perfect, or some flowers female only; **sepals** enclosing flower except for a small opening from which stamens and style branches protrude; petals absent. Seeds 1 mm long. Aug-Oct.—Shores, seeps and ditches; soils brackish. *Minnesota at eastern limit of species' range.*

Salicornia rubra

SALSOLA *Russian-Thistle*

Annual herbs. Leaves alternate, simple. Flowers small, perfect, axillary in the leaf axils and forming short to long spike-like inflorescences; perianth (4-)5-merous, the segments distinct and closely enveloping the ovary below, membranaceous and erect above, and with a median horizontal protuberance that in fruit develops into a winglike projection in some speies; stamens (3)5, exserted; stigmas 2(3). Fruit enveloped by the persistent calyx, obovoid, depressed at the tip, usually honzontally wmged; seeds horizontal.

1   Bracts appressed, only the tips arching outwards, strongly imbricate at maturity; spikes dense, not interrupted at
    maturity . . . . **S. collina**
1   Bracts spreading from the base, not imbricate at maturity; spikes at maturity interrupted at least in lower half. .
    . . . . **S. tragus**

Salsola collina Pall.   MAP 133
SLENDER RUSSIAN-THISTLE   *introduced (naturalized)*
Similar to *Salsola tragus*; plants with long, narrow spikes of flowers with appressed bracts.—Dry, open, disturbed places. *The long, narrow spikes of flowers with appressed bracts are distinctive.*

131. *Dysphania botrys*   132. *Froelichia floridana*   133. *Salsola collina*   134. *Salsola tragus*

Salsola tragus L.   MAP 134
PRICKLY RUSSIAN-THISTLE   *introduced (naturalized)*
  Salsola kali L. subsp. *tenuifolia* Moq.
Annual herb. **Stems** much branched, 3-8 dm tall, glabrous or pubescent, pink or
reddish striped. **Lower leaves** cylindric; **upper leaves** shorter, stiff, dilated at base,
long-spined at tip, each subtending a solitary flower or a short spike of 2 or 3
flowers. **Flowers** perfect, single or few in axils of the shorter and spinier upper
leaves, each subtended by a pair of bractlets; **calyx** deeply 5-lobed, the segments
at maturity incurved over the fruit; stamens usually 5; styles 2. Variable. Late
summer.—Dry, sandy, disturbed places. *Eurasian native; first collected in Minn in
1890 (Hennepin County).*

Salsola tragus

SUAEDA *Sea-Blite*

Suaeda calceoliformis (Hook.) Moq.   MAP 135
PLAINS SEA-BLITE   *introduced*
Annual taprooted herb. **Stems** upright to sprawling, usually branched, 0.5-6 dm
long. **Leaves** alternate, linear, flat on 1 side and convex on other, green, succulent,
5-30 mm long and 1 mm wide, reduced to wider bracts 1-5 mm long in the head;
petioles absent. **Flowers** small, perfect, or staminate or pistillate flowers separate,
green or sometimes red-tinged, in dense clusters of 3-7 flowers in bract axils;
sepals joined, deeply 5-lobed, the lobes unequal and hooded; stamens 5. **Fruit** a
utricle enclosed by the sepals; seeds black, shiny, about 1 mm wide. July-Sept.
—Brackish wetlands and along salted highways.

Suaeda calceoliformis

Anacardiaceae SUMAC FAMILY

Woody plants, juice often milky. Leaves alternate, chiefly compound. Flowers small, regular, perfect
or unisexual, 5-merous. Stamens 5, inserted beneath a disk surrounding the ovary. Pistil 1, 3-carpellary.
Ovary 1-celled, sessile on the disk; styles 3. Fruit a 1-seeded, dry or fleshy drupe.

1   Flowers in dense inflorescences, these either terminal or lateral on previous year's twigs; fruit red, glandular-hairy
    . . . . **Rhus**
1   Flowers in loose clusters from leaf axils; fruit whitish, nearly smooth . . . . **Toxicodendron**

RHUS *Sumac*

Trees or shrubs. Leaves pinnately compound, of 3 to many leaflets. Flowers lateral or terminal,
polygamo-dioecious. Calyx 5-lobed. Petals 5, white or greenish. Stamens 5. Ovary 1-celled. Fruit a
drupe.

HYBRIDS
Rhus × borealis Greene, *R. glabra* and *R. typhina*, MAP 136.

1   Bushy shrubs with 3 sessile leaflets . . . . **R. aromatica**
1   Sparsely branched shrubs or small trees; leaflets several to many 2
  2   Twigs and leaf petioles glabrous . . . . **R. glabra**
  2   Twigs and petioles densely hairy . . . . **R. typhina**

135. Suaeda calceoliformis   *136. Rhus × borealis*   *137. Rhus aromatica*   *138. Rhus glabra*

Rhus aromatica Ait.
SQUAW-BUSH

MAP 137
native

Bushy shrub, often forming thickets. **Leaflets** 3, all sessile or nearly so, the terminal elliptic to rhombic-ovate, 4-8 cm long, with usually 3-6 coarse rounded teeth on each side in the distal half, the lateral smaller, elliptic to ovate lance-shaped, with similar teeth, at least the outer margin rounded to the petiole. **Flowers** in several short (1-2 cm) spike-like clusters, forming a panicle about 1 dm long, opening before or with the leaves, sessile or on pedicels no longer than the calyx. Bracts glabrescent just below the strongly ciliate apex. **Drupes** bright red, densely pubescent. April-May.—Dry woods, hills, sand dunes, and rocky soil.

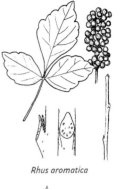

Rhus glabra L.
SMOOTH SUMAC

MAP 138
native

Rhus aromatica

Usually a sparsely branched shrub, but sometimes to 6 m tall, the younger branches and petioles glabrous and somewhat glaucous. **Leaflets** 11-31, lance-shaped to narrowly oblong, 5-10 cm long, commonly serrate, much paler beneath. **Panicle** dense, often 2 dm long. **Fruit** bright red, densely beset with minute obovoid hairs about 0.2 mm long. June-July.—Dry soil; old fields, roadsides.

Rhus typhina L.
STAGHORN SUMAC
　　Rhus hirta (L.) Sudw.

MAP 139
native

Tall shrub or small tree to 10 m tall. Younger branches, petioles, and leaf-rachis densely and softly hirsute. **Leaflets** 9-29, lance-shaped to narrowly oblong, 5-12 cm long, finely or coarsely serrate, paler beneath. **Fruit** red, densely covered with slender hairs 1-2 mm long. June-July.—Dry soil.

Rhus glabra

TOXICODENDRON *Poison-Ivy*

Shrubs or vines, with axillary, rather loose inflorescences often drooping in fruit; otherwise much like *Rhus*, and sometimes included in that genus. Fruit a white or yellowish drupe, shining and glabrous or inconspicuously short-hairy. *All parts of these plants may cause an allergic skin reaction.*

1　Leaflets 7-13, margins entire . . . . *T. vernix*
1　Leaflets 3, margins entire, toothed or lobed 2
　　2　Climbing or trailing vine, with aerial roots . . . . *T. radicans*
　　2　Somewhat erect shrubs without aerial roots, not climbing . . . . *T. rydbergii*

Toxicodendron radicans (L.) Kuntze
COMMON POISON-IVY
　　Rhus radicans L.

MAP 140
native

Plants of diverse habit varying from dwarf and erect to straggling or climbing by aerial rootlets and attaining a trunk diameter of 15 cm. **Leaflets** 3, ovate to subrotund, varying to rhombic or elliptic, acute to acuminate, rounded to cuneate at base, entire to irregularly serrate or crenate, glabrous or thinly pubescent. **Panicles** up to 1 dm long. **Fruit** grayish white, 5-6 mm wide.—Moist to dry woods, thickets, and open places.

Toxicodendron rydbergii (Small) Greene
WESTERN POISON-IVY
　　Rhus radicans L. var. *rydbergii* (Small ex Rydb.) Rehder

MAP 141
native

Strongly rhizomatous shrub, forming colonies. **Stems** to 1(-3) m tall, nearly erect, simple or sparingly branched. **Leaflets** broadly ovate, tending to be openly folded

Toxicodendron radicans

139. *Rhus typhina*　　　　140. *Toxicodendron radicans*　　　141. *Toxicodendron rydbergii*　　　142. *Toxicodendron vernix*

along the midrib rather than flat, glabrous on both sides or strigose beneath and often with a line of minute, curly hairs along the midrib above. **Inflorescence** unbranched or sparingly branched, usually with fewer than 25 flowers. **Fruit** 4-7 mm thick, smooth, sessile or subsessile and crowded in an erect inflorescence; otherwise much like *T. radicans*.—Dunes, shores; open, sandy or rocky places.

Toxicodendron vernix (L.) Kuntze
POISON-SUMAC
  Rhus vernix L.

MAP 142
native

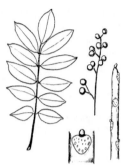

Shrub or small tree to 5 m tall, often branched from base. **Leaves** alternate, divided into 7-13 leaflets, the leaflets oblong to oval, 4-6 cm long, tapered to a pointed tip; margins entire, smooth. **Flowers** small, white or green, in panicles to 2 dm long; sepals 5, joined at base; petals 5, not joined; stamens 5. **Fruit** a round, gray-white drupe, 4-5 mm wide. June-July.—Tamarack swamps, thickets, floating bog mats and bog margins, often in partial shade.

Toxicodendron vernix

Apiaceae CARROT FAMILY

Biennial or perennial aromatic herbs with hollow stems, some very toxic. Leaves alternate and sometimes also from base of plant, mostly compound; petioles sheathing stems. Flowers small, perfect (with both staminate and pistillate parts), regular, in flat-topped or rounded umbrella-like clusters (umbels); sepals 5 or absent; petals 5, white or greenish. Fruit 2-chambered, separating into 2, 1-seeded segments when mature.

ADDITIONAL SPECIES
• *Cymopterus glomeratus* (Nutt.) Raf. (Plains spring-parsley), historical record from Clay County where species at eastern limit of its range.

KEY TO APIACEAE GROUPS

1 Inflorescence neither a true umbel nor a compound umbel . . . . **Group A**
1 Inflorescence a true umbel or a compound umbel 2
  2 Leaves all simple . . . . *Oxypolis rigidior*
  2 Leaves, or many of them, compound, dissected, or deeply divided 3
    3 Ovary and fruit pubescent, tuberculate, bristly, or prickly . . . . **Group B**
    3 Ovary and fruit glabrous 4
      4 Leaves divided into distinct and separate leaflets of about uniform shape, these often more than 2 cm
         wide . . . . **Group C**
      4 Leaves much dissected or 2 or more times compound, the segments ovate, oblong, linear, or thread-
         like and less than 1 cm wide 5
        5 Plants flowering . . . . **Group D**
        5 Plants fruiting . . . . **Group E**

GROUP A

Inflorescence neither a true umbel nor a compound umbel.

1 Inflorescence of dense heads, each flower subtended by a small spine-tipped bract . . . . *Eryngium*
1 Inflorescence otherwise; small bracts absent, or forming an a small involucre, not spine-tipped 2
  2 Stem leaves deeply palmately divided . . . . *Sanicula*
  2 Stem leaves pinnately dissected . . . . *Torilis japonica*

GROUP B

Inflorescence a true umbel or compound umbel; most leaves compound, dissected, or deeply divided; fruit and ovary pubescent, covered with small bumps, or bristly or prickly.

1 Principal leaves palmately or once-pinnately compound or divided, the leaflets sometimes again divided 2
  2 Leaflets large, mostly 1 dm wide or more; fruit pubescent . . . . *Heracleum maximum*
  2 Leaflets less than 1 dm wide; fruit bristly or spiny 3
    3 Leaves palmately divided into 3-7 wide segments, the segments toothed or incised . . . . *Sanicula*
    3 Leaves once-pinnate, some of the segments again divided . . . . *Torilis japonica*

1   Principal leaves twice or more compound 4
   4   Leaves with sharply toothed leaflets, the leaflets 1 cm wide or more 5
      5   Umbel branches 2-8; fruit not winged . . . . *Osmorhiza*
      5   Umbel branches 18-35; fruit winged . . . . *Angelica atropurpurea*
   4   Leaves highly dissected into segments less than 1 cm wide 6
      6   Branches of main umbel 20 or more; involucre of several conspicuous bracts . . . . *Daucus carota*
      6   Umbel branches 1-3; involucral bracts absent, or of only a few small linear bracts . . . .
        . . . . *Chaerophyllum procumbens*

GROUP C

Inflorescence a true umbel or a compound umbel; fruit and ovary glabrous; leaves divided into distinct leaflets of uniform shape, these often more than 2 cm wide.

1   Principal leaves once-compound (or sometimes simple in *Zizia* and *Thaspium*) 2
   2   Upper leaf-sheaths expanded, 1 cm or more wide when flattened; flowers white; fruit flattened and wing-margined . . . . *Heracleum maximum*
   2   Upper leaf sheaths not expanded, less than 1 cm wide; flowers and fruit various 3
      3   Taprooted introduced weeds of waste places and disturbed areas 4
        4   Flowers yellow; fruit wing-margined (sometimes wing nearly absent) . . . . *Pastinaca sativa*
        4   Flowers white; fruit not winged . . . . *Pimpinella saxifraga*
      3   Native species with fibrous or tuberous-thickened roots, most common in woods or wetlands 5
        5   Leaves with 3 leaflets (or the basal ones simple and toothed) 6
          6   Flowers white or greenish-white 7
            7   Leaflets linear . . . . *Oxypolis rigidior*
            7   Leaflets much wider . . . . *Cryptotaenia canadensis*
          6   Flowers yellow or cream-colored or purple 8
            8   Central flower of each umbellet sessile; fruit ribbed but not winged . . . . *Zizia*
            8   Flowers all on pedicels; fruit winged . . . . *Thaspium*
        5   Leaves with 5 or more leaflets; flowers white 9
          9   Leaflets entire, or with 5 or fewer coarse teeth on each side; fruit winged . . . . *Oxypolis rigidior*
          9   Leaflets with numerous teeth, or irregularly deeply toothed; fruit not winged 10
            10   Ribs of the fruit faint; leaflets of the upper leaves irregularly deeply toothed . . . . *Berula erecta*
            10   Ribs of the fruit prominent; leaflets of the upper leaves usually regularly sharply toothed *Sium suave*
1   Main leaves twice or three-times compound 11
 11   Leaflets entire; flowers yellow . . . . *Taenidia integerrima*
 11   Leaflets toothed or lobed; flowers yellow or white 12
   12   Plants flowering 13
     13   Flowers yellow or cream-colored 14
       14   Central flower of each umbellet sessile . . . . *Zizia*
       14   Flowers all on pedicels 15
         15   Native perennial herb with fibrous or fleshy roots, not weedy; sepals present (check with a hand lens) . . . . *Thaspium*
         15   Introduced biennial herb, taprooted weedy; sepals absent . . . . *Pastinaca sativa*
     13   Flowers white 16
      16   Sheaths of the upper leaves expanded, 1 cm or more wide when flattened . . *Angelica atropurpurea*
      16   Sheaths of the upper leaves less than 1 cm wide 17
        17   Rachis of the leaf conspicuously leafy-winged below each cluster of 3 leaflets . *Falcaria vulgaris*
        17   Rachis of the leaf not leafy-winged 18
          18   Main lateral veins of the leaflets oriented toward the sinuses between the teeth; some of the roots tuberous-thickened; base of stem thickened, hollow and cross-partitioned . . . . *Cicuta*
          18   Main lateral veins mostly oriented toward the teeth on the margin; stem and roots not modified as in *Cicuta* . . . . *Aegopodium podagraria*
   12   Plants fruiting 19
     19   Fruit evidently winged 20
       20   Dorsal and lateral ribs winged; fruit not much compressed . . . . *Thaspium*
       20   Dorsal ribs wingless, only the lateral ribs winged; fruit dorsally compressed 21
         21   Dorsal ribs prominent; plants taprooted . . . . *Angelica atropurpurea*
         21   Dorsal ribs very slender, only slightly raised above the fruit surface . . . . *Pastinaca sativa*
     19   Fruit not winged, or only slightly so 22

22 Rachis of the leaf broadly winged below each group of 3 leaflets; fruit linear . . . . . *Falcaria vulgaris*

22 Rachis of the leaf not winged; fruit various, often wider 23

    23 Main lateral veins of the leaflets oriented toward the sinuses between the teeth; base of the stem thickened, hollow and cross-partitioned . . . . *Cicuta*

    23 Main lateral veins mostly oriented toward the teeth on the margin, or more net-like and oriented toward neither the teeth or sinuses; base of stem not modified as in *Cicuta* 24

        24 Stylopodium (disk-like swelling at base of style) absent; stem from fibrous or fleshy roots . . *Zizia*

        24 Stylopodium well developed; rhizomes present . . . . *Aegopodium podagraria*

GROUP D

Inflorescence a true umbel or a compound umbel; fruit and ovary glabrous; leaves dissected or 2 or more times compound, the segments ovate, oblong, linear, or thread-like and less than 1 cm wide; plants flowering.

1 Flowers yellow 2

  2 Introduced, often weedy plants; sepals absent . . . . *Anethum graveolens*

  2 Native, non-weedy perennials; sepals evident (check with a hand lens) 3

    3 Plants taprooted . . . . *Polytaenia nuttallii*

    3 Plants with a cluster of fibrous or fleshy roots . . . . *Thaspium*

1 Flowers white (or rarely pink) 4

  4 Stem purple-spotted; plants coarse, well-branched, biennial herbs to 3 m high . . . . *Conium maculatum*

  4 Stem not purple-spotted 5

    5 Plants annual or biennial 6

      6 Bractlets fringed with hairs . . . . *Anthriscus sylvestris*

      6 Bractlets with entire margins, or bractlets absent 7

        7 Involucel (secondary umbels which make up the larger umbel) absent or scarcely developed . . . . *Carum carvi*

        7 Involucel well developed 8

        8 Bractlets arranged all around the umbellet . . . . *Chaerophyllum procumbens*

        8 Bractlets all on the outer side of the umbellet . . . . *Aethusa cynapium*

    5 Plants perennial 9

        9 Plants small, less than 2 dm tall when in flower . . . . *Erigenia bulbosa*

        9 Plants taller, well over 2 dm when in flower 10

          10 Plants with bulblets in axils of some of the upper leaves . . . . *Cicuta*

          10 Plants not with bulblets in upper leaf axils 11

            11 Umbel branches few, mostly 3-10 in number; bractlets lance-ovate, fringed with hairs . . . . *Anthriscus sylvestris*

            11 Umbel branches often more than 10; bractlets narrow and linear, not fringed with hairs . . . . *Conioselinum chinense*

GROUP E

Inflorescence a true umbel or a compound umbel; fruit and ovary glabrous; leaves dissected or 2 or more times compound, the leaf segments ovate, oblong, linear, or thread-like and less than 1 cm wide; plants fruiting.

1 Fruit dorsally flattened 2

  2 Garden escape with thread-like leaf segments . . . . *Anethum graveolens*

  2 Native perennial herbs, not weedy; the leaf segments mostly wider 3

    3 Plants taprooted; stylopodium absent; carpophore (prolonged part of receptacle, extending between the carpel segments) 2-parted to the base . . . . *Polytaenia nuttallii*

    3 Plants with a cluster of fibrous or fleshy-fibrous roots 4

      4 Carpophore and stylopodium (disk-like swelling at base of style) absent . . . . *Thaspium*

      4 Carpophore present, deeply 2-parted nearly to its base; stylopodium cone-shaped . . . . *Conioselinum chinense*

1 Fruit nearly round in cross-section or somewhat compressed laterally 5

  5 Stems purple-spotted; coarse, branched, biennial herb to 3 m high . . . . *Conium maculatum*

  5 Stems not purple-spotted 6

    6 Fruit lance-shaped or linear and with a beak 1-3 mm long, ribs absent; bractlets fringed with hairs . . . . *Anthriscus sylvestris*

    6 Fruit not beaked, the ribs evident; bractlets entire or absent 7

AEGOPODIUM *Goutweed*

Aegopodium podagraria L.
BISHOP'S GOUTWEED

MAP 143
introduced (invasive)

Perennial herb from a creeping rhizome. **Stems** erect, branched, 4-9 dm tall. **Lower leaves** long-petioled, mostly 1- or 2-times parted with 9 leaflets but often irregular; **leaflets** oblong to ovate, 3-8 cm long, margins sharply serrate; **upper leaves** reduced, short-petioled, chiefly once-parted. **Flowers** in dense umbels, these terminal and lateral, 6-12 cm wide, long-peduncled, rising above the leaves; primary rays 15-25, nearly equal; petals white. **Fruit** oblong-ovoid, 3-4 mm long, flattened laterally, tipped by the 2 conspicuous stylopodia.—Eurasian; cultivated and sometimes escaped, especially where moist and partially shaded.

Aegopodium podograria

AETHUSA *Fool's-Parsley*

Aethusa cynapium L.
FOOL'S-PARSLEY

MAP 144
introduced

Annual herb. **Stems** freely branched, 2-7 dm tall. **Leaves** shining, broadly triangular in outline, 2-3x pinnately dissected into narrow acute segments. **Flowers** in terminal and lateral compound umbels 2-5 cm wide; primary rays 10-20; sepals absent; petals white. **Fruit** broadly ovoid, nearly terete in cross-section, about 3 mm long and 2 mm wide; ribs corky, prominent, wider than the intervals or contiguous. June-Sept.—Native of Eurasia; weedy in waste places; toxic.

Aethusa cynapium

ANETHUM *Dill*

Anethum graveolens L.
DILL

MAP 145
introduced

Strongly scented annual herb. **Stems** to 15 dm tall, branched above, glabrous and more or less glaucous throughout. **Leaves** pinnately dissected into numerous filiform segments, the lower long-petioled, the upper shorter-petioled and smaller. **Flowers** in terminal and lateral compound umbels, overtopping the leaves; primary rays usually 30-40, widely spreading, about equal; sepals absent; petals yellow. **Fruit** oblong or elliptic, flattened; ribs prominent, the lateral conspicuously winged. July-Aug.—Native of s Europe; cultivated commercially and in kitchen gardens and escaped into waste ground.

Anethum graveolens

143. Aegopodium podograria   *144. Aethusa cynapium*   *145. Anethum graveolens*   *146. Angelica atropurpurea*

ANGELICA _Angelica_

Angelica atropurpurea L.
PURPLE-STEM ANGELICA

MAP 146
native

Perennial herb. **Stems** stout, 2-3 m tall, more or less smooth, often streaked with purple and green. **Leaves** alternate, lower leaves 3-parted, 1-3 dm long, on long petioles; upper leaves smaller, less compound, on shorter petioles, or reduced to bladeless sheaths; leaflets ovate to lance-shaped, smooth, 4-10 cm long; margins sharp toothed. **Flowers** in rounded small clusters (umbelets), these grouped into large rounded umbels 1-2 dm wide; petals white to green-white. **Fruit** oval, 4-6 mm long, winged. May-July.—Springs, calcareous fens, streambanks, shores, marshes, sedge meadows, wet depressions in forests; often where calcium-rich.

Angelica atropurpurea

ANTHRISCUS _Chervil_

Anthriscus sylvestris (L.) Hoffmann
WILD CHERVIL

MAP 147
introduced

Annual or biennial herb. **Stems** freely branched, to 1 m tall. **Leaves** 2-3x compound; leaflets dentate to incised. **Flowers** in large compound umbels, terminal and from the upper axils, with 6-10 primary rays up to 4 cm long; umbellets few-flowered; bractlets ovate lance-shaped, 3-6 mm long; sepals absent; petals white. **Fruit** lance-shaped, about 6 mm long, the beak about 1 mm long. May-July.—Native of Europe; rarely established in waste places.

BERULA _Water-Parsnip_

Berula erecta (Huds.) Coville
CUT-LEAF WATER-PARSNIP
    Berula pusilla (Nutt. ex Torr. & A. Gray) Fernald

MAP 148
❥_threatened_ | _native_

Perennial herb. **Stems** erect to trailing, sparsely branched, 4-8 dm long, often rooting along trailing portion. **Leaves** alternate, once-pinnate, basal leaves larger and less dissected than stem leaves, oblong, 5-20 cm long and 2-10 cm wide; leaflets lance-shaped to ovate; margins toothed or lobed. **Flowers** grouped into 5-15 small clusters (umbelets) 1 cm wide, these grouped into umbels 3-6 cm across; flowers white, 1-2 mm wide; sepals small or absent. **Fruit** oval or round, slightly flattened, 1-2 mm long, but seldom maturing. July-Sept.—Shallow water, springs, spring-fed streams, marshes, swamps, often where calcium-rich.

Berula erecta

CARUM _Caraway_

Carum carvi L.
CARAWAY

MAP 149
introduced

Glabrous biennial herb, from a taproot. **Stems** to 1 m tall. **Leaflets** pinnately dissected into linear segments 5-15 mm long. **Flowers** in terminal and lateral compound umbels; primary rays several to many; peduncles 5-13 cm long; primary rays 7-14, commonly 2-4 cm long; umbellets small; involucel of a few minute bracts or none; pedicels very unequal; sepals absent; petals white or rarely pink. **Fruit** elliptic to oblong, 3-4 mm long, about half as wide, prominently ribbed. June-Aug.—Native of Eurasia; sometimes cultivated and often weedy in waste places.

147. Anthriscus sylvestris

148. Berula erecta

149. Carum carvi

150. Cicuta bulbifera

CICUTA *Water-Hemlock*

Biennial or perennial toxic herbs. The tuberous roots, chambered stem base and young shoots of common water-hemlock (*Cicuta maculata*) are especially toxic. Leaves alternate, 2-3-pinnate; leaflets narrow or lance-shaped, entire or toothed; leaf veins ending in the lobes (sinuses) and not at teeth as in other members of this family. Flowers white or green, in few to many umbels; umbels usually without bracts, umbellets bracted. Fruit oval or round, flattened, ribbed.

1   Upper leaflet axils usually with bulblets; leaflets to 5 mm wide . . . . *C. bulbifera*
1   Bulblets absent; leaflets usually much more than 5 mm wide . . . . *C. maculata*

Cicuta bulbifera L.

BULBLET-BEARING WATER-HEMLOCK

MAP 150
native

Biennial or perennial herb, toxic; fibrous-rooted or with a few thickened, tuberlike roots. **Stems** slender, upright, 3-10 dm tall, not thickened at base. **Leaves** alternate along stem, to 15 cm long and 10 cm wide, pinnately divided; leaflets mostly linear, 1-5 mm wide, margins sparsely toothed to entire; upper leaves reduced in size, undivided or with few segments, with 1 to several bulblets 1-3 mm long, in axils. **Flowers** white, in umbels 2-4 cm wide. **Fruit** round, 1-2 mm wide, but rarely maturing. Aug-Sept.—Streambanks, lake and pond shores, marshes, swamps, open bogs, thickets, springs, streambanks and ditches.

Cicuta maculata L.

COMMON WATER-HEMLOCK

MAP 151
native

Biennial or perennial herb. **Stems** single or several together, often branched, 1-2 m long, distinctly hollow above the chambered and tuberous-thickened base. **Leaves** from base of plant and alternate on stem, mostly 10-30 cm long and 5-20 cm wide; basal leaves larger and longer stalked than stem leaves; leaflets linear to lance-shaped, 3-10 cm long and 5-35 mm wide; margins toothed. **Flowers** white, in several to many umbels, these 6-12 cm wide in fruit, on stout stalks 5-15 cm long. **Fruit** round to ovate, 2-4 mm long, with prominent ribs. June-Sept.—Wet meadows, marshes, swamps, moist to wet forests, thickets, shores, streambanks, springs. *Considered the most toxic plant in North America.*

Cicuta bulbifera

CONIUM *Poison-Hemlock*

Conium maculatum L.

POISON-HEMLOCK

MAP 152
introduced (invasive)

Biennial herb with a strong, unpleasant odor. **Stems** stout, branched, purple-spotted, 1-2 m long. **Leaves** alternate, 2-4 dm long, 3-4x pinnately divided, the leaflets toothed or sharply lobed. **Flowers** white, in many umbelets, these grouped in umbels to 6 cm wide. **Fruit** ovate, ribbed, 3 mm long. June-July. —Weed of shores, streambanks, waste ground and roadsides, especially on moist, fertile soil. *Very toxic, fatal if eaten.*

Cicuta maculata

CRYPTOTAENIA *Honewort*

Cryptotaenia canadensis (L.) DC.

CANADIAN HONEWORT

MAP 153
native

Perennial glabrous herb. **Stems** branched, 3-8 dm tall. **Leaves** 3-foliate, lower leaves long-petioled, the upper on short petioles dilated as far as the leaflets.

Conium maculatum

151. *Cicuta maculata*   152. *Conium maculatum*   153. *Cryptotaenia canadensis*

Leaflets lance-shaped to obovate, 4-15 cm long, irregularly often doubly serrate or sometimes lobed. **Flowers** in numerous loose, irregular, compound umbels arising terminally and from the upper axils; primary rays 2-7, ascending, 1-5 cm long, somewhat unequal; umbellets few-flowered; involucel none or of 1-3 minute bractlets; pedicels very unequal; sepals low or obsolete; corolla white. **Fruit** dark, slightly flattened, tipped by the slender stylopodium, 5-8 mm long; the ribs evident but low and obtuse. June-July.—Moist rich woods, swamps.

Cryptotaenia canadensis

DAUCUS *Carrot*

Daucus carota L.   MAP 154
QUEEN ANNE'S-LACE; WILD CARROT   *introduced (invasive)*
Biennial herb, with a stout taproot. **Stems** 5-10 dm tall, glabrous, scabrous, or commonly rough-hairy. **Leaves** pinnately compound, the ultimate divisions linear or lance-shaped. **Umbels** compound, terminal and from the upper axils, long-peduncled, usually many-rayed; terminal umbel erect, commonly 7-15 cm wide, the lateral ones usually smaller; the outer primary rays curve inward after anthesis, producing a congested cluster. **Flowers** white or rarely pinkish, the central one of each umbellet often purple. **Fruit** 3-4 mm long, flattened dorsally, the primary ribs low and inconspicuous, bearing a row of short bristles, the four secondary ribs prominently winged, divided into a row of hooked or straight spines. June-Sept.—Native of Eurasia; established as a weed in fields, roadsides, waste ground, and open woods. *The cultivated carrot is a race of this species.*

Daucus carota

ERYNGIUM *Eryngo*

Eryngium yuccifolium Michx.   MAP 155
RATTLESNAKE MASTER   *native*
Glabrous perennial herb. **Stems** erect, to 1 m high or more, unbranched except near the inflorescence. **Leaves** alternate, blue-green, mostly near base of plant and oftendownward-curved; narrowly lance-shaped, parallel-veined, succulent, clasping stem; **lower leaves** to 1 m long and 1-3cm wide; **upper leaves** similar but gradually reduced; margins with small prickles or spines. **Flowers** in spherical, thistle-like heads 2-3 cm wide, the flowers numerous, petals 5, green-white; each head subtended by bracts (involucre); each flower subtended by a separate bractlet. Fruit globose to obovoid, more or less tuberculate or papillate, not flattened or ribbed. July-Aug.—Moist or dry sandy soil, open woods and prairies.

Eryngium yuccifolium

HERACLEUM *Cow-Parsnip*

Heracleum maximum Bartr.   MAP 156
AMERICAN COW-PARSNIP   *native*
   Heracleum lanatum Michx.
   Heracleum sphondylium L. subsp. *montanum*
Large perennial herb. **Stems** stout, hairy, 1-2 m long. **Leaves** alternate, nearly round in outline, divided into 3 leaflets; leaflets 1-4 dm long and as wide, margins coarsely toothed. **Flowers** white, in large umbels, the terminal umbel 1-2 dm wide. **Fruit** obovate, 8-12 mm long and nearly as wide, often hairy. May-July. —Streambanks, thickets, wet meadows, moist forest openings and disturbed places.

Heracleum maximum

154. Daucus carota   *155. Eryngium yuccifolium*   *156. Heracleum maximum*

LOMATIUM *Desert-Parsley*

Lomatium orientale J.M. Coult. & Rose
DESERT-PARSLEY

MAP 157
native

Taprooted perennial herb; plants to 4 dm tall, covered with soft grayish hairs. **Leaves** chiefly basal, tripinnate, ultimate divisions linear, to 12 mm long and 0.5-2 mm wide. **Inflorescence** of loose compound umbels; **peduncles** usually solitary and terminal, longer than the leaves; involucel of linear-lanceolate to obovate, scarious-margined bractlets, about equaling the flowers. **Flowers** white or pinkish-white. **Fruit** ovate-oblong, 5-9 mm long, glabrous, wings narrower than body. April-June.—Dry prairies

Lomatium orientale

OSMORHIZA *Sweet-Cicely*

Erect perennial herbs from thickened roots and glabrous to pubescent stems 4-8 dm tall; our 3 species similar in general appearance and foliage. Leaves ternate; leaflets several, the lower petioled, the upper subsessile, the ultimate segments ovate to lance-shaped, serrate or lobed. Flowers in terminal and lateral umbels, these usually surpassing the leaves; primary rays of the umbel mostly 3-6, widely ascending; involucre present or absent. Umbellets few-flowered; involucel present or lacking. Sepals none; petals white or greenish white. Fruit elongate, slightly flattened, ribbed, the base prolonged into bristly tails.

ADDITIONAL SPECIES
• *Osmorhiza depauperata* Phil. (Blunt-seed sweet-cicely); Cook County.

1 Umbels without bracts at base of umbel branches	*O. chilensis*
1 Umbels with bracts at base of umbel branches	2
2 Plants anise-scented; styles 2 mm long, becoming 3-4 mm long in fruit	*O. longistylis*
2 Plants unscented; styles less than 1.5 mm long (even in fruit)	*O. claytonii*

Osmorhiza chilensis Hook. & Arn.
MOUNTAIN SWEET-CICELY
Osmorhiza berteroi DC.

MAP 158
endangered | native

Involucel lacking. **Fruit** concavely narrowed to the acute summit, 14-18 mm long. Stylopodium ovoid-conic, commonly longer than thick; styles at maturity outwardly curved, 0.4-0.7 mm long including the stylopodium. June.—Moist woods.

Osmorhiza claytonii (Michx.) C.B. Clarke
HAIRY SWEET-CICELY

MAP 159
native

Stems commonly sparsely villous, but vary from densely villous to nearly glabrous. Styles at anthesis distinctly shorter than the petals, in fruit nearly straight and parallel, 1.2-1.5 mm long including the stylopodium. **Mericarps** 2-2.5 cm long. May-June.—Moist woods.

Osmorhiza claytonii

Osmorhiza longistylis (Torr.) DC.
ANISEROOT

MAP 160
native

Styles at anthesis about 2 mm long, much exceeding the petals, in fruit nearly straight and parallel, 3-3.5 mm long including the stylopodium. **Mericarps** about 2 cm long. May-June.—Moist woods.

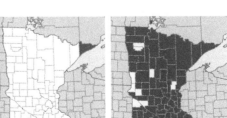

157. *Lomatium orientale*   158. *Osmorhiza chilensis*   159. *Osmorhiza claytonii*   160. *Osmorhiza longistylis*

OXYPOLIS *Cowbane*

Oxypolis rigidior (L.) Raf.   MAP 161
STIFF COWBANE   *native*
Glabrous perennial herb from a cluster of tuberous roots. **Stems** stout or slender, erect, to 1.5 m long, with few branches and leaves. **Leaves** once-pinnate or reduced to bladeless phyllodes; leaflets 5-9, linear to oblong, 5-15 cm long and 5-40 mm wide; margins entire or with scattered coarse teeth. **Flowers** on stalks 5-20 mm long, in loose umbels to 15 cm wide; sepals minute or none; petals white; bracts and bractlets few, threadlike, or lacking. **Fruit** rounded at ends, 4-6 mm long and 3-4 mm wide, strongly flattened, with 5 narrow ribs. July-Sept.—Swamps, thickets, marshes, moist or wet prairie, calcareous fens. *Similar to **water-parsnip** (Sium suave) but differs in having entire to irregularly toothed leaves and a slightly grooved stem, while Sium has finely toothed leaf margins and a more deeply grooved stem.*

Oxypolis rigidior

PASTINACA *Parsnip*

Pastinaca sativa L.   MAP 162
WILD PARSNIP   *introduced (invasive)*
Stout biennial herb, to 1.5 m tall. Lower **leaves** long-petioled, the upper on shorter, wholly sheathing petioles, all typically 1-pinnate; leaflets 5-15, usually oblong to ovate, 5-10 cm long, variously serrate or lobed, or in vigorous plants sometimes completely divided into 2-5 segments. **Umbels** large, 1-2 dm wide, compound, the terminal soon overtopped by the lateral ones; primary rays unequal, 15-25; involucre and involucel usually lacking; sepals minute or none; petals yellow. **Fruit** broadly elliptic or obovate, strongly flattened, 5-7 mm long, with low ribs, the lateral ribs broadly and thinly winged.—Native of Eurasia; long in cultivation and thoroughly established as a weed in waste places, fields, and roadsides. *Skin irritant if handled.*

Pastinaca sativa

PIMPINELLA *Burnet Saxifrage*

Pimpinella saxifraga L.   MAP 163
BURNET SAXIFRAGE   *introduced*
Perennial herb. **Stems** 3-6 dm tall, filled with pith. Lower stem **leaves** 1-pinnate, the leaflets varying from ovate or subrotund and merely serrate to deeply pinnately dissected. Upper leaves much reduced, the uppermost consisting of sheaths only or of sheaths with a few small linear leaflets at the summit. **Umbels** peduncled, terminal and lateral, compound; involucre none or rarely of 1-few bracts; primary rays 8-20; sepals minute or lacking; petals white. **Fruit** glabrous, ovoid, 2-2.5 mm long, the ribs 5, narrow.—Native of Eurasia; escaped or adventive in waste places.

SANICULA *Black-Snakeroot*

Biennial or perennial herbs; stems arising from a cluster of fibrous or sometimes tuberous roots. Leaves palmately divided into 3-5 segments, the basal long-petioled, the cauline progressively reduced, and the uppermost short-petioled to nearly sessile. Umbels irregular, with spreading primary branches of unequal length, the umbellets dense or almost capitate, commonly with 3 sessile or short-pediceled

161. *Oxypolis rigidior*   162. *Pastinaca sativa*   163. *Pimpinella saxifraga*   164. *Sanicula canadensis*

perfect flowers, their hypanthium bristly, and several staminate flowers with smooth hypanthium, all or mostly on much longer pedicels; sepals narrow, joined at base, persistent; petals greenish white to greenish yellow. Fruit ovoid to subglobose, slightly flattened laterally, ribs absent, densely covered with hooked bristles.

1   Styles longer than bristles of the fruit; staminate flowers 12-25 in each umbellet 2
    2   Staminate flowers longer than the fruit; sepals awl-shaped, 1-2 mm long . . . . ***S. marilandica***
    2   Staminate flowers shorter than the fruit; sepals lance-shaped or ovate, 0.5 mm long . . . . ***S. odorata***
1   Styles shorter than bristles of the fruit; staminate flowers 2-7 3
    3   Calyx lobes of perfect flowers conspicuous, equal to or longer than bristles; pedicels of staminate flowers 2-4 times length of their sepals . . . . ***S. trifoliata***
    3   Calyx lobes of perfect flowers inconspicuous, shorter than the bristles; pedicels of staminate flowers 1-2 times length of their sepals . . . . ***S. canadensis***

Sanicula canadensis L.
CANADA SANICLE

MAP 164
native

Leaves 3-parted, or 5-parted by division of the lateral leaflets. Bractlets of the involucel resembling the bracts but smaller. **Flowers** white, the fertile on pedicels 0.5-1 mm long, the sterile few, mostly concealed by the fertile; calyx lobes subulate, surpassing the petals. Anthers white. **Fruit** subglobose, 2-5 mm long, on pedicels 1-1.5 mm long, the bristles exceeding the inconspicuous styles and about equaling the sepals. June-Aug.—Moist or dry woods.

Sanicula marilandica L.
MARYLAND BLACK-SNAKEROOT

MAP 165
native

Leaves 5-parted, often appearing 7-parted, serrate, doubly serrate, or toward the apex incised. Bractlets of the involucel resembling the bracts but smaller. **Flowers** greenish white, the fertile ones sessile; calyx lobes lance-subulate, 1-1.5 mm long, equaling or slightly shorter than the petals. Anthers greenish white. **Fruit** nearly sessile, 4-6 mm long, narrowed and with shorter bristles toward the base. Styles recurved, exceeding the bristles. June-Aug.—Moist or dry woods.

Sanicula marilandica

Sanicula odorata (Raf.) Pryer & Phillippe
CLUSTERED BLACK-SNAKEROOT
Sanicula gregaria Bickn.

MAP 166
native

Leaves 3-5-parted, the segments sharply serrate to incised. Bractlets of the involucel small, subscarious. **Flowers** greenish yellow, the fertile on pedicels 0.5-1 mm long; calyx lobes ovatelance-shaped to ovate, obtuse or subacute, much shorter than the petals. Anthers bright yellow. **Fruit** subglobose, about 3 mm long. Styles conspicuous, recurved, exceeding the bristles. June-Aug.—Moist or dry woods.

Sanicula trifoliata Bickn.
LARGE-FRUIT BLACK-SNAKEROOT

MAP 167
native

Leaves 3-parted, the leaflets coarsely and doubly serrate to incised, the lateral often deeply lobed. Bractlets ovate, subscarious. **Flowers** white, the fertile sessile, the staminate few, on slender pedicels up to 8 mm long and much exceeding the fertile ones; sepals lance-subulate, exceeding the petals. **Fruit** ovoid to oblong, 6-8 mm long including the comparatively few bristles, the sepals lance-shaped, connivent, exceeding the bristles, forming a conspicuous beak 2-2.5 mm long. June-Aug.—Moist or dry woods.

Sanicula odorata

165. *Sanicula marilandica*

166. *Sanicula odorata*

167. *Sanicula trifoliata*

168. *Sium suave*

SIUM *Water-Parsnip*

Sium suave Walt.   MAP 168
HEMLOCK WATER-PARSNIP   *native*
Perennial emergent herb. **Stems** single, smooth, 5-20 dm long, strongly ribbed
upward; stem base thickened and hollow with cross-partitions. **Leaves** once-
pinnate, on long, hollow stalks (shorter stalked above); leaflets 7-17 per leaf, linear
to lance-shaped, 5-10 cm long and 3-15 mm wide; margins with fine, sharp,
forward-pointing teeth; finely dissected underwater leaves often present from
spring to midsummer. **Flowers** white or green-white, 1-2 mm wide, in stalked
umbels 4-12 cm wide at ends of stems and from side branches. **Fruit** oval, 2-3
mm long, with prominent ribs. July-Sept.—Wet forest depressions, marshes,
swamps, streambanks, lakeshores, ditches; usually in shallow water.

Sium suave

TAENIDIA *Pimpernel*

Taenidia integerrima (L.) Drude   MAP 169
YELLOW-PIMPERNEL   *native*
Perennial herb. **Stems** branched, 4-11 dm tall, glabrous and somewhat glaucous.
Lower **leaves** long-petioled, commonly 3x compound, the upper 1-2x compound,
with short, wholly sheathing petioles; leaflets normally entire, ovate to oblong
or elliptic. **Umbels** terminal and lateral, loose and irregular, primary rays
numerous, the outer elongate, to 9 cm long, the inner often much shorter;
involucre none; umbellets many-flowered, involucel none. Inner flowers of each
umbellet staminate and short-pediceled, the marginal long-pediceled and fertile;
calyx teeth tiny or none; petals yellow. **Fruit** elliptic to broadly ovate-oblong, 3-
4 mm long, flattened; ribs faint. May-June.—Dry woods and rocky hillsides.

Taenidia integerrima

THASPIUM *Meadow-Parsnip*

Thaspium barbinode (Michx.) Nutt.   MAP 170
HAIRY-JOINT MEADOW-PARSNIP   *native*
Perennial herb. **Stems** to 1 m tall, branched above, always pubescent around the
upper nodes with tiny stiff hairs. Basal and principal stem **leaves** 2-3x pinnate,
the leaflets ovate to lance-shaped, serrate or incised. **Umbels** terminal and lateral,
large, compound, commonly 3-6 cm wide, at anthesis scarcely surpassing the
leaves; involucre none; umbellets small, all flowers pedicellate. **Flowers** pale
yellow or cream-color. **Fruit** ellipsoid, 4-6 mm long, the lateral ribs and some of
the dorsal and intermediate ribs broadly winged. May-June.—Moist or dry woods
and woodland edges. *Minnesota at northern edge of species' range.*

Thaspium barbinode

TORILIS *Hedge-Parsley*

Torilis japonica (Houtt.) DC.   (NO MAP)
ERECT HEDGE-PARSLEY   *introduced (invasive)*
Annual herb. **Stems** much branched, 3-8 dm tall, hispidulous with appressed
hairs, as are also the peduncles and petioles. **Leaves** ovate or triangular in outline,
pinnately compound, the primary segments long-stalked; the ultimate divisions
lance-shaped to linear, to 6 cm long, sharply serrate. **Umbels** lateral or also
terminal, peduncles 3-12 cm long; primary rays 5-10, usually 1-3 cm long;

Torilis japonica

169. Taenidia integerrima   *170. Thaspium barbinode*   *171. Zizia aptera*   *172. Zizia aurea*

involucre of a few small bracts or none; umbellet pedicels very short, densely strigose, mostly exceeded by the narrow bractlets; petals white. **Fruit** body ovoid, flattened laterally, 2-4 mm long, densely covered by rough hooked bristles concealing the ribs.—Native of Europe; weedy in fields and waste ground. *First Minnesota collection in 2009 (Ramsey County).*

ZIZIA *Alexanders*

Branched perennial herbs 3-8 dm tall, glabrous or nearly so, from a cluster of thickened roots. Leaves mostly 1-3x compound. Umbels compound; primary rays several to many, the inner often much shorter; involucre none. Umbellets many-flowered; involucel of a few short linear lance-shaped bractlets; pedicels very unequal, the central flower commonly sessile. Sepals short, triangular. Petals bright yellow. Fruit ovate to oblong, flattened laterally; ribs 5 on each mericarp, varying from low and narrow to narrowly winged.

1 Basal leaves simple, with heart-shaped blades; stem leaves with 3 leaflets . . . . **Z. aptera**
1 Basal leaves compound and similar to the stem leaves, with 5-11 leaflets . . . . **Z. aurea**

Zizia aptera (Gray) Fern.   MAP 171
HEART-LEAF ALEXANDERS   *native*
Perennial herb. **Basal leaves** and occasionally the lower stem leaves simple, long-petioled, deltoid-ovate or round-ovate to oblong-ovate, 4-12 cm long, cordate at base. **Stem leaves** once or twice 3-parted, the leaflets ovate lance-shaped to obovate-oblong. Primary rays at anthesis 1-3 cm long, at maturity ascending, up to 5 cm long. **Fruit** oblong-ovate, 3-4 mm long. May-June.—Moist meadows and open woods.

Zizia aurea (L.) W.D.J. Koch   MAP 172
GOLDEN ALEXANDERS   *native*
Perennial herb. **Lower leaves** twice 3-parted, the **upper leaves** once 3-parted or irregularly compound; leaflets ovate to lance-shaped, finely serrate with ascending teeth averaging 5-10 per centimeter of margin. Primary rays commonly 10-18, the outer ones of the terminal umbel becoming 3-5 cm long and stiffly ascending at maturity of the fruit. **Fruit** oblong-ovoid, 3-4 mm long and about half as wide. May-June.—Moist fields and meadows.

Zizia aurea

Apocynaceae DOGBANE FAMILY

Our species herbs or twining woody vines; most species have milky juice. Leaves opposite, alternate, or sometimes whorled. Flowers 5-merous, regular, perfect. Fruit a capsule or follicle; seeds often bearing long hairs. *Family now includes former members of* **Asclepiadaceae;** *Apocynum differs by having corolla lobes overlapping and twisted in bud, and stamens without a crown.*

1 Plants trailing, subwoody, evergreen; flowers solitary in leaf axils; corolla blue; seeds glabrous. . . . . **Vinca**
1 Plants erect or twining, herbaceous and not evergreen; flowers in terminal or axillary cymes or umbels; corolla various colors, not blue; seeds with tuft of silky hairs. 2
  2 Plant a climbing vine, strongly twining at least apically; corolla lobes spreading or ascending, dark purple to nearly black . . . . **Vincetoxicum**
  2 Plant erect or ascending, not twining; corolla lobes strongly reflexed at maturity, except in *Apocynum*, white, pink, purple, yellow, orange, or greenish 3
    3 Corolla lobes erect to spreading; flowers in small terminal (and sometimes axillary) cymes; mature fruits 3-5 mm wide. . . . . **Apocynum**
    3 Corolla lobes strongly reflexed at maturity; flowers in umbels; mature fruits 6-35 mm in diameter. . . . . **Asclepias**

APOCYNUM *Dogbane*

Perennial herbs with tough fibrous stems. Leaves opposite, mucronate. Flowers small, white or pink, in branched terminal cymes. Calyx deeply divided into triangular or lance-shaped lobes. Corolla white or pinkish, campanulate or short-cylindric, with 5 short lobes, bearing within a tooth or scale near the base of the tube opposite each lobe. Anthers lance-shaped, joined, adherent to the stigma and prolonged into a cone beyond it. Ovaries 2, subtended by 5 nectaries; style none; stigma large, 2-lobed. Fruit a cylindric follicle, pendulous; seeds numerous, bearing long soft hairs (coma).

1   Corolla pink, 5-8 mm long; leaves widely spreading or drooping . . . . *A. androsaemifolium*
1   Corolla white, 3-4 mm long; leaves ascending . . . . *A. cannabinum*

Apocynum androsaemifolium L.
SPREADING DOGBANE
MAP 173
native

Perennial herb. **Stems** more or less inclined from tbe vertical, the branches chiefly alternate. **Leaves** petiolate, more or less drooping, oblong lance-shaped to ovate, commonly 3-8 cm long, pilose beneath. Principal cymes terminal; secondary cymes of smaller size in the upper axils; calyx lobes triangular, a third to half as long as the corolla tube; corolla campanulate, 6-10 mm long, pink to nearly white, marked with red within, the lobes spreading or recurved. May-Aug.—Upland woods, occasionally in fields and roadsides.

Apocynum cannabinum L.
INDIAN-HEMP
MAP 174
native

Apocynum sibiricum Jacq.

Apocynum androsaemifolium

Perennial herb. **Stems** erect, branched above, 1-1.5 m tall. **Leaves** varying from oblong lance-shaped to ovate or broadly elliptic, acute to rounded at the mucronate apex and base, glabrous or pubescent beneath, regularly on conspicuous petioles commonly 5-10 mm long. **Flowers** white or greenish white. **Follicles** usually 10-15 cm long; seed-coma 2-2.5 cm long. June-Sept.—Dry or moist open places.

ASCLEPIAS *Milkweed*

Perennial herbs from a thick root or deep rhizome and with milky juice (except in *A. tuberosa*). Stems usually simple. Leaves opposite (in some species whorled or rarely alternate), entire. Flowers small or medium-sized, in peduncled, terminal or axillary umbels; calyx lobes, corolla lobes, and stamens each 5; corolla lobes usually meeting in bud without overlapping; corolla deeply divided, at anthesis reflexed and concealing the calyx; anthers united with stigma forming an organ known as the gynostegium; pollen of each anther-sac united into a waxy mass known as a pollinium; ovaries 2; styles 2; stigma 1. Fruit a pod-like follicle, normally produced in pairs, commonly erect, lance-shaped or linear lance-shaped, acuminate; seeds with long silky hairs (coma).

ADDITIONAL SPECIES
• *Asclepias stenophylla* A. Gray (Narrow-leaf milkweed), plants with linear, widely spaced, opposite leaves, and white to greenish flowers; dry hill prairie in Houston County (☙*endangered*).

Asclepias flower anatomy

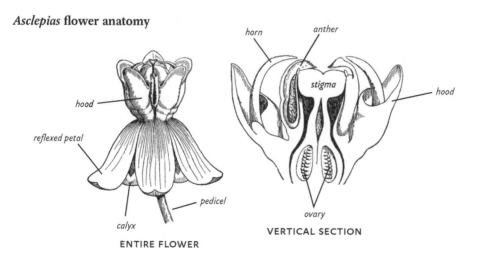

ENTIRE FLOWER

VERTICAL SECTION

1   Leaves linear, less than 4 mm wide, mostly whorled . . . . *A. verticillata*
1   Leaves more than 5 mm wide, alternate or opposite 2
   2   Leaves mostly alternate, linear to narrowly oblong 3
      3   Flowers orange; juice not milky . . . . *A. tuberosa*
      3   Flowers green, tinged with purple; juice milky 4
         4   Umbels single and terminal . . . . *A. lanuginosa*
         4   Umbels 2 or more from leaf axils . . . . *A. hirtella*
   2   Leaves opposite, oblong to ovate 5
      5   Leaves heart-shaped or clasping at base, sessile or nearly so 6
         6   Pedicels glabrous; horns (flattened or slender projections) shorter than hoods and mostly hidden . . .
             . . . . *A. sullivantii*
         6   Pedicels hairy; horns longer than hoods . . . . *A. amplexicaulis*
      5   Leaves rounded or tapered at base, petioles present although often short 7
         7   Reflexed corolla lobes red-purple, mostly less than 5 mm long . . . . *A. incarnata*
         7   Reflexed corolla lobes various colors, 5 mm or more long 8
            8   Hoods without horns; corolla lobes pale green 9
               9   Plants small, stems up to 25 cm high; umbels single and terminal . . . . *A. lanuginosa*
               9   Plants larger, stems more than 25 cm high; umbels 2 or more from leaf axils . . . . . *A. viridiflora*
            8   Hoods with slender horns; corolla lobes only rarely pale-green 10
              10 Umbels nodding; flowers white or greenish . . . . *A. exaltata*
              10 Umbels mostly erect; flowers cream-colored or tinged with red or purple 11
                 11 Upper stems, peduncles and pedicels densely white-woolly; hoods 1 cm long or more . . . . .
                     . . . . *A. speciosa*
                 11 Pubescence varies but not white-woolly; hoods less than 1 cm long 12
                    12 Plants small, slender, to 60 cm high; umbels usually single . . . . *A. ovalifolia*
                    12 Plants large and coarse, more than 60 cm high; umbels usually 2 or more . . *A. syriaca*

Asclepias amplexicaulis Sm.
CLASPING MILKWEED

MAP 175
🦫*threatened | native*

Stems simple, erect or sometimes decumbent, 3-8 dm tall, bearing 2-5 pairs of leaves and a single (rarely 2) long-peduncled, terminal umbel. **Leaves** oval or broadly oblong, 7-15 cm long, obtuse or rounded at the summit, broadly rounded or commonly cordate at the sessile or subsessile base. Peduncle 1-3 dm long. **Umbel** large, usually many-flowered; corolla greenish purple, 8-11 mm long. **Hoods** pink, about 5 mm long, about equaling the gynostegium, the lateral margins adjacent, the broad summit truncate, entire or with a few low obtuse lobes. Horns subulate, much exsert. **Pods** 10-13 cm long, erect on deflexed pedicels. June-Aug.—Dry fields, prairies, and open woods, usually in sandy soil.

Asclepias exaltata L.
POKE MILKWEED

MAP 176
native

Stems 8-15 dm tall, glabrous or puberulent in narrow lines. **Leaves** thin, broadly elliptic, 1-2 dm long, acuminate at both ends, glabrous, or puberulent beneath, on petioles 1-2 cm long. **Umbels** several from the upper axils, loosely few-flowered, the slender pedicels spreading or often drooping; corolla white to pale dull purple, 7-10 mm long. **Hoods** white or pink, about 4 mm long, about equaling the gynostegium, the lateral margins adjacent, each terminating in an erect tooth 1-1.5 mm long, the rest of the hood truncate. Horns subulate, nearly erect, conspicuously exsert. **Pods** erect on deflexed pedicels, puberulent, about 15 cm long. June-July.—Moist upland woods.

Asclepias exaltata

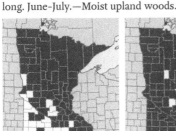

173. *Apocynum androsaemifolium*   174. *Apocynum cannabinum*   175. *Asclepias amplexicaulis*   176. *Asclepias exaltata*

Asclepias hirtella (Pennell) Woods.

(NO MAP)

GREEN MILKWEED •/*threatened* | *native*

   Asclepias longifolia var. *hirtella* (Pennell) B.L. Turner

Stems stout, 4-10 dm tall. **Leaves** linear or linear lance-shaped, 1-2 dm long, scabrellate. **Umbels** 2-10, densely flowered (flowers often 30-100), on peduncles commonly 1-2, rarely 3 cm long; pedicels hirsutulous with spreading hairs; petals about 6 mm long. **Hoods** 2-2.5 mm high, the base separated from the corolla by a distinct column, appressed to the gynostegium, obtuse at the summit, reaching to just above the base of the anther-wings. June-Aug.—Dry sandy soil; Mower County in se Minnesota.

Asclepias incarnata L.

MAP 177

SWAMP MILKWEED *native*

Perennial herb, from thick rhizomes; plants with milky juice. **Stems** stout, to 1.5 m long, branched above, smooth except for short, appressed hairs on upper stem. **Leaves** opposite, simple, mostly lance-shaped, 6-15 cm long and 1-5 cm wide, tapered to a sharp tip, margins entire, petioles short. **Flowers** pink to purple-red, numerous in umbels at ends of stems and from upper leaf axils, perfect, regular; sepals 5, spreading; petals 5, 4-6 mm long and curved downward; stamens 5; flowers with 5 petal-like "hoods", each with an awl-shaped "horn" projecting from the opening. **Fruit** a follicle (1-chambered and opening on 1 side only) with many seeds, the seeds having tufts of white hairs. June-Aug.—Openings in conifer swamps, marshes, streambanks, ditches, open bogs and fens; often in shallow water.

Asclepias incarnata

Asclepias lanuginosa Nutt.

MAP 178

SIDE-CLUSTER MILKWEED *native*

Stems 1.5-3 dm tall, villous. **Leaves** linear-oblong to more commonly lance-shaped, 4-7 cm long, obtuse, sparsely villous on both sides. **Umbel** solitary, erect, terminal, short-peduncled; pedicels hirsute; corolla lobes 4-5 mm long. **Hoods** 2.5-3.5 mm long, erect, appressed to the gynostegium, the base adjacent to the corolla, the obtuse summit reaching distinctly beyond the projecting angle of the anther-wings or nearly to the top of the gynostegium. May-June.—Dry upland hillside prairies.

Asclepias lanuginosa

Asclepias ovalifolia Dcne.

MAP 179

DWARF MILKWEED *native*

Stems slender, 2-5 dm tall. **Leaves** firm in texture, ovate lance-shaped to oblong or elliptic, commonly 3-6 cm., rarely to 10 cm long, cuneate to rounded at base, finely pubescent beneath; petioles 2-8 mm long. **Umbels** solitary and terminal, or a few in the upper axils, loosely few-flowered; corolla greenish white to greenish purple, 6-7 mm long. **Hoods** as in *A. syriaca* but smaller, 4.5-5 mm long. **Pods** merely thinly pubescent. June-July.—Dry prairies.

Asclepias speciosa Torr.

MAP 180

SHOWY MILKWEED *native*

Stems stout, to 1 m tall, pubescent. **Leaves** ovate, ovate lance-shaped, or ovate-oblong, 10-15 cm long, acute, broadly rounded or subcordate at base, pubescent beneath; petioles 3-6 mm long. **Umbels** usually few, terminal and subterminal but also in the upper axils, 5-7 cm wide; peduncles stout, 3-7 cm long; corolla greenish purple, 10-12 mm long. **Hoods** 11-15 mm long, abruptly narrowed below

Asclepias speciosa

177. *Asclepias incarnata*   178. *Asclepias lanuginosa*   179. *Asclepias ovalifolia*   180. *Asclepias speciosa*

the middle into an oblong-linear tip. Horns short, inflexed. **Pods** densely tomentose and beset with soft filiform processes. July-Aug.—Moist prairies.

Asclepias sullivantii Engelm.   MAP 181
SMOOTH MILKWEED   ❧*threatened | native*

Glabrous throughout; much resembling *A. syriaca* in habit. **Leaves** firm, ovate-oblong, 8-14 cm long, obtuse or rounded to the minutely apiculate summit, smooth on the cartilaginous margin, broadly rounded or subcordate at the sessile or subsessile base. **Umbels** 1-few, terminal or subterminal, compactly many-flowered, on peduncles 1-5 cm long; corolla dull pale purple, 9-12 mm long. **Hoods** much surpassing the gynostegium, about 6 mm long, the lateral margins entire, each hood flanked by a minute process at base. Horns horizontally inflexed. **Pods** glabrous or slightly verrucose, erect on deflexed pedicels. June-July.—Moist prairies.

Asclepias syriaca L.   MAP 182
COMMON MILKWEED   *native*

Stems tall and stout, mostly simple, pubescent. **Leaves** thick, narrowly or broadly elliptic to ovate or oblong, 10-15 cm long, acute or apiculate, softly pubescent beneath, on distinct petioles 5-15 mm long. **Umbels** often numerous, terminal and in the upper axils, compactly many-flowered; peduncles stout, 3-10 cm long; corolla green suffused with purple, varying from almost purple to almost green, 8-10 mm long. **Hoods** pale purple, somewhat divergent, 6-8 mm long, surpassing the gynostegium, the lateral margins bearing a prominent, sharp, triangular lobe at or near the middle. Horns short, inflexed. **Pods** erect on deflexed pedicels about 1 dm long, tomentose and beset with soft filiform to conic processes.—Fields, meadows, and roadsides; often weedy.

Asclepias syriaca

Asclepias tuberosa L.   MAP 183
BUTTERFLY WEED   *native*

Stems ascending or erect, 3-7 dm tall, villous or hirsute, simple to much branched above, the branches ascending or widely spreading, often flexuous. **Leaves** alternate or on the branches opposite, linear to lance-shaped or oblong lance-shaped, 5-10 cm long, pubescent, cuneate to truncate or subcordate at base. **Umbels** varying from solitary and terminal to numerous, often from most of the axils of divergent branches; corolla yellow to orange-red, 7-10 mm long. **Hoods** yellow to orange, 5-7 mm long, greatly exceeding the gynostegium, nearly straight, erect, the lateral margins bearing an obscure tooth below the middle. **Pods** 8-12 cm long, erect. June-Aug.—Dry or moist prairies and upland woods, especially in sandy soil. *Our only Asclepias without milky juice; plants variable in form and shades of flower color.*

Asclepias tuberosa

Asclepias verticillata L.   MAP 184
WHORLED MILKWEED   *native*

Stems slender, erect, 2-5 dm tall, simple to the inflorescence, pubescent in lines. **Leaves** very numerous in whorls of 3-6, narrowly linear, 2-5 cm long, 1-2 mm wide, revolute. **Umbels** several from the upper nodes; peduncles 1-3 cm long; petals white or greenish, 4-5 mm long. **Hoods** white or greenish white, somewhat divergent, 1.5-2 mm long, about equaling the gynostegium, their margins entire. Horns subulate, much surpassing the hoods, slightly narrowed over the stamens. **Pods** slender, erect on erect pedicels, 4-5 cm long. June-Aug.—Dry or moist fields, roadsides, upland woods, and prairies.

Asclepias verticillata

181. *Asclepias sullivantii*   182. *Asclepias syriaca*   183. *Asclepias tuberosa*   184. *Asclepias verticillata*

Asclepias viridiflora Raf.   MAP 185
GREEN COMET MILKWEED   *native*
Stems erect, ascending, or even prostrate, 3-8 dm long, thinly pubescent. **Leaves** vary from lance-shaped (most common) to broadly oblong, elliptic or obovate-oblong, thinly pubescent beneath, scabrous on the margin. **Umbels** lateral, densely flowered, sessile or on peduncles to 2 cm long; pedicels pubescent; corolla lobes 6-8 mm long. **Hoods** narrowly elliptic-oblong, 4.5-5.5 mm high, appressed to the gynostegium, the base adjacent to the corolla, the obtuse or subacute summit reaching well beyond the salient angle of the anther-wings or even to the top of the gynostegium. July-Aug.—Dry upland woods, prairies, and barrens, especially in sandy soil.

Asclepias viridiflora

VINCA *Periwinkle*

Vinca minor L.   (NO MAP)
LESSER PERIWINKLE   *introduced (invasive)*
Perennial trailing herb. **Stems** trailing or scrambling, to 1 m long, forming mats. **Leaves** leathery, opposite, lance-elliptic, 3-5 cm long, entire, petiolate. **Flowers** blue or rarely white, solitary in 1 axil only of a pair of leaves; calyx deeply 5-parted; corolla large, salverform, corolla tube 8-12 mm long, the limb 2-3 cm wide; ovaries 2, accompanied by 2 nectaries. **Fruit** a linear, few-seeded follicle; seeds naked. April-May.—Native of s Europe, planted as a groundcover and rarely escaped to roadsides and open woods; reported for Minnesota.

Vinca minor

VINCETOXICUM *Swallow-Wort*

Vincetoxicum nigrum (L.) Moench   MAP 186
BLACK SWALLOW-WORT   *introduced (invasive)*
  Cynanchum nigrum (L.) Pers. non Cav.
Perennial twining herb, climbing 1-2 m tall. **Leaves** short-petioled, oblong to ovate, 5-10 cm long, acuminate, rounded to subcordate at base. **Flowers** in peduncled umbel-like clusters from the axils of the leaves; corolla purple-brown and dark purple, its lobes about 3 mm long, much exceeding the cuplike corona. **Follicles** slender, 4-6 cm long. June-Sept.—Native of s Europe; occasionally cultivated and locally established in woods and on roadsides.

Vincetoxicum nigrum

Aquifoliaceae HOLLY FAMILY

ILEX *Holly*

Shrubs. Leaves usually alternate, toothed or entire, not lobed. Flowers from leaf axils, 4-8-parted, usually either staminate or pistillate, sometimes perfect, on same or different plants. Fruit a fleshy berrylike drupe with 4-9 stones.

1 Leaves tipped with a short, sharp point, margins mostly entire or with a few scattered teeth; petals linear; sepals tiny or absent . . . . ***Ilex mucronata***
1 Leaves not tipped with a short, sharp point, margins toothed; petals oblong; sepals evident . . . . ***Ilex verticillata***

Aralia hispida

185. Asclepias viridiflora   *186. Vincetoxicum nigrum*

Ilex mucronata (L.) Powell, Savolainen & Andrews   MAP 187
MOUNTAIN HOLLY; CATBERRY   *native*
   Nemopanthus mucronatus (L.) Loes.

Much-branched shrub to 3 m tall; young twigs purple-tinged. **Leaves** deciduous, alternate, oval or ovate, 3-6 cm long and 2-3 cm wide, bright green above, dull and paler below, tip of leaf with a small, sharp point; margins entire or with small scattered teeth, on purple-red stalks 1 cm long. **Flowers** very small, yellow-white, on threadlike stalks from leaf axils; staminate flowers usually in small groups, pistillate flowers single. **Fruit** a purple-red berrylike drupe, 5-6 mm wide. May-June.—Open bogs (especially along outer moat), swamps, thickets, wet depressions in forests, lakeshores.

Ilex mucronata

Ilex verticillata (L.) Gray   MAP 188
WINTERBERRY   *native*
Shrub to 5 m tall; twigs smooth, finely ridged. **Leaves** deciduous, alternate, obovate to oval, tapered to a tip, dull green above, paler below; margins with incurved teeth. **Flowers** small, green-white, on short stalks from leaf axils, opening before leaves fully expanded in spring; staminate flowers in crowded clusters, pistillate flowers 1 or several in a group. **Fruit** a berrylike drupe, orange or red, 5-6 mm wide and persisting into winter. June.—Swamps, open bogs, thickets, shores and streambanks.

Ilex verticillata

Araliaceae GINSENG FAMILY

Shrubs or herbs, rarely trees. Leaves usually alternate, compound or rarely simple, the petiole not sheathing at base and usually adnate to the stipules; flowers small, umbellate. Flowers regular, epigynous, perfect or unisexual, 5-10-merous. Calyx small, its limb truncate to denticulate. Petals valvate or scarcely imbricate, usually distinct, deciduous at maturity. Stamens usually as many as the petals, rarely more. inserted on a tusk within the calyx; anthers short, longitudinally dehiscent. Ovary inferior, 2-12-celled, with one pendulous ovule in each cell. Styles as many as the cells of the ovary, distinct or more or less connate. Fruit a berry or a leathery drupe.

1 Leaves compound 2
    2 Leaves alternate or basal, mostly 2-3 times compound; carpels 5 . . . . *Aralia*
    2 Leaves in 1 whorl, once-palmately compound; carpels 2 or 3 . . . . *Panax*
1 Leaves simple, palmately lobed . . . . *Hydrocotyle*

ARALIA *Sarsaparilla*

Herbs or shrubs (or rarely trees). Stems herbaceous or slightly woody at the base only, rarely thorny (*A. hispida* bristly at the base). Leaves pinnately or 3-partedly compound. Flowers white or greenish, in 2-many umbels in each inflorescence. Petals and stamens each 5. Cells of the ovary 4-6, usually 5. Styles 4-6, usually 5, free or somewhat connate at base. Fruit a berry, tipped by the persistent styles; seeds usually 5.

1 Plants with flowers on a leafless scape . . . . *A. nudicaulis*
1 Plants with leafy stems 2
    2 Lower stems bristly; umbels several (3-13) in a loose cluster . . . . *A. hispida*
    2 Stems smooth; umbels very many, in a large terminal panicle . . . . *A. racemosa*

187. *Ilex mucronata*   188. *Ilex verticillata*   189. *Aralia hispida*   190. *Aralia nudicaulis*

Aralia hispida Vent.

BRISTLY SARSAPARILLA

MAP 189
native

Perennial herb from a stout rhizome. **Stems** to 1 m tall, bristly near the base with sharp slender spines and often decreasingly so above. **Leaves** few, on petioles usually shorter than the blade, bipinnate; **leaflets** oblong to ovate or lance-shaped, up to 10 cm long but usually much smaller, acute or short-acuminate, sharply serrate. **Umbels** several, in a loose, open, terminal inflorescence; styles connate about half their length. **Berry** globose, nearly black. June-July.—Dry woods, especially in sandy or sterile soil.

Aralia nudicaulis

Aralia nudicaulis L.

WILD SARSAPARILLA

MAP 190
native

Acaulescent perennial herb, the leaves and peduncle arising from a long rhizome. Petiole erect, to 5 dm tall. **Leaves** 3-parted, each division pinnately 3-5-foliolate; **leaflets** lance-elliptic to obovate, up to 15 cm long and 8 cm wide, acuminate, finely serrate, the lateral ones asymmetric at base. Peduncles usually much shorter than the petioles, bearing 2-7, commonly 3 umbels; styles distinct to the base. **Fruit** nearly black. May-June.—Moist or dry woods.

Aralia racemosa L.

SPIKENARD

MAP 191
native

Stout perennial herb to 2 m tall, lacking thorns or bristles. **Leaves** few, widely spreading, up to 8 dm long, the three primary divisions pinnately compound; **leaflets** ovate, variable in size in the same leaf, the larger up to 15 cm long, sharply and often doubly serrate, acuminate, obliquely cordate at base. **Inflorescence** a large panicle with numerous umbels; styles connate at base only. **Fruit** dark purple. July.—Rich woods.

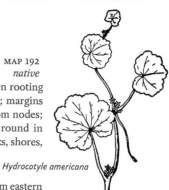
Aralia racemosa

HYDROCOTYLE *Pennywort*

Hydrocotyle americana L.

AMERICAN MARSH-PENNYWORT

MAP 192
native

Small perennial herb. **Stems** slender and creeping, 10-20 cm long, often rooting at nodes. **Leaves** round to kidney-shaped, 1-5 cm wide; petioles long; margins with 7-12 shallow lobes. **Flowers** white, in nearly stalkless umbels from nodes; umbels 2-7-flowered. **Fruit** of 2 compressed carpels, more or less round in outline, 1-2 mm wide, ribbed. June-Sept.—Conifer swamps, streambanks, shores, wet forest depressions. *Formerly included in Apiaceae.*

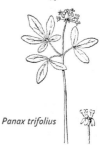
Hydrocotyle americana

ADDITIONAL SPECIES

Hydrocotyle ranunculoides L.f. (Floating marsh-pennywort); disjunct from eastern Ohio and Tenn, possibly introduced in Minn; known only from Scott County (Shakopee-Mdewakanton tribal lands).

PANAX *Ginseng*

Perennial herbs, the unbranched stems rising from a deep-seated, thickened or tuber-like root, bearing a single whorl of once-palmately compound leaves, usually 3 in number. Flowers in usually a single long-peduncled terminal umbel. Petals and stamens each 5; petals white or greenish; ovary 2-3 celled; styles 2 or 3. Fruit a small, 3-angled or flattened, 2-3-seeded berry.

Panax trifolius

191. Aralia racemosa *192. Hydrocotyle americana* *193. Panax quinquefolius* *194. Panax trifolius*

1 Leaflets long-stalked; uncommon .... *P. quinquefolius*
1 Leaflets sessile; common .... *P. trifolius*

Panax quinquefolius L.
AMERICAN GINSENG

MAP 193
native

Perennial herb. **Stems** 2-6 dm tall, root fusiform. **Leaflets** 3-7, usually 5, obovate to obovate, 6-15 cm long, conspicuously serrate, on long petiolules. **Flowers** greenish white, all or mostly perfect; peduncle 1-12 cm long; styles usually 2. **Fruit** a bright red berry, about 1 cm wide. June-July.—Rich deciduous woods, now rare due to heavy collecting.

Panax trifolius L.
DWARF GINSENG

MAP 194
native

Perennial herb. **Stems** 1-2 dm tall; root globose. **Leaflets** 3-5, sessile or nearly so, lance-shaped to elliptic or oblong lance-shaped, 4-8 cm long, finely serrate. **Flowers** white or tinged with pink, often unisexual; peduncle 2-8 cm long; styles usually 3. **Fruit** a yellow berry, about 5 mm wide. April-May.—Rich woods.

Panax quinquefolius

Aristolochiaceae BIRTHWORT FAMILY

ASARUM *Wild Ginger*

Asarum canadense L.
CANADIAN WILD GINGER

MAP 195
native

Perennial herb; rhizome slender, branched, pubescent; producing annually a pair of leaves, between which arises the solitary, short-peduncled flower. **Leaves** 2, cordate, entire, at anthesis commonly 8-12 cm wide, larger at maturity, pubescent, especially on the long petiole. **Flowers** axillary, red-brown, 2-4 cm long, on a stout, pubescent pedicel 2-5 cm long; calyx tubular at base, deeply 3-lobed, the lobes spreading to reflexed, purple inside; petals absent or tiny and awl-shaped; ovary inferior, 6-celled. **Fruit** a capsule, bursting irregularly; seeds large, ovoid, wrinkled. April-May.—Rich woods, usually in small colonies.

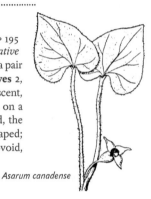

Asarum canadense

Asteraceae ASTER FAMILY

Annual, biennial or perennial herbs. Leaves simple or compound, opposite, alternate, or whorled. Flowers perfect (with both staminate and pistillate parts) or single-sexed (sometimes sterile) and of 2 types: ray (or ligulate) and disk (or tubular). Ray flowers joined at base and have a long, flat, segment above (the ray); disk flowers tube-shaped with 5 lobes or teeth at tip.

Flowers are clustered in 1 of 3 types of heads resembling a single flower and attached to a common surface (receptacle): ray flowers only (as in dandelion, *Taraxacum*); disk flowers only (discoid, as in tansy, *Tanacetum*); and heads with both ray and disk flowers (radiate), the ray flowers surrounding the disk flowers (as in sunflower, *Helianthus*).

In addition to flowers, the receptacle may also have scales called chaff; if no scales present, the receptacle is termed naked. Each head is surrounded by involucral bracts (sometimes called phyllaries); collectively, the bracts are termed the involucre, comparable to the group of sepals (calyx) subtending an individual flower. Fertile flowers have 1 pistil tipped by a 2-cleft style (undivided in sterile flowers); stamens 5; ovary (and achene) often topped by several to many scales, awns or hairs (the pappus). Fruit a seedlike achene (sometimes termed *cypsela* in Asteraceae).

ADDITIONAL SPECIES

A number of other members of the Aster Family occur in Minn, and, if not included in further described genera, are listed below. Many are introduced garden escapes, and most are adventive and not truly established in the state's flora.

• *Canadanthus modestus* (Lindl.) Nesom (Canada-aster), native; mostly ne Minn (Cook, Lake, St. Louis counties) plus Becker County.

• *Cosmos bipinnatus* Cav. (Garden Cosmos), introduced annual, leaves opposite, rays about 8, rose or lilac; cultivated and occasionally escaped; reported for Minn; see Tribe 8 key.

• *Dieteria canescens* (Pursh) Nutt. (Hoary tansy-aster), native to nw Great Plains; in Minn, known only from Blue Earth County.

• *Dyssodia papposa* (Vent.) A.S. Hitchc. (Fetid-marigold), native of central Great Plains; in Minn, Houston and Rock counties; see Tribe 8 key.

• *Leontodon autumnalis* L., introduced, reported from St. Louis County; see Tribe 4 key.

• *Leucanthemella serotina* (L.) Tzvelev (Giant daisy), introduced from e Europe; reported from Cass and St. Louis counties.

• *Logfia arvensis* (L.) Holub (Field cottonrose, syn. *Filago arvensis* L.), native to Eurasia and nw Africa; St. Louis County.

• *Madia glomerata* Hook (Mountain tarplant), coarse glandular annual herb, leaves alternate, rays yellow; native in w USA, adventive in Carlton and St. Louis counties; see Tribe 8 key.

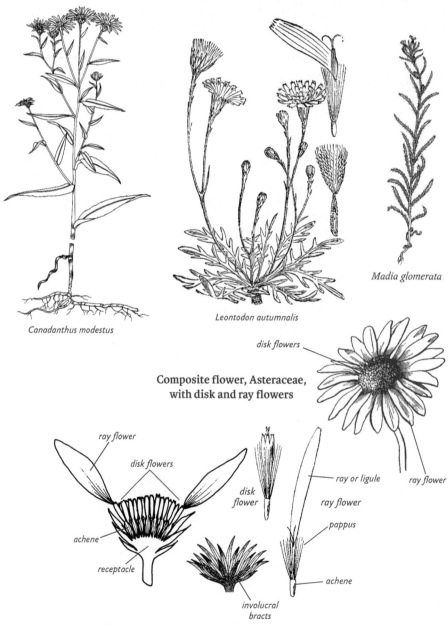

Madia glomerata

Canadanthus modestus

Leontodon autumnalis

disk flowers

Composite flower, Asteraceae, with disk and ray flowers

ray flower

disk flowers

ray or ligule

ray flower

disk flower

ray flower

pappus

achene

achene

receptacle

involucral bracts

Typical Aster Family inflorescence, with both disk and ray flowers.

KEY TO ASTERACEAE TRIBES

Because of its large size, the Asteraceae is often divided into smaller groups of related species called tribes. In Minn, 11 tribes (and one subtribe) occur, and are identified in the following key. The tribal key is adapted from Kowal (2007).

1 Flowers wind-pollinated, not showy; rays absent; florets and most heads unisexual; anthers not united; involucral bracts typically connate, at least basally, where free (*Iva*), only 3-5 . . . . **Tribe 8a. HELIANTHEAE**
. . . . **(Subtribe AMBROSIINAE, Ragweed subtribe)**

1 Flowers insect-pollinated, usually showy; rays present or absent; heads and most florets bisexual; anthers united; involucral bracts free; if wind-pollinated, involucral bracts free, scarious and more than 5 (*Artemisia*) 2

  2 Plants with milky juice; heads ligulate (florets bisexual and with a 5-toothed ligule) . . **Tribe 4. CICHORIEAE**
  . . . . **(Lettuce Tribe)**

  2 Plants with watery juice; heads radiate (with disk florets surrounded by ray florets), or disciform but with ray florets without rays, or discoid (only disk florets) 3

    3 Plants and/or heads usually prickly; heads discoid and corolla lobes of the disk florets at least 4 times longer than wide; receptacle densely bristly (naked in the prickly *Onopordum*); leaves alternate; style with a ring of hairs (sometimes merely with a thickened ring) below the branches; anthers tailed at base . . . .
    . . . . **Tribe 3. CARDUEAE (Thistle Tribe)**

    3 Plants and heads not prickly; heads various, corolla lobes of the disk florets less than 4 times longer than wide; receptacle various, rarely bristly; leaves various; style otherwise; anthers (except in Gnaphalieae and Inuleae) not tailed 4

      4 Heads discoid and corollas never yellow; style-branches long and slender (thread-like), conspicuously protruding from the corolla and often attractive; receptacle naked 5

        5 Style-branches hispidulous, acute or acuminate at tip; corollas purple; inflorescence corymbose; leaves alternate . . . . **Tribe 11. VERNONIEAE (Ironweed Tribe)**

        5 Style-branches merely papillate, blunt (to acutish) and sometimes thickened (clavate) towards the tip; corollas white, pink, rose or blue- violet; inflorescence various; leaves alternate, opposite or whorled . . . . **Tribe 5. EUPATORIEAE (Boneset Tribe)**

    4 Heads various, but if discoid, corollas yellow (or at least creamy); style- branches much shorter (relative to their widths); receptacle various 6

      6 Pappus of hairs or bristles; leaves alternate (in some Senecioneae directly from a rhizome) 7

        7 Involucral bracts equal and in 1 row (sometimes with a few small bractlets below them); rays yellow or absent; style-branches mostly truncate, with a tuft of hairs at the end . . . .
        . . . . **Tribe 10. SENECIONEAE (Groundsel Tribe)**

        7 Involucral bracts in 2-5 rows, equal or unequal, if (rarely) in 1 row, with conspicuous white, pink, purple, or blue rays 8

          8 Heads discoid or disciform; involucral bracts scarious, either virtually entirely or at least at the tip for a third of their lengths (styles and anthers as in Inuleae) **Tribe 6. GNAPHALIEAE**
          . . . . **(Pussytoes Tribe)**

          8 Heads radiate (rays minute in *Conyza*); involucral bracts not scarious or scarious only on margins. 9

            9 Giant perennial herb 1-3 m tall, with basal leaves often 1 m long, disk of head more than 2 cm wide, and rays more than 4 cm long, which are yellow, numerous, and narrowly linear; style branch slightly clavate and glabrous; anthers tailed at base; infrequent adventive. .
            . . . . **Tribe 9. INULEAE (Elecampane Tribe)**

            9 Plant smaller in all parts; rays of various colors and shapes; style branch with a lanceolate or elongate-deltoid hairy appendage; anthers rounded at base . . . . . **Tribe 2. ASTEREAE**
            . . . . **(Aster Tribe)**

      6 Pappus absent or of awns, scales, or teeth; leaves alternate or opposite. 10

        10 Involucral bracts with scarious or hyaline margins; leaves alternate. 11

          11 Leaves entire, not aromatic; receptacle naked; style branch with a lanceolate or elongate-deltoid hairy appendage (*Boltonia*). . . . . **Tribe 2. ASTEREAE (Aster Tribe)**

          11 Leaves toothed, lobed, or finely divided, often aromatic; receptacle chaffy or naked; style-branches mostly truncate, with a tuft of hairs at the end (like Senecioneae). . . . .
          . . . . **Tribe 1. ANTHEMIDEAE (Chamomile Tribe)**

        10 Involucral bracts not scarious or hyaline, or if so, leaves opposite; leaves alternate or opposite 12

          12 Receptacle naked; rays present, widest at the prominently 3-lobed apex; leaves alternate (opposite in *Arnica*), lanceolate to ovate . . . . **Tribe 7. HELENIEAE (Sneezeweed Tribe)**

          12 Receptacle chaffy (absent in *Dyssodia*, with unremarkable rays and opposite pinnatisect leaves); rays present or absent, but when present usually not as above, but if so, then the leaves opposite and either lobed or pinnatifid . . **Tribe 8. HELIANTHEAE (Sunflower Tribe)**

TRIBE 1. ANTHEMIDEAE (CHAMOMILE TRIBE)

GENERA: *Achillea, Anthemis, Artemisia, Leucanthemum, Matricaria, Tanacetum*

1   Receptacle chaffy; heads radiate 2
   2   Heads small, 5 mm or less in diameter, densely corymbose; receptacle flat; achenes compressed . . . ***Achillea***
   2   Heads rather large, 1-4 cm in diameter, solitary and terminal on long peduncles; receptacle conic at maturity; achenes terete or angled 3
      3   Ray florets white; disk 0.5-1.2 cm wide . . . . ***Anthemis***
      3   Ray florets yellow; disk 1-2 cm wide . . . . ***Anthemis tinctoria***
1   Receptacle naked or villous; heads radiate, disciform or discoid 4
   4   Inflorescence paniculate, racemose or spike-like, with inconspicuous (2-8 mm long) disciform or discoid heads; florets green . . . . ***Artemisia***
   4   Inflorescence corymbose or heads terminal on long peduncles; ray florets showy, yellow or white (sometimes obsolete) 5
      5   Receptacle conic at maturity; leaves pinnatisect . . . . ***Matricaria***
      5   Receptacle flat or low-convex 6
         6   Heads several or numerous, in corymbs, disk 4-9 mm wide, with or without rays; leaves often highly lobed . . . . ***Tanacetum***
         6   Heads solitary at tips of stem or long branches, large, disk 1-2.5 cm wide, with conspicuous white rays; leaves toothed to lobed . . . . ***Leucanthemum***

TRIBE 2. ASTEREAE (ASTER TRIBE)

GENERA: *Bellis, Boltonia, Conyza, Doellingeria, Eurybia, Erigeron, Euthamia, Grindelia, Heterotheca, Solidago, Symphyotrichum, Xanthisma*

1   Ray corollas yellow, conspicuous; disk corollas yellow 2
   2   Pappus of 2-8 caducous awns; involucre more or less glutinous . . . . ***Grindelia***
   2   Pappus of numerous capillary bristles or hairs; involucre not glutinous 3
      3   Pappus of 2 series, the outer distinctly shorter than the inner 4
         4   Receptacle with obvious chaffy scales among the achenes . . . . ***Xanthisma***
         4   Receptacle naked, without chaffy scales . . . . ***Heterotheca***
      3   Pappus with a single series of capillary bristles of nearly uniform size 5
         5   Inflorescence corymbiform; leaves glandular punctate, linear to narrowly oblong, only slightly reduced upwards on stem; ray florets more numerous than the disk florets . . . . ***Euthamia***
         5   Plants not with both inflorescence corymbiform and ray florets more numerous than the disk florets; leaves usually broader, not glandular punctate . . . . ***Solidago***
1   Ray corollas white, pink, violet, bluish or purple; disk corollas various 6
   6   Pappus absent or inconspicuous (2-4 awns up to 2 mm long and several minute bristles); receptacle conic or hemispherical 7
      7   Plant 3-15 dm tall, with numerous heads; pappus inconspicuous; receptacle low-conical or hemispherical
         . . . . ***Boltonia***
      7   Plant 1.5 dm or less tall, with one head on a scape; pappus absent; receptacle conic . . . . ***Bellis***
   6   Pappus of long capillary bristles or hairs; receptacle flat 8
      8   Rays tiny, shorter than the corolla tube and barely longer than the pappus; heads small with involucres less than 4 mm long, disks no more than 4 mm wide, and disk florets numbering no more than 21 . . . . . ***Conyza***
      8   Rays conspicuous, larger; heads larger 9
         9   Involucral bracts approximately in one series, neither chartaceous at base nor with herbaceous green tip; style appendages roundish or obtuse, no longer than 0.3 mm; rays very numerous and narrowly linear (mostly 1.3 mm or less wide); plants blooming chiefly in spring and early summer (when later, plants also with heads past fruiting) . . . . ***Erigeron***
         9   Involucral bracts clearly imbricated or with a foliaceous outer series; style appendages longer and more acute; rays in one or two series and relatively broader; plants blooming in late summer and fall 10
            10   Middle and lower stem leaves distinctly petioled; most of the petioles more than 1 cm long, wingless, or winged but less than 1/4 as wide as the blades; blades (except the uppermost) more than 12 mm wide, abruptly narrowed to a truncate or cordate base 11
               11   Involucral bracts narrowly to broadly ovate-lanceolate, outer ones 1.0-2.5 mm wide, less than 2.5x as long as wide; inflorescence corymbiform . . . . ***Eurybia***
               11   Involucral bracts linear-deltoid to lanceolate, outer ones 0.2-1.0 mm wide, greater than 2.5x as long as wide; inflorescence elongate (paniculate or racemose) . . . . ***Symphyotrichum***

10 Middle and lower stem leaves not distinctly petioled; sessile, or subsessile on petioles less than 0.5 cm long, or apparently on broad-winged petioles more than ¼ as wide as the blades, or with long narrow tapering petiole-like bases, but the blades not more than 12 mm wide 12

    12 Pappus double, the inner of long capillary bristles, the outer of short bristles, ca. 1 mm long or less (very obscure); middle and upper involucral bracts with scarious margins extending to tip, central green line not or only slightly expanded towards tip; inflorescence corymbose . . . . ***Doellingeria umbellata***

    12 Pappus not double; involucral bracts various, but in most species with the central green line conspicuously dilated at tip; inflorescence various, but in most species not corymbose (*Symphyotrichum*) 13

        13 Rays much reduced or absent (heads "disciform"); pappus conspicuous at anthesis; plants annual, with taproots . . . . ***Symphyotrichum ciliatum***

        13 Rays present, heads conspicuously radiate; pappus inconspicuous at anthesis or at most barely overtopping disk corollas; plants perennial, tufted or with rhizomes . . . . . . ***Symphyotrichum***

TRIBE 3. CARDUEAE (THISTLE TRIBE)

GENERA: *Arctium, Carduus, Centaurea, Cirsium, Echinops, Onopordum*

1 Plants and heads not prickly, or involucral bracts spine-tipped and corollas yellow; achenes obliquely attached to the receptacle; marginal disk florets often enlarged and showy; involucral bracts often with margins scarious and deeply cleft at tip (laciniate); pappus hairs mostly less than 3 mm long or lacking . . . . ***Centaurea***

1 Plants and/or heads prickly; corollas not yellow; achenes attached by the base to the receptacle; florets all alike; involucral bracts not laciniate at tip; pappus hairs usually more than 5 mm long 2

    2 Leaves unarmed, broadly rounded at base; tip of phyllary a hook . . . . ***Arctium***

    2 Leaves prickly, lanceolate to ovate; tip of phyllary a straight spine or merely mucronate 3

        3 Heads 1-flowered, aggregated into globose secondary heads . . . . ***Echinops***

        3 Heads many-flowered, only rarely sessile 4

            4 Pappus plumose; involucral bracts with needle-like spiny tips or merely mucronate, often with a glutinous ridge on back . . . . ***Cirsium***

            4 Pappus barbellate to capillary; involucral bracts not glutinous 5

                5 Receptacle bristly; leaves and stem wings glabrous or nearly so; pappus capillary . . . . ***Carduus***

                5 Receptacle alveolate (pitted), not bristly; leaves and stem wings densely cottony-velutinous; pappus barbellate; rare adventive . . . . ***Onopordum***

TRIBE 4. CICHORIEAE (LETTUCE TRIBE)

GENERA: *Agoseris, Cichorium, Crepis, Hieracium, Krigia, Lactuca, Lapsana,Lygodesmia, Nothocalais, Prenanthes, Shinnersoseris, Sonchus, Taraxacum, Tragopogon*

1 Pappus absent. . . . . ***Lapsana communis***

1 Pappus present. 2

    2 Pappus of numerous simple hairlike (capillary) bristles only 3

        3 Achenes flattened or compressed 4

            4 Achenes not beaked, not enlarged at the tip; heads yellow with many florets (80 or more) . . ***Sonchus***

            4 Achenes beaked or unbeaked, but constricted below enlarged tip; heads yellow or blue, with relatively few florets (less than 56) . . . . ***Lactuca***

        3 Achenes cylindrical, fusiform or terete, not flattened. 5

            5 Corolla pink, purple, or white. 6

                6 Annual with the leaves opposite at the lower 4 or 5 nodes . . . . ***Shinnersoseris***

                6 Perennial; all leaves alternate. 7

                    7 Leaves linear or reduced to bracts; heads terminating the branches . . . . ***Lygodesmia***

                    7 Well-developed leaves more than 1 cm wide, not linear; inflorescence panicle-like with several to many heads . . . . ***Prenanthes***

            5 Corolla yellow to orange-red. 8

                8 Plants scapose; achenes beaked, or tapered and the beak lacking; pappus white; involucral bracts in more than one series 9

                    9 Achenes beakless or nearly so . . . . ***Nothocalais cuspidata***

                    9 Achenes clearly beaked. 10

                        10 Body of achene spinulose upwards; outer involucral bracts shorter than inner bracts and reflexed . . . . ***Taraxacum***

                        10 Body of achene at most striate but not spinulose; involucral bracts nearly equal . . . ***Agoseris***

8 Stems branched or unbranched and leafy or subscapose; achenes truncate or tapered, rarely short-beaked; pappus pale yellow, red-brown, tannish or white; involucral bracts in 1 or 2 series 11

11 Annuals or biennials with well developed, usually pinnatifid basal leaves; inflorescences open corymbs or panicles of yellow campanulate heads; pappus white; main involucral bracts uniseriate . . . . *Crepis*

11 Perennials; cauline leaves lanceolate to palmately lobed, or unlobed and dentate to entire; inflorescences branched racemes, panicles of cylindrical drooping heads, or corymbs with erect campanulate heads; pappus tawny to brown, not pure snowy white; main involucral bracts biseriate 12

12 Leaves lanceolate to palmately lobed; heads cylindrical, nodding; corolla pink, purplish to yellow or white; pappus pale yellow to red-brown; plants sometimes tomentose, not glandular . . . . *Prenanthes*

12 Leaves spatulate to oblanceolate, not lobed; heads campanulate, erect; corolla yellow to red-orange; pappus tannish; plants usually glandular-pubescent . . . . *Hieracium*

2 Pappus otherwise (plumose bristles, scales, scales mixed with bristles, or a ring of many minute bristles). . . 13

13 Pappus of plumose (feathery) bristles only 14

14 Plants leafy stemmed, branched, not scaly-bracted above; leaves cauline, grasslike . . . . . . *Tragopogon*

14 Plants scapose, scaly bracted above; leaves basal, coarsely dentate . . . . *Leontodon**

13 Pappus of scales and/or bristles (sometimes minute) 15

15 Pappus of 5 to numerous outer scales alternating with 5 to numerous scabrous hairs; plants scapose or sub-scapose, branched or not branched; corolla yellow . . . . *Krigia*

15 Pappus a ring of numerous minute (0.2 mm) scales or bristles; plants profusely branched; corolla blue, rarely pink or white . . . . *Cichorium*

TRIBE 5. EUPATORIEAE (BONESET TRIBE)

GENERA: *Ageratina, Brickellia, Eupatorium, Eutrochium, Liatris*

1 Leaves alternate; plants from a stout taproot or enlarged corm; achenes 10-ribbed; pappus of plumose or barbellate bristles; involucral bracts weakly or strongly ribbed 2

2 Plants from stout taproots; pappus plumose; involucral bracts strongly ribbed; inflorescence corymbiform, the heads creamy-white . . . . *Brickellia*

2 Plants from enlarged corms; pappus plumose or barbellate; involucral bracts weakly ribbed; inflorescence spicate or racemose, the heads purple and often very showy . . . . *Liatris*

1 Leaves opposite or whorled; roots fibrous; achenes 5-angled; pappus of capillary bristles; involucral bracts not ribbed 3

3 Leaves in whorls of 3, 4 or 5; heads purple or dull rose; involucres cylindric with involucral bracts in 5-6 series . . . . *Eutrochium*

3 Leaves opposite (rarely in 3s in *E. perfoliatum*); heads white (rarely purple in *E. perfoliatum*); involucres short-cylindric with involucral bracts in 2-3 series 4

4 Leaves long-petioled, ovate; involucral bracts nearly uniseriate, narrowly linear, any basal ones usually much less than half the length of the longest; heads with 15-30 florets; amber resin glands absent . . . . . *Ageratina*

4 Leaves sessile (except *E. serotinum*), narrowly ovate or lanceolate; involucral bracts in 2-3 series, not narrowly linear, many roughly half the length of the longest; heads with 15 or fewer florets; tiny amber resin glands on leaf undersides, involucral bracts, corollas, and achenes . . . . *Eupatorium*

TRIBE 6. GNAPHALIEAE (PUSSYTOES TRIBE)

GENERA: *Anaphalis, Antennaria, Gnaphalium, Pseudognaphalium*

1 Stem leaves few, much smaller than those of the persistent basal rosette, strongly ascending; stolons present; plants either staminate or pistillate, populations dioecious . . . . *Antennaria*

1 Stem leaves many, about the same size as the basal leaves, which soon wither; stolons absent. 2

2 Involucral bracts pure white, with conspicuous, longitudinal creases creating the appearance of wrinkled tissue paper; populations dioecious, although pistillate plants often with heads having a few staminate florets in the center; dried plants without a strong odor . . . . *Anaphalis*

2 Involucral bracts grayish white, yellow or brown, scarious, with very small longitudinal ridges but no conspicuous creases; heads bisexual, with pistillate florets marginally and staminate heads in center; dried plants with strong tobacco-like odor. 3

3 Heads 2-3 mm long, in capitate leafy-bracted clusters; upper stems very densely white floccose-tomentose, obvious to the naked eye; stems usually much branched, 1-2 dm tall . . . . *Gnaphalium uliginosum*

3 Heads 4-6 mm long, capitate or corymbose; upper stems with appressed or nearly microscopic loose-spreading tomentum; stems erect, seldom branching except within a corymbose inflorescence, 1-10 dm tall . . . . *Pseudognaphalium*

TRIBE 7. HELENIEAE (SNEEZEWEED TRIBE)

GENERA: *Arnica, Gaillardia, Helenium*

1 Leaves opposite . . . . *Arnica*
1 Leaves alternate 2
    2 Receptacle naked; style branches truncate, without an appendage . . . . *Helenium*
    2 Receptacle bristly; style branches with a subulate appendage . . . . *Gaillardia*

TRIBE 8. HELIANTHEAE (SUNFLOWER TRIBE)

GENERA: *Bidens, Coreopsis, Echinacea, Eclipta, Galinsoga, Helianthus, Heliopsis, Parthenium, Polymnia, Ratibida, Rudbeckia, Silphium*

1 Involucral bracts (some or all) highly modified, either infolding outer achenes or united into a cup or tube; strongly scented annuals; very rare adventives or escapes from cultivation 2
    2 Involucral bracts free, outer (or larger) laterally compressed and infolding the laterally compressed achene; cauline leaves mostly alternate and unlobed; stems viscid and glandular pubescent . . . . *Madia**
    2 Involucral bracts (at least innermost) united into a cup or tube, none inclosing the opposite flower or achene; cauline leaves mostly opposite and pinnately lobed; stems glabrous or glabrate . . . . *Dyssodia**
1 Involucral bracts not highly modified, free and not infolding outer achenes; annuals and perennials, not strongly scented 3
    3 Involucre distinctly double, the outer larger (or minute, less than 2 mm long), foliaceous, somewhat spreading, the inner broader and appressed, nearly membranous. 4
       4 Pappus absent or of a few teeth . . . . *Coreopsis*
       4 Pappus of 2 to 4 barbed awns. 5
          5 Achenes beakless, flattened or slender and 4-sided (rarely subterete) . . . . *Bidens*
          5 Achenes long-beaked, slenderly fusiform, 5-angled and subterete . . . . *Cosmos**
    3 Involucre not double, involucral bracts all about equal in length, the inner and outer similar in texture 6
       6 Rays white or absent, if present, 1-10 mm long; disk small, 3-10 mm wide. 7
          7 Leaves alternate; heads whitish; leaves large, rough. . . . . *Parthenium*
          7 Leaves opposite 8
             8 Lower leaves deeply lobed, with connate-perfoliate expanded blade tissue at the nodes. . *Polymnia*
             8 Leaves not lobed, toothed, without such a foliaceous expansion at the nodes 9
                9 Leaves, except the uppermost, petioled, blades less than 3 times longer than wide . . *Galinsoga*
                9 Leaves tapered to the base, not distinctly petioled, the blades more than 3 times longer than wide; near Mississippi River, rare in Minn . . . . *Eclipta*
       6 Rays yellow, orange or purple, generally 1-6 cm long; disk generally large, 1-4 cm wide 10
          10 Rays purple, the receptacular bracts spiny-pointed . . . . *Echinacea*
          10 Rays yellow or orange. 11
             11 Disk florets staminate; ray florets pistillate, their large achenes broadly ovate, winged, strongly flattened parallel with the adjoining involucral bracts; plants large, usually resinous . . . . . *Silphium*
             11 Disk florets bisexual; ray florets neuter or pistillate; achenes wingless, sub-terete or angled 12
                12 At least some of the leaves opposite or all basal 13
                    13 Outer involucral bracts shorter than the inner; ray florets neuter, their rays thin and easily wilting, deciduous . . . . *Helianthus*
                    13 Outer involucral bracts longer than the inner; ray florets pistillate, their rays marcescent (thickish and persistent after flowering) . . . . *Heliopsis*
                12 Leaves all alternate 14
                    14 Disk flat or convex; leaves neither lobed nor divided . . . . *Helianthus*
                    14 Disk conical, hemispheric or columnar; leaves simple in *Rudbeckia hirta*, otherwise lobed, cleft, laciniate or pinnately parted 15
                        15 Leaves simple, 3-lobed, 3-cleft, or laciniate; rays not subtended by receptacular bracts; achenes 4-sided . . . . *Rudbeckia*
                        15 Leaves pinnately divided; rays subtended by receptacular bracts; achenes laterally flattened
Ratibida

TRIBE 8A. HELIANTHEAE (AMBROSIINAE, RAGWEED SUBTRIBE)

GENERA: *Ambrosia, Arnica, Iva, Xanthium*

1 Staminate and pistillate florets in the same head; ray florets pistillate, disk florets staminate . . . . *Iva*
1 Staminate and pistillate florets borne in separate heads 2

  2 Pistillate heads 2-flowered and with many, sharply-hooked spines; staminate heads lacking involucral bracts
  . . . . *Xanthium*
  2 Pistillate heads 1 (-2) -flowered with a few vestigial spines or none; staminate heads with involucres of connate
  involucral bracts. . . . . *Ambrosia*

TRIBE 9. INULEAE (ELECAMPANE TRIBE)

ONE GENUS: *Inula*

TRIBE 10. SENECIONEAE (GROUNDSEL TRIBE)

GENERA: *Arnoglossum, Erechtites, Hasteola, Packera, Petasites, Senecio, Tephroseris*

1 Perennials with green leaves arising individually from the ground from an underground rhizome; stems consisting
  of scaly bracted flowering scapes arising as the leaves develop in early spring . . . . *Petasites*
1 Habit various but with well developed stem leaves (though these may differ from the basal leaves) 2
  2 Corollas yellow to orange; heads usually with rays 3
    3 Cauline leaves progressively reduced upward and lobed (unlike the basal leaves); perennials, usually with
      obvious vegetative reproduction . . . . *Packera*
    3 Leaves more or less equal in size up the stem; annuals (perhaps rarely biennials) 4
      4 Rays conspicuous; leaves entire to weakly toothed; pubescence often copious . . . . *Tephroseris*
      4 Rays inconspicuous or absent; leaves, or some of them, lobed to pinnatifid; pubescence short and often
        sparse; introduced weeds . . . . *Senecio*
  2 Corollas whitish or creamy; heads without rays 5
    5 Annuals; heads disciform, with 2 to several marginal rows of pistillate florets with filiform corollas; leaves
      roughly the same size up the stem . . . . *Erechtites*
    5 Perennials; heads discoid, containing only bisexual florets with 5-lobed corollas 6
      6 Heads with ca. 13 involucral bracts and 20-40 florets; receptacle flat; larger leaves hastate; leaves roughly
        the same size up the stem . . . . *Hasteola*
      6 Heads with ca. 5 involucral bracts and ca. 5 florets; receptacle with a short conic projection in the center;
        leaves not hastate; leaves largest at base of the stem and becoming smaller upwards . . . . . . *Arnoglossum*

TRIBE 11. VERNONIEAE (IRONWEED TRIBE)

ONE GENUS: *Vernonia*

ACHILLEA *Yarrow*

Perennial herbs. Leaves alternate, subentire to pinnately dissected. Inflorescence more or less
corymbiform, of several to many relatively small heads. Heads radiate or rarely discoid, the rays
mostly 5-12, pistillate and fertile, rarely neutral, white, sometimes pink or rarely yellow. Involucral
bracts imbricate in 3-4 series, dry, with scarious or hyaline margins and often greenish midrib.
Receptacle conic or convex, chaffy throughout. Disk flowers about 10-75, perfect and fertile. Fruit a
compressed achene; pappus none.

ADDITIONAL SPECIES
• *Achillea alpina* L. (Siberian yarrow), southern range limit; Marshall and Roseau cos (✿*threatened)*; see key.
• *Achillea nobilis* L. (Noble yarrow); native to Europe; Sherburne and Stearns counties; likely introduced in
wildlife plantings.

1 Leaves finely dissected; ubiquitous . . . . *A. millefolium*
1 Leaves nearly entire to incised, not dissected 2
  2 Rays 3-5 mm long; leaves nearly entire or shallowly serrate; introduced in ne Minn . . . . *A. ptarmica*
  2 Rays 1-2 mm long; leaves incised; rare boreal species in nw Minn . . . . *A. alpina**

Achillea millefolium L.

COMMON YARROW
MAP 196
native

Aromatic rhizomatous perennial, sparsely to rather densely villous throughout.
Stems about 2-10 dm tall. **Leaves** pinnately dissected, the blade about 3-15 cm
long and to 2.5 cm wide, the basal petiolate, all but the lowermost stem leaves
sessile. **Heads** numerous in a flat or round-topped, short and broad, paniculate-
corymbiform inflorescence, the disk about 2-4 mm wide; involucre in ours
mostly 4-5 mm high; rays about 5, white or occasionally pink, 2-3 mm long; disk
flowers about 10-30. June-Oct. Common in fields, prairies, lawns, beaches, and
waste places.

Achillea millefolium

Achillea ptarmica L.

MAP 197

SNEEZEWEED   *introduced*

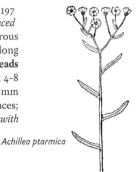

Rhizomatous perennial. **Stems** 3-6 dm tall, villous above, often nearly glabrous below. **Leaves** glabrous or nearly so, linear or lance-linear, about 3-10 cm long and 2-6 mm wide, sessile, closely and rather shallowly serrate to subentire. **Heads** several or numerous in an open corymbiform inflorescence, the disk about 4-8 mm wide; involucre about 4-5 mm high; rays commonly 8-10, white, 3-5 mm long; disk flowers about 50-75. July-Sept.—Beaches, roadsides, and waste places; native to n Europe and Asia. *Forms escaped from cultivation are often "double," with more than the usual number of ray flowers.*

Achillea ptarmica

AGERATINA *Snakeroot*

Ageratina altissima (L.) R. M. King & H. Rob.

MAP 198

WHITE SNAKEROOT   *native*

   Eupatorium rugosum Houtt.

Perennial herb. **Stems** 3-15 dm tall, glabrous or pubescent with short spreading hairs. **Leaves** opposite, ovate to broadly ovate, contracted to subcordate at base, 6-15 cm long and 3-12 cm wide, smaller upward; petiolate; margins serrate. Inflorescence flat-topped or flat dome-shaped; involucre 3-5 mm long, involucral bracts acuminate to obtuse, all about the same length; florets 12-24, corolla white. Aug-Oct.—Floodplain forests, cedar swamps, thickets, streambanks, wooded ravines, sometimes where disturbed. *A toxic substance in this plant can cause "trembles," a fatal disease of cattle which have browsed on it and transmittable to humans by their milk; the consequent "milk sickness" caused many deaths in the 19th century.*

Ageratina altissima

AGOSERIS *False Dandelion*

Agoseris glauca (Pursh) Raf.

MAP 199

PALE AGOSERIS   *native*

Taprooted, scapose perennial, mostly less than 5 dm tall, glabrous or nearly so, often glaucous. **Leaves** all basal, narrowly lance-shaped, 5-30 cm long and to 3 cm wide; marginsentire or irregularly toothed or shallowly lobed, flat and not undulate or crisped. **Heads** single at ends of long scapes; involucral bracts nearly equal or imbricate in several poorly defined series, mostly acute, sometimes purplish or spotted with purple; **flowers** all ligulate and fertile; **corolla** yellow. **Achenes** 10-nerved, the body tapering to a striate beak up to 1/2 the length of the body; pappus of numerous capillary bristles. May-June.—Moist prairies.

Agoseris glauca

AMBROSIA *Ragweed*

Coarse annual or perennial herbs. Leaves opposite or alternate, mostly lobed or dissected. Heads unisexual, small. Staminate heads in a spike-like or raceme-like bractless inflorescence; involucre 5-12-lobed; receptacle flat, its bracts slender. Pistillate heads borne below the staminate ones, in the axils of leaves or bracts; involucre closed, nut-like, usually with a single series of tubercles or short erect spines near the apex; pistil solitary, without corolla; pappus absent. *The pollen is wind-borne, and some species are among the most important causes of hay-fever in the USA.*

ADDITIONAL SPECIES

Ambrosia acanthicarpa Hook. (Flat-spine burr ragweed); native to w USA, Hennepin County.

195. Asarum canadense   *196. Achillea millefolium*   *197. Achillea ptarmica*   *198. Ageratina altissima*

1 Leaves palmately 3-5 lobed or unlobed; large annual plant to 2 m or more tall . . . . **A. trifida**

1 Leaves 1-2 times pinnately lobed or divided; plants usually less than 1 m tall 2

   2 Plants perennial, forming colonies from creeping underground roots; leaves usually coarsely lobed . . . .
     . . . . **A. psilostachya**

   2 Plants taprooted annuals; leaves finely divided . . . . **A. artemisiifolia**

Ambrosia artemisiifolia L.

COMMON RAGWEED
MAP 200
native

Annual weed. **Stems** branching at least above, variously hairy or subglabrous, mostly 3-10 dm tall. **Leaves** opposite below, alternate above, petiolate, 1-2x pinnatifid, ovate or elliptic in outline, commonly 4-10 cm long. Sterile heads short-pedunculate. Fruiting involucre short-beaked, about 3-5 mm long, with several short sharp spines. Aug-Oct.—Waste places.

Ambrosia psilostachya DC.

PERENNIAL RAGWEED
MAP 201
native

Similar to *A. artemisiifolia*. Perennial from a creeping rhizome. **Leaves** thicker, short-petiolate or subsessile, usually only once pinnatifid, averaging narrower in outline, sometimes 10 cm long. Fruiting involucre tuberculate above, sometimes obscurely so. July-Oct.—Waste places, usually in dry or sandy soil.

Ambrosia trifida L.

GIANT RAGWEED
MAP 202
native (invasive)

Annual weed, of various heights to sometimes 5 m tall. **Stems** spreading-hirsute or hispid above, often glabrous or glabrate below. **Leaves** opposite, petiolate, broadly elliptic to more commonly ovate or suhorbicular, serrate, palmately 3-5-lobed, or, especially in depauperate specimens, lobeless, often 2 dm long or more, more or less scabrous on both sides. Sterile involucres unilaterally 3-nerved. Fertile involucres about 5-10 mm long in fruit, several-ribbed, each rib bearing a short spine at the tip. July-Oct.—Moist soil and waste places.

Ambrosia trifida

ANAPHALIS *Pearly-Everlasting*

Anaphalis margaritacea (L.) Benth.

PEARLY-EVERLASTING
MAP 203
native

White-woolly perennial herbs. **Stems** erect, simple or branched, commonly 3-9 dm tall, leafy, loosely white-woolly. **Leaves** alternate, lance-shaped or linear, to about 12 cm long and 1.5 cm wide, sessile, commonly less pubescent above than beneath, or green and glabrous above, the margins entire and often revolute, basal leaves soon deciduous. **Heads** 1 cm wide or less, numerous and crowded in a short broad inflorescence; some flowers bearing both stamens and pistils. Involucre about 5-7 mm high, the bracts pearly white. **Achenes** papillate; pappus, in both staminate and pistillate flowers, of distinct capillary bristles. Variable. July-Aug.—Chiefly in dry woods and clearings.

Anaphalis margaritacea

ANTENNARIA *Pussytoes*

Perennial woolly herbs. Leaves basal and alternate on the stem. Flowers dioecious, rarely incompletely so. Heads many-flowered, disciform or discoid, solitary to many in a crowded inflorescence. Involucral bracts imbricate in several series, scarious at least at the tip, often colored. Receptacle naked, flat or convex. Staminate flowers with scanty pappus, the bristles commonly barbellate or

199. Agoseris glauca

200. Ambrosia artemisiifolia

201. Ambrosia psilostachya

202. Ambrosia trifida

clavate. Pistillate flowers with filiform-tubular corolla, bifid style, and copious bristles slightly united at the base. Achenes terete or slightly compressed. Most of our species are partly or wholly apomictic, producing seeds without fertilization.

1 Underside of basal leaves with 3-5 prominent longitudinal veins; widest leaves mostly 1.7-4 cm wide. 2
    2 Basal leaves glabrous or tomentose on upper surface, underside green-glabrous; pistillate involucres 8-13 mm long; staminate corollas 3.5-5 mm long; pistillate corollas 4-7 mm; widespread in Minn . . . . **A. parlinii**
    2 Underside of basal leaves tomentose; pistillate involucres 5-7 mm long; staminate corollas 2-3.5 mmlong; pistillate corollas 3-4 mm; se Minn . . . . **A. plantaginifolia**
1 Blades of all leaves with only 1 prominent longitudinal vein; widest leaves to 1.7 cm wide. 3
    3 Tips of phyllaries rose-pink; n Minn . . . . **A. rosea**
    3 Tips of phyllaries white; widespread 4
        4 Basal leaves not over 6 mm wide, ± equally and densely pubescent on both surfaces; involucre of pistillate heads ca. 8-10 mm long. . . . . **A. parvifolia**
        4 Basal leaves at least 6 mm wide, or less pubescent (even glabrous) above, or usually both conditions present; involucre of pistillate heads ca. 5.5-8 (rarely 10) mm long 5
            5 Middle and upper stem leaves merely acute or with firm subulate tip (bracts in inflorescence may have an appendage) . . . . **A. howellii**
            5 Middle and upper stem leaves with a flat (often ± curled or involute) scarious appendage at the tip. . . 6
                6 New basal leaves of the season essentially glabrous above or very soon becoming so (may appear hairy along the margin from tomentum of underside) . . . . **A. howellii**
                6 New basal leaves pubescent above when young (becoming glabrous only in age) . . . . . . **A. neglecta**

Antennaria howellii Greene
SMALL PUSSYTOES
MAP 204
native

Antennaria neglecta var. *howellii* (Greene) Cronquist

Plants mostly with pistillate flowers only, staminate plants rare; spreading by short stolons. **Stems** to 35 cm tall, sometimes with gland-tipped hairs. **Basal leaves** oblanceolate to ovate, 2-5 cm long, tips mucronate, upper surface tomentose, underside green-glabrous or gray-pubescent. **Stem leaves** linear, 1-4 cm long. **Heads** 3-15 in corymbiform clusters. Involucral bracts white, cream, or light brown, sometimes rose at base.—Many types of dry, open places, including rock ledges and outcrops, openings in sandy or rocky woods; sometimes on moist shores, roadsides, and in fields and lawns.

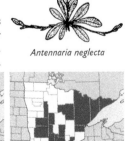

Antennaria howellii

Antennaria neglecta Greene
FIELD PUSSYTOES
MAP 205
native

Antennaria neodioica Greene

Plants 1-4 dm tall, with short and leafy or longer and merely bracteate stolons. Basal **leaves** and those at the ends of the stolons densely and persistently tomentose beneath, only sparsely so (and eventually glabrate) above, or the upper side glabrous from the first, relatively small, mostly under 1.5 cm wide, 1-nerved or obscurely 3-nerved. Pistillate involucres 7-10 mm long; variously sexual or apomictic. April-June.—Dry woods and open places.

Antennaria parlinii Fernald
PARLIN'S PUSSYTOES
MAP 206
native

Antennaria plantaginifolia var. *parlinii* Cronquist

Similar to *A. plantaginifolia* and sometimes included in it. See key for distinctions between the 2 taxa. **Stems** usually with purple glandular hairs (especially near tops of young flowering stems).—Dry open places, including rock outcrops, banks, grassy roadsides, hillsides, and open woods; sometimes in shaded forests.

Antennaria neglecta

203. *Anaphalis margaritacea*   204. *Antennaria howellii*   205. *Antennaria neglecta*   206. *Antennaria parlinii*

Antennaria parvifolia Nutt.
SMALL-LEAVED PUSSYTOES

MAP 207
native

Tomentose perennial, mat-forming and stoloniferous. **Flowering stems** erect, to 15 cm tall. **Basal leaves** and those at end of stolons about equally hairy above and below, becoming glabrate only in age; blades spatulate, 1-3.5 cm long and to 1 cm wide; stolons short, decumbent, leafy. **Heads** closely to somewhat loosely aggregated in a cyme; pistillate involucres 7-11 mm long, outer involucral bracts obtuse or rounded, the inner becoming lanceolate, the conspicuous scarious portion bright white (rarely dull white or pinkish). **Achenes** 1-1.3 mm long, minutely papillate, olive to yellowish-brown. May-July.—Prairies, open woods, pastures, roadsides. *Similar to **Antennaria rosea**, but A. parvifolia usually with larger leaves and heads and shorter flowering stems.*

Antennaria plantaginifolia (L.) Richards.
PLANTAIN-PUSSYTOES

MAP 208
native

Stoloniferous perennial, the stolons sparsely leafy or sometimes merely bracteate. **Stems** about 10-40 cm tall. **Basal leaves** and those at the ends of the stolons sooner or later glabrate above, relatively large, 3-5-nerved, evidently petiolate, the blade ovate to elliptic or obovate, mucronate, the larger ones 2-6 cm long and 1.5-5 cm wide; **stem leaves** reduced, mostly linear or lance-shaped. **Heads** several in a small cyme; some purplish glandular hairs often present in the inflorescence. Pistillate involucre 5-10 mm high, the bracts white-tipped, often pinkish toward the base; staminate involucres generally a little smaller than the pistillate, with broader and more conspicuous white bract-tips. Styles often crimson. Spring-early summer. —Dry, open, woodlands, banks, bluff tops. *Similar to **Antennaria parlinii** except for smaller heads, underside of basal leaves gray-pubescent, and restricted range in se Minn.*

Antennaria plantaginifolia

Antennaria rosea Greene
ROSY PUSSYTOES
Antennaria microphylla Rydb.

MAP 209
native

Tomentose perennial, mat-forming from short stolons. **Flowering stems** erect, to 30 cm tall, with narrowly lanceolate leaves. **Basal leaves** and those at tips of stolons spatulate, mostly 8-25 mm long and 2-7 mm wide, the upper surfaces nearly as densely hairy as the lower, glabrate in extreme age; base of leaves often somewhat petiolate. **Heads** several in a compact or rather loose cyme, pistillate involucres usually 4-7 mm long; involucral bracts obtuse or acute at tip, the upper scarious portion bright to dull white or deep pink, sometimes with pink striations. **Achenes** about 1 mm long, olive to brownish, sometimes lustrous, smooth or rarely minutely papillate. May-July.—Prairies, open woodlands, bluffs, roadsides.

ANTHEMIS *Chamomile*

Annual or perennial, usually aromatic herbs. Leaves alternate, dissected. Flowers in campanulate or nearly hemispheric heads terminating the branches. Heads radiate or rarely discoid, the rays elongate, white or yellow, pistillate or neutral; involucral bracts subequal or more commonly imbricate in several series, the margins more or less scarious or hyaline; receptacle convex to conic or hemispheric, chaffy at least toward the middle. Disk flowers numerous, perfect, yellow. Fruit a terete, angled, or somewhat compressed achene; pappus a short crown, or more commonly none. *Anthemis* and *Matricaria* are very similar, separated on the receptacle chaffy in *Anthemis* and naked in *Matricaria*.

207. *Antennaria parvifolia*   208. *Antennaria plantaginifolia*   209. *Antennaria rosea*   210. *Anthemis arvensis*

1　Ray flowers yellow . . . . *A. tinctoria*
1　Ray flowers white 2
　　2　Ray flowers pistillate and fertile; receptacle chaffy throughout . . . . *A. arvensis*
　　2　Ray flowers usually neutral, sterile; receptacle chaffy only near middle . . . . *A. cotula*

Anthemis arvensis L.
CORN CHAMOMILE

MAP 210
introduced

More or less branching annual, 1-5 dm tall, often with several stems from the base, more or less finely hairy. **Leaves** about 2-5 cm long, bipinnatifid, with narrowly winged rachis. **Heads** several or numerous, pedunculate at the ends of the branches; involucre thinly villous or villous-tomentose; disk about 6-12 mm wide, becoming ovoid in age; rays about 15-20, pistillate, white, about 6-13 mm long; receptacle chaffy throughout, its bracts thin, the pale cuspidate awn-tips equaling or shorter than the disk-flowers. **Achenes** quadrangular, about 10-nerved. Pappus a minute border, or obsolete. May-Aug.—Native of Europe; fields and waste places.

Anthemis cotula L.
STINKING CHAMOMILE; DOGFENNEL

MAP 211
introduced

More or less branched, usually subglabrous, ill-smelling annual, 1-6 dm tall. **Leaves** about 2-6 cm long, 2 or 3x pinnatifid, with very narrow segments. **Heads** more or less numerous, short-pedunculate at the ends of the branches, the disk about 5-10 mm wide, becoming ovoid or short-cylindric at maturity; involucre sparsely villous; rays about 10-20, white, neutral, 5-11 mm long; receptacle chaffy only toward the middle, its bracts narrow, tapering to the apex, scarcely awned. **Achenes** subterete, about 10-ribbed, glandular-tuberculate. Pappus none. May-Oct.—Native of Europe; fields and waste places.

Anthemis cotula

Anthemis tinctoria L.
GOLDEN CHAMOMILE
　　Cota tinctoria (L.) J. Gay ex Guss.

MAP 212
introduced

Short-lived perennial. **Stems** 3-7 dm tall, sparingly branched above or simple, finely hairy at least above. **Leaves** pinnatifid, about 2-5 cm long, with winged rachis and deeply toothed or pinnatifid segments, villous or almost floccose beneath. **Heads** solitary and long-pedunculate at the ends of the branches, the disk about 12-18 mm wide; involucre thinly tomentose; rays about 20-30, pistillate, yellow, about 7-15 mm long receptacle chaffy throughout, its bracts narrow, with firm yellow awn-tips equaling the disk-flowers. **Achenes** compressed-quadrangular, more or less striate-nerved. Pappus a very short crown. June-July.—Native of Europe; fields and waste places.

Anthemis tinctoria

ARCTIUM　*Burdock*

Coarse biennial herbs. Leaves large, alternate, heart-shaped, entire or toothed. Flowers all tubular and perfect, the corolla pink or purplish, with long slender lobes; involucre subglobose, its bracts multiseriate, narrow, appressed at the base, with a spreading, subulate, inwardly hooked tip. Receptacle flat, densely bristly. Achenes oblong, slightly compressed, few-angled, many-nerved, truncate at the apex, glabrous. Pappus of numerous short, separately deciduous bristles. *Any of the introduced species will hybridize with any of the others.*

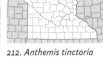

211. Anthemis cotula　　　*212. Anthemis tinctoria*　　　*213. Arctium lappa*

1 Heads 1-1.5 cm long, sessile or on short peduncles; common weed .... ***A. minus***
1 Heads 1.5-2.5 cm long; on long peduncles; uncommmon 2
2 Heads about 1.5 cm long; bracts densely cottony-hairy .... ***A. tomentosum***
2 Heads about 2.5 cm long; bracts glabrous .... ***A. lappa***

Arctium lappa L. MAP 213
GREATER BURDOCK *introduced*
Commonly to 1.5 m or sometimes even 3 m tall. **Leaves** petiolate, the petioles mostly solid, progressively shorter upwards, the blade ovate or broader, cordate, to 5 dm long and 3 dm wide, thinly tomentose beneath, nearly glabrous above. **Inflorescence** corymbiform, with long, glandular or glandular-hairy peduncles; heads large, the involucre commonly greenish-stramineous, 2.5-4 cm wide, generally equaling or surpassing the flowers, glabrous or slightly glandular, and often with a few long cobwebby hairs. Aug-Oct.—Native of Eurasia, sparingly established as a weed along along roadsides and in waste places.

Arctium lappa

Arctium minus Bernh. MAP 214
LESSER BURDOCK *introduced (invasive)*
Biennial, to 1.5 m tall or rarely taller. **Leaves** petiolate, the lower petioles mostly hollow; blade narrowly to very broadly ovate, to about 5 dm long and 4 dm wide, thinly tomentose and often eventually glabrate beneath, nearly glabrous above. Branches of the **inflorescence** ascending to widely spreading, raceme-like, the heads mostly short-pedunculate or subsessile, 1.5-3 cm thick, glabrous or slightly glandular to sometimes tomentose, usually a little shorter than the flowers, stramineous or purplish, the inner bracts often more flattened than the others and scarcely hooked.—Roadsides, railroads, fields, fencerows, farmyards, around old buildings, disturbed places.

Arctium tomentosum P. Mill. MAP 215
WOOLLY BURDOCK *introduced*
Similar to *A. lappa*, but smaller, seldom over 1.3 m tall; lower petioles mostly hollow; involucre mostly 2-3 cm thick, more or less strongly arachnoid-tomentose, and only weakly or scarcely hooked at the tip. June-Oct.—Native of Eurasia, sparingly established on roadsides and in waste places.

Arctium minus

ARNICA *Arnica*

Arnica lonchophylla Greene MAP 216
LONG-LEAVED ARNICA *threatened | native*
Perennial herb to 4 dm tall, stipitate-glandular and also covered with spreading hairs. **Stems** erect to somewhat lax, single or loosely clustered from a scaly, branching rhizome. **Lowermost leaves** narrowly elliptic to ovate, prominently several-veined, petiolate, 5-15 cm long and 1-3 cm wide; **upper leaves** strongly reduced, sessile. **Heads** 1-7, erect, campanulate; involucral bracts 1-2 cm long; ray florets ca. 8(6-10), ligule yellow-orange, 1-2 cm long; disk corollas 6-9 mm long, the lower part slender and tubular, 3-4 mm long. **Achenes** 4.5-6 mm long, pubescent; pappus of many white capillary bristles. June-July.—Rock cliffs of slate, diabase or basalt bedrock, on mossy ledges or in crevices, and where cool and shaded. *Arnica formerly in tribe Senecioneae, then placed (tentatively) in tribe Heliantheae; tribal assignment remains unresolved.*

Arnica lonchophylla

ARNOGLOSSUM *Indian Plantain*

Large perennial herbs with basal or alternate leaves. Flower heads with white disk flowers only, the ray flowers absent. Fruit an achene, tipped by a pappus of numerous, slender bristles.

1 Main leaves clearly longer than wide, margins nearly entire to toothed (sometimes double-toothed) .... ***A. plantagineum***
1 Main leaves broadly ovate to kidney-shaped, about as wide as long, margins coarsely toothed or undulate .... ***A. reniforme***

Arnoglossum plantagineum Raf.
GROOVE-STEM INDIAN-PLANTAIN
MAP 217
threatened | *native*
Cacalia plantaginea (Raf.) Shinners
Cacalia tuberosa Nutt.

Glabrous perennial herb with a short tuberous-thickened base and fleshy-fibrous roots. **Stems** stout, erect, 6-18 dm tall, striate-angled. **Leaves** thick and firm, entire or slightly toothed, with several prominent longitudinal nerves converging toward the summit; **basal and lowermost stem leaves** conspicuously long-petioled, the blade 6-20 cm long and 2-10 cm wide, commonly elliptic and tapering to the base, sometimes ovate and subtruncate at the base in robust plants; **stem leaves** few, conspicuously reduced upwards, becoming sessile or subsessile. June-July.—Moist to sometimes dry prairies; prairie remnants along railroads.

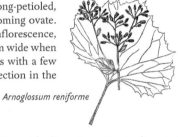
Arnoglossum plantagineum

Arnoglossum reniforme (Hook.) H.Rob.
GREAT INDIAN-PLANTAIN
MAP 218
threatened | *native*
Arnoglossum muhlenbergii (Schultz-Bip.) H.E. Robins.
Cacalia muhlenbergii (Schultz-Bip.) Fern.

Perennial herb with fibrous roots. **Stems** stout, usually 1-3 m tall, glabrous, conspicuously grooved. **Leaves** glabrous or nearly so, green on both sides, irregularly dentate and sometimes shallowly lobed, ciliolate in the sinuses, palmately veined, the lower ones kidney-shaped, very large and long-petioled, sometimes as much as 8 dm wide; **upper leaves** reduced and becoming ovate. **Heads** numerous in a short and broad, more or less flat-topped inflorescence, ordinarily 5-flowered, narrowly cylindric, the disk becoming 3-7 mm wide when pressed; involucre 7-12 mm high, the principal bracts 5, sometimes with a few minute outer ones at the base. Receptacle with a short conic projection in the center. June-Sept.—Moist woods and clearings.

Arnoglossum reniforme

ARTEMISIA *Wormwood; Sage*

Annual, biennial, or perennial herbs, or shrubs, usually aromatic, with alternate, entire to dissected leaves and few to numerous small, ovoid to campanulate or hemispheric heads in a spiciform, raceme-like, or panicle-like inflorescence. Heads discoid, sometimes with only perfect flowers, sometimes the outer pistillate, the central ones then sometimes sterile. Involucral bracts dry, imbricate, at least the inner scarious or with scarious margins. Receptacle flat to convex or hemispheric, naked or densely beset with long hairs. Achenes ellipsoid or obovoid to nearly prismatic, scarcely compressed, usually glabrous. Pappus none.

ADDITIONAL SPECIES
Artemisia abrotanum L. (Southern wormwood), introduced; reported from Cass, Kittson, and St. Louis cos.

1 Plants perennial and somewhat woody at base; leaves covered with silky hairs; receptacle hairy 2
  2 Leaves to 2 cm long, the segments thread-like, to 1 mm wide; flowering stems ascending, to 5 dm tall . . . . .
  . . . . ***A. frigida***
  2 Leaves 5-15 cm long, the segments 2-3 mm wide; flowering stems erect, to 9 dm tall . . . . ***A. absinthium***
1 Plants annual, biennial, or perennial; leaves hairy to glabrous; receptacle naked. 3
  3 Disk flowers sterile; mature plants usually glabrous 4
    4 First-year lower leaves in a basal rosette; leaves usually densely hairy; common in sandy habitats . . . . . .
    . . . . ***A. campestris***
    4 Lower leaves not in a rosette; leaves glabrous; uncommon . . . . ***A. dracunculus***

214. *Arctium minus*

215. *Arctium tomentosum*

216. *Arnica lonchophylla*

217. *Arnoglossum plantagineum*

3 Disk flowers fertile 5
5 Leaves glabrous or nearly so, pinnately divided or dissected . . . . . ***A. biennis***
5 Leaves densely hairy at least on one surface, simple or dissected 6
6 Leaves linear lance-shaped, unlobed, margins regularly toothed to entire, densely white hairy on underside . . . . . ***A. serrata***
6 Leaves deeply lobed or cut, or entire with irregular teeth on margin 7
7 Leaves finely divided into thread-like segments; uncommon garden escape . . . . . ***A. pontica***
7 Leaves entire or the leaf segments broader 8
8 Leaves green and nearly glabrous above, white hairy below; uncommon weed . . . . . ***A. vulgaris***
8 Leaves hairy on upper and lower sides 9
9 Leaves entire or irregularly toothed; common . . . . . ***A. ludoviciana***
9 Leaves obtusely lobed; uncommon garden escape near Lake Superior . . . . . ***A. stelleriana***

Artemisia absinthium L. MAP 219
COMMON WORMWOOD *introduced*

Fragrant perennial herb or shrub. **Stems** 4-10 dm tall, finely sericeous or eventually glabrate. **Leaves** silvery-sericeous on both sides, or eventually nearly glabrous above, the lower long-petiolate and 2-3 times pinnatifid, with mostly oblong segments about 1.5-4 mm wide, the blade rounded-ovate in outline, about 3-8 cm long; upper leaves progressively less divided and shorter-petiolate, the divisions often more acute. **Inflorescence** ample, leafy; involucre about 2-3 mm high, finely and densely sericeous; flowers all fertile, the marginal pistillate; receptacle beset with numerous long white hairs between the flowers. **Achenes** glabrous, nearly cylindric, but narrowed to the base and rounded at the summit. July-Sept.—Native of Europe; fields and waste places.

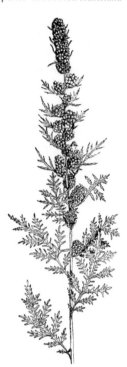

Artemisia biennis

Artemisia biennis Willd. MAP 220
BIENNIAL WORMWOOD *introduced*

Taprooted, annual or biennial herb. **Stems** erect, to 1 m or more long, often branched, smooth, only faintly scented. **Leaves** alternate, pinnately dissected nearly to middle, 5-12 cm long and 2-5 cm wide, the segments linear and toothed. **Flowers** in stalkless heads from upper leaf axils; the heads composed of many small green disk flowers, grouped into spike-like inflorescences, with leafy bracts much longer than the clusters of heads; pappus none. **Fruit** a small oblong achene. Aug-Sept. Sandy lakeshores, streambanks, ditches, mud flats, disturbed areas; often where seasonally flooded.—Native to nw USA, weedy throughout Minn.

Artemisia campestris L. MAP 221
FIELD SAGEWORT *native*

Scarcely odorous perennial with a taproot and generally several glabrous to villous **stems** 1-10 dm tall from a branching caudex. **Basal leaves** crowded, about 2-10 cm long including the petiole, 0.7-4 cm wide, 2x or 3x pinnatifid or 3-parted, with mostly linear-filiform divisions seldom more than 2 mm wide, glabrous to sericeous, persistent, or, especially in the larger forms, sometimes deciduous; **cauline leaves** similar but smaller and less divided, the uppermost often 3-parted or simple. **Inflorescence** small and spike-like to diffuse and panicle-like; involucre glabrous to densely villous-tomentose, 2-4.5 mm high; outer flowers pistillate and fertile; disk-flowers sterile, with abortive ovary; receptacle glabrous. **Achenes** subcylindric, glabrous, those of the disk flowers abortive. July-Sept.—Open places, often in sandy soil.

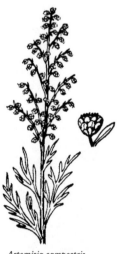

Artemisia campestris

Artemisia dracunculus L. MAP 222
DRAGON WORMWOOD *native*

Nearly odorless to strongly odorous perennial herb from a stout rhizome. **Stems** 5-15 dm tall, glabrous or occasionally puberulent. **Leaves** narrowly linear, 3-8 cm long and 1-6 mm wide, mostly entire, but sometimes 1-3-cleft, the lower generally deciduous by flowering time. **Inflorescence** panicle-like, usually open and ample; involucre glabrous or nearly so, 2-3 mm high; receptacle naked; outer flowers pistillate and fertile, with short tubular corolla; disk flowers sterile. **Achenes** glabrous, ellipsoid, those of the disk flowers abortive. July-Sept.—Dry open places.

Artemisia frigida Willd.
MAP 223
PRAIRIE SAGEWORT   *native*
Fragrant mat-forming perennial with a stout caudex or woody crown, often shrubby at the base. **Stems** 1-4 dm tall, white- or tawny-tomentose. **Leaves** small and numerous, clustered at the base and well distributed along the stem, tomentose throughout, short-petiolate, or the cauline subsessile, the blade about 5-12 mm long, 2-3x divided into linear or filiform divisions about 1 mm wide, commonly with a pair of stipule-like divisions at the base. **Inflorescence** panicle-like, or raceme-like in depauperate plants; involucre 2-3 mm high, loosely tomentose; flowers all fertile, the marginal ones pistillate; receptacle beset with numerous long hairs between the flowers. **Achenes** glabrous, narrowed to the base, truncate at the summit, obscurely if at all nerved. July-Sept.—Prairies and dry open places.

Artemisia frigida

Artemisia ludoviciana Nutt.
MAP 224
WHITE SAGE   *native*
Aromatic rhizomatous perennial. **Stems** about 3-10 dm tall, simple to the inflorescence, more or less white-tomentose, at least above. **Leaves** narrowly to broadly lance-shaped, 3-11 cm long and 4-15 mm wide, entire or irregularly toothed, or sometimes deeply lobed, but the lobes generally at least 2 mm wide or more, densely and persistently white-tomentose beneath and often also above, or more thinly hairy and soon glabrate above. **Inflorescence** ample or narrow; involucre tomentose, 2.5-4 mm high; flowers all fertile, the outer pistillate; disk corollas 2-3 mm long; receptacle glabrous. **Achenes** ellipsoid, not nerved or angled, essentially glabrous. July-Oct.—Prairies, dry ground, and waste places.

Artemisia pontica L.
(NO MAP)
ROMAN WORMWOOD   *introduced*
Perennial with a creeping rhizome. **Stems** 4-10 dm tall, fragrant, simple or nearly so, the twigs puberulent or eventually glabrate. **Leaves** 1-3 cm long, white-tomentose on both sides, more thinly so and sometimes eventually glabrate above, twice or thrice pinnatifid, with short divergent segments scarcely 1 mm wide, ordinarily with a pair of stipule-like lobes or auricles at the base. **Inflorescence** relatively narrow, elongate; involucre 2-3 mm high, tomentulose; receptacle glabrous; flowers all fertile, the outer pistillate. Achenes glabrous, 4-5-angled, broadest at or near the truncate summit. Aug-Sept.—Native of Europe; dry open places, Isanti County.

Artemisia ludoviciana

Artemisia serrata Nutt.
MAP 225
TOOTHED SAGE   *native*
Aromatic perennial herb from a stout rhizome. **Stems** 1-3 m tall, strict, glabrous or nearly so below the inflorescence. **Leaves** numerous, lance-shaped or lance-linear, acuminate, sharply and regularly serrate, 8-15 cm long and 8-25 mm wide, green and essentially glabrous above, densely white-tomentose beneath, sometimes with a pair of small stipule-like lobes at the base. **Inflorescence** ample, generally leafy; involucre 2.5-3.5 mm high, thinly tomentose; receptacle glabrous; flowers all fertile, the outer pistillate; disk corollas about 2 mm long. **Achenes** ellipsoid, not nerved or angled, essentially glabrous. Aug-Oct.—Prairies and low ground.

Artemisia stelleriana

218. *Arnoglossum reniforme*   219. *Artemisia absinthium*   220. *Artemisia biennis*   221. *Artemisia campestris*

Artemisia stelleriana Bess.
(NO MAP)
DUSTY MILLER
introduced

Perennial from a creeping rhizome, inodorous. **Stems** 3-7 dm tall, simple to the inflorescence, densely white-tomentose. **Leaves** white-tomentose on both sides more densely so beneath, obovate, 3-10 cm long, including the petiole, and 1-5 cm wide, with a few rounded relatively broad lobes, which may be again slightly lobed. **Inflorescence** narrow and often dense, elongate; heads relatively large, the involucre 6-7.5 mm high, the disk corollas 3-4 mm long; receptacle glabrous; flowers all fertile, the outer pistillate. **Achenes** glabrous, subterete, but narrowed to the base and rounded at the summit. May-Sept.—Sandy places; native of Asia, escaped from cultivation, St. Louis County.

Artemisia vulgaris L.
MAP 226
MUGWORT
introduced

Aromatic perennial herb with a stout rhizome. **Stems** 0.5-1.5 m tall, simple or branched above, glabrous or nearly so below the inflorescence. **Leaves** green and glabrous or nearly so above, densely white-tomentose beneath, chiefly obovate or ovate in outline, about 5-10 cm long and 3-7 cm wide, the principal ones cleft nearly to the midrib into ascending, unequal segments which are again toothed or more deeply cleft, and ordinarily with one or two pairs of stipule-like lobes at the base. **Inflorescence** generally ample and leafy; involucre 3.5-4.5 mm high, more or less tomentose; receptacle glabrous; flowers all fertile, the outer pistillate; disk corollas about 2.0-2.8 mm long. **Achenes** ellipsoid, not nerved or angled, essentially glabrous. July-Oct.—Fields, roadsides, and waste places; Old World native, now established throughout most of e North America.

Artemisia vulgaris

BELLIS *English Daisy*

Bellis perennis L.
(NO MAP)
LAWN DAISY; ENGLISH DAISY
introduced

Perennial, more or less spreading-hairy. **Leaves** basal, elliptic or obovate to orbicular, the blades dentate or denticulate, to 3.5 cm long and 2 cm wide, narrowed to margined petioles of equal or greater length. **Heads** solitary atop a scape 5-15 cm high; involucral bracts herbaceous, equal; receptacle conic, naked. Rays many, pistillate, white to pink or purple; disk flowers yellow. **Achenes** compressed, mostly 2-nerved; pappus absent. April-Nov.—Weedy in lawns or waste places; St. Louis County.

Bellis perennis

BIDENS *Beggarticks*

Weedy annual herbs; perennial in the aquatic *B. beckii*. Leaves opposite (or whorled in *B. beckii*), simple, lobed, or pinnately divided. Flower heads with both disk and ray flowers, or with disk flowers only; ray flowers often about 8, yellow; involucral bracts in 2 series, the outer row leaflike and spreading, the inner row much shorter and erect; receptacle more or less flat and chaffy. Fruit a flattened achene; pappus of 2-5 barbed awns which persist atop the achene; the body of achene barbed or with stiff hairs (at least on the angles), the "stick-tights" facilitating dispersal of seed by animals.

1   Plants aquatic; underwater leaves whorled, dissected into narrow segments . . . .***B. beckii***
1   Plants not aquatic (sometimes emergent); leaves not as above 2
   2   Leaves simple and toothed, or sometimes lobed; achenes 3-4-awned 3

222. Artemisia dracunculus   *223. Artemisia frigida*   *224. Artemisia ludoviciana*   *225. Artemisia serrata*

3 Leaves mostly sessile 4
   4 Heads nodding when mature; outer involucral bracts widely spreading . . . . *B. cernua*
   4 Heads mostly upright; outer involucral bracts erect or nearly so . . . . *B. tripartita*
3 Leaves with a petiole 1-4 cm long 5
   5 Disk flowers 4-lobed, pale yellow, the stamens shorter than the lobes; achenes mostly 3-awned . . . .
      . . . . *B. tripartita*
   5 Disk flowers 5-lobed, yellow-orange, the stamens longer than the lobes; achenes mostly 4-awned . . .
      . . . . *B. connata*
2 Leaves all (or mostly) pinnately divided or compound; achenes 2-awned 6
   6 Heads with disk flowers only, or with short rays less than 5 mm long 7
      7 Outer involucral bracts 2-5 (usually 4), not fringed with hairs . . . . *B. discoidea*
      7 Outer involucral bracts 6 or more, fringed with hairs (at least near base) 8
         8 Disk flowers orange; outer involucral bracts mostly 6-8 . . . . *B. frondosa*
         8 Disk flowers yellow; outer involucral bracts 10 or more . . . . *B. vulgata*
   6 Heads with both disk and ray flowers, the rays over 1 cm long 9
      9 Achenes broad and ovate, mostly more than 3 mm wide . . . . *B. aristosa*
      9 Achenes narrow and nearly straight-sided, less than 3 mm wide . . . . *B. trichosperma*

Bidens aristosa (Michx.) Britt.
BEARDED BEGGARTICKS
(NO MAP) *native*

Annual or biennial herb. **Stems** 3-12 dm long, much-branched, more or less smooth. **Leaves** pinnately divided, 5-15 cm long, the segments narrowly lance-shaped, hairy on underside; margins with coarse, forward-pointing teeth or shallow lobes; petioles 1-3 cm long. **Flower heads** 2-5 cm wide, numerous on leafless stalks; rays yellow, usually 8, 1-2.5 cm long; the outer involucral bracts 8-10, 5-10 mm long, margins smooth or fringed with hairs. **Fruit** a flattened achene, 5-7 mm long; pappus of 2 (rarely 4) barbed awns, or sometimes absent. Aug–Sept. Marshy areas, ditches, disturbed wetlands. Reported for Minn.

Bidens aristosa

Bidens beckii Torr. ex Spreng.
BECK'S WATER-MARIGOLD
Megalodonta beckii (Torr.) Greene
MAP 227 *native*

Perennial aquatic herb. **Stems** 0.4-2 m long, little-branched. **Underwater leaves** opposite or whorled, dissected into threadlike segments; **emersed leaves** simple, opposite, lance-shaped to ovate, margins with forward-pointing teeth, petioles absent. **Flower heads** single or few at ends of stems; rays 6-10, gold-yellow, 1-1.5 cm long, notched at tip; involucral bracts smooth. **Fruit** an achene, more or less round in section, 10-15 mm long; pappus of 3-6 slender awns, longer than achenes, the upper portion of awn with downward-pointing barbs. June–Sept. — Quiet, shallow to deep water of lakes, ponds, rivers and streams.

Bidens beckii

Bidens cernua L.
NODDING BUR-MARIGOLD
MAP 228 *native*

Annual herb. **Stems** often branched, to 1 m long, smooth or with spreading hairs. **Leaves** opposite, smooth, lance-shaped to oblong lance-shaped, 3-16 cm long and 0.5-5 cm wide; margins with sharp, forward-pointing teeth and often rough-to-touch; petioles absent, the leaves usually clasping at base. **Flower heads** many, globe-shaped, 1.5-3 cm wide, usually nodding after flowering; rays yellow, 6-8, to 1.5 cm long, or absent; outer involucral bracts 4-8, unequal in length, the margins often fringed with hairs. **Fruit** a more or less straight-sided achene, 5-7 mm long, with downward-pointing barbs on margins; pappus with 4 (sometimes 2) awns, the awns with downward-pointing barbs. July–Oct.—Exposed, sandy or muddy shores, streambanks, marshes, forest depressions, wet meadows, ditches and other wet places.

Bidens cernua

Bidens connata Muhl.
PURPLE-STEM BEGGARTICKS
(NO MAP) *native*

Annual herb. **Stems** green-purple, to 2 m long, usually branched, smooth. **Leaves** opposite, smooth, the lower leaves sometimes deeply lobed, 3-15 cm long and 1-4 cm wide; margins with coarse, forward-pointing teeth; petioles present on lower leaves, upper leaves short-petioled or stalkless. **Flower heads** several to many, 1-2 cm wide, upright; disk flowers orange-yellow; rays absent, or few and 3-4 mm long; outer involucral bracts 4-9, usually not much longer than the head. **Fruit** an achene, 3-7 mm long; pappus of 2-4 downwardly barbed awns, about half as long as achene. Aug-Oct.—Exposed muddy shores, streambanks, marshes, pond, forest depressions, wet meadows, ditches and other wet places. *Sometimes included in* **Bidens tripartita.**

Bidens discoidea

Bidens discoidea (Torr. & Gray) Britt.
MAP 229
SMALL BEGGARTICKS
native

Annual herb. **Stems** smooth, 3-10 dm long. **Leaves** opposite, smooth, divided into 3-leaflets, the leaflets lance-shaped, the terminal leaflet largest, to 10 cm long and 4 cm wide; margins with coarse, forward-pointing teeth; petioles slender, 1-6 cm long. **Flower heads** many on slender stalks, the disk to 1 cm wide; rays absent; outer involucral bracts usually 4, leaflike, much longer than disk. **Fruit** a flattened achene, 3-6 mm long; pappus of 2 awns to 2 mm long, with short, upward pointing bristles. Aug-Sept.—Hummocks or logs in swamps, exposed muddy shores; usually where shaded.

Bidens frondosa

Bidens frondosa L.
MAP 230
DEVIL'S-PITCHFORK
native

Annual herb. **Stems** erect, 2-10 dm tall, branched, purple-tinged, more or less smooth. **Leaves** pinnately divided into 3-5 segments, the segments lance-shaped, to 10 cm long and 3 cm wide, underside sometimes with short hairs; margins with coarse, forward-pointing teeth; petioles slender, 1-6 cm long. **Flower heads** many on long, leafless stalks; disk flowers orange, the disk to 1 cm wide; rays absent or very small; the outer involucral bracts usually 8, green and leaflike, longer than disk, fringed with hairs on margins. **Fruit** a flattened, nearly black achene, 5-10 mm long; pappus of 2 slender awns with downward-pointing barbs. July-Oct. —Wet, sandy or gravelly shores, forest depressions, streambanks, pond margins; weedy in wet disturbed areas.

Bidens trichosperma (Michx.) Britton
MAP 231
CROWNED BEGGARTICKS
native
    Bidens coronata (L.) Britt.

Annual or biennial herb. **Stems** branched, 3-15 dm tall, smooth, often purple. **Leaves** opposite, smooth, to 15 cm long, pinnately divided into 3-7 narrow leaflets; margins coarsely toothed or deeply lobed to sometimes entire; petioles 3-15 mm long. **Flower heads** with both disk and ray flowers, large and numerous on slender stalks; rays about 8, gold-yellow, 1-2.5 cm long; outer involucral bracts 6-10, to 1 cm long, short-hairy on margins, inner bracts shorter. **Fruit** a flattened achene, 5-9 mm long, with long, stiff hairs on margins; pappus of 2 short, scale-like awns, 1-2 mm long. July-Oct.—Fens, tamarack swamps, sandy shores, marshes.

Bidens trichosperma

Bidens tripartita L.
MAP 232
THREE-LOBE BEGGARTICKS
native
    Bidens acuta (Wieg.) Britt.
    Bidens comosa (Gray) Wieg.

Bidens tripartita

Annual herb. **Stems** yellow, 1-12 dm tall, branched, smooth. **Leaves** opposite, lance-shaped to oval, 3-15 cm long and 0.5-5 cm wide, margins with coarse, forward-pointing teeth, rough-to-touch; petioles absent, or leaves tapered to a short, winged petiole. **Flower heads** 1-2.5 cm wide, several to many, remaining

226. *Artemisia vulgaris*   227. *Bidens beckii*   228. *Bidens cernua*   229. *Bidens discoidea*

erect after flowering; disk flowers yellow-green; rays absent; outer involucral bracts leaflike, 5-10 or more, 2-4x longer than head. **Fruit** an achene, 3-7 mm long, downwardly barbed on the margins; pappus of 3 downward-pointing barbed awns, the awns shorter than the achenes. Aug-Oct.—Exposed shores, streambanks, mudflats, forest depressions, pond, wet meadows, ditches and other wet places.

Bidens vulgata Greene
TALL BEGGARTICKS
　Bidens puberula Wieg.

MAP 233
native

Annual herb. **Stems** to 2 m tall, smooth or upper stem and leaves short-hairy. **Leaves** opposite, pinnately divided into 3-5 segments, the segments lance-shaped, to 15 cm long and 5 cm wide, with prominent veins; margins with sharp, forward-pointing teeth; petioles present. **Flower heads** on stout, leafless stalks, disk flowers yellow; ray flowers usually present, small, yellow; outer involucral bracts about 13, leaflike. **Fruit** a flattened, olive-green or brown achene, 10-12 mm long; pappus of 2 awns with downward-pointing barbs. Aug-Oct.—Streambanks, wet meadows, wet forests; weedy in moist disturbed places. *Similar to Bidens frondosa, but usually larger.*

Bidens vulgata

BOLTONIA *Doll's Daisy*

Boltonia asteroides (L.) L'Hér.
WHITE BOLTONIA

MAP 234
native

Perennial herb, fibrous-rooted, sometimes with shallow rhizomes. **Stems** stout, erect, 3-15 dm long, smooth. **Leaves** alternate, lance-shaped or oval, 5-16 cm long and 0.5-2 cm wide, becoming smaller in the head, narrowed to stalkless or slightly clasping base; margins entire but rough-to-touch. **Flower heads** many, with both disk and ray flowers, 1.5-2.5 cm wide; disk flowers yellow; rays white, pink, or lavender, 5-15 mm long; involucres 2.5-5 mm high, the bracts overlapping, chaffy on outer margins, with a green midvein. **Fruit** a flattened, obovate achene, 1-2 mm long, with a winged margin; pappus of 2 awns and 2-4 shorter bristles. Aug-Sept.—Seasonally flooded muddy shores, wet meadows, marshes, low prairie.

Boltonia asteroides

BRICKELLIA *Brickellbush*

Brickellia eupatorioides (L.) Shinners
FALSE BONESET
　Kuhnia eupatorioides L.

MAP 235
native

Perennial herbs from a stout taproot. Plants 3-13 dm tall, densely puberulent to subglabrous. **Leaves** mostly alternate, lance-shaped, the principal ones mostly 2.5-10 cm long and 5-40 mm wide, gland-dotted beneath, entire or toothed, sessile or the lower short-petiolate. **Heads** discoid, the flowers all tubular and perfect, mostly in small corymbiform clusters terminating the branches; involucre 7-14 mm high, imbricate, the inner bracts mostly linear or oblong, the outer lance-shaped with a slender attenuate tip. **Flowers** 7-33 in each head, creamy-white. **Fruit** a ribbed achene; pappus bristles 20. Aug-Oct.—Dry open places, especially in sandy soils.

Brickellia eupatorioides

CARDUUS *Thistle*

Annual, biennial, or perennial spiny herbs. Stems generally winged by the decurrent leafbases. Leaves alternate, serrate to more often pinnately lobed or pinnatifid. Heads discoid, the flowers all tubular

230. Bidens frondosa　　*231. Bidens trichosperma*　　*232. Bidens tripartita*　　*233. Bidens vulgata*

and perfect, or the plants sometimes dioecious by abortion, clustered or solitary at branch tips. Involucral bracts imbricate in several series, mostly spine-tipped. Receptacle flat or convex, densely bristly. Corollas purple or reddish to white or rarely yellow. Achenes glabrous, obovate, quadrangular or somewhat flattened; 5-10-nerved or nerveless. Pappus of many capillary bristles, deciduous in a ring. Closely related to *Cirsium*, from which it is distinguished primarily by the non-plumose pappus.

ADDITIONAL SPECIES
Carduus crispus L. (Curly plumeless thistle); Eurasian native, reported for Minn.

1 Heads nodding; involucral bracts 2 mm wide or more ....*C. nutans*
1 Heads not nodding; involucral bracts narrow, less than 2 mm wide ....*C. acanthoides*

Carduus acanthoides L.
SPINY PLUMELESS-THISTLE

MAP 236
introduced (invasive)

Biennial herb 3-10 dm tall, very strongly spiny, the stem tough. **Leaves** deeply lobed or pinnatifid, to 25 cm long and 8 cm wide, loosely villous beneath, chiefly along the midrib and main veins, with long multicellular hairs, or glabrous, glabrous or similarly hairy over the surface above. **Heads** clustered or solitary at the ends of the branches, erect, small, the disk mostly 1.5-2.5 cm wide when pressed; involucral bracts narrow, rarely any of them as much as 2 mm wide, erect or loosely spreading, the usually middle and outer spine-tipped, the inner softer and flatter, large, scarcely spiny. July-Oct.—Roadsides, pastures, and waste places; native of Europe.

Carduus nutans L.
MUSK THISTLE

MAP 237
introduced (invasive)

Biennial or rarely annual herb 3-10 dm or rarely 20 dm tall. **Leaves** glabrous, or long-villous chiefly along the midrib and main veins beneath, deeply lobed, to 25 cm long and 10 cm wide. **Heads** mostly solitary and nodding at the ends of the branches, usually large, the disk 4-8 cm wide when pressed, sometimes smaller and scarcely more than 1.5 cm; middle and outer involucral bracts conspicuously broad (2-8 mm), with long, flat, spreading or reflexed, spine-pointed tip; inner bracts narrower and softer, scarcely spiny, often purplish. June-Oct.—Native of Europe and w Asia, established on roadsides and waste places.

Carduus nutans

CENTAUREA *Knapweed; Star-Thistle*

Annual, biennial, or perennial herbs with alternate or all basal, entire to pinnatifid leaves, and solitary to numerous, small to large heads. Heads discoid, the flowers sometimes all tubular and perfect, or more commonly the marginal ones sterile, with enlarged, irregular, falsely radiate corolla. Involucral bracts imbricate in several series, either spine-tipped or more often some of them with enlarged appendages. Receptacle nearly flat, densely bristly. Corollas purple or blue to yellow or white, with slender tube and long narrow lobes. Achenes obliquely or laterally attached to the receptacle. Pappus of several series of graduated bristles or narrow scales, often much reduced, or wanting.

ADDITIONAL SPECIES
Centaurea phrygia L. (Wig knapweed), native to Europe; St. Louis County.

1 Involucral bracts tipped by short to long spines ....*C. solstitialis*
1 Involucral bracts not tipped by long spines; leaf bases not decurrent 2
  2 Leaves pinnately divided into linear-elliptic lobes; common weed ....*C. stoebe*
  2 Leaves entire or toothed, sometimes few-lobed 3
    3 Margins of involucral bracts entire or nearly so ....*C. repens*

234. Boltonia asteroides   *235. Brickellia eupatorioides*   *236. Carduus acanthoides*   *237. Carduus nutans*

3 Margins of involucral bracts toothed, jagged or fringed 4
   4 Plants annual (or winter-annuals); leaves linear, less than 1 cm wide .... *C. cyanus*
   4 Plant perennial; leaves wider, at least some lower leaves more than 1 cm wide .... *C. jacea*

Centaurea cyanus L.

GARDEN CORNFLOWER; BACHELOR'S BUTTON

MAP 238
introduced

Annual or winter-annual, 2-12 dm tall. Herbage loosely white-tomentose when young, the leaf undersides often persistently so. **Leaves** linear, entire, or the lower ones slightly toothed or with a few lobes, to 13 cm long and 8 mm wide (excluding the lobes). **Heads** terminating the branches; involucre mostly 11-16 mm high, its bracts striate, with a pectinate or lacerate fringe near the tip; flowers mostly blue, sometimes purple or white, the marginal ones with enlarged irregular corolla; pappus mostly 2-3 mm long. May-Oct.—Native to the Mediterranean region, cultivated as an ornamental, and now weedy in fields, roadsides, and waste places.

Centaurea cyanus

Centaurea jacea L.

BROWN-RAY KNAPWEED

MAP 239
introduced (naturalized)

Perennial, to 12 dm tall, glabrous or somewhat arachnoid. **Leaves** toothed or shallowly lobed to entire, the basal ovate or lance-shaped to elliptic, long-petiolate, the cauline reduced upwards and becoming sessile. **Heads** terminating the often numerous branches; involucre mostly 12-18 mm high, a little narrower to a little broader than high; appendages of the involucral bracts well developed, broad, tan to dark brown, the middle and outer ones rather irregularly lacerate, the inner less so and often deeply bifid; marginal flowers almost always enlarged. Pappus none. June-Sept.—Fields, roadsides, and waste places; native of Europe.

Centaurea repens L.

RUSSIAN KNAPWEED

MAP 240
introduced (invasive)

  Acroptilon repens (L.) DC.
  Rhaponticum repens (L.) Hidalgo

Coarse, bushy-branched perennial from a deep-seated rhizome, mostly 4-8 dm tall. Herbage finely arachnoid-tomentose, later nearly glabrate. **Leaves** glandular-punctate, the lower stem leaves to 6 cm long and 1.5 cm wide, often few-lobed, the others leaves smaller, entire or few-toothed. **Heads** numerous, terminating the branches; involucre greenish straw-colored, 9-15 mm high, the middle and outer bracts broad, with large rounded, subentire hyaline tips, the inner bracts narrower and more tapering, with plumose-hairy tips; flowers purple, the marginal ones not enlarged. Larger pappus bristles plumose above, mostly 6-11 mm long. June-Sept.—Native of Asia; fields, roadsides, and waste places.

Centaurea solstitialis L.

YELLOW STAR-THISTLE

(NO MAP)
introduced

Annual or biennial, 2-8 dm tall, thinly but persistently tomentose, the stem appearing winged by the decurrent leaf-bases. **Basal leaves** lyrate or pinnatifid, mostly less than 20 cm long and 5 cm wide, the middle and upper ones smaller, becoming linear and entire. **Heads** few to numerous, broad-based; involucre mostly 10-15 mm high; middle and outer bracts spine-tipped, the larger central spines commonly 11-22 mm long; inner bracts with a small hyaline appendage; flowers yellow, the marginal ones not enlarged. Pappus of the marginal flowers wanting, that of the others mostly 3-5 mm long.—Native to the Mediterranean region; weedy in fields and waste places; probably ephemeral in Minnesota (Clay County).

Centaurea solstitialis

238. *Centaurea cyanus*

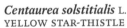

239. *Centaurea jacea*

240. *Centaurea repens*

241. *Centaurea stoebe*

Centaurea stoebe L.

MAP 241

SPOTTED KNAPWEED   *introduced (invasive)*

   Centaurea maculosa Lam.

Biennial or short-lived perennial, mostly 3-12 dm tall. Herbage with a thin and loose, soon deciduous tomenturn, also sparsely scabrous-puberulent. **Leaves** obscurely to evidently glandular-punctate, pinnatifid with narrow lobes, or the reduced ones of the inflorescence entire. **Heads** terminating the numerous branches, constricted upwards; involucre mostly 10-13 mm high, its bracts striate, the middle and outer ones with short, dark, pectinate tips; flowers pink-purple, the marginal ones enlarged. Pappus to 2 mm long, or rarely wanting. June-Oct. —Native of Europe; aggressive weed of fields, roadsides, and waste places.

Centaurea stoebe

CICHORIUM *Chicory*

Cichorium intybus L.

MAP 242

CHICORY   *introduced (invasive)*

Perennial with milky juice, from a long deep taproot. **Stems** branching, hirsute or glabrous, 3-17 dm tall. **Leaves** alternate, lower leaves oblong lance-shaped, petiolate, toothed or pinnatifid, 8-25 cm long and 1-7 cm wide, becoming reduced, sessile, and entire or merely toothed upwards. **Heads** sessile or short-pedunculate, borne 1-3 together in the axils of the much reduced upper leaves. Flowers all ligulate and perfect, blue or occasionally white; involucral bracts biseriate, the outer shorter. **Achenes** glabrous, 2-3 mm long, 5-angled, or the outer slightly compressed; pappus of 2-3 series of scales, sometimes minute. July-Oct. —Roadsides, fields, and waste places; native of Eurasia, now a cosmopolitan weed. *The root is sometimes roasted and used as an adulterant or substitute for coffee.*

Cichorium intybus

CIRSIUM *Thistle*

Biennial or perennial herbs. Stems and leaves often spiny. Leaves from base of plant or alternate on stem. Flower heads of pink to purple disk flowers only; involucral bracts tipped with spines. Fruit a smooth achene; pappus of many slender bristles.

1 Involucral bracts tipped by spines mostly more than 2 mm long 2
  2 Leaves coarsely hairy, with cobwebby hairs on underside 3
    3 Stem leaves decurrent at base, forming conspicuous spiny wings on stem . . . . *C. vulgare*
    3 Stem leaves not decurrent; stems not appearing winged 4
      4 Leaves green, with coarse hairs; stems 3-5 dm tall from persistent basal rosettes; dry to mesic prairies;
        rare in dry or mesic prairies . . . . *C. hillii*
      4 Leaves densely white-hairy on underside; stems 6 dm tall or more, the basal rosettes not persistent . 5
        5 All leaves deeply lobed, the lobes tipped with stout spines 3-7 mm long; open habitats . *C. discolor*
        5 Leaves mostly only shallowly lobed, tipped with small weak spines; wooded habitats . *C. altissimum*
  2 Leaves densely white-hairy on both sides, especially on underside 6
    6 Leaves narrowed to their base, rarely clasping . . . . *C. flodmanii*
    6 Leaves broadest near base, partially clasping . . . . *C. undulatum*
1 Involucral bracts tipped by short spines to only 1 mm long 7
  7 Colony-forming perennial herb from deep, creeping rhizomes; common weed of dry to moist places *C. arvense*
  7 Biennial herbs; moist to wet habitats 8
    8 Leaf bases not decurrent; stem not winged; involucral bracts usually with cobwebby hairs; flowers deep
      rose-purple; native and not weedy . . . . *C. muticum*

242. *Cichorium intybus*   243. *Cirsium altissimum*   244. *Cirsium arvense*

8 Leaf bases decurrent, forming spiny wings on stem; involucral bracts usually without cobwebby hairs; flowers pale pink-purple; introduced and weedy .... ***C. palustre***

Cirsium altissimum (L.) Spreng.

TALL THISTLE

MAP 243

native

Robust perennial 1-3 m tall. **Stems** crisply spreading-hirsute to subglabrate, sometimes slightly tomentose in the inflorescence. **Leaves** large, broadly oblong lance-shaped to obovate or elliptic, densely white-tomentose beneath, scabrous-hirsute to subglabrous on the upper surface, merely spiny-toothed on the margin to coarsely toothed or even shallowly lobed, the reduced ones of the inflorescence sometimes more evidently so. **Heads** several or numerous on the more or less leafy peduncles; involucre mostly 2.5-3.5 (rarely 2-4) cm high; middle and outer bracts tipped with spines 2-5 mm long; inner bracts merely attenuate, or sometimes with scarious, slightly dilated and erose tips; flowers mostly pink-purple. **Achenes** mostly 4.5-6.5 mm long. July-Oct.—Fields, waste places, river bottoms, and open woods.

Cirsium altissimum

Cirsium arvense (L.) Scop.

CANADIAN THISTLE

MAP 244

introduced (invasive)

Perennial with deep-seated rhizomes, mostly 3-15 (or 20) dm tall, subglabrous, or the leaves more or less white-tomentose beneath. **Heads** more or less numerous, polygamo-dioecious, the pappus of the pistillate heads surpassing the corollas, that of the starninate heads surpassed by the corollas; involucre 1-2 cm high, its bracts all innocuous, or the outer with weak spine-tips about 1 mm long; flowers pink-purple or occasionally white. **Achenes** about 4 mm long. July-Aug.—A noxious weed of fields and waste places; native of Eurasia, now statewide.

Cirsium arvense

Cirsium discolor (Muhl.) Spreng.

FIELD THISTLE

MAP 245

native

Similar to *Cirsium altissimum* and intergrading with it; perhaps not specifically distinct. Differs chiefly in its deeply pinnatifid, generally firmer and spinier **leaves**; plants averaging smaller (mostly 1-2 m) than *C. altissimum*, the peduncles tending to be a little leafier, and the **heads** often a little broader-based. July-Oct.—Fields, open woods, river bottoms, and waste places.

Cirsium flodmanii (Rydb.) Arthur

PRAIRIE THISTLE

MAP 246

native

Similar to *C. undulatum*, but smaller and more delicate, mostly 3-8 dm tall, and vigorously spreading by slender, often short-lived creeping roots. **Stem leaves** usually rather deeply pinnatifid, the lobes commonly lance-triangular, seldom over 7 mm wide; **basal leaves** sometimes similarly lobed, sometimes oblong lance-shaped and merely spinose-ciliate. **Heads** often more numerous; involucre mostly 2-2.5 (rarely approaching 3) cm high, the spine-tips of the bracts sometimes less than 3 mm long. **Achenes** mostly 3-4 mm long. June-Sept.—Prairies, dry meadows; common in Great Plains.

Cirsium flodmanii

Cirsium hillii (Canby) Fern.

HILL'S THISTLE

MAP 247

native

Perennial, producing basal rosettes of leaves the first year, followed by flowers one or two years later. Very similar to *Cirsium pumilum* in general form (a species of ne USA), and sometimes treated as a subspecies of it. **Achenes** mostly 4-5 mm long. June-Aug.—Prairies and other open places.

245. *Cirsium discolor*

246. *Cirsium flodmanii*

247. *Cirsium hillii*

248. *Cirsium muticum*

Cirsium muticum Michx.

SWAMP THISTLE

MAP 248
native

Stout biennial herb. **Stems** 0.5-2 m long, branched in head, with long, soft hairs when young, becoming more or less smooth. **Leaves** deeply lobed into pinnate segments, 1-2 dm long, underside often with matted, cobwebby hairs, becoming more or less smooth with age; margins toothed and often tipped with spines; petioles present on lower leaves, stem leaves sessile. **Flower heads** of purple or pink disk flowers only, single on leafless stalks over 1 cm long at ends of stems; involucre 2-3.5 cm high; the involucral bracts overlapping, densely hairy with cottony hairs (especially on margins), sometimes tipped with a short spine 0.5 mm long. **Achenes** 5 mm long; pappus of long, slender bristles. Aug-Oct. —Swamps, thickets, calcareous fens, sedge meadows, streambanks, shores.

Cirsium muticum

Cirsium palustre (L.) Scop.

EUROPEAN SWAMP THISTLE

(NO MAP)
introduced

Biennial herb. **Stems** 0.5-2 m tall, spiny. **Leaves** to 20 cm long, deeply lobed into pinnate segments, covered with loosely matted hairs or more or less smooth, tapered at base and continued downward on stem as spiny wings; margin teeth spine-tipped. **Flower heads** of purple disk flowers only, on short stalks mostly less than 1 cm long; involucre 1-2 cm high; the involucral bracts overlapping, not spine-tipped. **Achenes** 3 mm long; pappus of slender bristles to 1 cm long. June-Aug. Roadside ditches and adjacent wetlands, including swamps, thickets and fens; resembling the native *C. muticum* in these habitats.—In Minn, reported from Houston County; in adjacent states, spreading into wetlands, especially where disturbed.

Cirsium palustre

Cirsium undulatum (Nutt.) Spreng.

WAVY-LEAF THISTLE

(NO MAP)
introduced

Stout perennial 3-12 dm tall, seldom creeping belowground; lower surfaces of the leaves densely and persistently white-tomentose; upper surfaces thinly so and sometimes eventually glabrate. **Leaves** coarsely toothed to pinnatifid, the lobes ovate, deltoid, or occasionally oblong, seldom less than 7 mm wide. **Heads** several or occasionally solitary; involucre mostly 2.5-4 (rarely nearly 5) cm high, its bracts somewhat tomentose especially marginally, the inner with attenuate and often crisped tips, the others with spine-tips mostly 3-5 mm long; **flowers** commonly pink-purple, occasionally creamy. **Achenes** mostly 4-7 mm long. June-Sept. —Prairies, railroad tracks, and other open places; Dakota County.

Cirsium vulgare (Savi) Ten.

BULL THISTLE

MAP 249
introduced (invasive)

Biennial weed mostly 5-15 dm tall. **Stems** conspicuously spiny-winged by the decurrent leaf-bases, copiously spreading-hirsute to sometimes arachnoid. **Leaves** pinnatifid, the larger ones with the lobes again toothed or lobed, scabrous-hispid above, thinly white-tomentose to sometimes green and merely hirsute beneath. **Heads** several, purple; involucre 2.5-4 cm high, its bracts all spine-tipped, without any well developed glutinous dorsal ridge. **Achenes** less than 4 mm long. June-Oct.—Pastures, fields, roadsides, and waste places; native of Eurasia, now widely established as a weed in North America.

Cirsium vulgare

CONYZA *Horseweed*

Annual or perennial herbs, often weedy, with alternate leaves and several to numerous, mostly rather small heads. Involucral bracts more or less imbricate, scarcely herbaceous. Pistillate flowers very numerous and slender, without rays, or in some species (all ours) with very short, narrow, and inconspicuous white or purplish rays barely or scarcely exceeding the pappus. Disk-flowers few, in ours not more than about 20; style-appendages short, as in *Erigeron*. Receptacle flat or nearly so, naked. Achenes 1-2-nerved, or nerveless. Pappus of capillary bristles, sometimes with a short outer series. *The genus is closely related to* **Erigeron**.

1 Plants with spreading branches from base of plant; plants less than 3 dm tall . . . . *C. ramosissima*
1 Plants unbranched to the inflorescence; plants normally more than 3 dm tall . . . . *C. canadensis*

Conyza canadensis (L.) Cronq.

HORSEWEED

Erigeron canadensis L.
Leptilon canadense (L.) Britt.

MAP 250
introduced

Coarse annual, 1–15 dm tall, simple or nearly so to the inflorescence. **Stems** coarsely spreading-hirsute to nearly coarsely ciliate near the base, numerous, oblong lance-shaped, toothed, especially the lower, or entire, glabrous. **Leaves** more or less pubescent, or at least gradually reduced upwards, the cauline ones to about 8 cm long and 8 mm wide, the basal ones larger and relatively broader, but generally deciduous before flowering time. **Heads**, except in depauperate plants, numerous in a long and open inflorescence. Involucre about 3–4 mm high, glabrous or nearly so, the bracts strongly imbricate, brown or with distinct brown midvein. Rays white or sometimes pinkish, about equaling the pappus. Late summer and autumn.—A weed in waste places.

Conyza ramosissima Cronq.

DWARF FLEABANE

Erigeron divaricatus Michx.
Leptilon divaricatum (Michx.) Raf.

MAP 251
native

Conyza canadensis

Diffusely branched, slender, more or less hairy annual, 1–3 dm tall, with no well-defined central axis. **Leaves** narrowly linear, seldom more than 4 cm long and 2 cm wide, the upper most mere bracts. **Heads** numerous. Involucre about 3–4 mm high, the bracts strongly imbricate, sharply acute, the outer hairy, the inner glabrous. Rays minute, purplish, about equaling or slightly exceeding the pappus. Summer, fall.—A weed in waste places, particularly in sandy soil or along streams.

COREOPSIS *Tickseed*

Annual or perennial herbs or subshrubs. Leaves opposite or rarely alternate, entire to pinnatifid or 3-parted. Heads radiate, the rays conspicuous, usually neutral, yellow or rarely pink or white, sometimes marked with reddish brown at the base. Involucral bracts biseriate and dimorphic, all joined at the base, the outer narrower, usually shorter than the inner. Receptacle flat or slightly convex, its bracts thin and flat. Disk flowers tubular and perfect. Achenes flattened parallel to the bracts of the involucre, usually winged, not beaked. Pappus of 2 smooth or upwardly barbed, short awns or teeth, or a minute crown, or obsolete.

1   Stems with less than 5 pairs of leaves, the leaves clustered on the lower two-thirds of the stem, simple or
     sometimes with 1 or 2 lobes . . . . **C. lanceolata**
1   Stems with 5 or more pairs of leaves, the main leaves with 3 or more lobes or divisions 2
     2   Leaves stiffly 3-pronged, the blade tissue decurrent along the leaf midrib . . . . **C. palmata**
     2   Leaves not stiffly 3-pronged, divided to the midvein into 3 or more narrow leaflets . . . . **C. tinctoria**

Coreopsis lanceolata L.

LANCE-LEAF TICKSEED

MAP 252
native

Perennial with a short woody caudex. **Stems** usually several, 2–6 dm tall, glabrous, or, especially near the base, spreading-villous, leafy below, subnaked and elongate above. **Leaves** spatulate to linear or lance-linear, simple or with 1 or 2 pairs of small lateral lobes, glabrous to villous or hirsute, the lower long-petiolate, to 20 cm long (including petioles) and 17 mm wide, the others reduced and sessile or nearly so. **Heads** few or solitary on long naked peduncles, the disk about 1–2 cm wide; outer involucral bracts about 8–10, lance-shaped to oblong-ovate, glabrous

249. Cirsium vulgare   *250. Conyza canadensis*   *251. Conyza ramosissima*   *252. Coreopsis lanceolata*

except sometimes near the tip, more or less scarious-margined, about 5-10 mm long; inner involucral bracts longer and broader than the outer; rays about 1.5-3 cm long, often over 1 cm broad, yellow; receptacular bracts flat and chaffy below, somewhat awn-like above. **Achenes** with thin flat wings, orbicular, about 2-3 mm long, black. Pappus of 2 short chaffy teeth. May-July.—Dry, often sandy places.

Coreopsis palmata Nutt.   MAP 253
STIFF TICKSEED   *native*
Perennial from a creeping rhizome. **Stems** erect, 5-9 dm tall, glabrous, or hairy at the nodes. **Leaves** rather numerous, firm, glabrous except for the scabrous-ciliate margins, narrow, 3-8 cm long, essentially sessile, deeply 3-lobed at or below the middle, the lobes linear-oblong, about 2-7 mm wide, the central one sometimes again lobed. **Heads** few or solitary, short-pedunculate, the disk about 8-15 mm wide; outer involucral bracts 8-12, linear-oblong, glabrous except for the scabrous-ciliate margins, nearly equaling the much wider inner ones; rays about 1.5-3 cm long; receptacular bracts linear. **Achenes** oblong, blackish, narrowly winged, about 5-6.5 mm long. Pappus obsolete or of 2 callous teeth. June-July.—Prairies and open woods.

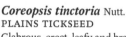

Coreopsis lanceolata

Coreopsis tinctoria Nutt.   MAP 254
PLAINS TICKSEED   *introduced*
Glabrous, erect, leafy and branching annual, mostly 4-12 dm tall. **Leaves** subsessile or short-petiolate, mostly 5-10 cm long, once or twice pinnatifid, the ultimate segments linear or lance-linear, mostly 0.5-4 mm wide. **Heads** numerous, the disk mostly 5-12 mm wide; outer involucral bracts very short, about 2 mm long, the inner ones about 5-8 mm long, deltoid-oblong to ovate, rays yellow with red-brown base, 0.7-1.5 cm long; receptacular bracts linear-subulate, few-striate; disk corollas red-purple. **Achenes** narrowly oblong, or somewhat cuneate, black, wingless, about 14 mm long. Pappus obsolete. June-Aug.—Dry ground and waste places.

Coreopsis tinctoria

CREPIS *Hawk's-Beard*

Taprooted annual or perennial herbs with milky juice; glabrate to glandular or pubescent. Basal leaves well-developed, entire to pinnatifid; stem leaves alternate and reduced, the uppermost leaves bractlike. Heads few to many in an open corymbiform inflorescence; involucre with an outer series of reduced involucral bracts and an inner 1 or 2 series of prominent, elongate involucral bracts; receptacle naked or ciliate. Florets all ligulate, perfect and fertile, corolla yellow. Achenes terete, prominently ribbed, constricted or tapered upward; pappus of numerous white capillary hairs.

1   Native perennial, not weedy . . . . *C. runcinata*
1   Introduced annual or weakly biennial weed of lawns and disturbed places . . . . *C. tectorum*

Crepis runcinata (James) Torr. & A. Gray   MAP 255
FIDDLE-LEAF HAWK'S-BEARD   *native*
Perennial herb with milky juice. **Stems** 2-6 dm long, glabrous or sparsely hairy, the stem leaves small and bractlike. **Leaves** in a rosette at base of plant, oblong lance-shaped to oval, 5-20 cm long and 1-4 cm wide, rounded at tip, tapered to a petiolelike base, margins entire or with widely spaced teeth. **Flower heads** 1-10, 1-2 cm wide, of yellow ray flowers only; involucre 8-15 mm high, with gland-tipped hairs, the involucral bracts in 2 series, the outer bracts shorter than inner.

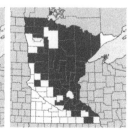

253. *Coreopsis palmata*   254. *Coreopsis tinctoria*   255. *Crepis runcinata*   256. *Crepis tectorum*

Achenes round in section, 4–5 mm long; pappus of many white slender bristles. June–July.—Wet meadows, low prairie, shores and swales, especially where alkaline.

Crepis tectorum L.

MAP 256

NARROW-LEAF HAWK'S-BEARD   *introduced (naturalized)*

Annual taprooted herb with milky juice, glabrous or pubescent. **Stems** mostly 1–10 dm tall. **Basal leaves** well-developed, petiolate, the blade lance-shaped or oblong lance-shaped, denticulate to pinnately parted, to 15 cm long and 4 cm wide; **stem leaves** sessile, auriculate, linear or nearly so. **Heads** several, 30–70-flowered; involucre cylindric or campanulate, the principal bracts in 1 or 2 series, the outer bracts 12–15, subulate, about 1/3 as long as the inner bracts, finely tomentose and sometimes also glandular. **Flowers** all ligulate and perfect, yellow. **Achenes** 2.5–4.5 mm long, dark purplish brown when mature, 10-ribbed; pappus of many whitish bristles. June–July.—Native of Eurasia; naturalized in waste places.

Crepis tectorum

DOELLINGERIA *White-Top*

Doellingeria umbellata (P. Mill.) Nees

MAP 257

TALL FLAT-TOPPED WHITE ASTER   *native*
     Aster pubentior Cronq.
     Aster umbellatus P. Mill.

Perennial herb, from thick rhizomes. **Stems** 0.5–2 m long, upper stem with appressed, short hairs. **Leaves** alternate, lance-shaped to oblong lance-shaped, 4–15 cm long and 1–4 cm wide, rough-to-touch above, densely short-hairy below; margins entire; petioles short, or absent on upper leaves. **Flower heads** usually many, 1–1.5 cm wide, in a ± flat-topped inflorescence; involucre 3–5 mm high, the involucral bracts short-hairy and overlapping; rays 5–10, white, 5–8 mm long. **Fruit** a nerved achene; pappus whitish. July–Sept.—Openings in swamps and moist forests, thickets, streambanks, sedge meadows, calcareous fens, roadside ditches.

Doellingeria umbellata

ECHINACEA *Coneflower*

Echinacea angustifolia DC.

MAP 258

NARROW-LEAVED PURPLE CONEFLOWER   *native*

Perennial 1–6 dm tall Stems simple or branched, hirsute. **Leaves** simple, alternate, entire, mostly 3-nerved; lower leaf blades narrowly lanceolate, 5–30 cm long and 1–4 cm wide, petiolate; upper leaves progressively smaller and becoming sessile. **Heads** solitary or few, mostly long-pedunculate; radiate; rays light pink to light purplish, spreading, 2–4 cm long and 5–8 mm wide; involucral bracts in 2–4 nearly equal or slightly imbricate series, with spreading or reflexed green tips; receptacle conic, its bracts partly enclosing the achenes, with stout spine-like tips exceeding the disk corollas; disk corollas slightly bulbous-thickened at base, not narrowed to a tube. **Achenes** 4–5 mm long, 4-angled, glabrous or sparsely pubescent on the angles; pappus a short toothed crown. June–July.—Well-drained prairies. *Similar to **Echinacea pallida**, common south of Minn, except with longer, narrower leaves and shorter, spreading rays in the heads. Many nursery plants sold as "purple coneflower" are **E. purpurea**, which is native further south and east.*

ECHINOPS *Globe-Thistle*

Echinops sphaerocephalus L.

(NO MAP)

GREAT GLOBE-THISTLE   *introduced*

Coarse perennial. **Stems** sometimes branching, to 2.5 m tall, spreading-hairy, and also tomentose above. **Leaves** alternate, white-tomentose beneath, green and scabrous or hirsute above, sessile and clasping (at least the middle and upper), not decurrent, pinnatifid, to 35 cm long and 20 cm wide. **Heads** 1-flowered, numerous, closely aggregated into globose secondary heads, the flowers all tubular and perfect; secondary heads naked-pedunculate; corolla blue to purple or white pale bluish; involucre 1.5–2 cm long, the subtending tuft of hairs seldom

Echinacea angustifolia

half as long. **Achenes** elongate, quadrangular or subterete, generally hairy; pappus of numerous short scales, free or more or less united, forming a crown. July–Sept. —Native of Eurasia, several species are cultivated and casually established in waste places; Dodge County in se Minn.

ADDITIONAL SPECIES
Echinops exaltatus Schrad. (Tall globe-thistle), native to Siberia; St. Louis County in former agricultural test plots.

ECLIPTA

Eclipta prostrata (L.) L.   (NO MAP)
FALSE DAISY; YERBA-DE-TAJO   *native*
   Verbesina alba L.
Annual herb. **Stems** spreading, branched, 5-8 dm long, with rough, appressed hairs, often rooting at the nodes. **Leaves** opposite, lance-shaped, 2-10 cm long and 0.5-2.5 cm wide, margins with shallow teeth; petioles absent, or short on lower leaves. **Flower heads** with both disk and ray flowers, in clusters of 1-3 at ends of stems or from leaf axils, on stalks or nearly stalkless; the disk 4-6 mm wide; rays short, nearly white. **Fruit** a flat-topped achene, 2-3 mm long; pappus a crown of very short bristles. July-Oct.—Mud flats, muddy streambanks and ditches, where somewhat weedy; Washington County.

ERECHTITES *Fireweed*

Erechtites hieraciifolius (L.) Raf. ex DC.   MAP 259
FIREWEED   *native*
   Senecio hieraciifolius L.

Eclipta prostrata

Fibrous-rooted annual herb. **Stems** erect, 0.1-2.5 m tall, slightly succulent. **Leaves** alternate, of various sizes to sometimes 20 cm long and 8 cm wide, sharply serrate with callous-tipped teeth, sometimes also irregularly lobed. **Heads** cylindric to ovoid, several to many in a flat-topped or elongate inflorescence, or in depauperate plants often solitary; discoid, whitish; involucre about 1-1.5 cm high, the bracts glabrous or finely strigose, green with pale margins, 0.5-2 mm wide. **Achenes** about 2-3 mm long, finely strigose between the mostly 10-12 ribs, with a white annular ring at the tip; pappus of numerous bright white bristles, eventually deciduous. Aug, Sept.—Various habitats, including dry woods, marshes, and waste places, often abundant after fires.

ERIGERON *Daisy; Fleabane*

Erechtites hieraciifolia

Biennial to perennial herbs with simple, alternate leaves. Flower heads with both disk and ray flowers; disk flowers yellow; rays white to pink, very narrow, only to about 0.5 mm wide; involucral bracts in 1-2 series, linear, about equal in length, green in middle and at base, translucent at tip and on upper margins. Fruit a flattened achene; pappus of 20-30 slender, rough bristles.

1 Pistillate flowers numerous, the corolla filiform with narrow, short erect rays, these sometimes not exceeding the involucre, or the inner pistillate corollas tubular 2
   2 Pistillate florets that are tubular, filiform, and essentially lacking rays present between the bisexual disk flowers and the outer pistillate flowers with rays; inflorescence more or less corymbiform. . . . . **E. acris**
   2 Pistillate florests all with rays; inflorescence more or less raceme-like or heads sometimes solitary . . . .
      . . . . **E. lonchophyllus**

257. *Doellingeria umbellata*

258. *Echinacea angustifolia*

259. *Erechtites hieraciifolia*

1 Pistillate florets few to many, corolla tube cylindrical with rays well-developed and spreading or somewhat reduced, but not short, very narrow and erect. 3

   3 Pappus of the ray flowers short, less than 1 mm long; weedy annual herbs 4

      4 Plants 6 dm or more tall; stems leafy; pubescence on middle of stem long and spreading . . . . . ***E. annuus***

      4 Plants to 7 dm tall; stem leaves few; pubescence mostly short and appressed . . . . ***E. strigosus***

   3 Pappus of long bristles; biennial or perennial herbs 5

      5 Disk flowers less than 4 mm long; rays very narrow, less than 1 mm wide . . . . ***E. philadelphicus***

      5 Disk flowers 4-6 mm long; rays about 1 mm wide 6

         6 Plants with shallow rhizomes or stolons; rays 50-100 . . . . ***E. pulchellus***

         6 Plants without rhizomes or stolons; rays 125 or more . . . . ***E. glabellus***

Erigeron acris L.

BITTER FLEABANE

MAP 260

🌱*endangered* | *native*

Perennial or biennial herb; plants nearly glabrous to spreading hairy and somewhat glandular, especially in the inflorescence. **Stems** 3-8 dm tall, from a simple or branched caudex. **Basal leaves** spatulate, to 10 cm long and 1.5 cm wide, entire or shallowly toothed; **stem leaves** numerous and well-developed, narrowly lance-shaped. **Heads** several to many, on upright peduncles; involucre 5-10 mm long, finely glandular and/or hirsute; involucral bracts nearly equal or the outermost somewhat shorter; pistillate flowers numerous, of 2 types, the outer with the corolla a long slender tube and an erect, narrow, pinkish ray 2.5-5 mm long; the inner with a tubular corolla lacking rays. **Achenes** 2-nerved, sparsely hairy; pappus of many slender bristles, white to sometimes reddish tinged. June-Aug.—Open, often rocky woods.

Erigeron annuus (L.) Pers.

EASTERN DAISY FLEABANE

MAP 261

native

Annual or rarely biennial. **Stems** 6-15 dm tall, amply leafy, more or less hirsute, the hairs spreading except near the top. **Basal leaves** elliptic to suborbicular, coarsely toothed, to 10 cm long and 7 cm wide, more or less abruptly long-petiolate; **stem leaves** numerous, broadly lance-shaped, all except sometimes the uppermost sharply toothed, or rarely nearly entire. **Heads** several to very numerous; involucre 3-5 mm high, finely glandular, and sparsely hairy with long, flattened, transparent hairs; disk 6-10 mm broad. Rays about 80-125, white or rarely pinkish or bluish, about 4-10 mm long and 0.5-1.0 mm wide; disk corollas 2.0-2.8 mm long. **Achenes** 2-nerved; pappus of the disk-flowers double, of 10-15 fragile bristles and several very short slender scales less than 1 mm long; pappus of the ray flowers of short scales only, lacking the longer bristles. Chiefly early and middle summer. *A weed over most of n USA and s Canada.*

Erigeron annuus

Erigeron glabellus Nutt.

STREAMSIDE FLEABANE

MAP 262

native

Biennial or perennial herb with nearly simple caudex and fibrous roots. **Stems** hairy, 1-5 dm tall, rarely more. **Leaves** hairy, the lower ones oblong lance-shaped, to 15 cm long and 15 mm wide, or rarely more, the middle and upper ones linear or lance-shaped, evidently reduced, sometimes bract-like. **Heads** solitary or several; disk 10-20 mm broad; involucre 5-9 mm high, hairy. Rays 125-175, 8-15 mm long, about 1 mm wide, blue, pink, or white; disk corollas 4.0-5.5 mm long. **Achenes** 2-nerved; pappus double.—Meadows, prairies, and open ground.

Erigeron glabellus

260. *Erigeron acris*

261. *Erigeron annuus*

262. *Erigeron glabellus*

263. *Erigeron lonchophyllus*

Erigeron lonchophyllus Hook.
SHORT-RAY FLEABANE

MAP 263
❧*threatened* | *native*

Biennial or short-lived perennial herb. **Stems** 1-6 dm tall, spreading-hirsute,from a weak, fibrous root. **Leaves** sparsely to moderately hirsute or the lower leaves glabrate, margins often ciliate; **basal leaves** spatulate, to 15 cm long and 12 mm wide; **stem leaves** narrower, becoming linear, but generally long and conspicuous. **Heads** borne on erect peduncles and at least the lower ones equaled or surpassed by their subtending leaves; involucre 4-9 mm long, disk 7-17 mm wide; involucral bracts thin and light green, commonly purplish near the tip, usually imbricated; pistillate florets numerous, rays about 2-3 mm long, white or sometimes pinkish; disk florets with corolla 3.5-5 mm long. **Achenes** 2-nerved, sparsely hairy; pappus with 20-30 obvious whitish bristles, equaling or surpassing the disk corolla. July-Aug.—Moist meadows and prairies.

Erigeron philadelphicus L.
PHILADELPHIA DAISY

MAP 264
native

Biennial or short-lived perennial herb. **Stems** 1 to several, branched in head, 2-7 dm long, usually long-hairy. **Leaves** alternate, lower leaves spatula-shaped, 5-15 cm long and 1-4 cm wide, tapered to a short petiole; upper leaves smaller, lance-shaped, clasping at base, hairy to nearly smooth, rounded at tip; margins entire or with rounded teeth. **Flower heads** few to many, with both disk and ray flowers, 1.5-2.5 cm wide; involucre 3-6 mm high, the involucral bracts hairy, of more or less equal length; rays many, white to deep pink, 5-10 mm long and to 0.5 mm wide. **Fruit** a short-hairy achene; pappus of long rough bristles. May-Aug. —Wet meadows, shores, streambanks, wet woods, floodplains, springs; also weedy in open disturbed areas and lawns.

Erigeron lonchophyllus

Erigeron pulchellus Michx.
ROBIN'S PLANTAIN

MAP 265
native

Biennial or short-lived perennial, with a simple caudex and slender stoloniform rhizomes. **Stems** 1.5-6 dm tall. **Basal leaves** oblong lance-shaped to suborbicular, mostly 2-12 cm long and 6-50 mm wide, commonly more or less toothed; **stem leaves** ovate to lance-shaped or oblong, reduced upwards. **Heads** solitary or few; involucre 5-7 mm high; disk 10-20 mm wide. Rays 50-100, 6-10 mm long, about 1 mm wide or a little more, blue, or sometimes pink or white; disk corollas 4.0-6.0 mm long. **Achenes** 2-4-nerved; pappus simple. Spring.—Woodlands and streambanks. *Var. tolsteadii Cronq.* is considered endemic to Minn and known from several s Minn counties.

Erigeron philadelphicus

Erigeron strigosus Muhl.
ROUGH FLEABANE

MAP 266
native

Erigeron ramosus (Walt.) B.S.P.

Annual or rarely biennial. **Stems** 3-7 dm tall, sparsely leafy, more or less hairy, the hairs spreading or usually appressed. **Basal leaves** mostly oblong lance-shaped to elliptic, entire or toothed, the blade and petiole together not more than 15 cm long and 2.5 cm wide; **stem leaves** linear to lance-shaped, entire, or the lower ones slightly toothed, rarely the middle ones slightly toothed also. **Heads** several to very numerous, involucre 2-5 mm high, obscurely glandular and more or less hairy, the hairs long or short; disk about 5-12 mm broad. Rays about 50-100, white, or sometimes pinkish or bluish, to 6 mm long, 0.4-1.0 mm wide; disk corollas 1.5-2.6 mm long. **Achenes** 2-nerved; pappus as in *E. annuus*. Early and mid-summer. *A weed in much of the USA and s Canada.*

264. *Erigeron philadelphicus*   265. *Erigeron pulchellus*   266. *Erigeron strigosus*

Erigeron strigosus

EUPATORIUM *Joe-Pye-Weed; Boneset*

Perennial herbs from a thick rhizome. Stems stout, erect. Leaves opposite and joined at base, the stem passing through the joined leaves; lower leaves smaller; margins toothed. Flower heads of pink, purple or white disk flowers only, usually many in a more or less flat-topped head at ends of stems; involucral bracts overlapping or nearly equal length. Fruit an angled achene; pappus of many slender bristles.

1 Leaf bases (except sometimes the uppermost) joined around the stem . . . . *E. perfoliatum*
1 Leaf bases entirely free and separate from the stem 2
   2 Leaves with distinct petioles; florets 8-50 (or more) per head . . . . *E. serotinum*
   2 Leaves sessile or nearly so (at most tapering to a narrow, winged base); florets fewer than 8 (usually 5) per head 3
      3 Stem densely puberulent on middle internodes; leaves tapered to narrow base (or short-winged petiole), with 3 prominent longitudinal veins (at least on basal half). . . . . *E. altissimum*
      3 Stem glabrous on middle internodes (or sparsely puberulent); leaves truncate to broadly rounded at the base, with only 1 long vein (the midrib) prominent beneath . . . . *E. sessilifolium*

Eupatorium altissimum L.

TALL BONESET

MAP 267
native

Erect perennial, pubescent with loose, soft, spreading hairs, glabrate below. **Stems** to 2 m tall. **Leaves** many, opposite, narrowly lance-shaped, prominently 3-veined, glandular-punctate; margins serrate; narrowed at base to a short petiole. **Inflorescence** broad and many-headed; involucral bracts imbricate, rounded or obtuse; florets 5 per head, corolla white. Aug-Sept.—Pastures, along railroads and roads, disturbed places.

Eupatorium perfoliatum L.

BONESET

MAP 268
native

Perennial herb. **Stems** 3-15 dm tall, with long, spreading hairs. **Leaves** opposite, mostly joined at the broad base and perforated by the stem (upper leaves sometimes separate), lance-shaped, 6-20 cm long and 1.5-5 cm wide, upper surface sparsely hairy, underside hairy, both sides dotted with yellow glands; margins finely toothed and rough-to-touch; petioles absent. **Flower heads** of dull white disk flowers only, in a flat-topped inflorescence; **involucre** 3-6 mm high, the involucral bracts green with white margins, hairy, overlapping in 3 series. **Fruit** a black achene, 1-2 mm long; pappus of long slender bristles. July-Sept.—Marshes, wet meadows, low prairie, shores, streambanks, ditches, cedar swamps, thickets, calcareous fens. *Often growing with* **spotted joe-pye-weed** *(Eutrochium maculatum).*

Eupatorium serotinum Michx.

LATE-FLOWERING THOROUGHWORT

MAP 269
introduced

Fibrous-rooted perennial 5-15 dm tall. **Stems** puberulent especially above. **Leaves** lance-shaped to ovate, petiolate, serrate (often coarsely and sharply so), 5-20 cm long and 1.5-10 cm wide, 3-5-nerved, commonly less hairy than the stem, the upper surface often nearly glabrous. **Involucre** 3-4 rnm high, its bracts imbricate, broadly rounded to obtuse, pubescent; flowers 9-15 (mostly 13) in each head, the corolla white, 2.7-3.7 mm long. **Achenes** nearly glabrous. Aug-Oct.—Mostly in bottomlands and moist woods, sometimes in drier or more open places.

Eupatorium altissimum

Eupatorium perfoliatum

267. *Eupatorium altissimum*   268. *Eupatorium perfoliatum*   269. *Eupatorium serotinum*   *Eupatorium serotinum*

Eupatorium sessilifolium L.

MAP 270

UPLAND BONESET *threatened | native*

Fibrous-rooted perennial. **Stems** 6-15 dm tall, puberulent in the inflorescence, otherwise glabrous. **Leaves** gland-dotted, opposite, sessile or subsessile, lance-shaped, usually broadly rounded at the base, serrate, acuminate, mostly 7-18 cm long and 1.5-5 cm wide, 2.5-7 times as long as wide, the lower smaller and deciduous. **Involucre** 4.5-6.5 mm high, its imbricate, broadly rounded to merely obtuse bracts finely hairy and usually also glandular; flowers 5 or sometimes 6 in each head, white. Aug.-Sept.—Dry to mesic, open oak woods, often on slopes or blufftops.

Eupatorium sessilifolium

EURYBIA *Wood-Aster*

Eurybia macrophylla (L.) Cass.

MAP 271

LARGE-LEAF WOOD-ASTER *native*

Aster macrophyllus L.

Perennial with creeping rhizomes, sometimes also with a short branched caudex, producing abundant clusters of basal leaves on short sterile shoots. **Stems** typically simple. 2-12 dm tall, glandular in the inflorescence or sometimes throughout, often also spreading-hairy. **Leaves** basal and alternate on stems, thick and firm, varying from essentially glabrous on both sides to scabrous above and hairy beneath, and sometimes glandular; margins crenate or serrate; basal and lower stem leaves cordate, 4-20 cm long and 3-15 cm wide, long-petiolate, the middle and upper leaves gradually or abruptly reduced, becoming sessile. **Inflorescence** corymbiform, flat or round-topped, its bracts commonly few and broad; involucre 7-11 mm high, usually glandular and sometimes also short-hairy, its bracts firm, imbricated, the green tips sometimes obscure; rays commonly 9-20, lilac- or purple-tinged, 7-15 mm long. Pappus persistent and bristly. July-Oct. —Woods of all types, often increasing after disturbance.

Eurybia macrophylla

EUTHAMIA *Flat-Topped Goldenrod*

Perennial herbs, spreading by rhizomes. Stems leafy. Leaves alternate, covered with resinous dots; margins entire; petioles absent or very short. Flower heads small, of yellow disk and ray flowers, in a more or less flat-topped cluster at ends of stems; involucre somewhat sticky. Fruit an achene; pappus of slender white bristles.

1　Largest stem leaves 4 mm or more wide, with 3 conspicuous longitudinal veins; leaves and upper stem short-hairy; upper leaves dull, glandular dots usually indistinct. . . . . *E. graminifolia*

1　Largest stem leaves less than 3 mm wide, with single longitudinal vein (midrib) and sometimes with faint pair of longitudinal veins; leaves and upper stem smooth; upper leaves shiny, with conspicuous glandular dots. . . . .
. . . . *E. gymnospermoides*

Euthamia graminifolia (L.) Greene

MAP 272

COMMON FLAT-TOPPED GOLDENROD *native*

Solidago graminifolia (L.) Salisb.

Perennial herb, spreading by rhizomes. **Stems** erect, 5-15 dm tall, smooth to hairy, usually branched in head. **Leaves** alternate, linear to narrowly lance-shaped or oval, 3-15 cm long and 3-10 mm wide, 3-veined, with small glandular dots; margins entire, smooth or rough-to-touch; petioles absent or very short. **Flower heads** small, in flat-topped clusters at ends of stems; with yellow disk and ray flowers, the rays small, to 1 mm long; involucre 3-5 mm high, somewhat sticky, the involucral bracts overlapping in several series, yellow or green-tipped. **Fruit** a finely hairy achene, 1 mm long; pappus of many white, slender bristles. Aug.-Sept. —Shores, wet meadows, low prairie, springs, fens, swamps, interdunal wetlands, streambanks, often where sandy or gravelly; also weedy in abandoned fields.

Euthamia gymnospermoides Greene

MAP 273

TEXAS GOLDENTOP *native*

Solidago gymnospermoides (Greene) Fern.

Perennial from branched creeping rhizomes. **Stems** 4-10 dm tall, glabrous. **Leaves** glabrous except for the slightly scabrous margins, densely and strongly glandular-

Euthamia graminifolia

punctate, obscurely to sometimes evidently 3-nerved, without any additional lateral nerves, the basal and lower cauline ones soon deciduous, the others numerous, not much reduced upwards, linear, mostly 4-9 cm long and 1.5-5 mm wide. **Inflorescence** terminal, corymbiform, the heads sometimes sessile in small glomerules, but not infrequently more pedunculate; involucre 4.5-6.5 mm high, glutinous; heads mostly 14-20-flowered, the short rays 10-14, the disk-flowers 4-6. **Achenes** hairy; pappus of bristles. Aug.-Oct.—Open, often sandy places.

Euthamia gymnospermoides

EUTROCHIUM *Joe-Pye-Weed*

Perennial herbs from a thick rhizome. Stems stout, erect. Leaves whorled, the stem passing through the joined leaves; lower leaves smaller; margins toothed. Flower heads of pink, purple or white disk flowers only, usually many in a more or less flat-topped head at ends of stems; involucral bracts overlapping or nearly equal length. Fruit an angled achene; pappus of many slender bristles.

1   Stems green, purple only at nodes, not purple-spotted; heads with usually 3-6 flowers; dry woods . ***E. purpureum***

1   Stems purple throughout or purple-spotted; heads with more than 8 flowers; common and widespread in wet habitats . . . . ***E. maculatum***

Eutrochium maculatum (L.) E. Lamont
SPOTTED JOE-PYE-WEED
   Eupatorium maculatum L.

MAP 274
native

Perennial herb. **Stems** 5-20 dm long, spotted or tinged with purple, short-hairy above, especially on branches of head. **Leaves** in whorls of mostly 4-5, lance-shaped to ovate, 5-20 cm long and 2-7 cm wide, upper surface with sparse short hairs, underside often densely short-hairy; margins with sharp, forward-pointing teeth; petioles to 2 cm long. **Flower heads** of light pink to purple disk flowers only, the inflorescence more or less flat-topped; involucres 6-9 mm high, purple-tinged, the involucral bracts overlapping. **Fruit** a black, angled achene, 2-4 mm long; pappus of long, slender bristles. July-Sept.—Wet meadows, marshes, low prairie, shores, streambanks, ditches, cedar swamps, bogs, calcareous fens.

Eutrochium maculatum

Eutrochium purpureum (L.) E. Lamont
PURPLE-NODE JOE-PYE-WEED
   Eupatorium purpureum L.

MAP 275
native

Fibrous-rooted perennial. **Stems** mostly 6-20 dm tall, slightly glaucous, usually purple only at the nodes, otherwise greenish, the pith usually remaining intact. **Leaves** mostly in 3s or 4s, lance-shaped or ovate to elliptic, mostly 8-30 cm long and 2.5-15 cm wide, gradually or sometimes rather abruptly narrowed to the short petiole, pinnately veined, usually sharply and coarsely toothed, loosely soft-pubescent to subglabrous beneath, usually minutely glandular as well. **Inflorescence** convex; involucre imbricate, 6.5-9 mm high, mostly 4-7-flowered; corolla generally very pale pinkish or purplish, but variable, 4.5-7.5 mm long. July-Sept.—Thickets and open woods, often in drier habitats than *E. maculatum*.

Eutrochium purpureum

270. *Eupatorium sessilifolium*

271. *Eurybia macrophylla*

272. *Euthamia graminifolia*

273. *Euthamia gymnospermoides*

GAILLARDIA *Blanket-Flower*

Gaillardia aristata Pursh
COMMON BLANKET-FLOWER

MAP 276
native

Commonly perennial. **Stems** 1 or several from the base, simple or not much branched, pubescent, about 2-7 dm tall. **Leaves** narrow, rarely as much as 15 cm long and 2.5 cm wide, sometimes all basal in depauperate plants, entire to coarsely toothed, hairy. **Heads** solitary or few, long-pedunculate, the disk commonly 1.5-3 cm wide, purple or brownish purple, rarely yellow; involucral bracts mostly acuminate or attenuate-acuminate, usually loosely hairy; rays yellow, or more or less suffused with purple at the base, about 1-3 cm long; disk corollas densely woolly toward the summit. Receptacle convex to subglobose, with chaffy or spinelike setae. **Achenes** partly or wholly covered by a basal tuft of long ascending hairs; pappus of 6-10 awned scales. May-Sept.—Plains, meadows, and other open places.

Gaillardia aristata

ADDITIONAL SPECIES
Gaillardia pulchella Foug. (Firewheel); native to southern USA.

GALINSOGA *Quickweed*

Annual herbs. Leaves opposite. Flower heads small, campanulate or hemispheric; radiate, the rays few, short, broad, only slightly surpassing the disk, white or pink, pistillate and fertile; involucral bracts few, broad, membranous but greenish in part, each subtending a ray, and sometimes joined at the base; receptacle conic, chaffy throughout, its bracts membranous, nearly flat. Disk-flowers perfect; style-branches flattened, with short, minutely hairy appendages. Achenes 4-angled; pappus of several to many scales, often fimbriate or awn-tipped, that of the rays often reduced or absent.

1   Leaves nearly entire to shallowly toothed; pappus of ray flowers absent . . . . *G. parviflora*
1   Leaves all sharply toothed; ray flowers with well developed pappus . . . . *G. quadriradiata*

Galinsoga parviflora Cav.
GALLANT-SOLDIER

MAP 277
introduced

Freely branching annual. **Stems** 2-7 dm tall, glabrous or sparsely pubescent with appressed hairs. **Leaves** ovate or lance-ovate, petiolate, 2-7 cm long and 1-4 cm wide, serrulate or crenulate, nearly glabrous or sparsely appressed-hairy. Peduncles appressed-hairy, or with spreading gland-tipped hairs. **Heads** numerous in leafy cymes, small, the disk about 3-6 mm wide; rays white; pappus nearly absent; pappus-scales of the disk-flowers conspicuously fimbriate, nearly as long as the corolla. **Achenes** of the disk sparsely hairy or glabrous. June-Nov. —Waste places.

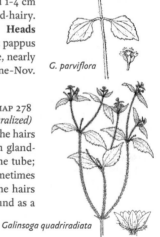

G. parviflora

Galinsoga quadriradiata Cav.
SHAGGY-SOLDIER

MAP 278
introduced (naturalized)

Similar to and more common than *G. parviflora*. **Stems** more pubescent, the hairs coarser and spreading. **Leaves** more coarsely toothed. Peduncles with gland-tipped hairs. Rays with well developed pappus scales about equaling the tube; pappus-scales of the disk-flowers less fimbriate than in *G. parviflora*, sometimes evidently shorter than the corolla. **Achenes** of the disk finely hairy, the hairs appressed or spreading.—Native of South and Central America; now found as a weed.

Galinsoga quadriradiata

274. *Eutrochium maculatum*   275. *Eutrochium purpureum*   276. *Gaillardia aristata*   277. *Galinsoga parviflora*

GNAPHALIUM *Cudweed*

Gnaphalium uliginosum L.   MAP 279
MARSH CUDWEED   *introduced (naturalized)*

Annual herb. **Stems** 5-25 cm tall, branching, densely and often loosely white-woolly, the leaves sparsely so. **Leaves** alternate, entire, numerous, linear, to 4 cm long and 5 mm wide. **Heads** disciform, glomerate in numerous small clusters in axils and at ends of the branches, overtopped by their subtending leaves; flowers yellow or whitish, the numerous outer ones slender and pistillate, the few inner ones coarser and perfect; involucre about 2-3 mm high, woolly at the base; bracts greenish or brown, often with lighter-colored tips. **Achenes** terete or slightly compressed; pappus of capillary bristles, these falling separately. July-Oct. —Streambanks and waste places, wet or dry.

Gnaphalium uliginosum

GRINDELIA *Gumweed*

Grindelia squarrosa (Pursh) Dunal   MAP 280
CURLY-TOP GUMWEED   *introduced*

Biennial or sometimes perennial. **Stems** branched above and sometimes also at base, 1-10 dm tall, sometimes woody at base. **Leaves** alternate, punctate and resinous, finely serrulate to entire, or, sometimes coarsely toothed; middle and upper leaves ovate or oblong, 3-7 cm long, 4-20 mm wide. **Heads** several to many, radiate or occasionally discoid, the rays mostly 15-45, yellow, pistillate and fertile; the disk about 1-2 cm wide; disk-flowers yellow, the inner and often also the outer sterile. Receptacle flat or convex, naked. Involucral bracts strongly sticky-resinous, imbricate in several series, the green tips reflexed, especially the outer. Rays 20-35, 7-15 mm long, or absent. **Fruit** a compressed to 4-angled achene, scarcely nerved, 2-3 mm long; pappus awns 2-8. July-Sept.—Open or waste places.

HASTEOLA *False Indian Plantain*

Hasteola suaveolens (L.) Pojark.   MAP 281
FALSE INDIAN PLANTAIN   ❦*endangered | native*
    Cacalia suaveolens L.

Perennial herb, from fleshy roots. **Stems** more or less smooth, grooved, 1-2.5 m tall, leafy to the inflorescence. **Leaves** alternate, smooth; lower leaves triangular with a pair of outward-pointing lobes at base, 5-20 cm long and nearly as wide; upper leaves smaller and often not lobed; margins sharply and irregularly toothed; petioles winged. **Flower heads** of disk flowers only, in a more or less flat-topped inflorescence, the disk about 1 cm wide; disk flowers white or light pink; involucre 1 cm long, the main involucral bracts 10-15. **Fruit** an achene; pappus of many soft, white bristles. July-Sept.—Riverbanks, shores, calcareous fens, wet low areas.

Grindelia squarrosa

Hasteola suaveolens

HELENIUM *Sneezeweed*

Annual or perennial herbs. Leaves alternate, glandular-dotted, usually decurrent on stem. Flower heads solitary to numerous, radiate or rarely discoid, the rays pistillate or neutral, yellow or sometimes partly purple, 3-lobed, not very numerous; involucral bracts in 2-3 series, subequal or the inner shorter, soon deflexed, the outer sometimes joined at the base; receptacle convex to ovoid or conic, naked. Disk flowers numerous, perfect, the corolla lobes glandular-puberulent. Achenes 4-5-angled, generally pubescent on the angles and ribs; pappus of several scarious or hyaline, often awn-tipped scales.

278. *Galinsoga quadriradiata*   279. *Gnaphalium uliginosum*   280. *Grindelia squarrosa*   281. *Hasteola suaveolens*

1 Disk flowers yellow, 5-lobed at tip; stem leaves more than 1 cm wide; common . . . . *H. autumnale*
1 Disk flowers dark brown, 4-lobed; stem leaves to 1 cm wide; rare . . . . *H. flexuosum*

Helenium autumnale L.

MAP 282
COMMON SNEEZEWEED   *native*

Perennial herb. **Stems** single or clustered, erect, 3-13 dm tall, smooth or finely hairy, branched in head. **Leaves** alternate, bright green, lance-shaped to oval, 4-12 cm long and 0.5-3.5 cm wide, glandular-dotted, usually short-hairy; margins entire to shallowly toothed; petioles absent, the blades tapered to a narrow base extending downward as wings on stem. **Flower heads** more or less round, 1.5-4 cm wide; few to many on slender stalks in a leafy inflorescence, with both disk and ray flowers, the disk flowers yellow to brown, the rays yellow and drooping, 1.5-2.5 cm long; involucral bracts in 2-3 series, linear, short-hairy, bent downward with age. **Fruit** a finely hairy, 4-5-angled achene, 1-2 mm long; pappus of several translucent, awn-tipped scales. July-Sept.—Wet meadows, shores, streambanks, marshes, fens, tamarack swamps.

Helenium autumnale

Helenium flexuosum Raf.

MAP 283
PURPLE-HEAD SNEEZEWEED   *introduced (naturalized)*

Fibrous-rooted perennial. **Stems** 2-10 dm tall, finely hairy, winged by the decurrent leaf-bases. **Leaves** smaller, less numerous, and more erect than in *H. autumnale*, entire or nearly so, densely glandular-dotted and also finely hairy, the lowermost oblong lance-shaped, commonly deciduous by flowering time, the others lance-shaped, sessile, not much reduced upwards except in the inflorescence, 3-12 cm long and 5-20 mm wide. **Heads** numerous, occasionally few or even solitary, in an open, leafy-bracteate inflorescence; involucral bracts lance-shaped, finely hairy, soon deflexed; rays yellow, sometimes tinged with purple at the base, 5-20 mm long, 3-lobed; disk purple or brownish purple, 6-14 mm wide, subglobose, a little more elongate than in *H. autumnale*. Pappus scales ovate or lance-shaped, awn-tipped. June-Oct.—Moist ground and waste places.

Helenium flexuosum

HELIANTHUS *Sunflower*

Large perennial herbs (annual in several species), with fibrous or fleshy roots and short to long rhizomes. Stems unbranched or branched above. Leaves usually opposite on lower part of stem and alternate above, lance-shaped, margins entire or with forward-pointing teeth; petioles present. Flower heads large, mostly 1 to several (rarely many), at ends of stems and branches, with yellow disk and ray flowers, the rays large and showy; involucre of several series of narrow, overlapping bracts; receptacle chaffy. Fruit a flattened achene; pappus of 2 deciduous, awn-tipped scales.

ADDITIONAL SPECIES & HYBRIDS

· *Helianthus nuttallii subsp. rydbergii* (Britt.) R.W. Long (Nuttall's sunflower); most similar to *H. grosseserratus*, but *H. nuttallii* has shorter petioles and smaller leaf blades, which are less than 4 cm wide; leaf margins of *H. nuttallii* usually entire or are only shallowly toothed. Rare in mesic to wet-mesic prairies; only verified Minn population at Foxhome Prairie in Wilkin County.

· Three *Helianthus* hybrids are reported for Minn: *H. × intermedius* R.W. Long, *H. × laetiflorus* Pers. (pro sp.), and *H. × luxurians* E.E. Wats. (pro sp.).

1 Plants annual; leaves mostly alternate; disk flowers red-purple to brown; receptacle flat or nearly so 2
   2 Involucral bracts lance-shaped, gradually tapered to a tip; chaff of receptacle bearded at tip with white hairs
      . . . . *H. petiolaris*
   2 Involucral bracts ovate, abruptly narrowed to a slender tip; chaff not with white hairs . . . . *H. annuus*
1 Plants perennial; leaves opposite or alternate; disk flowers yellow, or rarely red-brown or purple; receptacle convex to conical 3
   3 Disk flowers reddish-brown or yellow; stem leaves few to several, reduced in size upward on the stem . . . 4
      4 Disk flowers reddish brown; stems with more than 6 pairs of leaves, the leaves only gradually reduced in size upward on the stem . . . . *H. pauciflorus*
      4 Disk flowers yellow; stems with less than 6 pairs of leaves, greatly reduced in size upward on stem . . . . .
         . . . . *H. occidentalis*
   3 Disk flowers yellow; stem leaves numerous, well developed 5
      5 Stems glabrous or nearly so, sometimes glaucous; fine hairs may be present within the inflorescence . . 6

6 Stem leaves alternate, firm-textured, undersides pale and densely hairy . . . . *H. grosseserratus*

6 Leaves opposite, the undersides glabrous to finely hairy . . . . *H. strumosus*

  5 Stems pubescent 7

7 Leaves lance-shaped, less than 3.5 cm wide, mostly alternate 8

8 Leaves often somewhat folded along their midrib; stems pubescent, the hairs fine, white, and appressed . . . . *H. maximiliani*

8 Leaves not folded; stems pubescent, the hairs coarse and spreading . . . . *H. giganteus*

7 Leaves ovate, often more than 3.5 cm wide, the upper leaves opposite or alternate 9

9 Upper leaves alternate, tapered at base to a winged petiole more than 1.5 cm long; involucral bracts becoming dark with age, especially near their base . . . . *H. tuberosus*

9 Leaves opposite, tapered at base to an unwinged petiole less than 1.5 cm long; involucral bracts remaining green . . . . *H. hirsutus*

Helianthus annuus L.
COMMON SUNFLOWER

MAP 284
introduced (naturalized)

Coarse annual herb. **Stems** branching, more or less hirsute or hispid, 1-3 m tall, or much smaller and simpler in depauperate forms. **Leaves**, except the lowermost, chiefly alternate, ovate or broader, at least the lower ones cordate except in depauperate plants, acute to acuminate, mostly toothed, petiolate, scabrous on both sides. **Heads** mostly several or numerous, large, the disk 2 cm wide or more, smaller when depauperate; involucral bracts chiefly ovate or ovate-oblong and abruptly narrowed above the middle to the acuminate tip, occasionally narrower and more tapering, commonly more or less hispid or hirsute, and ciliate on the margins, sometimes merely shortly scabrous-hispid; disk red-purple (yellow in some cultivated forms); receptacle flat or nearly so, its bracts merely pubescent at the tip. July-Sept.—Prairies and dry places.

Helianthus giganteus L.
GIANT SUNFLOWER

MAP 285
native

Perennial herb, with short rhizomes and thick, fleshy roots. **Stems** 1-3 m long, often purple, with coarse hairs or sometimes nearly smooth, often branched in head. **Upper leaves** generally alternate, **lower leaves** opposite; lance-shaped, 6-20 cm long and 1-4 cm wide, base with 3 main veins, upper surface very rough-to-touch, underside with short, stiff hairs; margins toothed to more or less entire; petiole short or absent. **Flower heads** 3-6 cm wide, several to many, on long stalks in an open inflorescence; with yellow disk and ray flowers, the rays 1.5-3 cm long; involucral bracts narrow, awl-shaped, green or dark near base, hairy or margins fringed with hairs. **Fruit** a smooth achene; pappus of 2 awl-shaped scales. July-Sept.—Wet meadows, low prairie, sedge meadows, fens, floodplain forests, streambanks.

Helianthus grosseserratus Martens
SAWTOOTH SUNFLOWER

MAP 286
native

Perennial herb, with fleshy roots, spreading by rhizomes and forming colonies. **Stems** 1-3 m tall, short-hairy in head, smooth and often waxy below, purple or blue-green. **Upper leaves** alternate, **lower leaves** opposite; lance-shaped, 10-20 cm long and 2-5 cm wide, rough-to-touch on both sides, also densely short hairy on the paler underside; margins with coarse, forward-pointing teeth, upper leaves often entire; petioles 1-4 cm long. **Flower heads** 3-8 cm wide, several to many at ends of stems and branches; with yellow disk flowers and deep yellow ray

Helianthus annuus

Helianthus giganteus

282. *Helenium autumnale*

283. *Helenium flexuosum*

284. *Helianthus annuus*

285. *Helianthus giganteus*

flowers, the rays 2.5-4 cm long; involucral bracts narrowly lance-shaped, fringed with hairs and sometimes hairy on back. **Fruit** a smooth achene, 3-4 mm long; pappus of 2 lance-shaped scales. July-Oct.—Wet meadows, low prairie, streambanks, swamps, ditches, roadsides.

Helianthus hirsutus Raf.
MAP 287
HAIRY SUNFLOWER
native

Stems with coarse spreading hairs that are enlarged at the base, and often also with some shorter appressed hairs. **Leaves** ascending with short petioles mostly 5-15 mm long, occasionally subcordate at the base in robust plants, densely hairy beneath. Disk often 2 cm wide, the rays 10-15, 1.5-3.5 cm long. July-Oct.—Dry wooded or open places.

Helianthus maximiliani Schrad.
MAP 288
MAXIMILIAN SUNFLOWER
introduced (naturalized)

Perennial from short rhizomes and thickened, often fleshy roots. **Stems** 0.5-3 m tall, conspicuously pubescent, especially upwards, with mostly short, white, appressed hairs. **Leaves** lance-shaped, gradually narrowed to the short winged petiole, commonly 7-15 cm long and 1-3 cm wide, subentire or occasionally evidently toothed, pinnately veined, not 3-nerved, strongly scabrous on both sides, usually some of them falcate, the upper mostly alternate (all opposite in depauperate forms). **Heads** several or occasionally solitary, the disk 1.5-2.5 cm wide, yellow; involucral bracts narrow, often much exceeding the disk, canescent with short white hairs; rays 10-25, 1.5-4 cm long. June-Sept.—Prairies and waste ground, often in sandy soil.

Helianthus occidentalis Riddell
MAP 289
NAKED-STEMMED SUNFLOWER
native

Rhizomatous perennial. **Stems** 0.5-1.5 m tall, sparsely hairy, often becoming densely villous near the base. **Leaves** mostly opposite, 3-8 pairs below the inflorescence, the lower ones much the largest, long-petiolate; blades 3-nerved, ovate, to 15 cm long and 7 cm wide, entire or minutely and sparsely toothed, short-hairy on both sides or eventually nearly glabrous; middle and upper leaves reduced and distant, the stem often appearing almost naked. **Heads** solitary to numerous, generally few, the disk 1-1.5 cm wide, yellow; involucral bracts imbricate, lance-shaped, at least the inner with loose acuminate tips; rays about 10-20, 1-3 cm long. Aug-Oct.—Dry soil.

Helianthus pauciflorus Nutt.
MAP 290
STIFF SUNFLOWER
native

Perennial with well developed stout creeping rhizomes. **Stems** stout, 0.5-2 m tall, more or less scabrous or hispid to subglabrous. **Leaves** nearly all opposite, 9-15 pairs below the inflorescence (fewer in depauperate plants), lance-shaped, broadest below the middle, mostly 3-nerved, tapering to the short petioles, toothed or nearly entire, mostly 5-15 cm long and 1.5-6 cm wide, the middle ones seldom much smaller than the lowermost ones present at flowering time, scabrous on both sides. **Heads** several or solitary, the disk purple, rarely yellow, 1-2.5 cm wide; involucral bracts imbricate, appressed, ovate, conspicuously ciliolate, generally otherwise glabrous; rays commonly 15-20, about 1.5-3 cm long; pappus nearly always with some short bristles in addition to the 2 longer awns. Aug-Sept.—Dry prairies and plains.

Helianthus grosseserratus

Helianthus hirsutus

Helianthus pauciflorus

286. *Helianthus grosseserratus*

287. *Helianthus hirsutus*

288. *Helianthus maximiliani*

289. *Helianthus occidentalis*

Helianthus petiolaris Nutt.
PLAINS SUNFLOWER

MAP 291
native

Annual, similar to *H. annuus*, but smaller, seldom over 1 m tall, with narrower, more often entire, rarely cordate **leaves**, which may be more densely hairy beneath, and with smaller heads, the disk 1-2.5 cm wide. Involucral bracts lance-shaped, tapering gradually to the tip, shortly scabrous-hispid, seldom at all ciliate or with any long hairs. Central receptacle bracts conspicuously white-bearded at the tip. June-Sept.—Prairies, plains, and waste places.

Helianthus strumosus L.
PALE-LEAF WOODLAND SUNFLOWER

MAP 292
native

Perennial with rather woody roots and well developed rhizomes. **Stems** 1-2 m tall, short-hairy in the inflorescence, otherwise glabrous or with only a few scattered long hairs, often glaucous. **Leaves** opposite, or the uppermost alternate, broadly lance-shaped, 8-20 cm long and 2.5-9 cm wide, shallowly toothed or subentire, more or less abruptly contracted or sometimes broadly rounded at base, commonly with a short decurrence on the 6-30 mm petiole, scabrous-hispidulous above, some of the hairs with broad, white, slightly raised base (strumose), lower surface green and moderately short-hairy to nearly glabrous and glaucous, 3-nerved near the base, pinnately veined above. **Heads** several or solitary; disk yellow, 1-2 cm wide; involucral bracts lance-shaped, somewhat loose, especially the long acuminate tips, ciliolate on the margins; rays 8-15, 1.5-4 cm long. July-Sept.—Chiefly in woodlands.

Helianthus strumosus

Helianthus tuberosus L.
JERUSALEM-ARTICHOKE

MAP 293
native

Perennial with tuber-bearing rhizomes. **Stems** stout, 1-3 m tall, pubescent with mostly spreading hairs. **Leaves** alternate, or sometimes all but the uppermost opposite, broadly lance-shaped, 10-25 cm long and 4-12 cm wide, on winged petioles 2-8 cm long; margins serrate; densely and coarsely rough-hairy on the upper surface, sparsely to densely velvety-hairy on the lower surface, 3-nerved near the base, pinnately veined above. **Heads** usually several or numerous; disk 1.5-2.5 cm wide, yellow; involucral bracts usually rather dark, especially near the base, narrowly lance-shaped, loose especially above the middle, ciliate on the margins; rays 10-20, 2-4 cm long. Aug.-Oct.—Moist soil and waste places; native and also escaped from cultivation. *Cultivated since pre-Columbian times for its edible tubers.*

Helianthus tuberosus

HELIOPSIS *Sunflower-Everlasting*

Heliopsis helianthoides (L.) Sweet
SUNFLOWER-EVERLASTING

MAP 294
native

Short-lived perennial, generally with a short caudex and fibrous roots. **Stems** 5-15 dm tall, glabrous or more or less scabrous. **Leaves** opposite, ovate, serrate, often subtruncate at base, 5-15 cm long and 2.5-8 cm wide, borne on petioles about 5-35 mm long. **Heads** solitary or several, sometimes numerous, naked-pedunculate; radiate, the rays yellow, pistillate, fertile or rarely sterile, persistent on the achenes and becoming papery; receptacle conic, chaffy throughout, its bracts concave and clasping, subtending the rays as well as the disk-flowers; disk-flowers perfect and fertile; the disk about 1-2.5 cm wide; rays 8-15, pale yellow, 1.5-4 cm long. **Achenes**

Heliopsis helianthoides

290. *Helianthus pauciflorus*   291. *Helianthus petiolaris*   292. *Helianthus strumosus*   293. *Helianthus tuberosus*

quadrangular, glabrous; pappus none, or of a short irregular crown or a few teeth. June–Oct.—Dry woodlands, prairies, and waste places.

HETEROTHECA _Golden Aster_

Heterotheca villosa (Pursh) Shinners
HAIRY GOLDEN ASTER

MAP 295
native

  Chrysopsis villosa (Pursh) Nutt.

Perennial herb, pubescent throughout with long or short, appressed or spreading hairs. **Stems** several, 2–10 dm tall. **Leaves** numerous, nearly alike, oblong-elliptic to oblong lance-shaped, 2–7 cm long and 3–15 mm wide, entire or denticulate, the lower short-petiolate. **Heads** several, radiate, the rays yellow, pistillate and fertile; disk flowers yellow, disk 0.8–2.5 cm wide; receptacle flat or a little convex, naked; involucre strigose or hirsute and sometimes also glandular, the bracts commonly purple-tipped. **Achenes** narrowly obovate, 3–5-nerved; outer pappus of coarse bristles. July–Oct.—Dry, open, often sandy places.

Heterotheca villosa

ADDITIONAL SPECIES
Heterotheca stenophylla (A. Gray) Shinners (Stiff-leaf golden aster); Pipestone Co.

HIERACIUM _Hawkweed_

Fibrous-rooted perennial herbs with milky juice, with a rhizome which may be elongate or shortened into a caudex. Leaves alternate or all basal, entire or more or less toothed. Heads solitary to numerous, small or large, in a corymbiform or panicle-like inflorescence. Flowers all ligulate and perfect, yellow to red-orange. Involucre cylindric to hemispheric, its bracts imbricate. Achenes terete, mostly narrowed toward the base, truncate or occasionally narrowed toward the summit, strongly ribbed. Pappus of numerous whitish to brownish capillary bristles.

ADDITIONAL SPECIES
Two additional introduced _Hieracium_ species are reported for Minnesota:
• _Hieracium lachenalii_ K.C. Gmel.; Otter Tail and St. Louis counties.
• _Hieracium pilosella_ L.; Lake and St. Louis counties.

1 Plants with flowers on a naked stalk (scape); leaves clustered at base 2
  2 Flowers bright orange-red . . . . **_H. aurantiacum_**
  2 Flowers yellow 3
    3 Leaves glabrous, narrowly oblong lance-shaped; stolons absent . . . . **_H. piloselloides_**
    3 Leaves with tan or white hairs, oblong lance-shaped; stolons present, arching . . . . **_H. caespitosum_**
1 Flowers not with on a scape; leaves not clustered at base 4
  4 Leaves mostly basal, strongly reduced in size upwards, stems and leaves long-hairy; peduncles with yellow gland-tipped hairs . . . . **_H. longipilum_**
  4 Leaves mostly on stem; plants glabrous or hairy; peduncles various 5
    5 Leaves broadly elliptic, coarsely toothed, tapered to long, hairy petioles; stems glabrous . . . **_H. lachenalii_**
    5 Leaves various, petioles short or absent; stems glabrous or hairy 6
      6 Leaves spatula-shaped, lower leaves with petioles, upper leaves sessile; involucres and peduncles with black glands . . . . **_H. scabrum_**
      6 Leaves lance-shaped to oblong lance-shaped, sessile, toothed; involucres and peduncles without glands . . . . **_H. umbellatum_**

Hieracium aurantiacum L.
ORANGE KING-DEVIL; DEVIL'S-PAINTBRUSH

MAP 296
introduced (invasive)

Perennial with slender stolons and normally with a slender elongate rhizome, commonly 1–6 dm tall, the stem naked or with a single (rarely 2) more or less reduced leaf, conspicuously long-setose, also becoming stellate-tomentose and hispid with gland-tipped hairs above. **Basal leaves** oblong lance-shaped or narrowly elliptic, blunt, 4–20 cm long (including the petiole), 1–3.5 cm wide, long-setose on both sides, or nearly glabrous above; leaves of the stolons few, similar but much smaller. **Heads** 5–25 in a compact corymbiform inflorescence; flowers red-orange, becoming deeper red in drying; involucre 5–8 mm high, long-setose, hispid with blackish gland-tipped hairs. **Achenes** about 2 mm long; pappus slightly sordid. June–Sept.—Native of Europe; fields, roadsides, and meadows.

Hieracium aurantiacum

Hieracium caespitosum Dumort.

MAP 297
YELLOW KING-DEVIL; MEADOW HAWKWEED   *introduced (naturalized)*
    Hieracium pratense Tausch

Perennial with a short or more often elongate rhizome and commonly with short
stout stolons, the stem 2.5-9 dm tall, sparsely to rather densely long-setose,
becoming stellate-tomentose and hispid with blackish gland-tipped hairs above,
naked or with only one or two (rarely 3) reduced leaves. **Basal leaves** oblong lance-
shaped or narrowly elliptic, 4-25 cm long (including the petiole), 1-3 cm wide,
long-setose on both sides, sometimes sparsely so above, commonly slightly
stellate beneath. **Heads** several or rather numerous in a compact corymbiform
inflorescence, the involucre 6-8 mm high, hispid with blackish, gland-tipped
hairs, commonly also sparsely long-setose and slightly stellate. **Achenes** 1.5-2 mm
long; pappus slightly sordid. May-Sept.—Native of Europe; weedy in fields,
pastures, and along roadsides, occasionally in dry woods.

Hieracium caespitosum

Hieracium longipilum Torr.

MAP 298
HAIRY HAWKWEED   *native*

Perennial from a short stout caudex or crown. **Stems** mostly 6-20 dm tall, densely
long-hairy below, the hairs mostly 1 cm long or more, sometimes 2 cm, becoming
glabrous or nearly so above. **Leaves** pubescent like the stem, or the hairs shorter,
the basal and lower stem leaves rather numerous, oblong lance-shaped or narrowly
elliptic, 9-30 cm long, 1.5-4.5 cm wide, crowded, the lowest ones often deciduous,
the others progressively reduced upwards, the upper half of the stem commonly
naked or merely bracteate. **Inflorescence** elongate, cylindric, the branches and
peduncles stellate, long-stipitate-glandular and sometimes sparsely setose; heads
mostly 40-90-flowered; involucre 7-10 mm high, stellate-puberulent and hispid
with blackish, gland-tipped hairs. **Achenes** 3-4.5 mm long; pappus tawny. July-
Aug.—Dry prairies, open woodlands, and fields, especially in sandy soil.

Hieracium longipilum

Hieracium piloselloides Vill.

MAP 299
TALL HAWKWEED   *introduced (invasive)*
    Hieracium florentinum All.

Perennial from a usually rather short praemorse rhizome. **Stems** 2-10 dm tall,
naked or with 1 or 2, rarely as many as 5, reduced leaves. Herbage glaucous,
sparsely long-setose or subglabrous, the peduncles becoming stipitate-glandular
and somewhat stellate. **Basal leaves** oblong lance-shaped, mostly 3-18 cm long
(including the petiole) and 5-18 mm wide, 5-12 times as long as wide. **Heads**
mostly 3-75 in a corymbiform inflorescence, the involucre 6-8 mm high, hispid
with blackish, mostly gland-tipped hairs and somewhat stellate. **Achenes** 1.5-2
mm long; pappus slightly sordid. June-Sept.—Native of Europe; mostly in fields,
meadows, pastures, roadsides, and waste places.

Hieracium piloselloides

Hieracium scabrum Michx.

MAP 300
ROUGH HAWKWEED   *native*

Perennial from a short mostly simple caudex. **Stems** 2-14 dm tall, setose with
spreading hairs seldom as much as 5 mm long, at least near the base, becoming
stellate and glandular upwards, densely so in the inflorescence. **Leaves** sparsely
or moderately setose on both sides, more densely so on the petiole and midrib
beneath; basal and often also the lowermost stem leaves ordinarily deciduous,
the lower leaves oblong lance-shaped to elliptic, 5-20 cm long (including the

294. *Heliopsis helianthoides*

295. *Heterotheca villosa*

296. *Hieracium aurantiacum*

297. *Hieracium caespitosum*

usually short petiole), 1-4.5 cm wide, the others progressively reduced upwards, soon becoming sessile. **Inflorescence** open-corymbiform (especially in smaller specimens) to more elongate and cylindric; heads mostly 40-100-flowered; involucre 6-9 mm high, hispid with blackish mostly gland-tipped hairs, especially toward the base. **Achenes** 2-3 mm long; pappus tawny. July-Sept.—Open ground and dry woods, especially in sandy soil.

Hieracium umbellatum L.
NARROW-LEAF HAWKWEED
   Hieracium canadense Michx.
   Hieracium kalmii L.
   Hieracium scabriusculum Schwein.

MAP 301
native

Hieracium scabrum

Perennial from a short caudex. **Stems** 1.5-15 dm tall, often spreading-hairy below, sometimes stellate-puberulent above. **Leaves** stellate-puberulent to subglabrous, and often long-hairy beneath, the basal and lowermost stem ones small and soon deciduous, the others, except for the strongly reduced upper ones, mostly rather numerous, nearly alike in size and shape, sessile and tending to be broadly rounded and somewhat clasping at the base, elliptic to ovate, mostly 3-12 cm long and 7-40 mm wide, usually with a few irregularly spaced sharp teeth. **Inflorescence** loosely corymbiform to often umbel-like, or the heads occasionally solitary, the peduncles stellate-puberulent, occasionally with some longer spreading hairs as well; heads mostly 40-110-flowered; involucre 6-13 mm high, its bracts imbricate in several series, glabrous or obscurely puberulent, occasionally with a few longer hairs. **Achenes** 2.5-3.5 mm long; pappus tawny or yellowish. July-Sept.—Woodlands, beaches, and fields, especially in sandy soil.

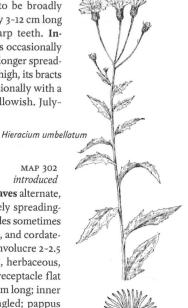
Hieracium umbellatum

INULA *Elecampane*

Inula helenium L.
ELECAMPANE

MAP 302
introduced

Coarse perennial herb. **Stems** to 2 m tall, finely spreading-hairy. **Leaves** alternate, irregularly and shallowly dentate, densely velvety beneath, sparsely spreading-hairy or subglabrous above, the lower long-petioled and elliptic; blades sometimes 5 dm long and 2 dm wide, the upper leaves becoming ovate, sessile, and cordate-clasping. **Heads** few, pedunculate, large, the disk 3-5 cm wide, the involucre 2-2.5 cm high, the bracts imbricate in several series; outer bracts broad, herbaceous, densely short-hairy; inner bracts narrow, subscarious, glabrous; receptacle flat or convex, naked. Outer flowers pistillate, with yellow rays over 1 cm long; inner flowers perfect, tubular, yellow. **Achenes** slender, glabrous, 4-angled; pappus bristles few to many. July-Aug.—Introduced from Europe; cultivated and escaped to fields and waste places where sometimes forming large colonies.

IVA *Marsh-Elder*

Iva xanthifolia Nutt.
CARELESSWEED
   Cyclachaena xanthiifolia (Nutt.) Fresen.

MAP 303
native

Coarse, branching annual weed. **Stems** 4-20 dm tall, the glabrous below, becoming viscid-villous in the inflorescence. **Leaves** opposite, except the upper, ovate, scaberulous above, paler and often finely hairy beneath, mostly 5-20 cm long and 2.5-15 cm wide, coarsely and often doubly serrate, long-petiolate.

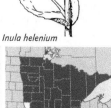
Inula helenium

298. *Hieracium longipilum*

299. *Hieracium piloselloides*

300. *Hieracium scabrum*

301. *Hieracium umbellatum*

Inflorescence large, panicle-like, the heads discoid, numerous, subsessile, not subtended by leaves; involucre viscid-hairy or subglabrous, about 1.5-3 mm high, the 5 herbaceous outer bracts larger than the 5 more membranous inner; corolla of the pistillate flowers nearly obsolete. **Achenes** glabrous or glandular, obovate, compressed; pappus none. Aug-Oct.—Bottomlands and moist waste places.

Iva xanthifolia

ADDITIONAL SPECIES
Iva axillaris Pursh, reported for Minn.

KRIGIA *Dwarf-Dandelion*

Krigia biflora (Walt.) Blake   MAP 304
ORANGE DWARF-DANDELION   *native*
Fibrous-rooted perennial, with milky juice. **Stems** 2-8 dm tall. Herbage glabrous, except often for some spreading glandular hairs under the heads, somewhat glaucous. **Basal leaves** oblong lance-shaped to elliptic, 3-25 cm long, including the petiole, 7-50 mm wide, entire or toothed to sometimes lobed or pirmatifid; **stem leaves** few, sessile and clasping, often much reduced, the uppermost often subopposite and with several long peduncles in their common axil. **Heads** several; flowers all ligulate and perfect, orange; involucre mostly 7-14 mm high, its bracts 9-18, narrow, becoming reflexed in age. **Achenes** nerved or ribbed, transversely rugulose; pappus of 20-35 fragile bristles and some short inconspicuous scales. May-Oct.—Woodlands, roadsides, and fields.

Krigia biflora

LACTUCA *Lettuce*

Annual, biennial, or perennial herbs with milky juice. Leaves alternate, entire to pinnatifid. Heads usually numerous in a panicle-like inflorescence. Flowers all ligulate and perfect, yellow, blue, or white, the corolla tube generally more than half as long as the ligule. Involucre cylindric, often broadening at the base in fruit, generally imbricate. Achenes compressed, winged or strongly nerved marginally, with 1-several lesser nerves on each face, expanded at the summit where the pappus is attached. Pappus of capillary bristles.

1   Achenes with one central nerve on each side 2
     2   Leaves with small spines on margins and underside midrib; involucre relatively large, 15-22 mm wide; achenes 7-10 mm long . . . . ***L. ludoviciana***
     2   Leaves without spines; involucre smaller, to 15 mm wide; achenes to 6 mm long . . . . ***L. canadensis***
1   Achenes with several prominent nerves on each face. 3
     3   Plants perennial, heads large, the involucre 15-20 mm wide; flowers blue or purple; leaves thickened, entire or with backward-pointing clefts, not sagittate . . . . ***L. pulchella***
     3   Plants annual or biennial; heads smaller; leaves various, sagittate in L. saligna 4
         4   Achene tipped by a slender beak as long as or longer than achene body . . . . ***L. serriola***
         4   Achene with a short beak, shorter than body, or the beak absent 5
             5   Leaves with petioles, the margins lobed; flowers blue; pappus white . . . . ***L. floridana***
             5   Leaves sessile, lower leaves lobed, upper entire; flowers pale blue to creamy white; pappus brown . . . . ***L. biennis***

Lactuca biennis (Moench) Fern.   MAP 305
TALL BLUE LETTUCE   *native*
Robust annual or biennial. **Stems** glabrous, 6-20 dm tall. **Leaves** glabrous, or hairy on the main veins beneath, sometimes sagittate at the base, commonly 10-40 cm

Lactuca biennis

302. *Inula helenium*

303. *Iva xanthifolia*

304. *Krigia biflora*

long and 4-20 cm wide. **Heads** numerous in an elongate, rather narrow, panicle-like inflorescence, often crowded, mostly 15-34-flowered (rarely to 54); fruiting involucre 10-14 mm high. **Achenes** 4-5.5 mm long, thin-edged, prominently several-nerved on each face, tapering to the beakless or shortly beaked tip; pappus light brown. July-Sept.—Moist places.

Lactuca canadensis L.
TALL LETTUCE

Annual, or usually biennial. **Stems** 3-25 dm tall, the herbage glabrous or occasionally coarsely hirsute, often more or less glaucous. **Leaves** entire or toothed to pinnately lobed, sagittate or sometimes narrowed to the base, mostly 10-35 cm long and 1.5-12 cm wide. **Heads** numerous, relatively small, mostly 13-22-flowered, flowers yellow; fruiting involucre mostly 10-15 mm long. **Achenes** blackish, very flat, with a median nerve on each face, rugulose, the body 3-4 mm long, beaked; pappus 5-7 mm long. July-Sept.—Fields, waste places, woods.

MAP 306
native

Lactuca canadensis

Lactuca floridana (L.) Gaertn.
WOODLAND LETTUCE
Robust annual or biennial. **Stems** 5-20 dm tall. **Leaves** mostly petiolate and not sagittate at the base, often hairy along the main veins beneath, otherwise glabrous or nearly so, toothed and often also pinnatifid, the blade mostly 8-30 cm long and 2.5-20 cm wide. **Heads** numerous in an ample panicle, mostly 11-17-flowered, the flowers blue or bluish, fruiting involucre 9-14 mm high. **Achenes** 4-6 mm long, narrowed upwards, with a stout beak or beakless, several-nerved on each face, thickened on the margins; pappus white. June-Sept.—Thickets, woodlands, and moist open places.

MAP 307
native

Lactuca floridana

Lactuca ludoviciana (Nutt.) Riddell
PRAIRIE LETTUCE
Lactuca campestris Greene
Biennial or possibly short-lived perennial. **Stems** glabrous, mostly 3-15 dm tall. **Leaves** prickly or coarsely hairy on the midrib and sometimes also on the main veins beneath, more or less prickly toothed on the margins, usually also pinnately lobed, commonly 7-30 cm long and 3-20 cm wide, reduced upwards. **Heads** relatively large, mostly 20-56-flowered, the flowers yellow, (rarely blue); involucre 15-22 mm long in fruit. **Achenes** strongly flattened, blackish, with a median nerve on each face, rugulose, 7-10 mm long, with a slender beak; pappus mostly 7-10 mm long at maturity. July-Sept.—Prairies and other open places.

MAP 308
native

Lactuca pulchella (Pursh) DC.
BLUE LETTUCE
Lactuca tatarica (L.) C.A. Mey. subsp. *pulchella*
Perennial from a deep-seated creeping root. **Stems** mostly 2-10 dm tall, glabrous, or slightly arachnoid when young. **Leaves** elongate, mostly 5-18 cm long and 6-35 mm wide, entire, or the lower ones commonly more or less pinnately lobed, often glaucous beneath, not sagittate. **Heads** several or numerous in a corymbiform or more elongate inflorescence, mostly 18-30-flowered, the flowers blue, very showy; involucre 15-20 mm high in fruit. **Achenes** 4-7 mm long, the slender body compressed, several-nerved on each face, tapering to the stout, often whitish beak. June-Sept.—Mostly in meadows, thickets, and other moist low places.

MAP 309
native

305. *Lactuca biennis*

306. *Lactuca canadensis*

307. *Lactuca floridana*

308. *Lactuca ludoviciana*

Lactuca serriola L.
PRICKLY LETTUCE
Lactuca scariola L.

MAP 310
introduced (naturalized)

Biennial or winter annual. **Stems** 3-15 dm tall, often prickly below, otherwise glabrous. **Leaves** prickly on the midrib beneath, and more finely prickly toothed on the margins, otherwise generally glabrous, pinnately lobed, commonly twisted at base to lie in a vertical position, sagittate-clasping, oblong or oblong lance-shaped in outline, mostly 5-30 cm long and 1-10 cm wide, the upper much reduced. **Heads** numerous in a long, often diffuse inflorescence, commonly 18-24-flowered (rarely 13-27), the flowers yellow, often drying blue; involucre 10-15 mm high in fruit. **Achenes** gray or yellowish gray, the body compressed, 3-4 mm long and a third as wide, prominently several-nerved on each face, spinulose above, at least marginally, the slender beak about equaling the body. July-Sept. —A weed in fields and waste places; native of Europe, naturalized throughout most of USA.

Lactuca serriola

LAPSANA *Nipplewort*

Lapsana communis L.
COMMON NIPPLEWORT

MAP 311
introduced (naturalized)

Branching annual herb with milky juice, hirsute to nearly glabrous. **Stems** 1.5-15 dm tall. **Leaves** alternate, thin, petiolate; blade ovate, toothed or occasionally basally lobed, 2.5-10 cm long and 2-7 cm wide, progressively less petiolate and narrowed upwards. **Heads** several or numerous in a corymbiform or panicle-like inflorescence, naked-pedunculate, mostly 8-15-flowered. **Flowers** all ligulate and perfect, yellow; involucre cylindric-campanulate, 5-8 mm high; bracts nearly equal, uniseriate, keeled. **Achenes** curved, narrowed to both ends, 3-5 mm long, glabrous; pappus none. June-Sept.—Native of Eurasia; now established in woods, fields, and waste ground.

Lapsana communis

LEUCANTHEMUM *Ox-Eye Daisy*

Leucanthemum vulgare Lam.
OX-EYE DAISY
Chrysanthemum leucanthemum L.

MAP 312
introduced (invasive)

Rhizomatous perennial. **Stems** 2-8 dm tall, simple or nearly so, glabrous or sparsely hairy. **Leaves** alternate, glabrous or hairy; basal leaves oblong lance-shaped or spatulate, petiolate, 4-15 cm long, crenate and often also lobed or cleft; stem leaves reduced and becoming sessile, pinnatifid or nearly entire. **Heads** hemispheric or flattened, solitary at the ends of the branches, naked-pedunculate, radiate; involucral bracts imbricate in 2-4 series, dry, scarious or hyaline at least at the margins and tips, the midrib sometimes greenish; receptacle flat or convex, naked; disk about 1-2 cm wide; rays about 15-30, white, 10-20 mm long; disk flowers tubular and perfect, the corolla with 4 or more commonly 5 lobes. **Achenes** terete, about 10-ribbed; pappus none. May-Oct.—Fields, roadsides, and waste places; native of Europe and Asia, naturalized throughout most of temperate North America.

Leucanthemum vulgare

309. Lactuca pulchella   *310. Lactuca serriola*   *311. Lapsana communis*   *312. Leucanthemum vulgare*

LIATRIS *Blazing Star; Gay Feather*

Perennial herbs, mostly with an evident corm, rarely from a more elongate caudex or stout rhizome. Leaves alternate, entire, more or less punctate, the basal ones usually the largest. Inflorescence spike-like. Heads discoid, the flowers all tubular and perfect, 3–100 or more in each head. Involucral bracts imbricate in several series. Receptacle naked. Corollas pink-purple or occasionally white. Achenes about 10-ribbed, pubescent. Pappus of 1 or 2 series of barbellate or plumose capillary bristles.

ADDITIONAL SPECIES

Liatris squarrosa (L.) Michx. (Scaly blazing star; Plains blazing star), native to central Great Plains and southeastward; reported from Sherburne National Wildlife Refuge, Sherburne County (where probably introduced in wildlife plantings).

1 Pappus bristles covered with short, stiff hairs less than 0.5 mm long 2
   2 Inflorescence a dense spike, heads with mostly 5-10 flowers; leaves mostly less than 1 cm wide . . . .
      . . . . *L. pycnostachya*
   2 Inflorescence an open spike or raceme; heads with 14 or more flowers; larger leaves 1-4 cm wide 3
      3 Heads with 30 or more flowers; terminal head distinctly larger than the others . . . . *L. ligulistylis*
      3 Heads with 14-35 flowers; heads similar in size . . . . *L. aspera*
1 Pappus bristles with softer feather-like hairs 0.5-1 mm long, the hairs with lateral branches 4
   4 Flowers 10-35 per head; corolla lobes coarsely hairy on inner surface . . . . *L. cylindracea*
   4 Flowers 4-6 per head; corolla lobes glabrous . . . . *L. punctata*

Liatris aspera Michx.

MAP 313

TALL GAYFEATHER   *native*

Plants 4-12 dm tall, the herbage short-hairy, or glabrous throughout. **Leaves** 25-90 below the inflorescence, the lowermost ones 5-40 cm long (including the long petiole) and 7-45 mm wide, the middle and upper ones gradually reduced and becoming sessile. **Heads** generally numerous in an elongate spiciform inflorescence, or the peduncles occasionally more elongate and to 5 cm long; terminal head not evidently enlarged; involucre 8-15 mm high, campanulate or subhemispheric, glabrous, its bracts loosely spreading, often purplish upwards, with conspicuous, lacerate, often crisped margins; flowers 16-35 in each head, the corolla hairy within toward the base; pappus barbellate. Aug-Oct.—Dry open places and thin woods, especially in sandy soil.

Liatris cylindracea Michx.

MAP 314

FEW-HEADED BLAZING STAR   *native*

Perennial from a well developed corm, 2-6 dm tall, glabrous or rarely short-hairy. **Leaves** more or less numerous, firm, linear or nearly so, the lowermost small and subsheathing, the next longer, mostly 10-25 cm long and 2-12 mm wide, the rest reduced upwards. **Heads** few or solitary, stiffly pedunculate or sessile; involucre 11-20 mm high, broadly cylindric, its bracts firm, appressed, generally broadly rounded and shortly mucronate, occasionally more tapering or without the mucro; **flowers** 10-35 in each head, the corolla lobes coarsely hairy within; pappus evidently plumose. July-Sept.—Dry open places.

Liatris ligulistylis (A. Nels.) K. Schum.

MAP 315

NORTHERN PLAINS BLAZING STAR   *native*

Plants 2-11 dm tall, glabrous below the inflorescence, or sometimes pubescent. **Leaves** 8-100 below the inflorescence, the lowermost ones 8-27 cm long and 5-40 mm wide, the others rather abruptly reduced and becoming sessile. **Heads** mostly 3-10, rarely solitary or to 35, evidently pedunculate to occasionally subsessile, the terminal one obviously the largest; involucre 13-20 mm high, broadly campanulate or hemispheric, glabrous, its bracts seldom much squarrose, with conspicuous, lacerate, scarious margins, seldom at all crisped, often purplish upwards; **flowers** mostly 30-100 in each head, the corolla glabrous within; pappus barbellate. Aug, Sept.—Mostly in damp low places, occasionally in drier soil.

Liatris aspera

Liatris punctata Hook.

MAP 316

DOTTED GAYFEATHER *native*

Perennial from a well developed corm, or a more elongate, thickened caudex, or even a stout horizontal rhizome, the stem glabrous, 1-8 dm tall. **Leaves** numerous, punctate, glabrous except for the often coarsely ciliate margin, linear or narrowly lance-shaped, the lowermost smaller than those just above and often deciduous. **Heads** several or numerous in a spiciform inflorescence, sessile or nearly so; involucre subcylindric, 10-18 mm high, its bracts punctate, mostly mucronate, commonly some of them more or less ciliate-margined; **flowers** mostly 4-6 in each head, the corolla lobes glabrous, the tube hairy toward the base within; pappus evidently plumose. July-September.—Dry open places, Sandy and gravelly prairies, roadsides.

Liatris pycnostachya Michx.

MAP 317

THICK-SPIKE BLAZING STAR *native*

Perennial from a woody corm or rootstock, 6-15 dm tall, more or less hirsute in the inflorescence or throughout. **Leaves** numerous, linear or nearly so, the lowermost ones 10-50 cm long and 3-13 mm wide, reduced upwards. **Heads** sessile, crowded in an elongate, densely spiciform inflorescence; involucre subcylindric or narrowly turbinate, 8-11 mm high, its bracts tapering to an acuminate, conspicuously squarrose tip, or the inner ones sometimes merely loosely erect; **flowers** mostly 5-7, or reputedly to 12, the corolla glabrous or nearly so within; pappus strongly barbellate. July-Sept.—Moist or dry prairies, open woods.

LYGODESMIA *Skeleton-Plant*

Lygodesmia juncea (Pursh) D. Don ex Hook.

MAP 318

RUSH SKELETON-PLANT *native*

Perennial herb with yellow milky juice, from a woody rhizome-bearing rootstock. **Stems** to 7 dm tall, erect or semidecumbent and arching upward, glabrous or glaucous, much branched from the base, often with numerous spherical galls, ca. l cm across, produced by solitary wasps, **Leaves** few, the lower leaves linear, usually shorter than 4 cm; **stem leaves** reduced to subulate scales. **Heads** numerous, terminal; involucre 1.3-1.6 cm long, cylindrical; principal involucral bracts 5-7, linear. subtended by about 3 series of short, linear bracts; florets mostly 5, ligulate and fertile, corolla pink to lavender or sometimes whitish. **Achenes** cylindrical, 6- 10 mm long. obscurely striate; pappus of numerous capillary bristles, 6-9 mm long. Jun-Sep.—Prairies, often where alkaline. *Seeds rarely produced; plants persisting via asexual means.*

Liatris pycnostachya

MATRICARIA *Mayweed*

Annual or perennial herbs. Leaves alternate, pinnatifid or pinnately dissected. Inflorescence corymbiform, terminating the branches. Heads radiate or discoid, the rays white, pistillate and usually fertile, or sometimes absent. Involucral bracts dry, 2-3-seriate, not much imbricate, with scarious or hyaline margins. Receptacle naked, hemispheric to more commonly conic, or elongate. Disk corollas yellow, 4-5-toothed. Achenes generally nerved on the margins and ventrally, nerveless dorsally. Pappus a short crown or none.

1 Heads with greenish disk flowers only; common . . . . *M. discoidea*
1 Heads with white rays; disk flowers yellow 2

313. *Liatris aspera*

314. *Liatris cylindracea*

315. *Liatris ligulistylis*

316. *Liatris punctata*

2   Receptacle hemispheric; achenes with wing-like ribs. . . . . **M. maritima**

2   Receptacle cone-shaped at maturity; achenes ribbed but these not enlarged and wing-like . . . **M. chamomilla**

Matricaria chamomilla L.
WILD CHAMOMILE
   Matricaria recutita L.

MAP 319
introduced

Glabrous branching aromatic annual about 2-8 dm tall. **Leaves** about 2-6 cm long, bipinnatifid, the ultimate segments linear or filiform. **Heads** numerous, the disk 6-10 mm wide; rays 10-20, white, 4-10 mm long; disk corollas 5-toothed; receptacle conic. **Achenes** with 2 nearly marginal and 3 ventral, raised but not at all wing-like ribs, smooth on the back and between the ribs; pappus a short crown or more commonly none. May-Sept.—Native of Europe and Asia, now on road-sides and in waste places; pollen causes allergies. *Similar to **Anthemis cotula**.*

Matricaria discoidea DC.
PINEAPPLE-WEED
   Matricaria matricarioides (Less.) Porter

MAP 320
native

Pineapple-scented glabrous annual. **Stems** leafy, branching, 5-40 cm tall. **Leaves** 1-5 cm long, 1-3x pinnatifid, the ultimate segments short, linear or filiform. **Heads** several or numerous, rayless, the disk about 5-9 mm wide; involucral bracts with broad hyaline margins; disk corollas 4-toothed; receptacle conic, pointed. **Achenes** with 2 marginal and 1 or several weak nerves; pappus a short crown. May-Sept.—Roadsides and waste places.

Matricaria maritima L.
SCENTLESS CHAMOMILE
   Chamomilla inodora (L.) Gilib.
   Tripleurospermum maritimum ssp. *inodorum* (L.) Appleq.
   Tripleurospermum perforata (Merat) M. Lainz

MAP 321
introduced

Matricaria discoidea

Annual, biennial, or occasionally perennial, nearly scentless herb 1-6 dm tall, glabrous or nearly so. **Leaves** 2-8 cm long, bipinnatifid, the ultimate segments mostly elongate, linear or linear-filiform. **Heads** several or numerous, the disk 8-15 mm wide; rays 12-25, white, 6-13 mm long; disk corollas 5-toothed; receptacle hemispheric, rounded. **Achenes** with 2 marginal and 1 ventral, thickened, almost wing-like ribs, minutely rugose on the back and between the ribs; pappus a short crown. July-Sept.—Native of Europe; established in roadsides and waste places.

NOTHOCALAIS *False Dandelion*

Nothocalais cuspidata (Pursh) Greene
FALSE DANDELION
   Agoseris cuspidata (Pursh) Raf.
   Microseris cuspidata (Pursh) Schultz-Bip.

MAP 322
native

Scapose, taprooted perennial with milky juice, 5-35 cm tall; the scape glabrous or often villous-tomentose upwards. **Leaves** crowded, entire to pinnatifid, narrow, 7-30 cm long and 3-20 mm wide, the margins lined with tiny hairs and often crinkled. **Flowers** all ligulate and perfect, on the ends of long naked peduncles; rays yellow, truncate at tips and with 5 teeth; disk flowers absent. Involucre 17-25 mm high, its bracts subequal or slightly imbricate, the inner and often also the outer long-acuminate. **Achenes** 8 mm long, strongly striate throughout, tapering slightly to the truncate beakless apex; pappus of numerous mixed capillary bristles

Nothocalais cuspidata

317. Liatris pycnostachya   *318. Lygodesmia juncea*   *319. Matricaria chamomilla*   *320. Matricaria discoidea*

and very slender, gradually attenuate scales. May-June.—Prairies, bluff tops, hillsides and other dry open places, often in gravelly soil. *The combination of leaves all basal and grasslike, and the yellow, blunt-tipped or fringed, ray flowers distinguish this species.*

ONOPORDUM *Scotch-Thistle*

Onopordum acanthium L.
SCOTCH-THISTLE

MAP 323
introduced

Coarse, branching, strongly spiny biennial. **Stems** 3-20 dm tall, broadly winged, the herbage sparsely to very densely tomentose. **Leaves** alternate, toothed and shallowly lobed, sessile and decurrent, or the lower petiolate, the blade 6-35 cm long and 3-20 cm wide. **Heads** discoid, the flowers all tubular and perfect, solitary at the ends of the branches or sometimes clustered, 2.5-5 cm wide; involucre globose, the involucral bracts all tapering to a spine-tip; corollas purple to violet or white. **Achenes** glabrous, 4-5 mm long, slightly compressed, rugulose; pappus of numerous reddish bristles, deciduous in a ring. July-Oct.—Native of Europe and e Asia; waste places; known from Pipestone and Rock counties but probably not persisting in the flora.

Onopordum acanthium

PACKERA *Groundsel*

Erect perennial, biennial, or annual herbs. Leaves alternate or from base of plant, stalked near base, stalkless and usually smaller upward. Flower heads with both disk and ray flowers, few to many in clusters at ends of stems; disk flowers perfect and yellow, the rays yellow; involucral bracts in 1 series and not overlapping, of equal lengths; receptacle flat or convex, not chaffy. Fruit an achene, nearly round in section; pappus of slender bristles.

ADDITIONAL SPECIES
• *Packera cana* (Hook.) W.A. Weber & A. Löve (Woolly groundsel); se range limit in Polk Co. (🖤*endangered*).
• *Packera pauciflora* (Pursh) A. Löve & D. Löve (Alpine groundsel), native to w North America and n Canada; Cook and Lake counties.

1 Plants with persistent covering of dense woolly hairs, especially on stem and leaf undersides . . . . . *P. plattensis*
1 Plants not persistently woolly hairy, except sometimes in leaf axils 2
  2 Heads with disk flowers only; Apostle Islands . . . . *P. indecora*
  2 Heads with both ray and disk flowers 3
    3 Basal leaves mostly oblong lance-shaped or elliptic, tapered at base to petiole . . . . *P. paupercula*
    3 Basal leaves ovate or heart-shaped 4
      4 Basal leaves heart-shaped at base. . . . . *P. aurea*
      4 Basal leaves ovate. . . . . *P. pseudaurea*

Packera aurea (L.) Á. & D.Löve
HEART-LEAVED GROUNDSEL
  Senecio aureus L.

MAP 324
native

Perennial herb, from a spreading crown or rhizome. **Stems** single or clumped, 3-8 dm long, slightly hairy when young, soon becoming smooth. **Basal leaves** heart-shaped, 5-10 cm long and to as wide, often purple-tinged, on long petioles, the margins with rounded teeth; **stem leaves** much smaller and more or less pinnately lobed, becoming sessile. **Flower heads** several to many, the disk 5-10 mm wide, rays gold-yellow, 6-13 mm long involucre 5-8 mm high, the involucral

321. *Matricaria maritima*

322. *Nothocalais cuspidata*

323. *Onopordum acanthium*

324. *Packera aurea*

bracts often purple-tipped. **Fruit** a smooth achene; pappus of slender white bristles. May–July.—Floodplain forests, wet forest depressions, swamp openings and hummocks, sedge meadows, thickets, fens, ditches. *Leaves and roots possibly toxic to humans, fatal if eaten by horses or cattle.*

Packera indecora (Greene) Á. & D.Löve
RAYLESS MOUNTAIN GROUNDSEL
Senecio indecorus Greene

NC MAP 325
❦ *endangered | native*

Fibrous-rooted perennial with a simple or slightly branched crown. Herbage glabrous or soon glabrate except sometimes for sparse tomentum in the axils. **Stems** 3-8 dm tall. **Leaves** relatively thin, the basal ones elliptic or broadly ovate, tapering or subtruncate at the base, serrate, evidently petiolate, the blade to 6 cm long and 4 cm wide; **stem leaves** sharply incised, the lobes irregularly again few-toothed, reduced and becoming sessile upwards. **Heads** mostly 6-40, rarely fewer, yellow, discoid or rarely with short rays; involucre mostly 7-10 mm high, its bracts often purple-tipped. **Achenes** glabrous. July–Aug.—Rare in moist woodlands, streambanks, swales, and bogs.

Packera paupercula (Pursh) Á. & D.Löve
RAYLESS ALPINE GROUNDSEL
Senecio pauperculus Michx.

MAP 326
native

Fibrous-rooted perennial with a short, simple or slightly branched crown, occasionally also with very short slender stolons. **Stems** 1-5 dm tall, the herbage lightly floccose-tomentose when young, generally soon glabrate, except frequently at the very base and in the leaf-axils. **Basal leaves** mostly oblong lance-shaped to elliptic, occasionally suborbicular, generally tapering to the petiolar base, crenate or serrate to subentire, seldom over 12 cm long and 2 cm wide, generally much smaller; **stem leaves** more or less pinnatifid, the lower sometimes larger than the basal, the others reduced and becoming sessile. **Heads** relatively few, seldom more than 20, the disk 5-12 mm wide; involucre 4-7 mm high, its bracts carinate-thickened or thin and flat, often purple-tipped; rays 5-10 mm long, yellow, rarely wanting. **Achenes** glabrous or hispidulous. May–July.—Meadows, prairies, streambanks, beaches, and cliffs.

Packera aurea

Packera plattensis (Nutt.) W.A. Weber & Á. Löve
PRAIRIE GROUNDSEL
Senecio plattensis Nutt.

MAP 327
native

Perennial with a short caudex and fibrous roots, sometimes also stoloniferous. **Stems** about 2-7 dm tall. Herbage more or less persistently floccose-tomentose until flowering time or later, at least on the stems, lower leaf-surfaces, and involucres. **Basal leaves** elliptic or ovate to suborbicular, tapering or abruptly contracted to the petiole or petiolar base, crenate-serrate, or some of them more deeply lobed, the blade and petiole sometimes as much as 10 cm long and 3 cm wide, generally much smaller; **stem leaves** conspicuously reduced upwards, becoming sessile, more or less pinnatifid. **Heads** several or rather numerous, the disk 6-12 mm wide; involucre 4-6 mm high. **Achenes** generally hispidulous. May–July.—Mostly in dry open places. *Leaves and roots possibly toxic to humans, fatal if eaten by horses or cattle.*

Packera paupercula

325. *Packera indecora*

326. *Packera paupercula*

327. *Packera plattensis*

328. *Packera pseudaurea*

Packera pseudaurea (Rydb.) W.A. Weber & Á. & D.Löve　　　MAP 328
WESTERN HEART-LEAVED GROUNDSEL　　　　　　　　　*native*
　　Senecio pseudaureus Rydb.
Perennial herb, from a crown or short rhizome. **Stems** single or few, solid, 2-5 dm
long, smooth or with tufts of woolly hairs in leaf axils when young. **Basal leaves**
ovate to oval, 2-4 cm long and 1-2 cm wide, underside often purple, margins with
rounded teeth, petioles long and slender; **stem leaves** 2-6 cm long and 0.5-2 cm
wide, pinnately cleft at least near base, stalkless and often clasping. **Flower heads**
1-1.5 cm wide, few to many in a single cluster; with both disk and ray flowers, the
rays pale yellow, 6-10 mm long; involucre 4-7 mm high, the involucral bracts green.
Achenes smooth, 1-2 mm long; pappus of white bristles. May-July.—Wet
meadows, low prairie, fens. *Ours var. semicordata (Mack. & Bush) Trock &
T.M.Barkley.*

Packera pseudaurea

PARTHENIUM　*Feverfew*

Parthenium integrifolium L.　　　　　　　　　　MAP 329
EASTERN PARTHENIUM; WILD QUININE　　　　🖝*endangered* | *native*
Perennial from a tuberous-thickened, usually short root. **Stems** simple or
branched above, finely hairy, 5-10 dm tall. **Leaves** alternate, large and sometimes
few, crenate-serrate, scabrous to nearly glabrous above, or sometimes hirsute
along the midrib and main veins, sparsely scaberulous beneath, the basal long-
petiolate, with ovate blades 7-20 cm long and 4-10 cm wide; **stem leaves** with
progressively shorter petioles and more or less reduced, the upper leaves often
sessile and clasping. **Heads** radiate, several or numerous in a flat-topped or slightly
rounded inflorescence; involucre of 2-4 series of imbricate dry bracts, the disk
4-7 mm wide; rays scarcely 2 mm long, white or whitish. **Achenes** obovate, black,
3 mm long, their subtending bracts joined at base to the 2 or 3 adjacent
receptacular bracts and partly enclosing the achene, the whole falling as a unit.
June-Sept.—Rare in prairies, dry woods, roadsides, and along railroads. *Minn at
northwestern edge of species' range.*

Parthenium integrifolium

PETASITES　*Sweet Colt's-Foot*

Perennial herbs, spreading by rhizomes. Leaves mostly from base of plant on long petioles,
arrowhead-shaped or palmately lobed, with white woolly hairs on underside; stem leaves alternate,
reduced to bracts. Flowering before or as leaves expand in spring, the heads white, the flowers mostly
staminate and pistillate and on different plants, the heads sometimes with both staminate and pistillate
flowers, the staminate heads usually with disk flowers only, the pistillate heads with all disk flowers
or sometimes with short rays; several to many in the inflorescence; involucral bracts in a single series;
receptacle not chaffy. Fruit a linear, ribbed achene; pappus of many white, slender bristles.

1　Leaf blades palmately lobed . . . . *P. frigidus*
1　Leaf blades arrowhead-shaped, toothed and not lobed . . . . *P. sagittatus*

Petasites frigidus (L.) Fries　　　　　　　　　　MAP 330
NORTHERN SWEET COLT'S-FOOT　　　　　　　　　*native*
　　Petasites palmatus (Ait.) Gray
Perennial herb, spreading by rhizomes. **Stems** 1-6 dm long, smooth or short-hairy
in the head. **Leaves** mostly from base of plant, triangular to nearly round in
outline, palmately lobed, 5-30 cm wide, upper surface green and smooth,
underside densely white-hairy, sometimes becoming smooth with age; margins
coarsely toothed; petioles of basal leaves 1-3 dm long; stem leaves small and
bractlike, 2-6 cm long. **Flower heads** nearly white, staminate and pistillate flowers
mostly on separate plants; rays of pistillate heads to 7 mm long, involucre 4-9
mm high. **Fruit** a narrow achene; pappus of many slender bristles. May-June.
—Wet conifer forests and swamps, wet trails and clearings, aspen woods.

Petasites frigidus

Petasites sagittatus (Banks) Gray
ARROW-LEAF SWEET COLT'S-FOOT
Petasites frigidus var. *sagittatus* (Banks ex Pursh) Cherniawsky

MAP 331
native

Perennial herb. **Stems** 3-6 dm tall, sparsely covered with woolly white hairs. **Leaves** mostly from base of plant, arrowhead-shaped, 10-30 cm long and 3-30 cm wide, upper surface smooth to sparsely hairy, densely white hairy below; margins wavy with outward-pointing teeth; petioles 1-3 dm long; the stem leaves reduced in size. **Flower heads** more or less white; rays of pistillate heads 8-9 mm long. **Fruit** a linear achene; pappus of slender bristles. May–June.—Wet meadows, marshes, sedge meadows, open swamps. *Now often treated as a variety of P. frigidus.*

Petasites sagittatus

POLYMNIA *Leafcup*

Polymnia canadensis L.
WHITE-FLOWER LEAFCUP
Polymnia radiata (Gray) Small

MAP 332
native

Coarse perennial herb. **Stems** about 6-15 dm tall, glabrous or nearly so below, becoming viscid-villous or stipitate-glandular above. **Leaves** opposite (or the upper alternate), to 3 dm long, broadly oblong to ovate in outline, pinnately few-lobed, margins dentate or denticulate, the petiole wingless, or winged only near the blade. **Heads** several or numerous in congested cymes at the ends of the branches; disk 6-13 mm wide; receptacle flat or nearly so, chaffy throughout; involucre a single series of green bracts; corolla of the pistillate flowers minute and tubular, or expanded into a short whitish ray which sometimes becomes 10 or 12 mm long. **Achenes** glabrous, 3-ribbed and 3-angled, not striate; pappus none. June–Oct.—Moist woodlands.

Polymnia canadensis

PRENANTHES *Rattlesnake-Root*

Perennial herbs with milky juice and tuberous-thickened roots. Leaves alternate. Inflorescence corymbiform or panicle-like to thyrsoid, the heads in most species nodding. Flowers all ligulate and perfect, pink or purple to white, cream-color, or pale yellow. Involucre of 4-15 principal bracts and several much reduced outer ones, or the outer occasionally better developed and almost passing into the inner. Achenes elongate, cylindric or slightly tapering to the summit, glabrous, mostly reddish brown, in our species ribbed-striate. Pappus of numerous deciduous capillary bristles. *Our species sometimes placed in genus **Nabalus**.*

1 Inflorescence an open panicle; lower leaves on long petioles, broadly ovate to triangular ....*P. alba*
1 Inflorescence a narrow raceme-like panicle; lower leaves spatula-shaped, gradually narrowed to petiole......2
  2 Flowers purplish to white; stem and leaves glabrous ....*P. racemosa*
  2 Flowers creamy-yellow; stem and leaf undersides rough-hairy ....*P. aspera*

Prenanthes alba L.
WHITE RATTLESNAKE-ROOT

MAP 333
native

Perennial herb. **Stems** stout, commonly 4-15 dm tall, the herbage more or less glaucous. **Leaves** glabrous above, paler and often hairy beneath, very variable in size and shape, the lower ones long-petioled, palmately few-lobed to sagittate and merely coarsely toothed, becoming smaller, less cut, and less petiolate upwards, the upper leaves often entire. **Inflorescence** elongate panicle-like, the heads nodding, 10-15-flowered, the flowers fragrant, greenish or yellowish white;

involucre 11-14 mm long, generally somewhat purplish, its principal bracts 8, glabrous, but more or less densely papillate with white, waxy-appearing cells; pappus cinnamon-brown. Aug-Sept.—Woodlands.

Prenanthes aspera Michx.

MAP 334
ROUGH RATTLESNAKE-ROOT   *native*

Perennial herb. **Stems** 7-15 dm tall, rough-hairy at least above. **Leaves** scabrous or coarsely hirsute on the lower and often also the upper surface, dentate or serrate to entire, the lower well developed, somewhat obovate, tapering to the petiole, but soon deciduous, the others sessile or nearly so and often clasping, narrowly to broadly oblong or elliptic, or lance-shaped, gradually reduced upwards, the larger commonly 4-10 cm long and 1-4 cm wide. **Inflorescence** narrow and elongate, thyrsoid, the heads crowded, mostly rather weakly ascending, but scarcely nodding, 11-14-flowered (mostly 13), the flowers creamy; involucre 12-17 mm long, coarsely and usually densely hairy, its principal bracts 8; pappus sordid or stramineous. Aug-Oct.—Dry prairies, generally on lower slopes.

Prenanthes racemosa Michx.

MAP 335
GLAUCOUS WHITE LETTUCE   *native*

Perennial herb. **Stems** slender, erect, ridged, 4-18 dm tall, smooth and somewhat waxy, hairy in the head. **Leaves** thick, smooth and waxy; lower leaves oval to obovate, 10-20 cm long and 2-10 cm wide; margins shallowly toothed; petioles long and winged; stem leaves becoming smaller upwards, stalkless and partly clasping the stem. **Flower heads** many in a narrow, elongate inflorescence, of ray flowers only, pink or purplish; involucre 9-14 mm high, purple-black, long-hairy. **Achenes** linear; pappus of straw-colored bristles. Aug-Sept.—Sandy or gravelly shores, streambanks, wet meadows, low prairie, fens.

Prenanthes alba

PSEUDOGNAPHALIUM *Rabbit-Tobacco*

Biennial glandular herbs (ours), sometimes aromatic. Stems usually erect, woolly-tomentose, sometimes glandular. Leaves basal and along the stem or mostly cauline, alternate, usually sessile; blades mostly narrowly lance-shaped, bases often clasping the stem, margins entire. Inflorescence corymbiform or panicle-like, sometimes a terminal cluster; heads disciform. Corollas yellowish. Fruit a glabrous achene. Pappus of 10-12 barbellate bristles.

1 Leaves decurrent at base; stems glandular-hairy . . . . *P. macounii*
1 Leaves not decurrent at base; stems woolly hairy, not glandular except sometimes near base . . . . *P. obtusifolium*

Pseudognaphalium macounii (Greene) Kartesz

MAP 336
CLAMMY RABBIT-TOBACCO   *native*
Gnaphalium macounii Greene

Similar to *P. obtusifolium*. **Stems** glandular-hairy, becoming woolly in the inflorescence, rarely somewhat woolly to near the base, as well as glandular. **Leaves** distinctly decurrent at the base, the upper surface glandular-hairy, the lower surface usually woolly, or sometimes glandular-hairy. July-Sept.—Open places.

Pseudognaphalium obtusifolium (L.) Hilliard & Burtt

MAP 337
FRAGRANT RABBIT-TOBACCO   *native*
Gnaphalium obtusifolium L.

Annual or perhaps sometimes biennial, fragrant, 1-8 dm tall, erect. **Stems** thinly

333. Prenanthes alba   *334. Prenanthes aspera*   *335. Prenanthes racemosa*   *Pseudognaphalium obtusifolium*

white-woolly, commonly becoming subglabrous or sometimes a little glandular toward the base. **Leaves** numerous, linear lance-shaped, up to about 10 cm long and 1 cm wide, sessile, white-woolly beneath, green and from glabrous to slightly glandular or slightly woolly above. **Inflorescence** branched and many-headed except in depauperate plants, flat or round-topped and often elongate, the final clusters with the heads somewhat glomerate. Involucre yellowish white or somewhat dingy, campanulate, woolly only near the base, 5-7 mm high; pappus bristles distinct, falling separately. **Achenes** glabrous. July-Oct.—Open, often sandy places. *When crushed, plants have a characteristic maple syrup scent.*

RATIBIDA *Coneflower*

Perennial herbs (ours). Leaves alternate, pinnatifid. Heads naked-pedunculate, radiate, the rays neutral, yellow or sometimes purple. Involucre a single series of green, subherbaceous, linear or lance-linear bracts. Receptacle columnar, its chaffy bracts subtending the rays as well as the disk-flowers more or less clasping the achenes. Disk-flowers perfect and fertile, their corollas short, cylindric, scarcely narrowed at the base. Achenes compressed at right angles to the involucral bracts, often also evidently quadrangular, glabrous except for the sometimes ciliate margins. Pappus with 1 or 2 prolonged awn-like teeth, or of awn-teeth only, or absent.

1 Disk columnar, 2-4 times longer than wide; plants taprooted . . . . *R. columnifera*
1 Disk less than 2 times longer than wide; plants fibrous-rooted . . . . *R. pinnata*

Ratibida columnifera (Nutt.) Woot. & Standl.
COLUMNAR CONEFLOWER

MAP 338
introduced

Perennial with a taproot and short caudex. **Stems** usually several, branching 3-12 dm tall, coarsely strigose. **Leaves** strigose or shortly hirsute, the segments linear or lance-shaped, entire or nearly so. **Heads** several or numerous, the disk columnar, dark, mostly 1.5-4 cm long and one-fourth to half as wide; rays about 3-7, yellow, or partly or wholly purple, 1.5-3 cm long, spreading or reflexed. Style-appendages short and blunt. **Achenes** ciliate and usually slightly winged on the inner margin; pappus an evident awn-tooth on the inner angle of the achene, often also with a shorter one on the outer angle. June-Aug.—Prairies and waste ground; also along railroads.

Ratibida pinnata (Vent.) Barnh.
GLOBULAR CONEFLOWER

MAP 339
native

Perennial from a stout woody rhizome or sometimes a short caudex. **Stems** mostly 4-12 dm tall, strigose above, strigose or more commonly spreading-hirsute below. **Leaves** loosely hirsute, the segments lance-shaped, coarsely toothed to entire. **Heads** several or occasionally solitary, the disk about 12-20 mm high and 0.6-0.9 times as thick, much shorter than the rays; rays about 5-10, pale yellow, mostly 2.5-6 cm long, spreading or reflexed; style-appendages elongate, acuminate. **Achenes** smooth; pappus none. June-Aug.—Prairies and dry woods.

Ratibida pinnata

RUDBECKIA *Coneflower*

Perennial herbs. Stems and leaves rough-hairy. Leaves alternate. Flower heads with both disk and ray flowers, the rays yellow to orange; involucral bracts green, overlapping; receptacle rounded, chaffy. Fruit a smooth, 4-angled achene; pappus none or a short crown. *The genus includes the well-known black-eyed Susan (Rudbeckia hirta), widespread on dry sites.*

336. *Pseudognaphalium macounii*   337. *Pseudognaph. obtusifolium*   338. *Ratibida columnifera*   339. *Ratibida pinnata*

1   Main leaves deeply lobed 2
   2   Disk yellow; stems glabrous or nearly so; largest leaves 5-7 lobed . . . . ***R. laciniata***
   2   Disk dark purple-red; stems pubescent; largest leaves 3-lobed 3
      3   Rays usually orange at base; chaff of receptacle tapered to a sharp point, glabrous . . . . ***R. triloba***
      3   Rays yellow; chaff rounded at tip and with fine glandular hairs at apex . . . . ***R. subtomentosa***
1   Leaves unlobed. 4
   4   Leaves ovate, margins toothed; chaff of receptacle glabrous, tapered to a sharp prolonged point . . ***R. triloba***
   4   Leaves and margins various; chaff of receptacle not tapered to a sharp point . . . . ***R. hirta***

Rudbeckia hirta L.

BLACK-EYED SUSAN

MAP 340

native

Biennial or short-lived perennial, sometimes flowering the first year. **Stems** 3-10 dm tall, more or less hirsute throughout. **Leaves** variable in size and shape, toothed or subentire, the basal and lower stem leaves mostly oblong lance-shaped to elliptic and long-petiolate, the others lance-linear to oblong or ovate, mostly sessile. **Heads** several or solitary, mostly long-pedunculate, the disk hemispheric or ovoid, 12-20 mm wide, dark purple or brown, rarely yellow; involucral bracts copiously hirsute, nearly equal, green, spreading, sometimes elongate and equaling the rays; rays about 8-20, orange or orange-yellow, sometimes darker or marked with purple near the base, commonly 2-4 cm long; receptacular bracts more or less hispid near the tip, often also ciliate on the margins. **Achenes** quadrangular; pappus none. June-Oct.—Various habitats, chiefly in disturbed or waste places and roadsides.

Rudbeckia hirta

Rudbeckia laciniata L.

CUTLEAF CONEFLOWER

MAP 341

native

Perennial herb, from a woody base. **Stems** branched, 5-30 cm tall, smooth and often waxy. **Leaves** alternate, to 30 cm wide, deeply lobed, nearly smooth to hairy on underside; margins coarsely toothed as well as lobed, or entire on upper leaves; petioles long on lower leaves, becoming short above. **Flower heads** several to many at ends of stems, with both disk and ray flowers, disk flowers green-yellow, rays lemon-yellow, drooping, 3-6 cm long; involucral bracts of unequal lengths; receptacle round at first, becoming cylindric. **Fruit** a 4-angled achene; pappus a short toothed crown. July-Sept.—Floodplain forests, swamps, streambanks, thickets, ditches; usually in partial or full shade.

Rudbeckia laciniata

Rudbeckia subtomentosa Pursh

SWEET CONEFLOWER

(NO MAP)

native

Perennial from a stout woody rhizome. **Stems** mostly 6-20 dm tall, glabrous below, densely pubescent above with short usually spreading hairs. **Leaves** firm, densely pubescent on both sides with short loosely spreading hairs, ovate to sometimes lance-elliptic, petiolate, serrate, some of the larger ones deeply 3-lobed. **Heads** several, the disk dark purple or brown, about 8-16 mm wide; involucral bracts narrow, spreading or reflexed, nearly equal, green, more or less canescent-strigose; rays about 12-20, yellow, 2-4 cm long; receptacular bracts obtuse or acutish, canescent near the tip with short white hairs. **Achenes** quadrangular; pappus a minute crown. July-Sept.—Prairies and low ground; in Minn, known from railway in Mower County.

Rudbeckia triloba L.

THREE-LOBED CONEFLOWER

MAP 342

👎*threatened | native*

Short-lived perennial. **Stems** mostly 5-15 dm tall, moderately spreading-hirsute to subglabrous. **Leaves** thin, sharply toothed to subentire, moderately appressed hairy or nearly glabrous, the basal leaves broadly ovate or subcordate and long-petiolate, the stem leaves mostly narrower and short-petiolate or sessile, usually some of the larger leaves deeply 3-lobed. **Heads** several or numerous, the disk dark purple, hemispheric or ovoid, 8-15 mm wide; involucral bracts narrow, nearly equal, green and more or less leafy, spreading or reflexed, mostly strigose and ciliate-margined; rays 6-12, yellow, or partly or wholly orange, 1-3 cm long; receptacular bracts glabrous, equaling or usually a little exceeding the disk corollas, abruptly narrowed to a distinct awn-point. **Achenes** equably

Rudbeckia triloba

quadrangular; pappus a minute crown. July-Oct.—Woodlands and moist soil. *Our form is var. triloba, with the larger leaves merely 3-lobed.*

SENECIO *Groundsel; Ragwort*

Erect annual herbs (ours). Leaves alternate or from base of plant, stalked near base, stalkless and usually smaller upward. Flower heads with both disk and ray flowers, few to many in clusters at ends of stems; disk flowers perfect and yellow, the rays yellow; involucral bracts in 1 series and not overlapping, of equal lengths; receptacle flat or convex, not chaffy. Fruit an achene, nearly round in section; pappus of slender bristles. *Several former members of this genus now placed in* **Packera.**

ADDITIONAL SPECIES
Senecio viscosus L. (Sticky ragwort), introduced, St. Louis County.

1   Annual herb; leaves about equally distributed on the stem . . . . *S. vulgaris*
1   Biennial or perennial herb; leaves progressively reduced in size upward on the stem . . . . *S. integerrimus*

Senecio integerrimus Nutt.   MAP 343
LAMB'S-TONGUE RAGWORT   *native*

Biennial or perennial herb, arachnoid villous with crisp jointed hairs when young, usually glabrate in age but with hairs remaining in and near the axils of the leaves and among the heads. **Stems** single, 2-7 dm tall from a short, buttonlike caudex with numerous fleshy, fibrous roots. **Basal and lowermost stem leaves** entire to irregularly dentate, lanceolate, petiolate or with the blade tapering to a broadly winged petiole; the petiole, when distinct, about equaling the blade; **upper stem leaves** strongly and progressively reduced, becoming mere bracts upwards. **Inflorescence** a corymbiform cyme of usually 6-20 heads, central terminal head often on a distinctly shortened peduncle; involucral bracts 7-15 mm long, often with small, faint black tips; ray florets ca. 13 or 8, the ligule 6-15 mm long, or sometimes ray florets absent. **Achenes** glabrous. May-June.—Moist, grassy prairies.

Senecio vulgaris L.   MAP 344
OLD-MAN-IN-THE-SPRING   *introduced*

Simple or strongly branched annual herb with a more or less evident taproot. **Stems** 1-4 dm tall, leafy throughout; herbage sparsely crisp-hairy or subglabrous. **Leaves** coarsely and irregularly toothed or more often pinnatifid, 2-10 cm long and 5-45 mm wide, the lower tapering to the petiole, the upper sessile and clasping. **Heads** several or numerous, strictly discoid, the flowers all tubular and perfect; disk usually 5-10 mm wide; involucre about 5-8 mm high; bracteoles well developed, black-tipped; pappus very copious, equaling or generally surpassing the corollas. **Achenes** strigillose, chiefly along the angles. May-Oct.—Native of the Old World; now in waste places. *Leaves and roots possibly toxic to humans, fatal if eaten by horses or cattle.*

Senecio vulgaris

SHINNERSOSERIS *Beaked Skeleton-Weed*

Shinnersoseris rostrata (A. Gray) Tomb   (NO MAP)
BEAKED SKELETON-WEED   *threatened | native*
    Lygodesmia rostrata (A. Gray) A. Gray

Taprooted annual herb, with cream-colored milky juice. **Stems** 1-6 dm tall, glabrous, green, paniculately branched in the upper 2/3. **Leaves** opposite in the

340. *Rudbeckia hirta*   341. *Rudbeckia laciniata*   342. *Rudbeckia triloba*   343. *Senecio integerrimus*

lowest 5- 8 nodes, not formmg a basal rosette, linear, 6-10 cm long and 2-4 mm wide, entire; upper leaves similar but alternate and smaller, the uppermost reduced to mere bracts. **Heads** terminal, involucre 12-15 mm long, narrowly cylindrical; principal involucral bracts 7 or 9, subtended by ca. 2 series of bracts; florets 8-11, all ligulate and fertile, corolla lavender with yellow tips, ca. 6 mm long, erect and not reflexed at anthesis. **Achenes** subcylindrical, 8-10 mm long, abruptly contracted below the tip; pappus of numerous capillary bristles 6-8 mm long, white, somewhat joined at their base. July Sept.—Sandy prairies and sand dunes. *A Great Plains species reaching eastern range limit in w Minnesota (Norman, Polk, and Sherburne counties).*

SILPHIUM *Rosinweed*

Tall perennial herbs, with resinous juice. Leaves opposite or all from base of plant, broadly ovate. Flower heads with yellow disk and ray flowers, in clusters at ends of stems; involucral bracts overlapping, receptacle more or less flat, chaffy. Fruit an achene; pappus none or of 2 small scales from top of achene.

1   Main leaves all opposite . . . . **S. perfoliatum**
1   Main leaves alternate . . . . **S. laciniatum**

Silphium laciniatum L.
COMPASS-PLANT

MAP 345
native

Coarse perennial with a woody taproot. **Stems** 1.5-3 m tall, hispid with spreading hairs, sometimes also slightly glandular. **Leaves** alternate, deeply pinnatifid, hirsute chiefly along the midrib and main veins beneath, the lower very large, sometimes 4 dm long, progressively reduced upwards, the uppermost entire and less than 1 dm long. **Heads** several or numerous in a narrow raceme-like inflorescence, large, the disk commonly 2-3 cm wide; involucre scabrous- hispid, commonly 2-4 cm long, exceeding the disk, its bracts ovate, squarrose, not much imbricate; rays about 15-30, 2-5 cm long. July-Sept.—Prairies. *The large basal leaves tend to align themselves facing in an east-west direction.*

Silphium laciniatum

Silphium perfoliatum L.
CUP-PLANT

MAP 346
native

Perennial herb, spreading by rhizomes. **Stems** erect, 4-angled, smooth, 1-2.5 m tall. **Leaves** opposite, broadly ovate, 8-30 cm long and 4-15 cm wide, rough-to-touch, margins coarsely toothed, the lower leaves often short-stalked and joined by wings on the petioles; upper leaves joined at base, forming a cup around stem. **Flower heads** several to many in an open inflorescence, with both disk and ray flowers, the disk 1.5-2.5 cm wide, the rays yellow, 1.5-2.5 cm long; involucre 1-2.5 cm high, the involucral bracts ovate, nearly equal, fringed with hairs on margins; receptacle flat, chaffy. **Achenes** flat, obovate, 8-10 mm long and 5-6 mm wide, the margins narrowly winged; pappus none. July-Sept.—Floodplain forests, streambanks, springs.

Silphium perfoliatum

344. Senecio vulgaris

345. Silphium laciniatum

346. Silphium perfoliatum

347. Solidago mollis

SOLIDAGO *Goldenrod*

Erect perennials, spreading by rhizomes or from a crown. Leaves alternate, margins entire or toothed. Flower heads small, many, in flat-topped (corymb-like), rounded (panicle-like) or spike-like clusters at ends of stems; the flowers sometimes mostly on 1 side of inflorescence branches (secund) in species with panicle-like heads; the heads with yellow disk and ray flowers; involucral bracts in several overlapping series, papery at base and tipped with green; receptacle flat or convex, not chaffy. Fruit an achene, angled or nearly round in cross-section; pappus of many slender white bristles.

ADDITIONAL SPECIES
Solidago mollis Bartl. (Velvet goldenrod, MAP 347), Great Plains native, w Minnesota.

1 Heads in a more or less flat-topped cluster at end of stem 2
  2 Leaf blades of middle and upper stem ovate to elliptic; stems and leaves densely hairy; common species of dry
    to mesic habitats, mostly south of tension zone . . . . ***S. rigida***
  2 Leaf blades linear to lance-shaped or oblong lance-shaped, glabrous apart from rough leaf margins; stems
    glabrous or nearly so, or slightly hairy below inflorescence 3
    3 Rays white, 12 or more; upper stem leaves broadest above their middle . . . . ***S. ptarmicoides***
    3 Rays yellow, 10 or less; upper stem leaves broadest at or below middle . . . . ***S. riddellii***
1 Heads in an elongate or pyramid-shaped cluster 4
  4 Inflorescence terminal, usually more or less pyramid-shaped and slightly nodding at top; inflorescence branches
    curving; the heads mostly on upper side of the branches 5
    5 Stem leaves with 3 prominent veins (midrib plus 2 distinct lateral veins) 6
      6 Lower leaves linear lance-shaped; inflorescence branches and pedicels glabrous; prairies south of tension
        zone . . . . ***S. missouriensis***
      6 Lower leaves elliptic, much larger than leaves of middle stem; inflorescence branches and pedicels at
        least sparsely hairy, the hairs short 7
        7 Stem pubescent for all or most of its length 8
          8 Involucres 2-3 mm long . . . . ***S. canadensis***
          8 Involucres 3-6 mm long 9
            9 Mid to upper leaves serrate, glabrous or scabrous above, pubescent on the veins beneath;
              stem pilose chiefly above the middle . . . . ***S. canadensis***
            9 Mid to upper leaves minutely serrate to entire, scabrous above, densely pubescent beneath;
              stem grayish with close hairs throughout, except sometimes near the base . . . . . ***S. altissima***
        7 Stem glabrous (or nearly so) below inflorescence 10
          10 Basal leaves absent; stem leaves elliptic, withering by flowering time, numerous, not reduced in
            size; distinctly 3-nerved; inflorescence branches densely hairy; plants flowering Aug-Sept. . . .
            . . . . ***S. gigantea***
          10 Basal leaves present; basal and lower stem leaves oblong lance-shaped to elliptic, with long petioles,
            persistent; middle and upper stem leaves few, smaller than basal leaves; leaves obscurely 3-nerved;
            inflorescence branches glabrous or nearly so; plants begin flowering in July . . . . ***S. juncea***
    5 Stem leaves with prominent midrib and weaker lateral veins 11
    11 Stems pubescent, at least on upper half . . . . ***S. nemoralis***
    11 Stems glabrous (or sometimes with fine hairs in inflorescence) 12
    12 Bases of lowest stem leaves clasping stem; wet habitats . . . . ***S. uliginosa***
    12 Lower leaf bases not clasping stem 13
      13 Basal and lower stem leaves much larger than leaves of middle stem, persistent; flowering begins
        early (July) . . . . ***S. juncea***
      13 Basal and lower stem leaves not much larger than leaves of middle stem, withered by flowering
        time; flowering late (August-September) . . . . ***S. ulmifolia***
  4 Flower heads spiraled around branches of inflorescence and not all on one side of branch 14
    14 Basal and lower stem leaves smaller than mid-stem leaves; middle and upper stem leaves with sharp teeth,
      longer than the axillary inflorescences . . . . ***S. flexicaulis***
    14 Basal and lower stem leaves larger than mid-stem leaves; middle and upper stem leaves entire or with
      rounded teeth, not longer than inflorescences 15
      15 Stem and leaves pubescent . . . . ***S. hispida***
      15 Stems glabrous or nearly so, sparse fine hairs may be present in inflorescence 16
        16 Lower stem leaves (including petioles) mostly 7-16 times longer than wide; petioles clasping stem;
          wet habitats . . . . ***S. uliginosa***
        16 Lower stem leaves usually 3-8 times longer than wide; petioles not clasping stem; dry, often sandy
          habitats 17

17 Basal and lower stem leaves broadly spatula-shaped to obovate; achenes short-hairy . . . .
. . . . **S. sciaphila**

17 Basal and lower stem leaves ovate to oblong lance-shaped; achenes glabrous . . . . **S. speciosa**

Solidago altissima L.

MAP 348
native

TALL GOLDENROD

Solidago canadensis var. *scabra* Torr. & Gray

Perennial from creeping rhizomes. **Stems** 5-20 dm tall, usually short-hairy throughout. **Lower stem leaves** usually withered by flowering; sessile or subpetiolate; blades oblong lance-shaped, 5-15 cm long and 7-20 mm wide, relatively thick and firm, entire to finely serrate, strongly 3-nerved, upper surface finely strigose, underside scabrous; much reduced upwards. **Heads** many, in a secund, pyramidal, panicle-like inflorescence, branches divergent and recurved; involucres narrowly campanulate, 2.5-4.5 mm long, the bracts in 3 series, unequal; ray florets 8-13; disk florets 3-6; corollas 2-4 mm long. **Achenes** sparsely to moderately hairy.—Found in many dry to wet habitats. *Solidago altissima is sometimes treated as S. canadensis var. scabra. The short hairs on the leaves give fresh plants a gray-green color not seen in S. canadensis. Subject to insect galls on the stems.*

Solidago altissima

Solidago canadensis L.

MAP 349
native

COMMON GOLDENROD

Perennial from creeping rhizomes, without a well-developed caudex. **Stems** 3-13 dm tall, more or less puberulent at least above the middle. **Leaves** thin, sharply serrate to subentire, glabrous or slightly scabrous above, commonly finely hairy on the midrib and main veins beneath; basal leaves absent, or, like the lower stem leaves, reduced and soon deciduous; mid- and upper **stem leaves** numerous and crowded, only gradually reduced upwards, lance-linear, tapering to the sessile base, 3-nerved, 5-13 cm long and 5-18 mm wide. **Inflorescence** terminal, panicle-like, with conspicuously recurved-secund branches; involucre about 2-3 mm high, its bracts imbricate in several series, yellowish, without well defined green tips; rays mostly 10-17, only about 1-1.5 mm long. **Achenes** short-hairy. July-Sept. —Open, moist or dry places.

Solidago canadensis

Solidago flexicaulis L.

MAP 350
native —

ZIGZAG GOLDENROD

Perennial with creeping rhizomes. **Stems** 3-12 dm tall, grooved, glabrous below the inflorescence. **Leaves** sharply and often coarsely serrate or dentate, hirsute beneath, at least on the midrib and main veins, or rarely glabrous, glabrous or sparsely hairy above; basal and lowermost stem leaves deciduous by flowering time; **upper leaves** ovate to elliptic, 7-15 cm long and 3-10 cm wide, abruptly contracted to the winged petiole. **Inflorescence** a series of short raceme-like clusters, the lower in the axils of ordinary scarcely reduced foliage leaves, these progressively reduced upwards, the uppermost becoming inconspicuous and shorter than their axillary clusters; involucre 4-6 mm. high, its bracts strongly imbricate, glabrous; rays 3-4. **Achenes** short-hairy. Aug-Oct.—Woodlands.

Solidago flexicaulis

Solidago gigantea Ait.

MAP 351
native

SMOOTH GOLDENROD

Solidago serotina Ait. non Retz.

Perennial herb, from stout rhizomes, often forming colonies. **Stems** 0.5-2 m tall, mostly smooth, sometimes waxy, short-hairy on upper branches. **Leaves** lance-

348. *Solidago altissima*   349. *Solidago canadensis*   350. *Solidago flexicaulis*   351. *Solidago gigantea*

shaped to oval, 6-15 cm long and 1-4 cm wide, prominently 3-veined, tapered to
a stalkless or short petiolelike base, glabrous or sparsely hairy on underside veins;
margins with sharp, forward-pointing teeth. **Flower heads** many, in large panicle-
like clusters, on 1 side of the spreading branches (secund), with yellow disk and
ray flowers, the rays 2-3 mm long; involucre 2-5 mm high, the involucral bracts
linear. **Achenes** 1-2 mm long. July-Sept.—Wet meadows, streambanks, swamps,
floodplain forests, thickets, marshes, calcareous fens, ditches; also in moist to dry
open woods and roadsides. *Canada goldenrod (Solidago canadensis) is similar but
generally smaller and densely short-hairy on leaf undersides and upper stem.*

Solidago hispida Muhl.   MAP 352
HAIRY GOLDENROD   *native*
Perennial with a stout branched caudex and fibrous roots. **Stems** 1-10 dm tall, the
herbage generally spreading-hirsute throughout. Basal and lowermost stem **leaves**
well developed and generally persistent, broadly oblong lance-shaped, crenate or
serrate to entire, petiolate, the blade and petiole 3-20 cm long and 1-5 cm wide;
stem leaves reduced upwards and becoming sessile. **Inflorescence** terminal, elongate and narrow, generally more or less leafy-bracteate toward the base, the lower
clusters often elongate and stiffly ascending, but not secund; involucre 4-6 mm
high, the bracts imbricate in several series, yellowish; rays about 7-14, usually
deep yellow. **Achenes** glabrous, at least when mature. July-Oct.—Dry woodlands
and rocky shores.

Solidago gigantea

Solidago juncea Ait.   MAP 353
EARLY GOLDENROD   *native*
Perennial with a stout branched caudex and fibrous roots, frequently with long
creeping rhizomes as well. **Stems** 3-12 dm tall, essentially glabrous throughout
except for the scabrous or ciliate leaf-margins, but sometimes short-hairy on one
or both surfaces or in the inflorescence. **Basal leaves** tufted and persistent, 15-40
cm long and 2-7.5 cm wide, with narrowly elliptic, serrate blades tapering to the
long petiole; **stem leaves** progressively reduced, becoming sessile. **Inflorescence**
terminal, panicle-like, dense, generally about as wide as long or even wider, with
recurved-secund branches; involucre glabrous, 3-5 mm high, its bracts imbricate;
rays minute, usually 7-12. **Achenes** persistently short-hairy. June-Oct.—Dry open
places and open woods, especially in sandy soil. *One of our earliest goldenrods to
flower.*

Solidago hispida

Solidago missouriensis Nutt.   MAP 354
MISSOURI GOLDENROD   *native*
Perennial from creeping rhizomes, sometimes with a caudex as well. **Stems** 3-10
dm tall, glabrous throughout, even in the inflorescence. **Leaves** firm, glabrous,
strongly 3-nerved (at least the middle and lower), entire, or some of them
(especially the lower) serrate; basal and lowermost stem leaves oblong lance-
shaped and conspicuously petiolate, but mostly soon deciduous, the others
reduced upwards, numerous or rather few, lance-elliptic. **Inflorescence** terminal,
panicle-like, with strongly recurved-secund branches, mostly short and wide;
involucre glabrous, about 3-5 mm high, its bracts imbricate; rays usually 7-13.
Achenes glabrous or sparsely hairy. July-Oct.—Prairies and other dry, open or
sparsely wooded places.

Solidago juncea

352. *Solidago hispida*

353. *Solidago juncea*

354. *Solidago missouriensis*

Solidago nemoralis Ait.
GRAY GOLDENROD

MAP 355
native

Perennial with a branchmg caudex and fibrous roots. **Stems** 1-10 dm tall, the herbage densely puberulent with loosely spreading hairs. **Leaves** weakly 3-nerved; basal leaves well-developed, tufted and persistent, oblong lance-shaped, long-petiolate, 5-25 cm long and 8-40 mm wide, toothed; **stem leaves** progressively reduced, less petiolate, and less toothed upwards, the lowermost similar to the basal, but often deciduous. **Inflorescence** terminal, panicle-like, sometimes elongate and nodding at the apex; sometimes larger with long, recurved, secund branches; involucre 3-6 mm high, its bracts imbricate in several series, glabrous except for the ciliolate margins; rays short, 5-9. **Achenes** pubescent. Aug-Oct.—Dry woods and open places, especially in sandy soil.

Solidago ptarmicoides (Nees) Boivin
PRAIRIE FLAT-TOPPED GOLDENROD

MAP 356
native

   Aster ptarmicoides (Nees) Torr. & Gray
   Oligoneuron album (Nutt.) Nesom

Solidago nemoralis

Perennial with a branched caudex and fibrous roots, the old leaf-bases persisting and becoming chaffy-fibrous. **Stems** 1-7 dm tall, scabrous at least above. **Leaves** firm, glabrous or scabrous, entire or with a few remote teeth, commonly 3-nerved, 3-20 cm long and 1.5-10 mm wide, the lower narrowly lance-shaped and petioled, sometimes tufted, persistent, and larger than those above; **upper leaves** becoming sessile and linear. **Heads** 3-60 in an open, minutely bracteate, corymbiform inflorescence; involucre 4-7 mm high, glabrous, its bracts imbricate, often with strongly thickened; rays 10-25, white, 5-9 mm long. **Achenes** several-nerved, glabrous. July-Sept.—Prairies and other open, usually dry places.

Solidago riddellii Frank
RIDDELL'S FLAT-TOPPED GOLDENROD

MAP 357
native

   Oligoneuron riddellii (Frank) Rydb.

Perennial herb, from a crown and sometimes also with rhizomes. **Stems** 2-10 dm tall, smooth but sometimes sparsely hairy in head. **Leaves** glabrous, largest at base of plant, these often early-deciduous, lance-shaped to linear, 10-20 cm long and 5-30 mm wide, becoming smaller upward, the upper leaves sickle-shaped and folded along midrib; margins entire; petioles of lower leaves long and winged, upper leaves sessile and clasping stem. **Flower heads** many, crowded in a branched, rounded to flat-topped inflorescence, the heads not confined to 1 side of the branches, with yellow disk and ray flowers, the rays 1-2 mm long; involucre 5-6 mm high, its bracts rounded at tip. **Achenes** glabrous, 1-2 mm long. Aug-Oct.—Wet meadows, calcareous fens, low prairie, lakeshores, streambanks.

Solidago rigida L.
STIFF GOLDENROD

MAP 358
native

   Oligoneuron rigidum (L.) Small

Solidago ptarmicoides

Perennial from a stout branched caudex. **Stems** 2.5-15 dm tall. Herbage densely pubescent with short spreading hairs, but sometimes nearly glabrous. **Leaves** firm, slightly toothed or entire, the basal and lowermost cauline leaves well developed and usually persistent, with elliptic, or broadly lance-shaped blades 6-25 cm long and 2-10 cm wide, often exceeded by the long petiole; **stem leaves** progressively reduced and less petiolate upwards, the middle ones sessile or nearly so. **Inflorescence** terminal, dense, corymbiform; heads large and many-

Solidago riddellii

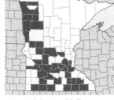

355. *Solidago nemoralis*   356. *Solidago ptarmicoides*   357. *Solidago riddellii*

flowered; involucre 5-9 mm high, its bracts conspicuously striate; rays 8-14.
Achenes 10-15 nerved, glabrous, or hairy at the tip. July-Oct.—Prairies and other
dry open places, especially in sandy soil.

Solidago sciaphila Steele
MAP 359
DRIFTLESS AREA GOLDENROD
native

Perennial with a branched caudex and fibrous root-system, glabrous except for
fine hairs in the inflorescence. **Stems** 4-11 dm tall. **Leaves** slightly succulent, the
basal and lowermost stem leaves largest and usually persistent, these with obovate
blades to 15 cm long and 8 cm wide, tapering to the petiole, margins toothed or
rarely nearly entire; middle and upper stem leaves progressively reduced,
becoming sessile or nearly so. **Inflorescence** an elongate, bracteate, terminal
thyrse, rarely branched; involucre about 5-7 mm high, the bracts strongly
imbricate, glabrous; rays 7-8, 2.5-4 mm long. **Achenes** short-hairy. Aug.-Sept.
—Calcareous or sandy cliffs, mostly se Minn and adjacent sw Wisc, Ill, and Iowa.

Solidago speciosa Nutt.
MAP 360
SHOWY GOLDENROD
native

Perennial with a stout woody caudex and fibrous roots. **Stems** 3-15 dm tall,
coarsely puberulent in the inflorescence, otherwise glabrous or slightly scabrous.
Leaves thick and firm, numerous, entire or the lower slightly toothed, sometimes
gradually increasing in size toward the base, the persistent lower ones abruptly
petiolate, to as much as 30 cm long and 10 cm wide, sometimes all smaller and
nearly uniform in size, the lower then generally deciduous. **Inflorescence**
terminal, not secund, usually with crowded, stiffly ascending branches,
sometimes becoming looser and more open; the heads conspicuously pedicellate;
involucre 3-5 mm high, its bracts imbricate, glutinous, yellowish; rays 6-8, 3-5
mm long. **Achenes** glabrous, seldom over 2 mm long. Aug.-Oct.—Open woods,
fields, prairies, and plains.

Solidago speciosa

Solidago uliginosa Nutt.
MAP 361
NORTHERN BOG-GOLDENROD
native

Perennial herb, from a branched crown. **Stems** stout, 5-15 dm long, glabrous but
finely hairy in the inflorescence. **Leaves** largest at base of plant, 5-35 cm long and
1-5 cm wide, becoming smaller upwards, lance-shaped to oblong lance-shaped,
glabrous; lower leaves tapered to long petioles, somewhat clasping stem, upper
leaves stalkless; margins finely toothed, or entire on upper leaves, rough-to-touch.
Inflorescence long, crowded, and spike-like, the branches ascending, straight or
curved downward at tip, the heads sometimes secund; involucre 3-5 mm high.
Achenes more or less glabrous. Aug.-Sept.—Conifer swamps, fens, open bogs,
low prairie, wet meadows, interdunal wetlands, Lake Superior rocky shore.

Solidago ulmifolia Muhl.
MAP 362
ELM-LEAVED GOLDENROD
native

Perennial with a branching caudex and fibrous roots. **Stems** 4-12 dm tall, glabrous
or nearly so below the inflorescence. **Leaves** thin, sharply and usually rather
coarsely serrate, glabrous to more commonly hirsute above, loosely hirsute on
the midrib and main veins beneath, and usually rather sparsely so over the surface
as well; basal leaves elliptic-ovate, abruptly contracted to the petiole, but usually
deciduous by flowering time; lowermost stem leaves soon deciduous and smaller
than the persistent ones just above, these 6-12 cm long and 1.2-5.5 cm wide,

Solidago uliginosa

358. Solidago rigida   *359. Solidago sciaphila*   *360. Solidago speciosa*   *361. Solidago uliginosa*

becoming reduced and nearly sessile upwards. **Inflorescence** terminal, panicle-like, with recurved-secund branches, these generally few, long, and divergent; involucre 2.5-4.5 mm high, its bracts imbricate; rays 3-5, minute. **Achenes** persistently short-hairy. Aug-Oct.—Woodlands.

SONCHUS *Sow-Thistle*

Annual or perennial herbs with milky juice. Leaves alternate or all basal, entire to pinnatifid or dissected, mostly auriculate, often prickly-margined Heads solitary to usually several or many in an irregular corymb-like inflorescence. Flowers all ligulate and perfect, yellow, few to more often numerous (our species with usually ca. 120-160 flowers in each head). Involucre ovoid or campanulate, its bracts generally imbricate in several series. Achenes flattened, about 6-20-ribbed, beakless, glabrous. Pappus of numerous white capillary bristles which tend to fall connected, sometimes with a few stouter ones which fall separately. *The perennial* **Sonchus arvensis** *is a troublesome, widespread farm weed.*

1   Perennial with creeping rhizomes; leaf bases auriculate and clasping stem, the auricles small .... *S. arvensis*
1   Taprooted annuals; leaf bases auriculate and clasping stem, the auricles large and conspicuous 2
   2   Leaf margins sparsely prickly .... *S. oleraceus*
   2   Leaf margins with numerous spine-tipped teeth .... *S. asper*

Sonchus arvensis L.
PERENNIAL SOW-THISTLE   MAP 363 · *introduced (naturalized)*

Perennial with long vertical roots, and extensively spreading by horizontal, rhizomelike, often deep-seated roots. **Stems** 4-20 dm tall, glabrous below the inflorescence and often somewhat glaucous. **Leaves** prickly-margined, the lower and middle ones usually pinnately lobed or pinnatifid, commonly 6-40 cm long and 2-15 cm wide, becoming less lobed and often more strongly auriculate upwards, the upper reduced and distant. **Heads** several in an open corymbiform inflorescence, relatively large, commonly 3-5 cm wide in flower, the fruiting involucre 15-22 mm long; involucre and peduncles more or less copiously provided with coarse, spreading, gland-tipped hairs, the involucre with some small and obscure tufts of tomenturn as well. **Achenes** about 2.5-3.5 mm long, with 5 or more prominent longitudinal ribs on each face, strongly rugulose. July-Oct.—A cosmopolitan weed of European origin.

Sonchus arvensis

Sonchus asper (L.) Hill
SPINY-LEAF SOW-THISTLE   MAP 364 · *introduced (naturalized)*

Similar to *S. oleraceus*, but usually more prickly. **Leaves** pinnatifid, or frequently obovate and lobeless, with rounded, not acute auricles. **Achenes** with 3 or rarely 4-5 evident longitudinal ribs on each face, not rugulose, although there may be minute projections from the marginal ribs. July-Oct.—A cosmopolitan weed; native of Europe.

Sonchus oleraceus

Sonchus oleraceus L.
COMMON SOW-THISTLE   MAP 365 · *introduced (naturalized)*

Annual with a short taproot. **Stems** 1-10 dm tall, glabrous except sometimes for a few spreading gland-tipped hairs on the involucre and peduncle. **Leaves** pinnatifid to occasionally merely toothed, the margins rather weakly or scarcely prickly, 6-30 cm long and 1-15 cm wide, all but the lowermost prominently auriculate, the auricles with well rounded margins but eventually sharply acute; leaves progres-

362. *Solidago ulmifolia*   363. *Sonchus arvensis*   364. *Sonchus asper*   365. *Sonchus oleraceus*

sively less divided upwards, and more or less reduced. **Heads** several in a corymbiform inflorescence, relatively small, only about 1.5-2.5 cm wide in flower; receptacle expanding and becoming conspicuously pale and indurate in fruit; fruiting involucre mostly 9-13 mm high. **Achenes** 2.5-3 mm long, rugulose and 3-5-ribbed on each face. July-Oct.—A cosmopolitan weed; native of Europe.

SYMPHYOTRICHUM *Wild Aster*

Mostly perennial herbs (annual in *S. ciliatum*). Leaves simple, alternate. Flower heads with both ray and disk flowers (disk flowers only in *S. ciliatum*); ray flowers white, pink, blue or purple, usually more than 0.5 mm wide (in contrast to the very narrow rays in *Erigeron*); disk flowers red, purple or yellow; involucral bracts in 2 or more series, usually overlapping; receptacle naked (not chaffy), flat or nearly so; pappus of numerous hairlike bristles. *The traditional genus* **Aster** *has been split into several segregate genera to reflect differences with European species. Most species native to e USA are now placed within the genus* **Symphyotrichum**, *with the following exceptions for Minnesota species:* **Aster umbellatus** *in the genus* **Doellingeria**, *and A.* **macrophyllus** *in the genus* **Eurybia**. *Initially controversial, this classification is now widely accepted and is followed here.*

1   Leaves, at least the lower ones, heart-shaped at base and with petioles 2
   2   Leaves entire or nearly so; involucral bracts with a short, diamond-shaped green tip 3
      3   Nearly all leaves below the inflorescence heart-shaped or nearly so . . . . *S. shortii*
      3   Only the lower leaves heart-shaped . . . . *S. oolentangiense*
   2   Leaves toothed; involucral bracts various 4
      4   Inflorescence with relatively few heads, often less than 50; peduncles and inflorescence branches with only a few bracts . . . . *S. ciliolatum*
      4   Inflorescence with many heads, often over 100; peduncles and inflorescence branches with many bracts 5
         5   Plants glabrous or nearly so (sometimes slightly finely hairy in the inflorescence) . . . . . . *S. urophyllum*
         5   Plants hairy to rough-hairy, at least in part 6
            6   Leaf margins with large, sharp teeth; petiole not winged or only slightly so; involucral bracts often strongly purple-tinged, rounded at tip . . . . *S. cordifolium*
            6   Leaf margins with only shallow, usually rounded teeth; petioles of stem leaves often strongly winged; involucral bracts green, tapered to a sharp tip 7
               7   Rays bright blue; plants often densely hairy . . . . *S. drummondii*
               7   Rays pale-blue, pale-purple, or white; plants thinly hairy . . . . *S. urophyllum*
1   Leaves not both heart-shaped and petioled 8
   8   Involucre strongly glandular 9
      9   Base of leaf strongly clasping stem . . . . *S. novae-angliae*
      9   Base of leaf not clasping stem or only slightly so . . . . *S. oblongifolium*
   8   Plants not glandular 10
      10 Base of leaf strongly clasping stem 11
         11 Involucral bracts (at least the inner), long-tapered to a slender tip . . . . *S. puniceum*
         11 Involucral bracts rounded or short-tapered to the tip 12
            12 Perennial herbs from an enlarged base or short rhizome; involucral bracts appressed and strongly overlapping; plants glabrous or with lines of hairs in the inflorescence, often glaucous . . . . *S. laeve*
            12 Perennial herbs from long creeping rhizomes; involucral bracts equal lengths or overlapping, not appressed, often loose; plants glabrous or hairy, not glaucous . . . . *S. prenanthoides*
      10 Base of leaf not clasping stem (or only slightly so) 13
         13 Leaves densely silvery-hairy; margins entire . . . . *S. sericeum*
         13 Leaves glabrous or pubescent, not silvery-hairy; margins entire to toothed 14
            14 Taprooted annual herb; rays absent . . . . *S. ciliatum*
            14 Perennial herbs with fibrous roots and from rhizomes or crowns; rays well developed 15
               15 Most involucral bracts with a slender green tip, the margins inrolled . . . . *S. pilosum*
               15 Involucral bracts flat, the margins not inrolled 16
                  16 Involucre 7-12 mm long; rays violet or blue . . . . *S. praealtum*
                  16 Involucre 3-6 mm long; rays usually white, sometimes pink or blue 17
                     17 Tips of outer involucral bracts loose or recurved, tapered to a very small spine-tip; leaves entire 18
                        18 Heads many, often arranged on 1 side of the branches; rays 8-20 . . . . *S. ericoides*

18 Heads fewer, solitary or clustered at branch ends; rays 20-35 . . . . *S. falcatum*

17 Involucral bracts appressed or only slightly loose, the tips not spine-tipped; leaves various
. . . . 19

19 Leaves hairy on underside, at least along the midvein 20

20 Leaf underside hairy; plants with creeping rhizomes . . . . *S. ontarionis*

20 Leaf underside glabrous except for hairs on the midvein; plants without creeping
rhizomes . . . . *S. lateriflorum*

19 Leaf underside glabrous (except sometimes hairy in *S. praealtum*) 21

21 Heads very small and numerous, the rays 3-6 mm long; heads often arranged on 1-
side of the inflorescence branches . . . . *S. lanceolatum*

21 Heads larger or few in number, not arranged on 1 side of the branches 22

22 Underside leaf venation forming a distinct net-like pattern, the spaces enclosed
by the secondary veins of about equal length and width . . . . *S. praealtum*

22 Underside leaf venation not clearly net-veined, or if so, the spaces enclosed by
the secondary veins longer than wide 23

23 Rays bright blue-violet; stem leaves ± clasping (most bases, especially lower
on the stem, circling more than half the circumference of the stem);
involucral bracts nearly equal in length (or the outer ones over half as long
as the inner ones) . . . . *S. robynsianum*

23 Rays usually white; stem leaves not clasping (all bases circling half or less
the circumference of the stem); involucral bracts of different lengths,
imbricate. 24

24 Slender plants of bogs and other wetlands; inflorescence short-stalked
and wide in outline . . . . *S. boreale*

24 Plants stouter, not occurring in bogs; inflorescence elongate . . . .
. . . . *S. lanceolatum*

Symphyotrichum boreale (Torr. & Gray) A.& D. Löve

NORTHERN BOG-ASTER

MAP 366
native

Aster borealis (Torr. & Gray) Prov.
Aster junciformis Rydb.

Perennial herb, from rhizomes 1-2 mm wide. **Stems** erect, slender, 3-8 dm tall
and to 2 mm wide, unbranched below, usually branched in the head; smooth
except for lines of short, appressed hairs below base of upper leaves. **Leaves**
alternate, linear, 4-12 cm long and 2-6 mm wide, sometimes slightly clasping at
base, margins rough-to-touch, petioles absent. **Flower heads** usually few to rarely
many, in an open, broad inflorescence; the heads 1.5-2 cm wide; involucre 5-7
mm high, the involucral bracts overlapping, often purple at tips and on margins;
ray flowers 20-50, white to light blue or lavender, 1-1.5 cm long. **Fruit** an achene;
pappus of pale hairs. Aug-Sept.—Conifer swamps, calcareous fens, open bogs,
wet meadows, shores and seeps.

Symphyotrichum ciliatum (Ledeb.) Nesom

WESTERN ANNUAL ASTER

MAP 367
native

Aster brachyactis Blake

Symphyotrichum boreale

Taprooted annual herb. **Stems** unbranched and erect, to branched and spreading,
2-6 dm long, smooth. **Leaves** alternate, linear, 2-10 cm long and mostly 2-5 mm
wide, margins fringed with scattered hairs, petioles absent. **Flower heads** several
to many, in an open inflorescence which forms much of plant; flower heads bell-
shaped, 1-2 cm wide, involucre 5-10 mm high, the involucral bracts mostly green,
linear, of equal length or slightly overlapping; ray flowers absent. **Achenes**
flattened, 1-2 mm long; pappus of many long, soft hairs. Aug-Sept.—Shores
(including along Great Lakes), streambanks, wet meadows, roadside ditches,
usually where brackish.

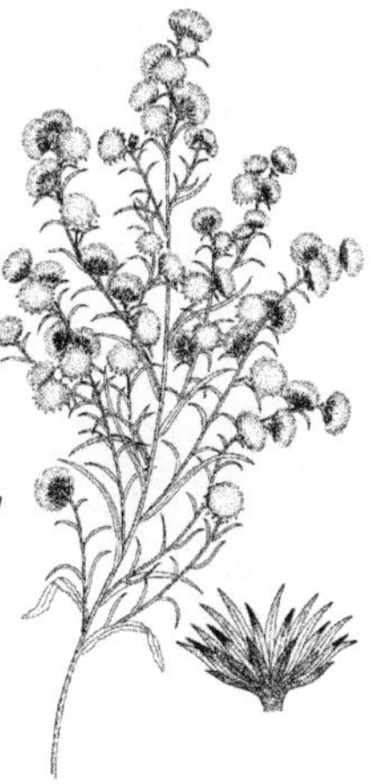

Symphyotrichum ciliatum

Symphyotrichum ciliolatum (Lindl.) A. & D. Löve
NORTHERN HEART-LEAVED ASTER
Aster ciliolatus Lindl.
Aster lindleyanus Torr. & Gray

MAP 368
native

Perennial with long creeping rhizomes, sometimes also with a short branched caudex. **Stems** 2-12 dm tall, hirsute, especially in the inflorescence and on the lower leaf surfaces, sometimes glabrous throughout. Basal and lower stem **leaves** petiolate and cordate or subcordate, 4-12 cm long and 2-6 cm wide, sharply serrate, often deciduous, those above abruptly narrowed to the broadly winged petiole, and often less toothed, or the **upper leaves** sessile and entire. **Inflorescence** open, relatively few-headed, the heads often less than 50, rarely more than 100, the branches and peduncles sparsely or scarcely bracteate, the bracts narrow, the peduncles of very unequal length, generally some of them over 1 cm long; involucre 5-8 mm high, its slender bracts slightly or moderately imbricate, glabrous except for the sometimes ciliolate margins, their green tips relatively narrow and elongate; rays mostly 12-25, blue, 8-15 mm long. **Achenes** glabrous or nearly so, gray or stramineous, 3-6-nerved. July-Oct.—Woodlands and clearings.

Symphyotrichum ciliolatum

Symphyotrichum cordifolium (L.) Nesom
COMMON BLUE HEART-LEAVED ASTER
Aster cordifolius L.

MAP 369
native

Perennial with a branched caudex or short rhizome and numerous fibrous roots, occasionally with long creeping rhizomes as well. **Stems** 2-12 dm tall, glabrous below the inflorescence or occasionally loosely pubescent with the hairs chiefly in lines. **Leaves** relatively thin, sharply toothed, acuminate, scabrous above, at least toward the margins, and hirsute beneath with appressed or spreading hairs, ovate, the larger ones 3.5-12 cm long and 2.5-7 cm wide, all but the reduced ones of the inflorescence cordate and petiolate, the petioles shorter upwards but only slightly if at all winged. **Inflorescence** panicle-like, with loosely ascending to widely spreading branches and often very numerous heads, the peduncles usually well developed and more or less bracteolate, sometimes as much as 1.5 cm long; involucre 3-6 mm high, glabrous, its narrow bracts imbricate in several series, their green tips short and broad (or in the innermost more elongate), the green usually replaced or obscured by anthocyanin (visible to the naked eye in some of them) rays commonly 8-20, blue or purple (rarely white), mostly 5-10 mm long. **Achenes** pale, glabrous, 3-5-nerved. Aug.-Oct.—Woodlands.

Symphyotrichum drummondii (Lindl.) Nesom
HAIRY HEART-LEAVED ASTER
Aster drummondii Lindl.

MAP 370
native

Perennial with a branched caudex or short rhizome and numerous fibrous roots. **Stems** 4-12 dm tall, usually densely pubescent at least above the middle with minute, stiffly spreading hairs. **Leaves** relatively firm, shallowly toothed, scabrous above, densely pubescent with short spreading hairs beneath, the lowermost ones ovate or lance-ovate, cordate, 6-14 cm long and 2.5-6.5 cm wide, long-petiolate, those above progressively less cordate (or the upper merely broadly rounded) at the base and with shorter, usually broadly winged petioles. **Inflorescence** panicle-like, with spreadmg or ascending bracteate branches, the heads often numerous, on bracteate peduncles usually less than 1 cm long; involucre glabrous or puberulent, 4.5-7 mm high, its bracts firm, imbricate, the green tips rhombic; rays

Symphyotrichum cordifolium

366. *Symphyotrichum boreale*   367. *Symphyotrichum ciliatum*   368. *Symphyotrich. ciliolatum*   369. *Symphyotri. cordifolium*

mostly 10-20, bright blue, 5-10 mm long. **Achenes** pale, minutely hairy especially toward the tip, or glabrous, with several weak nerves. Sept-Oct.—Clearings and open woodland.

Symphyotrichum ericoides (L.) Nesom
WHITE HEATH ASTER
  Aster ericoides L.

MAP 371
native

Perennial from well developed creeping rhizomes, pubescent with appressed or spreading hairs, or the leaves sometimes subglabrous. **Stems** 3-10 dm tall, occasionally more. **Leaves** numerous, linear, sessile, rarely as much as 6 cm long and 7 mm wide, the lower and often also the middle ones soon deciduous, those of the branches reduced and divaricate, often becoming mere bracts. **Heads** numerous, small, commonly somewhat secund on the divergent or recurved branches; involucre about 3-5 mm high, its bracts more or less strongly imbricate in several series, the outer spinulose and more or less squarrose, some or all of the bracts coarsely ciliolate-margined; rays 8-20, white, rarely blue or pink, 3-5 mm long. **Achenes** hairy.—Dry, open places.

Symphyotrichum ericoides

Symphyotrichum falcatum (Lindl.) Nesom
WHITE PRAIRIE ASTER
  Aster falcatus Lindl.
  Aster commutatus (Torr. & Gray) Gray

MAP 372
native

Similar to *S. ericoides* but smaller, seldom over 6 dm tall, with fewer and larger heads. **Stems** with appressed hairs. **Heads** solitary or clustered at the ends of the not at all secund branches, or the stem scarcely branched and the inflorescence subracerniform; involucre 5-7 mm high, its bracts seldom much imbricated, the outer often acute as well as the inner; rays mostly 20-30, 4-8 mm long.—Prairies and other open places.

Symphyotrichum laeve (L.) A. & D. Löve
SMOOTH BLUE ASTER
  Aster laevis L.

MAP 373
native

Perennial from a short stout rhizome or branched caudex, occasionally with short creeping red rhizomes as well. **Stems** 3-10 dm tall. Herbage glabrous throughout, except occasionally for some puberulent lines in the inflorescence, commonly somewhat glaucous. **Leaves** thick and firm, variable in size and shape but the larger ones over 1 cm wide, entire or sometimes toothed, sessile and more or less strongly clasping, or the lower tapering to winged petioles and scarcely clasping; leaves of the inflorescence reduced and often bractlike, clasping at their base. **Heads** several or numerous in an open inflorescence; involucre 5-9 mm high, its appressed bracts imbricate in several series, with short, commonly with rhombic green tips; rays mostly 15-25, blue or purple, 8-15 mm long. **Achenes** nearly glabrous; pappus reddish or sometimes white. Aug-Oct.—Open, usually dry places.

Symphyotrichum laeve

Symphyotrichum lanceolatum (Willd.) Nesom
EASTERN LINED ASTER
  Aster lanceolatus Willd.
  Aster interior Wieg.
  Symphyotrichum simplex (Willd.) A.& D. Löve

MAP 374
native

Perennial herb, forming colonies from long rhizomes. **Stems** 0.5-1.5 m long, upper stems with lines of hairs. **Leaves** alternate, all on stem, lance-shaped to linear, 8-

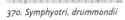

370. Symphyotri. drummondii   *371. Symphyotrichum ericoides*   *372. Symphyotrichum falcatum*   *373. Symphyotrichum laeve*

15 cm long and 3-30 mm wide, upper surface smooth or slightly rough-to-touch, margins toothed or sometimes entire; petioles absent or blades tapered to petiolelike base, sometimes slightly clasping stem. **Flower heads** many in an elongate leafy inflorescence; the involucre 3-6 mm high, the involucral bracts tapered to a green tip, smooth or margins fringed with hairs, strongly overlapping; ray flowers 20-40, usually white, sometimes lavender or blue, 4-12 mm long. **Fruit** an achene; pappus white. Aug-Oct.—Marshes, wet meadows, fens, swamp openings, low prairie, streambanks and shores. *One of our most common asters.*

Symphyotrichum lateriflorum (L.) A.& D. Löve   MAP 375
GOBLET-ASTER; FAREWELL-SUMMER   *native*
   Aster hirsuticaulis Lindl.
   Aster lateriflorus (L.) Britt.

Symphyotrichum lanceolatum

Perennial from a branching caudex or short stout rhizome, with numerous fibrous roots. **Stems** several, 3-12 dm tall, curly-villous to glabrous. **Leaves** scabrous or nearly glabrous above, glabrous beneath except for the usually puberulent midrib; basal and lower stem leaves soon deciduous, or the basal occasionally persistent, obovate to lance-shaped, tending to taper from the middle to both ends, entire or serrate, mostly 5-15 cm long and 5-30 mm wide, petiolate; upper leaves sessile or nearly so. **Heads** numerous in a widely branched or sometimes more simple inflorescence; involucre glabrous, mostly 4-5.5 mm high, its bracts imbricate in few series, with broad green tips, often suffused with purple upwards; rays 9-14, white or slightly purple-tinged, 4-6.5 mm long; lobes of the disk corollas recurved. **Achenes** few-nerved, somewhat hairy. Aug.-Oct.—Various habitats, most commonly in open woodlands, dry open places, and on beaches.

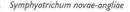

Symphyotrichum novae-angliae (L.) Nesom   MAP 376
NEW ENGLAND ASTER   *native*
   Aster novae-angliae L.

Symphyotrichum lateriflorum

Perennial herb, from a short rhizome or crown. **Stems** stout, erect, 4-10 dm long, with stiff, spreading, sometimes gland-tipped hairs. **Leaves** alternate, lance-shaped, 3-7 cm long and 1-2.5 cm wide, upper surface rough-to-touch or with short hairs, underside soft hairy, base of leaf strongly clasping stem, margins entire, petioles absent. **Flower heads** several to many, in clusters at ends of branches, 1.5-3 cm wide; involucre 7-12 mm high, the involucral bracts awl-shaped, glandular-hairy, sometimes purple; ray flowers 40 or more, blue-violet to less often red or pink, 1-2 cm long. **Achenes** hairy; pappus red-tinged. Aug-Oct.—Wet meadows, low prairie, shores, thickets, calcareous fens, roadsides.

Symphyotrichum oblongifolium (Nutt.) Nesom   MAP 377
AROMATIC ASTER   *native*
   Aster oblongifolius Nutt.

Perennial from creeping rhizomes, sometimes with a short caudex as well. **Stems** rigid, brittle, seldom over 4 dm tall, usually much branched, glandular upwards, and sometimes also hairy or scabrous. **Leaves** firm, entire, sessile and obscurely to evidently auriculate-clasping, oblong or lance-oblong, rarely as much as 8 cm long and 2 cm wide, often much smaller, more or less scabrous, or sometimes glabrous except for the margins, the lower leaves similar to those above but soon deciduous, those of the branches numerous and reduced, becoming mere spreading bracts. **Heads** several or numerous, terminating the branches, the

Symphyotrichum novae-angliae

374. *Symphyotri. lanceolatum*   375. *Symphyotri. lateriflorum*   376. *Symphyotr. novae-angliae*   377. *Symphyo. oblongifolium*

involucre densely glandular, 5-8 mm high, its bracts in several series but not much imbricate, with chartaceous base, and long, green, spreading tip; rays commonly 20-40, blue or purple, rarely rose, mostly 1-1.5 cm long. **Achenes** several-nerved, finely hairy. Aug-Oct.—Dry, usually open places.

Symphyotrichum ontarionis (Wieg.) Nesom

MAP 378
ONTARIO ASTER   *native*
  Aster ontarionis Wieg.

Perennial herb, from long creeping rhizomes. **Stems** branched, 3-8 dm long, upper stems with short spreading hairs. **Leaves** alternate, thin, oblong lance-shaped, 5-10 cm long and 1-3 cm wide (upper leaves smaller), upper surface rough-hairy to nearly smooth, underside finely to densely hairy; margins with sharp, forward-pointing teeth above middle of blade; petioles absent. **Flower heads** 1-2 cm wide, on short stalks from short leafy branches; involucre smooth to finely hairy, 5-7 mm high, the involucral bracts overlapping; ray flowers white, 9 or more. **Fruit** an achene. Sept-Oct.—Floodplain forests, river terraces, thickets. *Similar to S. lateriflorum, but with long rhizomes rather than a crown or short rhizomes.*

Symphyotrichum oblongifolium

Symphyotrichum oolentangiense (Riddell) Nesom

MAP 379
PRAIRIE HEART-LEAVED ASTER   *native*
  Aster oolentangiensis Riddell

Perennial from a branched caudex or short rhizomes, with numerous fibrous roots. **Stems** 2-15 dm tall, scabrous-puberulent to occasionally nearly glabrous. **Leaves** thick and firm, entire or occasionally shallowly serrate, scabrous-hispid above, the hairs on the lower surface softer, and usually longer and looser than those on the upper; basal and usually also the lower stem leaves long-petiolate, cordate, lance-shaped or ovate, 4-13 cm long and 1.2-6 cm wide, those above abruptly smaller, narrower, less petiolate, and generally not at all cordate, the **upper leaves** sessile and lance-shaped or linear. **Inflorescence** open, panicle-like, with narrow and usually numerous bracts, the peduncles often very long; involucre 4.5-8 mm high, its bracts imbricate in several series, with a diamond-shaped green tip, glabrous except for the often ciliolate margins; rays commonly 10-25, blue, or rarely pink, 5-12 mm long. **Achenes** glabrous or nearly so, 3-5-nerved, usually pale. Aug-Oct.—Prairies and dry open woods.

Symphyotrichum ontarionis

Symphyotrichum pilosum (Willd.) Nesom

MAP 380
WHITE OLDFIELD ASTER   *native*
  Aster pilosus Willd.

Perennial herb, from a large crown. **Stems** to 1.5 m long, more or less smooth (var. *pringlei*) or stems and leaves with spreading hairs (var. *pilosum*). **Lower leaves** oblong lance-shaped, 5-10 cm long and 1-2 cm wide, petioled; upper leaves smaller, linear, stalkless; margins entire or slightly toothed; petioles fringed with hairs; basal leaves and lower stem leaves soon deciduous (or basal leaves persistent). **Flower heads** at ends of small branches, forming an open inflorescence; involucre urn-shaped, narrowed near middle and flared upward, 3-5 mm high, smooth, involucral bracts overlapping to nearly equal in length, green-tipped; ray flowers 15-35, white. **Fruit** an achene.—Sandy and gravelly shores, interdunal swales, wet meadows; often where calcium-rich; sometimes weedy in disturbed fields and roadsides.

S. oolentangiense

Symphyotrichum pilosum

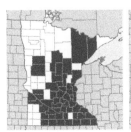
378 *Symphyotri. ontarionis*

379. *Symphyo. oolentangiense*

380. *Symphyotri. pilosum*

381. *Symphyotri. praealtum*

Symphyotrichum praealtum (Poir.) Nesom   MAP 381
WILLOW-LEAF ASTER   *native*
   Aster praealtus Poir.

Perennial herb, spreading by rhizomes and forming colonies. **Stems** to 1 m long,
with lines of hairs, especially in upper stem. **Leaves** alternate, firm, lance-shaped,
6-12 cm long and 1-2 cm wide, upper surface rough-to-touch to nearly smooth,
underside smooth or finely hairy, with conspicuous netlike veins surrounding
lighter colored areas (areole); margins more or less entire; petioles absent, the
base of leaves often slightly clasping. **Flower heads** at ends of short leafy
branches; involucre 5-7 mm high, the involucral bracts overlapping; rays 5-15
mm long, blue-purple (rarely white). **Fruit** an achene. Sept-Oct.—Wet meadows,
low prairie, moist fields, thickets.

Symphyotrichum prenanthoides (Muhl.) Nesom   MAP 382
ZIGZAG ASTER   *native*
   Aster prenanthoides Muhl.

Symphyotrichum praealtum

Perennial from long creeping rhizomes. **Stems** 2-10 dm tall, often zigzag,
pubescent in lines decurrent from the leaf-base, becoming uniformly so under
the heads and glabrate toward the base. **Leaves** scabrous to glabrous above,
glabrous or loosely hairy along the midrib beneath, the principal ones 6-20 cm
long and 1-5 cm wide, with ovate or lance-shaped, serrate blades abruptly
contracted or tapering to a long, winged, strongly auriculate-clasping petiolar
base; lower leaves similar but reduced and soon deciduous, the reduced leaves of
the inflorescence becoming sessile and entire. **Heads** several or numerous in an
open, sparsely leafy-bracteate inflorescence; involucre glabrous, mostly 5-7 mm
high, its bracts seldom much imbricate, often with spreading tips; rays mostly
20-35, blue or pale purple, occasionally white, 7-15 mm long; pappus yellowish.
Achenes strigose, several-nerved. Aug-Oct.—Streambanks, meadows, and moist
woodlands.

Symphyotrichum puniceum (L.) A. & D. Löve   MAP 383
PURPLE-STEM ASTER   *native*
   Aster firmus Nees
   Aster puniceus L.

Large perennial herb, from a short rhizome or crown, sometimes also with short
stolons. **Stems** stout, red-purple, 0.5-2 m long, unbranched, or branched in head,
with long stiff hairs or sometimes nearly smooth. **Leaves** alternate, lance-shaped
to oblong lance-shaped, 6-18 cm long and 1-4 cm wide, rough-to-touch to nearly
smooth above, underside smooth or with long hairs on midvein; margins with
scattered sharp teeth or sometimes entire; petioles absent, base of leaf clasping.
Flower heads numerous, 1.5-2.5 cm wide; involucre 6-10 mm high, involucral
bracts about equal in length, smooth or fringed with hairs, green and spreading;
ray flowers 20-50, blue (rarely white). **Fruit** a smooth achene; pappus more or
less white. Aug-Sept.—Swamps, sedge meadows, thickets, calcareous fens,
streambanks, shores, springs, roadside ditches.

Symphyotrichum robynsianum (J.Rousseau) Brouillet & Labrecque (NO MAP)
LONG-LEAVED ASTER   *native*
   Aster longifolius sensu Semple & Heard, non Lam.

Symphyotrichum puniceum

Perennial, forming colonies from long-creeping rhizomes. **Stems** 10-80 cm tall,
single, erect, often red-tinged, glabrous, upper portion with lines of hairs. **Leaves**
stiff, glabrous to scabrous, lower leaves withering by flowering, long-petiolate,
petioles narrowly winged, blades lance-shaped, 20 cm long and 3-5 mm wide,
bases clasping the stem; margins sparsely serrulate or entire, somewhat revolute;
upper stem leaves sessile, smaller, slightly clasping or not, margins entire.
Inflorescence elongate, open, panicle-like or raceme-like; branches ascending,
with 1-3 heads per branch; branch leaves small; peduncles glabrous or densely
pilose in lines. Involucre 5-8.5 mm long, its bracts in 3-4 series, their margins
scarious, erose, and hyaline. Rays 20-35; corollas dark blue-violet, seldom white;
disk florets 23-40; corollas yellow. **Achene** tan, obovoid, 5-6-nerved; pappus
pinkish.—Moist open sandy, gravelly, or rocky places, including shores, limestone

alvars, seasonally wet swales. *The long leaves usually overtop most or all of the inflorescence. Presence in Minn not verified, reported from Clearwater County.*

Symphyotrichum sericeum (Vent.) Nesom
WESTERN SILVERY ASTER
    Aster sericeus Vent.

MAP 384
native

Perennial from a short branched caudex, with numerous fibrous roots. **Stems** 2-7 dm tall, several, wiry, branched upwards, thinly sericeous, or glabrate below. **Leaves** sericeous on both sides, entire, the basal leaves oblong lance-shaped and petiolate, but these and the leaves on the lower half of the stem soon deciduous, the others sessile, lance-shaped to elliptic, to 4 cm long and 1 cm wide. **Heads** several or numerous in a widely branched inflorescence, often clustered at the ends of the branches; involucre sericeous, 6-10 mm high, its broad bracts in several series but seldom much imbricate, their leafy tips often loose or spreading; rays 15-25, deep violet to rose-purple or rarely white, 8-15 mm. long. **Achenes** glabrous, closely 8-12-nerved. Aug-Oct.—Dry prairies and other open places.

Symphyotrichum sericeum

Symphyotrichum shortii (Lindl.) Nesom
SHORT'S ASTER
    Aster shortii Lindl.

MAP 385
native

Perennial from a short branched caudex, with numerous fibrous roots. **Stems** 3-12 dm tall, striate, glabrous or nearly so below, spreading-hairy above. **Leaves** entire or occasionally few-toothed, glabrous or scaberulous above, spreading-hairy beneath, lance-shaped, petiolate, nearly all of those below the inflorescence cordate, the lower stem leaves usually deeply so, 6-15 cm long and 2-6 cm wide; basal leaves, if persistent, often shorter, broader, and somewhat toothed; middle and upper stem leaves only gradually reduced. **Inflorescence** open, panicle-like, with numerous, usually narrow bracts, the bracteate peduncles often very long; involucre 4-6 mm high, its bracts narrow, imbricate in several series, minutely pubescent, with small, somewhat diamond-shaped green tips shorter than the chartaceous portion; rays mostly 10-20, blue, or rarely rose-red or white, 5-14 mm long. **Achenes** pale, glabrous, 3-5-nerved. Aug-Oct.—Woodlands.

Symphyotrichum shortii

Symphyotrichum urophyllum (Lindl.) Nesom
ARROW-LEAVED ASTER
    Aster sagittifolius Willd.

MAP 386
native

Perennial with a branched caudex or short rhizome and numerous fibrous roots. **Stems** 4-12 dm tall, glabrous or nearly so below the inflorescence, or the upper part occasionally puberulent in lines. **Leaves** rather thick, shallowly toothed, glabrous or scabrous above, glabrous or hirsute beneath; lowermost leaves lance-ovate, cordate, 6-15 cm long and 2-6 cm wide, long-petiolate; upper leaves narrowed to the often broadly winged petiole, or sessile. **Inflorescence** panicle-like, elongate, with ascending bracteate branches; the heads often very numerous, borne on branches rarely more than 1 cm long, thus appearing crowded; involucre 4-6 mm high, its imbricate bracts glabrous except for the sometimes ciliolate margins, slender with elongate green tips; rays 8-20, usually pale blue or lilac, sometimes white, 4-8 mm long. **Achenes** pale, glabrous, 4-5-nerved. Aug-Oct.—Streambanks, woodlands, and less often in open places.

382. Symphyo. prenanthoides   *383. Symphyotri. puniceum*   *384. Symphyotrichum sericeum*   *385. Symphyotrichum shortii*

TANACETUM *Tansy*

Annual or perennial herbs, sometimes somewhat woody at the base. Leaves alternate, pinnately dissected. Heads small, corymbiform or solitary, hemispheric to campanulate; discoid or nearly so, the outer flowers pistillate, with a short tubular corolla in some species expanded into a short yellow ray, or the pistillate flowers rarely wanting. Involucral bracts imbricate, dry, the margins and tips commonly scarious. Receptacle flat or convex, naked. Disk-flowers perfect, with 5-toothed tubular yellow corolla. Achenes mostly 5-ribbed, commonly glandular. Pappus a short crown, or none.

1 Rays present, white . . . . *T. parthenium*
1 Rays absent . . . . *T. vulgare*

Tanacetum parthenium (L.) Schultz-Bip.   MAP 387
FEVERFEW   *introduced*
> *Chrysanthemum parthenium* (L.) Bernh.
> *Matricaria parthenium* L.

Perennial with a taproot or stout caudex. **Stems** 3-8 dm tall, generally glabrous below, puberulent above. **Leaves** finely puberulent at least beneath, pinnatifid, with rounded, incised or again pinnate segments, evidently petiolate, the blade to 8 cm long and 6 cm wide. **Heads** several or numerous in a corymbiform inflorescence, the disk 5-9 mm wide; involucral bracts narrow, the inner with sharply marked hyaline tips; rays 10-20, or more numerous in double forms, 4-8 mm long, white. **Achenes** subterete, about 10-ribbed; pappus a minute crown, or obsolete. June-Sept.—Native of Europe, sometimes escaping from cultivation to waste places.

Tanacetum parthenium

Tanacetum vulgare L.   MAP 388
COMMON TANSY   *introduced (invasive)*

Coarse aromatic perennial with a stout rhizome, glabrous or nearly so throughout. **Stems** about 4-15 dm tall. **Leaves** numerous, 1-2 dm long and nearly half as wide, sessile or short-petiolate, punctate, pinnatifid, with evidently winged rachis, the pinnae again pinnatifid or deeply lobed, with broadly winged rachis, the pinnules often again toothed. **Heads** discoid, numerous, commonly about 20-200, the disk about 5-10 mm wide; pappus a minute crown, almost obsolete. Aug-Oct.—Native of the Old World, escaped from cultivation to roadsides, fields and waste places.

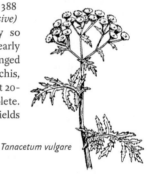

Tanacetum vulgare

TARAXACUM *Dandelion*

Perennial, scapose, taprooted herbs with milky juice. Leaves all basal, forming a rosette, entire to pinnatifid. Flowers all ligulate and perfect, mostly numerous. Heads solitary, erect; involucral bracts biseriate, the outer usually shorter than the inner and often reflexed. Fruit a columnar achene, longitudinally ribbed. Pappus of numerous capillary bristles.

1 Leaves generally deeply lobed or cut to midrib; mature achenes red-brown . . . . *T. erythrospermum*
1 Leaves various, deeply lobed to entire; mature achenes tan or olive-green . . . . *T. officinale*

Taraxacum erythrospermum Andrz. ex Besser   MAP 389
RED-SEED DANDELION   *introduced (naturalized)*
> *Taraxacum laevigatum* (Willd.) DC.

Similar to *T. officinale*, often more slender. **Leaves** generally very deeply cut for

386. Symphyotri. urophyllum   *387. Tanacetum parthenium*   *388. Tanacetum vulgare*   *389. Taraxacum erythrospermum*

their whole length, the lobes narrow, the terminal one seldom much larger than the lateral ones. **Heads** a little smaller, the involucre mostly 1-2 cm high, its inner bracts mostly 11-13, often somewhat corniculate, the outer bracts appressed to reflexed, a third to a little more than half as long as the inner. Body of the **achene** becoming bright red or reddish purple at maturity, commonly somewhat rugulose below as well as muricate above; beak usually stramineous, from more than twice as long to occasionally only half as long as the body. April-June.—Native of Eurasia, now established throughout much of Minn in fields, pastures, lawns, and other disturbed places, but less common than *T. officinale*.

Taraxacum officinale G.H. Weber   MAP 390
COMMON DANDELION   *introduced (naturalized)*

Leaves commonly sparsely hairy beneath and on the midrib, otherwise generally glabrous, or sometimes completely so, oblong lance-shaped, mostly 6-40 cm long and 0.7-15 cm wide, pinnatifid or lobed, the terminal lobe tending to be larger than the others, tapering to a narrow, scarcely or obscurely winged petiolar base. **Scape** 5-50 cm tall, glabrous or more or less villous, especially upwards. **Heads** usually large, the involucre mostly 1.5-2.5 cm high, the inner bracts mostly 13-20, these at first erect, finally reflexed, the mature achenes and pappus then forming a conspicuous ball easily disintegrated by the wind; outer bracts a little shorter and scarcely wider than the inner, reflexed. Body of the **achene** 3-4 mm long, pale gray-brown to olive-brown, muriculate above or sometimes to near the base, about half or a third as long as the slender beak; pappus white. March-Dec. —Native of Europe and adjacent Asia, now a cosmopolitan weed of lawns and disturbed sites.

Taraxacum officinale

TEPHROSERIS *Fleabane*

Tephroseris palustris (L.) Reichenbach   MAP 391
MARSH FLEABANE   *native*
> *Senecio congestus* (R. Br.) DC.
> *Senecio palustris* (L. Hook.

Annual or biennial herb, from a densely fibrous-rooted caudex, covered with loose arachnoid tomentum, especially among the heads in the inflorescence. **Stems** single, stout, to 1 m tall, hollow, sometimes pinkish. **Leaves** about equally distributed on the stem, somewhat larger on lower 1/2 of stem, oblanceolate, coarsely dentate to weakly pinnatifid, sometimes nearly entire, petiole short or absent, 5-15 cm long and 1-3(5) cm wide. Inflorescence of 6-20(40) heads in an open corymbiform cyme; involucral bracts ca. 21, 5-10 mm long, sometimes pink-tipped, ray florets ca. 21 or less, the ray to 8 mm long. **Achenes** glabrous but with many long pappus hairs. May-July.—Marshes, muddy shores, streambanks.

Tephroseris palustris

TRAGOPOGON *Goat's-Beard*

Biennial or perennial lactiferous herbs with a taproot. Leaves alternate, linear, entire, clasping, commonly grass-like. Heads solitary at the ends of the branches. Flowers all ligulate and perfect, yellow or purple. Involucre cylindric or campanulate, the bracts uniseriate, equal. Achenes linear, terete or angled, 5-10-nerved, narrowed at the base, slender-beaked, or the outer occasionally beakless. Pappus of a single series of plumose bristles, united at the base, the plume-branches interwebbed, several of the bristles commonly longer than the others and naked at the apex. *Our species may hybridize with the others where they grow together.*

1 Peduncle enlarged or inflated below the head; leaf tips not recurved . . . . **T. dubius**
1 Peduncle not enlarged; leaf tips recurved . . . . **T. pratensis**

Tragopogon dubius Scop.   MAP 392
MEADOW GOAT'S-BEARD   *introduced (naturalized)*
> *Tragopogon major* Jacq.

Similar to *T. porrifolius* but with yellow flowers and often smaller and less robust. **Leaves** averaging narrower. Involucral bracts sometimes more numerous.

Achenes (including beak) seldom over 3.5 cm long. May-July.—Native of Europe; roadsides and waste places.

Tragopogon pratensis L.
JACK-GO-TO-BED-AT-NOON

MAP 393
introduced (naturalized)

Glabrous perennial 1.5-8 dm tall. **Leaves** to 30 cm long and nearly 2 cm wide, often much narrower. Peduncles not at all enlarged in flower, scarcely so in fruit. Involucral bracts most commonly 8, mostly 12-24 mm long in flower, equaling or shorter than the yellow rays, elongating to 18-38 mm in fruit. **Achenes** 12-24 mm long, relatively shorter beaked, the body nearly or quite as long as in the other two species. May-Aug.—Native of Europe; roadsides, fields, waste places.

VERNONIA *Ironweed*

Vernonia fasciculata Michx.
SMOOTH IRONWEED

MAP 394
native

Stout perennial herb, from a thick rootstock. **Stems** erect, usually simple to the inflorescence, single or clumped, 5-12 dm long, red or purple, smooth but short-hairy on branches of the head. **Leaves** alternate, lance-shaped, 5-15 cm long and 1-4 cm wide, smooth above, underside finely pitted, margins serrate, petioles short. **Flower heads** usually many, crowded in flat-topped cymes to 10 cm wide, with purple disk flowers only (discoid), the limb 5-cleft; involucre 6-9 mm high, the involucral bracts overlapping, green with purple tips; receptacle flat, not chaffy. Achenes ribbed, 3-4 mm long; pappus of purple to brown, slender bristles. July-Sept.—Marshes, low prairie, streambanks.

ADDITIONAL SPECIES
Vernonia baldwinii Torr. (Western ironweed), Crow Wing and Goodhue counties.

Tragopogon pratensis

XANTHISMA

Xanthisma spinulosum (Pursh) D.R. Morgan & R.L. Hartman
LACY TANSY-ASTER
  Haplopappus spinulosus (Pursh) DC.

MAP 395
native

Perennial herb, finely glandular and tomentose, especially in the upper stem, or sometimes glabrous. **Stems** usually numerous, arising from a woody caudex, simple and erect below but branching upward, 5-8 dm tall. **Leaves** oblong to spatulate, 1.5-6 cm long and 2-10 mm wide, sessile or nearly so, margins dentate, the teeth bristle-tipped, or sometimes pinnately divided with bristle-tipped lobes; uppermost leaves smaller. **Heads** solitary at the ends of the branches; involucral bracts imbricate in 4 -6 series, acute and usually minutely bristle-tipped; **ray florets** 15-50 or more, the ligule yellow, to 1 cm long; **disk florets** numerous, corolla yellow, 4-5 mm long. **Achenes** narrow, ca. 2 mm long, weakly striate, sparsely appressed-hairy; pappus of scant yellow-brown bristles. May-Sep.—Dry prairies.

Vernonia fasciculata

Xanthisma spinulosum

XANTHIUM *Cocklebur*

Xanthium strumarium L.
COMMON COCKLEBUR

MAP 396
native

Weedy taprooted annual herb; plants variable in size and habit, rough-to-touch or sometimes nearly smooth. **Stems** 2-15 dm long, often brown-spotted. **Leaves**

390. *Taraxacum officinale*

391. *Tephroseris palustris*

392. *Tragopogon dubius*

393. *Tragopogon pratensis*

alternate, ovate to nearly round, sometimes with 3-5 shallow lobes, 3-15 cm long and 2-20 cm wide, margins with blunt teeth; petioles 3-10 cm long. **Flower heads** either staminate or pistillate, the staminate flowers brown, in clusters of small round heads at ends of stems above the larger pistillate heads; pistillate heads in several to many clusters from leaf axils, each head with 2 flowers, with a spiny involucre enclosing the head; petals absent. **Fruit** a brown bur formed by the involucre, 1.5-3 cm long, covered with hooked prickles; achenes thick, 1 in each of the 2 chambers of the bur; pappus none. Aug-Sept.—Shores, streambanks, wet meadows, sand bars, dried depressions, often where disturbed; also in cultivated and abandoned fields, roadsides and waste places.

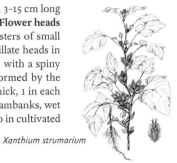

Xanthium strumarium

Balsaminaceae TOUCH-ME-NOT FAMILY

IMPATIENS *Touch-Me-Not*

Smooth annual herbs with hollow, succulent stems and shallow, weak roots. Leaves simple, alternate, the blades shallowly toothed. Flowers with both staminate and pistillate parts, irregular, yellow to orange-yellow, pouchlike and spurred, hanging from the petioles in few-flowered racemes from upper leaf axils; sepals 3, petal-like; petals 3; stamens 5. Fruit a 5-valved capsule; the mature capsules splitting when jarred or touched, scattering the seeds away from parent plants. *Small, cleistogamous (self-fertile) flowers lacking petals are sometimes produced in summer and are often the only flowers on plants growing in shaded situations.*

ADDITIONAL SPECIES
Impatiens glandulifera Royle (Policeman's helmet), native to Himalayan region;Lake County, in milder climates can be highly invasive.

1   Flowers orange-yellow, usually with red-brown spots; common . . . . *I. capensis*
1   Flowers pale yellow, spots faint or absent; uncommon . . . . *I. pallida*

Impatiens capensis Meerb.
SPOTTED TOUCH-ME-NOT; JEWELWEED
  Impatiens biflora Walt.

MAP 397
native

Annual herb. **Stems** 3-10 dm long, usually branched above. **Leaves** ovate to oval, 3-9 cm long and 1.5-4 cm wide, tapered to tip or rounded and tipped with a short slender point, margins shallowly and irregularly toothed; petioles longest on lower leaves, shorter upward, 0.5-5 cm long. **Flowers** orange-yellow, 1.5-3 cm long, usually mottled with red-brown spots, with a spur recurved parallel to the sac and to half its length. **Fruit** a capsule about 2 cm long, splitting when mature to forcefully eject the seeds. July-Sept.—Swamps, low areas in woods, floodplain forests, thickets, streambanks, shores, marshes, fens, springs; often where disturbed.

Impatiens pallida Nutt.
PALE TOUCH-ME-NOT

MAP 398
native

Impatiens capensis

Annual herb, similar to orange touch-me-not (*I. capensis*) but less common. *I. pallida* is typically larger, the leaves to 12 cm long and 8 cm wide, and more finely toothed than those of *I. capensis*. **Flowers** pale yellow, unspotted or with faint red-brown spots, 2-4 cm long, the spur recurved at a right angle to sac, and to 1/4 length of sac. July-Sept.—Floodplain forests, low spots in woods, swamps, streambanks, shores; often where somewhat disturbed.

394. *Vernonia fasciculata*   395. *Xanthisma spinulosum*   396. *Xanthium strumarium*   397. *Impatiens capensis*

Berberidaceae BARBERRY FAMILY

Herbs or shrubs. Leaves alternate or basal, simple, lobed, or compound. Flowers solitary, racemose or cymose; perfect, all parts free and distinct. Sepals 4 or 6, sometimes early deciduous, in some genera petal-like. Petals as many as or more than the sepals, petaloid or reduced to nectaries. Stamens as many as the petals. Ovary 1-celled. Fruit a berry or capsule.

1 Plants spiny shrubs . . . . *Berberis*
1 Plants smooth perennial herbs 2
  2 Flowers in a small panicle-like cyme . . . . *Caulophyllum thalictroides*
  2 Flowers single 3
    3 Leaves all basal, the flowering stem naked . . . . *Jeffersonia diphylla*
    3 Flowering stem with a pair of opposite leaves below inflorescence . . . . *Podophyllum peltatum*

BERBERIS *Barberry*

Spiny shrubs. Leaves of the shoots reduced to alternate, simple or 3-branched spines, with clusters of small foliage leaves in their axils. Flowers yellow, in elongate racemes, umbel-like clusters, or sometimes solitary. Sepals 6, petal-like, subtended by 2 or 3 small bracts. Petals 6, usually smaller than the sepals and with 2 glands at their base. Stamens 6, appressed to the sepals until irritated, when they rapidly bend toward the center. Fruit a red, one to few-seeded berry.

1 Leaves entire; flowers single or in clusters of 2-4 . . . . *B. thunbergii*
1 Leaves tipped by a small spine; flowers in racemes of 10-20 flowers . . . . *B. vulgaris*

Berberis thunbergii DC.
JAPANESE BARBERRY   MAP 399
                                 introduced (invasive)
Densely and divaricately branched shrub to 2 m tall; spines usually simple. **Leaves** obovate to spatulate, usually obtuse, entire, narrowed at base to a short petiole. **Flowers** solitary or in small clusters of 2-4, about 8 mm wide. **Fruit** about 1 cm long. May.—Native of Japan; planted for low hedges and sometimes escaped along roadsides and in thickets.

Berberis vulgaris

Berberis vulgaris L.
EUROPEAN BARBERRY   MAP 400
                                 introduced (invasive)
Freely branched shrub to 3 m tall. **Leaves** obovate to obovate-oblong, 2-5 cm long, obtuse or acute, finely spinulose-denticulate, the veinlets prominently reticulate beneath. **Racemes** usually 3-6 cm long, with 10-20 flowers on pedicels 5-10 mm long; petals entire. **Fruit** about 1 cm long.—Native of Europe. *Formerly widely planted and frequently escaped along roadsides and fences and in open woods; now largely purposefully exterminated as the alternate host of black rust of wheat.*

CAULOPHYLLUM *Blue Cohosh*

Caulophyllum thalictroides (L.) Michx.
BLUE COHOSH   MAP 401
                                 native
Smooth perennial herb. **Stems** erect, 3-8 dm tall, glaucous when young, bearing above the middle a single large, sessile, 3-parted leaf, and another smaller leaf just below the panicle. **Leaflets** obovate-oblong, 2-5-lobed above the middle, 5-8 cm long when fully grown. **Flowers** yellowish green or greenish purple, nearly 1 cm

Caulophyllum thalictroides

398. *Impatiens pallida*   399. *Berberis thunbergii*   400. *Berberis vulgaris*   401. *Caulophyllum thalictroides*

wide, in a panicle 3-6 cm long; sepals 6, petal-like, subtended by 3 or 4 sepal-like bracts; petals 6, reduced to small gland-like bodies much shorter than the sepals and opposite them; stamens 6; ovary soon ruptured by the enlarging seeds, which ripen exposed on short stout stalks and resembling drupes; seeds dark blue, 5-8 mm long, on stalks of nearly the same length. April-May.—Rich moist woods.

JEFFERSONIA *Twinleaf*

Jeffersonia diphylla (L.) Pers.   MAP 402
TWINLEAF   *native*

Smooth perennial herb. **Leaves** basal, deeply divided into 2 half-ovate segments; petioles at first shorter than the scapes, elongating to 3-5 dm; blades immature at anthesis, eventually 8-15 cm long. **Flowers** 2-3 cm wide, solitary on a naked scape; scape at anthesis 1-2 dm tall, later elongating; sepals usually 4, early deciduous; petals white, usually 8, narrowed at base; stamens as many as the petals; ovary ovoid,, tapering to a broad sessile stigma. **Fruit** capsular, 2-3 cm long, obovoid, opening in the upper portion by a horizontal cleft extending halfway around it, the top forming a lid; seeds numerous. April-May.—Rich woods, preferring calcareous soil.

Jeffersonia diphylla

PODOPHYLLUM *May-Apple*

Podophyllum peltatum L.   MAP 403
MAY-APPLE   *native*

Herb, from a perennial rhizome, usually colony-forming. **Flowering stem** 3-5 dm tall, bearing a pair of leaves and a short-peduncled, solitary, terminal flower. **Sterile plants** bearing a single, large, peltate, deeply radially lobed, terminal leaf; **fertile plants** bearing 2 half-round, similarly lobed leaves. **Flowers** 3-5 cm wide, on a short nodding peduncle; sepals 6, falling early; petals 6-9, white; stamens 2x as many as the petals; ovary ovoid, with a large sessile stigma. **Fruit** a yellow, ovoid, fleshy, many-seeded berry 4-5 cm long. May; fruit ripe in Aug.—Moist, preferably open woods. *The ripened fruit is edible in small amounts, toxic if consumed in large quantities; rhizome, leaves and seeds toxic.*

Podophyllum peltatum

Betulaceae BIRCH FAMILY

Medium to large trees, or shrubs. Leaves deciduous, simple, alternate, with toothed margins and pinnate veins. Flowers small, staminate and pistillate flowers separate on same plant, crowded into catkins (aments) that open in spring before leaves fully open; staminate catkins hang downward; conelike pistillate catkins erect or drooping. Fruit a small, 1-seeded, winged nutlet.

1   Plants in flower 2
  2   Pistillate flowers 1 or several in a cluster . . . . *Corylus*
  2   Pistillate flowers in catkins 3
    3   Each bract of staminate catkin with 1 flower, this without sepals 4
      4   Staminate catkins in groups of 1 . . . . *Carpinus caroliniana*
      4   Staminate catkins usually in clusters of 3 . . . . *Ostrya virginiana*
    3   Each bract of staminate catkin with 3-6 flowers, each with sepals 5
      5   Pistillate bracts 3-lobed; stamens 2 . . . . *Betula*
      5   Pistillate bracts 5-lobed; stamens 3-5 . . . . *Alnus*
1   Plants in fruit 6
  6   Each fruit (nut) subtended by leaf-like bracts 7
    7   Shrubs; nut 1 cm long or more . . . . *Corylus*
    7   Trees; nut to 6 mm long 8
      8   Bark furrowed and shredding, gray-brown, bracts saclike, enclosing the nut . . . . *Ostrya virginiana*
      8   Bark smooth and gray; bracts not enclosing the nut . . . . *Carpinus caroliniana*
  6   Fruit without leafy bracts, in the axil of a small scaly bract 9
    9   Bracts woody, widely spreading from rachis of cone . . . . *Alnus*
    9   Bracts papery, ascending . . . . *Betula*

ALNUS *Alder*

Thicket-forming shrubs, or an introduced tree. Leaves deciduous, ovate, toothed on margins. Staminate and pistillate flowers separate on same plant, staminate flowers in long, drooping catkins which fall after shedding pollen; pistillate flowers in short, persistent conelike clusters. Fruit a flattened achene with winged or thin margins.

1 Introduced tree (reported for Minn); leaves broadly rounded, tip rounded to blunt or notched .... *A. glutinosa*
1 Shrubs; leaves ovate to oval, tapered to a sharp tip 2
  2 Twigs and young leaves sticky, leaves with small sharp teeth; catkins on long stalks; fruit broadly winged ..
  .... *A. viridis*
  2 Twigs and young leaves not sticky, leaves unevenly double-toothed; catkins stalkless or on short stalks; fruit narrowly winged .... *A. incana*

Alnus glutinosa (L.) Gaertn.
EUROPEAN ALDER

(NO MAP)
introduced (invasive)

Tree to 20 m tall; twigs, young leaves and fruit sticky. **Leaves** oval to nearly round, tip rounded or with a small notch, veins 5-8 on each side of midvein, dark green and more or less shiny above, paler below, margins finely toothed. Staminate and pistillate **flowers** separate on same tree; **pistillate catkins** drooping from leaf axils, 1.5-2.5 cm long and 10-12 mm wide. April–May. Floodplain forests, riverbanks; also in drier places.—Introduced from Eurasia and planted as an ornamental; occasionally escaping; reported for Minn.

Alnus glutinosa

Alnus incana (L.) Moench
SPECKLED ALDER; TAG ALDER
  Alnus rugosa (Du Roi) Spreng.

MAP 404
native

Thicket-forming shrub to 5 m tall; twigs red-brown, waxy, with conspicuous pale lenticels. **Leaves** ovate to oval, broadest near or below middle, 6-14 cm long and 4-7 cm wide, dark green and smooth above, paler and hairy below; margins sharply toothed and shallowly lobed; petioles 1-2.5 cm long. **Flowers** in catkins clustered at ends of branches; **staminate catkins** developing in late summer, short-stalked, elongate, 4-9 cm long; **pistillate catkins** appear in late summer, stalkless, rounded, 1-2 cm long and to 1 cm wide, the scales unlobed, becoming conelike, persistent. **Fruit** a flat nutlet, narrowly winged on margin, 2-4 mm long. April–June.—Swamps, thickets, bog margins, shores and streambanks.

Alnus incana

Alnus viridis (Vill.) Lam. & DC.
GREEN ALDER
  Alnus crispa (Ait.) Pursh

MAP 405
native

Thicket-forming shrub to 4 m tall; bark red-brown to gray; twigs brown, sticky, somewhat hairy, lenticels pale and scattered. **Leaves** round-oval, bright green above, slightly paler and shiny below, sticky when young, margins wavy with small, sharp teeth; petioles 6-12 mm long. **Flowers** in catkins; **staminate catkins** stalked, slender, developing in late summer and expanding in spring; **pistillate catkins** appear in spring, becoming long-stalked, blunt and conelike, persistent, 1-2 cm long. **Fruit** a nutlet, 2-3 mm long, with a pale, thin wing.—Lakeshores, wet depressions in woods, rock outcrops, beaches along Lake Superior.

Alnus viridis

402. *Jeffersonia diphylla*   403. *Podophyllum peltatum*   404. *Alnus incana*   405. *Alnus viridis*

BETULA *Birch*

Trees or shrubs, often with multiple stems from base; bark sometimes peeling in thin layers. Leaves deciduous, alternate, sharply toothed. Staminate and pistillate flowers separate on same plant, catkins appearing in fall, opening the following spring, staminate flowers in drooping slender catkins; pistillate flowers in erect conelike catkins. Fruit an wing-margined achene (samara).

ADDITIONAL SPECIES AND HYBRIDS

· *Betula × purpusii* Schneid., hybrid between *B. alleghaniensis* and *B. pumila*; mostly east-central Minn.

· *Betula × sandbergii* Britt., hybrid between *B. papyrifera* and *B. pumila*; common, especially n and c Minn.

1 Shrub to 2 m tall; bark not shredding; leaves to 5 cm long . . . . *B. pumila*
1 Small to large trees; bark shredding with age 2
  2 Bark white; samara wings as wide or wider than body . . . . *B. papyrifera*
  2 Bark red-brown or yellow-gray; samara wings narrower than body 3
    3 Bark red-brown; leaves wedge-shaped at base, margins wavy-toothed . . . . *B. nigra*
    3 Bark yellow-gray; leaves rounded at base, margins not wavy-toothed . . . . *B. alleghaniensis*

Betula alleghaniensis Britt.

YELLOW BIRCH

Betula lutea Michx. f.

MAP 406
native

Medium to large tree to 25 m tall; **bark** on young trees thin and smooth with conspicuous horizontal lenticels, becoming yellow-gray and shredding into thin, shaggy horizontal strips; bark of old trees breaking into large plates; **twigs** hairy when young, becoming smooth and shiny, wintergreen-scented when crushed. **Leaves** alternate, simple, ovate, tapered to a short, sharp tip, dark green above, paler yellow-green below, 6-12 cm long, margins coarsely double-toothed, petioles grooved and hairy. Staminate and pistillate **flowers** in catkins, separate on same tree, appearing before leaves in spring; **staminate catkins** drooping, yellow-purple, 7-10 cm long; **pistillate catkins** erect, green, 2-4 cm long, more or less stalkless. **Fruit** a winged nutlet, 3-5 mm wide. April-May.—Moist forests with sugar maple; also occasional in swamps, thickets, and forest depressions with red maple, black ash, black spruce, eastern hemlock and *Alnus incana*.

Betula alleghaniensis

Betula nigra L.

RIVER BIRCH

MAP 407
native

Small or medium tree to 20 m tall, trunk to 6 dm wide, crown rounded; bark red-brown, shredding and curly; twigs slender, red-brown; buds pointed, hairy. **Leaves** alternate, simple, ovate, 4-8 cm long, upper surface smooth, lower surface paler and densely hairy; margins coarsely double-toothed, except untoothed near base; petioles with woolly hairs. Staminate and pistillate flowers small, separate but on same tree; **staminate flowers** in slender drooping clusters; **pistillate flowers** in short, woolly clusters. **Fruit** a small hairy nutlet with a 3-lobed, winged margin, crowded in a cylindrical cone 1.5-3 cm long. May.—Floodplain forests, riverbanks, swamps.

Betula nigra

Betula papyrifera Marsh.

WHITE BIRCH; PAPER BIRCH

MAP 408
native

Trees, usually 20 m or shorter; trunks single or sometimes 2 or more. Bark of young trunks and branches dark reddish brown, smooth; in maturity creamy to chalky white, peeling in paper-thin sheets; lenticels pale, horizontal, in maturity dark, much expanded. **Twigs** without strong odor and taste of wintergreen,

406. *Betula alleghaniensis*

407. *Betula nigra*

408. *Betula papyrifera*

409. *Betula pumila*

slightly to moderately pubescent, infrequently with small, scattered, resinous glands. Leaf blade ovate, with 9 or fewer pairs of lateral veins, 5-9 cm long and 4-7 cm wide, base rounded or truncate; lower surface pubescent, often velvety-hairy along major veins and in vein axils; margins coarsely or irregularly doubly serrate. **Flowers** in pendulous, cylindric catkins, 2.5-5 cm long, readily shattering with fruits in late fall; scales pubescent to glabrous. **Samaras** with wings as wide as or slightly wider than body. Late spring.—Moist, open, upland forest, especially where rocky; also on sand dunes swamps and sometimes in swampy woods; especially characteristic after fire or timber harvests, when seedlings are often abundant. *Includes **B. papyrifera Marsh. var. cordifolia (Regel) Fern.**, sometimes considered a separate species (B. cordifolia Regel), and present in ne Minn. The bark, which has a high oil content making it waterproof, was used for a wide variety of building and clothing purposes by Native Americans.*

Betula papyrifera

Betula pumila L.

MAP 409

BOG BIRCH

native

  Betula glandulosa var. *glandulifera* (Regel) Gleason

Shrub 1-3 m tall; bark dull gray or brown; twigs gray, short-hairy and dotted with resin glands, becoming red-brown and waxy with age. **Leaves** leathery, rounded to obovate, 2-4 cm long and 1-3 cm wide, dark green above, paler and often waxy below; margins coarsely toothed, the teeth blunt or sharp; petioles 3-6 mm long. **Flowers** in catkins; **staminate catkins** stalkless, cylindric, 15-20 mm long and 2-3 mm wide; **pistillate catkins** stalked, cylindric, 1-2 cm long and 5 mm wide; scales 3-lobed. **Fruit** a flat, winged, rounded nutlet, 2-3 mm long and 2-4 mm wide. May.—Swamps, bogs, fens, seeps; often where calcium-rich.

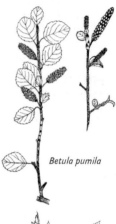

Betula pumila

CARPINUS *Hornbeam*

Carpinus caroliniana Walt.

MAP 410

HORNBEAM; IRONWOOD

native

Tall shrub or small tree up to 10 m tall, with fluted trunk and smooth, blue-gray or ashy gray bark. **Leaves** oblong to oblong-ovate, 5-12 cm long; margins sharply and often doubly serrate. **Staminate catkins** slender, pendulous; scales ovate, each subtending a single naked flower composed of several stamens. **Pistillate catkins** slender, 2-5 cm long; scales ovate, deciduous; pistillate flowers in pairs, each subtended by a minute bract adnate at base to 2 minute bractlets; calyx minute. **Fruit** a small ribbed nutlet.—Moist woods.

Carpinus caroliniana

CORYLUS *Hazelnut*

Shrubs or small trees. Leaves doubly serrate. Staminate catkins elongate, cylindric, emerging in autumn, reaching anthesis in early spring. Stamens 4, the filaments deeply bipartite, each division bearing a half-anther. Pistillate catkins small, ovoid, resembling a leaf-bud, the few closely imbricate scales concealing the flowers, except the elongate protruding stigmas. Flower subtended by a minute bract and 2 bractlets, becoming greatly enlarged at maturity and enclosing the hard-shelled edible nut. Ovary inferior, surmounted by the minute calyx.

1 Twigs and leaf petioles with glandular bristles . . . . **C. americana**
1 Twigs and petioles not glandular-bristly . . . . **C. cornuta**

Corylus americana Walt.

MAP 411

AMERICAN HAZELNUT

native

Shrub 1-3 m tall, the young twigs and petioles more or less pubescent (hairs red when young) and normally beset with stout stipitate glands. **Leaves** broadly ovate to obovate, finely doubly serrate, broadly rounded to cordate at base, paler and more or less pubescent beneath. Involucral bracts pubescent but not bristly, closely surrounding the nut and prolonged beyond it into a broadly dilated, flattened beak, cut at the summit into broadly triangular lobes, the whole 1.5-3 cm long. **Nut** compressed, 1-1.5 cm long.—Dry or moist woods and thickets.

Corylus americana

Corylus cornuta Marsh.
BEAKED HAZELNUT

MAP 412
native

Shrub 1-3 m tall, the young twigs villous, later nearly glabrous. **Leaves** oblong or obovate, broadly rounded to subcordate at base, pale green beneath, pubescent, especially on the veins and in the vein-axils beneath; margins coarsely doubly serrate. Involucre usually densely bristly toward the base, closely surrounding the nut and prolonged beyond it into a long slender beak cut at the summit into narrowly triangular lobes, the whole 4-7 cm long. **Nut** short-ovoid, scarcely compressed, 1-1.5 cm long.—Moist woods and thickets.

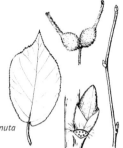
Corylus cornuta

OSTRYA *Hop-Hornbeam*

Ostrya virginiana (P. Mill.) K. Koch
HOP-HORNBEAM

MAP 413
native

Tree or tall shrubs to 20 m tall, with light brown scaly bark; twigs and petioles at first pilose, eventually nearly glabrous, occasionally also stipitate-glandular. **Leaves** alternate, narrowly to broadly oblong or ovate; margins sharply and often doubly serrate. **Catkins** opening with the leaves in spring; **staminate catkins** elongate, densely flowered, composed of spirally arranged scales, tipped with a sharp point and each subtending a cluster of several stamens; filaments shortdivided at the summit, each branch bearing a half-anther; **pistillate catkins** short-cylindric, 3-5 cm long, loosely flowered, the ovate, hairy bracts early deciduous; calyx minute. **Fruit** a flattened-ovoid nutlet about 5 mm long.—Moist or dry woods and banks.

Ostrya virginiana

Bignoniaceae TRUMPET-CREEPER FAMILY

CATALPA *Catalpa*

Catalpa speciosa Warder
NORTHERN CATALPA

MAP 414
introduced

Tree to 30 m tall, with well developed central trunk. **Leaves** simple, opposite or whorled, broadly ovate, to 3 dm long, distinctly acuminate, pubescent beneath, entire or shallowly lobed. **Flowers** perfect, 5-merous, in terminal panicles to 2 dm long; calyx closed in bud, at anthesis usually splitting into 2 unequal lobes; corolla large, campanulate, with 5 spreading lobes erose or crisped on the margin, white, marked with 2 yellow stripes and faintly spotted with purple, the limb 5-6 cm wide and shorter than the tube; stamens commonly 2, about as long as the corolla tube. **Capsule** linear, nearly terete 2-5 dm long and 1-1.5 cm thick; seeds flat, about 25 mm long, the 2 wings rounded and bearing a flat fringe of hairs. May-June.—Alluvial forests; native to sc USA, adventive in Minn.

ADDITIONAL SPECIES
Catalpa ovata G. Don (Chinese catalpa), introduced, Houston County.

Catalpa speciosa

Catalpa ovata

410. Carpinus caroliniana

411. Corylus americana

412. Corylus cornuta

413. Ostrya virginiana

Boraginaceae BORAGE FAMILY

Annual or perennial herbs with usually bristly stems and alternate, bristly leaves; plants glabrous in eastern bluebells (*Mertensia virginica*). Flowers typically in a spirally coiled, spike-like head that uncurls as flowers mature; flowers perfect (with both staminate and pistillate parts), with 5 petals, 4-5 sepals, and 5 stamens. Fruit a dry capsule with 4 nutlets. *Ellisia and **Hydrophyllum** previously included in Hydrophyllaceae and lack the deeply 4-lobed ovary of other Boraginaceae.*

ADDITIONAL SPECIES

• *Borago officinalis* L. (Borage), annual herb, 2-6 dm tall, with hirsute stem and bright blue flowers in large terminal cymes; sometimes cultivated as a salad herb; rarely escaped in waste places and roadsides; see key.

• *Buglossoides arvensis* (L.) I.M. Johnston (Corn-gromwell), annual from a slender taproot; flowers solitary in axils of the crowded upper leaves, white or bluish white; native of Eurasia, introduced as a weed in waste places; reported for Minn.

• *Phacelia franklinii* (R. Br.) A. Gray (Franklin's phacelia, MAP 415); rare in ne Minn on cliffs, talus, and rocks. Leaves pinnately parted with many lacerate lobes; flowers (June-July) bluish to white, subsessile, many in a hairy spiraled raceme (❧*threatened*).

1   Leaves shallowly palmately lobed to deeply pinnately divided 2
   2   Flowers on solitary pedicels opposite alternate leaves; stem leaves at lowest nodes opposite. . *Ellisia nyctelea*
   2   Flowers in terminal inflorescences; stem leaves all alternate. . . . . *Hydrophyllum*
1   Leaves simple, entire 3
   3   Plants glabrous . . . . *Mertensia virginica*
   3   Plants hairy 4
      4   Plants in flower 5
         5   Corolla rotate, the upper portion of the corolla lobes reflexed and disk-like . . . . *Borago officinalis**
         5   Corolla not rotate 6
           6   Flowers irregular; stamens conspicuously exserted . . . . *Echium vulgare*
           6   Flowers regular; stamens not longer than corolla 7
              7   Corolla blue or purple, or leaf base extending downward along stem (decurrent) 8
                8   Flowers more than 1 cm long 9
                   9   Leaf bases decurrent along stem . . . . *Symphytum*
                   9   Leaf bases not decurrent along stem . . . . *Mertensia paniculata*
                8   Flowers less than 1 cm long; leaf bases not decurrent 10
                  10   Leaves 2 cm or more wide, or calyx lobes 5 mm long or more 11
                     11   Calyx lobes downy-hairy . . . . *Cynoglossum*
                     11   Calyx lobes coarsely hairy . . . . *Anchusa*
                  10   Leaves less than 2 cm wide and calyx lobes less than 5 mm long 12
                    12   Flowers all subtended by bracts . . . . *Lappula*
                    12   Only lowest flowers with bracts 13
                       13   Calyx much longer than pedicel and with coarse appressed hairs . . . .
                           . . . . *Plagiobothrys hispidulus*
                     13   Calyx shorter or longer than pedicel, with spreading or glandular hairs . . *Myosotis*
              7   Corolla not blue or purple; the leaf bases not decurrent along the stem 14
             14   Style well-exserted beyond corolla . . . . *Lithospermum onosmodium*
             14   Style included or only slightly exserted from corolla 15
                15   Style 2-lobed, stigmas 2 . . . . *Lithospermum*
                15   Style not lobed, stigma 1 16
                  16   Corolla yellow . . . . *Amsinckia lycopsoides*
                  16   Corolla white 17
                    17   Leaves 2 cm or more wide . . . . *Hackelia*
                    17   Leaves less than 2 cm wide 18
                      18   Flowers with subtending bracts . . . . *Lappula*
                      18   Most flowers without subtending bracts . . . . *Myosotis*
      4   Plants in fruit 19
        19   Nutlets covered with bristly hairs, the hairs hooked at tip 20
        20   Leaves less than 1 cm wide . . . . *Lappula*
        20   Leaves more than 1 cm wide 21
          21   Sepals when mature more than 5 mm long . . . . *Cynoglossum*
          21   Sepals when mature less than 5 mm long . . . . *Hackelia*

ANCHUSA *Bugloss*

Anchusa arvensis (L.) Bieb.
SMALL BUGLOSS
  Lycopsis arvensis L.

MAP 416
introduced

Perennial herb; stems and leaves hirsute or hispid. **Stems** erect or ascending, usually branched, 2-6 dm tall. **Leaves** narrowly oblong, 4-8 cm long, dentate or entire. **Flowers** small, blue, in numerous, elongating, bracteate cymes or racemes, these usually paired at ends of ascending axillary branches; calyx divided to the middle or below; corolla salverform, 6-8 mm long, about 5 mm wide, barely surpassing the calyx, with conspicuous appendages in the throat; stamens and style short, included in the corolla tube; style 1, simple; stigma 1. Nutlets ovoid, angular and wrinkled. June-Sept.—Introduced as a weed in waste places.

Anchusa arvensis

CYNOGLOSSUM *Hound's-Tongue*

Biennial or perennial herbs. Leaves large, usually pubescent. Flowers pediceled in elongating, bractless, axillary and terminal racemes. Calyx deeply parted, in fruit reflexed by the growth of the nutlets. Corolla broadly funnelform, the short tube closed by 5 appendages at the throat. Stamens included in the corolla tube. Style slender; stigma 1. Nutlets with conspicuous, stout, hooked bristles.

1 Flowers red-purple; leaves many, continuing upward on stem into inflorescence, not clasping stem . *C. officinale*
1 Flowers blue; leaves few, not in inflorescence, the upper leaves clasping at base . . . . *C. boreale*

Cynoglossum boreale Fern.
WILD COMFREY
  Cynoglossum virginianum subsp. *boreale* (Fern). A. Haines

MAP 417
native

Perennial herb. **Stems** erect, unbranched, 4-8 dm tall. **Basal leaves** elliptic-oblong, the blades 1-2 dm long, tapering at base and decurrent upon the long petiole; **stem**

414. *Catalpa speciosa*

415. *Phacelia franklinii*

416. *Anchusa arvensis*

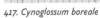

417. *Cynoglossum boreale*

leaves sessile, progressively smaller, some broadly clasping at base, some often narrowed below and more or less expanded at the very base. **Racemes** 1-4, usually 3, at maturity 1-2 dm long, terminating a long, erect, terminal peduncle; calyx at anthesis 3-4 mm long; corolla blue, 8-12 mm wide, its broadly rounded lobes more or less overlapping; fruiting pedicels 5-15 mm long, recurved. **Nutlets** 6-8 mm long, uniformly bristly over the exterior surface. May-June.—Upland woods.

Cynoglossum officinale L.   MAP 418
HOUND'S-TONGUE   *introduced (naturalized)*
Biennial herb, the stem and foliage finely and usually softly pubescent. **Stems** erect, branched above, 6-10 dm tall. Basal and lower **leaves** oblong or oblong lance-shaped, to 3 dm long, tapering to a long petiole-like base; **upper leaves** progressively shorter and proportionately narrower, the uppermost sessile. **Racemes** numerous, divaricate, eventually 1-2 dm long; mature pedicels spreading; corolla dull red or red-purple, rarely white, about 8 mm wide. **Nutlets** 5-8 mm long, uniformly bristly, surrounded by a low ridge with crowded bristles. May-Aug.—Native of Eurasia; established in fields, meadows, and open woods.

ECHIUM *Viper's-Bugloss*

Echium vulgare L.   MAP 419
COMMON VIPER'S-BUGLOSS   *introduced (naturalized)*

Cynoglossum officinale

Biennial, very hispid herb. **Stems** erect, simple or branched, 4-8 dm tall. **Leaves** linear-oblong to oblong lance-shaped, the basal to 15 cm long, the upper progressively smaller, the uppermost bract-like. **Cymes** numerous, in the axils of the upper foliage leaves, at first coiled, straightening with age. **Flowers** sessile, crowded, subtended by linear bracts; calyx deeply parted; corolla blue, rarely white, pubescent, narrowly campanulate, somewhat curved, conspicuously longer on the upper side, 12-20 mm long; stamens inserted near the middle of the corolla tube, the slender filaments unequal in length, long-exsert; style elongate, usually pubescent, shortly 2-cleft at the summit. **Nutlets** ovoid, 3-angled, rough.—Native of s Europe, weedy in waste places, roadsides, and meadows, usually where sandy or gravelly.

ELLISIA *Aunt Lucy*

Echium vulgare

Ellisia nyctelea (L.) L.   (NO MAP)
WATER-POD   *native*
Annual herb. **Stems** weak, ascending or spreading, 1-4 dm long, usually branched from the base, glabrous or sparsely hispid. **Leaves** 3-8 cm long, pubescent, deeply pinnatifid, divided almost to the midvein into 7-13 widely spreading, oblong, entire or more commonly coarsely few-toothed lobes, petioled. **Flowers** solitary on short pedicels arising opposite the leaves; sepals triangular-lance-shaped, united at base; corolla white, 5-8 mm long, narrowly campanulate, about equaling the calyx, and the ovate lobes distinctly shorter than the tube; stamens 5, glabrous, inserted at the base of the corolla and shorter than the tube. Fruiting pedicels drooping, becoming 2 cm long; fruiting calyx star-shaped, about 2 cm wide. **Capsule** globose, much exceeded by the calyx. May.—Moist alluvial woods; reported for Minn.

Ellisia nyctelea

HACKELIA *Stickseed; Beggar's-Lice*
Perennial herbs with numerous, usually paired racemes terminating the axillary branches; racemes bracteate for at least part of their length; flowers small, blue or white. Corolla deeply 5-cleft into narrow lobes. Corolla salverform or broadly funnelform, the tube shorter than to scarcely surpassing the calyx, the throat nearly closed by the small appendages. Stamens and style short, included in the corolla tube. Fruiting pedicels short, recurved or reflexed. Nutlets attached by a lance-shaped to ovate area occupying the middle third only, the terminal third free, the basal third free and often with 2 low divergent keels; dorsal area lance-shaped, bordered by a row of hooked bristles and in some species bearing similar bristles on the surface.

1   Corolla blue; widest stem leaves to 2.5 cm broad .... *H. deflexa*
1   Corolla white; widest stem leaves to 3-5 cm broad .... *H. virginiana*

Hackelia deflexa (Wahlenb.) Opiz
NODDING STICKSEED

MAP 420
native

Stems to 1 m tall, freely branched above, the branches all terminated by racemes (usually paired). Lower **leaves** long-tapering to a petiole-like base; middle and upper leaves oblong-elliptic, to 10 cm long, sharply pointed at both ends. **Racemes** eventually 5-10 cm long, spreading; bracts linear or lance-shaped, reduced above and often absent beyond the middle of the raceme, opposite the flowers or alternate with them; fruiting pedicels 2-4 mm long, abruptly deflexed at base; corolla white or pale blue, about 2 mm wide. **Nutlets** with an ovate dorsal area 2-3 mm long, with a few short bristles on the back, bearing a marginal row of flat hooked bristles. May-Aug.—Moist woods, thickets, and hillsides.

Hackelia virginiana (L.) I. M. Johnston
BEGGAR'S-LICE

MAP 421
native

Stems to 1 m tall, freely branched above and bearing numerous racemes. Lower **leaves** narrowed to a petiole, to 2 dm long; middle and upper leaves oblong-elliptic, 5-10 cm long, about 1/4 to 1/3 as wide, sharply narrowed to both ends, sessile; uppermost leaves, above the lowest flowering branch, progressively reduced and passing into the small, lance-shaped to linear bracts. **Racemes** eventually 5-15 cm long, spreading; bracts often alternate with the flowers, those beyond the middle of the raceme minute or lacking; fruiting pedicels 2-5 mm long, reflexed or recurved; corolla white or pale blue, about 2 mm wide. **Nutlets** forming a globose cluster of 4, bearing about 10-15 erect bristles as long as the marginal ones. July-Sept.—Dry or moist upland woods.

Hackelia virginiana

HYDROPHYLLUM   *Waterleaf*

Perennial herbs from horizontal rhizomes. Leaves large, lobed or divided. Flowers several to many in a repeatedly forked cyme. Sepals separate to below the middle or nearly to the base. Corolla campanulate to tubular, lobed to or below the middle, the lobes erect or somewhat spreading, white to purple. Stamens equaling the corolla or exsert, the slender filaments usually villous. Style 1, shortly bifid at the summit. Ovary 1-celled. Capsule globose, hispid or pubescent.

1   Leaves pinnately compound, divided into 5-7 leaflets or lobes .... *H. virginianum*
1   Leaves palmately lobed .... *H. appendiculatum*

Hydrophyllum appendiculatum Michx.
GREAT WATERLEAF

MAP 422
native

Stems at anthesis 3-6 dm tall, the upper portion and inflorescence densely pubescent with short hairs 0.3-0.5 mm long and also conspicuously hirsute with longer hairs 2-3 mm long. **Stem leaves** mostly overtopped by the cymes, orbicular in outline, 6-15 cm wide at anthesis, shallowly 5-7 lobed; sepals separate nearly to the base, lance-shaped, densely hirsute, alternating with small but conspicuous reflexed appendages; corolla lavender or pink-purple, 9-13 mm long, the lobes about equaling the tube; stamens as long as or slightly longer than the corolla. May-June.—Rich moist woods.

Hydrophyllum appendiculatum

418. Cynoglossum officinale   *419. Echium vulgare*   *420. Hackelia deflexa*   *421. Hackelia virginiana*

Hydrophyllum virginianum L.

MAP 423

EASTERN WATERLEAF

native

Stems 3-8 dm tall at anthesis, the upper portion, cymes, pedicels, and back of the sepals strigose with short hairs rarely to 0.5 mm long. **Stem leaves** broadly ovate triangular in outline, 1-2 dm long and usually somewhat wider, pinnately lobed almost to the midvein, the segments usually 5, occasionally 7 or 9, the terminal one and the basal pair often 2-3-lobed, all with sharply acute apex and similar, strongly ascending teeth. **Cymes** very dense at anthesis; sepals sparsely hirsute; corolla white to pale pink-purple, 7-10 mm long; stamens long-exsert. May-June. —Moist or wet woods, or open wet places.

Hydrophyllum virginianum

LAPPULA *Stickseed; Beggar's-Lice*

Roughly pubescent annual herbs. Stems erect, freely branched, each branch terminating in an elongate bracteate raceme of small blue or occasionally white flowers. Calyx deeply 5-cleft into narrow lobes. Corolla salverform or broadly funnelform, the tube about as long as the calyx, the throat closed by 5 scales. Stamens and style short, included in the calyx. Fruiting pedicels erect or spreading. Nutlets bearing near each margin one or two rows of hooked prickles. *Our species can be distinguished accurately only when in fruit; fruit is also necessary for the separation of Lappula from* **Hackelia**. *A single nutlet viewed from the end will show whether the bristles are in a single or double row on each margin.*

1   Nutlets with a single row of bristles, these usually joined at their base . . . .**L. redowskii**
1   Nutlets with a double row of bristles, the bristles distinct . . . .**L. squarrosa**

Lappula redowskii (Hornem.) Greene

MAP 424

WESTERN STICKSEED

native

Lappula occidentalis (S. Wats.) Greene

Very similar to *L. squarrosa* in habit, size, leaf-shape, and inflorescence. Pubescence of the stem tending to spreading-hirsute. **Leaves** more softly pubescent. **Nutlets** 2-3 mm long, the oval face surrounded by a single row of marginal bristles which are nearly or completely separate to their bases.—Waste places and along railways.

Lappula squarrosa (Retz.) Dumort.

MAP 425

TWO-ROW STICKSEED

introduced (naturalized)

Stems usually simple to above the middle, thence freely branched, 2-8 dm tall, tending to be appressed-pubescent. **Leaves** linear, or linear-oblong lance-shaped, 2-5 cm long, usually ascending, acute or obtuse, narrowed to a sessile base, roughly hirsute. **Racemes** numerous, eventually 5-10 cm long; pedicels at maturity erect or ascending, 5-10 mm apart, 1-2 mm long; bracts linear or lance-shaped, 3-10 mm long; corolla blue, 2-3 mm wide. **Nutlets** 3-4 mm long, the lance-shaped face surrounded by 2 rows of bristles, those of the inner row usually the longer. May-Sept.—Native of Asia and the Mediterranean region; established as a weed in waste places.

Lappula squarrosa

LITHOSPERMUM *Gromwell; Puccoon; Stoneseed*

Perennial herbs (ours) with pubescent stem and foliage. Leaves narrow. Flowers solitary in the axils or crowded into a terminal leafy-bracted cyme. Calyx lobes narrow, separate nearly to the base. Corolla funnelform or salverform; the tube slender or wide, appendaged at the summit. Stamens

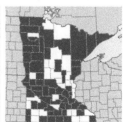

422. Hydro. appendiculatum   *423. Hydrophy. virginianum*   *424. Lappula redowskii*   *425. Lappula squarrosa*

inserted in the corolla tube, the anthers included or partly exsert. Style shortly 2-lobed. Nutlets bony, ovoid to nearly globose, smooth or pitted, usually only 1 or 2 ripening in each flower.

1 Corolla cylindrical, the lobes acute, barely if at all spreading . . . . **L. onosmodium**
1 Corolla funnelform, the lobes (especially if corolla over 10 mm long) usually spreading, not pointed 2
    2 Flowers light to deep yellow or yellow-orange in a terminal inflorescence 3
        3 Leaves linear, mostly less than 4 mm wide; corolla lobes fringed . . . . **L. incisum**
        3 Leaves wider; corolla lobes entire 4
            4 Plants soft-hairy; calyx lobes less than 5 mm long . . . . **L. canescens**
            4 Plants stiffly hairy; corolla lobes more than 5 mm long . . . . **L. caroliniense**
    2 Flowers white to pale yellow from leaf axils 5
        5 Largest leaves 2-4 cm wide; stem leaves below inflorescence number 20 or fewer . . . . **L. latifolium**
        5 Largest leaves less than 2 cm wide; stem leaves 25 or more . . . . **L. officinale**

Lithospermum canescens (Michx.) Lehm.
HOARY PUCCOON

MAP 426
native

Perennial herb. **Stems** often several from a thickened vertical root, at anthesis 1-4 dm tall, usually simple. **Leaves** ascending, lance-shaped, 2-6 cm long (or the lowest greatly reduced), softly and densely canescent, obtuse. **Inflorescence** of 1-3 densely flowered, terminal or subterminal, leafy-bracted cymes; calyx lobes linear, 3-6 mm long, densely villous; corolla bright yellow, the tube about 8 mm long, the limb 10-15 mm wide. **Nutlets** yellowish white, smooth and shining. April-May.—Moist or dry prairies and dry open woods.

Lithospermum caroliniense (Walt.) MacM.
PLAINS PUCCOON

MAP 427
native

Perennial herb. **Stems** erect from a stout woody root, at anthesis 3-6 dm tall, very leafy, simple or branched above, villous or hirsute. **Leaves** linear to lance-shaped, 3-6 cm long, roughly hirsute, the hairs often papillate at base. **Cymes** at first dense, leafy-bracted, becoming elongate and racerniform after anthesis; calyx lobes linear, 9-11 mm long, hirsute; corolla tube 10-14 mm long, pubescent at the base within; corolla-limb bright orange-yellow, 15-25 mm wide. **Nutlets** ivory-white, smooth and shining. May-July.—In dry, moist or preferably sandy soil, upland woods, shores, and prairies.

Lithospermum canescens

Lithospermum incisum Lehm.
NARROW-LEAVED PUCCOON

MAP 428
native

Perennial herb. **Stems** one or few, erect from a hardy woody root, 1.5-4 dm tall, at first simple, later much branched. **Leaves** narrowly lance-shaped, 3-7 cm, long, 3-5 or rarely 8 mm wide, densely strigose. **Early flowers** crowded in leafy terminal cymes, apparently always sterile; calyx lobes linear, 5-10 mm long; corolla tube very slender, 13-20 mm long, glabrous within; corolla-limb 12-20 mm wide, bright orange-yellow, the lobes denticulate. **Later flowers** fertile and cleistogamous, the corolla about 3 mm long, shorter than calyx lobes. **Nutlets** shining, ivory-white, conspicuously pitted. April-May.—Dry prairies and barrens.

Lithospermum latifolium Michx.
AMERICAN GROMWELL

MAP 429
native

Perennial from a thick root. **Stems** erect, simple or branched above, 4-8 dm tall, strigose, the principal internodes commonly 3-6 cm long. **Leaves** nearly sessile, lance-shaped to ovate lance-shaped, usually 2-4 cm wide, distinctly acuminate,

Lithospermum incisum

426. *Lithospermum canescens*   427. *Lithospermum caroliniense*   428. *Lithospermum incisum*   429. *Lithospermum latifolium*

scabrous above, with 2 or 3 prominent lateral veins on each side of the midvein. **Flowers** solitary in the axils of the upper leaves, becoming distant at maturity, yellowish-white, 5-7 mm long and nearly as wide; calyx lobes nearly as long as the corolla. **Nutlets** ovoid, white, shining, 3.5-5 mm long, smooth or remotely pitted. May-June.—Dry woods and thickets.

Lithospermum latifolium

Lithospermum officinale L.

(NO MAP)

EUROPEAN GROMWELL *introduced*

Perennial from a thick root. **Stems** erect, usually much branched above, to 1 m tall, strigose, the principal internodes usually less than 2 cm long, often only 5 mm. **Leaves** nearly sessile, lance-shaped to oblong, mostly 6-15 mm wide, scabrous above, with 2 or 3 conspicuous veins on each side of the midvein. **Flowers** solitary in the axils of the crowded upper leaves, 3-15 mm apart at maturity, white or nearly so, 4-5 mm long; calyx lobes nearly as long as the corolla. **Nutlets** ovoid, 3-3.5 mm long, white to pale brown, shining, smooth or sparsely pitted. May-Aug.—Native of Eurasia; a weed of waste places; reported for Minnesota.

Lithospermum onosmodium J. Cohen

MAP 430

FALSE GROMWELL *native*

  Lithospermum molle (Michx.) Muhl.
  Onosmodium bejariense A. DC.
  Onosmodium molle Michx.

Roughly pubescent perennial herbs. **Stems** stout, erect, 5-10 dm tall, densely hirsute; hairs of the stem either partly spreading and partly appressed, or all spreading. **Leaves** entire, lance-shaped to oblong, 5-10 cm long, midvein has 2 or 3 strong lateral veins which extend parallel to it nearly or quite to the tip; bracteal leaves and calyx densely sericeous, the slender soft hairs appressed and concealing the surface. **Flowers** many, sessile or nearly so, in terminal, bracteate scorpoid spikes or racemes which are coiled in anthesis but later elongate and straighten; calyx densely pubescent, deeply 5-parted into linear lobes; corolla dull white, tubular, 8-13 mm long, only slightly enlarged distally, pubescent externally, not appendaged within; stamens inserted on the corolla tube, the anthers included. **Nutlets** ovoid to subglobose, white to pale brown, 3-4 mm long. May-June.—Dry limestone hills and barrens.

Lithospermum officinale

MERTENSIA *Bluebells*

Perennial herbs; plants smooth or hairy. Leaves alternate and entire. Flowers usually blue (pink in bud), tube-, funnel- or bell-shaped, petals widened and shallowly lobed at tip; in small clusters at ends of stems and branches. Fruit a smooth or wrinkled nutlet.

1   Leaves and sepals hairy . . . . *M. paniculata*
1   Leaves and sepals without hairs . . . . *M. virginica*

Mertensia paniculata (Ait.) G. Don

MAP 431

NORTHERN BLUEBELLS *native*

Perennial herb. **Stems** erect, 3-10 dm long, branched above, smooth or with sparse hairs. **Basal leaves** ovate, rounded at base; **stem leaves** lance-shaped to ovate, 5-15 cm long, tapered to a tip, hairy, entire; petioles short on lower leaves, upper leaves more or less stalkless. **Flowers** blue-purple, narrowly bell-shaped, 10-15 mm long, on slender stalks, in few-flowered racemes at ends of stems and

Mertensia paniculata

430. *Lithosperm. onosmodium*   431. *Mertensia paniculata*   432. *Mertensia virginica*

branches; sepal lobes lance-shaped, 3-6 mm long, with dense, short hairs. **Fruit** a nutlet. June-July.—Conifer swamps, streambanks, seeps.

Mertensia virginica (L.) Pers.   MAP 432
VIRGINIA BLUEBELLS   *native*

Perennial herb; plants smooth. **Stems** upright, 3-7 dm long. **Leaves** oval to obovate, entire, 5-15 cm long, rounded or blunt at the tip; upper leaves stalkless, lower leaves with winged petioles. **Flowers** showy, blue-purple, trumpet-shaped, 5-lobed at tip, 2-3 cm long, stalked, in a cluster at end of stem; sepals rounded at tip, 3 mm long. **Fruit** a nutlet. April-May.—Floodplain forests, moist deciduous forests, streambanks; sometimes escaping from gardens where grown as an ornamental.

Mertensia virginica

MYOSOTIS *Forget-Me-Not; Scorpion Grass*

Perennial (sometimes annual) herbs; plants with short, appressed hairs. Leaves alternate and entire. Flowers blue, tube-shaped and abruptly flared outward at tip, in a 1-sided raceme. Fruit a nutlet.

1   Calyx hairs all straight-tipped, appressed 2
    2   Plants without stolons; lobes of sepals as long or longer than corolla tube; flowers up to 6 mm wide; nutlets longer than style . . . . *M. laxa*
    2   Plants creeping and spreading by stolons; lobes of sepals shorter than corolla tube; flowers mostly 6 mm or more wide; nutlets shorter than style . . . . *M. scorpioides*
1   Calyx hairs mostly hooked at tip, spreading 3
    3   Pedicels shorter than calyx; corolla 1-2 mm wide . . . . *M. stricta*
    3   Pedicels equal to length of calyx (when in full-flower or fruit); corolla 3 mm or more wide 4
       4   Expanded part of petal cupped, less than 4 mm wide . . . . *M. arvensis*
       4   Expanded part of petal flat, 5-10 mm wide . . . . *M. sylvatica*

Myosotis arvensis (L.) Hill   MAP 433
ROUGH FORGET-ME-NOT   *introduced*

Annual or biennial. **Stems** simple or branched, eventually 3-5 dm long. **Leaves** firm, oblong, varying to lance-shaped or oblong lance-shaped, the larger 2-5 cm long. **Racemes** becoming 1-2 dm long, usually completely bractless; fruiting pedicels 5-15 mm apart, divergent, 5-9 mm long; mature calyx 3-4.5 mm long, pubescent with both hooked and appressed hairs, the lobes slightly longer than the tube; corolla blue or white, broadly funnelform, the limb 2-3 mm wide. **Nutlets** 1.3-1.7 mm long. Summer.—Native of Eurasia; established in fields and roadsides.

Myosotis laxa Lehm.   MAP 434
SMALLER FORGET-ME-NOT   *native*

Short-lived perennial (sometimes annual) herb. **Stems** slender, 1-4 dm long, often lying on ground at base, but not creeping, with fine, short, appressed hairs. **Leaves** oblong or spatula-shaped, 2-6 cm long. **Flowers** blue, on stalks usually much longer than the flower, in 1-sided clusters at ends of stems, the clusters becoming open; sepals covered with short hairs, sepal lobes shorter than the tube; petal lobes shorter or slightly longer than the tube. **Fruit** a nutlet distinctly longer than the style. June-Sept.—Cedar swamps, wet shores and streambanks.

Myosotis laxa

433. Myosotis arvensis   *434. Myosotis laxa*   *435. Myosotis scorpioides*   *436. Myosotis sylvatica*

Myosotis scorpioides L.
TRUE FORGET-ME-NOT
Myosotis palustris (L.) Hill

MAP 435
introduced (invasive)

Perennial herb. **Stems** 2-6 dm long, with short, appressed hairs, often creeping
at base and producing stolons. **Leaves** 3-8 cm long and 0.5-2 cm wide, lower leaves
oblong lance-shaped, upper leaves oblong or oval; stalkless or the lower leaves
on short petioles. **Flowers** blue with a yellow center, tube-shaped, abruptly flared
at tip, in a 1-sided raceme at ends of stems, becoming open; flower stalks
spreading in fruit; sepals with short, appressed hairs, sepal lobes equal or shorter
than the tube. **Fruit** a nutlet shorter than the style. May-Sept.—Streambanks,
shores, ditches, swamps, wet depressions in forests.

Myosotis sylvatica Ehrh.
GARDEN FORGET-ME-NOT

MAP 436
introduced (invasive)

Perennial. **Stems** eventually to 5 dm long, bearing several racemes. **Leaves** oblong
to lance-shaped or spatulate, thin and soft, the larger 3-7 cm long. **Racemes**
bractless, seldom more than 1 dm long; fruiting pedicels 5-15 mm apart, ascending
or spreading, to 9 mm long; mature calyx 4-5 mm long, much shorter than the
pedicel, densely pubescent with hooked hairs, the narrowly triangular lobes
much longer than the tube; corolla blue or rarely white, salverform, the limb 5-
8 mm wide. **Nutlets** 1.5-2 mm long. April-Sept.—Native of Eurasia; commonly
cultivated for ornament and sometimes escaped near gardens.

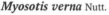

Myosotis scorpioides

Myosotis verna Nutt.
SPRING FORGET-ME-NOT
Myosotis virginica auct. non (L.) B.S.P.

MAP 437
native

Stems erect, often branched from the base, sometimes beginning to flower when
only 1 dm tall, eventually to 4 dm tall. **Leaves** linear to oblong, oblong lance-
shaped, 1-6 cm long. **Racemes** commonly bracteate at base or as far as the middle;
pedicels at maturity shorter than the fruiting calyx, nearly straight, erect or
appressed, usually less than 1 cm apart, the calyx itself ascending or spreading
from the axis, at maturity 4-6 mm long, hirsute, 3 of its lobes distinctly shorter
than the others; corolla white, 1-2 mm wide. **Nutlets**, 1.2-1.5 mm long. April-July.
—Dry soil of upland woods and fields.

PLAGIOBOTHRYS *Popcorn-Flower*

Plagiobothrys hispidulus (Greene) I.M. Johnston
POPCORN-FLOWER

MAP 438
native

Slender annual herb. **Stems** several or many, prostrate or ascending, to 20 cm
long, terminating in an elongate, loosely flowered false raceme or spike. **Leaves**
essentially all cauline, linear, to 6 cm long and 5 mm wide, the lower 1-4 pairs
opposite. Calyx 2-4 mm long in fruit, corolla small, white, salverform, the limb
mostly 1-2 mm wide. **Nutlets** ovate or lance-ovate, 1.5-2.2 mm long, usually
roughened. May-Aug.—Native to w USA; local in sw Minn.

Myosotis verna

SYMPHYTUM *Comfrey*

Symphytum officinale L.
COMMON COMFREY

MAP 439
introduced

Perennial pubescent herb. **Stems** erect, branched, 5-10 dm tall, sparsely to densely
hirsute. **Leaves** large, the lower to 2 dm long, lance-shaped or ovate lance-shaped,
narrowed at base to a winged petiole and decurrent as two wings on the stem;
upper leaves progressively smaller, on shorter petioles or sessile. **Flowers**
numerous, nodding, in dense scorpioid cymes; calyx deeply parted into linear
lobes; corolla tubular-campanulate, 12-18 mm long, the tube wide, the limb little
expanded above the throat, the lobes erect or spreading at the tip, dull blue or
dull yellow; stamens inserted at the summit of the corolla tube; appendages
shorter than to nearly equaling the stamens. **Nutlets** brown, shining, smooth or
slightly wrinkled. June-Aug.—Garden herb, sometimes escaped to waste places.

Symphytum officinale

Brassicaceae MUSTARD FAMILY

Annual, biennial or perennial herbs. Leaves simple or compound, alternate on stems or basal, smooth or hairy, some species with branched or star-shaped hairs. Flowers in terminal or lateral clusters (racemes), the lower portion often fruiting while tip in flower, the stalks elongating in fruit. Flowers perfect (with both staminate and pistillate parts), cross-shaped, with 4 sepals and 4 yellow, white, pink or purple petals; stamens 6, the outer 2 stamens shorter than the inner 4; pistil 1, style 1, ovary superior. Fruit a cylindrical (silique) or round (silicle) pod with 2 chambers and 1 to many seeds in 1 or 2 rows in each chamber.

ADDITIONAL SPECIES
Lobularia maritima (L.) Desv. (Sweet-alyssum), native to Mediterranean region; Hennepin and St. Louis counties; see key.

1 Petals pale to deep yellow 2
  2 Leaves (at least the middle or lower ones) ± deeply lobed (sinuses at least halfway to midrib), pinnatifid, or dissected 3
    3 Stem leaves mostly deeply pinnatifid, appearing dissected (almost parsley-like), the ultimate segments mostly less than 2 mm broad; stem pubescence in our common species largely of forked, stellate, and/or glandular hairs. . . . . ***Descurainia***
    3 Stem leaves at most once-pinnatifid, at least the terminal segment more than 2 mm broad (except sometimes in *Sisymbrium altissimum*); stem pubescence absent or of simple hairs, not glandular 4
      4 Pedicels (at least lower ones) subtended by pinnatifid bracts. . . . . ***Erucastrum***
      4 Pedicels all bractless 5
        5 Stem leaves strongly clasping the stem with well developed auricles. 6
          6 Petals less than 3 mm long; fruit less than 5 times as long as broad . . . . ***Rorippa***
          6 Petals 4-14 (-16) mm long; fruit becoming over 10 times as long as broad. 7
            7 Distal leaves mostly ± pinnatifid (with at least 1 pair of narrow lobes) or with angular teeth; fruit with beak not over 3.1 mm long. . . . . ***Barbarea***
            7 Distal leaves entire to obscurely toothed or scalloped; fruit with beak 5-15 mm long. ***Brassica***
        5 Stem leaves sessile to petioled but not clasping. 8
          8 Petals 10-20 mm long; style at least 1.5 mm long, elongating into a prominent beak on fruit. . 9
            9 Ovary and fruit on a short stalk 0.5-1 mm long; fruit indehiscent, strongly constricted (and ultimately breaking) between the ripe seeds . . . . ***Raphanus raphanistrum***
            9 Ovary and fruit sessile; fruits dehiscent at maturity, slightly if at all swollen around the seeds . . . . ***Sinapis***
        8 Petals less than 10 mm long; style usually shorter than 1.5 mm or absent, elongating at most into a beak 2 mm long (longer in *Brassica*). 10
          10 Fruit (and maturing ovary) nearly spherical to oblong or cylindrical, less than 5 times as long as wide. . . . . ***Rorippa***
          10 Fruit (and maturing ovary) slender, ± linear, attaining a length at least 10 times as great as the width 11
            11 Petals less than 5.5 mm long; fruit in common species less than 2 cm long 12
              12 Plant usually in moist ground, the stem usually ± lax or prostrate, reproducing vegetatively (ripe seeds not formed); terminal lobe of most leaves scarcely if at all broader than lateral lobes. . . . . ***Rorippa sylvestris***
              12 Plant usually in dry ground, the stem erect, reproducing by seed; terminal lobe of most leaves much broader than lateral lobes . . . . ***Sisymbrium***
            11 Petals 5.5-9.5 mm long; fruit often longer than 2 cm. 13
              13 Beak of fruit 7-14 mm long at maturity, the style longer than 4 mm after flowering. . 14

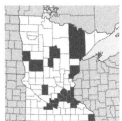

437. Myosotis verna   *438. Plagiobothrys scouleri*   *439. Symphytum officinale*   *440. Alliaria petiolata*

    14 Uppermost leaves entire or nearly so, narrow (including petiole if any, 5-10 times longer than wide); fruit without parallel nerves besides margins and mid-nerves (additional nerves, if any, ± looped or anastomosing), glabrous; petals 7-10 mm long . . . . *Brassica*

    14 Uppermost leaves (e.g., at base of main branches of inflorescence) coarsely toothed, 2-4 times longer than wide; valves of fruit each with 2 or 4 distinct parallel nerves besides the midnerves and margins or fruits densely hispid; petals 10-15 mm long . . . . *Sinapis*

   13 Beak of fruit less than 4 mm long, or none 15

    15 Buds overtopping open flowers; pedicels and fruit becoming closely appressed to axis of inflorescence . . . . *Brassica nigra*

    15 Buds mostly overtopped by open flowers; pedicels and fruit spreading *Sisymbrium*

2 Leaves all unlobed, entire or toothed 16

  16 Stem leaves sagittate- or auriculate-clasping at the base 17

    17 Body of fruit ± spherical or obovoid; distal leaves (like the proximal) with forked or stellate and/or simple hairs (at least a few on margins) 18

      18 Axis of inflorescence glabrous; petals 3.5-5 mm long; fruit dehiscent, several-seeded, 4-5 mm wide, the body weakly if at all reticulate . . . . *Camelina*

      18 Axis of inflorescence at least sparsely pubescent; petals up to 2.5 mm long; fruit indehiscent, 1-2-seeded, less than 2.5 mm wide, the body strongly reticulate . . . . *Neslia*

    17 Body of fruit elongate, linear (the shape evident as ovary matures); leaves mostly glabrous. 19

      19 Stem and leaves glabrous; petals 8-12 mm long; leaves broadly rounded at apex. . . . . *Conringia*

      19 Stem and leaves pubescent at very base of plant; petals < 7 mm long; leaves acute . . *Turritis glabra*

  16 Stem leaves merely sessile, not clasping 20

    20 Plant glabrous or with simple hairs; fruit a linear silique 1-4.5 cm long 21

      21 Distalmost leaves entire or nearly so, narrow (including petiole if any, ca. 5-10 times as long as wide); fruit without parallel nerves besides margins and mid-nerves (additional nerves, if any, ± looped or anastomosing), glabrous; petals 7-10 mm long . . . . *Brassica*

      21 Distalmost leaves (e.g., at base of main branches of inflorescence) coarsely toothed, ca. 2-4 times as long as broad; valves of fruit each with 2 or 4 distinct parallel nerves besides the midnerves and margins or fruits hispid; petals (8-) 10-15 mm long . . . . *Sinapis*

    20 Plant pubescent with stellate or forked hairs; fruit various. 22

      22 Fruit 4-sided or ± terete, at least 15 mm long; petals 3.5-10 mm long . . . . *Erysimum*

      22 Fruit strongly flattened (parallel to the septum), less than 10 mm long; petals less than 5 mm long. 23

        23 Fruit elongate (3-5 times as long as broad), 5-9 mm long; ovules and seeds numerous in each locule; leaves slightly toothed, ovate to elliptic . . . . *Draba*

        23 Fruit round or nearly so, 5 mm or less long; ovules and seeds 1-2 in each locule; leaves entire, linear to oblanceolate . . . . *Alyssum*

1 Petals white to purple, or none. 24

  24 Principal stem leaves deeply lobed (e.g., lyrate or pinnatifid) or compound (uppermost leaves or bracts, at the inflorescence, or above water in aquatics, may be simple). 25

    25 Leaves palmately compound or deeply palmately divided, the stem leaves only 2 or 3 (-4) . . . . *Cardamine*

    25 Leaves pinnately lobed or divided, the stem often more than 3. 26

      26 Plants aquatic, the submersed leaves dissected in a bipinnate pattern into filiform segments (midvein present, the lateral segments again dissected), easily detaching from the stem . . . . . . *Rorippa aquatica*

      26 Plants terrestrial or aquatic but if in water the leaves with definite flat lobes (not bipinnately dissected) and not falling from the stem 27

        27 Leaf blades or leaflets with short stiff hairs to 0.5 mm long on margins or undersides; petals at least 10 mm long; mature fruit elongate, 3-12 mm thick, indehiscent . . . . *Raphanus*

        27 Leaf blades or leaflets glabrous or with finer smaller hairs, or if blades ciliate, the petals much less than 10 mm long; mature fruit narrower or round, dehiscent. 28

          28 Fruit less than twice as long as broad, with 1-2 seeds in each locule; plant an erect weed of usually dry places 29

            29 Petals less than 4 mm long; fruit strongly flattened; habitat dry . . . . *Lepidium*

            29 Petals at least 5 mm long; fruit ± spherical; habitat dry to wet . . . . *Armoracia*

          28 Fruit soon becoming more than twice as long as broad, many-seeded; plant often ± lax, usually in wet ground or water. 30

            30 Petals at least 7 mm long . . . . *Cardamine pratensis*

            30 Petals less than 6 mm long 31

31 Fruit straight, ± erect, on ascending pedicels; seeds smooth; plants often with a basal rosette (at least when young and if not submersed), the stems not forming extensive creeping mats; petals 0-4 mm long . . . . *Cardamine*

31 Fruit often ± curved, spreading (the pedicels soon divergent after flowering); seeds reticulate; plants without basal rosette, the stems elongated and prostrate or ascending, forming mats; petals (2.5-) 3.5-5.7 mm long. . . . . *Nasturtium*

24 Principal stem leaves (if any) simple, unlobed (except for clasping base in some species), entire or toothed. . 32

32 Stems and/or leaves (especially beneath and along margins) pubescent with many or all of the hairs stellate or forked (check especially lower leaves). 33

33 Stem leaves sagittate- or auriculate-clasping 34

34 Fruit strongly flattened at right angles to the septum, ± triangular to obcordate, less than twice as long as broad; petals less than 3 mm long . . . . *Capsella*

34 Fruit plump or flattened parallel to the septum, linear (straight or curved), becoming at least 10 times as long as broad; petals usually at least 4 mm long (less than 3 mm in *Boechera dentata*). 35

35 Fruiting pedicels ± spreading, divaricate, or reflexed; fruits straight or somewhat curved and clearly spreading from the axis or even pendent . . . . *Boechera*

35 Fruiting pedicels strongly ascending to appressed; fruits straight, erect and closely appressed to the stem 36

36 Stem and leaves entirely glabrous or with a very few scattered simple and/or appressed medifixed hairs at the very base of the plant (especially on leaf margins and petioles); sepals ca. half as long as the petals; mature fruit 1.4-3 mm wide, with seeds in 2 rows in each locule . . . . *Boechera stricta*

36 Stem and leaves pubescent, at least at the base, with spreading simple or stellate hairs; sepals ca. 2/3 as long as the petals; mature fruit less than 1.3 mm wide, with seeds crowded into 1 row in each locule 37

37 Fruit rather strongly flattened; style-beak clearly narrower than mature fruit; stem pubescent with simple and/or forked (or stellate) hairs on at least the lower half or third, and leaves on the same portion ± pubescent (often stellate) . . . . *Arabis pycnocarpa*

37 Fruit ± terete or 4-angled, slightly if at all flattened at maturity; style-beak nearly or quite as wide as the fruit; stem pubescence only on the lowermost 1-3 full-grown internodes, and only the lowermost leaves pubescent . . . . *Turritis glabra*

33 Stem leaves (if any) petioled or sessile but not clasping the stem. 38

38 Body of fruit (and maturing ovary) slender, ± linear, maturing to a length at least 10 times longer than wide 39

39 Petals 15-25 mm long, purple, lavender, pink, or white . . . . *Hesperis*

39 Petals less than 10 mm long, white or slightly tinged with color 40

40 Fruit curved, pendent on reflexed pedicels; leaves (at least lower ones) (4-) 6-12 (-16) cm long; basal rosette absent at flowering time . . . . *Boechera canadensis*

40 Fruit straight, on ascending pedicels; leaves less than 3.5 (-4.5) cm long, basal rosette of usually toothed or lyrate-lobed blades often present at flowering time. . . . . *Arabidopsis*

38 Body of fruit (and maturing ovary) never linear, but short-oblong, ovate to narrowly elliptic, or round, less than 6 (-8) times longer than wide 41

41 Petals deeply bilobed . . . . *Berteroa*

41 Petals entire or slightly notched at apex (or absent) 42

42 Pubescence mostly (or entirely) of appressed medifixed hairs (evident on leaves, stems, and inflorescences); seed 1 in each locule . . . . *Lobularia**

42 Pubescence mostly of branched (or stellate) or simple hairs, without appressed medifixed ones; seeds 2-many in each locule. 43

43 Fruit round or nearly so, ca. 4 mm or less long; ovules and seeds 2 in each locule; leaves all entire, all from the stem (or on short basal shoots), without basal rosette . . . *Alyssum*

43 Fruit elongate, elliptic or narrowly oblong to ovate (2.5-8 times longer than wide), at least 5 mm long; ovules and seeds numerous in each locule; leaves mostly in a basal rosette or toothed (or both) . . . . *Draba*

32 Stems and leaves glabrous or with only simple hairs (rarely a few forked hairs may be intermixed) 44

44 Stem leaves sagittate- or auriculate-clasping 45

45 Fruit (and maturing ovary) linear, becoming at least (1.5-) 3 cm long; petals ca. 3-12 mm long. . . 46

46 Stem and leaves pubescent (at least at base), some leaves basal, leaves toothed, and/or leaves acute . . . . *Boechera*

46 Stem and leaves completely glabrous; leaves all stem, entire and broadly rounded at the apex . . . . *Conringia*

45 Fruit (and maturing ovary) round to obovate (flattened to nearly spherical), less than twice as long as broad and not over 1.5 (-2) cm long; petals not over 4 mm long (or absent) 47

   47 Plant slightly to densely pubescent; ovules and seeds 1 per locule; fruit less than 5.5 mm wide at maturity . . . . *Lepidium*

   47 Plant glabrous; ovules and seeds 5-7 in each locule; fruit ca. 9-12 (-20) mm wide at maturity . . . . *Thlaspi*

44 Stem leaves (if any) sessile or petioled, but not clasping the stem 48

   48 Small aquatic plant; leaves all basal and awl-shaped, usually flowering and fruiting underwater . . . . *Subularia*

   48 Plant with leafy stem, of moist or dry ground, not flowering underwater 49

      49 Middle stem leaves with toothed, triangular-ovate blades little if at all longer than broad, on slender petioles; bruised plant with odor of onion or garlic. . . . . *Alliaria*

      49 Middle stem leaves with blades toothed or entire, distinctly longer than broad, sessile or tapered into petiole; plant without onion-garlic odor 50

         50 Fruit (and maturing ovary) linear, becoming at least 10 times longer than wide 51

            51 Petals 8-14 (-16) mm long; basal leaves distinctly with a rounded blade and long slender petiole, arising from a tuberous root; pubescence (if any) of strictly simple hairs. . . . . *Cardamine*

            51 Petals 4-8 (-9) mm long; basal leaves (if any) not distinctly petioled, arising from a slender root; pubescence (if any) usually including a few stellate hairs. 52

               52 Fruit straight, mostly 2-4 cm long, less than 1.3 mm wide, on ascending pedicels; leaves less than 4 cm long, including those in a basal rosette of usually toothed or lyrate-lobed blades (normally present at flowering time); stem often branched at base. . . . . *Arabidopsis lyrata*

               52 Fruit curved, 4.5-7 cm long, (2-3.2 mm wide, pendent on reflexed pedicels; leaves (at least lower ones) 6-12 cm long, with no basal rosette present at flowering time; stem simple . . . . *Boechera canadensis*

         50 Fruit round or spherical, or nearly so, less than 2x longer than wide 53

            53 Largest stem and basal leaves usually 3.5-30 cm broad, with ± rounded or obtuse teeth; basal leaves long-petioled; fruit ± ellipsoid-obovoid (not flattened), not notched at the apex, the several ovules not ripening into seeds . . . . *Armoracia*

            53 Largest leaves less than 2.5 (-3.5) cm wide, entire or sharply toothed; basal long-petioled leaves absent; fruit round or nearly so, strongly flattened, notched at apex, with 1 seed in each locule. . . . . *Lepidium*

ALLIARIA *Garlic-Mustard*

Alliaria petiolata (Bieb.) Cavara & Grande
GARLIC-MUSTARD
   Alliaria alliaria (L.) Britt.
   Alliaria officinalis Andrz.

MAP 440
introduced (invasive)

Biennial, garlic-scented herb, glabrous or nearly so, the hairs simple. **Stems** erect, to 1 m tall, simple or little branched. **Basal leaves** in more or less evergreen rosettes; **lower leaves** kidney-shaped; **stem leaves** deltoid, 3-6 cm long and wide, coarsely toothed. **Petals** white, spatulate, 5-6 mm long; pedicels at maturity stout, about 5 mm long. **Fruit** widely divergent, 4-6 cm long; seeds black, nearly cylindric, about 3 mm long. May-June.—Native of Europe; invasive in rich, moist, shaded soil; also on roadsides or rarely in swamps.

Alliaria petiolata

ALYSSUM *Madwort*

Alyssum alyssoides (L.) L.
PALE MADWORT

MAP 441
introduced

Annual herb. Stem, leaves, inflorescence, and fruits stellate-pubescent. **Stems** 5-25 cm tall, simple and erect, or branched from the base only. **Leaves** oblong lance-shaped, 6-15 mm long, entire, obtuse. **Flowers** pale yellow or nearly white, about 2 mm wide; petals narrowly oblong. **Fruit** on widely divergent pedicels, circular, 3-4 mm long, flat at the margin, convex toward the center; seeds 2 in each cell. May-June.—Native of Europe; weedy in waste places.

ADDITIONAL SPECIES
Alyssum desertorum Stapf (Desert madwort) native to Eurasia; Freeborn County.

ARABIDOPSIS *Thalecress*

Arabidopsis lyrata (L.) O'Kane & Al-Shehbaz   MAP 442
LYRE-LEAF ROCKCRESS   *native*
    Arabis lyrata L.

Biennial herb, more or less pubescent with branched hairs. **Stems** erect or ascending, branched from the base, 1-4 dm tall, hirsute below (very rarely glabrous), glabrous or glabrescent above. **Leaves** mostly in a basal rosette; **basal leaves** spatulate, 2-4 cm long, entire to pinnately lobed; **stem leaves** linear to narrowly spatulate, the lowest sometimes with a few teeth or shallow lobes. **Petals** white, spatulate, 3-8 mm long; pedicels at maturity widely ascending, 6-15 mm long. **Fruit** linear, nearly terete, many-seeded, maintaining about the same direction as the pedicel, 2-4.5 cm long, occasionally shorter, about 1 mm wide; seeds oblong to elliptic, wingless, about 1 mm long. April-June.—Dry woods and fields, especially in sandy soil; sand dunes.

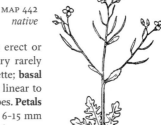

Arabidopsis lyrata

ARABIS *Rockcress*

Arabis pycnocarpa M. Hopkins   MAP 443
HAIRY ROCK CRESS   *native*
    Arabis hirsuta (L.) Scop.

Biennial herb. **Stems** erect, 2-8 dm tall, pubescent at least at base with simple or branched hairs. **Stem leaves** oblong to linear lance-shaped, 1-3 cm long, sessile and more or less clasping, at least the lower pubescent. Mature pedicels erect, slender, 7-10 mm long; petals white. **Fruit** erect, flat, linear, 3-5 cm long, about 1 mm wide; seeds in one row, flattened and narrowly winged, 1-1.2 mm long. May-June.—Sandy and rocky places; shores and riverbanks. *Other native former members of genus Arabis now placed in* **Boechera***, with either broader fruit (if tightly appressed) or the fruit spreading, reflexed or pendent; Arabis glabra (L.) Bernh. placed in genus* **Turritis***.*

Arabis pycnocarpa

ARMORACIA *Horse-Radish*

Armoracia rusticana P.G. Gaertn. B. Mey. & Scherb.   MAP 444
HORSE-RADISH   *introduced*

Glabrous perennial herb from thick roots. **Stems** erect, to 1 m tall. **Lower leaves** long-petioled, the blade oblong, 1-3 dm long, cordate at base; **upper leaves** smaller, short-petioled to sessile, lance-shaped. **Racemes** several, terminal and from the upper axils; petals white, obovate, 6-8 mm long; pedicels after anthesis ascending, 8-12 mm long. **Fruit** obovoid, inflated, 2-celled, eventually up to 6 mm long but usually falling early; seeds apparently never maturing. May-July.—Native of se Europe and w Asia; commonly cultivated and escaped into moist soil of ditches, shores, roadsides, and disturbed places. *Toxic to livestock.*

BARBAREA *Yellow-Rocket*

Biennial herbs, smooth or with a few simple hairs. Basal leaves pinnatifid with a large terminal lobe and 2 to several small lateral lobes; stem leaves smaller, entire to pinnatifid. Petals yellow, spatulate to obovate. Short stamens partly surrounded at base by a semicircular gland; long stamens separated by a short erect gland. Ovary cylindric, narrowed to a slender style. Fruit linear, terete or obscurely 4-angled, several-seeded, tipped by the persistent style.

441. Alyssum alyssoides

442. Arabidopsis lyrata

443. Arabis pycnocarpa

Armoracia rusticana

1 Petals 6-8 mm long; beak of fruit 2-3 mm long . . . . *B. vulgaris*
1 Petals to 5 mm long; beak of fruit less than 2 mm long . . . . *B. orthoceras*

Barbarea orthoceras Ledeb.

MAP 445

AMERICAN YELLOW-ROCKET   *native*

Biennial herb; plants smooth or with sparse covering of unbranched hairs. **Stems** 3-8 dm long, unbranched, or branched above. **Leaves** simple or with 1-4 pairs of lateral lobes, the middle and upper leaves deeply lobed. **Flowers** in racemes; on short stalks to 1 mm long, the stalks clublike at tip; petals yellow, 3-5 mm long. **Fruit** upright, 2-4 cm long, with a beak 0.5-2 mm long. June-July.—Rocky shores, swamps and wet woods.

Barbarea vulgaris Ait. f.

MAP 446

GARDEN YELLOW-ROCKET   *introduced (naturalized)*

Stems erect, branched above, 2-8 dm tall. **Basal leaves** petioled, with 1-4 pairs of small, elliptic to ovate, lateral lobes and a large ovate to rotund terminal lobe; **stem leaves** progressively shorter petioled and with fewer lobes, the upper sessile or clasping, angulately toothed, repand, or entire. **Flowers** yellow, about 8 mm wide, crowded at anthesis; pedicels at maturity 3-6 mm long, about 0.5 mm thick. **Fruit** 1.5-3 cm long, the beak 2-3 mm long. April-June.—Native of Europe; naturalized as a weed in damp soil of fields, roadsides, and gardens.

Barbarea vulgaris

BERTEROA *Hoary Alyssum*

Berteroa incana (L.) DC.

MAP 447

HOARY ALYSSUM   *introduced (naturalized)*

Annual herb. Stem, foliage, and inflorescence finely canescent, the hairs stellate with radiating branches. **Stems** stiffly erect, usually branched above, to 7 dm tall. **Leaves** oblong lance-shaped, 2-5 cm long, acute, entire. Sepals ascending; petals white, 2-lobed, about 3 mm wide. **Fruit** elliptic, thinly pubescent, 5-8 mm long, 3-4 mm wide; seeds 3-6 in each cell. May-Sept.—Native of Europe; weedy.

Berteroa incana

BOECHERA *Rockcress*

Biennial or perennial herbs. Basal leaves petioled, the stem leaves smaller and usually sessile; pubescence usually present, of simple, forked, or stellate hairs. Sepals erect or spreading, the outer pair sometimes saccate at base. Petals white, yellowish, or pink, spatulate to oblong or obovate. Ovary cylindric. Fruit linear, elongate, flat or subterete, many-seeded. Seeds flattened, often with a marginal wing. *Includes former native members of genus Arabis.*

ADDITIONAL SPECIES

Boechera retrofracta (Graham) A. Löve & D. Löve (Holboell's rockcress), dry cliff crevices in ne Minn (Cook and Lake counties), dry prairies and sand dunes in nw Minn (Kitson County); ☛*threatened;* see key.

1 Leaves not clasping at base . . . . *B. canadensis*
1 Upper leaves clasping at their base 2
  2 Pedicels becoming distinctly reflexed before the petals wither, the fruit pendent; sepals ca. half as long as mature petals or a little shorter 3
    3 Stems with stellate pubescence only at the very base, otherwise glabrous; sepals glabrous; mature fruit spreading to loosely pendent, the pedicels more arched than reflexed . . . . *B. grahamii*
    3 Stems with stellate pubescence at least on lower half; sepals at least sparsely stellate-pubescent; mature fruit strongly pendent, the pedicels sharply reflexed . . . . *B. retrofracta**

444. Armoracia rusticana

445. Barbarea orthoceras

446. Barbarea vulgaris

447. Berteroa incana

2   Pedicels spreading or ascending to strongly appressed, even after anthesis, the fruit spreading to erect; sepals various **4**

     4   Fruiting pedicels strongly ascending to appressed, the fruit straight, erect and closely appressed to the stem . . . . *B. stricta*

     4   Fruiting pedicels ± spreading, the fruit straight or somewhat curved and clearly spreading from the axis **5**

         5   Upper stem leaves (i.e., below the lowermost pedicels or branches) ± dentate and pubescent on both surfaces . . . . *B. dentata*

         5   Upper stem leaves entire or nearly so, glabrous **6**

             6   Basal leaves lyrate-pinnatifid, with at least a few simple hairs at the tips of the teeth or lobes; stem leaves below the inflorescence many (ca. 30-40); sepals ca. half as long as the petals . . . . *B. missouriensis*

             6   Basal leaves entire or merely serrate (or absent at anthesis), completely glabrous or stellate-pubescent on both surfaces; stem leaves various; sepals various **7**

                 7   Stem leaves ca. 25-35 or more below the inflorescence, the longest 2.5-5 cm; stem at the base and both surfaces of basal leaves ± stellate-pubescent; petals pink or pale purple; sepals at most barely more than half as long as the petals . . . . *B. grahamii*

                 7   Stem leaves ca. 10-15 (-20) below the inflorescence, the longest 9-15 cm; stem and leaves completely glabrous at base of plant (and elsewhere); petals white; sepals much more than half as long as petals . . . . *B. laevigata*

Boechera canadensis (L.) Al-Shehbaz

SICKLEPOD

Arabis canadensis L.

MAP 448
native

Biennial herb. **Stems** stout, erect, to 1 m tall, sparsely pubescent at base, glabrous for most of its length. **Stem leaves** lance-shaped to elliptic or oblong, 3-10 cm long, narrowed to the base, chiefly sharply and remotely dentate, more or less pubescent. **Petals** 3-5 mm long; pedicels erect in bud, becoming widely divergent at anthesis and deflexed at maturity, 7-12 mm long. **Fruit** pendent, flat, more or less curved, 7-11 cm long, 2-3.5 mm wide, prominently veined; seeds in 1 row, about 3 mm long, as wide as the valve, the conspicuous wing 0.5-1 mm wide. May-July.—Moist or dry woods.

Boechera canadensis

Boechera dentata (Raf.) Al-Shehbaz & Zarucchi

SHORT'S ROCKCRESS

Arabis shortii (Fern.) Gleason

MAP 449
native

Perennial herb. **Stems** 2-5 dm tall, branched at the base, often decumbent, thinly pubescent with mostly forked hairs. **Stem leaves** oblong lance-shaped to obovate, 2-6 cm long, even the uppermost usually sharply toothed, somewhat narrowed to the clasping base, pubescent with simple hairs above, with stellate ones beneath. **Petals** white, little exceeding the sepals; pedicels at anthesis hirsute, at maturity 2-4 mm long, usually glabrous. **Fruit** widely spreading, linear, flat, 1.5-3 cm long, about 1 mm wide, often minutely pubescent; seeds in 1 row, wingless. April-May.—Rich moist woods.

Boechera grahamii (Lehmann) Windham & Al-Shehbaz

SPREADING ROCKCRESS

Arabis divaricarpa A. Nels.

MAP 450
native

Biennial herb. **Stems** erect, to 1 m tall, glabrous except at the very base. **Basal leaves** oblong lance-shaped, finely stellate-pubescent on both sides; **stem leaves** linear lance-shaped, erect or nearly so, 2-5 cm long, sessile, auriculate at base, entire, glabrous on both sides. **Petals** pinkish or white, 5-8 mm long; pedicels at maturity widely spreading, 6-12 mm long. **Fruit** at first erect, soon widely spreading, linear, straight or nearly so, 3-9 cm long, 1.2-2.2 mm wide, the valves 1-nerved to or beyond the middle; seeds in 1 row and broadly quadrate to orbicular, or in 2 rows and oblong. June-July.—Sandy or rocky soil.

Boechera dentata

Boechera laevigata (Muhl. ex Willd.) Al-Shehbaz

SMOOTH BANK CRESS

Arabis laevigata (Muhl.) Poir.

MAP 451
native

Biennial herb. Glabrous and glaucous throughout, except the sparsely hirsute, spatulate, basal leaves. **Stems** to 1 m tall. **Stem leaves** narrowly lance-shaped, usually 5-10 cm long, serrate to entire, usually sagittate at the sessile base. **Petals** white, 3-5 mm long, equaling to one-fourth longer than the sepals; pedicels at maturity widely spreading, 7-12 mm long. **Fruit** widely spreading, horizontal, or somewhat decurved, rarely straight, linear, flat, 5-10 cm long, 1.2-2 mm wide; seeds in 1 row, oblong, narrowly winged. May-June.—Moist or dry woods.

Boechera missouriensis (Greene) Al-Shehbaz (NO MAP)
GREEN ROCKCRESS *native*
  Arabis missouriensis Greene

Biennial herb. **Basal leaves** long persistent, usually present at anthesis, dentate to pinnatifid; **stem leaves** numerous, erect, lance-shaped to linear, the lower commonly with a few sharp teeth, the upper mostly entire. Stem and leaves sparsely pubescent with simple hairs; pubescence of the leaves chiefly on the midvein and margin. **Racemes** at maturity elongate; pedicels ascending, 5-10 mm long; petals creamy white, 6-8 mm long, nearly or quite 2x as long as the sepals. **Fruit** erect when young, soon becoming widely divergent, 5-9 cm long, 1.2-2 mm wide, flat; seeds in 1 row, 1.5-2 mm long, conspicuously winged. May-June.—In Minnesota, known from a a single roadside population in Pine County.

Boechera stricta (Graham) Al-Shehbaz MAP 452
DRUMMOND'S ROCKCRESS *native*
  Arabis drummondii A. Gray

Biennial herb. **Stems** erect, 3-9 dm tall, glabrous, or at base very thinly pubescent with 2-pronged hairs, often glaucous. **Stem leaves** sessile, lance-shaped to narrowly oblong, 2-8 cm long, acute, entire or with a few teeth, auriculate at base, usually wholly glabrous. **Petals** 5-9 mm long; fruiting pedicels erect, 10-15 mm long. **Fruit** straight, erect, flat, 4-7 cm long or rarely longer, 1.5-2.5 mm wide or occasionally wider; seeds in 2 rows. May-Aug.—Moist or dry, acid or calcareous soil, in various habitats.

Boechera stricta

BRASSICA *Mustard*

Coarse annual or biennial herbs. Leaves (at least the lower) pinnatifid. Sepals erect or spreading, often sac-like at base. Petals yellow (ours), varying to nearly white in some cultivated species, obovate, clawed. Ovary nearly cylindric, scarcely narrowed to the short style. Fruit nearly terete to angled, more or less elongate, few-several-seeded, terminated by a conspicuous beak sometimes containing a seed at its base. Seeds nearly globose, in one row. Many species have been long-cultivated, and may persist in gardens overwinter, blooming the second year. *The oilseeds known as canola are sometimes varieties of* **Brassica rapa** *but are mostly* **B. napus** *and* **B. juncea.**

ADDITIONAL SPECIES
Brassica napus L. (Turnip), native to Mediterranean region; cultivated and sometimes escaping but doubtfully persisting; city weeds in Pennington and St. Louis counties.

1 Middle and upper leaves clasping stem . . . . *B. rapa*
1 Leaves not clasping stem 2
    2 Fruit to 2 cm long, strongly appressed . . . . *B. nigra*
    2 Fruit becoming more than 2 cm long, not strongly appressed . . . . *B. juncea*

Brassica juncea (L.) Czern. MAP 453
BROWN MUSTARD; CHINESE MUSTARD *introduced (naturalized)*
Annual herb, glabrous, often somewhat glaucous. **Stems** branched, 3-10 dm tall.

448. Boechera canadensis   *449. Boechera dentata*   *450. Boechera grahamii*   *451. Boechera laevigata*

Lower leaves to 2 dm long, pinnatifid and dentate, the upper progressively reduced, short-petioled to sessile. **Flowers** 12-15 mm wide. Pedicels at maturity ascending, 10-15 mm long. **Fruit** ascending, nearly terete, 1.5-4 cm long; beak slender, subulate, 6-9 mm long; seeds brown, about 2 mm long, conspicuously and evenly reticulate. June-Oct.—Established as a weed in waste ground and fields.

Brassica nigra (L.) W.D.J. Koch
BLACK MUSTARD

MAP 454
introduced

Annual herb. **Stems** simple or branched, to 15 dm tall, usually bristly below, glabrate or glabrous above. **Leaves** all petioled, ovate to obovate, the lower commonly lobed, the upper merely dentate. **Flowers** 8-10 mm wide. Pedicels at maturity erect, 3-4 mm long. **Fruit** erect, quadrangular, 1-2 cm long, smooth; beak slender, 2.5-4 mm long; seeds brown, 1.5-2 mm long, minutely roughly reticulate. Summer and fall.—Naturalized in fields and waste places.

Brassica rapa L.
FIELD MUSTARD; TURNIP
   Brassica campestris L.

MAP 455
introduced

Annual or biennial herb, green or glaucous, glabrous or nearly so. **Stems** branched, to 8 dm tall. **Lower leaves** petioled, more or less pinnately lobed; **upper leaves** oblong to lance-shaped, dentate or entire, sessile and clasping. **Flowers** about 10 mm wide; pedicels at maturity widely ascending, 1-2 cm long. **Fruit** ascending to nearly erect, terete or nearly so, 3-5 cm long; ; beak slender, 8-15 mm long; seeds dark brown, 1.5-2 mm long, minutely roughened. May-Oct. —Naturalized as a weed of fields and waste ground.

Brassica nigra

CAMELINA *False Flax*

Annual or winter-annual herbs, bearing both simple and branched hairs; stems branched above. Basal leaves narrowly spatulate; stem leaves linear to lance-shaped, clasping by a sagittate-auriculate base. Sepals erect, obtuse, the outer slightly saccate at base. Petals yellow, spatulate. Short stamens flanked at base by a pair of semicircular glands. Style slender, persistent. Fruit obovoid or pyriform, somewhat keeled, narrowed to the base and short-stipitate.

1   Fruit to 7 mm long and 5 mm wide; lower stem pubescent with both spreading and appressed hairs . . . .
. . . . **C. microcarpa**

1   Fruit more than 7 mm long and more than 5 mm wide; stem glabrous or with tiny hairs . . . . **C. sativa**

Camelina microcarpa DC.
LITTLE-POD FALSE FLAX

MAP 456
introduced

Stems erect, 3-7 dm tall, rough-pubescent, as is also the foliage, with both simple and branched hairs, the former 1-2 mm long. **Fruit** erect, 5.5-8 mm long, 3-4.5 mm wide, obscurely rugulose. April-June.—Fields and waste places, usually in sandy soil.

Camelina sativa (L.) Crantz
LARGE-SEED FALSE FLAX

MAP 457
introduced

Similar to *C. microcarpa* in foliage and habit. Stems and leaves glabrous to sparsely pubescent, the simple hairs not projecting beyond the stellate. **Fruit** commonly 7-10 mm long, 5-7 mm wide, inconspicuously veiny. May-June.—Fields and waste places, usually where sandy.

Camelina sativa

452. *Boechera stricta*

453. *Brassica juncea*

454. *Brassica nigra*

455. *Brassica rapa*

CAPSELLA *Shepherd's-Purse*

Capsella bursa-pastoris (L.) Medik.   MAP 458
SHEPHERD'S-PURSE   *introduced (naturalized)*
Annual herb, pubescent with stellate hairs. **Stems** 1-6 dm tall, sparingly branched.
Basal leaves oblong, 5-10 cm long, pinnately lobed; **stem leaves** much smaller,
lance-shaped to linear, entire or denticulate, auriculate at base. **Racemes** at
anthesis congested, at maturity greatly elongate, often forming half the total height
of the plant; pedicels at maturity widely spreading, 1-2 cm long; sepals short-
oblong, ascending; petals white, obovate, about 2 mm wide and about 2x as long
as the sepals. **Fruit** oblong cordate, flattened, 5-8 mm long, truncate to notched
at the tip. Spring.—Weedy in lawns, gardens, and waste places. *Where sheltered,
one of the first plants to bloom in spring.*

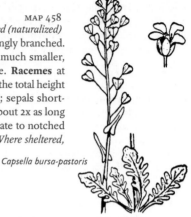

Capsella bursa-pastoris

CARDAMINE *Bittercress; Toothwort*

Annual, biennial or perennial herbs, smooth or with short hairs near base of stem. Leaves simple to
pinnately divided, the basal leaves often different in shape than stem leaves. Flowers in racemes or
umbel-like clusters; sepals green to yellow, early deciduous; petals usually white. Fruit a 2-chambered,
linear pod (silique), the seeds in a single row in each chamber.

ADDITIONAL SPECIES
Cardamine impatiens L. (Arrow-leaf bittercress), Eurasian native with explosively dehiscent fruits; first
collected in Minn in 2008 along Mississippi River (Dakota and Ramsey counties).

1 Leaves palmately divided into 4-7 linear segments . . . . **C. concatenata**
1 Leaves simple to pinnately compound 2
    2 Leaves simple; plants from a shallow tuber-like rhizome 3
        3 Petals pink to purple; sepals purple, turning brown with age . . . . **C. douglassii**
        3 Petals white; sepals green, turning yellow with age . . . . **C. bulbosa**
    2 Stem leaves pinnately dissected, with 2 or more deep lobes; plants without a tuber-like base 4
        4 Petals 8 mm or more long . . . . **C. pratensis**
        4 Petals to 4 mm long 5
            5 Leaflets of stem leaves linear . . . . **C. parviflora**
            5 Leaflets ovate . . . . **C. pensylvanica**

Cardamine bulbosa (Schreb.) B.S.P.   MAP 459
BULBOUS BITTERCRESS   *native*
Cardamine rhomboidea (Pers.) DC.
Perennial herb. Stems 1 to several from a short thick tuber, 2-6 dm long,
unbranched or with a few branches above, smooth or with short hairs on lower
stems. **Leaves** simple, sparsely to densely covered with short hairs; basal leaves
round or heart-shaped, on long petioles, withering before anthesis; stem leaves
4-8, oblong to oval, 2-7 cm long and 0.5-2.5 cm wide; petioles shorter upward on
stem. **Flowers** in racemes; sepals green, turning yellow after flowering, 2-4 mm
long; petals white (rarely pink), 6-15 mm long. **Fruit** a silique, 1-2.5 cm long and
1-2 mm wide, with a style beak 2-4 mm long, on spreading stalks 1-3 cm long,
the pod often falling before mature. May-June.—Wet forest depressions,
floodplain forests, streambanks, wet meadows, swamps, calcareous fens.

Cardamine bulbosa

456. *Camelina microcarpa*   457. *Camelina sativa*   458. *Capsella bursa-pastoris*   459. *Cardamine bulbosa*

Cardamine concatenata (Michx.) Sw.   MAP 460
CUT-LEAF TOOTHWORT   *native*
  Dentaria laciniata Muhl.

Perennial herb; rhizome constricted at intervals, the segments 2-3 cm long. **Stems** 2-4 dm tall, pubescent above and on the rachis. Basal and stem leaves similar, **basal leaves** usually absent at anthesis, **stem leaves** typically in a whorl of 3 above the middle of the stem, deeply 3-parted, the segments linear or lance-shaped, nearly entire to laciniately toothed, the segments often deeply bifid, the whole leaf appearing 5-parted. Sepals 5-8 mm long; petals 12-19 mm long. April-May. —Moist rich woods.

Cardamine douglassii Britt.   (NO MAP)
LIMESTONE BITTERCRESS   *native*

Perennial herb, spreading by shallow rhizomes; plants with dense to sparse hairs. **Stems** to 6 dm long. **Leaves** simple, **basal leaves** round or heart-shaped, deciduous before anthesis; **stem leaves** 3-5, narrowly oblong to ovate; petioles long on lower leaves, becoming shorter above. **Flowers** in a raceme; sepals purple, turning brown with age; petals pink, purple, or rarely white. **Fruit** an upright silique, 2-3 cm long and 2-3 mm wide, on a stalk 1-2 cm long. April-May.—Floodplain forests and low deciduous woods, often in shade; reported for Minnesota.

Cardamine douglassii

Cardamine parviflora L.   MAP 461
SMALL-FLOWERED BITTERCRESS   *native*
  Cardamine arenicola Britt.

Annual herb. **Stems** usually solitary, simple to much branched, 1-3 dm tall. Terminal leaflet of the basal leaves oblong to broadly cuneate-obovate. **Stem leaves** 2-4 cm long, with 3-6 pairs of segments, the terminal linear to cuneate-oblong, entire or toothed, the lateral not much smaller, linear or oblong, usually 1-3 mm wide and entire, not decurrent. Pedicels and fruit as in *C. pensylvanica*. — Usually in dry soil.

Cardamine pensylvanica Muhl.   MAP 462
PENNSYLVANIA BITTERCRESS   *native*

Biennial herb. **Stems** erect or spreading, to 6 dm long, usually hairy on lower stem. **Leaves** pinnately divided into 2-5 pairs of lateral leaflets and a single terminal segment, 4-8 cm long and 1-4 cm wide, the leaflets entire or with a few teeth or lobes; the terminal leaflet largest, 1-4 cm long and 1-2 cm wide; petioles shorter than blades, becoming shorter upward. **Flowers** in a raceme; sepals 1-2 mm long; petals white, 2-4 mm long. **Fruit** an upright silique, 2-3 cm long and to 1 mm wide, with a style-beak to 2 mm long, on stalks 5-15 mm long. May-Sept. —Streambanks, swamps, and wet forests (often where seasonally flooded); wet, disturbed areas.

Cardamine pensylvanica

Cardamine pratensis L.   MAP 463
CUCKOO-FLOWER   *threatened | native*

Perennial upright herb. **Stems** 2-5 dm long. **Basal leaves** on long petioles, divided into 3-8 broad leaflets, 5-20 mm long, the terminal segment largest and more or less entire; **lower stem leaves** similar to basal ones, becoming shorter and with shorter petioles upward on stem; **stem leaves** with 7-17 oval to linear leaflets. **Flowers** in a crowded raceme; petals white, 8-15 mm long. **Fruit** an upright silique, 2.5-4 cm long, with a style-beak 1-2 mm long, on stalks 8-15 mm long.

Cardamine pratensis

460. *Cardamine concatenata*   461. *Cardamine parviflora*   462. *Cardamine pensylvanica*   463. *Cardamine pratensis*

May-June.—Peatlands, tamarack and cedar swamps, wet depressions in forests.
Flowers in cultivated European strains, escaped in some areas south and east of Minn,
are usually pink.

CONRINGIA *Hare's-Ear-Mustard*

Conringia orientalis (L.) Dumort.   MAP 464
HARE'S-EAR-MUSTARD   *introduced (naturalized)*
Annual glabrous herb, often glaucous. **Stems** erect, branched above or simple, up
to 8 dm tall. **Leaves** entire, pale green, the lower narrowed to the base, the upper
oval or oblong, cordate-clasping. Sepals erect, saccate at base; petals yellowish
white, narrowly obovate, 10-12 mm long, long-clawed; ovary cylindric, gradually
tapering to the short style; pedicels and fruit widely divergent, the **fruit** elongate,
slender, 8-12 cm long, 2-3 mm thick, 4-angled; seeds in 1 row, oblong, 2-3 mm
long, granular-roughened. May-Aug.—Native of Eurasia; naturalized or adventive
in waste places.

DESCURAINIA *Tansy-Mustard*

Annual or biennial herbs, more or less pubescent or canescent with wholly or partly branched hairs;
leaves 1-3-pinnate with very numerous small segments. Sepals ovate, obtuse. Petals yellow or pale
yellow, small, sometimes barely surpassing the calyx, obovate or spatulate. Filaments slender; anthers
ovate or oblong. Staminal glands minute or none. Ovary cylindric; style very short, as thick as the
ovary; stigma capitate; ovules numerous. Fruits linear or clavate, terete or slightly 4-angled, tipped
with the very short persistent style; valves with a prominent midnerve. Seeds elliptic or oblong, in
one or two rows.

1   Plants green, with glandular hairs; fruit less than 13 mm long . . . . **D. pinnata**
1   Plants gray-green, with stellate hairs, the hairs not glandular; fruit 13 mm or more long . . . . **D. sophia**

Descurainia pinnata (Walt.) Britt.   MAP 465
TANSY-MUSTARD   *native*
Annual herb. **Stems** erect, simple, or abundantly branched below, or branched at
the inflorescence, 2-7 dm tall. **Leaves** oblong in outline, the lower leaves largest,
bipinnate, or pinnate with deeply pinnatifid segments; the upper leaves
progressively reduced, less divided, the uppermost 1-pinnate. **Flowers** 2-4 mm
wide.; raceme after anthesis elongate, up to 3 dm long; pedicels at maturity widely
divergent, 5-20 mm long. **Fruit** narrowly clavate, 5-13 mm long, 1-2 mm wide;
seeds in 2 rows.—Usually in disturbed places; roadsides, railroads, fields, gravel
pits, shores.

Descurainia sophia (L.) Webb   MAP 466
HERB-SOPHIA   *introduced (naturalized)*
Annual herb, plants canescent throughout. **Stems** erect, usually much branched,
3-8 dm tall. **Leaves** ovate to obovate in outline, or the upper narrower, 2 to 3x
pinnate into linear segments. **Flowers** about 3 mm wide; raceme after anthesis
loose and open; pedicels widely ascending, 8-14 mm long. **Fruit** narrowly linear,
15-25 mm. long, 0.5-1 mm wide; seeds in 1 row.—Disturbed places, roadsides,
railroads.

Descurainia pinnata

DRABA *Whitlow-Grass*

Annual, biennial, or perennial herbs, in some species woody at base. Leaves entire or dentate, more
or less pubescent with simple, branched, or stellate hairs, or with 2 types of hairs together. Sepals
ascending or erect, blunt. Petals yellow or white, rounded, sometimes bifid, narrowed below to a
claw, or in certain species sometimes reduced or absent. Fruit a 2-valved silicle, rarely as much as 5x
longer than wide.

ADDITIONAL SPECIES
Draba norvegica Gunnerus (Norwegian whitlow-grass), disjunct in Cook County from the high-arctic of
Canada; ☛*endangered*.

Draba arabisans Michx.
ROCK WHITLOW-GRASS

MAP 467
native

Perennial. Stems 1-4 dm tall, simple to branched above, glabrous to stellate-pubescent. **Basal leaves** narrowly oblong lance-shaped to spatulate, up to 6 cm long, often sharply toothed, uniformly stellate-pubescent; **stem leaves** few to several, oblong to obovate, narrowed or acute at base, often dentate. Mature racemes loose, up to 10 cm long, commonly glabrous or nearly so; petals white, 4-6 mm long. **Fruit** glabrous, lance-shaped to narrowly oblong, 7-12 mm long, about one-fourth as wide, soon twisted, in poorly grown examples shorter, ovate, and straight. May-June.—Rocks and cliffs.

Draba cana Rydb.
HOARY WHITLOW-GRASS

MAP 468
⬤*endangered* | *native*

Perennial. **Stems** 1-3 dm tall. Basal rosettes very dense, the numerous spatulate, densely stellate-pubescent leaves commonly less than 3 cm long; **stem leaves** lance-shaped to ovate, usually 5-20 mm long. **Raceme** elongate, at maturity constituting 1/2 to 3/4 of the total plant height; lower flowers remote, often axillary, only the upper crowded; petals white, about 4 mm long. **Fruit** oblong, 5-12 mm long, usually 1.5-2 mm wide, stellate-pubescent. May-July.—Rocky limestone ledges, cliffs, and gravelly or rocky soil; rare in ne Minn; more common in Rocky Mtns.

Draba nemorosa L.
WOODLAND WHITLOW-GRASS

MAP 469
introduced

Annual or winter-annual, to 3 dm tall. **Basal leaves** ovate lance-shaped to oval, elliptic, or obovate, 1-2.5 cm long; **stem leaves** similar, few to several, all below the middle of the stem, often dentate, pubescent with both simple and branched hairs. **Raceme** at maturity loose and elongate, up to 2 dm long, glabrous; petals pale yellow, becoming white in age, about 2 mm long; pedicels at maturity widely spreading or ascending, to 3 cm long, glabrous. **Fruit** ascending to erect, oblong-linear, 5-10 mm long.—Dry soil, prairies and hillsides.

Draba reptans (Lam.) Fern.
CAROLINA WHITLOW-GRASS

MAP 470
native

Annual or winter-annual. **Stems** simple or branched at the base, 5-15 cm tall. **Basal leaves** spatulate or obovate, 1-3 cm long, blunt, entire, pubescent with mostly simple hairs above, stellate beneath; **stem leaves** few and near the base of the stem. **Racemes** at maturity congested, the glabrous axis 5-20 mm long, or rarely longer; petals white, to 5 mm long, or smaller or lacking; pedicels glabrous, ascending. **Fruit** ascending or erect, usually 1-2 cm long, glabrous or strigulose. April-May.—Dry, sterile or sandy soil.

Draba reptans

464. *Conringia orientalis*

465. *Descurainia pinnata*

466. *Descurainia sophia*

467. *Draba arabisans*

ERUCASTRUM *Dog-Mustard*

Erucastrum gallicum (Willd.) O.E. Schulz   MAP 471
COMMON DOG-MUSTARD   *introduced (naturalized)*

Annual or biennial, with the general aspect of a *Brassica;* pubescence of simple
hairs or none. **Stems** erect or ascending, 3-6 dm tall, branched from the lower
nodes. Basal and lower **leaves** oblong lance-shaped in outline, to 15 cm long,
sparsely pubescent, deeply pinnatifid, the segments dentate, the terminal segment
largest; **stem leaves** progressively reduced, the uppermost only 1-2 cm long;
Mature **racemes** greatly elongate; pedicels slender, ascending; sepals ascending;
petals yellow, spatulate, about 7 mm long. **Fruit** 4-angled, usually upwardly
curved, the body 2-2.5 cm long, the beak about 3 mm long; seeds numerous, in 1
row. May-Sept.—Waste places.

Erucastrum gallicum

ERYSIMUM *Wallflower*

Annual to perennial herbs, with narrow, entire, dentate, or pinnatifid leaves, more or less pubescent
with appressed, 2-4-pronged hairs. Petals yellow to orange (in our species), obovate or spatulate,
abruptly or gradually narrowed to a long claw. Ovary linear-cylindric, pubescent; style very short;
stigma capitate, 2-lobed. Fruits elongate, more or less 4-angled, thinly to densely pubescent; valves
with a prominent midnerve. Seeds numerous, in one row. *All our species are more or less densely
pubescent on the stem, leaves, sepals, and fruit, and more or less so on the back of the petals, especially at the
base of the blade. The 2-pronged hairs lie lengthwise; V-shaped hairs have the single prong directed backward.*

1   Petals 15-25 mm long; fruit 5-10 cm long . . . . ***E. capitatum***
1   Petals 10 mm long or less 2
    2   Petals less than 6 mm long; fruit to 3 cm long . . . . ***E. cheiranthoides***
    2   Petals 6 mm or more long . . . . ***E. inconspicuum***

Erysimum capitatum (Dougl.) Greene   MAP 472
WESTERN WALLFLOWER   *introduced*
Erysimum asperum (Nutt.) DC.

Biennial herb. **Stems** erect, simple or branched above, 2-10 dm tall. **Leaves** linear
to oblong lance-shaped, entire or with a few low teeth, thinly to densely
pubescent. **Racemes** at maturity greatly elongate, the stout pedicels divergent, 7-
15 mm long; sepals 10 mm long; petals bright yellow to orange-yellow, 15-25 mm
long, the blade about half as long as the very slender exserted claw. **Fruit**
ascending, 4-10 cm long, 4-angled. May-June.—Prairies, sand hills, open woods.

Erysimum cheiranthoides L.   MAP 473
WORM-SEED WALLFLOWER   *introduced (naturalized)*

Annual herb. **Stems** erect, simple or sparingly branched, 2-10 dm tall. **Leaves**
linear to oblong lance-shaped, entire or barely sinuate, thinly pubescent hut bright
green, tapering to the base. Mature **racemes** elongate, the rachis straight, the
pedicels very slender, widely divergent, 6-14 mm, commonly 8-12 mm long;
sepals 2-3.5 mm long; petals bright yellow, 3.5-5.5 mm long. **Fruit** ascending to
erect, 12-25 mm, commonly 15-20 mm long. June-Aug.—Usually in wet soil, but
also appearing as a weed in fields and roadsides.

Erysimum cheiranthoides

468. Draba cana   *469. Draba nemorosa*   *470. Draba reptans*   *471. Erucastrum gallicum*

Erysimum inconspicuum (S. Wats.) MacM.   MAP 474
SHY WALLFLOWER   *introduced (naturalized)*
Perennial herb. **Stems** erect, commonly simple, occasionally sparingly branched,
3-8 dm tall. **Leaves** mostly erect or ascending, linear to oblong lance-shaped,
entire or obscurely and remotely sinuate-dentate, the stem leaves rarely more
than 5 mm wide, canescent. Mature **racemes** elongate and wand-like, the stout
ascending pedicels 3-9 mm long; sepals densely stellate, 5-7 mm long; petals pale
yellow, 6-10 mm long. **Fruit** erect or nearly so, 1.5-4 cm long. May-Aug.—Dry soil
of prairies, plains, and upland woods.

Erysimum inconspicuum

HESPERIS *Dame's Rocket*

Hesperis matronalis L.   MAP 475
DAME'S ROCKET   *introduced (invasive)*
Perennial herb. **Stems** erect, 5-10 dm tall, simple or branched above. **Leaves** lance-
shaped, short-petioled or sessile, remotely and sharply denticulate, pubescent
above with simple hairs, below chiefly with branched hairs. **Flowers** fragrant;
sepals erect, the outer narrow; the inner broad, saccate at base; petals purple,
varying to pink or white, 2-2.5 cm long, the blade obovate; ovary cylindric; stigma
2-lobed. **Fruit** widely spreading on stout pedicels, linear, terete or nearly so, 5-10
cm long, somewhat constricted between the seeds; seeds numerous, large, 3-4
mm long, angularly fusiform, in 1 row. May-June.—Formerly cultivated for
ornament; frequently escaped along roads and fencerows and in open woods.

IODANTHUS *Purple-Rocket*

Iodanthus pinnatifidus (Michx.) Steud.   MAP 476
PURPLE-ROCKET   ✽*endangered | native*
Perennial herb; plants smooth. **Stems** to 1 m long, unbranched except in head.
Leaves lance-shaped to oval or oblong, leaf base often with lobes which clasp
stem; **lower leaves** often divided at base into 1-4 pairs of small segments; margins
deep-toothed; petioles short. **Flowers** in a branched raceme, on stalks 5-10 mm
long, pale violet to white; sepals rounded at tip, 3-5 mm long; petals 10-13 mm
long. **Fruit** a linear, cylindric silique, 2-4 cm long and 1-2 mm wide, on spreading
stalks. June-July.—Wet or moist floodplain forests.

Hesperis matronalis

LEPIDIUM *Pepperwort*

Annual, biennial, or perennial herbs. Leaves linear to elliptic, entire, toothed, or pinnatifid. Sepals
blunt. Petals small, white (rarely yellowish), linear to spatulate, sometimes notched at tip. Stamens 6,
or by abortion 4 or 2. Ovary flat. Fruit a flattened silicle, thin or somewhat distended over the seeds,
ovate to circular or obovate, often winged, commonly notched at tip, tipped by the persistent style
or stigma.

ADDITIONAL SPECIES
Lepidium sativum L. (Gardencress pepperweed), Eurasian native; Hennepin and St. Louis counties.

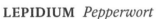

1   At least upper stem leaves sessile and auriculate, sagittate, or clasping at base 2
     2   Plants annual, not rhizomatous; fruit broadly winged at apex; racemes elongated in fruit . . . . . . *L. campestre*
     2   Plants perennial, rhizomatous; fruit wingless at apex; racemes not elongated in fruit. 3
         3   Fruit pubescent, inflated, spherical, valves not veined. . . . . *L. appelianum*
         3   Fruit glabrous, flattened, cordate, valves veined . . . . *L. draba*

472. Erysimum capitatum   *473. Erysimum cheiranthoides*   *474. Erysimum inconspicuum*   *475. Hesperis matronalis*

1   Stem leaves petiolate or subsessile, never auriculate, sagittate, or clasping at base 4
    4   Fruit obovate, widest above middle; petals absent or often rudimentary; rachis of raceme puberulent with cylindrical or clavate hairs.. ***L. densiflorum***
    4   Fruit orbicular, widest at middle; petals present or rarely rudimentary; rachis of raceme puberulent with curved hairs, rarely glabrous .... ***L. virginicum***

Lepidium campestre (L.) Ait. f.

FIELD-CRESS

MAP 477
introduced (naturalized)

Biennial herb; densely short-pubescent. **Stems** erect, 2–5 dm tall, simple to much branched. **Basal leaves** elongate, oblong lance-shaped, entire to shallowly lobed; **stem leaves** erect or ascending, lance-shaped to narrowly oblong, 2–4 cm long, entire or denticulate, sessile, clasping by acute auricles. **Racemes** dense, up to 15 cm long at maturity; fruiting pedicels 4–8 mm long, widely divergent. **Fruit** oblong-ovate, 5–6 mm long, about three-fourths as wide, convex below, concave above, broadly winged distally, the short style barely exsert. May–June.—Native of Europe; a weed of sandy waste ground, fields, and roadsides.

Lepidium campestre

Lepidium densiflorum Schrad.

PRAIRIE PEPPERWORT

MAP 478
native

Annual herb. Stems 2–5 dm tall, thinly short-pubescent. **Basal leaves** 4–7 cm long or rarely longer, coarsely dentate or pinnatifid; **stem leaves** shorter, linear or narrowly oblance-shaped, mostly entire, sharply acute. **Racemes** at maturity erect, 5–10 cm long; petals none, or shorter than the sepals, linear to narrowly spatulate. **Fruit** broadly oval to obovate, 2–3.3 mm long, narrowly winged distally; stigma included in the notch. May–June.—Dry, sandy or gravelly disturbed places.

Lepidium densiflorum
capsule

Lepidium draba L.

HEART-POD HOARYCRESS
    Cardaria draba (L.) Desv.

MAP 479
introduced

Perennial herb. **Stems** erect, up to 6 dm tall, commonly simple below, much branched above. **Stem leaves** oblong to ovate, ascending or erect, sessile, auriculate at base. **Racemes** numerous, dense; pedicels at maturity 10–15 mm long. **Fruit** about 3 mm long, 3–5 mm wide, rounded to subcordate at base, subacute at the summit, the surface finely reticulate; style persistent, about 1 mm long. May–July.—Fields, roadsides, and waste places.

Lepidium virginicum L.

POOR-MAN'S PEPPER

MAP 480
native

Annual herb. **Stems** erect, 1–5 dm tall, simple to much branched. **Basal leaves** oblong lance-shaped in outline, sharply toothed to pinnatifid, occasionally bipinnatifid. **Upper leaves** smaller, oblong lance-shaped to linear, dentate to entire, acute, narrowed to the base. **Racemes** numerous, many-flowered, up to 1 dm long; petals present, equaling to twice as long as the sepals. **Fruit** broadly elliptic to circular, 2.5–4 mm long, narrowly winged across the top; style included in the notch. May–June.—Dry fields, gardens, roadsides and waste places.

Lepidium virginicum

LESQUERELLA *Bladderpod*

Lesquerella ludoviciana (Nutt.) S. Wats.

LOUISIANA BLADDERPOD
    Physaria ludoviciana (Nutt.) O'Kane & Al-Shehbaz

MAP 481
endangered | native

Perennial herb, more or less canescent with stellate hairs. **Stems** several, 1–3 dm

476. *Iodanthus pinnatifidus*   477. *Lepidium campestre*   478. *Lepidium densiflorum*   479. *Lepidium draba*

tall, erect or ascending from a stout caudex. **Basal leaves** narrowly oblong lance-shaped, to 10 cm long, entire to rarely dentate, the stem leaves progressively narrower and shorter. **Racemes** at maturity to 15 cm long, many-flowered; pedicels 10-15 mm long, strongly recurved; sepals erect, obtuse; petals yellow, obovate,about 7 mm long; style persistent, 3-4.5 mm long. **Fruit** subglobose or obovoid, 4.5-6 mm long, including the short stalk; seeds 4-6 in each cell. May-July.—Rare on dry dolomitic bluff edges along the Mississippi River.

NASTURTIUM *Watercress*

Nasturtium officinale R.Br.
WATERCRESS

Rorippa nasturtium-aquaticum (L.) Hayek

MAP 482
introduced (invasive)

Perennial herb; plants smooth, often forming large, tangled colonies. **Stems** underwater, floating, or trailing on mud; rooting from lower nodes. **Leaves** 4-12 cm long and 2-5 cm wide, pinnately divided into 3-9 segments, the lateral segments round to ovate in outline, the terminal segment largest; margins entire or with a few shallow rounded teeth; petioles present. **Flowers** in 1 to several racemes per stem, flat-topped and elongating in fruit; flowers 5 mm wide, sepals green-white, oblong, 1-3 mm long; petals white, sometimes purple-tinged, obovate, 4-5 mm long. **Fruit** a linear, often curved pod (silique), 1-2.5 cm long and 2 mm wide, tipped with a short style beak to 1 mm long. May-Sept.—Seeps, slow-moving streams, ditches, cedar swamps, especially in cold spring-fed waters. Naturalized throughout most of USA and s Canada.

Nasturtium officinale

ADDITIONAL SPECIES

Nasturtium microphyllum (Boenn. ex Rchb.) Rchb., introduced perennial known from scattered Minn locations; very similar to *N. officinale* (sometimes treated as a variety) and found in same aquatic habitats; distinguished by narrower mature fruit and 2 rows of seeds under each valve rather than one row.

Neslia paniculata

NESLIA *Ball-Mustard*

Neslia paniculata (L.) Desv.
YELLOW BALL-MUSTARD

MAP 483
introduced

Annual herb. **Stems** much branched, to 8 dm tall, pubescent with branched hairs. **Stem leaves** lance-shaped, 3-6 cm long, entire or nearly so, sessile, clasping, scabrous with 2-pronged hairs. **Flowers** small, to about 1.5 mm wide; sepals oblong, obtuse; petals yellow, spatulate; fruiting pedicels 10-15 mm long. **Fruit** obliquely ovoid, 7-10 mm long, slightly compressed, reticulate and pitted. June-July.—Introduced and weedy, sometimes in cultivated fields.

RAPHANUS *Radish*

Raphanus raphanistrum L.
WILD RADISH

MAP 484
introduced (naturalized)

Coarse annual herb from a stout taproot, pubescence of simple hairs. **Stems** stout, 3-8 dm tall, usually sparsely hispid. **Lower leaves** obovate in outline, 1-2 dm long, pinnatifid into 5-15 oblong segments, the lower very small, the upper progressively larger; **upper leaves** much smaller, oblong to lance-shaped, entire, dentate, or few-lobed. Sepals obtuse, somewhat saccate at base; petals yellow, becoming white in age, 10-15 mm long; mature pedicels ascending, 8-15 mm long.

Raphanus raphanistrum

480. *Lepidium virginicum*   481. *Lesquerella ludoviciana*   482. *Nasturtium officinale*   483. *Neslia paniculata*

Fruit nearly cylindrical when fresh, when dry becoming prominently several-ribbed and constricted between the 4-10 seeds, the body 2-4 cm long, the beak 1-3 cm long. June-Aug.—Native of Eurasia; weedy on roadsides, fields, waste places.

ADDITIONAL SPECIES
Raphanus sativus L. (Radish), cultivated and rarely escaping from gardens.

RORIPPA *Yellowcress*

Annual, biennial or perennial herbs; plants smooth or with unbranched hairs. Leaves sometimes in a basal rosette in young plants, toothed to pinnately divided, petioles short or absent. Flowers small, in racemes at ends of stems or from lateral branches; sepals green to yellow, deciduous by fruiting time; petals yellow or white, shorter to longer than sepals. Fruit a short-cylindric to linear pod (silique), mostly 2-chambered, the seeds in 2 rows.

ADDITIONAL SPECIES
Rorippa austriaca (Crantz) Bess. (Austrian yellowcress); perennial from a rhizome; native of Europe; weedy in fields where the plants spread by fragments of the rhizome; Lincoln and Pipestone counties.

1   Plant truly aquatic, the submersed leaves dissected in a bipinnate pattern into filiform segments (midvein present, the lateral segments again dissected), frequently detaching readily from the stem; petals white . . . . . *R. aquatica*
1   Plant terrestrial or aquatic but even if in water the leaves with definite flat lobes (not bipinnately dissected) and not falling from the stem; petals yellow 2
  2   Plants annual or biennial, taprooted; petals shorter than or equal to sepals 3
    3   Pedicels of mature fruit curved or arching downwards; petals 1 mm long or shorter; leaves all glabrous beneath; mature fruit ca. 2-5.2 mm long, up to 1.7 mm thick, mostly broadest well below the middle, strongly tapering to the acute tip . . . . *R. curvipes*
    3   Pedicels of mature fruit usually ± straight, ascending or spreading; petals 1.5-2.3 mm long; leaves glabrous or hispid beneath; mature fruit wider, the largest 2-2.7 mm wide at or near the middle, not strongly tapering, the tip blunter . . . . *R. palustris*
  2   Plants perennial, roots creeping; petals longer than sepals 4
    4   Stems sprawling or spreading; lateral leaf segments entire or with a few shallow teeth; beak of fruit 1-2 mm long . . . . *R. sinuata*
    4   Stems erect or nearly so; lateral leaf segments with sharp teeth; beak of fruit to 1 mm long . . *R. sylvestris*

Rorippa aquatica (Eaton) E.J. Palmer & Steyerm.   MAP 485
LAKECRESS   *native*
    Armoracia aquatica (Eaton) Wieg.
    Armoracia lacustris (Gray) Al-Shehbaz & Bates
    Neobeckia aquatica (Eaton) Greene
Perennial, fibrous-rooted herb. Stems and leaves smooth, usually underwater. **Underwater leaves** pinnately dissected into many threadlike segments; **emersed leaves**, if present, lance-shaped, 3-7 cm long, coarsely toothed. **Flowers** on spreading stalks to 1 cm long; sepals turning upright; petals white, 6-8 mm long. **Fruit** oval, 5-8 mm long, 1-chambered, tipped by a persistent slender style 2-4 mm long, but apparently rarely maturing. June-Aug.—Quiet water in lakes, rivers and streams; muddy shores.

Rorippa curvipes Greene   MAP 486
BLUNT-LEAF YELLOW CRESS   *native*
Annual or biennial taprooted herb. **Stems** 1 to several, prostrate to erect, 2-5 dm tall, glabrous. **Basal and lower stem leaves** sessile, somewhat auriculate to

Rorippa aquatica

484. *Raphanus raphanistrum*   485. *Rorippa aquatica*   486. *Rorippa curvipes*

nonauriculate at base but not clasping stem, oblong or spatulate, 2.5-7 cm long and to 2 cm wide, usually pinnatifid with toothed lobes, glabrous or sparsely hirsute above, glabrous below. **Racemes** terminal and axillary, 0.5-1.1 dm long; sepals to 1.5 mm long, early deciduous; petals yellow, to 1.2 mm long. **Fruit** a cylindrical silique, slightly to strongly curved upward and inward toward the raceme axis, tapering to the apex, somewhat constricted in the center, 2.5-5 mm long, style in the fruit straight to mm long; fruiting pedicels 2.5-5 mm long; seeds 20-50 per silique. July-Sept.—Wet meadows, muddy shores of drying ponds and rivers.

Rorippa palustris (L.) Bess.

COMMON YELLOWCRESS

MAP 487
native

Annual or biennial herb. **Stems** erect, usually 1, to 1 m long, unbranched or branched upward. **Leaves** lance-shaped to obovate, mostly pinnately divided; the blades oblong to oblong lance-shaped, 5-30 cm long and 2-6 cm wide, middle stem leaves usually with basal lobes and clasping stem, smooth to densely hairy on lower surface; margins deeply lobed and slightly wavy; petioles short or absent. **Flowers** in racemes at ends of stems and from leaf axils, the terminal raceme flowering and fruiting first, the oldest siliques on lowest portions of raceme; sepals green, 1-3 mm long, early deciduous; petals yellow, drying white, 2-3 mm long. **Fruit** a round to short-cylindric pod, 3-10 mm long and 1-3 mm wide, straight-sided or slightly tapered to tip, on stalks 3-10 mm long. June-Sept. —Marshes, wet meadows, shores, streambanks, ditches and other wet places.

Rorippa palustris

Rorippa sinuata (Nutt.) A.S. Hitchc.

SPREADING YELLOWCRESS

MAP 488
native

Perennial herb, spreading by rhizomes. **Stems** usually several, sprawling, 1-4 dm long, sparsely to densely pubescent. **Leaves** all from stem (basal leaves absent), 2-8 cm long and 0.5-2 cm wide, oblong, pinnately divided into 5-7 pairs, sometimes with basal lobes clasping stem, margins entire or with a few teeth. **Flowers** in racemes at ends of stems and from upper leaf axils, all flowering at about same time or flowers from axils first; sepals yellow-green, 3-5 mm long, early deciduous; petals yellow, 4-6 mm long, longer than sepals. **Fruit** a linear pod (silique), 5-12 mm long and 1-2 mm wide, tapered to the style beak, on upright to spreading stalks 4-10 mm long. June-Aug.—Stream and riverbanks, ditches, and other low places, especially where sandy.

Rorippa sylvestris (L.) Bess.

CREEPING YELLOWCRESS

MAP 489
introduced (naturalized)

Perennial herb, spreading by rhizomes and sometimes stolons. **Stems** erect, branched above, 2-6 dm long; smooth, or sparsely hairy on lower stem; basal rosettes present on young plants. **Stem leaves** pinnately divided, oblong in outline, 3-15 cm long and 2.5 cm wide, gradually reduced in size upward on stem, margins usually toothed; petioles present on lower leaves, absent on upper leaves. **Flowers** in racemes at ends of stems and from upper leaf axils, all flowering at about same time or the oldest siliques on lower portion of terminal racemes; sepals yellow-green, 2-3 mm long; petals yellow, 3-5 mm long. **Fruit** a linear pod (silique), 4-10 mm long and to 1 mm wide, usually upright on spreading stalks 5-10 mm long. June-Aug. Introduced from Europe.—Wet forests, lakeshores, muddy streambanks and ditches; sometimes weedy.

Rorippa sylvestris

487. Rorippa palustris

488. Rorippa sinuata

489. Rorippa sylvestris

490. Sinapis arvensis

SINAPIS *White-Mustard*

Sinapis arvensis L.   MAP 490
CORN-MUSTARD   *introduced (naturalized)*
   Brassica arvensis Rabenh. non L.
   Brassica kaber (DC.) L.C. Wheeler

Annual herb. **Stems** 2-8 dm tall, usually sparsely hirsute. **Leaves** obovate in outline, the lower sometimes lobed but more often merely coarsely toothed; upper leaves progressively smaller, coarsely toothed, roughly pubescent to nearly glabrous. **Flowers** about 15 mm wide; pedicels at maturity ascending, about 5 mm long. **Fruit** ascending, linear, nearly terete, the body 1-2 cm long, 1.5-2.5 mm thick, smooth or somewhat pubescent; beak commonly about half as long as the body, flattened-quadrangular; seeds dark brown, smooth, 1-1.5 mm wide. May-July. —Established as a weed in fields, gardens, and waste ground. *Similar to Brassica (and previously included in that genus) but the flowers tend to be larger.*

Sinapis arvensis

SISYMBRIUM *Hedge-Mustard*

Our species annual or winter-annual herbs, with simple hairs. Leaves (at least the lower) deeply pinnatifid. Sepals obtuse, ascending. Petals small, yellow, obovate. Ovary cylindric; style short, scarcely differentiated. Fruits elongate, linear, terete or slightly quadrangular, tipped with the minute persistent style. Seeds in one row, oblong, nearly or quite smooth.

1   Fruit erect, appressed; pedicels erect, 2-3 mm long . . . . **S. officinale**
1   Fruit widely spreading; pedicels spreading, 5 mm long or more 2
   2   Fruit 5 cm long or more; pedicels about as thick as fruit . . . . **S. altissimum**
   2   Fruit to 5 cm long; pedicels thinner than fruit . . . . **S. loeselii**

Sisymbrium altissimum L.   MAP 491
TUMBLING MUSTARD   *introduced (naturalized)*
Stems erect, usually much branched, to 1 m tall, glabrous or sparsely pilose. **Leaves** petioled, deeply pinnately parted, the lower into 5-8 pairs, the upper into 2-5 pairs of segments; segments varying from linear and entire to lance-shaped and serrate. **Racemes** greatly elongate after anthesis; pedicels nearly or quite as thick as the fruit, ascending, 5-10 mm long; petals pale yellow, 6-8 mm long. **Fruit** ascending or spreading, slender, linear, 5-10 cm long, 1-1.5 mm wide. June-July. —Native of Eurasia; established as a weed in fields, roadsides, and waste ground.

Sisymbrium loeselii L.   MAP 492
TALL HEDGE-MUSTARD   *introduced*
Stems 5-10 dm tall, hirsute toward the base with reflexed hairs. **Lower leaves** lyrate-pinnatifid and dentate, usually hirsute, the lateral segments triangular to ovate, acute, spreading or reflexed, the terminal larger, triangular. **Flowers** rising above the young fruits; pedicels at maturity divergent, 5-10 mm long. **Fruit** narrowly linear, 1.2-3.5 cm long. June-July.—Native of se Europe and w Asia; occasionally adventive.

Sisymbrium altissimum

Sisymbrium officinale (L.) Scop.   MAP 493
HEDGE-MUSTARD   *introduced (naturalized)*
Stems erect, 3-8 dm tall, branched above or simple. **Lower leaves** petioled, deeply pinnatifid; segments oblong to ovate or the terminal sometimes rotund, angularly toothed; **upper leaves** sessile or nearly so, few-lobed or 3-lobed or entire, the lateral lobes widely divergent. **Flowers** bright yellow, about 3 mm wide. Racemes erect, simple or with straight, widely divergent branches; pedicels at maturity 2-3 mm long, closely appressed, distally thickened and as wide as the fruit at the summit. **Fruit** closely appressed, subulate, 10-15 mm long, 1-1.5 mm wide at base. May-Oct.—Native of Europe; weedy in gardens, roadsides, and waste ground.

Sisymbrium officinale

SUBULARIA *Water-Awlwort*

Subularia aquatica L.
WATER-AWLWORT

MAP 494
🌿*threatened* | *native*

Small, annual aquatic herb; plants underwater or sometimes on muddy shores. **Stems** 3-10 cm long. Leaves all basal, awl-shaped or linear, 1-5 cm long. **Flowers** small, 2-10, widely separated in a raceme; sepals persistent, petals white. **Fruit** a short, oval or oblong pod (silicle), 2-4 mm long. June-Aug.—Cold lakes in shallow water to 1 m deep; usually where sandy.

Subularia aquatica

THLASPI *Pennycress*

Thlaspi arvense L.
FIELD PENNYCRESS

MAP 495
introduced (naturalized)

Glabrous annual herb. **Stems** 1-5 dm tall, simple to much branched. **Stem leaves** sessile, oblong to lance-shaped, entire or few-toothed, with 2 narrow auricles at base 1-5 mm long. **Petals** white, spatulate to obovate, about 3 mm wide, 2x as long as the sepals; pedicels at maturity ascending. **Fruit** circular to broadly elliptic, 10-14 mm long, strongly flattened and distended over the seeds, keeled or winged at the margin, tip deeply (2-3 mm) notched. April-June.—Native of Europe; roadsides and waste ground.

TURRITIS *Tower-Mustard*

Turritis glabra L.
TOWER-MUSTARD
    Arabis glabra (L.) Bernh.

MAP 496
native

Biennial herb. **Stems** commonly hirsute near the base with mostly simple hairs, occasionally with some or many branched hairs, glabrous and glaucous above. **Lower leaves** more or less pubescent, usually with Y-shaped hairs; **stem leaves** overlapping in the lower part of the stem, more remote above, all lance-shaped or lance-oblong, sessile and auriculate-clasping, usually glabrous and glaucous. **Petals** 3-6 mm long; mature pedicels erect, 7-16 mm long. **Fruit** erect, nearly terete, overlapping, 5-9 cm long, 0.8-1.3 mm wide; seeds angular, very narrowly winged. May-June.—Usually in dry sandy soil of fields, barrens, gravel pits, savannas, roadsides, rarely on gravelly shores.

Thlaspi arvense

Cabombaceae WATERSHIELD FAMILY

BRASENIA *Watershield*

Brasenia schreberi J.F. Gmel.
WATERSHIELD

MAP 497
native

Perennial aquatic herb; underwater portions of plant with a slippery, jellylike coating. **Stems** to 2 m long. **Leaf blades** floating, oval, 4-12 cm long and half as wide; petiole attached to center of blade underside. **Flowers** perfect (with both staminate and pistillate parts), dull-purple, on emergent stalks to 15 cm long from leaf axils; sepals 3, petals 3, 12-15 mm long. **Fruit** an oblong capsule, 3-5 mm long. July.— Quiet ponds and lakes; water usually acid.

Brasenia schreberi

491. *Sisymbrium altissimum*

492. *Sisymbrium loeselii*

493. *Sisymbrium officinale*

494. *Subularia aquatica*

Cactaceae CACTUS FAMILY

Perennial succulent herbs. Stems simple or segmented, the segments termed joints; globose to flattened (ours); spiny from aereoles, with central spines projecting from the stem axis and radial spines oriented more or less parallel to the surface of the stem. In *Opuntia*, also with small barbed spines (glochids) borne among the larger spines. Flowers showy. Fruit fleshy or dry, naked or spiny.

1 Stems jointed into segments, these cylindric or bilaterally flattened; areoles with spmes and glochids . . **Opuntia**
1 Stems not jointed into into segments, prominently wrinkled; aereoles with spines only . . . . **Escobaria**

ESCOBARIA *Fox-Tail Cactus*

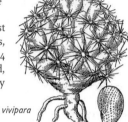

Escobaria vivipara (Nutt.) Buxb.
SPINYSTAR
    Coryphantha vivipara (Nutt.) Britton & Rose

MAP 498
❧*endangered* | *native*

Perennial cactus. Stems 1 several, more or less globose, to o 7cm tall. Most tubercles with a groove on the upper side; areoles with usually 3-4 central spines, one of them turned downward, and ca 12-40 smaller radial spines. Flowers 2.5-4 cm long, pink to reddish purple. Mature fruit green, naked, oblong to club-shaped, to 2.5 cm long; seeds brown, 1.5-2 mm wide. May-Aug.—Dry sandy or rocky prairies. *Minnesota at eastern edge of species' range.*

Escobaria vivipara

OPUNTIA *Prickly Pear*

Branched and jointed perennial plants, the joints ("pads") varying from cylindric to greatly flattened, with conspicuous yellow flowers (ours), and with short prickles from the areoles (glochids). Flowers regular, perfect, sepals and petals numerous in several series. Stamens numerous, shorter than the petals. Ovary 1-celled. Fruit a dry, pulpy, or juicy berry. Seeds wingless.

1 Spines 1-2, borne at only a few areoles . . . . **O. humifusa**
1 Spines several per cluster, borne at most areoles . . . . **O. fragilis**

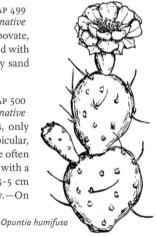

Opuntia fragilis (Nutt.) Haw.
LITTLE PRICKLY PEAR

MAP 499
native

Stems spreading, forming dense mats to 5 dm wide; **joints** orbicular to obovate, very turgid, 2-5 cm long, easily detached; **areoles** crowded, nearly all armed with 3-7 spines. **Flowers** about 5 cm wide. **Fruit** dry, inedible. May-July.—Dry sand prairies and shallow, dry soil over rock outcrops.

Opuntia humifusa (Raf.) Raf.
EASTERN PRICKLY PEAR

MAP 500
native

Stems rostrate or spreading, forming large mats; roots mostly fibrous, only seldom tuberous-thickened; **joints** of the stem flattened, oblong to suborbicular, 4-12 cm at maturity; **areoles** commonly 10-25 mm apart, spineless, or some often with 1 (rarely 2) spines 1.5-3 cm long. **Flowers** 4-8 cm wide, yellow, often with a red center; outer sepals subulate to lance-shaped. **Fruit** red or purple, 2.5-5 cm long, edible; seeds discoid, with an indurate, regular margin. June-July.—On rocks, shores, sand dunes, or sandy prairies.

Opuntia humifusa

495. *Thlaspi arvense*

496. *Turritis glabra*

497. *Brasenia schreberi*

498. *Escobaria vivipara*

Campanulaceae BELLFLOWER FAMILY

Perennial herbs. Stems usually with milky juice. Leaves simple, alternate. Flowers in racemes at ends of stems or single from upper leaf axils, perfect (with both staminate and pistillate parts), 5-parted, regular and funnel-shaped (*Campanula*) or irregular (*Lobelia*); petals blue, white or scarlet; stamens separate or joined into a tube around style. Fruit a many-seeded capsule. *Lobelia is sometimes placed in the Lobeliaceae, but that family discontinued under APG III.*

1   Flowers irregular; stamens joined to form a tube around the style . . . . *Lobelia*
1   Flowers regular; stamens separate 2
  2   Plants annual; flowers sessile in leaf axils; leaves clasping stem . . . . *Triodanis perfoliata*
  2   Plants biennial or perennial; flowers on slender pedicels; leaves not clasping stem 3
    3   Flowers rotate (flattened and disk-like) . . . . *Campanulastrum americanum*
    3   Flowers bell-shaped or funnel-shaped . . . . *Campanula*

CAMPANULA *Bellflower; Harebell*

Annual, biennial, or perennial herbs. Leaves alternate. Flowers conspicuous, solitary or in various types of inflorescence. Sepals 5, triangular to linear. Corolla rotate, campanulate, or funnelform, deeply or shallowly 5-lobed, in our species blue or violet to white. Stamens attached at the very base of the corolla; filaments widened at the base; anthers distinct. Ovary 3-5-celled with elongate style. Capsule short, usually conspicuously ribbed, opening by 3 or 5 lateral pores; seeds numerous. *Several species are cultivated for their handsome flowers.*

ADDITIONAL SPECIES
• *Campanula cervicaria* L. (Bristly bellflower), native to Europe; Lake and St. Louis counties.
• *Campanula glomerata* L. (Clustered bellflower), native to Europe; reported from former agricultural test plots in St. Louis County.
• *Campanula persicifolia* L. (Peachleaf bellflower), native to Asia; St. Louis County (Duluth area).

1   Stems weak, reclining on other plants . . . . *C. aparinoides*
1   Stems upright 2
  2   Flowers on short pedicles in an erect, 1-sided raceme . . . . *C. rapunculoides*
  2   Flowers solitary or in loose, open clusters on slender pedicels . . . . *C. rotundifolia*

Campanula aparinoides Pursh
MARSH BELLFLOWER

MAP 501
native

Perennial herb, spreading by slender rhizomes. **Stems** slender, weak, usually reclining on other plants, 2-6 dm long, 3-angled, rough-to-touch. **Leaves** linear or narrowly lance-shaped, larger below and smaller upward on stem, 2-8 cm long and 2-8 mm wide, tapered to a sharp tip; margins and midvein on leaf underside often rough; petioles absent. **Flowers** single on long slender stalks from upper leaf axils, funnel-shaped, sepals triangular to lance-shaped, 2-5 mm long; petals pale blue to white, 5-12 mm long. **Fruit** a capsule, opening near its base to release seeds. July-Sept.—Sedge meadows, marshes, calcareous fens, conifer swamps (cedar, tamarack), thickets, open bogs; soils often calcium-rich.

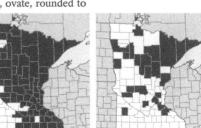

Campanula aparinoides

Campanula rapunculoides L.
CREEPING BELLFLOWER

MAP 502
introduced (invasive)

Erect perennial herb. **Stems** 4-10 dm tall from a creeping rhizome, usually unbranched, smooth or sparsely pubescent. **Leaves** coarse, irregularly serrate, usually sparsely pubescent beneath, the lower long-petioled, ovate, rounded to

499. Opuntia fragilis   *500. Opuntia humifusa*   *501. Campanula aparinoides*   *502. Campanula rapunculoides*

subcordate at base, the upper progressively narrower, short-petioled or subsessile. **Inflorescence** strict, unbranched, secund, forming a 1-sided raceme with much reduced bracts; lower pedicels sometimes elongate to 5 cm long, the upper 1-5 mm long; calyx lobes reflexed; corolla blue, somewhat nodding, 2-3 cm long. **Capsule** opening from pores near base. July-Aug.—Native of Eurasia, forming persistent weedy colonies on roadsides, railroads, and in disturbed places.

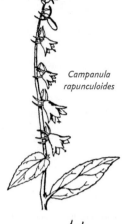

Campanula rapunculoides

Campanula rotundifolia L.   MAP 503
BLUEBELL-OF-SCOTLAND   *native*

Perennial herb. **Stems** simple or branched from the base, 1-5 dm tall, smooth or nearly so, bearing 1 to several spreading or drooping flowers. **Basal leaves** broadly ovate or subcordate, seldom persistent to the flowering season; **stem leaves** linear, 2-10 cm long, decreasing above; pedicels slender. Sepals linear, 4-10 mm long; corolla blue (rarely white), bell-shaped, 12-20 mm long or occasionally somewhat larger, its lobes much shorter than the tube. **Capsule** turbinate or short-cylindric, opening by pores near the base. June-Sept.—Dry woods, meadows, cliffs and beaches. *Variable in habit, stature, and number and size of flowers.*

CAMPANULASTRUM *American-Bellflower*

Campanulastrum americanum (L.) Small   MAP 504
AMERICAN-BELLFLOWER   *native*
  Campanula americana L.

Biennial herb. **Stems** erect, simple or with a few branches, to 2 m tall, smooth or hairy. **Leaves** thin, lance-shaped to ovate-oblong, 7-15 cm long including the margined petiole, serrate, tapering at the base. **Spike** 1-4 dm long or even longer, the lower bracts leaf-like, the upper reduced. **Flowers** blue, solitary or in small clusters, the rotate corolla about 2.5 cm wide; sepals linear, spreading, 5-40 mm long; style curved downward. **Capsule** 7-12 mm long, opening by round pores near the summit. July-Sept.—Moist woods and streambanks, especially in openings, and in disturbed areas such as trails, field edges and railroads.

Campanula rotundifolia

LOBELIA *Lobelia*

Mostly perennial herbs. Stems single, usually with milky juice. Leaves alternate. Flowers irregular, in racemes at ends of stems; white, bright red, or pale to dark blue, often with white or yellow markings; 2-lipped, the 3 lobes of lower lip spreading, the 2 lobes of upper lip erect or pointing forward, divided to base, the anthers projecting through the split; stamens 5, joined to form a tube around style, the lower 2 anthers hairy at tip and shorter than other 3. Fruit a capsule. *Most species toxic if eaten.*

1 Stem leaves narrow, to 4 mm wide, margins entire or with a few small teeth; or leaves all from base of plant . . 2
　2 Leaves all from base of plant, hollow, round in cross-section; plants usually underwater . . . . . . **L. dortmanna**
　2 Leaves all from stem, flat and linear; wetland habitats . . . . **L. kalmii**
1 Stem leaves broader, 1-5 cm wide, margins toothed 3
　3 Flowers small, to 1.5 cm long 4
　　4 Inflorescence usually branched; hypanthium about equalling the corolla, much inflated in fruit . **L. inflata**
　　4 Inflorescence unbranched; hypanthium shorter than corolla, not much inflated in fruit . . . . **L. spicata**
　3 Flowers larger, 2-4 cm long 5
　　5 Flowers bright red (rarely white), 3 cm or more long . . . . **L. cardinalis**
　　5 Flowers blue with white stripes on lower lip, less than 2.5 cm long . . . . **L. siphilitica**

503. Campanula rotundifolia　*504. Campanulas. americanum*　*505. Lobelia cardinalis*　*506. Lobelia dortmanna*

Lobelia cardinalis L.
MAP 505
CARDINAL-FLOWER
native

Perennial herb. **Stems** erect, usually unbranched, 5-15 dm long, hairy to smooth. **Leaves** lance-shaped to oblong, 10-15 cm long and 3-5 cm wide, margins toothed; lower leaves on short petioles, upper leaves more or less stalkless. **Flowers** bright scarlet (rarely white), in racemes 1-4 dm long, the racemes with small, leafy, linear bracts; flowers 2-4 cm long, on hairy pedicels 5-15 mm long. July-Sept. —Floodplain forests, swamps, shores and ditches; sometimes in shallow water.

Lobelia dortmanna L.
MAP 506
WATER LOBELIA
native

Perennial herb; plants usually underwater or sometimes on exposed shores. **Stems** upright, hollow, smooth, with milky juice. **Leaves** in dense rosettes at base of plants, fleshy, hollow, linear, 3-8 cm long, rounded at tip; **stem leaves** tiny. **Flowers** pale blue or white, 1-2 cm long, in a few-flowered raceme; sepals 2 mm long. July-Sept. Shallow water of acid lakes and ponds; wet, sandy shores.

Lobelia inflata L.
MAP 507
INDIAN-TOBACCO
native

Annual or biennial herb. **Stems** erect, usually branched, villous, to 1 m tall. Leaves sessile or subsessile, obovate, 5-8 cm long, 1.5-3.5 cm wide, more or less serrate, usually pubescent. **Racemes** terminating the branches, 1-2 dm long; lower bracts foliaceous, the upper gradually reduced; pedicels 3-8 mm long, glabrous or puberulent, bracteolate at the base. **Flowers** 7-10 mm long; sepals linear, 3-5 mm long; corolla blue or white, the lower lip pubescent; hypanthium much inflated in fruit. July-Oct.—Open woods in moist or dry soil, disturbed places such as roadsides, ditches, borrow pits, trails, utility line clearings. *The long, irregular hairs at base of stem are distinctive. Long used in herbal medicine.*

Lobelia kalmii L.
MAP 508
BROOK LOBELIA
native

Small perennial herb. **Stems** erect, smooth, 1-4 dm long, unbranched or with a few branches above, sometimes with a rosette of small, obovate leaves at base of plant. **Stem leaves** linear, 1-5 cm long and 1-5 mm wide, blunt to sharp-tipped, margins with a few small teeth. **Flowers** blue with a white center, 6-10 mm long, in an open raceme, the flowers on pedicels 4-10 mm long. July-Oct.—Wet, sandy or gravelly shores, wet meadows, interdunal wetlands, conifer swamps (cedar, tamarack), rock ledges and crevices; usually where calcium-rich.

Lobelia siphilitica L.
MAP 509
GREAT BLUE LOBELIA
native

Perennial herb. **Stems** stout, erect, 3-12 dm long. **Leaves** oblong or oval, smaller upward, 6-12 cm long and 1-3 cm wide, tip sharp or blunt, margins irregularly toothed, petioles absent. **Flowers** dark blue, in crowded racemes 1-3 dm long; the lower lip blue and white-striped, 1.5-2.5 cm long, on ascending stalks 4-10 mm long; sepals triangular to lance-shaped, 5-20 mm long, usually with narrow lobes near base. Aug-Sept.—Swamps, floodplain forests, thickets, streambanks, calcareous fens, wet meadows.

Lobelia spicata Lam.
MAP 510
SPIKED LOBELIA
native

Perennial herb. **Stems** unbranched, 3-10 dm long, hairy toward base. **Leaves**

Lobelia cardinalis

Lobelia kalmii

507. Lobelia inflata   508. Lobelia kalmii   509. Lobelia siphilitica   510. Lobelia spicata

obovate to lance-shaped, 5-10 cm long, hairy, becoming smaller above. **Flowers** pale blue to white, 6-10 mm long, on stalks 2-4 mm long, in a slender, crowded raceme; base of sepals often with distinct, curved lobes (auricles), 1-2 mm long. May-Aug.—Moist to wet prairie (sometimes where disturbed), wet meadows, swamp margins.

TRIODANIS *Venus' Looking-Glass*

Triodanis perfoliata (L.) Nieuwl.

MAP 511

CLASPING-LEAF VENUS'-LOOKING-GLASS

native

Annual herb. **Stems** erect, simple or sparingly branched, 1-10 dm tall, the angular stems glabrous to finely rough-hairy. **Leaves** numerous, orbicular or broadly ovate, 1-3 cm long, cordate-clasping at the sessile base, usually toothed, often pubescent, palmately veined. **Flowers** in sessile axillary cymes, the lower flowers usually cleistogamous with minute corolla; the upper with a blue, deeply 5-lobed, subrotate corolla about 15 mm wide; sepals 5; stamens 5; ovary 3-celled; stigmas 3, pubescent. **Capsule** ellipsoid, 5-8 mm long, opening near the middle to expose 1-3 linear pores; seeds lenticular. May-June.—Open woods, old fields, roadsides.

ADDITIONAL SPECIES

Triodanis leptocarpa (Nutt.) Nieuwl. (MAP 512); flower bracts linear to lanceolate, at least 6x longer than wide; capsules of cleistogamous flowers usually sickle-shaped; in *T. perfoliata*, the bracts ovate and capsules of cleistogamous flowers straight.

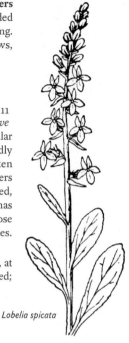

Lobelia spicata

Cannabaceae HEMP FAMILY

Trees (*Celtis*), erect herbs (*Cannabis*), or twining herbs (*Humulus*). Leaves alternate or opposite, simple to palmately lobed or compound. Inflorescences axillary to the upper (often reduced) leaves, the staminate relatively loose, branched, and many-flowered, the pistillate more compact and few-flowered. Flowers unisexual, small and inconspicuous, the staminate with 5 erect stamens opposite the 5 sepals, the pistillate with a short, entire, membranous calyx enclosing the ovary (*Humulus*), or the calyx often much reduced in *Cannabis*; petals absent; style short, with 2 elongate, filiform stigmas. Fruit a drupe (*Celtis*) or an achene, in *Humulus* invested by the persistent calyx.

1 Trees or shrubs; leaves simple; fruits pediceled drupes . . . . **Celtis occidentalis**
1 Herbs or herbaceous vines; larger leaves compound or lobed; fruits sessile achenes subtended by bracts 2
   2 Plants erect; leaves compound . . . . **Cannabis sativa**
   2 Plants twining; leaves not compound . . . . **Humulus**

CANNABIS *Hemp*

Cannabis sativa L.

MAP 513

HEMP; MARIJUANA

introduced (naturalized)

Erect annual herb. **Stems** slender, 1-2 m tall. **Leaves** parted to the base into 5-9 serrate leaflets, the lower commonly opposite, the upper smaller, usually alternate, with fewer leaflets or undivided; leaflets linear to narrowly lance-shaped, pubescent, 5-15 cm long, petioled. **Flowers** green, ordinarily dioecious; **staminate flowers** numerous in small clusters from the upper axils, forming a leafy panicle; sepals 5, imbricate; stamens 5; **pistillate flowers** in small clusters

511. Triodanis perfoliata   *512. Triodanis leptocarpa*   *513. Cannabis sativa*   *514. Celtis occidentalis*

on short lateral leafy branches from the upper axils, each flower closely surrounded by an abruptly acuminate bract; calyx barely lobed, surrounding only the base of the ovary; stigmas 2, elongate, filiform. **Fruit** a thick-lenticular achene, 3-4 mm long, enclosed within the expanding bract.—Native of Asia; cultivated for its valuable fiber in many parts of the world and frequently escaped. *The pistillate inflorescence is the source of the narcotic marijuana.*

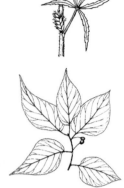

Cannabis sativa

CELTIS *Hackberry*

Celtis occidentalis L.
COMMON HACKBERRY

MAP 514
native

Medium tree; bark cork-like with wart-like protuberances. **Leaves** alternate, simple, ovate lance-shaped to broadly ovate, distinctly asymmetrical at base, 3-nerved; those of fertile branches 6-12 cm long, conspicuously serrate, abruptly acuminate to very long-acuminate. Plants monoecious or polygamous; **staminate flowers** in small clusters near the base of the twigs of the season; calyx deeply 5-parted; stamens 5, opposite the calyx lobes, exsert; **fertile flowers** solitary or sometimes paired from the upper axils of the same twigs; stamens present or none; ovary ovoid, 1-celled; style very short; bearing 2 elongate, recurved stigmas. **Fruit** an ellipsoid drupe 7-13 mm long, dark red to nearly black at maturity, with thin sweet pulp and a hard stone. Variable. May (appearing after the leaves). —Usually in rich moist forests, on riverbanks, and in ravines. *Trees sometimes with "witch's brooms" when disease causes a proliferation of branch tips.*

Celtis occidentalis

HUMULUS *Hops*

Twining, herbaceous, annual or perennial vines with rough stems, broad, opposite, usually lobed leaves, and axillary clusters of small flowers. Dioecious. Staminate flowers numerous, paniculate. Sepals 5, distinct. Stamens 5. Pistillate flowers in short spikes, in pairs, each pair subtended by a foliaceous bract. Calyx membranaceous, unlobed. Style prolonged into 2 filiform stigmas. Fruit an achene enclosed within the persistent calyx and covered by the expanded bracts.

1   Main leaves with 3 lobes; plants perennial . . . . *H. lupulus*
1   Main leaves with 5-7 lobes; plants annual . . . . *H. japonicus*

Humulus japonicus Sieb. & Zucc.
JAPANESE HOPS

(NO MAP)
introduced

Annual vine. **Stems** rough. Uppermost **leaves** usually 3-5-lobed; petioles commonly longer than the 5-7-lobed blades. Bracts of the **pistillate spikes** all densely spinulose-ciliate, dull green at maturity, conspicuously and abruptly acuminate, scarcely glandular.—Native of eastern Asia; escaped from cultivation, Fillmore and Houston counties.

Humulus lupulus L.
COMMON HOPS

MAP 515
native

Perennial vine to 10 m long. Stems rough. **Principal leaves** as wide as long, cordate at base, 3-lobed to below the middle, the lateral lobes obliquely ovate-oblong, the terminal lance-shaped, constricted at base; **upper leaves** commonly broadly ovate, unlobed. **Staminate panicles** 5-15 cm long; **pistillate spikes** about 1 cm long at anthesis, with conspicuous slender stigmas. **Fruit** (hops) cylindric, straw-color, 3-6 cm long, the bracts entire and mostly blunt, very glandular at base. July-Aug. —Moist soil. *Yellow glands secreting a bitter substance, lupulin, occur on many parts of the plant but are most numerous on the fruit, which is important in beer-making.*

Humulus lupulus

Caprifoliaceae HONEYSUCKLE FAMILY

Shrubs or vines, with opposite, mostly simple leaves. Flowers perfect (with both staminate and pistillate parts), mostly 5-parted. Fruit a fleshy berry or dry capsule. Family now includes members of the former Valerianaceae (*Valeriana, Valerianella*); herbs with opposite, simple or divided leaves, and numerous small flowers in terminal, panicled or capitate cymes.

1   Flowers numerous, in rather dense terminal inflorescences (at ends of stem and branches) . . . . *Valeriana*
1   Flowers axillary or on paired pedicels on a peduncle. 2
  2   Plants small, creeping, evergreen; flowers paired and nodding at tips of slender stalks . . . . . *Linnaea borealis*
  2   Plants larger shrubs or coarse herbs, upright, deciduous 3
    3   Plants herbaceous; flowers from leaf axils . . . . *Triosteum*
    3   Plants woody vines or shrubs; flowers various 4
      4   Leaf margins toothed or lobed . . . . *Diervilla lonicera*
      4   Leaf margins entire 5
        5   Corolla bell-shaped, less than 1 cm long . . . . *Symphoricarpos*
        5   Corolla tube-shaped or tubular at base with long lobes, mostly more than 1 cm long . . . . *Lonicera*

DIERVILLA *Bush-Honeysuckle*

Diervilla lonicera P. Mill.
NORTHERN BUSH-HONEYSUCKLE

MAP 516
native

Shrub to 12 dm tall, at first simple, branched in age. **Leaves** opposite, oblong lance-shaped, 8-15 cm long, finely serrate, usually ciliate, otherwise nearly glabrous; petioles 3-10 mm long. Peduncles 3-7-flowered, the terminal flower usually sessile, the lateral pediceled; sepals narrowly linear, 2-7 mm long, persistent and accrescent in fruit; corolla funnelform, nearly regular, 5-lobed, 12-20 mm long, at first yellow, becoming reddish in age, hairy within; stamens 5, about equaling the corolla; ovary 2-celled; style exsert. **Capsule** slender, beaked, 10-15 mm long, tardily dehiscent. June-July.—Dry or rocky soil.

Diervilla lonicera

LINNAEA *Twinflower*

Linnaea borealis L.
TWINFLOWER

MAP 517
native

Low, evergreen, trailing vine. **Stems** slightly woody, to 1-2 m long, with numerous short, erect, leafy branches to 10 cm long; branches green to red-brown, finely hairy; older stems woody, 2-4 mm wide. **Leaves** opposite, simple, evergreen, oval to round, 1-2 cm long, blunt at tip, upper surface and margins with short, straight hairs; margins rolled under, with a few rounded teeth near tip; petiole short, short-hairy. **Flowers** small, pink to white, bell-shaped, shallowly 5-lobed, slightly fragrant, in nodding pairs atop a Y-shaped stalk to 10 cm long, the stalk with gland-tipped hairs and 2 small bracts at the fork and a pair of smaller bracts at base of each flower. **Fruit** a small, dry, 1-seeded capsule. June-Aug.—Hummocks in cedar swamps and thickets, moist conifer woods, on rotten logs and mossy boulders.

Linnaea borealis

LONICERA *Honeysuckle*

Shrubs or woody vines. Leaves opposite, simple, entire. Flowers long and tubular or funnel-shaped, in pairs from leaf axils. Fruit a few-seeded, blue or red berry.

HYBRIDS
· *Lonicera* × *bella* Zabel, hybrid between *L. morrowii* and *L. tatarica*, common and invasive statewide; see key.
· *Lonicera* × *salicifolia* Dieck ex Zabel (*L. ruprechtiana* × *L. xylosteoides*); native to Asia; St. Louis County.

1   Flowers in opposite, sessile, 3-flowered clusters, producing a whorl of 6 flowers; plants woody, climbing vines 2
  2   Leaves hairy on upper surface . . . . *L. hirsuta*
  2   Leaves glabrous on upper surface 3

515. Humulus lupulus   *516. Diervilla lonicera*   *517. Linnaea borealis*   *518. Lonicera caerulea*

Lonicera caerulea L.

MAP 518

WATERBERRY

native

    Lonicera villosa (Michx.) J. A. Schultes

Shrub to 1 m tall; **branches** upright, red-brown to gray, outer thin layers soon peeling to expose red-brown inner layers; **twigs** purple-red, with long, soft hairs. **Leaves** opposite, oval to oblong, 2-6 cm long and 1-3 cm wide, blunt or rounded at tip, upper surface dark green, underside paler and hairy, especially on veins; margins fringed with hairs and often rolled under; petioles absent or to 1-2 mm long. **Flowers** yellow, tubular to funnel-shaped, 10-15 mm long, in pairs on short hairy stalks from axils of lower leaves. **Fruit** an edible dark blue berry consisting of the 2 joined ovaries. May-July.—Cedar and tamarack swamps, fens, shores.

Lonicera caerulea

Lonicera canadensis Bartr.

MAP 519

FLY-HONEYSUCKLE

native

Shrub to 2 m tall, with straggling branches. **Leaves** ovate to oblong, 3-12 cm long, acute or obtuse, ciliate, glabrous to sparsely pubescent beneath. Peduncles 2-3 cm long; bracts linear or subulate, from much shorter than to slightly exceeding the ovaries; bractlets to 0.5 mm long, or obsolete; **corolla** yellowish, 12-22 mm long, distinctly saccate at base, glabrous, its lobes a third to a half as long as the tube; ovaries glabrous, strongly divergent at anthesis; style glabrous. **Berries** red. May-June.—Dry or moist woods, occasionally swamps.

Lonicera canadensis

Lonicera dioica L.

MAP 520

LIMBER HONEYSUCKLE

native

Climbing woody vine with glabrous branches. **Leaves** ovate or obovate, 5-12 cm long, rounded or narrowed at base, glaucous beneath; uppermost one or two pairs united into a rhombic or doubly ovate disk narrowed to an obtuse or acute tip or rounded and mucronate. **Spike** short-peduncled (usually 5-20 mm); corolla yellow to deep maroon, 1.5-2.5 cm long, abruptly bulging just above the base, hairy inside. **Berries** red, 8-12 mm long, in clusters surrounded by leafy cup-like bracts, inedible and extremely bitter. May-June.—Moist woods and thickets, occasionally on dunes or in swamps.

Lonicera dioica

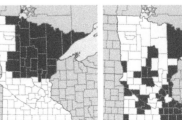

519. Lonicera canadensis   *520. Lonicera dioica*   *521. Lonicera hirsuta*   *522. Lonicera morrowii*

Lonicera hirsuta Eat.
HAIRY HONEYSUCKLE

MAP 521
native

Twining woody vine, the younger **stems** pubescent and glandular. **Leaves** dull green, sessile or short-petioled, broadly oval, 6-12 cm long, more or less pubescent on both sides, underside also glaucous; upper 1 or 2 pairs acuminate, connate into a rhombic-elliptic to subrotund disk. **Spikes** bearing 1-4 crowded whorls of flowers; corolla usually yellow, corolla tube 10-18 mm long, the pubescent tube slightly bulging near the base. **Berries** orange to red, sessile, subtended by a pair of saucer-shaped bracts. June-July.—Moist woods, particularly on margins and in clearings, often where sandy or rocky; occasionally in white cedar swamps. *The pubescent upper surface of the leaves distinguish this species from* **Lonicera dioica** *and* **L. reticulata** *which also have connate terminal leaves.*

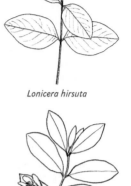

Lonicera hirsuta

Lonicera morrowii Gray
MORROW'S HONEYSUCKLE

MAP 522
introduced (invasive)

Tall shrub, the older branches hollow. **Leaves** ovate to oblong, 3-6 cm long, rounded at base to a short petiole, softly pubescent beneath. Peduncles 5-15 mm long; bracts linear lance-shaped, 1-3 times as long as the ovary; bractlets half as long as to equaling the ovary; sepals ciliate; **corolla** white, fading yellow, pubescent, saccate at base, the lips equaling or longer than the tube; upper lip 4-lobed to its base; style hirsute. **Fruit** a dark red berry 7-8 mm wide; seeds numerous. May-June.—Native of Asia; escaping and invasive on forest margins and along roads and railroads.

Lonicera morrowii

Lonicera oblongifolia (Goldie) Hook.
SWAMP FLY-HONEYSUCKLE

MAP 523
native

Thicket-forming shrub 1-1.5 m tall; **branches** upright, with shredding bark and solid pith; **twigs** green to purple, smooth. **Leaves** opposite, oblong or oval, 3-8 cm long and 1-4 cm wide, rounded or blunt at tip, underside hairy when young, becoming smooth; margins entire, not fringed with hairs; petioles absent or to 1-2 mm long. **Flowers** yellow-white, tube-shaped with 2 spreading lips, 10-15 mm long, in pairs at ends of slender stalks up to 4 cm long from leaf axils. **Fruit** an orange-red to red (or sometimes purple), few-seeded berry composed of the 2 joined ovaries. May-June.—Cedar and tamarack swamps, fens, open bogs, wet streambanks and shores; often over limestone.

Lonicera reticulata Raf.
GRAPE HONEYSUCKLE

MAP 524
native

Lonicera prolifera (Kirchn.) Booth

Woody climber with glabrous stems to 5 m long. **Leaves** thinly hairy beneath, the lower broadly oval, sessile or nearly so, 4-8 cm long; upper 2-4 pairs more or less connate, the uppermost completely so into a suborbicular disk rounded or retuse at the ends and glaucous above. **Spike** short-peduncled, the whorls of flowers usually crowded; hypanthium glabrous and glaucous; **corolla** 2-3 cm long, glabrous outside, hairy inside, gradually enlarged above the base. **Berries** orange-red to red, seeds about 3 mm long. May-June.—Moist woods and thickets.

Lonicera oblongifolia

Lonicera tatarica L.
TARTARIAN HONEYSUCKLE

MAP 525
introduced (invasive)

Tall shrub, the older branches hollow. **Leaves** ovate to oblong, 3-6 cm long, rounded to subcordate at base, glabrous. Peduncles 15-25 mm long; bracts

523. Lonicera oblongifolia   *524. Lonicera reticulata*   *525. Lonicera tatarica*   *526. Lonicera xylosteum*

subulate, shorter than to exceeding the ovary; bractlets broadly ovate, about a third as long as the ovary; sepals entire; **corolla** white to pink, glabrous, barely gibbous at base, the lips equaling or exceeding the tube; upper lip 4-lobed to its base; style hirsute. **Fruit** a shiny orange or red berry to 1 cm wide. May-June. —Native of e Europe and Asia, an old favorite in cultivation and frequently escaped and invasive.

Lonicera xylosteum L.

MAP 526

EUROPEAN FLY-HONEYSUCKLE   *introduced*

Shrub to 3 m tall, the young stems pubescent. **Leaves** oval, 2-6 cm long, usually more than half as broad, pubescent beneath. Peduncles 6-12 mm long; bracts subulate, equaling or surpassing the ovaries; bractlets rotund, shorter than the separate glandular ovaries; **corolla** yellowish, pubescent, 7-12 mm long, the lips more than twice as long as the tube; lateral clefts of the upper lip twice as long as the central one; style hirsute. **Berries** red. May-June.—Native of Eurasia.

Lonicera tatarica

SYMPHORICARPOS　*Snowberry*

Low bushy shrubs. Leaves ovate-oblong to rotund, short-petioled, entire or sometimes crenate on the rapidly growing branches. Flowers small, white or pink, terminating the stem or also in the upper axils. Corolla funnelform or campanulate, regular or nearly so, 4- or 5-lobed, usually bearded within. Calyx short, 4-5-toothed. Stamens (4 or) 5. Ovary 4-celled. Fruit a 2-seeded white or red berry.

1　Fruit red; corolla to 4 mm long; presence in Minn not verified (native s of state) . . . . **S. orbiculatus**
1　Fruit white; corolla 5 mm or more long; native species 2
　2　Style exserted, 4 mm or more long . . . . **S. occidentalis**
　2　Style included, to 3 mm long　. . . . . **S. albus**

Symphoricarpos albus (L.) Blake

MAP 527

SNOWBERRY   *native*

Shrub to 1 m tall, or sometimes dwarf, the younger branches pubescent or glabrous. **Leaves** ovate or oval, usually 2-3 cm long. **Flowers** in pairs on short pedicels or in short, few-flowered, interrupted spikes; corolla campanulate, slightly ventricose, 6-8 mm long, the lobes from half as long as to sometimes equaling the tube; style glabrous, 2-3 mm long. **Fruit** white; seeds 5 mm long. —Dry or rocky soil.

Symphoricarpos occidentalis Hook.

MAP 528

WESTERN SNOWBERRY   *native*

Symphoricarpos albus

Shrub to 1 m tall, the younger parts finely pubescent. **Leaves** ovate to ovate-oblong, usually 3-6 cm long, often coarsely crenate. **Flowers** several to many, sessile in short dense spikes, terminal or from the upper axils; corolla funnelform, 6-8 mm long, its lobes equaling the tube; stamens exserted; style mostly 4-8 mm long, typically pilose near the middle. **Fruit** white; seeds narrowly elliptic, 5 mm long. June-Aug.—Dry or rocky soil.

Symphoricarpos orbiculatus Moench

MAP 529

CORALBERRY   *introduced*

Freely branched shrub, the slender purplish stems to 15 dm tall, pubescent toward the summit. **Leaves** oval or ovate, usually 2-4 cm long, obtuse or rounded at both ends, pubescent beneath. **Flowers** in dense clusters from most upper axils, sessile or nearly so; corolla 3-4 mm long, its lobes half as long as the tube. **Fruit** red,

Symphoricarpos occidentalis

527. *Symphoricarpos albus*　　528. *Symphoricarpos occidentalis*　529. *Symphoricarpos orbiculatus*　530. *Triosteum aurantiacum*

persistent through the winter; seeds 3 mm long. June-Aug.—All Minn collections are likely from planted populations.

TRIOSTEUM *Feverwort; Horse-Gentian*

Coarse, erect, pubescent, perennial herbs. Leaves large, connate or united by a ridge around the stem. Flowers greenish yellow to dull red, solitary or in small clusters in their axils. Corolla narrowly campanulate, gibbous at the base, unequally 5-lobed. Sepals 5, linear, elongate. Stamens 5. Ovary 3-5-celled; style slender, included or exserted; stigma capitate. Fruit a yellow, red, or greenish dry berry, crowned by the persistent sepals, enclosing a few hard oblong seeds.

1 Main leaves joined at base and perforated by stem; hairs on stem short, less than 0.5 mm long . . . *T. perfoliatum*
1 Leaves not joined at base or perforated by stem, mostly tapered to a narrow base; hairs on stem longer, more than 0.5 mm long . . . . *T. aurantiacum*

Triosteum aurantiacum Bickn.
HORSE-GENTIAN

MAP 530
native

Much like *T. perfoliatum*, and not always clearly separable, but the **leaves** distinct, tapering to a narrow base (or seldom 1-3 pairs with connate base 1-2 cm wide), the hairs of the stem mostly over 0.5 mm long, the corolla purplish-red, the style about equaling the corolla or shortly included, and the **fruit** bright orange-red. May-July, flowering a little after *T. perfoliatum*.—Rich woods, thickets.

Triosteum perfoliatum L.
FEVERWORT

MAP 531
native

Coarse herb to 13 dm tall. **Stems** crisp-hairy, the abundant hairs rnostly less than 0.5 mm long. **Leaves** obovate, ovate-oblong, or subrhombic, the main ones 10-30 cm long and 4-15 cm wide, narrowed below the middle but broadly connate-perfoliate at base (3-9 cm wide where united), sparsely setose above. usually densely and softly hairy beneath. **Flowers** usually 3-4 per axil; sepals 10-18 mm long, finely and uniformly hairy on the back and margin, often also glandular; corolla 8-17 mm long, crisp-hairy, purplish to dull greenish-yellow, the style exserted about 2 mm. **Fruit** subglobose, dull orange-yellow. May-July.—Woods and thickets, often in shallow or rocky soils.

Triosteum aurantiacum

Triosteum perfoliatum

VALERIANA *Valerian*

Perennial, strongly scented herbs. Leaves from base of plant and opposite along stem, simple to pinnately divided. Flowers somewhat irregular, in branched heads at ends of stems; calyx inrolled when young, later expanding and spreading; petals joined into a tube-shaped, 5-lobed corolla; stamens 3. Fruit a 1-chambered achene.

1 Basal and stem leaves mostly with 6 or more pairs of leaflets . . . . *V. officinalis*
1 Basal leaves entire or with a single pair of lobes at base; stem leaves sparse, with only 1-5 pairs of lobes . . . . . .
. . . . *V. edulis*

Valeriana edulis Nutt. ex Torr. & Gray
COMMON VALERIAN; TOBACCO-ROOT
    Valeriana ciliata Torr. & Gray
    Valeriana edulis Nutt. subsp. *ciliata* (Torr. & Gray) F.G. Mey.

MAP 532
❦ *threatened | native*

Perennial herb, from a stout taproot. **Stems** smooth, 3-12 dm long. **Leaves** thick, more or less parallel-veined, often hairy when young, becoming smooth or with the margins fringed with hairs when mature; **basal leaves** oblong lance-shaped, 1-3 dm long and 1-2 cm wide, margins entire or with several lobes, tapered to a winged petiole; **stem leaves** sessile, pinnately divided into lance-shaped segments. **Flowers** both perfect and single-sexed, the different types often on different plants; perfect and staminate flowers 2-4 mm wide, pistillate flowers to 1 mm wide, in widely branched panicles at ends of stems; corolla 5-lobed, yellow-white. **Fruit** an ovate achene, 3-4 mm long. May-June.—Wet meadows, calcareous fens, low prairie.

Valeriana edulis

Valeriana officinalis L.

ALLHEAL

MAP 533
introduced

Perennial herb. **Stems** stout, erect, 6-15 dm tall, usually pubescent at the nodes. Basal and stem **leaves** similar, pinnately divided into 11-21 lance-shaped dentate segments; petioles of the upper leaves progressively shorter. **Panicle** large and open, its lower branches often remote (to 10 cm) from the upper, to 10 cm long; corolla obconic, the tube about 4 mm, the lobes about 1 mm long. **Fruit** lance-oblong, 4.5-5 mm long by about half as wide, glabrous. May–Aug. Native of Europe and Asia; escaped from gardens, where it is commonly cultivated, to roadsides, ditches, fields, shores, and forest margins.

Valeriana officinalis

Caryophyllaceae PINK FAMILY

Annual or perennial herbs. Leaves simple, entire, mostly opposite but sometimes alternate or whorled. Stems often swollen at nodes. Flowers perfect (with both staminate and pistillate parts) or imperfect, in open or compact heads at ends of stems or from leaf axils; sepals usually 5, separate or joined into a tube; petals 5 (sometimes 4), separate, often lobed or toothed, sometimes absent; stamens 3-10, anthers often distinctly colored. Fruit a few- to many-seeded capsule.

1 Leaves with chaffy or membranous stipules 2
  2 Flowers with petals; fruit a several-seeded capsule 3
  2 Flowers without petals; fruit a 1-seeded utricle . . . . *Paronychia*
    3 Leaves whorled; styles 5 . . . . *Spergula arvensis*
    3 Leaves opposite; styles 3 . . . . *Spergularia*
1 Leaves without stipules 4
  4 Sepals joined to form a lobed tube 5
    5 Styles 2 6
      6 Calyx subtended by 1-3 pairs of bracts 7
        7 Calyx with 20 or more nerves . . . . *Dianthus*
        7 Calyx 5-nerved . . . . *Petrorhagia saxifraga*
      6 Calyx not subtended by bracts 8
        8 Flowers to 1 cm long . . . . *Gypsophila*
        8 Flowers 2 cm long or more 9
          9 Calyx tube-shaped, nerved . . . . *Saponaria officinalis*
          9 Calyx ovoid, angled and wing . . . . *Vaccaria hispanica*
    5 Styles 3-5 10
      10 Styles mostly 3 . . . . *Silene*
      10 Styles mostly 5 11
        11 Lobes of calyx much longer than tube formed by sepals . . . . *Agrostemma githago*
        11 Lobes of calyx much shorter than tube . . . . *Silene*
  4 Sepals not joined, distinct from one another 12
    13 Petals absent, or entire or somewhat fringed at tip 13
      14 Petals absent; fruit a 1-seeded utricle . . . . *Scleranthus*
      14 Petals usually present; fruit a several- to many-seeded capsule 14
        15 Styles 4 or 5, equaling the number of sepals . . . . *Sagina procumbens*
        15 Styles (or style-branches) 3, fewer than the sepals 15
          16 Leaves linear-subulate, the principal stem leaves subtending dense axillary clusters; plant entirely glabrous; capsule dehiscing into 3 valves . . . . *Minuartia*

531. *Triosteum perfoliatum*   532. *Valeriana edulis*   533. *Valeriana officinalis*   534. *Agrostemma githago*

16 Leaves ovate to elliptic or lanceolate, mostly without axillary tufts; plants puberulent at least on the stem; capsule with the 3 valves again split, resulting in a total of 6 teeth 17

    17 Ripe seeds minutely and regularly roughened (tuberculate) and unappendaged; leaves ovate-elliptic, acute to acuminate, but not over 7 (-9) mm long; petals shorter than sepals; annuals. . . . . ***Arenaria serpyllifolia***

    17 Ripe seeds smooth and shiny, with a pale appendage at the point of attachment; leaves lance-shaped to elliptic, mostly over 10 mm long; petals exceeding sepals; perennials. . . . . ***Moehringia***

13 Petals deeply cleft at tip into 2 segments 18

    18 Fruit cylindric; styles usually 5 (3 in *Cerastium nutans*) . . . . ***Cerastium***

    18 Fruit ovoid or oblong; styles usually 3 (5 in *Myosoton aquaticum*) . . . . ***Stellaria***

AGROSTEMMA *Corncockle*

Agrostemma githago L.

COMMON CORNCOCKLE

MAP 534
introduced

Annual herb. **Stems** to 1 m tall, thinly hairy. **Leaves** opposite, entire, linear or lance-shaped, 8-12 cm long and 5-10 mm wide. **Flowers** reddish. solitary at the ends of the branches, on pedicels to 2 dm long; calyx tube 12-18 mm long, 10-ribbed, calyx lobes 5, much longer than the tube; petals 5, 2-3 cm long, oblong lance-shaped stamens 10; styles (4)5. **Capsule** 14-18 mm long, dehiscent by (4)5 ascending teeth. July-Sept.—Native of Europe, originally a weed in grainfields and waste places, but becoming less common due to herbicide use and improved seed screening; seeds toxic and contain saponin.

Agrostemma githago

ARENARIA *Sandwort*

Arenaria serpyllifolia L.

THYME-LEAF SANDWORT

MAP 535
introduced (naturalized)

Finely hairy annual herb. **Stems** diffuse, 5-20 cm long, the internodes usually much longer than the leaves. **Leaves** usually 8-10 pairs, 3-5 mm long, 3-4 mm wide, ovate, sparsely rough hairy, often pustulate, 3-5-nerved. **Inflorescence** a terminal cyme, short or extending to the middle of the stem; bracts leaf-like; pedicels subcapillary, 4-8 mm long; sepals 5, 2.5-3.5 mm long, ovate lance-shaped, frequently glandular; petals 5, obovate, usually shorter than the sepals; stamens normally 10. **Capsule** ovoid, exceeding the sepals, dehiscent by 6 nearly equal teeth; seeds numerous, about 0.5 mm wide, kidney-shaped, gray-black.—Native of Eurasia; sandy or rocky places.

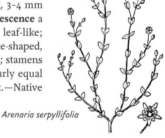

Arenaria serpyllifolia

CERASTIUM *Mouse-Ear Chickweed*

Low annual or perennial herbs. Leaves opposite. Flowers solitary or more commonly in terminal cymes. Sepals 5. Petals 5, notched at tip to bifid, seldom entire. Stamens normally 10, sometimes 5. Styles normally 5, sometimes 4 or 3. Capsule usually exceeding the sepals, cylindric, membranous, dehiscent by 10 short teeth, frequently curved. Ovary 1-celled. Seeds numerous, kidney-shaped, papillate.

1 Petals large and showy, longer than the sepals . . . . ***C. arvense***

1 Petals about equal to the sepals 2

    2 Bracts of inflorescence green and herbaceous . . . . ***C. nutans***

    2 Bracts of upper inflorescence with papery, non-green margins and tips . . . . ***C. fontanum***

Cerastium arvense L.

FIELD CHICKWEED

MAP 536
native

Matted perennial. **Stems** ascending or erect, glabrous to densely villous, glandular or nonglandular, mostly 1.5-4 dm tall. **Leaves** linear to lance-shaped, 2-7 cm long, 1-15 mm wide, glabrous or pubescent, glandular or nonglandular; primary leaves usually subtending conspicuous axillary fascicles or short sterile shoots. **Inflorescence** with few to many flowers, the pedicels very slender; sepals lance-shaped, mostly 5-8 mm long, 2-3x exceeded by the conspicuous white petals. **Capsule** cylindric, somewhat to much exceeding the sepals; seeds papillate-tuberculate, reddish brown. April-Aug.—Rocky, gravelly, or sandy areas, chiefly in calcium- or magnesium-rich soils, weedy in abandoned fields and meadows.

Cerastium arvense

Cerastium fontanum Baumg.
MOUSE-EAR CHICKWEED
Cerastium vulgatum L.

MAP 537
introduced (naturalized)

Perennial. Stems tufted, spreading or erect, viscid-pubescent, 1.5-5 dm long. **Leaves** oblong to lance-shaped, 1-2 cm long, 3-12 mm wide, 1-nerved, sparingly pubescent, the lower leaves oblong lance-shaped. **Inflorescence** at length rather open, the mature pedicels 5-12 mm long; sepals 4.5-6 mm long, oblong lance-shaped, pubescent, rather strongly 1-nerved toward the base, scarious-margined; petals about as long as the sepals. **Capsule** 8-10 mm long, 2-3 mm wide, cylindric, sometimes curved; seeds rugose-papillate, reddish brown. April-Oct.—Native of Eurasia; widely naturalized in fields, woods, and waste places and frequently a troublesome weed, especially in lawns.

Cerastium nutans Raf.
NODDING MOUSE-EAR CHICKWEED
Cerastium brachypodum (Engelm.) B.L. Robins.

MAP 538
native

Cerastium fontanum

Annual. **Stems** weak or ascending, usually branched, viscid-pubescent, 1-4.5 dm long. **Leaves** narrowly oblong lance-shaped or oblong lance-shaped, commonly 1.5-5 cm long, 5-10 mm wide. **Inflorescence** open and loosely cymose; sepals lance-shaped, 4-5 mm long, acute or obtusish, scarious-margined; petals more or less equaling, frequently conspicuously exceeding the sepals; occasionally lacking. **Capsule** 8-15 mm long, cylindric, straight or curved; seeds coarsely papillose, pale reddish brown. April-June.—Moist or dry woods or open places. *C. brachypodum* sometimes treated as separate species, and can be distinguished as follows:

1 Pedicels straight or only slightly curved with age;in flower, to 1.25x length of calyx...........*C. brachypodum*
1 Pedicels sharply curved below the calyx with age; in flower, 1-3x length of calyx.................*C. nutans*

DIANTHUS *Pink*
Biennial or perennial, usually glaucous herbs. Leaves narrow. Flowers solitary or in paniculate or capitate cymes. Calyx subtended by 1-3 pairs of bracts, cylindric, with 30 or more nerves. Petals 5, without auricles or appendages. Stamens 10. Styles 2. Capsule dehiscent by 4 or 5 teeth. Seeds disc-shaped, apiculate. Many species are well known in cultivation; the carnation is *D. caryophyltus* L.

1 Leaves not linear, more than 9 mm wide ....*D. barbatus*
1 Leaves linear, less than 9 mm wide 2
  2 Annual; calyx and bracts hairy ....*D. armeria*
  2 Perennial; calyx and bracts glabrous or only very finely hairy ....*D. deltoides*

Dianthus armeria L.
DEPTFORD PINK

MAP 539
introduced

Biennial. **Stems** 2-6 dm tall, usually strigose below the nodes, otherwise glabrous. **Basal leaves** numerous; **stem leaves** 5-10 pairs, linear to linear lance-shaped, 3-8 cm long, puberulent, ciliate. **Cymes** congested, 3-9-flowered, the lower, lance-subulate, erect bracts frequently surpassing the flowers; calyx 12-18 mm long, 20-25-nerved; petals 2-2.5 cm long, the blades 4-5 mm long, pink or rose, dentate. **Capsule** equaling the calyx, dehiscent by 4 recurved teeth. Summer.—Native of Europe, established as a weed.

Dianthus armeria

535. *Arenaria serpyllifolia*   536. *Cerastium arvense*   537. *Cerastium fontanum*   538. *Cerastium nutans*

Dianthus barbatus L.

MAP 540
SWEETWILLIAM *introduced*

Glabrous perennial. **Stems** stout, 3-6 dm tall. **Stem leaves** 5-19 pairs, lance-shaped to oblong lance-shaped, 6-10 cm long, 1-1.8 cm wide; **basal leaves** somewhat wider. **Cymes** densely corymbose; primary bracts leaflike; secondary bractlets awn-tipped, ciliolate; calyx 15-18 mm long, about 40-nerved; petals 15-25 mm long, the blades dark red, pink, or whitish, crenate-denticulate. **Capsule** about 1 cm long. Summer.—Native of the Old World; rarely escaped from cultivation.

Dianthus deltoides L.

MAP 541
MAIDEN PINK *introduced*

Perennial with a very slender creeping rootstalk. **Stems** slender, branched, 1-4 dm tall, glabrous or hispidulous-puberulent. **Basal leaves** oblong lance-shaped, 1.5-3 cm long, 1.5-3 mm wide; **stem leaves** 5-10 pairs, linear lance-shaped, acute, 2-4 cm long. **Flowers** solitary on pedicels 1-4 cm long; calyx 12-15 mm long, with 30-40 nerves, subtended by 1 or 2 pairs of obovate, abruptly acuminate or awned bracts; petals purple-red, lavender, or white, 1.5-2 cm long, the blades 4-8 mm long, sharply denticulate. **Capsule** narrowly ellipsoid-lance-shaped, about equaling the calyx. Summer.—Native of Europe; often cultivated and locally escaped into waste places.

Dianthus deltoides

GYPSOPHILA *Baby's-Breath*

Annual or perennial Eurasian herbs. Cymes paniculately much branched or the flowers solitary. Calyx campanulate to turbinate, short, 5-nerved, ebracteate. Petals white to pinkish, scarcely differentiated into claw and blade, without auricles or appendages. Styles 2. Capsule globose to ovoid-oblong, dehiscent by 4-6 ascending teeth. Seeds obovoid, ovoid, or kidney-shaped.

1 Plants annual . . . . *G. muralis*
1 Plants perennial . . . . *G. paniculata*

Gypsophila muralis L.

MAP 542
LOW BABY'S-BREATH *introduced*

Annual herb. **Stems** slender, diffusely branched 5-15 cm tall, glabrous or puberulent. **Leaves** 5-15 mm long, 1-2 mm wide, linear. Pedicels capillary, 1-2 cm long, spreading or ascending from the axils of all but the lower leaves; calyx 5-nerved, 3-4 mm long; petals oblong lance-shaped, 6-10 mm long, emarginate, pink or purplish. **Capsule** ellipsoid-ovoid, 3-4 mm long;seed about 0.6 mm long, low-tuberculate. June-Sept.—Native of Eurasia; established locally as a weed.

Gypsophila paniculata L.

MAP 543
TALL BABY'S-BREATH *introduced (invasive)*

Perennial herb; plants large and tumbleweed-like, much-branched and covered with tiny flowers. **Inflorescence** paniculate, diffusely branched; petals petals white or rarely pinkish, about 3 mm long. **Capsule** globose.—Sandy roadsides, fields, ditches and railroad embankments, a troublesome weed of sand dunes.

Gypsophila muralis

MINUARTIA *Stitchwort*

Previously included in genus *Arenaria*.

539. Dianthus armeria   *540. Dianthus barbatus*   *541. Dianthus deltoides*   *542. Gypsophila muralis*

1 Petals clearly longer than the sepals; seeds 0.7-0.8 mm wide . . . . *M. michauxii*
1 Petals shorter than to equaling the sepals; seeds ca. 0.6-0.7 mm wide . . . . *M. dawsonensis*

Minuartia dawsonensis (Britt.) House
ROCK STITCHWORT
MAP 544
🌷*threatened* | *native*

Perennial herb, sometimes mat-forming, similar to *M. michauxii* but typically smaller and less common. **Stems** erect to ascending, green, to 30 cm long, glabrous. **Leaves** overlapping or crowded near base, with a small sheath around the stem; blades straight to slightly curved, 1-veined, linear, 4-15 mm long and to 2 mm wide, shiny; axillary leaves present among lower stem leaves. **Inflorescence** 7-15-flowered in open cymes; bracts subulate; sepals 3-veined, ovate, 2.5-4 mm long, tips green to purple; petals lanceolate to spatulate, or petals absent. **Capsules** ovoid, 3.5-4.5 mm long, longer than the sepals; seeds dark brown to black, suborbiculate, tuberculate. Late spring-summer.—Crevices on dry outcrops of sedimentary rock.

Minuartia michauxii (Fenzl) Farw.
MICHAUX'S STITCHWORT
Arenaria michauxii (Fenzl) Hook. f.
(NO MAP)
native

Perennial or annual herb, diffuse, completely glabrous or sometimes pubescent, the prostrate branches with numerous short sterile shoots or the plants merely cespitose. **Stems** 1-4 dm long, leafy for 1/3 to 2/3 of their length, the primary leaves with short, leafy, fascicle-like sterile shoots in their axils. **Primary leaves** 8-30 mm, usually 10-20 mm long, subulate, somewhat involute, 3-nerved. **Inflorescence** open, forked; pedicels slender, 5-20 mm long; sepals 3.5-6.5 mm long, broadly lance-shaped, scarious-margined, 3-nerved or rarely 1-nerved; petals oblong lance-shaped, 5-8 mm long, entire. **Capsule** equaling or somewhat exceeding the sepals, the 3 valves dehiscent from near the middle to the base; seed kidney-shaped, brown-black, low-tuberculate. July-Sept.—Not known from Minn but may occur as present in Iowa, Wisc, and S Dakota; likely habitat includes calcareous gravels and ledges.

Minuartia michauxii

MOEHRINGIA *Grove-Sandwort*

Perennial herbs. Stems prostrate or ascending to erect. Leaves not congested at or near base of flowering stem; blades lanceshaped to elliptic or ovate. Inflorescence an open cyme. Fruit a capsule. Seeds with strophioles, spongy seed appendages that attract ants; foraging ants gather the seeds, eat only the strophiole, and "plant" the seeds in their nests.

1 Leaves acute; sepals often longer than the petals . . . . *M. macrophylla*
1 Leaves mostly blunt-tipped; sepals much shorter than the petals . . . . *M. lateriflora*

Moehringia lateriflora (L.) Fenzl
BLUNT-LEAF GROVE-SANDWORT
Arenaria lateriflora L.
MAP 545
native

Perennial with slender, rhizomes; spreading vegetatively and forming extensive colonies. **Stems** 5-20 cm tall, leafy, sparingly to densely puberulent. **Leaves** 1-2 cm long, 5-10 mm wide, usually ovate or elliptic obtuse. **Cymes** 1-5-flowered, from the axils of the middle or upper leaves or terminal; peduncle slender, 1-3 cm long; pedicels usually 5-15 mm long, slender, puberulent or occasionally glabrous; sepals 2-2.5 mm long, ovate or obovate, obtuse, sometimes acutish, faintly 3-5-nerved, glabrous, scarious-margined; petals commonly 4-6 mm long, obovate-oblong, entire. **Capsule** 3-5 mm long, ovoid-oblong, dehiscing nearly to the base; seed obliquely kidney-shaped, smooth, glossy. May-July.—Woodlands or sometimes open areas.

Moehringia macrophylla (Hook.) Fenzl
LARGE-LEAF GROVE-SANDWORT
Arenaria macrophylla Hook.
MAP 546
🌷*threatened* | *native*

Moehringia lateriflora

Similar in habit and pubescence to *M. lateriflora*. **Leaves** lance-shaped to elliptic, 2-5 cm long, 3-8 mm wide. Sepals mostly 3-5 mm long, broadly lance-shaped. **Capsule** shorter than the sepals, globose-oblong, the 6 segments dehiscing halfway or nearly to the base, the teeth recurved; seed obliquely kidney-shaped, smooth, glossy, reddish brown. May-Aug.—Open to partly shaded rocks and cliffs.

MYOSOTON *Giant Chickweed*

Myosoton aquaticum (L.) Moench   MAP 547
GIANT CHICKWEED   *introduced (naturalized)*
  Stellaria aquatica (L.) Scop.
Perennial herb, spreading by rhizomes. **Stems** sprawling and matted, to 8 dm long, rooting at nodes, covered with gland-tipped hairs. **Leaves** ovate to lance-shaped, 2-8 cm long and 1-4 cm wide, petioles short or absent. **Flowers** in open, leafy clusters at ends of stems; sepals 5-9 mm long; petals white, much longer than sepals. **Fruit** a capsule; seeds 0.8 mm long, covered with small bumps. June-Oct.—Streambanks, ponds, wet or moist disturbed areas, often in partial shade.

Myosoton aquaticum

PARONYCHIA *Nailwort*

Annual or perennial herbs. Leaves small, opposite, entire, with conspicuous hyaline stipules. Flowers perfect, often remaining closed. Sepals distinct or united at the base, more or less strongly cucullate. Stamens usually 5, inserted at the base of the calyx. Ovary maturing as an ovoid or obovoid membranous utricle. Style 2-parted. Seed smooth, reddish black.

1 Stems glabrous; sepals oval . . . .*P. canadensis*
1 Stems finely hairy; sepals ovate . . . .*P. fastigiata*

Paronychia canadensis (L.) Wood   MAP 548
SMOOTH FORKED NAILWORT   🖤*endangered | native*
Annual, completely glabrous, with slender, erect, forking **stems** and almost capillary ultimate branches. **Leaves** 5-30 mm long, 2-8 mm wide, elliptic to oval, thin, entire, usually punctate; petioles about 1 mm long. Inflorescence diffuse; calyx 1-1.5 mm long; sepals oblong-ovate, scarious-margined, 1-nerved, the apiculate hood very short; styles short, free nearly to the base, recurved. **Utricle** exceeding the sepals, obovate. June-Sept.—Rare in dry sandy woods; Minn at western edge of species' range.

Paronychia fastigiata (Raf.) Fern.   (NO MAP)
FORKED CHICKWEED   🖤*endangered | native*
Annual, with forked, erect or low-spreading and diffuse, puberulent **stems**, 5-25 cm tall. **Leaves** of the primary branches narrowly lance-shaped to oblong lance-shaped, 5-20 mm long, frequently white-punctate or granular-punctate; foliar bracts extending through the repeatedly forked cymes. Calyx 2-3 mm long, glabrous or slightly puberulent; sepals linear lance-shaped, 1-3-nerved, the tips of the hooded apex abruptly short-awned. **Utricle** glabrous; seed plump, oval, about 0.8 mm long, dark red and smooth. July-Sept.—Sandy open woods; Washington County.

Paronychia canadensis

PETRORHAGIA *Saxifrage-Pink*

Petrorhagia saxifraga (L.) Link   MAP 549
SAXIFRAGE-PINK   *introduced*
Cespitose perennial. **Stems** decumbent at base, 1-4 dm tall, glabrous or sparsely hispidulous. **Leaves** linear-subulate, 5-10 mm long, 1 mm wide. **Flowers** solitary

543. *Gypsophila paniculata*

544. *Minuartia dawsonensis*

545. *Moehringia lateriflora*

546. *Moehringia macrophylla*

or in cymes; calyx 4-5 mm long, 5-ribbed, closely subtended by 2 or 3 pairs of lance-shaped scarious bracts; petals purple to pink, 5-6 mm long, the blades broadly notched; stamens 10; styles 2. **Capsule** globose-ovoid, dehiscent by 4 teeth; seeds disciform. Summer.—Native of Europe; rarely escaped from cultivation and established mostly as a roadside weed.

Petrorhagia saxifraga

SAGINA *Pearlwort*

Small, tufted perennial herbs. Leaves filiform, subulate. Flowers small, inconspicuous, terminal or axillary; petals 4 or 5 white, entire or notched; styles as many as the sepals; capsules many-seeded.

1   Petals distinctly longer than the sepals; styles 1-1.5 mm long. . . . . *S. nodosa*
1   Petals much shorter than the sepals, inconspicuous; styles less than 0.5 mm long . . . . *S. procumbens*

Sagina nodosa (L.) Fenzl
KNOTTY PEARLWORT
MAP 550
⬥*endangered* | *native*

Tufted, mat-forming, perennial herb, 5-15 cm high. **Stems** erect, ascending, or decumbent.**Lower stem leaves** triangular in cross-section, 5-20 mm long; **upper leaves** paired, scale-like; some leaf-pairs there may have a small, sterile shoot at their base. **Flowers** small, white, delicate, borne singly at ends of slender branches; sepals to 2 mm long; petals to 4 mm long. **Capsules** with several black, rough-surfaced seeds.—In Minn, known from only several locations along rocky shores of Lake Superior; disjunct from arctic Canada.

Sagina procumbens L.
BIRD-EYE PEARLWORT
MAP 551
introduced

Branched perennial or perhaps sometimes annual herb. **Stems** prostrate, spreading, or ascending, 2-10 cm long, glabrous or minutely puberulent; short shoots or leaf-fascicles often conspicuous at the nodes. **Leaves** opposite, linear, 3-15 mm long, mucronate, often minutely ciliolate. **Flowers** lateral or in terminal cymes, on filiform pedicels, often nodding after anthesis, at length becoming erect; sepals 4, sometimes 5, broadly ovate, 2-2.5 mm long, spreading at maturity; petals white, shorter than the sepals or lacking; stamens 5 or 4; styles 5 or 4, alternate with the sepals. **Capsule** about equaling the sepals, the valves 4, sometimes 5; seeds many, 0.5 mm wide, grooved, dark reddish brown. May-Sept. —Moist soil and rocky places, weedy in paths and pavements.

Sagina procumbens

SAPONARIA *Soapwort; Bouncing-Bet*

Saponaria officinalis L.
BOUNCING-BET
MAP 552
introduced (naturalized)

Perennial herb from a horizontal rhizome and forming colonies. **Stems** coarse, erect, 4-8 dm tall, simple or branched, glabrous. **Leaves** 7-10 cm long, 2-4 cm wide, elliptic to elliptic-ovate, glabrous, rarely puberulent. **Inflorescence** congested and subcapitate to open and oblong-pyramidal, to 15 cm long; primary bracts foliaceous, the ultimate ones scarious. **Flowers** fragrant, frequently double; calyx 1.5-2.5 cm long, 20-nerved, the lobes long triangular, the tube often deeply

Saponaria officinalis

547. *Myosoton aquaticum*   548. *Paronychia canadensis*   549. *Petrorhagia saxifraga*   550. *Sagina nodosa*

bilobed; petals white or pinkish, appendages conspicuous, awl-shaped; stamens exsert; styles 2 (rarely 3). **Capsule** elliptic-oblong, dehiscent by 4 (rarely 6) teeth; seeds uniformly reticulate. Summer.—Native of the Old World; formerly in cultivation and now commonly weedy on roadsides, railways and waste places. *Name from the Latin, sapo, soap, alluding to the mucilaginous juice (but toxic as contains saponin) which forms a lather with water.*

SCLERANTHUS *Knawel*

Scleranthus annuus L.   MAP 553
ANNUAL KNAWEL   *introduced (naturalized)*
Annual herb; plants low, diffuse, spreading, glabrous or puberulent, to 15 cm tall; stems forked. **Leaves** opposite, subulate, joined at the base. **Flowers** perfect, sessile or subsessile; calyx 5-lobed, the lobes equal or exceeding the calyx tube; the tube becoming thick and indurate, enclosing the membranous utricle; stamens usually 5-10, inserted on a disc in the throat of the calyx tube. Seeds ovoid, beaked, 1-1.3 mm long, straw-colored. Summer.—Native of Eurasia; a weed of dry, usually sandy fields, roadsides, and waste places.

Scleranthus annuus

SILENE *Catchfly; Campion*

Annual or perennial herbs. Leaves opposite, entire. Inflorescence simple or branched, sometimes reduced to a few-flowered or 1-flowered cyme. Flowers perfect or sometimes unisexual. Calyx sometimes inflated. Petals 5, the claw narrow, expanded distally into more or less prominent auricles, provided ventrally with a pair of appendages; blade usually exsert, entire, lobed or dissected. Stamens normally 10. Styles normally 3, sometimes 4, or occasionally 5. Ovary usually stipitate. Capsule 3-celled (or 1-celled), dehiscent normally by 6 teeth. Seeds kidney-shaped to globose, sometimes covered with small bumps.

ADDITIONAL SPECIES
· *Silene dioica* (L.) Clairville (Red catchfly), native to Europe; Kittson and Wabasha counties.
· *Silene drummondii* Hook. (Drummond's campion, MAP 553A), Great Plains species reaching eastern range limit in Minnesota.
· *Silene flos-cuculi* (L.) Clairville (Ragged robin), native to Europe; Aitkin County.

1 Calyx not glandular or inflated . . . . *S. chalcedonica*
1 Calyx glabrous, glandular, or hairy, typically inflated 2
  2 Styles 5 . . . . *S. latifolia*
  2 Styles 3 3
    3 Main leaves whorled; petals fringed . . . . *S. stellata*
    3 Leaves opposite; petals not fringed 4
      4 Calyx glabrous 5
        5 Corolla pink . . . . *S. armeria*
        5 Corolla white 6
          6 Annual; calyx tight around capsule . . . . *S. antirrhina*
          6 Perennial; calyx somewhat inflated 7
            7 Flowers 5 or fewer, single in leaf axils . . . . *S. nivea*
            7 Flowers in clusters of more than 5 8
              8 Perennial; calyx very inflated . . . . *S. vulgaris*
              8 Biennial; calyx only slightly inflated . . . . *S. csereii*
      4 Calyx hairy or glandular 9

551. Sagina procumbens   *552. Saponaria officinalis*   *553. Scleranthus annuus*   *553A. Silene drummondii*

     9 Flowers in long, upright, often one-sided racemes . . . . *S. dichotoma*
     9 Flowers in an open cyme, often nodding . . . . *S. noctiflora*

Silene antirrhina L.
SLEEPY CATCHFLY   MAP 554
                                       native

Annual, glabrous or more or less puberulent. **Stems** 2-8 dm tall, simple or branched, erect or sometimes decumbent, usually with glutinous zones below the upper nodes. **Basal leaves** oblong lance-shaped; **stem leaves** oblong lance-shaped to linear, usually 3-6 cm long, 2-12 mm wide, glabrous or puberulent, the margins ciliate near the base. **Inflorescence** open, strict or with divaricate branches. **Flowers** numerous, rarely few or solitary; calyx 4-10 mm long, 10-nerved; petals white or pink, equaling or exceeding the calyx, frequently obsolete, 2-lobed; appendages minute or lacking. **Capsule** ovoid, 4-10 mm long, 3-celled; seeds with 3 or 4 rows of dorsal papillae. Summer.—In waste places or sandy soil.

Silene armeria L.
NONE-SO-PRETTY   MAP 555
                                 introduced

Annual with glabrous or rarely sparsely puberulent stems about 3 dm tall. **Leaves** ovate lance-shaped; basal leaves 2-5 cm long, 5-15 mm wide, sessile; upper leaves clasping. **Inflorescence** simple or open and compound, the ultimate cymes congested; calyx tubular, 13-17 mm long, 10-nerved; corolla pink or lavender; auricles lacking; appendages linear, 2-3 mm long; blades 4-7 mm long, obovate. **Capsule** nearly completely 3-celled; seeds 0.6 mm wide, rugose; carpophore (the stalk supporting the fruit) 7-8 mm long. June-July.—Native of Europe; once popular in cultivation; escaped as a weed in waste places.

Silene antirrhina

Silene chalcedonica (L.) E.H.L. Krause
MALTESE CROSS   MAP 556
   Lychnis chalcedonica L.   *introduced*

Perennial with hirsute **stems** 5-10 dm tall. **Basal leaves** spatulate or lance-shaped; **stem leaves** 10-20 pairs, lance-shaped to ovate lance-shaped, 5-12 cm long, 2-5 cm wide, sparingly pubescent or glabrate, serrulate-ciliate. **Inflorescence** terminal, congested; **flowers** numerous, red, rose, or white; calyx tubular, 12-17 mm long at maturity, coarsely 10-ribbed, the ribs strigose-hirsute, the lobes lance-shaped, 2.5-3.5 mm long; petals 14-18 mm long, the claws ciliate; appendages tubular, 2-3 mm long; blades 7-9 mm long, deeply bilobed. **Capsule** about 1 cm long. June-Sept.—Native of Asia; escaped from cultivation and occasionally spontaneous.

Silene csereii Baumg.
BALKAN CATCHFLY   MAP 557
                      introduced (naturalized)

Robust glaucous perennial; **leaves** 2-4 cm wide. **Inflorescence** narrow, raceme-like; calyx 7-9 mm long, in fruit becoming 10-12 mm long, but little inflated and the veins not conspicuously reticulate; petals as in *S. vulgaris* but root much stouter and inflorescence more elongate. Seeds conspicuously papillate. Summer. —Native of Europe; disturbed places. *Often confused with **Silene vulgaris**.*

Silene dichotoma Ehrh.
FORKED CATCHFLY   MAP 558
                      introduced (naturalized)

Annual, with simple or sparingly branched, strongly hirsute **stems** 3-8 dm tall. **Leaves** lance-shaped to oblong lance-shaped, 3-8 cm long, 3-35 mm wide, the lower leaves usually with ciliate petioles, the upper sessile. **Inflorescence** usually

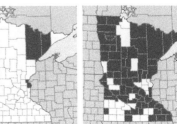

Silene csereii

554. *Silene antirrhina*   555. *Silene armeria*   556. *Silene chalcedonica*   557. *Silene csereii*

once or several times dichotomous, the ultimate branches racemose. **Flowers** mostly perfect; calyx narrowly tubular, 10-15 mm long, the 10 green nerves stiffly hirsute; corolla white to reddish; auricles lacking; appendages truncate, about 0.2 mm long; blades cuneate, 5-9 mm long, deeply 2-lobed; stamens usually exsert but sometimes vestigial. **Capsule** 3-celled; seeds 1-1.3 mm wide, finely and regularly rugose; carpophore 2-4 mm long. Summer.—Native of Eurasia; disturbed places such as fields, roadsides, and railways.

Silene latifolia Poir.   MAP 559
WHITE CAMPION   *introduced (naturalized)*
   Lychnis alba Mill.

Dioecious annual or perennial from a stout root. **Stems** 4-12 dm tall, coarsely pubescent, glandular above. **Stem leaves** as many as 10 pairs, lance-shaped to broadly elliptic, 3-10 cm long, 1-4 cm wide, 3-5-nerved, puberulent to hirsute, the lower petiolate, the upper sessile. **Inflorescence** usually much branched, the primary bracts foliar; **flowers** white, characteristically unisexual, opening in the evening; calyx 15-20 mm long, tubular in anthesis, becoming distended at maturity, 10-nerved in the staminate flower, 20-nerved in the pistillate, the lobes lance-shaped, 3-5 mm long; petals 2-4 cm long, the claw exsert, auriculate, the appendages 1-1.5 mm long, erose, the blade deeply bilobed. **Capsule** ovoid, 10-15 mm long, dehiscent by 10 erect or spreading teeth. Summer.—Native of Europe; a common weed.

Silene latifolia

Silene nivea (Nutt.) Muhl.   MAP 560
SNOWY CATCHFLY   ❧*threatened* | *native*

Perennial herb, spreading by rhizomes; plants smooth or with a few short hairs. **Stems** 2-3 dm long. **Leaves** mostly on stem, opposite, lance-shaped or oblong, 5-10 cm long and 1-3 cm wide, sessile or on short petioles. **Flowers** few, mostly in leaf axils; sepals joined to form a tube 1.5 cm long; petals white, stamens 10, styles 3. **Fruit** a 1-chambered capsule. June-July.—Streambanks, wooded ravines, calcareous fens.

Silene nivea

Silene noctiflora L.   MAP 561
NIGHT-FLOWERING CATCHFLY   *introduced (naturalized)*

Annual, 2-8 dm tall, with simple or branched, coarsely hirsute stems and leaves. **Leaves** ovate lance-shaped, 5-12 cm long, 2-4 cm wide; **basal leaves** somewhat narrowed to a petiole; **stem leaves** narrower, sessile. **Inflorescence** loosely branched; **flowers** often unisexual; calyx about 15 mm long in anthesis, in fruit 2.5-5 cm long, the 10 nerves glandular, the lobes linear lance-shaped, 5-9 mm long; corolla white or pink; auricles 1-1.5 mm long; appendages broad, 0.5-1.5 mm long, entire or erose; blades 7-10 mm long, deeply 2-lobed. **Capsule** 3-celled; seeds to 1 mm wide, uniformly rugose-papillate; carpophore 1-3 mm long. July-Sept. —Native of Europe; disturbed places such as roadsides, railways, fields. *Plants superficially resemble* **Silene latifolia** *which normally has 5 styles.*

Silene stellata (L.) Ait. f.   MAP 562
STARRY CAMPION   *native*

Perennial, with several simple, more or less puberulent **stems** 3-8 dm tall. **Stem leaves** usually in whorls of 4, lance-shaped, 3-10 cm long, to 4 cm wide. **Inflorescence** loosely paniculate; calyx campanulate, 5-12 mm long, more or less finely puberulent; petals white, 8-11 mm long, lanate at the base; auricles and

Silene noctiflora

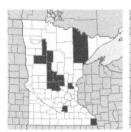

558. Silene dichotoma   *559. Silene latifolia*   *560. Silene nivea*   *561. Silene noctiflora*

appendages lacking; blades fimbriately 8-12-lobed. Seeds about 1 mm long, uniformly rugose-papillate; carpophore 2-3 mm long.—Dry oak woods.

Silene vulgaris (Moench) Garcke   MAP 563
BLADDER-CAMPION   *introduced (naturalized)*

Robust perennial. **Stems** 2-8 dm tall, from a creeping rhizome, usually glabrous and glaucous, often decumbent. **Leaves** ovate lance-shaped, 3-8 cm long, 1-3 cm wide, abruptly acuminate, sometimes ciliolate; **stem leaves** often clasping. **Inflorescence** open, 5-30-flowered; calyx campanulate, 1 cm long, papery in texture with reticulate veins, in fruit becoming much inflated; corolla white; auricles lacking; appendages inconspicuous or lacking; blades 3.5-6 mm long, deeply bilobed. **Capsule** 3-celled; seeds 1-1.5 mm, warty; carpophore 2-3 mm long. Summer.—Native of Europe, weedy in waste places.

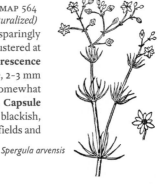
Silene stellata

SPERGULA *Spurry*

Spergula arvensis L.   MAP 564
CORN SPURRY   *introduced (naturalized)*

Fleshy annual herb. **Stems** simple or much-branched, to 40 cm long, sparingly glandular-puberulent. **Leaves** whorled, 2-5 cm long, narrowly linear, clustered at the nodes in two opposite sets of 6-8; stipules small, connate. **Inflorescence** terminal, dichotomously branched, the pedicels reflexed; sepals 5, ovate, 2-3 mm long, obtuse, glandular-puberulent; petals 5, white, shorter than or somewhat surpassing the sepals; stamens 10 or sometimes 5; styles normally 5. **Capsule** broadly ovoid, somewhat longer than the sepals; seeds 1-1.5 mm wide, blackish, minutely roughened. May-Aug.—Native of Europe; weedy in cultivated fields and waste places.

Spergula arvensis

SPERGULARIA *Sandspurry*

Low-growing succulent herbs, often where salted in winter. Leaves opposite, linear or reduced to bristles. Flowers in branched terminal cymes. Sepals and petals each 5. Stamens 2-10. Styles normally 3. Fruit a 3-valved capsule.

1 Stamens 2-5 . . . . *S. salina*
1 Stamens usually 10 . . . . *S. rubra*

Spergularia rubra (L.) J.& K. Presl   MAP 565
ROADSIDE SANDSPURRY   *introduced (naturalized)*

Simple or much branched annual or short-lived perennial with slender, prostrate or ascending **stems** 5-30 cm long, glabrous, or sparsely glandular-pubescent below the inflorescence. **Leaves** linear-filiform, mucronate, scarcely fleshy, 4-25 mm long, to 1 mm wide; stipules conspicuous, triangular-acuminate, 2.5-5 mm long. Sepals 3.5-5 mm long, lance-shaped; petals pink, shorter than the sepals; stamens 6-10, more often 10. **Capsule** 3.5-5 mm long; seeds tiny, dark brown, papillate, not winged. May-Sept.—Native of Europe; sandy or gravelly soil.

Spergularia rubra

Spergularia salina J.& K. Presl   (NO MAP)
SALTMARSH SANDSPURRY   *introduced*
   Spergularia marina (L.) Griseb.

Annual herb. **Stems** upright, or sprawling, to 30 cm long, smooth or with gland-tipped hairs. **Leaves** fleshy, 5-40 mm long and to 1.5 mm wide, tipped with a short

562. Silene stellata   *563. Silene vulgaris*   *564. Spergula arvensis*   *565. Spergularia rubra*

spine. **Flowers** pink or white; stamens 2–5; seeds less than 1 mm wide, usually not winged. Summer.—Highway ditches where salted; Washington County.

STELLARIA *Chickweed*

Low, spreading or erect perennials (ours), mostly without hairs. Stems slender, 4-angled. Flowers single in forks of stems or in few-flowered clusters at ends of stems; sepals green with translucent margins; petals white, lobed or deeply cleft (sometimes absent in *S. borealis*); stamens 10 or less; styles 3. Fruit an ovate or oblong capsule.

ADDITIONAL SPECIES
Stellaria alsine Grimm (Bog stitchwort); native to e North America, adventive in Ramsey and Winona counties.

1　Leaves wider, not linear, mostly more than 1 cm wide . . . . ***S. media***
1　Leaves narrow, linear or lance-shaped, less than 1 cm wide 2
　　2　Flowers in branched cymes 3
　　　　3　Petals usually absent, or shorter than the sepals . . . . ***S. borealis***
　　　　3　Petals much longer than sepals 4
　　　　　　4　Inflorescence open and branched; pedicels spreading 5
　　　　　　　　5　Flowers numerous; sepals 4.5–5.5 mm long, with 3 prominent nerves; seeds bumpy . . ***S. graminea***
　　　　　　　　5　Flowers few; sepals to 4.5 mm long, only weakly 3-nerved; seeds smooth . . . . ***S. longifolia***
　　　　　　4　Inflorescence less open; pedicels erect or ascending . . . . ***S. longipes***
　　2　Flowers single in forks of stems 7
　　　　6　Stems 25 cm or more long; seeds smooth . . . . ***S. borealis***
　　　　6　Stems to 20 cm long; seeds rough . . . . ***S. crassifolia***

Stellaria borealis Bigelow
NORTHERN STITCHWORT
MAP 566
native

Perennial herb, spreading by rhizomes. **Stems** sprawling, to 5 dm long, branched, angled. **Leaves** lance-shaped, narrowed at base, 1–5 cm long and 2–8 mm wide, margins hairy. **Flowers** in clusters at ends of stems; sepals 2–4 mm long; petals usually absent. **Fruit** a dark capsule, longer than sepals; seeds 0.8 mm long, with very small bumps. June–Aug.—Openings and hollows in conifer forests, margins of ponds and marshes.

Stellaria borealis

Stellaria crassifolia Ehrh.
FLESHY STITCHWORT
MAP 567
native

Perennial herb. **Stems** sprawling and matted to erect, freely branched, 8–30 cm long, fleshy, glabrous. **Leaves** soft, oval to lance-shaped, narrowed at base, 1–3 cm long and 1–3 mm wide. **Flowers** single in forks of stem, nodding on stalks 1–3 cm long; sepals 2–4 mm long; petals longer than sepals. **Fruit** an ovate capsule, to 5 mm long and longer than the sepals; seeds red-brown, to 1 mm long. June–July. —Streambanks and wet shores.

Stellaria graminea L.
GRASS-LEAF STITCHWORT
MAP 568
introduced (naturalized)

Perennial herb. **Stems** 3–5 dm long, weak, 4-angled, the angles prominent and sometimes scabrous. **Leaves** 1.5–5 cm long, 1.5–7 mm wide, linear to linear lance-shaped, the base often obtuse and ciliate. **Inflorescence** terminal, many-flowered, diffuse, frequently extending to the middle of the stem; bracts scarious, ciliolate; pedicels slender, spreading or reflexed; sepals lance-shaped, in fruit 4.5–5.5 mm long, strongly 3-nerved, the margins scarious, commonly ciliolate, at least at the

566. Stellaria borealis　　　*567. Stellaria crassifolia*　　　*568. Stellaria graminea*　　　*569. Stellaria longifolia*

base; petals exceeding the sepals. **Capsule** straw-colored, more or less equaling or somewhat surpassing the sepals; seeds 0.8-1.2 mm long, kidney-shaped, dark reddish brown, covered with small bumps. May-July.—Native of Europe; introduced in grassy places, fields, roadsides, and waste land.

Stellaria longifolia Muhl.
MAP 569
LONG-LEAVED STITCHWORT
native

Perennial herb. **Stems** sprawling, prominently 4-angled, usually freely branched, 1-5 dm long. **Leaves** spreading to ascending, linear to lance-shaped, 2-5 cm long and 1-6 mm wide, widest at or above middle, tapered at both ends. **Flowers** in branched clusters at ends of stems; sepals 3-5 mm long; petals longer than sepals. **Fruit** a green-yellow to brown capsule, usually longer than the sepals; seeds light brown, about 1 mm long. May-July.—Wet meadows and marshes, shrub thickets, swamps, streambanks, pond margins.

Stellaria graminea

Stellaria longipes Goldie
MAP 570
LONG-STALK STARWORT
native

Perennial herb, spreading by rhizomes. **Stems** erect, or sprawling and matted, 5-30 cm long. **Leaves** upright, stiff and shiny-waxy, linear or lance-shaped, 1-4 cm long and 1-4 mm wide, widest near base, tapered to tip. **Flowers** in branched clusters at ends of stems or appearing lateral from stem; sepals 4-5 mm long; petals slightly longer than sepals. **Fruit** a straw-colored to shiny purple capsule, longer than the sepals; seeds reddish brown, about 1 mm long. May-July.—Wet meadows, ditches and thickets.

Stellaria media (L.) Vill.
MAP 571
COMMON CHICKWEED
introduced (naturalized)

Weakly tufted annual. **Stems** to 4 dm long, with ascending branches, puberulent in lines. **Leaves** usually 1-3 cm long, ovate or obovate, glabrous, frequently pustulate; **upper leaves** sessile; **lower leaves** with petioles that may exceed the length of the blade, often ciliate toward the base or on the petioles. **Flowers** solitary or in few-flowered, terminal, leafy cymes; pedicels ascending, reflexed, frequently pubescent; sepals oblong, 3.5-6 mm long, pubescent and pustulate; petals shorter than the sepals; stamens 3-5. **Capsule** ovoid, somewhat surpassing the sepals; seeds 1-1.2 mm long, suborbicular, reddish brown, conspicuously covered with small bumps. Summer.—Introduced from the Old World but often appearing to be native; now a cosmopolitan weed of waste places, cultivated areas, meadows, and woodlands.

Stellaria longifolia

VACCARIA *Cowcockle*

Vaccaria hispanica (P. Mill.) Rauschert
MAP 572
COWCOCKLE
introduced

Annual herb from a slender taproot. **Stems** branching above, 2-6 dm tall, glabrous and glaucous. **Stem leaves** 5-10 cm long, 24 cm wide, lance-shaped to ovate lance-shaped, clasping or the lower connate. **Inflorescence** a loose, open, paniculate cyme; calyx strongly 5-ribbed, 12-17 mm long, ovoid; petals 18-22 mm long, pink, without auricles or appendages, the blades 6-8 mm long, obovate, retuse; stamens exsert. **Capsule** 6-8 mm long, dehiscent by 4 teeth; seeds 2-2.5 mm long, minutely tuberculate, reddish brown to black.—Native of Europe; often a weed in grain-fields.

Stellaria media

Celastraceae BITTERSWEET FAMILY

Shrubs (*Euonymus*), vines (*Celastrus*), or glabrous perennial herbs (*Parnassia*), with simple, evergreen or deciduous, opposite or alternate leaves, and small, axillary or terminal, solitary or clustered flowers. Flowers perfect or unisexual, regular, polypetalous, usually 4-5-merous. Stamens as many as the petals and alternate with them; in *Parnassia*, staminodes (infertile stamens) attached to base of petals and divided into threadlike segments tipped with glandular knobs. Pistil 1, inserted on or surrounded by the disk; ovary 2-5-celled. Fruit a capsule. *Celastraceae now includes members of genus Parnassia.*

1   Perennial herbs; leaves basal with a single stem leaf. . . . . *Parnassia*
1   Shrubs or twining vines; leaves cauline, alternate or opposite 2
  2   Twining vines; leaves alternate . . . . *Celastrus*
  2   Shrubs; leaves opposite . . . . *Euonymus*

CELASTRUS *Bittersweet*

Woody twiners. Leaves deciduous, alternate, serrulate. Flowers dioecious or polygamo-dioecious, small, whitish or greenish, 5-merous. Staminate flowers with 5 stamens about as long as the petals, inserted on the margin of the cup-shaped disk. Pistillate flowers with rudimentary stamens and a well developed ovary, stout columnar style, and 3-lobed stigma. Fruit 3-valved, each valve covering 1 or 2 seeds enclosed in a fleshy bright red-orange aril.

1   Leaves obovate to nearly round; inflorescences from leaf axils . . . . *C. orbiculatus*
1   Leaves ovate; inflorescences at ends of new twigs . . . . *C. scandens*

Celastrus orbiculatus Thunb.   (NO MAP)
ASIAN BITTERSWEET   *introduced (invasive)*
Similar to *C. scandens* in fruit and general habit. **Leaves** suborbicular to obovate. **Flowers** few in small axillary cymes much shorter than the subtending leaves. —Sometimes cultivated, but can be aggressive if escaped near homes and into woods; Anoka and Hennepin counties.

Celastrus scandens L.   MAP 573
AMERICAN BITTERSWEET   *native*
Climbing several meters high. **Leaves** elliptic or oblong to ovate, acuminate, serrulate, 5-10 cm long. **Panicles** terminal, 3-8 cm long. **Fruit** red-orange, several in a cluster, subglobose, nearly 1 cm long; seeds ellipsoid, 6 mm long. May-June.— Roadsides and thickets, usually in rich soil; occasionally cultivated and now established in open woods and thickets.

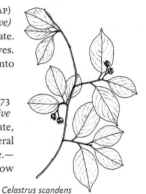

Celastrus scandens

EUONYMUS *Spindletree*

Shrubs or small trees, prostrate, erect, or climbing by rootlets, with opposite, deciduous or evergreen, finely serrate leaves and small flowers solitary or cymose in the leaf-axils. Flowers perfect, 4-5-merous. Petals widely spreading. Stamens very short, inserted at the margin of the broad disk which apparently covers and conceals the 3-5-celled ovary. Style none; stigma 3-5-lobed. Fruit 3-5-lobed, colored; aril completely covering the seed.

1   Branches with corky wings; petals yellowish; fruit completely divided into 1-4 lobes . . . . *E. alatus*
1   Branches without corky wings; petals purple; fruit only partially divided into 4 lobes . . . . *E. atropurpureus*

Euonymus alatus (Thunb.) Sieb.   (NO MAP)
WINGED SPINDLETREE   *introduced (invasive)*
Shrub to 2.5 m; twigs with 2-4 conspicuous corky wings. **Leaves** subsessile, elliptic to obovate, to 6 cm long, sharply serrulate, turning bright red in autumn, then deciduous. **Flowers** 4-merous, green, 6-8 mm wide. **Fruit** smooth, purplish; aril orange. May-June.—Native of e Asia, cultivated and locally escaped; St. Louis County.

570. Stellaria longipes   *571. Stellaria media*   *572. Vaccaria hispanica*   *573. Celastrus scandens*

Euonymus atropurpureus Jacq.

MAP 574
native

BURNING BUSH

Erect shrub to 6 m tall. **Leaves** elliptic to ovate lance-shaped, 6-12 cm long, acuminate, finely serrulate, acute at the base, glabrous above, finely pubescent beneath; petioles 1-2 cm long. **Flowers** few to many in divergently branched cymes 2-4 cm wide on axillary peduncles 2-5 cm long, 4-merous, brownish purple, 6-8 mm wide. **Fruit** red, depressed-obovoid, smooth, about 1.5 cm wide, 4-lobed, or by abortion with 1-3 small defective lobes. Aril bright red. June. —Moist woods.

Euonymus atropurpureus

PARNASSIA *Grass-of-Parnassus*

Glabrous perennial herbs. Leaves all from base of plant but often with 1 stalkless leaf near middle of stalk, margins entire; petioles present. Flowers large, white, single at ends of stalks; calyx 5-lobed; petals white, veined, spreading; fertile stamens 5, alternating with petals; staminodes (infertile stamens) attached to base of petals and divided into threadlike segments tipped with glandular knobs; stigmas 4. Fruit a 4-chambered capsule with numerous seeds.

1   Sepals with narrow translucent margins; staminodes (sterile stamens) 3-parted, not widened at base; petals 12-16 mm long; leaves leathery and somewhat succulent . . . . **P. glauca**
1   Sepal margins green; staminodes 5 to many-parted; petals 8-13 mm long; leaves thin and membranous . . . . **P. palustris**

Parnassia glauca Raf.

MAP 575
native

FEN GRASS-OF-PARNASSUS

Smooth perennial herb. **Leaves** from base of plant and usually with 1, more or less sessile stem leaf; broadly ovate to nearly round, 2-7 cm long and 1-5 cm wide; margins entire; petioles long. **Flowers** single atop a stalk 1-4 dm long; sepals ovate, 2-5 mm long, with a narrow, translucent margin; petals white with green veins, 1-2 cm long; staminodes 3-parted from near base, shorter than to equal to stamens. **Fruit** a capsule about 1 cm long. Aug-Sept.—Calcareous fens and wet meadows.

Parnassia palustris L.

MAP 576
native

ARCTIC GRASS-OF-PARNASSUS

Smooth perennial herb. **Leaves** from base of plant and usually with 1, clasping, heart-shaped leaf below middle of stalk; ovate to nearly round, 1-3 cm long; margins entire; petioles long and slender. **Flowers** single atop a stalk 1.5-4 dm long; sepals lance-shaped, to 1 cm long, green throughout; petals white with green veins, ovate, 1-1.5 cm long, longer than sepals; staminodes many-parted from the widened tip, 5-9 mm long. **Fruit** a capsule. July-Sept.—Calcareous fens, shores, streambanks and wet, seepy meadows.

Parnassia glauca

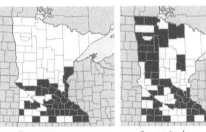

574. *Euonymus atropurpureus*   575. *Parnassia glauca*

Parnassia palustris

Ceratophyllaceae HORNWORT FAMILY

CERATOPHYLLUM *Coon's-Tail; Hornwort*

Aquatic perennial herbs, often forming large patches; roots absent, but plants usually anchored to substrate by pale, modified leaves. Stems slender,

branched. Leaves in whorls, with more than 4 leaves per node, whorls crowded at ends of stems, dissected 2-3 times into narrow segments. Flowers small, inconspicuous in leaf axils, staminate and pistillate flowers separate on same plant, staminate usually above pistillate on stems. _Our only aquatic vascular genus with whorled, forked leaves._

1 Leaves usually stiff, forked 1-2 times, margins coarsely toothed; achenes with 2 spines near base . . **C. demersum**
1 Leaves limp, some larger leaves forked 3-4 times, margins not toothed; achenes with 2 spines near base and several
  spines on margin . . . . **C. muricatum**

Ceratophyllum demersum L.
COON'S-TAIL

MAP 577
native

Aquatic perennial herb. **Stems** long, branched. **Leaves** in whorls of 5-12 at each node, stiff, 1-3 cm long, 1-2-forked; leaf segments linear, 0.5-1 mm wide, coarsely toothed. **Fruit** an oval achene, 4-6 mm long, with 2 spines at base.—Shallow to deep water of lakes, ponds, backwater areas, ditches; water typically neutral or alkaline.

Ceratophyllum muricatum Cham.
SPINELESS HORNWORT
   Ceratophyllum echinatum Gray

MAP 578
native

Aquatic perennial herb. Similar to _C. demersum_, but leaves usually limp, larger **leaves** usually 3- or sometimes 4-forked, the segments narrower and mostly without teeth. **Fruit** an achene with 2 spines at base and several unequal spines on achene body.—Lakes, ponds and quiet water of rivers and streams; water typically acid.

Ceratophyllum demersum

Cistaceae ROCK-ROSE FAMILY

Herbs or shrubs. Leaves simple, alternate, opposite or appearing whorled. Flowers cymose, perfect, regular except the calyx, 3-5-merous. Sepals 5, the outer 2 much smaller than the inner 3. Petals small to large, soon deciduous, or lacking in some flowers. Stamens irregular in number, often very numerous, the filaments distinct. Ovary 1-celled; style 1, short or elongate. Fruit a capsule, usually separating completely to the base and enclosed by the persistent calyx.

1 Plants shrubby; leaves small and scale-like . . . . **Hudsonia tomentosa**
1 Plants herbaceous; leaves linear to ovate 2
  2 Leaves densely white-hairy, the hairs branched; petals 5, yellow, conspicuous . . . . **Crocanthemum**
  2 Leaves nearly glabrous to densely hairy, the hairs unbranched; petals 3, dark red, tiny . . . . **Lechea**

CROCANTHEMUM _Frostweed_

Perennial herbaceous or suffrutescent plants from short or elongate rhizomes. Stems and leaves with stellate-pubescence. Leaves narrow. Sepals 3 or 5; when 5, the outer two much narrower than the inner. Petals yellow, 5 in the first flowers of the season, soon deciduous; petals mostly absent in the later flowers. Stamens numerous. Ovary 1-celled; style short; stigmas large, capitate. Capsule short. At the beginning of the blooming season, plants have one or a few flowers with petals 1-2 cm long. Later, plants produce numerous smaller apetalous flowers. Both types are normally followed by mature capsules, those from apetalous flowers usually much smaller, containing similar seeds. _Our species formerly included in genus Helianthemum._

576. Parnassia palustris   _577. Ceratophyllum demersum_   _578. Ceratophyllum muricatum_   _579. Crocanthemum bicknellii_

1   Petal-bearing flowers 1 . . . . *C. canadense*
1   Petal-bearing flowers 3 or more . . . . *C. bicknellii*

Crocanthemum bicknellii (Fernald) Janch.   MAP 579
HOARY FROSTWEED   *native*
   Helianthemum bicknellii Fern.

Perennial herb. **Stems** solitary or few together, erect or nearly so, simple or
sparsely branched at first anthesis, later producing numerous floriferous branches
from the upper axils. **Leaves** linear-oblong to oblong lance-shaped, 2-3 cm long
on the main axis, much smaller on the branches. **Petaliferous flowers** 5-12 in a
loose terminal raceme, 15-25 mm wide; sepals densely stellate, the outer nearly
or quite as long as the inner. **Capsules** of the petaliferous flowers 4-5 mm wide.
Apetalous flowers numerous and crowded on short axillary branches, their
capsules about 2 mm wide, strongly triquetrous; seeds minutely net-veined. June-
July; flowering 2-3 weeks later than *C. canadense.*—Dry, usually sandy soil. *The
terminal flowers are not much surpassed by the lateral branches, and their capsules, if
persistent in late summer, are near the top of the plant.*

Crocanthemum canadense (L.) Britton   MAP 580
LONG-BRANCH FROSTWEED   *native*
   Helianthemum canadense (L.) Michx.

Perennial herb. Resembling *C. bicknellii* in habit and foliage. **Petaliferous flowers**
solitary or occasionally 2, 2-4 cm wide; sepals densely stellate and also villous with
apparently simple hairs 1-1.5 mm long, the outer about two-thirds as long as the
inner. **Capsules** of the petaliferous flowers 4-6 mm wide. **Apetalous flowers** fewer
and less crowded than in *C. bicknellii*, their capsules commonly 3-3.5 mm wide
with convex sides; seeds minutely papillose. Late May-June.—Dry sandy soil, open
upland woods. *The terminal flowers are soon surpassed by the lateral branches and
their capsules, usually long persistent, are then far below the top of the plant.*

Crocanthemum canadense

HUDSONIA *Golden-Heather*

Hudsonia tomentosa Nutt.   MAP 581
SAND GOLDEN-HEATHER   🠾 *threatened | native*

Perennial. **Stems** prostrate, much branched, woody at base, forming dense mats
or bushes 2-6 dm across **Leaves** scale-like, lance-shaped, 1-4 mm long, closely
appressed and imbricate, the entire surface nearly concealed by the pubescence.
Flowers 6-10 mm wide, each solitary at the end of a short, leafy, lateral branch;
petals 5, yellow, narrowly elliptic, early deciduous; stamens 10-30; ovary 1-celled,
glabrous. **Capsule** ovoid, glabrous, much shorter than the mature calyx, few-
seeded. May-July.—Rare on beaches, sand dunes, sandy prairies.

Hudsonia tomentosa

LECHEA *Pinweed*

Perennial herbs, with solitary or few erect stems. Leaves small, alternate (occasionally appearing
opposite or whorled), entire, sessile or short-petioled, 1-nerved. Flowers many, tiny, red, in leafy
panicles. Sepals 5. Petals 3, smaller than the sepals. Stamens commonly 5-15. Ovary 1-celled; style
none; stigmas 3, plumose. Capsule 3-valved, maturing 1-6 seeds, enclosed wholly or largely by the
persistent calyx. Flowering in mid-late summer but rarely seen with expanded petals; at anthesis the
sepals spread widely but soon return to an erect position. Late in the season basal shoots with
numerous crowded leaves are produced.

   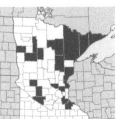   

580. Crocanthemum canadense   *581. Hudsonia tomentosa*   *582. Lechea intermedia*   *583. Lechea stricta*

1 Outer sepals narrow, equal to or longer than the wider inner sepals . . . . ***L. tenuifolia***
1 Outer sepals narrow, shorter than the wider inner sepals 2
    2 Branches stiffly ascending to nearly erect; leaves densely gray-hairy . . . . ***L. stricta***
    2 Branches mostly widely spreading from main stem; leaves hairy on underside but less densely so . . . .
      . . . . ***L. intermedia***

Lechea intermedia Leggett

MAP 582
native

SAVANNA PINWEED

Stems 2-6 dm tall, thinly appressed-pubescent. **Leaves** of the basal shoots oblong lance-shaped to narrowly elliptic, 3-7 mm long, sparsely pilose on the midrib and margin beneath or essentially glabrous; **stem leaves** linear-oblong, very sparsely pubescent on the midrib beneath or glabrous. **Panicle** occupying 1/3 to 1/2 of the plant, slenderly cylindric, the lateral branches seldom more than 5 cm long; pedicels equaling or surpassing the sepals; calyx and capsule together subglobose. **Capsule** subglobose, barely exceeding the sepals; seed shaped like a section of orange, pale brown, partly and irregularly invested with a gray membrane.—Dry sterile or sandy soil.

Lechea stricta Leggett

MAP 583
native

PRAIRIE PINWEED

Plants canescent. **Stems** commonly procumbent for 1-5 cm at base, thence abruptly erect, 1-4 dm tall. **Leaves** of the basal shoots crowded but not conspicuously whorled, 3-5 mm long, more or less canescent beneath with hairs on the surface as well as the midrib and margin; **stem leaves** similarly pubescent, narrowly lance-shaped to oblong lance-shaped, up to 15 mm long. **Panicle** forming a 1/3 to 1/2 of the plant, its suberect branches diverging at an angle of 30 degrees or less, the ultimate branchlets crowded; pedicels equaling or exceeding the calyx, very pubescent; sepals densely pubescent, about equaling the subglobose **capsule**.—Dry sandy woods, prairies, and shores.

Lechea intermedia

Lechea tenuifolia Michx.

MAP 584
☙*endangered* | *native*

NARROW-LEAF PINWEED

Stems 1-3 dm tall, sparsely pubescent with erect or ascending hairs. Leaves of the basal shoots linear, crowded, 3-6 mm long; **stem leaves** linear, to 2 cm long, usually less than 1 mm wide, glabrous above, sparsely pilose beneath, soon deciduous. **Panicle** occupying 1/2 the plant or more, its numerous branches often secund; inner sepals concave, not keeled but with a conspicuous midvein, more or less pilose over all or most of the surface; outer sepals linear, usually distinctly exceeding the inner. **Capsule** subglobose, usually slightly shorter than the sepals and enclosed by them.—Dry soil, upland woods and barrens.

Lechea tenuifolia
calyx and capsule

Cleomaceae CLEOME FAMILY

Annual herbs. Leaves alternate, compound. Flowers regular or irregular, in terminal bracteate racemes. Sepals 4, separate or slightly united at base. Petals 4, equal or unequal, commonly long-clawed at base. Stamens 6 to many; filaments elongate, exsert. Ovary of 2 carpels, 1-celled with 1 style. Fruit an elongate capsule, dehiscent by 2 valves. Seeds numerous, kidney-shaped.

1 Petals entire; stamens 6 . . . . ***Cleome***
1 Petals notched at tip; stamens more than 6 . . . . ***Polanisia***

CLEOME *Beeplant*

Cleome serrulata Pursh

MAP 585
native

ROCKY MOUNTAIN BEEPLANT

   Peritoma serrulata (Pursh) DC.

Annual herb. **Stems** 5-8 dm tall, branched above, pale and glabrous. **Leaves** palmately compound; **leaflets** 3, narrowly lance-shaped, 3-6 cm long, sharply acuminate or cuspidate, entire, glabrous at maturity, sometimes finely and sparsely villosulous when young. **Flowers** in elongating terminal racemes; **petals**

Cleome serrulata

white to pink, oblong, about 1 cm long, the blade much exceeding the claw.; stamens normally 6, the filaments very slender and elongate. **Capsule** 3-5 cm long, glabrous, reticulately veined. July-Aug.—Native of w USA, uncommon in Minnesota.

POLANISIA *Clammyweed*

Viscid-pubescent, branched, annual herbs. Leaves trifoliolate. Flowers small, white or pinkish, in terminal racemes. Petals unequal, long-clawed, notched at tip. Stamens 6-many, unequal in length. Receptacle bearing a large, fleshy, 2-lobed gland on the upper side. Ovary sessile or short-stipitate, glandular-viscid. Capsule linear, reticulate-veined. Seeds finely net-veined.

1   Leaflets to 4 mm wide; bracts 3-parted . . . . *P. jamesii*
1   Leaflets 5 mm or more wide; bracts simple . . . . *P. dodecandra*

Polanisia dodecandra (L.) DC.   MAP 586
LARGE CLAMMYWEED   *native*
Stems 2-5 dm tall. **Leaflets** oval, elliptic, or oblong, 2-5 cm long, acute; petiole about as long as blade. **Inflorescence** crowded at anthesis; petals 4-8 mm long, the blade usually exceeding the claw; stamens little exsert, the longest rarely 2 mm longer than the petals. **Capsule** 2-4 cm long; seeds net-veined. July-Sept. —Dry sandy or gravelly soil, especially along streams, also in waste places and along railroads.

Polanisia jamesii (Torr. & Gray) Iltis   MAP 587
JAMES' CLAMMYWEED   ❦*endangered* | *native*
Stems simple or branched, 1-4 dm tall. **Leaflets** linear or linear lance-shaped, 2-4 cm long, short-petioled. **Racemes** short and few-flowered, the flowers appearing axillary; bracts mostly trifoliolate; petals 4, white to ochroleucous, strongly dimorphic, the larger pair 4-5 mm long, the smaller 2-3 mm long; stamens 6-9. **Capsule** flattened, 2-3 cm long. June-July.—A Great Plains species, rare in Minn on sandy or sandy-gravelly deposits associated with eroding slopes and fluvial deposits.

Polanisia dodecandra

Convolvulaceae MORNING-GLORY FAMILY

Herbs (ours), often twining, with alternate simple leaves and small to very large flowers. Flowers regular, perfect, mostly 5-merous. Sepals usually distinct to the base, imbricate, often of unequal size. Corolla rotate, funnelform, salverform, or tubular, entire or deeply to shallowly lobed. Stamens as many as the corolla lobes and alternate with them, inserted near the base of the corolla. Ovary usually 2-3-celled; styles 1 or 2; stigmas linear to capitate. Fruit in most genera a capsule.

1   Plants leafless, non-green, annual parasitic vines. . . . . *Cuscuta*
1   Plants leafy, green, not parasitic 2
    2   Bracts leaf-like, attached just below the calyx and nearly concealing it . . . . *Calystegia*
    2   Bracts small, attached much below the calyx . . . . *Convolvulus arvensis*

CALYSTEGIA *Bindweed*

Much like *Convolvulus*, but the bracts usually large, inserted just beneath the calyx, and more or less

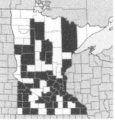

584. Lechea tenuifolia   *585. Cleome serrulata*   *586. Polanisia dodecandra*   *587. Polanisia jamesii*

concealing it; ovary more or less 1-chambered, the partition incomplete; stigmas oblong, cylindric, blunt; flowers usually solitary; ours rhizomatous perennials.

1 Petioles of leaves subtending flowers with petiole more than half length of blade midvein . . . . **C. sepium**
1 Petioles of leaves subtending flowers with petiole much less than half length of midvein . . . . **C. spithamaea**

Calystegia sepium (L.) R. Br.
HEDGE-BINDWEED
MAP 588
native

Stems twining or occasionally trailing, to 3 m long. **Leaves** long-petioled, triangular to oblong in outline, hastate or sagittate, 5-10 cm long, 1/4 to 3/4 as wide. Peduncles 5-15 cm long; bracts ovate or oblong, 1-2 cm long, nearly cordate at the base; corolla pink or white, 4-7 cm long.—Fields and waste places.

Calystegia spithamaea (L.) Pursh
LOW BINDWEED
MAP 589
native

Stems erect, at least to and including the flowering portion, the remainder often elongating and eventually declined. **Leaves** obovate-oblong, 3-8 cm long, acute to obtuse or rounded, at base rounded, truncate, or cordate, always more or less pubescent. Peduncles few, 2-8 cm long, produced 5-20 cm above the base of the plant; bracts oblong or ovate, very rarely cordate at base; corolla white or pink, 4-7 cm long. May-July.—Dry rocky or sandy soil, fields and open woods.

Calystegia sepium

CONVOLVULUS *Bindweed*

Convolvulus arvensis L.
FIELD BINDWEED
MAP 590
introduced (invasive)

Perennial, deeply rooted herb. **Stems** trailing or climbing, to 1 m long, often forming dense tangled mats. **Leaves** variable, triangular to oblong in outline, 2-5 cm long, cordate-ovate or hastate, glabrous or finely pubescent, the basal lobes spreading or descending. **Flowers** borne mostly 1-2 together on axillary peduncles exceeding the subtending leaves; bracts borne 5-20 mm below the flower; sepals elliptic, 3-5 mm long; corolla funnelform, usually white, sometimes pink, 15-20 mm long; stamens included, inserted near the base of the corolla. **Capsule** globose, 2-4-celled. May-Sept.—Native of Europe; naturalized in fields, roadsides, and waste places; often a troublesome weed.

Convolvulus arvensis

CUSCUTA *Dodder*

Ours annual, yellow or brown, parasitic, twining vines. Leaves reduced to minute scales. Flowers small, yellow or whitish, in cymose clusters, mostly 4-5-merous. Corolla campanulate to cylindric, lobed. Stamens inserted at the sinuses of the corolla, usually shorter than its lobes. Opposite each stamen near the base of the corolla tube is (in almost all species) a usually toothed or fringed scale. Ovary 2-celled. Fruit a capsule. Only a few species of the genus cause serious damage to crop plants, but all members of the genus are considered noxious weeds. Dodder seeds germinate in the soil like autonomous plants. If young plants contact a suitable species, they soon attach themselves to a host-plant by means of numerous haustoria borne along the stem. Connection with the soil is then soon lost. Our species bloom in late summer and most of them live on a wide variety of host-plants. Identification of dodders is easiest using flowering rather than fruiting plants, although the corolla and stamens often persist around the capsule. Distribution of our species is not well known.

588. Calystegia sepium   *589. Calystegia spithamaea*   *590. Convolvulus arvensis*

ADDITIONAL SPECIES
Cuscuta indecora Choisy (Big-seed alfalfa dodder, MAP 591); n Minnesota.

1 Each flower subtended by 1 or several bracts; sepals free to their bases 2
  2 Flowers without pedicels, in dense, rope-like clusters . . . . **C. glomerata**
  2 Flowers on pedicels in loose panicles . . . . **C. cuspidata**
1 Individual flowers without bracts; sepals joined at base 3
  3 Flowers 5-parted 4
    4 Corolla lobes acute . . . . **C. pentagona**
    4 Corolla lobes obtuse . . . . **C. gronovii**
  3 Flowers 4-parted 5
    5 Corolla lobes obtuse or rounded . . . . **C. cephalanthi**
    5 Corolla lobes acute 6
      6 Tips of corolla lobes erect . . . . **C. polygonorum**
      6 Tips of corolla lobes bent inward . . . . **C. coryli**

Cuscuta cephalanthi Engelm.
BUTTONBUSH DODDER

MAP 592
native

Flowers mostly 4-merous, about 3 mm long, sessile or short-pediceled in loose clusters; calyx shorter than the corolla tube, its lobes obtuse; corolla lobes ovate, obtuse, erect to spreading, about half as long as the tube.

Cuscuta coryli Engelm.
HAZEL DODDER

MAP 593
native

Flowers 4-merous, about 2.5 mm long, in dense or loose clusters, some or all distinctly pediceled; calyx about half as long as the corolla, its lobes acute; corolla cylindric, its lobes narrowly triangular with acute inflexed tips, about as long as the tube.

Cuscuta cuspidata Engelm.
CUSP DODDER

(NO MAP)
native

Flowers 3-4 mm long, pediceled or subsessile in loose open panicles. Bracts 1-3, broadly round-ovate, appressed, much shorter than the calyx; sepals ovate, very obtuse, sometimes minutely cuspidate; corolla lobes ovate, about 2 mm long. **Capsule** globose or depressed-globose, 2.5-3.5 mm wide. Ramsey County.

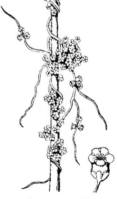
Cuscuta coryli

Cuscuta glomerata Choisy
ROPE DODDER

MAP 594
native

Flowers in dense, twisted, rope-like masses, sessile or nearly so, 4-5 mm long. Bracts oval or oblong, erect or loosely ascending, about equaling the calyx, their tips squarrose or recurved; corolla lobes ovate, subacute, about 2 mm long. **Capsule** concealed by the withering corolla, globose with a short terminal neck.

Cuscuta gronovii Willd.
COMMON DODDER

MAP 595
native

Flowers 2.5-4 mm long, sessile or subsessile in dense clusters; calyx short, its lobes broadly round-ovate to subrotund, overlapping, scarcely reaching the middle of the corolla tube; corolla lobes broadly ovate, obtuse, spreading, shorter than the tube. Scales commonly copiously fringed, reaching to the sinuses of the corolla. Styles nearly as long as the ovary. **Capsule** commonly globose-ovoid, about 3 mm wide; seeds about 1.5 mm long.

Cuscuta gronovii

591. *Cuscuta indecora*

592. *Cuscuta cephalanthi*   593. *Cuscuta coryli*   594. *Cuscuta glomerata*

Cuscuta pentagona Engelm. MAP 596
FIELD DODDER *native*
Flowers 1.5-2 mm, long, short-pediceled in loose clusters; calyx about as long as
the corolla tube, its lobes very broadly ovate or depressed, often broader than
long; corolla lobes usually spreading, about equaling the broad tube, the acute
tips often inflexed. *Found on a wide variety of hosts.*

Cuscuta polygonorum Engelm. MAP 597
SMARTWEED DODDER *native*
Flowers mostly 4-merous, about 2 mm long, sessile or subsessile in small but
dense clusters; calyx as long as or longer than the corolla tube, its lobes very
obtuse; corolla lobes triangular, acute, erect or ascending, commonly as long as
the tube or longer. Often on *Persicaria*, but also on *Cephalanthus* and likely other
genera. *Distinctive among our species by its very short style.*

Cuscuta pentagona

Cornaceae DOGWOOD FAMILY

CORNUS *Dogwood*
Shrubs, or herbaceous shoots from a woody rhizome in bunchberry (*Cornus canadensis*). Leaves
opposite, simple, entire. Flowers in a rounded or flat-topped cluster, 4-parted, sepals and petals small.
Fruit a berrylike drupe with 1-2 hard seeds.

1 Plants herbaceous from a woody rhizome, less than 3 dm tall; leaves whorled . . . . *C. canadensis*
1 Taller shrubs, 5 dm or more tall; leaves opposite or alternate 2
  2 Leaves alternate on stems . . . . *C. alternifolia*
  2 Leaves opposite 3
    3 Twigs yellow or yellow-green with purple spots; leaves round in outline or nearly so . . . . *C. rugosa*
    3 Twigs not yellow, or if yellow not spotted; leaves longer than wide 4
      4 Fruit white; young twigs densely short-hairy . . . . *C. obliqua*
      4 Fruit blue; young twigs smooth or nearly so 5
        5 Twigs gray; leaves with fewer than 5 pairs of lateral veins . . . . *C. racemosa*
        5 Twigs red; leaves with 5 or more pairs of lateral veins . . . . *C. alba*

Cornus alba L. MAP 598
RED OSIER-DOGWOOD *native*
  *Cornus seri*cea L.; *Cornus stolonifera* Michx.
Many-stemmed shrub, 1-3 m tall, forming thickets; **branches** upright or prostrate
and rooting; **twigs** and young branches red; pith white. **Leaves** opposite, green,
ovate to oval, mostly 5-15 cm long and 2-7 cm wide, tapered to a tip, soft hairy
on underside; margins entire; petioles to 2.5 cm long. **Flowers** small, white, many
in flat-topped or slightly rounded clusters. **Fruit** a round, white or blue-tinged,
berrylike drupe, 6-9 mm wide. May-Aug.—Swamps, marshes, shores,
streambanks, floodplain forests, shrub thickets, calcareous fens; also on sand
dunes.

Cornus alternifolia L. f. MAP 599
PAGODA DOGWOOD; ALTERNATE-LEAF DOGWOOD *native*
  Swida alternifolia (L. f.) Small
Shrub, to 5 m tall; **twigs** red-green or brown, somewhat shiny, alternate on stems,
pith white. **Leaves** alternate, sometimes crowded and appearing whorled near

Cornus alba

595. *Cuscuta gronovii*   596. *Cuscuta pentagona*   597. *Cuscuta polygonorum*   598. *Cornus alba*

ends of stems, oval to ovate, 5-12 cm long and 3-7 cm wide, tapered to a sharp tip, underside finely hairy; lateral veins 4-5 pairs, these curving toward tip of blade; margins entire; petioles to 5 cm long. **Flowers** small, creamy-white, in crowded, flat-topped or rounded clusters at ends of stems. **Fruit** a round, blue, berrylike drupe, 6 mm wide, atop a red stalk. May-July.—Swamps, thickets, streambanks and springs; also in drier deciduous and mixed forests.

Cornus canadensis L.
MAP 600
BUNCHBERRY; DWARF CORNEL
native

Perennial from horizontal, woody rhizomes, often forming large colonies. **Stems** erect, green, 1-2 dm tall, with a pair of small bracts on lower stem, topped with a whorl-like cluster of 4-6 leaves. **Leaves** oval to obovate, 4-7 cm long, tapered at both ends; lateral veins 2-3 pairs, arising from midvein below middle of blade; margins entire; petioles short or absent. **Flowers** small, yellow-green or creamy-white in a single cluster at end of a stalk 1-3 cm long; flowers surrounded by 4 white or pinkish, petal-like showy bracts, 1-2 cm long, these soon deciduous. **Fruit** a cluster of round, bright red berrylike drupes, the drupes 6-8 mm wide. June-July.—Cedar swamps, thickets and moist conifer forests, often on hummocks or rotting logs; also in drier, mixed conifer-deciduous forests.

Cornus alternifolia

Cornus obliqua Raf.
MAP 601
SILKY DOGWOOD
native
  Cornus amomum P. Mill. subsp. *obliqua* (Raf.) J.S. Wilson

Shrub, 1-3 m tall; older **branches** red and gray-streaked, young **twigs** gray, finely hairy; pith brown. **Leaves** opposite, oval to ovate, 5-12 cm long and 2-5 cm wide, usually less than half as wide as long, tapered to a sharp tip, lateral veins 4-6 on each side, underside finely hairy; margins entire; petioles 1-2 cm long, often curved and causing the leaves to droop. **Flowers** small, creamy-white, in flat-topped or slightly rounded, hairy clusters. **Fruit** a round, blue or blue-white, berrylike drupe, 8 mm wide, atop a long stalk. June-July (our latest flowering dogwood).—Conifer swamps, marshes, bogs, calcareous fens, shores, streambanks, wet dunes.

Cornus canadensis

Cornus racemosa Lam.
MAP 602
GRAY DOGWOOD
native
  Cornus foemina subsp. *racemosa* (Lam.) J.S. Wilson

Shrub, 1-3 m tall, often forming dense thickets; **twigs** red, becoming gray or light brown; pith usually brown. **Leaves** opposite, lance-shaped to oval, 4-9 cm long and 2-4 cm wide, abruptly tapered to a rounded tip, underside with short hairs; lateral veins 3 or 4 on each side of midvein; margins entire; petioles to 1 cm long. **Flowers** small, creamy-white, ill-scented, in numerous, open, elongated clusters. **Fruit** a round, berrylike drupe, at first lead-colored, becoming white, 5 mm wide, on red stalks. June-July.—Lakeshores, streambanks, swamps, thickets, marshes, moist woods, low prairie.

Cornus racemosa

Cornus rugosa Lam.
MAP 603
ROUND-LEAF DOGWOOD
native

Shrub 1-3 m tall, the younger **branches** yellow-green, often mottled with red; pith white. **Leaves** ovate to rotund, usually 7-12 cm long, abruptly acuminate, broadly cuneate or usually rounded at base, minutely scaberulous above, softly white-pubescent beneath with erect, curled or curved hairs usually 0.5-1 mm long; lateral

Cornus rugosa

599. Cornus alternifolia   *600. Cornus canadensis*   *601. Cornus obliqua*   *602. Cornus racemosa*

veins 7 or 8 on each side. **Inflorescence** flat or slightly convex. **Drupes** light blue, about 6 mm wide. May-July.—Moist or dry, sandy or rocky soil.

Crassulaceae STONECROP FAMILY

Usually succulent plants of diverse habit and aspect. Leaves simple. Flowers usually cymose, regular, 4–5-merous or occasionally more, usually perfect.

1   Aquatic annual; flowers 4- merous; rare in Rock and St. Louis counties . . . . *Crassula aquatica*
1   Succulent terrestrial perennials; flowers 4-5-merous 2
   2   Leaves cauline, not forming rosettes, dying back in winter to rootstock or tuberous base; leaf blades laminar, margins entire or toothed; rare in se Minn . . . . *Rhodiola integrifolia*
   2   Leaves clustered in persistent rosettes or not, sometimes with scattered, smaller, cauline leaves; leaf blades flat to terete, margins entire or irregularly toothed; introduced species . . . . *Sedum*

CRASSULA *Pygmyweed*

Crassula aquatica (L.) Schönland   MAP 604
WATER PYGMYWEED   ❤'*threatened | native*
   Tillaea aquatica L.

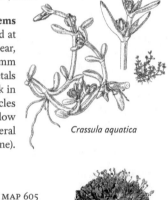

Aquatic annual herb, sometimes stranded on muddy shores. **Stems** decumbent, later ± erect if stranded, reddish in age, usually branched at base, to 15 cm long and rooting at basal nodes. **Leaves** oblanceolate to linear, 2-6 mm long. **Inflorescence** lax; **flowers** one per node; pedicels 1-20 mm long; flowers 4-merous; seas to 1.5 mm long, tip obtuse to rounded; petals ovate to oblong, 1-2 mm long, whitish in the deepwater form and pink in the dwarf form. **Fruit** an erect, oblong follicle, 6-17-seeded; old follicles spreading; seeds dull, minutely rugulose. July-Aug.—In muck in shallow water (to 1 m deep) of lakes; in water and muddy margins of ephemeral rainwater pools (plants disappear when the mud dries, usually by late June).

Crassula aquatica

RHODIOLA *Rosewort*

Rhodiola integrifolia Raf.   MAP 605
LEDGE STONECROP   ❤'*endangered | native*
   Sedum integrifolium (Raf.) A. Nelson
   Sedum rosea var. *integrifolium* (Raf.) A. Berger

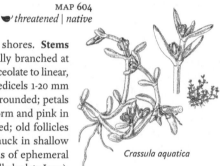

Succulent, glabrous perennial, with thick, scaly rhizomes; plants dioecious (male and female flowers on separate plants); **stems** to 50 cm tall. **Leaves** usually bright green, sometimes glaucous, varying from elliptic to ovate to linear, to 5 cm long and 1.5 cm wide; margins entire or toothed. **Inflorescence** densely flowered flat-topped clusters (cymes); pedicels ca. 2 mm; **flowers** 4-5-merous; sepals lanceolate to ovate, 1.5-3 mm long; petals mostly dark red, sometimes yellowish at base or yellow with upper 1/3 red, 1.5-5 mm long, shorter than the stamens. **Fruit** a follicle 4-9 mm long, with a spreading beak. Seeds winged, 1-3 mm long. June.—Shallow cracks and moist ledges on north-facing dolomite cliffs in se Minn. There are 3 western North American subspecies, but none of these are present in Minn; ours are subsp. *leedyi* (Rosendahl & Moore) Kartesz; federally listed as threatened, and known from 7 locations (4 in Minn, 3 in New York).

Rhodiola integrifolia

603. *Cornus rugosa*   604. *Crassula aquatica*   605. *Rhodiola integrifolia*   606. *Sedum acre*

SEDUM *Stonecrop*

Succulent perennial herbs. Leaves thick or terete, alternate, opposite, or whorled. Flowers yellow or red-purple, 4-5-merous. Sepals united at base. Petals separate, often lance-shaped. Stamens 8 or 10, the epipetalous ones usually adnate to the petals at base. Nectarial scales short, at the base of the ovaries. Pistils distinct or nearly so, tapering into a stout style. Fruit a group of follicles; seeds numerous, small.

ADDITIONAL SPECIES

• *Sedum aizoon* L. (Orange stonecrop); native to Asia; rarely escaped from cultivation in Lake Superior region.

• *Sedum spurium* M.Bieb. (Two-row stonecrop); native to the Caucasus Mtns; Lake and St. Louis counties.

1   Petals deep pink . . . . *S. purpureum*
1   Petals yellow . . . . *S. acre*

Sedum acre L.   MAP 606
MOSSY STONECROP   *introduced (naturalized)*

Perennial from creeping stems, forming dense mats. **Flowering stems** 5-10 cm long. **Leaves** crowded, imbricate, terete, ovoid, 2-5 mm long, blunt. Inflorescence of a few short branched cymes. **Flowers** yellow, 8-10 mm wide; petals lance-shaped, spreading, about twice as long as the sepals. June-July.—Native of Eurasia; cultivated and escaped in dry, sandy soil.

Sedum purpureum (L.) J.A. Schultes   MAP 607
LIVE FOREVER   *introduced*
   Hylotelephium telephium (L.) H. Ohba.
   Sedum telephium L. subsp. *purpureum* (L.) Schinz & Keller

Perennial from a thick caudex. **Stems** stout, erect, 3-6 dm tall. **Leaves** fleshy, green or bluish green, not glaucous, oblong to obovate, 3-6 cm long, commonly with several to many conspicuous irregular teeth, varying to entire. **Inflorescence** repeatedly branched, convex to hemispheric, the branchlets narrowly winged. **Flowers** densely crowded, red-purple, 6-8 mm wide; sepals triangular, about a third as long as the ovate lance-shaped petals. Late summer.—A variable Eurasian species, cultivated for ornament and occasionally escaped.

Sedum acre

Cucurbitaceae CUCUMBER FAMILY

Annual or perennial vines, trailing or climbing by tendrils, with small to large, mostly white or yellow or greenish flowers, and simple, alternate, often lobed leaves. Flowers monoecious or dioecious, regular. Calyx 4-6 (usually 5)-lobed, sometimes to the very base of the tube. Stamens 1-5, distinct or wholly or partly united, usually 3. Ovary 1- or 3-celled; styles united, with a thick stigma. Fruit a dry or fleshy pepo, few-many-seeded.

1   Leaves divided about halfway to petiole; corolla 6-lobed; fruit 3-5 cm long, inflated, with weak prickles, 4-seeded
    . . . . *Echinocystis lobata*
1   Leaves divided less than half distance to petiole; corolla 5-lobed; fruit to 1.5 cm long, bur-like, spiny, 1-seeded .
    . . . . *Sicyos angulatus*

ECHINOCYSTIS *Wild Cucumber*

Echinocystis lobata (Michx.) Torr. & Gray   MAP 608
WILD CUCUMBER   *native*

Annual vining herb, to 5 m or more long. **Leaves** round in outline, with 3-7 (usually 5) sharp, triangular lobes; petioles 3-8 cm long. **Flowers** white; **staminate flowers** 8-10 mm wide, with lance-shaped lobes, in long, upright racemes; **pistillate flowers** 1 to several on short stalks from leaf axils. **Fruit** green, ovate, inflated, 3-5 cm long, with soft prickles. Aug-Sept.—Floodplain forests, wet deciduous forests, streambanks, thickets, and waste ground.

Echinocystis lobata

SICYOS *Bur-Cucumber*

Sicyos angulatus L.   MAP 609
ONE-SEED BUR-CUCUMBER   *native*
Annual vining herb, to 2 m long. **Stems** angled, sticky-hairy, with branched
tendrils. **Leaves** round in outline, with 3-5 shallow, toothed lobes, rough on both
sides; petioles hairy, 3-10 cm long. **Flowers** monoecious, 5-merous, green or
white; **staminate flowers** 8-10 mm wide, 5-lobed, in corymbiform racemes on
stalks 10 cm or more long; **pistillate flowers** in small capitate clusters on stalks to
8 cm long. **Fruit** yellow, ovate, 1.5 cm long, hairy and covered by prickly bristles.
Aug-Sept.—Floodplain forests, wet deciduous forests, streambanks, thickets and
waste ground.

Sicyos angulatus

Dipsacaceae TEASEL FAMILY

Herbs. Leaves opposite, simple or divided. Flowers in dense heads subtended by a many-leaved
involucre; each flower also often subtended by a receptacular bract. Flowers perfect or polygamo-
monoecious, more or less zygomorphic, 4-5-merous. Sepals minute, but sometimes with conspicuous
appendages. Corolla tubular to narrowly campanulate. Stamens 4 or 2. Ovary 1-celled; style 1, slender.
Included in **Caprifoliaceae** *in the 2009 Angiosperm Phylogeny Group III system.*

1   Stems prickly . . . . *Dipsacus*
1   Stems not prickly . . . . *Knautia arvensis*

DIPSACUS *Teasel*

Coarse, tall, biennial or perennial herbs, little branched, with prickly stems. Leaves large, sessile or
connate. Flowers small, in dense ovoid to cylindric heads. Calyx short, 4-angled or 4-lobed. Corollas
4-lobed, the marginal ones not enlarged. Bracts of the involucre linear, often elongate. Receptacular
bracts ovate or lance-shaped, acuminate into an awn surpassing the flowers. Involucel 4-angled,
truncate or 4-toothed at the summit. True calyx very short, hairy, without appendages.

1   Flowers white; leaves deeply pinnately lobed . . . . *D. laciniatus*
1   Flowers purple; leaves not divided . . . . *D. fullonum*

Dipsacus fullonum L.   (NO MAP)
FULLER'S TEASEL   *introduced (naturalized)*
    Dipsacus sylvestris Huds.
Stems stout, erect, 0.5-2 m. tall, increasingly prickly above. **Basal leaves** oblong
lance-shaped, crenate; **stem leaves** lance-shaped, entire, sessile or connate, prickly
on the midvein beneath. **Heads** ovoid to cylindric, 3-10 cm long, terminating long
naked peduncles; involucral bracts curved-ascending, linear, prickly, some of
them surpassing the head; bracts of the head exceeding the flowers, ending in a
straight awn. Calyx silky, 1 mm long; corolla slender, pubescent, 10-15 mm long,
the tube white, the short (1 mm) lobes pale purple. July-Sept.—Naturalized from
Europe; roadsides and waste ground; Winona County.

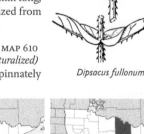

Dipsacus laciniatus L.   MAP 610
CUT-LEAF TEASEL   *introduced (naturalized)*
Resembling *D. fullonum* in habit and flowers. **Stem leaves** irregularly pinnately
lobed or divided, more or less bristly. July-Aug. Native of Europe.

Dipsacus fullonum

607. *Sedum purpureum*   608. *Echinocystis lobata*   609. *Sicyos angulatus*   610. *Dipsacus laciniatus*

KNAUTIA *Bluebuttons*

Knautia arvensis (L.) Coult.   MAP 611
BLUEBUTTONS   *introduced*
Perennial herb. **Stems** erect, pubescent, 4-8 dm tall, the upper internodes
progressively longer. **Leaves** pinnately divided into 5-15 narrowly lance-shaped
segments, the upper pairs progressively reduced. **Flowers** in dense hemispheric
heads terminating elongate peduncles; heads 2-4 cm wide; involucral bracts ovate
lance-shaped, 10-15 mm long; calyx with 8-12 setaceous teeth; corolla lilac-purple,
4-lobed, more or less irregular, the marginal ones distinctly so, 9-12 mm long.
Achenes hairy, 4-ribbed; calyx-limb about 1 mm long, bearing 8-12 setaceous
appendages. June-Sept.—Native of Europe; fields, roadsides, waste places.

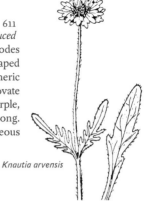

Knautia arvensis

Droseraceae SUNDEW FAMILY

DROSERA *Sundew*

Perennial herbs. Leaves all from base of plant, covered with stalked, sticky glands that trap and digest
insects. Flowers white, several, on 1 side of erect, leafless stalks, the stalks nodding at tip; with 5
petals and 5 sepals; stamens mostly 5, styles 3. Fruit a dry, many-seeded capsule.

HYBRIDS
Drosera × obovata Mert. & Koch (Obovate-leaved sundew), hybrid between *D. anglica* and *D. rotundifolia*;
disjunct from west coast; in Minn known from Beltrami County.

1   Leaves widely spreading, the blades round, wider than long .... *D. rotundifolia*
1   Leaves upright, blades linear or broad at tip and tapered to base, longer than wide 2
  2   Leaf blades linear, 10-20 times longer than wide; young petals pink......................... *D. linearis*
  2   Leaf blades broad near tip and narrowed to base, 2-7 times longer than wide; young petals white 3
    3   Blades 2-3 times longer than wide, petioles without hairs; flower stalks from side of plant base and curving
        upward .... *D. intermedia*
    3   Blades 5-7 times longer than wide, petioles with some hairs; flower stalks erect from center of plant base
        .... *D. anglica*

Drosera anglica Huds.   MAP 612
ENGLISH SUNDEW   *native*
Perennial insectivorous herb. **Leaf blades** obovate to spatula-shaped, 15-35 mm
long and 3-4 mm wide, upper surface covered with gland-tipped hairs; petioles 3-
6 cm long, smooth or with few glandular hairs. **Flowers** 1-9 in a racemelike cluster
atop a stalk 6-25 cm tall; flowers 6-7 mm wide; sepals 5-6 mm long; petals white,
6 mm long, spatula-shaped. **Seeds** black, 1 mm long, with fine lines. June-Aug.
—Floating sphagnum mats, calcareous fens, wet areas between dunes. *Similar to*
Drosera intermedia but rarely occurring together; plants of D. anglica are generally
larger, with shorter petioles (1-3x as long as blades vs. 2.5-3.5x as long in D. intermedia).

Drosera anglica

Drosera intermedia Hayne   MAP 613
SPOON-LEAF SUNDEW   *native*
Perennial insectivorous herb. **Leaves** in a basal rosette and also usually along
lower stem; spatula-shaped, 2-4 mm wide, upper surface covered with long,
gland-tipped hairs; petioles smooth, 2-5 cm long. **Flowers** on stalks to 20 cm tall;
sepals 3-4 mm long; petals white, 4-5 mm long. **Seeds** red-brown, to 1 mm long,
covered with small bumps. July-Sept.—Low spots in open bogs, sandy shores,
often in shallow water.

Drosera linearis Goldie   MAP 614
SLENDER-LEAF SUNDEW   *native*
Perennial insectivorous herb. **Leaf blades** linear, 2-5 cm long and 2 mm wide;
petioles smooth, 3-7 cm long. **Flowers** 1-4 atop stalks 6-15 cm tall; flowers 6-8
mm wide; sepals 4-5 mm long; petals obovate, 6 mm long, white. **Seeds** black,
less than 1 mm long, with small craterlike pits on surface. June-Aug.—Calcareous
fens, wet areas between dunes near Great Lakes; rarely in sphagnum moss.

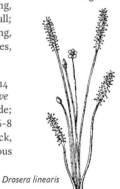

Drosera linearis

Drosera rotundifolia L.
ROUND-LEAF SUNDEW

MAP 615
native

Small, perennial insectivorous herb. **Leaf blades** more or less round, wider than long, 2-10 mm long and as wide or wider, covered with long, red, gland-tipped hairs; abruptly tapered to a petiole longer than blade; petioles 2-5 cm long covered with gland-tipped hairs. **Flowers** 2-15 in a more or less 1-sided, racemelike cluster, on a leafless stalk 10-30 cm tall; flowers 4-7 mm wide, sepals 5, 4-5 mm long; petals white to pink, longer than sepals; stamens 5, shorter than petals. **Seeds** light brown, shiny and with fine lines, 1-1.5 mm long. July-Aug.—Swamps and open bogs, usually in sphagnum; wet sandy shores and openings.

Drosera rotundifolia

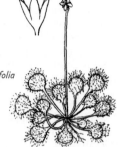

Elaeagnaceae OLEASTER FAMILY

Shrubs or trees. Leaves opposite or alternate, covered with small scales (lepidote). Flowers small, solitary or clustered, perfect or unisexual, regular, usually 4-merous. Hypanthium in the staminate flowers saucer-shaped to cup-shaped, in perfect or pistillate flowers prolonged into a short or elongate tube and persistently enclosing the ovary. Sepals present, often colored. Petals none. Stamens inserted at or just below the summit of the hypanthium, as many or twice as many as the sepals. Ovary 1-celled. Fruit drupe-like, the dry mature ovary enclosed by the base of the hypanthium.

1 Leaves alternate; stamens 4 .... *Elaeagnus*
1 Leaves opposite; stamens 8 .... *Shepherdia*

ELAEAGNUS *Russian-Olive; Silver-Berry*

Shrubs or small trees. Leaves alternate. Flowers perfect or unisexual in small lateral clusters on twigs of the current year. Hypanthium tubular, in the perfect or pistillate flowers constricted above the ovary. Disk present or none. Stamens 4, inserted near the summit of the hypanthium, scarcely exsert.

1 Shrub to 4 m tall; upper leaf surface green and nearly glabrous .... *E. umbellata*
1 Shrub or small tree to 7 m tall; upper and lower leaf surfaces covered with silvery scales 2
    2 Leaves lanceolate, 3-8 x longer than wide; branchlets and petioles silvery-gray; small branches often spine-tipped .... *E. angustifolia*
    2 Leaves oblong, 2-3 x longer than wide; branchlets and petioles with golden-brown scales; branches not spine-tipped .... *E. commutata*

Elaeagnus angustifolia L.
RUSSIAN-OLIVE

MAP 616
introduced

Shrub or small tree to 7 m tall, the twigs densely silvery. **Leaves** narrowly elliptic, 3-10 cm long, silvery on both sides. **Flowers** short-pediceled in small clusters at the base of twigs of the current season, 12-15 mm long, densely silvery; sepals spreading, about 4 mm long, yellow within; the style surrounded by a short tubular disk just above the constriction of the hypanthium. **Fruit** yellow with silvery scales. June-July.—Native of Eurasia; planted for ornament and in shelterbelts, and escaped to fields, riverbanks, and other places, especially in w Minnesota.

Elaeagnus angustifolia

611. *Knautia arvensis*   612. *Drosera anglica*   613. *Drosera intermedia*   614. *Drosera linearis*

Elaeagnus commutata Bernh. ex Rydb.
SILVERBERRY
MAP 617
native

Shrub or rarely treelike, to 5 m tall, compactly branched, unarmed; **young twigs** with brown-scurfy scales, **older branches** dark gray. **Leaves** light green, densely silvery scrufy on both sides, ovate to oblong, 2-8 cm long, entire, the scurfy-brown scales extending from the petiole on the underside of the leaf blade along the midvein to ca. 1/ 2 the distance to the tip; petiole 2-6 mm long. **Flowers** fragrant, 1-4 in lateral and axillary clusters near the base of twigs of the current season; sepals 4, joined below and enclosing the pistil, 6-10 mm long. the lobes 2-4 mm long, spreading at maturity, yellow on the inside, the outside with a dense silvery-gray pubescence; stamens 4, alternate with the lobes. **Fruit** ovate to ellipsoid, 1-1.5 cm long, the covering dry and mealy, the achene striate. June-July. —Dry to moist sandy soils, streambanks, hillsides.

Elaeagnus commutata

Elaeagnus umbellata Thunb.
AUTUMN OLIVE
(NO MAP)
introduced (invasive)

Shrubby tree to 5 m. **Leaves** soon green and glabrescent above; hypanthium tube about twice as long as the sepals. **Fruit** red, finely dotted with pale scales, juicy and edible, 6-8 mm wide, on pedicels about 1 cm long. May-June.—Native of e Asia, originally introduced as an ornamental shrub and for wildlife habitat, now spreading to many dry and wet habitats; in Minn, reported from Brown County.

Elaeagnus umbellata

SHEPHERDIA *Buffalo-Berry*

Shrubs or small trees. Leaves opposite, usually silvery and scaly (lepidote). Flowers dioecious, in small clusters on twigs of the previous season, the pistillate flowers usually few. Sepals 4, greenish yellow within. Stamens 8, alternating with the lobes of the disk. Fruit a red or yellow-red berry.

1   Upper surface of leaf green and nearly glabrous . . . . **S. canadensis**
1   Upper and lower leaf surfaces covered with silvery scales . . . . **S. argentea**

Shepherdia argentea (Pursh) Nutt.
SILVER BUFFALO-BERRY
MAP 619
native

Widely branched shrub or small tree to 6 m tall, the stiff branches often ending in short stout spines. **Leaves** silvery-lepidote on both sides, oblong lance-shaped to oblong, 2-5 cm long, usually 7-12 mm wide, obtuse at the tip, narrowed to the base. **Flowers** similar to those of the preceding species, usually somewhat smaller with erect sepals. **Fruit** scarlet, about 5 mm long, edible but sour.—April-May. Riverbanks. *Native of Great Plains, reaching eastern range limit in Minnesota.*

Shepherdia canadensis (L.) Nutt.
RUSSET BUFFALO-BERRY
MAP 620
native

Unarmed shrub 1-3 m tall. **Leaves** ovate lance-shaped to ovate, varying to narrowly lance-shaped or elliptic, 3-5 cm long, obtuse, obtuse to rounded or subcordate at base, green and nearly glabrous above, densely lepidote beneath. **Staminate flowers** 4-6 mm wide; sepals ovate, spreading, much exceeding the erect stamens; **pistillate flowers** similar, the mouth of the hypanthium closed by a dense tomentum. **Fruit** yellowish red, inedible, 5-7 mm long. April-May.—Dry, sandy or stony, calcareous soil.

Shepherdia argentea

615. *Drosera rotundifolia*   616. *Elaeagnus angustifolia*   618. *Elaeagnus commutata*   619. *Shepherdia argentea*

Elatinaceae WATERWORT FAMILY

ELATINE *Waterwort*

Small, branched, annual herbs of shallow water, shores and mud flats. Leaves simple, opposite, entire or toothed, with small membranous stipules. Flowers small, 1 to several from leaf axils, perfect; sepals, petals and stamens 2-3 (ours); styles 3; ovary superior, 3-4-chambered. Fruit a capsule with numerous small seeds.

1 Flowers with 2 sepals and 2 petals, seeds all at base of fruit . . . . ***E. minima***
1 Flowers with 3 sepals and 3 petals; seeds at differing levels in fruit . . . . ***E. rubella***

Elatine minima (Nutt.) Fisch. & C.A. Mey.
SMALL WATERWORT

MAP 621
native

Annual herb, forming small mosslike mats on mud; plants small, smooth, with branches to 5 cm long. **Leaves** opposite, oblong to obovate, rounded at tip, to 4 mm long, petioles absent. **Flowers** small, single and stalkless in leaf axils, sepals 2, petals 2. **Fruit** a round capsule; seeds with rows of small, rounded pits.— Shallow water and wet shores along lakes and ponds, usually where sandy or mucky.

Elatine minima

Elatine rubella Rydb.
RED-STEM WATERWORT
Elatine triandra auct. non Schkuhr p.p.

MAP 622
native

Annual herb; plants small, matted, to 15 cm long, somewhat fleshy, smooth, branched from base, the branches sprawling or floating, often rooting at nodes. **Leaves** opposite, linear to obovate, 3-10 mm long and 1-3 mm wide, margins entire, petioles absent; stipules very small. **Flowers** small, single and stalkless in leaf axils, 1.5-2 mm wide, sepals 3, petals 3. **Fruit** a round capsule, 1-2 mm wide; seeds 0.5 mm long, ridged and with tiny angled pits. July-Sept.—Mud flats or in shallow water of lakes and ponds.

Ericaceae HEATH FAMILY

Ericaceae now includes former members of Monotropaceae and Pyrolaceae. The traditional Ericaceae are shrubs or scarcely woody shrubs. Leaves evergreen or deciduous, mostly alternate, simple, with entire or toothed margins. Flowers usually perfect (with both staminate and pistillate parts), urn- or vase-shaped, mostly white, pink, or cream-colored; stamens as many (or 2x as many) as petals. Fruit a berry or dry capsule.

Former **Monotropaceae** (*Monotropa, Pterospora*) are mycotropic perennial herbs without chlorophyll, variously white to pink, red, purple, yellow or brown in color. Leaves much-reduced, scale-like, alternate. Flowers solitary or in a bracteate raceme, regular, perfect, mostly 4-5-merous; petals distinct or connate into a lobed tube, commonly about the same color as the stem; stamens mostly 6-10, mostly twice as many as the sepals or petals, distinct or shortly connate at base. Fruit a capsule or berry; seeds numerous and tiny.

Former **Pyrolaceae** (*Moneses, Orthilia, Pyrola*) are perennial herbs or half-shrubs, most dependent on wood-rotting fungi (mycotrophic). Leaves alternate to sometimes opposite or nearly whorled, often shiny, evergreen or deciduous. Flowers perfect, 5-parted, waxy and nodding. Fruit a capsule.

620. *Shepherdia canadensis*   621. *Elatine minima*   622. *Elatine rubella*   623. *Andromeda glaucophylla*

1 Leaves reduced to non-green scales; plants entirely white, yellow, reddish, orange, or maroon . . . . . . *Monotropa*
1 Leaves green (these sometimes small and needle- or scale-like); plants normal green color 2
  2 Leaves needle-like, less than 1.5 mm wide . . . . *Empetrum*
  2 Leaves with expanded flat blades, more than 1.5 mm wide 3
    3 Leaves in a basal rosette; plants herbaceous 4
      4 Style ± strongly bent downward, at least 4 mm long; inflorescence a ± symmetrical raceme. . . . *Pyrola*
      4 Style straight, short or long; inflorescence various (usually 1-flowered or a 1-sided raceme) 5
        5 Inflorescence 1-flowered, the corolla 15-20 (-22) mm broad, flat (petals widely spreading); anthers prolonged into a short cylindrical tube below the pore; valves of capsule glabrous; style (not including prominent stigma lobes) 3-5 mm long . . . . *Moneses uniflora*
        5 Inflorescence racemose, the corolla 3-7 mm broad, ± bell-shaped (petals close about reproductive parts); anthers not prolonged into tubes; valves of capsule with cobwebby fibers on the margins when dehiscing; style various (but stigma only very shallowly lobed) 6
          6 Raceme 1-sided; style 2.5-6 (-6.5) mm long, protruding at maturity from the corolla; sepal margins finely toothed or erose . . . . *Orthilia secunda*
          6 Raceme symmetrical; style ca. 1.5 mm or less long, scarcely if at all protruding beyond the corolla; sepal margins entire . . . . *Pyrola minor*
    3 Leaves opposite, alternate, or whorled; plants woody (sometimes small subshrubs woody only at the base or prostrate creepers) 7
      7 Leaves opposite or whorled; flowers 8-20 mm broad 8
        8 Leaves coarsely few-toothed; subshrub woody only at base, forming colonies by rhizomes . . . . *Chimaphila umbellata*
        8 Leaves entire; true woody, clump forming shrub . . . . *Kalmia polifolia*
      7 Leaves all alternate; flowers in most species less than 8 mm wide 9
        9 Leaves narrow, linear to linear lance-shaped, more than 7 times longer than wide; margins revolute . . . . *Andromeda glaucophylla*
        9 Leaves ovate to oblong; margins various 10
          10 Leaves less than 7 times longer than wide, dark green and leathery on upper surface, densely covered with woolly rust-red hairs on underside; margins revolute . . . . *Rhododendron groenlandicum*
          10 Leaves never both revolute and with rust colored hairs on underside 11
            11 Leaves scurfy, densely covered with scales, especially on upper surface . . . . *Chamaedaphne calyculata*
            11 Leaves various but not scurfy 12
              12 Fruit fleshy; leaves evergreen or deciduous 13
                13 Plants trailing; leaves evergreen 14
                  14 Leaves with small bristles; fruit white . . . . *Gaultheria hispidula*
                  14 Leaves glabrous; fruit red when ripe 15
                    15 Wet habitats; leaves small, to 15 mm long . . . . *Vaccinium* (**Cranberries**)
                    15 Drier habitats; leaves 2 cm long or more . . . . *Gaultheria procumbens*
                13 Upright shrubs; leaves deciduous 16
                  16 Leaves with shiny, orange-yellow resinous glands (especially on underside) . . . . *Gaylussacia baccata*
                  16 Leaves without glands . . . . *Vaccinium* (**Blueberries**)
              12 Fruit dry or mealy; leaves evergreen 17
                17 Plants with stiff hairs; leaves ovate to broadly elliptic . . . . *Epigaea repens*
                17 Plants nearly glabrous or only finely hairy; leaves spatula-shaped, mostly widest above middle . . . . *Arctostaphylos uva-ursi*

ANDROMEDA *Bog-Rosemary*

Andromeda glaucophylla Link
BOG-ROSEMARY
Andromeda polifolia L. var. *glaucophylla* (Link) DC.

MAP 623
native

Low upright or trailing shrub, 3-6 dm tall. **Stems** gray to blackish; twigs brown, with hairs in lines running down stems, or sometimes smooth. **Leaves** evergreen and leathery, often blue-green, linear or narrowly oval, 2-5 cm long and 3-10 mm wide, the tip sharp-pointed and tipped with a small spine, the base tapered to the stem or a short petiole, dark green above and whitened below by short stiff hairs; margins entire and distinctly rolled under. **Flowers** in drooping clusters at ends of branches, white or often pink, urn-shaped, 5-parted, 5-6 mm long, on curved stalks to 8 mm long. **Fruit** a rounded capsule to 5 mm wide, the style persistent from indented top of capsule; fruit drooping at first, but erect when mature. May-June.—Sphagnum bogs, black spruce and tamarack swamps.

Andromeda glaucophylla

ARCTOSTAPHYLOS *Bearberry*

Arctostaphylos uva-ursi (L.) Spreng.   MAP 624
RED BEARBERRY   *native*

Shrub, forming low mats to 1 m wide. **Stems** prostrate, freely branched. **Leaves** leathery, evergreen, alternate, entire, obovate, 1-3 cm long, obtuse or rounded at tip, tapering to the base. **Flowers** 5-merous, in short terminal racemes; calyx saucer-shaped, the sepals imbricate, distinct to the base, about 1.5 mm long; corolla white or tinged with pink, 4-6 mm long, the 5 rounded lobes spreading or recurved; stamens 10, much shorter than the corolla; ovary 5-celled, subtended by a 10-lobed disk. **Fruit** a bright red drupe, dry or mealy, 6-10 mm wide, with 5 bony nutlets. May-June.—Sandy or rocky soil. *Bearberry has a long history of medicinal uses, especially amongst American Indians; it was also the main component of a smoking mix known as kinnikinnick.*

Arctostaphylos uva-ursi

CHAMAEDAPHNE *Leatherleaf*

Chamaedaphne calyculata (L.) Moench   MAP 625
LEATHERLEAF   *native*

Upright shrub to 1 m tall. Older **stems** gray, the outer bark shredding to expose the smooth, red inner bark; **twigs** brown, with fine hairs and covered with small, round scales. **Leaves** evergreen and leathery, becoming smaller toward ends of flowering branches, oval to ovate, 1-5 cm long and 3-15 mm wide, the tip rounded or pointed, brown-green and smooth above, pale brown with a covering of small, round scales below; margins entire or with small rounded teeth; petioles short. **Flowers** white, urn-shaped or cylindric, in 1-sided, leafy racemes, hanging from axils of reduced leaves near ends of branches; 5-parted, 5-7 mm long, on stalks 2-5 mm long. **Fruit** a brown, rounded capsule to 6 mm wide, the hairlike style persistent from indented top of capsule; capsules persisting on branches for several years. May-June.—Open bogs, lakeshores, often forming low, dense thickets.

Chamaedaphne calyculata

CHIMAPHILA *Prince's Pine*

Chimaphila umbellata (L.) W. Bart.   MAP 626
PRINCE'S PINE; PIPSISSEWA   *native*

Low, perennial, evergreen half-shrubs, from a creeping rhizome. **Stems** spreading, the flowering branches erect, 1-3 dm tall. **Leaves** thick, oblong lance-shaped, 3-6 cm long, acute or mucronate, sharply dentate especially toward the tip, nearly entire below the middle, tapering to a short petiole. **Flowers** 4-8, 10-15 mm wide, white or pink, corymbose on long peduncles; petals 5, distinct, widely spreading; stamens 10; ovary 5-celled, depressed-globose. **Capsule** erect, globose, opening from the top downward. June-Aug. Dry woods, especially in sandy soil.

Chimaphila umbellata

624. *Arctostaphylos uva-ursi*   625. *Chamaedaphne calyculata*   626. *Chimaphila umbellata*   627. *Epigaea repens*

EMPETRUM *Crowberry*

Much-branched dwarf shrubs, often mat-forming, with small permanently revolute leaves. Flowers usually unisexual, 3-parted, axillary and nearly sessile, pinkish to purplish. Fruit dark-purple to blackish. *Previously placed in its own family (**Empetraceae**), but now considered a wind-pollinated member of the Ericaceae.*

Empetrum atropurpureum Fernald & Wiegand   (NO MAP)
CROWBERRY   🍂*endangered* | *native*
> *Empetrum eamesii* subsp. *atropurpureum* (Fernald & Wiegand) D.Löve
> *Empetrum nigrum* var. *atropurpureum* (Fernald & Wiegand) B. Boivin

Much-branched low shrub to 3 dm tall; sometimes forming mats 1-2 m wide. **Leaves** evergreen and needlelike, dark green and leathery, linear-oblong, only 4-8 mm long, rounded or blunt at tip, narrowed at base to a short stalk, margins rolled under. **Flowers** small, pink to purple, single in axils of upper leaves. **Fruit** purple-black, berrylike, 4-6 mm wide, somewhat juicy, with 6-9 hard nutlets. July-Aug. *E. atropurpureum* and *E. nigrum* are closely related and often considered part of a single species. However, in *E. atropurpureum*, the branchlets are white and tomentose (with dense, woolly hairs) but not glandular; the leaves spread outward from the stem at right angles or are directed forward; also, the fruit is purple. In *E. nigrum*, the branchlets are not tomentose but are minutely glandular, the leaves soon becoming reflexed, and the fruit is black. All of the known Minn *E. atropurpureum* locations are from a small group of islands in Lake Superior where plants occur on the rocky shores.

Empetrum nigrum

ADDITIONAL SPECIES

Empetrum nigrum L. (Black crowberry), known only from an island in Lake Superior (but last collected 1948), 🍂*endangered*; also known from Michigan's Isle Royale and Upper Peninsula.

EPIGAEA *Trailing Arbutus*

Epigaea repens L.   MAP 627
TRAILING ARBUTUS   *native*

Prostrate, creeping, evergreen shrub, often dioecious. **Stems** branched, 2-4 dm long, hirsute. **Leaves** leathery, alternate, entire, ovate or oblong, 2-10 cm long, apiculate, rounded to cordate at base, more or less pilose, especially when young; on pubescent petioles about half as long as the blade. **Flowers** pink to white, fragrant, perfect or unisexual, 5-merous, each closely subtended by 2 ovate bracts nearly or quite as long as the calyx, in short, crowded, terminal and axillary spikes 2-5 cm long; sepals distinct to the base, strongly imbricate; corolla salverform, the tube 8-15 mm long, densely pubescent within, the lobes 6-8 mm long; stamens included; ovary 5-celled. **Capsule** depressed-globose, hirsute, subtended by the persistent calyx and bracts, white-pulpy within. April-May.—Sandy or rocky soil.

Epigaea repens

GAULTHERIA *Teaberry*

Shrubs of diverse aspect, with alternate persistent leaves and usually white flowers in racemes or particles or (in our species) solitary in or just above the axils and closely subtended by 2 bracteoles. Flowers 4-5-merous. Calyx campanulate to saucer-shaped, deeply divided. Corolla tubular to campanulate, shallowly lobed. Stamens included. Ovary 4-5-celled. Capsule thin-walled, completely enclosed in the fleshy, white or colored, expanded calyx, forming a dry or mealy berry.

1 Leafy stems upright; flowers 5-parted; berries red . . . . ***G. procumbens***
1 Leafy stems prostrate; flowers 4-parted; berries white . . . . ***G. hispidula***

Gaultheria hispidula (L.) Muhl.   MAP 628
CREEPING SNOWBERRY   *native*

Low, creeping, matted shrub. **Stems** 2-4 dm long, covered with brown hairs. Leaves crowded, evergreen, oval to nearly round, 4-10 mm long and to 5 mm wide, abruptly tapered to tip, green above, underside paler, with brown, bristly hairs; margins rolled under; petioles short. **Flowers** few, single in leaf axils, white, bell-shaped, 4-parted, 2-4 mm long, on curved stalks 1 mm long. **Fruit** a translucent, juicy, white berry 5-10 mm wide, slightly wintergreen-flavored. May-June.—Open bogs, swamps, wet conifer woods, often in moss on hummocks or downed logs.

Gaultheria procumbens L.
WINTERGREEN

MAP 629
native

Low, creeping shrub. Leafy **stems** erect from a horizontal rhizome, 1-2 dm tall, bearing a few leaves crowded near the summit. **Leaf blades** elliptic or oblong, 2-5 cm long, entire or crenulate, glabrous; petioles 2-5 mm long. **Flowers** 5-merous, on nodding pedicels 5-10 mm long; calyx saucer-shaped; corolla barrel-shaped, 7-10 mm long, the rounded lobes about 1 mm long. **Berry** bright red, 7-10 mm wide, wintergreen-flavored. July-Aug.—Dry or moist woods in acid soil.

Gaultheria hispidula

GAYLUSSACIA *Huckleberry*

Gaylussacia baccata (Wangenh.) K. Koch
BLACK HUCKLEBERRY

MAP 630
🍂*threatened | native*

Medium shrub. **Stems** upright, much-branched, 3-10 dm long; branches brown, finely hairy when young, dark and smooth with age. **Leaves** alternate, deciduous, leathery, oval, 2-5 cm long and 1-2.5 cm wide; dark green above, paler below, both sides with shiny, orange-yellow resinous dots; margins entire, often fringed with small hairs; petioles 2-4 mm long. **Flowers** yellow-orange or red-tinged, cylindric, 5-lobed, 4-6 mm long, in more or less 1-sided racemes from lateral branches, the flowers on short, gland-dotted stalks 4-5 mm long. **Fruit** a red-purple to black, berrylike drupe, 6-8 mm long, with 10 nutlets; edible but seedy. May-June.—Open bogs, usually with tamarack and leatherleaf (*Chamaedaphne calyculata*); more common in dry, acid, sandy or rocky habitats.

Gaultheria procumbens

KALMIA *Laurel*

Kalmia polifolia Wangenh.
BOG-LAUREL

MAP 631
native

Low evergreen shrub to 6 dm tall. Older **stems** dark; **twigs** swollen at nodes, flattened and 2-edged in section, smooth, pale brown when young. **Leaves** opposite, evergreen and leathery, linear to narrowly oval, 1-4 cm long and 6-12 mm wide, tip blunt or narrowed to an abrupt point; dark green and smooth above, white below with a covering of short, white hairs, midrib on underside with large purple, stalked glands; margins entire and rolled under; petioles absent. **Flowers** showy, pale to rose-pink, in terminal clusters at ends of current year's branches, saucer-shaped, 5-parted, 8-11 mm wide, on stalks to 3 cm long. **Fruit** a rounded capsule to 6 mm wide, tipped by the persistent style, the capsules in upright clusters. May-June.—Sphagnum peatlands, black spruce and tamarack swamps.

Kalmia polifolia

MONESES *Single-Delight*

Moneses uniflora (L.) Gray
ONE-FLOWERED SHINLEAF
  Pyrola uniflora L.

MAP 632
native

Low perennial herb from a very slender creeping rhizome. **Stems** to 10 cm long. **Leaves** deciduous, mostly at base of plant, opposite or in whorls of 3, nearly round, margins entire or finely toothed. **Flowers** white, single at end of long stalk,

Moneses uniflora

628. *Gaultheria hispidula*   629. *Gaultheria procumbens*   630. *Gaylussacia baccata*

nodding, 1-2 cm wide; petals 5 distinct, widely spreading; stamens 10; ovary subglobose, concave at the summit, 5-celled. **Capsule** subglobose, opening from top downward. July-Aug.—Cedar swamps, wet conifer or mixed conifer and deciduous forests.

MONOTROPA *Indian-Pipe*

White, yellow, pink, or red plants, turning black in drying, parasitic on soil-fungi. Stems erect. Leaves small, scale-like Flowers nodding, of the same color as the stem. Corolla urn-shaped or broadly tubular; petals 4 or 5, distinct, all or some saccate at base. Sepals none, or 2-5. Stamens 8 or 10; filaments slender, pubescent. Ovary 4-5-celled; style short, thick. Capsules erect, ovoid to subglobose.

1 Flowers single . . . . *M. uniflora*
1 Flowers few to many in a raceme . . . . *M. hypopithys*

Monotropa hypopithys L.
PINESAP
   Hypopitys americana (DC.) Small

MAP 633
native

Stems 1-3 dm tall, often gregarious, yellow, tawny, pink, or red, never pure white, more or less pubescent. **Raceme** dense, at first nodding, erect at anthesis. **Flowers** 8-12 mm long, the lower usually 4-merous, the terminal often 5-merous and larger; sepals lance-shaped, erect; style shorter than the ovary; stigma more or less villous at the margin.—Moist or dry woods, soils usually acid.

Monotropa uniflora L.
ONE-FLOWER INDIAN-PIPE

MAP 634
native

Stems 1-2 dm tall, usually solitary, commonly pure waxy white, rarely pink or red. **Flower** solitary, nodding, odorless, 10-17 mm long; sepals often absent; petals broadly oblong, slightly widened distally; style longer than the ovary; stigma glabrous. June-Aug.—Rich woods in leaf-mold.

Monotropa hypopithys (l)
M. uniflora (r)

ORTHILIA *Sidebells*

Orthilia secunda (L.) House
ONE-SIDED SHINLEAF
   Pyrola secunda L.

MAP 635
native

Perennial herb. **Leaves** elliptic to subrotund, 1.5-4 cm long, entire to crenulate, often separated by conspicuous internodes. **Scape** 8-20 cm tall, bearing a crowded secund raceme; sepals semicircular to ovate, 0.5-1 mm long; petals white or greenish, about 5 mm long; style elongate, exsert at anthesis, 5-lobed. June-July.— Moist woods and mossy bogs. *Separated from other members of family by its ovary subtended by a 10-lobed hypogynous disk, and petals with 2 rounded projections at base.*

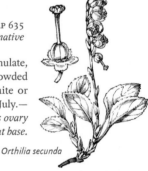

Orthilia secunda

PYROLA *Wintergreen; Shinleaf*

Perennial herbs from creeping rhizomes. Leaves few, broad, petiolate, nearly basal. Flowers in an erect, terminal, long-peduncled raceme; regular, 5-merous. Stamens 10. Ovary 5-celled; style short or elongate; stigma 5-lobed. Capsule dehiscent from the base upward.

1 Style straight, the stamens closely surrounding style . . . . *P. minor*
1 Style curved downward; anthers of stamen not surrounding style 2

631. Kalmia polifolia   *632. Moneses uniflora*   *633. Monotropa hypopithys*   *634. Monotropa uniflora*

2   Sepal lobes longer than wide 3
   3   Leaves to 3 cm long; sepals ovate . . . . *P. chlorantha*
   3   Leaves 3-7 cm long; sepals triangular . . . . *P. elliptica*
2   Sepal lobes shorter than wide 4
   4   Petals white; sepals oblong . . . . *P. americana*
   4   Petals pink; sepals triangular . . . . *P. asarifolia*

Pyrola americana Sweet
AMERICAN WINTERGREEN
   Pyrola rotundifolia L.

MAP 636
native

Perennial herb. **Leaves** firm in texture, broadly elliptic to subrotund, rarely somewhat ovate or obovate, 2.5-7 cm long, broadly rounded above, rounded, truncate, or short-cuneate at base; always somewhat decurrent on the petioles. **Scapes** 1.5-3 dm tall, usually with 1 or 2 scale-leaves below the raceme; sepals oblong or ovate-oblong, nearly twice as long as wide, erose or undulate, not overlapping at base; petals white. July-Aug.—Dry or moist woods and bogs.

Pyrola asarifolia Michx.
PINK SHINLEAF

MAP 637
native

Perennial herb. **Stems** to 3 dm long. **Leaves** persisting over winter, all near base of plant, kidney-shaped, 3-4 cm long and 3-5 cm wide, margins shallowly rounded-toothed; flower stalk with 1-3 small, scale-like leaves. **Flowers** nodding in a raceme; sepals triangular, 2-3 mm long; petals 5, 5-7 mm long, pink to pale purple. **Fruit** a capsule opening from base upward. June-Aug.—Cedar swamps, peatlands, marly wetlands, and interdunal wetlands.

Pyrola asarifolia

Pyrola chlorantha Sw.
GREEN-FLOWER WINTERGREEN

MAP 638
native

Perennial herb. **Leaves** obovate or broadly elliptic to subrotund, 1-3 cm long, often shorter than the petiole, rounded to truncate at the summit, rounded to broadly cuneate at base but scarcely decurrent. **Scapes** 1-2.5 dm tall; petals white, more or less veined with green; sepals broadly ovate-triangular, broader than long, obtuse or subacute. June-Aug.—Dry woods.

Pyrola elliptica Nutt.
ELLIPTIC SHINLEAF

MAP 639
native

Perennial herb. **Leaves** broadly elliptic, broadly oblong, or somewhat obovate, 3-7 cm long, commonly longer than the petiole, subacute to rounded at the summit, acute to rounded at base but always decurrent partway down the petiole. **Scapes** 1.5-3 dm tall; petals white, more or less veined with green; sepals triangular, about as broad as long, very shortly acuminate. June-Aug.—Dry upland woods.

Pyrola elliptica

Pyrola minor L.
LITTLE SHINLEAF

MAP 640
native

Perennial herb. **Leaves** elliptic or round-oblong, 2-4 cm long, rounded or truncate at both ends. **Scape** 5-15 cm tall, bearing a loose, non-secund raceme of 5-15 nodding flowers; petals white, about 5 mm long; style at anthesis about 2 mm long, about equaling the petals; stigma deeply 5-lobed. June-Aug.—Moist, northern boreal forests near Lake Superior. *Minnesota at southern edge of species' range.*

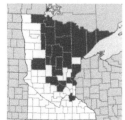

636. *Pyrola americana*   637. *Pyrola asarifolia*   638. *Pyrola chlorantha*   639. *Pyrola elliptica*

RHODODENDRON

Rhododendron groenlandicum (Oeder) Kron & Judd
RUSTY LABRADOR-TEA
Ledum groenlandicum Oeder

MAP 641
native

Medium shrub, to 1 m tall. Older **stems** gray or red-brown; twigs covered with woolly, curly brown hairs. **Leaves** alternate, evergreen and leathery, fragrant when rubbed, narrowly oval to oblong, 2.5–5 cm long and 5–20 mm wide, rounded at tip; dark green and smooth above, the midvein sunken; underside covered with tan to rust-colored curly hairs; margins entire and rolled under; petioles short. **Flowers** creamy-white, in rounded clusters at ends of branches, to 1 cm wide, on finely hairy stalks 1–2 cm long; calyx 5-lobed, the lobes much shorter than the corolla; corolla campanulate, 5-lobed. **Fruit** a lance-shaped capsule 5–6 mm long, the style persistent and hairlike; capsules splitting at base to release numerous small seeds, the empty capsules persistent on stems for several years. May-June.—Sphagnum bogs, swamps and wet conifer forests.

Rhododendron groenlandicum

VACCINIUM *Blueberry*

Deciduous or evergreen shrubs. Leaves alternate, simple. Flowers 4- or 5-parted, single in leaf axils or in clusters in axils or at ends of branches; ovary inferior. Fruit a many-seeded, red, blue, or black berry. *The genus may be divided into 3 subgroups:* **blueberries** *(V. angustifolium, V. myrtilloides),* **cranberries** *(V. macrocarpon, V. oxycoccos, V. vitis-idaea), and* **bilberries** *(V. caespitosum, V. uliginosum).*

ADDITIONAL SPECIES

Vaccinium uliginosum L. (Alpine bilberry), leaves similar to those of bearberry (*Arctostaphylos uva-ursi*), common in similar habitats; flowers white or pinkish, with 4 or 5 lobes on the urn-shaped corolla; berries blue or blackish and somewhat waxy.—In Minnesota, known from a single location—a large rhyolite outcrop along Lake Superior in Cook County (✔*endangered*).

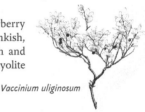

Vaccinium uliginosum

1   Leaves deciduous; berries blue to blue-black 2
   2   Leaves less than 2.5 cm long; flowers solitary in leaf axils or 2–3 from axillary buds . . . . ***V. caespitosum***
   2   Leaves 2.5 cm long or more; flowers many in terminal or lateral clusters 3
      3   Leaf margins with small bristle-tipped teeth . . . . ***V. angustifolium***
      3   Leaves entire; margins sometimes finely hairy . . . . ***V. myrtilloides***
1   Leaves evergreen; berries red 4
   4   Leaf underside with black bristly glands . . . . ***V. vitis-idaea***
   4   Leaf underside without black glands 5
      5   Leaves blunt or rounded at tip (and sometimes notched), pale below; bracts on flower stalk green and
         leaflike (more than 1 mm wide) . . . . ***V. macrocarpon***
      5   Leaves tapered to pointed tip, white below; bracts on flower stalk red and narrow (less than 1 mm wide)
         . . . . ***V. oxycoccos***

Vaccinium angustifolium Ait.
LOWBUSH BLUEBERRY

MAP 642
native

Low shrub 1–6 dm tall, forming colonies from surface runners. Older **stems** red-brown to black; **twigs** green-brown, with hairs in lines down stems, or sometimes smooth. **Leaves** deciduous, bright green oval, 2–5 cm long and 5–15 mm wide, smooth on both sides or sparsely hairy on veins; margins finely toothed with bristle-tipped teeth; petioles very short. **Flowers** in clusters, opening before or

635. Orthilia secunda

640. Pyrola minor

641. Rhododen. groenlandicum

642. Vaccinium angustifolium

with leaves, white or pale pink, narrowly bell-shaped, 5-parted, 4-6 mm long. **Fruit** blue and wax-covered, 5-12 mm wide, edible and sweet. Flowering April-June, fruit ripening July-Aug.—Sphagnum peatlands and wetland margins; also in dry, sandy openings and forests.

Vaccinium angustifolium

Vaccinium caespitosum Michx.
DWARF BILBERRY
MAP 643
native

Shrub. **Stems** branched, 1-2 dm tall. **Leaves** deciduous, thin, subsessile, oblong lance-shaped or cuneate to obovate, 1-3 cm long, obtuse or rounded at the summit, finely aristate-serrulate, tapering to the base. **Flowers** solitary in the axils of the lower leaves of the current season's branches, on decurved pedicels about 3 mm long; sepals very short and broad; corolla about 5 mm long, usually pink. **Berries** blue, 6-8 mm wide. May-June, fruit ripens in Aug.—Openings in pine barrens, often with bracken fern.

Vaccinium macrocarpon Ait.
LARGE CRANBERRY
MAP 644
native

Evergreen trailing shrub. **Stems** slender, to 1 m or more long, with branches to 2 dm tall. **Leaves** leathery, oblong-oval, 5-15 mm long and 2-5 mm wide, rounded or blunt at tip, pale on underside; margins flat or slightly rolled under; petioles absent or very short. **Flowers** white to pink, 1 cm wide, 4-lobed, the lobes turned back at tips, single or in clusters of 2-6, on stalks 1-3 cm long, the stalks with 2 bracts above middle of stalk, the bracts green, 2-4 mm long and 1-2 mm wide. **Fruit** red, 1-1.5 cm wide, edible but tart, often over-wintering. Flowering June-July, fruit ripening Aug-Sept.—Sphagnum bogs, swamps and peaty pond margins. *V. macrocarpon is the cultivated cranberry.*

Vaccinium macrocarpon

Vaccinium myrtilloides Michx.
VELVET-LEAF BLUEBERRY
MAP 645
native

Low shrub, often forming colonies. **Stems** 3-6 dm long, red-brown to black with numerous wartlike lenticels; young twigs green-brown, densely velvety white-hairy. **Leaves** deciduous, thin and soft, oval, 2-5 cm long and 1-2.5 cm wide, dark green above, paler and soft hairy below, not waxy; margins entire and finely hairy; petioles very short. **Flowers** in clusters at ends of short, leafy branches, opening with leaves, creamy or green-white, tinged with pink, bell-shaped or short-cylindric, 5-parted, 4-5 mm long. **Fruit** blue, wax-covered, 6-9 mm wide; edible but tart. Flowering May-July, fruit ripening July-Sept.—Sphagnum bogs and swamps; also in dry to moist woods and clearings.

Vaccinium myrtilloides

Vaccinium oxycoccos L.
SMALL CRANBERRY
MAP 646
native

Evergreen trailing shrub. **Stems** slender, 0.5 m or more long, with upright branches 1-2 dm tall. **Leaves** leathery, ovate to oval or narrowly triangular, 2-10 mm long and 1-3 mm wide, pointed or rounded at tip, strongly whitened on underside; margins flat or strongly rolled under; petioles absent or very short. **Flowers** pale pink, 1 cm wide, 4-lobed, the lobes turned back at tips, single or in clusters of 2-4, on stalks 1-3 cm long, the stalks with 2 bracts at or below middle of stalk, the bracts red, scale-like, to 2 mm long and less than 1 mm wide. **Fruit** pale and red-speckled when young, becoming red, 6-12 mm wide, edible but tart. Flowering June-July, fruit ripening Aug-Sept.—Wet, acid, sphagnum bogs.

Vaccinium oxycoccos

643. *Vaccinium caespitosum* 644. *Vaccinium macrocarpon* 645. *Vaccinium myrtilloides* 646. *Vaccinium oxycoccos*

Vaccinium vitis-idaea L.

MAP 647
LINGONBERRY; MOUNTAIN-CRANBERRY   *native*

Low evergreen, trailing shrub. Older **stems** brown-black with peeling bark, branching, the branches upright, slender, 1-2 dm long, often forming mats; twigs green-brown to red, more or less smooth. **Leaves** alternate, leathery, oval to oval, 0.5-2 cm long and 4-15 mm wide, rounded or slightly indented at tip; upper surface dark green, shiny and smooth, paler and with dark bristly glands below; margins entire and rolled under; petioles hairy, 1-2 mm long. Flowers white to pink, bell-shaped and 4-lobed, style longer than petals, several in 1-sided clusters at ends of branches, the flowers on short glandular stalks, the stalks with 2 small bracts at base. **Fruit** a dark red berry, to 1 cm wide, persisting over winter, tart but edible, especially the following spring. June-July.—Sphagnum bogs; also in drier, sandy or rocky places; Minn at south edge of range. *Mountain cranberry can be distinguished from the more common cranberries (V. macrocarpon and V. oxycoccos) by the black, bristly, glandular dots on leaf underside. Gathered in Europe (where known as lingen or red whortleberry) and North America (where available) and cooked and eaten like commercial cranberries.*

Vaccinium vitis-idaea

Euphorbiaceae SPURGE FAMILY

Herbs (ours). Leaves usually alternate and simple. Flowers mostly tiny but in some species subtended by conspicuous bracts or involucral appendages. Plants monoecious or dioecious. Flowers commonly unisexual, very rarely perfect, regular. Calyx present or absent; petals absent in most genera. Stamens 1 to many, the filaments sometimes branched. Pistil 1; ovary usually 3-celled. Fruit usually a dehiscent capsule. Seeds with copious endosperm.

A large, chiefly tropical family, with about 6,500 species, some of which are of economic importance. Species of the Amazonian genus *Hevea* are the chief source of rubber; *Manihot esculenta* Crantz, native of Brazil, yields cassava (tapioca), a staple food in the tropics. Many species toxic and a few are used in medicine.

1   Stem and leaves with some (or all) hairs forked or stellate . . . . *Croton glandulosus*
1   Stem and leaves glabrous or with only simple hairs 2
  2   Plant with watery juice; stem pubescent with incurved hairs . . . . *Acalypha rhomboidea*
  2   Plant with milky juice; stems glabrous or variously pubescent . . . . *Euphorbia*

ACALYPHA *Copperleaf*

Acalypha rhomboidea Raf.

MAP 648
RHOMBIC COPPERLEAF   *native*
   Acalypha virginica L. var. *rhomboidea* (Raf.) Cooperrider

Annual herb, plants monoecious. **Stems** erect, simple or branched, 2-6 dm tall, glabrous, puberulent in lines, or puberulent throughout with incurved hairs, often with a few spreading hairs also. **Leaves** alternate, ovate lance-shaped to ovate, commonly with a distinct tendency to rhombic; petioles slender, divaricate, those of the larger leaves regularly more than half as long as the blades. **Flowers** minute

Acalypha rhomboidea

647. *Vaccinium vitis-idaea*   648. *Acalypha rhomboidea*   649. *Euphorbia corollata*

in clusters in the axils of the leaves, each fascicle of flowers subtended by a bract; petals none; sepals of the staminate flowers 4; **staminate spikes** little if any exceeding the bracts; sepals of the pistillate flowers 3-5; **pistillate bracts** 5-7-lobed, usually stipitate-glandular (visible under 10x lens). Capsule 3-celled; seeds solitary in each cell. July-Sept.—Dry or moist soil of open woods, roadsides, waste places, and gardens.

CROTON *Croton*

Croton glandulosus L.

(NO MAP)

TOOTH-LEAVED CROTON

native

Branched annual herb, densely covered with rough stellate hairs; plants monoecious or dioecious. **Stems** 2-6 dm tall; lower branches and leaves alternate; upper leaves tending to be opposite or whorled. **Leaves** narrowly oblong to oblong-ovate, 3-7 cm long, coarsely serrate, with 1 or 2 glands at the summit of the petiole. The terminal inflorescences are soon surpassed by the branches and appear lateral. **Staminate flowers** 4-merous, petaliferous, with 8 stamens; **pistillate flowers** 5-merous, apetalous, each of the styles 2-cleft nearly to the base. **Capsule** usually pubescent; seeds with a caruncle. July-Oct.—Dry or sandy soil; Fillmore and Goodhue counties.

Croton glandulosus

EUPHORBIA *Spurge*

Annual or perennial herbs of diverse form; with milky, often highly acrid juice. Flowers greatly reduced, the staminate flowers consisting of a single stamen only, the pistillate flowers of a single pistil only. Several staminate flowers surround one pistillate flower inserted at the base of a cup-shaped involucre to form an inflorescence termed a cyathium. Around the margin of the cyathium are 4-5 glands, and in some species these have petal-like appendages, so that the whole cyathium mimics a single flower. Ovary 3-celled; styles 3, each bifid. Capsule 3-lobed, 3-seeded. *The milky juice is poisonous and for some people produces a dermatitis similar to that caused by poison-ivy.*

ADDITIONAL SPECIES

Euphorbia hexagona Nutt. ex Spreng. (Six-angle spurge), native; Goodhue County.

1 Annual herbs; leaf bases symmetrical; glands of cyathium 1, without appendages; stems erect, with ascending branches 2
   2 Plants glabrous or upper stems softly hairy; leaves all alternate or nearly so, linear to narrowly lance-shaped, the margins entire . . . . ***E. cyathophora***
   2 Plants usually with hairs, especially on upper stems and leaf undersides; leaves all opposite or nearly so, ovate to linear, the margins toothed . . . . ***E. davidii***
1 Annual or perennial herbs; leaf bases various; glands of cyathium 4 or 5, not appendaged or with petal-like appendages; stems erect to prostrate 3
   3 Annual herbs, the stems prostrate or ascending; leaves all opposite; leaf bases typically unequal 4
      4 Stems with long soft hairs; capsules with stiff appressed hairs . . . . ***E. maculata***
      4 Stems glabrous or pubescent; capsules glabrous 5
         5 Leaves entire; seeds round, smooth, with a white seed coat . . . . ***E. geyeri***
         5 Leaves finely toothed, at least along upper portion of blade; seeds angular, smooth, bumpy, or ridged, the seed coat brown or blackish 6
            6 Stems pubescent (at least upper portions); leaves mostly more than 1 cm long, margins toothed . 7
               7 Stems erect or ascending, nearly glabrous or with lines of hairs; mature leaves more than 15 mm long . . . . ***E. nutans***
               7 Stems prostrate or nearly so, sparsely hairy; mature leaves less than 15 mm long ***E. vermiculata***
            6 Stems glabrous; leaves mostly less than 1 cm long, the margins toothed only near leaf tip and along one side near leaf base 8
               8 Leaves linear-oblong, finely sharp-toothed, rounded at tip; seeds with small ridges . . . .
                     . . . . ***E. glyptosperma***
               8 Leaves oblong to ovate, the lower two-thirds of the blade entire, finely toothed at the blunt tip; seeds smooth, or faintly wrinkled or pitted . . . . ***E. serpyllifolia***
   3 Annual or perennial herbs, the stems erect, leaves mostly alternate; leaf bases equal or nearly so 9

9　Inflorescence glands with conspicuous white, petal-like appendages 10

　　10　Upper leaves and bracts green with conspicuous white patches; capsules pubescent; plants annual ..
　　　　...***E. marginata***

　　10　Leaves and bracts green; capsules glabrous; plants perennial ....***E. corollata***

9　Inflorescence glands without white, petal-like appendages 11

　　11　Leaves finely sharp-toothed 12

　　　　12　Capsules smooth; seeds with strong raised reticulate pattern; principal inflorescences of 5 umbellate
　　　　　　rays and cyathia glabrous on the outside.......................................***E. helioscopia***

　　　　12　Capsules tuberculate with prominent bumps; seeds smooth; principal inflorescences of 3 rays and
　　　　　　outside of cyathia glabrous...***E. spathulata***

　　11　Leaves entire 13

　　　　13　Main stem leaves slender and linear, 1-3 cm long and 1-3 mm wide, crowded ....***E. cyparissias***

　　　　13　Main stem leaves 3-7 cm long, mostly 3-10 mm wide, less crowded ....***E. virgata***

Euphorbia corollata L.

FLOWERING SPURGE

MAP 649
native

Perennial from a deep root, glabrous to villous on stem and leaves. **Stems** 3-10
dm tall, usually simple below, umbellately or paniculately branched above. **Stem
leaves** alternate, linear to elliptic, usually 3-6 cm long; leaves subtending the
primary branches similar, whorled; leaves of the inflorescence smaller, opposite
or alternate. **Involucres** numerous, forming a panicle-like cyme often 3 dm wide;
pedicels, except a few lower ones, less than 1 cm long; petal-like appendages white
(very rarely green), conspicuous, ovate to obovate, 1.5-4 mm long. June-Sept.—
Dry woods and old fields. Highly variable. *May cause severe skin irritation.*

Euphorbia cyathophora Murr.

FIRE-ON-THE-MOUNTAIN

Poinsettia cyathophora Murr.

MAP 650
native

Erect annual, to 1 m tall, usually branched, glabrous or nearly. **Leaves** mainly or
all alternate (or the uppermost opposite), variable, even on the same plant, from
linear to broadly oblong or ovate or pandurate, entire or serrate to lobed; the
upper mostly lobed and blotched with red or white at base. **Involucral gland**
solitary, bilabiate, cupulate, usually wider than high. **Fruit** smooth, 6-8 mm thick;
seeds tuberculate, 3-3.5 mm long, without a caruncle. Summer.—Moist soil, often
in shade; cultivated and sometimes escaped.

Euphorbia cyparissias L.

CYPRESS SPURGE

MAP 651
introduced (invasive)

Perennial by horizontal rhizomes, gregarious. **Stems** 2-4 dm tall. **Stem leaves** very
numerous, crowded, linear, 1-3 cm long, 1-nerved; leaves subtending the umbel
similar; leaves of the umbel broadly cordate. **Rays** of the umbel usually 10 or more.
Capsule about 3 mm long, slightly granular-roughened; seeds plump, smooth,
1.5-2 mm long. April-July.—Native of Eurasia; established on roadsides and waste
ground. *Fruit is seldom produced.*

Euphorbia davidii Subils

DAVID'S SPURGE

MAP 652
introduced

Erect annual, 2-6 dm tall, often branched, with hairy herbage. **Leaves** all or mostly
opposite, petiolate, linear to ovate. coarsely toothed to subentire. **Inflorescence**
congested, mingled with reduced green leaves; **involucres** 2-3 mm long, with
fimbriate lobes and a conspicuous, fleshy, flattened, bilabiate gland; styles bifid

Euphorbia corollata

Euphorbia cyparissias

650. Euphorbia cyathophora　　　*651. Euphorbia cyparissias*　　　*652. Euphorbia davidii*　　　*653. Euphorbia geyeri*

half their length or deeper. **Fruit** smooth, 5 mm thick; seeds ovoid, rough-tuberculate, 2.5-3 mm long, usually carunculate. July-Sept.—Dry soil; established as a weed on roadsides and waste places, especially in cindery soil.

Euphorbia geyeri Engelm.
MAP 653
DUNE SPURGE
native
   Chamaesyce geyeri (Engelm.) Small

Annual, glabrous throughout. **Stems** branched from the base, usually prostrate, 1-3 dm long. **Leaves** oblong to broadly elliptic, 5-10 mm long, entire, broadly rounded to shallowly retuse at the apex. Petal-like appendages inconspicuous, short-ovate, rarely more than 2x as long as the gland; stamens in each involucre 5-17. **Capsule** about 2 mm long; seeds not compressed, smooth, roundly 3-angled, about 1.5 mm long.—Sandy prairies and dunes.

Euphorbia glyptosperma

Euphorbia glyptosperma Engelm.
MAP 654
RIB-SEED SANDMAT
native
   Chamaesyce glyptosperma (Engelm.) Small

Annual, glabrous throughout. **Stems** mostly prostrate, freely branched, 1-3 dm long, often forming mats. **Leaves** oblong or ovate, 4-15 mm long, strongly inequi-lateral, minutely serrulate, especially on the rounded summit (may need a lens to see the teeth). Appendages rather conspicuous. **Capsule** depressed-ovoid, sharply 3-angled, about 1.5 mm long; seeds about 1 mm long, sharply 4-angled, marked with 3 or 4 conspicuous transverse ridges.—Dry sandy soil.

Euphorbia helioscopia L.
(NO MAP)
WARTWEED; MAD-WOMAN'S-MILK
introduced

Annual glabrous herb. **Stems** 2-5 dm tall, the upper internodes usually progressively longer. **Stem leaves** spatulate, 1.5-5 cm long, very blunt or retuse, finely and sharply serrulate; leaves subtending the primary umbel similar but proportionately wider; leaves of the umbel somewhat oblique, broadly elliptic to obovate. Rays of the primary umbel 5, on well grown plants repeatedly branched. **Involucres** about 2 mm long. **Capsule** smooth, about 3 mm long; seeds ovoid, 2-2.5 mm long, conspicuously areolate.—Native of Europe; fields, Winona County.

Euphorbia helioscopia

Euphorbia maculata L.
MAP 655
SPOTTED SANDMAT
native
   Chamaesyce maculata (L.) Small

Annual. **Stems** prostrate or nearly so, to 4 dm long, often forming circular mats, sparsely to densely villous. **Leaves** dark green, often with a red spot, oblong or ovate-oblong, varying to linear-oblong, usually 5-15 mm long, almost always widest below the middle. **Involucre** cleft on one side; ovary and capsule strigose. **Capsule** about 1.5 mm long; seeds 4-angled, about 1 mm long, with a few inconspicuous transverse ridges.—Common weed in lawns, gardens, and waste places, also in meadows and open woods. *May cause severe skin irritation if handled.*

Euphorbia marginata Pursh
MAP 656
SNOW-ON-THE-MOUNTAIN
native

Annual herb. **Stems** erect, 3-8 dm tall, softly villous, especially above. **Stem leaves** alternate, sessile, broadly ovate to elliptic or obovate-oblong, 4-10 cm long; leaves subtending the inflorescence whorled; those of the usually 3-rayed inflorescence smaller, margined with white or entirely white. **Cymes** crowded; involucres pubescent, the 5 lobes deeply fimbriate, the 5 petal-like appendages white,

Euphorbia maculata

654. *Euphorbia glyptosperma*   655. *Euphorbia maculata*   656. *Euphorbia marginata*   657. *Euphorbia nutans*

conspicuous, kidney-shaped to broadly ovate. **Capsule** 3-lobed, 6-7 mm wide; seeds ovoid, about 4 mm long, tuberculate. Summer.—Native of Great Plains; cultivated for ornament and sometimes escaped farther east. *The milky juice is extremely acrid.*

Euphorbia nutans Lag.
MAP 657
EYEBANE
native
   Chamaesyce nutans (Lag.) Small

Annual herb. **Stems** to 8 dm tall, obliquely ascending at least in the upper half; the lower half often erect; the younger parts puberulent, often in a single longitudinal strip, with usually incurved hairs to 0.3 mm. the older parts glabrous or nearly so. **Leaves** opposite, oblong or oblong-ovate, 1-3.5 crn long and about a third as wide, serrulate, usually conspicuously inequilateral. **Fruit** 2-2.5 mm long, strongly 3-lobed, glabrous; seeds gray or pale brown, 1-1.5 mm long. June-Oct. —Dry or moist soil; weedy in lawns and gardens.

Euphorbia serpyllifolia Pers.
MAP 658
THYME-LEAVED SPURGE
introduced
   Chamaesyce serpyllifolia (Pers.) Small

Annual glabrous herb. **Stems** usually prostrate and much branched, 1-3 dm long. **Leaves** linear-oblong to obovate, 6-12 mm long, very inequilateral, minutely serrulate on the rounded summit. Petal-like appendages of the involucre minute. **Capsule** sharply 3-angled, 1.5-2 mm long; seeds quadrangular, 1-1.4 mm long, smooth or very minutely rugulose.—Dry rocky soil.

Euphorbia serpyllifolia

Euphorbia spathulata Lam.
MAP 659
WARTY SPURGE
native

Annual glabrous herb. **Stems** erect, to 50 cm tall, main stems 1-3 or more from base, branches several above, alternate. **Leaves** alternate, mostly oblong-spatulate, 1-4.5 cm long, sessile, obtuse at tip, tapering to base, serrulate at least on upper 1/2; stipules absent; leaves of the umbel shorter and wider. Rays of primary **umbel** usually 3, repeatedly dichotomous in well-developed plants. **Cyathia** solitary in forks of inflorescence; **involucre** ca. 1 mm long; glands 4(5), minute; appendages and horns absent; staminate flowers 5-8per cyathium. **Capsule** 2-5 mm long, smooth except for warts near tip and along lobes; seeds brown, roundish, to 2 mm long, with low irregular reticulate ridges. May-June.—Rocky open woods, prairies, roadsides, waste places.

Euphorbia vermiculata Raf.
(NO MAP)
WORM-SEED SANDMAT
introduced
   Chamaesyce vermiculata (Raf.) House

Annual. **Stems** prostrate to ascending, to 4 dm long, hirsute more or less uniformly from base to tip with spreading hairs 0.5-1.5 mm long. **Leaves** obliquely ovate-oblong to ovate, 0.5-2 cm long, serrulate. **Capsule** 1.5-2 mm long, strongly 3-lobed, glabrous; seeds gray or pale brown, 1-1.3 mm long.—Fields, roadsides, and waste ground. Native in ne USA; considered adventive in Minn (Steele Co.).

Euphorbia virgata Waldst. & Kit.
MAP 660
LEAFY SPURGE
introduced (invasive)
   Euphorbia esula L.

Perennial from a deep root. **Stems** erect, 3-7 dm tall, glabrous, usually with numerous alternate flowering branches below the umbel. **Stem leaves** linear to

Euphorbia virgata

658. *Euphorbia serpyllifolia*   659. *Euphorbia spathulata*   660. *Euphorbia virgata*   661. *Amorpha canescens*

narrowly oblong, 3-7 cm long, obtuse to mucronate; leaves subtending the umbel shorter and broader, lance-shaped to ovate; leaves of the umbel broadly cordate or kidney-shaped. Rays of the primary umbel 7 or more. **Capsule** 2.5-3 mm long, finely granular; seeds brown, globose-ovoid, about 2 mm long. Summer.—Native of Eurasia; widely established in North America; a troublesome noxious weed sometimes infesting large areas. *May cause severe skin irritation if handled.*

Fabaceae PEA FAMILY

Perennial herbs, shrubs and trees. Leaves alternate, pinnately divided, the terminal leaflet sometimes modified as a tendril (*Lathyrus, Vicia*). Flowers in simple or branched racemes, perfect (with both staminate and pistillate parts), irregular, 5-lobed (only 1 lobe in *Amorpha*), the upper lobe (banner) larger than the other lobes, with 2 outer, lateral petals (wings), and 2 inner petals which are partly joined (the keel), and enclosing the 10 stamens and style; pistil 1, ovary 1-chambered, maturing into a pod.

ADDITIONAL SPECIES
Glycine max (L.) Merr. (Soybean), occasionally adventive following cultivation but not persisting in Minn's flora.

18 Pods 1-several-jointed and -seeded; leaflets usually petiolulate; flowers purple or white . . . . ***Desmodium***

18 Pods of a single 1-seeded joint (the lower joint when present empty and stalk-like); leaflets without stipules, usually prominently veined . . . . ***Lespedeza***

17 Fruit a legume (like a pea pod), not breaking into 1-seeded segments 19

19 Leaflets without stipule-like appendages at their base; plants not twining or vining . . 20

20 Flowers in heads; pods small, often included in the calyx . . . . ***Trifolium***

20 Flowers in racemes, or solitary . . . . ***Baptisia***

19 Leaflets with stipule-like appendages at their base; plants twining or vining 21

21 Style glabrous . . . . ***Amphicarpaea bracteata***

21 Style pubescent on upper surface . . . . ***Strophostyles***

12 Leaves with 5 or more leaflets 22

22 Leaves dotted with small pits or depressions 23

23 Pods covered with hooked prickles; flowers whitish; stamens 10 . . . . ***Glycyrrhiza lepidota***

23 Pods without hooked prickles 24

24 Corolla of 1 petal; stamens 10 . . . . ***Amorpha***

24 Corolla of 5 petals . . . . ***Dalea***

22 Leaves not dotted with small pits 25

25 Leaflets 5-11 26

26 Flowers yellow, borne in umbels . . . . ***Lotus***

26 Flowers not yellow, borne in axillary or terminal racemes 27

27 Stems twining or climbing; leaflets 5-7; flowers in axillary racemes . . . . ***Apios americana***

27 Stems erect; leaflets 7-11; flowers blue (or pink or white), in terminal racemes . . ***Lupinus***

25 Leaflets 11-31 28

28 Flowers in terminal racemes . . . . ***Tephrosia virginiana***

28 Flowers in axillary racemes or head-like umbels 29

29 Flowers in umbel-like clusters; pods linear, 4-angled, jointed . . . . ***Securigera varia***

29 Flowers in racemes; pods neither 4-angled nor jointed 30

30 Keel of flower tipped with a sharp point . . . . ***Oxytropis***

30 Keel of flower not tipped with a sharp point . . . . ***Astragalus***

AMORPHA *Indigo-Bush*

Shrubs. Leaves pinnately compound, stipules linear. Flowers small, blue, rarely white, terminal and from the upper axils in dense spike-like racemes. Calyx tube obconic, the lobes equal or the lowest one slightly larger. Standard obovate, more or less folded about the stamens; wings and keel absent. Stamens 10, exsert. Pod oblong, often curved, slightly compressed, indehiscent, 1-2-seeded. *The foliage, pods, and often the calyx are glandular-punctate; the glands on the pod are especially conspicuous.*

1 Plants usually 1-3.5 m tall; leaflets 2-5 cm long . . . . ***A. fruticosa***

1 Plants less than 1 m tall; leaflets 0.5-1.5 cm long 2

2 Leaves and calyx conspicuously pubescent; racemes usually several in axils of upper leaves . . . . ***A. canescens***

2 Leaves and calyx glabrous or nearly so; racemes usually one at tips of stem and branches . . . . ***A. nana***

Amorpha canescens Pursh — MAP 661

LEADPLANT — *native*

Shrub. **Stems** 5-10 dm tall, erect or ascending, simple or sparingly branched, the whole plant ordinarily canescent with a close pubescence. **Petioles** 1-2 mm long. **Leaflets** about 15-25 pairs, 8-15 mm long. **Racemes** several, usually crowded, the terminal 5-12 cm long, the lower usually shorter; calyx lobes lance-shaped, about half as long as the tube. **Pod** canescent, about 4 mm long.—Sandy open woods and dry prairies.

Amorpha canescens

Amorpha fruticosa L. — MAP 662

FALSE INDIGO-BUSH — *native*

Much-branched shrub. **Stems** mostly 1-3 m tall; **twigs** tan to gray. **Leaves** pinnately divided, 5-15 cm long; **leaflets** 9-27, oval to obovate, 1-4 cm long and 0.5-3 cm wide, upper surface smooth, underside short-hairy, margins entire, petioles 2-5 cm long, stipules absent. **Flowers** dark purple, in dense spike-like racemes 2-15 cm long at ends of stems; petals 1-lobed, only the banner present,

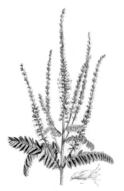

3-5 mm long, folded to enclose the 10 stamens. **Pod** oblong, curved near tip, 5-7 mm long, spotted with glands, with 1-2 seeds. June-July.—Moist to wet prairies, wet meadows, shores, streambanks, ditches.

Amorpha nana Nutt.   MAP 663
DWARF FALSE INDIGO   *native*
Erect or upright shrub mostly 3-6 (10) dm tall, branched above, sometimes rhizomatous. **Stems** moderately strigulose, becoming glabrate with age. **Leaves** alternate, odd-pinnate, 3-7 cm long; petioles 4-8 cm long; stipules 3-5 mm long; leaflets usually 6-13 pairs plus one leaflet at tip, 6-13 mm long, leaflet apex with a short sharp point to 1.5 mm long. **Flowers** in racemes, these solitary, 3-9 cm long, at tips of current year's growth; pedicels 2-3 mm long; calyx with punctate glands; petals dark purple; stamens 10. **Pod** 4-6 mm long, 2-3 mm wide, glabrous, punctate-glandular in upper 2/3, tipped by short, persistent base of style ca. 0.5 mm long; seeds olive-brown, 2.5-3 mm long. May-July.—Dry prairies; soils often sandy or rocky.

Amorpha fruticosa

AMPHICARPAEA *Hog-Peanut*

Amphicarpaea bracteata (L.) Fern.   MAP 664
AMERICAN HOG-PEANUT   *native*
Annual to short-lived perennial, twining herb. **Stems** to 1 m long. **Leaves** pinnately compound into 3 petioled leaflets. **Flowers** in racemes or panicles peduncled from many of the axils, each pedicel subtended at base by a striate-veined bractlet, bearing several to many pale purple to whitish flowers 12-18 mm long; calyx slightly irregular, the tube short-cylindric, the lobes apparently 4 through the fusion of the upper two; standard obovate, narrowed to the base, sometimes auricled below the middle; wings and keel slightly shorter, with elongate slender claws exceeding the blades. **Pods** (of petaliferous flowers) flat, oblong, pointed at both ends, usually 3-seeded, coiled after dehiscence. Aug-Oct.—Woods and thickets. *Besides the pod-producing petaliferous flowers, the plants bear nearly or completely apetalous flowers near the base of the stem, producing, often under the ground, small 1-seeded pods.*

Amphicarpaea bracteata

APIOS *Groundnut*

Apios americana Medik.   MAP 665
GROUNDNUT   *native*
Perennial herbaceous vine, rhizomes with a necklace-like series of 2 or more edible tubers; plants with milky juice. **Stems** to 1 m long, climbing over other plants. **Leaves** pinnately divided; main leaves with 5-7 leaflets; leaflets ovate, 4-6 cm long, tapered to a point, smooth to short-hairy beneath, margins entire. **Flowers** brown-purple, 10-13 mm long, single or paired, in crowded racemes from leaf axils. **Pods** linear, 5-10 cm long. July-Aug. Floodplain forests, thickets, shores, wet meadows, low prairie.

Apios americana

ASTRAGALUS *Milk-Vetch*

Ours perennial herbs from a stout taproot, caudex, or rhizome. Leaflets numerous. Flowers white, yellowish white, or purple, in long or short axillary racemes. Calyx tube campanulate to cylindric;

662. *Amorpha fruticosa*

663. *Amorpha nana*

664. *Amphicarpaea bracteata*

665. *Apios americana*

calyx lobes short, triangular or subulate. Standard obovate to rotund, usually exceeding the wings. Stamens 10. Fruit a pod of various forms. Seeds few to many.

Astragalus are most common in arid or semiarid regions of Asia and w North America. Many species of the genus produce an alkaloid toxic to livestock. From their erratic movements, animals so affected were termed *loco* (mad) and the name locoweed is commonly used for these plants in the West. Other species are able to accumulate the element selenium, when growing on seleniferous soils in the western states; such plants, if eaten by animals, cause sickness or death.

ADDITIONAL SPECIES

• *Astragalus cicer* L. (Chickpea milk-vetch), native of Europe, Ramsey and St. Louis counties.

• *Astragalus tenellus* Pursh (Loose-flower milk-vetch), native; eastern range limit in Otter Tail County; see key.

1 Pubescence of leaves dolabriform (hairs attached to surface at their center, 'T-shaped') or mostly so. 2
   2 Plants definitely caulescent; stipules (at least those at lower nodes), joined opposite the petiole 3
      3 Flowers greenish-white or tinged with purple, angled downward; stems from rhizomes. . . . ***A. canadensis***
      3 Flowers purplish, upright; stems from a crown. . . . . ***A. adsurgens***
   2 Plants without distinct stems or stems shorter than inflorescence and leaves; stipules distinct, not joined
      opposite leaves 4
      4 Banner 16-22 mm long; calyx tube 6-9 mm long. . . . . ***A. missouriensis***
      4 Banner less than 14 mm long; calyx tube 2-4.5 mm long . . . . ***A. lotiflorus***
1 Pubescence of leaves basifixed (hairs attached to surface at their base). 5
   5 Stipules distinct, not joined 6
      6 Stems erect; flowers white or pale yellow . . . . ***A. neglectus***
      6 Stems sprawling or ascending; flowers purple or pinkish . . . . ***A. crassicarpus***
   5 Stipules (at least those at lower nodes), joined to form a bidentate sheath. 7
      7 Flowers large, calyx tube 4.5 mm long or more; banner 13 mm long or longer. . . . . ***A. agrestis***
      7 Flowers smaller, calyx tube to 4.3 mm long; banner to 12.6 mm long 8
         8 Pod strongly compressed, 2-sided . . . . ***A. tenellus****
         8 Pod terete, not strongly compressed 9
            9 Pod short-stalked; rare in Lake County. . . . . ***A. alpinus***
            9 Pod sessile; w Minn . . . . ***A. flexuosus***

Astragalus adsurgens Pall.
MAP 666
PRAIRIE MILK-VETCH
native
   Astragalus laxmannii Jacq.

Tufted perennial from woody taproot and branching woody crown. **Stems** 1-4 dm tall, herbage grayish-strigulose with dolabriform hairs (hairs attached at their center). **Leaves** alternate, odd-pinnate, 4-15 cm long, lower leaves with petioles, uppr leaves sessile, **leaflets** 9-25, narrowly oblong, 1-2 cm long and 3-8 mm wide, strigose; stipules 5-15 mm long, joined for 1/3 or more of their length. **Flowers** in congested, somewhat spike-like racemes with ca. 15-50 flowers, on peduncles 4-14 cm long from the leaf axils; pedicels ca. 1 mm long; **calyx** 5-9 mm long, covered with mixed black and white hairs; **corolla** varying from dark purple, dull blue, or whitish; banner 13-19 mm long; wings 10-17 mm long; stamens 10. **Pod** nearly sessile, 7-12 mm long and 3-4 mm wide, strigulose with white basifixed hairs, seeds ca. 2 mm long, brown, smooth. June-Sept.—Dry, often rocky prairies; pastures, roadsides.

Astragalus adsurgens

Astragalus agrestis Dougl. ex G. Don
MAP 667
PURPLE MILK-VETCH
native

Low taprooted perennial. **Stems** decumbent to weakly erect, 1-3 dm tall, from a crown, thinly strigulose with basifixed hairs or nearly glabrous. **Leaves** alternate, pinnate, with short petioles or nearly sessile; stipules linear to ovate, 2-10 mm long, usually joined at their base; **leaflets** 11-21, lance-shaped to oblong, 4-20 mm long. **Flowers** in ovoid heads of 5-15 flowers; peduncles longer or shorter than leaves; pedicels to 1.5 mm long; **calyx tube** 5-8 mm long, covered with black and white hairs, **corolla** varying from purplish, bluish, whitish, or yellowish; banner, 17-22 mm long, shallowly or deeply notched; wings 15-18 mm long; stamens 10. **Pod** nearly sessile, erect, straight, 8-10 mm long, densely pubescent with white hairs; seeds ca. 2 mm long, brown, smooth. May-Aug.—Moist prairies, roadsides.

Astragalus agrestis

Astragalus alpinus L.
ALPINE MILK-VETCH

(NO MAP)

☙ *endangered | native*

Stems arising from slender rhizomes, more or less decumbent, 2-5 dm tall, glabrous or nearly so. **Leaflets** 15-29, narrowly oblong to oval, 1-2 cm long, 2-10 mm wide, sparsely pilosulous on both sides or glabrous above. **Racemes** long-peduncled, 2-4 cm long, loosely few-flowered, much elongate at maturity. **Flowers** purple or purplish, about 1 cm long; calyx tube broad, about 2 mm long; **calyx lobes** triangular, about 1 mm long; keel petals exceeding the wings and about as long as the standard. **Pods** reflexed, curved and densely pilose, lance-oblong, 10-13 mm long, more or less falcate, deeply sulcate on the lower side, on a petiole 3-4 mm long. May-Aug.—Sandy or gravelly, sparsely wooded lakeshores and riverbanks; rare in Lake County.

Astragalus canadensis L.
CANADIAN MILK-VETCH

MAP 668
native

Stems erect, to 15 dm tall, glabrous to thinly strigose. **Stipules** connate, lance-shaped to deltoid, 3-6 mm long. **Leaflets** 13-29, oblong or elliptic, 1-3 cm long, 5-15 mm wide, glabrous or rarely strigose above, strigose beneath with T-shaped hairs. **Racemes** long-peduncled, 5-12 cm long. **Flowers** white or yellowish white, spreading or somewhat reflexed, 12-15 mm long. **Pods** numerous in a crowded raceme, ovoid or oblong, 10-18 mm long, 2-celled, glabrous, nearly terete in cross-section. May-Aug.—Open woods, river banks, shores, usually in moist soil.

Astragalus crassicarpus Nutt.
GROUND-PLUM

MAP 669
native

Stems commonly several, clustered from a stout caudex, sparsely pilose, 2-5 dm tall. **Leaflets** 15-23, oblong lance-shaped to elliptic, 8-15 mm long, cuneate at base, appressed-pilose on both sides or glabrous above. **Flowers** about 2 cm long; calyx tube pubescent, 6-7 mm long; standard exceeding the wings and keel. **Pods** subglobose, about 2 cm wide, abruptly pointed, thick-walled, indehiscent, glabrous. April-May.—Dry prairies and bluffs.

Astragalus flexuosus (Hook.) Don
FLEXIBLE MILK-VETCH

MAP 670
native

Perennial caulescent herb. **Stems** slender, decumbent with ascending tips; 1.5-6 dm long, from a branched crown; plants greenish or silky-canescent, with basifixed hairs. **Leaves** alternate, odd-pinnate; petiolate below to nearly sessile above; stipules 1.5-7 mm long, joined near their base; leaflets 11-25, linear, obtuse. **Flowers** in racemes of ca. 12-26 flowers; peduncles axillary, 2.5-6 cm long; **calyx tube** ca 2.5 mm long; **corolla** pale purple; banner 7-9 mm long; wings 7-8 mm long. **Pod** nearly sessile, oblong, slightly compressed; seeds 2.-2.5 mm long, pale brown, smooth. June-July.—Prairies, roadsides.

Astragalus lotiflorus Hook.
LOTUS MILK-VETCH

MAP 671
native

Low, loosely to densely tufted perennial; taprooted and with a short crown; plants with dolabriform (T-shaped) pubescence, varying to hirsute. **Stems** 1-several, short, to only ca. 12 cm long; outer stems decumbent to prostrate; central stems more or less erect. **Leaves** alternate, odd-pinnate, 2-9 cm long; petioles absent or to 2 cm long; stipules 2-8 mm long, not joined; leaflets 7-17, elliptic, oblanceolate, or obovate, 4-15 mm long, variously pubescent. **Flowers** 3-17 in ovoid or

Astragalus alpinus

Astragalus canadensis

Astragalus crassicarpus

666. *Astragalus adsurgens*

667. *Astragalus agrestis*

668. *Astragalus canadensis*

669. *Astragalus crassicarpus*

subcapitate heads; **calyx tube** 3-4.5 mm long; **corolla** whitish or yellowish, sometimes purplish-tinged; banner 8-14 mm long; wings 7.5-12 mm long. **Pod** ascending to prostrate; 1.2-4 cm long, straight or curved, pubescent; seeds 1.5-2.5 mm long, brownish and often with purplish spots. April-June.—Prairies, shores, roadsides, waste places. *Cleistogamous flowers sometimes produced, usually on separate plants or later in the season.*

Astragalus missouriensis Nutt.
MISSOURI MILK-VETCH

MAP 672
native

Low perennials, loosely tufted or prostrate, with a taproot and branched crown; densely strigose throughout with dolabriform (T-shaped) hairs; plants silvery-white to greenish-gray. **Stems** short or sometimes nearly absent, 1-4 cm long, becoming prostrate in fruit. **Leaves** alternate, odd-pinnate, 4-10 cm long; stipules 2-9 mm long, lanceolate, distinct; **leaflets** usually 9-17, elliptic to narrowly obovate, 7-13 mm long. **Flowers** 3-15 in a raceme, on peduncles equaling or exceeding the leaves; pedicels to 2 mm long; **calyx tube** 6.5-9.5 mm long, grayish and usually blackish-strigulose; **corolla** rose-purple; banner 14-24 mm long; wings 13-19 mm long. **Pod** 1.5-3 cm long, 6-8 mm wide, sessile, straight or nearly so, subcylindric but laterally compressed when mature, crossocorrugated and strigulose, abruptly contracted at tip to a beak to 4 mm long; seeds 2-3 mm long, satiny brown, wrinkled. April-July.—Prairies, bluffs, roadsides.

Astragalus lotiflorus

Astragalus neglectus (Torr. & Gray) Sheldon
COOPER'S MILK-VETCH

MAP 673
native

Stems erect, 4-7 dm tall, nearly or quite glabrous. **Leaflets** 11-17, oblong to elliptic or obovate, 1-3 cm long, a fourth to a third as wide, glabrous above, strigose beneath. **Racemes** several, scarcely surpassing the subtending leaf, many-flowered; **calyx tube** cylindric, 4-6 mm long, strigose, the lobes about a third as long; **corolla** commonly white, 11-14 mm long. **Pods** erect, sessile, straight, ovoid, inflated, 1-2 cm long, glabrous. June.—Riverbanks and lakeshores, especially on limestone; disturbed forests and fields.

Astragalus neglectus

BAPTISIA *Wild Indigo*

Perennial herbs from thick rhizomes. Stems usually much branched and the lateral branches often surpassing the central axis in length, bearing conspicuous white, yellow, or violet flowers in long or short racemes terminating central axis and often also the lateral branches. Calyx bilabiate, the upper lip entire, notched, or 2-lobed, the lower deeply 3-lobed. Standard kidney-shaped to nearly circular; wings and keel nearly equal. Stamens 10. Pod papery to woody in texture, globose to cylindric, terminating in a curved beak, elevated on a distinct petiole. *Some species turn black when dried.*

ADDITIONAL SPECIES
Baptisia australis (L.) R. Br. (Blue wild indigo); native to e and se USA; adventive in St. Louis County (Duluth area) where a likely garden escape.

1   Bract at base of each pedicel 1-3 cm long, persistent and leaf-like, distincly net-veined . . . . ***B. bracteata***
1   Bracts smaller, less than 1 cm long, usually soon deciduous, not net-veined . . . . ***B. alba***

Baptisia alba (L.) Vent.
WHITE WILD INDIGO
  Baptisia lactea (Raf.) Thieret

MAP 674
native

Plants to 1.5 m tall, much branched, glabrous or nearly so throughout. **Stipules**

670. *Astragalus flexuosus*   671. *Astragalus lotiflorus*   672. *Astragalus missouriensis*   673. *Astragalus neglectus*

minute, soon deciduous. **Petioles** slender, 5-10 mm long. **Leaflets** oblong lance-shaped, 2-4 cm long, 8-15 mm wide, obtuse to rounded at the summit. **Racemes** single or few, erect, 2-5 dm long; bracts early deciduous, about 5 mm long. Pedicels usually 3-6 mm long. **Flowers** white, 12-18 mm long; calyx about 7 mm long, the upper lip entire, the lobes of the lower triangular-ovate. **Pod** cylindric, brown, 2-3 cm long, mm wide, on a petiole scarcely exceeding the calyx.—Dry sandy woods, mostly on the coastal plain.

Baptisia bracteata Muhl.   MAP 675
PLAINS WILD INDIGO   *native*
Plants 4-8 dm tall, pubescent throughout. **Stipules** persistent, foliaceous, lance-shaped, those of the lower leaves up to 4 cm long, the upper gradually reduced. **Petioles** 2-5 mm long. **Leaflets** oblong lance-shaped, the larger ones up to 8 cm long. **Raceme** usually single, more or less declined, 1-2 dm long, secund; bracts persistent, lance-shaped or oblong, 1-3 cm long, reticulately veined; pedicels 1.54 cm long. **Flowers** white or cream-color, 20-28 mm long. **Pod** ellipsoid, 3-5 cm long, pubescent, tapering to a conspicuous beak.—Prairies, open dry woods.

Baptisia alba

CARAGANA *Peashrub*

Caragana arborescens Lam.   MAP 676
SIBERIAN PEASHRUB   *introduced*
Shrub or small tree to 6 m tall, young branches pubescent. **Leaves** alternate or fascicled, even-pinnate, petiolate; stipules spiny, to 9 mm long; **leaflets** 8-12, obovate to elliptic-oblong, 1-3 cm long, rounded at tip and mucronate, pubescent when young, later glabrescent. **Flowers** 1-4, fascicled on short spur branches, yellow, on pedicels 1-4 cm long; **calyx tube** 5-5.5 mm long; banner to 20 mm long, notched at tip. **Pod** 3.5-5 cm long, to 5 mm wide, sessile, narrowed at tip to a slender beakbeak;seeds 4.5-5 mm long, dark brown. smooth. May-June. —Commonly planted in shelter belts, occasionally escaping; native to Siberia.

CHAMAECRISTA *Sensitive-Pea*

Chamaecrista fasciculata (Michx.) Greene   MAP 677
PARTRIDGE-PEA   *native*
Annual. **Stems** erect, ascending, or rarely spreading, pubescent. Petiolar gland saucer-shaped, sessile or nearly so. **Leaflets** 6-18 pairs, oblong, usually 1-2 cm long, acute to obtuse, mucronate. **Flowers** 1-6 in short, axillary, bracted racemes; pedicels 1-2 cm long; petals bright yellow, nearly equal, 1-2 cm long; stamens 10, very unequal, the two largest up to 10 mm long. **Pod** linear-oblong, flat, straight; seeds quadrate, faintly marked with shallow pits in rows. July-Sept. Variable in size and pubescence.—Moist or dry prairie, open woods, roadsides; especially in sandy soil.

Chamaecrista fasciculata

CROTALARIA *Rattlebox*

Crotalaria sagittalis L.   MAP 678
ARROW-HEAD RATTLEBOX   *native*
Annual herb. **Stems** simple or branched above, 1-4 dm tall, pubescent with spreading hairs. **Stipules** present, at least on the upper leaves, decurrent on the stem. **Leaves** pubescent, sessile or nearly so, lance-shaped to linear, 3-8 cm long,

Crotalaria sagittalis

674. *Baptisia alba*

675. *Baptisia bracteata*

676. *Caragana arborescens*

677. *Chamaecrista fasciculata*

up to 1.5 cm wide. **Racemes** 2-4-flowered, terminating the stem and branches; calyx villous, about 9 mm long; lower sepals linear lance-shaped. Standard about 8 mm long, yellow. **Pod** oblong, 2-3 cm long, much inflated, nearly sessile in the calyx. June-Sept.—Dry open soil and waste places.

DALEA *Prairie-Clover*

Annual or perennial herbs. Leaves small, odd-pinnate, glandular-punctate; stipules setaceous. Flowers numerous, small, each subtended by a bract, in dense terminal spikes. Calyx campanulate to tubular, usually sharply ribbed; calyx lobes about equal, triangular to lance-shaped. Corolla apparently of 5 petals, actually of only 1; the standard, with an obovate to rotund blade on an elongate capillary claw, the other apparent petals actually staminodes. Stamens 9; 5 stamens fertile, long-exsert, alternating with 4 petal-like staminodes. Pod enclosed by the persistent calyx, somewhat compressed, obovate, 1-2-seeded.

1   Flowers white. 2
    2   Plants annual; calyx tube pilose . . . . *D. leporina*
    2   Plants perennial; calyx tube glabrous . . . . *D. candida*
1   Flowers purple or violet; calyx tube densely hairy 3
    3   Main leaves with mostly 5 leaflets . . . . *D. purpurea*
    3   Main leaves with mostly 11-17 leaflets . . . . *D. villosa*

Dalea candida Michx.   MAP 679
WHITE PRAIRIE-CLOVER   *native*
   Petalostemum candidum (Willd.) Michx.

Perennial herb; foliage and erect stems glabrous. **Leaflets** 5-9, commonly 7, linear to oblong, 1-3 cm long, 2-5 mm wide, flat, often mucronate, glandular punctate beneath. **Spikes** 1 to few, the terminal one cylindric, 2-8 cm long; bracts glabrous, the oblong lance-shaped body about equaling the calyx tube, tapering to an acuminate tip much surpassing the calyx lobes; **calyx tube** sharply 10-ribbed, glabrous to short-villous; calyx lobes finely ciliate; **corolla** white. **Pod** 2.6-4.5 mm long, usually exserted, glandular; seeds 1.5-2.5 mm long May-Aug.—Dry prairies or dry upland woods.

Dalea leporina (Aiton) Bullock   MAP 680
FOXTAIL PRAIRIE-CLOVER   *native*

Erect annual herb with a slender taproot. **Stems** 1.5-10 dm tall, branching from near base to more often at midstem, glabrous, glandular above. Principal stem **leaves** with 8-24 pairs of leaflets; **leaflets** oblong-lanceolate, 3-12 mm long, gland-dotted on underside, glabrous, margins sometimes red-tinged. **Spikes** densely flowered, ovoid or cylindric, 2-8 cm long, on peduncles 3-10 cm long at end of branches and opposite leaves; calyx tube 2 mm long, pilose; **corolla** white or tinged with blue. **Pod** 2.5-3 mm long; seeds 2 mm long, smooth and shiny brown. July-Sept.—Roadsides, fields, streambanks, open woods.

Dalea candida

Dalea purpurea Vent.   MAP 681
PURPLE PRAIRIE-CLOVER   *native*
   Petalostemum purpureum (Vent.) Rydb.

Perennial herb; foliage and stems usually glabrous. **Stems** single or few from the same base. **Leaves** numerous, often with smaller ones clustered in the axils; **leaflets** 3-7, usually 5, involute when dry, linear, 8-20 mm long, 1-2 mm wide,

678. Crotalaria sagittalis   *679. Dalea candida*   *680. Dalea leporina*   *681. Dalea purpurea*

glandular-punctate beneath. **Spikes** cylindric, 2-6 cm long; bracts shorter than the calyx, the oblong lance-shaped body villous at the tip, tapering into a dark, subulate, glabrous tip; calyx densely villous; **corolla** rose-purple, rarely varying to white. **Pod** 2-2.5 mm long; seeds 1.5-2 mm long, brown, smooth. June-Aug.— Dry prairies.

Dalea villosa (Nutt.) Spreng.   MAP 682
DOWNY PRAIRIE-CLOVER   *native*
  Petalostemum villosum Nutt.

Perennial herb. **Stems** softly and densely villous, very leafy. **Leaflets** 11-17, oblong, 5-10 mm long, glandular-punctate beneath, softly villous, usually flat even when dry. **Spikes** cylindric, 3-10 cm long; bracts narrowly lance-shaped, somewhat surpassing the calyx, villous, quickly deciduous; **calyx** densely villous; **corolla** rose-purple, varying to white. **Pod** 2.5-3 mm long, densely villous; seeds 2-2.5 mm long, brown, smooth. Aug.—Sandy prairies.

DESMANTHUS *Bundle-Flower*

Desmanthus illinoensis (Michx.) MacM.   MAP 683

Dalea purpurea

PRAIRIE BUNDLE-FLOWER   *native*
Perennial herb. **Stems** 1-2 m tall, strongly angled, glabrous to finely hairy. **Stipules** filiform, 6-10 mm long. **Leaves** 2-pinnate, 5-10 cm long; pinnae 6-12 pairs, 2-4 cm long; **leaflets** 20-30 pairs, oblong, 3-5 mm long, often ciliate. **Flowers** whitish or greenish in long-peduncled axillary heads; calyx campanulate, 5-toothed; petals 5, about 2 mm long; stamens 5, usually long-exsert. **Pods** strongly curved or some- what twisted together in a dense subglobose head, thin, 1-2.5 cm long, 4-7 mm wide; seeds 3-5 mm long, nearly as wide. Summer. Our species usually with one or more round glands on the leaf-rachis between the bases of the pinnae.—Moist or dry soil, riverbanks, prairies, and pastures.

Desmanthus illinoensis

DESMODIUM *Tick-Trefoil*

Ours perennial herbs. Leaves petioled, 3-parted. Flowers small, white to purple or violet, sometimes marked with yellow, often greenish in age, in elongate, simple or panicled racemes. Calyx tube more or less 2-lipped, slightly oblique; upper 2 calyx lobes connate for all or most of their length, the lower 3 separate. Standard oblong to nearly orbicular, narrowed at base; wings oblong; keel nearly straight. Fruit an indehiscent pod, elevated on a stalk above the persistent calyx and stamens, more or less beset with hooked hairs.

1 Pods conspicuously long-stalked, the stalk 2-3 times the length of the calyx 2
  2 Flowers in a panicle on a leafy stem . . . . ***D. glutinosum***
  2 Panicle on a long leafless stalk . . . . ***D. nudiflorum***
1 Pods sessile or short-stalked 3
  3 Stipules small, awl-shaped, soon deciduous . . . . ***D. canadense***
  3 Stipules large, persistent, lance-shaped to ovate, persistent 4
    4 Joints of the pod oval-shaped . . . . ***D. illinoense***
    4 Joints of the pod diamond-shaped, longer than wide 5
      5 Leaflets rounded at tip, about same length as petiole . . . . ***D. canescens***
      5 Leaflets tapered to a tip, longer than petiole . . . . ***D. cuspidatum***

Desmodium canadense (L.) DC.   MAP 684
SHOWY TICK-TREFOIL   *native*
Stems erect, branched above, to 2 m tall, pubescent. **Stipules** linear-subulate, to 8 mm long, ciliate, otherwise glabrous. **Petioles** 2-20 mm, usually about 10 mm long, the petiole and leaf-rachis together up to 1/2 as long as the terminal leaflet. **Leaflets** oblong or lance-oblong, appressed-pubescent beneath, the terminal 5-9 cm long. **Racemes** densely flowered, with conspicuous ovate lance-shaped bracts. **Flowers** 10-13 mm long; calyx 5-7 mm long; petiole of the fruit 2-4 mm long; joints commonly 3-5. July-Aug.—Moist soil, thickets, and riverbanks.

Desmodium canescens (L.) DC.   (NO MAP)
HOARY TICK-TREFOIL   *native*

Stems erect, 1-1.5 m tall, more or less pubescent. **Stipules** long persistent, ovate, acuminate, up to 12 mm long, ciliate, otherwise nearly glabrous. **Petioles** nearly as long as the lateral leaflets. **Leaflets** thin, ovate lance-shaped to ovate, inconspicuously reticulate, nearly smooth, the terminal usually 6-11 cm long. **Panicle** of several racemes, the axis more or less villous or hirsute. **Flowers** about 10 mm long; calyx about 5 mm long, sparsely hirsute; petiole of the fruit 2-5 mm long; joints usually 4-6. July-Aug.—Moist or dry soil; Chisago County.

Desmodium cuspidatum (Muhl.) DC.   MAP 685
BIG TICK-TREFOIL   ❧*threatened | native*

Stems erect, stout, leafy, to 2 m tall. **Stipules** lance-shaped, 8-17 mm long, usually persistent. **Petioles** of the principal leaves flattened distally, commonly 5-8 cm long, those of the upper leaves shorter. **Leaflets** thin, bright green above, paler beneath, the lateral ovate lance-shaped, the terminal ovate, 6-12 cm long, sharply acuminate. **Inflorescence** a simple raceme or a sparsely branched panicle. **Flowers** 10-12 mm long; calyx 4-5 mm long; petiole of the fruit 2-5 mm long; joints 3-7. July-Aug.—Mesic woods of oak, sugar maple and basswood.

Desmodium canadense

Desmodium glutinosum (Muhl.) Wood   MAP 686
POINTED-LEAF TICK-TREFOIL   *native*

Stems erect, 1-4 dm tall, bearing near the summit several long-petioled leaves and prolonged into a terminal panicle 3-8 dm long. **Lateral leaflets** asymmetrically ovate, acuminate; **terminal leaflet** round-ovate, 7-15 cm long and nearly as wide, long-acuminate. **Flowers** 6-8 mm long; calyx 2.5-3 mm long; petiole of the fruit 6-12 mm long, glabrous; joints seldom more than 3. July.—Rich woods.

Desmodium illinoense Gray   MAP 687
ILLINOIS TICK-TREFOIL   *native*

Stems erect, 1-2 m tall, pubescent with hooked hairs, commonly bearing a single elongate, terminal raceme. **Stipules** ovate, 10-15 mm long, persistent, ciliate, glabrous above, pubescent beneath. **Petiole** much longer than the stalk of the terminal leaflet, pubescent with hooked hairs and sparsely hirsute. **Leaflets** ovate lance-shaped, rough on both sides with hooked hairs, strongly reticulate beneath, the terminal commonly 6-10 cm long. Axis of the panicle softly villous to hirsute. **Flowers** 8-10 mm long; petiole of the fruit 2-4 mm long; joints 3-6. July-Aug.—Rich prairie soil.

Desmodium glutinosum

Desmodium nudiflorum (L.) DC.   MAP 688
NAKED-FLOWER TICK-TREFOIL   ❧*threatened | native*
   Hylodesmum nudiflorum (L.) H. Ohashi & R.R. Mill

Stems normally forked from the base, the one branch sterile, 1-3 dm tall, naked below, bearing a crowded cluster of leaves at the summit, the other fertile, leafless, ascending, 4-10 dm tall. **Lateral leaflets** ovate to ovate-oblong; **terminal leaflet** elliptic to ovate, 4-10 cm long. **Flowers** 6-8 mm long on capillary pedicels usually 1-2 cm long; petiole of the fruit glabrous, 10-18 mm long; joints 2-4. July-Sept.—Rich woods, especially with red oak (*Quercus rubra*).

Desmodium illinoense

682. *Dalea villosa*

683. *Desmanthus illinoensis*

684. *Desmodium canadense*

685. *Desmodium cuspidatum*

GLEDITSIA *Honey-Locust*

Gleditsia triacanthos L.
HONEY-LOCUST   MAP 689
native

Tree, commonly to 20 m tall, stems and branches usually thorny. **Leaves** often closely crowded on short branches, pinnate or 2-pinnate even on the same tree, the pinnate with 9-14 pairs of leaflets, the bipinnate with 4-7 pairs of pinnae; **leaflets** oblong lance-shaped, obscurely crenate, 2-4 cm long on pinnate leaves, 1-2 cm long on bipinnate leaves. **Flowers** unisexual or rarely perfect, greenish yellow, in spike-like racemes; **staminate racemes** 4-10 cm long, densely many-flowered; **pistillate racemes** looser with fewer flowers; petals and sepals each 3-5, almost alike; stamens 3-10, inserted at the base of the perianth, exsert. **Pods** curved and usually twisted, 1-4 dm long, 3-4 cm wide, dark brown, rather papery in texture, indehiscent, pubescent when young, eventually glabrous, the seeds about 2 cm apart and separated by a sweetish pulp.—Rich moist woods.

Gleditsia triacanthos

GLYCYRRHIZA *Licorice*

Glycyrrhiza lepidota Pursh
AMERICAN LICORICE   MAP 690
native

Glandular-dotted perennial herb. **Stems** to 1 m tall, the younger parts and lower side of the leaflets dotted with minute glands. **Leaves** odd-pinnate; leaflets 11-19, oblong or lance-shaped. **Flowers** in dense axillary racemes shorter than the subtending leaves; pale yellow, 12-15 mm long; calyx bilabiate, the tube campanulate, the upper two lobes united for part of their length; petals usually acute, the standard obovate, the wings and keel shorter. **Pods** brown, about 15 mm long, 1-celled, few-seeded, densely beset with hooked prickles. May-June. —Moist prairies, along railroads and in waste places.

Glycyrrhiza lepidota

GYMNOCLADUS *Coffeetree*

Gymnocladus dioicus (L.) K. Koch
KENTUCKY COFFEETREE   MAP 691
native

Tree to 30 m tall, polygamo-dioecious. Single **leaves** sometimes nearly 1 m long, with 3-7 pairs of pinnae, each with several pairs of ovate, abruptly acuminate leaflets, or the lowest pinnae replaced by single leaflets. **Flowers** regular, perfect or unisexual, greenish-white, softly pubescent, in terminal panicles 6-20 cm long; petals and sepals each 5, nearly alike, oblong or oblong lance-shaped, 8-10 mm long, exceeding the stamens. **Pods** 8-15 cm long, 3-5 cm wide, shed in early spring; seeds thick, very hard, nearly black, 10-15 mm wide and long. May.—Rich moist woods. *Seeds toxic to livestock.*

Gymnocladus dioicus

LATHYRUS *Vetchling; Wild Pea*

Perennial herbs (ours). Leaves terminated by a tendril. Flowers few to many in a raceme; corolla small or medium-sized, red-purple to white or yellow; standard broadly obovate; wings obovate; keel upwardly curved. Pods flat to terete, 2–many-seeded. Most of our species superficially resemble *Vicia*.

ADDITIONAL SPECIES
Lathyrus sylvestris L. (Narrow-leaf vetchling), introduced; Grant and St. Louis counties.

686. *Desmodium glutinosum*   687. *Desmodium illinoense*   688. *Desmodium nudiflorum*   689. *Gleditsia triacanthos*

1   Leaflets 1-pair; introduced species 2
   2   Stem winged . . . . *L. latifolius*
   2   Stem not winged . . . . *L. tuberosus*
1   Leaflets 2 or more pairs; native species 3
   3   Flowers yellow-white . . . . *L. ochroleucus*
   3   Flowers purple, rarely white 4
     4   Stipules leafy, nearly as large as the adjacent leaflets . . . . *L. japonicus*
     4   Stipules much smaller than leaflets 5
       5   Stems usually winged; racemes with usually 10-20 flowers; moist habitats . . . . *L. palustris*
       5   Stems not winged; racemes with 2-6 flowers; dry woods . . . . *L. venosus*

Lathyrus japonicus Willd.
BEACH-PEA   MAP 692 *native*
    Lathyrus maritimus Bigelow

Perennial, plants typically glabrous. **Stems** stout, decumbent to nearly erect, up to 1 m long. **Stipules** foliaceous, broadly ovate, 1.5-4 cm long, 1-2.5 cm wide, essentially symmetrical and therefore attached at the middle of the broadly truncate base. **Leaflets** 3-6 pairs, oblong to obovate, 3-5 cm long; about half as wide, the lowest pair near the base of the petiole. Peduncles equaling or shorter than the subtending leaves, bearing usually 5-10 purple flowers about 2 cm long; calyx irregular, the lowest lobe linear lance-shaped, nearly 2x as long as the triangular upper ones. June-Aug.—Beaches and lakeshores.

Lathyrus latifolius L.
EVERLASTING-PEA   MAP 693 *introduced*

Perennial. **Stems** climbing or trailing, to 2 m long, broadly winged, 5-10 mm wide. **Stipules** lance-shaped, with a basal lobe, foliaceous, 1.5-4 cm long, usually wider than the stem. **Petiole** broadly winged, about as wide as the stem. **Leaflets** 2, lance-shaped to elliptic, 4-8 cm long, 1-3 cm wide. Peduncles 10-20 cm long, bearing a raceme of 4-10 handsome flowers 1.5-2.5 cm long; corolla purple, varying to pink or white; calyx lobes very unequal. June-Aug.—Native of s Europe; cultivated and escaping to roadsides and vacant land.

Lathyrus ochroleucus

Lathyrus ochroleucus Hook.
CREAM VETCHLING   MAP 694 *native*

Glabrous perennial. **Stems** to 8 dm long. **Stipules** semi-ovate, 1.5-3 cm long, the larger ones toothed, usually shorter than the petiole. **Leaflets** 3-5 pairs, thin, elliptic to ovate lance-shaped, 2.5-5 cm long. **Racemes** shorter than the subtending leaf, bearing 5-10 yellowish white flowers 12-18 mm long; calyx irregular, the upper lobes triangular, to half as long as the lower. May-July.—Dry upland woods and thickets.

Lathyrus palustris L.
MARSH VETCHLING   MAP 695 *native*

Perennial vining herb, spreading by rhizomes. **Stems** to 1 m long, strongly winged, climbing and clinging to surrounding plants by tendrils. **Leaves** pinnately divided, with 4-8 leaflets and a terminal leaflet modified into a tendril; **leaflets** linear to lance-shaped, 2-7 cm long and 3-20 mm wide; **stipules** prominent, more or less arrowhead-shaped, 1-3 cm long; margins entire; petioles absent. **Flowers** in racemes from leaf axils, 2-6 flowers per raceme, red-purple, drying blue to blue-violet; sepals irregular, 7-10 mm long; petals 12-20 mm long. **Fruit** a flat,

Lathyrus palustris

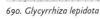

many-seeded pod, 3-5 cm long. June-Aug.—Conifer swamps, wet meadows, marshes, streambanks, calcareous fens, low prairie.

Lathyrus tuberosus L.

EARTH-NUT VETCHLING

MAP 696
introduced

Perennial, with tuberously thickened roots. **Stems** wingless, 4-angled, to 8 dm long, branched above. **Stipules** lance-shaped, 5-12 mm long, with a single short basal lobe. **Leaflets** 2, oblong lance-shaped to elliptic, 1.5-3 cm long. Peduncles 5-8 cm long, bearing a crowded raceme of 2-5 red-purple flowers about 15 mm long, the standard broader than long; calyx lobes broadly triangular, shorter than the tube. June-Aug.—Native of Europe and w Asia.

Lathyrus venosus Muhl.

VEINY VETCHLING

MAP 697
native

Perennial. **Stems** stout, to 1 m long, glabrous or sparsely pubescent. **Stipules** narrowly lance-shaped to semi-ovate in outline. **Leaflets** commonly 8, 10, or 12, narrowly to broadly elliptic, 3-6 cm long, rounded to the mucronate tip. Peduncles stout, shorter than to equaling the subtending leaves, bearing a dense raceme of 10-30 purple flowers about 15 mm long; calyx oblique, the lower teeth much exceeding the upper but shorter than the tube. June-July.—Moist woods and thickets.

Lathyrus venosus

LESPEDEZA *Bush-Clover*

Annual or perennial herbs, or some exotic species shrubs. Leaves small, trifoliolate. Flowers purple to yellowish white, in sessile or peduncled axillary clusters, each flower subtended at base by 2 (sometimes 4) small bractlets; some species produce 2 types of flowers, with and without petals. Calyx tube short, campanulate; calyx lobes equal in length, separate or the 2 uppermost joined for part of their length. Standard short-clawed; wings straight, clawed and auriculate, connivent with the keel. Stamens equal. Fruit oval to elliptic, indehiscent, 1-seeded. *The genus differs from* **Desmodium** *by its 1-seeded fruits and in the absence of leaflet petioles.*

ADDITIONAL SPECIES

Lespedeza violacea (L.) Pers., native species usually on sandstone bluffs, Wabasha and Winona counties, more common south and east of the state; leaflets glabrous; flowers purple, in loose racemes.

1 Plants woody, at least at base, 1-3 m tall . . . . *L. cuneata*
1 Plants entirely herbaceous . . . . *L. virginica*
   2 Leaflets linear; spikes slender, loosely flowered . . . . *L. leptostachya*
   2 Leaflets elliptic; flowers in densely flowered rounded heads . . . . *L. capitata*

Lespedeza capitata Michx.

ROUND-HEAD BUSH-CLOVER

MAP 698
native

Stems usually erect, 6-15 dm tall, simple or branched above, sparsely to densely villous. **Leaflets** oblong, to 4.5 cm long and 1.8 cm wide, glabrous to sericeous above, thinly to densely sericeous or velutinous beneath. **Petioles** 2-5 mm long. **Spikes** numerous, forming a thyrsoid inflorescence, subglobose to short-ovoid, 12-25 mm long, with densely crowded flowers; peduncles rarely longer than the spikes and usually shorter than the subtending leaves. **Flowers** 8-12 mm long; calyx lobes villous, 6-10 mm long. **Fruit** pubescent, conspicuously shorter (about 2 mm long) than the calyx. July-Sept.—Open dry woods, sand dunes, and prairies. Plants growing on sand dunes are occasionally prostrate.

694. Lathyrus ochroleucus   *695. Lathyrus palustris*   *696. Lathyrus tuberosus*   *697. Lathyrus venosus*

Lespedeza cuneata (Dum.-Cours.) G. Don   (NO MAP)
CHINESE BUSH-CLOVER   *introduced*

Stems erect, somewhat shrubby, with numerous elongate virgate branches, very leafy. **Leaflets** ascending or erect, linear-cuneate, 10-25 mm long, truncate and mucronate at the tip, glabrous above, sericeous beneath. Branches pubescent on the angles. **Petioles** 2-5 mm long. **Flowers** mostly solitary in the upper axils, white marked with purple or pink, 7-9 mm long; calyx sericeous, the lobes lance-subulate, about 3 mm long. **Pod** oval, about 3 mm long. Sept-Oct.—Native of e Asia; introduced into cultivation and reported from Green County.

*Lespedeza
capitata*

Lespedeza leptostachya Engelm.   MAP 699
PRAIRIE BUSH-CLOVER   ☙*threatened | native*

Stems erect, nearly simple, 5-10 dm tall, sericeous. Leaflets narrowly oblong, 2-4 cm long, 3-7 mm wide, obtuse and mucronate, sparsely appressed pubescent above, sericeous beneath. Petioles 4-10 mm long. Spikes slender, interrupted, 2-3 cm long, on peduncles 1-2 cm long. Flowers about 4 mm long, the corolla about equaling the Calyx lobes. Fruit densely villous, as long as the Calyx lobes. July-Aug.—Dry, gravelly or sandy hillside prairies. *State and Federally threatened.*

Lespedeza virginica (L.) Britt.   (NO MAP)
SLENDER BUSH-CLOVER   *native*

Stems erect or nearly so, simple or virgately branched above, 3-9 dm tall. **Leaves** usually erect to strongly ascending; **leaflets** linear to narrowly oblong, 3-5 mm wide, usually 4-6 times as long, sparsely short-strigose above or rarely glabrous. **Flowers** purple, 6-8 mm long, the apetalous flowers mostly along the middle of the stem in small sessile clusters, the petaliferous flowers in short few-flowered racemes from the axils of the upper leaves, on peduncles shorter than the leaves, forming a crowded leafy inflorescence; calyx lobes of the petaliferous flowers 2-3 mm long, the 2 uppermost connate for up to 2/3 of their length. **Fruit** thinly strigose. Aug-Sept.—Dry prairies, open upland woods, red cedar glades; Winona County. *Similar to* **Lespedeza capitata** *except the leaves are more crowded, and the leaflets are longer and more hairy on upper surface.*

Lespedeza leptostachya

LOTUS *Bird's-foot Trefoil*

Herbaceous or suffrutescent herbs. Leaves pinnately compound. Flowers solitary or umbellate. Calyx campanulate or obconic, the elongate teeth nearly equal. Petals clawed; standard obovate, not auriculate; keel petals usually distinctly beaked. Pod several-seeded, oblong to linear, terete (ours).

1 Leaflets 5 . . . . **L. corniculatus**
1 Leaflets 3 . . . . **L. unifoliolatus**

Lotus corniculatus L.   MAP 700
BIRD'S-FOOT-TREFOIL   *introduced (invasive)*
    Lotus corniculatus var. *arvensis* (Schkuhr) Ser.

Perennial herb. **Stems** prostrate, ascending, or erect, to 6 dm long. **Leaves** nearly sessile, without stipules; **leaflets** 5, elliptic to oblong lance-shaped, 5-15 mm long, the terminal one sessile. **Flowers** in long-peduncled head-like umbels from the upper axils; pedicels 1-3 mm long; calyx lobes linear-triangular, about equaling the tube; corolla yellow to brick-red, about 14 mm long. **Pods** 2-4 cm long. June-Aug.—Native of Europe; established in fields, meadows, and roadsides.

698. *Lespedeza capitata*   699. *Lespedeza leptostachya*   700. *Lotus corniculatus*   701. *Lotus unifoliolatus*

Lotus unifoliolatus (Hook.) Benth.
SPANISH CLOVER

MAP 701
native

Acmispon americanus (Nutt.) Rydb.
Lotus purshianus F.E. & E.G. Clem.

Annual herb. **Stems** erect, branched, 2-6 dm tall. **Leaves** almost sessile; stipules represented by minute glands; **leaflets** 3, lance-shaped to ovate, 1-2 cm long, the terminal one stalked. **Flowers** solitary in the upper axils; peduncles about equaling the subtending leaves, bearing a terminal bract as long as the flower; calyx lobes hirsute, linear, exceeding the tube; corolla pink, 5-7 mm long. **Pods** deflexed, 2-3 cm long. Summer.—Dry prairies.

Lotus corniculatus

LUPINUS *Lupine*

Perennial herbs. Leaves palmately compound. Flowers white, yellow, pink, or blue, in terminal racemes or spikes. Calyx deeply bilabiate, the upper lip 2-toothed, the lower entire or 3-lobed. Standard suborbicular with strongly reflexed sides; wings united toward the summit; keel petals strongly convex on the lower side, prolonged into a beak-like tip. Stamens 10, forming a closed tube for about half their length. Pods oblong, flattened, with 2-several seeds. *Several species cultivated for ornament; toxic to humans and livestock if eaten.*

1   Plants large, to 1 m or more tall; leaflets 11-17; inflorescence 2-4 dm long . . . .**L. polyphyllus**
1   Plants smaller, 3-6 dm tall; leaflets 7-11; inflorescence 1-2 dm long . . . .**L. perennis**

Lupinus perennis L.
SUNDIAL-LUPINE

MAP 702
native

Perennial herb. **Stems** erect, 2-6 dm tall, thinly pubescent. **Leaflets** 7-11, oblong lance-shaped, 2-5 cm long. **Petioles** 2-6 cm long. **Racemes** erect, 1-2 dm long, with numerous attractive blue flowers, varying to pink or white. Lower lip of the calyx entire, about 8 mm long; upper lip about half as long. Standard 12-16 mm long and about as wide. **Pods** pubescent, 3-5 cm long. May-June.—In dry or moist sandy soil of prairies, clearings, and savannas.

Lupinus polyphyllus Lindl.
BLUE-POD LUPINE

MAP 703
introduced

Perennial herb. Plants taller and coarser than *L. perennis,* to 1 m or more tall; **leaflets** 11-17; **inflorescence** 2-4 dm long.—Escape from cultivation, especially along roadsides.

Lupinus perennis

MEDICAGO *Alfalfa; Medick*

Herbs with 3-foliolate serrulate leaves, the terminal leaflet stalked. Flowers in axillary heads or short head-like racemes of small yellow or blue flowers. Calyx tube campanulate, the 5 lobes nearly equal. Standard obovate or oblong, longer than the oblong erect wings; keel blunt, shorter than the wings. Stamens all free from the corolla. Pod straight or coiled, glabrous or spiny, usually indehiscent, 1-several-seeded.

1   Plants perennial from a long taproot; flowers blue-violet or sometimes yellow . . . .**M. sativa**
1   Plants annual or biennial; flowers yellow . . . .**M. lupulina**

702. *Lupinus perennis*   703. *Lupinus polyphyllus*   704. *Medicago lupulina*   705. *Medicago sativa*

Medicago lupulina L.

BLACK MEDICK

MAP 704
introduced (naturalized)

Annual herb. **Stems** prostrate, widely spreading, or ascending, to 8 dm long; 4-angled. **Leaflets** elliptic to obovate, 1-2 cm long. **Stipules** lance-shaped, entire or toothed. Peduncles slender, much exceeding the subtending leaves, bearing a globose to short-cylindric head up to 1 cm long; peduncles and calyx glandular. **Flowers** yellow, 2-4 mm long. **Pods** nearly black, 2-3 mm long, kidney-shaped, 1-seeded, the conspicuous veins tending to be longitudinal. May–Sept.—Native of Europe and w Asia; common as a troublesome weed of roadsides, lawns, fields, railroads, and disturbed places.

Medicago sativa L.

ALFALFA

MAP 705
introduced

Perennial herb. **Stems** erect or decumbent, to 1 m tall. **Leaflets** oblong lance-shaped, 1.5-3 cm long, toothed at the tip. **Stipules** ovate lance-shaped, toothed. Peduncles erect, about equaling the subtending leaves, with a subglobose to short-cylindric head 1-3 cm long. **Flowers** blue, nearly 1 cm long, on pedicels 2-3 mm long; sepals linear lance-shaped, 2-3 mm long, about equaling the tube. **Pod** coiled into a loose spiral of 1-3 complete turns, finely pubescent. June–Sept.—Native probably of c and w Asia; long in cultivation and valued for hay and forage; commonly escaped or introduced on roadsides, fields, and disturbed places.

Medicago lupulina (top)
Medicago sativa (bottom)

MELILOTUS *Sweet-Clover*

Annual or biennial herbs. Leaves 3-foliolate, serrulate, the terminal leaflet stalked. Flowers white or yellow, in elongate peduncled racemes from the upper axils; stipules partially adnate to the petiole. Calyx eventually deciduous, the tube campanulate, the lobes nearly equal. Petals separate; standard oblong to obovate, usually longer than the others; wings and keel coherent. Ovary short, sessile or somewhat stipitate. Pod ovate to rotund, slightly compressed to nearly globose, 1-4-seeded.

1   Flowers white .... *M. albus*
1   Flowers yellow .... *M. officinalis*

Melilotus albus Medik.

WHITE SWEET-CLOVER

(NO MAP)
introduced (invasive)

Stems erect, 1-3 m tall. **Leaflets** lance-shaped or oblong lance-shaped to narrowly oblong or rarely ovate, 1-2.5 cm long. **Racemes** numerous, 5-20 cm long, including the peduncles. Pedicels 1-2 mm long. **Flowers** white, 4-6 mm long. Summer and fall.—Native of Europe and w Asia; throughout Minn in waste places and along roads, especially in calcareous soil. *Sometimes treated as only a color variant of Melilotus officinalis.*

Melilotus officinalis (L.) Lam.

YELLOW SWEET-CLOVER

MAP 706
introduced (invasive)

Stems erect or ascending, 5-15 dm tall. **Leaflets** oblong lance-shaped to obovate, 1-2.5 cm long. **Racemes** 5-15 cm long including the peduncle. Pedicels 1.5-2 mm long, decurved. **Flowers** yellow, 5-7 mm long. Summer.—Native of Eurasia; established as a weed of waste places.

Melilotus officinalis

706. *Melilotus officinalis*   707. *Oxytropis campestris*   708. *Oxytropis lambertii*    709. *Pediomelum argophyllum*

OXYTROPIS *Locoweed*

Tufted, taprooted perennials; acaulescent. Leaves odd-pinnately divided into leaflets. Flowers in pedunculate spikes or racemes; calyx usually campanulate; petals usually reddish-purple (our species); stamens 10. Pod several-seeded.

ADDITIONAL SPECIES
Oxytropis viscida Nutt. (Sticky locoweed), ☙*endangered;* in Minn, known from a single north-facing cliff site in Cook County; disjunct from western North America and the arctic.

1 Pubescence of herbage with dolabriform hairs (hairs T-shaped, attached to surface at their center) **O. lambertii**
1 Pubescence of basifuced hairs (hairs attached to surface at their base) . . . . **O. campestris**

Oxytropis campestris (L.) DC.
FASSETT'S LOCOWEED
MAP 707
native
Leaflets lance-shaped, 8-25 mm long, densely to sparsely villous or nearly glabrous. **Scapes** villous or sericeous. **Spikes** dense, 2-4 cm long, much longer in fruit; bracts lance-shaped, densely villous, not glandular; **calyx** tubular, villous, the tube 5-7 mm long, the lance-shaped lobes 2-3 mm long; **corolla** purple, 15-20 mm long. **Pods** ovoid, pubescent, 2-2.5 cm long including the prominent beak. May-July.—Prairies, open woodlands.

Oxytropis lambertii Pursh
PURPLE LOCOWEED
MAP 708
native
Leaves usually strongly dimorphic; principal leaves 10-17 cm long; **leaflets** 7-19, linear or sometimes falcate, 0.5-4 cm long, 1-4 mm wide. **Scapes** usually erect, 5-30 cm long. **Racemes** mostly 10-20-flowered, flowers spreading to erect; **calyx** cylindric, the tube ca. 6-7 mm long, silky-strigose, sometimes with intermixed blackish hairs; **corolla** usually reddish purple or various shades of rose, blue, or purple, 15-25 mm long. **Pod** oblong or ovoid, the body 8-15 mm long, with a beak 4-5 mm long. May-Aug.—Prairies, bluffs, open wooded hillsides, roadsides; poisonous to livestock. *Pubescence of stem and leaves with dolabriform (T-shaped) hairs, with one branch usually very short.*

Oxytropis campestris

PEDIOMELUM *Indian-Breadroot*

Perennial herbs from rhizomes or thickened roots, more or less glandular-punctate. Leaves compound with mostly 3 or 5 leaflets. Flowers in peduncled spikes or racemes from the upper axils, usually blue. Calyx campanulate, often gibbous; calyx lobes equal or the lower longer. Standard obovate to rotund, usually clawed at base; wings exceeding the keel. Stamens 10 (rarely 9). Fruit short, flattened or turgid, 1-seeded, sometimes terminated by the persistent style.

1 Inflorescence a dense spike-like raceme; bracts of raceme 5-15 mm or more long; calyx (including longest tooth)
   8-17 mm or more long at anthesis . . . . **P. esculentum**
1 Inflorescence a slender loose raceme or narrow interrupted spike; bracts of raceme to 4 mm long: calyx including
   longest tooth 2-7 mm long at anthesis 2
   2   Flowers at anthesis in well-separated whorls, not pedicellate. . . . . **P. argophyllum**
   2   Flowers at anthesis in loose to dense racemes, distinctly pedicelled . . . . **P. tenuiflorum**

Pediomelum argophyllum (Pursh) J. Grimes
SILVER-LEAF INDIAN-BREADROOT
MAP 709
native
   Psoralea argophylla Pursh
Plant much branched, densely white-sericeous throughout. **Stems** 3-6 dm tall. **Leaflets** 3 or 5, narrowly elliptic to oblong lance-shaped, 2-5 cm long. **Petioles** 1-3 cm long. **Spikes** 2-8 cm long, interrupted, composed of 2-5 fascicles of flowers, or reduced to a single fascicle only. **Flowers** dark blue, sessile, 8-10 mm long; calyx tube 2-3 mm long; lower calyx-lobe linear lance-shaped, 4.5-7 mm long, about twice as long as the upper four. **Pods** densely silky. June-Aug.—Dry prairies.

Pediomelum esculentum (Pursh) Rydb.
LARGE INDIAN-BREADROOT
MAP 710
native
   Psoralea esculenta Pursh

Pediomelum argophyllum

Stems arising from a fusiform to subglobose root 5-10 cm long, much branched, 1-4 dm tall, villous. **Leaflets** 5, oblong to oblong lance-shaped or narrowly

obovate, 2-6 cm long. **Petioles** of the principal leaves 5-10 cm long. **Spikes** dense, leafy-bracted, 3-8 cm long. **Flowers** blue, nearly or quite sessile, 16-20 mm long; calyx tube gibbous, 5-6.5 mm long, glabrous to sparsely hirsute; calyx lobes nearly equal, linear lance-shaped, 7-10 mm long, ciliate. **Pods** hirsute, terminated by a long beak. May-July.—Dry prairies and plains.

Pediomelum tenuiflorum (Pursh) A.N. Egan
SLENDER-FLOWER INDIAN-BREADROOT

MAP 711
❧*endangered* | *native*

   Psoralea tenuiflora Pursh
   Psoralidium tenuiflorum (Pursh) Rydb.

Stems erect or ascending, much branched, 1 several from base, 4-6 dm tall, striate, sparsely to densely strigose and sometimes with spreading or ascendmg hairs, sparsely glandular or glands absent. **Lower leaves** usually palmately divided into 5 leaflets, becoming 3(4)-foliolate above and on branches; **leaflets** linear to elliptic to oblanceolate, 1-5 cm long, glabrate above, strigose below, conspicuously glandular on upper surface. **Petioles** 3-15 mm long. **Racemes** loose or dense, in clusters of 2 or 3 or some single; **flowers** light blue, purple, or rarely white with keel purple-tipped; pedicels 1-2 mm long; calyx tube campanulate, 1.5-2 mm long, conspicuously glandular and with appressed or spreading hairs, not enlarging in fruit, the two middle teeth of upper lobe united. **Pods** 7-9 mm long with an abruptly tapering short beak, body slightly compressed, often asymmetric, elliptic to ovoid, glabrous, conspicuously glandular. May-July.—Prairies, bluffs, roadsides.

Pediomelum esculentum

ROBINIA *Locust*

Trees or shrubs. Leaves odd-pinnate, stipules setaceous or modified into spines. Flowers white, pink, or purple, in axillary racemes. Calyx tube broadly campanulate, bilabiate; lower 3 calyx lobes about equal; upper 2 lobes connate for a third or more of their length. Corolla large; standard more or less reflexed; wings and keel long-clawed with a rounded lobe at base of the blade; the keel petals strongly upwardly curved. Pods elongate, flat, many-seeded.

1   Tree to 25 m tall; twigs and petioles glabrous; flowers white . . . . *R. pseudoacacia*
1   Shrubs to 3 m tall; stems gummy or bristly; flowers pink or rose-colored 2
    2   Stems gummy or sticky . . . . *R. viscosa*
    2   Stems bristly with short stiff hairs . . . . *R. hispida*

Robinia hispida L.
BRISTLY LOCUST

MAP 712
introduced

Stoloniferous shrub 1-2 m tall. Stems, peduncles, and calyx densely or sparsely hispid with glandular hairs up to 5 mm long, those of the stem persisting and becoming indurate. **Leaflets** 7-13, ovate-oblong to nearly rotund, commonly 3-6 cm long. **Racemes** usually 3-6-flowered. **Flowers** rose or pink-purple, 2.5-3 cm long; ovary densely glandular. **Pods** densely hispid, rarely developed. June-July. — Sometimes planted and occasionally escaped to roadsides and open woods.

Robinia pseudoacacia L.
BLACK LOCUST

MAP 713
introduced (invasive)

Tree up to 25 m tall, the younger stems and peduncles finely pubescent. **Stipules** frequently modified into stout woody thorns. **Leaflets** 7-19, oval or elliptic, 2-4 cm long, mucronate at the truncate or rounded apex. **Racemes** drooping, many-flowered, 1-2 dm long. **Flowers** white, very fragrant, 2-2.5 cm long; calyx finely pubescent, the upper lip truncate or broadly notched; ovary glabrous. **Pods** very

Robinia hispida

710. *Pediomelum esculentum*   711. *Pediomelum tenuiflorum*   712. *Robinia hispida*   713. *Robinia pseudoacacia*

flat, smooth, 5-10 cm long. June.—Commonly planted and escaped to roadsides, open woods, and waste land.

Robinia viscosa Vent.
CLAMMY LOCUST

(NO MAP)
introduced

Tall shrub or small tree, the younger stems and peduncles viscid with numerous large, sessile or subsessile glands. **Stipules** setaceous. **Leaflets** 13-25, ovate-lance-shaped to oval, obtuse to rounded, usually mucronate. **Flowers** pink, with a yellow spot on the standard, about 2.5 cm long; calyx finely pubescent, the upper lip cleft into 2 sharp triangular lobes shorter than the body of the lip. **Pods** hispid with stipitate glandular hairs. June.—Ramsey County.

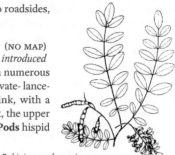

Robinia pseudoacacia

SECURIGERA *Crown-Vetch*

Securigera varia (L.) Lassen
PURPLE CROWN-VETCH
Coronilla varia L.

MAP 714
introduced

Perennial herb. **Stems** ascending, 3-5 dm long. **Leaves** sessile, 6-15 cm long; **leaflets** 11-21, oblong to obovate, 1-2 cm long, acute to rounded or retuse at the summit. Peduncles stout, equaling or surpassing the subtending leaves. **Flowers** in long-peduncled axillary umbels of 10-15 flowers, pink, the keel tipped with purple; calyx tube campanulate, bilabiate, the broad lower lip with 3 short triangular teeth, the upper lip narrow, triangular, shallowly cleft; petals about equal in length, clawed; standard orbicular; wings ovate-oblong; keel-petals upwardly curved. **Pods** linear, 4-angled, 2-4 cm long, with 3-7 joints. May-Sept. —Native of Eurasia and n Africa; introduced or escaped on roadsides.

Securigera varia

STROPHOSTYLES *Fuzzy-Bean*

Annual herbs. Stems twining or trailing, to 1 m long or more. Leaves pinnately compound, 3-foliolate. Flowers pink-purple to white, in a short, head-like, long-peduncled raceme, each subtended at base of the calyx by a pair of striate-veined bracteoles. Calyx irregular, 4-lobed; lowest lobe the longest. Standard orbicular, its sides at base folded over the other petals; wings much shorter than the keel, curved upward; keel petals broadest near the middle, beyond the middle contracted and curved upward into a beak. Style bearded along the upper side. Pods subterete, elongate, coiled after dehiscence, bearing several woolly seeds.

1 Leaflets all entire; pods to 5 cm long . . . . *S. leiosperma*
1 At least some leaflets with shallow lobes; pods 5-9 cm long . . . . *S. helvula*

Strophostyles helvula (L.) Ell.
TRAILING FUZZY-BEAN

MAP 715
native

Annual vine. **Leaflets** commonly ovate or ovate-oblong, rarely varying to oblong, 2-6 cm long, sparsely pilose on both sides or glabrous above, some leaflets commonly with a lateral lobe on one or both sides, or with distinctly concave lateral margins. **Flowers** few or several, 8-14 mm long; calyx tube glabrous or with a few appressed hairs; bracteoles lance-olate, acute, usually glabrous, extending to or beyond the sinuses of the calyx. **Pods** 4-9 cm long, sparsely appressed-pubescent; seeds 5-10 mm long, persistently woolly. Late summer.—Dry or sandy uplands.

Strophostyles helvula

714. *Securigera varia*

715. *Strophostyles helvula*

716. *Strophostyles leiosperma*

717. *Tephrosia virginiana*

Strophostyles leiosperma (Torr. & Gray) Piper   MAP 716
SLICK-SEED FUZZY-BEAN   *native*
Annual vine. **Leaflets** narrowly to broadly oblong or lance-shaped, 3-5 cm long,
pilose on both sides, more densely beneath, with stiff hairs 1-2 mm long. **Heads**
bearing a few flowers 5-8 mm long; calyx and bracteoles hirsute, the bracteoles
lance-shaped, variable in length. **Pods** 2-4 cm long, pubescent with spreading
hairs; seeds 2.5-3 mm long, the pubescence easily detached. Late summer.—Dry
or moist sandy soil, upland woods, dunes, and shores.

TEPHROSIA *Goat's-Rue*

Tephrosia virginiana (L.) Pers.   MAP 717
GOAT'S-RUE   *native*
Perennial herb. **Stems** erect or ascending, simple or branched from the base only,
2-5 dm tall, villous. **Leaflets** 9-27, commonly about 21, narrowly oblong to elliptic,
2-3 cm long. **Flowers** in single (or rarely compound), terminal racemes, 4-8 cm
long, compactly flowered; pedicels 3-10 mm long; bracts setaceous, deciduous;
calyx tube hemispheric, villous; calyx lobes lance-shaped, exceeding the tube;
standard yellow, 15-20 mm long; wings pink or pale purple; wings and keel
connivent, broadly auriculate on the upper side above the short claw, the wings
obovate-oblong, the keels semicircular; stamens 10. **Pods** linear, terete, 3-5 cm
long, several-seeded, villous. June-July.—Old fields, open woods, dunes, often in
sandy soil. *Leaf and stem pubescence varies; may cause skin irritation if handled.*

Tephrosia virginiana

TRIFOLIUM *Clover*

Annual, biennial, or perennial herbs. Leaves 3-foliolate, serrulate. Flowers in heads, spikes, or head-like
racemes or umbels. Calyx tube campanulate to tubular. Petals all separate or more or less united into a
tube, usually withering and persistent after anthesis; standard ovate to obovate, often folded about the
wings or with only the tip outwardly curved. Fruit short, straight, often included in the persistent calyx,
1-6-seeded. Valuable for forage and several species extensively cultivated. *In the absence of fruit, our yellow-
flowered species may be distinguished from* **Medicago** *by their strongly bilabiate calyx.*

ADDITIONAL SPECIES
Several other clovers are introduced and reported for Minn: ***Trifolium dubium*** Sibthorp (Suckling clover) and
T. incarnatum L. (Crimson clover); see key.

1 Flowers white, pink, or purple 2
  2 Flowers on short pedicels, these becoming reflexed with age 3
    3 Flowers white; very common . . . . ***T. repens***
    3 Flowers pink or purple-tinged . . . . **T. hybridum**
  2 Flowers sessile or nearly so 4
    4 Heads cylindric-shaped 5
      5 Flowers white, shorter than the calyx . . . . ***T. arvense***
      5 Flowers crimson, longer than the calyx . . . . **T. incarnatum***
    4 Heads nearly globose to ovoid . . . . ***T. pratense***
1 Flowers yellow, turning brown with age 6
  6 Leaflets sessile; stipules linear . . . . ***T. aureum***
  6 Terminal leaflet on a short petiole; stipules ovate to lance-shaped 7
    7 Heads with 20-40 flowers; the banner (upper, larger petal) distinctly finely striped . . . . **T. campestre**
    7 Heads with 3-15 flowers; banner only faintly striped . . . . ***T. dubium****

718. Trifolium arvense   *719. Trifolium aureum*   *720. Trifolium campestre*   *721. Trifolium hybridum*

Trifolium arvense L.
MAP 718
RABBIT-FOOT CLOVER *introduced (naturalized)*
Annual. **Stems** erect, freely branched, 1-4 dm tall, softly pubescent. **Petioles** 4-10
mm long, exceeded by the subulate tips of the stipules. **Leaflets** narrowly oblong
lance-shaped, 1-2 cm long, serrulate only at the tip. **Heads** gray to pale brown,
densely flowered, ovoid to cylindric, 1-3 cm long, on peduncles 1-3 cm long; calyx
densely villous with hairs up to 2 mm long, the tube to 2 mm long, the lobes 3-5
mm long, exceeding and partly concealing the small whitish or pinkish corolla.
May-Sept.—Native of Eurasia and n Africa; a weed of sterile soil, roadsides, old
fields, and waste places.

Trifolium arvense

Trifolium aureum Pollich
MAP 719
GREATER HOP CLOVER *introduced (naturalized)*
Annual or biennial. **Stems** much-branched, mostly erect, 2-5 dm tall, appressed-
hairy. **Leaflets** all sessile or nearly so, oblong lance-shaped, 1-2 cm long; petioles
5-12 mm long, about equaling the lance-oblong stipules. **Heads** short-cylindric,
1-2 cm long, on peduncles 1-4 cm from the upper axils; pedicels 0.5 mm. **Flowers**
5-7 mm long; calyx strongly 2-lipped, glabrous, the tube 5-nerved, 1 mm, the lobes
lance-linear; corolla yellow; the standard obovate, conspicuously striate in age,
usually serrulate; the wings somewhat spreading at the tip. May-Sept.—Native of
Eurasia, weedy on roadsides and in waste places.

Trifolium campestre Schreb.
MAP 720
LESSER HOP CLOVER *introduced (naturalized)*
Annual. **Stems** much-branched, 1-4 dm tall, pubescent. **Leaflets** obovate, 8-15 mm
long, the terminal one on a stalk 1-3 mm long; heads globose to short-cylindric,
8-15 mm long, compact, with usually 20-30 flowers; petioles 8-12 mm long, 2x as
long as the stipules. **Flowers** 3.5-5 mm long; calyx as in *T. aureum*; corolla yellow,
the standard obovate, with 5 conspicuous diagonal veins on each side, much
exceeding the spoon-shaped, slightly divergent wings. May-Sept.—Native of
Eurasia and n Africa; weedy on roadsides and in waste places.

Trifolium hybridum L.
MAP 721
ALSIKE CLOVER *introduced (naturalized)*
Perennial. **Stems** erect or ascending, 3-8 dm tall. **Stipules** ovate lance-shaped,
tapering to a long slender point. **Leaflets** oval to elliptic, broadly rounded to retuse
at the summit. **Heads** numerous, not involucrate, globose, on peduncles 2-8 cm
long. **Flowers** distinctly pediceled, 7-10 mm long; calyx glabrous, the linear lobes
somewhat unequal, 1.7-2.5 mm long, slightly exceeding the tube; corolla white
and pink, turning brown after anthesis; the standard obovate, about 2 mm longer
than the obtuse wings. Summer.—Native of Eurasia, commonly escaped.

Trifolium hybridum

Trifolium pratense L.
MAP 722
RED CLOVER *introduced (invasive)*
Perennial. **Stems** erect, decumbent, or ascending, to 8 dm tall, sparsely to densely
appressed-pubescent. **Stipules** oblong, the free portion abruptly narrowed to a
short awn. **Lower leaves** long-petioled; **upper leaves** short-petioled to sessile.
Heads sessile or on peduncles up to 2 cm long, globose or round-ovoid. **Flowers**
13-20 mm long; calyx glabrous to sparsely pilose, the tube 3-4 mm long, the lobes
setaceous, one 4-7 mm long, four 2-5 mm long; corolla magenta, varying to nearly
white; standard obovate, equaling or slightly exceeding the oblong obtuse wings.
May-Aug.—Native of Europe, commonly planted for forage and escaped to fields
and on roadsides.

Trifolium repens L.
MAP 723
WHITE CLOVER *introduced (naturalized)*
Perennial. **Stems** creeping, sending up long-petioled leaves and long-peduncled
heads without involucres. **Leaflets** broadly elliptic to obovate, rounded or
notched at the tip, 1-2 cm long. **Flowers** distinctly pediceled, 7-11 mm long; calyx
glabrous, the tube to 3 mm long, its lobes narrowly triangular, unequal, the longest
about equaling the tube; corolla white or tinged with pink; the standard elliptic-

Trifolium pratense

obovate, rounded at the summit, exceeding the obtuse wings. Summer.—Native of Eurasia, commonly planted and escaped to lawns and roadsides.

VICIA *Vetch*

Annual or perennial herbs. Leaves 1-pinnate, with small stipules, the terminal leaflets in most species metamorphosed into tendrils. Flowers in short or elongate racemes from the axils, or in sessile few-flowered, axillary clusters. Calyx regular or irregular, often swollen at base. Standard with a broad claw overlapping the wings, its blade obovate to subrotund; wings oblong or narrowly obovate, adherent to and usually exceeding the keel. Ovary sessile or short-stipitate. Pods flat to terete. Seeds 2 to many.

1 Flowers single or in pairs, sessile from leaf axils .... *V. sativa*
1 Flowers in racemes on stalks from leaf axils 2
    2 Flowers white or white tinged with purple, 3-7 mm long .... *V. tetrasperma*
    2 Flowers blue or white, 8 mm long or more 3
       3 Calyx with a large swollen bump on one side of base .... *V. villosa*
       3 Calyx only slightly swollen on one side of base..................................... 4
          4 Margins of stipules sharply toothed; flowers 15-30 mm long .... *V. americana*
          4 Margins of stipules entire; flowers to 13 mm long 5
             5 Flowers white, in loose racemes .... *V. caroliniana*
             5 Flowers blue, in dense racemes .... *V. cracca*

Vicia americana Muhl.
AMERICAN VETCH

MAP 724
native

Perennial. **Stems** trailing or climbing, to 1 m long. **Leaflets** usually 4-7 pairs, elliptic to oblong, 1.5-3 cm long, 5-12 mm wide, obtuse to broadly rounded at the mucronate tip. **Stipules** all or mostly sharply serrate. **Racemes** shorter than the subtending leaves, loose, bearing 2-9 blue-purple flowers 17-27 mm long; calyx tube 3.5-5.5 mm long. May-July.—Moist woods.

Vicia caroliniana Walt.
CAROLINA VETCH

(NO MAP)
native

Perennial. **Stems** slender, trailing or climbing, to 1 m long. **Leaflets** usually 5-9 pairs, elliptic or oblong lance-shaped, 1-2 cm long, rounded or obscurely notched at the tip, mucronate, with usually 5-7 lateral veins on each side. **Stipules** lance-shaped, entire. **Racemes**, including the peduncle, 6-10 cm long, bearing 7-20 white flowers 7.5-12 mm long; calyx nearly regular, the tube 2-2.7 mm long, the lobes equal, broadly triangular, less than 1 mm long. **Pod** 1.5-3 cm long. May-June.—Moist woods and thickets. Reported for Minn.

Vicia americana

Vicia cracca L.
BIRD-VETCH

MAP 725
introduced (naturalized)

Perennial. **Stems** climbing or trailing, to 1 m long. **Leaflets** usually 5-10 pairs, linear, 1.5-3 cm long, mucronate. **Stipules** entire. **Racemes** long-peduncled, dense, secund, equaling or exceeding the subtending leaf, bearing numerous crowded blue flowers 9-13 mm long; calyx tube swollen at base, 2-3 mm long. Blade of the standard about as long as the claw. June-Aug.—Fields, roadsides.

Vicia sativa L.
COMMON VETCH

MAP 726
introduced

Annual. **Stems** slender, to 1 m long, ascending, erect, or tending to climb. **Leaflets**

Vicia cracca

722. *Trifolium pratense*   723. *Trifolium repens*   724. *Vicia americana*   725. *Vicia cracca*

commonly 4-8 pairs, oblong to elliptic or obovate, 3-5 cm long, mucronate. **Stipules** often sharply serrate, bearing a glandular spot beneath. **Flowers** commonly paired in the axils, nearly sessile, violet or purple, rarely white, 2-3 cm long; calyx tube campanulate, 5-7 mm long; lobes nearly equal, the upper 3-7 mm, the lower 4-9 mm long. **Pod** flattened, brown; seeds flattened.—Native of Europe; in cultivation since antiquity; may persist after cultivation or escape into fields and roadsides.

Vicia tetrasperma (L.) Schreb.
LENTIL VETCH

(NO MAP)
introduced

Annual. **Stems** slender, branched, decumbent or climbing, 3-6 dm long. **Leaflets** commonly 3 or 4 pairs, occasionally more, linear-oblong, 1-2 cm long. Peduncles very slender, 1-3 cm long, bearing usually 1 or 2, sometimes 3 or 4, light purple to white flowers 4-6.5 mm long. Lowest calyx-lobe linear, about equaling the tube, the upper much shorter and triangular. **Pod** flat, glabrous, 1-1.5 cm long, usually 4-seeded. May-Aug.—Eurasian introduction, St. Louis County (Duluth area).

Vicia sativa

Vicia villosa Roth
HAIRY VETCH

MAP 727
introduced (naturalized)

Annual. **Stems** to 1 m long, more or less villous throughout, always softly villous above and in the racemes with hairs 1-2 mm long. **Leaflets** usually 5-10 pairs, narrowly oblong to linear lance-shaped, obtuse and mucronate to acute, 1-2.5 cm long. **Racemes** long-peduncled, dense, secund, bearing usually 10-30 flowers; calyx irregular, villous, the tube 2-4 mm long, swollen at base; upper lobes linear-triangular, 0.8-1.5 mm long; lateral and lower lobes linear above a triangular base, the lowest 3-5 mm long, long-villous; corolla slender, 12-20 mm long, the spreading blade of the standard less than 1/2 as long as the claw. June-Aug.—Native of Europe; introduced in fields, roadsides, and waste places.

Vicia villosa

Fagaceae BEECH FAMILY

QUERCUS OAK

Deciduous trees (or rarely shrubby). Leaves alternate, simple, lobed, pinnately veined. Plants monoecious (staminate and pistillate flowers separate but on same tree). Staminate flowers in slender naked catkins, catkins appearing with the leaves. Calyx divided to the base into 3-7 (usually 6) segments. Stamens 3-12. Pistillate flowers solitary or in small spikes, each subtended by a bract and surrounded by an involucre of many scales. Ovary 3-celled. Fruit a nut (acorn) partially enclosed by a cuplike structure (cupule). *Acorns are important food for many mammals and birds but are usually avoided by humans because of their tannin content.*

HYBRIDS
- *Quercus × bebbiana* C.K.Schneid., *Q. alba* and *Q. macrocarpa,* east-central Minn.
- *Quercus × hawkinsiae* Sudw., *Q. rubra* and *Q. velutina,* Houston County.
- *Quercus × palaeolithicola* Trel., *Q. ellipsoidalis* and *Q. velutina,* Houston and Wabasha counties.
- *Quercus × schuettei* Trel., *Q. bicolor* and *Q. macrocarpa,* Dakota and Hennepin counties.

1   Leaves not deeply lobed .... *Q. bicolor*
1   Leaves deeply lobed 2
   2   Lobes rounded, not tipped by bristles 3

726. *Vicia sativa*   727. *Vicia villosa*   728. *Quercus alba*

   3   Acorn 1.5-3 cm long within a deep, fringed cup; branches often with corky ridges . . . . *Q. macrocarpa*

   3   Acorn 1.3-2 cm long, only about one-quarter covered by warty cup; branches not corky-ridged . . *Q. alba*

 2 Lobes acute, bristle-tipped 4

   4   Leaf underside hairy . . . . *Q. velutina*

   4   Leaf underside glabrous or nearly so 5

     5   Acorn cup covering lower one-third to lower one-half of acorn . . . . *Q. ellipsoidalis*

     5   Acorn cup saucer-shaped; covering only base of acorn . . . . *Q. rubra*

Quercus alba L.
WHITE OAK

MAP 728
native

Tall tree with light gray bark and widely spreading branches; **twigs** soon glabrescent. **Leaves** obovate, glabrous or very sparsely and obscurely pubescent beneath at maturity; lobes variable, 3, 4, or rarely 5 pairs, ascending, oblong to ovate, rounded or rarely acute. **Acorns** sessile or on peduncles to 4 cm long; **cup** deeply saucer-shaped, pubescent within, covering a fourth to a third of the nut; **nut** ovoid to cylindric-ovoid, 1.5-2.5 cm long.—Upland woods of oak-hickory and beech-maple, sometimes on sandy plains with other oaks and jack pine.

Quercus alba

Quercus bicolor Willd.
SWAMP WHITE OAK

MAP 729
native

Medium tree to 20 m tall; trunk to 1 m wide; bark gray-brown, deeply furrowed, becoming flaky; **twigs** gray to yellow-brown. **Leaves** broadest above middle, to 15 cm long and 10 cm wide, smooth or hairy on upper surface, white and soft hairy on underside; margins with coarse, rounded teeth or shallow lobes; petioles 2-3 cm long. **Staminate flowers** in slender, drooping catkins, **pistillate flowers** in groups of 2-4. **Acorns** paired, on stalks 2-3 cm long, the **cup** rough and hairy, covering about 1/3 of the nut; **nut** ovate, pale brown, 2.5-4 cm long. May. —Floodplain forests, low woods and swamps.

Quercus bicolor

Quercus ellipsoidalis E.J. Hill
NORTHERN PIN OAK

MAP 730
native

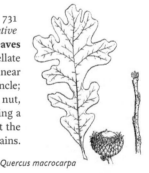

Medium-sized tree, the twigs soon glabrescent. **Leaves** smooth on both sides except for small tufts of stellate hairs in the vein-axils beneath; lateral lobes 2-3 pairs, separated by rounded sinuses, usually extending more than half-way to the midvein, sometimes broadest at the base, but usually widened and several-toothed distally, the sinuses then elliptic. **Acorn cup** turbinate, 9-14 mm wide, with closely appressed puberulent scales, covering about a third of the nut; **nut** ovoid to ellipsoid, 12-20 mm long.—Dry upland soil.

Quercus ellipsoidalis

Quercus macrocarpa Michx.
BUR-OAK

MAP 731
native

Low shrub to tall tree, the latter with rough, deeply furrowed bark. **Leaves** obovate to obovate, cuneate at base, pale beneath with a close, fine, stellate pubescence, with 4-7 pairs of blunt or acute lateral lobes, a pair of sinuses near the middle usually deeper than the others. **Acorns** sessile or on a stout peduncle; **cup** deeply saucer-shaped to sub-globose, covering 1/3 to nearly all the nut, pubescent within, the marginal scales acuminate into slender awns forming a terminal fringe; **nut** depressed-ovoid, broadly rounded to almost retuse at the summit, to narrowly ovoid, 1-4 cm wide.—Moist woods and alluvial floodplains.

Quercus macrocarpa

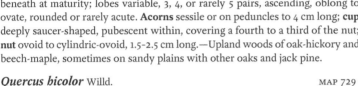

729. *Quercus bicolor*   730. *Quercus ellipsoidalis*   731. *Quercus macrocarpa*   732. *Quercus rubra*

Quercus rubra L.
MAP 732
NORTHERN RED OAK
native

Medium to large tree. Young **twigs** glabrous, dark reddish brown. **Leaves** dull green, 10-20 cm long, soon glabrous throughout or with small tufts of pubescence persistent in the leaf-axils, 7-11-lobed, lobes roughly triangular in outline, broadest at the base, bristle-tipped and usually with a few lateral teeth, little if any longer than the central body of the blade. **Acorn cup** saucer-shaped or almost turbinate, 1.5-2 cm wide, enclosing about 1/4 to 1/3 of the nut; **nut** ovoid, 2-2.5 cm long. —Rich mesic forests, ridges, sandy plains with jack pine.

Quercus rubra

Quercus velutina Lam.
MAP 733
BLACK OAK
native

Tree to 40 m tall, with very dark rough bark; inner bark orange. **Leaves** variable in shape and pubescence, shallowly or deeply lobed, glabrous above or pubescent along the midvein, pubescent in the vein-axils beneath, glabrous on the surface or retaining a loose stellate pubescence when mature, commonly thinly pubescent on the petioles and twigs of the season. **Buds** 4-angled, densely pubescent. **Acorn cup** turbinate, covering about 1/2 the nut, the scales comparatively few and large, pubescent, the uppermost loose, prominently projecting and forming a marginal fringe; **nut** 1.5-2 cm long.—Usually in dry or sterile upland soil and on dunes.

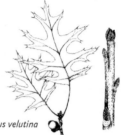

Quercus velutina

Gentianaceae GENTIAN FAMILY

Annual, biennial or perennial herbs; plants usually glabrous. Leaves simple, entire, opposite or whorled, stem leaves without petioles. Flowers often showy, perfect (with both staminate and pistillate parts), regular, single at end of stems or in clusters; petals 4-5, blue, purple, white or green, joined for at least part of their length; stamens 4 or 5. Fruit a 2-chambered, many-seeded capsule enclosed by the withered, persistent petals.

1 Leaves reduced to small, narrow scales less than 3 mm long . . . . *Bartonia virginica*
1 Leaves not scale-like, well developed 2
  2 Flowers pink . . . . *Centaurium pulchellum*
  2 Flowers blue, green tinged with purple, or white 3
    3 Petals 4, spurred at base; flowers green, tinged with purple . . . . *Halenia deflexa*
    3 Petals 4, with fringed lobes; or petals 5 and not spurred; blue, purple or white 4
      4 Petals 4, fringed; flowers on pedicels longer than the flowers; seeds covered with small bumps . . . . .
      . . . . *Gentianopsis*
      4 Petals 5, not fringed; flower pedicels short or absent; seeds smooth 5
        5 Flowers 2.5-4 cm long, on short pedicels; seeds flattened and winged . . . . *Gentiana*
        5 Flowers 1-2 cm long, sessile; seeds round . . . . *Gentianella*

BARTONIA *Screwstem*

Bartonia virginica (L.) B.S.P.
MAP 734
YELLOW SCREWSTEM
♥*endangered* | *native*

Annual or biennial herb. **Stems** slender, erect, yellow-green, 1-4 dm long. **Leaves** mostly opposite, small and scale-like, 1-2 mm long. **Flowers** 4-parted, bell-shaped, green-yellow or green-white, 3-4 mm long, in a slender terminal raceme or

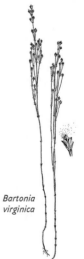

Bartonia virginica

733. Quercus velutina   *734. Bartonia virginica*   *735. Centaurium pulchellum*

panicle, the branches and flower stalks opposite and upright; sepals awl-shaped; petals oblong, tapered to a rounded tip. **Fruit** a capsule 2-3 cm long. Aug-Sept. —Swamps (often in sphagnum moss), open bogs, wet woods and depressions, sandy shores and ditches.

CENTAURIUM *Centaury*

Centaurium pulchellum (Sw.) Druce   MAP 735
BRANCHED CENTAURY   *introduced*
Annual herb. **Stems** much branched, often from the base, 1-2 dm tall. **Leaves** sessile, lance-shaped or ovate lance-shaped, 1-2 cm long. **Inflorescence** a many-flowered terminal cyme; bracteal leaves linear. **Flowers** 4-merous; calyx tubular, about 9 mm long, deeply cleft into narrow segments; corolla tube slightly exceeding the calyx; corolla lobes pink, about 4 mm long; stamens inserted in the throut of the corolla; filaments slender, exsert; ovary elongate, 1-celled. **Capsule** oblong, thin-walled, invested by the persistent calyx and withered corolla. June-Sept.—Native of Europe; local in fields and waste places, often where salted in winter.

Centaurium pulchellum

GENTIANA *Gentian*

Perennial herbs, with thick, fibrous roots. Leaves opposite or whorled, simple, margins entire, petioles absent. Flowers large, blue, green-white or yellow, 5-parted, in clusters near ends of stems; petals forming a tubelike, shallowly lobed flower, the lobes alternating with a folded membrane as long or longer than petal lobes; stamens 5. Fruit a 2-chambered capsule.

1 Flowers blue (rarely white), remaining closed, the corolla lobes absent or reduced to small points . *G. andrewsii*
1 Flowers blue, white or yellowish, opening, the corolla lobes prominent 2
  2 Corolla lobes spreading; flowers deep blue 3
    3 Corolla less than 3 cm long . . . . *G. affinis*
    3 Corolla more than 3 cm long. . . . . *G. puberulenta*
  2 Corolla lobes erect; flowers vary from white or yellow to blue or purple; stems glabrous 4
    4 Flowers yellowish or white, with greenish veins; leaves 5-veined; mostly s eMinn . . . . *G. alba*
    4 Flowers blue to purple; leaves 1-5-veined; mostly n Minn . . . . *G. rubricaulis*

Gentiana affinis Griseb.   MAP 736
PLEATED GENTIAN; NORTHERN GENTIAN   *native*
Glabrous perennial herb. **Stems** 1-3.5 dm tall. **Leaves** lance-ovate, 1-3.5 cm long and to 1.5 cm wide. **Inflorescence** of several flowers in clusters from upper leaf axils; **calyx** 7-15 mm long, the lobes narrowly linear, less than 1 mm wide, sometimes obsolete; **corolla** blue-purple, narrowly funnelform, open, 2-3 cm long, the lobes ovate, extending past the tips of the plaits. July-Aug.—Moist prairies.

Gentiana alba Muhl.   MAP 737
YELLOW GENTIAN   *native*
  Gentiana flavida Gray
Perennial herb. **Stems** stout, 5-9 dm tall, almost always unbranched. **Leaves** divaricately spreading, lance-shaped or ovate lance-shaped, 5-13 cm long, 1.5-5 cm wide, long-acuminate, widest near the broadly rounded or subcordate sessile base, often distinctly 3-nerved. **Inflorescence** usually compact and many-

Gentiana affinis

736. *Gentiana affinis*   737. *Gentiana alba*   738. *Gentiana andrewsii*   739. *Gentiana puberulenta*

flowered; **calyx lobes** ovate lance-shaped or ovate, 4-10 mm long, 2.5-5 mm wide, often spreading; **corolla** greenish white or yellowish white, 3-4.5 cm long, the broadly ovate lobes commonly 4-6 mm longer than the erose plaits. **Seeds** winged. Aug-Sept.—Clay soils in wooded ravines, open woodlands and woodland edges, bluffs, wet sandy prairies, and along railroads and in roadside ditches.

Gentiana andrewsii Griseb.
MAP 738
BOTTLE-GENTIAN
native

Perennial herb. **Stems** erect, single or few together, 2-8 dm long, unbranched, smooth. **Leaves** opposite, lance-shaped, 4-12 cm long and 1-3 cm wide, margins entire. **Flowers** 1 to many, stalkless in upper leaf axils, 3-5 cm long; **sepals** forming a tube around petals, the sepal lobes unequal, fringed with hairs; **petals** forming a tubelike flower, usually remaining closed, the folds between petal lobes finely fringed (use hand lens to see this) and longer than the petal lobes. **Fruit** a capsule; seeds winged. Aug-Sept.—Wet meadows, swamps and wet woods, thickets, low prairie, shores, ditches.

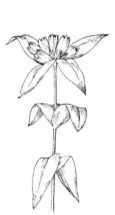

Gentiana andrewsii

Gentiana puberulenta J. Pringle
MAP 739
DOWNY GENTIAN
native

Perennial herb. **Stems** mostly simple, 2-5 dm tall, commonly scaberulous above. **Leaves** firm, lance-shaped or oblong lance-shaped, 2-5 cm long, 8-15 mm wide, broadly obtuse or rounded at the sessile base. **Flowers** several in a dense terminal cluster, with or without others in the upper axils, sessile or on pedicels to 1 cm long; calyx lobes linear to linear lance-shaped, 5-15 mm long, broadest near the base; corolla blue, 3.5-5 cm long; free lobes, above the fimbriate plaits, 4-8 mm long, broadly ovate, acute. Seeds winged. Aug-Oct.—Dry upland woods and prairies.

Gentiana rubricaulis Schwein.
MAP 740
GREAT LAKES GENTIAN
native
    Gentiana linearis var. *lanceolata* A. Gray

Perennial herb. **Stems** smooth, 3-7 dm long. **Leaves** pale green, lance-shaped, 4-8 cm long and 2-3 cm wide, margins entire. **Flowers** 3-5 cm long, green-blue below, blue above, narrowly open, in a cluster at end of stem; sepal lobes oblong, 4-12 mm long, chaffy and translucent near base. **Fruit** a capsule; seeds winged. —Wet meadows, peatlands, streambanks, thickets, conifer swamps, Lake Superior rocky shores; soils usually calcium-rich.

Gentiana rubricaulis

GENTIANELLA *Gentian*

Annual or biennial herbs. Leaves opposite, stalkless, margins entire. Flowers 4-5-parted, blue to white, funnel-shaped or tubular; in clusters from ends of stems or upper leaf axils; petals withering and persistent around capsule.

1 Petal lobes with fringe of hairs at base; nw Minn . . . . ***G. amarella***
1 Petal lobes not fringed with hairs at base; se Minn . . . . ***G. quinquefolia***

Gentianella amarella (L.) Boerner
MAP 741
AUTUMN DWARF GENTIAN
native

Annual or biennial herb. **Stems** unbranched, 1-6 dm long. **Leaves** lance-shaped, 2-6 cm long; margins entire. **Flowers** blue, 10-15 mm long, 5-parted (rarely 4-parted); single from middle leaf axils, several in a cluster from upper axils, on stalks less than 1 cm long; sepal lobes linear, 3-5 mm long; petals forming a tubelike to flared, funnel-like flower, petal lobes 3-5 mm long, the base of lobe fringed with hairs 2 mm long. **Fruit** a capsule. July-Aug.—Wet or moist sandy or gravelly soil.

Gentianella quinquefolia (L.) Small
MAP 742
STIFF GENTIAN
native

Annual or biennial herb. **Stems** 4-angled, 2-8 dm long, usually branched. **Leaves** opposite, without petioles; lower leaves spatula-shaped, upper leaves lance-ovate, 2-7 cm long; margins entire. **Flowers** 4-5-parted, blue (rarely white), 15-25 mm long, in clusters of 1-7 flowers at ends of stems or upper leaf axils, on stalks to 1 cm long; sepal lobes lance-shaped; petals forming a narrowly funnel-shaped

Gentianella quinquefolia

flower, petal lobes 4-6 mm long, not fringed with hairs at base. Aug-Sept.—Wet meadows, streambanks, moist woods; often where calcium-rich.

GENTIANOPSIS *Fringed-Gentian*

Smooth, taprooted, annual or biennial herbs. Leaves opposite, stalkless, margins entire. Flowers 1 to several, showy, blue, sometimes tinged with white on outside, long-stalked at ends of stems and branches, 4-parted; sepals oblong cone-shaped; petals deeply lobed, forming a tubular or bell-shaped flower, the lobes ragged or fringed at tips and sometimes on sides, without a folded membrane between the lobes (present in *Gentiana*); stamens 4. Fruit a capsule; seeds covered with bumps.

1   Upper leaves lance-shaped to ovate; petal lobes long-fringed across tip and sides, the fringes 2-5 mm long . . . .
. . . . *G. crinita*

1   Upper leaves linear; tips of petal lobes ragged with short, fine teeth, and often fringed on sides . . . . . *G. virgata*

Gentianopsis crinita (Froel.) Ma
MAP 743
GREATER FRINGED-GENTIAN
native

Annual or biennial herb. **Stems** erect, 2-7 dm long, usually branched above. **Basal leaves** spatula-shaped, smaller than stem leaves; **stem leaves** ovate, 2-6 cm long and 1-2.5 cm wide, the base usually clasping stem; margins entire. **Flowers** bright blue, 3-6 cm long, 4-parted, single at ends of main stems and branches, on stalks 5-20 cm long; sepals forming a tube, 1-2 cm long; petals joined to form a funnel-like to bell-shaped flower, the petal lobes fringed across tip and part way down sides with linear fringes 2-6 mm long. **Fruit** a capsule, broadest at middle. Aug-Oct.—Wet meadows, streambanks, ditches, wet woods; soils usually calcium-rich and sandy or gravelly.

Gentianopsis crinita

Gentianopsis virgata (Raf.) Holub
MAP 744
LESSER FRINGED-GENTIAN
native
   Gentianopsis procera (Holm) Ma

Annual herb, similar to *G. crinita* but smaller. **Stems** simple or few-branched, 1-5 dm long. **Basal leaves** spatula-shaped; **stem leaves** linear to linear lance-shaped, 2-5 cm long and 2-7 mm wide, tapered to a blunt tip, the base not clasping stem; margins entire. **Flowers** bright blue, 2-5 cm long, mostly 4-parted, single on stalks at ends of stems; sepal tube 6-15 mm long; petals forming a tubelike flower, flared toward tip, petal lobes ragged toothed across tips, often fringed on sides. **Fruit** a capsule. Sept-Oct.—Sandy and gravelly shores, wet meadows, fens; soils usually calcium-rich.

HALENIA *Spurred Gentian*

Halenia deflexa (Sm.) Griseb.
MAP 745
SPURRED GENTIAN
native

Annual herb. **Stems** erect, simple or few-branched, rounded 4-angled, 15-40 cm long. **Leaves** opposite, lower leaves spatula-shaped, narrowed to a petiole; stem leaves lance-shaped to ovate, 2-5 cm long and 1-2.5 cm wide, sessile; margins entire. **Flowers** green, tinged with purple, 10-12 mm long, 4-parted, on stalks to 4 cm long, in loose clusters of 5-9 flowers at ends of stems; petals lance-shaped, usually with downward-pointing spurs at base, the spurs to 5 mm long. **Fruit** an oblong capsule. July-Aug.—Cedar swamps, moist conifer woods (especially along shores), old logging roads.

Halenia deflexa

740. *Gentiana rubricaulis*   741. *Gentianella amarella*   742. *Gentianella quinquefolia*   743. *Gentianopsis crinita*

Geraniaceae GERANIUM FAMILY

Annual or perennial herbs. Leaves usually opposite, simple or compound, palmately toothed, lobed, or divided. Flowers 5-merous, regular or nearly so, perfect or part of them sterile. Sepals 5. Petals 5, pink to purple. Mature fruit a beaked carpel and eventually separating; seed 1 in each carpel.

1 Leaves simple, palmately lobed, or 3-parted; anthers usually 10 . . . . *Geranium*
1 Leaves pinnately compound; anthers 5 . . . . *Erodium cicutarium*

ERODIUM *Stork's Bill; Filaree*

Erodium cicutarium (L.) L'Hér.   MAP 746
REDSTEM-FILAREE   *introduced (naturalized)*

Winter-annual or biennial herb. **Stems** at first anthesis short, the leaves mostly basal, later diffusely branched, to 4 dm long. **Leaves** alternate, oblong lance-shaped in outline, pinnately compound, with several sessile, deeply and irregularly cleft pinnae each 1-2.5 cm long. **Flowers** in long-peduncled, 2-8 flowered cymes; pedicels 1-2 cm long; sepals 5; petals 5, obovate, the 2 upper often differing in size from the lower 3; glands 5, minute, alternating with the petals; ovary 5-celled, each carpel containing a single seed and prolonged into a long beak which separates from the other carpels and becomes spirally twisted when dry. April-Sept.—Native of the Mediterranean region; weedy, especially in fallow fields.

Erodium cicutarium

GERANIUM *Wild Geranium; Crane's-Bill*

Annual or perennial herbs. Leaves palmately lobed, cleft, or divided, the stem leaves chiefly opposite. Flowers small or medium-sized, usually pink to purple, usually pedicellate in pairs at the ends of axillary peduncles. Sepals 5, imbricate. Petals 5, imbricate, alternating at base with 5 glands. Stamens 10. Axis of the ovary prolonged at maturity into a long beak.

ADDITIONAL SPECIES
· *Geranium pratense* L., introduced in St. Louis County.
· *Geranium sanguineum* L. (Bloody crane's-bill), introduced in St. Louis County.

1 Perennial, spreading by rhizomes; petals more than 11 mm long; leaves few, large . . . . *G. maculatum*
1 Annuals or short-lived perennials; petals less than 11 mm long; stem leaves several to many 2
   2 Sepals rounded or acute, not awn-tipped . . . . *G. pusillum*
   2 Sepals narrowed to long, awn-like tips 3
      3 Leaves divided to their base . . . . *G. robertianum*
      3 Leaves deeply divided but not to their base 4
         4 Flower pedicels covered with glandular, spreading hairs . . . . *G. bicknellii*
         4 Pedicel hairs without glands 5
            5 Pedicels less than twice length of calyx . . . . *G. carolinianum*
            5 Pedicels mostly more than twice length of calyx . . . . *G. sibiricum*

Geranium bicknellii Britt.   MAP 747
NORTHERN CRANE'S-BILL   *native*

Annual. **Stems** erect, usually with many ascending branches, eventually to 5 dm long. **Leaves** pentagonal in outline, the principal ones cleft nearly to the base with usually 5 segments, these deeply incised with several parrowly oblong lobes. Peduncles 2-flowered, the elongate pedicels glandular-villous; sepals at anthesis

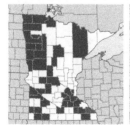

744. Gentianopsis virgata   *745. Halenia deflexa*   *746. Erodium cicutarium*   *747. Geranium bicknellii*

7-9 mm long, including the conspicuous subulate tips; petals pink-purple, about equaling the sepals. Mature **fruit**, including the calyx, 20-25 mm long, the beak 4-5 mm long, the body 3 mm long, sparsely hirsute. May-Sept.—Open woods and fields, usually where sandy or gravelly.

Geranium carolinianum L.   MAP 748
CAROLINA CRANE'S-BILL   *native*

Annual. **Stems** several from the base, freely branched, eventually to 6 dm long, villous with spreading or somewhat retrorse hairs, becoming glandular in the inflorescence. **Principal leaves** kidney-shaped, 3-7 cm wide, deeply cleft into 5-9 oblong to obovate, deeply toothed or lobed segments. **Flowers** in compact, many-flowered, umbel-like, terminal clusters Peduncles mostly 2-flowered, the pedicels to twice as long as the calyx; sepals to 1 cm long, about equaling the pink petals. **Fruit** about 2.5 cm long, the stylar beak 1-2 mm long, the body hirsute with long antrorse hairs; seeds very obscurely reticulate. May-Aug.—Dry, barren, rocky or sandy soil and disturbed places.

Geranium bicknellii

Geranium maculatum L.   MAP 749
SPOTTED CRANE'S-BILL   *native*

Perennial from a thick rhizome. **Stems** erect, 3-7 dm long. **Basal leaves** long-petioled, pedately 5-7-cleft into wedge-like segments; **stem leaves** a single pair, resembling the basal but short-petioled. **Flowers** few to several, rose-purple, 2.54 cm wide; calyx and pedicels pubescent but not glandular. **Fruit** erect, the beak 2-3 cm long; seed minutely reticulate. April-June.—Dry or moist woods.

Geranium pusillum L.   (NO MAP)
SMALL-FLOWER CRANE'S-BILL   *introduced*

Annual or biennial. **Stems** to 5 dm long, diffusely branched, spreading or ascending. **Basal leaves** long-petioled, the blades rotund, 3-6 cm wide, deeply 7-9 cleft, the divisions cuneate, palmately lobed at the summit; **upper leaves** progressively smaller, shorter-petioled, 7-3-cleft. **Flowers** numerous on densely but minutely glandular pedicels; sepals at anthesis 2.5-4 mm long, more or less hirsute, especially at the margin, nearly as long as the red-violet corolla. **Fruit**, including the calyx, 9-12 mm long, the body closely but minutely strigose. Summer.—Native of Europe; in Minn, known only from Stearns Co. (historical collection from 1902).

Geranium carolinianum

Geranium robertianum L.   (NO MAP)
HERB-ROBERT   *native*

Weak annual or winter-annual. **Stems** to 6 dm long, branched, spreading, villous. **Leaves** triangular in outline, 3-divided, the lateral segments often again divided and all segments pinnately lobed or cleft. Peduncles from most of the upper nodes, usually 2-flowered. **Flowers** pink to red-purple, 10-15 mm wide. **Carpels** detached from the cauline beak, each terminating in 2 slender filaments. May-Sept.—Moist woods; St. Louis County.

Geranium maculatum

Geranium sibiricum L.   MAP 750
SIBERIAN CRANE'S-BILL   *introduced*

Annual or biennial. **Stems** spreading, ascending, or erect, to 1 m long, villous. **Stem leaves** kidney-shaped in outline, 4-7 cm wide, palmately 3-5-cleft, the divisions coarsely toothed or lobed, chiefly beyond the middle. Peduncles bearing

748. *Geranium carolinianum*   749. *Geranium maculatum*   750. *Geranium sibiricum*   751. *Ribes americanum*

1 or occasionally 2 flowers, on villous pedicels; calyx villous, 5-7 mm long; corolla
pink, scarcely surpassing the calyx. Mature **fruit**, including the calyx, 15-20 mm
long, the beak about 1 mm long, the body finely pubescent on the sides, pilose
on the back. July-Sept.—Introduced; native of Asia.

Grossulariaceae CURRANT FAMILY

RIBES *Currant; Gooseberry*

Medium shrubs. Stems upright to spreading, smooth, or with spines at nodes and sometimes also
with bristles between nodes. Leaves alternate, palmately veined and palmately 3-5-lobed, margins
toothed. Flowers 1 to several in short clusters, or few to many in racemes; green to white or yellow,
perfect, regular, ovary inferior; sepals 5; petals 5, shorter than sepals; stamens 5, alternate with petals,
styles 2. Fruit a many-seeded berry, usually topped by persistent, dry flower parts. *Ribes are of two
types:* **currants** *and* **gooseberries.** *Currants lack spines and bristles (except in R. lacustre) and the stalk of
berry is jointed at its tip so that berries detach from stalks. Gooseberries have spines and bristles and the berry
stalk is not jointed so that stalks remain attached to berries when picked.*

1 Stems with spines or bristles, at least at the nodes; flowers single or in corymb-like clusters of 2-3 (**gooseberries**)
     2
     2 Ovary and fruit usually bristly; calyx lobes shorter than hypanthium . . . . *R. cynosbati*
     2 Ovaries and fruit smooth (or bristly in the rare *R. oxyacanthoides*); calyx lobes longer than corolla tube 3
         3 Flowers whitish; stamens exserted, about 2 times longer than calyx lobes; spines at nodes stout . . . .
         . . . . *R. missouriense*
         3 Flowers greenish or purplish; stamens not exserted; spines at nodes absent, or if present, weak and slender
         4
             4 Leaves with glands, at least on underside veins; fruit bristly or with gland-tipped hairs to sometimes
             smooth. . . . . *R. oxyacanthoides*
             4 Leaves without glands; fruit smooth . . . . *R. hirtellum*
1 Flowers in racemes of 5 or more; stems without spines or bristles (except in *R. lacustre*; **currants**) 5
     5 Ovary and fruit bristly with gland-tipped hairs 6
         6 Stems densely bristly . . . . *R. lacustre*
         6 Stems unarmed . . . . *R. glandulosum*
     5 Ovary and fruit neither bristly nor with gland-tipped hairs 7
         7 Leaf underside dotted with shiny resinous glands; fruit black 8
             8 Flowers yellow to greenish; calyx glabrous or sparsely hairy; inflorescence bracts longer than pedicels
             . . . . *R. americanum*
             8 Flowers white to greenish-white; calyx hairy; inflorescence bracts much shorter than pedicels 9
                 9 Flowers and fruit in upright racemes; native species . . . . *R. hudsonianum*
                 9 Flowers and fruit in drooping racemes; occasional garden escape . . . . *R. nigrum*
         7 Leaf underside without resinous glands 10
             10 Flowers golden-yellow; fruit black . . . . *R. aureum*
             10 Flowers yellow-green; fruit red 11
                 11 Pedicels with scattered hairs and short-stalked glands . . . . *R. triste*
                 11 Pedicels glabrous . . . . *R. rubrum*

Ribes americanum P. Mill.   MAP 751
WILD BLACK CURRANT   *native*

Shrub, 1-1.2 m tall. **Stems** without spines or bristles, young stems finely hairy;
branches upright to spreading; twigs gray-brown and smooth, black with age.
Leaves 3-8 cm long and 3-10 cm wide, 3-lobed and usually with 2 additional
shallow lobes at base, dotted with shiny, yellow to brown resinous glands,
especially on underside, smooth or short-hairy above, hairy below; margins
coarsely toothed; petioles hairy and resin-dotted, 3-6 cm long. **Flowers** creamy-
white to yellow, bell-shaped, 8-12 mm long; 6-15 in drooping racemes 3-8 cm
long; each flower with a linear bract longer than the flower stalk, the stalks 2-3
mm long; sepals 4-5 mm long, rounded; petals blunt, 2-3 mm long; stamens about
equaling petals. **Fruit** an edible, smooth, black berry. April-June.—Moist to wet
forests, swamps, marsh and lake borders, streambanks.

Ribes americanum

Ribes aureum Pursh
BUFFALO-CURRANT
Ribes odoratum H. Wendl.

MAP 752
introduced

Erect shrub. **Leaves** orbicular to cuneate-obovate in outline, broadly cuneate to truncate at base, deeply 3-lobed or rarely 5-lobed, ciliate, finely puberulent to glabrate beneath, the lobes entire in their lower half, entire or few-toothed across the summit. **Flowers** golden yellow; hypanthium above the ovary tubular, 11-15 mm long; sepals obovate, 5-6.5 mm long, broadly rounded above; petals 2.5-3.5 mm long, erose at the summit. **Fruit** yellow or black, edible. Apr-June.—Cliffs and rocky hillsides; native of w North America; considered adventive in Minn.

Ribes cynosbati L.
EASTERN PRICKLY GOOSEBERRY

MAP 753
native

Shrub to 6-9 dm tall, branches upright to spreading. **Stems and branches** with 1-3 spines at nodes, outer bark peeling off, inner bark brown-purple to black; **young stems** brown-gray, finely hairy. **Leaves** 3-8 cm long and 3-7 cm wide, 3-5-lobed, the lobes rounded at tips; upper surface dark green, sparsely hairy, underside paler, finely hairy and with gland-tipped hairs along veins; margins with coarse, round teeth; petioles 2.5-4 cm long, finely hairy and with scattered gland-tipped hairs. **Flowers** green-yellow, bell-shaped, 6-9 mm long, in clusters of 2-3 from spurs on old wood, on stalks with gland-tipped hairs. **Fruit** a red-purple berry, covered with stiff, brown spines. May-June.—Occasional in wet woods, swamps, thickets and streambanks; more typical in moist hardwood forests (where our most common gooseberry).

Ribes cynosbati

Ribes glandulosum Grauer
SKUNK CURRANT
Ribes ruizii Rehder

MAP 754
native

Shrub to 8 dm tall. **Stems** sprawling, spines and bristles absent. **Stems and leaves** with skunklike odor when crushed; **older stems** smooth and dark as outer bark peels off; **young stems** smooth to finely hairy, brown-gray. **Leaves** 2-8 cm long and 4-8 cm wide, 3-5-lobed, smooth above, paler and finely glandular hairy below (at least along veins); margins toothed or double-toothed; petioles 3-6 cm long, finely hairy. **Flowers** yellow-green to purple, saucer-shaped, in loose upright clusters 3-6 cm long, on slender stalks; bracts very small, the stalks and bracts with gland-tipped hairs; sepals 2 mm long; petals 1-2 mm long. **Fruit** a dark red berry with bristles and gland-tipped hairs, 6 mm wide. June.—Cedar and tamarack swamps, cool wet woods, thickets and streambanks.

Ribes glandulosum

Ribes hirtellum Michx.
HAIRY-STEM GOOSEBERRY

MAP 755
native

Shrub to 9 dm tall. **Stems** upright, outer bark pale, soon peeling to expose dark inner layer; **young stems** gray and smooth, or with 1-3 slender spines at nodes and scattered bristles between nodes. **Leaves** 2.5-5 cm long and 2-5 cm wide, with 3 or 5 pointed lobes, upper surface dark green, smooth to sparsely hairy, lower surface paler, hairy at least along veins, without glands; margins coarsely toothed and fringed with hairs; petioles 1-3 cm long, hairy, some of which are gland-tipped. **Flowers** green-yellow to purple, bell-shaped, 6-9 mm long, in clusters of 2-3 on short, smooth stalks; stamens as long or longer than sepals, the bracts fringed with long hairs. **Fruit** an edible, smooth, dark blue-black berry. June. —Cedar and tamarack swamps, thickets, shores, rocky openings.

Ribes hirtellum

752. *Ribes aureum*   753. *Ribes cynosbati*   754. *Ribes glandulosum*   755. *Ribes hirtellum*

Ribes hudsonianum Richards.

MAP 756
HUDSON BAY CURRANT *native*

Shrub, 6–9 dm tall. **Stems** upright, spines and bristles absent; bark gray, with scattered yellow resin dots, peeling to expose inner purple-black bark. **Leaves** 5–9 cm long and 6–13 cm wide, 3–5-lobed, with unpleasant odor when rubbed, upper surface dark green and mostly hairless, underside paler, smooth to hairy and with yellow resin dots; margins coarsely toothed, the teeth with a hard tip; petioles 2.5–8 cm long, with fine hairs and resin dots. **Flowers** white, bell-shaped, 4–5 mm long, in small clusters on threadlike stalks. **Fruit** a smooth, blue-black berry, barely edible. June.—Cedar swamps, wet conifer woods and streambanks.

Ribes hudsonianum

Ribes lacustre (Pers.) Poir.

MAP 757
BRISTLY BLACK GOOSEBERRY *native*

Shrub to 1 m tall. **Stems** upright or spreading, densely bristly, long-spiny at nodes; older bark gray, peeling to expose dark inner bark. **Leaves** 4–8 cm long and 4–7 cm wide, with 3–5 deeply parted, pointed lobes, upper surface dark green and mostly smooth, underside paler with scattered gland-tipped hairs; margins cleft into rounded teeth; petioles 2.5–4 cm long, with gland-tipped hairs. **Flowers** yellow-green to pinkish, saucer-shaped, 4–5 mm wide, on stalks with dark, gland-tipped hairs, in arching or drooping clusters. **Fruit** palatable but insipid, red, becoming black or dark purple, covered with gland-tipped hairs. May–June.—Moist conifer woods, swamps, thickets, and rock outcrops.

Ribes missouriense Nutt.

MAP 758
MISSOURI GOOSEBERRY *native*

Shrub. **Stems** usually with stout nodal spines. **Leaves** rotund in outline, the two principal sinuses extending nearly to the middle, glabrous to villosulous above, softly pubescent beneath or glabrous in age. Peduncles 1–2 cm long, commonly much exceeding the pedicels; ovary glabrous; hypanthium nearly cylindric; sepals oblong lance-shaped, pale green to white, 5–7 mm long; petals obovate, 2.5–3.5 mm long, pale green to nearly white; stamens 10–12 mm long. **Fruit** red to purple, glabrous, edible. May.—Moist or dry upland woods.

Ribes lacustre

Ribes nigrum L.

MAP 759
GARDEN BLACK CURRANT *introduced*

Shrub. **Leaves** 3–5-lobed about to the middle, dotted with resinous glands beneath. Racemes drooping, the pedicels (2–8 mm long) much exceeding the minute ovate bracts; hypanthium above the ovary short-campanulate; sepals greenish purple within; ovary commonly with sessile resinous glands. **Fruit** black, glabrous, sweet-tasting.—Native of Eurasia; occasionally planted and rarely escaped.

Ribes oxyacanthoides L.

MAP 760
NORTHERN GOOSEBERRY 🌱 *threatened | native*

Shrub to 1 m tall. **Stems** upright with 1–3 spines to 1 cm long at nodes and smaller spines scattered between nodes; **young stems** gray-brown and finely hairy. **Leaves** 2.5–5 cm long and 2–5 cm wide, with 3–5 blunt or rounded lobes, upper surface sparsely hairy, some hairs tipped with glands, underside resin-dotted, hairy, some gland-tipped, especially along veins; margins coarsely toothed and hairy; petioles 0.5–3 cm long, with short hairs and scattered glands. **Flowers** green-yellow, bell-shaped, 6–9 mm long, in clusters of 2–3 on short stalks; stamens shorter than

Ribes oxyacanthoides

756. *Ribes hudsonianum*   757. *Ribes lacustre*   758. *Ribes missouriense*   759. *Ribes nigrum*

petals. **Fruit** a smooth, edible, blue-black berry. June.—Rocky and sandy shores, rocky openings, cold moist woods.

Ribes rubrum L.
GARDEN RED CURRANT
   Ribes sativum Syme

MAP 761
introduced

Erect shrub. **Stems** erect, nearly glabrous, crisped-puberulent; spines at nodes absent; prickles on internodes absent. **Leaves** commonly 5-lobed, the lateral lobes spreading. **Flowers** cream to pinkish. **Fruit** a bright red berry, glabrous, sour. —Native of the Old World; long in cultivation and occasionally escaped.

Ribes triste Pallas
SWAMP RED CURRANT

MAP 762
native

Low shrub, 0.4-1 m tall. **Stems** spreading or lying on ground and rooting at nodes, spines and bristles absent; **older stems** smooth, purple-black, **young stems** short-hairy. **Leaves** 4-10 cm long and 4-10 cm wide, with 3-5 broad lobes, dark green and mostly smooth above, paler and usually finely hairy below; margins with both rounded and sharp teeth, the teeth with a hard tip; petioles 2.5-6 cm long, with scattered gland-tipped hairs. **Flowers** green-purple, 4-5 mm wide, on stalks 1-4 mm long, in drooping clusters of 5-12. **Fruit** a red berry, glabrous, sour-tasting. May-June.—Wet woods swamps, alder thickets, seeps.

Ribes triste

Haloragaceae WATER-MILFOIL FAMILY

MYRIOPHYLLUM *Water-Milfoil*

Perennial aquatic herbs. Stems submerged, sparsely branched, freely rooting at lower nodes. Leaves mostly whorled (alternate in *M. farwellii*), pinnately divided into threadlike segments (scale-like in *M. tenellum*), upper leaves often reduced to bracts. Flowers small, mostly imperfect, stalkless in axils of upper emersed leaves (the floral bracts) or axils of underwater leaves; staminate flowers above pistillate flowers; perfect flowers (if present) in middle portion of spike; sepals inconspicuous; petals 4 or absent; stamens 4 or 8; pistil 4-chambered. Fruit nutlike, 4-lobed, each lobe (mericarp) with 1 seed, rounded on back or with a ridge or row of small bumps.

1 Leaves simple, reduced to small, blunt-tipped scales; stems erect and crowded from creeping rhizomes . . . . . .
   . . . . **M. tenellum**
1 Leaves dissected into narrow segments 2
  2 Leaves alternate, opposite, or scattered on stem . . . . **M. farwellii**
  2 Foliage leaves all whorled (or appearing so in *M. heterophyllum*). 3
    3 Flowers and bracts below flowers alternate on stem . . . . **M. alterniflorum**
    3 Flowers and bracts below flowers whorled 4
      4 Bracts surrounding staminate flowers deeply cleft . . . . **M. verticillatum**
      4 Bracts surrounding staminate flowers sharply toothed or entire 5
        5 Bracts sharply toothed and much longer than flowers . . . . **M. heterophyllum**
        5 Bracts surrounding staminate flowers entire and not longer than flowers 6
          6 Leaf segments mostly 5-12 on each side of midrib; small bulbs (turions) produced at ends of stems
            and in upper leaf axils . . . . **M. sibiricum**
          6 Leaf segments many, 12-20 on each side of midrib; turions absent . . . . **M. spicatum**

760. *Ribes oxyacanthoides* 761. *Ribes rubrum* 762. *Ribes triste* 763 *Myriophyllum alterniflorum*

Myriophyllum alterniflorum DC.
ALTERNATE-FLOWER WATER-MILFOIL   *native*
Perennial herb. **Stems** very slender. **Leaves** in whorls of 3-5, usually less than 1 cm long and shorter than the stem internodes, pinnately divided. **Flower spikes** raised above water surface, 2-5 cm long; bracts mostly alternate, linear, shorter than the flowers; staminate flowers with 4 pink petals; stamens 8. **Fruit segments** 1-2 mm long, rounded on back and base.—Acidic lakes, Lake Superior coastline.

Myriophyllum farwellii Morong
MAP 764
FARWELL'S WATER-MILFOIL   *native*
Perennial herb; plants entirely underwater, turions present at ends of stems. **Leaves** 1-3 cm long, dissected into threadlike segments, all or most leaves alternate, or more or less opposite, or irregularly scattered on stems. **Flowers** underwater, single in axils of foliage leaves; **pistillate flowers** with 4 purple petals; stamens 4, tiny. **Fruit** 2 mm long, each fruit segment with 2 small, bumpy, longitudinal ridges.—Ponds and small lakes.

Myriophyllum heterophyllum Michx.
MAP 765
TWO-LEAF WATER-MILFOIL   *native*
Perennial herb. **Stems** stout, to 3 mm wide, often red-tinged, to 1 m or more long. **Leaves** appearing whorled due to the very short internodes, 1.5-4 cm long, divided into threadlike segments. **Flowers** in spikes raised above water surface, 5-30 cm long; floral bracts whorled, smaller than foliage leaves, ovate, sharply toothed, spreading or curved downward. Flowers both perfect and imperfect; petals of staminate and perfect flowers 1-3 mm long; stamens 4. **Fruit** olive, more or less round, 2 mm long; **fruit segments** rounded or with 2 small ridges, beaked by the curved stigma. June-Aug.—Lakes, ponds and pools in streams; sometimes where calcium-rich.

Myriophyllum sibiricum Komarov
MAP 766
COMMON WATER-MILFOIL   *native*
   Myriophyllum exalbescens Fern.
Perennial herb; plants often whitish when dried. **Stems** to 1 m or more long. **Leaves** in whorls of 3-4, 1-4 cm long, with mostly 5-10 threadlike segments on each side of midrib; internodes between whorls about 1 cm long. **Flowers** in spikes with whorled flowers and bracts, raised above water surface, red, clearly different than underwater stems, 4-10 cm long; flowers imperfect, the upper staminate, the lower pistillate; floral bracts much smaller than the leaves, oblong to obovate; **staminate flowers** with pinkish petals (absent in pistillate flowers), 2-3 mm long; stamens 8, the yellow-green anthers conspicuous when flowering. **Fruit** more or less round, 2-3 mm long, the segments rounded on back. June-Sept.—Shallow to deep water of lakes, ponds, marshes, ditches and slow-moving streams; sometimes where calcium-rich. *When flowering, the numerous red spikes of this species are conspicuous on water surface.* **M. spicatum**, *introduced from Eurasia, is similar but has more finely divided leaves (12-24 threadlike segments on each side of midrib) and larger floral bracts.*

Myriophyllum spicatum L.
MAP 767
EURASIAN WATER-MILFOIL   *introduced (invasive)*
Perennial herb, similar to *M. sibiricum*. **Stems** widening below head and curved to a horizontal position, usually many-branched near water surface, internodes

Myriophyllum alterniflorum (l)
M. farwellii (r)

Myriophyllum spicatum

764. *Myriophyllum farwellii*   765. *Myriophy. heterophyllum*   766. *Myriophyllum sibiricum*   767. *Myriophyllum spicatum*

between leaves mostly 1-3 cm long, turions absent. **Leaves** with more leaf segments per side (mostly 12-20) than in *M. sibiricum*; lower flower bracts often divided into comblike segments and often longer than the flowers. **Fruit segments** 2-3 mm long. Aug-Sept. Lakes and ponds. Introduced from Europe and spreading in lakes throughout eastern USA.

Myriophyllum tenellum Bigelow
SLENDER WATER-MILFOIL

MAP 768
native

Perennial herb. Stems slender, 10-30 cm long, mostly upright and unbranched. **Leaves** absent or reduced to a few spaced scales. **Flowers** in spikes raised above water surface, 2-5 cm long; flower bracts mostly alternate, oblong to obovate, entire, shorter to slightly longer than the flowers. **Fruit segments** rounded on back and at base, 1 mm long.—Acidic lakes; often forming large colonies, especially in deep water.

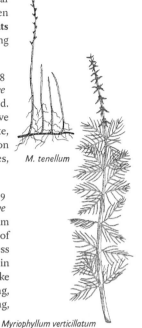

M. tenellum

Myriophyllum verticillatum L.
WHORLED WATER-MILFOIL

MAP 769
native

Perennial herb, similar to *M. sibiricum*, but plants often larger. **Stems** 5-25 dm long. **Leaves** in whorls of 4-5, with 9-17 threadlike segments along each side of midrib, 1-5 cm long; lower and middle internodes between whorls mostly less than 1 cm long. **Flowers** perfect, or the lower pistillate and upper staminate; in spikes 4-12 cm long, the floral bracts much smaller than the leaves, with comblike segments, mostly longer than the flowers; petals blunt-tipped, 2-3 mm long, smaller in pistillate flowers; stamens 8. **Fruit** more or less round, 2-3 mm long, the segments rounded on back. July-Sept.—Lakes, ponds, quiet rivers.

Myriophyllum verticillatum

Hamamelidaceae WITCH-HAZEL FAMILY

HAMAMELIS *Witch-Hazel*

Hamamelis virginiana L.
AMERICAN WITCH-HAZEL

MAP 770
🌢*threatened | native*

Tall shrub to 5 m, with scurfy or glabrous twigs. **Leaves** broadly obovate, with several to many rounded teeth, base broadly rounded or subcordate, green on both sides, glabrous or stellate-pubescent beneath. **Flowers** in short-pediceled axillary clusters; 4-merous; sepals small, triangular, dull yellowish brown within; petals bright yellow or suffused with red, spreading, 1.5-2 cm long; stamens 4, opposite the sepals and much shorter than them, alternating with 4 small scale-like staminodia; styles 2. **Fruit** ovoid before dehiscence, 1-1.5 cm long, the hypanthium often bearing the persistent sepals; seeds black, eventually discharged explosively from the capsule. Oct-Nov; fruit ripe a year later.—Dry to moist deciduous woods of oak, sugar maple or basswood. *Witch hazel extract is derived from the bark.*

Hamamelis virginiana

Hypericaceae ST. JOHN'S-WORT FAMILY

Glabrous annual or perennial herbs (shrubby in *Hypericum kalmianum* and *H. prolificum*). Stems usually unbranched below, branched in head. Leaves simple, opposite, dotted with dark or translucent glands (visible when held to a light), especially on underside; margins entire; petioles absent. Flowers few to many in clusters at ends of stems or from upper leaf axils, perfect (with both staminate and pistillate parts), regular, sepals 5, petals 5, yellow or pink to green or purple; stamens 9-35, separate or joined near base into 3 or more groups; styles 3, ovary superior. Fruit a 3-chambered, many-seeded capsule.

1 Petals yellow; stamens 15-many . . . . *Hypericum*
1 Petals pink or purple; stamens 9 . . . . *Triadenum*

HYPERICUM *St. John's-Wort*

Shrubs or herbs. Leaves opposite, sometimes dotted with black and/or small transparent glands; margins entire. Flowers in clusters at ends of stems and upper leaf axils, yellow, perfect, regular, sepals

5, petals 5, stamens 5-many, separate or joined into 3 or 5 bundles. Fruit a capsule.

ADDITIONAL SPECIES
Hypericum maculatum Crantz (Spotted St. John's-wort), native to Europe; St. Louis County (Duluth area).

1 Styles joined at base, persisting on capsule as a straight beak; stamens many, distinct 2
  2 Small shrubs to 1 m tall . . . . ***H. kalmianum***
  2 Perennial herbs, slightly woody at base . . . . ***H. ellipticum***
1 Styles free to base, the capsules not beaked; stamens few to many, joined at base into 3 or 5 bundles 3
  3 Plants 1-2 m tall; leaves 5 cm long or more; flowers 4 cm or more wide; styles 5 . . . . ***H. pyramidatum***
  3 Plants usually less than 1 m tall; leaves less than 5 cm long; flowers to 3 cm wide; styles 3 4
    4 Petals spotted with black dots; stamens in 3 weak groups 5
      5 Flowers 15 mm or more wide, petals black-dotted only on margins; capsules oblong cone-shaped;
        common introduced weed . . . . ***H. perforatum***
      5 Flowers 6-10 mm wide, petals and sepals with black dots and lines; capsules nearly round to ovate;
        native species . . . . ***H. punctatum***
    4 Petals not spotted with black dots; stamens in 5 weak groups 6
      6 Leaves reduced to tiny scales to 3 mm long; dry, sandy habitats; reported for Minn . . . ***H. gentianoides***
      6 Leaves larger, linear to elliptic-ovate 7
        7 Sepals broadest near or above middle; capsule rounded at tip 8
          8 Bracts leafy and oval, uppermost 0.5-2 mm wide; sepals much shorter than fruit . . . ***H. boreale***
          8 Bracts awl-shaped, uppermost to 0.2 mm wide; sepals same length as fruit . . . . ***H. mutilum***
        7 Sepals lance-shaped, broadest below middle; capsule tapered to tip . . . . ***H. majus***

Hypericum boreale (Britt.) Bickn.   MAP 771
NORTHERN ST. JOHN'S-WORT   *native*
Perennial herb, from slender rhizomes. **Stems** 1-4 dm long, round or slightly 4-angled, branched above. **Leaves** oval or oblong, rounded at ends and nearly clasping stem, 3-5-nerved, larger leaves 1-2 cm long and 0.5-1 cm wide; petioles absent. **Flowers** in clusters at ends of stems and from upper leaf axils; sepals blunt-tipped; petals yellow, 3 mm long; stamens 8-15; styles 3 (sometimes 4), less than 1 mm long. **Fruit** a 1-chambered purple capsule, 3-5 mm long. July-Sept.—Pond and marsh margins, low areas between dunes, open bogs.

Hypericum ellipticum Hook.   MAP 772
PALE ST. JOHN'S-WORT   *native*
Perennial herb, spreading by rhizomes. **Stems** 2-5 dm long, branched only in head. **Leaves** oval, 1-4 cm long and 1-1.5 cm wide, rounded at tip, narrowed at base and sometimes clasping stem; petioles absent. **Flowers** few to many, in clusters at ends of stems; sepals to 6 mm long; petals pale yellow, 6-7 mm long; stigmas 3 (sometimes 4), small. **Fruit** a 1-chambered capsule, 5-6 mm long, rounded to a short beak formed by the persistent styles. July-Aug.—Streambanks, sandy shores and flats, thickets, bogs.

Hypericum gentianoides (L.) B.S.P.   (NO MAP)
ORANGE-GRASS   *native*
Annual herb. **Stems** 1-4 dm tall, repeatedly branched into very numerous, filiform, erect branches. **Leaves** appressed, scale-like, 1-3 mm long. **Flowers** nearly sessile, chiefly solitary at the nodes, about 3 mm wide; sepals linear lance-shaped, 2-2.5 mm long. **Capsule** slenderly conic, 5-7 mm long; seeds about 0.5 mm long, pale brown, obscurely areolate. June-Sept.—Sterile often sandy soil; reported for Minn.

Hypericum boreale

Hypericum ellipticum

768. Myriophyllum tenellum   *769. Myriophyllum verticillatum*   *770. Hamamelis virginiana*

Hypericum kalmianum L.
KALM'S ST. JOHN'S-WORT   (NO MAP) *native*

Branched shrub to 1 m tall; **branches** 4-angled, **twigs** flattened. **Leaves** linear, 2-4 cm long and 3-8 mm wide, often waxy on underside; margins sometimes rolled under; petioles absent. **Flowers** in clusters of 3-7 at ends of stems, yellow, 2-3.5 cm wide; stamens many, not joined; styles 5. **Fruit** a 5-chambered, ovate capsule, 7-10 mm long, beaked by the persistent style base. June-Sept.—In Minn, known only from a wilderness entry trailhead in Lake County.

Hypericum majus (Gray) Britt.
GREATER CANADIAN ST. JOHN'S-WORT   MAP 773 *native*

Perennial herb, spreading from rhizomes or stolons. **Stems** upright, unbranched or branched above, 1-6 dm long. **Leaves** lance-shaped, 2-4 cm long and 3-10 mm wide, dotted with brown sunken glands, 5-7-nerved from base; leaf tip rounded, leaf base rounded or heart-shaped and weakly clasping; petioles absent. **Flowers** few to many in clusters at ends of stems and from upper leaf axils; sepals lance-shaped, 4-6 mm long; petals yellow, equal to sepals but then shriveling to half the length of sepals; stamens 14-21, not joined; styles to 1 mm long. **Fruit** a red-purple ovate capsule, 5-7 mm long. July-Sept.—Streambanks, sandy, mucky or calcareous shores, low areas between dunes, marshes, wetland margins.

Hypericum majus

Hypericum mutilum L.
DWARF ST. JOHN'S-WORT   (NO MAP) *native*

Annual or perennial herb. **Stems** 1-8 dm long, branched above. **Leaves** lance-shaped to oval, 1-4 cm long, 3-5 nerved from base, petioles absent. **Flowers** in branched, leafy clusters at ends of stems and from upper leaf axils, upper leaves bractlike and 1-4 mm long; sepals linear and pointed at tip; petals pale orange-yellow, 2-3 mm long; stamens 5-16; styles 3, less than 1 mm long. **Fruit** a green capsule, 2-4 mm long. July-Sept.—Streambanks, wet meadows, marshes, ditches; usually where sandy. Reported for Minn.

Hypericum mutilum

Hypericum perforatum L.
COMMON ST. JOHN'S-WORT   MAP 774 *introduced (invasive)*

Perennial herb. **Stems** 4-6 dm tall, with numerous very leafy decussate branches. **Leaves** sessile, linear-oblong, commonly 2-4 cm long, on the main axis, about half as large on the branches. **Flowers** numerous, forming a large rounded or flattened compound cyme; sepals narrowly lance-shaped, acuminate, 4-6 mm long, with few or no black glands; petals oblong, 8-10 mm long, black-dotted near the margin. Seeds 1-1.3 mm long. June-Sept.—Native of Europe; common as a weed in fields, meadows, and roadsides.

Hypericum perforatum

Hypericum punctatum Lam.
SPOTTED ST. JOHN'S-WORT   MAP 775 *native*

Perennial herb. **Stems** erect, 5-10 dm tall, with few branches below the inflorescence. **Leaves** oblong-elliptic, the larger ones commonly 4-6 cm long, and more than 1 cm wide, blunt or even retuse. **Inflorescence** usually small, compact and crowded. **Flowers** short-pediceled, 8-15 mm wide; sepals heavily dotted and lined with black, ovate or oblong, obtuse or broadly acute, 2.5-4 mm long; petals copiously dotted with black; styles 2-4 mm long, often persistent. **Capsule** ovoid, 4-6 mm long; seeds less than 1 mm long. June-Aug.—Moist or dry soil, fields and open woods.

771. *Hypericum boreale*   772. *Hypericum ellipticum*   773. *Hypericum majus*

Hypericum punctatum

Hypericum pyramidatum Ait.
GREAT ST. JOHN'S-WORT

Hypericum ascyron L.

MAP 776
native

Perennial herb. **Stems** upright, branched, 6-20 dm long. **Leaves** lance-shaped to oval, 4-10 cm long and 1-4 cm wide, base often clasping stem; petioles absent. **Flowers** few, 4-6 cm wide, mostly single on stalks from upper leaf axils; stamens numerous, joined at base into 5 bundles; petals bright yellow; styles 5, not persisting. **Fruit** an ovate, 5-chambered capsule, 15-30 mm long. July-Aug. —Streambanks, ditches, fen and marsh margins.

Hypericum pyramidatum

TRIADENUM *Marsh St. John's-Wort*

Triadenum fraseri (Spach) Gleason
FRASER'S MARSH-ST. JOHN'S-WORT

Hypericum virginicum L. var. *fraseri* (Spach) Fern.

MAP 777
native

Glabrous perennial herb, with creeping rhizomes. **Stems** upright, mostly unbranched, red, smooth, 3-6 dm long. **Leaves** opposite, entire, oval or ovate, 3-6 cm long and 1-3 cm wide, pinnately veined, rounded at tip, rounded or heart-shaped and clasping at the base, with dark dots and transparent glands on underside. **Flowers** in clusters at ends of stems and from leaf axils; sepals 3-5 mm long, rounded at tip; petals 5, pink to green-purple, 5-8 mm long; stamens 9, joined at base into 3 bundles, the bundles alternating with orange glands; styles 1-2 mm long. **Fruit** a purple, cylindric capsule, 7-12 mm long, abruptly narrowed to the 1 mm long persistent style-beak. July-Aug.—Marshes, sedge meadows, open bogs, fens, sandy and calcium-rich shores.

Triadenum fraseri

Juglandaceae WALNUT FAMILY

Trees. Leaves alternate, odd-pinnate. Flowers monoecious. Staminate flowers in elongate catkins, each composed of a 2-6-lobed calyx, subtended by a narrow bract, and bearing few to many stamens on its upper side. Pistillate flowers terminating the young branches, each subtended by a perianth-like, cup-shaped involucre formed of connate bracts. Ovary 1-celled, tipped with 2 plumose stigmas. Fruit large, consisting of a fleshy or woody exocarp enclosing a nut; embryo large and oily, without endosperm.

1 Leaflets mostly 5-9, the terminal leaflet largest . . . . *Carya*
1 Leaflets 11-23, the lateral leaflets largest . . . . *Juglans*

CARYA *Hickory*

Trees with hard, heavy wood. All species are more or less stellate-pubescent, at least when young, and leaves, buds, and fruit also copiously covered with resin when young. Leaves odd-pinnate, the 3 terminal leaflets the largest. Flowers appear in spring as the leaves open. Staminate catkins slender, elongate, borne in peduncled groups of 3 at the summit of the previous year's growth or the base of that of the current year. Staminate calyx 2- or 3-lobed. Stamens 3-10, commonly 4. Pistillate flowers solitary or in spikes of 2-10, terminating the branches, each subtended by a cup-shaped, 4-lobed, perianth-like involucre. Fruit a hard-shelled nut, enclosed within the expanded, 4-valved involucre.

774. Hypericum perforatum   *775. Hypericum punctatum*   *776. Hypericum pyramidatum*   *777. Triadenum fraseri*

1   Leaflets 7-9; bud scales sulfur-yellow; bark smooth or with shallow ridges .... ***C. cordiformis***
1   Leaflets 5; bud scales not yellow; bark shaggy .... ***C. ovata***

Carya cordiformis (Wangenh.) K. Koch   MAP 778
BITTERNUT HICKORY   *native*

Tree; bark scaly. **Winter-buds** bright orange-yellow. **Leaflets** commonly 7 or 9, occasionally 5, rarely 11, the lateral lance-shaped to ovate lance-shaped, the terminal commonly long-cuneate at base and nearly or quite sessile. **Fruit** obovoid to subglobose, often somewhat flattened, 2.5-3.5 cm long, winged chiefly above the middle, splitting about to the middle. Nut subglobose to obovoid, 1.5-3 cm long, at least two-thirds as thick, obscurely angled, otherwise smooth, tipped with a slender persistent point. Kernel bitter.—Dry or moist forests.

Carya cordiformis

Carya ovata (P. Mill.) K. Koch   MAP 779
SHAGBARK HICKORY   *native*
Tree; bark light gray, soon separating into long plates. **Leaflets** 5, or 7 on sprouts, pubescent beneath when young, soon becoming nearly or wholly glabrous, the terminal obovate, much larger and proportionately wider than the lateral. **Fruit** subglobose to broadly obovoid, 3.5-5 cm long, thick-walled, eventually splitting to the base; **nut** compressed, 2-3 cm long, rounded at base, usually sharp-pointed.—Rich moist soil. *Variable in the size and shape of the nuts and in the pubescence of the leaves.*

Carya ovata

JUGLANS *Walnut*
Trees. Leaves glandular-pubescent, odd-pinnate, the median lateral leaflets the largest. Staminate catkins protruding from the buds in autumn, elongating in spring, densely flowered, pendulous. Calyx spreading, 3-6-lobed, with 8-40 stamens on its upper side. Pistillate flowers in short spikes terminating the branches, composed of a 3-lobed, cup-shaped involucre. Fruit clammy-glandular. Nut indehiscent but 2-valved.

1   Leaflets 11-17, terminal leaflet usually present; pith of twigs brown; fruit sticky-downy .... *J. cinerea*
1   Leaflets 13-23, terminal leaflet often absent; pith of twigs cream colored; fruit globose, not sticky-downy .....
              .... *J. nigra*

Juglans cinerea L.   MAP 780
BUTTERNUT; WHITE WALNUT   *endangered | native*
Tree, to 30 m tall; bark grayish brown, with smooth ridges; pith dark brown. **Leaflets** commonly 11-17, oblong lance-shaped, somewhat pointed at tip. **Nut** ovoid, ovoid-oblong, or short-cylindric, very rough, marked with 2 or 4 obscure longitudinal ridges.—Rich moist soil.

Juglans nigra L.   MAP 781
BLACK WALNUT   *native*
Tree, to 40 m tall; bark nearly black, with rough ridges; pith light brown. **Leaflets** commonly 11-23, oblong-ovate, acuminate. **Fruit** 5-8 cm wide; **nut** subglobose and slightly flattened, very rough, distinctly 2-valved.—Rich moist soil. Its handsome durable wood is highly prized and the commercial supply of walnut is scarce. The nuts vary considerably in shape and size. *Moderately toxic to dogs and horses (as when the bark or wood shavings are used as bedding).*

Juglans cinerea

778. *Carya cordiformis*

779. *Carya ovata*

780. *Juglans cinerea*   781. *Juglans nigra*

Lamiaceae   MINT FAMILY

Perennial, often aromatic, herbs. Stems usually 4-angled. Leaves simple, opposite, sharply toothed or deeply lobed. Flowers in leaf axils or in heads or spikes at ends of stems, perfect (with both staminate and pistillate parts), nearly regular to irregular; sepals 5-toothed or sometimes 2-lipped; petals white, pink, blue or purple, often 2-lipped; stamens 2 or 4; ovary 4-lobed, splitting into 4, 1-seeded nutlets when mature.

ADDITIONAL SPECIES

Hyssopus officinalis L. (Hyssop), introduced, known from several e-c Minn locations; see Group D key.

Thymus pulegioides L. (Lemon thyme), introduced and known from several Minn locations.

1 Calyx with a distinct cap or protuberance on the upper side of the tube . . . . *Scutellaria*
1 Calyx without a cap or protuberance on the tube 2
  2 Upper lip of the corolla very short, or its lobes adjacent to the margins of the lower lip, the corolla thus appearing to be 1-lipped 3
    3 Lower lip 5-lobed, the 2 lobes nearest its base representing the upper lip . . . . *Teucrium canadense*
    3 Lower lip 3-lobed, or appearing 4-lobed if the center lip is notched . . . . *Ajuga genevensis*
  2 Upper lip of the corolla well developed, entire or 2-lobed, or the corolla regular or nearly so 4
    4 Stamens included and hidden within the corolla tube 5
      5 Calyx lobes 10, awl-shaped and hooked at the tip . . . . *Marrubium vulgare*
      5 Calyx lobes 5, broader and not hooked at tip . . . . *Glechoma hederacea*
    4 Stamens exserted beyond the throat of the corolla 6
      6 Stamens 2 . . . . **Group A**
      6 Stamens 4 7
        7 Inflorescence appearing axillary, the verticils (whorls of flowers around the stem) several to many, subtended by normal leaves and separated from one another by normal interodes, or the uppermost subtending leaves smaller and internodes shorter (not including plants with axillary spikes or racemes) . . . . **Group B**
        7 Inflorescence appearing terminal, the verticils 1 to many, all or mostly subtended by bract-like leaves different from the main leaves, or separated by much shorter internodes (and including plants with lateral or axillary spikes) 8
          8 Flowers single in the axils of each bract-like leaf, the verticils with 1 or 2 flowers . . . . . . **Group C**
          8 Flowers 2-many in the axil of each bract-like leaf, the verticils with 4 or more flowers . **Group D**

GROUP A

1 Calyx distinctly 2-lipped 2
  2 Flowers in loose, few-flowered verticils in the axils of foliage leaves, blue, 3-4 mm long . . . . *Hedeoma*
  2 Flowers in terminal inflorescences 3
    3 Flowers single or paired at each node of the slender raceme . . . . *Salvia*
    3 Flowers 3 or more at each flower-bearing node (but not all blooming at the same time) 4
      4 Verticils usually numerous, the flowers at each node usually less than 12, not tightly clustered . . . . *Salvia*
      4 Verticils 1-5, dense and head-like, of numerous crowded flowers . . . . *Blephilia*
1 Calyx regular or nearly so, the lobes alike in size and shape 5
  5 Corolla very irregular, 15-50 mm long . . . . *Monarda*
  5 Corolla regular or nearly so, to 5 mm long . . . . *Lycopus*

GROUP B

1 Calyx regular or nearly so, the lobes of the upper and lower lips similar in shape and size 2
  2 Corolla about equally 4- or 5-lobed 3
    3 Flowers 1-3 in each axil, and 2-6 in each verticil . . . . *Trichostema brachiatum*
    3 Flowers many in each axil . . . . *Mentha*
  2 Corolla strongly 2-lipped, the upper lip concave and arched over the stamens 4
    4 Flowers distinctly pediceled, forming loosely flowered cymules (the clusters making up a cyme) . . . . *Glechoma hederacea*
    4 Flowers sessile in the cymules 5
      5 Calyx lobes tapered to a slender tip but not spiny . . . . *Lamium*
      5 Calyx lobes prolonged into short but stiff spines 6

      6 Lower corolla lip with 2 yellow or white protuberances at its base . . . . *Galeopsis*
      6 Lower corolla lip without protuberances . . . . *Leonurus*
1 Calyx distinctly 2-lipped, the lobes of the upper and lower lips of different size and shape 7
  7 Stamens projecting beyond the corolla . . . . *Mentha*
  7 Stamens ascending under the upper lip of the corolla but not longer than the lip . . . . *Clinopodium*

GROUP C

1 Main leaves linear to narrowly oblong, sessile or nearly so; corolla usually pink-purple . . . *Physostegia virginiana*
1 Main leaves broadly ovate to oblong-ovate, with long petioles; lower corolla lip blue to white . *Perilla frutescens*

GROUP D

1 Stamens ascending under the upper corolla lip but not longer than the lip 2
  2 Calyx distinctly 2-lipped and irregular 3
    3 One calyx lobe (the upper center lobe) longer and wider than the other 4 . . . . *Dracocephalum*
    3 Three calyx lobes (which form the upper lip) differing from the other 2 lobes 4
      4 Bracts broadly rounded, abruptly tapered at the tip to a short sharp point . . . . *Prunella vulgaris*
      4 Bracts awl-shaped, coarsely hairy . . . . *Clinopodium*
  2 Calyx regular or nearly so, the lobes all alike or differing in size only 5
    5 Leaves linear, entire, sessile 6
      6 Stems finely pubescent . . . . *Clinopodium*
      6 Stems glabrous, or with small hairs on the angles only . . . . *Stachys*
    5 Leaves wider than linear, or the margins toothed, or petioled 7
      7 Calyx 15-nerved; lower verticils often with distinct peduncles . . . . *Nepeta cataria*
      7 Calyx 5-10-nerved; lower verticils sessile . . . . *Stachys*
1 At least some of the stamens protruding from the corolla 8
  8 Inflorescence a dense or loose raceme in which the component verticils are plainly visible; flowers on distinctly
      short pedicels 9
    9 Main foliage leaves entire . . . . *Hyssopus officinalis**
    9 Main foliage leaves toothed . . . . *Mentha*
  8 Inflorescence otherwise 10
    10 Inflorescence a group of terminal heads or crowded cymes, often with secondary heads or cymes in some
       of the upper axils, never a spike or raceme . . . . *Pycnanthemum*
    10 Inflorescence a dense spike, or with one or 2 lower verticils sometimes separate from the others; flowers
       sessile or nearly so . . . . *Agastache*

AGASTACHE *Giant-Hyssop*

Perennial herbs. Flowers small, numerous in dense verticils subtended by inconspicuous bracteal leaves, forming terminal, continuous or interrupted spikes. Calyx nearly regular, the tube cylindric, slightly longer on the upper side, the lobes 3-nerved, similar in size and shape. Corolla surpassing the calyx, the upper lip shallowly 2-lobed; the lower lip 3-lobed. Stamens 4, exsert beyond the corolla lobes, the 2 lower stamens curved upward under the upper corolla-lip, the 2 upper stamens curved downward. Nutlets minutely pubescent at their tip.

1 Flowers blue; leaf underside densely covered with white felt-like hairs . . . . *A. foeniculum*
1 Flowers rose, purple or yellow; leaf underside smooth to hairy, the pubescence if present not dense and felt-like
  2
  2 Flowers rose or purple; stems often red-tinged . . . . *A. scrophulariifolia*
  2 Flowers yellow; stems green . . . . *A. nepetoides*

Agastache foeniculum (Pursh) Kuntze
BLUE GIANT-HYSSOP

MAP 782
native

Stems erect, to 1 m tall, simple or branched above. **Leaves** ovate,, the larger to 9 cm long, rounded or truncate at base, coarsely serrate, glabrous above, beneath whitened with a very fine pubescence, the hairs scarcely visible under a 10x lens; petioles less than 1.5 cm long. **Spikes** solitary and terminal, or with additional spikes from short axillary branches, cylindric, to 15 cm long, 2-2.5 cm wide including the corollas, commonly interrupted at base; bracteal leaves broadly ovate; calyx puberulent at anthesis, 5-7 mm long, its lobes blue, 1.5-2 mm long; corolla blue, almost 1 cm long. July-Aug.—Dry upland woods and prairies.

Agastache foeniculum

Agastache nepetoides (L.) Kuntze   MAP 783
YELLOW GIANT-HYSSOP   *native*

Stems erect, 1-1.5 m tall, branched above. **Leaves** thin, green, ovate, to 15 cm long, reduced in size upwards, rounded or subcordate at base, coarsely serrate, finely pubescent beneath, the hairs visible under a 10x lens; petioles of the larger leaves to 6 cm long, those of the upper leaves reduced to 5 mm long. **Spikes** nearly cylindric, to 2 dm long, 1-1.5 cm wide, continuous or occasionally somewhat interrupted at base; bracteal leaves inconspicuous, broadly ovate; calyx at anthesis glabrous, about 6 mm long; calyx lobes 1-1.5 mm long. July-Oct.—Open woods and woodland edges.

Agastache scrophulariifolia (Willd.) Kuntze   MAP 784
PURPLE GIANT-HYSSOP   *native*

Similar to *A. nepetoides* in habit, size, and foliage. **Leaves** varying from glabrous to villous beneath. **Spikes** cylindric to somewhat tapering, to 15 cm long, 1.5-2 cm wide (including the corollas), usually continuous, occasionally with 1 or 2 separate verticils at base; bracteal leaves often projecting, round-ovate; calyx glabrous at anthesis, 7-9 mm long; calyx lobes 2-2.5 mm long. Aug-Sept.—Dry woods.

Agastache scrophulariifolia

AJUGA *Bugle*

Ajuga genevensis L.   MAP 785
BLUE BUGLE   *introduced*

Perennial herb, without basal stolons. **Flowering stems** erect, 1-3 dm tall, villous. **Leaves** ovate to spatulate, 2-5 crn long, the larger leaves usually sinuate-dentate; lower leaves tapering to a petiole; upper leaves narrowed or rounded to a sessile base. **Flowers** in whorls of 4-6 in the axils of bracteal leaves, forming a terminal leafy spike; calyx villous, 6-8 mm long, its lobes linear lance-shaped, somewhat longer than the tube, one lobe slightly shorter than the other four; corolla blue, 10-15 mm long; upper lip very short, 2-lobed; lower lip dilated immediately beyond the upper lip, the lateral lobes reaching to the middle of the median lobe; stamens 4, unequal in length, reaching to the end of the lateral lobes; ovary shallowly 4-lobed. April-June.—Native of Europe and n Asia; cultivated for ornament and escaped in lawns, gardens, and roadsides.

Ajuga genevensis

BLEPHILIA *Pogoda-Plant*

Blephilia hirsuta (Pursh) Benth.   MAP 786
HAIRY PAGODA-PLANT   *native*

Perennial aromatic herb. **Stems** erect or ascending, sparingly branched, 4-8 dm tall, hirsute, especially above, with spreading hairs 1-2 mm long. Principal **leaves** ovate, 4-8 cm long, more or less serrate, obtuse to rounded or subcordate at base, on petioles 1-2 cm long. **Flowers** pale purple, crowded in usually 3-5 dense glomerules in axils of upper leaves, all separated by well developed internodes or the upper pair contiguous, subtended by several ciliate bracts; calyx tubular, distinctly 2-lipped, the upper lip longest; calyx lobes narrowly triangular. Corolla 2-lipped, villous; tube much longer than the lobes, gradually widened distally; upper lip straight, entire; lower lip about as long as the upper, spreading, with 2 broad lateral lobes and an oblong median lobe; stamens 2, ascending under the upper lip and eventually exsert. May-Aug.—Rich forests, swamps, floodplains, usually in moist shaded places.

Blephila hirsuta

782. *Agastache foeniculum*   783. *Agastache nepetoides*   784. *Agastache scrophulariifolia*   785. *Ajuga genevensis*

CLINOPODIUM *Wild Basil*

Clinopodium vulgare L.
WILD BASIL
     Satureja vulgaris (L.) Fritsch

MAP 787
native

Perennial from short stolons. **Stems** erect, simple or occasionally branched above, 2-6 dm tall. **Leaves** ovate, 2-4 cm long, entire or with a few low teeth, on petioles to 1 cm long or the upper nearly sessile. **Flowers** numerous in a dense, subglobose, terminal, head-like glomerule, or in vigorous plants with 1 or 2 similar glomerules in the uppermost axils, mingled with numerous hirsute bracts about as long as the calyx; **calyx** tubular, hirsute throughout and conspicuously 10-13-nerved, 9-10 mm long, the lips nearly as long as the tube; upper lip cleft about half its length, its lobes subulate above a triangular base; lower lip cleft to its base into subulate lobes; **corolla** pale purple, rose-purple, or pink, varying to white, upper lip flat or slightly concave, straight to somewhat spreading, entire; lower lip deflexed, 3-lobed; stamens 4, ascending under the upper lip of the corolla, the upper pair distinctly shorter than the lower. **Nutlets** smooth.—Dry or moist upland woods.

Clinopodium vulgare

DRACOCEPHALUM *Dragonhead*

Dracocephalum parviflorum Nutt.
AMERICAN DRAGONHEAD

MAP 788
native

Erect perennial herb. **Stems** simple or branched, 2-8 dm tall, finely pubescent to nearly glabrous. **Leaves** lance-shaped, 3-8 cm long, several-nerved from the base, sharply serrate with a few teeth. **Flowers** in dense glomerules aggregated into a terminal, globose or short-cylindric spike 2-10 cm long and 2-3 cm wide, sometimes also with a separate lower glomerule; bracts lance-shaped, about equaling the calyx, the few teeth ending in short awns; **calyx** at anthesis 10-14 mm long, the tube villous, 2-lipped, the 4 lower lobes similar, the uppermost lobe much wider, with 5 long-villous protuberances at the sinuses; calyx lobes nearly as long as the tube, sharply tipped, strongly 3-nerved. **Corolla** blue, barely longer than the calyx, weakly bilabiate, the tube elongate, gradually widened upwards, the limb much shorter; upper lip straight, 2-lobed; lower lip deflexed, 3-lobed, the median lobe notched; stamens 4, ascending under the upper corolla-lip. **Nutlets** oblong, smooth.—Fields, roadsides, rocky places.

Dracocephalum parviflorum

GALEOPSIS *Hemp-Nettle*

Galeopsis tetrahit L.
BRITTLE-STEM HEMP-NETTLE

MAP 789
introduced (naturalized)

Annual herb. **Stems** simple or branched, 3-8 dm tall, swollen at the nodes, hispid, often densely so, with long, straight, somewhat reflexed hairs. **Leaves** lance-shaped to ovate, 5-10 cm long, acuminate, crenate-serrate, pubescent on both sides, on petioles 1-3 cm long. **Flowers** white or pink or variegated, commonly with two yellow spots, borne in 2-6 dense verticils in the axils of the upper foliage leaves; **calyx** with 10 conspicuous ribs and usually 10 intermediate ones, enlarged in fruit; calyx lobes all equal, narrowly triangular, the strong midnerve excurrent as a prominent spine. **Corolla** strongly 2-lipped, the tube exceeding the calyx, the upper lip entire, erect, concave, the lower lip 3-lobed, bearing 2 protuberances at its base; stamens 4, ascending under the upper corolla lip, the lower pair slightly

Galeopsis tetrahit

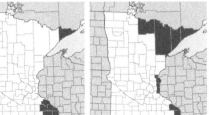

786. Blephilia hirsuta   *787. Clinopodium vulgare*   *788. Dracocephalum parviflorum*   *789. Galeopsis tetrahit*

the longer. **Nutlets** broadly obovate, smooth, 3-4 mm long. June-Sept.—Native of Eurasia; introduced as a weed of gardens, roadsides, waste places, and forests. Variable in density of pubescence, presence of glandular hairs, shape of leaf, and size of calyx and corolla. *Sometimes treated as* **Galeopsis bifida** Boenn.

GLECHOMA *Ground-Ivy*

Glechoma hederacea L.
GROUND-IVY

MAP 790
introduced (invasive)

Perennial herb. **Stems** slender, creeping, eventually to 1 m long, villous to nearly glabrous. **Leaves** rotund to kidney-shaped, 1.5-4 cm wide, conspicuously crenate, long-petioled. **Flowers** lavender to purple-blue, usually 3 in each axil; bractlets subulate, shorter than the calyx; calyx tubular, 5.5-9 mm long, 15-nerved, the 5 lobes triangular, about equal, about a 1/3 as long as the tube, with 3 nerves subtending each lobe, the middle one excurrent into a short awn; corolla much-surpassing the calyx, 2-lipped, upper lip shallowly 2-lobed; lower lip much larger, the lateral lobes short and rounded, the median lobe dilated; stamens 4, ascending under the upper corolla lip, and about equaling it. April-June.—Native of Eurasia; widely naturalized in yards, roadsides, cemeteries, and moist woods.

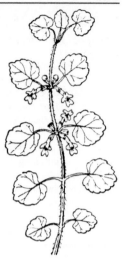

Glechoma hederacea

HEDEOMA *False Pennyroyal*

Hedeoma hispida Pursh
ROUGH FALSE PENNYROYAL

MAP 791
native

Small, strongly scented, annual herb. **Stems** simple or branched from the base, occasionally branched above, 5-20 cm tall, pubescent with recurved hairs. **Leaves** linear, 1-2 cm long, sessile, entire. **Flowers** small, blue, pediceled, in axillary few-flowered verticils; calyx tubular at anthesis, flask-shaped in fruit, strongly 13-ribbed, 2-lipped, villous in the throat; upper lip of the calyx cleft to or below the middle into narrow ciliate teeth. **Corolla** tubular, weakly 2-lipped, the upper lip erect, the lower spreading, 3-lobed; stamens 2, ascending under the upper corolla-lip and about equaling it. **Nutlets** ovoid, smooth. May-Aug.—Dry soil, sand dunes and barrens.

Hedeoma hispida

LAMIUM *Dead Nettle*

Annual or perennial herbs, commonly spreading or decumbent. Leaves broad, crenate. Flowers white to red or purple, in verticils of 6-12, subtended by scarcely reduced leaves, forming a short, crowded or somewhat interrupted, terminal spike. Calyx campanulate, almost regular, 5-nerved, the lobes nearly equal, nearly as long as to longer than the tube, triangular at base, tapering to a long, slender, but not spine-like tip. Corolla tube very slender at base, near the summit abruptly dilated, the upper lip erect, constricted at base; lateral lobes of the lower lip essentially obsolete; lowest median lobe constricted at base, as broad as long or broader, emarginate to deeply 2-lobed. Stamens 4, ascending under the upper corolla-lip, the lower pair the longer.

ADDITIONAL SPECIES
• *Lamium album* L. (Snowflake); native to Eurasia; Ramsey County.
• *Lamium galeobdolon* (L.) L. (Yellow archangel); native to Europe; St. Louis County (Duluth area).

1   Upper leaves sessile and clasping stem, lower leaves on long petioles . . . . *L. amplexicaule*
1   All leaves with petioles . . . . *L. maculatum*

Lamium amplexicaule L.
HENBIT

MAP 792
introduced

Annual. **Stems** branched from the base, weak, ascending or decumbent, 1-4 dm long, bearing a few small long-petioled leaves at the base, usually with 1 or 2, rarely 3, greatly elongate internodes, above which the internodes are much shorter and subtended by sessile leaves. **Leaves** subrotund, 1-3 cm wide, deeply crenate. **Flowers** in dense verticils in the axils of the upper leaves, the uppermost verticils often adjacent; **calyx** 5-7 mm long, densely villous, its setaceous lobes directed forward, about equaling the tube; corolla pink to purplish, 12-18 mm long, the upper lip a fourth to a third as long as the tube. March-Nov.—Native of Eurasia and n Africa; introduced as a weed in fields, gardens, and waste places, especially in moist fertile soil.

Lamium maculatum L.
SPOTTED DEAD NETTLE

(NO MAP)
introduced

Perennial. **Stems** erect or ascending from a decumbent base, 2-6 dm tall. **Leaves** all petioled, usually with a white stripe along the midvein, ovate or deltoid. **Calyx** 8-10 mm long, the lobes mostly shorter than to equaling the tube; corolla red-purple, sometimes white, 2-2.5 cm long, the upper lip more than 1/2 as long as the tube, densely short-pubescent, the tube with a transverse constriction near the base. April-Sept.—Native of Eurasia, escaped from cultivation on roadsides and waste places; in Minn known from St. Louis Co. (cemetery population).

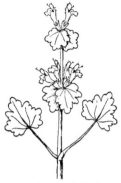

Lamium amplexicaule

LEONURUS *Motherwort*

Erect, biennial or perennial, strongly scented herbs. Leaves dentate to laciniate, petiolate. Flowers white to pink, crowded in dense verticils subtended by bracteal leaves and by linear bracts, forming long, interrupted, terminal spikes. Calyx tube 5-10-nerved, calyx lobes prolonged into stiff slender spines, the lower 2 often slightly larger or deflexed. Corolla strongly bilabiate; upper lip erect, entire, pubescent; lower lip spreading or deflexed, 3-lobed. Stamens 4, about equal, ascending under the upper lip of the corolla. Nutlets obpyramidal, 3-4-angled, truncate and pubescent at their tips.

ADDITIONAL SPECIES
Leonurus sibiricus L. (Siberian motherwort), native to Asia; Brown and Dakota counties.

1   Main leaves palmately divided and coarsely toothed; calyx glabrous or nearly so, with 2 calyx teeth usually strongly deflexed   . . . . **L. cardiaca**
1   Main leaves entire to coarsely toothed; calyx pubescent, none of the teeth strongly deflexed . **L. marrubiastrum**

Leonurus cardiaca L.
MOTHERWORT

MAP 793
introduced (naturalized)

Perennial. **Stems** stout, erect, to 1.5 m tall, finely pubescent on the angles and nodes. **Leaves** long-petioled, the larger broadly ovate, palmately lobed and sharply toothed, the upper progressively smaller and narrower, those subtending verticils commonly oblong and merely 3-toothed; **bracts** subulate, rarely 1/2 as long as the calyx; **calyx tube** 5-angled, 5-ribbed, nearly glabrous, 3-4 mm long; calyx lobes nearly as long as the tube, the lower two somewhat the larger and strongly deflexed; **corolla** pale pink, the upper lip white-villous. June-Aug.—Native of c Asia; formerly cultivated as a home remedy and now established in waste places, roadsides, and gardens.

Leonurus marrubiastrum L.
LION'S-TAIL

MAP 794
introduced

Chaiturus marrubiastrum (L.) Reichenb.

Biennial. **Stems** 1-1.5 m tall, finely pubescent. **Leaves** ovate lance-shaped to ovate, sharply or crenately serrate, those subtending verticils smaller and narrower, few-toothed to entire; **bracts** 1/2 as long as to longer than the inconspicuously 10-nerved calyx tube; **corolla** scarcely longer than the sepals. June-Sept.—Native of Europe and n Asia; introduced in waste places.

Leonurus cardiaca

790. *Glechoma hederacea*   791. *Hedeoma hispida*   792. *Lamium amplexicaule*   793. *Leonurus cardiaca*

LYCOPUS *Water-Horehound*

Perennial, unscented herbs. Stems erect, 4-angled. Leaves opposite, coarsely toothed or deeply lobed, smaller on upper stems; petioles short or absent. Flowers small, in clusters in middle and upper leaf axils, often appearing whorled; white to pink, the sepals and petals often dotted on outer surface, 4-lobed, stamens 2. Fruit a nutlet.

HYBRIDS

Lycopus × *sherardii* Steele, hybrid between *L. uniflorus* and *L. virginicus* (MAP 795).

1   Sepal lobes broad, triangular to ovate, to 1 mm long, shorter than to about as long as nutlets, the midvein not prominent 2
    2   Leaves mostly less than 3 cm wide; stamens and styles visible, longer than petals; outer rim of nutlets taller than the inner rim . . . . *L. uniflorus*
    2   Larger leaves 3 cm or more wide; stamens and styles hidden by petals; inner and outer rim of nutlets same height, the 4 nutlets appearing flat-topped across tops . . . . *L. virginicus*
1   Sepal lobes slender, 1-3 mm long, longer than nutlets, the midvein prominent 3
    3   Main leaves sessile . . . . *L. asper*
    3   Leaves with petioles . . . . *L. americanus*

Lycopus americanus Muhl.   MAP 796
CUT-LEAF WATER-HOREHOUND   *native*

Perennial herb, spreading by rhizomes, tubers absent. **Stems** erect, often branched, 2-8 dm long, upper stems smooth or short-hairy. **Leaves** opposite, lance-shaped, 3-8 cm long and 1-4 cm wide, with glandular dots, smooth or rough on upper surface, underside veins short-hairy; margins coarsely and irregularly deeply toothed or lobed, the lowest teeth largest; nearly stalkless or on short petioles. **Flowers** in dense, whorled clusters in leaf axils; sepal lobes narrow, sharp-tipped, 1-3 mm long, longer than fruit; petals white, sometimes pink to purple-dotted, 4-lobed, the upper lobe wider and notched. **Fruit** a nutlet, 1-2 mm long. July-Sept.—Marshes, wet meadows, shores, streambanks, ditches, calcareous fens, wetland margins. *Our most common water-horehound.*

Lycopus asper Greene   MAP 797
ROUGH WATER-HOREHOUND   *introduced*

Perennial emergent herb, spreading by rhizomes (tubers present) and also usually stolons. **Stems** erect, 2-8 dm long, simple or sometimes branched, hairy, at least on stem angles. **Leaves** opposite, oval to oblong lance-shaped, 3-10 cm long and 0.5-3 cm wide, smooth or rough; margins coarsely toothed; stalkless. **Flowers** in dense, whorled clusters in leaf axils; sepal lobes narrow, firm, sharp-tipped, 1-3 mm long, longer than nutlets; petals white, 4-lobed, only slightly longer than sepals. **Fruit** a nutlet, 1-2 mm long. July-Sept.—Shores and ditches, especially where disturbed, often with *L. americanus*.

Lycopus uniflorus Michx.   MAP 798
NORTHERN WATER-HOREHOUND   *native*

Perennial herb, similar to rough water-horehound (*L. asper*). **Stems** smooth or short-hairy, 1-5 dm long. **Leaves** opposite, lance-shaped to oblong, 3-6 cm long and 1-3 cm wide, margins with a few outward-pointing teeth, petioles short or nearly absent. **Flowers** in dense, whorled clusters in leaf axils; sepal lobes broad, triangular to ovate, soft, rounded at tip, to 1 mm long, shorter to as long as nutlets; petals white or pink, 2-3 mm long, 5-lobed, longer than sepals. **Fruit** a nutlet 1-

Lycopus americanus

794. *Leonurus marrubiastrum*

795. *Lycopus* × *sherardi*

796. *Lycopus americanus*

797. *Lycopus asper*

1.5 mm long. Aug.-Sept. Hybrids common with *L. virginicus* where ranges overlap producing a hybrid swarm known as *L.* × *sherardii* Steele.—Swamps, streambanks, thickets, wet meadows, open bogs, calcareous fens, ditches; often with *L. americanus.*

Lycopus virginicus L.
VIRGINIA WATER-HOREHOUND

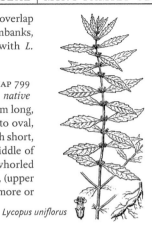

MAP 799
native

Perennial herb, spreading by stolons (tubers usually absent). **Stems** 2-6 dm long, with dense covering of appressed hairs. **Leaves** opposite, lance-shaped to oval, 5-10 cm long and 1.5-5 cm wide, long-hairy, lower surface usually also with short, feltlike hairs; margins coarsely toothed, the lowest tooth just below middle of blade, the margin below tooth concave and petiolelike. **Flowers** in whorled clusters from leaf axils; sepals shorter than nutlets; petals white, 4-lobed, (upper lobe often notched). **Fruit** a nutlet, 1-2 mm long, the group of 4 nutlets more or less flat across tips. July-Sept.—Floodplain forests.

Lycopus uniflorus

MENTHA *Mint*

Perennial herbs, spreading by rhizomes or stolons, with erect stems, serrate leaves, and small, blue to lavender flowers borne in the axils of the leaves or in terminal spikes or heads. Calyx regular or weakly 2-lipped, tubular to campanulate, 10-13-nerved, the lobes broadly triangular to subulate. Corolla tube slightly widened to the summit; corolla limb nearly regular and apparently 4-lobed; upper lobe, corresponding to the upper lip, usually somewhat wider than the others. Stamens 4, essentially uniform in length, straight, somewhat divergent, exsert from the corolla. Nutlets ovoid, smooth or roughened. All species bloom in summer.

ADDITIONAL SPECIES
Mentha × *gracilis* Sole (pro sp.), hybrid between *M. arvensis* and *M. spicata*, occasional in Minn.

1   Flowers in axillary whorls separated by internodes of normal length . . . . *M. arvensis*
1   Flowers in terminal spikes or heads, the internodes short 2
    2   Main leaves with petioles; peppermint-scented . . . . *M.* × *piperita*
    2   Main leaves sessile or nearly so; spearmint-scented . . . . *M. spicata*

Mentha arvensis L.
AMERICAN WILD MINT

MAP 800
native

Perennial herb, strongly mint-scented, spreading by rhizomes and often also by stolons. **Stems** 2-8 dm long, 4-angled, hairy at least on stem angles. **Leaves** opposite, ovate to lance-shaped, 2-7 cm long and 0.5-3 cm wide, smooth or hairy; margins with sharp, forward-pointing teeth; petioles short. **Flowers** small, white or light pink to lavender, hairy, crowded in whorled clusters in middle and upper leaf axils; sepals 2-3 mm long, hairy and glandular; petals more or less regular to slightly 2-lipped, 4-6 mm long, glandular on outside, 4- or 5-lobed; stamens and style longer than petals. **Fruit** a smooth nutlet to 1 mm long, enclosed by the persistent sepals. July-Sept.—Wet meadows, marshes, swamps, thickets, streambanks, ditches, springs and other wet places.

Mentha × *piperita* L.
PEPPERMINT

(NO MAP)
introduced

Perennial herb. **Stems** erect, glabrous or very nearly so, to 1 m. tall. **Leaves** lance-shaped or oblong lance-shaped, 4-8 cm long, sharply serrate, obtuse or rounded at base, glabrous; petioles of the principal leaves 4-15 mm long, those on the

Mentha arvensis

798. Lycopus uniflorus   *799. Lycopus virginicus*   *800. Mentha arvensis*   *801. Mentha spicata*

branches much shorter. **Spikes** 1 to several, terminating the stem and the upper lateral branches, 2-8 cm long, continuous, about 1 cm wide (excluding the corollas); calyx tubular, 3-4 mm long, the tube glabrous, the lance-subulate lobes glabrous or sparsely pilose. Considered to have originated by hybridization between *M. aquatica* and *M. spicata*; resembling the former in its large tubular calyx and blunt spikes, the latter in its elongate spikes and narrow leaves.—Of European origin; cultivated as an herb and commercially for its oil; escaped in wet soil; reported for Minn.

Mentha spicata L.
SPEARMINT

MAP 801
introduced

Perennial herb. **Stems** erect, to 5 dm tall, nearly or quite glabrous. **Leaves** sessile or subsessile, oblong lance-shaped, 2-6 cm long, sharply serrate, rounded or obtuse at base, nearly or quite glabrous. **Spikes** several, terminating the stem and short branches from the upper axils, 3-12 cm long, about 6 mm wide (excluding the corollas), continuous or somewhat interrupted, often tapering; calyx campanulate, 1.5-2 mm long, the tube glabrous, the lobes more or less pilose. —Native of Europe; commonly cultivated as an aromatic herb; reported from several Minn locations.

Mentha spicata

MONARDA *Beebalm*

Erect perennial herbs (ours). Leaves lance-shaped to ovate, sessile or petiolate. Flowers conspicuous, densely aggregated into head-like clusters terminating the branches or also borne in the upper axils, subtended by foliaceous bracts and with linear bractlets. Calyx tubular, 13-15-nerved, regular, the 5 lobes alike or nearly so, much shorter than the tube. Corolla strongly bilabiate, the upper lip narrow, entire, straight or curved, the lower somewhat broader, spreading or deflexed, 3-lobed or with a central projecting tooth. Stamens 2, ascending under the upper corolla lip. Nutlets oblong, smooth.

1   Flowers yellowish, dotted with purple; stamens and style not exserted . . . . *M. punctata*
1   Flowers lavender, white or scarlet; stamens and style strongly exserted beyond corolla; heads 2 or more and forming an interrupted spike 2
  2   Corolla lavender (rarely white) . . . . *M. fistulosa*
  2   Corolla bright scarlet . . . . *M. didyma*

Monarda didyma L.
SCARLET BEEBALM; OSWEGO TEA

MAP 802
introduced

Perennial. **Stems** 7-15 dm tall, simple or branched, glabrous or sparsely pilose, especially at the nodes. **Leaves** thin, ovate, deltoid-ovate, or nearly lance-shaped, 7-15 cm long, 2.5-6 cm wide, acuminate, serrate, broadly acute to commonly rounded at base, on petioles 1-4 cm long. **Heads** 2-4 cm wide (excluding the corollas); bracteal leaves lance-shaped, longer than the calyx, usually tinged with red; calyx 10-14 mm, long, glabrous to minutely puberulent, nearly or quite glabrous in the throat; calyx lobes 1-2 mm long, subulate above a triangular base; corolla bright crimson, 3-4.5 cm long, the upper lip about half as long as the tube. July-Sept.—Moist woods and thickets. *Often cultivated as an ornamental.*

Monarda fistulosa L.
WILD BERGAMOT

MAP 803
native

Perennial. **Stems** erect, often branched, 5-12 dm tall, usually pubescent, at least above, rarely glabrous. **Leaves** 6-10 cm long, commonly deltoid-lance-shaped, varying to lance-shaped or rarely ovate, more or less serrate; rounded, truncate, or broadly acute at base, pubescent or essentially glabrous above or canescent beneath, on petioles 1-1.5 cm long. **Heads** 1.5-3 cm wide (excluding the corollas); bracteal leaves lance-shaped or ovate; calyx 7-10 mm long, puberulent, its throat densely hirsute within; calyx lobes subulate, 1-2 mm long; corolla pale lavender, 2-3 cm long, the upper lip densely villous at the summit. June-Sept.—Upland woods, thickets, and prairies; our most abundant species of *Monarda*.

Monarda punctata L.
HORSE-MINT

MAP 804
native

Perennial. **Stems** simple or branched, 3-10 dm tall, thinly canescent. **Leaves** lance-

Monarda fistulosa

shaped or narrowly oblong, 2-8 cm long, more or less pubescent. **Glomerules** 2-5, or solitary on depauperate plants, the bracteal leaves lance-shaped to ovate, much exceeding the calyx, spreading or reflexed, often pale green to nearly white, or tinged with purple; calyx 5-9 mm long, densely villous in the throat, more or less villous externally at the summit, its lobes 1-1.5 mm long; corolla pale yellow, spotted with purple, the upper lip arched. June-Sept.—Sandy fields and dunes, dry oak and pine woods; roadsides, railroads, and disturbed places.

Monarda punctata

NEPETA *Catnip*

Nepeta cataria L.
CATNIP

MAP 805
introduced (naturalized)

Perennial herb; stems, undersides of leaves, and inflorescences covered with grayish hairs. **Stems** erect, much branched, to 1 m tall. **Leaves** narrowly to broadly deltoid, 3-8 cm long, truncate or subcordate at base, coarsely crenate-dentate, on petioles about 1/2 as long as the blade. **Flower clusters** continuous or interrupted, 2-6 cm long, rather loosely many-flowered; calyx tubular, weakly 2-lipped, at anthesis about 7 mm long, its lobes about 1/2 as long as the tube; upper 3 lobes each 2-3-nerved, somewhat longer and wider than the 1-nerved lower lobes; corolla 10-12 mm long, dull white, the lower lobe dotted with pink or purple; stamens 4, ascending under the upper corolla lip and nearly equaling it, the upper pair slightly longer. July-Oct.—Native of se Europe and sw Asia, formerly cultivated for reputed medicinal properties; established in waste places and roadsides.

Nepeta cataria

PERILLA *Perilla-Mint*

Perilla frutescens (L.) Britt.
PERILLA-MINT

(NO MAP)
introduced

Annual herbs, often purple or suffused with purple. **Leaves** ovate-oblong to broadly ovate, 8-15 cm long, coarsely serrate or incised, cuneate at the summit of the long petiole. **Flowers** purple or white, borne singly in the axils of small bracteal leaves, forming a loose, elongate, spike-like raceme 5-15 cm long, terminal and from the upper axils; bracteal leaves folded; calyx campanulate, 10-nerved, at anthesis 3 mm long; fruiting calyx enlarged, 9-12 mm long, distinctly 2-lipped and hairy within; corolla tube shorter than the calyx; corolla lips about equal in length, the 5 lobes broadly rounded; stamens 4, nearly equal, straight, about as long as the corolla. **Nutlets** globose, areolate. Aug.-Sept.—Native of India; cultivated for its ornamental foliage; reported from Martin County.

Perilla frutescens

PHYSOSTEGIA *False Dragonhead*

Physostegia virginiana (L.) Benth.
OBEDIENCE

MAP 806
native

Perennial herb, spreading by rhizomes. **Stems** erect, 5-15 dm long, often branched near top, 4-angled. **Leaves** opposite, oval to oblong lance-shaped, 2-15 cm long and 1-4 cm wide, sometimes smaller upward; margins with sharp teeth; sessile, not clasping. **Flowers** in several racemes 5-20 cm long, the stalks short-hairy; sepals 4-8 mm long, often with some gland-tipped hairs; petals pink-purple or white with purple spots, 1.5-3 cm long, short-hairy to smooth. **Fruit** a nutlet, 2-3 mm long. July-Sept.—Sedge meadows, low prairie, shores, swamps, floodplain forests, thickets and ditches. *Sometimes cultivated for its attractive flowers.*

802. Monarda didyma

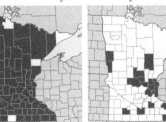

803. Monarda fistulosa   *804. Monarda punctata*

Physostegia virginiana

PRUNELLA *Self-Heal*

Prunella vulgaris L.
SELF-HEAL

MAP 807
native-introduced

Perennial herb. **Stems** upright or sometimes spreading, 1-5 dm long, 4-angled. **Leaves** opposite, lance-shaped to oval or ovate, 2-8 cm long and 1-4 cm wide; lower leaves wider than upper; margins entire or with a few small teeth; petioles present. **Flowers** in dense spikes 2-5 cm long and 1-2 cm wide, with obvious bracts; sepals to 1 cm long, green or purple, with spine-tipped teeth; corolla 2-lipped, the upper lip hoodlike and entire, lower lip shorter and 3-lobed; petals blue-violet (rarely pink or white), 1-2 cm long; stamens 4, about as long as petals. **Fruit** a smooth nutlet. Subsp. *vulgaris*, introduced from Europe and found in mostly disturbed places, has broad leaves half as wide as long. The native subsp. *lanceolata* has narrower leaves, 1/3 as wide as long. June-Oct.—Common in many types of wetlands (especially where disturbed): swamps, wet forest depressions, wet trails, streambanks; also in drier forests, fields and lawns.

Prunella vulgaris

PYCNANTHEMUM *Mountain-Mint*

Erect herbs, perennial from rhizomes, simple to the inflorescence or branched. Leaves linear to ovate, sessile or petioled, entire to serrate. Flowers small, in crowded or head-like cymes terminating the stem and its branches, or also sessile or peduncled in the axils of the upper leaves. Calyx tubular, 10-13-nerved, regular or more or less 2-lipped; calyx lobes erect, triangular, commonly shorter than the tube. Corolla 2-lipped, only slightly irregular, purple to white, the lower lip commonly spotted with purple; upper lip entire, lower lip 3-lobed. Stamens 4, exsert. Nutlets smooth, or pubescent at the summit. *Our species all bloom in summer.*

1 Stems and leaves glabrous .... *P. tenuifolium*
1 Stems pubescent on the angles, leaves rough-to-touch .... *P. virginianum*

Pycnanthemum tenuifolium Schrad.
NARROW-LEAF MOUNTAIN-MINT

(NO MAP)
introduced

Perennial barely scented herb. **Stems** 5-8 dm tall, glabrous, very leafy by the production of numerous short axillary branches. **Leaves** linear, entire, glabrous, those of the central axis 2-5 cm long, 2-4 mm wide, those of the axillary branches smaller; lateral veins 1 or 2, rarely 3, on each side of the midvein, all arising in the basal 1/4 of the leaf. **Heads** numerous, dense, hemispheric, 3-8 mm wide, on peduncles 3-15 mm long. Outer bracts lance-shaped, glabrous, sometimes exceeding the heads; inner bracts closely appressed, about as long as the calyx, the conspicuous midvein prolonged into a awl-like point. Calyx lobes narrowly triangular, puberulent, usually 1-1.5 mm long.—Chiefly in dry soil of upland woods and prairies. Reported for Anoka County.

Pycnanthemum virginianum (L.) T. Dur. & B.D. Jackson
VIRGINIA MOUNTAIN-MINT

MAP 808
native | NC | MW

Perennial, strongly scented herb. **Stems** to 1 m long, branched above, 4-angled, angles short-hairy. **Leaves** numerous, opposite, narrowly lance-shaped, 3-4 cm long and to 1 cm wide (leaves in heads much smaller), upper surface smooth, with 3-4 pairs of lateral veins, undersides often finely hairy on midvein; margins entire but fringed with short, rough hairs; more or less sessile. **Flowers** small, 2-lipped, in branched, crowded clusters at ends of stems and branches from upper leaf

Pycnanthemum virginianum

805. Nepeta cataria   *806. Physostegia virginiana*   *807. Prunella vulgaris*   *808. Pycnanthem. virginianum*

axils; sepals short woolly hairy; petals white, purple-spotted. **Fruit** a 4-parted nutlet. July-Sept. Wet meadows, marshes, tamarack swamps, calcareous fens, low prairie.

SALVIA *Sage*

Salvia reflexa Hornem.
LANCE-LEAF SAGE

MAP 809
native

Annual herb. **Stems** erect, much branched, 3-6 dm tall, the stem minutely pubescent with recurved hairs. **Leaves** lance-shaped, 3-5 cm long, 4-12 mm wide, entire or with a few low teeth, gradually narrowed to the base; petioles of the principal leaves to 2 cm long. **Racemes** erect, 5-10 cm long, the internodes 8-15 mm long; bracteal leaves linear lance-shaped, 1-3 mm long; **flowers** 2, rarely 3 or 4, at each node, subtended by usually much reduced bracteal leaves; calyx about 7 mm long, 2-lipped, the upper lip entire, 5-nerved, about half as long as the tube; corolla blue, 6-8 mm long, its tube no longer than the calyx, 2-lipped, the upper lip straight or arched, the lower 3-lobed; stamens 2, ascending under the upper lip and in some species surpassing it. June-Sept.—Adventive in dry sandy or gravelly soil of hillsides and prairies.

Salvia reflexa

SCUTELLARIA *Skullcap*

Perennial herbs, spreading by rhizomes. Stems erect or spreading, 4-angled. Leaves opposite, ovate to lance-shaped, margins toothed, petioled or nearly sessile. Flowers blue or blue with white markings, single on short stalks in axils of middle and upper leaves, or in racemes from leaf axils; calyx 2-lipped, with a rounded bump on upper side; corolla 2-lipped, pubescent on outer surface, upper lip hoodlike, lower lip more or less flat, 3-lobed; stamens 4, ascending into the upper corolla lip. Fruit a 4-parted nutlet.

1 Flowers single in leaf axils 2
  2 Corolla 15-20 mm long; leaves 2 or more times longer than wide. . . . . *S. galericulata*
  2 Corolla to 10 mm long; leaves less than 2 times longer than wide . . . . *S. parvula*
1 Flowers in racemes from end of stem or leaf axils 3
  3 Flowers in racemes from axils of stem leaves . . . . *S. lateriflora*
  3 Flowers mainly in terminal racemes, with smaller racemes from axils of upper leaves . . . . *S. ovata*

Scutellaria galericulata L.
HOODED SKULLCAP
    Scutellaria epilobiifolia A. Hamilton

MAP 810
native

Perennial. **Stems** erect or spreading, 2-8 dm long, unbranched or branched, 4-angled, short-hairy at least on angles of upper stem. **Leaves** opposite, lance-shaped to narrowly ovate, 2-6 cm long and 0.5-2.5 cm wide, upper surface smooth, underside short-hairy; margins with low, rounded, forward-pointing teeth; petioles very short. **Flowers** 2-lipped, single in leaf axils (and paired at nodes), on stalks 1-3 mm long; sepals 3-6 mm long; petals blue, marked with white, 15-25 mm long. **Fruit** a nutlet. June-Sept.—Shores, streambanks, marshes, wet meadows, swamps, thickets, bogs, ditches.

Scutellaria lateriflora L.
BLUE SKULLCAP

MAP 811
native

Perennial. **Stems** 2-6 dm long, usually branched, 4-angled, short-hairy on upper stem angles or smooth. **Leaves** opposite, ovate to lance-shaped, 3-8 cm long and 1.5-5 cm wide, smooth; margins coarsely toothed; petioles 0.5-2 cm long. **Flowers** 2-lipped, in elongate racemes from leaf axils; sepals 2-4 mm long; petals blue (rarely pink or white), 5-8 mm long. **Fruit** a nutlet. July-Sept.—Shores, streambanks, wet meadows, marshes, swamps, shaded wet areas.

Scutellaria ovata Hill
FOREST SKULLCAP

MAP 812
❧ *threatened* | *native*

Scutellaria galericulata

Perennial. **Stems** usually stout and erect, to 7 dm tall, usually conspicuously and softly pubescent with spreading glandular hairs. **Leaves** ovate to round-ovate, cordate at base, crenate (the teeth usually more than 12 on each margin), long-petioled. **Racemes** one or more, to 1 dm long, even the lowest bracteal leaves very different from the adjacent foliage leaves; corolla blue, 15-25 mm long. June-July.—Moist or dry woods, often with silver maple, oaks, basswood, and elms.

Scutellaria parvula Michx.   MAP 813
LITTLE SKULLCAP   *native*

Small perennial. **Stems** erect, often several from the end of a rhizome, 1-2 dm tall, pubescent, usually densely so, with spreading glandular hairs, puberulent on the angles also with minute recurved eglandular hairs. Principal **stem leaves** sessile, ovate, usually 10-15 mm long, distinctly hirsute on the whole upper surface; lateral veins 3-5 on each side of the midvein, not anastomosing or scarcely so. **Flowers** axillary, blue, 7-9 mm long, the short pedicels pubescent, the hairs of the pedicels spreading; calyx glandular-pubescent. May-June.—Upland woods, dry prairies, sandstone bluffs. *Includes plants sometimes separated as **Scutellaria leonardii** Epling.*

Scutellaria lateriflora

STACHYS *Hedge-Nettle*

Erect perennial herbs, spreading by rhizomes; plants usually hairy. Stems 4-angled. Leaves opposite, margins entire or toothed, stalkless or with short petioles. Flowers in interrupted spikes at ends of stems, appearing whorled in more or less evenly spaced clusters; sepals more or less regular, with 5 equal teeth; corolla 2-lipped, petals pink, often with purple spots or mottles, upper lip concave, entire, lower lip spreading, 3-lobed; stamens 4, ascending under the upper lip. Fruit a dark brown, 4-lobed nutlet, loosely enclosed by the persistent sepals.

1   Plants glabrous; leaf petioles 8-25 mm long . . . . ***S. tenuifolia***
1   Plants pubescent on the stem angles; leaves with petioles to 10 mm long . . . . ***S. pilosa***

Stachys pilosa Nutt.   MAP 814
HEDGE-NETTLE   *native*

Perennial herb **Stems** erect, rarely branched, 5-10 dm tall, villous on the sides and angles; hairs of the stem widely spreading. **Leaves** lance-shaped to ovate, 5-10 cm long, 2-4 cm wide, softly pubescent on both sides, usually with short fine hairs and longer bristles mingled, sharply serrate, sessile or nearly so. **Verticils** usually 6-flowered, the subtending leaves narrowly lance-shaped; calyx tube densely glandular-pubescent and also hirsute, the tube 3.5-5 mm long; calyx lobes glandular-hirsute, narrowly triangular, nearly as long as the tube, tapering to a stiff subulate tip. July-Aug.—Damp ground, ditch banks, beaches, and wet prairies.

Stachys tenuifolia Willd.   MAP 815
SMOOTH HEDGE-NETTLE   *native*

Perennial herb. **Stems** 4-10 dm long, 4-angled, smooth, or with downward-pointing, bristly hairs on stem angles. **Leaves** opposite, lance-shaped to ovate, 6-14 cm long and 2-6 cm wide, more or less smooth; margins with sharp, forward-pointing teeth; petioles slender, 1-2 cm long or absent. **Flowers** in interrupted spikes at ends of stems or also in upper leaf axils; sepals 5-7 mm long, glabrous; petals pale red to purple, 1.5-2.5 cm long. **Fruit** a nutlet. July-Sept.—Floodplain forests, shores, streambanks, thickets, wet meadows.

Stachys tenuifolia

809. Salvia reflexa   *810. Scutellaria galericulata*   *811. Scutellaria lateriflora*   *812. Scutellaria ovata*

TEUCRIUM *Germander*

Teucrium canadense L.
MAP 816
AMERICAN GERMANDER
native

Perennial herb, spreading by rhizomes. **Stems** 3-10 dm long, mostly unbranched, 4-angled, long-hairy. **Leaves** opposite, lance-shaped or oblong, 4-12 cm long and 1.5-5 cm wide, upper surface smooth or sparsely hairy, underside with dense, matted hairs, margins irregularly finely toothed, petioles 5-15 mm long. **Flowers** in a dense spike-like raceme, 5-20 cm long; bracts present and narrowly lance-shaped; pedicels 1-3 mm long; sepals more or less regular, purple or green, 4-7 mm long, covered with long silky hairs and very short glandular hairs; corolla irregular, 10-16 mm long, with short gland-tipped hairs, upper lip absent, lower lip large; petals pink to purple; stamens 4, arched over the corolla. **Fruit** a golden nutlet. July-Sept.—Marshes, wet meadows, streambanks, floodplain forests, ditches.

Teucrium canadense

TRICHOSTEMA *False Pennyroyal*

Trichostema brachiatum L.
MAP 817
FALSE PENNYROYAL
native
　Isanthus brachiatus (L.) B.S.P.

Annual herb. **Stems** erect, much branched, 2-4 dm tall, finely puberulent, becoming glandular in the inflorescence. **Leaves** acute, narrowed to the base, short-petioled. **Flowers** 1-3 from the axils of the scarcely reduced nearly linear bracteal leaves, forming a leafy panicle; calyx campanulate, nearly regular, the lobes narrowly triangular, exceeding the tube, at anthesis 2-3 mm, in fruit 3-5 mm long; corolla blue, the tube included in the calyx, upper 4 corolla lobes spreading or ascending, the lower lobe deflexed, usually slightly longer; stamens 4, somewhat exsert from the corolla tube. **Nutlets** obovoid, 2.5-3 mm long, prominently reticulate. Aug-Sept.—Dry soil.

Trichostema brachiatum

Lentibulariaceae BLADDERWORT FAMILY

Insectivorous herbs. Leaves in a basal rosette (*Pinguicula*), or floating, or in peat, muck, or wet soil (*Utricularia*). Flowers perfect (with both staminate and pistillate parts), irregular, 2-lipped, sometimes with a spur, 1 to several on an erect stem; stamens 2. Fruit a capsule.

1　Leaves ovate or oval, in a basal rosette; flowers single on a bractless stalk . . . . ***Pinguicula vulgaris***
1　Leaves linear or dissected into narrow segments; flowers 1, or several in a raceme, each flower subtended by a
　bract　. . . . . ***Utricularia***

PINGUICULA *Butterwort*

Pinguicula vulgaris L.
MAP 818
COMMON BUTTERWORT
native

Perennial herb. **Leaves** 3-6 in a basal rosette, ovate or oval, 2-5 cm long, blunt-tipped, narrowed to base, upper surface sticky; margins inrolled. **Flowers** single atop a leafless stalk (scape) 5-15 cm long; corolla violet-purple, spurred, 2-lipped, the upper lip 3-lobed, the lower lip 2-lobed, 1.5-2 cm long (including spur). **Fruit**

813. *Scutellaria parvula*

814. *Stachys pilosa*

815. *Stachys tenuifolia*

816. *Teucrium canadense*

a 2-chambered capsule. June-July.—Mostly in rock crevices in cool sandstone cliffs along Lake Superior; usually occurring with Mistassini primrose (*Primula mistassinica*). *Small insects are trapped by the sticky, slimy surface of the leaves.*

Pinguicula vulgaris

UTRICULARIA *Bladderwort*

Mostly aquatic, annual or perennial herbs. Leaves underwater, alternate, entire or dissected into many linear segments, some with bladders which trap tiny aquatic invertebrates; or leaves in wet soil and rootlike or absent. Flowers perfect, irregular, 1 to several in a raceme atop stalks raised above water or soil surface, each flower subtended by a small bract; corolla yellow or purple, similar to a snapdragon flower, 2-lipped, the upper lip erect, entire or slightly 2-lobed, lower lip entire or 3-lobed, the corolla tube extended backward into a sac or spur, stamens 2. Fruit a many-seeded capsule.

1 Flowers purple or pink 2
  2 Flowers 2-5 atop a stout stalk; plants floating in water, masses of leaves present . . . . ***U. purpurea***
  2 Flowers single atop a slender stalk; plants not free-floating, rooted in peat or muck, appearing leafless . . . .
   . . . . ***U. resupinata***
1 Flowers yellow 3
  3 Scapes appearing leafless; leaves simple or absent; plants of peat or moist sand or marl . . . . ***U. cornuta***
  3 Scapes with leaves at base, the leaves dissected and with bladderlike traps; plants mostly floating in water 4
    4 Leaf divisions flat in cross-section 5
     5 Bladders borne on leaves; smallest leaf divisions entire (visible with a 10x hand lens); flower with a sac or spur much shorter than lower lip . . . . ***U. minor***
     5 Bladders on branches separate from leaves; smallest leaf divisions finely toothed, the teeth spine-tipped; flower with a spur as long as lower lip . . . . ***U. intermedia***
    4 Leaf divisions round in cross-section or threadlike 6
     6 Plants large; leaves floating; scapes 1 mm or more wide; flowers 13 mm or more long, 5 or more per head; larger bladders more than 2 mm wide . . . . ***U. macrorhiza***
     6 Plants smaller; leaves floating or creeping; scapes threadlike; flowers to 12 mm long, 1-3 per head; larger bladders mostly less than 2 mm wide 7
      7 Plants forming tangled masses, creeping on bottom in shallow water, or on muck or drying pond edges; often with emergent scapes with at least 1 normal flower; cleistogamous flowers absent . .
       . . . . ***U. gibba***
      7 Plants forming a delicate mass of floating leaves; emergent scapes with normal flowers rare; cleistogamous flowers common, on stalks 4-8 mm long . . . . ***U. geminiscapa***

Utricularia cornuta Michx.
HORNED BLADDERWORT
                             MAP 819
                                native
Annual or perennial herb. **Stems and leaves** underground, roots with tiny bladders. **Flowers** yellow, with a downward-pointing spur 6-15 mm long, on stalks 1-2 mm long, 1-6 atop an erect stalk 10-25 cm long; bracts ovate, 1-2 mm long. **Fruit** a rounded capsule. June-Sept.—Acidic lakes, shores, peatlands, calcareous pools between dunes, borrow pits.

Utricularia geminiscapa Benj.
HIDDEN-FRUIT BLADDERWORT
                              MAP 820
                    ✔*threatened | native*
Annual or perennial herb, similar to *U. macrorhiza* but smaller. **Stems** floating below water surface, sparsely branched. **Leaves** alternate, 1-2 cm long, branched into 4-7 segments and without bladders, or unbranched with bladders. **Flowers** yellow, 2-5 atop a slender stalk, 5-15 cm long, bracts below flowers 2-3 mm long; individual flower stalks 4-8 mm long, these arched when plants fruiting; cleistogamous flowers without petals more commonly produced, these single on leafless stalks 5-15 mm long along stems and often 1 at base of scape. July-Aug. —Acidic lakes, pools in open bogs.

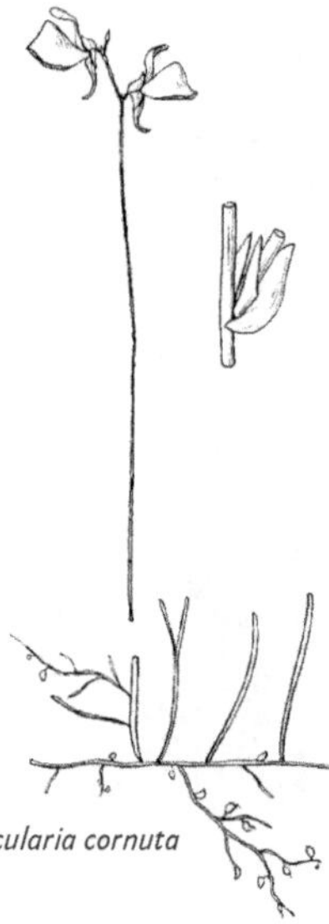

Utricularia cornuta

Utricularia gibba L.　　　MAP 821
CREEPING BLADDERWORT　　　　　　*native*

Annual or perennial herb. **Stems** creeping on bottom in shallow water, mostly less than 10 cm long, radiating from base of flower stalk (scape) and forming mats. **Leaves** alternate, scattered, to 5 mm long, 1-2-forked into threadlike segments; bladders present. **Flowers** 1-3, yellow, 5-6 mm long, with a thick, blunt spur shorter than lower lip, atop a single stalk 5-10 cm long. **Fruit** a rounded capsule. July-Sept.—Exposed shores, lakes, ponds, marshes, fens.

Utricularia gibba

Utricularia intermedia Hayne　　　MAP 822
FLAT-LEAF BLADDERWORT　　　　　　*native*

Annual herb. **Stems** very slender, creeping along bottom in shallow water. **Leaves** alternate, 0.5-2 cm long, mostly 3-parted near base, then again divided 1-3x, the segments linear and flat, margins with small, bristly teeth; bladders 2-4 mm wide, borne on branches separate from leaves. **Flowers** yellow, 2-4 atop an emergent stalk 5-20 cm long; individual flower stalks to 15 mm long, remaining erect in fruit; spur nearly as long as lower lip. **Fruit** a capsule. June-Aug.—Shallow water (usually alkaline), marly pools between dunes, calcareous fens, marshes, ponds and rivers. bogs and swamps.

Utricularia macrorhiza Le Conte　　　MAP 823
GREATER BLADDERWORT　　　　　　*native*
　　Utricularia vulgaris L.

Perennial herb. **Stems** floating below water surface, sparsely branched, often forming large mats. **Leaves** alternate, 1-5 cm long, 2-forked at base and repeatedly 2-forked into segments of unequal length, the segments more or less round in section, becoming smaller with each branching, the final segments threadlike; bladders 1-4 mm wide, borne on leaf segments. **Flowers** yellow, 6-20 atop a stout stalk 6-25 cm long; lower flower lip 1-2 cm long, sometimes much smaller on late-season flowers, upper lip more or less equal to lower lip; spur about 2/3 as long as lower lip; stalks bearing individual flowers curved downward in fruit. **Fruit** a capsule. June-Aug.—Shallow water of lakes, ponds, peatlands, marshes and rivers. *Our most common bladderwort.*

Utricularia intermedia

Utricularia minor L.　　　MAP 824
LESSER BLADDERWORT　　　　　　*native*

Perennial herb. **Stems** few-branched, 10-30 cm long, creeping on bottom in shallow water or on wet soil. **Leaves** alternate, to 1 cm long, with few divisions, the segments slender, flat, the smallest segments strongly tapered to tip, margins entire; bladders 1-2 mm wide, 1-5 on leaves. **Flowers** pale yellow, 2-8 atop a threadlike stalk 4-15 cm long; individual flower stalks to 1 cm long, curved downward in fruit; lower lip of flower 4-8 mm long, 2x longer than upper lip; spur small, to half length of lower lip. **Fruit** a capsule. June-Aug.—Fens, open bogs, sedge meadows and marshes; often in shallow water and where calcium-rich.

Utricularia macrorhiza

Utricularia purpurea Walt.　　　MAP 825
PURPLE BLADDERWORT　　　🌢*endangered* | *native*
　　Vesiculina purpurea (Walt.) Raf.

Annual or perennial herb. **Stems** underwater, to 1 m long. **Leaves** in whorls of 5-7, branched into threadlike segments, many segments tipped by a bladder. **Flowers** red-purple, 1-4 atop a stalk 3-15 cm long; corolla 1 cm long, lower lip 3-lobed, with

Utricularia purpurea

817. *Trichostema brachiatum*

818. *Pinguicula vulgaris*

819. *Utricularia cornuta*

820. *Utricularia geminiscapa*

a yellow spot near base; spur short and appressed to lower lip. **Fruit** a capsule. July-Sept.—Acidic lakes and ponds in water to 1 m deep, peatlands, marshes.

Utricularia resupinata B.D. Greene   MAP 826
LAVENDER BLADDERWORT   🐦*threatened* | *native*

Annual or perennial herb. **Stems** delicate, on water surface in shallow water or creeping just below soil surface. **Leaves** alternate, 3-parted from base, the middle segment erect and linear, to 3 cm long; the 2 lateral segments slender, rootlike, with bladders. **Flowers** purple, 1 cm long, single atop an erect stalk 2-10 cm long; bract tubelike, surrounding the stem, its margin notched; flower tipped backward on stalk and facing upward; lower lip 3-lobed; spur more or less horizontal. **Fruit** a rounded capsule. July-Aug. Shallow to deep water, wet lake and pond shores where sandy or mucky.

Utricularia resupinata

Limnanthaceae MEADOWFOAM FAMILY

FLOERKEA *False Mermaidweed*

Floerkea proserpinacoides Willd.   MAP 827
FALSE MERMAIDWEED   🐦*threatened* | *native*

Annual herb. **Stems** weak, diffuse or decumbent, 1-3 dm long. **Leaves** deeply divided into 3-7 linear, oblong lance-shaped, or narrowly elliptic lobes each 1-2 cm long. Peduncles from the upper axils, at first about equaling the petiole, becoming much longer in fruit; sepals ovate lance-shaped, about 3 mm long at anthesis, up to 7 mm at maturity; petals white, oblong lance-shaped, about 2 mm long; stamens (3 or) 6. **Carpels** (2-) 3, tuberculate. April-May.—Seepage areas and depressions in moist woods. *Distinct among our dicots in its completely 3-merous flowers, and distinguished from our monocots by the deeply pinnately lobed leaves.*

Floerkea proserpinacoides

Linaceae FLAX FAMILY

LINUM *Flax*

Annual or perennial herbs. Leaves simple, alternate or opposite, narrow, margins entire, petioles absent. Flowers regular, perfect, 5-parted. Sepals separate, imbricate. Petals yellow or blue. Stamens as many as the petals. Fruit a 5 or 10-chambered capsule.

ADDITIONAL SPECIES
Linum perenne L. (Wild blue flax), introduced perennial from Europe; introduced in roadside plantings in Goodhue County; petals blue, 15-20 mm long.

1 Petals blue; pedicels becoming more than 1 cm long 2
   2 Margins of inner sepals fringed with short hairs, the sepal tips long-tapered . . . . ***L. usitatissimum***
   2 Margins of inner sepals entire, the sepal tips rounded or only short-pointed . . . . ***L. lewisii***
1 Petals yellow; pedicels to 1 cm long 3
   3 Styles distinct or nearly so; fruit dehiscing into ten 1-seeded segments. . . . . ***L. sulcatum***
   3 Styles unired to above rhe middle; fruit dehiscmg into five 2-seeded segments . . . . ***L. rigidum***

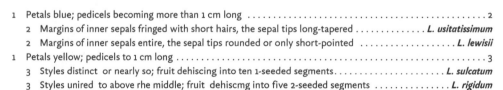

821. *Utricularia gibba*

822. *Utricularia intermedia*

823. *Utricularia macrorhiza*

824. *Utricularia minor*

Linum lewisii Pursh
LEWIS' FLAX

MAP 828
native

Linum perenne L. var. *lewisii* (Pursh), Eat. & Wright

Glabrous perennial. **Stems** branched at base, 2-8 dm tall. **Leaves** linear ro linear-lanceolate, 1-3 cm long, usually crowded below, alternate above; stipular glands absent. **Inflorescence** paniculate, few-branched, pedicels spreading to recurved; sepals 3.5-5 mm long, entire; petals blue (rarely white), 10-15 mm long; styles distinct, 4-9 mm long. **Capsules** ovoid, 5-7 mm long, separating into 10 segments; seeds 4-5 mm long. May-Aug.—Prairies, open rocky slopes.

Linum lewisii

Linum rigidum Pursh
LARGE-FLOWER YELLOW FLAX

MAP 829
native

Erect annual, glabrous throughout or finely hairy near the base. **Stems** 5-50 cm tall. **Leaves** alternare or the lower ones apparently opposite, linear to linear-lanceolate, entire or the upper leaves with a few teeth, 1-3 cm long and to 4 mm wide; stipular glands sometimes present. **Inflorescence** open, paniculate to ± flat-topped; sepals lanceolate, 5-10 mm long, conspicuously glandular· toothed; petals yellow, or orange to red toward the base, ovate, mostly 7-16 mm long; styles united to above the middle. **Capsule** triangular-ovate, 3.5-4.5 mm long, separating into five 2-seeded segments; seeds brownish, ca. 3 mm long. May-Sept.—Sandy or gravelly prairies.

Linum sulcatum Riddell
GROOVED YELLOW FLAX

MAP 830
native

Annual. **Stems** erect, branched above, 2-8 dm tall. **Leaves** narrow, all or chiefly alternate, 1-2 cm long, with a pair of minute dark glands at base. Branches of the **inflorescence** slender and raceme-like; pedicels to 8 mm long but averaging much shorter. Sepals persistent, 5-6 mm long, long-acuminate, conspicuously glandular-ciliate; petals yellow, 5-8 mm long. **Capsule** subglobose, about 3 mm long. June-July.—Dry sandy soil, prairies.

Linum sulcatum

Linum usitatissimum L.
CULTIVATED FLAX

MAP 831
introduced

Annual. **Stems** erect, usually solitary from a slender root, to 1 m tall. **Leaves** linear lance-shaped, 3-nerved. Sepals 7-9 mm long at maturity, the inner ciliate on the scarious margin; petals blue, 10-15 mm long. **Capsule** globose, 6-8 mm long, separating into 10 segments. Summer.—Of unknown origin; cultivated since prehistoric times for its fiber (linen) and more recently for its oil (linseed); sometimes escaped or adventive in fields and roadsides.

Linderniaceae LINDERNIA FAMILY

LINDERNIA *False Pimpernel*

Lindernia dubia (L.) Pennell
YELLOW-SEED FALSE PIMPERNEL

MAP 832
native

Annual herb. **Stems** smooth, 1-2 dm long, widely branched. **Leaves** opposite, ovate to obovate, 5-30 mm long and 3-10 mm wide, the upper leaves smaller; margins entire or with small, widely spaced teeth; petioles absent. **Flowers** single, on slender stalks 0.5-2.5 cm long from leaf axils; sepals 5, linear; corolla pale blue-purple, 5-10 mm long, 2-lipped, the upper lip 2-lobed, the lower lip 3-lobed and

Lindernia dubia

825. Utricularia purpurea   *826. Utricularia resupinata*   *827. Floerkea proserpinacoides* *828. Linum lewisii*

wider than upper lip; fertile stamens 2, staminodes (sterile stamens) 2. **Fruit** an ovate capsule, 4-6 mm long. June-Sept.—Mud flats, sandbars, shores of temporary ponds and marshes, streambanks.

Lythraceae LOOSESTRIFE FAMILY

Annual or perennial herbs, sometimes woody at base (*Decodon*). Leaves simple, opposite, or both opposite and alternate, or whorled, margins entire, more or less stalkless. Flowers 1 or several in leaf axils or in spike-like heads at ends of stems; perfect (with both staminate and pistillate parts), regular or irregular; sepal lobes 4 or 6; petals 4 or 6, separate, pink or purple, deciduous; stamens usually 2 times number of petals. Fruit a dry, many-seeded capsule.

1 Plants arching, woody near base; leaves with petioles and mostly whorled . . . . *Decodon verticillatus*
1 Plants annual or perennial herbs; leaves opposite, or if whorled, leaves without petioles 2
   2 Plants perennial; flowers in spike-like heads at ends of stems; petals and sepals 6 . . . . *Lythrum*
   2 Plants annual; flowers from leaf axils; petals and sepals 4 or 5 (when present) 3
      3 Flowers mostly 2-5 per leaf axil; flowers purple-tinged . . . . *Ammannia*
      3 Flowers mostly 1 per axil, not purple 4
         4 Leaves lance-shaped, broadest at base, less than 3 mm wide . . . . *Didiplis diandra*
         4 Leaves oval, widest near middle, larger leaves 3 mm or more wide . . . . *Rotala ramosior*

AMMANNIA *Redstem*

Annual glabrous herbs. Stems 1-10 dm tall. Leaves decussate (the opposite pairs oriented perpendicular from one another), linear to lance-shaped, sessile. Flowers in sessile or pedunculate axillary cymes, 1-5 flowers per cyme, 4-merous. Floral tubes campanulate to urn-shaped, globose in fruit; calyx lobes 4, alternating with appendages shorter than to equaling the lobes. Petals 4, early deciduous. Stamens 4(8). Fruit a many-seeded smooth capsule. *Plants of **Ammannia** and **Rotala** are often strongly flushed with red; petals in both are quickly deciduous, but are a little larger in Ammannia than in Rotala.*

1 Inflorescence peduncled, flowers mostly 3-5 per axil; petals rose-purple or rose with purple midvein; anthers deep yellow; capsule 3.5-5 mm wide . . . . *A coccinea*
1 Inflorescence sessile; flowers mostly 1-3 per axil; petals pale lavender; anthers yellow; capsule 4-6 mm wide. .
     . . . . *A. robusta*

Ammannia coccinea Rottb.
VALLEY REDSTEM

MAP 833
native

Stems erect, 2-8 dm long, often branched from base. **Leaves** opposite, linear, 2-8 cm long and 3-15 mm wide, heart-shaped and clasping at base; margins entire; petioles absent. **Flowers** peduncled, in clusters of 3-5 per leaf axil; petals 4 (rarely 5), 2-3 mm long, rose-purple, sometimes with a purple midvein at base; stamens 4, deep yellow, exserted. **Capsule** round, 4-parted, 3.5-5 mm wide, tipped by the persistent style. July-Oct.—Exposed mud flats and marshes, disturbed open wet areas; sometimes where calcium-rich.

Ammannia coccinea
stem detail

Ammannia robusta Heer & Regel
GRAND REDSTEM

MAP 834
native

Ammannia coccinea subsp. *robusta* (Heer & Regel) Koehne

Stems to 10 dm tall, unbranched or branched, the lowest branches decumbent from the base, often equaling the height of the main stem, the upper branches

829. Linum rigidum

830. Linum sulcatum

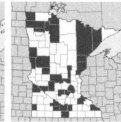

831. Linum usitatissimum

832. Lindernia dubia

few, short. **Leaves** linear lance-shaped, to 8 cm long and 15 mm wide, clasping at base. **Flowers** sessile in axillary cymes, 1-3 (5) flowers per cyme; floral tube prominently 4-ridged, 3-5 mm long; calyx lobes alternating with thickened appendages equaling the lobes; petals 4(8), pale lavender, sometimes with deep rose midvein at base, 2-3 mm long; stamens 4 (5-12), exserted, pale yellow to yellow. **Capsules** at maturity 4-6 mm wide, enclosed within or equaling the calyx lobes. July-Oct.—Marshy ground and muddy flats, especially in wet disturbed areas with bare soil.

Ammannia coccinea

DECODON *Water-Willow*

Decodon verticillatus (L.) Ell.   MAP 835
SWAMP-LOOSESTRIFE   *native*

Perennial herb, woody near base. **Stems** slender, angled, smooth or slightly hairy, 1-3 m long, arching downward and rooting at tip when in contact with water or mud. **Leaves** in whorls of 3-4 or opposite, lance-shaped, 5-15 cm long and 1-3 cm wide, smooth above, sparsely hairy below; margins entire; petioles short. **Flowers** in dense clusters in upper leaf axils; sepals 5-7, short, triangular; petals pink-purple, tapered to base, 10-15 mm long; stamens 10 (rarely 8), alternately longer and shorter than petals. **Fruit** a more or less round capsule, 5 mm wide. July-Sept.—Shallow water and margins of lakes, ponds, bogs, swamps and marshes; soils mucky.

Decodon verticillatus

DIDIPLIS *Water-Purslane*

Didiplis diandra (Nutt.) Wood   (NO MAP)
WATER-PURSLANE   *native*
    Peplis diandra (Nutt.) ex DC.

Annual herb; plants underwater or on exposed shores. **Stems** weak, branched, 1-4 dm long. **Leaves** numerous, opposite; underwater leaves linear, straight across base, 1-2.5 cm long; emersed leaves shorter and wider, tapered at base; petioles absent. **Flowers** few, inconspicuous, green. **Fruit** a small round capsule. July-Aug.—Shallow water and muddy pond margins; Mower County. *Plants somewhat resemble **water-starwort** (Callitriche), but in water-starwort the underwater leaves have a shallow notch at tip and the capsule is flattened.*

Didiplis diandra

LYTHRUM *Loosestrife*

Perennial herbs. Stems erect, sometimes rather woody at base, usually with ascending branches above, upper stems 4-angled. Leaves entire, opposite, alternate, or rarely whorled, lance-shaped, stalkless, reduced to bracts in the head. Flowers in showy, spike-like heads, 1 to several in axils of upper leaves, regular or somewhat irregular, the stamens and styles of 2 or 3 different lengths. Sepals joined into a tube, the calyx tube cylinder-shaped, green-striped with 8-12 nerves; petals 6, purple, not joined; stamens 6 or 12; ovary 2-chambered. Fruit an ovate capsule, enclosed by the calyx tube.

1   Flowers single in upper leaf axils; stamens usually 6 . . . . ***L. alatum***
1   Flowers many in spike-like heads at ends of stems; stamens usually 12 (6 long and 6 short) . . . . ***L. salicaria***

833. Ammannia coccinea   *834. Ammannia robusta*   *835. Decodon verticillatus*   *836. Lythrum alatum*

Lythrum alatum Pursh
WINGED LOOSESTRIFE

MAP 836
native

Smooth perennial herb, spreading by rhizomes. **Stems** usually branched above, 2-8 dm long, somewhat woody at base. **Lower leaves** usually opposite, **upper leaves** alternate; lance-shaped, 1-4 cm long, 3-10 mm wide, rounded at base; margins entire; sessile. **Flowers** single in axils of upper, reduced leaves (bracts), short-stalked; calyx tube 4-6 mm long, glabrous; petals 6, deep purple, 3-7 mm long; stamens usually 6. **Fruit** a capsule enclosed by the sepals. June-Aug. —Shores, wet meadows, marshes, low prairie, calcareous fens, ditches; especially where sandy.

Lythrum alatum

Lythrum salicaria L.
PURPLE LOOSESTRIFE

MAP 837
introduced (invasive)

Perennial herb, spreading and forming colonies by thick, fleshy roots which send up new shoots. **Stems** erect, 6-15 dm long, 4-angled, with many ascending branches. **Leaves** opposite or sometimes in whorls of 3, becoming alternate and reduced to bracts in the head; lance-shaped, 3-10 cm long and 0.5-2 cm wide, mostly heart-shaped and clasping at base; margins entire; petioles absent. **Flowers** large and showy, 2 or more in axils of reduced upper leaves (bracts), in spikes 1-4 dm long at ends of branches; sepals joined, the calyx tube 4-6 mm long, hairy; petals 6, purple-magenta, 7-10 mm long; stamens usually 12, the stamens and styles of 3 different lengths. **Fruit** a capsule enclosed by the sepals. June-Sept. —Introduced from Europe and sometimes planted as an ornamental, escaping to marshes, wet ditches, streambanks, cranberry bogs and shores, where a serious threat to our native flora and of little value to wildlife. In addition to spreading vegetatively, a single plant may produce thousands of seeds each year. To limit the spread of this species, plants should be pulled (including roots), bagged, and removed from infested sites. *First collected in Minn in Ramsey County in 1924.*

ROTALA *Toothcup*

Lythrum salicaria

Rotala ramosior (L.) Koehne
LOWLAND TOOTHCUP

MAP 838
❦ *threatened | native*

Small, annual herb. **Stems** smooth, 4-angled, to 4 dm long, unbranched or branched from base, the branches spreading to upright. **Leaves** opposite, linear to oblong, 1-5 cm long and 2-12 mm wide; margins entire; stalkless or tapered to a short petiole. **Flowers** single and stalkless in leaf axils, calyx tube bell-shaped to cylindric, 2-5 mm long, not strongly nerved, the lobes alternating with appendages of same length; petals small, white to pink, 4, slightly longer than sepals; stamens 4. **Fruit** a round capsule enclosed by the sepals. July-Oct.—Muddy or sandy shores, marshes (especially those that dry during growing season), low spots in fields, ditches and other seasonally flooded places.

Rotala ramosior

Malvaceae MALLOW FAMILY

Annual or perennial herbs with upright stems; trees in *Tilia*. Leaves alternate, entire to lobed or dissected, often round or kidney-shaped, palmately veined. Flowers single or in small, narrow clusters from leaf axils, with 5 united sepals (separate in *Tilia*) and 5 petals; stamens many and joined near base, forming a tube around the style. Fruit a capsule.

1 Trees; with inflorescence apparently borne at the middle of a tongue-shaped bract . . . . *Tilia*
1 Herbs or shrubs; inflorescences various, but never with a large, tongue-shaped bract 2
  2 Calyx subtended by a series of 2 or more bracts 3
    3 Involucral bracts 6 or more 4
      4 Styles 5; involucral bracts narrow and linear . . . . *Hibiscus*
      4 Styles many; involucral bracts triangular . . . . *Althaea officinalis*
    3 Involucral bracts 5 or less 5
      5 Flower petals straight across at tip, the tip finely fringed . . . . *Callirhoe*
      5 Petals obovate, rounded at tip, not fringed . . . . *Malva*

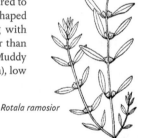

ABUTILON *Velvetleaf*

Abutilon theophrasti Medik.   MAP 839
VELVETLEAF   *introduced (naturalized)*
Annual herb, softly pubescent throughout with stellate hairs. **Stems** stout, branched, 1-1.5 m tall. **Leaves** cordate, 10-15 cm long and as wide, toothed, on petioles of about the same length. Peduncles jointed above the middle, at first short, at maturity 2-3 cm long. **Flowers** yellow, 15-25 mm wide. Head of **fruit** 2-3 cm wide; **carpels** commonly 10-15, densely pubescent, with conspicuous, horizontally spreading beaks. July-Oct.—Native of s Asia; established as a weed in fields and waste places but more common south of Minn.

Abutilon theophrasti

ALTHAEA *Marsh-Mallow*

Althaea officinalis L.   (NO MAP)
COMMON MARSH-MALLOW   *introduced*
Pubescent perennial herb. **Stems** erect, branched, 5-12 dm tall. **Leaves** ovate, 5-10 cm long, coarsely and irregularly serrate, commonly shallowly 3-lobed, velvety-pubescent. **Flowers** several in a peduncled cluster from the axil of the upper leaves, pink, about 3 cm wide; bractlets narrowly lance-shaped. **Carpels** numerous, usually 15 or more, 1-seeded. July-Sept.—Native of Europe, Winona County. *The thick mucilaginous roots are used in confectionery.*

Althaea officinalis

CALLIRHOE *Poppy-Mallow*

Callirhoe triangulata (Leavenworth) Gray   MAP 840
CLUSTERED POPPY-MALLOW   *native*
Perennial herb; stems, leaves, pedicels, and calyx harshly stellate-pubescent; stipules oblong, about 5 mm long. **Leaves** triangular, truncate to cordate at base, crenate, the upper much narrower; a few leaves sometimes lobed. **Flowers** several, crowded at the end of axillary peduncles, about 5 cm wide, the petals entire or inconspicuously erose; bractlets spatulate or obovate; calyx deeply 5-parted, each lobe commonly with 3 conspicuous nerves, densely stellate-pubescent. **Carpels** 10-20 pubescent, not rugose. June-Aug.—Dry sandy prairies.

ADDITIONAL SPECIES
Callirhoe involucrata (Torr. & A. Gray) A. Gray (Purple poppymallow), native, reported from Nobles County.

Callirhoe triangulata

HIBISCUS *Rose-Mallow*

Large, upright perennial herbs. Leaves alternate, smooth or hairy, palmately divided. Flowers large and showy, pink to white; ovary divided into 5 segments (carpels). Fruit an ovate capsule.

991. Lythrum salicaria

992. Rotala ramosior

993. Abutilon theophrasti

996. Callirhoe triangulata

1   Annual herbs to 6 dm tall; petals pale yellow with purple center . . . . **H. trionum**
1   Tall perennial herbs to 1 m tall or more; petals pink, 5-9 cm long . . . . **H. laevis**

Hibiscus laevis All.   (NO MAP)
SMOOTH ROSE-MALLOW   *introduced*

Perennial herb; stems and leaves smooth. **Stems** upright, 1-2 m long. **Leaves**
triangular in outline, heart-shaped at base, sometimes with outward pointing basal
lobes; margins with rounded teeth; petioles 3-15 cm long. **Flowers** large, from
leaf axils or clustered at ends of stems or branches; petals pink with darker center,
5-8 cm long. **Fruit** an ovate capsule, enclosed by the calyx; seeds silky-hairy. Aug-
Sept.—Marshes, muddy shores and shallow water; native to se USA, considered
adventive in Minn (Ramsey and Winona counties).

Hibiscus laevis

Hibiscus trionum L.   MAP 841
FLOWER-OF-AN-HOUR   *introduced*

Annual herb. **Stems** branched from the base, 3-5 dm tall, more or less hirsute.
Leaves deeply 3-parted, the segments oblong to obovate, coarsely serrate or lobed;
long-petioled. **Calyx** conspicuously veined, hispid on the nerves with spreading
simple hairs from swollen bases; petals 1.5-4 cm long, pale yellow, purple at the
base, expanded for but a few hours. Fruiting calyx inflated, 5-angled, enclosing
the hirsute **capsule**; seeds finely verrucose. July-Sept.—Native of Europe; fields,
roadsides, and waste places, often a troublesome weed.

MALVA *Mallow*

Annual, biennial, or perennial herbs. Leaves broad, serrate, crenate, lobed, or parted. Flowers solitary
or fascicled in the axils. Bractlets of the involucel 3, linear to obovate. Calyx 5-lobed. Petals truncate,
notched, or obcordate at tip. Carpels 10-20, beakless, 1-seeded, glabrous, pubescent, or rugose.

ADDITIONAL SPECIES
Malva verticillata L., introduced from Asia, reported from Kittson County, but doubtfully persisting.

1   Leaves deeply divided into 3-7 segments . . . . *M. moschata*
1   Leaf margins entire or only shallowly lobed 2
   2   Petals purple or pink, more than 1.5 cm long; stems erect . . . . *M. sylvestris*
   2   Petals white or purple-tinged, less than 1.5 cm long; stems ascending or prostrate 3
      3   Stems glabrous or nearly so; petals only slightly longer than calyx lobes . . . . *M. pusilla*
      3   Stems pubescent; petals about 2 times longer than calyx lobes . . . . *M. neglecta*

Malva moschata L.   (NO MAP)
MUSK MALLOW   *introduced (naturalized)*

Perennial herb. **Stems** erect, 4-10 dm tall, roughly pubescent. **Leaves** orbicular in
outline, 5-7-parted, the segments of the upper leaves again deeply pinnatifid.
Flowers partly solitary on long pedicels from the upper axils but chiefly crowded
in terminal clusters; bractlets linear to narrowly lance-shaped or oblong lance-
shaped, ciliate, glabrous or nearly so on the back; petals white to pale purple,
triangular, 2.4-3 cm long. Mature **carpels** rounded on the back, not rugose,
densely pubescent. June-Sept.—Native of Europe; escaped from cultivation along
roadsides and in lawns and waste places; St. Louis County.

Malva moschata

Malva neglecta Wallr.   MAP 842
COMMON MALLOW   *introduced (naturalized)*

Biennial herb. **Stems** prostrate, procumbent, or ascending, to 1 m long, usually
branched from the base. **Leaves** long-petioled, orbicular or kidney-shaped, 3-6
cm wide, shallowly 5-9-lobed, crenate, cordate at base. **Flowers** fascicled in the
axils, on pedicels to 3 cm long; bractlets narrow; petals obcordate, 6-12 mm long,
white or slightly tinged with pink or purple. Mature **carpels** usually 12-15,
rounded on the back, not rugose or reticulate, usually finely pubescent, the whole
ring of carpels presenting a crenate outline, the depressed central portion of the
head about a 1/3 as wide as the head. May-Oct.—Native of Eurasia and n Africa;
common as a weed in gardens and waste places.

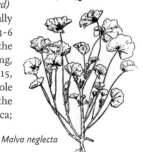

Malva neglecta

Malva pusilla Sm.　　　　　　　　　　　　　MAP 843
DWARF MALLOW　　　　　　　　　　*introduced (naturalized)*
　Malva rotundifolia L.
Biennial herb; resembling *M. neglecta* in habit and foliage. Pedicels often little
longer than the calyx. Mature **carpels** 5-11, commonly 10, glabrous or pubescent,
conspicuously rugose-reticulate on the back, the margins sharply angled, the
whole head of carpels circular in outline; central depressed area about 1/5 the
diameter of the whole head.—Native of Europe; occasional as a weed.

Malva sylvestris L.　　　　　　　　　　　　MAP 844
HIGH MALLOW　　　　　　　　　　　　　*introduced*
Biennial herb. **Stems** erect, 4-10 dm tall, sparsely hirsute to glabrate. **Leaves**
orbicular or kidney-shaped in outline, shallowly 3-7-lobed, the lobes broadly
rounded, serrate; petioles pubescent only or chiefly in a single line on the upper
side; bractlets oblong to ovate or obovate. **Flowers** fascicled in the upper axils,
on peduncles to 5 cm long; petals red-purple, 2-2.5 cm long. Mature **carpels**
rugose-reticulate on the back, glabrous or sparsely pubescent. June-Aug.—Native
of Eurasia; occasionally escaped from cultivation.

Malva sylvestris

NAPAEA　*Glade-Mallow*

Napaea dioica L.　　　　　　　　　　　　　MAP 845
GLADE-MALLOW　　　　　　　　　　*threatened | native*
Large perennial herb. **Stems** erect, 1-2 m long. **Leaves** round in outline, 1-3 dm
wide, deeply 5-9 lobed, the lobes coarsely toothed, on long petioles; **upper leaves**
smaller, with short petioles. **Flowers** either staminate or pistillate and on separate
plants; many in large panicles at ends of stems; petals white, obovate, petals of
staminate flowers 5-9 mm long, petals of pistillate flowers smaller. **Fruit** a 10-
parted capsule, the segments (carpels) 5 mm long, ribbed, and irregularly
separating when mature. June-Aug.—Moist floodplain forests, riverbanks.

Napaea dioica

TILIA　*Basswood; Linden*

Tilia americana L.　　　　　　　　　　　　MAP 846
BASSWOOD; LINDEN　　　　　　　　　　　*native*
Tree to 35 m tall; bark gray to light brown, with narrow, well-defined fissures;
twigs smooth, reddish-green, becoming light to dark gray, marked with dark wart-
like bumps. **Leaves** broadly ovate to subrotund, palmately veined, cordate or
truncate at the oblique base, sharply serrate, green beneath and glabrous to
sparsely stellate-pubescent on the surface, with conspicuous tufts of hairs in the
vein axils. **Flowers** fragrant, perfect, 5-merous, white or cream-colored in axillary
cyme-like clusters, the long peduncle adnate about to the middle of a narrow,
elongate, short-petioled, foliaceous bract; bracts glabrous or nearly so on both
sides; sepals separate to the base; petals narrowly oblong, 7-12 mm long, tapering
to the base; stamens numerous, either all distinct or united into 5 bundles, one
in front of each petal; ovary tomentose, 5-celled. **Fruit** nutlike, tomentose, 1-2-
seeded. July.—Moist fertile soil. *The dried flowers have a long history of medicinal
uses, and bees produce a fragrant honey from the blossoms.*

Tilia americana

ADDITIONAL SPECIES
Tilia europaea L. (European linden), European native; Anoka and Hennepin cos.

841. Hibiscus trionum

842. Malva neglecta

843. Malva pusilla

844. Malva sylvestris

Menispermaceae MOONSEED FAMILY

MENISPERMUM *Moonseed*

Menispermum canadense L.
CANADIAN MOONSEED

MAP 847
native

Dioecious woody twiners climbing 2-4 m high. **Leaves** simple, alternate, broadly ovate to nearly orbicular, 10-15 cm wide and long, palmately veined, shallowly 3-7-lobed to entire; slender-petioled. **Flowers** small, unisexual, usually 3-merous, regular, in racemes or panicles that arise just above the leaf-axils; perianth segments scarcely differentiated into calyx and corolla, normally in 4 alternating whorls, the 2 outer (calyx) exceeding the 2 inner (corolla); sepals 4-8, longer than the 4-8 petals; stamens 12-24. **Drupe** bluish-black, 6-10 mm long; stone flattened, thickened into 3 rough ridges over most of its margin. June-July.—Moist woods and thickets. *The drupes, suspected to be toxic, resemble wild grapes.*

Menispermum canadense

Menyanthaceae BUCKBEAN FAMILY

MENYANTHES *Buckbean*

Menyanthes trifoliata L.
BUCKBEAN

MAP 848
native

Perennial glabrous herb, with thick rhizomes covered with old leaf bases. **Leaves** alternate along rhizomes, palmately divided into 3 leaflets, the leaflets oval to ovate, 3-10 cm long and 1-5 cm wide, entire or sometimes wavy-margined; petioles 5-30 cm long, the base of petiole expanded and sheathing stem. **Flowers** in racemes on leafless stalks 2-4 dm long and longer than the leaves; bracts mostly 3-5 mm long; individual flowers on stalks 5-20 mm long; flowers perfect, regular, 5-parted, often of 2 types, some with flowers with long stamens and a shorter style, others with a long style and shorter stamens; sepal lobes 2-3 mm long; corolla funnel-shaped, 8-12 mm long, petals white, often purple-tinged, bearded with white hairs on inner surface; stamens 5. **Fruit** a rounded capsule, 6-10 mm wide; seeds shiny, yellow-brown. May-July.—Open bogs and fens (especially in pools and in outer moat), cedar swamps, wet thickets.

Menyanthes trifoliata

Molluginaceae CARPETWEED FAMILY

MOLLUGO *Carpetweed*

Mollugo verticillata L.
GREEN CARPETWEED

MAP 849
introduced (naturalized)

Annual herb. **Stems** prostrate or ascending, repeatedly forked, forming mats to 4 dm wide. **Leaves** in whorls of 3-8, narrowly to broadly oblong lance-shaped, 1-3 cm long, long-tapering to a short, scarcely differentiated petiole. **Flowers** perfect, 2-5 from each node, on pedicels 5-15 mm long, sepals 5; petals 5, pale green to white, 4-5 mm wide; stamens 3 or 4. **Capsules** ovoid, 3 mm long, many-seeded. June-Sept.—Apparently native of tropical America; now a common weed in moist soil.

Mollugo verticillata

845. *Napaea dioica* | 846. *Tilia americana* | 847. *Menispermum canadense* | 848. *Menyanthes trifoliata*

Montiaceae MONTIA FAMILY

The family Montiaceae includes our 3 genera formerly within Portulacaceae.

ADDITIONAL SPECIES
Montia chamissoi (Ledeb. ex Spreng.) Greene (Water miner's-lettuce), ➥*endangered;* disjunct from Rocky Mountains; in Minnesota, known from a single population in Winona County.

1   Leaves clustered at base of stem . . . . *Phemeranthus*
1   Leaves not all clustered at base of stem, in a single pair, opposite on stem *Claytonia*

Montia chamissoi

CLAYTONIA *Springbeauty*

Glabrous perennial herbs from rounded tubers (ours). Leaves one or few from base and a single opposite pair on the stem below the loose terminal raceme; the raceme with 5-15 long-pediceled flowers and sometimes a small bract below the lowest flower. Sepals ovate, persistent in fruit. Petals 5, white or pale pink with pink veins, oval or elliptic, spreading. Stamens 5, opposite the petals. Capsule ovoid, opening by inrolling valves. Flowers open from March to May, with stems and leaves withered by early summer.

1   Leaves with distinct petiole; blades less than 5 times longer than wide . . . . *C. caroliniana*
1   Petiole not distinct; blades 5 times or more longer than wide; . . . . *C. virginica*

Claytonia caroliniana Michx.
CAROLINA SPRINGBEAUTY
Perennial herb. **Stem leaves**, including the petiole, commonly 3-6 cm long, rarely to 9 cm long, the blade usually 10-15 mm wide, acute at base, clearly distinguished from the petiole.—Cool woods.

MAP 850
native

Claytonia virginica L.
VIRGINIA SPRINGBEAUTY
Perennial herb. **Stem leaves** long-tapering to base, the blade sessile or merging gradually into the short, poorly differentiated petiole, commonly 4-10 mm wide, rarely less than 7 cm long, including the petiole.—Damp woods and fields.

MAP 851
native

Claytonia virginica

PHEMERANTHUS *Fameflower*

Perennial herbs (ours), often with fleshy tuberous roots. Stems glabrous, succulent. Leaves fleshy. alternate or nearly opposite, entire, terete. Flowers showy, on peduncled terminal cymes. Sepals 2; petals 5, both early deciduous. Stamens 5-many; style 3-lobed at tip. Fruit a 1-celled, many-seeded capsule; seeds flattened, rounded kidney-shaped.

1   Stamens 4-8; capsule ellipsoidal . . . . **P. parviflorus**
1   Stamens 12-25; capsule globose . . . . **P. rugospermus**

Phemeranthus parviflorus (Nutt.) Kiger
SUNBRIGHT
    Talinum parviflorum Nutt.
Stems to 20 cm tall, from fleshy roots. **Leaves** terete or nearly so, linear, 1.5-3 cm long and ca. 1-2.5 mm thick, broadened at the base. **Flowers** in a terminal bracteate cyme; **sepals** ovate, 3-4 mm long, deciduous; **petals** 5, pink to purplish, 5-7 mm long; stamens 4-8: style longer than the stamens. **Capsule** 3.5-4.5 mm long; seeds smooth. April-Aug.—Sandy acidic soil.

MAP 852
native

849. *Mollugo verticillata*   850. *Claytonia caroliniana*   851. *Claytonia virginica*   852. *Phemeranthus parviflorus*

Phemeranthus rugospermus (Holz.) Kiger

PRAIRIE FAMEFLOWER

Talinum rugospermum Holz.

MAP 853

◤*threatened* | *native*

Stems to 25 cm tall, usually simple for about half its length and branched above.
Leaves crowded, succulent, terete, 3-6 cm long, sessile. **Flowers** in long-
peduncled bracted cymes 1-2 dm long; **sepals** 2, early deciduous; **petals** 5, pink,
6-8 mm long; stamens 10-25. **Capsule** 4-5 mm long, many-seeded; seeds minutely
roughened and strongly wrinkled. July-Aug.—Thin soil overlying sandstone and
on sand prairies.

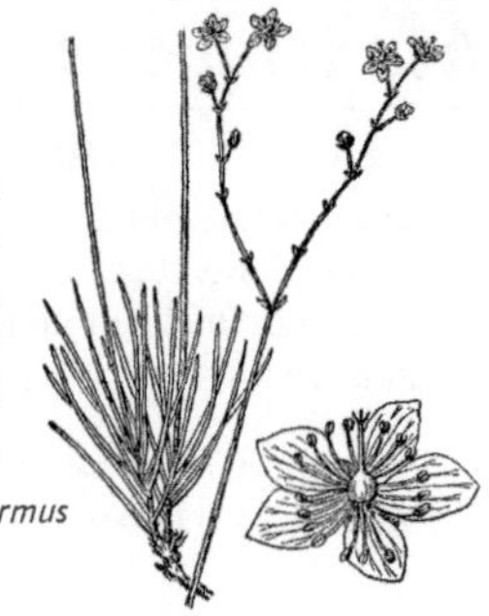

Phemeranthus rugospermus

Moraceae   MULBERRY FAMILY

Trees (rarely herbs), juice milky or watery. Leaves alternate, simple or compound. Flowers small,
crowded in dense clusters or heads, their receptacles often confluent, especially in fruit; unisexual,
the plants monoecious or dioecious. Calyx of 2-6, usually 4, separate sepals, or 2-6-lobed. Corolla
none. Stamens usually as many as the sepals or calyx lobes and opposite them, rarely fewer or only
1, often incurved in the bud. Ovary bicarpellate; styles 1 or 2. Fruits diverse.

ADDITIONAL SPECIES

Fatoua villosa (Thunb.) Nakai, annual weed introduced from Asia, reported from Anoka County.

MORUS *Mulberry*

Monoecious or dioecious trees. Leaves alternate, serrate or lobed, palmately veined. Flowers in
cylindric catkins, the staminate longer and more loosely flowered than the pistillate. Calyx deeply 4-
parted. Stamens 4. Style deeply 2-parted. Fruit white or colored, edible, resembling a blackberry,
composed of the juicy calyx, each enclosing a small seed-like achene, with the remains of the styles
protruding.

1   Leaves pubescent on underside, often unlobed . . . . *M. rubra*
1   Leaves glabrous or with scattered hairs on underside veins, often with 3-5 lobes . . . . *M. alba*

Morus alba L.

WHITE MULBERRY

MAP 854

introduced (naturalized)

Tree to 15 m tall. **Leaves** rotund in outline, serrate, often irregularly several-lobed,
often cordate at base, glabrous or nearly so on both sides, or sparsely pubescent
with white spreading hairs along the veins beneath. **Fruit** white, pink, or pale
purple to nearly black.—Apparently native of Asia; long cultivated in Europe and
America for its fruit or fiber or as food for the silkworm, and now used for
ornament in several horticultural forms; escaped along roadsides, in vacant land,
and open woods.

Morus rubra L.

RED MULBERRY

MAP 855

native

Forest tree to 20 m tall, with dark scaly bark. **Leaves** thin, broadly ovate, obovate,
or subrotund, coarsely serrate, occasionally 2-5-lobed, abruptly acuminate into a
conspicuous point up to 4 cm long, glabrous to scabrous above, softly pubescent
beneath. **Fruit** dark purple, 2-3 cm long.—Rich woods.

Morus alba

Myricaceae   BAYBERRY FAMILY

Monoecious or dioecious shrubs, with alternate simple leaves; leaves resinous-dotted and fragrant.
Flowers unisexual, without perianth, solitary in the axils of small bracts, aggregated into globose to
cylindric catkins. Stamens 2-many, usually 4-8, the short filaments free or connate. Ovary 1-celled,
subtended by 2-8 usually minute braetlets; ovule 1, basal, orthotropous; style very short; stigmas 2,
linear, elongate.

1   Leaves entire or nearly so; wet habitats . . . . *Myrica gale*
1   Leaves pinnately lobed; dry sandy habitats . . . . *Comptonia peregrina*

COMPTONIA *Sweet-Fern*

Comptonia peregrina (L.) Coult.
SWEET-FERN

MAP 856
native

Shrub. **Stems** much branched, to 1 m tall. **Leaves** linear-oblong, 6-12 cm long, about 1 cm wide, deeply pinnately lobed, resinous-dotted, more or less pubescent. **Staminate catkins** clustered, cylindric, 1-3 cm long, nodding; bracts quadrangular, resinous, villous, acuminate; **pistillate catkins** subglobose; bracts similar but concealed by the linear-subulate bractlets. **Nutlets** ellipsoid, blunt, 3-5 mm long, subtended by the elongate bractlets, the whole fruit bur-like, 1-2 cm wide. April-May.—Dry, especially sandy soil.

Comptonia peregrina

MYRICA *Bayberry*

Myrica gale L.
SWEET GALE
    Gale palustris Chev.

MAP 857
native

Much-branched shrub, 6-15 dm tall; **bark** dark gray to red-brown with small pale lenticels; twigs hairy, dotted with glands. **Leaves** alternate, deciduous, wedge-shaped, tapered to base, broadest above middle, 3-6 cm long and 1-2 cm wide, tip rounded and toothed, dark green on upper surface, paler below, dotted with shiny yellow glands, fragrant when rubbed; petioles short, 1-3 mm long. Staminate and pistillate flowers separate and on different plants, appearing before or with unfolding leaves; **staminate flowers** in catkins 1-2 cm long, with dark brown, shiny triangular scales; **pistillate flowers** in conelike, brown clusters 10-12 mm long. **Fruit** a flattened, ovate achene, resin-dotted, 2-3 mm long. April-May.—Lakeshores, marshes, swamps and bogs.

Myrica gale

Nelumbonaceae LOTUS-LILY FAMILY

NELUMBO *Lotus-Lily*

Nelumbo lutea Willd.
AMERICAN LOTUS-LILY

MAP 858
native

Perennial aquatic herb, from a large, horizontal rootstock. **Leaves** large and shield-shaped, 3-7 dm wide, ribbed, floating on water surface or held above water, smooth above, somewhat hairy below; petioles thick, attached at center of blade. **Flowers** pale yellow, single, 15-25 cm wide; petals obovate, blunt-tipped; receptacle flat-topped, to 1 dm wide; seeds acornlike, 1 cm thick. July-Aug.—Lakes, ponds, backwater areas, marshes; mostly near Mississippi River.

Nelumbo lutea

853. Phem. rugospermus   *854. Morus alba*   *855. Morus rubra*   *856. Comptonia peregrina*

Nyctaginaceae FOUR-O'CLOCK FAMILY

MIRABILIS *Four-O'clock*

Perennial herbs, or woody at base. Leaves opposite. Flowers many in terminal panicles. Calyx funnelform, 5-lobed, the short tube closely surrounding the ovary and constricted above it, the ovary apparently inferior. Stamens 3-5. Flowers rose to pink-purple, open in the morning, solitary or in clusters of 2-4, nearly sessile, subtended by a 5-lobed, saucer-shaped or cup-shaped involucre. Fruit prismatic to obovoid, 5-ribbed, mucilaginous when wet. *Early in the season plants commonly produce a few solitary peduncled flowers from the forks of the stem; the large panicles appear later.*

ADDITIONAL SPECIES

Mirabilis linearis (Pursh) Heimerl (Narrow-leaf four-o'clock), native; Houston and Stevens counties in disturbed rocky or gravelly places.

1   Leaves ovate, heart-shaped or truncate at base; inflorescence not glandular . . . . **M. nyctaginea**
1   Leaves linear to lance-shaped, tapered to the base; inflorescence glandular hairy . . . . **M. albida**

Mirabilis albida (Walter) Heimerl

HAIRY FOUR-O'CLOCK

MAP 859
native

Mirabilis hirsuta (Pursh) MacM.

Stems erect or decumbent, to 1 m tall, more or less hirsute, especially about the nodes, with spreading hairs 1-2 mm long, becoming glandular-pubescent in the inflorescence. **Leaves** linear lance-shaped to ovate lance-shaped, the larger commonly 1-2 cm wide. **Involucre** about 5 mm long, glandular-pubescent, becoming 1-2 cm long at maturity; calyx pink, about 1 cm long. **Fruit** narrowly obovoid, 4-5 mm long, pubescent, rugose on the sides and ridges. Summer.—Dry prairies, hills, and barrens.

Mirabilis nyctaginea (Michx.) MacM.

HEART-LEAF FOUR-O'CLOCK

MAP 860
native

Stems nearly smooth, branched above, to 1 m tall. **Leaves** ovate to deltoid-ovate, cordate or truncate at base, glabrous or nearly so, petioles 1-3 cm long. **Involucre** saucer-shaped, about 1 cm wide, densely ciliate, accrescent in fruit; calyx pinkish-purple, about 10 mm long. **Fruit** narrowly obovoid, densely pubescent, rough on the sides and on the 5 prominent ribs. May-Aug.—Dry soil, waste places.

Mirabilis nyctaginea

Nymphaeaceae *Water-Lily Family*

Aquatic, perennial herbs. Stems long and fleshy, from horizontal rhizomes rooted in bottom mud. Leaves large, leathery, mostly floating or emergent above water surface, heart-shaped to shield-shaped, notched at base, margins entire. Flowers showy, single on long stalks and borne at or above water surface, perfect, white or yellow, sepals 4-6, green or yellow; petals numerous, small to large and showy. Fruit a many-seeded, berrylike capsule, opening underwater when mature.

1   Flowers yellow, often red-tinged, sepals petal-like, true petals small; leaf blades oblong to oval or heart-shaped
. . . . **Nuphar**
1   Flowers white (rarely pink), sepals green, true petals large and showy; leaf blades nearly round . . . .
. . . . **Nymphaea odorata**

857. Myrica gale   *858. Nelumbo lutea*   *859. Mirabilis albida*   *860. Mirabilis nyctaginea*

NUPHAR *Yellow Water-Lily*

Aquatic herbs. Leaves mostly large and floating or emergent. Sepals 5-6, yellow and petal-like, forming a saucer-shaped flower; petals small and numerous.

1 Disk at base of stigma green; anthers longer than filaments . . . . *N. variegata*
1 Disk at base of stigma red; anthers shorter than the filaments 2
   2 Leaf sinus 2/3 or more length of the midrib; sepals 5; anthers 1-3 mm long . . . . *N. microphylla*
   2 Leaf sinus about ½ length of midrib; sepals 5 or 6; anthers 3-6 mm long . . . . *N.* × *rubrodisca*

Nuphar microphylla (Pers.) Fern.
YELLOW POND-LILY
  Nuphar pumila (Timm) DC.

MAP 861
native

Leaves both underwater and floating; **floating leaves** 5-10 cm long and 3-8 cm wide, notch at base usually more than half as long as midvein; petioles flattened on upper side; **underwater leaves** membranous, somewhat larger. **Flowers** 1.5-2 cm wide, sepals 5, yellow on inner surface; petals small and many; disk at base of stigma red, 3-6 mm wide, with 6-10 rays. **Fruit** ovate, 15 mm long. July-Aug. —Lakes, ponds and slow-moving streams.

Nuphar × *rubrodisca* Morong
YELLOW POND-LILY
  Nuphar lutea (L.) Sm. subsp. *rubrodisca* (Morong) Hellquist & Wiersema

MAP 862
native

Leaves both submersed and floating, the latter commonly 10-15 cm long, the sinus averaging half as long as the midvein; petioles flattened on the under side. **Flowers** 3-4 cm wide, yellow within or suffused with red; anthers 3-6 mm long; stigmatic disk red, 7-10 mm wide at anthesis, somewhat wider in fruit, 8-13-rayed. **Fruit** 20-25 mm long, scarcely constricted below the disk. Summer. *Considered a hybrid between Nuphar microphylla and N. variegata.*

Nuphar microphylla

Nuphar variegata Dur.
YELLOW POND-LILY

MAP 863
native

Leaves mostly floating, 10-25 cm wide, notch usually less than half as long as midvein, petioles flattened on upper side and narrowly winged; **underwater leaves** absent or few. **Flowers** 2.5-5 cm wide; sepals usually 6, yellow, red-tinged on inner surface; petals small and numerous; anthers 4-7 mm long, longer than filaments; disk at base of stigma green, 1 cm wide, with 10-15 rays. **Fruit** ovate, 2-4 cm long. June-Aug.—Ponds, lakes, quiet streams.

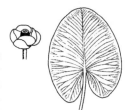

Nuphar variegata

NYMPHAEA *Water-Lily*

Large aquatic plants, from stout rhizomes, these sometimes with lateral tubers. Leaves floating, round, notched to the petiole, petioles not flattened or winged. Flowers white and showy; sepals 4, green; petals white or pink, showy, numerous and overlapping; stamens many, the outer stamens with broadened, petal-like filaments, anthers yellow, ovary depressed at tip with a rounded projection from the center, stigmas 10-25. Fruit round, covered with persistent petal and stamen bases, maturing underwater; seeds numerous, each enclosed within a sac (aril).

1 Leaves round in outline, narrowly notched; flowers large and showy, usually fragrant; common . . . .
   . . . . *Nymphaea odorata*
1 Leaves oval in outline, notch more widely spreading; flowers smaller and scarcely fragrant; rare in n Minn . . . .
   . . . . *Nymphaea leibergii*

861. *Nuphar microphylla*

862. *Nuphar x rubrodisca*

863. *Nuphar variegata*

864. *Nymphaea leibergii*

Nymphaea leibergii Morong
DWARF WATER-LILY
  Nymphaea tetragona Georgi

MAP 864
♥'*threatened* | *native*

Aquatic perennial herb, rhizomes ascending. **Stems** arising from tip of rhizomes.
Leaves 7-12 cm long and to 3/4 as wide, notch fairly wide, upper surface green,
green or purple below. **Flowers** white, usually not fragrant, 4-8 cm wide, reported
to open in afternoon; sepals 4, green, 2-3 cm long; petals 8-17, about as long as
sepals; stamens 20-40. **Fruit** not covered by the erect sepals. Summer.—Shallow
water of ponds and lakes.

Nymphaea leibergii

Nymphaea odorata Ait.
WHITE WATER-LILY
  Nymphaea tuberosa Paine

MAP 865
native

Aquatic perennial herb, rhizomes sometimes with knotty tubers. **Leaves** floating,
round, 1-3 dm wide, with a narrow notch, green and shiny on upper surface,
usually purple or red below. **Flowers** large and showy, white (rarely pink), usually
fragrant, 7-20 cm wide, often opening in morning and closing in late afternoon
(or remaining open on cool, cloudy days); sepals 4, green, 3-10 cm long; petals
17-25, about as long as sepals, oval, tapered to a rounded tip; stamens 40-100. **Fruit**
round, mostly covered by sepals; seeds 2-4 mm long. June-Aug.—Shallow water
of ponds and lakes, quiet water of rivers.

Nymphaea odorata

Oleaceae   Olive Family

Trees or shrubs with opposite, simple or compound leaves. Flowers perfect or unisexual, regular,
usually 4-merous. Calyx small or in some genera lacking. Corolla in our genera partially or wholly
fused, or lacking (*Fraxinus*). Stamens 2-4, usually 2, inserted on the corolla tube if the corolla is present.
Ovary 2-celled; seeds 2-several or rarely 1 in each cell. Fruit a drupe, capsule, or samara. *Includes the
widely cultivated Olea europaea L., the olive, native of the e Mediterranean region.*

1   Trees; leaves pinnately compound .... *Fraxinus*
1   Shrubs; leaves simple .... *Syringa*

FRAXINUS *Ash*

Medium trees. Leaves deciduous, opposite, pinnately divided into leaflets. Flowers in clusters from
axils of previous year's twigs, mostly single-sexed, staminate and pistillate flowers on different trees,
rarely perfect, petals absent. Fruit a 1-seeded, winged samara.

1   Twigs densely hairy 2
    2   Lateral leaflets tapered at base to a short winged petiole, or the leaflets sessile .... *F. pennsylvanica*
    2   Lateral leaflets rounded at base, short petioles present .... *F. americana*
1   Twigs glabrous 3
    3   Leaflets pale or waxy on underside, margins often entire; lateral leaflets on short petioles 5 mm or more long
        .... *F. americana*
    3   Leaflets not waxy on underside, margins usually finely toothed; lateral leaflets sessile or on short petioles to
       3 mm long 4
        4   Lateral leaflets usually number 8, sessile; body of fruit flat in cross-section .... *F. nigra*
        4   Lateral leaflets usually 4-6, on short petioles; body of fruit round in section .... *F. pennsylvanica*

Fraxinus americana L.
WHITE ASH

MAP 866
native

Tree to 40 m. tall. **Leaflets** 5-9, usually 7, oblong to ovate or obovate, usually
abruptly acuminate, entire or serrulate toward the summit, rounded to broadly
acute at base, paler beneath, on wingless leaflet petioles. **Samaras** linear or oblong,
3-5 cm long, obtuse to retuse at the tip, the wing extending about 1/3 of the length
of the terete body; the free portion, above the apex of the body, longer than the
body itself; subtending calyx 1-1.5 or rarely 2 mm long, seldom cleft on one side
only.—Rich moist woods; a valuable timber tree.

Fraxinus americana

Fraxinus nigra Marsh.
BLACK ASH

MAP 867
native

Tree to 15 m tall, crown open and narrow; **bark** gray, thin, flaky; **twigs** smooth, round in section, dark green, becoming gray. **Leaves** opposite, pinnately divided into 7-11 stalkless (except for terminal) leaflets; **leaflets** lance-shaped to oblong, 7-13 cm long and 2.5-5 cm wide, long-tapered to a tip; margins with sharp, forward-pointing teeth. **Flowers** appear in spring before leaves, in open clusters on twigs of previous year; some perfect, some single-sexed, staminate and pistillate flowers on different trees. **Fruit** a 1-seeded samara, 2.5-4 cm long and 6-10 mm wide, the wing broad and rounded at tip, deciduous or persisting until following spring. April-May.—Floodplain forests, cedar swamps, wet depressions in forests.

Fraxinus nigra

Fraxinus pennsylvanica Marsh.
GREEN ASH

MAP 868
native

Tree to 15 m tall; **bark** dark gray or brown, thick, with shallow furrows and netlike ridges; **twigs** usually hairy for 1-3 years, becoming light gray or red-brown. **Leaves** opposite, pinnately divided into 7-9 leaflets; leaflets oblong lance-shaped to ovate, 7-13 cm long and 2.5-4 cm wide, upper surface smooth, underside smooth or hairy; margins entire or with few forward-pointing teeth; leaflet petioles short, smooth or hairy. **Flowers** appear in spring before or with leaves, in compact, hairy clusters on twigs of previous year; single-sexed, staminate and pistillate flowers on different trees. Fruit a 1-seeded, slender samara, 2.5-5 cm long, in open clusters persisting until following spring. April-May.—Floodplain forests, swamps, shores, streambanks. *Both smooth and hairy forms of Fraxinus pennsylvanica occur, with trees becoming less hairy as one moves w across the Great Lakes region.*

SYRINGA *Lilac*

Fraxinus pennsylvanica

Syringa vulgaris L.
COMMON LILAC

MAP 869
introduced

Much-branched deciduous shrub to 6 m tall, spreading and forming thickets. **Leaves** opposite, simple, entire, ovate, 5-10 cm long, short-acuminate, truncate to cordate at base. **Flowers** fragrant, in dense panicles 1-2 dm long; 4-merous; calyx small, campanulate, truncate to 4-toothed; corolla salverform, usually lilac, about 1 cm wide; stamens 2, included in the corolla tube. **Fruit** a 2-celled capsule with 2 seeds in each cell. May.—Native of se Europe, found near abandoned farms. *Lilac apparently does not spread by seed but is very long-lived and persists indefinitely after planting.*

ADDITIONAL SPECIES

Syringa vulgaris

- *Syringa reticulata* (Blume) H. Hara, native to n Japan and China; St. Louis County.
- *Syringa villosa* Vahl (Japanese tree lilac), native to China; St. Louis County (Duluth area).

Onagraceae EVENING-PRIMROSE FAMILY

Annual or perennial herbs. Leaves opposite to alternate, simple to pinnately divided, stalkless or short-petioled. Flowers usually large and showy, perfect (with both staminate and pistillate parts), regular, borne in leaf axils or in heads at ends of stems; sepals 8 or 4; petals 4, white, yellow, or pink to rose-purple. Fruit a 4-chambered capsule; seeds many, with or without a tuft of hairs (coma).

865. *Nymphaea odorata*   866. *Fraxinus americana*   867. *Fraxinus nigra*   868. *Fraxinus pennsylvanica*

1 Petals 2, small, white; leaves opposite; fruit with bristly hairs . . . . **Circaea**
1 Petals 4 (rarely absent), white, pink, or yellow; leaves alternate or opposite; fruit without bristly hairs 2
   2 Hypanthium prolonged beyond ovary into a tube below the petals; leaves alternate 3
      3 Petals pink or white; fruit broadest in middle, tapering to each end, to 1 cm long . . . . **Gaura**
      3 Petals yellow (white in *Oenothera nuttallii*); fruit linear, usually more than 1 cm long 4
         4 Stigma 4-parted . . . . **Oenothera**
         4 Stigma peltate (i.e., umbrella-like, the style attached to center of stigma underside) **Calylophus serrulatus**
   2 Hypanthium scarcely if at all prolonged beyond ovary, not tube-like; leaves alternate or opposite 5
      5 Petals pink or rose-purple; seeds with a tuft of hairs (coma) . . . . **Epilobium**
      5 Petals yellow (or absent); seeds without a tuft of hairs . . . . **Ludwigia**

CALYLOPHUS *Sundrops*

Calylophus serrulatus (Nutt.) Raven
YELLOW SUNDROPS
Oenothera serrulata Nutt.

MAP 870
native

Perennial herb. **Stems** simple or branched from the base, often somewhat woody, 2-4 dm tall, glabrous to canescent. **Leaves** numerous, linear, 2-6 cm long, entire or commonly sharply serrulate, glabrous to canescent. **Flowers** sessile in the axils of the upper leaves; hypanthium above the ovary 6-8 mm long, funnelform, 4-angled, more or less pubescent, sometimes on the angles only; sepals triangular-ovate, reflexed at anthesis; petals yellow, 8-12 mm long; stamens glabrous, of two lengths. **Fruit** linear, canescent, roundly 4-angled, 1.5-3 cm long. June-July.—Dry prairies.

Calylophus serrulatus

CIRCAEA *Enchanter's Nightshade*

Perennial herbs with opposite petioled leaves and small white flowers in one to few terminal racemes. Flowers 2-merous. Hypanthium shortly prolonged above the ovary, tubular. Petals obcordate or deeply notched. Stamens 2. Ovary 1-2-celled. Fruit reflexed, obovoid or pear-shaped, usually slightly compressed, beset with soft or stiff hooked bristles.

1 Plants to 6 dm tall; flowers and fruit well-spaced on stalk; calyx lobes more than 1.5 mm long; leaves rounded at base, the margins very shallowly toothed . . . . **C. lutetiana**
1 Plants smaller, to 3 dm tall; open flowers clustered near top of stem; calyx lobes less than 1.5 mm long; leaves usually heart-shaped at base, margins sharply toothed . . . . **C. alpina**

Circaea alpina L.
ALPINE ENCHANTER'S NIGHTSHADE

MAP 871
native

Perennial herb, spreading from rhizomes thickened and tuberlike at ends. **Stems** weak, 1-3 dm long, mostly smooth. **Leaves** opposite, ovate, 2-5 cm long and 1-3 cm wide; margins coarsely toothed; petioles flat on upper side, underside thin-winged along center. **Flowers** white, in short racemes of 10-15 flowers, becoming 1 dm long in fruit; sepals 1-2 mm long; petals to 2 mm long. **Fruit** a 1-seeded capsule, 2-3 mm long, covered with soft hooked bristles. June-Aug.—Cedar swamps (where often on rotting logs), low spots in forests.

Circaea lutetiana L.
COMMON ENCHANTER'S NIGHTSHADE
Circaea canadensis (L.) Hill

MAP 872
native

Stems erect, to 1 m tall, glabrous below, becoming minutely villosulous in the inflorescence. **Leaves** oblong-ovate, commonly 6-12 cm long, acuminate, very

Circaea alpina

869. Syringa vulgaris   *870. Calylophus serrulatus*   *871. Circaea alpina*   *872. Circaea lutetiana*

shallowly sinuate-denticulate, rounded or barely subcordate at base; petioles rounded or angled on the lower side. **Racemes** commonly many-flowered, to 2 dm long; petals 2.5-3.5 mm long. **Fruit** 3.5-5 mm long, beset with stiff bristles, equally 2-celled, 2-seeded, each half bearing normally 3 large and 2 small rounded ridges separated by narrow furrows. June-Aug.—Moist woods.

EPILOBIUM *Willow-Herb; Fireweed*

Perennial herbs, often producing leafy rosettes or bulblike offsets (turions) at base of stem late in growing season. Leaves simple, opposite, alternate, or opposite below and becoming alternate above; stalkless or short-petioled. Flowers white to pink, single in axils of upper reduced leaves, or in spike or racemes at ends of stems; sepals 4; petals 4; stamens 8, the inner 4 stamens shorter than outer 4; ovary 4-chambered, maturing into a linear, 4-parted capsule, splitting from tip to release numerous brown seeds which are tipped with a tuft of fine hairs (coma).

1   Flowers showy in a terminal raceme; petals 8-16 mm long; stigma 4-parted . . . . *E. angustifolium*
1   Flowers single from upper leaf axils; petals 3-8 mm long 2
   2   Stigma 4-parted . . . . *E. brachycarpum*
   2   Stigma entire, not 4-parted 3
      3   Leaves entire or nearly so, the margins often revolute; stems round in cross-section, without lines of hairs on stem below base of each leaf 4
         4   Stems with soft, straight hairs . . . . *E. strictum*
         4   Stems finely hairy, the hairs appressed to stem 5
            5   Upperside of leaves finely hairy . . . . *E. leptophyllum*
            5   Upper surface of leaves glabrous or nearly so . . . . *E. palustre*
      3   Leaf margins conspicuously toothed; stems 4-angled in section, with lines of hairs down stems below leaf bases 6
         6   Tuft of hairs attached to tip of seeds (coma) white or nearly so, seeds with a broad, short beak; margins of stem leaves with mostly 10-30 teeth on a side . . . . *E. ciliatum*
         6   Coma brown, seeds beakless; leaf margins with more than 30 teeth on a side . . . . *E. coloratum*

Epilobium angustifolium L.

MAP 873
native

FIREWEED
Chamerion angustifolium (L.) Holub

Perennial herb. **Stems** erect, to 2 m or more tall. **Leaves** lance-shaped or linear lance-shaped, to 2 dm long, narrowed to a sessile or obscurely petioled base, glabrous beneath; veinlets conspicuous. **Racemes** elongate, many-flowered, the lower flowers often exceeded by the subtending leaves, the upper with short bracts or none; petals purple, or rarely white, 10-15 mm long, clawed at base; style pubescent at base; stigmas soon revolute. **Capsules** 2.5-7 cm long. June-Sept. —In a variety of habitats, preferring moist soils rich in humus; often abundant after fire.

Epilobium brachycarpum K. Presl

(NO MAP)
introduced

TALL ANNUAL WILLOWHERB

Annual from a slender taproot. **Stems** 1-6 dm tall, terete, glabrous, the bark exfoliating near the base. **Leaves** linear or nearly so, rarely more than 3 mm wide, entire or nearly so, not revolute; lateral veins obsolete or very obscure. **Petals** about 5 mm long. **Capsules** about 2 cm long, much longer than their pedicels. —More common in w USA; Clay County.

Epilobium ciliatum Raf.

MAP 874
native

AMERICAN WILLOWHERB
Epilobium glandulosum Lehm.

Perennial herb, with over-wintering leafy rosettes. **Stems** often branched, 3-10 dm long, smooth below, short-hairy above, especially in the head (where often with gland-tipped hairs). **Leaves** opposite, usually alternate near top; lance-shaped to ovate, 3-10 cm long and to 3 cm wide; margins with few, small, forward-pointing teeth; sessile or with short, winged petioles to 6 mm long. **Flowers** usually nodding when young, on stalks 3-10 mm long, on branches from upper leaf axils; sepals ovate, 2-5 mm long; petals white (or pink), notched at tip, 2-8

Epilobium angustifolium

mm long. **Fruit** a linear capsule, 4-8 cm long, with gland-tipped hairs; seeds 1 mm long, the coma white. July-Sept.—Shores, streambanks, marshes, wet meadows, seeps, ditches and other wet places.

Epilobium coloratum Biehler
PURPLE-LEAF WILLOWHERB

MAP 875
native

Perennial herb, producing basal, leafy rosettes in fall; similar to American willowherb (*E. ciliatum*) but larger. **Stems** 5-10 dm long, much-branched in the head, smooth below, short-hairy above with hairs often in lines; stems and leaves often purple-tinged. **Leaves** mostly opposite, becoming alternate and smaller above, lance-shaped, 5-15 cm long and 0.5-3 cm wide, long-tapered to a pointed tip; margins finely toothed, with irregular sharp teeth; short-petioled to sessile. **Flowers** many on branches from upper leaf axils; sepals lance-shaped, 2-3 mm long; petals pink or white, 3-5 mm long, notched at tip; individual flowers on stalks to 10 mm long. **Fruit** a linear capsule, 3-5 cm long; seeds 1.5 mm long, the coma brown when mature. July-Sept.—Shores, seeps, swamps and wet woods, wet meadows, fens, ditches.

Epilobium ciliatum

Epilobium leptophyllum Raf.
BOG WILLOWHERB

MAP 876
native

Perennial herb, similar to marsh willowherb (*E. palustre*) but somewhat larger and more hairy. **Stems** simple or branched, 2-10 dm long, with short, incurved hairs. **Leaves** opposite or alternate, linear or linear lance-shaped, 2-7 cm long and 1-6 mm wide, upper surface hairy, underside hairy, at least on midvein, lateral veins indistinct; margins entire and rolled under; petioles short or more or less absent. **Flowers** erect in upper leaf axils on short, slender stalks to 1 cm long; petals light pink, 3-5 mm long, entire or slightly notched at tip. **Fruit** a linear, finely hairy capsule, 4-5 cm long; the coma yellow-white. July-Sept.—Swamps, marshes, open bogs, sedge meadows, shores, streambanks and springs.

Epilobium coloratum

Epilobium palustre L.
MARSH WILLOWHERB

MAP 877
native

Perennial herb, from slender rhizomes or stolons. **Stems** simple or with a few branches above, 1-6 dm long, upper stem hairy with small incurved hairs. **Leaves** mostly opposite, lance-shaped, erect or ascending, 2-6 cm long and 3-15 mm wide, tapered to a rounded tip, upper surface smooth or with sparse hairs along midvein, underside smooth or finely hairy along midvein, lateral veins distinct; margins entire and often rolled under; sessile. **Flowers** few in upper leaf axils, on short stalks; petals white to pink, 3-5 mm long, notched at tip. **Fruit** a linear, finely hairy capsule; coma pale. July-Aug.—Open bogs and swamps.

Epilobium strictum Muhl.
DOWNY WILLOWHERB

MAP 878
native

Perennial herb, spreading by slender rhizomes; plants densely soft white-hairy. **Stems** erect, simple or branched above, 3-6 dm long. **Lower leaves** opposite, **upper leaves** alternate; lance-shaped, ascending, 2-4 cm long and 3-8 mm wide, tapered to a rounded tip; margins mostly entire, rolled under; sessile. **Flowers** on slender stalks from upper leaf axils; petals pink, 5-8 mm long, notched at tip. **Fruit** a linear, densely hairy capsule; coma pale brown. July-Aug.—Conifer swamps, sedge meadows, calcareous fens, marshes.

Epilobium palustre

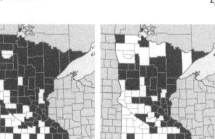

GAURA *Gaura; Beeblossom*

Annual or perennial herbs with alternate, entire, sinuate or dentate leaves and long terminal spikes or racemes of small flowers. Flowers 4-merous, usually somewhat irregular. Hypanthium tubular, prolonged above the ovary in a tube about equaling the fertile basal portion and deciduous from the fruit. Sepals reflexed at anthesis. Petals narrow, ephemeral. Stamens 8. Ovary 4-celled, or 1-celled by abortion of the partitions, with 1 ovule in each cell. Fruit a hard, 1-4-seeded capsule.

1   Leaves narrowly lance-shaped, less than 5 mm wide and to 3 cm long; fruit densely hairy, the hairs appressed; plants to 5 dm high . . . . *G. coccinea*

1   Leaves lance-shaped, wider and longer than in *G. coccinea*; fruit finely hairy, the hairs spreading; plants 5 dm or more high . . . . *G. biennis*

Gaura biennis L.

BIENNIAL BEEBLOSSOM
Oenothera gaura W.L. Wagner & Hoch

MAP 879
native

Biennial herb. **Stems** erect, branched above, to 1.5 m tall, more or less pubescent. Leaves lance-shaped or oblong lance-shaped, to 12 cm long, narrowed to the base, remotely or obscurely denticulate or sinuate. **Spikes** several, many-flowered; sepals 6-8 mm long, reflexed in pairs; petals white, soon turning pink or red, 4-8 mm long. **Capsule** finely pubescent, 4-sided, with a prominent thick rib on each angle and a slender one on each face. Aug, Sept.—Moist or dry prairies and open woods.

Gaura coccinea Nutt. ex Pursh

SCARLET BEEBLOSSOM
Oenothera suffrutescens (Ser.) W.L. Wagner & Hoch

MAP 880
introduced

Perennial herb. **Stems** 2-5 dm tall, arising several together from the base, glabrous, strigose, or villous. **Leaves** lance-shaped to narrowly oblong, crowded, 2-3 cm long, entire or commonly with 2-4 sinuate teeth on each side, finely pubescent. **Spikes** 5-15 cm long; sepals 5-8 mm long, reflexed separately; petals pink to white, 3-6 mm long. **Capsule** narrowly obovoid, 5-7 mm long, finely pubescent. May-Aug.—Dry prairies and plains.

Gaura biennis

LUDWIGIA *Primrose-Willow*

Perennial herbs. Stems floating, creeping, or upright. Leaves simple, opposite or alternate, entire. Flowers single in leaf axils; sepals 4; petals 4 (or absent), yellow or green, large or very small; stamens 4; stigma unlobed. Fruit a 4-chambered, many-seeded capsule; seeds without a tuft of hairs at tip (coma).

1   Leaves opposite; stems floating, or creeping and rooting at nodes . . . . *L. palustris*

1   Leaves alternate; stems erect . . . . *L. polycarpa*

Ludwigia palustris (L.) Ell.

MARSH PRIMROSE-WILLOW

MAP 881
native

Perennial herb. **Stems** weak, creeping and rooting at nodes or partly floating, simple to branched, 1-5 dm long, succulent, smooth or with sparse scattered hairs. **Leaves** opposite, lance-shaped to ovate, 0.5-3 cm long and 0.5-2 cm wide, shiny green or red, margins entire, tapered at base to a winged petiole to 2 cm long. **Flowers** single in leaf axils, stalkless; sepals broadly triangular, 1-2 mm long; petals usually absent, or small and red. **Fruit** a capsule, 2-5 mm long and 2-3 mm wide,

Ludwigia palustris

877. *Epilobium palustre*

878. *Epilobium strictum*

879. *Gaura biennis*

somewhat 4-angled, with a green stripe on each angle. July-Sept.—Shallow water or exposed mud of pond margins, lakeshores, streambanks, ditches, springs.

Ludwigia polycarpa Short & Peter
MANY-FRUIT PRIMROSE-WILLOW

MAP 882
native

Perennial herb, producing leafy stolons from base in fall; plants smooth. **Stems** erect, 1-9 dm long, often branched, usually 4-angled. **Leaves** alternate, lance-shaped to oblong lance-shaped, 3-12 cm long and 5-15 mm wide; margins entire; more or less stalkless. **Flowers** single in leaf axils, stalkless; sepals triangular, 2-4 mm long, usually persistent; petals green and very small or absent. **Fruit** a short-cylindric, rounded 4-angled capsule, 4-7 mm long and 3-5 mm wide. July-Sept.—Borders of swamps and marshes, muddy shores, wet depressions.

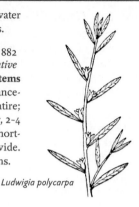

Ludwigia polycarpa

OENOTHERA *Evening-Primrose*

Annual, biennial, or perennial herbs with alternate, mostly narrow leaves and small to large, yellow, white, or pink flowers solitary in the axils or forming a terminal raceme. Flowers 4-merous. Hypanthium slenderly tubular (except one species), much prolonged above the ovary, deciduous from the fruit. Sepals at first connate, often with terminal or subterminal appendages, splitting at anthesis and reflexed. Petals commonly yellow, or in a few species white to pink, usually large and conspicuous but ephemeral. Stamens 8, equal or alternately unequal. Ovary 4-celled; stigma entire, 4-lobed, or deeply 4-cleft into elongate segments. Fruit a capsule; seeds numerous.

Four of our species can be considered part of an *Oenothera biennis* "complex," including closely related (and sometimes difficult to distinguish) *O. biennis*, *O. oakesiana*, *O. parviflora*, and *O. villosa*.

1   Flowers white, becoming pink . . . . ***O. nuttallii***
1   Flowers yellow 2
  2   Ovary 4-angled; fruit sharply 4-angled or 4-winged, tapered to the base . . . . ***O. perennis***
  2   Ovary round in cross-section or nearly so; fruit round or rounded 4-angled in cross-section, abruptly rounded
      at base 3
    3   Capsules linear, 2-3 mm wide and about same width throughout; stem leaves either pinnately lobed or
        linear to narrowly lance-shaped 4
      4   Leaves pinnately lobed; flowers few, from the axils of upper leaves . . . . ***O. laciniata***
      4   Stem leaves linear to lance-shaped, entire or nearly so; flowers many from leafy bracts in a terminal
          spike 5
        5   Petals 1.5-3 cm long; stigma elevated above anthers when in full-flower . . . . ***O. rhombipetala***
        5   Petals to 1.5 cm long; stigma surrounded by anthers at full-flower . . . . ***O. clelandii***
    3   Capsules tapered upward from base, 5-7 mm wide; stem leaves unlobed, lance-shaped, usually at least 1
        cm wide 6
      6   Bases of sepals contiguous 7
        7   Plant green in aspect, with mostly spreading long hairs and often shorter glandular ones   ***O. biennis***
        7   Plant, especially the upper portion and inflorescence, gray in aspect, with dense appressed non-
            glandular hairs . . . . ***O. villosa***
      6   Bases of awl-shaped sepals separate 8
        8   Calyx, ovary, capsule, and upper leaves or bracts densely pubescent with appressed whitish non-
            glandular hairs; largest leaves typically less than 15 mm wide, finely toothed . . . . ***O. oakesiana***
        8   Calyx, ovary, capsule, and other parts glabrate to sparsely pubescent, often with some long spreading
            hairs as well as shorter glandular hairs; largest leaves various, usually at least 15 mm wide, nearly
            entire . . . . ***O. parviflora***

881. Ludwigia palustris   *882. Ludwigia polycarpa*   *883. Oenothera biennis*   *880. Gaura coccinea*

Oenothera biennis L.

COMMON EVENING-PRIMROSE

MAP 883

native

Biennial herb. **Stems** 1-2 m tall, often suffused with red, terete or becoming somewhat angled in the inflorescence. **Leaves** lance-shaped to oblong, 1-2 dm long, acute or acuminate, entire to repand-dentate, often crisped on the margin, sessile or short-petioled, glabrous to sparsely pubescent but always green. **Flowers** several to many in a terminal raceme, the bracts resembling the leaves but much smaller; hypanthium tube 3-6 cm long; petals yellow, 15-25 mm long. July-Oct.—Fields, roadsides, and waste places.

Oenothera clelandii W. Dietr. Raven & W.L. Wagner

LESSER FOUR-POINT EVENING-PRIMROSE

MAP 884

native

Biennial herb. **Stems** erect or ascending, 4-10 dm tall. **Leaves** linear to narrowly lance-shaped, 3-8 cm long, entire or remotely and obscurely denticulate, short-hairy on both sides. **Flowers** numerous, crowded in a terminal, leafy bracteate spike 1-3 dm long; hypanthium 1.5-3 cm, sparsely strigose; sepals linear, 0.5-1.5 cm long, reflexed separately or somewhat connivent; petals yellow, 0.5-1.5 cm long, ovate. **Fruit** linear, 10-18 mm long, usually curved; seeds dark brown, obscurely pitted. June-Sept.—Sandy fields and prairies.

Oenothera biennis

Oenothera laciniata Hill

CUT-LEAF EVENING-PRIMROSE

(NO MAP)

native

Annual herb. **Stems** simple or branched from the base, erect or ascending. **Leaves** lance-shaped in outline, 3-8 cm long, tapering to the base, prominently sinuate-dentate to pinnatifid, green, sparsely puberulent to glabrous above; bracteal leaves resembling the stem leaves in shape and scarcely smaller. **Flowers** few, sessile in the axils of the upper foliage leaves, not forming a distinct spike; hypanthium tube hirsute; petals yellow. **Capsules** linear, straight or curved, 1.5-3.5 cm long; seeds pale brown, pitted.—Dry sandy soil; Anoka and Ramsey counties.

Oenothera nuttallii Sweet

WHITE-STEM EVENING-PRIMROSE

MAP 885

introduced

Perennial herb. **Stems** erect, 3-8 dm tall, with white bark exfoliating toward the base, glabrous below, minutely glandular-puberulent in the inflorescence. **Leaves** linear, 2-8 cm long, entire or nearly so, tapering to the base, glabrous above, puberulent with incurved hairs beneath. **Flowers** sessile in the upper axils, nodding in the bud; hypanthium tubular, prolonged 2-2.5 cm beyond the ovary; petals white, turning pink, about 2 cm long. **Capsule** linear-oblong, 1-3 cm long, minutely glandular; seeds in one row in each cell. June-July.—Prairies.

Oenothera laciniata

Oenothera oakesiana (Gray) J.W. Robbins ex. S. Wats. & Coult.

OAKES' EVENING-PRIMROSE

MAP 886

native

　Oenothera biennis L. var. *oakesiana* A. Gray
　Oenothera parviflora L. var. *oakesiana* (Robbins) Fern.

Biennial herb with a taproot. **Stems** erect to procumbent, 1-6 dm tall. **Leaves** narrowly oblanceolate, 4-20 cm long, 0.5-3 cm wide. **Flower petals** yellow. July-Sept. Very similar to *O. parviflora, O. biennis* and *O. clelandii*; differs from *O. parviflora* by its inflorescence lacking gland-tipped hairs; differs from *O. biennis* in having sepals separate at base (in *O. biennis* sepals close together at base); differs from *O. clelandii* by its seeds not being pitted and the fruit being broad at the base.—Sandy or rocky shores, dunes, and clearings along the Lake Superior; occasionally inland along railroads, sandy shores, or in disturbed places.

884. Oenothera clelandii　　*885. Oenothera nuttallii*　　*886. Oenothera oakesiana*　　*887. Oenothera parviflora*

Oenothera parviflora L.   MAP 887
SMALL-FLOWER EVENING-PRIMROSE   *native*
Biennial herb, similar to *O. laciniata and O. nuttallii* but plants usually smaller.
Leaves commonly narrowly oblong lance-shaped to almost linear, green, glabrous
or sparsely pubescent. **Raceme** crowded, the bracteal leaves commonly as long
as the hypanthium; calyx in anthesis densely strigose to nearly glabrous, the actual
end of the sepal represented by a prominent lobe or transverse ridge; petals
yellow, 10-15 mm long. June-Oct.—Shores, banks, sandy open places.

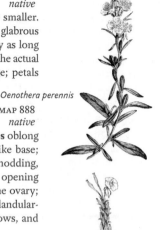

Oenothera perennis

Oenothera perennis L.   MAP 888
LITTLE SUNDROPS   *native*
Perennial herb. **Stems** erect, 2-6 dm tall, usually simple. **Principal leaves** oblong
lance-shaped to elliptic, 3-6 cm long, obtuse, narrowed to a petiole-like base;
bracteal leaves shorter and proportionately narrower. **Inflorescence** nodding,
the axis straightening during anthesis, the flowers becoming erect and opening
singly; hypanthium prolonged 3-10 mm., averaging 6.5 mm, beyond the ovary;
petals 5-9 mm long. **Capsule** 5-10 mm long, obovoid, at first minutely glandular-
puberulent, often glabrescent in age.—Moist or dry soil, fields, meadows, and
open woods. June-Aug.

Oenothera rhombipetala Nutt.   MAP 889
GREATER FOUR-POINT EVENING-PRIMROSE   *introduced*
Biennial herb. **Stems** erect, 4-10 dm tall. **Leaves** linear to narrowly lance-shaped
or linear-oblong, 3-8 cm long, acuminate, entire or remotely and obscurely
denticulate, short-pubescent on both sides. **Flowers** numerous, crowded in a
terminal spike 1-3 dm long, sessile, subtended by bracteal leaves resembling the
stem leaves in shape but much smaller; hypanthium tube prolonged 2-3 cm
beyond the ovary; sepals linear, 10-24 mm long, reflexed separately or more or
less connivent; petals yellow, 15-25 mm long. **Capsule** linear, 10-18 mm long,
usually curved. June-Sept.—Fields and prairies in sandy soil.

Oenothera villosa Thunb.   MAP 890
HAIRY EVENING-PRIMROSE   *native*
Biennial herb, appearing grayish due to pubescence. **Stems** 1-2 m tall, branching
above. **Leaves** oval, tapering to both ends, to 12 cm long and 2.5 cm wide, margins
weakly toothed; sessile; pubescent on both surfaces. **Flowers** in crowded terminal
and axillary spikes; sepals recurved; petals yellow. **Fruit** an elongate capsule to
2.5 cm long, weakly angled, opening by 4 sections separating at the tip and
recurving. July-August.—Fields, shores, roadsides, railroads.

Oenothera villosa

Orobanchaceae   BROOM-RAPE FAMILY

Annual, biennial, or perennial herbs; some genera fleshy, without green color, parasitic on the roots
of other plants. Leaves opposite, alternate, or the leaves reduced to scales. Flowers mostly perfect,
single or few from leaf axils, or numerous in clusters at ends of stems or leaf axils, usually with a
distinct upper and lower lip; calyx 2-5-lobed or toothed, persistent in fruit; ppetals 4-5 (petals
sometimes absent); stamens usually 4, inserted on the corolla tube. Fruit a several- to many-seeded
2-valved capsule. *Includes many former members of **Scrophulariaceae**.*

AGALINIS *False Foxglove*

Annual hemiparasitic herbs. Stems slender, erect, branched, usually 4-angled. Leaves opposite, linear, stalkless, smooth, or rough-to-touch on upper surface. Flowers showy, in clusters at ends of branches; sepals joined, the calyx 5-lobed, bell-shaped; petals united, corolla 5-lobed, bell-shaped, and nearly regular, only slightly 2-lipped, pink to purple; stamens 4, of 2 different lengths. Fruit a nearly round, many-seeded capsule.

1 Leaves lanceolate or broader, the uppermost often with a pair of basal lobes; stem terete, with stiff retrorse hairs longer than the very short pubescence; calyx pubescent . . . . **A. auriculata**
1 Leaves narrowly linear (up to 3.5 mm wide), without basal lobes; stem usually angled (not in *A. gattingeri*), glabrous or antrorse-scabrous; calyx glabrous. 2
   2 Pedicels less than 6 mm long, shorter than or equaling the calyx 3
      3 Corolla 2-3 cm long; calyx lobes less than half length of calyx tube. . . . . **A. purpurea**
      3 Corolla less than 2 cm long; calyx lobes nearly as long as calyx tube . . . . **A. paupercula**
   2 Longer pedicels more than 6 mm long, equaling or longer than the calyx 4
      4 Plants yellow-green, remaining so when dried; leaves about 1 mm wide; seeds yellow-brown **A. gattingeri**
      4 Plants deep green, often tinged with purple, tending to darken when dried; leaves to 6 mm wide; seeds dark 5
         5 Flowers on slender, widely spreading pedicels; the calyx lobes v-shaped . . . . **A. tenuifolia**
         5 Flowers on stout upright pedicels; the calyx lobes broadly rounded . . . . **A. aspera**

Agalinis aspera (Dougl.) Britt.   MAP 891
TALL FALSE FOXGLOVE   *native*
Annual herb. **Leaves** narrowly linear, very scabrous above, often accompanied by small axillary fascicles of reduced leaves. Calyx tube 3-5 mm long; calyx lobes triangular, acuminate, 1.5-3 mm long; corolla 2-2.5 cm long. **Capsule** ellipsoid, about 1 cm long. Aug.-Sept.—Dry prairies.

Agalinis aspera
calyx and capsule

Agalinis auriculata (Michx.) Blake   MAP 892
EAR-LEAF FALSE FOXGLOVE   ☙ *endangered* | *native*
Annual herb; separated from our other species by broader, dull or dark green lance-shaped leaves, the uppermost often with a pair of basal lobes; the terete stem; and the pubescent calyx; corolla rose-purple or pink. Aug.-Sept.—Dry prairies.

Agalinis gattingeri (Small) Small   MAP 893
ROUND-STEM FALSE FOXGLOVE   ☙ *endangered* | *native*
Annual herb. **Stems** very much branched, the very slender lateral branches bearing a few small leaves and rarely more than a single, apparently terminal flower; flowers also very few on the central axis and a terminal raceme scarcely developed. Pedicels at anthesis 5-25 mm long; calyx tube 2.5-3.5 mm long; calyx lobes broadly triangular, 0.6-1 mm long; corolla 12-18 mm long. **Capsule** subglobose, 4-5 mm wide. Aug.-Sept.—Dry prairies and sparsely wooded glades and openings; sites usually with shallow soils and exposed bedrock.

Agalinis gattingeri
calyx

888. *Oenothera perennis*   889. *Oenothera rhombipetala*   890. *Oenothera villosa*   891. *Agalinis aspera*

Agalinis paupercula (A. Gray) Britton   MAP 894
SMALL-FLOWER FALSE FOXGLOVE   *native*
  Gerardia purpurea var. *paupercula* Gray

Annual herb. **Stems** erect, 30-70 cm long, 4-angles, simple or branching. **Stem leaves** opposite, sessile, linear 2-4 mm wide; **branch leaves** may be alternate. **Flowers** in racemes from upper leaf axils; calyx 5-lobed, joined to form a tube at base, separating into lobes above, the lobes nearly as long as the tube; corolla 1.5-2 cm long. Aug-Sept.—Open, sandy wet places. *Very similar to Agalinis purpurea and perhaps best considered a variety of that species; A. paupercula has smaller flowers and longer calyx lobes than those of A. purpurea.*

Agalinis purpurea (L.) Pennell   MAP 895
PURPLE FALSE FOXGLOVE   *native*
  Gerardia purpurea L.

Annual herb. **Stems** slender, 2-8 dm long, 4-angled, smooth to slightly rough, branched and spreading above. **Leaves** opposite, spreading, linear, 1-5 cm long and 1-3 mm wide; margins entire; petioles absent. **Flowers** on spreading stalks 2-5 mm long, in racemes on the branches; calyx 4-6 mm long, the lobes less than half the length of the tubular base; corolla purple, 2-3 cm long, the lobes spreading, 5-10 mm long. **Fruit** a round capsule, 4-6 mm wide. Aug-Sept.—Wet meadows, fens, shores of Great Lakes and along inland lakes and ponds, moist areas between dunes, ditches; usually where sandy, often where calcium-rich.

Agalinis purpurea

Agalinis tenuifolia (Vahl) Raf.   MAP 896
COMMON FALSE FOXGLOVE   *native*
  Agalinis besseyana (Britt.) Britt.
  Gerardia tenuifolia var. *parviflora* Nutt.

Annual herb. **Stems** slender, erect, 2-6 dm tall, smooth, usually with many branches. **Leaves** opposite, spreading, linear, 1-5 cm long and 1-3 mm wide, upper surface slightly rough; margins entire; petioles absent. **Flowers** on slender, ascending stalks, 1-2 cm long; calyx 3-5 mm long, with short teeth; corolla purple (rarely white), often spotted, 10-15 mm long, the lobes 3-5 mm long. **Fruit** a round capsule, 4-6 mm wide. Aug-Sept.—Wet meadows, low prairie, fens, shores, streambanks and ditches, usually where sandy.

Agalinis tenuifolia

AUREOLARIA *False Foxglove*

Large, branched, annual or perennial herbs; partially parasitic on roots of oaks. Principal leaves opposite, entire to deeply lobed, the upper ones reduced in size; the uppermost often irregularly alternate, subtending large, yellow, solitary, pediceled flowers. Calyx tube campanulate to cup-shaped, calyx lobes triangular to linear, often unequal. Corolla campanulate, the 5 lobes shorter than the tube, all distinct, broadly rounded. Stamens 4. Style slender; stigma 1. Capsule ovoid to ellipsoid; seeds few to several.

1   Corolla and pedicels glandular hairy; stems and leaves with scattered, sticky glandular hairs . . . . ***A. pedicularia***
1   Corolla glabrous; pedicels, stems and leaves without glandular, sticky hairs . . . . ***A. grandiflora***

Aureolaria grandiflora (Benth.) Pennell   MAP 897
WESTERN FALSE FOXGLOVE   *native*

Perennial. **Stems** about 1 m tall, widely branched, pubescent. **Lower leaves** ovate in outline, more or less pinnatifid, the upper progressively reduced. **Upper and bracteal leaves** sharply serrate to deeply laciniate, finely pubescent on both sides. Pedicels stout, 4-10 mm long at anthesis, abruptly upwardly curved, densely but

892. *Agalinis auriculata*   893. *Agalinis gattingeri*   894. *Agalinis paupercula*   895. *Agalinis purpurea*

minutely pubescent; calyx similarly pubescent, the tube hemispheric, longer than the lance-shaped lobes; corolla yellow, about 4 cm long. **Capsule** glabrous, ovoid, 15-20 mm long. July-Sept.—Upland woods.

Aureolaria grandiflora

Aureolaria pedicularia (L.) Raf.

MAP 898

ANNUAL FALSE FOXGLOVE ❧*threatened* | *native*

Annual, partly parasitic on oak roots. **Stems** much branched, to 1 m tall, finely pubescent and usually densely stipitate-glandular. **Principal stem leaves** 3-6 cm long, sessile or subsessile, lance-shaped or ovate in outline, pinnatifid, the 5-8 pairs of pinnae irregularly serrate. Pedicels curved upward, usually 1-2 cm long at anthesis, stipitate-glandular; calyx stipitate-glandular, the lobes spreading, 7-10 mm long, usually entire, the tube stipitate-glandular; corolla usually yellow, 2.5-4 cm long. **Capsule** ellipsoid or ovoid, 10-15 mm long. Aug-Sept.—Dry sandy oak woods.

Aureolaria pedicularia

CASTILLEJA *Indian-Paintbrush*

Annual or perennial hemiparasitic herbs. Leaves alternate, often pinnatifid. Flowers in dense terminal spikes, each subtended by a large, entire or pinnatifid, sometimes brightly colored, bracteal leaf. Calyx tubular, divided into two lateral halves. Corolla tube slender, usually surpassing the lips, scarcely dilated; upper corolla lip acuminate; lower corolla lip much shorter than the upper. Stamens 4, ascending under the upper corolla lip and not exsert. Capsule ovoid or oblong, many-seeded.

1 Floral bracts red, scarlet, orange or yellow; plants annual or biennial . . . . *C. coccinea*
1 Floral bracts green, cream-colored or yellowish; plants perennial 2
   2 Floral bracts cream-colored or yellowish (lower ones often purplish); rare in ne Minn . . . . . *C. septentrionalis*
   2 Floral bracts green; widespread in w and s Minn . . . . *C. sessiliflora*

Castilleja coccinea (L.) Spreng.

MAP 899

SCARLET INDIAN-PAINTBRUSH *native*

Annual, more or less pubescent. **Stems** usually simple, 2-6 dm tall. **Principal stem leaves** diverse, varying from rarely entire to commonly 3-5-cleft, the segments linear, the lateral segments almost always shorter or narrower than the terminal; **bracteal leaves** wholly or mostly scarlet (rarely pale), commonly deeply 3-lobed, occasionally 5-lobed. **Spike** at first dense, 4-6 cm long, elongating to as much as 2 dm in fruit; calyx 2-3 cm long, thin and membranous, often more or less scarlet, deeply divided into two lateral halves; each half gradually widened distally and at the summit broadly rounded or truncate; corolla greenish yellow, little surpassing the calyx, the minute lower lip less than 1/3 as long as the upper. May-Aug.—Meadows, moist prairies, calcareous sandy or gravelly shores, swamps.

Castilleja septentrionalis Lindl.

(NO MAP)

LABRADOR INDIAN-PAINTBRUSH ❧*endangered* | *native*

Pubescent perennial. **Stems** to 50 cm tall. **Leaves** linear-lanceolate, sessile; **bracteal leaves** white, often tinged with purple (especially the lower bracts). June-July. —Rock ledges, openings, open forests, and sandy places near Lake Superior in Cook County; more common northward and in the Rocky Mtns.

Castilleja sessiliflora Pursh

MAP 900

GREAT PLAINS INDIAN-PAINTBRUSH *native*

Perennial, softly pubescent. **Stems** usually several from one base, simple, 1-4 dm tall, very leafy. **Principal stem leaves** 3-5 cm long, cleft to below the middle into

Castilleja coccinea

896. *Agalinis tenuifolia*   897. *Aureolaria grandiflora*   898. *Aureolaria pedicularia*   899. *Castilleja coccinea*

3 lance-linear divergent lobes, of which the middle one may be again cleft; bracteal leaves resembling the stem leaves but somewhat smaller, green. **Spikes** dense, 3-5 cm long; calyx 3-4 cm long, cleft about to the middle into two lateral halves, each half also cleft into two linear segments about 1 cm long; corolla curved, exsert from the bracts, yellowish or white, 4-5.5 cm long, the upper lip about 12 mm long, the lower about 6 mm long, 3-lobed, deflexed. May-July.—Dry prairies and plains.

EUPHRASIA *Eyebright*

Low annual herbs. Leaves opposite, lobed or toothed. Flowers in axils of leaf-like bracts. Calyx 4-lobed. Corolla 2-lipped. Fruit a flattened capsule.

1   Calyx, bracts, and leaves glabrous (sometimes scabrous on the nerves); calyx lobes and leaf teeth tapered into prolonged bristle tips. . . . . **E. stricta**
1   Calyx, bracts, and leaves pubescent; calyx lobes acute to somewhat bristle-tipped . . . . **E. hudsoniana**

Euphrasia hudsoniana Fernald & Wiegand
HUDSON BAY EYEBRIGHT

MAP 901
native

Low annual herb. **Stems** erect, to 30 cm tall, simple or branching, minutely villous. **Leaves** opposite, ovate or elliptic, 1-2 cm long, puberulent, sessile. **Flowers** from the upper axils of slightly smaller bracts, 7-9 mm long; calyx about equally 4-lobed with acute, ciliate teeth; corolla white to pale lilac, with veins of deeper purple, the upper lip 2-lobed, the lower lip 3-lobed, each lobe notched; stamens included. **Capsule** compressed, pubescent, widened toward the tip; style base short-persistent; seeds wing-edged, ribbed, finely cross-striate.—Rocky shores and crevices along Lake Superior.

Euphrasia stricta D. Wolff ex J.F.Lehm.
DRUG EYEBRIGHT

MAP 902
introduced

Euphrasia nemorosa (Pers.) Wallr.
Euphrasia officinalis L.

Low annual herb. **Stems** 1-3 dm tall, usually freely branched below the middle. **Leaves** glabrous, opposite, sessile, ovate, conspicuously longer than wide, sharply 3-5-toothed on each margin, the teeth tipped with a hair-like bristle; upper bracteal leaves tending to become alternate. **Flowers** small, sessile or nearly so; calyx 4-lobed (the upper median lobe lacking); corolla bilabiate, 6-8 mm long; lower lip 3-lobed, the lateral lobes diverging at an angle of about 60 degrees, white with violet lines; upper lip shallowly 2-lobed or merely notched, suffused with purple; stamens 4, ascending under the upper corolla-lip and not exsert. **Capsule** usually laterally compressed, truncate or retuse at the tip; seeds several, with about 10 narrow longitudinal wings.—Eurasian species, spreading into dry fields, lawns, clearings, trails, roadsides, old railroad grades.

Euphrasia stricta

MELAMPYRUM *Cow-Wheat*

Melampyrum lineare Desr.
AMERICAN COW-WHEAT

MAP 903
native

Annual herb, partially parasitic on other plants, often red-tinged when in open habitats. **Stems** usually branched, 1-4 dm long. **Leaves** opposite, lower leaves oblong lance-shaped, upper leaves linear or lance-shaped, often toothed near base; petioles short or absent. **Flowers** from upper leaf axils; calyx tube cup-

Melampyrum lineare

900. Castilleja sessiliflora   *901. Euphrasia hudsoniana*   *902. Euphrasia stricta*   *903. Melampyrum lineare*

shaped, calyx lobes 4 or 5, longer than the tube; corolla about 1 cm long, 2-lipped, the upper lip white, the lower pale yellow; stamens 4, ascending under the upper lip and not exsert. **Fruit** a capsule to 1 cm long. June-Aug.—In a wide variety of habitats, ranging from wet to dry forests and openings; in wetlands occasional in swamps and on hummocks in open fens.

OROBANCHE *Broom-Rape*

Plants of diverse aspect with white to yellowish or purple flowers in racemes or spikes, or apparently solitary. Flowers perfect. Calyx campanulate, variously lobed. Corolla tubular, bilabiate, the tube usually curved downward, much longer than the rounded or acute lobes. Stamens 4, about as long as the corolla tube and inserted below its middle. Capsule 2-valved, many-seeded, enclosed by the withering corolla.

1 Flowers many, sessile or nearly so, in a dense spike . . . . *O. ludoviciana*
1 Flowers 1 or several on long pedicels 2
    2 Flowers solitary, white, cream or lilac; the leaves scale-like and glabrous . . . . *O. uniflora*
    2 Flowers 2 or more, purple; the scale-like leaves pubescent . . . . *O. fasciculata*

Orobanche fasciculata Nutt.
CLUSTERED BROOM-RAPE
MAP 904
❦ *threatened* | *native*

Parasitic on many species of plants, but only known host plant in Minn is *Artemisia campestris*. **Stem** proper 5-1.9 cm long. **Scale-leaves** ovate lance-shaped, pubescent, all or at least the upper acuminate. Pedicels 3-10, 2-6 cm long, erect, without bractlets, each bearing a solitary purple flower 1.5-2 cm long; calyx lobes triangular-acuminate, equaling or somewhat exceeding the calyx tube. June. —Dry soil, prairies and plains, and especially on sand dunes.

Orobanche ludoviciana Nutt.
PRAIRIE BROOM-RAPE
MAP 905
❦ *threatened* | *native*

Parasitic on members of Asteraceae, most commonly on *Artemisia* and *Ambrosia*. Plant 1-3 dm tall, simple or rarely branched, with numerous appressed scale-leaves. **Spikes** many-flowered, dense, constituting usually 1/3 to 2/3 of the plant. **Flowers** mostly sessile, or the lower on erect appressed pedicels to 15 mm long; calyx bilabiate, the upper lip with a single lobe, the lower with 4; calyx lobes linear, 8-12 mm long; corolla often purplish, 1.5-2.5 cm long. June-Aug.—Sandy soil.

Orobanche uniflora L.
NAKED BROOM-RAPE
MAP 906
❦ *threatened* | *native*

Parasitic on numerous plant species. **Stem** proper only 1-3, or rarely 5 cm long, all or mostly underground, bearing a few overlapping, obovate, glabrous scales. Pedicels 1-4, usually 2, 6-20 cm long, erect, finely glandular-pubescent, without bractlets, each bearing a single white to violet flower about 2 cm long; calyx lobes 5, about equal, triangular-acuminate, slightly longer than the calyx tube.—Moist woods and streambanks.

Orobanche
uniflora

Orobanche fasciculata

ORTHOCARPUS *Owl-Clover*

Orthocarpus luteus Nutt.
YELLOW OWL-CLOVER
MAP 907
native

Annual herb, hemiparasitic, glanular-pubescent. **Stems** slender, erect 1-3 dm tall, usually unbranched. **Leaves** alternate, sessile, narrowly lance-shaped, 1.5-3.5 cm

904. *Orobanche fasciculata*   905. *Orobanche ludoviciana*   906. *Orobanche uniflora*   907. *Orthocarpus luteus*

long, entire or the uppermost 3-lobed. **Inflorescence** a narrow spike or spike-like raceme, subtended by green, 3-lobed bracts. **Flowers** strongly bilabiate; calyx 6–8 mm long, 4-lobed; corolla yellow, 9–12 mm long, finely hairy, the upper lip hood-like and erect, the lower lip pouch-like and inflated; stamens 4. **Capsule** elliptic-ovoid, with several seeds. July-Aug.—Prairies, dry meadows, open woods.

PEDICULARIS *Lousewort*

Perennial herbs (ours). Leaves either opposite, alternate, or scattered, sharply toothed to 2-pinnatifid. Flowers yellow or purple in terminal spikes or racemes, each subtended by a bracteal leaf. Calyx campanulate to tubular, entire or variously lobed, but usually longer on the upper side. Corolla tube gradually enlarged distally; upper lip as long as or longer than the lower, very concave or arched, often laterally compressed; lower lip more or less expanded, with two longitudinal folds below the sinuses. Stamens 4, ascending under the upper corolla-lip and not exsert. Capsule compressed, ovate to oblong, pointed. Seeds several, not winged.

1   Stems glabrous or nealy so; leaves opposite; flowering in late summer . . . . *P. lanceolata*
1   Stems usually long-hairy; leaves alternate; flowering in early summer . . . . *P. canadensis*

Pedicularis canadensis L.
WOOD BETONY
MAP 908
native

Perennial herb. **Stems** several, erect, 1.5–4 dm tall, sparsely villous. **Leaves** chiefly basal, lance-shaped to oblong lance-shaped, pinnately lobed usually more than halfway to the midvein; **lower leaves** on petioles often longer than the blade; **stem leaves** progressively reduced, short-petioled to nearly sessile; bracteal leaves usually toothed only at the tip. **Spikes** commonly solitary, at anthesis 3–5 cm, in fruit to 20 cm long; corolla yellow, maroon, or yellow on the lower lip and maroon on the upper; the upper lip bearing 2 slender teeth just below the rounded tip; lower lip shorter than the upper. **Capsule** oblong, about 15 mm long, 2x as long as the mature calyx, opening along the upper side. April-June.—Dry forests and savannas, moist hardwood forests, especially in openings; less often in conifer swamps, meadows, and grasslands.

Pedicularis canadensis

Pedicularis lanceolata Michx.
SWAMP LOUSEWORT
MAP 909
native

Perennial herb; plants at least partially parasitic on other plants. **Stems** 3–8 dm long, more or less smooth, unbranched or few-branched. **Leaves** opposite, or in part alternate, mostly lance-shaped, 4–9 cm long and 1–2 cm wide, pinnately lobed; margins with small rounded teeth; **lower leaves** short-petioled, **upper leaves** sessile. **Flowers** more or less sessile, in spikes at ends of stems and from upper leaf axils; the spikes 2–10 cm long; calyx 2-lobed; corolla yellow, about 2 cm long, the upper lip entire and arched, lower lip upright. **Capsule** unequally ovate, mostly shorter than the calyx. July-Sept.—Wet meadows, calcareous fens, wetland margins, springs, streambanks.

Pedicularis lanceolata

Oxalidaceae WOOD-SORREL FAMILY

OXALIS *Wood-Sorrel*

Perennial herbs (ours). Leaves basal or alternate on the stem, 3-foliolate, leaflets obcordate. Flowers solitary on axillary peduncles or in cymose or umbel-like clusters; perfect, regular, 5-merous, white, yellow, pink, or purple. Sepals usually imbricate. Stamens 10, alternately long and short. Ovary 5-celled; styles 5. Fruit a capsule.

1   Plants with leaves from stems; flowers yellow 2
    2   Pubescence largely of septate hairs, mostly spreading on the stem (or stem glabrate) and pedicels, the capsules glabrous or with only septate ± spreading hairs; pedicels remaining erect or ascending in fruit; stipules absent
        . . . . *O. stricta*
    2   Pubescence without or with very few septate hairs, appressed at least on pedicels, the capsules with minute retrorse non-septate hairs; pedicels usually becoming ± strongly reflexed in fruit (but the capsules erect); stipules often evident, ± oblong, adnate to base of petiole . . . . *O. corniculata*

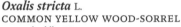

1 Plants without stems, the leaves and scapes all from plant base; flowers white to purple 3
    3 Peduncles with 1 flower . . . . *O. montana*
    3 Peduncles with 2 or more flowers . . . . *O. violacea*

Oxalis corniculata L.
CREEPING YELLOW WOOD-SORREL

MAP 910
introduced

Perennial herb. **Stems** creeping, rooting at the nodes, more or less villous. **Leaflets** 8-15 mm wide. Peduncles about equaling the leaves; pedicels more or less pubescent with either appressed or spreading hairs, often but not always deflexed at maturity. **Flowers** yellow, 2-several or sometimes solitary, 5-8 mm long. **Capsules** 10-15 mm long, densely pubescent with minute hairs 0.1-0.3 mm long and occasionally mingled with some longer ones.—Weedy in lawns and fields.

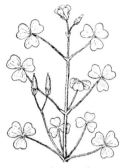

Oxalis montana Raf.
NORTHERN WOOD-SORREL
    Oxalis acetosella L.

MAP 911
native

Perennial herb, from slender, scaly rhizomes. **Leaves** single or 3-6 together, all from base of plant, on stalks 4-15 cm long, these joined at base; palmately divided into 3 leaflets, the leaflets notched at tips, sparsely hairy. **Flowers** perfect, broadly bell-shaped, single atop stalks 6-15 cm long (usually slightly taller than leaves), with a pair of small bracts above middle of stalk; sepals 5, much shorter than petals; petals 5, white or pink and with pink veins, 10-15 mm long. **Fruit** a smooth, nearly round capsule. May-July.—Hummocks in swamps, wet depressions in forests, moist wetland margins.

Oxalis corniculata

Oxalis stricta L.
COMMON YELLOW WOOD-SORREL
    Oxalis dillenii Jacq.
    Oxalis fontana Bunge

MAP 912
native

Perennial herb. **Stems** erect or eventually decumbent, to 5 dm tall, more or less pubescent with ascending or incurved hairs. **Leaflets** 1-2 cm wide. Pedicels similarly pubescent, at maturity commonly abruptly divaricate or deflexed. **Inflorescence** umbel-like. **Flowers** yellow, 5-10 mm long, rarely more than 3 to a peduncle. **Capsules** 1-3 cm long, densely to thinly gray-pubescent with mostly retrorse hairs 0.1-0.3 mm long, or with longer ones intermingled, or wholly or partly glabrous.—In many different habitats, mostly a common weed of roadsides, railroads, gardens, lawns, fields, and disturbed places; also in forests, especially along trails.

Oxalis montana

Oxalis violacea L.
VIOLET WOOD-SORREL

MAP 913
native

Perennial herb from a scaly bulbous base. **Leaves** glabrous. Peduncles erect, 1-2 dm tall, much surpassing the leaves, bearing an umbel-like cluster of pediceled flowers subtended by small bracts. **Flowers** commonly rose-violet, 10-18 mm long; sepals callous-tipped. April-June and occasionally later.—Dry upland woods and prairies.

Oxalis stricta

908. *Pedicularis canadensis*

909. *Pedicularis lanceolata*

910. *Oxalis corniculata*

911. *Oxalis montana*

Papaveraceae POPPY FAMILY

Herbs or vines (*Adlumia*), with watery, milky, or colored juice. Leaves alternate or rarely opposite. Flowers regular, perfect. Sepals 2 or 3, early deciduous. Petals 4 or more (rarely absent), separate, conspicuous. Stamens 6, or 12 or more. Ovary 1-celled or falsely 2-celled, of 2 or more carpels. Fruit a capsule, dehiscent by terminal valves or longitudinally (rarely otherwise). *The Fumariaceae, now included here, were previously recognized as a separate family, differing in bilateral symmetry of the flowers and watery juice. All of our members of Papaveraceae in the strict sense have colored juice (yellow to red-orange or milky).*

ADDITIONAL SPECIES

Eschscholzia californica Cham. (California poppy); native to sw USA; known from Cass County, an uncommon annual escape from roadside plantings but not persisting in the flora.

1　Corolla bilaterally symmetrical; juice watery, clear 2
　　2　Delicate vine . . . . *Adlumia fungosa*
　　2　Upright herbaceous plants 3
　　　　3　Corolla with 2 spurs, white; leaves basal . . . . *Dicentra*
　　　　3　Corolla 1-spurred, pink, yellow or red-purple; leave alternate 4
　　　　　　4　Flowers pink, yellow-tipped; seeds ca. 1-1.5 mm wide; plants ± erect, the terminal inflorescences definitely surpassing the leaves. . . . . *Capnoides*
　　　　　　4　Flowers yellow or purple; seeds ca. 1.8-2.2 mm wide; plants ± spreading or sprawling, the terminal inflorescences barely if at all surpassing the leaves. . . . . *Corydalis*
1　Corolla regular, juice colored whitish to yellow or red-orange 5
　　5　Leaf 1 from base of plant; petals 8 or more . . . . *Sanguinaria canadensis*
　　5　Plants with leafy stems; petals 4 8
　　　　6　Flowers yellow . . . . *Chelidonium majus*
　　　　6　Flowers red, purple, or white . . . . *Papaver*

ADLUMIA *Allegheny-Vine*

Adlumia fungosa (Ait.) Greene   MAP 914
ALLEGHENY-VINE   *native*
Biennial vine, climbing by the upper part of the rachis of the 3-parted leaves, During the first year acaulescent, with several ascending, non-prehensile, decompound **leaves**; climbing to 3 m high the second year, with slender elongate **stems** and large, delicate, prehensile **leaves**, their rachis elongate and the **uppermost leaflets** greatly reduced. **Flowers** pearly pink, in drooping axillary panicles; sepals 2, scale-like, quickly deciduous; corolla bilateral, narrowly flattened-ovoid, the outer petals constricted near the summit to form an ovate appendage, the inner narrow, dilated at the summit into an oval appendage; corolla after anthesis persistent with little change of color, becoming spongy, enclosing the slender 2-valved **capsule**. June–Sept.—Woods, rocky shores, thickets; sometimes where soil has been disturbed.

Adlumia fungosa

CAPNOIDES *Rock-Harlequin*

Capnoides sempervirens (L.) Borkh.   MAP 915
ROCK-HARLEQUIN   *native*
　　Corydalis sempervirens (L.) Pers.
Biennial herb, glaucous. **Stems** slender, erect, 3-6 dm tall, divaricately branched

912. *Oxalis stricta*　　　913. *Oxalis violacea*　　　914. *Adlumia fungosa*　　　915. *Capnoides sempervirens*

above; principal internodes 4-8 cm long. **Lower leaves** petioled, **upper leaves** nearly sessile. **Flowers** in small panicles at the end of the branches; bracts minute, lance-shaped; corolla pink, tipped with yellow, 12-17 mm long, the tube 8.5-12 mm, the spur 2.5-5 mm long; sepals broadly ovate, 2-4 mm long. **Capsule** erect or nearly so, 2-4 cm long; seed 1.3-1.5 mm long.—Dry or rocky woods, gravelly shores, especially where disturbed.

CHELIDONIUM *Celandine*

Chelidonium majus L.
CELANDINE
MAP 916
introduced (invasive)

Biennial herb with saffron-colored juice. **Stems** branched, 3-8 dm tall. **Stem leaves** several, alternate, deeply pinnately parted (usually to the midrib) into 5-9 segments; lateral segments often alternate, variously toothed or lobed, the lowest often with a secondary basal division; terminal segments broadly obovate, 3-lobed. **Umbel** peduncled, several-flowered; sepals 2, deciduous, glabrous; petals 4, yellow, about 1 cm long; stamens numerous, with long slender filaments. **Capsule** cylindric, glabrous, 3-5 cm long. April-Sept.—Native of Eurasia; established in moist soil.

Capnoides sempervirens

CORYDALIS *Fumewort*

Annual or biennial herbs. Leaves cauline, alternate, 2-pinnately dissected. Flowers short-pediceled, in bracted racemes. Sepals 2, small, appressed. Petals elongate, more or less connivent, the upper spurred at base, at the apex somewhat dilated and keeled or winged, the lower narrower, similarly dilated and keeled, the 2 inner slender at base, at the apex dilated, keeled or winged. Capsule slender, 2-valved, terminated by the slender persistent style. Seeds black, shining, minutely low-tuberculate.

Chelidonium majus

1   Outer petals with well developed wings . . . . *C. micrantha*
1   Outer petals not winged . . . . *C. aurea*

Corydalis aurea Willd.
GOLDEN CORYDALIS
MAP 917
native

Biennial herb. **Stems** 2-6 dm tall, erect or ascending, branched above. **Racemes** dense, 1-3 cm long, often surpassed by the upper leaves; bracts lance-shaped; sepals broadly ovate, 1.5-2 mm long, erose; corolla yellow, 12-15 mm long, of which the spur constitutes less than 1/3; outer petals folded distally along the median line into a conspicuous but wingless keel. **Capsules** smooth, spreading or drooping, 1-2 cm long; seeds 2-2.5 mm wide.—Rocky banks or sandy soil.

Corydalis micrantha (Engelm.) Gray
SLENDER CORYDALIS
MAP 918
native

Corydalis aurea

Annual herb, glaucous or nearly green. **Stems** erect or ascending, 1-3 dm tall. **Racemes** usually well-surpassing the leaves; bracts narrowly lance-shaped; corolla pale yellow, 11-15 mm long, including the 4-6 mm long spur; crest of the upper petal low, entire. **Fruit** erect, 1-2 cm long seeds 1.5 mm wide, without a ring-margin. Often some or all flowers cleistogamous, these 1-5 in a raceme, inconspicuous, often with smaller fruit.—Moist, especially sandy soil.

916. Chelidonium majus   *917. Corydalis aurea*   *918. Corydalis micrantha*

Dicentra cucullaria
flowers

DICENTRA *Bleedinghearts*

Perennial herbs from rhizomes or a cluster of small tubers. Leaves basal or alternate, compound. Flowers white to red-purple, scapose or in axillary racemes or panicles. Sepals 2, minute. Corolla ovate or cordate, bilaterally symmetrical; petals weakly united, the outer two large, saccate or spurred at base, spreading or ascending at the summit, the inner much narrower and more or less dilated at the summit. Ovary slender, gradually tapering into the long style. Fruit a capsule.

1   Corolla sac-like, with small rounded spurs about as long as wide; leaves waxy on underside . . . . . . **D. canadensis**
1   Corolla with widely spreading spurs, these longer than wide; leaves green or only slightly waxy . . . **D. cucullaria**

Dicentra canadensis (Goldie) Walp.

MAP 919
SQUIRREL-CORN   *native*

Very similar to *D. cucullaria* in foliage, size, and habit. **Tubers** fewer and about 2x larger; corolla narrowly ovate, the spurs short, broadly rounded, scarcely divergent. April-May.—Rich deciduous forests, rarely in swampy or dry forests.

Dicentra cucullaria (L.) Bernh.

MAP 920
DUTCHMAN'S-BREECHES   *native*

Scapes and leaves from a dense cluster of small, white, grain-like tubers. **Leaves** broadly triangular in outline, compound, the ultimate segments linear, long-petioled. **Scapes** 1-3 dm tall, bearing a terminal raceme of 3-12 nodding white flowers, suffused with yellow at the summit; corolla 15-20 mm long; spurs subacute, divergent. April-May.—Rich deciduous forests, rarely in swampy or drier woods.

Dicentra canadensis

PAPAVER *Poppy*

Annual herbs (ours), with colored juice and large, usually long-peduncled flowers terminating the stem and branches. Sepals 2, deciduous. Petals normally 4, white or colored, thin in texture. Stamens numerous. Ovary of 4 to many carpels. Capsule opening by small valves near the margin of the disk.

1   Stem leaves clasping at base . . . . *P. somniferum*
1   Stem leaves not clasping . . . . *P. rhoeas*

Papaver rhoeas L.

MAP 921
CORN POPPY   *introduced*

Stems sparsely branched, to 1 m tall, hirsute. **Leaves** pinnately divided, the pinnae usually lobed or incised. **Flowers** usually scarlet, varying to purple or white. **Capsule** subglobose to broadly obovoid, glabrous; stigmatic rays 8-14, usually 10.—Native of Eurasia and n Africa; escaped but seldom abundant.

Papaver somniferum L.

(NO MAP)
OPIUM POPPY   *introduced*

Stems rather stout, to 1 m tall. **Leaves** sessile, cordate-clasping, oblong in outline, coarsely toothed or shallowly lobed. **Flowers** purple or red to white. **Fruit** subglobose or broadly ovoid, glabrous; stigmatic rays 8-12. June-Aug.—Native of Eurasia, cultivated for ornament and sometimes escaped; St. Louis County. *The seeds are commonly used in baking; opium is derived from the milky juice of the capsule.*

Sanguinaria canadensis

SANGUINARIA *Bloodroot*

Sanguinaria canadensis L.

MAP 922
BLOODROOT   *native*

Perennial herb with red juice, from a stout rhizome which sends up a single lobed leaf and a large white scapose flower. **Leaves** orbicular in outline, 3-9-lobed, the lobes undulate to coarsely toothed. **Scape** 5-15 cm tall at anthesis. **Flowers** white, varying rarely to pink, 2-5 cm wide; sepals 2; petals typically 8, often more and as many as 16; 4 petals usually longer than the others and the flower quadrangular in outline; stamens numerous. **Capsule** 3-5 cm long, crowned by the persistent style, dehiscent longitudinally. March-April.—Rich deciduous and floodplain forests. *The leaves continue to expand after anthesis and may grow to 2 dm wide.*

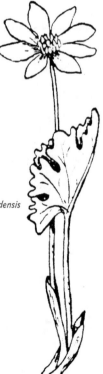

Penthoraceae PENTHORUM FAMILY

PENTHORUM *Ditch-Stonecrop*

Penthorum sedoides L.

DITCH-STONECROP

MAP 923
native

Perennial herb, spreading by rhizomes; plants often red-tinged. **Stems** 1-6 dm long, smooth and round in section below, **upper stem** often angled and with gland-tipped hairs. **Leaves** alternate, lance-shaped, 2-10 cm long and 0.5-3 cm wide, tapered to tip and base; margins with small, forward-pointing teeth; sessile or on petioles to 1 cm long. **Flowers** star-shaped, perfect, 3-6 mm wide, on short stalks, in branched racemes at ends of stems; sepals 5, green, triangular, 1-2 mm long; petals usually absent; stamens 10; pistils 5, joined at base and sides to form a ring. **Fruit** a many-seeded capsule, the seeds about 0.5 mm long. July-Sept. —Streambanks, muddy shores and ditches.

Penthorum sedoides

Phrymaceae LOPSEED FAMILY

Perennial herbs. Calyx tubular, 5-lobed. Fruit a dehiscent capsule. Previously, this family was monotypic with only genus *Phryma*; now includes *Mimulus*.

1 Flowers nearly sessile in pairs in terminal spike-like racemes, subtended by tiny bracts; upper calyx teeth bristle-like; fruit an achene, strongly reflexed . . . . *Phryma*
1 Flowers peduncled, borne singly in the axils of opposite leaves or bracts with expanded blades; fruit a capsule, not strongly reflexed . . . . *Mimulus*

MIMULUS *Monkey-Flower*

Perennial herbs (ours). Leaves opposite, margins shallowly toothed. Flowers often large and showy, single on stalks from leaf axils or in leafy racemes at ends of stems; sepals joined, the calyx tube-shaped; corolla 2-lipped, the upper lip 2-lobed, the lower lip 3-lobed, yellow or blue-violet; stamens 4, of 2 different lengths; stigmas 2. Fruit a cylindric capsule.

1 Flowers blue to violet; leaves lance-shaped or oblong lance-shaped . . . . *M. ringens*
1 Flowers yellow; leaves nearly round . . . . *M. glabratus*

Mimulus glabratus Kunth

ROUND-LEAF MONKEY-FLOWER

MAP 924
native

Perennial herb, spreading by stolons and often forming large mats. **Stems** succulent, smooth, 0.5-5 dm long, creeping and rooting at nodes, the stem ends angled upward. **Leaves** opposite, nearly round to broadly ovate, 1-2.5 cm wide, palmately veined, hairy when young, becoming glabrous; margins shallowly toothed or entire; petioles short and winged, or the upper leaves sessile. **Flowers** yellow, on stalks from leaf axils and at ends of stems; calyx 5-9 mm long, barely toothed, irregular, the upper lobe large, the other lobes smaller; corolla 2-lipped, 9-15 mm long, the throat open and bearded on inner surface. **Fruit** an ovate capsule, 5-6 mm long. June-Aug.—Cold springs, seeps, and banks of spring-fed streams; usually where calcium-rich.

Mimulus glabratus

919. *Dicentra canadensis*

920. *Dicentra cucullaria*

921. *Papaver rhoeas*

922. *Sanguinaria canadensis*

Mimulus ringens L.
ALLEGHENY MONKEY-FLOWER

MAP 925
native

Smooth perennial herb, from stout rhizomes. **Stems** usually erect, 3–8 dm long, 4-angled and sometimes winged. **Leaves** opposite, oblong to lance-shaped, 4–12 cm long and 1–3.5 cm wide, **upper leaves** smaller; margins with forward-pointing teeth; petioles absent, the base of leaf clasping stem. **Flowers** single from upper leaf axils, on slender stalks 1–5 cm long and longer than the sepals; calyx regular, angled, 1–2 cm long, the lobes awl-shaped, 3–5 mm long; corolla blue-violet, 2-lipped, 2–3 cm long, the throat nearly closed, the upper lip erect and bent upward, lower lip longer and bent backward. **Fruit** a capsule, about as long as calyx tube. July–Aug.—Streambanks, oxbow marshes, swamp openings, floodplain forests, muddy shores, ditches; sometimes where disturbed.

Mimulus ringens

PHRYMA *Lopseed*

Phryma leptostachya L.
AMERICAN LOPSEED

MAP 926
native

Perennial herb. **Stems** erect, 5–10 dm tall, simple or with a few divergent branches. **Leaves** opposite, ovate, 6–15 cm long; lower petioles to 5 cm long, the upper shorter or the uppermost sessile. **Flowers** pale purple to white, in elongate, long-peduncled, interrupted spike-like racemes terminating the stem and also from a few upper axils, opposite and horizontal; calyx 2-lipped, the upper 3 lobes bristle-like, with hooked tips when mature, about equaling the tube, the lower 2 very short, broadly triangular; corolla tube scarcely widened upward, the upper lip straight, the lower much longer, spreading, 3-lobed; stamens 4, included. **Fruit** an achene, contained in the persistent calyx. June–Aug.—Rich deciduous forests, especially moist areas in beech-maple woods, but also in drier forests with oak and sometimes with conifers. *Recognized by the distant paired flowers, reflexed fruit, and broad, opposite, petioled leaves.*

Phryma leptostachya

Plantaginaceae PLANTAIN FAMILY

Annual or perennial herbs. Leaves simple, entire, all from base of plant. Flowers perfect in a narrow spike (*Plantago*), each flower subtended by bracts, or single-sexed, the staminate and pistillate flowers on same plant (*Littorella*); flower parts mostly in 4s. Fruit a capsule opening at tip. *Plantaginaceae is the correct name for the family that encompasses not only the plantains with their reduced flowers, but also the related larger-flowered genera formerly placed in the Scrophulariaceae as well as highly reduced aquatics, such as* Hippuris *(Hippuridaceae) and* Callitriche *(Callitrichaceae).*

ADDITIONAL SPECIES
Limosella aquatica L. (Mudwort, MAP 926A), a small, glabrous, annual or perhaps perennial herb, producing stolons, with tiny (2–4 mm long), white, 5-petaled flowers at ends of slender pedicels; associated with rainwater pools on rock outcrops and muddy depressions in wet prairies; see key.

1   Plants aquatic or exposed on wet shores 2
   2   Leaves in a basal rosette 3
      3   Leaves terete, linear . . . . *Littorella uniflora*
      3   Leaves long-petioled, spatula-shaped . . . . *Limosella aquatica**

923. *Penthorum sedoides*

924. *Mimulus glabratus*

925. *Mimulus ringens*

926. *Phryma leptostachya*

BACOPA *Water-Hyssop*

Bacopa rotundifolia (Michx.) Wettst.

DISK WATER-HYSSOP

MAP 927

🌿*threatened* | *native*

Bacopa rotundifolia

Perennial succulent herb, spreading by stolons. **Stems** creeping, 0.5-4 dm long, rooting at leaf nodes, smooth when underwater, usually hairy when emersed. **Leaves** opposite, obovate to nearly round, 1-3.5 cm long and 1-2.5 cm wide, smooth, palmately veined, rounded at tip, clasping at base; margins entire or slightly wavy; petioles absent. **Flowers** 1-2 from leaf axils, on hairy pedicels to 1.5 cm long and shorter than the leaves; sepals 5, unequal, 4-5 mm long; corolla white with a yellow throat, 2-lipped, bell-shaped, 5-10 mm long, the 5 lobes shorter than the tube; stamens 4. **Fruit** a round capsule, about as long as sepals. Aug-Sept.—Mud flats and shallow water of ponds and marshes.

BESSEYA *Kitten-Tails*

Besseya bullii (Eat.) Rydb.
MAP 928
KITTEN-TAILS ✿*threatened* | *native*

Perennial herb. Scape unbranched, 2-4 dm tall, hirsute or villous, with several reduced leaves and a dense, terminal, spike-like raceme of small yellow flowers. **Leaves** in a basal rosette; **basal leaves** ovate, 6-12 cm long, crenate or obtusely serrate, long-petioled; **stem leaves** smaller, alternate, sessile or nearly so, ovate or oblong. Spike-like **raceme** dense, cylindric, 5-15 cm long; bracts nearly as long as the flowers; pedicels 1-2 mm long; calyx nearly regular, deeply 4-lobed, the lobes about 5 mm long, villous; corolla strongly bilabiate, yellow, the upper lip surpassing the calyx, the lower lip shallowly or irregularly 3-lobed, the middle lobe the smallest; with 2 exserted stamens. **Capsule** nearly orbicular, 4-8 mm long and nearly as wide, slightly flattened, many-seeded. April-June.—Sandy soil of prairies, open woods, bluffs, barrens, and hillsides.

Besseya bullii

CALLITRICHE *Water-Starwort*

Small, perennial aquatic herbs with weak, slender stems and fibrous roots. Leaves simple, opposite, all underwater or upper leaves floating; underwater leaves linear, 1-nerved, entire except for shallowly notched tip; floating leaves mostly in clusters at ends of stems, obovate to spatula-shaped, 3-5-nerved, rounded at tip. Flowers tiny, staminate and pistillate flowers usually separate on same plant, each flower with 1 stamen or 1 pistil; single and stalkless in middle and upper leaf axils, or 1 staminate and 1 pistillate flower in each axil, subtended by a pair of thin, translucent, deciduous bracts, or the bracts absent; ovary flattened, oval to round, 4-chambered, separating when mature into 4 nutlets.

ADDITIONAL SPECIES
Callitriche stenoptera Lansdown (Narrow-wing water-starwort), reported for Traverse County in w Minn.

1 Leaves all underwater, 1-veined, linear . . . . *C. hermaphroditica*
1 Leaves both underwater and floating; floating leaves 3-veined, spatula-shaped or obovate 2
 2 Margins of fruit without wings; pits on fruit not in rows . . . . *C. heterophylla*
 2 Margins of fruit with small wings; fruit pitted in rows . . . . *C. palustris*

Callitriche hermaphroditica L.
MAP 929
AUTUMN WATER-STARWORT *native*

Stems 10-30 cm long. **Leaves** all underwater, alike, linear, 1-nerved, 3-12 mm long and to 1.5 mm wide, shallowly notched at tip, clasping at base, the opposite leaf bases not connected; darker green than our other species. **Flowers** either staminate or pistillate; single in leaf axils, not subtended by translucent bracts. **Fruit** flattened, rounded, 1-2 mm long, deeply divided into 4 segments. June-Sept.—Shallow to deep water of lakes, ponds, marshes, ditches and streams.

Callitriche heterophylla Pursh
MAP 930
LARGE WATER-STARWORT ✿*threatened* | *native*

Stems 10-20 cm long. Leaves of 2 types; **underwater leaves** linear, 1-2 cm long and to 1.5 mm wide, 1-nerved, notched at tip, the leaf pairs connected at base by a narrow wing; **floating leaves** in clusters at ends of stems or opposite along upper stems, 3-5-nerved, obovate to spatula-shaped, rounded at tip, 6-15 mm long and 3-7 mm wide; leaves intermediate between underwater and floating leaves often present. **Flowers** either staminate or pistillate; usually 1 staminate and 1 pistillate flower together in leaf axils, subtended by a pair of translucent, deciduous bracts.

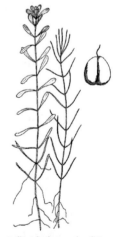
Callitriche hermaphroditica

926A. Limosella aquatica

927. Bacopa rotundifolia

928. Besseya bullii

929. Callitr. hermaphroditica

Fruit about 1 mm long and not more than 0.1 mm longer than wide, often broadest above middle, not wing-margined, pits on surface not in rows. May-Aug. Shallow water or mud of springs, stream pools, ponds and wet depressions.

Callitriche palustris L.
VERNAL WATER-STARWORT

MAP 931
native

Stems 10-20 cm long. Leaves of 2 types; **underwater leaves** mostly linear, 1-2 cm long and to 1 mm wide, shallowly notched at tip, the leaf pairs connected at base by a narrow wing; **floating leaves** in clusters at ends of stems or opposite along upper stems, 3-5-nerved, obovate to spatula-shaped, rounded at tip, 5-15 mm long and 2-5 mm wide; leaves intermediate between underwater and floating leaves usually present. **Flowers** either staminate or pistillate; usually 1 staminate and 1 pistillate flower together in leaf axils, subtended by a pair of translucent bracts, these soon deciduous. **Fruit** 1-1.5 mm long and about 0.2 mm longer than wide, broadest above middle, narrowly winged near tip, pitted in vertical rows. June-Sept.—Shallow water of lakes, ponds, streams; exposed mudflats.

CHAENORHINUM *Dwarf-Snapdragon*

Chaenorhinum minus (L.) Lange
DWARF-SNAPDRAGON

MAP 932
introduced (naturalized)

Annual herb. Stems erect, branched, 1-3 dm tall, glandular-pubescent. **Leaves** linear, 1-2 cm long, obtuse, narrowed to the base but scarcely petiolate. Pedicels 10-15 mm long, arising from many or most leaf-axils; sepals linear-spatulate, unequal, about 3 mm long; corolla 5-6 mm long, blue-purple, with yellow on the palate; spur 1.5-2 mm long. **Capsule** subglobose, about 5 mm long. June-Sept. —Native of Europe; established in waste places, especially on railway-ballast.

Callitriche palustris

CHELONE *Turtlehead*

Chelone glabra L.
WHITE TURTLEHEAD

MAP 933
native

Perennial herb. Stems erect, 5-10 dm long, rounded 4-angled, unbranched or sometimes branched above. **Leaves** opposite, lance-shaped, to 15 cm long and 1-3 cm wide, tapered to a sharp tip; margins with sharp, forward-pointing teeth; petioles very short or absent. **Flowers** in dense spikes at ends of stems, 3-8 cm long; sepals 5; corolla white or light pink, 2.5-3.5 cm long. **Fruit** an ovate capsule. Aug-Sept.—Swamp openings, thickets, streambanks, shores, wet meadows, marshes, calcareous fens.

Chelone glabra

DIGITALIS *Foxglove*

Introduced perennial herbs (ours). Leaves alternate. Flowers showy, in terminal racemes. Calyx 5-lobed. Corolla short lobed. Stamens 4. in pairs. *Some species are a source of cardiac medicines, but plants can be highly toxic or even fatal if consumed.*

1   Corolla yellow, 3-5 cm long, the lower lip with middle lobe scarcely longer than the lateral lobes; inflorescence (pedicels and axis) densely covered with short hairs (less than 0.5 mm long) . . . . **D. grandiflora**
1   Corolla white with red veins, 2-3 cm long, the lower lip with very greatly prolonged middle lobe; inflorescence densely covered with long (over 1 mm) hairs. . . . . **D. lanata**

930. *Callitriche heterophylla*   931. *Callitriche palustris*   932. *Chaenorhinum minus*   933. *Chelone glabra*

Digitalis grandiflora P. Mill.
YELLOW FOXGLOVE

(NO MAP)
introduced

Perennial herb. **Stems** to 12 dm tall. **Leaves** glossy. **Flowers** bell-shaped, pale yellow; **inflorescence** with dense covering of short, gland-tipped hairs.—Native to Europe and western Asia; in Minn, escaped from cultivation and reported from St. Louis County (Duluth area). *Toxic, potentially fatal if eaten.*

Digitalis lanata Ehrh.
GRECIAN FOXGLOVE

(NO MAP)
introduced

Perennial herb. **Stems** pubescent, to 6 dm tall. **Leaves** with woolly hairs, especially on underside. **Flowers** bell-shaped with broad, prolonged lower lip, cream-colored with purple-brown venation. June-July.—Native to southern Europe; potentially invasive into disturbed areas and considered a noxious weed in Minn; known from Washington County (and from scattered locations in north-central and northeastern USA). *Toxic, potentially fatal if eaten.*

Digitalis lanata

GRATIOLA *Hedge-Hyssop*

Gratiola neglecta Torr.
CLAMMY HEDGE-HYSSOP

MAP 934
native

Annual herb. **Stems** erect to horizontal, 5-25 cm long, usually branched, glandular-hairy above. **Leaves** opposite, linear to lance-shaped, 5-25 mm long, 1-10 mm wide, clasping at base; margins entire to wavy-toothed; petioles absent. **Flowers** single in the leaf axils, on slender pedicels 1-2 cm long, subtended by a pair of small narrow bracts; sepals 5, unequal, 3-6 mm long, enlarging after flowering; corolla white, tube-shaped, slightly 2-lipped, 6-10 mm long; stamens 2. **Fruit** an ovate 4-chambered capsule, 3-5 mm long. June-Sept.—Mud flats, shores of ponds and marshes.

Gratiola neglecta

HIPPURIS *Mare's-Tail*

Hippuris vulgaris L.
COMMON MARE'S-TAIL

MAP 935
native

Perennial herb, from large, spongy rhizomes. **Stems** 2-6 dm long, unbranched, underwater and lax, or emersed and upright, densely covered by the closely spaced whorls of leaves. **Leaves** numerous, in whorls of 6-12, linear, 1-2.5 cm long and 1-3 mm wide, stalkless. **Flowers** very small, perfect, stalkless and single in upper leaf axils, or often absent; sepals and petals lacking; stamen 1, style 1, ovary 1-chambered. **Fruit** nutlike, oval, 2 mm long. June-Aug.—Shallow water or mud of marshes, lakes, streams and ditches.

Hippuris vulgaris

LINARIA *Toadflax*

Perennial herbs (ours), almost always glabrous, with erect flowering stems. Leaves numerous, narrow. Flowers several to many in terminal racemes. Calyx deeply 5-parted. Corolla irregular, strongly bilabiate, spurred at base, the upper lip erect, 2-lobed, the lower 3-lobed. Stamens 4. Capsule ovoid to globose.

1   Leaves 6 mm wide or more, ovate, the upper leaves clasping stem . . . . *L. dalmatica*
1   Leaves less than 5 mm wide, linear, sessile or with petioles . . . . *L. vulgaris*

Linaria dalmatica (L.) P. Mill.
DALMATIAN TOADFLAX

MAP 936
introduced

Stout, glaucous perennial, spreading by rhizomes and forming colonies. **Stems** 4-12 dm tall, branched above. **Leaves** numerous, ovate or lance-ovate, 2-5 cm long, palmately veined, sessile and clasping. **Flowers** short-pedicellate or nearly sessile in elongate racemes, bright yellow, with well developed, orange-bearded palate, the spur about as long as the rest of the corolla. **Capsule** broadly ovoid-cylindric, 6-8 mm long; seeds irregularly wing-angled. July-Aug.—Native of Europe; roadsides and other disturbed sites.

Linaria dalmatica

Linaria vulgaris P. Mill.   MAP 937
BUTTER-AND-EGGS   *introduced (invasive)*
Perennial; spreading by rhizomes and forming colonies. **Stems** erect, 3-8 dm tall.
Leaves very numerous, pale green, 2-5 cm long, 2-4 mm wide, narrowed below
to a petiolelike base. **Flowers** numerous in a compact spike, yellow with orange
palate, 2-3 cm long, including the spur. **Capsule** round-ovoid, 8-12 mm long, the
seeds winged. May-Sept.—Native of Europe; fields, roadsides, and waste places.

Linaria vulgaris

LITTORELLA

Littorella uniflora (L.) Aschers.   NC MAP 938
AMERICAN SHOREWEED   *native*
   Littorella americana Fernald
Low perennial herb; plants clumped, often forming mats. **Leaves** bright green,
linear, to 5 cm long and 2-3 mm wide, succulent; margins entire. **Flowers** only
from emersed plants, single-sexed, staminate and pistillate flowers on same plant;
staminate flowers 1-2 on stalks to 4 cm long; **pistillate flowers** stalkless among
the leaves; sepals 4 (sometimes 3 in pistillate flowers), lance-shaped, 2-4 mm long,
with a dark green midrib and lighter margins; petals joined, 4-lobed; stamens 4,
longer than the petals. **Fruit** a 1-seeded nutlet, 2 mm long and 1 mm wide. July-
Aug.—Sandy or mucky lakeshores, or in water 1 m or more deep.

Littorella uniflora

NUTTALLANTHUS *Oldfield-Toadflax*

Nuttallanthus canadensis (L.) D.A. Sutton   MAP 939
OLDFIELD-TOADFLAX   *native*
   Linaria canadensis (L.) Chaz.
Annual herb. **Stems** erect, 2-6 dm tall, glabrous, with several procumbent or
widely spreading sterile shoots from the base. **Leaves** narrowly linear, 1-3 cm
long, those of the erect stems widely scattered, alternate, those of the sterile
shoots smaller, crowded, often opposite or whorled. **Racemes** congested at
anthesis, later elongate; pedicels 2-4 mm long; corolla blue, the lips much longer
than the tube; lower lip with 2 short white ridges. **Capsule** 3-4 mm wide. May-
Aug.—Dry, open, sandy or rocky sterile ground; oak savanna, jack pine plains,
dried lake beds. *Sometimes misidentified as the less common **Lobelia kalmii**, with which
it shares narrow leaves and blue bilaterally symmetrical flowers, but L. kalmii is found
in wetlands and has milky juice.*

Nuttallanthus canadensis

PENSTEMON *Beardtongue*
Perennial herbs (ours), the erect stems rising from a rosette of petioled basal
leaves, the stem leaves sessile and often clasping, the upper progressively
reduced in size (the leaves of all our species are about alike and are of little
value in distinguishing species). Flowers white to blue-violet or red-violet,
in terminal clusters. Calyx herbaceous, deeply 5-parted, the lobes usually
unequal. Corolla tubular or trumpet-shaped, the tube much longer than the
lobes, bilabiate, the upper lip erect, 2-lobed, the lower equaling or longer
than the upper, 3-lobed. Fertile stamens 4; sterile stamen present, about as
long as the fertile stamens. Capsule ovoid or conic, many-seeded.

934. Gratiola neglecta   *935. Hippuris vulgaris*   *936. Linaria dalmatica*   *937. Linaria vulgaris*

ADDITIONAL SPECIES

Penstemon laevigatus Aiton (Long-sepal beardtongue), native to se USA; Stearns County, where possibly a garden escape.

1 Upper leaves clasping stem, nearly round; stems glabrous and glaucous . . . . *P. grandiflorus*
1 Leaves sessile or with petioles, lance-shaped to oblong lance-shaped; stems various 2
   2 Stems glabrous toward the base . . . . *P. digitalis*
   2 Stems finely hairy to villous toward the base 3
      3 Corolla violet . . . . *P. gracilis*
      3 Corolla white 4
         4 Stems and leaves usually appearing velvety; stems glandular-hairy near base . . . . *P. pallidus*
         4 Stems and leaves finely hairy near base, not appearing velvety . . . . *P. albidus*

Penstemon albidus Nutt.
WHITE PENSTEMON   MAP 940
                                                                                     native

Stems 1.5-5.5 dm tall, finely hairy below and glandular-pubescent near the inflorescence; plants with 1-5 stems arising from a short-branched crown. **Leaves** entire to serrate, nearly glabrous to finely hairy or scabrous; **basal leaves** oblong lance-shaped to obovate, 2-9 cm long and, 0.5-2 cm wide, petiolate; **stem leaves** slightly smaller, sessile and clasping. **Inflorescence** to 30 cm long, individual cymes 2- to 7-flowered, peduncles appressed or erect; calyx glandular-pubescent, 4-7 mm long; corolla 16-20 mm long, funnelform, weakly bilabiate, white to pale pink or violet, glandular-pubescent externally, glandular internally; staminode included, flattened only slightly at the tip, the distal 2-6 mm bearded with yellowish hairs to 1 mm long. **Capsule** 8-12 mm long. April-July.—Sandy to gravelly prairies.

Penstemon digitalis Nutt.
FOXGLOVE BEARDTONGUE   MAP 941
                                                                  introduced (naturalized)

Stems to 1.5 m tall, typically glabrous and shining, often suffused with purple or somewhat glaucous. **Stem leaves** narrowly oblong to narrowly triangular, strictly glabrous beneath, the larger commonly 10-15 cm long. **Panicle** 1-3 dm long, with erect or strongly ascending branches; calyx at anthesis 6-7 mm long; corolla white or very faintly suffused with violet, usually marked with purple lines within, 23-30 mm long, the tube abruptly dilated near the middle into a wide throat. May-July.—Moist open woods and prairies.

Penstemon gracilis Nutt.
SLENDER BEARDTONGUE   MAP 942
                                                                                     native

Stems 3-5 dm tall, finely puberulent with minute reflexed hairs, often in two longitudinal strips, varying to glabrous. **Stem leaves** lance-shaped, 5-10 cm long, glabrous or sparsely finely pubescent. **Inflorescence** slender, the short lateral branches erect; calyx 6-9 mm long at anthesis; corolla 15-20 mm long, pale violet.—Prairies and open woods. *The typical var. gracilis has leaves glabrous on both sides.*

Penstemon grandiflorus Nutt.
LARGE-FLOWER BEARDTONGUE   MAP 943
                                                                                     native

Stems to 1 m tall; plants completely glabrous throughout. **Lower leaves** obovate, 2-4 cm wide, the upper progressively shorter but scarcely narrower, becoming broadly ovate, subcordate and somewhat clasping at base; **bracteal leaves** similar but smaller. **Flowers** 2-4 in each axil, short-pediceled, producing a raceme-like

Penstemon grandiflorus

938. Littorella uniflora   *939. Nuttallanthus canadensis*   *940. Penstemon albidus*   *941. Penstemon digitalis*

inflorescence about 2 dm long; calyx at anthesis 9-11 mm long; corolla 3.5-5 cm long, pale purple externally, the tube widely dilated. **Capsule** 1.5-2 cm long. May-June.—Dry prairies and barrens.

Penstemon pallidus Small
PALE BEARDTONGUE

MAP 944
native

Stems 5-40 dm tall, always pubescent or canescent throughout with hairs about 0.1 mm long, the same pubescence also on both sides of the narrowly lance-shaped leaves. **Calyx** at anthesis 3.5-5 mm long; corolla 17-22 mm long, white, marked with fine purple lines within the throat. April-June.—Dry woods and fields.

Penstemon pallidus

PLANTAGO *Plantain*

Perennial or annual herbs. Leaves all from base of plant, simple. Flowers small, perfect or single-sexed, green, more or less stalkless in axils of small bracts, grouped into crowded spikes; sepals and petals 4. Fruit a capsule.

1 Plants distinctly caulescent; leaves opposite . . . . *P. arenaria*
1 Plants acaulescent and leaves in a loose basal rosette, or if with short stems, then the leaves alternate 2
  2 Lower bracts of spike much longer than calyces 3
    3 Plants dark green; leaves glabrous on upper surface. . . . . *P. aristata*
    3 Plants yellowish-green; leaves pubescent on upper surface . . . . *P. patagonica*
  2 Lower bracts not evidently longer than calyces. 4
    4 Sepals appearing to be 3,the 2 next to the bract united into 1 and having a double midvein . . *P. lanceolata*
    4 Sepals 4, the lobes nearly distinct. 5
      5 Bracts and/or sepals pubescent to long-villous. . . . . *P. patagonica*
      5 Bracts and sepals glabrous or nearly so, sometimes finely ciliate 6
        6 Leaves narrowly lance-shaped or linear, to 2 mm wide . . . . *P. elongata*
        6 Leaves lance-shaped to ovate, usually well over 1 cm wide 7
          7 Leaf blades much longer than wide; crown usually brown woolly at summit; bracts and sepals scarcely keeled . . . . *P. eriopoda*
          7 Leaf blades ca. 1/2 to 2/3 as wide as long; crown not brown woolly; bracts and sepa s with prominent raised keels 8
            8 Petioles green; bracts broadly ovate . . . . *P. major*
            8 Petioles red-tinged at base; bracts narrowly lance-shaped . . . . *P. rugelii*

Plantago arenaria Waldst. & Kit.
SAND PLANTAIN

MAP 945
introduced

Pubescent annual herb. **Stems** erect, 1-5 dm tall. **Leaves** opposite, linear, 3-8 cm long. Peduncles several, opposite from the upper axils. **Heads** 1-1.5 cm long; lowest bracts rotund at base, abruptly narrowed to a slender point 2-5 mm long; median and upper bracts obovate, rounded at the summit, broadly scarious-margined. July-Aug.—Native of Eurasia; a weed of waste places, roadsides, and railways.

Plantago aristata Michx.
LARGE-BRACT PLANTAIN

MAP 946
introduced (naturalized)

Annual herb. Scapes pubescent to villous, to 25 cm long. **Leaves** linear, to 18 cm long, more or less villous. **Spikes** (excluding the bracts) cylindric, commonly 3-6 cm long, occasionally to 10 cm; **bracts** linear, more or less hirsute, the scarious margin very narrow and strictly basal, the lowest to 2 cm long, the upper

942. *Penstemon gracilis*   943. *Penstemon grandiflorus*   944. *Penstemon pallidus*   945. *Plantago arenaria*

progressively reduced. **Sepals** narrowly obovate; petals about 2 mm long, round-ovate, spreading after anthesis. Seeds 2, brown, elliptic, about 2.5 mm long, very convex on the outer side, concave on the inner.—Dry sterile or sandy soil. *Depauperate forms much smaller, with filiform leaves and few-flowered spikes.*

Plantago elongata Pursh
PRAIRIE PLANTAIN

MAP 947
native

Annual taprooted herb. **Leaves** linear, 3-7 cm long and 0.5-2 mm wide, glabrous or appressed hairy. **Spikes** 2-8 cm long, rather loosely flowered and the axis exposed, on 1-several sparsely pubescent peduncles from base of plant, these commonly longer than the leaves; bracts ovate, 2-2.5 mm long, glabrous, margins hyaline; sepals 2-2.5 mm long, ovate, with wide scarious margins; corolla lobes 0.5-1 mm long, spreading or reflexed with age; stamens 2. **Capsules** ovoid, 1.5-3.5 mm long; seeds usually 4 or 5 per capsule, ca. 2 mm long, dark brown and finely pitted. April-June.—In Minn, known from several moist, quartzite bedrock locations in the extreme sw portion of the state; more common westward in the USA.

Plantago eriopoda Torr.
RED WOOLLY PLANTAIN

MAP 948
native

Plantago aristata

Perennial taprooted herb, caudex usually conspicuously brown-woolly at summit. **Leaves** somewhat fleshy, oblong lance-shaped or elliptic, sometimes remotely denticulate; 3- to 9-nerved, pubescent, 0.5-2 dm long; petioles 1-6 cm long. **Spikes** 5-15 cm long, on peduncles 1-3 dm long, glabrous or nearly so; flowers dense above, looser below with axis exposed; bracts 2-4 mm long, ovate, somewhat keeled below, with narrow scarious margins; sepals subequal to bracts, with thin scarious margins; corolla lobes ovate, 1-2 mm long, reflexed at maturity. **Capsules** ovoid, 3-4 mm long, circumscissile below the middle; seeds 2-4 per capsule, 2-2.5 mm long, dark purplish-black, with thin hyaline margin at one or both ends. June-Sept.—Low, often alkaline or salty prairies, marshes, roadsides, and waste places.

Plantago lanceolata L.
ENGLISH PLANTAIN

MAP 949
introduced (naturalized)

Perennial herb. **Scapes** to 6 dm tall, strigose above. **Leaves** narrowly lance-shaped to oblong lance-shaped, to 3 dm long, including the petiole, gradually tapering to both ends. **Spikes** very dense, at maturity 1-10 cm long; **bracts** broadly ovate, with narrow herbaceous center and broad scarious margins, often caudate-tipped. Outer two sepals united into one, broadly obovate, truncate, with two midveins; inner sepals ovate; corolla lobes 2-3 mm long. **Capsule** ellipsoid, 3-4 mm long, circumscissile near the base; seeds 2, black, 2-3 mm long, deeply concave on the inner face. Variable.—Native of the Old World; a common weed of lawns, road-sides, and waste places.

Plantago lanceolata

Plantago major L.
COMMON PLANTAIN

MAP 950
introduced (naturalized)

Perennial herb, closely resembling *P. rugelii* in form and often confused with it. Petioles commonly green and pubescent at base. **Flowers** sessile; **bracts** shorter than the sepals, broadly ovate or elliptic, with prominent scarious margin and rounded elevated keel; **sepals** ovate, obtuse, the rounded keel about as wide as the scarious margins. **Capsule** ellipsoid, 2-4 mm long, circumscissile near the

Plantago major

middle; seeds several, commonly 10 or more, about 1 mm long.—Native of Eurasia; naturalized in lawns, roadsides, and waste places.

Plantago patagonica Jacq.
MAP 951
WOOLLY PLANTAIN
native

Annual herb, gray-villous throughout. **Leaves** linear, to 15 cm long, 3-8 mm wide. **Scapes** 5-15 or rarely 20 cm long. **Spikes** very dense cylindric, obtuse, 3-10 cm long, 4-6 mm wide; bracts linear, even the lowest scarcely exceeding the flowers; sepals, petals, and seeds essentially as in *P. aristata*.—Dry prairies.

Plantago rugelii Dcne.
MAP 952
AMERICAN PLANTAIN
native

Perennial herb. **Leaves** broadly elliptic to oval, 5-20 cm long, many-nerved, narrowed at base; petiole margined, at base usually glabrous and tinged with purple. **Spikes** to 3 dm long, about 5 mm wide, comparatively loose, the axis frequently exposed; pedicels about 0.5 mm long. Bracts lance-shaped, 1/2 to 3/4 as long as the calyx; **sepals** ovate or oblong, the sharp keel much wider than the scarious margin; corolla lobes less than 1 mm long, reflexed after anthesis. **Capsule** narrowly ovoid, 4-6 mm long, dehiscent well below the middle; seeds 4-10, black, angular, about 2 mm long.—Lawns, gardens, roadsides, waste places.

Plantago patagonica

VERONICA *Speedwell*

Annual or perennial herbs. Leaves opposite, or becoming alternate in the head. Flowers single or in racemes from leaf axils or at ends of stems; sepals deeply 4-parted, enlarging after flowering; corolla blue or white, 4-lobed, somewhat 2-lipped, the tube shorter than the lobes; stamens 2. Fruit a flattened capsule, lobed or notched at tip; styles usually persistent on fruit.

ADDITIONAL SPECIES
Veronica verna L. (Spring speedwell), introduced; reported from Cook and Pine counties; see key.

1   Flowers in racemes from leaf axils, or leaves more than 4 cm long, or both; plants perennial 2
   2   Stems glabrous or nearly so; leaves toothed or entire 3
      3   Leaves with short petioles . . . . *V. americana*
      3   Leaves sessile 4
         4   Upper leaves lance-shaped, with wide, clasping bases; rachis of raceme stout and straight; capsules swollen . . . . *V. anagallis-aquatica*
         4   Leaves mostly linear, narrowed to a sessile base; rachis of raceme slender and zigzagged; capsules strongly flattened . . . . *V. scutellata*
   2   At least the upper stem pubescent; leaves toothed 5
      5   Flowers on long pedicels, the pedicels longer than the bracts . . . . *V. austriaca*
      5   Flowers sessile or on short pedicels shorter than the bracts 6
         6   Leaves more than 5 cm long, widest near base, on petioles 1 cm or more long; flowers in dense terminal spikes; styles persistent on capsule . . . . *V. longifolia*
         6   Leaves less than 5 cm long, widest near middle, sessile or nearly so; spikes from leaf axils, loosely flowered; styles deciduous . . . . *V. officinalis*
1   Flowers single in axils of leafy bracts, or in terminal spikes; leaves less than 3 cm long; plants annual or perennial 7
   7   Flowers and capsules on pedicels more than 4 mm long . . . . *V. persica*
   7   Flowers and capsules sessile or on short pedicels to 4 mm long 8
      8   Middle stem leaves pinnately divided . . . . *V. verna**
      8   Leaves entire or toothed, not divided 9

950. *Plantago major*   951. *Plantago patagonica*   952. *Plantago rugelii*   953. *Veronica americana*

9 Plants matted perennial herbs; stems finely hairy; leaves glabrous or nearly so (except when young) .
. . . . **V. serpyllifolia**

9 Plants erect annuals; stems and leaves glabrous or pubescent with mostly spreading hairs 10

   10 Flowers blue; the capsules only shallowly notched at tip; stems fleshy; plants glabrous **V. peregrina**

   10 Flowers white; the capsules deeply notched at tip; stems not fleshy; plants pubescent . **V. arvensis**

Veronica americana Schwein.

AMERICAN-BROOKLIME

MAP 953
native

Perennial, spreading by rhizomes; plants glabrous and succulent. **Stems** erect to creeping, 1-6 dm long. **Leaves** opposite, ovate to lance-shaped (or lower leaves oval), 2-8 cm long and 0.5-3 cm wide, **upper leaves** tapered to a tip, **lower leaves** often rounded; margins with forward-pointing teeth; petioles short. **Flowers** in stalked racemes from leaf axils; the racemes with 10-25 flowers and to 15 cm long; corolla 4-lobed, blue (sometimes white), often with purple stripes. **Fruit** a more or less round, compressed capsule, 3-4 mm long, slightly notched at tip, the styles persistent, 2-4 mm long. July-Sept.—Streambanks and wet shores, hummocks in swamps, springs.

Veronica anagallis-aquatica L.

BLUE WATER SPEEDWELL
Veronica catenata Pennell

MAP 954
native

Biennial or short-lived perennial, spreading by stolons or leafy shoots produced in fall; plants more or less glabrous. **Stems** erect to spreading, 1-6 dm long, often rooting at lower nodes. **Leaves** opposite, lance-shaped to ovate, 2-10 cm long and 0.5-5 cm wide, tapered to a blunt or rounded tip; margins entire or with fine, forward-pointing teeth; petioles absent, the leaves often clasping. **Flowers** in many-flowered racemes from leaf axils, the racemes 5-12 cm long; corolla 4-lobed, blue or striped with purple, about 5 mm wide. **Fruit** a round, compressed capsule, 2-4 mm long, notched at tip, the styles persistent, 1-2 mm long. June-Sept.—Wet, sandy or muddy streambanks and ditches; often in shallow water.

Veronica americana

Veronica arvensis L.

CORN SPEEDWELL

MAP 955
introduced (naturalized)

Annual, villous throughout. **Stems** erect or nearly so, simple or branched, 1-2 dm tall. **Foliage leaves** ovate, 6-12 mm long, obtuse, with 2-4 blunt teeth on each side, palmately veined, the lower short-petioled, the upper sessile. **Inflorescence** often constituting 2/3 of the plant, the bracteal leaves progressively reduced in length and width and mostly entire. Pedicels to 1.5 mm long; calyx lobes oblong, the lower pair 4-5 mm long, the upper pair 3/4 as long; corolla blue, about 2 mm wide. **Capsule** 3-4 mm wide, nearly as long, deeply notched; style extending about as far as the summit of the capsule lobes. April-June.—Native of Eurasia; established as an inconspicuous weed in gardens, lawns, and fields, and occasionally in open woods.

Veronica anagallis-aquatica

Veronica austriaca L.

BROAD-LEAF SPEEDWELL
Veronica teucrium L.

(NO MAP)
introduced

Perennial. **Stems** erect, 3-6 dm tall, finely pubescent. **Leaves** sessile or nearly so, lance-shaped to ovate, 2-4 cm long, obtuse, serrate, acute to rounded at base. **Racemes** commonly 2-4 from the upper axils, 5-10 cm long, on peduncles of about the same length, 30-60-flowered, compact at anthesis, later becoming loose;

954. Veronica anagallis-aquatica   *955. Veronica arvensis*   *956. Veronica longifolia*   *957. Veronica officinalis*

bracts lance-shaped, shorter than the pedicels; lower calyx lobes 2.5-4 mm long, the upper usually about 2/3 as long; corolla blue, about 12 mm wide; style (after corolla has fallen) 6-8 mm long. June-July.—Native of Eurasia; occasionally escaped from cultivation in waste places, roadsides and meadows; Lake County.

Veronica longifolia L.
LONG-LEAF SPEEDWELL
MAP 956
introduced

Perennial. **Stems** erect, to 1 m tall. **Leaves** opposite or in whorls of 3, lance-shaped, 4-10 cm long, very sharply serrate; short-petioled. **Racemes** 1 or few, erect, spike-like, the axis pubescent but not glandular; corolla blue, pubescent in the throat, its lobes 4-5 mm long. **Capsule** little flattened, 3 mm long, smooth or puberulent, about half as long as the persistent style. June-Aug.—Native of Europe; introduced in fields, roadsides, and waste places.

Veronica officinalis L.
COMMON SPEEDWELL
MAP 957
introduced

Perennial, pubescent throughout. **Stems** prostrate or reclining, the flowering branches erect or ascending, 2-3 dm long. **Leaves** elliptic, 2.5-5 cm long, obtuse or rounded, uniformly serrate except toward the base, narrowed below to a short petiole. **Racemes** few, solitary or opposite, spike-like, commonly 3-6 cm long, often interrupted below, on a peduncle of about their own length; bracts linear lance-shaped, about equaling the flowers; calyx lobes oblong, 2-3 mm long; corolla pale violet with darker lines, 5-7 mm wide. **Capsule** reverse-triangular, glandular-puberulent, 4.5-5 mm wide, truncate or with a broad and very shallow notch; style at maturity to 3 mm long. May-July.—Dry fields and upland woods. *At anthesis the main axis is often developed only slightly beyond the racemes, so that the inflorescence may appear terminal.*

Veronica officinalis

Veronica peregrina L.
PURSLANE SPEEDWELL
MAP 958
native

Small annual. **Stems** upright, 0.5-3 dm long, unbranched or with spreading branches, usually glandular-hairy. **Lower leaves** opposite, becoming alternate and smaller in the head, oval to linear, 5-25 mm long and 1-5 mm wide, rounded at tip; margins of lower leaves sparsely toothed, **upper leaves** entire; petioles short or absent. **Flowers** small, on short stalks from upper leaf axils; corolla 4-lobed, more or less white, about 2 mm wide. **Fruit** an oblong heart-shaped capsule, 2-4 mm long, notched at tip, the styles not persistent. May-July.—Mud flats, shores, ditches, temporary ponds, swales; also weedy in cultivated fields, lawns and moist disturbed areas.

Veronica peregrina

Veronica persica Poir.
BIRDSEYE SPEEDWELL
MAP 959
introduced (naturalized)

Annual. **Stems** prostrate or ascending, much branched, 1-3 dm long. **Leaves** broadly ovate, 8-15 or rarely 25 mm long, obtuse, bearing 3-5 sharp and usually coarse teeth on each side, broadly obtuse to truncate at base; petioles 1-5 mm long. Pedicels solitary in the axils, in fruit more or less recurved and to 2 cm long; calyx lobes ovate lance-shaped, 4-5 mm long at anthesis, to 8 mm long in fruit, conspicuously 3-nerved; corolla blue with deeper blue lines and pale orifice, 8-11 mm wide. **Capsule** 6.5-10 mm wide, reticulately veined, with a broad triangular notch; style surpassing the capsule. April-Aug.—Native of sw Asia; introduced in gardens, lawns, roadsides, and waste places.

958. *Veronica peregrina*   959. *Veronica persica*   960. *Veronica scutellata*   961. *Veronica serpyllifolia*

Veronica scutellata L.
GRASS-LEAF SPEEDWELL

MAP 960
native

Perennial, spreading by rhizomes or leafy shoots produced in fall; plants smooth (or sometimes with sparse hairs). **Stems** slender, erect to reclining, 1-4 dm long, often rooting at lower nodes. **Leaves** opposite, linear to narrowly lance-shaped, 3-8 cm long and 2-10 mm wide, tapered to a sharp tip; margins entire or with small, irregularly spaced teeth; petioles absent. **Flowers** in racemes from leaf axils, the racemes with 5-20 flowers, as long or longer than the leaves; corolla 4-lobed, blue, 6-10 mm wide. **Fruit** a strongly flattened capsule, 3-4 mm long, notched at tip, the style persistent, 3-5 mm long. June-Sept.—Marshes, pond margins, hardwood swamps, thickets, springs, streambanks, wet depressions.   *Veronica scutellata*

Veronica serpyllifolia L.
THYME-LEAF SPEEDWELL

MAP 961
introduced

Perennial. **Stems** creeping and forming mats, the flowering ones upwardly curved and erect, 1-2 dm tall. **Leaves** ovate, elliptic, or nearly rotund, mostly 1-1.5 cm, occasionally 2 cm long, obtuse, entire or obscurely crenate, the lower often somewhat narrowed to a short petiole, the upper sessile. **Racemes** at first short and compact, soon elongating, in fruit to 10 cm long; bracteal leaves elliptic, to 3 cm long; pedicels 2-4 mm long; calyx lobes obtuse. **Capsule** notched at the apex for about 1/4 of its length, 3-5 mm wide, distinctly wider than long, but much longer than the persistent style. Variable. May-July.—Native of Europe, established in fields, meadows, and lawns, extending into moist open woods where it often appears indigenous.

VERONICASTRUM *Culver's-Root*

Veronicastrum virginicum (L.) Farw.
CULVER'S-ROOT

MAP 962
native

Erect perennial herb. **Stems** 1-2 m tall, usually with several upright branches. **Leaves** in whorls of 3-6, lance-shaped; margins with fine, forward-pointing teeth; petioles to 1 cm long. **Flowers** in erect, spike-like racemes to 15 cm long, the flowers crowded and spreading; corolla white, nearly regular, 4-5 parted, the lobes shorter than the tube; stamens 2, long-exserted from the corolla mouth. **Fruit** a capsule, 4-5 mm long. June-Aug.—Moist to wet prairie, fens and streambanks; also in drier deciduous woods and sandy grasslands.

Veronicastrum virginicum

Polemoniaceae PHLOX FAMILY

Perennial herbs (ours). Leaves opposite (*Phlox*) or pinnately divided (*Polemonium*). Flowers perfect (with both staminate and pistillate parts), single or in clusters at ends of stems and from leaf axils; sepals and petals 5-parted and joined for part of length. Fruit a 3-chambered capsule, with usually 1 seed per chamber.

1 Leaves pinnately divided into leaflets . . . . *Polemonium*
1 Leaves undivided and entire 2
   2 Leaves opposite or mostly so . . . . *Phlox*
   2 Leaves alternate . . . . *Collomia linearis*

COLLOMIA *Mountain-Trumpet*

Collomia linearis Nutt.
NARROW-LEAF MOUNTAIN-TRUMPET

MAP 963
native

Annual herb. **Stems** simple or branched above, 1-4 dm tall, minutely pubescent below, increasingly so above. **Leaves** alternate, linear to narrowly lance-shaped, entire or pinnatifid, 2-6 cm long, very finely puberulent. **Flowers** in sessile cymes; several in the axils of the crowded upper leaves, forming a dense headlike cluster; calyx at anthesis about 6 mm long, at maturity about 10 mm long; corolla narrowly trumpet-shaped, blue-purple to white, 8-12 mm long, its limb 3-4 mm wide;

*Collomia
linearis*

stamens unequal lengths in the corolla tube and not protruding from it. **Capsule** obovoid, 3-lobed, surrounded by the persistent calyx; seeds 2.5-3 mm long, mucilaginous when wet. May-Aug.—Dry sandy or gravelly grasslands, shores, clearings and disturbed places.

PHLOX *Phlox*

Erect perennial herbs. Leaves opposite, margins entire. Flowers pink, purple or rarely white, in stalked clusters at ends of stems and from upper leaf axils; sepals joined and tubelike; corolla 5-lobed, tubelike but flared outward at tip; stamens 5. Fruit a 3-chambered capsule.

1 Calyx glabrous and stem (at least below the uppermost internodes) glabrous or nearly so. 2
    2 Leaves with evident anastomosing lateral veins and with hispidulous or ciliate margins; escapes from cultivation
    . . . . *P. paniculata*
    2 Leaves with lateral veins obscure or not at all visible and with smooth glabrous margins; native wetland species
    . . . . *P. maculata*
1 Calyx and stem finely hairy to pilose 3
    3 Stems somewhat woody, matted and trailing on ground . . . . *P. subulata*
    3 Stems herbaceous, upright 4
        4 Leaves lance-shaped to ovate, less than 5 times longer than wide . . . . *P. divaricata*
        4 Leaves linear to linear lance-shaped, more than 5 times longer than wide . . . . *P. pilosa*

Phlox divaricata L.
FOREST PHLOX   MAP 964
                                 native

Perennial herb. **Stems** erect or decumbent at base, 3-5 dm tall, emitting decumbent basal stolons. **Leaves** ovate lance-shaped to oblong, 3-5 cm long at anthesis, broadest usually below the middle. **Inflorescence** a loosely branched, glandular-pubescent cyrne, the branches on distinct peduncles, the pedicels often 5-10 mm long; corolla usually pale blue-purple, varying to red-purple or white, 2-3 cm wide, the glabrous tube 1-2 cm long. April-June.—Rich moist woods.

Phlox maculata L.
WILD SWEET WILLIAM   MAP 965
                                   native

Perennial herb. **Stems** erect, 3-8 dm long, simple or branched above, smooth or finely hairy, usually red-spotted. **Leaves** opposite, smooth, ± firm, lance-shaped, 5-12 cm long and 0.5-1.5 cm wide, long-tapered to a sharp tip; margins entire; petioles absent. **Flowers** 1-2 cm wide, in stalked clusters (cymes) at ends of stems and from several to many upper leaf axils, these short-stalked, forming a long, narrow head 10-20 cm long, the head finely hairy; sepals smooth, joined to form a sharp-tipped tube 6-8 mm long; petals pink or purple, rounded at tip; style elongated. **Fruit** a 3-chambered capsule. July-Sept.—Fens, sedge meadows, springs.

Phlox divaricata

Phlox paniculata L.
FALL PHLOX   MAP 966
                 introduced (naturalized)

Perennial herb. **Stems** erect, to 2 m tall. **Leaves** narrowly oblong or lance-shaped, 8-15 cm long, minutely ciliate, narrowed to an acute or obtuse base, usually glabrous above, the conspicuous lateral veins confluent to form a submarginal connecting vein. **Inflorescence** often large, of several panicled cymes, densely but minutely pubescent; calyx tube minutely puberulent or more commonly glabrous; calyx lobes glabrous; corolla red to purple, varying to white, 1.5-2 cm wide, its tube usually sparsely pubescent; one or more anthers at least partly

962. *Veronicastrum virginicum*

963. *Collomia linearis*

964. *Phlox divaricata*

965. *Phlox maculata*

exsert from the corolla tube. July-Sept.—Rich moist soil; cultivated in numerous horticultural varieties and escaped into roadsides and waste places.

Phlox pilosa L.

MAP 967
PRAIRIE PHLOX   *native*
Perennial herb. **Stems** erect, 3-6 dm tall, the sterile basal shoots also erect or ascending. **Leaves** linear to ovate, 3-8 cm long, narrowed to a sharp, stiff tip. **Inflorescence** a loosely branched cyme, the branches conspicuously stalked, the flowers all or mostly on distinct pedicels; corolla commonly pale red to purple, 1.5-2 cm wide, the tube usually sparsely to conspicuously pubescent (rarely glabrous). April-June.—Upland woods and prairies. *A highly variable species.*

Phlox subulata L.

MAP 968
MOSS-PINK   *introduced*
Perennial by a prostrate suffruticose **stem**, freely branched and producing numerous flowering branches 5-20 cm long. **Leaves** numerous and crowded, subulate, 5-20 mm long, usually ciliate, often with fascicles of smaller leaves in their axils. **Cymes** few-flowered; corolla rose-purple to pink or white, 12-20 mm wide, its lobes notched for 1/8 to 1/4 of their length. April-May.—Sandy or gravelly soil and rock-ledges; frequently cultivated and sometimes escaped.

Phlox pilosa

POLEMONIUM *Jacob's Ladder*

Perennial herbs. Leaves alternate, pinnately compound. Flowers blue, in terminal, panicle-like or thyrsoid clusters. Calyx herbaceous, campanulate, 5-lobed. Corolla funnelform to broadly campanulate, 5-lobed. Stamens inserted at the tip of the very short corolla tube, the filaments slender, all declined toward one side of the corolla. Capsule ovoid, 3-valved, enclosed by the persistent expanded calyx.

1   Plants flowering in spring; inflorescence loosely flowered . . . . *P. reptans*
1   Plants flowering in summer; inflorescence crowded . . . . *P. occidentale*

Polemonium occidentale Greene

MAP 969
WESTERN JACOB'S LADDER   ✔*endangered | native*
Perennial herb. **Stems** erect, to 10 dm long, single from upturned ends of short, unbranched rhizomes. **Leaves** pinnately divided with up to 27 leaflets, the leaflets 1-4 cm long, smaller upward; margins entire; petioles short or absent. **Flowers** blue, 10-15 mm wide, crowded in a long panicle composed of smaller clusters of flowers; sepals joined to form a tube; petal lobes longer than calyx tube; stamens shorter or equal to corolla; style longer than stamens. **Fruit** a 3-chambered capsule. July.—Rare in conifer swamps of black spruce, tamarack and northern white cedar. *Disjunct in Minnesota from main range of western North America.*

Polemonium reptans L.

MAP 970
SPREADING JACOB'S LADDER   *native*

Polemonium occidentale

Perennial herb. **Stems** slender, 2-4 dm long, erect, ascending, or eventually diffuse, branched above. **Basal leaves** long-petioled; **stem leaves** short-petioled or the upper sessile; leaflets lance-shaped to oblong or elliptic, usually 2-4 cm, occasionally to 7 cm long. **Panicles** few-flowered, loose and open, the pedicels at anthesis nearly as long to longer than the calyx; calyx 5-6 mm long, the broadly triangular lobes nearly as long as the tube; corolla 10-15 mm long, lobed about to the middle; stamens shorter than the corolla. May.—Rich moist woods.

966. *Phlox paniculata*   967. *Phlox pilosa*   968. *Phlox subulata*   969. *Polemonium occidentale*

Polygalaceae MILKWORT FAMILY

POLYGALA *Milkwort*

Annual, biennial, or perennial herbs. Leaves alternate or verticillate. Flowers perfect, in racemes. Sepals 5, the three outer small, the two inner (termed wings) much larger and often colored like the petals. Petals 3, all more or less united with each other and with the stamen-tube, the two upper ones similar, the lower one keel-shaped or boat-shaped with a fringe-like crest (in our species). Stamens 8 (or 6). Ovary 2-celled. Fruit a small capsule.

1   Flowers large, 13 mm long or more; stamens 6; leaves few, mostly near top of stem . . . . *P. paucifolia*
1   Flowers smaller, mostly less than 10 mm long; stamens 8; leaves distributed along stem or mostly near base . . 2
  2   Plants annual, the stems solitary from a small taproot 3
    3   Flowers in slender racemes, tapering to the tip . . . . *P. verticillata*
    3   Flowers in head-like or rounded racemes 4
      4   Leaves alternate . . . . *P. sanguinea*
      4   Leaves whorled . . . . *P. cruciata*
  2   Plants biennial or perennial 5
    5   Flowers white, in densely flowered spike-like racemes . . . . *P. senega*
    5   Flowers rose-purple to white, in loose racemes . . . . *P. polygama*

Polygala cruciata L.
DRUM-HEADS

MAP 971
🐛*endangered | native*

Annual. **Stems** erect, 4-angled, 1-4 dm long, usually branched above. **Leaves** mostly in whorls of 4, linear or oblong lance-shaped, 1-4 cm long and 1-5 mm wide, rounded and often with a short, sharp point at tip; margins entire; petioles short or absent. **Flowers** more or less stalkless in cylindric racemes, 1-5 cm long and 1-1.5 cm wide; pale purple or green purple; sepals 5, the 2 lateral sepals (wings) petal-like, 4-6 mm long and 3-4 mm wide at base; petals 3, joined into a tube; stamens 8 (sometimes 6). **Fruit** a 2-chambered capsule, with a single, more or less hairy seed in each chamber. July-Sept.—Rare in sandy or mucky lakeshores, wet areas between dunes.

Polygala cruciata

Polygala paucifolia Willd.
FRINGED POLYGALA

MAP 972
native

Triclisperma paucifolia (Willd.) Nieuwl.

Perennial from a slender rhizome. **Stems** 8-15 cm tall, bearing below several scattered scale-like leaves 2-8 mm long and near the summit 3-6 elliptic to oval leaves 1.5-4 cm long. **Flowers** 1-4, rose-purple varying to white, the obovate wings about 15 mm long; corolla about equaling the wings; stamens 6. **Capsule** suborbicular, about 6 mm long and wide, notched at the summit. May-June.—Moist rich woods. *Leaves usually pubescent only on the midrib and margin.*

Polygala polygama Walt.
RACEMED MILKWORT

MAP 973
native

Biennial. **Stems** several from base, decumbent, glabrous, 1-2.5 dm tall, simple at anthesis, later sparingly branched. **Lowest leaves** spatulate to obovate, about 1 cm long; **stem leaves** oblong lance-shaped, 1-3 cm long, 2-7 mm wide, obtuse to subacute. **Raceme** loose and open, 2-10 cm long. **Flowers** rose-purple, varying to white; wings obovate, 4-6 mm long, exceeding the corolla.—Dry, usually sandy soil.

Polygala paucifolia

970. *Polemonium reptans*   971. *Polygala cruciata*   972. *Polygala paucifolia*   973. *Polygala polygama*

Polygala sanguinea L.

MAP 974
PURPLE MILKWORT _native_

Annual. **Stems** 1-4 dm tall, erect, simple or branched above. **Leaves** linear or narrowly elliptic, 1-4 cm long, 1-5 mm wide. **Racemes** very dense, headlike, rounded or short-cylindric, about 1 cm thick, the floriferous portion 1-2 cm long, the whole axis to 4 cm long, sessile or short-peduncled. **Flowers** rose-purple, white, or greenish; wings oval, 3-5 mm long, or longer in fruit, blunt, with conspicuous midvein; corolla about half as long as the wings; seed pear-shaped, the two linear lobes of the aril extending beyond the middle. July-Sept.—Fields, meadows, and open woods.

Polygala senega L.

MAP 975
SENECA-SNAKEROOT _native_

Perennial. **Stems** commonly several from one base, 1-5 dm tall, usually unbranched, minutely puberulent. **Leaves** alternate, the lowest reduced or scale-like; **stem leaves** linear lance-shaped or wider. **Racemes** dense, 1.5-4 cm long, 6-8 mm thick, on a peduncle 1-3 cm long. **Flowers** white; wings broadly elliptic, 3-3.5 mm long, exceeding the corolla. **Capsule** suborbicular; seeds pubescent, 2-3 mm long; aril nearly or quite as long. May-June.—Dry or moist woods and prairies.

Polygala verticillata L.

MAP 976
WHORLED MILKWORT _native_

Annual. **Stems** erect, divergently branched, 1-4 dm tall. **Leaves** linear to linear-oblong, 1-2 (rarely 3) cm long, 1-3 mm wide, at least the lower and sometimes all in whorls of 2-5. Lower branches of the inflorescence usually opposite or whorled; peduncle elongate. **Racemes** not interrupted, conic or cylindric-conic, appearing truncate at base, the whole axis to 4 cm long. **Flowers** white, greenish, or occasionally pinkish, the lower dropping promptly at maturity of the fruit; wing 1/2 to 2/3 as long as the capsule. July-Oct.—Moist sandy soil, grasslands and woods.

Polygala sanguinea

Polygonaceae BUCKWHEAT FAMILY

Annual or perennial herbs, plants sometimes vining. Leaves alternate, simple, sometimes wavy-margined, otherwise entire; the nodes usually enlarged. Stipules joined to form a membranous or papery sheath (ocrea) around stem at each node. Flowers in spike-like racemes or small clusters from leaf axils (e.g., _Persicaria_, _Polygonum_), or in crowded panicles at ends of stems (_Rumex_). Flowers small, perfect (with both staminate and pistillate parts), regular, petals absent. In _Rumex_ the sepals herbaceous, green to brown, in inner and outer groups, each group with 3 sepals, the 3 inner enlarging after flowering, becoming broadly winged, persisting to enclose the achene; stamens 4-8; ovary 1-chambered, styles 2-3; in other genera of family, sepals more or less petal-like, white to pink or yellow, mostly 5 (sometimes 4). Fruit a 3-angled or lens-shaped achene. _Polygonaceae recognized by presence of a stipular sheath (ocrea), which surrounds the stem above the attachment of each leaf. The similar reduced structure in the inflorescence is called an ocreola._

ADDITIONAL SPECIES

• _Fagopyrum esculentum_ Moench (Garden buckwheat); native of China, occasional escape from cultivation or where seed spilled, but not persisting in our flora.

• _Rheum rhabarbarum_ L. (Garden rhubarb), native of Asia; commonly cultivated; occasionally escaping.

1 Tepals 6, greenish or reddish, scarcely petaloid, the 3 inner (but not the outer) ones enlarging in fruit and concealing the achene; stigmas a feathery tuft; plants in some species dioecious or polygamous and hence some flowers entirely staminate . . . . **_Rumex_**

1 Tepals 4-5, white to red and ± petaloid at least along the margins, uniform in size or the outer ones larger; stigmas usually not feathery and plants mostly with bisexual flowers 2

 2 Pedicels with a swollen joint near the middle (but not far above the sheathing ocreolae), solitary in each ocreola, the inflorescence thus composed of slender racemes, appearing jointed because of the overlapping ocreolae; leaves not over 1 (-1.1) mm wide; delicate-looking annual . . . . **_Polygonella_**

 2 Pedicels usually jointed near the summit (if at all), often crowded, the inflorescence various; leaves at least (1.5-) 2 mm wide; annual or perennial, not delicate 3

3   Stem and petioles with retrorse prickles; leaves hastate or sagittate (with acute basal lobes) . . . *Persicaria*
3   Stem and petioles without prickles; leaves various 4
    4   Outer tepals winged or keeled in fruit, or plant somewhat twining or vine-like, or both; leaves ovate-cordate to broadly sagittate . . . . *Fallopia*
    4   Outer tepals not winged or keeled; plant not twining; leaves various 5
        5   Flowers 1-4 at a node, sessile or pediceled in the axils of foliage leaves or bracts; leaf blades jointed at the base, less than 2 (-2.4) cm broad; summit of ocrea silvery white, becoming lacerate-shredded; annuals . . . . *Polygonum*
        5   Flowers (or bulblets in *Bistorta vivipara*) numerous in peduncled terminal or axillary spikes, racemes, or panicles, often densely crowded; leaves not jointed at base of blade, in some species over 2.5 cm broad; summit of ocrea tinged with brown, shattering at maturity but not shredding; annuals or perennials 6
           6   Leaves mostly basal, rapidly reduced in size up the stem and not more than 3 stem leaves present; many flowers in the single spike converted to bulblets; stems simple . . . . *Bistorta vivipara*
           6   Leaves cauline, more than 3, basal leaves absent; flowers in the often several to many spikes not converted to bulblets; stems usually branched, rarely simple in depauperate individuals . . . . . .
           . . . . *Persicaria*

BISTORTA *Bistort*

Bistorta vivipara (L.) Delarbre
ALPINE BISTORT
  Polygonum viviparum L.

MAP 977
🌓 *threatened | native*

Glabrous perennial herb from knotty, elongate rhizome; **stems** to 3.5 dm tall, simple, terminating in a spike-like raceme; **basal leaves** with long slender petioles and oblong blades; **stem leaves** linear lanceolate, pale green beneath, with prominent midvein, margins revolute; ocreae buff sparsely puberulent; **Racemes** bulbiliferous except for 1-3 staminate flowers toward the tip; bulbils maroon, pointed, rounded at base, 3-5 mm long; **sepals** pinkish, stamens 8 with reddish anthers; perfect flowers and fruits not present. Leaves of young plants ovate with very slender petioles. June-July.—Wet cobble beaches, and to a lesser extent in bedrock crevices, along the rocky shore of Lake Superior; often growing in the shade of shrubs such as alder (*Alnus*).

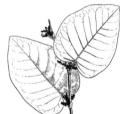

Bistorta vivipara

FALLOPIA *Black-Bindweed*

Annual or perennial, twining or stout and erect and forming large colonies. *In the past, our species typically included in genus Polygonum.*

ADDITIONAL SPECIES
Fallopia dumetorum (L.) Holub (Climbing false buckwheat); native to Eurasia; to be expected on disturbed sites along forest edges; reported from St. Louis County; often confused with *F. scandens.*

Fallopia sachalinensis (F. Schmidt) Ronse Decr. (Giant knotweed); native to e Asia; closely resembling *F. japonica* in habit, flower, and fruit; stems sometimes more than 4 m tall; leaf blades ovate, cordate at base, the basal lobes broadly rounded; unverified report from St. Louis County; see key.

Fallopia sachalinensis

1   Stems twining and slender 2
  2   Base of sheathing stipules with stiff, downward-pointing hairs . . . . *F. cilinodis*

974. Polygala sanguinea   *975. Polygala senega*   *976. Polygala verticillata*   *977. Bistorta vivipara*

2 Base of stipules not with stiff, downward-pointing hairs 3
  3 Plants annual; styles united; achenes dull and finely roughened . . . . *F. convolvulus*
  3 Plants perennial; styles divergent; achenes shiny and smooth . . . . *F. scandens*
1 Stems erect and stout, 1-3 m tall 4
  4 Leaf blades heart-shaped at base with rounded basal lobes, the blades often 20 cm or more long from leaf tip
    to lobe tip; flowers perfect . . . . *F. sachalinense**
  4 Leaf blades cut nearly straight across at base, the blades less than 20 cm long; flowers functionally either
    staminate or pistillate . . . . *F. japonica*

Fallopia cilinodis (Michx.) Holub

FRINGED BLACK BINDWEED
Polygonum cilinode Michx.

MAP 978
native

Perennial, pubescent, varying to nearly glabrous. **Stems** twining, trailing, or occasionally erect, to 2 m long, nearly terete. **Leaves** ovate, deeply cordate at base; ocreae very oblique, reflexed-bristly at base. **Racemes** long-peduncled, mostly branched, 4-10 cm long, the small flower clusters remote; perianth white, 1.5-2 mm long; styles separate, divergent. **Achenes** very glossy, black, scarcely surpassed by the calyx. July-Aug.—Dry woods and thickets. *Plants in open sun are often erect, with stouter red stems, the red color extending into the leaf veins.*

Fallopia convolvulus (L.) Á. Löve

BLACK BINDWEED
Polygonum convolvulus L.

MAP 979
introduced (naturalized)

Annual. **Stems** trailing or twining, to 1 m long, angled, minutely scabrous in lines, as are also the petioles and often the leaf veins. **Leaves** hastate to triangular-cordate, broadly V-shaped to cordate at base; ocreae smooth. **Racemes** interrupted, 2-6 cm long, naked or with a few small leaves at base; **flowers** in clusters of 3-6; pedicels 1-2 mm long, jointed near the summit; perianth 1.5-2 mm long, green without, white within; outer 3 sepals often narrowly winged on the midrib; styles united. **Achenes** dull black, 3-4 mm long, not exceeded by the calyx. June-Sept.—Native of Europe; roadsides, railway tracks, and waste ground.

Fallopia convolvulus

Fallopia japonica (Houtt.) Ronse Decr.

JAPANESE KNOTWEED
Polygonum cuspidatum Sieb. & Zucc.

MAP 980
introduced (invasive)

Perennial and spreading by long rhizomes. **Stems** stout, 1-3 m tall. **Leaves** broadly ovate, 8-15 cm long, 5-12 cm wide, abruptly acuminate, broadly truncate at base, the basal angles prominent. **Racemes** numerous from most of the upper axils, often branched, forming a series of panicles 8-15 cm long; perianth white or greenish white; outer sepals narrowly winged along the midrib; styles 3; stigmas minute. **Achenes** triangular, about 3 mm long, enclosed by the enlarged calyx. Aug-Sept.—Native of Japan; sometimes planted (not a good idea!) but later escaping to form large colonies.

Fallopia japonica

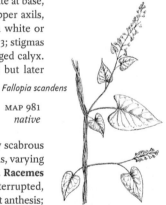

Fallopia scandens

Fallopia scandens (L.) Holub

FALSE BUCKWHEAT
Polygonum scandens L.

MAP 981
native

Perennial. **Stems** twining, to 5 m long, sharply angled, often minutely scabrous on the angles, as are also the petioles, peduncles, and often the leaf veins, varying to glabrous. **Leaves** ovate or broadly cordate; ocreae oblique, smooth. **Racemes** from most of the upper axils, 5-11 cm long, usually unbranched, interrupted, leafless or with 1-2 small leaves; pedicels winged above the joint, even at anthesis;

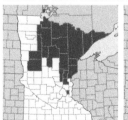

978. *Fallopia cilinodis*

979. *Fallopia convolvulus*

980. *Fallopia japonica*

981. *Fallopia scandens*

perianth 1.5-2.5 mm long, white; outer 3 sepals at maturity with broadly winged midrib. **Achenes** very glossy, black, 3-5 mm long, much exceeded by the calyx. Aug-Sept.—Moist woods, thickets, and roadsides. Variable in the shape of the wings and the length of the fruit.

PERSICARIA *Lady's-Thumb; Smartweed*

Annual and perennial herbs. Flowers pink or sometimes white, in terminal spikes. *The genus was formerly included in Polygonum.*

ADDITIONAL SPECIES
• *Persicaria bungeana* (Turcz.) Nakai (Bunge's smartweed), Eurasian native; Blue Earth and McLeod counties.

1 Tepals 4; styles elongate, persistent and becoming hard and stiff .... *P. virginiana*
1 Tepals usually 5 (4 in *P. hydropiperoides*); styles short, not persistent nor becoming hard and stiff 2
  2 Stems with downward-pointing prickles on the stem angles 3
    3 Basal lobes of leaves pointed downward; achenes 3-sided .... *P. sagittata*
    3 Basal lobes pointed outward; achenes 2-sided .... *P. arifolia*
  2 Stems smooth to hairy, but not prickly 4
    4 Perennial herbs from rhizomes or stolons 5
      5 Flowers in 1 or 2 terminal racemes .... *P. amphibia*
      5 Flowers in several to many terminal and axillary racemes 6
        6 Perianth dotted with glands .... *P. punctata*
        6 Perianth not dotted with glands .... *P. hydropiperoides*
    4 Taprooted annual herbs 7
      7 Sheathing stipules (ocreae) fringed with bristles at tip 8
        8 Perianth dotted with glands 9
          9 Tepals usually 4; achenes dull .... *P. hydropiper*
          9 Tepals 5; achenes shiny .... *P. punctata*
        8 Perianth not dotted with glands 10
          10 Leaves broadly ovate to heart-shaped, 5-10 cm wide .... *P. orientalis*
          10 Leaves linear to lance-shaped, usually less than 5 cm wide 11
            11 Small stipules at base of each inflorescence (ocreolae) fringed with long hairs 2-3 mm long .... *P. longiseta*
            11 Small stipules at base of each inflorescence entire, or with a few short hairs to 1 mm long .... *P. maculosa*
      7 Ocreae entire or irregularly cut, not fringed with bristles 12
        12 Outer sepals strongly 3-nerved, each nerve ending in an anchor shaped fork; racemes nodding to erect .... *P. lapathifolia*
        12 Outer sepals with faint, irregularly forked nerves; racemes erect .... *P. pensylvanica*

Persicaria amphibia (L.) Delarbre   MAP 982
WATER SMARTWEED   *native*
   Polygonum amphibium L.

Perennial floating or emergent herb, from spreading rhizomes. **Stems** to 1 m or more long, leaves and habit variable. **Submerged plants** smooth, usually branched, the branches floating, branch tips often upright and raised above water surface; leaves floating, leathery, oval, 4-20 cm long and 1-4 cm wide, rounded at tip; stipules (ocreae) membranous; petioles 1-8 cm long. **Exposed plants** hairy; leaves stalkless or with short petioles. **Flowers** pink to red, in 1-2 spike-like racemes from branch tips, the racemes 2-15 cm long and 1-2 cm wide; sepals 5-lobed to below middle, 4-5 mm long; stamens 5. **Achenes** lens-shaped, 2-4 mm long, shiny dark brown. June-Sept.—Ponds, lakes, marshes, bog pools, backwater areas, slow-moving streams.

Persicaria amphibia

Persicaria arifolia (L.) Haraldson   MAP 983
HALBERD-LEAF TEARTHUMB   *native*
   Polygonum arifolium L.

Annual herb, similar to arrow-leaf tearthumb (*P. sagittata*). **Leaves** to 20 cm long and 15 cm wide, arrowhead-shaped at base but the triangular-shaped basal lobes pointing outward rather than downward as in *P. sagittata*. **Flowers** in rounded heads at ends of stems or from leaf axils, flower stalks with glands; sepals pink,

2-3 mm long. **Achenes** lens-shaped, 4-5 mm long. July-Sept.—Swamps, wet woods, streambanks and shores.

Persicaria hydropiper (L.) Delarbre

MILD WATER-PEPPER
  Polygonum hydropiper L.

MAP 984
introduced

Annual herb. **Stems** red, erect to sprawling, 2-6 dm long, sometimes rooting at lower nodes, branched or unbranched, peppery-tasting. **Leaves** lance-shaped, 3-8 cm long and to 2 cm wide, hairless except for short hairs on veins and margins, nearly stalkless or with a short petiole; stipules (ocreae) membranous, 5-15 mm long, swollen and fringed with bristles. **Flowers** green and usually white-margined, continuous in slender racemes, often nodding at tip; sepals 5, 3-4 mm long, with glandular dots; stamens 4 or 6. Achenes dull, dark brown, 3-angled or lens-shaped, 2-3 mm long. July-Oct.—Muddy shores, streambanks, floodplains, marshes, ditches and roadsides.

Persicaria hydropiperoides (Michx.) Small

SWAMP SMARTWEED
  Polygonum hydropiperoides Michx.

MAP 985
native

Perennial herb, spreading by rhizomes. **Stems** erect to sprawling with upright tips, to 1 m long, usually branched, nearly smooth or with short hairs. **Leaves** linear to lance-shaped, 4-12 cm long and to 2.5 cm wide, petioles short; stipules (ocreae) membranous, 5-15 mm long, with stiff hairs and fringed with bristles. **Flowers** green, white or pink, in 2 to several slender racemes, 1-6 cm long, often interrupted near base; sepals 2-3 mm long, 5-lobed to just below middle, without glandular dots or only the inner sepals slightly glandular; stamens 8. **Achenes** black, shiny, 3-angled with concave sides, 2-3 mm long. July-Sept.—Shallow water or wet soil; ponds, marshes, swamps, bogs and fens, streambanks, shores, ditches.

Persicaria arifolia

Persicaria lapathifolia (L.) Delarbre

DOCK-LEAF SMARTWEED
  Polygonum lapathifolium L.

MAP 986
native

Annual herb. **Stems** erect to sprawling, unbranched or few-branched, 2-15 dm long. **Leaves** lance-shaped, 4-20 cm long and 0.5-5 cm wide, smooth above, often densely short-hairy on leaf undersides; petioles to 2 cm long, smooth to glandular; stipules (ocreae) 5-20 mm long, entire or with irregular, jagged margins. **Flowers** deep pink, white or green, crowded in erect or nodding racemes 1-5 cm long; sepals 3-4 mm long, 4- or 5-lobed to below middle, the outer 2 sepals strongly 3-nerved; stamens usually 6. **Achenes** brown, lens-shaped, 2-3 mm long. July-Sept.—Marshes, wet meadows, shores, streambanks, ditches and cultivated fields. Common and weedy.

Persicaria longiseta (Bruijn) Kitag.

BRISTLY LADY'S-THUMB
  Polygonum caespitosum Blume

MAP 987
introduced

Annual. **Stems** glabrous or nearly so, freely branched, soon decumbent, to 1 m long. **Leaves** thin, dark green, lance-shaped to elliptic or oblong lance-shaped; ocreae minutely strigose or glabrous, ciliate with bristles 5-10 mm long. **Racemes** dense 2-4 cm long, about 5 mm thick; ocreolae overlapping, their cilia 2-3.5 mm long, often equaling or surpassing the flowers. **Achenes** black, smooth and shining, trigonous, about 2 mm long.—Native of e Asia; waste places, preferably in moist soil.

Persicaria hydropiperoides

982. Persicaria amphibia   *983. Persicaria arifolia*   *984. Persicaria hydropiper*   *985. Persica. hydropiperoides*

Persicaria maculosa Gray
LADY'S-THUMB
Polygonum persicaria L.

MAP 988
introduced

Annual herb. **Stems** upright to spreading, 2-8 dm long, unbranched to branched, often red. **Leaves** lance-shaped, 3-15 cm long and 0.5-3 cm wide, smooth or with few hairs, underside usually dotted with small glands, leaves stalkless or on petioles to 1 cm long; ocreae 5-15 mm long, fringed with bristles, with short hairs. **Flowers** pink to rose, crowded in straight, cylindric racemes 1-4 cm long and 0.5-1 cm wide; sepals 2-4 mm long, 5-lobed to near middle; stamens 6. **Achenes** black, shiny achene, lens-shaped or sometimes 3-angled, 2-3 mm long. July-Sept. —Muddy shores, streambanks, ditches and cultivated fields, often weedy.

Persicaria orientalis (L.) Spach
PRINCE'S FEATHER
Polygonum orientale L.

MAP 989
introduced

Persicaria maculosa

Annual herb. **Stems** erect, branched, to 2.5 m tall, pubescent. **Leaves** ovate, broadly rounded at base, finely pubescent; ocreae villous, ciliate, often with spreading herbaceous border. **Inflorescence** large; peduncles densely pubescent. Racemes commonly drooping, dense, cylindric, 3-8 cm long. **Flowers** rose to crimson. **Achenes** flat, lenticular, 2.8-3.5 mm long and about as wide, beakless, smooth and shining.—Native of India; escaped in waste places near gardens.

Persicaria pensylvanica (L.) M. Gómez
PINKWEED
Polygonum pensylvanicum L.

MAP 990
native

Annual herb. **Stems** erect, 3-20 dm long, unbranched to widely branching. **Leaves** lance-shaped, 3-15 cm long and 1-4 cm wide, smooth except for short hairs on margins; petioles to 2.5 cm long; stipules (ocreae) 0.5-1.5 cm long, entire or with an irregular, jagged margin, hairless, not fringed with bristles. **Flowers** pink to white, in dense racemes 2-3 cm long, the flower stalks with gland-tipped hairs; sepals 3-5 mm long, 5-parted to below middle, the outer sepals faintly nerved; stamens 8 or less. **Achenes** dark brown to black, shiny, lens-shaped, to 3 mm long. June-Sept. —Streambanks, exposed shores, marshes, fens, ditches and cultivated fields.

Persicaria pensylvanica

Persicaria punctata (Elliott) Small
DOTTED SMARTWEED
Polygonum punctatum Ell.

MAP 991
native

Annual or perennial herb. **Stems** erect to spreading, 4-10 dm long, unbranched to branched. **Leaves** narrowly lance-shaped or oval, 4-15 cm long and 1-2 cm wide, smooth except for small short hairs on margins, underside usually dotted with small glands; petioles short; stipules (ocreae) 5-15 mm long, smooth or with stiff hairs and fringed with bristles. **Flowers** green-white; in numerous slender, loosely flowered racemes, interrupted in lower portion, to 10 cm long; sepals 3-4 mm long, with glandular dots, 5-parted to about middle; stamens 6-8. **Achenes** dark, shiny, lens-shaped or 3-angled, 2-3 mm long. Aug-Sept.—Floodplain forests, marshes, shores, streambanks and cultivated fields.

Persicaria punctata

Persicaria sagittata (L.) H.Gross
ARROW-LEAF TEARTHUMB
Polygonum sagittatum L.

MAP 992
native

Slender annual herb. **Stems** 4-angled, weak, usually supported by other plants, 1-2 m long, with downward pointing prickles on stem angles, petioles, leaf midribs

986. Persicaria lapathifolia   *987. Persicaria longiseta*   *988. Persicaria maculosa*   *989. Persicaria orientalis*

and flower **stalks.** Leaves lance-shaped to oval, arrowhead-shaped at base, 3-10 cm long and to 2.5 cm wide, the basal lobes pointing downward; petioles long on lower leaves, shorter above; stipules (ocreae) 5-10 mm long, with a few hairs on margins. **Flowers** white or pink; in round racemes to 1 cm long, on long slender stalks at ends of stems or from leaf axils; sepals 3 mm long, 5-parted to below middle. **Achenes** brown to black, shiny, 3-angled, 2-3 mm long. July-Sept. —Swamps, marshes, wet meadows and burned wetlands.

Persicaria sagittata

Persicaria virginiana (L.) Gaertn.
JUMPSEED
> Antenoron virginianum (L.) Roberty & Vautier
> Polygonum virginianum L.

MAP 993
native

Perennial herb. **Stems** erect from a rhizome, 5-10 dm tall. **Leaves** lance-shaped to ovate, to 15 cm long, acute to rounded at base, varying from roughly pubescent to glabrous on either or both sides; petioles to 2 cm long; ocreae pubescent and long-ciliate. **Racemes** very slender, terminal, 1-4 dm long, the ocreolae much separate toward the base, becoming contiguous or overlapping toward the summit, 1-3-flowered; pedicels divergent, jointed at the tip; sepals 4, greenish white, or suffused with pink, about 2.5 mm long, the 2 lateral exterior and somewhat smaller than the median, scarcely changed in fruit. **Achenes** lens-shaped, ovate, about 4 mm long; styles persistent, hooked at the tip. Aug-Sept. —Moist woods.

Persicaria virginiana

POLYGONELLA *Jointweed*

Polygonella articulata (L.) Meisn.
COASTAL JOINTWEED
> Polygonum articulatum L.

MAP 994
native

Annual herb. **Stems** slender, wiry, branched above, 1-4 dm tall. **Leaves** linear, revolute, 1 mm or less wide, 5-20 mm long; leaves jointed with the summit of the ocrea. **Flowers** perfect, or a few unisexual by abortion, each flower solitary from the axils of a sheathing bract, in several racemes; pedicels slender, decurved, jointed just above the base; sepals 5, persistent, petal-like, white or greenish to pink or red, 1.5-2 mm long, the outer 2 obovate, keeled toward the summit, the inner 3 elliptic; stamens 8; ovary 3-angled. **Fruit** a smooth, sharply 3-angled achene, subtended and loosely enclosed by the calyx. July-Aug. —Great Lakes sandy shores and dunes.

Polygonella articulata

POLYGONUM *Smartweed; Knotweed; Tearthumb*

Annual herbs (ours). Stems erect to sprawling, often swollen at nodes. Leaves arrowhead-shaped to lance-shaped or oval; stipules joined to form a tubular sheath (ocrea) around the stem above each node; the ocreae (plural) membranous or papery, entire or with an irregular, jagged margin or fringed with bristles. Flowers small, from leaf axils; sepals usually 5, petal-like, green-white to pink; stamens 8 or less; styles 2-3. Fruit a brown to black achene, lens-shaped or 3-angled.

1 Flowers in the axils of short bracts, all but the lowermost bracts less than 2x longer than the flowers, the inflorescence thus appearing to be a remotely flowered slender spike; plants stiffly erect with leaves mostly linear (rarely all nearly elliptic) and sharply acute. 2
   2 Flowers and fruit becoming strongly reflexed; leaves flat or with margins revolute but glabrous; fruiting perianth 3.5-4.5 mm long . . . . *P. douglasii*

990. *Persicaria pensylvanica*   991. *Persicaria punctata*   992. *Persicaria sagittata*   993. *Persicaria virginiana*

2 Flowers and fruit erect; leaves longitudinally folded or grooved (W-shaped in cross-section) with minutely
  ciliate margins; fruiting perianth 3-3.5 mm long . . . . ***P. tenue***

1 Flowers in the axils of foliage leaves, these mostly at least 2x longer than the flowers; plants erect to ascending
  or prostrate, with leaves acute to blunt 3

3 Perianth abruptly narrowed above achene ("bottle-shaped") 4

4 Leaves yellow-green; fruiting perianth divided for about three-fourths of its length . . . . ***P. erectum***

4 Leaves blue-green; fruiting perianth divided for about one-third its length . . . . ***P. achoreum***

3 Perianth not narrowed above achene 5

5 Outer 3 tepals flat, shorter than or equaling inner 2 tepals places . . . . ***P. aviculare***

5 Outer 3 tepals hood-like, longer than inner 2 tepals 6

6 Plants prostrate; leaves 2-4 times longer than wide . . . . ***P. aviculare***

6 Plants upright; leaves 4-12 times longer than wide . . . . ***P. ramosissimum***

Polygonum achoreum Blake

LEATHERY KNOTWEED

MAP 995
native

Annual, closely resembling *P. erectum*. **Stems** erect or ascending, freely branched,
1-5 dm tall. **Leaves** elliptic to obovate, thin, bright- or bluish green, 1-3 cm long,
broadly rounded at the tip; ocreae to 1 cm long, mostly scarious, 3-nerved.
Pedicels about equaling the calyx; calyx about 3 mm long, green, unequally 5-
lobed to above the middle; outer lobes at maturity distinctly exceeding the inner,
cucullate at the tip, exceeding the achene. **Achenes** dull yellow-brown, finely and
uniformly granular.—Sandy and gravelly roadsides, barnyards, gardens, railroads.

Polygonum achoreum

Polygonum aviculare L.

YARD KNOTWEED

MAP 996
native

Annual. **Stems** erect to prostrate, much branched, the branches commonly
equaling the central axis, or the latter suppressed. **Leaves** linear to elliptic or
oblong, 1-3 cm long, 1-8 mm wide, narrowed to the base, veinless or faintly
veined. **Flowers** short-pediceled, included in the ocrea or barely exsert; calyx 2-
3 mm long, lobed to below the middle; sepals oblong or ovate, green with white
or pink margins, appressed at maturity. **Achenes** ovoid, dark brown, 2-2.5 mm
long, finely puncticulate.—Common weed of waste ground, streets, and lawns;
also common on beaches and around salt marshes.

Polygonum aviculare

Polygonum douglasii Greene

DOUGLAS' KNOTWEED

MAP 997
native

Slender taprooted annual. **Stems** to 4 dm tall, the branches few, ascending and
sometimes crowded. **Leaves** not crowded, inclined, the lower ones to 4 cm long
and 8 mm wide, linear to lanceolate, the petiole very short; leaves smaller above.
Inflorescences terminal on the branches, of spike-like racemes, or the racemes
in a small panicle, the flowers 2-4 at the nodes. **Flowers** pedicellate, the pedicels
becoming reflexed in fruit; perianth 5-lobed, connate only at the base, green with
white (pinkish) margins. **Achene** black, 3-angled, the sides concave, sometimes
flattened on 1 or 2 sides. July-Sept.—Open, rocky places.

Polygonum erectum L.

ERECT KNOTWEED

MAP 998
native

Annual. **Stems** erect or ascending, 1-5 dm tall, with numerous branches. **Leaves**
oval to obovate, 1-4 cm long, thin, bright- or bluish green, broadly rounded, acute
at base; ocreae to 1 cm long, 3-5-nerved. Pedicels shorter than to equaling the calyx;

Polygonum erectum

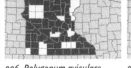

994. *Polygonella articulata*   995. *Polygonum achoreum*   996. *Polygonum aviculare*   997. *Polygonum douglasii*

calyx about 3 mm long, green, unequally 5-lobed to below the middle; outer lobes at maturity distinctly exceeding the inner, narrowly keeled. **Achenes** dimorphic; either shining, punctate, dark brown, broadly ovoid, included, about 2.5 mm long; or dull brown, ovoid, exsert, 3-3.5 mm long.—Weedy in waste ground.

Polygonum ramosissimum Michx.
MAP 999
YELLOW-FLOWER KNOTWEED
native
Annual. **Stems** erect, 3-10 dm tall, freely branched; lower internodes to 5 cm long, the upper progressively shorter. **Leaves** linear, mostly 1-6 cm long, 2-5 mm wide, flat; lateral veins inconspicuous or obsolete. **Flowers** from the upper ocreae only, 1-3 together, exsert on pedicels longer than the calyx, forming racemes to 15 cm long; calyx about 3 mm long, 5-parted nearly to the base, the outer 3 sepals notably exceeding the inner, especially in fruit. **Achenes** black, ovoid, 3 mm long, smooth and shining.—Sandy or gravelly fields, meadows, and shores.

Polygonum tenue Michx.
MAP 1000
PLEAT-LEAF KNOTWEED
native
Annual. **Stems** very slender, wiry, erect, 1-4 dm tall, with ascending or erect branches. **Leaves** linear, 1-3 cm long, subulate-tipped, plicate in two folds near the midvein; margins with tiny, spine-tipped teeth. **Flowers** remote, mostly solitary in each ocrea; calyx cleft nearly to the base, the oblong sepals connivent over the achene. **Achenes** ovoid, black, sharply trigonous, about 2.5 mm long. —Dry, sandy open hills and old fields, roadsides.

Polygonum tenue

RUMEX *Dock; Sorrel*

Perennial, sometimes weedy herbs (annual in *R. fueginus*). Leaves large and clustered at base of plants, or leafy-stemmed; mostly oblong to lance-shaped, flat to wavy-crisped along margins, usually with petioles. Membranous sheaths around stems present at nodes (ocreae). Flowers in crowded whorls in panicles at ends of stems; flowers small and numerous, green but turning brown; sepals in 2 series of 3, the inner 3 sepals (valves) enlarging, becoming winged and loosely enclosing the achene, giving the appearance of a 3-winged fruit, the midvein of the valve often swollen to produce a grainlike tubercle on the back; stamens 6; styles 3. Fruit a brown, 3-angled achene, tipped with a short slender beak.

ADDITIONAL SPECIES
• *Rumex alpinus* L. (Monk's-rhubarb); native to Eurasia; Cook County.
• *Rumex occidentalis* S. Watson (Western dock) reported for w Minnesota but not verified; frequently misidentified as the similar *R. longifolius*.

1   At least some of the leaves arrowhead-shaped, the basal lobes pointing backward or outward 2
  2   Basal lobes pointing backward; valves with a conspicuous grain at base . . . . *R. acetosa*
  2   Basal lobes pointing outward; valves without grains . . . . *R. acetosella*
1   Leaves not arrowhead-shaped with basal lobes 3
  3   At least 1 of the valves with a prominent grain 4
    4   Margins of mature valves entire or shallowly lobed, not toothed 5
      5   Flower pedicels without a large swollen joint; base of grain distinctly above base of valve   *R. britannica*
      5   Flower stalks with a large swollen joint below the middle or near base; base of grain even with base of valve 6
        6   Fruit with 1 grain, the grain small, less than half as long as the valve . . . . *R. patientia*
        6   Fruit with 1-3 grains, the larger grains at least half as long as the valve 7
          7   Fruit with 3 grains; flower pedicels 2-5 times longer than fruit . . . . *R. verticillatus*
          7   Fruit with 1-3 grains, the grains not projecting below the valves; flower stalks 1-2 times longer than fruit 8
            8   Leaves crisp-margined (crinkled); grains two-thirds as wide as long . . . . *R. crispus*
            8   Leaf margins flat; grains narrower, up to half as wide as long 9
              9   Grains usually 1 (sometimes 2-3); leaves mostly less than 4 times longer than wide . . . . .
                . . . . *R. altissimus*
              9   Grains usually 3; leaves mostly more than 4 times longer than wide . . . *R. triangulivalvis*
    4   Margins of mature valves with coarse or spine-tipped teeth 10
      10   Plants annual from fibrous roots; valve teeth spinulose; grains 3; leaves all along the stem   *R. fueginus*

10 Plants perennial from a stout taproot; grain 1; valves coarsely toothed; leaves basal and along the stem 11

    11 Base of larger leaves cordate (heart-shaped); usually only 1 valve with a grain . . . . . . ***R. obtusifolius***

    11 Leaf base not cordate; all valves with a grain . . . . ***R. stenophyllus***

3 Valves without grains 12

    12 Mature valves 2-3 cm wide . . . . ***R. venosus***

    12 Mature valves less than 1 cm wide 13

        13 Leaf blades 15-30 cm long and to 4 cm wide; inner tepals usually 3-5 mm wide; achenes reddish brown, usually 1-1.5 mm wide . . . . ***Rumex pseudonatronatus***

        13 Leaf blades 25-60 cm long and wider than 7 cm; inner tepals 5-7 mm wide; achenes brown to dark brown, normally 1.5-2 mm wide . . . . ***R. longifolius***

Rumex acetosella

Rumex acetosa L.

GREEN SORREL

MAP 1001

introduced

Perennial herb. **Stems** stout, erect, 3-9 dm tall, usually simple to the inflorescence. **Leaves** oblong, all or chiefly sagittate, the lower long-petioled, the upper subsessile with triangular basal lobes directed backward. **Panicle** 1-2 dm long, usually leafless; sepals of the staminate flowers 2-3 mm long; outer sepals of the pistillate flowers soon reflexed, nearly 2 mm long; inner sepals in fruit 4-6 mm long and about as wide, reticulate-veined, the midrib conspicuously dilated at base into a tubercle-like appendage. **Achenes** dark brown, 2-2.5 mm long.—Native of Eurasia; occasionally cultivated for greens and sparsely naturalized.

Rumex acetosella L.

COMMON SHEEP SORREL

MAP 1002

introduced (invasive)

Perennial herb. **Stems** erect, simple or branched, 1-4 dm tall. **Leaves** variable, usually 3-lobed, the terminal lobe narrowly elliptic to oblong, the lateral much smaller, triangular, divergent; leaf base below the lobes truncate to long-cuneate. **Inflorescence** sometimes half as long as the plant; outer sepals lance-shaped; inner sepals in the staminate flower 1.5-2 mm long, obovate, in the pistillate flower broadly ovate. **Achenes** ca. 1.5 mm long, shining golden brown. —Naturalized from Eurasia in fields, lawns, and waste places, soils acidic; often a troublesome weed.

Rumex altissimus Wood

PALE DOCK

MAP 1003

native

Perennial herb, similar to willow-leaf dock (*R. triangulivalvis*). **Stems** 3-10 dm long, usually branched from base and with short branches above. **Leaves** all from stem, ovate to lance-shaped, 6-20 cm long and 2-6 cm wide, margins flat or slightly wavy. **Flowers** in panicles 1-3 dm long, the panicle branches short and more or less upright; flower stalks short, 3-5 mm long, swollen and jointed near base; valves rounded, 4-6 mm long and as wide, flattened across base, margins smooth or irregularly toothed; grains usually well developed on only 1 of the 3 valves, although sometimes present on 2-3 valves; the largest grain lance-shaped. **Fruit** a brown achene, 2-3 mm long. May-Aug.—Marshes, shores, streambanks, ditches, disturbed areas.

Rumex brittannica L.

GREAT WATER-DOCK

Rumex orbiculatus Gray

MAP 1004

native

Rumex altissimus

Perennial herb. **Stems** stout, unbranched, 2-2.5 m long. **Leaves** lance-shaped or oblong lance-shaped, lower leaves 30-60 cm long, upper leaves 5-15 cm long;

998. Polygonum erectum *999. Polygon. ramosissimum* *1000. Polygonum tenue* *1001. Rumex acetosa*

margins flat. **Flowers** in panicles to 5 dm long; valves rounded, flat at base, 5-8 mm long and as wide, smooth or with small teeth; grains 3, narrowly lance-shaped, the base distinctly above base of valve. June–Aug.—Marshes, fens, streambanks and ditches, often in shallow water.

Rumex brittannica

Rumex crispus L.
CURLY DOCK

MAP 1005
introduced (naturalized)

Perennial herb, from a thick taproot. **Stems** stout, upright, usually single, 5-15 dm long. **Basal leaves** large, 10-30 cm long and 1-5 cm wide, on long petioles, often drying early in season; **stem leaves** smaller and with shorter petioles, oval to lance-shaped, margins strongly wavy-crisped (crinkled). **Flowers** in large branched panicles, the panicle branches more or less upright; flower stalks drooping at tips, 5-10 mm long, swollen-jointed near base; valves heart-shaped to broadly ovate, 4-5 mm long and as wide, margins more or less smooth; grains 3, swollen, often of unequal size, rounded at ends. **Fruit** a brown achene, 2-3 mm long. July–Sept.—Wet meadows, shores, ditches, old fields, and other wet and disturbed areas; weedy.

Rumex fueginus Phil.
GOLDEN DOCK

MAP 1006
native

Annual herb. **Stems** hollow, to 8 dm long, much-branched. **Leaves** mostly on stems, smaller upward, lance-shaped to linear, 5-20 cm long and 0.5-4 cm wide, wedge-shaped or heart-shaped at base, margins flat to wavy-crisped. **Flowers** in large open panicles, the panicle branches more or less upright, leafy, the flower stalks jointed near base; valves triangular-ovate, 2-3 mm long, the margins lobed into 2-3 spine-tipped teeth on each side; grains 3. **Fruit** a light brown achene, 1-2 mm long. July–Aug.—Marshes, shores, streambanks and ditches, sometimes where brackish.

Rumex longifolius DC.
DOOR-YARD DOCK

MAP 1007
introduced

Perennial herb. **Stems** erect, to 1 m tall. Lower **leaves** narrowly oblong, broadest near middle, tapering to an acute base. Mature pedicels visibly jointed near the base; valves rotund to nearly kidney-shaped, 4-6 mm long, 5-7 mm wide, entire or toothed, reticulate-veined, without grains.—Native of Europe; waste places.

Rumex crispus

Rumex obtusifolius L.
BITTER DOCK

MAP 1008
introduced (naturalized)

Perennial herb. **Stems** stout, to 12 dm long, usually unbranched. **Lower leaves** oblong or ovate, to 30 cm long and 15 cm wide, heart-shaped or rounded at base; **upper leaves** smaller. **Flowers** in much-branched panicles, flower stalks longer than fruit, jointed near base; valves triangular-ovate, 4-5 mm long, with 2-4 spine-tipped teeth on each side; grains large and with tiny wrinkles. **Fruit** a shiny, red-brown achene. June–Aug.—Floodplain woods and openings, cultivated fields and disturbed areas.

Rumex patientia L.
PATIENCE DOCK

MAP 1009
introduced

Perennial herb. **Stems** erect, simple to the inflorescence, to 1.5 m tall. **Leaves** somewhat crisped, oblong to lance-shaped, to 15 cm wide, the larger truncate to subcordate at base, the smaller acute. **Inflorescence** to 5 dm long, with stout

Rumex fueginus

1002. *Rumex acetosella*

1003. *Rumex altissimus*

1004. *Rumex brittannica*

1005. *Rumex crispus*

ascending branches subtended by reduced leaves, otherwise leafless, the verticils eventually contiguous; pedicels 5-10 mm long, visibly jointed near the base; valves broadly rounded, 6-9 mm long, very blunt, deeply cordate, usually dentate; grain 1 or none, 1/3 as long as the valve or shorter.—Native of Europe; waste places.

Rumex pseudonatronatus (Borbás) Murbeck

FIELD DOCK   MAP 1010
       introduced

Perennial herb, nearly glabrous. **Stems** erect, branched from above middle, to 1.2 m tall. **Leaves** lance-shaped or linear lance-shaped, 15-30 cm long and 1-4 cm wide, tapering toward the stem. **Inflorescences** terminal, normally dense in upper part and interrupted at base, branches usually straight or slightly arching. **Flowers** 15-25 in each whorl; tubercles normally absent; pedicels usually with a small tiny swelling about a third of the way up from the base. **Achenes** reddish brown, 2-2.5 mm long. Late spring-summer. Alluvial habitats, soils often somewhat saline; waste places, roadsides, shores of rivers and lakes, meadows, cultivated fields. — Native to Eurasia; frequently misidentified as *R. longifolius* and sometimes *R. crispus*. *The erect, dense fruiting heads turn brown in late summer and are conspicuous in fields and on roadsides.*

Rumex patientia

Rumex stenophyllus Ledeb.

NARROW-LEAF DOCK   MAP 1011
       introduced

Perennial taprooted herb. **Stems** 1 m or more tall, simple or few branched below the inflorescence.. **Leaves** narrowly lance-shaped, to ca. 20 cm long, narrowed at both ends; margins flat or undulate; petioles long; stem leaves somewhat reduced. **Inflorescence** narrow, somewhat leafy at base; **fruiting valves** toothed on the margins and bearing a tubercle on each valve, the tubercle about 1/2 as long as the valve. **Achenes** light reddish brown, ca. 2 mm long. May-July.—Damp meadows, ditches, streambanks.

Rumex triangulivalvis (Danser) Rech. f.

WILLOW-LEAF DOCK   MAP 1012
       native
    Rumex salicifolius Weinm.

Perennial taprooted herb. **Stems** smooth, 3-10 dm long, usually branched from base and with short branches on stem. **Leaves** mostly on stems, not much smaller upward, narrowly lance-shaped, tapered at both ends, pale waxy green, 5-16 cm long and 1-3 cm wide, margins mostly flat. **Flowers** in panicles 1-3 dm long, panicle branches few and more or less upright, with small linear leaves at base; flower stalks 2-4 mm long, swollen and jointed near base; valves thick, triangular, 3-6 mm long and wide, margins smooth or shallowly toothed; grains usually 3. **Fruit** a brown achene, 2 mm long. June-Aug.—Wet meadows, marshes, shores, streambanks, ditches and other low areas, sometimes where brackish.

Rumex venosus Pursh

VEINY DOCK   (NO MAP)
       introduced

Glabrous rhizomatous perennial herb. **Stems** 2-6 dm tall. **Leaves** ovate to oblong or lance-shaped, flat, entire, 4-12 cm long. **Inflorescence** very dense in fruit; mature wings 2-3 cm wide and reticulately veined.—Uncommon adventive in waste places and along railways; reported for Minn.

Rumex verticillatus L.

SWAMP DOCK   MAP 1013
       native

Perennial taprooted herb. **Stems** stout, 1-1.5 m long, with many short branches

Rumex verticillatus

1006. *Rumex fueginus*   1007. *Rumex longifolius*   1008. *Rumex obtusifolius*   1009. *Rumex patientia*

from leaf axils. **Leaves** narrowly lance-shaped, tapered to base, margins flat. **Flowers** in leafless panicles 2-4 dm long, the panicle branches few and more or less upright; flower stalks 10-15 mm long, jointed near base; valves triangular-ovate, 4-6 mm long and wide, thickened at center; grains 3, lance-shaped, the base blunt and projecting 0.5 mm below base of valve. June-Sept.—Marshes, swamps, wet forests, backwater areas and muddy shores, often in shallow water.

Portulacaceae PURSLANE FAMILY

PORTULACA *Purslane*

Ours succulent annual herbs. Leaves cauline, mostly alternate, the uppermost crowded and forming an involucre to the flowers. Flowers ephemeral, opening only in the sunshine, solitary or glomerate at the end of the stem and branches, sessile or nearly so. Sepals 2. Petals 4-6, commonly 5. Stamens 8-many. Styles 3-several. Capsule opening near the middle, many-seeded.

1 Plants prostrate, glabrous; leaves obovate; flowers yellow . . . . ***P. oleracea***
1 Plants upright or spreading, hairy at nodes; leaves terete; flowers bright red to yellow . . . . ***P. grandiflora***

Portulaca grandiflora Hook.
MOSS-ROSE

(NO MAP)
introduced

Stems diffusely branched, ascending or spreading, 2-4 dm long, hairy at the nodes. **Leaves** linear, 1-3 cm long, nearly terete; **stem leaves** alternate, long persistent, the terminal crowded, forming an involucre mingled with long hairs. **Flowers** white or of various brilliant shades of red or yellow, 2-4 cm wide; stamens about 40. All summer.—Native of Argentina; cultivated for ornament and possibly occasionally escaped; reported for Minn.

Portulaca oleracea L.
COMMON PURSLANE

MAP 1014
introduced (naturalized)

Stems prostrate, fleshy, usually purplish red, glabrous, repeatedly branched, forming large mats. **Leaves** succulent, flat, spatulate, 1-3 cm long, commonly rounded at the tip; **stem leaves** usually alternate, occasionally opposite. **Flowers** yellow, sessile, 5-10 mm wide, solitary or in small terminal glomerules; stamens 6-10. **Seeds** with low blunt tubercles. All summer.—Reputedly native of w Asia, but now widely distributed as a familiar weed; sometimes cooked for greens.

Portulaca oleracea

Primulaceae PRIMROSE FAMILY

Annual or perennial herbs. Leaves simple, opposite (sometimes whorled in *Lysimachia*), or leaves all basal. Flowers perfect (with both staminate and pistillate parts), regular, single from leaf axils, or in clusters at ends of stems; sepals 4-5, petals mostly 5 (varying from 4-9), joined, tube-shaped below and flared above, deeply cleft to shallowly lobed at tip; ovary superior, style 1; stamens 5. Fruit a 5-chambered capsule.

1 Leaves all from base of plant, inflorescence an umbel at end of naked stalk 2
  2 Lobes of corolla strongly reflexed . . . . ***Dodecatheon***
  2 Lobes of corolla spreading or ascending 3
    3 Corolla tube longer than the calyx . . . . ***Primula mistassinica***

1010. Rumex pseudonatronatus   *1011. Rumex stenophyllus*   *1012. Rumex triangulivalvis*   *1013. Rumex verticillatus*

3   Corolla tube shorter than the calyx .... *Androsace*

1   Leaves from stem; inflorescence various 4

     4   Leaves in a single whorl near end of stem; flowers 7-merous .... *Trientalis borealis*

     4   Leaves opposite or in several whorls; flowers 5-6-merous 5

         5   Perennial of mostly wetland habitats; flowers yellow .... *Lysimachia*

         5   Annual weed; flowers rusty red .... *Anagallis arvensis*

ANAGALLIS *Pimpernel*

Anagallis arvensis L.

PIMPERNEL

    Lysimachia arvensis (L.) U. Manns & Anderb.

MAP 1015
introduced (naturalized)

Annual herb. **Stems** usually much branched, diffuse, ascending, or erect, 1-3 dm long, 4-angled. **Leaves** opposite, entire, sessile, decussate, elliptic to ovate, 1-2 cm long. **Flowers** solitary in the axils, on slender pedicels, ascending at anthesis, recurved in fruit, usually, but not always, exceeding the leaves; sepals distinct, 3-4 mm long; corolla deeply 5-parted, usually scarlet or brick-red, varying to white, opening only in fair weather. **Fruit** a globose capsule about 4 mm wide, circumscissile near the middle. May-Aug.—Native of Eurasia, now in much of the USA and s Canada on roadsides, lawns, gardens, and waste places.

Anagallis arvensis

ANDROSACE *Rock-Jasmine*

Small annual herbs; roots fibrous; with 1 to several, erect, leafless scapes, bearing terminal umbels of flowers. Leaves in basal rosettes, linear-lanceolate to oblanceolate, slightly petiolate. Flowers very small, subtended by bracts. Calyx tube hemispherical to subglobose, equaling or exceeding the 5 triangular lobes. Corolla 5-parted, salverform or funnelform, inflated around the ovary, constricted at the throat, shorter than calyx, white to pinkish; stamens 5, attached opposite corolla lobes below the middle of the tube, ovary 1-celled. Capsule more or less globose, few- to many-seeded; seeds ovoid to elliptical, brown, minutely pitted.

1   Involucral bracts lanceolate-ovate to obovate; calyx lobes linear to narrowly triangular, equal to or slightly longer than calyx tube .... *A. occidentalis*

1   Involucral bracts lanceolate; calyx lobes broadly triangular, much shorter than the calyx tube . *A. septentrionalis*

Androsace occidentalis Pursh

WESTERN ROCK-JASMINE

MAP 1016
native

Small annual herb; scapes leafless, 1-several, each with a terminal umbel subtended by several bracts. **Leaves** oblong lance-shaped to oblong or obovate, 6-15 mm long, usually entire. **Scapes** 3 to many, 2-5 cm tall; bracts resembling the leaves in shape, 3-6 mm long. **Flowers** white or pink; pedicels 5-9, to 3 cm long; **calyx tube** equaling or exceeding the triangular lobes, pale and nearly glabrous; **corolla** salverform, white, 2.5 mm wide; corolla tube inflated around the ovary, constricted at the throat, not exceeding the calyx; stamens inserted in the corolla tube. **Capsule** about as long as the persistent, enclosing calyx. April.— Dry, sandy soil.

Androsace occidentalis

Androsace septentrionalis L.

PYGMY-FLOWER ROCK-JASMINE

MAP 1017
native

Erect annual herb to 25 cm tall; scapes several, erect, the central scape well-developed, the surrounding scapes smaller and of unequal lengths. **Leaves** in a basal rosette, linear to lanceolate, 1-3 cm long and to 6 mm wide, often reddish

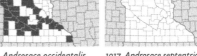

1014. *Portulaca oleracea*   1015. *Anagallis arvensis*   1016. *Androsace occidentalis*   1017. *Androsace septentrionalis*

green. Flowers small, few to many in terminal umbels, these bracted at base; calyx 2.5-4 mm long; calyx lobes shorter than tube; corolla tube about as long as the calyx; corolla lobes 0.5-1.0 mm long, white. May-July.—Dry prairies, hillsides, roadsides, open woods; weedy in cultivated fields.

DODECATHEON *Shooting Star*

Perennial glabrous herbs. Leaves in a basal rosette. Flowers in a terminal bracted umbel of attractive nodding flowers on ascending or erect pedicels, atop a solitary, erect, leafless scape. Calyx deeply 5-parted, persistent in fruit. Corolla 5-cleft almost to the base, the lobes reflexed. Capsule ovoid to cylindric, erect, opening by 5 short terminal valves.

1   Flowers deep rose-purple; plants slender, to 35 cm high . . . . ***D. amethystinum***
1   Flowers white to lilac; plants stout, to 60 cm high . . . . ***D. meadia***

Dodecatheon amethystinum (Fassett) Fassett   MAP 1018
WESTERN SHOOTING STAR   *native*
> *Dodecatheon radicatum* Greene
> *Dodecatheon pulchellum* (Raf.) Merrill
> *Primula fassettii* Mast & Reveal

Similar to *D. meadia*, but usually smaller and blooming about 2 weeks later, and restricted to ne Minn. **Leaves** not tinged with red toward the base; corolla lobes deep rose-purple or rarely white, smaller than in *D. meadia*. **Capsule** ellipsoid to cylindric, pale brown, thickest near the middle. April-June.—Moist meadows.

Dodecatheon meadia L.   MAP 1019
EASTERN SHOOTING STAR   ☙*endangered* | *native*
> *Primula meadia* (L.) Mast & Reveal

Leaves oblong to oblong lance-shaped or rarely ovate, 6-20 cm long, usually tinged or marked with red at the base. **Scapes** 2-6 dm tall. **Flowers** few to many; corolla lobes narrow, white to lavender or lilac, 1-2.5 cm long. **Capsules** dark reddish brown, 7-18 mm long, thickest near the base. May-June.—Moist or dry woods and prairies.

Dodecatheon meadia

LYSIMACHIA *Loosestrife*

Perennial herbs, spreading by rhizomes. Stems erect. Leaves mostly opposite (sometimes appearing whorled), ovate or lance-shaped. Flowers 5-parted, single on stalks from leaf axils or in racemes or panicles; sepals green; petals bright to pale yellow. Fruit a capsule. *Purple loosestrife (Lythrum salicaria), an introduced weed of wetlands, is a member of Lythraceae.*

ADDITIONAL SPECIES
Lysimachia maritima (L.) Galasso, Banfi & Soldano (Sea-milkwort), in Minn known only from Kittson County; ☙*endangered*.

1   Plants creeping; leaves opposite, nearly round . . . . ***L. nummularia***
1   Plants upright; leaves opposite or whorled, longer than wide 2
  2   Flowers in terminal racemes or panicles 3
    3   Plants pubescent . . . . ***L. vulgaris***
    3   Plants glabrous . . . . ***L. terrestris***
  2   Flowers solitary or in clusters or spikes from the leaf axils 4
    4   Leaves rounded or heart-shaped at base; petioles 1-3 cm long, fringed with hairs . . . . ***L. ciliata***
    4   Leaves tapered to their base; petioles absent or short, smooth or fringed with hairs 5
      5   Flowers many in racemes from leaf axils; flowers mostly 6-merous . . . . ***L. thyrsiflora***
      5   Flowers 1 to several from the leaf axils, 5-merous 6
        6   Leaves narrowly linear, to 5 mm wide . . . . ***L. quadriflora***
        6   Leaves lance-shaped to ovate, usually more than 8 mm wide 7
          7   Main leaves in whorls of 3 or more leaves; corolla lobes entire . . . . ***L. quadrifolia***
          7   Leaves opposite or whorled; corolla lobes ragged-toothed at tip . . . . ***L. hybrida***

Lysimachia ciliata L.   MAP 1020
FRINGED YELLOW-LOOSESTRIFE   *native*
Perennial herb, spreading by rhizomes. **Stems** upright, 3-12 dm long, unbranched

or with few branches above. **Leaves** ovate to lance-shaped, 4-15 cm long and 2-6 cm wide, rounded to heart-shaped at base, green above, slightly paler below; margins fringed with short hairs; petioles 0.5-5 cm long, fringed with hairs. **Flowers** yellow, single from upper leaf axils, on stalks 2-7 cm long; sepal lobes lance-shaped, often with 3-5 parallel red-brown veins; petal lobes rounded and finely ragged at tip, 4-10 mm long and 3-9 mm wide, with a short slender tip. **Fruit** a capsule, 4-7 mm wide. June-Aug.—Usually shaded wet areas, such as shores, streambanks, wet meadows, ditches, floodplains, wet woods and thickets.

Lysimachia hybrida Michx.
LOWLAND YELLOW-LOOSESTRIFE
MAP 1021
native

Perennial herb, spreading by rhizomes. **Stems** usually erect, 2-8 dm long, unbranched or sometimes branched from base, usually branched above. **Leaves** narrowly lance-shaped to ovate, 3-10 cm long and 1-2 cm wide, tapered to base, upper surface green, underside green or slightly paler; **lower leaves** opposite, stalked, withering, petioles fringed with hairs at least near base; **upper leaves** more or less whorled and stalkless, persistent. **Flowers** yellow, single from leaf axils but often appearing crowded, on stalks 1-4 cm long; sepal lobes lance-shaped; petal lobes rounded and finely fringed at tip, 5-10 mm long and 4-10 mm wide, with a short slender tip. **Fruit** a capsule, 4-6 mm wide. July-Aug.—Wet meadows, marshes, streambanks, ditches and shores, sometimes in shallow water.

Lysimachia ciliata

Lysimachia nummularia L.
CREEPING-JENNY
MAP 1022
introduced (naturalized)

Perennial herb, often forming mats. **Stems** creeping, to 5-6 dm long. **Leaves** opposite, dotted with black glands, round or broadly oval, 1-2.5 cm long; petioles short. **Flowers** single in leaf axils, on stalks to 2.5 cm long; sepals leaflike, triangular; petals yellow, dotted with dark red, 10-15 mm long. **Fruit** a capsule, shorter than sepals. June-Aug.—Swamps, floodplain forests, streambanks, shores, meadows and ditches.

Lysimachia hybrida

Lysimachia quadriflora Sims
FOUR-FLOWER YELLOW-LOOSESTRIFE
MAP 1023
native

Perennial herb, spreading by rhizomes which form clusters of basal rosettes. **Stems** upright, 3-10 dm long. **Leaves** opposite, sometimes appearing whorled; **stem leaves** stalkless, often ascending, linear, 3-8 cm long and 2-7 mm wide, margins smooth or rolled under, sometimes fringed with a few hairs near base. **Flowers** yellow, single in clusters at ends of stems and branches, on stalks 1-4 cm long; sepal lobes lance-shaped; petal lobes oval, 7-12 mm long, entire or finely ragged at tip. **Fruit** a capsule, 3-5 mm wide. July-Aug.—Wet meadows, pond and marsh margins, low prairie, calcareous fens; often where sandy and calcium-rich.

Lysimachia quadrifolia L.
WHORLED YELLOW-LOOSESTRIFE
MAP 1024
native

Perennial herb. **Stems** erect, 3-9 dm tall, glabrous or sparsely pubescent, rarely branched. **Leaves** chiefly in whorls of 4 (3-6), lance-shaped, 5-10 cm long, widely spreading. **Flowers** from many of the median nodes, usually one from the axil of each leaf, on spreading pedicels 2-5 cm long; sepals oblong lance-shaped; petals yellow with dark lines, oblong or elliptic, 6-8 mm long. June-July.—Moist or dry upland soil, chiefly in open woods.

Lysimachia nummularia

1018. *Dodecath. amethystinum*   1019. *Dodecatheon meadia*   1020. *Lysimachia ciliata*   1021. *Lysimachia hybrida*

Lysimachia terrestris (L.) B.S.P.
SWAMPCANDLES

MAP 1025
native

Perennial herb, spreading by shallow rhizomes. **Stems** smooth, 4-8 dm long, usually branched. **Leaves** opposite, dotted with glands, narrowly lance-shaped, 5-10 cm long and 2-4 cm wide, with small bulblike structures produced in leaf axils late in season; bracts awl-like, 3-8 mm long. **Flowers** yellow, in a single, crowded, upright raceme, 1-3 dm long; sepals lance-shaped; petal lobes oval, 5-7 mm long, with dark lines, on stalks 8-15 mm long. **Fruit** a capsule, 2-3 mm wide. June-Aug.—Marshes, fens, thickets, muddy shores, and ditches.

Lysimachia thyrsiflora L.
SWAMP LOOSESTRIFE

MAP 1026
native

Perennial upright herb, spreading by rhizomes; plants conspicuously dotted with dark glands. **Stems** smooth or with patches of brown hairs, 3-7 dm long, unbranched or branched on lower stem. **Leaves** opposite, linear to lance-shaped, 4-12 cm long and 0.5-4 cm wide, smooth above, smooth or sparsely hairy below; petioles absent. **Flowers** yellow, crowded in dense racemes from leaf axils, on spreading stalks 2-5 cm long; mostly 6-parted; sepal lobes awl-shaped; petal lobes linear, 3 mm long; stamens 2x longer than petals. **Fruit** a capsule, 2-4 mm wide. June-Aug.—Many types of wetlands: thickets, shores, fens and bogs, marshes, low places in conifer and deciduous swamps, often in shallow water.

Lysimachia vulgaris L.
GARDEN YELLOW-LOOSESTRIFE

MAP 1027
introduced

Perennial herb. **Stems** erect, to 1 m tall, densely softly pubescent. **Leaves** either whorled or opposite, lance-shaped or ovate lance-shaped, 8-12 cm long, softly pubescent beneath. **Inflorescence** a terminal raceme and a series of peduncled short racemes or panicles from the upper axils, forming a terminal leafy panicle; sepals about 3 mm long; corolla yellow, about 2 cm wide, its lobes entire. July-Sept.—Native of Eurasia; escaped from cultivation, occasional on mudflats along rivers and in wet meadows.

Lysimachia quadriflora

Lysimachia terrestris

PRIMULA *Primrose*

Primula mistassinica Michx.
MISTASSINI PRIMROSE

MAP 1028
native

Perennial herb. **Stems** to 25 cm long. **Leaves** all at base of plant, oblong lance-shaped, 2-7 cm long, long tapered to base, smooth on upper surface, smooth or often white-yellow powdery below; margins with outward pointing teeth; bracts below flowers awl-shaped, 3-6 mm long. **Flowers** 1-2 cm wide, 2-10 in a cluster atop a leafless stalk; sepals joined, shorter than petals; petals joined, tubelike and flared at ends, pink and sometimes with a yellow center. **Fruit** an oblong, upright capsule to 1 cm long. May-June.—Moist ledges near Lake Superior and also inland; often found with common butterwort (*Pinguicula vulgaris*).

Primula mistassinica

Lysimachia thyrsiflora

1022. *Lysimachia nummularia*

1023. *Lysimachia quadriflora*

1024. *Lysimachia quadrifolia*

1025. *Lysimachia terrestris*

TRIENTALIS *Starflower*

Trientalis borealis Raf.
STARFLOWER
   Lysimachia borealis (Raf.) U. Manns & Anderb.

MAP 1029
native

Trientalis borealis

Low perennial herb, with slender rhizomes. **Stems** 1-2 dm tall, usually with a small scale-leaf near the middle and at the summit a whorl of lance-shaped acuminate **leaves** 4-10 cm long, from the axils of which appear 1 or several white flowers on slender pedicels 2-5 cm long. **Flowers** ordinarily 7-merous; calyx deeply divided into nearly separate lance-shaped sepals; corolla rotate, 8-14 mm wide, with very short tube and lance-shaped to ovate lobes; stamens inserted at base of the corolla. **Fruit** a 5-valved, many-seeded capsule. May-June.—Rich woods, hummocks in swamps and bogs.

Ranunculaceae BUTTERCUP FAMILY

Annual or perennial, aquatic or terrestrial herbs (or vines in *Clematis*). Leaves simple to compound, usually alternate, sometimes opposite or whorled, or all at base of plant. Flowers mostly white or yellow, usually with 5 (occasionally more) separate petals and sepals, or petals absent and then with petal-like sepals; flowers perfect (with both staminate and pistillate parts), stamens usually numerous; pistils several to many, ripening into beaked achenes or dry capsules (follicles).

ADDITIONAL SPECIES
• *Aconitum napellus* L. (Venus' chariot), native to Europe; occasional on roadsides in ne Minn.
• *Consolida ajacis* (L.) Schur (Doubtful knight's-spur), introduced garden escape; Clay and Polk cos; see key.

1 Vines; leaves opposite; fruit with a long, feathery style . . . . *Clematis*
1 Herbs; leaves alternate or from base of plant; fruit not with a long, feathery style 2
  2 Leaves linear, to 2 mm wide, all from base of plant; achenes in a spike-like cluster to 6 cm long . . . .
    . . . . *Myosurus minimus*
  2 Leaves not linear, petioles usually distinct; achenes in round to short-cylindric heads 3
    3 Flowers spurred or strongly irregular 4
      4 Flowers reddish . . . . *Aquilegia canadensis*
      4 Flowers blue with a single spur 5
        5 Plants perennial; pistils 3 . . . . *Delphinium carolinianum*
        5 Plants annual; pistil 1 . . . . *Consolida ajacis**
    3 Flowers regular and unspurred 6
      6 Stem leaves whorled. . . . . *Anemone*
      6 Stem leaves alternate, or all leaves from base of plant 7
        7 Flowers yellow, or leaves simple and not lobed, or plants aquatic 8
          8 Leaves all alike, unlobed; sepals yellow, large and petal-like; petals absent . . . . *Caltha*
          8 Leaves usually of 2 types (stem leaves different from basal leaves), or leaves deeply lobed or
            divided; sepals green; petals yellow or white 9
          9 Receptacle becoming long and cylindric; achenes covered with woolly hairs, tipped by a sharp
            beak 2-3 mm long; small annual herb with pinnately dissected basal leaves . . . .
            . . . . *Ceratocephala testiculata*
          9 Receptacle globose to short-cylindric; achenes neither woolly hairy nor sharp-beaked; leaves
            various . . . . *Ranunculus*

1026. Lysimachia thyrsiflora   *1027. Lysimachia vulgaris*   *1028. Primula mistassinica*   *1029. Trientalis borealis*

7 Flowers not yellow; leaves compound or 3-lobed; plants not aquatic 10
10 Plants with a naked scape and solitary flowers, the leaves basal 11
11 Leaves glabrous, parted into 3 leaflets; sepals white ...... ***Coptis trifolia***
11 Leaves hairy, 3 lobed but not divided into leaflets; sepals white, pink, or blue .. ***Hepatica***
10 Plants with leafy stems; flowers 1 to several 12
12 Flowers several to many in terminal racemes or panicles 13
13 Fruit an achene ...... ***Thalictrum***
13 Fruit berry-like, white or red ...... ***Actaea***
12 Flowers solitary or few, not in racemes or panicles 14
14 Leaves divided into leaflets; flowers on long slender peduncle; fruit a cluster of 4 follicles ...... ***Enemion biternatum***
14 Leaves deeply palmately lobed; flower solitary on short stout peduncle; fruit a dense cluster of red berries ...... ***Hydrastis canadensis***

ACTAEA *Baneberry*

Perennial herbs, plants toxic. Leaves 2-3 times compound, the leaflets sharply toothed. Flowers small, white, in a dense, long-peduncled, terminal raceme; the raceme at anthesis short and congested with short-pediceled flowers; the axis and pedicels elongating later, the pedicels becoming widely divergent. Sepals 3-5, obovate, petal-like. Petals 4-10, deciduous, obovate, clawed at base. Stamens numerous; filaments usually distinctly widened toward the summit. Pistil 1; stigma broad, sessile, 2-lobed. Fruit a several-seeded berry.

1 Fruit red, on slender pedicels ...... ***A. rubra***
1 Fruit white, on thicker pedicels ...... ***A. pachypoda***

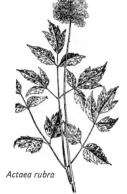

Actaea pachypoda Ell.

MAP 1030
WHITE BANEBERRY; DOLL'S EYES
native

Stems 4-8 dm tall. **Leaflets** usually completely glabrous beneath. **Petals** 2.5-4 mm long, usually spatulate; stigma wider than the diameter of the ovary. Fruiting pedicels red, 1-2 mm thick; **berries** globose, normally white, with persistent stigma. May-June.—Rich woods.

Actaea rubra (Ait.) Willd.

MAP 1031
RED BANEBERRY
native

Stems 4-8 dm tall. **Leaflets** commonly pubescent on the veins beneath. **Petals** 2.5-4 mm long, spatulate to obovate; stigma not so wide as the diameter of the ovary. Fruiting pedicels slender, 0.4-0.7 mm thick; **berries** usually red, ellipsoid. May-June.—Rich woods.

Actaea rubra

ANEMONE *Thimbleweed*

Perennial herbs from a rhizome or caudex. Basal leaves few to several, deeply palmately divided; stem erect with a whorl of 3 or more involucral leaves subtending one or more elongate peduncles. Flowers white to blue or red or greenish. Sepals 4-20, petal-like. Petals none. Stamens numerous. Pistils numerous, in a subglobose to cylindric head, pubescent. Achenes flattened, clavate, or fusiform, tipped with the persistent style.

ADDITIONAL SPECIES

• ***Anemone halleri*** All. (Glacial anemone), native to Europe; introduced with a prairie planting in Freeborn Co.

1 Styles elongating to 2 cm or more at maturity, becoming plumose ...... ***A. patens***
1 Styles much shorter, not becoming plumose 2
2 Achenes hidden by long, cottony hairs 3
3 Involucral leaves sessile or nearly so 4
4 Sepals 4-9 stems from a stout caudex ...... ***A. multifida***
4 Sepals 10-35; stems from a tuberous rhizhome ...... ***A. caroliniana***
3 Involucral leaves with petioles 5
5 Involucral leaves 2 or 3; main leaflets thin and shallowly divided; achenes borne in an ovoid cluster ...... ***A. virginiana***
5 Involucral leaves 4 or more; main leaflets thickened and deeply divided; achenes borne in an cylindrical cluster ...... ***A. cylindrica***

2 Achenes nearly glabrous or only short-hirsute 6

   6 Involucral leaves with petioles; basal leaves absent or few . . . . *A. quinquefolia*

   6 Involucral leaves without petioles; basal leaves usually many . . . . *A. canadensis*

Anemone canadensis L.
ROUND-LEAF THIMBLEWEED

MAP 1032
native

Perennial herb, from slender rhizomes, often forming large patches. **Stems** erect, 1-6 dm long, unbranched below the head. **Leaves** all from base of plant and with long petioles except for 2-3 stalkless leafy bracts below the head; 4-15 cm wide, deeply 3-5-lobed, round to kidney-shaped in outline, underside with long silky hairs, margins sharp-toothed. **Flowers** mostly single at ends of stalks, white and showy, 2-5 cm wide; sepals 5, petal-like, 1-2 cm long; petals absent; stamens and pistils many. **Achenes** clustered in a round, short-hairy head; achene body flat, 3-5 mm long and wide, beak 2-4 mm long. May-Aug.—Wet openings, streambanks, thickets, low prairie, ditches and roadsides.

Anemone caroliniana Walt.
CAROLINA THIMBLEWEED

MAP 1033
native

Perennial herb. **Stems** 1-4 dm tall, from a short, erect, tuber-like rhizome 1-3 cm long; commonly glabrous below. **Basal leaves** deeply 3-parted, the segments deeply and irregularly incised into few or several acute divisions. **Involucre** much below the middle, 1-flowered, its leaves resembling the basal but sessile. Peduncle villous; sepals 10-20, white to rose, 10-22 mm long, narrowly oblong, 3-5 times as long as wide. Head of **fruit** narrowly ovoid to subcylindric 17-25 mm long. April-May.—Dry sandy and gravelly prairies, barrens, bluff tops.

Anemone canadensis

Anemone cylindrica Gray
LONG-HEAD THIMBLEWEED

MAP 1034
native

Perennial herb. **Stems** stiffly erect, 3-10 dm tall. Basal and involucral **leaves** similar, the basal few to several, the involucral 3-10 and commonly 2x as many as the peduncles, both types petioled, broadly rounded in outline, deeply 5-parted into segments which are incised or sharply toothed only above the middle. **Inflorescence** usually of 2-6 erect peduncles 1-3 dm long, some of them often bearing a secondary involucre. **Flowers** greenish white, about 2 cm wide. **Fruit** a dense cylindric spike 20-35 mm long. **Achenes** and style densely woolly, the style about 0.5 mm long, outwardly curved. June-Aug.—Dry open woods and prairies.

Anemone multifida Poir.
CUT-LEAF ANEMONE

MAP 1035
native

Perennial herb, from a stout (about 5 mm thick), erect or ascending, often branched caudex. **Stems** 1-6 dm tall, villous below the involucre. **Basal leaves** several, long-petioled, deeply 3-parted, the segments deeply incised or lobed into acute linear-oblong divisions; **involucral leaves** similar but sessile, usually near the middle, 1-flowered or in vigorous plants emitting also 1 or 2 other peduncles each bearing a small involucre and a flower; sepals white, yellowish, or red. May-June.—Limestone bluffs, open cliffs, hillside prairies, rocky banks in calcareous soil.

Anemone cylindrica

1030. Actaea pachypoda

1031. Actaea rubra

1032. Anemone canadensis

1033. Anemone caroliniana

Anemone patens L.

PASQUE-FLOWER

Pulsatilla patens (L.) P. Mill.

MAP 1036
native

Perennial herb, from a short, branched, erect or ascending caudex. **Stems** 1-4 dm tall, villous throughout. **Basal leaves** several, long-petioled, kidney-shaped in outline, the segments deeply and repeatedly incised into linear-oblong divisions; **involucral leaves** similar but smaller and sessile, produced variously from near the base to near the summit of the stem. **Sepals** 5-7, blue or purple to white, elliptic to oblong, 25-35 mm long, villous on the back; style filiform, flexuous, 2-4 cm long, villous. **Achenes** clavate, 3-4 mm long. April.—Dry prairies and barrens.

Anemone patens

Anemone quinquefolia L.

WOOD-ANEMONE

MAP 1037
native

Delicate perennial herb from a slender horizontal rhizome. **Stems** 1-2 dm tall. **Basal leaf** solitary, long-petioled; **leaflets** 3 or apparently 5, coarsely and unevenly toothed or incised, chiefly above the middle; **involucral leaves** similar but smaller, the lateral leaflets commonly incised on the outer margin. Peduncle villous; sepals white or suffused with red beneath, usually 5, 10-22 mm long. **Achenes** fusiform, 3-4 mm long. April-June.—Moist woods.

Anemone virginiana L.

TALL THIMBLEWEED

Anemone riparia Fern.

MAP 1038
native

Perennial herb. **Leaf segments** cuneate at base, the margins straight or nearly so. **Flowers** white, greenish white, or even red, 2-3 cm wide. **Head of fruit** slenderly ovoid or nearly cylindric, usually about 8 mm thick. **Achenes** densely woolly, the styles 1-1.5 mm long, strongly ascending, the stigma often incurved. June-Aug. —Rocky banks and open woods.

Anemone quinquefolia

AQUILEGIA *Columbine*

Aquilegia canadensis L.

RED COLUMBINE

MAP 1039
native

Perennial herb from a stout caudex-like rhizome. **Stems** at anthesis 3-10 dm tall, with few to several large basal leaves. **Leaves** compound, stem leaves gradually reduced upward, with fewer leaflets, the uppermost 3-foliolate or simple; leaflets broadly obovate, crenately toothed or lobed. **Flowers** nodding, 3-4 cm long; sepals 5, red; petals 5, the blade yellow, prolonged backward from the base into an elongate red spur; stamens numerous, projecting in a column; pistils usually 5, erect, each prolonged into a slender style. **Fruit** a several-seeded follicle. April-June.—Dry woods, rocky cliffs and ledges.

Aquilegia canadensis

CALTHA *Marsh-Marigold*

Succulent perennial herbs. Leaves simple, heart-shaped, mostly from base of plant, becoming smaller upward; margins entire or rounded-toothed. Flowers single at ends of stalks, mostly bright yellow (*C. palustris*), to pink or white (*C. natans*); sepals large and petal-like; petals absent; stamens many. Fruit a follicle.

1 Flowers bright yellow; stems upright; widespread . . . . **C. palustris**
1 Flowers pink or white; stems floating; rare in ne Minn . . . . **C. natans**

1034. Anemone cylindrica   *1035. Anemone multifida*   *1036. Anemone patens*   *1037. Anemone quinquefolia*

Caltha natans Pallas

MAP 1040

FLOATING MARSH-MARIGOLD   🌱*endangered | native*

Perennial herb. **Stems** floating or creeping, branched, rooting at nodes. **Leaves** heart- or kidney-shaped, 2-5 cm wide, notched at base, upper leaves smaller. **Flowers** pink or white, 1 cm wide; sepals oval; petals absent; stamens 12-25. **Fruit** a follicle, 4-5 mm long, in dense heads of 20-40. July-Aug.—Rare in shallow water and shores of ponds and slow-moving streams; St. Louis County.

Caltha palustris L.

MAP 1041

COMMON MARSH-MARIGOLD   *native*

Loosely clumped perennial herb. **Stems** smooth, 2-6 dm long, hollow. **Leaves** heart-shaped to kidney-shaped, 4-10 cm wide, usually with 2 lobes at base; margins smooth or shallowly toothed; lower leaves with long petioles, stem leaves with shorter petioles. **Flowers** bright yellow, showy at ends of stems or in leaf axils, 2-4 cm wide; sepals 4-9, petal-like, 12-20 mm long; petals absent; stamens many; pistils 4-15, with short styles. **Fruit** a follicle, 10-15 mm long. March-June.—Shallow water, swamps, wet woods, thickets, streambanks, calcareous fens, marshes, springs.

Caltha palustris

CERATOCEPHALA *Butterwort*

Ceratocephala testiculata (Crantz) Bess.

MAP 1042

CURVESEED-BUTTERWORT   *introduced*

Ranunculus testiculatus Crantz

Small, stemless annual to 1 dm tall, thinly silky-tomentose. **Leaves** 1-4 cm long, 3-parted, the segments narrow. **Sepals** greenish, ovate lance-shaped, persistent, expanding to 5-6 mm long; **petals** narrow, 4-8 mm long, pale yellow, fading to whitish with pink veins. **Achenes** usually 35-70, the abrupt stiff beak longer than the body, spreading, forming a cylindric bur-like head 1.5-2.5 cm long.—Spring ephemeral Eurasian weed, widespread in w USA and occasional in Minn.

Ceratocephala testiculata

CLEMATIS

Herbaceous or woody plants, erect, or climbing by the prehensile leaf-rachis. Leaves opposite, simple or compound. Flowers solitary or panicled, usually dioecious. Sepals petal-like, commonly 4. Petals none. Stamens numerous. Pistils numerous; style elongate. Fruit a flattened achene, terminated by the elongate persistent style.

ADDITIONAL SPECIES

Clematis terniflora DC. (Sweet autumn virgin's-bower); native to eastern Asia; St. Louis Co. (Duluth area).

1 Sepals whitish, less than 1 cm long, in a branched inflorescence . . . . ***C. virginiana***
1 Sepals purple, 4-5 cm long, solitary . . . . ***C. occidentalis***

Clematis occidentalis (Hornem.) DC.

MAP 1043

PURPLE CLEMATIS   *native*

Clematis verticillaris DC.

Perennial, woody vine. **Stems** trailing or climbing, to 2 m long. **Leaflets** 3, long-stalked, ovate in outline; entire, crenately toothed, or lobed. **Flowers** chiefly axillary, solitary, on peduncles about equaling the subtending petiole; sepals 4, blue, ovate lance-shaped, 3-5 cm long, softly villous. **Achenes** villous, in a dense globular head; styles long-villous, 3-4 cm long. May. Rocky woods and streambanks. The purple flowers open early in spring with the unfolding leaves.

1038. Anemone virginiana   *1039. Aquilegia canadensis*   *1040. Caltha natans*   *1041. Caltha palustris*

Clematis virginiana L.
VIRGIN'S BOWER

MAP 1044
native

Perennial, woody vine. **Stems** slender, to 5 m long or more, trailing on ground or over shrubs, smooth, brown to red-purple. **Leaves** opposite, divided into 3 leaflets, the leaflets ovate, 4-8 cm long and 2.5-5 cm wide; margins sharp-toothed or lobed; petioles 5-9 cm long. Staminate and pistillate **flowers** separate and on separate plants, in many-flowered, open clusters from leaf axils, on stalks 1-8 cm long, usually shorter than leaf petioles; sepals 4, creamy-white, 6-10 mm long; petals absent. **Fruit** a rounded head of hairy brown achenes tipped with feathery, persistent styles 2.5-4 cm long. July-Sept.—Thickets, streambanks, moist to wet woods, rocky slopes. *May cause severe skin irritation if handled.*

Clematis virginiana

COPTIS *Goldthread*

Coptis trifolia (L.) Salisb.
THREE-LEAF GOLDTHREAD

MAP 1045
native

Coptis groenlandica (Oeder) Fern.

Perennial herb, with slender, bright yellow rhizomes. **Leaves** from base of plant on long petioles, evergreen, divided into 3-leaflets, the leaflets shallowly lobed, with rounded teeth tipped by an abrupt point. **Flowers** single, white, 10-15 mm wide, on a stalk 5-15 cm long from base of plant; sepals 4-7, petal-like; petals absent; pistils 3-7, narrowed to a short, slender style. **Fruit** a beaked follicle 8-13 mm long. May-June.—Wet conifer woods and swamps, often on mossy hummocks.

Coptis trifolia

DELPHINIUM *Larkspur*

Delphinium carolinianum Walt.
CAROLINA LARKSPUR

MAP 1046
native

Perennial herb. **Stems** 4-12 dm tall, pubescent throughout. **Leaves** well distributed on the stem, deeply dissected into linear segments 2-8 mm wide. **Flowers** in an elongate terminal raceme, often branched; flowers irregular, prevailingly blue; upper sepal prolonged backward into a long spur 13-18 mm long, usually equaling or exceeding the blade; petals normally 4, the 2 upper inequilateral, each prolonged backward into a spur extending into the spurred sepal; lower petals bifid, bearded; stamens numerous; pistils 1-5, ripening into as many follicles, these 10-15 mm long; **seeds** 2-2.5 mm long, obscurely 3-winged. May-June.—Dry woods, prairies, sandhills.

ENEMION *False Rue-Anemone*

Enemion biternatum Raf.
EASTERN FALSE RUE-ANEMONE

MAP 1047
native

Isopyrum biternatum (Raf.) Torr. & Gray

Perennial herb; roots bearing numerous small tuber-like thickenings. **Stems** slender, erect or ascending, 1-4 dm long. **Basal leaves** long-petioled, 2-3x 3-parted; **stem leaves** short-petioled or sessile, 1-2x 3-parted or the uppermost trifoliolate; **leaflets** broadly obovate, 3-lobed. **Flowers** white, 1.5-2 cm wide. **Follicles** commonly 4, ovoid, compressed, divergent. April-May.—Moist woods.

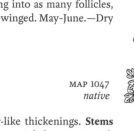

Enemion biternatum

1042. Ceratocephala testiculata   *1043. Clematis occidentalis*   *1044. Clematis virginiana*   *1045. Coptis trifolia*

HEPATICA

Perennial herbs with several 1-flowered scapes bearing a calyx-like involucre of 3 entire bracts immediately below the flower. Leaves basal, simple, lobed. Sepals 5-12, petal-like. Petals none. Stamens numerous. Pistils numerous; ovary tapering into a short style. Achenes conic to fusiform, pubescent. *The genus is very close to **Anemone** and often merged with it, differing only in the simple leaves and the position of the involucre (see species descriptions for synonyms). Leaves persist during the winter, the new leaves appearing after the very early blooming flowers.*

1   Leaves lobed nearly to middle of blade, the lobes rounded . . . . *H. americana*
1   Leaves lobed to more than middle of blade, the lobes acute . . . . *H. acutiloba*

Hepatica acutiloba DC.
MAP 1048
SHARP-LOBE HEPATICA
native
    Anemone acutiloba (DC.) G. Lawson
    Hepatica nobilis var. *acuta* (Pursh) Steyermark

Leaves 3-lobed or occasionally 5-7-lobed, deeply cordate at base, the lobes acute. **Scapes** 5-15 cm long, villous, as are also the petioles. **Bracts** acute, about equaling the sepals. **Flowers** 12-25 mm wide. March-April.—Dry or moist woods.

Hepatica americana (DC.) Ker-Gawl.
MAP 1049
ROUND-LOBE HEPATICA
native
    Anemone americana (DC.) Hara
    Hepatica nobilis var. *obtusa* (Pursh) Steyermark
    Hepatica triloba Chaix

Hepatica acutiloba

Very similar to *H. acutiloba* except in leaves and bracts. **Leaves** averaging smaller, 3-lobed, the lobes broadly obtuse or rounded, the terminal one often wider than long. **Bracts** obtuse. March-April.—Rich deciduous forests, as for *H. acutiloba*, but more often found on drier sites with aspen, oak, hickory, pine, or sometimes with spruce or cedar.

HYDRASTIS *Goldenseal*

Hydrastis canadensis L.
MAP 1050
GOLDENSEAL
endangered | native

Perennial herb. **Stems** 2-5 dm high, pubescent, bearing one basal leaf and two stem leaves near the summit. **Leaf blades** broadly cordate in outline, 5-lobed and palmately 5-nerved, at anthesis 3-10 cm wide, continuing their growth and eventually to 2.5 dm wide, the lobes incised, doubly serrate. **Flower** solitary, terminal, peduncle pubescent, about 1 cm long; sepals 3, petal-like, falling when the flower opens; petals none; stamens and pistils numerous; styles very short. **Fruit** a head of dark red, 1-2-seeded berries. April-May.—Deep rich woods. The knotty yellow rhizomes are used in medicine and have been collected so extensively that the plant is scarce. *Minnesota at northern edge of species' range.*

Hepatica americana

MYOSURUS *Mousetail*

Myosurus minimus L.
MAP 1051
TINY MOUSETAIL
introduced

Inconspicuous annual herb. **Stems** 4-15 cm long. **Leaves** in a basal tuft, hairless, linear, mostly less than 1 mm wide. **Flowers** few to many, in a spike atop a slender stalk to 6 cm long when mature; sepals 5, green, upright, with a spur at base;

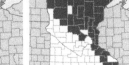
Hydrastis canadensis

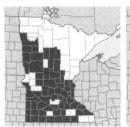

1046. Delphini. carolinianum   1047. Enemion biternatum   1048. Hepatica acutiloba   1049. Hepatica americana

petals 5 or sometimes absent, white or pink; stamens 5-10; pistils many, in an elongate receptacle. **Fruit** an achene, 2-3 mm long and 1 mm wide, with a small beak. April-June.—Wet to moist places such as streambanks and floodplains, sometimes temporarily in shallow water; also in disturbed drier areas.

Myosurus minimus

RANUNCULUS *Buttercup; Crowfoot; Spearwort*

Aquatic, semi-aquatic, or terrestrial annual and perennial herbs. Stems erect to sprawling, sometimes floating in water. Leaves simple, or compound and finely dissected, often variable on same plant; alternate on stem or all from base of plant; petioles short to long. Flowers borne above water surface in aquatic species; sepals usually 5, green; petals usually 5, yellow or white, often fading to white, usually with a small nectary pit covered by a scale near base of petal; stamens and pistils numerous. Achenes many in a round or cylindric head; achene body thick or flattened, tipped with a straight or curved beak.

1　Flowers white; leaves divided into linear or threadlike segments; plants typically aquatic . . . . *R. aquatilis*
1　Flowers yellow; leaves simple to deeply lobed or divided into narrow segments; plants aquatic or terrestrial . . 2
　　2　Sepals 3 (rarely 4) . . . . *R. lapponicus*
　　2　Sepals 5 (or rarely more) 3
　　　　3　All leaves simple and entire, or shallowly lobed with rounded teeth 4
　　　　　　4　Leaves ovate to round or kidney-shaped, shallowly lobed with rounded teeth; achenes with longitudinal ribs . . . . *R. cymbalaria*
　　　　　　4　Leaves oval to lance-shaped or linear, entire to sharp-toothed; achenes not ribbed . . . . . . *R. flammula*
　　　　3　All, or at least stem leaves, deeply lobed, divided, or compound 5
　　　　　　5　Basal and stem leaves distinctly different in shape, the basal leaves mostly entire or with rounded teeth, the stem leaves deeply divided 6
　　　　　　　　6　Flower petals 4-10 mm long, longer and wider than the sepals . . . . *R. rhomboideus*
　　　　　　　　6　Flower petals to 3 mm long, shorter and narrower than the sepals . . . . *R. abortivus*
　　　　　　5　Basal and stem leaves similar, all deeply lobed, divided, or compound 7
　　　　　　　　7　Achenes swollen, without a sharp-edged margin 8
　　　　　　　　　　8　Petals 2-4 mm long; achenes to 1.2 mm long, nearly beakless; plants terrestrial or in water only part of season . . . . *R. sceleratus*
　　　　　　　　　　8　Petals 4-14 mm long; achenes 1.2-2.5 mm long, beaked; plants underwater or exposed later in season 9
　　　　　　　　　　　　9　Petals more than 7 mm long; achene body more than 1.6 mm long, achene margin thickened and white-corky below the middle . . . . *R. flabellaris*
　　　　　　　　　　　　9　Petals less than 7 mm long; achene body less than 1.6 mm long, achene margin rounded but not thickened . . . . *R. gmelinii*
　　　　　　　　7　Achenes flattened, with a sharp or winglike margin 10
　　　　　　　　　　10　Petals 2-5 mm long 11
　　　　　　　　　　　　11　Beak of achene strongly hooked . . . . *R. recurvatus*
　　　　　　　　　　　　11　Beak of achene straight or only slightly curved 12
　　　　　　　　　　　　　　12　Petals shorter than sepals; achenes in cylindric heads longer than wide; widespread . . . . *R. pensylvanicus*
　　　　　　　　　　　　　　12　Petals equal or longer than sepals; heads ovate or round; uncommon in n Minn . . . . *R. macounii*
　　　　　　　　　　10　Petals 7-15 mm long 13
　　　　　　　　　　　　13　Style short and outcurved; introduced and weedy species 14
　　　　　　　　　　　　　　14　Stems creeping; terminal segment of the main leaves stalked . . . . *R. repens*
　　　　　　　　　　　　　　14　Stems upright; terminal segment of the main leaves not stalked, usually with green tissue extending to the lateral segments . . . . *R. acris*
　　　　　　　　　　　　13　Style elongate and nearly straight; native, non-weedy species 15
　　　　　　　　　　　　　　15　Main leaf blades mostly longer than wide; mature receptacle cone-shaped　*R. fascicularis*
　　　　　　　　　　　　　　15　Main leaf blades usually wider than long; mature receptacle often club-shaped and widest at tip . . . . *R. hispidus*

Ranunculus abortivus L.

MAP 1052

KIDNEY-LEAF BUTTERCUP   *native*

Biennial or perennial herb. **Stems** upright, 2-5 dm long, branched above, smooth
or with fine hairs. **Leaves** at base of plant round to kidney-shaped, margins with
rounded teeth, some leaves lobed; petioles long; stem leaves 3-5-divided into
linear segments, margins entire or broadly toothed, petioles absent. **Flowers**
yellow, petals 2-3 mm long, shorter than sepals. **Achenes** in a short, round head;
achene body swollen, 1-2 mm long, with a very short, curved beak. April-June.
—Wet to moist woods, floodplains, wet meadows, thickets, ditches; especially
where soils disturbed or compacted.   *Ranunculus abortivus*

Ranunculus acris L.

MAP 1053

MEADOW-BUTTERCUP   *introduced (naturalized)*

Perennial herb, with fibrous roots. **Stems** hairy, to 1 m long, with few branches,
most leaves on lower part of stem. **Leaves** kidney-shaped, deeply 3-7-divided, the
segments again lobed or dissected; branch leaves much smaller, 3-parted. **Flowers**
numerous; sepals 5, half length of petals; petals 5, bright yellow, 6-15 mm long,
obovate, often with a rounded notch at tip. **Achenes** in a round head; achene
body flat, 2-3 mm long, beak 0.5 mm long. June-Aug.—Common weed of fields,
thickets, ditches and shores.   *Ranunculus acris*

Ranunculus aquatilis L.

MAP 1054

LONG-BEAK WATER-CROWFOOT   *native*

Ranunculus longirostris Godr., *Ranunculus trichophyllus* Chaix

Perennial aquatic herb; plants mostly smooth. **Stems** underwater or floating, 3-
8 dm long, with a few branches, rooting from lower nodes. **Leaves** round to
kidney-shaped in outline, 2-3x divided into narrow threadlike segments 1-2 cm
long, stiff and not collapsing when removed from water; leaf segments tipped
with tiny transparent spine; petioles absent or to 4 mm long. **Flowers** at or below
water surface, single from upper leaf axils, 1-1.5 cm wide; sepals 5, purple-green,
spreading, 2-4 mm long; petals 5, white, yellow at base, 4-9 mm long. **Achenes**
15-25 in a round head; achene body obovate, ridged, the beak thin and straight,
1-1.5 mm long. May-Aug.—Ponds, lakes, streams, rivers and ditches.

Our plants ometimes treated as 2 species as follows:

1   Styles (at least the longest) and achene beaks 0.6-1.1 mm long, more than 1/3
    the length of the achene body. . . . . **R. longirostris**
1   Styles and achene beaks very short, less than 0.6 mm long, less than about 1/3
    the length of the body . . . . **R. trichophyllus**

Ranunculus aquatilis

Ranunculus cymbalaria Pursh

MAP 1055

ALKALI BUTTERCUP   *native*

Cyrtorhyncha cymbalaria (Pursh) Britton, *Halerpestes cymbalaria* (Pursh) Greene

Perennial herb, spreading by stolons and forming dense mats. **Stems** 3-20 cm
long, smooth. **Leaves** all from base of plant, ovate to kidney-shaped, 5-25 mm
long and 4-30 mm wide, heart-shaped at base; margins with rounded teeth, often
with 3 prominent lobes at tip; petioles sparsely hairy. **Flower stalks** longer than
leaves, unbranched or with a few branches, with 1 to several flowers; sepals 5,
green-yellow, 3-5 mm long, deciduous; petals usually 5, yellow, turning white
with age, 3-5 mm long; stamens 10-30. **Achenes** numerous in a cylindric head to
10 mm long; achene body 1.5-2 mm long, longitudinally nerved, beak short and

Ranunculus cymbalaria

1050. Hydrastis canadensis   *1051. Myosurus minimus*   *1052. Ranunculus abortivus*   *1053. Ranunculus acris*

straight. June-Sept.—Wet meadows, streambanks, sandy or muddy shores, ditches and seeps, often in wet mud or sand; often where brackish.

Ranunculus fascicularis Muhl.   MAP 1056
EARLY BUTTERCUP   *native*

Perennial herb. **Stems** 1-2, or at maturity 3 dm tall, usually 2-5 from one base, strigose. **Leaves** mostly basal, ovate in outline, distinctly longer than wide, the terminal segment stalked, all segments deeply lobed, the lobes incised or coarsely crenately toothed; **stem leaves** 1-3, smaller, sessile or nearly so, less divided. **Flowers** long-peduncled; petals elliptic or oblong, 8-14 mm long, 3-5.5 mm wide. **Achenes** rotund, 2-3.3 mm long, sharply margined; beak slender, straight or nearly so, 1.4-3 mm long. April-May.—Prairies and dry woods.

Ranunculus flabellaris Raf.   MAP 1057
GREATER YELLOW WATER BUTTERCUP   *native*

Perennial herb; plants smooth or sometimes hairy when growing out-of-water. **Stems** floating, or upright from a sprawling base when exposed, branched, rooting at lower nodes, 3-7 dm long. **Underwater leaves** 3-parted into linear segments 1-2 mm wide, **exposed leaves** (when present) round to kidney-shaped in outline, 2-10 cm long and 2-12 cm wide, divided into 3 segments, the segments again 3-divided. **Flowers** 1 to several at ends of stems; sepals 5, green-yellow, 4-8 mm long; petals 5-8, bright yellow, 6-15 mm long. **Achenes** 50-75 in a round to ovate head; achene body obovate, to 2 mm long, the margin thickened and corky below middle, beak broad, flat, 1-1.5 mm long. May-July.—Shallow water or muddy shores of ponds, quiet streams, swamps, woodland pools, marshes and ditches.

Ranunculus flabellaris

Ranunculus flammula L.   MAP 1058
CREEPING SPEARWORT   *native*

Perennial herb, spreading by stolons; plants often covered with appressed hairs. **Stems** sprawling, rooting at nodes, unbranched or few-branched, with upright shoots 4-15 cm long. **Leaves** in small clusters at nodes, simple, linear or threadlike, 1-5 cm long and 1.5 mm wide, margins more or less entire; upper leaves smaller and with shorter petioles than lower. **Flowers** single at ends of stems; sepals 5, yellow-green, 2-4 mm long, with stiff hairs; petals 5, yellow, obovate, 3-5 mm long. **Achenes** 10-25 in a round head; achene body swollen, obovate, 1-1.5 mm long, smooth, the beak short, to 0.5 mm long. June-Aug. Sandy, gravelly, or muddy shores; shallow to deep water, water usually acid.

Ranunculus flammula

Ranunculus gmelinii DC.   MAP 1059
LESSER YELLOW WATER BUTTERCUP   *native*

Perennial herb, similar to yellow water-crowfoot (*R. flabellaris*) but plants aquatic or at least partly underwater; smooth or sometimes with coarse hairs. **Stems** usually sprawling and rooting at nodes, 1-5 dm long, sparsely branched. **Leaves** all on stem or with a few basal leaves on long petioles, deeply 3-lobed or dissected, the segments again forked 2-3 times; underwater leaf segments 2-4 mm wide; exposed leaves to 2 cm long and 1.5-2.5 cm wide. **Flowers** usually 1 to several at ends of stems; sepals 5, green-yellow, 3-6 mm long; petals 5-8, yellow, 4-8 mm long. **Achenes** 50-70 in a round to ovate head; achene body obovate, 1-1.5 mm long, the margin rounded, not corky-thickened, the beak broad and thin, 0.4-0.7 mm long, somewhat curved. July-Aug.—Muddy streambanks and lakeshores, cold springs, pools in swamps and bogs.

Ranunculus gmelinii

1054. *Ranunculus aquatilis*

1055. *Ranunculus cymbalaria*

1056. *Ranunculus fascicularis*

1057. *Ranunculus flabellaris*

Ranunculus hispidus Michx.

MAP 1060
NORTHERN SWAMP BUTTERCUP　　　　　　　　　　*native*
Perennial herb; stems and leaves variable. **Stems** upright, 2-9 dm long, smooth
to coarsely hairy. **Leaves** from base of plant and on stems, the basal leaves larger
and with longer petioles than stem leaves; 3-lobed, heart-shaped in outline, 3-14
cm long and 4-20 cm wide, with appressed hairs on veins, upper leaves usually
strongly toothed. **Flowers** 1 to several; sepals 5, yellow-green, 5-11 mm long,
hairy; petals 5-8, yellow, fading to white, 7-15 mm long and 3-10 mm wide.
Achenes 15-30 or more in a round head; achene body obovate, 2-4 mm long,
smooth, winged on margin, the beak straight, 2-3 mm long. May-July.—Wet
woods, floodplains and swamps, thickets, lakeshores, wet meadows and fens.

Ranunculus lapponicus L.

MAP 1061
LAPLAND BUTTERCUP　　　　　　　　　　　　*native*
　　Coptidium lapponicum (L.) Tzvelev
Perennial herb, spreading by rhizomes. **Stems** prostrate, 1-2 dm long, sending up
1 shoot from each node, the shoots with 1-2 basal leaves, sometimes with a single
smaller leaf above. **Leaves** kidney-shaped, deeply 3-cleft, margins with rounded
teeth or shallowly lobed. **Flowers** single at ends of shoots; petals yellow with
orange veins, 8-12 mm wide; sepals 3, curved downward. **Achenes** in a round
head; achene body 2-3 mm long, swollen near base, flattened above, beak slender,
sharply hooked. June-July.—Cedar swamps and bogs. *Plants resemble **three-leaf
goldthread** (Coptis trifolia) but Lappland buttercup leaves are lobed, not compound,
lighter green and deciduous.*

Ranunculus hispidus

Ranunculus macounii Britton

MAP 1062
MACOUN'S BUTTERCUP　　　　　　　　　　　　*native*
Annual or short-lived perennial herb, similar to bristly crowfoot (*Ranunculus
pensylvanicus*) but less common; plants smooth to densely hairy. **Stems** erect or
reclining, hollow, 2-7 dm long, branched, the branches again branched. **Leaves**
from base of plant and on stems, the basal leaves larger and with longer petioles
than stem leaves; triangular in outline, 4-14 cm long and 6-16 cm wide, 3-lobed
or divided into 3 segments, the segments themselves 3-lobed and coarsely
toothed. **Flowers** several at ends of branches; sepals 5, yellow, 3-5 mm long; petals
5, yellow, 3-5 mm long, equal or longer than sepals; stamens 15-35. **Achenes** 30-
50 in an ovate to round head; achene body flat, 3 mm long, smooth or shallowly
pitted, with a stout, slightly curved or straight beak 1-2 mm long. June-Aug.
—Wet meadows, marshes, shores, streambanks and ditches.

Ranunculus lapponicus

Ranunculus pensylvanicus L. f.

MAP 1063
BRISTLY CROWFOOT　　　　　　　　　　　　*native*
Annual or short-lived perennial herb. **Stems** erect, hollow, 3-8 dm long, branched
or unbranched. **Leaves** at base of plant withering early, larger and with longer
petioles than the few stem leaves; 4-12 cm long and 4-15 cm wide, with appressed
hairs, 3- lobed and coarsely toothed, the terminal leaflet stalked. **Flowers** few, on
short stalks; sepals 5, yellow, 4-5 mm long; petals 5, pale yellow, fading to white,
shorter than the sepals, 2-4 mm long; stamens 15-20. **Achenes** many, in a rounded
cylindric head 10-15 mm long; achene body flattened, 2-3 mm long, smooth, the
beak stout, 0.5-1.5 mm long. July-Aug.—Marshes, wet meadows, ditches and
streambanks, often in muck.

Ranunculus pensylvanicus

1058. *Ranunculus flammula*　　1059. *Ranunculus gmelinii*　　1060. *Ranunculus hispidus*　　1061. *Ranunculus lapponicus*

Ranunculus recurvatus Poir.

MAP 1064
HOOKED CROWFOOT *native*

Perennial herb. **Stems** 2-7 dm long, usually hairy, branches few. **Leaves** broadly kidney-shaped or round in outline, 3-parted to below middle, covered with long, soft hairs; petioles present on all but uppermost leaves. **Flowers** on stalks at ends of stems; sepals curved downward, to 6 mm long; petals pale yellow, 4-6 mm long; styles strongly hooked. **Achenes** in a short-cylindric head; achene body flat, round, sharp-margined, to 2 mm long; beak 1 mm long, hooked or coiled. May-June.—Moist deciduous forests (especially in openings), swamps; also in drier woods; southward also in partial shade in calcareous fens.

Ranunculus repens L.

MAP 1065
CREEPING BUTTERCUP *introduced*

Perennial herb. **Stems** normally creeping and rooting at the nodes, rarely ascending or erect; hirsute, strigose, or rarely glabrous. **Leaves** 3-parted, petioled, the segments broadly obovate in outline, cleft or lobed, sharply toothed. **Petals** 8-15 mm long, about two-thirds as wide. **Achenes** obovate, 2.5-3.5 mm long, sharply but narrowly margined; beak triangular, usually somewhat curved, 0.8-1.5 mm long. May-July.—Native of Europe; introduced in fields, lawns, roadsides, and wet meadows. Plants vary in size, and in kind and amount of pubescence.

Ranunculus recurvatus

Ranunculus rhomboideus Goldie

MAP 1066
LABRADOR BUTTERCUP *native*

Perennial herb. **Stems** 8-20 cm tall at anthesis. **Basal leaves** ovate-oblong to broadly ovate, 1-5 cm long, long-petioled, crenate mostly above the middle, tapering to rounded or acute at base; **stem leaves** sessile or subsessile, cleft into a few linear divisions. **Flowers** few to several, on villous peduncles; petals oblong-elliptic, 5-9 mm long, much longer than the villous sepals. **Achenes** in a globose head, obovate, 2-2.8 mm long, flattened at the base, turgid above the middle; beak very short. April-May.—Dry open woods and prairies.

Ranunculus rhomboideus

Ranunculus sceleratus L.

MAP 1067
CURSED CROWFOOT *native*

Weedy annual herb; plants smooth, sometimes partly submersed in shallow water. **Stems** upright, hollow, 1-6 dm long, branched above and with many flowers. **Leaves** from base of plant less deeply parted and with longer petioles than stem leaves; upper stem leaves small; leaves deeply 3-parted, the main lobes again lobed, heart-shaped at base, rounded at tip, 1-6 cm long and 3-8 cm wide. **Flowers** numerous at ends of stalks from upper leaf axils and branches; sepals 5, 2-3 mm long, yellow-green, tips curved downward; petals 5, light yellow, fading to white, 3-5 mm long. **Achenes** numerous in a short-cylindric head 4-11 mm long; achene body obovate, 1 mm long, slightly corky-thickened on margins; beak tiny, blunt. May-Sept.—Muddy shores, streambanks, wet meadows, ditches, marshes and other wet places.

Ranunculus sceleratus

THALICTRUM *Meadow-Rue*

Perennial herbs. Leaves alternate, compound. Staminate and pistillate flowers separate, in panicles on separate plants; sepals 4-5, green or petal-like but soon deciduous; petals absent; stamens numerous, the stalks (filaments) long and slender; pistils several to many. Fruit a ribbed or nerved achene.

1062. *Ranuncul. macounii*   1063. *Ranuncul. pensylvanicus*   1064. *Ranunculus recurvatus*   1065. *Ranunculus repens*

1 Flowers few in an umbel .... ***T. thalictroides***
1 Flowers in racemes or panicles 2

    2 Upper stem leaves with long petioles; leaflets glabrous and not glandular; flowering in April or May before leaves fully expanded; plants less than 1m tall .... ***T. dioicum***

    2 Upper stem leaves sessile or nearly so (the 3 stalked leaflets appearing to arise together from the node); leaflets glabrous, or hairy, or with small, short-stalked glands; flowering in summer after leaves expanded; plants often more than 1 m tall 3

        3 Leaflets 3-lobed, each lobe tipped with 1-3 teeth .... ***T. venulosum***

        3 Leaflets usually 3-lobed, the lobes usually not toothed 4

            4 Underside of leaflets with very short hairs (rarely smooth), not glandular; leaves odorless; widespread .... ***T. dasycarpum***

            4 Underside of leaflets with small beads and hairs tipped with gray or amber exudate; leaves with strong odor when crushed; uncommon in ne Minn .... ***T. revolutum***

Thalictrum dasycarpum Fisch. & Avé-Lall.

PURPLE MEADOW-RUE

MAP 1068
native

Perennial herb, from a short rootstock. **Stems** purple-tinged, 1-2 m long, branched above. **Leaves** divided into 3-4 groups of leaflets; leaflets 15 mm or more long, mostly tipped with 3 pointed lobes, dark green above, underside sparsely short-hairy, not waxy and without gland-tipped hairs; margins usually slightly turned under; stem leaves mostly without petioles. **Flowers** in panicles at ends of stems; staminate and pistillate flowers separate and on different plants (sometimes with some perfect flowers); sepals 3-5 mm long, lance-shaped; anthers linear and sharp-tipped, 2-3 mm long, filaments white; stigmas straight, 2-4 mm long. **Achenes** 4-6 mm long, ribbed, in a round cluster. June-July.—Wet to moist meadows, low prairie, swamps, thickets, streambanks.

Thalictrum dasycarpum

Thalictrum dioicum L.

EARLY MEADOW-RUE

MAP 1069
native

Perennial herb, dioecious. **Stems** 3-7 dm tall at anthesis. **Leaves** all with long petioles, the uppermost 3-6 cm long and subtending the inflorescence; stipules of the upper leaves broadly ovate, mostly much wider than long. Filaments and anthers yellow or greenish yellow. Mature **achenes** sessile or subsessile, about 4 mm long, strongly ribbed, straight and essentially symmetrical.—Moist woods. *Flowering with or before the expansion of leaves on deciduous trees in spring.*

Thalictrum revolutum DC.

WAXY-LEAF MEADOW-RUE

MAP 1070
native

Perennial herb, from short rootstocks, with strong odor when crushed. **Stems** more or less smooth, often purple-tinged, 0.5-1.5 m long. Lowest **leaves** with petioles, middle and upper leaves stalkless; leaves divided into 3-4 groups of leaflets; **leaflets** variable in shape and size, usually 3-lobed, some 1-2 lobed, upper surface smooth, underside leathery and conspicuously net-veined, finely hairy with gland-tipped hairs, margins turned under. **Flowers** in panicles at ends of stems; staminate and pistillate flowers separate and on different plants (sometimes with some perfect flowers); anthers linear, 2-3 mm long, filaments threadlike, 2-5 mm long; pistils 6-12, stigmas 2-3 mm long. **Fruit** an oval or lance-shaped achene, 4-5 mm long, ridged, with tiny gland-tipped hairs. June-July. —Streambanks, thickets, moist meadows and prairies.

Thalictrum dioicum

Thalictrum revolutum

1066. Ranuncul. rhomboideus   *1067. Ranunculus sceleratus*   *1068. Thalictrum dasycarpum*   *1069. Thalictrum dioicum*

Thalictrum thalictroides (L.) Eames & Boivin
RUE-ANEMONE
Anemonella thalictroides (L.) Spach.

MAP 1071
native

Perennial herb. **Stems** slender, 1-2 dm tall. **Leaf segments** broadly ovate or oblong to subrotund, 1-3 cm long, 3-toothed distally, rounded to subcordate at base. **Sepals** white to pale pink-purple, 10-15 mm long. April-May.—Dry to moist woods. Color of the sepals sometimes approaches red, blue, or green; double flowers are often observed.

Thalictrum venulosum Trel.
VEINY-LEAF MEADOW-RUE

MAP 1072
native

Perennial herb, spreading by rhizomes; plants pale green, waxy. **Stems** erect, 3-10 dm long. **Leaves** divided into 3-4 groups of leaflets; leaflets firm, nearly circular or obovate in outline, tipped by 3-5 lobes, underside veiny, appearing wrinkled, usually sparsely covered with gland-tipped hairs; lower leaves on petioles, upper leaves stalkless. **Flowers** in narrow panicles at ends of stems, the panicle branches nearly erect; staminate and pistillate flowers separate and on different plants; stamens 8-20, anthers linear and pointed at tip, filaments slender. **Fruit** an ovate achene, 4-6 mm long, tapered to a short-beak. June-July.—Streambanks, thickets, wet shores.

Thalictrum venulosum

Rhamnaceae BUCKTHORN FAMILY

Shrubs, trees, or woody vines with simple, opposite or alternate leaves, and small flowers. Flowers perfect or unisexual, regular, 4-5-merous. Petals present or lacking, small, separate. Stamens as many as and alternate with the sepals, opposite and often enfolded by the petals. Ovary 1, sessile on the disk or immersed in it; styles 2-5, united for all or part of their length. Fruit a capsule or drupe.

1 Leaves 3-veined from base of leaf; flowers white in many-flowered, stalked clusters; fruit a capsule . . **Ceanothus**
1 Leaves not 3-veined from base; flowers greenish, single or few to a cluster; fruit a fleshy drupe 2
    2 Leaf margins entire or nearly so . . . . *Frangula alnus*
    2 Leaf margins toothed . . . . *Rhamnus*

CEANOTHUS *Ceanothus*

Low shrubs. Leaves alternate, 3-nerved, glandular-serrate. Flowers small, white, in sessile or short-peduncled umbels aggregated into terminal or axillary panicles. Sepals inflexed, at length deciduous above the hypanthium. Petals long-clawed. Stamens at anthesis free and exsert. Ovary 3-angled and 3-celled, immersed in the disk; style 3-lobed. Fruit a 3-lobed capsule-like drupe subtended by the persistent hypanthium. Many species highly ornamental. *Characteristic are the leaves with 3 pairs of prominent parallel veins extending from the leaf base to the outer margins of the leaf tips.*

1 Leaves elliptic, less than 2 cm wide; inflorescences at ends of current year's shoots . . . . *C. herbaceus*
1 Leaves ovate, mostly more than 2 cm wide; inflorescences from leaf axils . . . . *C. americanus*

Ceanothus americanus L.
NEW JERSEY-TEA

MAP 1073
native

Shrub to 1 m tall, often freely branched. **Leaves** narrowly to broadly ovate, 3-8 cm long, usually more than half as wide, broadly cuneate to rounded or subcordate at base, the lateral nerves commonly naked for 1-3 mm at base. **Inflorescences** on axillary peduncles, the lower peduncles progressively longer and to 2 dm long; panicle

1070. Thalictrum revolutum   *1071. Thalictrum thalictroides*   *1072. Thalictrum venulosum*   *1073. Ceanothus americanus*

short-cylindric to ovoid, occasionally branched, often subtended by 1-3 reduced leaves, the umbels usually separated by distinct internodes. **Fruit** depressed-obovoid, 5-6 mm long. June-July.—Upland woods, prairies, and barrens.

Ceanothus herbaceus Raf.

MAP 1074

PRAIRIE REDROOT

native

Bushy shrub to 1 m tall. **Leaves** oblong to elliptic, 2-6 cm long, 1-2 cm wide, the lateral nerves never naked and often arising unevenly 1-3 mm above the base of the leaf; leaf underside usually pubescent. **Panicles** several to many, terminating the leafy branches of the season, on peduncles rarely to 5 cm long, hemispheric to short-ovoid, the component umbels very close together. **Fruit** 4-5 mm long. May-June.—Sandy or rocky soil, prairies and plains.

Ceanothus americanus

FRANGULA *False Buckthorn*

Frangula alnus P. Mill.

MAP 1075

GLOSSY FALSE BUCKTHORN

introduced (naturalized)

    Frangula dodonei Ard.
    Rhamnus frangula L.

Shrub to 7 m tall. **Leaves** usually obovate-oblong, 5-8 cm long, commonly more than half as wide, acute to abruptly short-acuminate, entire or with a few marginal glands near the tip. **Umbels** sessile, 2-8-flowered; pedicels usually unequal, 3-10 mm long. **Flowers** perfect, 5-merous; petals broadly obovate, scarcely clawed, cleft at the tip, 1-1.4 mm long; styles connate to the tip. **Fruit** red, ripening to nearly black, 2-3-stoned. May-June.—Eurasian; escaped from cultivation, especially in wet soil.

Frangula alnus

RHAMNUS *Buckthorn*

Shrubs or small trees. Leaves simple, alternate or opposite, pinnately veined, usually with stipules. Flowers perfect, or staminate or pistillate, regular, single or few from leaf axils; sepals joined, 4- or 5-parted; petals 4 or 5. Fruit a purple-black, berrylike drupe with 2-4, 1-seeded stones.

1   Leaves with 2-4 obvious pairs of lateral veins .... *R. cathartica*
1   Leaves with mostly 5 or more pairs of lateral veins .... *R. alnifolia*

Rhamnus alnifolia L'Hér.

MAP 1076

ALDER-LEAF BUCKTHORN

native

Shrub to 1 m tall, forming low thickets. **Leaves** alternate, oval to ovate, 6-10 cm long and 3-5 cm wide, green above, paler green below; margins with low, rounded teeth; petioles grooved, 5-12 mm long; stipules linear, to 1 cm long, deciduous before fruit mature. **Flowers** appearing with leaves in spring, in clusters of 1-3 flowers from leaf axils; yellow-green, usually 5-parted, 3 mm wide, on short stalks, with both stamens and pistils but one or other is nonfunctional, sepals 1-2 mm long, petals absent. **Fruit** a purple-black, berrylike drupe, 6-8 mm wide, with 1-3 nutletlike stones. May-June.—Conifer swamps, thickets, sedge meadows, wet depressions in deciduous forests; usually where calcium-rich.

Rhamnus cathartica L.

MAP 1077

EUROPEAN BUCKTHORN

introduced (invasive)

Rhamnus alnifolia

Shrub or small tree to 5 m tall. **Stems** with pale lenticels. **Leaves** mostly alternate but some leaves often nearly opposite, oval or obovate, 5-8 cm long and 3-5 cm wide; margins entire or slightly wavy; petioles stout, 1-2 cm long. **Flowers**

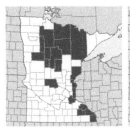

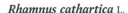

1074. *Ceanothus herbaceus*   1075. *Frangula alnus*   1076. *Rhamnus alnifolia*   1077. *Rhamnus cathartica*

appearing after leaves in spring, perfect, single or in clusters of 2-8 in leaf axils, green-yellow, 5-parted, to 5 mm wide; petals 1-2 mm long. **Fruit** a purple-black, berrylike drupe, 7 mm wide, with 2-3 nutlike stones. May-Aug. Conifer swamps, thickets, calcareous fens, lakeshores, moist to dry woods, especially where disturbed, heavily grazed, or cleared.—Introduced from Eurasia; escaping from cultivation in ne and c North America.

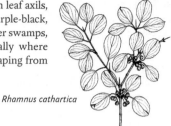

Rhamnus cathartica

Rosaceae   ROSE FAMILY

Shrubs and perennial, biennial, or annual herbs. Leaves evergreen or deciduous, mostly alternate and simple or compound. Flowers perfect (with both staminate and pistillate parts), regular, with 5 sepals and petals; stamens numerous. Fruit an achene, capsule, or fleshy fruit with numerous embedded seeds (drupe), or a fleshy fruit with seeds within (pome).

ADDITIONAL SPECIES
Cotoneaster acutifolius Turcz. var. *lucidus* (Schltdl.) L.T. Lu, native of se Asia; Cook and St. Louis counties.

1   Plants trees, shrubs, or erect to trailing, thorny to bristly brambles 2
    2   Leaves mostly compound; branches or stems often thorny or bristly 3
        3   Stems biennial, prickly or bristly; leaves 3-parted or palmately compound; fruit a tight cluster of juicy drupelets; flowers usually white . . . . *Rubus*
        3   Stems perennial, smooth or thorny; leaves pinnately compound; fruit various but not a cluster of drupelets; flowers white, pink, or yellow 4
            4   Flowers pink (rarely white or yellow), 2 cm or more wide; stems thorny; fruit fleshy, red to orange   *Rosa*
            4   Flowers white or yellow, mostly less than 2 cm wide; stems smooth; fruit various 5
                5   Flowers solitary or few in an inflorescence, the petals yellow; leaflets entire . . . *Potentilla fruticosa*
                5   Flowers many in a crowded inflorescence, the petals white; leaflets toothed 6
                    6   Colony-forming shrub, occasionally escaping from cultivation; inflorescence a panicle, much longer than wide; leaflets doubly-toothed (each main tooth with several smaller teeth) . . . . *Sorbaria sorbifolia*
                    6   Small trees; inflorescence much wider than long; leaflets not doubly toothed . . . . *Sorbus*
    2   Leaves simple; branches and stems smooth or only with long stout spines 7
        7   Style and ovary 1; fruit a drupe; leaves unlobed . . . . *Prunus*
        7   Styles 2 or more (1 in *Crataegus monogyna*); fruit a pome, or a cluster of drupelets or dry fruits 8
            8   Ovaries superior 9
                9   Leaves mostly 3-5 lobed; bark shredding into long strips . . . . *Physocarpus opulifolius*
                9   Leaves not lobed; bark not shredding into long strips . . . . *Spiraea*
            8   Ovary inferior 10
                10 Leaves with red or black glands along the midrib of the leaf upper surface . . . . *Aronia melanocarpa*
                10 Leaves without glands on midrib 11
                    11 Branches never thorny; flower petals white, lance-shaped and usually more than 2 times longer than wide . . . . *Amelanchier*
                    11 Branches sometimes with stout spines; petals less than 2 times longer than wide 12
                        12 Branches normally with spines; leaves toothed and often slightly lobed 13
                            13 Spines shiny; bud scales glabrous; petals white; seeds within hard nutlets . . . . *Crataegus*
                            13 Spines dull; bud scales hairy; petals pinkish; seeds within papery carpels . . . . *Malus*
                        12 Branches without spines; leaves toothed but not lobed 14
                            14 Young twigs densely hairy; petals pinkish; fruit an apple . . . . *Malus*
                            14 Young twigs glabrous; petals white; fruit a pear . . . . *Pyrus communis*
1   Plants herbs (sometimes woody at base), not thorny or bristly 15
    15 Leaves 3-parted or palmately compound 16
        16 Styles long, jointed near middle, the lower portion persistent on the achene as a long beak . . . . . . *Geum*
        16 Styles short, neither jointed nor persistent on the fruit 17
            17 Calyx with bractlets about as large as sepals, the calyx appearing 10-lobed 18
                18 Petals white; fruit fleshy and red; leaflets 3 . . . . *Fragaria*
                18 Petals yellow or white; fruit dry; leaflets 3, 5, or 7 19
                    19 Flowers yellow, leaflets 3, 5, or 7, regularly toothed, deciduous . . . . *Potentilla*

AGRIMONIA *Agrimony; Grooveburr*

Perennial herbs from stout rhizomes. Stems erect, simple or branched above. Leaves pinnately compound, mostly below middle of stem; stipules foliaceous, usually deeply toothed or laciniate. Flowers in long, interrupted, spike-like racemes, the short peduncle subtended by a laciniate bract, the very short pedicels by a pair of 3-lobed bractlets. Hypanthium obconic to hemispheric, with hooked bristles and small resinous glands. Sepals spreading at anthesis, later incurved and forming a beak on the fruit. Petals 5, yellow, 5-8 mm wide. Stamens 5-15. Pistils 2. Fruit an achene.

1 Inflorescence rachis covered with small glands, the pubescence sparse or absent . . . . *A. gryp, sepala*
1 Inflorescence rachis without glands or nearly so, but rachis covered with appressed to spreading hairs 2
   2 Leaflet underside velvety to touch, the hairs spreading . . . . *A. pubescens*
   2 Leaflet underside smooth or rough-to-touch, the hairs usually appressed . . . . *A. striata*

Agrimonia gryp250sepala Wallr.
TALL HAIRY AGRIMONY

MAP 1078
native

Perennial herb, roots fibrous. **Stems** stout, to 15 dm tall, glandular and sparsely or densely long-hirsute throughout. Principal **leaflets** of the larger leaves 5-9, ovate lance-shaped to elliptic or obovate, coarsely and often bluntly serrate, glabrous or or nearly so on the surface, sparsely hirsute on the veins; **stipules** large and leaflike, usually 1-2 cm wide. **Axis** glandular, hirsute with long spreading hairs; pedicel hirsute. **Hypanthium** glandular only, or also with a few short stiff hairs near the base, 3-5 mm long at maturity, expanded at the summit. July-Aug. —Moist or dry open woods.

Agrimonia gryposepala

1078. Agrimonia gryposepala   *1079. Agrimonia pubescens*   *1080. Agrimonia striata*

Agrimonia pubescens Wallr.
SOFT AGRIMONY

MAP 1079

native

Perennial herb, roots tuberously thickened. **Stems** stout, to 1 m tall or more, densely pubescent. Principal **leaflets** of the larger leaves 5-13, lance-shaped to elliptic or narrowly obovate, coarsely serrate, glabrous, scabrellate, or sparsely pubescent above, velvety-pubescent beneath; **stipules** lance-shaped to semi-ovate. **Axis** eglandular, densely pubescent. Mature **hypanthium** campanulate, 2.5-3 mm long, nearly as wide, more or less covered with short stiff ascending hairs, especially toward the base. July-Aug.—Dry open woods.

Agrimonia striata Michx.
WOODLAND AGRIMONY

MAP 1080

native

Perennial herb, roots fibrous. **Stems** stout and coarse, to 1 m tall or more, hirsute below, pubescent and glandular above. Principal **leaflets** of the larger leaves 7-11, the upper 5 commonly directed forwards, ovate lance-shaped, coarsely serrate, glabrous or nearly so above, sparsely pubescent beneath, especially on the veins; **stipules** lance-shaped, 1-2 cm long. **Axis** eglandular, densely pubescent with ascending hairs, commonly also with some long flexuous hairs. **Flowers** densely crowded; peduncle and pedicel short, the 3-cleft bractlet commonly surpassing the hypanthium; mature **hypanthium** reflexed, turbinate, 4-5 mm long, deeply furrowed. July-Aug.—Dry or moist woods.

Agrimonia striata

AMELANCHIER *Serviceberry*

Trees or shrubs, without thorns. Leaves simple, alternate, serrate. Flowers in short leafy racemes (except in *A. bartramiana*) terminating the branches of the season and opening with or before the leaves. Hypanthium obconic, campanulate, or saucer-shaped. Sepals 5, spreading to recurved, persistent. Petals 5, white, oblong to oval or obovate. Stamens usually 20, shorter than the petals. Ovary 5-celled; styles 5. *A confusing genus, similar to Crataegus in that hybridization, polyploidy, and asexual vegetative reproduction have created a wide variety of forms.*

HYBRIDS

• *Amelanchier* × *intermedia* Spach, cross between *A. arborea* × *A. canadensis;* see MAP 1082 for Minn distribution.
• *Amelanchier* × *neglecta* Eggl. ex G.N. Jones (pro sp.); cross between *A. bartramiana* and *A. laevis*, reported from several ne Minn locations.

1 Pedicels 1-3 in axils of leaves; petals less than twice as long as broad; leaves at least partly open and essentially glabrous (except margins and petioles) at flowering time, the blade tapering trough-like into raised petiole margins; petioles less than 8 (-15) mm long. . . . . ***A. bartramiana***
1 Pedicels 4 or more (at least scars present if some have fallen with fruit), the inflorescence a raceme; petals at least 2x as long as broad; leaves various (glabrous to tomentose) but the blade rounded or truncate to subcordate, not tapered at base; petioles usually longer than 8 mm 2
  2 Top of ovary glabrous; leaf blades short-acuminate, finely and closely serrate with 22-45 teeth per side . . . 3
    3 Leaves just beginning to unfold at flowering time, densely white-tomentose beneath, otherwise green, retaining some of the pubescence on petioles and along midrib beneath into maturity . . . . ***A. arborea***
    3 Leaves mostly half-grown at flowering time, usually bronze-red, glabrous or nearly so, completely glabrous at maturity . . . . ***A. laevis***
  2 Top of ovary tomentose; leaf blades variously shaped and toothed 4
    4 Larger leaves with ca. 25-50 fine teeth on a side (more than twice as many teeth as lateral veins), acute to short-acuminate, at flowering time open though not fully grown and often glabrous or soon becoming so. . . . . ***A. interior***
    4 Larger leaves with fewer than 20 (-25) teeth on a side (no more than 2x as many teeth as lateral veins), the blades at flowering time ± folded and white-tomentose beneath, when mature the tip acute to rounded . 5
      5 Most leaves finely toothed at least toward apex (5-8 teeth per cm when mature), the veins anastomosing and becoming indistinct near the margin, at most with weak veinlets ending in the teeth; petals ca. 5-9 mm long; plants typically spreading underground and forming colonies of low shrubs . . . ***A. spicata***
      5 Most leaves coarsely toothed (2-5 teeth per cm toward tip when mature), the veins prominent and running to tips of the teeth (or a principal fork into the teeth) at least toward tip of blade 6
        6 Pedicels short, mostly 6-8 mm long; petals less than 10 mm long . . . . ***A. alnifolia***
        6 Pedicels longer, the lower ones 15-20 mm long; petals 11 mm or more long . . . . ***A. sanguinea***

Amelanchier alnifolia (Nutt.) Nutt. ex M. Roem.

SASKATOON SERVICEBERRY

MAP 1083
native

Shrub or small tree, 1-4 m high, spreading via stolons. **Young branches** silky-pubescent, becoming glabrous or nearly so. **Older branches** smooth, reddish-brown to grayish **Leaves** longitudinally folded at anthesis, rounded at each end, 2-5 cm long and 2.5-4 cm wide; margins with a few serrate teeth at the tip. **Flowers** white, about 8-12 mm across, in racemes of 3-20 flowers quite early in the season. **Pome** globose, 6-10 mm wide, dark purple and very sweet and juicy when ripe; often with slight bloom; seeds 3-4 mm long. reddish-brown, often slightly hooked at one end, faintly striate. April-May.—Open woods, thickets, and shores. Distinguished from the similar and more eastern *A. sanguinea* by the usually broadly truncate or leaves, the blade broadly oval, the leaves unfolded but not fully grown at flowering time and soon becoming glabrous, and also by the shorter lower pedicels of the racemes. *Used by the Indians and early settlers as a constituent of pemmican; still used today in preserves, especially in the western USA.*

Amelanchier alnifolia

Amelanchier arborea (Michx. f.) Fern.

DOWNY SERVICEBERRY

MAP 1084
native

Tall shrub or small tree, rarely to 10 m tall. **Leaves** typically obovate, sharply and finely serrate nearly to the rounded or cordate base, densely pubescent beneath when young, at maturity nearly glabrous. **Racemes** drooping, many-flowered; pedicels 5-20 mm long, often covered with silky hairs; hypanthium glabrous; sepals 2-3 mm long, reflexed; petals narrowly oblong, 10-15 mm long. **Pomes** maroon-purple, 6-10 mm wide, insipid. April-May.—Usually in dry sandy open forests with red maple, aspen, oaks, or jack pine; sometimes in moist or swampy forests and borders.

Amelanchier arborea

Amelanchier bartramiana (Tausch) M. Roemer

OBLONG-FRUIT SERVICEBERRY

NC MAP 1085
native

Shrub to 2 m tall, often forming clumps; **twigs** purplish, more or less glabrous. **Leaves** alternate, ovate to oval, 2-5 cm long and 1-2.5 cm wide, often tipped with a small spine, green above, paler below, often purple-tinged when unfolding; margins with small, sharp, forward-pointing teeth; petioles to 1 cm long. **Flowers** 1 cm or more wide, single or in groups of 2-4 at ends of branches or on pedicels 1-2 cm long from leaf axils; sepals lance-shaped; petals white, oval to oblong, 6-10 mm long. **Pomes** dark purple, 1-1.5 cm wide, insipid. May-Aug.—Conifer swamps, open bogs, thickets, old dune or rock ridges; borders of hardwood forests; plants may be low and sprawling on bare rock shores and ledges, otherwise a tall shrub.

Amelanchier bartramiana

Amelanchier interior Nielsen

INLAND SERVICEBERRY
  Amelanchier wiegandii E.L. Nielsen

MAP 1086
native

Shrub or small tree. **Stems** 1-10 m tall, often straggling or arching; **twigs** glabrous at flowering. **Leaves** broadly ovate, 3-7 cm long and 2-5 cm wide, acute to short-acuminate, base rounded to subcordate, upper surface green, sparsely pubescent or glabrous by flowering time; margins serrate nearly to the base; petioles 1-3 cm long. **Inflorescence** 4-12-flowered, drooping or nodding; pedicels glabrous or nearly so; hypanthium campanulate, 3-6 mm wide; sepals recurving after flowering, 2-5 mm; petals white, obovate, 6-15 mm long; stamens 20; styles 5. **Pomes** purple-black, globose, 6-8 mm wide, sweet. May-June.—Sandy open

1082. Amelanch. × intermedia   1083. Amelanchier alnifolia   1084. Amelanch. arborea   1081. Amelanchier alnifolia

savannas and dunes, shallow soil on rock outcrops and shores; sometimes at borders of hardwood forests and conifer swamps.

Amelanchier laevis Wieg.
SMOOTH SERVICEBERRY

MAP 1087
native

Tall erect shrub or tree, to 10 m tall. **Leaves** elliptic to ovate, to 8 cm long at maturity, abruptly acute to short-acuminate, finely and sharply serrate nearly to the rounded or subcordate base, at anthesis about half grown and glabrous beneath or rarely with a few scattered hairs. **Racemes** many-flowered; pedicels glabrous, 1-3 cm long; hypanthium glabrous externally; sepals 3-4 mm long, reflexed; petals oblong, 10-18 mm long or rarely more; ovary glabrous at the tip. **Pomes** dark purple, mostly 10-15 mm wide, sweet. May.—Most often in dry sandy open forests and savannas, rocky sites, sandy bluffs and shores; also on river banks and forest and bog margins.

Amelanchier laevis

Amelanchier sanguinea (Pursh) DC.
NEW ENGLAND SERVICEBERRY
  Amelanchier humilis Wieg.

MAP 1088
native

Erect or straggling shrub or small tree, to 3 m tall, usually growing in clumps of several stems. **Leaves** about half grown at anthesis and then tomentose beneath, eventually glabrous, oblong to subrotund or subquadrate, to 7 cm long, finely or coarsely toothed, often only above the middle; veins often prominent and running to the teeth, especially in upper portion of blade. **Inflorescences** 4-10-flowered, soon arching or drooping; pedicels hairy; hypanthium saucer-shaped, 3.5-7.5 mm wide; sepals recurving or spreading after flowering, 3.5-5 mm; petals white, linear to narrowly spatulate, 11-18 mm long; stamens 20; styles 5; ovary summit rounded, densely hairy. **Pomes** dark purple or almost black, 5-8 mm wide, sweet. May-June.—Dry, open, sandy savannas and clearings; sandy thickets, borders of forests, gravelly shores, and low dunes.

Amelanchier sanguinea

Amelanchier spicata (Lam.) K. Koch
RUNNING SERVICEBERRY
  Amelanchier stolonifera Wieg.

MAP 1089
native

Stoloniferous shrub 3-10 or rarely 15 dm tall, forming colonies. **Leaves** a quarter to half grown at anthesis and then densely tomentose beneath, at maturity glabrous and much paler beneath, ovate to oblong, or obovate-oblong, usually 2-5 cm long, finely and sharply toothed; lateral veins curved forward, branched and anastomosing near the margin; teeth almost always more than twice as many as the veins. **Racemes** dense; pedicels thinly pubescent, soon glabrescent, the lowest 7-15 mm long. **Pomes** purple-black, glaucous, 7-12 mm wide, sweet. May. —Dry, sandy plains, dunes, and savannas, usually with jack pine or oaks, often little taller than the associated shrubby species of *Comptonia* and *Vaccinium*.

Amelanchier spicata

ARONIA *Chokeberry*

Aronia melanocarpa (Michx.) Elliott
BLACK CHOKEBERRY
  Photinia melanocarpa (Michx.) K.R. Robertson & J.B. Phipps

MAP 1090
native

Shrub, 1-2.5 m tall; plants glabrous; **twigs** gray to purple. **Leaves** alternate, oval or obovate, 3-8 cm long and 1-4 cm wide, upper surface dark green, underside paler; margins with small, rounded, forward-pointing teeth, the teeth gland-tipped;

Aronia melanocarpa

1085. Amelanch. bartramiana   1086. Amelanchier interior   1087. Amelanchier laevis

petioles to 1 cm long. **Flowers** 5-10 mm wide, in clusters of 5-15 at ends of stems and short, leafy branches; sepals usually glandular; petals white, 4-6 mm long. **Fruit** a dark purple to black, berrylike pome, 8-11 mm wide, not persisting into winter. May-June.—Tamarack swamps, open bogs, thickets, marshes and shores.

CHAMAERHODOS *Little-Rose*

Chamaerhodos erecta (L.) Bunge   MAP 1091
LITTLE-ROSE   *native*

Short-lived biennial or perennial herb from a taproot, usually reddish-tinged, glandular hairy throughout. **Stems** single, 1-3 dm tall, branched above. **Basal leaves** many, withering but not falling off, petiole slender, the blades 2-4x dissected into linear segments; **stem leaves** alternate, 2-3x dissected, sessile above. **Flowers** in dichotomously branched bracteate cymes; petals 5, white to purplish-tinged; stamens 5, opposite the petals; pistils 5-10 or more. **Fruit** an ovoid-pyriform achene, olive-green to blackish, ca. 1.5 mm long. June-July. —Gravelly prairies, open woodlands, waste places.

Chamaerhodos erecta

COMARUM *Marshlocks*

Comarum palustre L.   MAP 1092
MARSH CINQUEFOIL   *native*
   Potentilla palustris (L.) Scop.

Perennial herb, from long, stout rhizomes. **Stems** 3-8 dm long, ascending to sprawling or floating in shallow water, often rooting at nodes, more or less woody at base; lower stems smooth, upper stems sparsely hairy. **Leaves** all from stem, pinnately divided or nearly palmate, with 3-7 leaflets; **leaflets** oblong to oval, 3-10 cm long and 1-3 cm wide, mostly rounded at tip, underside waxy; margins with sharp, forward-pointing teeth; lower leaves long-petioled, upper leaves nearly sessile; **stipules** forming wings around petioles of lower leaves, becoming shorter upward. **Flowers** single or paired from leaf axils, or in open clusters; sepals dark red or purple (at least on inner surface), ovate to lance-shaped, 6-20 mm long; petals 5 (sometimes 10), very dark red, 3-5 mm long, with a short slender tip; stamens about 25, dark red. **Achenes** red to brown, smooth, 1 mm long. June-Aug.—Open bogs (especially in pools and wet margins), conifer swamps, shores.

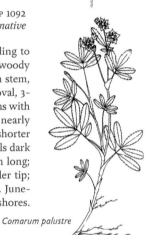

Comarum palustre

CRATAEGUS *Hawthorn*

Small trees or shrubs with usually spiny branches. Leaves simple, deciduous, alternate, serrate or dentate and otherwise entire or variously lobed. Flowers perfect, regular, in corymbs or rarely single or 2 or 3 together. Sepals 5. Petals 5, white or rarely pink. Stamens 5-20 or rarely 25. Ovary of 1-5 carpels; styles 1-5, persistent. Fruit a globose or ovoid pome, red or rarely yellow, blue, or black at maturity, with 1-5 bony, usually 1-seeded nutlets. The leaves of sterile shoots or of the ends of branches (vegetative leaves) are often differently shaped and more deeply incised than those of the flowering branchlets.

Because of the apparent instability of many species and their tendency to hybridize, there is no generally agreed upon consensus regarding Minnesota's hawthorns. Included in the key and descriptions are the most common, well-defined species reported for Minnesota; listed below are additional reported hawthorn species and hybrids not further treated in this Flora (excluded are species known only from one or several collections made more than 50 years ago):

1088. *Amelanchier sanguinea*   1089. *Amelanchier spicata*   1090. *Aronia melanocarpa*   1091. *Chamaerhodos erecta*

Crataegus schuettei Ashe (Schuette's hawthorn), Stearns County, see key.

Crataegus submollis Sarg. (Quebec hawthorn, MAP 1093), see key.

1 Nutlets with deep to shallow pits or depressions on their lateral surfaces; flowering in late May or later 2

  2 Mature fruit purplish black, glaucous; thorns mostly 1.5-2.5 cm long; inflorescence glabrous or very sparsely villous; stamens 10 or fewer; nutlets 3-4 (-5), rounded at the ends. . . . . ***C. douglasii***

  2 Mature fruit red or orange; thorns mostly 2.5-9.5 cm long; inflorescence densely villous (glabrous in *C. succulenta*); stamens ca. 10 or 20; nutlets 2-3, or if more, then acute at the ends 3

    3 Mature leaf blades thin, the veins (except sometimes for midrib) scarcely if at all impressed above, strigose above and usually pubescent beneath; inflorescences, branchlets of current year, and petioles all usually villous or lightly tomentose; thorns ca. 2.5-5 cm long, often sparse or even absent; stamens ca. 20; late flowering (usually early June) . . . . ***C. calpodendron***

    3 Mature leaf blades ± leathery, thickened at margins, the veins usually deeply impressed above, glabrous to pubescent on both surfaces; inflorescences, new branchlets, and petioles sparsely villous to glabrous (if inflorescence somewhat villous, at least the young branchlets nearly always glabrous, the veins deeply impressed, and/or the stamens ca. 10); thorns ca. 2.5-9.5 cm long, usually numerous; stamens ca. 20 or 10; mid-season flowering (mid- to late May in s Minn). . . . . ***C. succulenta***

1 Nutlets not pitted laterally; flowering in April–early June 4

  4 Blades of at least the floral leaves (in many species also the vegetative leaves) ± acute to broadly or (more commonly) narrowly tapered or cuneate at the base 5

    5 Blades (especially of floral leaves) mostly obovate to oblong-elliptic, broadest above or rarely at the middle, unlobed or very obscurely lobed near the apex, mostly 1.5-3 or more times as long as broad, usually thick or even stiff and leathery . . . . ***C. punctata***

    5 Blades (at least of floral leaves) mostly elliptic to ovate, broadest at or below the middle, often ± lobed, usually 1-1.5 times as long as broad, often thin . . . . ***C. chrysocarpa***

  4 Blades of both floral and vegetative leaves mostly broadly rounded, truncate, or subcordate at the base . . . 6

    6 Inflorescence, calyx, and leaves (at least along main veins) beneath ± densely villous-tomentose; fruit short-villous at least at the ends; stamens ca. 20, the anthers white or yellow (rarely pink) 7

      7 Stamens ca. 20, white or yellow; fruit nearly spherical . . . . ***C. mollis***

      7 Stamens ca. 10, pink; fruit pear-shaped or obovoid . . . . ***C. submollis****

    6 Inflorescence, calyx, and leaves glabrous or pubescent; fruit glabrous; stamens ca. 10 or 20 but anthers in most species pink to purple 8

      8 Stamens 10 or fewer; anthers pink to purple; young leaves strigose above; widespread in e Minn . . . .
. . . . ***C. macrosperma***

      8 Stamens ca. 15-20; anthers pink to purple or white to yellowish; young leaves glabrous to pubescent above; Stearns County . . . . ***C. schuettei****

Crataegus calpodendron (Ehrh.) Medik.

PEAR HAWTHORN

MAP 1094
native

Arborescent shrub or small tree; **branchlets** straight, slender, villous or tomentose while young. **Leaves** ovate or rhombic, 5-9 cm long, 4-8 cm wide, coarsely serrate except near the base and usually more or less divided above the middle into 3-5 pairs of shallow, often irregular, lateral lobes, short-villous above and pubescent or rarely glabrous beneath, dull yellow-green, thin but firm and with the veins slightly impressed above at maturity; petioles stout, 1-1.5 cm long, wing-margined sometimes nearly to base. **Flowers** 1.3-1.5 cm wide, in many-flowered tomentose corymbs; sepals coarsely glandular-serrate; stamens about 20, anthers pink or rarely white. **Fruit** oblong or obovoid or rarely subglobose, 7-9 mm thick, scarlet, glabrous when ripe, with a narrow elevated calyx, and 2-3 nutlets. May-June; fruit ripe Oct. Open woods and thickets, usually along small rocky streams.

Crataegus calpodendron

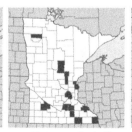

1092. Comarum palustre   *1093. Crataegus submollis*   *1094. Crataegus calpodendron*   *1095. Crataegus chrysocarpa*

Crataegus chrysocarpa Ashe
FIREBERRY HAWTHORN

MAP 1095
native

Stout, intricately branched shrub or rarely a small tree to 5-6 m tall; **branchlets** very spiny. **Leaves** elliptic, oval, or suborbicular, 4-6 cm long and 2-4 cm wide, lobed, serrate except near the base with gland-tipped teeth, roughened above with short appressed hairs while young; firm, dark yellow-green, the veins impressed above at maturity; petioles slender, sometimes slightly glandular, mostly 1/4 to 1/2 as long as the blades. **Flowers** 1.3-1.6 cm wide; stamens about 10, anthers white or pale yellow; sepals nearly entire or finely glandular-serrate. **Fruit** dull or dark red or rarely dull yellow, with thin flesh, remaining hard or dry or becoming mellow late in the season; nutlets 3-4. May; fruit ripe Sept-Oct.—Sandy hillsides, stream and river banks, forest borders, roadsides, fields, pastures; sometimes in wet places.

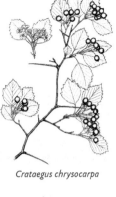

Crataegus chrysocarpa

Crataegus douglasii Lindl.
BLACK HAWTHORN

MAP 1096
native

Shrub or small tree to 10 m tall; old bark grayish brown with low sinuous ridges; young **twigs** reddish brown, glabrous, shiny, with conspicuous oval light-colored lenticels; winter buds glossy, reddish, ovoid to suborbicular; **spines** sharp-pointed, 2-3 cm long, or sometimes absent. **Leaves** obovate or ovate, to 10 cm long; blades often indented above or near the middle, sometimes with 3-4 pairs of ascending short lobes; upper surface somewhat lustrous, lightly pubescent with appressed hairs; lower surface glabrous or pilose on the veins; margins serrate; petioles reddish, about a third as long as the blades. **Flowers** 3-12, white or pinkish, in small corymbs; sepals triangular, narrowed to glandular serrate tips; stamens 10, anthers pale pink or white. **Fruit** purple-black, to about 13 mm long; pulp honey-colored; nutlets 3.5-5 mm long, with cavities on inner faces. June-July; fruit ripe Aug-Sept.—Rocky or gravelly lakeshores, shrub thickets, forest margins, rock outcrops; disjunct from western North America. Known mostly from near Lake Superior in ne Minn, but with populations also reported from inland locations. Distinguished by the combination of these characters: ripe fruit purplish-black; thorns to 3 cm long; underside of leaves with hairs only in axils of lateral veins; inflorescence glabrous.

Crataegus douglasii

Crataegus macrosperma Ashe
BIG-FRUIT HAWTHORN

MAP 1097
native

Crataegus roanensis Ashe

Shrub to 5 m tall, with ascending branches; **bark** of young branches pale gray, appearing twisted on older flexuous branches; **spines** numerous, 2-5 cm long. **Leaf blades** ovate, 3-7 cm long and 2-2.5 cm wide, appressed pubescent above, glabrous below; margins with 3-5 lobes and gland-tipped teeth; petioles slender, glabrous, with a few sessile glands. **Flowers** 12-18 mm wide, in corymbs of usually 6-10 flowers; the corymbs glabrous or with few pilose hairs; sepals lanceolate, slightly villous within, margins glandular-toothed; stamens 10, anthers pink. Ripe **fruit** crimson, 10-12 mm long, pulp firm and mellow.—Sandy woods and fields.

Crataegus mollis Scheele
DOWNY HAWTHORN

MAP 1098
native

Tree to 12 m tall, usually with a broad rounded top of widely spreading branches; **branchlets** sparingly spiny or nearly spineless, villous while young. **Leaves**

Crataegus macrosperma

1096. Crataegus douglasii   *1097. Crataegus macrosperma*   *1098. Crataegus mollis*   *1099. Crataegus punctata*

relatively large, variable in shape, sometimes 8-10 cm long and nearly as wide on vegetative shoots, thickly covered with short appressed hairs on the upper surface and densely white tomentose especially along the prominent veins beneath while young, firm, yellow-green, glabrate above and more or less pubescent beneath at maturity; petioles appearing stout at flowering time from the heavy tomentum, mostly 1/4 to 2/3 as long as the blades. **Flowers** in densely tomentose, many-flowered, compound corymbs; stamens about 20, anthers white, pale yellow, or rarely pink; calyx tube densely tomentose, the sepals pubescent on both sides, coarsely glandular-serrate. **Fruit** variable in shape and size and in the time of ripening, scarlet or bright crimson with pale dots, pubescent at least near the ends, with a broad shallow calyx, thick mellow flesh, and normally 5 small nutlets. April-May; fruit ripe Aug-Oct.—Open woods, usually in alluvial or fertile ground, and most common in limestone regions.

Crataegus mollis

Crataegus punctata Jacq.
DOTTED HAWTHORN

MAP 1099
native

Tree to 8-10 m tall with an open top of stiff spreading **branches**, armed with slender gray spines 4-6 cm long, and often with compound spines on trunk. **Leaves** obovate, or sometimes oblong-elliptic on shoots, dull yellowish green, mostly 2.5-6 cm long, 1.5-3 cm wide, cuneate or attenuate at base, serrate sometimes only above the middle, usually slightly lobed at least toward the apex, often deeply lobed on vegetative shoots, firm, the veins distinctly impressed on the upper surface at maturity; leaves covered with short appressed hairs above while young. **Flowers** in many-flowered corymbs; stamens about 20, anthers pink or pale yellow; corymbs and calyx tube gray-pubescent. **Fruit** subglobose or short-oblong, appearing pyriform while immature, usually 1.2-1.5 cm wide, dull red or orange-red, pale-dotted, with thick flesh becoming mellow or slightly succulent; nutlets usually 5, rounded and ridged on the back. May-June; fruit ripe Sept-Oct.—Thickets and borders of woods, often in rocky ground.

Crataegus succulenta Schrad.
FLESHY HAWTHORN
  Crataegus macracantha Lodd.

MAP 1100
native

Crataegus punctata

Tree to 7 or 8 m tall or sometimes an arborescent shrub, with slender **branchlets**, glabrous or rarely slightly hairy while young, often armed with long chestnut-brown spines becoming gray and compound on the larger branches. **Leaves** elliptic, rhombic or rarely ovate, finely serrate and usually indented with 4-6 pairs of shallow lobes above the middle, glabrous or slightly villous along the veins beneath, firm to nearly leathery, roughened with short appressed hairs on the upper surface while young; petioles 1-2 cm long, wing-margined above, usually eglandular. **Flowers** 1.3-1.7 cm wide, in many-flowered, slightly villous or glabrous corymbs stamens about 10-20, anthers white or pink; sepals glandular-serrate, reflexed after anthesis, usually deciduous from the mature fruit. **Fruit** subglobose, 0.7-1.2 cm wide, bright red, glabrous, lustrous; nutlets 2-3, rounded at the ends, grooved and ridged on the back and deeply pitted on the inner faces. May-June; fruit ripe Sept.—Thickets, pastures, and borders of woods, usually in dry or rocky ground.

Crataegus succulenta

1100. *Crataegus succulenta*   1101. *Drymocallis arguta*   1102. *Filipendula rubra*   1103. *Filipendula ulmaria*

DRYMOCALLIS *Woodbeauty*

Drymocallis arguta (Pursh) Rydb.
TALL WOODBEAUTY
Potentilla arguta Pursh

MAP 1101
native

Perennial from a stout rhizome, more or less viscid-pubescent throughout. **Stems** erect, 3-10 dm tall, simple to the inflorescence. **Leaves** pinnately compound, the basal leaves long-petioled; **leaflets** 7-11, or only 5 in the uppermost leaves. **Flowers** white, cream or pale yellow, 12-18 mm wide, crowded in a slender, elongate inflorescence; sepals ovate, much longer than the lance-shaped bractlets, nearly as long as the petals. **Achenes** obovoid, pale brown, 1 mm long, finely striate. June-July.—Dry woods and prairies.

Drymocallis arguta

FILIPENDULA *Queen-of-the-Prairie*

Perennial rhizomatous herbs. Leaves stipulate, pinnately compound. Flowers in large panicles, the lateral branches of the panicle surpassing the axis. Flowers white to pink, 5-7-merous. Hypanthium cup-shaped. Sepals ovate or oblong, reflexed. Petals spreading. Stamens 20-40, inserted at various levels in longitudinal rows opposite the perianth segments. Pistils 5-15, inserted in a circle. Fruit 1-seeded, resembling a follicle in appearance but indehiscent.

1   Petals white; leaves white-hairy on underside . . . . **F. ulmaria**
1   Petals rose-colored; leaves green on underside . . . . **F. rubra**

Filipendula rubra (Hill) B.L. Robins.
QUEEN-OF-THE-PRAIRIE

MAP 1102
native

Stems smooth, 1-2 m long. **Leaves** large, lower leaves to 8 dm long and to 2 dm wide, pinnately parted or divided into 5-9 segments, the segments opposite, stalkless, with 3-5 deep or shallow lobes; margins sharply toothed. **Flowers** pink-purple, fragrant, 7-10 mm wide, in a panicle 1-2 dm wide at ends of stems; petals 5, 2-4 mm long; stamens many. **Fruit** an erect, smooth capsule, 6-8 mm long. June-July.—Wet meadows and shores, calcareous fens; soils usually calcium-rich. *Native to ne North America but considered adventive in Minnesota.*

Filipendula rubra

Filipendula ulmaria (L.) Maxim.
QUEEN-OF-THE-MEADOW

MAP 1103
introduced

Stems 1-2 m tall. **Terminal leaflet** rotund in outline, 6-15 cm wide, deeply divided into 3-5 ovate or ovate-oblong, serrate lobes; **lateral leaflets** oblong to ovate, coarsely and sharply doubly serrate or occasionally shallowly lobed. **Flowers** white, about 8 mm wide; sepals ovate-triangular. **Capsules** glabrous, 3-4 mm long, each twisted about half a complete turn. June-Aug.—Native of Eurasia; occasionally planted for ornament and sometimes escaped. The leaves are usually pale beneath with a close tomentum.

Filipendula ulmaria

FRAGARIA *Strawberry*

Perennial herbs, usually spreading freely by runners and forming colonies. Leaves basal, 3-foliolate, serrate. Flowers several on peduncles. Hypanthium saucer-shaped. Sepals alternating with foliaceous bracts of nearly equal size. Petals white, obovate to subrotund. Stamens numerous, sometimes abortive. Pistils numerous. Fruit consisting of numerous minute achenes on the greatly enlarged, red, juicy receptacle, subtended by the persistent calyx and bracts.

1   Terminal center tooth of leaflets smaller than the tooth on either side of it; calyx lobes appressed to fruit . . . . .
       . . . . **F. virginiana**
1   Terminal center tooth of leaflets as large or larger than the tooth on either side of it; calyx lobes spreading away
       from fruit . . . . **F. vesca**

Fragaria vesca L.
THIN-LEAVED WILD STRAWBERRY

MAP 1104
native

Leaflets sessile or nearly so, ovate to obovate, more or less silky beneath; principal lateral veins diverging from the midvein at an angle of about 45 degrees; teeth sharp and divergent. Peduncles at anthesis usually shorter than the leaves, exceeding them at maturity; pedicels of unequal length, eventually forming a panicle-like **inflorescence**; **petals** commonly 5-7 mm long. April-June. —Deciduous and mixed forests, cedar and tamarack swamps, shores and forest edges. *In nearly all leaves, a line connecting the apices of the 2 uppermost lateral teeth passes across the projecting terminal tooth, which is usually more than half as wide as the lateral ones, measured from sinus to sinus.*

Fragaria virginiana Duchesne
THICK-LEAVED WILD STRAWBERRY

MAP 1105
native

Leaflets petioled, glabrate to sericeous beneath; principal lateral veins commonly divergent from the midrib at an angle of about 30 degrees; teeth blunter and less divergent than in *F. vesca*. **Inflorescence** with as many as 12 flowers on pedicels of about uniform length, forming a corymbiform cluster usually shorter than the leaves; **petals** usually 7-10 mm long. April-June.—Widespread in many habitats, in a diversity of deciduous, mixed, and coniferous forests, clearings, dry sandy forests, roadsides, and fields; more often in dry open sunny places than *F. vesca*. *In nearly all leaves, a line connecting the tips of the 2 uppermost lateral teeth passes above the tip of the small terminal tooth, which is usually less than half as wide as the adjacent lateral ones, measured from sinus to sinus.*

Fragaria vesca

Fragaria virginiana

GEUM *Avens*

Perennial herbs. Lower leaves pinnately lobed or divided, upper leaves smaller, less divided or entire. Flowers yellow, white or purple; 1 to many in clusters at ends of stems; petals 5; stamens 10 to many. Fruit an achene.

1 Leaves all 3-foliolate and basal . . . . *G. fragarioides*
1 Leaves mostly pinnately compound or divided, if 3-foliolate, then cauline 2
  2 Calyx bell-shaped; reddish; flowers nodding; petals yellow, tinged with purple 3
    3 Plant of wetlands; terminal leaflet much larger than lateral leaflets; style with distinct joint near its middle, lengthening to less than 2x length of perianth . . . . *G. rivale*
    3 Plant of dry habitats; terminal leaflet barely larger than lateral leaflets; style not jointed, elongating to 2x or more longer than perianth . . . . *G. triflorum*
  2 Calyx lobes spreading, green; flowers upright; petals white or yellow 4
    4 Plants flowering 5
      5 Petals white to pale yellow 6
        6 Petals equal to or longer than the sepals; stems glabrous or only sparsely hairy . . . . . *G. canadense*
        6 Petals shorter than the sepals; stems densely hairy, the hairs spreading . . . . *G. laciniatum*
      5 Petals bright yellow 7
        7 Terminal leaflet of basal leaves much larger than lateral segments; lower portion of style with short-stalked glands . . . . *G. macrophyllum*
        7 Terminal leaflet various; lower portion of style without glands . . . . *G. allepicum*
    4 Plants fruiting 8
      8 Receptacle glabrous or only sparsely hairy; plants with either the achene beak with short-stalked glands, or with the pedicels with dense long hairs over the much shorter hairs 9
        9 Achene beak not glandular; pedicels densely long-hairy . . . . *G. laciniatum*
        9 Achene beak with short-stalked glands, especially near base; pedicels finely hairy and with only scattered long hairs . . . . *G. macrophyllum*
      8 Receptacle densely hairy; achene beaks neither with glands nor the pedicels with dense long hairs 10
        10 Stem leaves pinnately compound; achenes many (150 or more) in each head, the achene beak with long hairs at base . . . . *G. allepicum*

1104. Fragaria vesca   *1105. Fragaria virginiana*   *1106. Geum aleppicum*   *1107. Geum canadense*

10 Stem leaves mostly 3-parted; achenes less than 100 in each head, the achene beak glabrous . . . . .
. . . . *G. canadense*

Geum aleppicum Jacq.

MAP 1106

YELLOW AVENS   *native*

Perennial herb. **Stems** erect or ascending, to 1 m long, branched above, covered with coarse hairs. **Leaves** variable, **basal leaves** pinnately divided into 5-7 oblong leaflets, wedge-shaped at base, petioles long-hairy; **stem leaves** divided into 3-5 segments, stalkless or short-petioled; margins coarsely toothed. **Flowers** 1 to several, short-stalked, on branches at ends of stems; **sepals** lance-shaped; **petals** 5, yellow; style jointed. **Achenes** usually long-hairy. June-July.—Swamps, wet forests, wet meadows, marshes, calcareous fens, ditches and roadsides.

Geum aleppicum

Geum canadense Jacq.

MAP 1107

WHITE AVENS   *native*

Perennial herb. **Stems** slender, 4-10 dm tall, glabrous or sparsely pubescent below, above and on the pedicels becoming densely velvety-puberulent, often with a few scattered longer hairs. **Basal leaves** long-petioled, commonly 3-foliolate with obovate leaflets; **upper leaves** short-petioled, 3-foliolate with oblong lance-shaped, sharply serrate leaflets; **uppermost leaves** mostly simple, lance-shaped, nearly sessile. Pedicels finely velvety hairy, with or without long scattered hairs; **petals** white, obovate, about as long as the sepals or distinctly exceeding them. Head of **fruit** obovoid, 10-15 mm long; receptacle densely bristly, the hairs protruding among the ovaries at anthesis but shorter than the mature achenes. **Achenes** 2.5-3.5 mm long, excluding the style. May-June.—Dry or moist woods.

Geum canadense

Geum fragarioides (Michx.) Smedmark

MAP 1108

BARREN STRAWBERRY   *native*

Waldsteinia fragarioides (Michx.) Tratt.

Perennial rhizomatous herb with the aspect of a strawberry. **Leaves** basal, 3-foliolate, 1-2 dm long including the petioles, ± winter-green; **leaflets** broadly obovate, rounded at tip, serrate with numerous broad teeth and commonly also shallowly and irregularly lobed, the lateral leaflets unsymmetrical. **Flowers** in a cyme on a naked or bracted peduncle, the peduncles about equaling the leaves; hypanthium obconic; **sepals** triangular; **petals** yellow, obovate, 5-10 mm long, obtuse or rounded, much exceeding the sepals; stamens numerous, the slender filaments erect and persistent after anthesis. **Fruit** an achene. April-May.—Moist or dry woods, thickets, thin soil over rock outcrops.

Geum fragarioides

Geum laciniatum Murr.

MAP 1109

ROUGH AVENS   *native*

Perennial herb. **Stems** 4-10 dm long, covered with long, mostly downward-pointing hairs. **Lower leaves** pinnately divided, the segments pinnately lobed; **upper leaves** divided into 3 leaflets or lobes; margins coarsely toothed; petioles hairy. **Flowers** mostly single at ends of densely hairy stalks from ends of stems; **sepals** triangular, 4-10 mm long; **petals** 5, white, 3-5 mm long. **Fruit** an achene, 3-5 mm long (excluding style), grouped into round heads 1-2 cm long. May-June.—Wet woods, floodplain forests, ditches.

Geum laciniatum

1108. *Geum fragarioides*

1109. *Geum laciniatum*

1110. *Geum macrophyllum*

1111. *Geum rivale*

Geum macrophyllum Willd.
BIG-LEAF AVENS

MAP 1110

native

Perennial herb. **Stems** to 1 m long, unbranched, or branched above, bristly-hairy. **Leaves** pinnately divided, **basal leaves** stalked, the terminal segment large, 3-7-lobed, with much smaller segments intermixed; **stem** leaves smaller, deeply 3-lobed or divided into 3 leaflets, short-stalked or stalkless; margins sharply toothed. **Flowers** 1 to several on branches at ends of stems; **sepals** triangular, bent backward; **petals** yellow, obovate, 4-7 mm long; style jointed. **Achenes** finely hairy. May-July.—Moist to wet forest openings, streambanks, wet meadows, ditches.

Geum macrophyllum

Geum rivale L.
PURPLE AVENS

MAP 1111

native

Perennial herb. **Stems** erect, 3-8 dm long, mostly unbranched, hairy. **Basal leaves** large, 1-4 dm long, pinnately divided, the terminal 1-3 leaflets much larger than other segments; **stem leaves** smaller, 2-5 on stem, pinnately divided or 3-lobed; margins shallowly lobed and coarsely toothed. **Flowers** mostly nodding, few on pedicels at ends of stems, the pedicels with short gland-tipped hairs and longer coarse hairs; **sepals** 5, purple, triangular, 6-10 mm long, ascending; **petals** 5, yellow to pink with purple veins, tapered to a clawlike base; stamens many; styles jointed above middle, the portion above joint deciduous, lower portion persistent and curved in fruit. **Fruit** a long-beaked, hairy achene, 3-4 mm long, grouped into round heads. May-July.—Conifer swamps, wet forests, bogs, fens, wet meadows; often where calcium-rich.

Geum triflorum Pursh
PRAIRIE SMOKE

MAP 1112

native

Perennial herb. **Stems** 2-4 dm tall, pubescent throughout. **Basal leaves** 1-2 dm long, oblong lance-shaped in outline, pinnately compound with 7-17 leaflets; lateral leaflets progressively increasing in size toward the tip, irregularly lobed; terminal leaflet similar but somewhat wider, often confluent with the upper lateral ones and scarcely larger than them; **stem leaves** few and small, laciniate. Peduncles eventually to 1 dm long; **sepals** triangular, much shorter than the linear bractlets; **petals** purplish, oblong lance-shaped, 8-12 mm long, about equaling the bractlets, nearly erect; styles at maturity 3-5 cm long, strongly plumose except the very tip. May-June.—Dry woods and prairies.

Geum triflorum

MALUS *Apple*

Trees or shrubs, sometimes thorny, with simple, alternate, toothed or lobed leaves. Flowers large, in simple umbels on dwarf lateral branches (fruit-spurs), blooming in April or May. Hypanthium globose to obovoid. Sepals 5, spreading or ascending or recurved. Petals 5, elliptic to obovate, short-clawed. Stamens 15-50, shorter than the petals. Ovary inferior, 3-5-celled (5-celled in our species); styles as many as the cells, separate or connate at base. Fruit a fleshy pome, each cell normally with 2 seeds.

ADDITIONAL SPECIES
• *Malus baccata* (L.) Borkh. (Siberian crabapple), introduced in St. Louis County.
• *Malus prunifolia* (Willd.) Borkh. (Plum-leaf crabapple), native to ne Asia; Becker and Goodhue counties.

1 Leaf margins toothed, the teeth sharp or rounded and not coarse . . . . **M. pumila**
1 Leaf margins irregularly double-toothed, often coarsely so 2
  2 Leaves thick and leathery, the upperside veins sunken into leaf surface; petioles and pedicels densely woolly hairy; se Minn . . . . **M. ioensis**
  2 Leaves thinner, the upperside veins not sunken; petioles and pedicels glabrous, or if hairy, the hairs thinning by end of flowering period; adventive in Dakota County . . . . **M. coronaria**

Malus coronaria (L.) P. Mill.
SWEET CRAB

(NO MAP)

introduced

Pyrus coronaria L.

Attractive tall shrub or low tree with thorny branches, occasionally to 10 m tall. **Leaves** usually ovate or in outline, varying to broadly lance-shaped, glabrous beneath or sparsely villous when young, serrate, or commonly with a few triangular lobes near the widest part. Hypanthium and calyx glabrous or sparsely villous; anthers pink or salmon-color. **Fruit** subglobose, greenish, about 2.5 cm wide.—Woods and thickets; adventive in Dakota County.

Malus ioensis (Wood) Britt.

PRAIRIE CRAB

MAP 1113
native

> *Pyrus ioensis* (Wood) Bailey

Tall shrub or low tree of irregular habit, to 10 m tall; **twigs** tomentose. **Leaves** firm, ovate-oblong to broadly elliptic, 6-10 cm long, coarsely serrate and usually also shallowly lobed, usually persistently pubescent beneath. **Flowers** 3.5-4 cm wide; hypanthium and pedicels densely tomentose; anthers pink or salmon-color. **Fruit** subglobose, green, about 2.5 cm wide.—Woods and thickets.

Malus ioensis

Malus pumila P. Mill.

CULTIVATED APPLE

MAP 1114
introduced

> *Pyrus malus* L.
> *Pyrus pumila* (P. Mill.) K. Koch

Widely spreading tree to 15 m tall. **Leaves** elliptic to ovate, finely serrate, permanently pubescent beneath. **Flowers** white, tinged with pink, about 3 cm wide; hypanthium densely tomentose, open at the mouth; anthers yellow; calyx persistent on the fruit.—Native probably of w Asia; long in cultivation and occasionally escaped. *Many wild apples are persistent from planted trees, but some trees have developed from seed and appear in old fields and along fences and roads.*

Malus pumila

PHYSOCARPUS *Ninebark*

Physocarpus opulifolius (L.) Maxim.

NINEBARK

MAP 1115
native

Much-branched shrub, 2-3 m tall; **twigs** greenish, slightly angled or ridged, smooth or finely hairy; **bark** of older stems shredding in long thin strips. **Leaves** alternate, ovate in outline, mostly 3-lobed, dark green above, paler and often sparsely hairy below; margins irregularly toothed; petioles 1-2 cm long, with a pair of small, deciduous stipules at base. **Flowers** 5-parted, white, 5-10 mm wide; many in stalked, rounded clusters at ends of branches. **Fruit** a red-brown pod, 5-10 mm long, in round clusters; **seeds** 1-2 mm long, shiny, 3-4 in each pod. June-July.—Streambanks, lakeshores, swamps, rocky shores of Lake Superior.

Physocarpus opulifolius

POTENTILLA *Cinquefoil*

Annual or perennial herbs, or woody in shrubby cinquefoil (*P. fruticosa*); stolons present in some species. Leaves pinnately or palmately divided, alternate or mostly from base of plant. Flowers perfect, regular; sepals 5, alternating with small bracts, the sepals and bractlets joined at base to form a saucer-shaped hypanthium; petals 5, yellow; stamens many; pistils numerous. Fruit a group of many small achenes, surrounded by the persistent hypanthium.

1   Plants shrubs; leaflets 5-7, 1-2 cm long .... *P. fruticosa*
1   Plants herbs (or woody only at base) 2
   2   Flowers solitary on naked pedicels from nodes of creeping stems 3
      3   Leaves palmately compound; surface of leaf underside visible through coare hairs .... *P. simplex*
      3   Leaves pinnately compound 4

1112. *Geum triflorum*   1113. *Malus ioensis*   1114. *Malus pumila*   1115. *Physocarpus opulifolius*

Potentilla anserina L.

SILVERWEED
         MAP 1116
         native

Argentina anserina (L.) Rydb.

Perennial herb, with a stout rootstock and spreading by stolons to 1 m long. **Leaves** all at base of plant except for a few clustered leaves on stolons, pinnately divided into 7-25 leaflets; **leaflets** oblong or obovate, 1.5-5 cm long and 0.5-2 cm wide, lower leaflets much smaller; upper surface green and smooth to gray-green and silky-hairy, underside densely white-hairy; margins with sharp, forward-pointing teeth; stipules brown, membranous, at base of petiole. **Flowers** single from leafy axils of stolons, on stalks 5-15 cm long; sepals white silky-hairy; petals yellow, oval to obovate, 5-10 mm long; stamens 20-25. **Fruit** a light brown achene. May-Sept.—Wet meadows, marshes, sandy and gravelly shores and streambanks; soils often calcium-rich.

Potentilla anserina

Potentilla argentea L.

SILVERY CINQUEFOIL
         MAP 1117
         introduced (naturalized)

Perennial herb, at first acaulescent, soon producing one or more long stolons which root and have small clusters of leaves at the nodes. **Leaves** erect, oblong lance-shaped in outline, to 3 dm long, pinnately compound with numerous leaflets often alternating with others much smaller; axis and peduncles villous; leaflets narrowly elliptic, to 4 cm long, sharply toothed, tomentose beneath and also with long appressed hairs. **Flowers** yellow, 15-25 mm wide, on naked peduncles, about as long as the leaves. **Achenes** about 2.5 mm long, deeply furrowed on the summit and back. May-Sept.—Wet sandy beaches.

Potentilla fruticosa L.

SHRUBBY CINQUEFOIL
         MAP 1118
         native

Dasiphora fruticosa (L.) Rydb.
Potentilla floribunda Pursh

Much-branched shrub, 0.5-1 m tall; **twigs** brown to red, covered with long, silky-white hairs; **bark** of older branches shredding. **Leaves** alternate, pinnately divided; leaflets 3-7 (mostly 5), the terminal 3 leaflets often joined at base, oval to

Potentilla argentea

1116. *Potentilla anserina*   1117. *Potentilla argentea*   1118. *Potentilla fruticosa*   1119. *Potentilla gracilis*

oblong, 1-2 cm long and 3-7 mm wide, tapered at each end, upper surface dark green, underside paler, with silky hairs on both sides or at least on underside; margins entire, often rolled under; short-stalked. **Flowers** 5-parted, bright yellow, 1-2.5 cm wide, 1 to few in clusters at ends of branches; bracts much narrower than the ovate sepals; stamens 15-20. **Fruit** a small head of hairy achenes surrounded by the 10-parted calyx. June-Sept.—Calcareous fens, lakeshores, open bogs, conifer swamps, wet meadows.

Potentilla gracilis Dougl.
SLENDER CINQUEFOIL
Potentilla flabelliformis Lehm.

MAP 1119
introduced

Perennial from a stout caudex, erect, 4-8 dm tall. **Basal leaves** long-petioled. palmately compound, with 5-7 leaflets; **stem leaves** much smaller, often with 3 leaflets, becoming bract-like in the inflorescence; **leaflets** oblong lance-shaped, densely tomentose beneath, green and often glabrous above, cleft into narrow segments. **Inflorescence** an open cyme with ascending branches; petals yellow, 6-10 mm long. July-Aug.—Prairies, rocky banks, and dry woods.

Potentilla fruticosa

Potentilla intermedia L.
DOWNY CINQUEFOIL

(NO MAP)
introduced

Perennial from a stout root. **Stems** erect or decumbent, leafy, 3-7 dm tall. **Leaves** digitate; **leaflets** of the principal leaves 5, oblong lance-shaped in outline, commonly 3-5 cm long, deeply and often irregularly serrate above the cuneate base, villous or sericeous beneath. **Inflorescence** much-branched, many-flowered; flowers 8-10 mm wide; petals yellow, about equaling the sepals. **Achenes** with prominent longitudinal ridges.—European; roadsides, waste places; reported for St. Louis County.

Potentilla norvegica L.
STRAWBERRY-WEED

MAP 1120
native

Annual herb. **Stems** stout and leafy, commonly branched and many-flowered, hirsute below. **Leaves** 3-foliolate; **leaflets** elliptic to broadly obovate, to 8 cm long, crenately toothed. **Flowers** yellow, nearly 1 cm wide; bractlets and sepals ovate lance-shaped, about equal at anthesis, the sepals expanding in fruit to 16 mm long; petals nearly as long as the sepals; stamens usually 20. **Achenes** pale brown, flattened, about 1 mm long, with curved longitudinal ridges. June-Aug.—In a wide variety of moist or dry habitats, usually where somewhat disturbed; roadsides, railroads, fields, shores, meadows, rock outcrops, gardens.

Potentilla norvegica

Potentilla recta L.
SULPHUR CINQUEFOIL

MAP 1121
introduced (naturalized)

Perennial herb. **Stems** erect, simple to the inflorescence, 4-8 dm tall, pubescent. **Leaves** digitately compound, the basal and lower long-petioled with 5-7 leaflets, the upper short-petioled to sessile, smaller, with only 3 leaflets; **leaflets** radially divergent, narrowly oblong lance-shaped, deeply toothed. **Inflorescence** many-flowered, flattened; sepals and bractlets ovate lance-shaped, about equal; petals yellow, about 1 cm long. **Achenes** striate with low curved ridges. June-Aug. —Native of Europe; weedy in dry soil, roadsides, fields, railroads, gravel pits; invading dry open forests. *Sessile or short-stalked glands are usually present on the leaflet underside.*

Potentilla recta

1120. *Potentilla norvegica*   1121. *Potentilla recta*   1122. *Potentilla rivalis*   1123. *Potentilla simplex*

Potentilla rivalis Nutt.
BROOK CINQUEFOIL
> *Potentilla millegrana* Engelm. ex Lehm.
> *Potentilla pentandra* Engelm.

MAP 1122
native

Annual or biennial herb, taprooted. **Stems** upright to spreading, 2-9 dm long, with soft, long hairs, unbranched or branched from base, upper stems branched. **Leaves** mostly on stems, palmately divided into 3-7 leaflets, or lower leaves pinnately divided; leaflets obovate to oval, 1.5-5 cm long and 0.5-2.5 cm wide, sparsely hairy; margins with coarse, forward- pointing teeth; stipules ovate, to 1.5 cm long; petioles present, but uppermost leaves nearly sessile. **Flowers** in leafy, branched clusters at ends of stems; sepals triangular, 3-6 mm long; petals yellow, obovate, 1-2 mm long, to half as long as sepals; stamens 10-15. **Achenes** yellow, less than 1 mm long, smooth. June-Aug.—Wet meadows, streambanks, shores, ditches.

Potentilla rivalis

Potentilla simplex Michx.
OLDFIELD CINQUEFOIL

MAP 1123
native

Perennial herb; stems and basal leaves from a short rhizome to 8 cm long. **Stems** at first erect or ascending, soon widely spreading or arching and rooting at the tips, to 1 m long, very slender, with long internodes, villous to glabrate. **Leaflets** 5, oblong lance-shaped to elliptic, to 7 cm long, usually less than half as wide, with numerous teeth in the upper 2/3. Peduncles slender, the lowest arising at the end of the second well developed internode. **Flowers** yellow, 10-15 mm wide. April-June.—Dry open sandy forests, fields, roadsides, and sandy barrens; also in moist thickets and deciduous forests, and on rocky ledges.

Potentilla supina L.
BUSHY CINQUEFOIL
> *Potentilla paradoxa* Nutt.

MAP 1124
native

Potentilla simplex

Annual or short-lived perennial herb, taprooted. **Stems** erect to reclining on ground with tip upright, 1-6 dm long, unbranched or branched from base, smooth below to long-hairy above. **Leaves** mostly on stem, pinnately divided into 7-11 leaflets; leaflets oval to obovate, 1-4 cm long and 0.5-2 cm wide, finely hairy; margins with rounded teeth; stipules ovate, to 1.5 cm long; lower leaves long-petioled, upper leaves with short petioles. **Flowers** usually many in leafy-bracted clusters at ends of stems; sepals ovate, 2-4 mm long; petals yellow, obovate, 2-3 mm long, about as long as sepals; stamens 15-20. **Achenes** brown, 1 mm long. June-Sept.—Shores, ditches, floodplains and flats, often where sandy or gravelly.

PRUNUS *Plum; Cherry*

Trees or shrubs. Leaves alternate, simple, serrate, often with petiolar glands. Flowers umbellate or solitary from axillary buds or short lateral branches, or racemose and terminal. Hypanthium cup-shaped, obconic, or urn-shaped. Sepals spreading or reflexed, usually soon deciduous. Petals 5, white to pink or red, elliptic to obovate, spreading. Stamens about 20, with slender exserted filaments. Pistil 1. Fruit a 1-seeded drupe, the exocarp fleshy or juicy, the endocarp hard. *Many members of the genus are important for their edible fruits or attractive flowers.*

ADDITIONAL SPECIES
• *Prunus tomentosa* Thunb. (Nanking cherry); native to Asia; Anoka and Washington counties; stems, leaves, and fruits downy hairy.

1 Flowers 20 or more in elongate racemes; inflorescence bracts absent 2
    2 Tree; leaves 2 times longer than wide, the margins with incurved teeth; fruit black . . . . *P. serotina*
    2 Shrub; leaves less than 2 times longer than wide, the margins with sharp, outward pointing teeth; fruit dark
      red to purple . . . . *P. virginiana*
1 Flowers 1 to several, in umbel-like clusters 3
    3 Plants in flower 4
        4 Sepals glabrous 5
            5 Leaf margins mostly entire below middle; leaves widest above middle; flower pedicels mostly less than
               1 cm long . . . . *P. pumila*
            5 Leaf margins finely toothed for their entire length; leaves widest at or below middle; pedicels mostly
               more than 1 cm long . . . . *P. pensylvanica*

 4 Sepals hairy, at least on upper surface near base 6
  6 Sepals entire or with a few small teeth at tip .... *P. americana*
  6 Sepal margins with gland-tipped teeth .... *P. nigra*
3 Plants in fruit and with fully developed leaves 7
 7 Leaves glabrous, obovate, distinctly widest above the middle; the margins entire or nearly so below the middle of the leaf .... *P. pumila*
 7 Leaves not as above 8
  8 Leaves finely toothed, the teeth much less than 1 mm long; leaves more than 2 times longer than wide, widest below middle .... *P. pensylvanica*
  8 Leaves coarsely toothed, the teeth 1 mm or more long; leaves less than 2 times longer than wide, widest at or above the middle 9
   9 Margin teeth sharp, often tipped with a short spine .... *P. americana*
   9 Margin teeth rounded or tapered to a tip, sometimes gland-tipped .... *P. nigra*

Prunus americana Marsh.
WILD PLUM

MAP 1125
native

Shrub or small tree to 8 m tall, spreading from the roots and forming thickets. **Leaves** obovate, 6-10 cm long at maturity, sharply acuminate, coarsely serrate, glandless, 1-2 mm long. **Flowers** 2-4 in an umbel; petals white, 10-12 mm long; sepals pubescent on the upper (inner) side, often toothed toward the end, nearly glandless. **Fruit** red, glaucous, about 2 cm wide; stone flattened. April-May. —Moist woods, roadsides, and fencerows.

Prunus americana

Prunus nigra Ait.
CANADIAN PLUM

MAP 1126
native

Small tree, occasionally to 10 m tall. **Leaves** obovate, 7-12 cm long at maturity, abruptly acuminate, coarsely and often doubly serrate with irregular, gland-tipped teeth often 2 mm long, more or less pubescent beneath, at least in the vein-axils. **Flowers** in clusters of 3 or 4, on reddish pedicels 1-2 cm long; sepals glandular on the margin, pubescent above, glabrous on the lower (outer) side; petals white, 10-15 mm long. **Fruit** ellipsoid, red varying to yellow, 2-3 cm long. May.—Moist woods and thickets.

Prunus pensylvanica L. f.
PIN-CHERRY

MAP 1127
native

Slender shrub or small tree to 10 m tall. **Leaves** mostly lance-shaped, 6-12 cm long, long-acuminate, finely and irregularly serrate with rounded teeth, the gland near the sinus; petioles usually glandular at the summit. **Flowers** in umbel-like clusters of 2-5, on pedicels 1-1.5 cm long; sepals glabrous; petals white, about 6 mm long, villous on the back near the base. **Fruit** red, juicy, about 6 mm wide; stone subglobose. April-May.—Woods and clearings, often abundant after fire.

Prunus nigra

Prunus pumila L.
SAND-CHERRY

MAP 1128
native

Low, diffusely branched, decumbent or prostrate shrub, seldom more than 1 m tall, rarely to 3 m. **Leaves** oblong lance-shaped, 4-10 cm long, long-tapering at base, the margin firm or cartilaginous, finely and remotely serrate with glandular teeth, glabrous, often glaucous beneath; petioles 5-12 mm long. **Flowers** in clusters of 2-4, on pedicels 4-12 mm long; sepals glandular-serrulate; petals white, elliptic, 4-8 mm long. **Fruit** nearly black, subglobose, 10-15 mm wide, edible. May.—Sand dunes and sandy soil, Great Lakes shores, dry or rocky woods.

Prunus pensylvanica

1124. Potentilla supina

1125. Prunus americana

1126. Prunus nigra

1127. Prunus pensylvanica

Prunus serotina Ehrh.   MAP 1129
WILD BLACK CHERRY   *native*

Tree to 25 m tall, but often blooming when less than 5 m tall. **Leaves** firm, lance-shaped to oblong, 6-12 cm long, finely serrate with slender or blunt incurved teeth. **Racemes** terminating leafy twigs of the current season, 8-15 cm long; pedicels 3-6 mm long; sepals oblong or triangular, 1-1.5 mm long, entire or sparsely glandular-erose, persistent under the fruit; petals white, subrotund, about 4 mm long. **Fruit** dark purple or black, 8-10 mm wide, edible when fully ripe. May.—Formerly a forest tree, now more common as a weedy tree of roadsides, waste land, and forest margins.

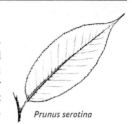

Prunus serotina

Prunus virginiana L.   MAP 1130
CHOKE-CHERRY   *native*

Usually a shrub, sometimes a tree to 10 m tall. **Leaves** thin, oblong to obovate, 5-12 cm long, sharply serrate with slender ascending teeth. **Racemes** terminating leafy twigs of the season, 6-15 cm long; pedicels usually 5-8 mm long; sepals broadly triangular, 1-1.5 mm long, conspicuously glandular-erose, deciduous soon after anthesis; petals white, subrotund, about 4 mm long. **Fruit** dark red or crimson, 8-10 mm wide, astringent, scarcely edible. May.—In a wide variety of habitats, from rocky hills and dunes to borders of swamps.

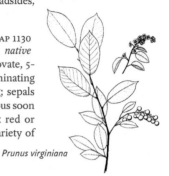

Prunus virginiana

ROSA *Rose*

Shrubs or woody vines, usually thorny. Leaves pinnately compound with 3-11 serrate leaflets, the stipules commonly large and adnate to the petiole. Hypanthium globose to urceolate with a constricted orifice. Sepals usually long-attenuate, often persistent in fruit. Petals large, spreading at anthesis, white to yellow or red. Stamens very numerous, inserted near the orifice of the hypanthium. Ovaries numerous, inserted on the bottom or also on the sides of the hypanthium; styles usually barely exsert, distinct or united. Fruit a bony achene; mature hypanthium commonly colored, pulpy or fleshy.

1 Styles joined to form a column, protruding from the hypanthium opening; Washington County . . . *R. multiflora*
1 Styles distinct, styles not exserted from hypanthium opening, only the stigmas protruding 2
  2 Young twigs densely hairy; petals 3-5 cm long; introduced species . . . . ***R. rugosa***
  2 Young twigs glabrous or nearly so; petals 2-3 cm long; native species except for *R. cinnamomea* 3
    3 Pedicel and hypanthium with stalked glands; sepals spreading and then deciduous; Ramsey Co. ***R. carolina***
    3 Pedicel and hypanthium glabrous; sepals persistent on fruit and typically upright 4
      4 Prickles at nodes below leaf stipules present and larger than internodal prickles . . . . ***R. woodsii***
      4 Prickles at nodes below leaf stipules absent or similar to internodal prickles 5
        5 Flowers from tips of currrent year's stems and also on lateral branches on stems from previous year; leaflets mostly 9 or 11 . . . . ***R. arkansana***
        5 Flowers only on lateral branches of previous year's stems; leaflets mostly 5 or 7 6
          6 Stems usually not prickly or bristly, or with slender prickles only on lower internodes ***R. blanda***
          6 Stems densely prickly on most internodes . . . . ***R. acicularis***

Rosa acicularis Lindl.   MAP 1131
BRISTLY ROSE   *native*
Rosa sayi Schwein.

Stems to 1 m tall, usually densely beset with straight slender thorns, even on the flowering lateral branches. **Stipules** pubescent, glandular on the margin, when young densely covered with short-stipitate glands, as are also the bracts; rachis

Rosa acicularis

1128. Prunus pumila

1129. Prunus serotina

1130. Prunus virginiana

usually pubescent and glandular; **leaflets** 3-7, usually 5, oblong-elliptic, coarsely serrate. **Flowers** usually solitary; hypanthium and pedicel glabrous; petals pink, 2-3 cm long **Fruit** ellipsoid to pyriform or globose. Upland woods, hills, and rocky banks; statewide.

Rosa arkansana Porter
MAP 1132
DWARF PRAIRIE-ROSE
native

Colonial, only half-shrubby. **Stems** under 1 m tall, usually densely prickly; prickles slender, straight, unequal. **Stipules** pubescent, usually entire, or glandular-dentate toward the tip, **leaflets** (7)9 or 11, 1-4 cm long, obovate, sharply serrate, very often pubescent beneath. **Flowers** corymbose, terminating the nearly herbaceous stems of the season and often also on short lateral branches from older stems; hypanthium and pedicel usually glabrous or nearly so; sepals persistent; petals pink to deep rose, 1.5-3 cm long. **Fruit** purplish or red, 10-15 mm wide.—Prairies and plains, or in open or brushy sites.

Rosa blanda Ait.
MAP 1133
SMOOTH ROSE
native

Stems to 1.5 m tall, unarmed or with few to many slender prickles toward the base, not extending upon the flowering branches. **Stipules** entire to glandular-dentate; **leaflets** commonly 5 or 7, narrowly oblong to oval, glabrous or nearly so, coarsely toothed, especially above the middle. **Flowers** solitary or corymbose; pedicel and hypanthium glabrous; petals pink, 2-3 cm long.—Dry woods, hills, prairies, and dunes. *Thorns may be entirely absent, or may extend a distance up the stem.*

Rosa blanda

Rosa carolina L.
(NO MAP)
PASTURE ROSE
native

Stems rarely more than 1 m tall, simple or little branched, usually armed with copious internodal thorns; thorns straight, slender and terete to the base, the infrastipular thorns scarcely differentiated. **Stipules** glandular-dentate to entire; **leaflets** 3, 5, or 7, oblong to oval or nearly rotund, often more than half as wide as long, coarsely toothed, in some forms glandular on the margin. **Flowers** usually solitary; pedicels and hypanthium stipitate-glandular; sepals attenuate into linear tips, or rarely with narrow foliaceous appendages; petals pink, 2-3 cm long. —Upland woods and prairies; Ramsey County.

Rosa multiflora Thunb.
(NO MAP)
MULTIFLORA ROSE
introduced (invasive)

Stems climbing or scrambling. **Stipules** conspicuously serrate and glandular-ciliate; **leaflets** commonly 7-9, elliptic to obovate, obtuse or merely acute. **Inflorescence** many-flowered; sepals often prolonged into lance-shaped appendages; petals commonly white, 1-2 cm long.—Native of Asia; previously cultivated as a hedgerow plant (mostly south of Minn); sometimes escaping as the seeds are readily spread by birds eating the fruit; Washington County.

Rosa carolina

Rosa rugosa Thunb.
MAP 1134
RUGOSA ROSE
introduced

Stems 1-2 m tall, densely thorny, the infrastipular thorns larger, decurved; younger parts of the stem, young thorns, and thorn bases densely pubescent. **Leaflets** usually 7-9, rugose above. Pedicel bristly and pubescent; hypanthium smooth.—Native of e Asia; commonly cultivated and rarely escaped. *Notable for its large "rose-hips" (fruit), rich in vitamin C.*

1131. *Rosa acicularis*

1132. *Rosa arkansana*

1133. *Rosa blanda*

1134. *Rosa rugosa*

Rosa woodsii Lindl.   MAP 1135
WESTERN ROSE; WOOD'S ROSE   *native*
Stems to 1 m tall, armed with straight, slender, infrastipular thorns 3-5 mm long.
Stipules rarely to 15 mm long, glandular on the margin, densely stipitate-
glandular; rachis glandular, often also bristly; **leaflets** 5-7, elliptic to oval, sparsely
glandular beneath, the teeth glandular on the longer margin. **Flowers** commonly
corymbose; pedicel and hypanthium glabrous; petals pink, 1.5-2 cm long.—Fields
and openings.

RUBUS   *Blackberry; Raspberry; Dewberry*

Perennials, woody at least at base, usually with bristly stems. Stems biennial in some species, the first
year's canes called primocanes, the second year's growth termed floricanes. Leaves alternate,
palmately lobed or divided. Flowers 5-parted, usually perfect, white to pink or rose-purple; stamens
many. Fruit a group of small, 1-seeded drupes forming a berry.

ADDITIONAL SPECIES
• *Rubus missouricus* L.H. Bailey (Missouri dewberry), Anoka and possibly Kanabec counties (❧*endangered*).

1 Stems without bristles or prickles 2
   2 Leaves simple (cloudberry, thimbleberry) 3
      3 Plants low (1–3 dm); leaves reniform, with rounded lobes and blunt teeth; flowers solitary *R. chamaemorus*
      3 Plants taller (0.3–2 m); leaves not reniform, the lobes and teeth sharp-pointed; flowers in open clusters of
         3–10 . . . . *R. parviflorus*
   2 Leaves with 3–5 leaflets 4
      4 Stems short and upright or trailing; flowers single or several in a cluster; fruit red. 5
         5 Flowering stems 1 or several from a short base; petals light to deep pink, 1–2 cm long . . . . . *R. arcticus*
         5 Flowering stems single from a creeping stem; petals green-white, 0.5–1 cm long.. . . . . *R. pubescens*
      4 Stems erect or arching; flowers many in long, bracted clusters; fruit black . . . . *R. canadensis*
1 Stems with bristles or prickles 6
   6 Leaves whitish or gray-hairy on underside; fruit separating easily from receptacle when ripe (raspberries) . 7
      7 Stems erect or spreading, with stiff straight bristles; fruit red . . . . *R. idaeus*
      7 Stems arching, often rooting at tip, with broad-based, recurved prickles; fruit black . . . . . . *R. occidentalis*
   6 Leaves green on both sides, underside veins hairy; fruit falling with receptacle when ripe (dewberries and
      blackberries) 8
      8 Plants low and trailing (less than 0.5 m tall), often rooting at nodes; flowers 1 to several in a cluster; fruit
         red to red-purple (dewberries) 9
         9 Stems with prickles, these hooked at tip and broad at base; leaves thin and deciduous; petals more than
            1 cm long . . . . *R. flagellaris*
         9 Stems with coarse hairs and slender bristles; leaves leathery and often evergreen; petals less than 1 cm
            long . . . . *R. hispidus*
      8 Plants tall, to 2 m; stems erect, neither rooting at nodes nor arching and rooting at tips; flowers numerous
         in elongate clusters; fruit black (blackberries) 10
         10 Stems smooth or with scattered prickles; leaves glabrous . . . . *R. canadensis*
         10 Stems glandular-hairy, with broad-based prickles or covered with spreading bristles; leaves hairy on
             underside veins 11
             11 Stems covered with stiff bristles, broad-based prickles absent . . . . *R. setosus*
             11 Stems with bristles, gland-tipped hairs, and scattered broad-based prickles 12
                 12 Petioles and pedicels covered with gland-tipped hairs . . . . *R. allegheniensis*
                 12 Petioles and pedicels without glandular hairs (or nearly so) . . . . *R. pensilvanicus*

Rubus allegheniensis Porter   MAP 1136
COMMON BLACKBERRY   *native*
Stems 0.5-3 m tall, mostly erect, the young primocanes often sparsely glandular.
Primocane leaves usually 5-foliolate with the intermediate pair long-petiolulate,
softly pubescent beneath; **terminal leaflet** usually 1-2 dm long, widest near the
middle, sharply serrate; **lateral leaflets** smaller; armature of the stem of nearly
straight spines spreading at right angles, much flattened at their base; armature
of the petioles, pedicels, and lower side of the midveins commonly present and
consisting of spines similarly flattened but prominently hooked. **Inflorescence**
racemose, many-flowered, the lower 1, 2, or rarely 3 flowers subtended by leaves,

the others by stipules only; pedicels glandular; **flowers** about 2 cm wide.—Forests and forest edges, clearings, old fields, roadsides; usually on dry uplands, occasional in marshy or swampy ground. *Our commonest tall blackberry.*

Rubus arcticus L.
MAP 1137
DWARF RASPBERRY
native
> *Rubus acaulis* Michx.

Stems herbaceous (woody at base), 5-10 cm long, bristles or prickles absent. **Leaves** divided into 3 leaflets, 1-4 cm long and 0.5-3 cm wide, **terminal leaflet** stalked, lateral pair of leaflets nearly sessile, **lateral leaflets** often with a shallow lobe, upper surface smooth, underside finely hairy; margins with blunt, forward-pointing teeth; petioles long, finely hairy; stipules small, ovate. **Flowers** single at ends of erect stems; sepals lance- shaped, to 1 cm long; petals 5, light to dark pink, 1-2 cm long. **Fruit** red, nearly round, 1 cm wide, edible. June-Aug.—Conifer swamps, open bogs. *Ours **subsp. acaulis (Michx.) Focke.***

Rubus allegheniensis

Rubus canadensis L.
MAP 1138
SMOOTH BLACKBERRY; DEWBERRY
native
Stems erect or nearly so, to 2 m tall, spineless, or occasionally beset with stout straight spines from expanded bases. **Primocane leaves** commonly 5-foliolate, typically glabrous beneath, rarely softly pubescent, the 3 central leaflets long-petiolulate, the lower pair subsessile to short-petiolulate; lateral leaflets lance-shaped to broadly oblong; terminal leaflet commonly 1-2 dm long, ovate, always conspicuously acuminate, sharply serrate. **Floricane leaflets** much smaller, the terminal one widest above the middle, always acute to short-acuminate, sometimes entire in the basal half. **Inflorescence** racemose, many-flowered, the flowers on glandless pedicels 2-4 cm long, subtended by stipules 1-2 cm long and serrate.—Woods, clearings, fields, roadsides; occasionally in moist soil.

Rubus chamaemorus L.
MAP 1139
CLOUDBERRY; BAKE-APPLE
☙ *threatened | native*
Stems upright, unbranched, and unarmed, 1-3 dm high, with leaves from the upper 1-3 nodes and stipules only at the lower nodes. **Leaves** alternate simple, and deciduous, the somewhat leathery blades rounded to reniform, 4-11 cm wide, with 5-7 rounded lobes and rather shallow sinuses; margins serrate with blunt teeth; petioles 2-8 cm long. **Flowers** unisexual, 2-3 cm wide, solitary and terminal on long peduncles; calyx lobes pubescent and glandular, sometimes lacerate or fringed; petals white. **Fruit** 1-2 cm in diameter, composed of a few large-seeded drupelets, at first reddish then turning amber to yellowish, soft and translucent when ripe, soon falling from the receptacle, edible and with a pleasant distinctive flavor. June-July.—Common across Canada with a few extensions southward into USA (first discovered in Minn in 1954). Usually on sphagnum moss hummocks in bogs. *The leaves are similar to those of **swamp red currant** (Ribes triste), but the lobes are more rounded.*

Rubus canadensis

Rubus flagellaris Willd.
MAP 1140
WHIPLASH DEWBERRY
native
> *Rubus baileyanus* Britt.

Stems long-trailing, 2-4 m long, often rooting at tip, brown to red-purple, with curved, broad-based prickles; bristles absent. **Primocane leaves** divided into 3-5 leaflets, the terminal leaflet 2-6 cm long and 1-5 cm wide, often with small lobes

Rubus chamaemorus

1135. *Rosa woodsii*

1136. *Rubus allegheniensis*

1137. *Rubus arcticus*

1138. *Rubus canadensis*

above middle; **floricane leaves** smaller, usually divided into 3 leaflets; **leaflets** ovate to obovate, upper and lower surface more or less glabrous, or underside veins with appressed hairs; margins with forward-pointing teeth; petioles finely hairy, with scattered, hooked prickles. **Flowers** mostly 2-7 (sometimes 1), on upright, finely hairy stalks, the stalks with scattered prickles; sepals joined, the lobes narrowed to dark tips; petals 5, white, 10-15 mm long. **Fruit** red, more or less round, composed of large, juicy drupelets, edible, not easily separating from receptacle. May-June.—Swamps, wetland margins; also in drier sandy woods, prairies and openings.

Rubus hispidus L.
BRISTLY DEWBERRY
Rubus fulleri L.H. Bailey

MAP 1141
threatened | native

Stems trailing or low-arching, often rooting at tip, with slender bristles or spines 2-5 mm long, these sometimes gland-tipped, not much widened at base. **Leaflets** 3 (rarely 5), ovate to obovate, 2-5 cm long and 1-3 cm wide, upper surface dark green and slightly glossy, slightly paler and more or less glabrous below, some leaves persisting through winter; margins with rounded teeth; petioles finely hairy and bristly; stipules linear, persistent. **Flowers** single in upper leaf axils or in open clusters of 2-8 at ends of short branches; sepals joined, the lobes ovate, tipped with a small dark gland; petals 5, white, 5-10 mm long. **Fruit** red-purple, less than 1 cm wide, sour, not easily separated from receptacle. June-Aug. —Conifer swamps, wet hardwood forests, thickets, wetland margins; usually where shaded.

Rubus hispidus

Rubus idaeus L.
WILD RED RASPBERRY
Rubus strigosus Michx.

MAP 1142
native

Stems erect or spreading, to 1.5 m long, biennial; young stems bristly with slender, often gland-tipped hairs; older stems brown, smooth. **Primocane leaves** divided into 3 or 5 leaflets, **floricane leaflets** usually 3; **leaflets** ovate to lance-shaped, upper surface dark green and smooth or sparsely hairy, underside gray-hairy; margins with sharp, forward-pointing teeth; petioles with bristly hairs; stipules slender, soon deciduous. **Flowers** in clusters of 2-5 at ends of stems and 1-2 from upper leaf axils; sepals with gland-tipped hairs; petals 5, white, shorter than the sepals. **Fruit** red, about 1 cm wide, edible, separating from receptacle when ripe. May-Aug.—Thickets, moist to wet openings, streambanks; often where disturbed. *Our native plants sometimes considered a variety (R. idaeus var. strigosus) of the cultivated red raspberry (R. idaeus L.) from Europe.*

Rubus idaeus

Rubus occidentalis L.
BLACK RASPBERRY

MAP 1143
native

Stems erect or ascending, or sometimes arching and rooting at the tip, not glandular, glaucous the first year, becoming glabrous the second, sparsely beset with stout, straight or hooked spines with expanded bases, as are also the petioles and especially the pedicels. **Leaflets** commonly 3, occasionally 5 on the primocanes ; uppermost leaves of the floricane often simple; terminal leaflet broadly ovate, rounded or subcordate at base, sharply and irregularly serrate; lower leaflets similar but smaller and narrower; all thinly gray-tomentose beneath. **Flowers** 3-7 in a dense umbel-like cluster; often 1 or 2 flowers also from the upper axils; petals white, shorter than the sepals, narrowly obovate, at first erect, soon

Rubus occidentalis

1139. Rubus chamaemorus   *1140. Rubus flagellaris*   *1141. Rubus hispidus*   *1142. Rubus idaeus*

deciduous. **Fruit** commonly black, rarely yellowish, about 1 cm wide. May-June.—Dry or moist woods, fields, and thickets. *Often cultivated in many horticultural varieties.*

Rubus parviflorus Nutt.
THIMBLEBERRY

MAP 1144
native

Stems unarmed, 1-2 in. tall, with shredding **bark**, the younger parts, petioles, and pedicels stipitate-glandular. **Leaves** rotund to kidney-shaped in outline, 1-2 dm wide, lobed to 1/3 of their width, the lobes serrate. **Flowers** few, white, in a long-peduncled cluster; sepals with a long caudate tip; petals elliptic-obovate, 1.5-2 cm long. **Fruit** edible, red, 1.5-2 cm wide, with pubescent coherent drupelets. May-July.—Open woods and thickets. *Sometimes harvested for use in jam.*

Rubus parviflorus

Rubus pensilvanicus Poir.
PENNSYLVANIA BLACKBERRY

MAP 1145
native

Stems usually stout, 1-3 m tall; armature of the primocanes of straight or spreading spines from expanded bases; shorter hooked spines usually occur on the petioles, often on the petiolules, and occasionally on the midveins and axis of the raceme. **Primocane leaves** softly pubescent beneath, 3-5-foliolate; terminal leaflet broadly ovate, 6-12 cm long at maturity, broadest well below the middle, distinctly acuminate, coarsely and irregularly serrate or doubly serrate. **Floricane leaflets** usually elliptic to obovate, coarsely toothed above the middle, many of them simple, ovate. **Racemes** usually short, few-flowered, well surpassing the leaves, sometimes loose and open.—Roadsides, fields, thickets, forests and forest borders; often in moist places such as borders of marshes and swamps. The spines on the primocane vary from numerous to few, from stout with broad bases to very slender. *The coarse serration, commonly accentuated beyond the middle of the leaflets, is characteristic, but forms with simpler serration occur.*

Rubus pubescens Raf.
DWARF RASPBERRY

MAP 1146
native

Low perennial. **Stems** long-creeping at or near soil surface, with upright, hairy branches 1-3 dm tall; the branches herbaceous but woody at base, bristles absent; **sterile branches** arching to trailing, often rooting at nodes; **flowering branches** erect, with few leaves. **Leaves** alternate, divided into 3 leaflets; **leaflets** oval, 2-6 cm long and 1-4 cm wide, tapered to a sharp point; margins with coarse, forward-pointing teeth, often entire near base; petioles hairy. **Flowers** on glandular-hairy stalks, 1-3 in loose clusters at ends of erect branches, sometimes with 1-2 flowers from leaf axils; petals 5, white or pale pink, to 1 cm long. **Fruit** bright red, round, 5-15 mm wide, the drupelets large, juicy, edible, not separating easily from receptacle. May-July.—Conifer swamps, wet deciduous woods, rocky shores.

Rubus pubescens

Rubus setosus Bigelow
BRISTLY BLACKBERRY
Rubus semisetosus Blanch.

MAP 1147
native

Stems erect to spreading or arching, to 1.5 m long; **branches** covered with spreading bristles 1-4 mm long; older canes red-brown, ridged, not rooting at tip. **Leaves** alternate; **primocane leaves** divided into 3-5 leaflets; **floricane leaves** 3-divided; **leaflets** ovate to obovate, upper and lower surface more or less smooth but often hairy on underside veins; margins with sharp, forward-pointing teeth; petioles bristly; stipules linear, 1-2 cm long. **Flowers** few to many in elongate

Rubus setosus

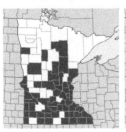

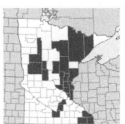

1143. Rubus occidentalis   *1144. Rubus parviflorus*   *1145. Rubus pensilvanicus*   *1146. Rubus pubescens*

clusters at ends of stems, with small, leafy bracts throughout the head; petals 5, white, to 1 cm long. **Fruit** red, ripening to black, round, to 1 cm wide, dry, poor eating quality. June-Aug.—Wetland margins, shores, occasional in open bogs; also in drier sandy prairie.

SIBBALDIA

Sibbaldia tridentata (Aiton) Paule & Soják   MAP 1148
SHRUBBY-FIVEFINGERS   *native*
  Potentilla tridentata Ait.
  Sibbaldiopsis tridenta (Aiton) Rydb.
Stems woody at base, from a caudex, often 2 or 3 together, 1-3 dm tall, sparsely strigose. **Leaves** mostly near the base, digitately compound; **leaflets** 3, firm in texture, oblong lance-shaped, 15-25 mm long, entire near base, 3-toothed at the truncate tip, glabrous above, obscurely strigose beneath. **Flowers** several in a flattened cyme, white, about 10 mm wide; bractlets lance-shaped, somewhat shorter than the ovate-triangular sepals; ovary and achenes villous. June-Aug. —Open sandy places, dry savannas of jack pine and oak; rocky and gravelly shores, rock outcrops.

Sibbaldia tridentata

SORBARIA *False Spiraea*

Sorbaria sorbifolia (L.) A. Braun   MAP 1149
FALSE SPIRAEA   *introduced*
Shrub 1-2 m tall, the younger parts covered with a flocculent, deciduous, stellate tomentum. **Leaves** 1-pinnate; stipules lance-shaped, about 1 cm long; **leaflets** lance-shaped, 3-7 cm long, sharply doubly serrate. **Flowers** 5-merous, in panicles 1-3 dm long, the branches ascending; hypanthium broadly cup-shaped; sepals to 1.5 mm long, soon reflexed, often erose; petals white, elliptic-obovate, 2.5-3 mm long; stamens numerous, to 8 mm long; pistils 5, opposite the sepals. **Fruit** a thin-walled follicle. July.—Native of e Asia; cultivated and escaped along roadsides and fencerows.

Sorbaria sorbifolia

SORBUS *Mountain-Ash*

Trees or shrubs. Leaves odd-pinnate with normally 11-17 serrate leaflets; flowers white, numerous, in repeatedly branched, round or flattened clusters. Hypanthium obconic. Sepals triangular, ascending. Petals 5, obovate to orbicular, rounded or cuneate at base, spreading. Stamens 15-20. Fruit a small pome, each cell with 1 or 2 elongate flattened seeds.

1 Leaflets tapered to a tip, 3-5 times longer than wide; petals obovate, to 4 mm long; fruit 5-6 mm wide . ***S. americana***
1 Leaflets rounded at tip or abruptly tapered to a tip, 2-3 times longer than wide; petals orbicular, 4-5 mm long; fruit 8-10 mm wide 2
  2 Leaflets glabrous, pale on underside; inflorescence branches and pedicels glabrous or nearly so . . . ***S. decora***
  2 Leaflets soft-hairy on underside; inflorescence branches and pedicels with soft hairs . . . . ***S. aucuparia***

Sorbus americana Marsh.   MAP 1150
AMERICAN MOUNTAIN-ASH   *native*
  Pyrus americana (Marsh.) DC.
Shrub or tree to 10 m tall, the young **twigs** glabrous or nearly so. **Winter buds** glutinous, with glabrous or sparsely ciliate scales. **Leaflets** lance-shaped to narrowly oblong, long-acuminate, 5-9 cm long, sharply serrate, paler and usually glabrous beneath. **Inflorescence** 6-15 cm wide; hypanthium and sepals glabrous;

Sorbus americana

1147. Rubus setosus

1148. Sibbaldia tridentata

1149. Sorbaria sorbifolia

petals obovate, 3-4 mm long, conspicuously longer than the stamens. **Fruit** bright red, 4-6 mm wide. May-June; fruit in late summer.—In moist or wet soil; swamps (both cedar and deciduous), streambanks, forest borders.

Sorbus aucuparia L.
EUROPEAN MOUNTAIN-ASH; ROWAN
MAP 1151
introduced
    Pyrus aucuparia (L.) Gaertn.

Tree to 10 m tall, the young **twigs** more or less villous. **Winter buds** white-villous, not glutinous. **Leaflets** oblong, 3-5 cm long, serrate, paler and usually long-villous beneath, at least when young. **Inflorescence** 10-20 cm wide; hypanthium densely white-villous; petals orbicular, 4-5 mm long, about equaling the stamens. **Fruit** bright red, about 10 mm wide. May-June.—Native of Europe; planted for ornament and escaped into moist woods; often mistaken for a native plant.

Sorbus decora (Sarg.) Schneid.
NORTHERN MOUNTAIN-ASH
MAP 1152
native
    Pyrus decora (Sarg.) Hyl.

Shrub or tree to 10 m tall, the young **twigs** glabrous or nearly so. **Winter buds** glutinous, the principal scales glabrous on the back, the inner usually conspicuously brown-ciliate. **Leaflets** oblong, 4-7 cm long, acute or very shortly acuminate, sharply serrate, paler and glabrous or sparsely pilose beneath. **Inflorescence** 6-15 cm wide; hypanthium glabrous or sparsely pilose; petals orbicular, 4-5 mm long, about equaling the stamens. **Fruit** bright red, 8-10 mm wide. May-June.—Moist or dry, often rocky soil; wooded dunes and bluffs, forest margins.

Sorbus decora

SPIRAEA *Meadowsweet*

Shrubs with simple leaves and terminal or lateral clusters of white, pink, or purple flowers. Flowers 5-merous. Hypanthium cup-shaped or turbinate. Petals small, widely spreading. Stamens 15 to many. Pistils commonly 5, alternate with the sepals; styles terminal; ovules 2–several. Follicles firm in texture, dehiscent along the ventral suture. *Most species are attractive flowering shrubs.*

1   Leaves glabrous on both sides; flowers white to pinkish ....**S. alba**
1   Leaf underside densely covered with light brown, woolly hairs; flowers rose-pink ....**S. tomentosa**

Spiraea alba Du Roi
MEADOWSWEET
MAP 1153
native

Much-branched shrub, often forming colonies. **Stems** somewhat angled or ridged, 0.5-1.5 m long, smooth or short-hairy when young, becoming red-brown and smooth. **Leaves** alternate, often crowded on stems, oval to oblong lance-shaped, 3-7 cm long and 1-2 cm wide, smooth on both sides; margins with sharp, forward-pointing teeth; petioles 2-8 mm long; stipules absent. **Flowers** small, 6-8 mm wide, many in a narrow, pyramid-shaped panicle 5-25 cm long at ends of branches; sepals 5; petals 5, white. **Fruit** a group of 5-8 small follicles, each with several seeds; the fruiting branches often persistent over winter. June-Aug.—Wet meadows, streambanks, lakeshores, conifer swamps; soils often sandy.

    Includes plants sometimes treated as *S. latifolia* (Aiton) Borkh., more common in ne USA, and here treated as var. *latifolia* (Aiton) Dippel; the inflorescence glabrous or nearly so, the stem red- to purple-brown, and leaves less than 3 times longer than wide, with margins coarsely and bluntly toothed. The more common

1150. Sorbus americana   *1151. Sorbus aucuparia*   *1152. Sorbus decora*   *Spiraea alba*

form in Minn, var. *alba*, has a densely pubescent inflorescence, yellow-brown stems, and leaves 4-8 times longer than wide, with margins finely and sharply toothed.

Spiraea tomentosa L.
MAP 1154
HARDHACK   *native*

Sparsely branched shrub to 1 m tall. Young **stems** covered with brown woolly hairs, becoming smooth and red-brown. **Leaves** alternate, lance-shaped to ovate, 2-5 cm long and 0.5-2 cm wide; more or less smooth above, underside gray-green to tan, densely covered with feltlike hairs, the veins prominent; margins with coarse, forward-pointing teeth; petioles 1-4 mm long or absent. **Flowers** small, 3-4 mm wide, in spirelike panicles 5-15 cm long at ends of stems, the panicle branches covered with reddish woolly hairs; petals 5, pink or rose (rarely white). **Fruit** a cluster of small, hairy follicles, often persisting over winter. July-Sept. —Open bogs, conifer swamps, thickets, lakeshores, wet meadows; soils often sandy.

Spiraea tomentosa

Rubiaceae MADDER FAMILY

Shrubs (*Cephalanthus*) or herbs. Leaves simple, opposite or whorled. Flowers small, perfect (with both staminate and pistillate parts), white to green, single or in loose or round clusters; petals joined, 3-4-lobed; stamens 3-4; ovary 2-chambered. Fruit a nutlet (*Cephalanthus, Diodia*), a capsule (*Galium, Houstonia*), or a berry (*Mitchella*).

1 Shrubs; flowers in spherical heads .... *Cephalanthus occidentalis*
1 Herbs; flowers not in spherical heads 2
  2 Leaves whorled .... *Galium*
  2 Leaves opposite 3
    3 Leaves evergreen; fruit a scarlet or white berry .... *Mitchella repens*
    3 Leaves deciduous; fruit not a berry .... *Houstonia*

CEPHALANTHUS *Buttonbush*

Cephalanthus occidentalis L.
MAP 1155
COMMON BUTTONBUSH   *native*

Shrub or small tree, 1-4 m tall. **Young stems** green-brown, with lighter lenticels; **older stems** gray-brown. **Leaves** opposite or in whorls of 3, oval to ovate, 8-20 cm long and to 7 cm wide, upper surface bright green and shiny, paler or finely hairy below; margins entire or slightly wavy; petioles grooved, to 2 cm long. **Flowers** small, perfect, in round, many-flowered heads 2-4 cm wide, on long stalks at ends of stems or from upper leaf axils; petals 4, creamy white, 5-8 mm long; styles longer than petals and swollen at tip. **Fruit** a round head of brown, cone-shaped nutlets, tipped by 4 teeth of persistent sepals. June-Aug.—Hardwood swamps, floodplain forests, thickets, streambanks, marshes, bogs; often in standing water or muck.

Cephalanthus occidentalis

GALIUM *Bedstraw*

Annual or perennial herbs, from slender rhizomes. Stems 4-angled, ascending to reclining, smooth

1153. *Spiraea alba*   1154. *Spiraea tomentosa*   1155. *Cephalanth. occidentalis*   1156. *Galium aparine*

or bristly. Leaves entire, in whorls of 4-6. Flowers small, perfect, regular, 1 to several from leaf axils or in clusters at ends of stems; sepals absent; petals joined, 3-4-lobed, white; stamens 3-4; styles 2, ovary 2-chambered and 2-lobed, maturing as 2 dry, round fruit segments which separate when mature.

ADDITIONAL SPECIES
• *Galium odoratum* (L.) Scop. (Sweet woodruff), native to Europe; Washington County.

1 Fruit with bristly hairs 2
  2 Main leaves in whorls of 5 or more 3
    3 Annual herb; leaves in whorls of 7 or more; flowers white, blooming completed by early summer; stems very rough-to-touch . . . . *G. aparine*
    3 Perennial herb; leaves in whorls of up to 6; flowers greenish, blooming beginning in early summer; stems rough or smooth . . . . *G. triflorum*
  2 Leaves in whorls of 4 or less 4
    4 Leaves linear to linear lance-shaped, usually less than 5 mm wide; flowers white in a large panicle . . . . . .
       . . . . *G. boreale*
    4 Leaves ovate, often more than 5 mm wide; flowers greenish to purple, in few-flowered clusters; reported from Houston County . . . . *G. circaezans*
1 Fruit smooth or nearly so 5
  5 Leaves tipped with a short spine or at least sharp-pointed 6
    6 Leaves linear, hairy on underside, the margins revolute; flowers yellow, in elongate terminal panicles . . .
       . . . . *G. verum*
    6 Leaves narrowly lance-shaped to ovate, glabrous or rough-hairy on underside; flowers white, the inflorescence various 7
      7 Leaves and stems with rough, downward-pointing hairs . . . . *G. asprellum*
      7 Leaves and stems smooth or with short, upward-pointing hairs 8
        8 Leaves in whorls of 7 or more, oblong lance-shaped; stems smooth or short-hairy . . . . *G. mollugo*
        8 Leaves in whorls of 6 or less, linear; stems usually rough-hairy on the angles . . . . *G. concinnum*
  5 Leaves rounded or blunt at tip 9
    9 Lobes of corolla 3, mostly wider than long 10
      10 Leaves in whorls of 4; flowers and fruit on long, curved, rough-hairy pedicels . . . . *G. trifidum*
      10 Leaves usually in whorls of 5 or more; flowers and fruit on straight glabrous pedicels 11
        11 Pedicels 0.5-4 mm long and often curved at maturity, solitary or in pairs in leaf axils or at ends of branches but not on a common peduncle; corolla less than 1 mm wide; mature fruit to 1 mm long; leaves mostly 2.5-7 mm long . . . . *G. brevipes*
        11 Pedicels (at least the longest) 3-8 mm long and nearly always straight at maturity, often on a peduncle; corolla ca. 1-1.8 mm wide; mature fruit 1-2 mm long; leaves 5-20 mm long *G. tinctorium*
    9 Lobes of corolla 4, mostly longer than wide 12
      12 Leaves linear, bent downward, less than 2 mm wide . . . . *G. labradoricum*
      12 Leaves linear to oblong, spreading but not angled downward, mostly more than 2 mm wide . . . .
       . . . . *G. obtusum*

Galium aparine L.
STICKY-WILLY; CLEAVERS

MAP 1156
native

Annual herb. **Stems** weak, prostrate or reclining on bushes, 3-10 dm long, with stiff, downward-pointing hairs. **Leaves** on the principal stems in whorls of 8, typically oblong lance-shaped, mostly 3-8 cm long, rounded to an apiculate tip, retrorsely hispid on the margins and midvein. Peduncles axillary, exceeding the subtending leaves, divaricately branched, few-flowered. **Fruit** with hooked bristly hairs, 2-4 mm long. May-June.—Damp ground, usually in shade. Variable.

Galium aparine

1157. *Galium asprellum*   1158. *Galium boreale*   1159. *Galium brevipes*

Galium asprellum Michx.

ROUGH BEDSTRAW

MAP 1157
native

Perennial herb. **Stems** spreading or reclining on other plants, much-branched, to 2 m long, 4-angled, with rough, downward-pointing hairs on stem angles (which cling tightly to clothing). **Leaves** 6 in a whorl or 5-whorled on branches, narrowly oval, usually widest above middle, 1-2 cm long and 4-6 mm wide, tapered to a sharp tip; underside midvein and margins with rough hairs; petioles absent. **Flowers** in loose, few-flowered clusters at ends of stems and from upper leaf axils; corolla 4-lobed, white, 3 mm wide. **Fruit** smooth. July-Sept.—Swamps, streambanks, thickets, marshes, wet meadows, calcareous fens.

Galium asprellum

Galium boreale L.

NORTHERN BEDSTRAW

MAP 1158
native

Perennial herb. **Stems** erect, 2-8 dm long, 4-angled, smooth or with short hairs at leaf nodes, sometimes slightly rough-to-touch. **Leaves** in whorls of 4, linear to lance-shaped, 1.5-4 cm long and 3-8 mm wide, 3-nerved, tapered to a small rounded tip; margins sometimes fringed with hairs; petioles absent. **Flowers** many, 3-6 mm wide, in branched clusters at ends of stems; corolla lobes 4, white. **Fruit** with short, bristly hairs, or smooth when mature. June-Aug.—Streambanks, shores, thickets, swamps, moist meadows; also in drier woods and fields.

Galium brevipes Fern. & Weig.

LIMESTONE SWAMP BEDSTRAW

MAP 1159
native

   Galium trifidum subsp. *brevipes* (Fernald & Wiegand) A. & D. Löve

Perennial herb. **Stems** scabrous, forming sprawling, tangled mats. **Leaves** whorled, 4 at each node. **Flowers** 1 per peduncle, the peduncles very short, to only 4 mm long. **Fruit** smooth, lacking bristles. July-Aug.—Marshes, thickets; exposed calcareous shores, interdunal hollows, ditches. The very small pedicels (usually ± recurved), fruits, corollas, and leaves, if all are present, are distinctive. *Often included within* **Galium trifidum**.

Galium boreale

Galium circaezans Michx.

FOREST BEDSTRAW

(NO MAP)
native

Perennial herb. **Stems** simple or branched from the base, erect or ascending, 2-6 dm tall, more or less pubescent. **Leaves** in whorls of 4, oval, elliptic, or ovate-oblong, broadest near the middle, 2-5 cm long, 1-2.5 cm wide, obtuse, 3-5-nerved. **Inflorescences** terminal and from the upper axils, simple or with 1 or 2 divaricate forks, the flowers remote, sessile or subsessile; corolla greenish-purple, pilose, its lobes acute. **Fruit** reflexed, hooked-hispid, about 3 mm long. June-July.—Dry woods and thickets; reported from Houston County.

Galium concinnum Torr. & Gray

SHINING BEDSTRAW

MAP 1160
native

Perennial herb. **Stems** slender, spreading or ascending, much branched, 2-5 dm long, sparsely retrorse-scabrous on the angles or smooth. **Principal leaves** in whorls of 6, those of the branches often in whorls of 4, linear or linear-elliptic, 1-2 cm long, acute or cuspidate, upwardly scabrous on the margin. **Inflorescences** terminal and divaricately spreading from the upper axils, 2-3 times branched, the branches and short pedicels very slender; corolla 4-lobed, white, 2.5-3 mm wide. **Fruit** smooth, 2 mm long. June-Aug.—Dry woods.

Galium circaezans

1160. Galium concinnum

1161. Galium labradoricum

1162. Galium mollugo

1163. Galium obtusum

Galium labradoricum (Wieg.) Wieg.
NORTHERN BOG BEDSTRAW

MAP 1161
native

Perennial herb. **Stems** simple or branched, 1-3 dm long, 4-angled, hairy at leaf nodes, smooth on stem angles. **Leaves** in whorls of 4, soon curved downward, oblong lance-shaped, 1-1.5 cm long and 1-2 mm wide, blunt-tipped; underside midvein and margins with short, bristly hairs; petioles absent. **Flowers** single or in small groups on stalks from leaf axils; corolla lobes 4, white. **Fruit** smooth, dark. June-July.—Conifer swamps, sphagnum bogs, fens, sedge meadows.

Galium labradoricum

Galium mollugo L.
FALSE BABY'S-BREATH

MAP 1162
introduced

Erect perennial from a decumbent base. **Stems** 3-10 dm tall, smooth to finely pubescent. **Leaves** in whorls of 6 or 8, narrow, oblong lance-shaped, 10-20 (rarely 25) mm long, acute or apiculate, scabrous on the margin. **Inflorescences** several from the upper axils, forming a loose, open, elongate, divaricately branched panicle 1-3 dm long; corolla lobes white, acuminate. **Fruit** smooth, 1.5 mm long. May-July.—Meadows, fields, roadsides, lawns.

Galium obtusum Bigelow
BLUNTLEAF BEDSTRAW

MAP 1163
native

Perennial herb. **Stems** branched, 2-6 dm long, 4-angled, hairy at leaf nodes, otherwise smooth. **Leaves** mostly in whorls of 4 (sometimes 5 or 6), ascending to spreading, linear to lance-shaped or oval, 1-3 cm long and 3-5 mm wide, blunt-tipped; margins with short, bristly hairs and often somewhat rolled under; petioles absent. **Flowers** in clusters at ends of stems; corolla lobes 4, white. **Fruit** smooth, dark, often with only 1 segment maturing. May-July.—Wet deciduous forests, wet meadows, streambanks, thickets, floodplains, moist prairie.

Galium tinctorium (L.) Scop.
STIFF MARSH BEDSTRAW

MAP 1164
native

Galium trifidum L. subsp. *tinctorium* (L.) Hara

Perennial herb. **Stems** slender, weak, 4-angled, with rough hairs on angles. **Leaves** in whorls of 4 or sometimes 5-6, linear to oblong lance-shaped, 1-2.5 cm long, tapered to a narrow base, dark green and dull; underside midvein and margins with rough hairs; petioles absent. **Flowers** in clusters of 2-3, on slender, smooth, straight stalks at ends of stems; corolla lobes 3, white. **Fruit** smooth. July-Sept. —Conifer swamps, open bogs, fens, thickets, wet shores and marshes. *Plants similar to* **Galium trifidum** *and sometimes considered a variety of that species.*

Galium tinctorium

Galium trifidum L.
NORTHERN THREE-LOBED BEDSTRAW

MAP 1165
native

Perennial herb. **Stems** slender, weak, 2-6 dm long, much-branched, sharply 4-angled, with rough, downward-pointing hairs on stem angles. **Leaves** in whorls of 4, linear to oblong lance-shaped, 5-20 mm long and 1-3 mm wide, blunt-tipped, dark green and dull on both sides; underside midvein and margins often rough-hairy; petioles absent. **Flowers** small, on 2-3 slender stalks from leaf axils or at ends of stems, the stalks much longer than the leaves; corolla lobes 3, white. **Fruit** dark, smooth. June-Sept.—Shores, streambanks, swamps, marshes, bogs, springs.

Galium trifidum

Galium triflorum Michx.
SWEET-SCENTED BEDSTRAW

MAP 1166
native

Perennial herb. **Stems** prostrate or scrambling, 2-8 dm long, 4-angled, smooth or

1164. *Galium tinctorium*   1165. *Galium trifidum*   1166. *Galium triflorum*   1167. *Galium verum*

with rough, downward-pointing hairs on stem angles. **Leaves** shiny, in whorls of 6 (or 4 on smaller branches), narrowly oval to oblong lance-shaped, 2-5 cm long and to 1 cm wide, l-nerved, tipped with a short, sharp point, slightly vanilla-scented, underside midvein with rough hairs, margins with rough, forward-pointing hairs; petioles absent. **Flowers** 2-3 mm wide, on slender stalks from leaf axils and at ends of stems, the stalks with 3 flowers or branched into 3 short stalks, each with 1-3 flowers; corolla lobes 4, green-white. **Fruit** 2-lobed, covered with hooked bristles. June-Aug.—Moist to wet woods, hummocks in cedar swamps, wetland margins and shores, clearings.

Galium triflorum

Galium verum L.   MAP 1167
YELLOW SPRING BEDSTRAW   *introduced*
Perennial herb. Stems erect from a horizontal rhizome, 3-8 dm tall, finely pubescent throughout or in the inflorescence. **Leaves** mostly in whorls of 8, linear, 1-3 cm long, often deflexed in age, sharply acute, usually pubescent beneath, often scabrellate above. **Inflorescences** numerous from the upper axils, compactly many-flowered, equaling or longer than the internodes below which they rise, forming a dense panicle; corolla yellow. **Fruit** smooth, about 1 mm long. June-Sept.—Fields and roadsides, usually in dry soil.

HOUSTONIA *Bluets*

Houstonia longifolia Gaertn.   MAP 1168
LONG-LEAF SUMMER BLUETS   *native*
   Hedyotis longifolia (Gaertn.) Hook.
Perennial herb. Stems numerous from a perennial base, simple or branched above, 10-25 cm tall, glabrous or finely pubescent, especially at the nodes. **Leaves** small, sessile, broadly linear to narrowly oblong, 10-30 mm long, 2-5 mm wide, narrowed to the base, glabrous or minutely scaberulous on the margin, 1-nerved, often with a few obscure veinlets. **Flowers** 4-merous, short-pediceled, numerous in loose or crowded cymes; sepals linear lance-shaped, 1-2 mm long, in fruit equaling or longer than the capsule; corolla purplish to white, funnelform, 5.5-9 mm long, the lobes about half as long as the tube, pubescent within; stamens 4; ovary 2-celled; stigmas 2. **Capsule** globose, 2.3-3.1 mm long, protruding beyond the hypanthium. June-Aug.—Dry to sometimes moist, sandy or gravelly soil; shallow soil over limestone; sandy fields.

Houstonia longifolia

MITCHELLA *Partridge-Berry*

Mitchella repens L.   MAP 1169
PARTRIDGE-BERRY   *native*
Creeping perennial herb. Stems rooting at the nodes, 10-30 cm long, forming mats. **Leaves** evergreen, petioled, round-ovate, 1-2 cm long. **Flowers** 4-merous, dimorphic, in pairs, their hypanthia united, mostly terminal, the common peduncle shorter than the subtending leaves; corolla white, funnelform, 10-14 mm long, with elongate tube and 4 short, spreading or recurved lobes villous on the inner face; ovary 4-celled; stigmas 4. **Fruit** a scarlet berry, composed of the ripened hypanthia and ovaries of the 2 flowers, 5-8 mm wide, crowned with the short sepals, edible but insipid, persistent through the winter; seeds 8. May-July.—Dry or moist woods.

Mitchella repens

1168. Houstonia longifolia

1169. Mitchella repens

1170. Zanthoxyl. americanum

1171. Populus × jackii

Rutaceae RUE FAMILY

Mostly trees or shrubs with alternate, simple or compound leaves and small flowers. Flowers perfect or unisexual, usually regular. Stamens usually as many or 2x as many as the petals. Carpels commonly as many as the petals, in some genera fewer, separate, or weakly united (often by the styles only), or completely connate into a compound ovary. Fruit commonly separating into segments, in some genera a capsule, drupe, or berry. Most parts of the plant contain oil-glands; those of the leaves *appear as translucent dots. The most important economic genus in the Rue Family is Citrus L., including cultivated varieties of orange, grapefruit, lemon, lime, citron, and tangerine; the two Minnesota species are the northernmost members of the family.*

ADDITIONAL SPECIES
• *Phellodendron chinense* C.K. Schneid (Chinese corktree) native to China; Winona County, where an escape from nearby ornamental plantings; potentially invasive.

1   Leaflets 3; Hennepin County . . . . *Ptelea trifoliata*
1   Leaflets 5–11; widespread in Minn . . . . *Zanthoxylum americanum*

PTELEA *Hop-Tree*

Ptelea trifoliata L.
COMMON HOP-TREE

(NO MAP)
native

Deciduous shrub or small tree, without spines. **Leaves** alternate, 3-foliolate, long-petioled; **leaflets** sessile, ovate, elliptic, or ovate-oblong, entire or serrulate. **Flowers** small, greenish white or yellowish white, with staminate, pistillate, and perfect flowers on the same plant, and produced together in terminal cymes 4–8 cm wide; sepals, petals, and stamens 4 or 5, the latter imperfect or abortive in the pistillate flowers; petals oblong, pubescent, 4–7 mm long. **Fruit** a thin, flat, circular samara, 15–25 mm wide, the broad wing completely surrounding the indehiscent 2-celled body, reticulately veined, with the odor of hops. May–June.—Moist woods; Hennepin County, where possibly planted; more common south of the state.

Ptelea trifoliata

ZANTHOXYLUM *Prickly Ash*

Zanthoxylum americanum P. Mill.
PRICKLY ASH

MAP 1170
native

Tall dioecious shrub or rarely a small tree to 8 m tall, foliage strongly aromatic. **Stems** thorny. **Leaves** alternate, odd-pinnately compound; **leaflets** 5–11, oblong to elliptic or ovate, crenate or entire, pubescent beneath, at least when young. **Flowers** greenish or whitish, in short-peduncled, sessile, axillary clusters on branches of the previous year; sepals none; petals 4 or 5, fringed at the tip; stamens 4 or 5, alternate with the petals; ovaries 3–5. **Fruit** (from each ovary) a firm-walled or somewhat fleshy follicle, about 5 mm long, the surface pitted, dehiscent across the top, with 1 or 2 seeds. April–May.—Moist woods and thickets.

Zanthoxylum americanum

Salicaceae WILLOW FAMILY

Deciduous trees or shrubs. Leaves alternate, margins entire or toothed; stipules often present at base of leaf petiole, these usually soon falling. Flowers borne in catkins near ends of branches. Flowers imperfect, the staminate and pistillate flowers on separate plants, usually appearing before leaves open, or in a few species after leaves open; flowers without petals or sepals, each flower with either 1 or 2 enlarged basal glands (*Salix*) or a cup-shaped disk (*Populus*). Fruit a dry, many-seeded capsule; seeds small, covered with long, silky hairs.

1   Large trees; leaves heart-shaped to ovate, mostly less than 2 times longer than wide; buds often sticky and covered by 2 or more overlapping scales; catkins drooping, flowers subtended at base by a cup-shaped disk; stamens many, 12–80 . . . . *Populus*
1   Shrubs and trees; leaves ovate, lance-shaped or linear, 2 or more times longer than wide; buds covered by 1 scale; catkins upright or drooping, flowers subtended by 1 or 2 enlarged glands; stamens 2–8 . . . . *Salix*

POPULUS *Aspen; Poplar; Cottonwood*

Trees with deciduous, ovate to triangular leaves. Flowers in drooping catkins that develop and mature before and with leaves in spring; staminate and pistillate flowers on separate trees; base of flower with a cup-shaped disk; stamens 10-80. Fruit a 2-4 chambered capsule with many small seeds, these covered with long, white hairs which aid in dispersal by the wind.

HYBRIDS
Populus × jackii Sarg. (Balm-of-Gilead), *P. balsamifera × P. deltoides,* MAP 1171.

1 Leaf petioles round in section, leaf underside often stained brown from resin . . . . *P. balsamifera*
1 Leaf petioles strongly flattened, leaf underside not stained brown 2
  2 Leaf underside and petioles densely woolly hairy . . . . *P. alba*
  2 Leaf underside and petioles glabrous 3
    3 Leaves strongly triangular in shape 4
      4 Leaf blades about as long or longer than wide, often with glands at tip of petiole; trees with broad
        crowns . . . . *P. deltoides*
      4 Leaf blades wider than long, never with glands on petiole; trees narrow and spire-like . . . . . . *P. nigra*
    3 Leaves ovate to nearly round 5
      5 Leaf margins coarsely wavy-toothed; leaves 7-13 cm long . . . . *P. grandidentata*
      5 Leaf margins finely sharp-toothed; leaves less than 7 cm long . . . . *P. tremuloides*

Populus alba L.
WHITE POPLAR
MAP 1172
introduced (invasive)

Tree with widely spreading branches and whitish gray bark; terminal bud and young twigs tomentose. **Leaves** white-tomentose beneath, palmately 3-7-lobed on the elongate shoots at the end of the branches, on the short lateral shoots ovate, irregularly dentate. **Pistillate catkins** 4-6 cm long. **Capsules** narrowly ovoid.—Native of Eurasia, commonly planted and spreading by root sprouts.

Populus balsamifera L.
BALSAM-POPLAR
MAP 1173
native

Medium to large tree to 20 m or more tall; trunk 30-60 cm wide; crown open, somewhat narrow; **bark** smooth when young, becoming dark gray and furrowed; twigs red-brown when young, becoming gray; leaf buds fragrant, very resinous and sticky. **Leaves** resinous, ovate, 8-13 cm long and 4-7 cm wide, tapered to a long tip, rounded or somewhat heart-shaped at base, dark green and somewhat shiny above, white-green or silvery and often stained with rusty brown resin below; margins with small, rounded teeth; petioles round in section, 3-4 cm long. **Catkins** densely flowered, drooping, appearing before leaves; scales fringed with long hairs, early deciduous; **pistillate catkins** 10-13 cm long; **pistillate flowers** with 2 spreading stigmas; stamens 20-30. **Capsules** ovate, 6-8 mm long, crowded on short pedicels. April-May.—Swamps, floodplain forests, shores, streambanks, forest depressions, moist dunes.

Populus balsamifera

Populus deltoides Bartr.
PLAINS COTTONWOOD
MAP 1174
native

Large tree to 30 m or more tall, with a large trunk (often 1 m or more wide) and a broad, rounded crown; **bark** gray to nearly black, deeply furrowed; **twigs** olive-brown to yellow, turning gray with age; **leaf buds** very resinous and sticky, shiny, covered by several tan bud scales. **Leaves** smooth, broadly triangular, 8-14 cm long and 6-12 cm wide, short-tapered to tip, heart-shaped or truncate at base;

Populus deltoides

margins with forward-pointing, incurved teeth, 2-5 large glands usually present at base of blade near petiole; petioles strongly flattened, 3-10 cm long; stipules tiny, early deciduous. **Catkins** loosely flowered, drooping, appearing before leaves; scales fringed, soon falling; flowers subtended by a cup-shaped disk 2-4 mm wide; **pistillate catkins** green, 7-12 cm long in flower, to 20 cm long in fruit; pistillate flowers with 3-4 spreading stigmas; **staminate catkins** dark red, soon deciduous; stamens 30-80. **Capsules** ovate, 6-12 mm long, on pedicels 3-10 mm long. April-May.—Floodplains, streambanks and bars, shores, wet meadows, ditches.

Populus grandidentata Michx.
MAP 1175
BIG-TOOTH ASPEN
native

Small or large tree; **bark** light greenish gray when young, becoming dark brown in age. Terminal buds dull brown, finely pubescent. **Leaf blades** broadly ovate in outline, 8-12 cm long, with 5-10 large, projecting, round-pointed teeth on each side, the lowest veins strongly ascending; petioles strongly flattened. Scales of the catkins shallowly cleft into 5-7 lance-shaped lobes; stamens 5-12; stigmas 4. **Capsules** slenderly conic, 3-5 mm long, on pedicels 1-2 mm long.—Dry or moist soil; common northward where it usually grows in drier soil than *P. tremuloides*.

Populus grandidentata

Populus nigra L.
(NO MAP)
LOMBARDY POPLAR
introduced

Tall tree, with dull gray branches and dark furrowed **bark** on the older trunks; a horticultural form is the Lombardy poplar with erect branches forming a narrowly conic crown. **Leaves** triangular-ovate, abruptly pointed, broadly cuneate to truncate at base, finely and bluntly serrate, 5-10 cm long and usually slightly broader, glandless at the base, pubescent when young; petioles distinctly flattened. Stamens 30 or fewer; stigmas 2, broadly dilated. **Capsules** ovoid, 7-9 mm long, 2-valved, twice as long as their pedicels.—Native of Eurasia, often planted and occasionally escaped; reported from Pipestone and Stearns counties.

Populus tremuloides Michx.
MAP 1176
QUAKING ASPEN
native

Slender tree with light grayish green **bark**, becoming dark and furrowed in age; terminal buds brown, shining, glabrous or nearly so. **Leaves** broadly ovate to orbicular, 3-10 cm long, abruptly pointed, broadly cuneate (rarely) to truncate or subcordate at base, finely and regularly serrate or crenate to nearly entire; lowest lateral veins strongly ascending, the venation hence apparently palmate; petioles strongly flattened. Scales of the **catkins** cleft to below the middle into 3-5 lance-shaped lobes; stamens, stigmas, and capsules as in *P. grandidentata*.—Dry or moist soil, especially in cut-over land.

Populus tremuloides

SALIX *Willow*

Shrubs and trees. Leaves variable in shape, petioles glandular in some species; stipules early deciduous or persistent, sometimes absent. Catkins (aments) stalkless or on leafy branchlets, usually shed early in season. Staminate and pistillate flowers on separate plants; staminate flowers with mostly 2-3 stamens (to 8 in some species). Fruit a 2-chambered, stalked or stalkless capsule.

ADDITIONAL SPECIES
· *Salix daphnoides* Vill. (Daphne willow); native to Eurasia; St. Louis Co. (Duluth area).
· *Salix pseudomonticola* Ball (False mountain willow), n Minn (MAP 1177).

1 Leaves opposite or nearly so; young branches often dark purple . . . . **S. purpurea**
1 Leaves alternate; branches various colors 2
  2 Leaf petioles with glands at or near base of blade 3
    3 Trees, usually with a single trunk; leaves narrow 4
      4 Leaves often curved sideways (scythe-shaped), tapered to a long, slender tip; vigorous shoots with large stipules; native species . . . . **S. nigra**
      4 Leaves not curved sideways, tapered to a short tip; stipules small and early deciduous; introduced species 5
        5 Twigs drooping, slender . . . . **S. × sepulcralis**

    5 Twigs not drooping, thicker 6

      6 Leaves glabrous; twigs easily broken at base . . . . ***S. × fragilis***

      6 Leaf underside usually silky-hairy; twigs not easily broken at base . . . . ***S. alba***

  3 Small trees or shrubs, usually with several to many stems; leaves broader 7

    7 Leaves waxy-coated on underside 8

      8 Leaf tips rounded or with a short point; leaf base heart-shaped or rounded; young leaves translucent; buds and leaves with a balsamlike scent . . . . ***S. pyrifolia***

      8 Leaves tapered to tip; leaf base blunt or rounded; young leaves not translucent; buds and leaves not balsam-scented 9

        9 Young leaves sparsely hairy; margins with small forward-pointing teeth; flowering in early summer . . . . ***S. amygdaloides***

        9 Young leaves without hairs; margins with small, gland-tipped, forward-pointing teeth; flowering summer or fall . . . . ***S. serissima***

    7 Leaves not waxy on underside 10

      10 Leaves short-tapered to tip; twigs and young leaves resin-scented; introduced species . . . . ***S. pentandra***

      10 Leaves long-tapered to tip; twigs and young leaves not resin-scented; native species . . . . ***S. lucida***

2 Petioles without glands 11

  11 Mature leaves hairy, at least on underside 12

    12 Leaves linear or narrowly lance-shaped 13

      13 Underside of leaves with felt-like covering of white tangled hairs; young twigs white-hairy; plant of peatlands, often where calcium-rich . . . . ***S. candida***

      13 Leaves not with felt-like hairs; twigs smooth or sparsely hairy 14

        14 Leaf margins entire and somewhat revolute; leaf underside pubescent . . . . ***S. pellita***

        14 Leaf margins with gland-tipped teeth; leaf underside sparsely hairy 15

          15 Leaf margins with widely spaced sharp teeth; petioles 1–5 mm long; colony-forming shrub of sandy banks . . . . ***S. interior***

          15 Leaf margins with small teeth at least above middle of blade; petioles 3–10 mm long; stems clustered but not forming large colonies . . . . ***S. petiolaris***

    12 Leaves broadly lance-shaped, oblong, or ovate 16

      16 Leaves rounded or heart-shaped at base; margins toothed; stipules present and persistent 17

        17 Twigs gray-brown to dark brown, closely gray-pubescent the first year and often into the second . . . . ***S. eriocephala***

        17 Twigs yellow or yellowish gray to yellowish brown, glabrous . . . . ***S. famelica***

      16 Leaves tapered to base; margins entire or toothed; stipules usually falling early 18

        18 Leaves narrowly to broadly lance-shaped, more than 5 times longer than wide, underside velvety with shiny white hairs . . . . ***S. pellita***

        18 Leaves obovate or elliptic, less than 5 times longer than wide, underside hairs not shiny 19

          19 Small branches widely spreading; young leaves with white hairs; catkins appearing with leaves in spring; catkin bracts yellow or straw-colored; capsules on pedicels 2–5 mm long . . . . ***S. bebbiana***

          19 Small branches not widely spreading; young leaves with some red or copper-colored hairs; catkins appearing before leaves in spring; catkin bracts dark brown to black; capsules on pedicels 1–3 mm long 20

            20 Leaf upperside smooth or the veins slightly raised, the underside sparsely hairy; twigs often shiny . . . . ***S. discolor***

            20 Leaf upperside somewhat wrinkled, the veins sunken, the leaf underside densely woolly hairy; twigs dull . . . . ***S. humilis***

  11 Mature leaves without hairs (sometimes hairy on petiole and midvein) 21

    21 Leaves green on both sides or slightly paler on underside, not glaucous or white-waxy below 22

      22 Single-stemmed tree; stipules large . . . . ***S. nigra***

      22 Many-stemmed shrub; stipules small or absent 23

        23 Many-stemmed, colony-forming shrub; upper leaf surface not conspicuously shiny; common . . . . ***S. interior***

        23 Clumped shrub, not forming colonies; upper leaf surface very shiny; rare in nw Minn . . . . ***S. maccalliana***

    21 Leaves glaucous or white-waxy on underside 24

      24 Leaf margins entire to shallowly lobed or with irregular teeth, sometimes revolute 25

      25 Leaf margins entire and somewhat revolute 26

26 Stems upright, to 1 m tall, or creeping and rooting in moss; upper surface of leaves with raised, net-like veins; catkins appearing with leaves; capsules not hairy . . . . *S. pedicellaris*

26 Stems upright, 1-4 m tall; leaf veins not net-like; catkins appearing before leaves; capsules hairy . . . . *S. planifolia*

25 Leaf margins irregularly toothed, the teeth sharp or rounded 27

27 Leaves dull green above, wrinkled below; catkins appearing with leaves; bracts of pistillate catkins green-yellow to straw-colored . . . . *S. bebbiana*

27 Leaves dark green and shiny above; catkins appearing before leaves; bracts of pistillate catkins dark brown to black 28

28 Stipules large on vigorous shoots; capsules on distinct stalks 2 mm or more long *S. discolor*

28 Stipules lance-shaped and soon deciduous, or absent; capsules sessile or on short stalks less than 2 mm long . . . . *S. planifolia*

24 Leaf margins distinctly toothed 29

29 Leaves balsam-scented (especially when dried), broadly elliptic, ovate, or obovate, rounded or somewhat abruptly short-tapered to tip . . . . *S. pyrifolia*

29 Leaves narrowly to broadly lance-shaped, long- or short-tapered to tip 30

30 Leaves more or less equally tapered from middle of blade to tip and base 31

31 Twigs from previous year glabrous and shining, often also somewhat waxy; young leaves with few to many coppery hairs mixed with white hairs; mature leaves smooth on both sides or hairy above; lateral veins not prominent; capsules lance-shaped . . . . *S. petiolaris*

31 Twigs from previous year finely hairy (or at least with some patches of fine hairs); young leaves densely silky-hairy, without copper-colored hairs; underside of mature leaves silky-hairy with conspicuous, riblike, lateral veins; capsules ovate and rounded at tip *S. sericea*

30 Leaves unequally tapered, the tip tapered to a point; base usually rounded or heart-shaped 32

32 Young twigs glabrous; stipules small or absent; bracts of pistillate catkins pale yellow and soon deciduous . . . . *S. amygdaloides*

32 Young twigs gray-hairy; stipules large; bracts of pistillate catkins dark brown to black, persistent . . . . *S. eriocephala*

Salix alba L.
WHITE WILLOW

MAP 1178
introduced (naturalized)

Tree to 20 m tall; **twigs** golden-yellow, often with long, silky hairs. **Leaves** lance-shaped, 4-10 cm long and 1-2.5 cm wide, dark green and shiny above, waxy white below, smooth to sparsely hairy on both sides, margins with small gland-tipped teeth; petioles 2-8 mm long, with silky hairs; stipules lance-shaped, 2-4 mm long, early deciduous. **Catkins** appearing with leaves in spring; **pistillate catkins** 3-6 cm long, on leafy branches 1-4 cm long; **staminate catkins** 3-5 cm long, stamens 2; catkin bracts pale yellow, hairy near base, early deciduous. **Capsules** ovate, 3-5 mm long, without hairs, stalkless or on stalks to 1 mm long. May-June. —Introduced from Europe, sometimes escaping to streambanks and other wet areas.

Salix alba

Salix amygdaloides

Salix amygdaloides Anderss.
PEACH-LEAF WILLOW

MAP 1179
native

Shrub or tree to 15 m tall, often with several trunks; **twigs** gray-brown to light yellow, shiny and flexible. **Leaves** smooth, lance-shaped, long-tapered to tip, 5-12 cm long and 1-3 cm wide, yellow-green above, waxy-white below, margins finely toothed; petioles 5-20 mm long and often twisted; stipules small and early deciduous. **Catkins** appearing with leaves, linear and loosely flowered; **pistillate catkins** 3-12 cm long, on leafy branches 1-4 cm long; catkin bracts deciduous, pale yellow, long hairy especially on inner surface; stamens 3-7 (usually 5). **Capsules**

1176. *Populus tremuloides*

1177. *Salix pseudomonticola*

1178. *Salix alba*

1179. *Salix amygdaloides*

smooth, ovate, 3-7 mm long, on pedicels 1-3 mm long. May-June.—Floodplains, streambanks, lake and pond borders.

Salix bebbiana Sarg.

MAP 1180

BEBB'S WILLOW; BEAKED WILLOW   *native*

Shrub or small tree to 8 m tall, stems 1 to several; **twigs** yellow-brown to dark brown, usually with short hairs. **Leaves** oval to ovate or obovate, tapered to tip, 4-8 cm long and 1-3 cm wide, dull gray-green, hairy or sometimes smooth on upper surface, waxy-gray, hairy and wrinkled below, the veins distinctly raised on lower surface; margins entire to shallowly toothed; petioles 5-15 mm long; stipules deciduous or persistent on vigorous shoots. **Catkins** appearing before leaves in spring; **pistillate catkins** loose, 2-6 cm long, on short leafy branches to 2 cm long; catkin bracts persistent, red-tipped when young, turning brown, long hairy; stamens 2. **Capsules** ovate, 5-8 mm long, finely hairy, on pedicels 2-6 mm long. May-June.—Swamps, thickets, wet meadows, streambanks, marsh borders.

Salix bebbiana

Salix candida Flueggé ex Willd.

MAP 1181

SAGE WILLOW   *native*

Low shrub to 1.5 m tall; **twigs** much-branched, covered with dense, matted white hairs. **Leaves** linear-oblong, tapered at tip, 4-10 cm long and 0.5-2 cm wide, dull, dark green and sparsely hairy above, veins sunken, densely white-hairy below; margins entire and rolled under; petioles 3-10 mm long; stipules persistent, 2-10 mm long, white-hairy. **Catkins** appearing with leaves in spring; **pistillate catkins** 1-5 cm long, on leafy branches 0.5-2 cm long; catkin bracts persistent, brown, hairy; stamens 2. **Capsules** ovate, 4-8 mm long, white-hairy, on pedicels to 1 mm long. May-June.—Fens, bogs, open swamps, streambanks, usually where calcium-rich.

Salix candida

Salix discolor Muhl.

MAP 1182

PUSSY-WILLOW   *native*

Shrub or small tree to 5 m tall; **twigs** yellow-brown to red-brown, dull, smooth with age or with patches of fine hairs. **Leaves** oval and short-tapered to tip, 3-10 cm long and 1-4 cm wide, dark green and smooth above, underside red-hairy when young, becoming white-waxy, smooth and not wrinkled; margins entire or with few rounded teeth; petioles without glands; stipules deciduous, or often persistent on vigorous shoots. **Catkins** appearing and maturing before leaves in spring; pistillate catkins 4-8 cm long, stalkless, sometimes with 2 or 3 small, brown, bractlike leaves at the base; stamens 2. **Capsules** ovate with a long neck, 6-10 mm long, densely gray-hairy, on pedicels 2-3 mm long. April-May.—Swamps, fens, streambanks, floodplains, marsh borders.

Salix eriocephala Michx.

MAP 1183

MISSOURI WILLOW   *native*

Salix cordata Muhl.
Salix rigida Muhl.

Shrub or small tree to 6 m tall; **twigs** red-brown to dark brown, hairy when young. **Leaves** lance-shaped or oblong lance-shaped, 5-12 cm long and 1-3 cm wide, red-purple and hairy when young, upper surface becoming smooth and dark green, underside becoming pale-waxy; margins finely toothed; petioles without glands, 3-15 mm long; stipules persistent (especially on vigorous shoots), ovate or kidney-shaped, to 12 mm long, hairless, toothed. **Catkins** appearing with

Salix discolor

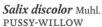

1180. Salix bebbiana   *1181. Salix candida*   *1182. Salix discolor*   *1183. Salix eriocephala*

or slightly before leaves in spring; **pistillate catkins** 2-6 cm long, on short leafy branches to 1 cm long; catkin bracts persistent, brown to black, hairy; stamens 2. **Capsules** ovate with a long neck, 4-6 mm long, without hairs, on pedicels 1-2 mm long. April-May.—Shores, streambanks, floodplains, ditches and wet meadows, especially along major rivers.

Salix famelica (C.R. Ball) Argus
YELLOW WILLOW
MAP 1184
native

> *Salix eriocephala* Michx. var. *famelica* (C. R. Ball) Dorn
> *Salix lutea* Nuttall var. *famelica* C. R. Ball

Shrubs or small tree, 1.5-7 m tall; **twigs** yellow-brown or red-brown, usually glabrous, sometimes pubescent or weakly glaucous; **older branches** yellow-brown to gray-brown. **Leaves** lance-shaped, base subcordate or rounded, midribs of both sides hairy; margins toothed. **Staminate catkins** flowering before leaves emerge; **pistillate catkins** flowering as leaves emerge, 1.5-8 cm long, floral bract dark brown, 0.8-1.6 mm long. **Capsules** 5-6 mm long. April-June.—Silty, sandy, or gravelly streambanks and floodplains, wet meadows, rich fens, prairie depressions. *Hybridizes with the closely related **Salix eriocephala**.*

Salix eriocephala

Salix × fragilis L.
CRACK WILLOW
MAP 1185
introduced (naturalized)

Large tree to 20 m tall and 1 m diameter; **twigs** greenish to dark red, glabrous, very brittle at base and deciduous in strong winds. **Leaves** large, lance-shaped, 7-12 or 15 cm long, 2-3.5 cm wide, with 5-6 glandular serrations per cm of margin, dark green above, glaucescent to glaucous beneath, glabrous at maturity; petioles 7-15 mm long, glandular above at the outer end; stipules wanting or small, semi-cordate, and early deciduous. **Catkins** appearing with leaves in spring, lax, 4-8 cm long, on leafy peduncles 1-3 or 5 cm long, bearing 2-5 small leaves; catkin bracts greenish yellow, crisp-villous, deciduous. **Capsules** narrowly conic, 4-5.5 mm long, glabrous; pedicels 0.5-1 mm long. April-May.—Introduced to North America from Europe in colonial times for ornament, shade, and gunpowder charcoal; common in farmyards and pastures and sometimes escaped. *Considered of hybrid orogin between S. alba × S. euxina.*

Salix × fragilis

Salix humilis Marsh.
UPLAND WILLOW
MAP 1186
native

Shrub 1-3 m tall; **twigs** yellowish to brown, pubescent to glabrate. **Leaves** oblong lance-shaped to narrowly obovate, 3-10 or 15 cm long, 1-2 or 3 cm wide, acute to abruptly short-acuminate, somewhat revolute, entire or sparingly undulate-crenate, dark green and often puberulent above; underside glaucous, somewhat rugose, and more or less gray-pubescent, becoming glabrate; stipules lance-shaped, acute, dentate, often deciduous. **Catkins** precocious, sessile or nearly so, oval-obovoid, 1.5-3 cm long, 1.5-2 cm wide; scales oblong lance-shaped, 1.5-2 mm long, blackish, long-villous; stamens 2; filaments long, free, glabrous. **Capsules** narrowly lance-shaped, 7-9 mm long, gray-pubescent; pedicels 1-2 mm long, pubescent. March-April.—Open woodlands, dry barrens, and prairies.

Salix humilis

Salix interior Rowlee
SANDBAR WILLOW
MAP 1187
native

> *Salix exigua* Nutt. subsp. *interior* (Rowlee) Cronq.

Shrub to 4 m tall, spreading by rhizomes and often forming dense thickets; **twigs** yellow-orange to brown, smooth. **Leaves** linear to lance-shaped, tapered at tip

1184. *Salix famelica*   1185. *Salix fragilis*   1186. *Salix humilis*   1187. *Salix interior*

and base, 5-14 cm long and 5-15 mm wide, green on both sides but paler below, at first hairy but soon usually smooth; margins with widely spaced, large teeth; petioles without glands, 1-5 mm long; stipules tiny or absent. **Catkins** appearing with leaves in spring on short leafy branches (and plants sometimes again flowering in summer); **pistillate catkins** loosely flowered, 2-8 cm long; catkin bracts deciduous, yellow; stamens 2. **Capsules** narrowly ovate, 5-8 mm long, hairy when young, smooth when mature, on pedicels to 2 mm long. May-June. —Shores, streambanks, sand and mud bars, ditches and other wet places; often colonizing exposed banks.

Salix interior

Salix lucida Muhl.
MAP 1188
SHINING WILLOW
native

Shrub or small tree to 5 m tall; **twigs** yellow-brown or dark brown, smooth and shiny. **Leaves** lance-shaped to ovate, long-tapered and asymmetric at tip, 4-12 cm long and 1-4 cm wide, shiny green above, pale below, red-hairy when young, but soon smooth; margins with small, gland-tipped teeth; petioles with glands near base of leaf; stipules often persistent, strongly glandular. **Catkins** appearing with leaves in spring; **pistillate catkins** 2-5 cm long, on leafy branches 1-3 cm long; catkin bracts deciduous, yellow, sparsely hairy; stamens 3-6. **Capsules** ovate with a long neck, 4-7 mm long, not hairy, on short pedicels to 1 mm long. May. —Swamps, shores, wet meadows, moist sandy areas.

Salix lucida

Salix maccalliana Rowlee
MAP 1189
MCCALLA'S WILLOW
native

Shrub 2-4 m tall; **twigs** upright, red- to yellow-brown, sparsely hairy or smooth, glossy. **Leaves** strap-shaped to narrowly oblong, to 8 cm long and 2.5 cm wide, dark green, upper surface glossy; leaf underside not waxy-coated; margins usually finely toothed; young leaves smooth or with white or reddish hairs; petioles sparsely hairy, without glandular dots; stipules small or leaflike. **Catkins** appearing with leaves in spring; female catkins 2-6 cm long, on leafy branches 1-2.5 cm long. **Capsules** densely hairy with age.—Uncommon in shrubby wetlands, fens, sedge meadows, soils usually sedge-derived peat and not strongly acid; typically found with other willows, dogwoods (*Cornus* spp.), and bog birch (*Betula pumila*). *Rare in n Minn; more common in central and western Canada.*

Salix maccalliana

Salix nigra Marsh.
MAP 1190
BLACK WILLOW
native

Medium tree to 15 m tall, trunks 1 or several, crown rounded and open; **bark** dark brown, furrowed, becoming shaggy; **twigs** bright red-brown, often hairy when young. **Leaves** commonly drooping, linear lance-shaped, 6-15 cm long and 0.5-2 cm wide, long-tapered to an often curved tip, green on both sides but satiny above and paler below, lateral veins upturned at tip to form a more or less continuous vein near leaf margin; margins finely toothed; petioles 3-8 mm long, hairy, usually glandular near base of blade; stipules to 12 mm long, heart-shaped, usually deciduous. **Catkins** appearing with leaves in spring; **pistillate catkins** 3-8 cm long, on leafy branches 1-3 cm long; stamens usually 6 (varying from 3-7); catkin bracts yellow, hairy, deciduous. **Capsules** ovate, 3-5 mm long, without hairs, on a short pedicel to 2 mm long. May.—Streambanks, lakeshores and wet depressions; not tolerant of shade.

Salix nigra

1188. *Salix lucida*

1189. *Salix maccalliana*

1190. *Salix nigra*

Salix pedicellaris Pursh
BOG WILLOW   MAP 1191
                          native

Short, sparsely branched shrub 4-15 dm tall; **twigs** dark brown and smooth. **Leaves** oblong lance-shaped to obovate, tapered to tip or blunt and often with a short point, 3-6 cm long and 0.5-2 cm wide, silky hairy when young, soon hairless, green on upper surface, white-waxy below, veins slightly raised on both sides; margins entire, often slightly rolled under; petioles without glands, 2-8 mm long; stipules absent. **Catkins** appearing with leaves in spring; **pistillate catkins** 2-4 cm long, on leafy branches 1-3 cm long; catkin bracts persistent, yellow-brown, hairy on inner surface near tip; stamens 2. **Capsules** lance-shaped, 4-7 mm long, without hairs, on pedicels 2-3 mm long. May-June.—Bogs, fens, sedge meadows, interdunal wetlands.

Salix pedicellaris

Salix pellita (Anderss.) Anderss.
SATINY WILLOW   MAP 1192
               threatened | native

Shrub, 3-5 m tall; **twigs** easily broken, yellow to olive-brown or red-brown, smooth or sparsely hairy when young, becoming waxy. **Leaves** lance-shaped, 4-12 cm long and 1-2 cm wide, short-tapered to a tip, upper surface without hairs, veins sunken, underside waxy and satiny hairy but becoming smooth with age, with numerous, parallel lateral veins; margins rolled under, entire or with rounded teeth; petioles to 1 cm long; stipules absent. **Catkins** appearing and maturing before leaves in spring; **pistillate catkins** 2-5 cm long, stalkless or on short branches to 1 cm long; catkin bracts black, long-hairy; **staminate catkins** rarely seen. **Capsules** lance-shaped, 4-6 mm long, silky hairy, more or less stalkless. May.—Streambanks, sandy shores and rocky shorelines.

Salix pellita

Salix pentandra L.
BAY-LEAF WILLOW   MAP 1193
                   introduced

Much like *S. serissima*, but the scales hairy only at the base outside, glabrous or nearly so distally. Shrub or small tree to 7 m tall. **Staminate catkins** mostly 3-6 cm or more long; **pistillate catkins** 3.5-7 cm; stamens 4-9, mostly 5. **Capsules** 5-8 mm long, on pedicels 0.5-1.5 mm long. May-June, the fruit maturing in mid- and late summer.—Native of Europe, cultivated and occasionally escaped.

Salix pellita

Salix petiolaris Sm.
MEADOW WILLOW   MAP 1194
                   native

Shrub to 5 m tall; **twigs** red-brown to dark brown, sometimes with short, matted hairs when young, smooth with age. **Leaves** narrowly lance-shaped, 4-10 cm long and 1-2.5 cm wide, hairy when young, becoming smooth, dark green above, white-waxy below; margins entire or with small, gland-tipped teeth; petioles without glands, 3-10 mm long; stipules absent. **Catkins** appearing with leaves in spring; **pistillate catkins** 1-4 cm long, stalkless or on short branches to 2 cm long; catkin bracts persistent, brown, with a few long, soft hairs; stamens 2. **Capsules** narrowly lance-shaped, 4-8 mm long, finely hairy, on pedicels 2-4 mm long. May.—Wet meadows, fens, streambanks, shores, open bogs, floating sedge mats, ditches.

Salix petiolaris

Salix planifolia Pursh
TEA-LEAF WILLOW   MAP 1195
                   native
     Salix phylicifolia subsp. *planifolia* (Pursh) Hiitonen

Shrub to 3 m tall; **twigs** dark red-brown, short hairy when young, soon smooth and shiny. **Leaves** oval to oblong lance-shaped, 3-6 cm long and 1-3 cm wide, short-

Salix planifolia

1191. *Salix pedicellaris*   1192. *Salix pellita*   1193. *Salix pentandra*   1194. *Salix petiolaris*

hairy when young, becoming smooth, green above, paler or waxy below; margins entire or with a few small, rounded teeth; petioles 3-6 mm long, without glands; stipules small and deciduous. **Catkins** appearing before leaves in spring; **pistillate catkins** 2-5 cm long, stalkless; catkin bracts 2-3 mm long, persistent, black, with long, soft hairs; stamens 2. **Capsules** lance-shaped, 4-8 mm long, finely hairy, stalkless or on short pedicels to 0.5 mm long. May.—Rocky lakeshores, cedar swamps, black spruce bogs, streambanks, margins of sedge meadows.

Salix purpurea L.

PURPLE WILLOW; BASKET WILLOW

(NO MAP)
introduced

Shrub to 2.5 m tall; **twigs** smooth, green-yellow to purple. **Leaves** more or less opposite (unique among our willows), smooth, linear to oblong lance-shaped, 4-9 cm long and 7-16 mm wide, purple-tinged, somewhat waxy below, veins raised and netlike on both sides; margins entire near base, irregularly toothed near tip; petioles short; stipules absent. **Catkins** appearing with and maturing before leaves in spring; **pistillate catkins** 2-3.5 cm long, stalkless; catkin bracts black; stamens 2 but often joined. **Capsules** ovate, 3-4 mm long, short-hairy, stalkless. May-June.—Introduced from Europe; St. Louis County.

Salix purpurea

Salix pyrifolia Anderss.

BALSAM WILLOW

MAP 1196
native

Shrub or small tree to 5 m tall; **twigs** smooth, yellow when young, becoming shiny red. **Leaves** smooth, ovate to lance-shaped, often rounded at tip, rounded to heart-shaped at base, 4-12 cm long and 2-4 cm wide, red-tinged and translucent when unfolding; green on upper surface, waxy and finely net-veined below; with balsam fragrance; margins with small gland-tipped teeth; petioles 1-2 cm long; stipules absent or small and 1-2 mm long. **Catkins** appearing with or after leaves in spring; **pistillate catkins** loosely flowered, 2-6 cm long, on leafy branches 1-3 cm long; catkin bracts red-brown, white-hairy, 2 mm long; stamens 2. **Capsules** lance-shaped, beaked at tip, 6-8 mm long, smooth, on pedicels 2-4 mm long. May-June.—Conifer swamps, bogs, rocky shores.

Salix pyrifolia

Salix sericea Marsh.

SILKY WILLOW

Salix petiolaris var. *sericea* (Marshall) Andersson

MAP 1197
native

Shrub to 4 m tall; **twigs** brown, brittle, densely gray or brown hairy when young, becoming smooth except at leaf nodes. **Leaves** lance-shaped, 6-12 cm long and 1-2.5 cm wide, upper surface dark green and smooth or finely hairy, waxy and with short silky hairs below; margins with small, gland-tipped teeth; stipules broadly lance-shaped, to 1 cm long, mostly deciduous. **Catkins** appearing before leaves in spring; **pistillate catkins** 1-4 cm long; catkin bracts black, long-hairy, 1 mm long; stamens 2. **Capsules** obovate, 3-5 mm long, short-hairy, on pedicels to 1 mm long. May.—Moist sandy or gravelly riverbanks and shores, sometimes in shallow water.

Salix sericea

Salix × sepulcralis Simonkai

WEEPING WILLOW

(NO MAP)
introduced

Tree to 12 m tall; **twigs** in cultivated plants slender, elongate, pendulous, yellowish to brownish, glabrous. **Leaves** linear lance-shaped, 8-12 cm long, 0.5-1.5 mm wide, mostly falcate, long-acuminate, finely but unevenly spinulose- serrulate, yellowish green above, glaucescent to glaucous beneath, glabrous; stipules lance-shaped, 2-7 mm long, or mostly wanting. **Catkins** appearing with leaves, small, 1-2.5 cm or

1195. *Salix planifolia*

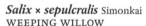

1196. *Salix pyrifolia*

1197. *Salix sericea*

1198. *Salix serissima*

the staminate to 4 cm long, on peduncles 0.5-1.5 cm long, bearing 2-4 tiny leaves; scales pale yellow, crinkly-pubescent, deciduous; stamens 3-5 or more, free, pubescent at base. **Capsules** narrowly ovoid, 1.5-2.5 mm long, sessile; styles almost obsolete; stigmas minute. April-May.—Early introduction from Europe, especially for cemeteries, and sparingly escaped; in Minn, known only from Anoka and Chisago counties. *Considered a hybrid between S. alba × S. babylonica. Formerly, all weeping willows were called S. babylonica, which is not cold hardy.*

Salix serissima (*Bailey*) Fern.

AUTUMN WILLOW   MAP 1198
                                                      native

Shrub to 4 m tall; **twigs** gray, yellow or dark brown, shiny and smooth. **Leaves** smooth, oval to lance-shaped, 4-10 cm long and 1-3 cm wide, red and hairless when young; green and shiny above, usually white-waxy below; margins with small gland-tipped teeth; petioles with glands near base of leaf; stipules usually absent. **Catkins** appearing with or after leaves in spring; **pistillate catkins** 2-4 cm long, on leafy branches 1-4 cm long; catkin bracts deciduous, light yellow, long hairy; stamens 3-7. **Capsules** narrowly cone-shaped, 7-10 mm long, smooth, on pedicels to 2 mm long. Late May-July (our latest blooming willow).—Fens, cedar and tamarack swamps, marshes, floating sedge mats, streambanks and shores, often where calcium-rich.

Salix serissima

Santalaceae SANDALWOOD FAMILY

Herbs (ours), usually root-parasites. Leaves simple, alternate or opposite. Flowers perfect or unisexual (plants usually monoecious or dioecious), in terminal or axillary clusters, or solitary. Hypanthium wholly or partly enclosing the ovary, with 3-several sepals on its margin and a conspicuous disc in its center. Stamens as many as the sepals, opposite them, inserted on their base. Ovary 1-celled. Fruit a nut or drupe, indehiscent, 1-seeded. *Santalum album* furnishes the fragrant sandalwood of the East Indies. Both *Comandra* and *Geocaulon*, though bearing green leaves, are hemiparasitic, and are apparently always attached (by means of modified roots, or haustoria) to some other plant. Both species also serve as alternate hosts for the canker-producing Comandra blister rust fungus (*Cronartium comandrae*), which in Minnesota infects trees of jack pine.

1 Plant an essentially leafless, non-green parasite on the branches of coniferous trees . . . . *Arceuthobium*
1 Plant leafy, green, terrestrial 2
    2 Flowers green-purple, 2-3 from leaf axils; fruit a juicy orange to red drupe . . . . *Geocaulon lividum*
    2 Flowers white, numerous in a terminal inflorescence; fruit a dry green or yellowish drupe . . . .
        . . . . *Comandra umbellata*

ARCEUTHOBIUM *Dwarf-Mistletoe*

Arceuthobium pusillum Peck

EASTERN DWARF-MISTLETOE   MAP 1199
                                                      native

Woody, parasitic plants on conifers, dioecious, attached to trees by haustoria, lacking ordinary roots, but with chlorophyll. **Stems** short, to 2 cm long, usually only 5-10 mm long, simple or with a few short branches, greenish brown. **Leaves** opposite, scale-like, about 1 mm wide. **Flowers** perfect or unisexual, regular, resembling short lateral branches until expanded, solitary or few in the axils of the leaves; perianth simple. **Fruit** united with the receptacle, berry-like or drupe-like, about 2 mm long, on a short recurved pedicel about equaling the subtending leaf. June-July.—Chiefly on trees of black spruce, rarely on tamarack or white spruce; reported on white pine. On spruce it often produces witches' brooms, and may become so abundant as to endanger the host tree. *Usually a single host tree supports only one sex of the mistletoe.*

1199. *Arceuthobium pusillum*

Arceuthobium pusillum

COMANDRA *Bastard Toadflax*

Comandra umbellata (L.) Nutt.
BASTARD TOADFLAX

MAP 1200
native

Stems 1-3 dm tall, from a rhizome near the surface of the soil. **Leaves** narrowly oblong to oval, 2-4 cm long, blunt or subacute, green on both sides, the lateral veins obscure and (except the basal) scarcely differentiated from the veinlets. **Flowers** white (rarely pinkish), bright green at their base; cymules terminal or subterminal, usually forming a flat-topped cluster; sepals oblong, 2-3 mm long. **Fruit** a dry or slightly fleshy green or yellowish drupe 4-6 mm long. May-July. —Prairies, shores, upland woods, and rock bluffs.

GEOCAULON *False Toadflax*

Geocaulon lividum (Richards.) Fern.
FALSE TOADFLAX
   Comandra livida Richards.

MAP 1201
native

Perennial herb, from a slender rhizome; at least partially parasitic on other plants. **Stems** smooth, 1-3 dm long. **Leaves** alternate, oval or ovate, 1-3 cm long and 1-1.5 cm wide, rounded at tip; margins entire; petioles short. **Flowers** greenish, usually 3 on slender stalks from leaf axils, the lateral 2 flowers typically staminate, the middle flower perfect; sepals 4-5, triangular, 1-2 mm long; petals absent. **Fruit** a round, orange or red drupe, about 6 mm wide. June-Aug.—Cedar swamps, open bogs; more commonly in sandy conifer woods and forested dune edges.

Geocaulon lividum

Sapindaceae SOAPBERRY FAMILY

Family now includes former members of Aceraceae and Hippocastanaceae.

1   Leaves simple and lobed or pinnately compound; fruit a 2-winged samara . . . .***Acer***
1   Leaves palmately compound; fruit a large capsule . . . .***Aesculus***

ACER *Maple*

Trees or shrubs. Leaves opposite, simple or compound. Staminate and pistillate flowers borne on same or separate plants. Flowers with 5 sepals and 5 petals (sometimes absent), clustered into a raceme or umbel. Fruit a samara with 2 winged achenes joined at base.

ADDITIONAL SPECIES
• *Acer ginnala* Maxim. (Amur maple, MAP 1202), a shrubby Asian species grown for its brilliant fall color, occasionally escaped throughout eastern half of Minnesota.

1   Leaves pinnately compound . . . .***A. negundo***
1   Leaves simple 2
   2   Leaf sinuses between main leaf lobes sharp at their base 3
      3   Leaves deeply lobed to middle of blade or below, the lobes long and narrow . . . .***A. saccharinum***
      3   Leaf lobes shorter and wider 4
         4   Leaves with downy white hairs on underside, tips of twigs with appressed hairs; shrubs or small trees; fruit persistent on plants until autumn . . . .***A. spicatum***
         4   Leaves not downy-hairy on underside; twigs glabrous; medium trees; fruit shed in early summer . . . .
            . . . .***A. rubrum***

1200. Comandra umbellata   *1201. Geocaulon lividum*   *1202. Acer ginnala*   *1203. Acer negundo*

2   Leaf sinuses rounded at their base 5

     5   Leaf undersides and petioles covered with downy hairs; margins of the lobes undulate or entire; blades drooping at their edges; base of petioles with stipules . . . . ***A. nigrum***

     5   Leaf undersides and petioles glabrous or nearly so; margins of the lobes coarsely toothed; blades not drooping at their edges; base of petioles without stipules 6

        6   Leaf petioles exuding milky juice when broken; twigs stout; samara wings widely divergent; bark becoming closely fissured, not scaly . . . . ***A. platanoides***

        6   Leaf petioles not exuding milky juice when broken; twigs slender; samara wings less divergent; bark becoming deeply furrowed and plate-like . . . . ***A. saccharum***

Acer negundo L.

BOXELDER

MAP 1203

native

Tree to 20 m tall, the trunk soon dividing into widely spreading branches; **bark** brown, ridged when young, becoming deeply furrowed; **twigs** smooth, green and often with waxy-coated. **Leaves** opposite, compound, **leaflets** 3–7, oval to ovate, coarsely toothed or shallowly lobed, upper surface light green and smooth, underside pale green and smooth or hairy. **Flowers** either staminate or pistillate and on separate trees, appearing with leaves in spring; petals absent; **staminate flowers** in drooping, umbel-like clusters, **pistillate flowers** in drooping racemes. **Fruit** a paired samara 3–4.5 cm long.—Floodplain forests, streambanks, shores; also fencerows, drier woods and disturbed areas. *Distinguished from the ashes (Fraxinus) by its paired fruit (vs. single in ash) and its green or waxy twigs.*

Acer negundo

Acer nigrum Michx. f.

BLACK MAPLE

MAP 1204

native

    Acer saccharum Marsh. var. *nigrum* (Michx. f.) Britt.

Resembling *A. saccharum* in habit and size, but with darker, thicker, more deeply furrowed bark. **Leaves** commonly with somewhat decurved or drooping sides, similarly lobed but the lobes with fewer and shorter, often obtuse or rounded teeth, darker and duller above than those of *Acer saccharum*. **Samaras** similar in shape, 2.7–4.5 cm, averaging 3.5 cm long.—In moist soil, often associated with *Acer saccharum*.

Acer nigrum

Acer platanoides L.

NORWAY MAPLE

(NO MAP)

introduced (naturalized)

Tree with widely spreading crown. **Leaves** resembling those of *Acer saccharum*, with 5–7 sharply acuminate lobes and a few large teeth; juice milky (best seen at the base of a detached petiole). **Flowers** yellow, in erect rounded corymbs, the obovate petals 5–6 mm long, widely spreading. **Samaras** 35–45 mm long, scarcely distended over the seed, the halves divergent at an angle of about 180 degrees. Apr.–May.—Native of Europe; planted as a shade tree and established as a weedy tree in vacant lots; Dakota and St. Louis (Duluth area) counties.

Acer rubrum L.

RED MAPLE

MAP 1205

native

Acer platanoides

Tree to 25 m tall; **bark** gray and smooth when young, becoming darker and scaly; **twigs** smooth, reddish with pale lenticels. **Leaves** opposite, 3–5-lobed (but not lobed to middle of blade), coarsely doubly toothed or with a few small lobes, upper surface green and smooth, underside pale green to white, smooth or hairy. **Flowers** either staminate or pistillate, usually on different trees but sometimes on same tree, in dense clusters, opening before leaves in spring; sepals oblong, 1

Acer rubrum

mm long, petals narrower and slightly longer. **Fruit** a paired samara, 1-2.5 cm long.—Floodplain forests, swamps; also common in drier forests. *Distinguished from **silver maple** (Acer saccharinum) by its shallowly lobed leaves vs. the deeply lobed leaves of silver maple.*

Acer saccharinum L.

SILVER MAPLE

MAP 1206
native

Tree to 30 m tall; **bark** gray or silvery when young, becoming scaly; **twigs** red-brown, smooth. **Leaves** opposite, deeply 5-lobed to below middle of blade, sharply toothed, upper surface pale green and smooth, underside silvery white; petioles usually red-tinged. **Flowers** either staminate or pistillate, usually on different trees but sometimes on same tree, in dense clusters, opening before leaves in spring. **Fruit** a paired samara, each fruit 3-5 cm long, falling in early to mid-summer.—Floodplain forests, swamps, streambanks, shores, low areas in moist forests.

Acer saccharinum

Acer saccharum Marsh.

SUGAR MAPLE

MAP 1207
native

Tree to 40 m tall, with straight central trunk when growing in a forest and a widely spreading network of branches when in the open. **Leaves** about as wide as long, 3-5-lobed, the lobes usually bearing a few large sharp teeth. **Flowers** unisexual in umbels from the terminal or uppermost lateral buds, appearing as the leafbude open, drooping on slender pedicels up to 8 cm long; calyx gamosepalous, campanulate, 2.5-6 mm long, more or less hirsute; petals none. **Samaras** 2.5-4 cm, averaging 3 cm long, the seed-bearing portions diverging at right angles to the pedicel, the wings curved forward. April-May.—Rich woods, especially in calcareous soils.

Acer saccharum

Acer spicatum Lam.

MOUNTAIN MAPLE

MAP 1208
native

Shrub or small tree, occasionally 10 m tall. **Leaves** 3-lobed or obscurely 5-lobed, softly pubescent beneath, coarsely and irregularly serrate, the teeth 2-3 per centimeter, each tipped with a minute sharp gland. **Flowers** mostly polygamo-monoecious, produced in fascicles of 2-4 along an erect axis, forming a slender, terminal, long-peduncled panicle, each flower long-pediceled, the terminal one of each fascicle usually perfect, the others sterile; petals greenish, very narrowly linear-oblong lance-shaped, about 3 mm long, much exceeding the sepals; stamens usually 8. **Samaras** 18-25 mm long, conspicuously reticulate-veined over the seed, the halves diverging at about a right angle. June.—Moist woods and swamps.

Acer spicatum

AESCULUS *Buckeye*

Aesculus glabra Willd.

OHIO-BUCKEYE

MAP 1209
introduced

Small to medium tree, 10-12 m tall; trunk 15-30 cm wide; **bark** thin, yellow-brown, smooth to scaly, dark brown and deeply furrowed with age, bark and leaves foul-smelling when bruised; **twigs** red-brown, becoming light gray. **Leaves** appearing early in spring, turning yellow in fall, opposite, smooth, palmately compound into usually 5 (rarely 7) leaflets; **leaflets** obovate, 7-15 cm long and 3-6 cm wide, tapered at both ends, margins finely toothed, petioles 10-15 cm long. **Flowers** perfect or either staminate or pistillate on same tree, numerous, yellow-green, appearing after leaves unfold in spring, in panicles 1-1.5 dm long and 6 cm wide at ends of branches; petals 4, pale yellow, hairy, 2 cm long, stamens 7, longer than the petals. **Fruit** a prickly, red-brown capsule, 2-3 cm wide, with 1 smooth, satiny brown seed. April-May.—Floodplain forests, streambanks, thickets. Local in Minn (and considered adventive), where reaching its northern range limit.

Aesculus glabra

ADDITIONAL SPECIES

• *Aesculus hippocastanum* L. (Horse-chestnut), reported from St. Louis County, where likely an uncommon escape from cultivation; leaves palmately 7-parted.

Sarraceniaceae PITCHERPLANT FAMILY

SARRACENIA *Pitcherplant*

Sarracenia purpurea L.　　　　　　　　　　MAP 1210
PITCHERPLANT　　　　　　　　　　　　　　　*native*
Perennial insectivorous herb. **Flower stalks** leafless, 3-6 dm long. **Leaves**
clumped, hollow and vaselike, curved and upright from base of plant, 1-2 dm long
and 1-5 cm wide, green or veined with red-purple, winged, smooth on outside,
upper portion of inside with downward-pointing hairs, tapered to a short petiole
at base. **Flowers** large and nodding, 5-6 cm wide, single at ends of stalks, perfect;
sepals 5; petals 5, obovate, dark red-purple, curved inward over yellow style;
ovary large and round. **Fruit** a 5-chambered capsule; seeds small and numerous.
May-July.—Sphagnum bogs, floating bog mats, occasionally in calcium-rich
wetlands.

Sarracenia purpurea

Saxifragaceae SAXIFRAGE FAMILY

Perennial herbs. Leaves alternate, opposite or basal. Flowers perfect (with both staminate and pistillate
parts), regular, single on stalks or in narrow heads. Sepals 5; petals 5 (sepals and petals 4 in
Chrysosplenium); stamens 5 or 10, stigmas 2 or 4. Fruit mostly a 2-parted capsule.

1　Leaves all from stem; petals absent, the flowers 4-merous . . . . *Chrysosplenium*
1　Leaves all (or nearly all) from base of plant; the flowers 5-merous 2
　2　Stamens 5 3
　　3　Petioles densely long-hairy; widespread in Minn . . . . *Heuchera richardsonii*
　　3　Petioles glabrous; local in se Minn . . . . *Sullivantia sullivantii*
　2　Stamens 10 3
　　3　Petals deeply pinnatisect; carpels in fruit spreading widely, exposing the seeds in a shallow flattish cup . .
　　　. . . . . *Mitella*
　　3　Petals entire; carpels in fruit not spreading but forming an elongate capsule or pair of follicles separate
　　　nearly to the base 4
　　　4　Leaf blades both lobed and irregularly toothed their entire length, strongly cordate, shorter than their
　　　　petioles; carpels very unequal; inflorescence a simple raceme . . . . *Tiarella cordifolia*
　　　4　Leaf blades 3-toothed at tip, or with teeth or crenulations of equal size or nearly entire, tapered at base
　　　　(petiole usually shorter than the blade or absent); carpels equal; inflorescence branched 5
　　　　5　Basal leaves minutely crenulate, nearly entire, or with green teeth; petals not dotted; flowering stem
　　　　　with only 1-2 small bracts between the inflorescence and basal leaves. . . . . *Micranthes*
　　　　5　Basal leaves with cartilaginous sharp teeth (either 3 spines at the end, or regular flat teeth with lime
　　　　　encrustations); petals usually dotted with red or purplish; flowering stem with several bracts or
　　　　　small leaves . . . . *Saxifraga*

CHRYSOSPLENIUM *Golden-Saxifrage*

Small, somewhat succulent perennial herbs. Leaves rounded, palmately veined, margins lobed.
Flowers small, yellow or yellowish-green. Sepals 4; petals 4. Fruit a capsule.

1　Leaves opposite, sometimes upper leaves alternate; mostly ne Minn (absent from se Minn) . . . . . *C. americanum*
1　Leaves alternate; inflorescences compact cymes; rare in extreme se Minn . . . . *C. iowense*

1207. Acer saccharum　　　　*1208. Acer spicatum*　　　　*1209. Aesculus glabra*　　　　*1210. Sarracenia purpurea*

Chrysosplenium americanum Schwein.
AMERICAN GOLDEN-SAXIFRAGE

MAP 1211
native

Small, perennial herb, often forming large mats. **Stems** creeping, branched, 5-20 cm long. **Lower leaves** opposite, the **upper leaves** often alternate, broadly ovate, 5-15 mm long and as wide, margins entire or with rounded teeth or lobes; petioles short. **Flowers** single and stalkless from leaf axils, 4-5 mm wide; sepals 4, green-yellow or purple-tinged; petals absent; stamens usually 8 from a red or green disk, anthers red. **Fruit** a 2-lobed capsule. April-June.—Springs, shallow streams, shady wet depressions; soils mucky.

Chrysosplenium iowense Rydb.
IOWA GOLDEN SAXIFRAGE

MAP 1212
endangered | native

Perennial herb, differing from *C. americanum* by having leaf margins with 5-7 large rounded teeth.—Disjunct from arctic regions in driftless area of se Minn and ne Iowa on cool, moist, mossy, talus slopes underlain by dolomitic limestone.

Chrysosplenium americanum

HEUCHERA *Alumroot*

Heuchera richardsonii R. Br.
PRAIRIE ALUMROOT

MAP 1213
native

Perennial herb. **Stems** more or less hirsute, becoming glandular in the inflorescence. **Leaves** broadly cordate-ovate, glabrous or nearly so above, sparsely hirsute on the veins beneath, shallowly 7-9-lobed, each lobe with 3-5 rountled or acute, mucronate lobes; petioles strongly hirsute. **Flowers** in relatively narrow and congested panicles; hypanthium very oblique, twice as long above as below; petals 3-4 mm long, about equaling the sepals and stamens and styles.—Prairies and dry woods.

Heuchera richardsonii

MICRANTHES *Pseudosaxifrage*

Perennial scapose herbs. Leaves in basal rosettes. Calyx 5-cleft. Petals 5. Stamens 10. Pistil 1, 2-carpellate. *Micranthes includes former members of* **Saxifraga** *having a leafless flowering stem (or at most tiny bracts), and (in our species) herbaceous-textured leaves.*

1   Larger leaves 10-35 cm long, obscurely crenulate-toothed, entire near the tip; petals 2-3 mm long; plants of swampy habitats . . . . ***M. pensylvanica***
1   Larger leaves 3-7.5 cm long, distinctly toothed, especially near the tip; petals 3-5 mm long; plants of rocky, drier habitats   . . . . ***M. virginiensis***

Micranthes pensylvanica (L.) Haworth
SWAMP SAXIFRAGE

MAP 1214
native

Saxifraga pensylvanica L.

Perennial herb. **Stems** stout, erect, 3-10 dm long, with sticky hairs. **Leaves** all from base of plant, ovate to oblong ovate, 1-2 dm long and 4-8 cm wide, smooth or hairy; margins entire to slightly wavy or with irregular rounded teeth; petioles wide. **Flowers** small, in clusters atop stem, the head elongating with age; sepals bent backward, 1-2 mm long; petals green-white or purple-tinged, lance-shaped, 2-3 mm long; stamens 10, the filaments threadlike. **Fruit** a follicle. May-June. —Swamps, wet deciduous forests, marshes, moist meadows and low prairie; often where calcium-rich.

Micranthes pensylvanica

1211. Chrysosple. americanum   *1212. Chrysosplenium iowense*   *1213. Heuchera richardsonii*

Micranthes virginiensis (Michx.) Small
EARLY SAXIFRAGE

MAP 1215

native

Saxifraga virginiensis Michx.

Perennial herb. **Stems** to 25 cm tall, usually glandular-villous; scapes naked, rarely minutely bracted. **Leaves** in basal tufts, often purplish beneath; blades oblanceolate, narrowing to flattened petioles. **Inflorescence** leafy-bracted, becoming paniculate, sometimes longer than the scape; **flowers** white, in congested cymules; petals oblanceolate, 5-6 mm long; tip of ovary becoming inflated and long-beaked; **seed** ellipsoid, not appendaged, less than 0.5 mm long. —Rocky openings and hilltops.

MITELLA *Mitrewort; Bishop's Cap*

Perennial rhizomatous herbs. Leaves basal or alternate from the rhizome; flowering stems leafless or few-leaved, with a terminal raceme of small white, greenish, or purple flowers. Flowers perfect, regular, 5-merous. Hypanthium turbinate to saucer-shaped, adnate to the base of the ovaries, bearing the sepals, petals, and stamens at its margin. Petals narrow, deeply pinnatifid or fimbriate to entire. Stamens 10 (in our species), shorter than the sepals. Pistils 2. Carpels short, dehiscent along the ventral suture.

1 Plants small, the scape naked; the basal leaves not lobed or only slightly so; flowers green-yellow . . . . *M. nuda*
1 Plants larger, with a pair of nearly sessile leaves on the scape below the inflorescence; the basal leaves clearly 3-lobed; flowers white . . . . *M. diphylla*

Mitella diphylla L.
TWO-LEAF MITREWORT

MAP 1216

native

*Mitella
diphylla*

Flowering stems 1-4 dm tall, sparsely pubescent below, glandular-puberulent above the stem leaves. **Basal leaves** long-petioled, ovate-rotund, shallowly 3-5-lobed, crenate, cordate at base, pubescent. **Stem leaves** 2, sessile, smaller, 3-lobed, the middle lobe elongate. **Raceme** 5-15 cm long; pedicels 1-2 mm long. **Flowers** white, 5-6 mm wide; petals deeply fimbriate-pinnatifid, about 2 mm long; seeds few, black, smooth, shining, 1-1.5 mm long. May-June.—Rich woods. *The follicles at dehiscence diverge and open widely, exposing the shiny seeds.*

Mitella nuda L.
NAKED MITREWORT

MAP 1217

native

Small perennial herb, spreading by rhizomes or stolons. **Leaves** all from base of plant, or with 1 small leaf on flower stalk, rounded heart-shaped, 1-3.5 cm wide, both sides with sparse coarse hairs; margins with rounded teeth; petioles 2-8 cm long. **Flowers** small, green, on short stalks, in racemes of 3-12 flowers, on a glandular-hairy stalk 10-25 cm tall; calyx lobes 5, 1-2 mm long; petals green, pinnately divided into usually 4 pairs of threadlike segments, the segments 2-4 mm long; stamens 10. **Fruit** a capsule, splitting open to reveal the black, shiny, 1 mm long seeds. June-July.—Hummocks in swamps and alder thickets, ravines, seeps, moist mixed conifer and deciduous forests.

SAXIFRAGA *Saxifrage*

Small perennial herbs of rocky places (ours). Leaves simple. Flowers solitary or in cymes. Sepals 5. Petals 5; stamens 10; carpels 2, fused at least at base to form 2-celled ovary. *Several of our former saxifrage species now segregated into* **Micranthes.**

Mitella nuda

1214. *Micranthes pensylvanica*   1215. *Micranthes virginiensis*   1216. *Mitella diphylla*   1217. *Mitella nuda*

1   Inflorescences with all or some flowers replaced by bulbils; rare in Cook County . . . . *S. cernua*
1   Inflorescences without bulbils; rare in Cook and Lake counties . . . . *S. paniculata*

Saxifraga cernua L.

NODDING SAXIFRAGE (NO MAP)
✿*endangered | native*

Perennial herb. **Stems** slender, ascending, pubescent, 8-25 cm tall, with bulblets at the base. Basal and lower stem **leaves** petioled, kidney-shaped, 5-7-lobed, 6-25 mm wide; upper stem leaves sessile, 3-lobed or entire, bearing bulblets in the axils. **Flower** usually single, often nodding; sepals about 3 mm long; petals 6-9 mm long. **Fruit** seldom developing. June.—Disjunct in Minn (Cook County) from northern Canada and the Rocky Mountains, and known from a single north-facing, diabase rock cliff. *Plants rarely produce seed, and reproduction is primarily from distinctive ruby-red bulblets in the axils of the leaves.*

*Saxifraga
cernua*

Saxifraga paniculata Mill.

ENCRUSTED SAXIFRAGE MAP 1218
native
    Saxifraga aizoon Jacq.

Perennial herb from short stolons. **Stems** erect, to 30 cm tall. **Leaves** clustered in ± hemispherical basal rosettes; obovate, 2-3 cm long, stiff, margins finely toothed, at the base of each tooth is a white, lime-encrusted pore; sessile. **Inflorescence** a small terminal panicle with glandular-hairy branches; petals 5, white to cream, sometimes red-spotted, 3-6mm long. **Fruit** a capsule. June-July.—Rock crevices and on small ledges on shady cliffs having cool, northerly aspects.

SULLIVANTIA *Coolwort*

Sullivantia sullivantii (Torr. & Gray) Britt.

SULLIVANT'S COOLWORT MAP 1219
✿*threatened | native*

Perennial herb. **Leaves** basal, long-petioled, rounded kidney-shaped, 3-7 cm wide, sparsely pubescent to nearly glabrous, with numerous shallow, rounded lobes each terminating in 2 or 3 short teeth. **Flowers** small, in an open panicle atop a scape-like flowering stem with a single foliage leaf near its base. Inflorescence reclining, 2-4 dm long, glandular-pubescent, its branches subtended by toothed bracts; flowers regular, perfect, 5-merous; hypanthium deeply cup-shaped, bearing the sepals, petals, and stamens at its margin; petals white, spatulate, about 3 mm long; stamens 5, opposite and much shorter than the sepals; pistils 2. **Follicles** dehiscent along the ventral suture; seeds numerous, winged. June-July. —Rare on moist shaded cliffs, usually of sandstone.

TIARELLA *Foam-Flower*

Tiarella cordifolia L.

FOAM-FLOWER (NO MAP)
introduced

Perennial herbs with long stolons. **Flowering stems** 1-3.5 dm tall, glandular-puberulent. **Leaves** basal, broadly cordate-ovate, shallowly 3-5-lobed, crenate, sparsely pubescent. **Flowers** in a raceme atop an erect, usually leafless stem; the raceme at first short and crowded, elongating to 1 dm; pedicels 5-10 mm long; hypanthium small, campanulate; sepals 2-3.5 mm long, blunt; petals white, elliptic, clawed, 3-5 mm long; stamens 10; pistils 2, united at base, unequal in length. **Follicles** 2, thin-walled, the larger about 10 mm long; seeds several, black,

Tiarella cordifolia

1218. *Saxifraga paniculata*   1219. *Sullivantia sullivantii*   1220. *Scrophularia lanceolata*   1221. *Scrophular. marilandica*

smooth, shining. May-early June.—Rich, mesic hardwood forests; Stearns
County, where considered adventive from main range of eastern USA.

Scrophulariaceae FIGWORT FAMILY

Annual, biennial, or perennial herbs. Leaves mostly opposite or alternate (*Verbascum*). Flowers single
or few from leaf axils, or numerous in clusters at ends of stems or leaf axils, perfect (with both
staminate and pistillate parts), usually with a distinct upper and lower lip; sepals and petals 4-5 (petals
sometimes absent); stamens usually 4; pistil 2-chambered. Fruit a several- to many-seeded capsule.
Formerly a much larger family, many of our genera now segregated into other families, especially
Orobanchaceae *and* **Plantaginaceae**.

1   Stem leaves of fertile stems mostly alternate (a basal rosette may be present and the lower leaves may sometimes
     be opposite) . . . . *Verbascum*
1   Stem leaves of fertile stems all opposite or nearly so, sometimes alternate below the flowers . . . . . *Scrophularia*

SCROPHULARIA *Figwort*

Perennial herbs. Stems 4-angled. Leaves opposite. Flowers 2-lipped, in open terminal clusters. Corolla
brownish, bilaterally symmetrical and ± 2-lipped. Stamens 5, 4 plus a staminodium (sterile filament)
under the upper corolla lobe.

ADDITIONAL SPECIES
Scrophularia nodosa L. (European figwort), native to Europe; St. Louis County (Duluth area).

1   Main leaves coarsely toothed or cleft, the teeth mostly long-tapered to their tip; leaf base tapered and extending
     downward along the petiole; sterile stamen green-yellow . . . . *S. lanceolata*
1   Main leaves evenly toothed, the teeth rounded at tip or abruptly tapered to a short point; leaf base rounded to
     heart-shaped, not extending downward along petiole; sterile stamen brown to purple . . . . *S. marilandica*

Scrophularia lanceolata Pursh
LANCE-LEAF FIGWORT

MAP 1220
native

Perennial herb, often forming dense colonies. **Stems** erect, to 2 m tall, glabrous,
or minutely glandular in the inflorescence, the sides flat or shallowly grooved.
Leaves ovate or ovate lance-shaped, 8-20 cm long, sharply serrate or incised or
doubly serrate, truncate to broadly rounded at the base, glabrous beneath; petioles
commonly 1.5-3 cm long, rarely as much as a third as long as the blade, narrowly
margined to the base. **Panicle** 1-3 dm long, tending to be cylindric, rarely more
than 8 cm wide; corolla 7-11 mm long, dull reddish brown except the yellowish
green lower lobe. **Capsule** dull brown, 6-10 mm long. Late May-July.—Roadsides,
railroads, old roads; forests, especially in clearings and edges; fields, fencerows,
shores, swamp borders.

Scrophularia marilandica L.
CARPENTER'S-SQUARE

MAP 1221
native

Perennial herb, often forming colonies. **Stems** erect, to 3 m tall, glabrous below,
becoming sparsely glandular in the inflorescence, the sides, especially in the older
portions, roundly angled and prominently grooved. **Leaves** ovate or ovate lance-
shaped, to 2.5 cm long, finely to coarsely serrate, broadly rounded to shallowly
cordate at base; petioles slender, not margined, 1.5-5 cm long, those of the principal leaves commonly to half as long as the blades. **Panicle** loosely and irregular
branched, tending to be pyramidal, often 10-15 cm wide; corolla 5-8 mm long,
reddish brown. **Capsule** 4-7 mm long, somewhat shining. July-Aug, its flowering
period rarely overlapping that of *S. lanceolata*.—Less common than *S. lanceolata*
but in similar habitats: riverbank thickets and floodplains; open woods, especially
in clearings and on margins; roadsides. *Not always easily distinguished from*
Scrophularia lanceolata, *though often taller and more branched*.

Scrophularia lanceolata

VERBASCUM *Mullein*

Biennial herbs (ours), producing a rosette of leaves the first year, from which the tall flowering stem rises the following season. Leaves alternate, entire, crenate, or rarely deeply toothed. Flowers yellow, white, or blue, in one to many spike-like racemes. Calyx regular, deeply 5-parted. Corolla rotate or saucer-shaped, nearly regular, the 3 lower lobes slightly larger than the 2 upper. Stamens 5, all fertile, more or less dimorphic. Capsule ovoid to globose, the 2 valves more or less cleft at the tip; seeds numerous, marked with longitudinal ridges.

1 Stems glabrous, or often glandular-hairy on upper stem and inflorescence; flowers yellow or white . **V. blattaria**
1 Stems densely woolly hairy; flowers yellow 2
    2 Base of leaves extending downward on stem to about next lower leaf . . . . **V. thapsus**
    2 Base of leaves not extending downward on stem (or only very shortly so) . . . . **V. phlomoides**

Verbascum blattaria L.

WHITE MOTH MULLEIN   (NO MAP)
                             introduced (naturalized)

Stems slender, to 1 m tall, simple or branched, glandular-pubescent above; branched hairs lacking. **Leaves** variable, narrowly triangular to oblong or lance-shaped, sessile, not decurrent, coarsely toothed to nearly entire, glabrous, the basal larger, oblong lance-shaped, tapering to the base. **Racemes** elongate, loose, bearing a single flower at each node on a pedicel 8-15 mm long; calyx glandular-pubescent; corolla yellow or white, about 2.5 cm wide, the filaments all about equally villous. June-Oct.—Eurasian weed of fields, roadsides, and waste places; Beltrami County.

Verbascum phlomoides L.

ORANGE MULLEIN   (NO MAP)
                             introduced (naturalized)

Stems 5-12 dm tall. **Leaves** oblong to ovate lance-shaped, tomentose on both sides, sessile, only slightly decurrent on the stem. **Raceme** at first dense and spike-like, at full maturity usually elongating and exposing the axis between the flower clusters; corolla as in *V. thapsus*, but commonly 25-35 mm wide; stamens as in *V. thapsus*. June-Sept.—Native of Europe, reported for Minn.

Verbascum thapsus L.

GREAT MULLEIN   MAP 1222
                             introduced (naturalized)

Plants usually densely gray-tomentose throughout. **Stems** stout and erect, 1-2 m tall. **Lower leaves** oblong or oblong lance-shaped, to 3 dm long, petioled; **upper leaves** progressively reduced, sessile, decurrent along the stem to the next leaf below. **Raceme** spike-like, very dense, 2-5 dm long, about 3 cm thick, usually solitary; corolla yellow, 12-22 mm wide; upper 3 filaments short, densely white-villous; lower 2 filaments much longer, glabrous or nearly so. June-Sept.—European weed of fields, roadsides, and disturbed places.

Verbascum thapsus

Solanaceae POTATO FAMILY

Herbs or shrubs, rarely climbing, or in the tropics small trees. Leaves alternate or appearing opposite. Flowers perfect, almost always 5-merous, regular (in most of our genera) or irregular. Calyx gamosepalous, persistent in fruit. Corolla rotate to funnelform or tubular. Stamens inserted on the corolla tube and alternate with its lobes, as many as the petals in most genera with regular flowers. Ovary commonly 2-celled (falsely 4-celled in *Datura*). Fruit a capsule or berry. *A large family, most numerous in tropical America, and with many plants, such as tomato, potato, eggplant, and peppers, of economic importance.*

1 Plants woody (at least at base), sprawling or climbing vines; fruit a red berry 2
    2 Leaves unlobed; stems mostly woody . . . . **Lycium barbarum**
    2 Main leaves 3-4 lobed; stems woody near base . . . . **Solanum dulcamara**
1 Plants herbs; fruit various 3
    3 Plants in flower 4
        4 Corolla with short tube and widely flared upper portion 5
            5 Anthers opening at tip . . . . *Solanum*
            5 Anthers opening along sides . . . . **Leucophysalis grandiflora**

DATURA *Jimsonweed*

Coarse annual herbs (ours). Leaves large, ovate, petioled. Flowers large, white to violet. Calyx elongate, tubular, unevenly 5-lobed at the tip. Corolla funnelform. Stamens barely exsert from the corolla tube. Fruit a many-seeded capsule, either 4-valved or bursting irregularly. *All species are toxic if eaten.*

1 Plants glabrous or nearly so; flowers less than 10 cm long .... *D. stramonium*
1 Plants covered with soft hairs; flowers more than 10 cm long .... *D. inoxia*

Datura inoxia P. Mill.
DOWNY THORN-APPLE
   Datura wrightii Regel.

MAP 1223
introduced

Stems to 2 m tall or rarely taller, the upper parts very finely and softly pubescent or almost velutinous, extending along the petioles and veins of the lower leaf-surface. **Leaves** ovate, rounded to cordate at base, mostly entire. **Flowers** 12-20 cm long, white. **Capsule** ovoid, spiny, about 5 cm in diameter. July-Oct.—Native of the sw states; occasionally escaped from cultivation in waste places.

Datura stramonium L.
JIMSONWEED

MAP 1224
introduced (naturalized)

Stems stout, hollow, green or purple, divaricately branched, to 1.5 m tall. **Leaves** thin, ovate, 5-20 cm long, coarsely serrate with a few large triangular teeth, long-petioled. **Flowers** white or pale violet, 7-10 cm long; calyx about half as long as the corolla. **Capsule** ovoid, 3-5 cm long, 4-valved at maturity, usually covered with short spines.—Widely distributed weed of fields, barnyards, and waste places.

Datura stramonium

LEUCOPHYSALIS *False Ground-Cherry*

Leucophysalis grandiflora (Hook.) Rydb.
LARGE FALSE GROUND-CHERRY
   Chamaesaracha grandiflora (Hook.) Fernald
   Physalis grandiflora Hook.

MAP 1225
native

Annual herb; thinly villous and more or less viscid. **Stems** to 1 m tall. **Leaves** ovate or ovate lance-shaped, 5-12 cm long, acute or short-acuminate, entire, at base rounded or broadly cuneate and decurrent along the petiole. **Flowers** commonly 2-4 from the upper nodes, on pedicels 10-15 mm long; calyx lobes narrowly triangular, acuminate; corolla white with pale yellow center, rotate, 3-4 cm wide; filaments slender; anthers about 3 mm long; fruiting calyx round-ovoid, open at

Leucophysalis grandiflora

1222. *Verbascum thapsus*   1223. *Datura inoxia*   1224. *Datura stramonium*   1225. *Leucophys. grandiflora*

the end, about 15 mm long, nearly filled by the berry; **berry** 8-14 mm long, ovoid, beaked, puberulent. June-Aug.—Dry sandy soil.

LYCIUM *Matrimony-Vine*

Lycium barbarum L.
MAP 1226
MATRIMONY-VINE   *introduced*
Glabrous shrub with long slender branches to 3 m long, arched or recurved, sometimes climbing, often spiny at the nodes, bearing alternate leaves on the young shoots, later bearing at each node a tuft of leaves of various sizes, often subtended by a thorn. **Leaves** grayish green, lance-shaped to spatulate, 2-5 cm long, 5-15 mm wide, sessile or petioled. **Flowers** in clusters of 1-4, slender-pediceled; calyx usually 3-lobed; corolla funnelform, 10-12 mm wide, dull pinkish violet, the 5 lobes spreading or ascending and slightly shorter than the tube, short-lived and fading the second day; stamens exsert. **Berry** scarlet, ellipsoid, 1-2 cm long. May-Aug.—Native of s Europe; cultivated in old gardens and now escaped in vacant lots, roadsides, fencerows, and at the edge of woods.

Lycium barbarum

PHYSALIS *Ground-Cherry*

Annual or perennial herbs, commonly widely branching. Leaves alternate or falsely opposite. Flowers solitary or few at the nodes, white, greenish yellow, or yellow, often with a darker center. Calyx at anthesis small, 5-lobed. Calyx tube enlarging promptly after anthesis, at maturity completely enclosing the berry or barely open at the summit, often greatly enlarged, commonly 5-angled, the calyx lobes scarcely enlarged. Corolla rotate to campanulate, shallowly lobed or entire. Stamens inserted near the base of the corolla. Berry many-seeded, pulpy.

ADDITIONAL SPECIES
• *Physalis grisea* (Waterfall) M. Martinez (Strawberry-tomato), adventive in e Minn; see key.
• *Physalis hispida* (Waterfall) Cronq.; possible presence in Minn in Isanti and Morrison counties.

1   Colony-forming perennial herbs, spreading by rhizomes; corolla 1-2 cm long 2
   2   Upper stems with soft, spreading hairs . . . . **P. heterophylla**
   2   Upper stems with short, stiff, appressed hairs or glabrous 3
      3   Leaves sparsely hairy on both sides; calyx tube with stiff hairs to 1.5 mm long . . . . **P. virginiana**
      3   Leaves nearly glabrous, hairs if present mostly along main veins; calyx tube with very short, appressed hairs, the hairs less than 0.5 mm long . . . . **P. longifolia**
1   Taprooted annual herbs; corolla less than 1 cm long (except in *P. philadelphica*) 4
   4   Leaves grayish due to hairs, leaves also with sessile glands . . . . **P. grisea***
   4   Leaves greenish, the pubescence less dense; sessile glands absent . . . . **P. pubescens**

Physalis heterophylla Nees
MAP 1227
CLAMMY GROUND-CHERRY   *native*
Perennial. **Stems** erect or spreading, often much branched; pubescence of the younger parts, pedicels, and calyx distinctly villous, composed of slender spreading hairs. **Leaves** ovate to rhombic, 3-8 cm long, shallowly and irregularly sinuate-dentate, varying to entire, at base broadly rounded or subcordate, often inequilateral, not decurrent, more or less pubescent on each side. Pedicels at anthesis about 1 cm long, to 3 cm in fruit; calyx lobes deltoid or ovate; corolla 15-20 mm long. **Fruiting calyx** ovoid, 3-4 cm long. June-Sept.—In dry or sandy soil, upland woods and prairies. *Our most common Physalis.*

Physalis heterophylla

1226. *Lycium barbarum*   1227. *Physalis heterophylla*   1228. *Physalis longifolia*   1229. *Physalis pubescens*

Physalis longifolia Nutt.
LONGLEAF GROUND-CHERRY

MAP 1228
native

Perennial. **Stems** erect, 4-8 dm tall, usually divergently branched, the younger parts nearly glabrous to densely puberulent, the hairs always ascending or appressed, rarely more than 0.5 mm long. **Leaves** thin, ovate to lance-shaped, entire to sinuate-dentate, glabrous or nearly so, long-petioled. Pedicels at anthesis 1-2 cm long; calyx minutely pubescent in longitudinal strips along the nerves; calyx lobes triangular or ovate, 3-4 mm long, densely ciliate; corolla about 15 mm long. **Fruiting calyx** ovoid or short cylindric, 3-4 cm long. July-Aug.—Moist or dry fields, open woods, and prairies.

Physalis longifolia

Physalis pubescens L.
DOWNY GROUND-CHERRY

MAP 1229
native

Annual. In habit, flowers, and fruit very like *P. grisea*, differing chiefly in its pubescence and leaves. Pubescence of the upper part of the stem and leaves shortly villous, the hairs soft and spreading, 0.2-0.5 mm long, not dense enough to interfere with the green color. **Leaves** uneven in size and shape, usually broadly ovate, 3-6 cm long, commonly abruptly acuminate to an obtuse tip, entire or somewhat sinuate-dentate, but never much toothed below the middle, broadly rounded at base but not decurrent, very often inequilateral; slender-petioled. **Fruiting calyx** enlarges as the fruit develops, becoming inflated, ribbed, lanternlike 2-4 cm long which contains the berry. May-Sept.—Moist soil. Sometimes cultivated for its fruit, and persisting around gardens.

Physalis virginiana P. Mill.
VIRGINIA GROUND-CHERRY

MAP 1230
native

Perennial. **Stems** usually forked with ascending branches, 3-6 dm tall; pubescence of the younger parts, including the petioles and often the pedicels, of more or less curved hairs. **Leaves** lance-shaped to ovate, sinuately toothed to entire, narrowed to the base and more or less decurrent on the long petiole, sparsely to abundantly finely hirsute on both sides, margins minutely ciliolate. Pedicels at anthesis 1-2 cm long; calyx with short spreading hairs, the lobes at anthesis 2.5-5 mm long, minutely ciliate; corolla 12-18 mm long. **Fruiting calyx** 5-angled, notably longer than thick.—Dry or moist fields, sandy upland woods, prairies.

Physalis virginiana

SOLANUM *Nightshade*

Herbs or vines. Corolla rotate or broadly campanulate, regular. Stamens 5. Fruit a many-seeded berry. *Our species bloom in summer, often continuing into the fall.*

ADDITIONAL SPECIES
• *Solanum physalifolium* Rusby (syn *Solanum sarrachoides* Rusby; Ground-cherry nightshade), introduced in several Minn locations; see key.
• *Solanum triflorum* Nutt. (Cut-leaf nightshade); native to w USA, adventive in Minn.
• *Solanum tuberosum* L. (Irish potato); native to Andes Mtns of South America; occasionally escaping from cultivation but not persisting for more than one or two years.

1   Plants with spines or prickles 2
   2   Corolla bright yellow; leaves 1-2 times pinnately compound; calyx covered with spines . . . . *S. rostratum*
   2   Corolla pale violet or white; leaves entire or toothed or lobed; calyx not spiny . . . . *S. carolinense*
1   Plants without spines or prickles 3
   3   Plants climbing or trailing vines, woody at base; flowers usually light blue or violet . . . . *S. dulcamara*
   3   Plants upright herbs; flowers white 4
     4   Plants sticky-hairy; calyx enlarging to cover lower half of berry . . . . *S. physalifolium**
     4   Plants glabrous to pubescent, the hairs appressed and not gland-tipped; calyx covering only bottom of berry . . . . *S. ptychanthum*

Solanum carolinense L.
HORSE-NETTLE

MAP 1231
introduced (naturalized)

Perennial. **Stems** erect, branched, to 1 m tall, spiny and loosely stellate-pubescent. **Leaves** ovate in outline, commonly 7-12 cm long and about half as wide, with 2-

5 large teeth or shallow lobes on each side, more or less spiny along the principal veins, stellate-pubescent on both sides, the hairs sessile with 4-8 branches, the central branch often elongate. **Inflorescence** several-flowered, elongating at maturity and forming a simple raceme-like cluster; corolla pale violet to white, about 2 cm wide. **Berry** yellow, 1-1.5 cm wide, subtended but not enclosed by the calyx.—Fields and waste places, especially in sandy soil.

Solanum carolinense

Solanum dulcamara L.
CLIMBING NIGHTSHADE

MAP 1232
introduced (naturalized)

Perennial vine, climbing 2-4 m high, the **stems** somewhat woody at base. **Leaves** either simple or deeply lobed, the simple ones and the terminal segment of the lobed ones ovate, 4-10 cm long, entire, rounded or subcordate at base; lobes, when present, 1 or 2, basal, divergent, lance-shaped or ovate, much smaller than the terminal segment. **Inflorescences** arising from the internodes or opposite the leaves, peduncled, loosely branched, the pedicels jointed at base; corolla pale violet or blue, varying to white, about 1 cm wide. **Berry** red.—Native of Eurasia; moist thickets.

Solanum ptychanthum Dunal
WEST INDIAN NIGHTSHADE
   Solanum nigrum L.

MAP 1233
native

Annual. **Stems** erect, 3-6 dm tall, often widely branched. **Leaves** thin, long-petioled, ovate lance-shaped or ovate, cuneately narrowed to the base. **Inflorescences** lateral from the internodes, peduncled, umbel-like, 2-10-flowered, the pedicels not jointed at base; corolla white or very pale violet, 5-9 mm wide. **Berries** globose.—Probably native of Eurasia, now a cosmopolitan weed.

Solanum ptychanthum

Solanum rostratum Dunal
BUFFALO-BUR

MAP 1234
introduced (naturalized)

Annual. **Stems** widely branched, to 6 dm tall, spiny and also stellate-pubescent. **Leaves** ovate or oblong in outline, usually spiny along the principal veins, deeply pinnately lobed, or the segments again lobed in the larger leaves, stellate-pubescent on both sides. Axis of the lateral inflorescences soon elongating and becoming raceme-like; calyx tube spiny at anthesis, later expanding, becoming 3 cm wide (including the long spines), completely enclosing the berry. **Flowers** yellow, 2-3 cm wide; anthers yellow, one of them much longer than the other 4.—Dry prairies.

Solanum rostratum

Staphyleaceae   BLADDERNUT FAMILY

STAPHYLEA *Bladdernut*

Staphylea trifolia L.
AMERICAN BLADDERNUT

MAP 1235
native

Erect shrub to 5 m tall, with striped bark. **Leaves** opposite, long-petioled, 3-foliolate; **leaflets** oblong to elliptic or ovate, 5-10 cm long at maturity, finely serrate, broadly acute to rounded at base, the terminal leaflet long-stalked, the lateral leaflets sessile or short-petioled and often oblique at base. **Inflorescence** a terminal drooping panicle 4-10 cm long including the peduncle. **Flowers** regular, perfect, 5-merous; sepals and petals distinct, imbricate, long-pediceled, greenish

Staphylea trifolia

1230. *Physalis virginiana*   1231. *Solanum carolinense*   1232. *Solanum dulcamara*

white, campanulate, 8-10 mm long; sepals nearly as long as the erect petals; ovary 3-lobed. **Fruit** a 3-lobed, thin-walled, inflated capsule about 5 cm long. May. —Moist deciduous forests and thickets, especially on riverbanks and floodplains.

Thymelaeaceae MEZEREUM FAMILY

DIRCA *Leatherwood*

Dirca palustris L.
EASTERN LEATHERWOOD

MAP 1236
native

Freely branched shrub 1-2 m tall, **bark** very tough and pliable, **twigs** jointed. **Leaves** alternate, entire, obovate, 5-8 cm long, 1/2 to 2/3 as wide, usually rounded at base, glabrous at maturity, on petioles 2-5 mm long. **Flowers** perfect, regular, pale yellow, 7-10 mm long, subtended by hairy bud scales in early spring before the leaves appear, in lateral clusters of 2-4; hypanthium narrowly funnelform, the limb slightly spreading; stamens 8, protruding about 3 mm from the top of the tube; sepals minute; petals none. **Fruit** an ellipsoid drupe, about 8 mm long. Spring.—Rich, moist, deciduous woods.

Dirca palustris

Ulmaceae ELM FAMILY

ULMUS *Elm*

Trees. Leaves alternate, simple, short-petioled or subsessile, inequilateral; margins usually doubly serrate. Flowers perfect, in short racemes or, by abbreviation of the axis, in fascicles. Calyx campanulate, 4-9-lobed. Corolla none. Stamens as many as the calyx segments, exsert. Ovary compressed, 1-celled. Fruit a flat, 1-seeded samara, usually short-stipitate and often surmounted by the persistent or enlarged styles. *Several exotic elm species are sometimes planted as street trees. Hackberry (Celtis), a former member of this family, now included in Cannabaceae.*

1   Leaf blades small, 3-7 cm long . . . . *U. pumila*
1   Leaf blades larger, 7-18 cm long 2
   2   Leaves smooth on each side; branches with corky wing-like ridges, the lowermost branches short and strongly drooping; main trunk usually not dividing into several large limbs . . . . *U. thomasii*
   2   Leaves roughened on one or both sides; branches not with corky wings, the lowermost branches longer and not strongly drooping; main trunk usually dividing into several large limbs, tree vase-shaped in outline . . . 3
      3   Leaves usually rough only on upperside; bark gray, deeply fissured . . . . *U. americana*
      3   Leaves usually rough on both sides; bark dark red-brown, shallowly fissured . . . . *U. rubra*

Ulmus americana L.
AMERICAN ELM

MAP 1237
native

Tree to 25 m tall, trunk to 1 m wide, crown broadly rounded or flat-topped, smaller **branches** usually drooping; **bark** gray, furrowed, breaking into thin plates with age; **twigs** brown, smooth or with sparse hairs, often zigzagged; **buds** red-brown. **Leaves** to 15 cm long and 7-8 cm wide, oval, pointed at tip, base strongly asymmetrical, upper surface dark green and smooth, lower surface pale and smooth or soft-hairy; margins coarsely double-toothed; petioles short, usually yellow. **Flowers** small, green-red, hairy, in drooping clusters of 3-4; appearing

1233. Solanum ptychanthum   *1234. Solanum rostratum*   *1235. Staphylea trifolia*   *1236. Dirca palustris*

before leaves unfold in spring. **Samaras** 1-seeded, oval, 1 cm wide, with a winged, hairy margin, notched at tip.—Floodplain forests, streambanks and moist, rich woods. *Less common now than formerly due to losses from Dutch elm disease.*

Ulmus pumila L.
SIBERIAN ELM

MAP 1238
introduced (invasive)

Tree 15 to 30 m; crowns open; **bark** gray to brown, deeply furrowed with interlacing ridges; **branches** not winged; **twigs** gray-brown, pubescent; **buds** dark brown, ovoid, glabrous; scales light brown, shiny, glabrous to slightly pubescent. **Leaves** narrowly elliptic to lanceolate, to 6.5 cm long and 2-3.5 cm wide, base generally not oblique, margins singly serrate; upper surface with some pubescence in axils of veins, lower surface glabrous; petioles 2-4 mm long. **Inflorescences** tightly clustered fascicles of 6-15 sessile flowers; flowers and fruit not pendulous, sessile; calyx shallowly 4-5-lobed, glabrous; stamens 4-8; anthers brownish red. **Samaras** yellow-cream, orbiculate, 10-14 mm wide, broadly winged, glabrous, tip notched 1/3-1/2 its length.—Escaping from cultivation to waste places, roadsides, fencerows. *Distinguished from our other elms by its singly serrate leaf margins.*

Ulmus rubra Muhl.
SLIPPERY ELM

MAP 1239
native

Tree, to 20 m tall; **twigs** scabrously pubescent; winter-buds densely covered with red-brown hairs. **Leaves** oblong to obovate, thick and stiff, usually 10-20 cm long, very rough above. **Flowers** fascicled, short-pediceled to nearly sessile. **Samaras** nearly circular, 1.5-2 cm long, entire, the sides smooth on the wing, pubescent over the seed, scarcely reticulate.—Moist woods. *The inner bark is very mucilaginous and has some medicinal value.*

Ulmus thomasii Sarg.
ROCK ELM

MAP 1240
native

Tree, to 30 m tall, with thinly pubescent **twigs** often becoming irregularly winged with 2 or more plates of cork after their second year; winter-buds thinly pubescent. **Leaves** oblong to obovate, 6-12 cm long, distinctly cordate on one side at base, glabrous above. **Flowers** in slender racemes to 4 cm long. **Samaras** elliptic, 1.5-2 cm long, ciliate, pubescent on the sides, the petiole about 1 mm long.—Rich upland woods. *The thick, corky-winged branches are distinctive.*

Ulmus americana

Ulmus pumila

Ulmus rubra

Urticaceae NETTLE FAMILY

Annual or perennial herbs with watery juice, sometimes with stinging hairs. Leaves alternate or opposite, simple, with petioles. Flowers small, green, in simple or branched clusters from leaf axils, staminate and pistillate flowers usually separate, on same or separate plants; sepals joined, 3-5-lobed; petals absent; ovary superior, 1-chambered. Fruit an achene, often enclosed by the sepals which enlarge after flowering.

1 Leaves alternate 2
    2 Plants large and coarse, with stiff stinging hairs, the leaves sharply toothed . . . . ***Laportea canadensis***
    2 Plants smaller, without stinging hairs; leaves entire . . . . ***Parietaria pensylvanica***
1 Leaves opposite 3

1237. Ulmus americana   *1238. Ulmus pumila*   *1239. Ulmus rubra*   *1240. Ulmus thomasii*

3   Plants with stinging hairs; leaves lance-shaped .... ***Urtica dioica***

3   Plants without stinging hairs; leaves ovate 4

     4   Stems translucent and fleshy; flowers in dense clusters from leaf axils; achene longer than sepals .. ***Pilea***

     4   Stems neither translucent nor fleshy; flowers in cylindric spikes from leaf axils; achene shorter than and hidden by the sepals .... ***Boehmeria cylindrica***

BOEHMERIA *False Nettle*

Boehmeria cylindrica (L.) Sw.
SMALL-SPIKE FALSE NETTLE

MAP 1241
native

Perennial, nettlelike herb, stinging hairs absent. **Stems** upright, 4-10 dm long, usually unbranched. **Leaves** opposite, rough-textured, ovate to broadly lance-shaped, narrowed to a pointed tip, with 3 main veins; margins coarsely toothed; petioles shorter than blades. **Flowers** tiny, green, staminate and pistillate flowers usually on separate plants, in small clusters along unbranched stalks from upper leaf axils, forming cylindric, interrupted spikes of staminate flowers or continuous spikes of pistillate flowers. **Fruit** an achene, enclosed by the enlarged bristly sepals and petals, ovate and narrowly winged. July-Aug.—Floodplain forests, swamps, marshes and bogs.

Boehmeria cylindrica

LAPORTEA *Wood-Nettle*

Laportea canadensis (L.) Weddell
CANADIAN WOOD-NETTLE

MAP 1242
native

Perennial herb, spreading by rhizomes. **Stems** somewhat zigzagged, 5-10 dm long. **Leaves** alternate, 8-15 cm long, ovate and narrowed to a tip, with small stinging hairs, margins coarsely toothed. **Flowers** small, green, staminate and pistillate flowers separate but borne on same plant; **staminate flowers** in branched clusters from lower leaf axils, shorter than leaf petioles; **pistillate flowers** in open, spreading clusters from upper axils, usually much longer than petioles. **Fruit** a flattened achene, longer than the 2 persistent sepals. July-Sept.—Floodplain forests, rich moist woods, low places in hardwood forests, streambanks. Differs from stinging nettle (*Urtica dioica*) by its shorter size, broader, alternate leaves, and the longer spike-like heads arising from upper leaf axils. *Caution-stinging hairs.*

Laportea canadensis

PARIETARIA *Pellitory*

Parietaria pensylvanica Muhl.
PENNSYLVANIA PELLITORY

MAP 1243
native

Annual pubescent herb; monoecious or polygamous. **Stems** erect, 1-4 dm tall, simple or rarely branched. **Leaves** alternate, entire, thin, lance-shaped, 3-8 cm long, 3-nerved from above the cuneate base, slightly scabrellate above, with a slender petiole. **Flowers** green, from the middle and upper axils, subtended and exceeded by narrow green bracts about 5 mm long; **staminate flowers** with deeply 4-parted calyx and 4 stamens; calyx of the pistillate flowers tubular at base, 4-lobed. **Fruit** a smooth, shining achene about 1 mm long, loosely enclosed by the expanded calyx. June-Sept.—Moist to dry forests, gravelly shores, disturbed sites.

Parietaria pensylvanica

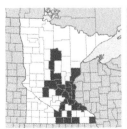

1241. Boehmeria cylindrica

1242. Laportea canadensis

1243. Parietaria pensylvanica

1244. Pilea fontana

PILEA *Clearweed*

Annual herbs, sometimes forming colonies from seeds of previous year. Stems erect to sprawling, smooth, translucent and watery. Leaves opposite, stinging hairs absent, thin and translucent, ovate, with 3 major veins from base of leaf, margins toothed. Flowers green, staminate and pistillate flowers separate, borne on same or different plants, in clusters from leaf axils; staminate flowers with 4 sepals and 4 stamens; pistillate flowers with 3 sepals, ovary superior. Fruit a flattened, ovate achene.

1 Achenes 1-1.5 mm wide, olive-green to dark purple with a narrow pale margin, covered with low bumps . . . . . .
. . . . ***P. fontana***

1 Achenes to 1 mm wide, green to yellow, often marked with purple spots, smooth . . . . ***P. pumila***

Pilea fontana (Lunell) Rydb.
LESSER CLEARWEED
MAP 1244
native

Annual herb. **Stems** 1-4 dm long, often sprawling. **Leaves** opposite, 2-6 cm long and 1-4 cm wide; petioles 0.5-5 cm long. **Flowers** in clusters, staminate flowers usually innermost when mixed with pistillate flowers. **Fruit** a dark olive-green to purple achene, 1-1.5 mm wide, with a narrow pale margin; sepals persistent, shorter to slightly longer than achene. Aug-Sept.—Lakeshores, riverbanks, swamps, marshes and springs.

Pilea pumila (L.) Gray
CANADIAN CLEARWEED
MAP 1245
native

Annual herb, similar to *P. fontana*, but sometimes taller (to 5 dm). **Leaves** opposite, usually larger (to 12 cm long and 8 cm wide), thinner and more translucent than in *P. fontana*; petioles to 8 cm long. July-Sept.—Swampy woods (often on logs), wooded streambanks, floodplain forests, wet depressions, rocky hollows; usually in partial shade.

Pilea pumila

URTICA *Stinging Nettle*

Urtica dioica L.
STINGING NETTLE
MAP 1246
native

Stout perennial herb, often forming dense patches from spreading rhizomes. **Stems** 8-20 dm tall, usually unbranched, with stinging hairs on stems and leaves, the hairs irritating to skin. **Leaves** opposite, ovate to lance-shaped, 5-15 cm long and 2-8 cm wide; margins coarsely toothed; petioles 1-6 cm long; stipules lance-shaped, to 15 mm long. **Flowers** small, green, staminate and pistillate flowers separate but mostly on same plants; flower clusters branched and spreading from leaf axils, the clusters usually longer than petioles, all of one sex or a mix of staminate and pistillate flowers, the **pistillate clusters** usually above the **staminate clusters** when both present on a plant. **Fruit** an ovate achene, 1-2 mm long, enclosed by the inner pair of sepals. July-Sept.—Moist woods, thickets, ditches, streambanks and disturbed areas. *Caution-stinging hairs.*

Urtica dioica

Verbenaceae VERBENA FAMILY

Perennial herbs with 4-angled, erect or prostrate stems. Leaves opposite, toothed. Flowers small, numerous, perfect (with both staminate and pistillate parts), in branched or unbranched spikes or heads at ends of stems or from upper leaf axils, the spikes elongating as flowers open upward from the base. Calyx 5-toothed (*Verbena*) or 2-parted (*Phyla*); corolla 5-lobed (*Verbena*) or 4-lobed (*Phyla*), somewhat 2-lipped; stamens 4, of 2 lengths. Fruit dry, enclosed by the sepals, splitting lengthwise into 2 or 4 nutlets when mature.

1 Flowers in dense rounded heads or short spikes, at ends of long, solitary peduncles from leaf axils; corolla 2-lipped . . . . ***Phyla lanceolata***

1 Flowers in short to long racemes or spikes, terminal or from upper leaf axils; corolla regular or nearly so . . . . .
. . . . ***Verbena***

PHYLA *Fogfruit*

Phyla lanceolata (Michx.) Greene
NORTHERN FOGFRUIT
   Lippia lanceolata Michx.

MAP 1247
native

Perennial herb, sometimes forming mats; plants smooth or with sparse, short, forked hairs. **Stems** slender, weak, 4-angled, creeping to ascending, often rooting at nodes, the stem tips and lateral branches upright. **Leaves** opposite, ovate to oblong lance-shaped, 2-7 cm long and 0.5-3 cm wide, bright green, tapered to a sharp tip; margins with coarse, forward-pointing teeth to below middle of blade; tapered to a short petiole. **Flowers** small, crowded in spikes from leaf axils, the spikes single, at first round, becoming short-cylindric, 0.5-2 cm long, on slender stalks 2-9 cm long; calyx 2-parted and flattened, about as long as corolla tube; corolla pale blue or white, 3-4 mm long, 4-lobed and 2-lipped, the lower lip larger than upper lip; withering but persistent in fruit. **Fruit** round, enclosed by the sepals, separating into 2 nutlets. June-Sept.—Margins of lakes, ponds, streams, ditches, mud flats; often where seasonally flooded.

Phyla lanceolata

VERBENA *Vervain*

Annual or perennial herbs. Leaves usually opposite, simple, entire to somewhat lobed. Inflorescence of terminal spikes, usually densely many-flowered, often flat-topped, sometimes elongate with scattered flowers. Flowers solitary in the axil of a usually narrow bractlet. Calyx usually tubular, 5-angled, 5-ribbed, unequally 5-toothed, not at all or but slightly changed in fruit. Corolla funnelform, the limb weakly 2-lipped, 5-lobed. Stamens 4, inserted in the upper half of the corolla tube, included. Ovary mostly 4-lobed. Fruit mostly enclosed by the mature calyx, separating at maturity into 4 linear-oblong nutlets.

1   Plants spreading; leaves incised and often somewhat 3-lobed .... *V. bracteata*
1   Plants erect; leaves unlobed or lobed only near base 2
     2   Leaves narrowly lance-shaped, less than 1.5 cm wide, tapered at base to an indistinct petiole; plants glabrous or with scattered appressed hairs .... *V. simplex*
     2   Leaves mostly ovate, 2 cm or more wide, with petioles or sessile; plants usually with at least some hairs .. 3
         3   Plants densely gray-hairy; leaves sessile .... *V. stricta*
         3   Plants not densely hairy; leaves with petioles 4
             4   Flowers blue to purple, densely overlapping on spike; leaves often lobed at their base ..... *V. hastata*
             4   Flowers white, not overlapping on spike; leaves not lobed .... *V. urticifolia*

Verbena bracteata Lag. & Rodr.
CARPET VERVAIN

MAP 1248
native

Annual or perennial. **Stems** usually several from a common base, diffusely branched, decumbent or ascending, rarely erect, coarsely hirsute. **Leaves** 1-6.5 cm long, pinnately incised or usually 3-lobed, narrowed at base into the short margined petiole, hirsute on both surfaces, the midrib and large veins slightly prominent beneath, the lateral lobes narrow and divaricate, the middle lobe large, obovate, incised or cleft. **Flowers** in terminal, sessile spikes usually 10-15 mm wide, conspicuously bracteose, harshly hispid-hirsute throughout; **bractlets** much longer than the calyx, conspicuous, 8-15 mm long, recurved in age, coarsely hirsute, the lowermost often incised and leaf-like, the upper linear lance-shaped, entire; **calyx** 3-4 mm long, hirsute particularly along the nerves, its lobes very

1245. Pilea pumila

1246. Urtica dioica

1247. Phyla lanceolata

Verbena bracteata

short; **corolla** bluish, violet, lavender, lilac, or purple, its tube protruding slightly beyond the calyx, finely pubescent outside the throat, the limb 2-3 mm wide. **Nutlets** linear, 2-2.5 mm long, sharply raised-reticulate above, striate below. April-Oct.—Prairies, fields, roadsides, and waste places.

Verbena hastata L.

COMMON VERVAIN

MAP 1249
native

Perennial herb; plants with short, rough hairs. **Stems** stout, erect, 4-12 dm tall, 4-angled, sometimes branched above. **Leaves** opposite, lance-shaped to oblong lance-shaped, 4-12 cm long and 1-5 cm wide; margins with coarse, forward-pointing teeth and sometimes lobed near base; petioles short. **Flowers** small, numerous, slightly irregular, in long, narrow spikes 5-15 cm long at ends of stems, the spikes elongating as flowers open upward from base; **calyx** unequally 5-toothed, 1-3 mm long; **corolla** dark blue to purple, 5-lobed, trumpet-shaped, slightly 2-lipped, 2-4 mm wide. **Fruit** 4-angled, splitting into 4 nutlets. July-Sept. —Marshes, wet meadows, shores, streambanks, openings in swamps, ditches.

Verbena hastata

Verbena simplex Lehm.

NARROW-LEAF VERVAIN

MAP 1250
native

Perennial. **Stems** chiefly erect, 1-5 dm tall, simple or sparingly branched above, the branches ascending, usually sparsely strigose. **Leaves** linear, narrowly oblong, or lance-shaped, 3-10 cm long, tapering into a subsessile base, distantly or coarsely serrate, reticulately rugose above, somewhat prominently veined beneath, glabrate or sparsely strigose on both surfaces. **Flowers** in slender spikes, solitary at the apex of the stem and branches, usually somewhat crowded; **bractlets** lance-shaped, commonly shorter than the calyx, glabrous or nearly so; mature calyx 4-5 mm long, sparsely pubescent; **corolla** deep lavender or purple, its tube scarcely longer than the calyx, with scattered hairs at the mouth, its limb 5-6 mm wide. **Nutlets** linear, 2.5-3 mm long, raised-reticulate above, striate toward base. June-Aug.—Dry soil of woods, fields, rocky places, and roadsides.

Verbena stricta

Verbena stricta Vent.

HOARY VERVAIN

MAP 1251
native

Perennial. **Stems** 2-12 dm tall, subterete, simple or branched above, rather densely pale-pubescent or hirsute. **Leaves** ovate, elliptic, or suborbicular, 3-10 cm long, sessile or nearly so, thick-textured, sharply serrate, or incised, hirsute and rugose above, densely hirsute and prominently veined beneath. **Flowers** in 1 or several spikes, usually quite densely compact at anthesis and in fruit; **bractlets** lance-shaped, about as long as the calyx, hirsute, ciliate; **calyx** 4-5 mm long, densely hirsute; **corolla** deep blue or purple, or white, its tube protruding slightly beyond the calyx, pubescent outside, its limb 8-9 mm wide. **Nutlets** ellipsoid, about 2.5 mm long, raised-reticulate above, striate below. June-Sept.—Prairies, barrens, fields, and roadsides.

Verbena urticifolia L.

WHITE VERVAIN

MAP 1252
native

Annual or perennial. **Stems** erect, 4-15 dm tall, solitary, simple or more often branching from near the base, finely hirsute or almost glabrous. **Leaves** broadly lance-shaped to obovate, petiolate, 8-20 cm long, rounded at base and decurrent into the petiole, coarsely and somewhat doubly crenate-serrate, often minutely pustulate above, hirsute on both surfaces, the hairs whitish, 1-1.3 mm long, or

Verbena urticifolia

1248. *Verbena bracteata*

1249. *Verbena hastata*

1250. *Verbena simplex*

1251. *Verbena stricta*

sometimes glabrous. **Flowers** in slender, usually stiffly ascending spikes, more or less sparsely flowered and remotely fruited; **bractlets** ovate, 1-1.5 mm long, ciliate; **mature calyx** 2-2.3 mm long, pubescent (especially along the nerves), the teeth short, subequal, subulate; **corolla** white, its tube scarcely exserted, its limb 2-3 mm wide, the lobes obtuse. **Nutlets** ellipsoid, about 2 mm long, corrugated or ribbed on the back. June-Oct.—In thickets, moist fields, meadows, and waste places.

Violaceae VIOLET FAMILY

Herbs. Leaves simple, stipulate, alternate or rarely opposite. Flowers perfect, 5-merous, usually irregular, axillary or basal, usually nodding. Sepals persistent. Lower petal usually spurred or larger than the others. Stamens 5. Pistil solitary; ovary 1-celled. Fruit a capsule; seeds numerous.

1 Leaves all from stem, 10 or more; plants 3-10 dm tall; corolla green or greenish-white . . . . . . ***Hybanthus concolor***
1 Leaves either all basal, or if from stem, then numbering less than 10; plants often less than 3 dm tall; corolla not green or greenish-white . . . . *Viola*

HYBANTHUS *Green-Violet*

Hybanthus concolor (T.F. Forst.) Spreng. (NO MAP)
EASTERN GREEN-VIOLET ☙*endangered* | *native*
Perennial herb. **Stems** solitary to several in a cluster, to 1 m tall, leafy, arising from a crown of fibrous roots, more or less pubescent. **Leaves** alternate, broadly elliptic to ovate-oblong, 7-16 cm long, abruptly acuminate, more or less pubescent, tapering below into slender petioles 1-2 cm long. **Flowers** greenish white, 4-5 mm long, on strongly recurved axillary peduncles jointed above the middle; sepals linear, nearly as long as the corolla; petals nearly equal in length, recurved at the tip, the lower one much the largest and spurred. **Capsules** oblong-ellipsoid, 3-valved, 1.5-2 cm long; seeds nearly globular, cream-color, about 5 mm wide. May-June.—Rich woods and ravines; local in Winona County, and a range extension from adjacent Iowa and Wisconsin.

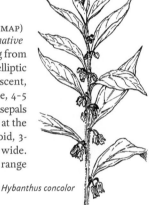

Hybanthus concolor

VIOLA *Violet*

Perennial herbs, with or without leafy stems. Leaves all at base of plant or alternate on stems; petioles with membranous stipules. Flowers perfect, nodding, and single at ends of stems, with 5 unequal sepals, 2 upper petals, 2 lateral, bearded petals, and 1 lower petal prolonged into a nectar-holding spur at its base. Fruit an ovate capsule which splits to eject the seeds.

ADDITIONAL SPECIES
Viola nuttallii Pursh (Nuttall's violet, MAP 1253), a species of dry gravelly prairie; w Minn at eastern edge of species' range (☙*threatened*); the only yellow-flowered violet found in Minnesota prairies.

1 Plants with stems; leaves and flowers borne on the upright stems 2
  2 Corolla solid yellow, or white with a yellow center; stipules entire or jagged-tooth on margins 3
    3 Corolla yellow; stipules ovate, widened above base before tapering to tip . . . . ***V. pubescens***
    3 Corolla white with yellow center; stipules long-tapered from base to tip . . . . ***V. canadensis***
  2 Corolla creamy-white to yellow-orange, or lavender to blue, with or without a yellow center; stipules fringed or deeply lobed 4
    4 Stipules deeply lobed near base into long oblong segments . . . . ***V. tricolor***
    4 Stipules fringed with short, slender segments 5
      5 Leaves narrowly ovate to triangular, tapered to a rounded tip, often densely pubescent, the hairs tiny; margins entire or nearly so; corolla dark blue . . . . ***V. adunca***
      5 Leaves ovate to kidney-shaped, glabrous or only slightly hairy; the margins with rounded or sharp teeth; corolla creamy-white, lavender or light blue . . . . ***V. labradorica***
1 Plants without stems; leaves and flowers borne directly from rootstock 6
  6 Corolla blue; petals not bearded within; spur more than 2 times longer than wide . . . . ***V. selkirkii***
  6 Corolla white or purple; petals sometimes bearded within; spur less than 2 times longer than wide 7
    7 Corolla white 8

8 Leaf blades more than 1.5 times longer than wide 9
   9 Leaves lance-shaped, tapered to a narrow base . . . . ***V. lanceolata***
   9 Leaves broader, ovate and narrowly heart-shaped at base . . . . ***V. primulifolia***
8 Leaf blades often wider than long 10
  10 Leaves dull, upper and lower surface without hairs, lower surface not paler than upper; margins nearly entire or with low rounded teeth; petioles often with long, soft hairs . . . . . ***V. macloskeyi***
  10 Leaves shiny and smooth on upper surface, or dull and hairy on either upper or lower surface; underside paler than upper surface; margins with sharp teeth 11
     11 Plants with stolons and horizontal rhizomes; upper and lower surface of leaves sparsely to densely hairy with short hairs less than 1 mm long . . . . ***V. blanda***
     11 Plants without stolons, rhizomes turned upright; leaves often shiny and smooth on upper surface, or densely hairy on upperside with hairs about 1-2 mm long and smooth on underside . . . . ***V. renifolia***
7 Corolla purple; lateral petals bearded within; stolons absent 12
  12 Leaf blades lobed or divided 13
   13 Leaf blades deeply divided into slender linear segments . . . . ***V. pedatifida***
   13 Leaf blades less deeply lobed or divided, the segments triangular to ovate 14
     14 Leaf blades much longer than wide; the spurred petal densely bearded within . . ***V. sagittata***
     14 Leaf blades about as long as wide; the spurred petal nearly glabrous within . . . . . . ***V. pedata***
  12 Leaf blades toothed on margin, not lobed or divided 15
   15 Leaf blades distinctly longer than wide 16
     16 Plants of wet places; leaves glabrous or nearly so; sepal margins not fringed with hairs . . 17
        17 Lateral petals with long, threadlike hairs on inner surface; spurred petal densely hairy within . . . . ***V. affinis***
        17 Lateral petals with short, knob-tipped hairs on inner surface; spurred petal without hairs . . . . ***V. cucullata***
     16 Plants of dry or rocky habitats; leaves sparsely to densely hairy; sepal margins usually fringed with hairs 18
        18 Hairs on leaves over 1 mm long; sepals ovate, rounded at tip . . . . ***V. novae-angliae***
        18 Hairs on leaves shorter, less than 1 mm long; sepals long-tapered to a sharp tip . . . . ***V. sagittata***
   15 Leaf blades as wide as or wider than long 19
     19 Sepals long-tapered to a sharp tip; lateral petals with short, knob-tipped hairs on inner surface; spurred petal without hairs . . . . ***V. cucullata***
     19 Sepals oblong to broadly lance-shaped, rounded at tip; lateral petals with long, threadlike hairs on inner surface 20
        20 Leaves and stems without hairs, leaves rounded at tip; the spurred petal densely hairy within; plants of wetlands . . . . ***V. nephrophylla***
        20 Leaves and stems usually hairy, leaves tapered to a pointed tip; spurred petal glabrous to only slightly hairy within; plants of moist forests . . . . ***V. sororia***

Viola adunca Sm.
HOOK-SPURRED VIOLET

MAP 1254
native

Perennial tufted herb. **Stems** several to many, 2-8 cm tall at anthesis, at first erect, later becoming prostrate and spreading and to 15 cm long. **Leaves** ovate to suborbicular, obtuse, crenulate, subcordate at base; stipules linear lance-shaped with fimbriate teeth. Peduncles long and slender; sepals narrowly lance-shaped; petals violet; spur 4-6 mm long, either straight and blunt or tapering to a sharp incurved point. **Capsules** 4-5 mm long, ellipsoid; seeds dark brown.—Dry sandy open places, often with jack pine and oaks; crevices in rock outcrops.

Viola adunca

1252. Verbena urticifolia   *1253. Viola nuttallii*   *1254. Viola adunca*

Viola affinis Le Conte
SAND VIOLET　　　　　　　　　　　　　　　　　　　(NO MAP)
　　　　　　　　　　　　　　　　　　　　　　　　native

Perennial herb, spreading by rhizomes. **Leaves** all from base of plant, hairless, narrowly heart-shaped; margins with rounded teeth. **Flowers** violet, bearded within with long, threadlike hairs, atop stalks slightly longer than leaves. **Fruit** a purple-flecked capsule on horizontal or arching stalks, seeds dark. April–May. —Swamps, floodplain forests, streambanks and lakeshores, low prairie; Fillmore County. *Sometimes treated as part of* **Viola sororia.**

Viola blanda Willd.
SWEET WHITE VIOLET　　　　　　　　　　　　　MAP 1255
　　　　　　　　　　　　　　　　　　　　　　　　native

Perennial herb, spreading by short rhizomes (and stolons later in season). **Stems** smooth. **Leaves** all from base of plant, heart-shaped, dark green and satiny, 2–5 cm wide, upper surface near base of blade usually with short, stiff white hairs; petioles usually red. **Flowers** white, fragrant, on stalks shorter than longer than leaves; lower 3 petals with purple veins near base, all more or less beardless; upper 2 petals narrow, twisted backward, 2 side petals forward-pointing. **Fruit** a purple capsule 4–6 mm long, seeds dark brown. April–May.—Hummocks in swamps and bogs, low wet areas in deciduous and conifer forests.

Viola blanda

Viola canadensis L.
TALL WHITE VIOLET　　　　　　　　　　　　　MAP 1256
　　　　　　　　　　　　　　　　　　　　　　　　native

Perennial herb, arising from a short, woody rhizome; plants glabrous or minutely pubescent. **Stems** numerous, 2–4 dm tall, with several long-petioled basal leaves. **Stem leaves** numerous, the lower widely spaced, the upper crowded toward the apex, the blades cordate, 5–10 cm long; **upper leaves** becoming shorter-petioled and with truncate or broadly cuneate base. Stipules lance-shaped, slightly sscarious; peduncles slende. Sepals lance-shaped, ciliate; petals white inside, with yellowish eye-spot and brown-purple veins near the base, purplish-tinged outside. **Capsules** globose-ellipsoid, 5–7 mm long; seeds brown.—Mesic deciduous woods.

Viola cucullata Ait.
MARSH BLUE VIOLET　　　　　　　　　　　　　MAP 1257
　　　　　　　　　　　　　　　　　　　　　　　　native

Perennial herb, spreading by short, branched rhizomes; plants smooth. **Leaves** all from base of plant, ovate to kidney-shaped, to 10 cm wide, heart-shaped at base; margins coarsely toothed; blade angled from the upright petioles. **Flowers** light purple or white, dark at center, on slender stalks longer than leaves; the 2 side petals densely bearded with short hairs, the hairs mostly knobbed or club-tipped. **Fruit** a cylinder-shaped capsule, seeds dark. April–June.—Swamps, sedge meadows, shady seeps; occasionally in bogs and low areas in forests.

Viola cucullata

Viola labradorica Schrank
ALPINE VIOLET　　　　　　　　　　　　　　　MAP 1258
　　　　　　　　　　　　　　　　　　　　　　　　native
　　Viola adunca Sm. var. *minor* (Hook.) Fern.
　　Viola conspersa Reichenb.

Perennial herb; plants smooth. **Leaves** in clumps from rhizomes, at first all from base of plants, later with leafy, horizontal stems to 15 cm long; light green, ovate to kidney-shaped, 1–2.5 cm wide; margins with rounded teeth; petioles 2–6 cm long. **Flowers** pale blue, side petals bearded on inner surface. **Fruit** 4–5 mm long, seeds dark brown. April–June.—Swamps, streambanks, moist hardwood forests.

1255. *Viola blanda*　　　　1256. *Viola canadensis*　　　　1257. *Viola cucullata*　　　　*Viola labradorica*

Viola lanceolata L.   MAP 1259
STRAP-LEAF VIOLET   ⚘ *threatened* | *native*

Perennial herb, spreading by rhizomes and stolons. **Leaves** from base of plant, narrowly lance-shaped, more than 2x longer than wide, tapered to base; margins toothed. **Flowers** white, all beardless; lower 3 petals purple-veined near base. **Fruit** a green capsule 5-8 mm long, seeds brown. April-June.—Rare in open bogs, sedge meadows; soils sandy or mucky. *The lance-shaped leaves are distinctive.*

Viola macloskeyi Lloyd   MAP 1260
WILD WHITE VIOLET   *native*
    Viola pallens (Banks) Brainerd

Small perennial herb (our smallest violet), spreading by rhizomes and stolons. **Leaves** all from base of plant, heart-shaped to kidney-shaped, 1-3 cm wide at flowering, later to 8 cm wide, underside orange-tinged; margins with rounded teeth. **Flowers** white, on upright stalks equal or longer than leaves, 3 lower petals purple-veined near base, 2 side petals beardless or with sparse hairs. **Fruit** a green capsule 4-6 mm long, seeds olive-black. April-July.—Marshes, sedge meadows, open bogs and swamps, alder thickets; sometimes in shallow water.

Viola lanceolata

Viola nephrophylla Greene   MAP 1261
NORTHERN BOG VIOLET   *native*

Low perennial herb, spreading by short rhizomes. **Leaves** all from base of plant, smooth, heart-shaped to kidney-shaped, 1-4 cm long and 2-6 cm wide, rounded at tip; margins with rounded teeth; petioles slender, 2-16 cm long. **Flowers** single, nodding on slender stalks, the stalks longer than leaves. Flowers violet, bearded near base on inside, or upper pair of petals not bearded. **Fruit** a capsule 5-10 mm long. May-sometimes again flowering in Aug or Sept.—Wet meadows, fens, calcium-rich wetlands, low areas between dunes, streambanks, rocky shores.

Viola macloskeyi

Viola novae-angliae House   MAP 1262
NEW ENGLAND BLUE VIOLET   *native*
    Viola sororia var. *novae-angliae* (House) McKinney

Perennial herb. **Leaves** ovate, longer than wide, cordate, crenate-serrate near the base, distantly so toward the acuminate apex; petioles and lower surface of the leaves villous or pubescent. **Flowers** violet-purple, the three lower petals villous at the base; sepals obtuse, glabrous; cleistogamous flowers on long ascending peduncles, their **capsules** nearly globose, mottled with purple; seeds light brown to buff.—Gravelly and sandy shores and in rock crevices along streams.

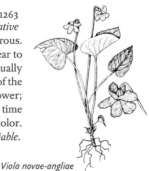

Viola nephrophylla

Viola pedata L.   MAP 1263
BIRD-FOOT VIOLET   *native*

Perennial herb, plants glabrous or nearly so; rhizome erect, not stoloniferous. **Leaves** primarily 3-parted, the lateral divisions 3-5-parted, the segments linear to lance-shaped, often 2-4-toothed near the tip; earliest and latest leaves usually smaller and less dissected. **Corolla** 2-4 cm wide, the petals all beardless; tips of the large orange stamens conspicuously exsert at the center of the flower; cleistogamous flowers absent; petaliferous flowers may be produced at any time during the summer and fall. **Capsules** green and glabrous; seeds copper-color. —Dry fields, sandy open woods of oak and jack pine. *Leaves and flowers variable.*

Viola novae-angliae

1258. *Viola labradorica*

1259. *Viola lanceolata*

1260. *Viola macloskeyi*

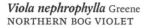

1261. *Viola nephrophylla*

Viola pedatifida G. Don
CROW-FOOT VIOLET

MAP 1264
native

Viola palmata L.

Perennial herb; plants glabrous to sparsely pilose; rhizome short, vertical. **Leaves** primarily 3-parted, each division again 3-parted or cleft into linear lobes, these often further cut into 2-4 lobes; earliest and latest leaves almost as deeply cut as the others. **Corolla** 2-4 cm wide, the three lower petals bearded, all bright violet; cleistogamous flowers on erect peduncles, their **capsules** yellowish when ripe; seeds light brown.—Prairies.

Viola pedatifida

Viola primulifolia L.
PRIMROSE-LEAF VIOLET

MAP 1265
native

Perennial herb, spreading by rhizomes and stolons. Leaves all from base of plant, oblong to ovate, rounded at tip, longer than wide; margins with small rounded teeth. Flowers white, on stalks shorter or equal to leaves, 3 lower petals purple-veined at base, 2 side petals beardless or with few hairs. Fruit a capsule 7-10 mm long; seeds red-brown to black. May.—Wet meadows and bogs, often in sphagnum moss; sandy streambanks. *Viola lanceolata* × *V. macloskeyi hybrid*.

V. primulifolia

Viola pubescens Ait.
YELLOW FOREST VIOLET

MAP 1266
native

Perennial herb; plants softly pubescent, with 1 or 2 (rarely more) stout upright stems arising from a brown woody rhizome bearing coarse fibrous roots. **Leaves** 2-4 near the summit, occasionally accompanied by a long-petioled kidney-shaped-cordate root leaf; **stem leaves** orbicular-ovate, short-pointed, crenate-dentate, cordate or truncate-decurrent at base, 4-10 cm long, and usually about 1 cm wider than long; stipules broadly ovate, the apex blunt or shallowly toothed. **Flowers** on downy pubescent peduncles rising little above the leaves; sepals lance-shaped, ciliate; petals clear yellow with brown-purple veins near the base, the lateral ones bearded. **Capsules** 10-12 mm long, woolly or glabrous; seeds pale brown.—Mesic woods.

Viola pubescens

Viola renifolia Gray
KIDNEY-LEAF WHITE VIOLET

MAP 1267
native

Perennial herb, spreading by long rhizomes. **Leaves** all from base of plant, mostly kidney-shaped, rounded at tip, varying from smooth and shiny above to hairy on lower surface only; margins with few rounded teeth. **Flowers** white, all bearded or beardless, 3 lower petals purple-veined at base. **Capsules** 4-5 mm long, seeds brown and dark-flecked. May-July.—Cedar swamps, sphagnum hummocks in peatlands.

Viola sagittata Ait.
ARROWHEAD VIOLET

MAP 1268
native

Perennial herb. **Leaves** lance-shaped to oblong lance-shaped, hastately or sagittately incised, lobed, or toothed at the subcordate or truncate base, otherwise distantly toothed; leaves of late summer often nearly deltoid and merely crenate at the base; petioles usually longer than the blades **Flowers** 2-2.5 cm across, violet-purple, the lower petals usually with prominent dark veining; sepals glabrous; cleistogamous flowers on erect peduncles; seeds numerous, brown. April-June. — Open, dry pine and oak woods, usually where sandy.

Viola renifolia

1262. *Viola novae-angliae*

1263. *Viola pedata*

1264. *Viola pedatifida*

Viola sagittata

Viola selkirkii Pursh
GREAT-SPUR VIOLET
Perennial herb; plants rather delicate, from a slender, elongate, non-stoloniferous rhizome. **Leaves** all from base of plant, with minute spreading hairs on the upper surface, otherwise glabrous, at anthesis 1.5-3 cm long, later becoming larger, broadly ovate-cordate, the basal sinus narrow, the basal lobes converging or overlapping. **Flowers** numerous, about 1.5 cm across; sepals lance-shaped; petals pale violet, beardless, the spur large and blunt, 5-7 mm long. **Capsules** ellipsoid, 4-6 mm long; seeds buff-colored.—Deciduous woods and shady ravines; preferring calcareous soils.

MAP 1269
native

Viola sororia Willd.
HOODED BLUE VIOLET
  Viola missouriensis Greene
  Viola septentrionalis Greene
Perennial herb, spreading by short rhizomes. **Leaves** all from base of plant, ovate to heart-shaped, sometimes expanding to 10 cm wide in summer, with long hairs; margins with rounded teeth; blades angled from the upright petioles. **Flowers** blue-violet, on stalks about as high as leaves, the 2 side petals densely bearded with hairs 1 mm long and not club-tipped. **Fruit** a purple-flecked capsule, seeds dark brown. April-June.—Moist hardwood forests; occasionally in swamps, floodplain forests and along rocky streambanks.

MAP 1270
native

Viola sororia

Viola tricolor L.
JOHNNY-JUMP-UP
Annual herb, plants glabrous or pubescent. **Stems** to 45 cm tall, often branched from the base. **Lowest leaves** orbicular or cordate; **upper leaves** oblong to elliptic, tapering to a blunt tip; margins crenate; stipules foliaceous, laciniate to lyrate-pinnatifid, the middle lobe oblong lance-shaped. **Flowers** 1.5-2 cm across; sepals about 2/3 as long as the petals; petals variously marked with yellow, purple, or white, the upper petals usually darker. **Capsules** ellipsoid, 6-10 mm long; seeds dark brown.—Native of the Old World; escaped from gardens in waste places, only rarely persistent. *The cultivated pansy is the product of long cultivation and hybridization of Viola tricolor with several allied European species.*

MAP 1271
introduced

Vitaceae   GRAPE FAMILY

Mostly woody vines, climbing by tendrils. Leaves alternate, simple or compound; tendrils and flower clusters produced opposite the leaves. Flowers regular, 4-5-merous, perfect or unisexual, with a hypanthium and usually with a cup-shaped disk. Calyx small or almost lacking. Petals small. Stamens as many as the petals and opposite them. Ovary 2-celled; style very short; stigma 1, slightly 2-lobed. Fruit a berry; seeds 4 or by abortion fewer.

1 Stems brown-pithy inside, the bark shredding into strips; leaves simple . . . . *Vitis*
1 Stems white-pithy, the bark tight, not shredding; leaves simple or palmately compound 2
  2 Leaves palmately compound, leaflets 5 . . . . *Parthenocissus*
  2 Leaves simple, the margins shallowly to deeply 3-5-lobed . . . . *Ampelopsis*

1265. Viola primulifolia   *1266. Viola pubescens*   *1267. Viola renifolia*   *1268. Viola sagittata*

PARTHENOCISSUS *Creeper*

Woody vines, trailing or climbing by tendrils. Leaves palmately compound with typically 5 leaflets (ours). Flowers small, in panicles borne opposite the leaves or aggregated into terminal clusters, perfect or unisexual, 5-merous. Disk none. Petals separate and spreading at anthesis. Stamens short, erect. Berries with thin flesh and 1-4 seeds.

1 Plants often climbing trees by means of adhesive disks on the tendrils; inflorescence with central axis . . . .
. . . . *P. quinquefolia*
1 Plants not climbing, without adhesive disks on tendrils; inflorescence branched, without an evident central axis
. . . . *P. vitacea*

Parthenocissus quinquefolia (L.) Planch.
MAP 1272
VIRGINIA-CREEPER
native

High-climbing vine, adhering to its support by numerous adhesive disks at the ends of the much-branched tendrils; pubescence variable. **Leaves** long-petioled; **leaflets** dull green above, elliptic to obovate, 6-12 cm long, abruptly acuminate, sharply serrate chiefly beyond the middle, cuneate to the base, subsessile or on petioles to 15 mm long. **Inflorescences** terminal and from the upper axils, forming a panicle usually longer than wide, with well marked axis and divergent branches, the flowers in terminal umbel-like clusters. **Berries** nearly black, about 6 mm wide. June.—Moist soil, thickets, swamps.

Parthenocissus vitacea (Knerr) A.S. Hitchc.
MAP 1273
THICKET-CREEPER
native
Parthenocissus inserta (Kerner) Fritsch

Parthenocissus quinquefolia

Very similar to *P. quinquefolia* in habit and foliage; tendrils few-branched, almost always without adhesive disks. **Leaflets** glossy green above, glabrous to thinly pubescent beneath. **Inflorescence** forked at the summit of the peduncle, the two branches both divergent, producing a broad rounded cluster. June.—Moist soil.

VITIS *Grape*

Woody vines, climbing by tendrils. Flowers actually or functionally unisexual, with a hypogynous disk, 5-merous. Calyx essentially none. Petals cohering at the tip, separating at the base, falling early. Sterile flower with 5 erect stamens and a rudimentary pistil. Fertile flower with a well developed pistil and 5 short, reflexed, functionless stamens. Fruit a juicy berry; seeds ovoid, 4, or fewer by abortion. Our species bloom in May or June.

1 Leaves white hairy on underside when young, becoming smooth and strongly blue-green waxy when fully developed, with persistent hairs on the prominent veins . . . . *V. aestivalis*
1 Leaves smooth and greenish on underside when fully developed, not waxy; often with persistent tufts of hairs in leaf axils . . . . *V. riparia*

Vitis aestivalis Michx.
MAP 1274
SUMMER-GRAPE
❧ *threatened | native*

High-climbing vine, the pith interrupted by a diaphragm; tendrils or panicles lacking opposite each third leaf. **Leaves** broadly cordate-ovate to subrotund in outline, with narrow (45 degrees) to broad basal sinus, rarely unlobed, usually shallowly 3-5-lobed, when young covered with a reddish or rusty cobwebby tomentum on both sides, sometimes also with straight hairs on the veins, persistently tomentose on the lower surface; petioles and stems glabrous or

1269. *Viola selkirkii*   1270. *Viola sororia*   1271. *Viola tricolor*   1272. *Parthenoc. quinquefolia*

sparsely pilose after disappearance of the tomentum. **Panicles** usually long (5-15 cm) and slender. **Berries** dark purple or black, 5-10 mm wide.—Rare in mesic hardwood forests of se Minnesota.

Vitis riparia Michx.
RIVERBANK GRAPE

MAP 1275
native

Vitis vulpina subsp. *riparia* (Michx.) R.T. Clausen

Woody, climbing vine to 5 m or more long; young **branches** green or red, hairy, becoming smooth. **Leaves** alternate, heart-shaped in outline, 1-2 dm long and as wide, with a triangular tip and 2 smaller lateral lobes, leaf base with a U-shaped indentation, upper surface smooth, bright green, underside paler and sparsely hairy along veins; margins with coarse, forward-pointing teeth; petioles shorter than blades. **Flowers** small, sweet-scented, green-white to creamy, in stalked clusters 5-10 cm long. **Berries** dark blue to black, 6-12 mm wide, with a waxy bloom, sour when young, becoming sweeter when ripe in fall. May-July. —Floodplain forests, moist sandy woods, streambanks, thickets, sand dunes.

Vitis aestivalis

Vitis riparia

Zygophyllaceae CREOSOTE-BUSH FAMILY

TRIBULUS *Puncturevine*

Tribulus terrestris L.
PUNCTUREVINE

MAP 1276
introduced

Prostrate annual herb. **Stems** hirsute, branched from the base, forming mats up to 1 m wide. **Leaves** opposite, evenly pinnate, short-petioled, 2-6 cm long, one of each pair distinctly the larger; **leaflets** usually 6-8 pairs, oblong, 5-15 mm long. **Flowers** yellow, 8-10 mm wide, solitary in the axils on peduncles 5-10 mm long; sepals deciduous after anthesis; ovary 5-celled. **Fruit** a capsule, splitting at maturity into 5 segments, each septate into 3-5 one-seeded compartments; body of the fruit about 1 cm thick, each segment with 2 stout divergent spines and a longitudinal row of tubercles. All summer. —Native of Europe; dry or sandy soil, along railroads and highways, in dry lawns, parking lots, and disturbed places. *Recognized by its prostrate habit, hairy stems and leaves, the leaves usually with 6-7 pairs of small leaflets, and the spiny nutlets.*

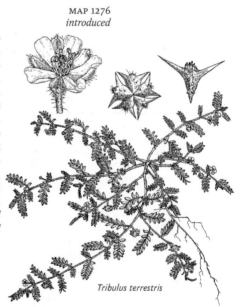

Tribulus terrestris

1273. Parthenocissus vitacea

1274. Vitis aestivalis

1275. Vitis riparia

1276. Tribulus terrestris

MONOCOTS

Acoraceae   CALAMUS FAMILY

ACORUS   *Sweetflag; Calamus*

Perennial herbs of wetlands, rhizomes and leaves pleasantly scented. Rhizomes branched, creeping at or near surface. Leaves sword-shaped, equitant, bright green, with 1-6 prominent veins parallel along length of leaf. Inflorescence a solitary spadix, borne from near midway of leaf, nearly cylindric, tapering, apex obtuse; true spathe absent. Flowers bisexual; tepals 6, light brown; stamens 6; ovaries 1, usually 3-locular. Fruit light brown to reddish berries with darker streaks. Seeds 1-6 (-14), embedded in a mucilagenous jelly.

1   Leaves lacking a single prominent raised midvein, but with 2-several clearly separate veins of ± equal strength along with numerous fainter veins, the leaf thus not obviously ridged to the naked eye; fruit maturing . . . . ***A. americanus***

1   Leaves with a single prominent raised midvein (best observed at about mid-portion of the leaf) that is much more conspicuous than any other veins, appearing as a ridge to the naked eye; fruit not maturing . . . . ***A. calamus***

Acorus americanus (Raf.) Raf.   MAP 1277
AMERICAN SWEETFLAG   *native*
   Acorus calamus var. *americanus* (Raf.) H.D. Wulff.

Similar to the less common, introduced *A. calamus* and long considered a variety of it. Best distinguished using leaf venation differences as described in the key and illustrations below.—Marshes, wet meadows, edges of rivers and streams.

Acorus calamus L.   MAP 1278
SWEETFLAG   *introduced (naturalized)*

Leaves linear, long and swordlike, leathery, 2-ranked, 5-15 dm long and 1-2 cm wide, sweet-scented when crushed; margins entire, sharp-edged, translucent near base. **Flowers** small, in a cylindric, yellow-green spadix, appearing lateral from a leaflike, tapered stalk; the spadix upright, 5-10 cm long and 1-2 cm wide; flowers perfect, yellow or brown, composed of 6 papery tepals and 6 stamens. **Fruit** a 1-3-seeded berry, dry outside and jellylike on inside. June-July.—Marshes (often with cat-tails), bogs, streambanks.

Acorus americanus

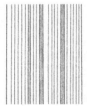

Acorus americanus
leaf venation

Acorus calamus
leaf venation

1277. *Acorus americanus*

1278. *Acorus calamus*

Alismataceae   WATER-PLANTAIN FAMILY

Perennial, aquatic or emergent herbs; plants swollen and tuberlike at base. Leaves all from base of plant and clasping an erect stem; underwater leaves often ribbonlike; emergent leaves broader. Flowers perfect (with both staminate and pistillate parts) or imperfect, in racemes or panicles at ends of stems, with 3 sepals and 3 petals; stamens 6 or more. Fruit a compressed achene, usually tipped by the persistent style.

1   Leaves often arrowhead-shaped; pistils or achenes in several series around a large, round receptacle, and forming a dense, round head . . . . ***Sagittaria***

1   Leaves never arrowhead-shaped; achenes in a single whorl on a small, flat receptacle . . . . ***Alisma***

ALISMA *Water-Plantain*

Perennial herbs, from cormlike rootstocks. Leaves emersed or floating, ovate to lance-shaped, never arrowhead-shaped; underwater leaves sometimes ribbonlike (in *A. gramineum*). Flowers perfect, in whorled panicles, sepals 3, green; petals 3, white or light pink; stamens 6. Fruit a flattened achene in a single whorl on a flat receptacle, style beak small or absent.

1 Leaves lance-shaped to oval, or if underwater, leaves long and ribbonlike; flower stalks rarely much longer than leaves; petals somewhat pink-tinged .... *A. gramineum*
1 Leaves ovate, rounded to truncate or heart-shaped at base; flower stalks usually much longer than leaves; petals white 2
   2 Flowers larger; petals about 4 mm long and to 4 mm wide .... *A. triviale*
   2 Flowers smaller; petals to 2.5 mm long and 2 mm wide .... *A. subcordatum*

Alisma gramineum Lej.

MAP 1279
native

NARROW-LEAF WATER-PLANTAIN
  Alisma geyeri Torr.

Stems upright to spreading, 0.5-3 dm tall. **Emersed leaves** lance-shaped to oval, 2-10 cm long and 1-3 cm wide, petioles mostly longer than blades; **underwater leaves** reduced to linear, ribbonlike petioles, to 6 dm long and 1 cm wide. **Flowers** many on spreading stalks, the stalks shorter to somewhat longer than the leaves; sepals 3; petals pink, 1-3 mm long. **Fruit** an achene, 2-3 mm long, with a central ridge and 2 lateral ridges. July-Sept.—Shallow, often brackish water, muddy shores, streambanks.

Alisma gramineum

Alisma subcordatum Raf.

MAP 1280
native

AMERICAN WATER-PLANTAIN
  Alisma plantago-aquatica L. var. *parviflorum* (Pursh) Torr.

Leaves ovate to oval, 3-15 cm long and 2-12 cm wide, rounded to nearly heart-shaped at base; petioles long. **Flowers** clustered on slender stalks 1-10 dm long, in whorls of 3-10; sepals 3; petals white, 3-5 mm long. **Fruit** an achene, 2-3 mm long, with a central groove. July-Sept.—Shallow water marshes, shores, ditches.

Alisma triviale Pursh

MAP 1281
native

NORTHERN WATER-PLANTAIN
  Alisma brevipes Greene
  Alisma plantago-aquatica L. var. *americanum* J.A. Schultes

Leaves usually long-petioled, the blade elliptic to broadly ovate, rounded to subcordate at base, 3-18 cm long. **Inflorescence** on a scape 1-10 dm long. **Flower pedicels** in whorls of 3-10; sepals obtuse, 2-3 mm long; petals white, about 4 mm long. **Fruit** an achene 2-3 mm long, usually with a median dorsal groove. June-Sept.—Marshes, ponds, and streams.

Alisma triviale

SAGITTARIA *Arrowhead*

Perennial or annual herbs, with fleshy or tuberous rootstocks. Leaves sheathing, all from base of plant, variable in shape and size. Emersed and floating leaves usually arrowhead-shaped with large lobes at base, or sometimes ovate to oval and without lobes; underwater leaves often linear in a basal rosette, normally absent by flowering time. Flowers in a raceme of mostly 3-flowered whorls; upper flowers usually staminate, lower flowers usually pistillate or sometimes perfect; sepals 3, green, persistent; petals 3, white, deciduous; stamens 7 to many; pistils crowded on a rounded receptacle.

1279. Alisma gramineum   *1280. Alisma subcordatum*   *1281. Alisma triviale*

Fruit a crowded cluster of achenes in more or less round heads, the achenes flattened and winged, beaked with a persistent style.

1   Emersed leaves not arrowhead-shaped, basal lobes absent 2
    2   Pistillate flowers and fruiting heads sessile or nearly so . . . . *S. rigida*
    2   Pistillate flowers and fruiting heads obviously stalked . . . . *S. graminea*
1   Emersed leaves all or mostly arrowhead-shaped, with large basal lobes 3
    3   Plants annual, rhizomes absent; sepals appressed to fruiting heads; stalks of fruiting heads stout . . . .
       . . . . *S. montevidensis*
    3   Plants perennial, with rhizomes; sepals reflexed on fruiting heads; stalks of fruiting heads slender 4
       4   Bracts below flowers mostly less than 1 cm long; achene beak projecting horizontally from tip of achene
       . . . . *S. latifolia*
       4   Bracts below flowers usually more than 1 cm long; achene beak erect or ascending 5
          5   Achene beak short, erect, to 0.4 mm long; basal lobes of leaves mostly shorter than terminal lobe . . .
          . . . . *S. cuneata*
          5   Achene beak larger, curved and ascending, 0.5 mm or more long; basal lobes of leaves usually equal or
          longer than terminal lobe . . . . *S. brevirostra*

Sagittaria brevirostra Mackenzie & Bush
SHORT-BEAK ARROWHEAD   MAP 1282
                                  ❦ *endangered* | *native*
    Sagittaria engelmanniana subsp. *brevirostra* (Mack. & Bush) Bogin
Perennial herb. **Leaves** arrowhead-shaped, mostly 10–30 cm long and to 20 cm wide; basal lobes lance-shaped and usually equal or longer than terminal lobe; petioles long. **Flowers** in heads 1–2 cm wide, on a mostly unbranched stalk usually longer than leaves, the **staminate flowers** above the pistillate flowers; bracts below flowers 1–5 cm long; **pistillate flowers** on ascending stalks 0.5–2 cm long; sepals bent backward in fruit; petals white, 1–2 cm long. **Fruit** a winged achene, 2–3 mm long, separated from style beak by a saddlelike depression, the beak usually curved-ascending. July–Sept.—Shallow water, muddy shores, marshes.

Sagittaria cuneata Sheldon
ARUM-LEAF ARROWHEAD   MAP 1283
                                      native
Perennial herb, with rhizomes and large, edible tubers. **Submerged leaves** (if present) often awl-shaped or reduced to bladeless, expanded petioles (phyllodes); **emersed leaves** long-stalked, usually arrowhead-shaped, 5–20 cm long and 2–15 cm wide, the basal lobes much shorter than terminal lobe; **floating leaves** often heart-shaped (unlike our other species of *Sagittaria*). **Flowers** imperfect, the staminate flowers above the pistillate, in more or less round heads 5–12 mm wide, with 2–10 whorls of heads on a stalk 1–6 dm tall, the stalks often branched at lowest node; bracts tapered to tip, 1–4 cm long; sepals ovate, bent backward in flower and fruit; petals white, 7–15 mm long. **Fruit** an achene, 2–3 mm long; beak erect, small, 0.1–0.4 mm long. June–Sept.—Shallow water, lakeshores and streambanks.

Sagittaria graminea Michx.
GRASS-LEAF ARROWHEAD   MAP 1284
                                      native
Perennial herb, with rhizomes. **Underwater plants** sometimes only a rosette of bladeless, ribbonlike petioles (phyllodes) to 1 cm wide; **emergent leaves** lance-shaped to oval, never arrowhead-shaped, 3–20 cm long and 0.5–3 cm wide, tapered to a blunt tip. **Flowers** imperfect, the staminate flowers usually above the pistillate, clustered in more or less round heads, 5–12 mm wide, the heads on

Sagittaria brevirostra

Sagittaria graminea

1282. *Sagittaria brevirostra*   1283. *Sagittaria cuneata*   1284. *Sagittaria graminea*

spreading stalks 1-4 cm long; with 2-10 whorls of flowers along an unbranched stalk mostly shorter than leaves; bracts broadly ovate, joined in their lower portion, 2-8 mm long; sepals ovate, bent backward in fruit; petals white, equal or longer than sepals. **Fruit** a winged achene, 1-2 mm long, beak small or absent. June-Sept.—Shallow water and shores.

S. *graminea* includes *Sagittaria graminea* Michx. var. *cristata* (Engelm.) Bogin, sometimes treated as a separate species, *Sagittaria cristata* Engelm., and distinguished as follows:

1 Achenes with beak 0.4-0.6 mm long; anthers clearly shorter than the filaments . . . .*S. cristata*
1 Achenes with beak minute, scarcely discernable, ca. 0.2 mm long; anthers as long as or longer than filaments. . . . .*S. graminea*

Sagittaria latifolia Willd.
DUCK-POTATO

MAP 1285
native

Perennial herb, with rhizomes and edible tubers in fall. **Leaves** variable; **emersed leaves** arrowhead-shaped, mostly 8-40 cm long and 1-15 cm wide, lobes typically narrow on plants in deep water to broad on emersed plants; plants sometimes with bladeless, expanded petioles (phyllodes). **Flowers** staminate above and pistillate below, clustered in more or less round heads 1-2.5 cm wide, at ends of slender, spreading stalks 0.5-3 cm long, in whorls of 2-15 along a stalk 2-10 dm tall; bracts tapered to a tip or blunt, 0.5-1 cm long; sepals ovate, bent backward by fruiting time; petals white, 7-20 mm long. **Fruit** a winged achene, 2-4 mm long, the beak projecting horizontally, 1-2 mm long. July-Sept.—Shallow water, shores, marshes and pools in bogs.

Sagittaria latifolia

Sagittaria montevidensis Cham. & Schltdl.
MISSISSIPPI ARROWHEAD
    Sagittaria calycina Engelm.

MAP 1286
🌱 *threatened | native*

Annual herb, rhizomes and tubers absent. **Leaves** erect to spreading; **emersed blades** arrowhead-shaped (the lobes sometimes outward spreading) or oval to ovate, 3-40 cm long and 2-25 cm wide, the basal lobes usually longer than terminal lobe; petioles and flower stalks spongy, round in cross-section. Lower flowers usually perfect; upper flowers usually staminate, in heads 1-2 cm wide **Flowers** from a stalk 1-10 dm tall, heads leaning when fruiting; bracts membranous, short and rounded at lower nodes, upper bracts longer (to 1 cm long) and tapered to a tip; sepals blunt-tipped, bent backward in flower but appressed to the head in fruit; petals white with a yellow base. **Fruit** an achene, 2-3 mm long, beak more or less horizontal from top of achene. July-Sept.—Muddy shores.

Sagittaria montevidensis

Sagittaria rigida Pursh
SESSILE-FRUIT ARROWHEAD

MAP 1287
native

Perennial herb, rhizomes present. **Stems** erect or lax. **Emersed leaves** lance-shaped to ovate, rarely with short, narrow basal lobes, (but not arrowhead-shaped), 4-15 cm long and to 7 cm wide; petioles sometimes bent near junction with blades; deep water plants often with only linear, bladeless, expanded petioles (phyllodes). **Flowers** in more or less round heads to 1.5 cm wide, the heads stalkless and bristly when mature due to achene beaks; in 2-8 whorls on a stalk 1-8 dm tall, the stalk often bent near lowest node; flowers imperfect, staminate flowers above the pistillate, **staminate flowers** on threadlike stalks 1-3 cm long,

Sagittaria rigida

1285. *Sagittaria latifolia*

1286. *Sagittaria montevidensis*

1287. *Sagittaria rigida*

pistillate flowers more or less stalkless; bracts ovate, 5 mm long, joined at base; sepals ovate, 4-7 mm long, bent backward when in fruit; petals white, 1-3 cm long. **Fruit** a narrowly winged achene, 2-4 mm long; beak ascending, 1-1.5 mm long. June-Sept.—Shallow water, shores and streambanks.

Araceae ARUM FAMILY

Traditionally, perennial herbs with alternate, simple or compound, often fleshy leaves. Flowers small and numerous, mostly single-sexed, staminate flowers usually above pistillate, crowded in a cylindric or rounded spadix subtended by a leaflike spathe; sepals 4-6 or absent; petals absent; stamens mostly 2-6; pistils 1-3-chambered. Fruit a usually fleshy berry, containing 1 to few seeds, or the entire spadix ripening as a fruit.

Now included in the Araceae are the tiny duckweeds (*Lemna, Spirodela,* and *Wolffia*), aquatic genera formerly treated as their own family (Lemnaceae). These are small perennial herbs, floating at or near water surface, single or forming colonies. Plants thallus-like (not differentiated into stems and leaves), the thallus (or frond) flat or thickened; the roots, if present, unbranched, 1 or several from near center of leaf underside; reproducing vegetatively by buds from 1-2 pouches on the sides, the parent and budded plants often joined in small groups. Flowers rare, either staminate or pistillate, in tiny reproductive pouches on margins (*Lemna, Spirodela*) or upper surface (*Wolffia*) of the leaves, subtended by a small spathe within the pouch; sepals and petals absent; staminate flowers 1-2, consisting of 1 anther on a short filament; pistillate flower 1 (a single ovary), in same pouch as staminate flowers. Fruit a utricle with 1 to several seeds.

1 Plants tiny, less than 1 mm long, floating or submerged in water, without differentiation into leaves or stems . 2
  2 Roots absent; leaves thickened, less than 1.5 mm long. . . . . ***Wolffia***
  2 One to several roots present on leaf underside; leaves flat, mostly more than 1.5 mm long 3
    3 Each leaf with 1 root; leaf underside green or purple-tinged . . . . ***Lemna***
    3 Each leaf with 3 or more roots; leaf underside solid purple . . . . ***Spirodela polyrhiza***
1 Plants large, with clearly differentiated normal leaves and with rhizomes or tubers 4
  4 Leaves compound . . . . ***Arisaema***
  4 Leaves simple, not divided 5
    5 Leaves arrowhead-shaped, lobes equaling 1/3 or more length of blade . . . . ***Peltandra virginica***
    5 Leaves heart-shaped or rounded at base 6
      6 Leaves broadly heart-shaped, abruptly tapered to a tip; spathe white, long-stalked; flowering in spring
        . . . . ***Calla palustris***
      6 Leaves rounded ovate, tapered to a rounded tip; spathe green-yellow to purple-brown, short-stalked
        or stalkless; flowering in late winter to early spring . . . . ***Symplocarpus foetidus***

ARISAEMA *Jack-in-the-Pulpit*

Perennial herbs. Leaves compound. Flowers either staminate or pistillate, on same or different plants; staminate flowers with 2-5, more or less stalkless stamens, above the pistillate flowers on a fleshy spadix, the spadix subtended by a green or purple-brown spathe; sepals and petals absent. Fruit a cluster of round, red berries, each berry with 1-3 seeds.

1 Leaflets 7-13; spadix longer than spathe; se Minn . . . . ***A. dracontium***
1 Leaflets usually 3; spathe arching over spadix; statewide . . . . ***A. triphyllum***

Arisaema dracontium (L.) Schott
GREENDRAGON

MAP 1288
native

Perennial herb, from corms. **Leaf** usually single, palmately branched into 7-15 leaflets, the leaflets oval to oblong lance-shaped, tapered to a point and narrowed at base, the central leaflets 1-2 dm long and to 8 cm wide, the outer leaflets progressively smaller; petioles 2-10 dm long. **Flowers** staminate or pistillate and on different plants, or plants with both staminate and pistillate flowers, the staminate above pistillate, on a long, slender spadix exserted 5-10 cm beyond spathe; the spathe green, slender, rolled inward, 3-6 cm long; the flower stalk shorter than the leaf petiole. **Fruit** a cluster of red-orange berries. May-July. —Wet woods and floodplain forests.

Arisaema dracontium

Arisaema triphyllum (L.) Schott

JACK-IN-THE-PULPIT

MAP 1289
native

Perennial herb, from bitter-tasting corms. **Stems** 3-12 dm long. **Leaves** usually longer than the flower stalk, mostly 2, divided into 3 leaflets, the terminal leaflet oval to ovate, the lateral leaflets often asymmetrical at base. **Flowers** staminate or pistillate and usually on separate plants, borne near base of a cylindric, blunt-tipped spadix, subtended by a green, purple-striped spathe, rolled inward below, expanded and arched over the spadix above, abruptly tapered to a tip. **Fruit** a cluster of shiny red berries, the fruit about 1 cm wide. April-July.—Moist forests, cedar swamps.

Arisaema triphyllum

CALLA *Water-Arum*

Calla palustris L.

WATER-ARUM

MAP 1290
native

Perennial herb, from thick rhizomes, the rhizomes creeping in mud or floating in water. **Leaves** broadly heart-shaped, abruptly tapered to a tip, 5-15 cm long and about as wide; petioles stout, 1-2 dm long (or longer when underwater). **Flowers** perfect or the uppermost staminate, on a short-cylindric spadix, 1.5-3 cm long, shorter than the spathe; the spathe white, ovate, tipped with a short, sharp point to 1 cm long; sepals and petals absent; stamens 6. **Fruit** a fleshy, few-seeded berry, turning red when ripe, 8-12 mm long. May-July.—Bog pools, swamps, shores and wet ditches.

Calla palustris

LEMNA *Duckweed*

Small perennial floating herbs, with 1 root per frond (or roots sometimes absent on oldest and youngest leaves). Blades single or 2 to several and joined in small colonies, floating on water surface or underwater (star-duckweed, *L. trisulca*), varying from round, ovate, to obovate or oblong, tapered to a long point (petiole) in *L. trisulca*; green or often red-tinged; upper surface flat to slightly convex, underside flat or convex. Reproductive pouches 2, on margins of frond. Flowers uncommon, consisting of 2 stamens (staminate flowers) and a single pistil (pistillate flower) in each pouch. Fruit an utricle with 1 to several seeds. Reproduction mostly by budding of new leaves from the reproductive pouches.

1 Fronds denticulate toward the tip, tapered to a slender stipitate base, the stipe often as long as the main body and commonly attached to the parent frond; colonies star-shaped, usually submersed . . . . **L. trisulca**

1 Fronds entire on the margin, nearly rounded and not obviously stipitate at the base, solitary or in tight colonies, these not star-shaped, floating on the water surface or stranded on mud 2

  2 Root sheath winged at the base; root tip sharply pointed; roots to 3 cm long; fronds completely green . . . . .
. . . . **L. perpusilla**

  2 Root sheath not winged at the base; root tip mostly rounded; roots often longer than 3 cm; fronds often red-tinged beneath or with red spots on either surface 3

    3 Fronds with several about equal sized, small papillae on the upper surface from the midline to the tip (often obscure), very often red-tinged on the lower surface, forming small, obovate to orbicular, rootless, dark green to brown turions under unfavorable conditions, these sinking to the bottom of the water . . . . **L. turionifera**

1288. Arisaema dracontium   *1289. Arisaema triphyllum*   *1290. Calla palustris*

3 Fronds lacking papillae or with one prominent papilla at the tip and another just above the node and with smaller papillae between them, rarely forming turions; if formed, the turionlike fronds have short roots and are slowly forming daughter fronds 4

    4 Papilla at tip of the frond very prominent; fronds often red beneath. . . . . ***L. obscura***

    4 Papilla at tip of the frond not very prominent; fronds never red beneath. . . . . ***L. minor***

Lemna minor L.
COMMON DUCKWEED

MAP 1291
native

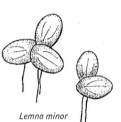

Lemna minor

Fronds nearly orbicular to elliptic-obovate, broadest near the middle, 2–4 mm long, symmetric or nearly so, green to yellowish green, never red-tinged or mottled on either surface (as in *L. turionifera*), obscurely 3 (5)-nerved; both surfaces flat to weakly convex, the upper surface with a low papilla at the apex and often one above the node, usually with a low median ridge or row of smaller papillae between them, the lower surface never inflated. **Turions** not produced. Root sheath not winged, root tip rounded. **Fruit** ovoid to ellipsoid, wingless, 1-seeded. July–Sept.—Quiet or stagnant water of ponds, oxbows, shores, slow-moving rivers, ditches.

Lemna obscura (Austin) Daubs
LITTLE DUCKWEED

(NO MAP)
native

Lemna obscura

Quite similar to *L. minor* and differing mainly as follows: **Fronds** obovate to oblong-orbicular, 1.5–3 mm long, slightly asymmetric, often reddish beneath, obscurely 3-nerved; upper surface flat to slightly convex, with a prominent papilla at the apex, the lower surface convex. Much less common than *L. minor*, Washington County.

Lemna perpusilla Torr.
MINUTE DUCKWEED

MAP 1292
native

Lemna perpusilla

Fronds oblong to obovate, asymmetrical and falcate, 2–2.5 mm long, 1.2–2.5 mm wide, obscurely 3-nerved, distinctly narrowed to the base, solitary or in groups of 2–6.

Lemna trisulca L.
IVY-LEAF DUCKWEED

MAP 1293
native

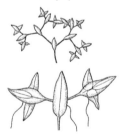

Lemna trisulca

Perennial floating herb, forming tangled colonies just below water surface, floating at surface only when flowering; roots single from underside of frond or absent. **Fronds** several to many, joined to form star-shaped colonies; oblong lance-shaped, 5–20 mm long, tapered to a slender base (petiole), flat on both sides. **Fruit** a 1-seeded utricle.—Ponds, streams, ditches.

Lemna turionifera Landolt
TURION DUCKWEED

MAP 1294
native

Fronds single or in groups of several, obovate, usually flat and not humped, 1–4 mm long and 1–1.5 times longer than wide, veins 3, small white dots (papillae) present on midline of upper surface (visible with naked eye but clearer with 10x hand lens); underside of frond usually red or purple and redder than upper side point of root, upper surface (especially near tip) sometimes red-spotted. **Turions** sometimes present, dark-green to brown, 1–1.6 mm wide, without roots, sinking to bottom and forming new plants.—Quiet water of ponds and lakes.

1291. *Lemna minor*   1292. *Lemna perpusilla*   1293. *Lemna trisulca*   1294. *Lemna turionifera*

PELTANDRA *Arrow-Arum*

Peltandra virginica (L.) Schott   (NO MAP)
GREEN ARROW-ARUM   *native*
Perennial herb, with thick, fibrous roots. **Leaves** all from base of plant on long
petioles, bright green, oblong to triangular in outline, 1-3 dm long and 8-15 cm
wide at flowering, to 8 dm long later; leaf base with a pair of lobes. **Flowers** in a
white to orange spadix about as long as the spathe, atop a curved stalk 2-4 dm
long; flowers either staminate or pistillate, the **staminate flowers** covering upper
3/4 of the spadix, the **pistillate flowers** covering lower portion; **spathe** green with
a pale margin, 1-2 dm long, the lower portion covering the fruit. **Fruit** a head of
green-brown berries, the berries with 1-3 seeds surrounded by a jellylike material.
June-July.—Shallow water, shores, bog pools; often where shaded; Cook County.

Peltandra virginica

SPIRODELA *Greater Duckweed*

Spirodela polyrrhiza (L.) Schleid.   MAP 1295
GREATER DUCKWEED   *native*
Perennial herb, floating on water surface; roots 5-12 per frond. **Fronds** usually in
clusters of 2-5, flat, round to obovate, 3-6 mm long, upper surface green,
underside red-purple. **Flowers** uncommon, comprised of 2-3 stamens (staminate
flowers) and 1 pistil (pistillate flower) in each pouch. **Fruit** a 1-2-seeded utricle.
Reproduction mainly by budding of new leaves from reproductive pouches (1
pouch on each margin of frond).—Stagnant or slow-moving water of lakes, ponds,
marshes and ditches, often with *Lemna*.

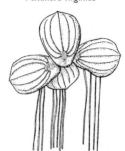

Spirodela polyrrhiza

SYMPLOCARPUS *Skunk-Cabbage*

Symplocarpus foetidus (L.) Salisb.   MAP 1296
SKUNK-CABBAGE   *native*
Perennial, foul-smelling herb, from thick rootstocks. **Leaves** all from base of plant,
ovate to heart-shaped, 3-8 dm long and to 3 dm wide, strongly nerved; petioles
short, channeled. **Flowers** appearing before leaves in late winter or early spring,
perfect; the spathe ovate, curved over spadix, 8-15 cm long, green-purple and
often mottled; sepals 4. **Fruit** round, 8-12 cm wide; seeds 1 cm thick. Feb-May
(our earliest flowering native plant).—Floodplain forests, swamps, streambanks,
calcareous fens, moist wooded slopes.

Symplocarpus foetidus

WOLFFIA *Watermeal*

Tiny perennial herbs, floating at or just below water surface, sometimes abundant and forming a
granular scum across surface, usually mixed with other aquatic species of this family, roots absent.
Leaves single or often paired, globe-shaped or ovate, flat or rounded on upper surface. Flowers
uncommon, consisting of 1 stamen (staminate flower) and 1 pistil (pistillate flower) in the pouch. Fruit
a round, 1-seeded utricle. Reproduction mainly by budding from the single pouch near base of frond.
*Watermeal is the world's smallest flowering plant. The blades feel granular or mealy and tend to stick to the
skin. The 3 species in Minn often occur together.*

1   Leaves rounded on upper surface, not brown-dotted . . . . **W. columbiana**
1   Leaves flattened on upper surface, brown-dotted (under 10x magnification). 2
    2   Leaves rounded at tip, with a wartlike bump in center of upper surface . . . . **W. brasiliensis**

1295. Spirodela polyrrhiza   *1296. Symplocarpus foetidus*   *1297. Wolffia borealis*   *1298. Wolffia brasiliensis*

2 Leaves with an upturned point at tip, wartlike bump absent . . . . *W. borealis*

Wolffia borealis (Engelm.) Landolt
MAP 1297
NORTHERN WATERMEAL
native
Wolffia punctata auct. non Griseb.

Fronds oval to oblong when viewed from above, 0.1-1 mm long and to 0.5 mm wide, with a raised pointed tip, usually brown-dotted; upper surface floating just above water surface, bright green, underside paler.—Quiet water of ponds, marshes and ditches, often with other species of *Wolffia* and *Lemna*.

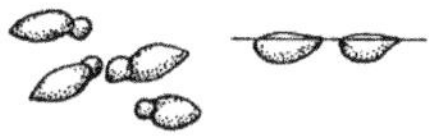

Wolffia borealis

Wolffia brasiliensis Weddell
MAP 1298
BRAZILIAN WATERMEAL
native
Wolffia papulifera C.H. Thompson
Wolffia punctata Griseb.

Fronds broadly ovate in outline, slightly asymmetrical, 1-1.5 mm long, about 1 mm wide, rounded beneath, the upper side floating above the water, punctate with brown pigment cells, elevated near the center into a conic papilla.

Wolffia brasiliensis

Wolffia columbiana Karst.
MAP 1299
COLUMBIAN WATERMEAL
native

Fronds float low in water, only small upper surface exposed, round to broadly ovate and 1-1.5 mm long when viewed from above; nearly round when viewed from side, not raised and pointed at tip; green, not brown-dotted.—Stagnant water of ponds and marshes.

Wolffia columbiana

Butomaceae FLOWERING RUSH FAMILY

BUTOMUS *Flowering-Rush*

Butomus umbellatus L.
MAP 1300
FLOWERING-RUSH
introduced (invasive)

Perennial herb, from creeping rhizomes. **Leaves** all from base of plant, erect when emersed, or floating when in deep water, linear, to 1 m long and 5-10 mm wide, parallel-veined; petioles absent. **Flowers** pink, perfect, 2-3 cm wide, stalked, in a many-flowered umbel, borne on a round stalk 1-1.2 m tall; with 4 lance-shaped bracts subtending the umbel; sepals 3, petal-like; petals 3; stamens 9; pistils 6. **Fruit** a dry, many-seeded capsule, splitting open on inner side. June-Aug. —Marshes and shores.

Butomus umbellatus

Commelinaceae SPIDERWORT FAMILY

Herbs, often succulent. Leaves parallel-veined, broad or narrow, dilated at base into a tubular sheath. Flowers cymose or rarely solitary, from the axils of foliaceous bracts or spathes; perfect, regular or irregular, 3-merous. Sepals free and distinct, usually green and herbaceous. Petals colored or white, ephemeral, free or united into a tube. Stamens typically in 2 whorls of 3 each, but in various genera may be fewer. Ovary in most genera 3-celled. Fruit a capsule.

1 Corolla irregular, with 2 blue petals and 1 smaller petal; inflorescence subtended by a wide bract less than 3 cm long . . . . *Commelina*
1 Corolla regular; the petals all alike; inflorescence subtended by long, narrow, leaflike bracts 4-20 cm long . . . . *Tradescantia*

COMMELINA *Day-Flower*

Annual or perennial herbs with succulent stems. Leaves alternate, linear to lance-shaped. Inflorescence a small cyme, closely subtended by a folded, heart-shaped spathe from which the pedicels protrude; flowers attractive but short-lived. Sepals 3, herbaceous, somewhat unequal, two usually somewhat united at base. Petals 3, the two upper blue, ovate to kidney-shaped, the lower one much smaller, usually white, sometimes absent. Fertile stamens 3; sterile stamens 3, smaller than the fertile, bearing imperfect cross-shaped anthers. Ovary sessile, morphologically 3-celled; upper median cell smaller, 1-ovuled, or empty, or abortive; lower two cells fertile, with 1 or 2 ovules. Fruit a 2- or 3-celled capsule. Our species bloom in summer and early autumn.

1   Plants erect; leaf blades lance-shaped or linear 7-10 times longer than wide .... *C. erecta*
1   Plants prostrate or creeping; leaf blades ovate, 2-4 times longer than wide .... *C. communis*

Commelina communis L.
COMMON DAY-FLOWER   MAP 1301   *introduced (naturalized)*

Annual. **Stems** at first erect, later diffuse and rooting from the lower nodes, to 8 dm long. **Leaves** ovate lance-shaped, 5-10 cm long, 1-3 cm wide. **Spathe** (folded) cordate, 15-25 mm long, about half as wide, glabrous or minutely pubescent, its margins free to the base. **Fruit** 2-celled, the upper cell abortive, 4-seeded.—Moist or shaded ground, often a weed in gardens.

Commelina communis

Commelina erecta L.
ERECT DAY-FLOWER   MAP 1302   ❦ *endangered | native*

Perennial from a cluster of thickened fibrous roots. **Stems** erect or ascending, usually branched, to 1 m tall. **Principal leaves** varying from linear to lance-shaped, 5-15 cm long, 5 mm to 4 cm wide; sheaths ciliate with white hairs, somewhat prolonged into rounded, often flaring auricles. **Spathes** arising near the summit of the culm, single or in small clusters, short-peduncled, broadly triangular, often with conspicuous radiating cross-veins, the margins connate for about 1/3 of their length; **upper petals** 10-25 mm long; **lower petal** white, much smaller.—Dry, usually sandy soil; se Minn. *Variable in the size of the leaves.*

Commelina erecta

TRADESCANTIA *Spiderwort*

Perennial herbs, usually somewhat succulent. Leaves alternate, elongate, linear to lance-shaped, dilated into conspicuous basal sheaths. Flowers in umbel-like cymes of several to many attractive flowers subtended by elongate foliaceous bracts. Sepals 3, herbaceous, green or suffused with purple or rose. Petals 3, all alike, obovate to elliptic, blue to pink, rarely white. Stamens 6, usually with villous filaments. Ovary 3-celled; style slender; stigma capitate. Fruit a capsule.

1   Sepals and pedicels glabrous or with only a few hairs at either tip or base of the sepal .... *T. ohiensis*
1   Sepals and pedicels distinctly pubescent 2
   2   Sepals and pedicels densely soft-hairy, with both gland-tipped and nonglandular hairs, the hairs often more than 1 mm long; sepals 10-15 mm long .... *T. bracteata*
   2   Sepals and pedicels sparsely hairy, the hairs all gland-tipped and shorter, to only 0.5 mm long; sepals to 10 mm long .... *T. occidentalis*

Tradescantia bracteata Small.
LONG-BRACT SPIDERWORT   MAP 1303   *native*

Stems rather stout, straight, rarely branched, at anthesis ordinarily 2-4 dm tall, glabrous or minutely puberulent. **Leaves** glabrous or sparsely pilose at the base, the larger leaves 8-15 mm wide; bracts often longer and wider than the leaves. **Cyme** usually solitary and terminal, rarely with an additional one from the upper node; pedicels and sepals densely and softly villous with glandular and nonglandular hairs mingled, the hairs commonly 1-1.5 mm long; **sepals** obtuse or subacute, 10-14 mm long; **petals** rose-color or blue, 15-20 mm long.—Prairies.

1299. Wolffia columbiana   *1300. Butomus umbellatus*   *1301. Commelina communis*

Tradescantia bracteata

Tradescantia occidentalis (Britt.) Smyth

MAP 1304

PRAIRIE SPIDERWORT   *native*

Stems slender, straight, often branched, at anthesis commonly 2-6 dm tall, glabrous and glaucous. **Leaves** firm, glabrous, involute, usually narrowly linear and less than 1 cm wide; bracts similar to the leaves. **Cyme** solitary and terminal, or accompanied by another peduncled cyme from the upper node; pedicels and sepals sparsely pubescent with entirely glandular hairs usually about 0.5 mm long; **sepals** acute to acuminate, 6-10 mm long; **petals** rose-color to blue, 12-16 mm long.—Dry prairies.

Tradescantia ohiensis Raf.

MAP 1305

BLUEJACKET   *native*

Stems slender, straight or nearly so, often branched, ordinarily 4-10 dm tall, glabrous and glaucous. **Leaves** narrowly linear, flat, firm, glabrous, glaucous, usually less than 1 cm wide, conspicuously dilated into the sheath. **Cymes** solitary, terminating the stem and its branches; pedicels 7-25 mm long, glabrous; **sepals** glaucous, usually 8-12 mm long, often red-margined, glabrous throughout, occasionally minutely pilose with non-glandular hairs at the apex, rarely sparsely pilose at the base; **petals** blue or rose, rarely white, 1-2 cm long.—Moist prairies and meadows.

Tradescantia ohiensis

Cyperaceae SEDGE FAMILY

Mostly perennial, grasslike, rushlike or reedlike plants. Stems 3-angled, or more or less round in section, solid or pithy. Leaves 3-ranked or reduced to sheaths at base of stem; leaf blades, when present, grasslike, parallel-veined, often keeled; sheaths mostly closed around the stem. Flowers small, perfect (with both staminate and pistillate parts), or single-sexed, each flower subtended by a bract (scale); perianth of 1 to many (often 6) small bristles, or a single perianth scale, or absent; stamens usually 3; ovary 2-3-chambered, contained in a saclike covering (perigynium) in *Carex*, maturing into an achene, stigmas 3 or 2. Flowers arranged in spikelets (termed spikes in *Carex*), the spikelets single as a terminal or lateral spike, or several to many in various types of heads, the head often subtended by 1 to several bracts.

1 Achenes enclosed in a closed sac (perigynium) subtended by a scale, the style protruding through the apex; flowers strictly unisexual (sedges with exclusively staminate flowers should be keyed here) . . . . *Carex*
1 Achenes not enclosed in a closed sac, naked beside the subtending scale; at least some flowers bisexual (except in *Scleria*) 2
  2 Achenes white, hard (bone-like), ± spherical; flowers all unisexual . . . . *Scleria*
  2 Achenes yellow, brown, or black, rarely whitish, not spherical; at least some flowers bisexual 3
    3 Scales of spikelets 2-ranked; spikelets ± flattened in cross-section and always more than one per inflorescence 4
      4 Stems usually ± angled, solid; inflorescences terminal; achenes without subtending bristles . . *Cyperus*
      4 Stems round, hollow; inflorescences in the axils of stem leaves; achenes with subtending bristles. . . . . *Dulichium*
    3 Scales of spikelets spirally arranged (or if 2-ranked, the spikelet solitary); spikelets round or several-angled in cross-section, solitary or several to many per inflorescence 5
      5 Spikelet or cluster of spikelets borne on one side of the stem at the base of a single ± erect to somewhat angled or curved involucral bract that appears to be a continuation of the stem 6

1302. Commelina erecta　　*1303. Tradescantia bracteata*　　*1304. Tradescan. occidentalis*　　*1305. Tradescantia ohiensis*

6 Stems less than 0.5 mm thick; plants tiny, less than 10 cm tall . . . . ***Lipocarpha***

6 Stems thicker than 0.5 mm; plants usually much taller than 10 cm . . . . ***Schoenoplectus***

5 Spikelet or spikelets terminating the stem or borne both terminally and laterally; if more than one spikelet, the inflorescence with (1-) 2 to several spreading to reflexed, leaflike involucral bracts 7

  7 Spikelet solitary and terminal on the stem (very rarely a few smaller accessory spikelets occur at the base of the terminal spikelet in the bladeless genus *Eleocharis*) 8

    8 Sheaths totally bladeless or at most with an apical tooth up to 1 mm long; achenes usually with an apical tubercle formed by the expanded and persistent base of the style . . . . ***Eleocharis***

    8 Upper sheaths with short green blades 0.3-12 cm long; achenes blunt at apex, tubercle absent. 9

      9 Achenes subtended by 1-8 bristles less than twice as long as the achenes, or bristles absent . . . . ***Trichophorum*** (in part)

      9 Achenes subtended by conspicuous silky, white or tawny, hair-like bristles many times as long as the achenes 10

        10 Bristles numerous, ca. (12-) 15-50 or more; rhizomes erect, very short . . . . . . ***Eriophorum***

        10 Bristles 6; rhizomes horizontal and short-creeping . . . . ***Trichophorum alpinum***

  7 Spikelets several to many on the stem, terminal or lateral 11

    11 Achenes subtended by (12-) 15-50 conspicuous, silky, white or tawny, hair-like bristles many times as long as the achenes . . . . ***Eriophorum***

    11 Achenes subtended by 1-8 bristles, or bristles absent 12

      12 Leaves flat or folded; with a definite, ± keeled midrib 13

        13 Achenes with a conspicuous tubercle formed by the expanded, persistent style base . . . . ***Rhynchospora***

        13 Achenes blunt at apex, without a tubercle; style base, if expanded, not persistent to maturity 14

          14 Widest leaves 4-15 mm wide; achenes subtended by 1-8 bristles 15

          14 Widest leaves 0.5-3 mm wide; achenes lacking bristles . . . . ***Fimbristylis***

            15 Spikelets (10-) 15-36 mm long; achenes 3-5 mm long, including apiculus; anthers 3-5 mm long; stems sharply 3-angled nearly or quite to the base; colonial from rhizomes with large corm-like thickenings . . . . ***Bolboschoenus***

            15 Spikelets 2-10 (-12) mm long, achenes 0.9-1.2 mm long; anthers 0.5-1.3 mm long; stems terete, obtusely 3-angled, or sharply 3-angled only toward summit; tufted or with rhizomes lacking corm-like enlargements . . . . ***Scirpus***

      12 Leaves inrolled and wiry; rounded on the back and without a definite midrib 16

      16 Styles 2-cleft; achenes subtended by slender bristles . . . . ***Rhynchospora***

      16 Styles 3-cleft; achenes lacking bristles 17

        17 Achenes 2.2-3.5 mm long; perennials 4-11 dm tall; colonial from elongated rhizomes . . . . ***Cladium***

        17 Achenes 0.7-0.8 mm long; tufted annuals 0.2-4 dm tall . . . . ***Bulbostylis***

BOLBOSCHOENUS *Club-Rush*

Former members of genus *Scirpus*, and sometimes included in *Schoenoplectus*.

1 Styles 3-parted; achenes 3-angled; perianth bristles strong, distinctly retrorse-barbed; leaf sheaths convex at tip . . . . ***B. fluviatilis***

1 Styles 2-parted; achenes lens-shaped; perianth bristles weak, scarcely half as long as achene, obscurely barbed; leaf sheaths straight or concave at tip . . . . ***B. maritimus***

Bolboschoenus fluviatilis (Torr.) Soják
RIVER CLUB-RUSH

  Schoenoplectus fluviatilis (Torr.) M.T. Strong
  Scirpus fluviatilis (Torr.) Gray

MAP 1306
native

Bolboschoenus fluviatilis

Perennial, spreading by rhizomes and often forming large colonies. **Stems** stout, erect, 6-15 dm long, sharply 3-angled, the sides more or less flat. **Leaves** several on stem, smooth, 6-15 mm wide, upper leaves often longer than the head; bracts 3-5, leaflike, erect to spreading, to 3-4 dm long. **Spikelets** 1-3 cm long and 6-12 mm wide, clustered in an umbel of 10-20 spikelets at end of stem, several of the spikelets nearly stalkless in 1-2 clusters, others single or in groups of 2-5 at ends of spreading or drooping stalks to 8 cm long; **scales** gold-brown, short-hairy on back, 6-10 mm long, the midvein extended into a curved awn 1-3 mm long; bristles 6, unequal, white to copper-brown, downwardly barbed, persistent, about as long as body of achene; style yellow, 3-parted. **Achenes** 3-angled, dull, tan to gray-green, 3-5 mm long, with a beak to 0.5 mm long. June-Aug.—Shallow water of streams, ditches, marshes, lakes and ponds; sometimes where brackish. *The sharply triangular leafy stems are distinctive.*

Bolboschoenus maritimus (L.) Palla
PRAIRIE BULRUSH
> *Schoenoplectus maritimus* (L.) Lye
> *Scirpus maritimus* L.
> *Scirpus paludosus* A. Nels.

MAP 1307
native

Perennial, from tuber-bearing rhizomes. **Stems** single, sharply 3-angled, 5-15 dm long. **Leaves** several on stem, smooth, to 1 cm wide; bracts 3-5, the longest bract sometimes erect, to 30 cm long. **Spikelets** cylindric, 10-25 mm long and 6-9 mm wide, in clusters of 3-20 in a dense, stalkless head, or some spikelets single or in groups of 2-4 on stalks to 4 cm long; scales ovate, notched at tip, pale brown, 5-7 mm long, with an awn to 2 mm long; bristles 2-6, coppery, about half as long as achene; style 2-parted. **Achenes** lens-shaped, brown to black, 3-4 mm long, the beak small, to 0.3 mm long. June-Aug.—Marshes, shores, ditches; especially where brackish. *Plants more slender than in* **B. fluviatilis**, *the inflorescence more congested and the scales paler brown.*

Bolboschoenus maritimus

BULBOSTYLIS *Hair Sedge*

Bulbostylis capillaris (L.) Kunth
HAIR SEDGE

MAP 1308
native

Small tufted annual. **Stems** threadlike, to 3 dm tall. **Leaves** short, filiform, involute, mostly at or near the base. **Cymes** capitate or umbel-like; longest bract usually exceeding the spikelets; peduncles none or to 1 cm long; **spikelets** few-flowered, ovoid, 3-6 mm long; **scales** boat-shaped, ovate, purple-brown with strong green midvein, minutely pubescent and ciliate. **Achenes** trigonous, to 1 mm long, straw-colored, obscurely rugose, capped with a tiny tubercle.—Wet sandy or muddy soil.

Bulbostylis capillaris

CAREX *Sedge*

Perennial grasslike plants. Stems mostly 3-angled. Leaves 3-ranked, margins often finely toothed. Flowers either staminate or pistillate, with both sexes in same spike, or in separate spikes on same plant, or the staminate and pistillate flowers on different plants. Staminate flowers with 3 or rarely 2 stamens; pistillate flowers with style divided into 2 or 3 stigmas. Achenes lens-shaped or flat on 1 side and convex on other (in species with 2 stigmas), or achenes 3-angled or nearly round (in species with 3 stigmas), enclosed in a sac called the perigynium (singular) or perigynia (plural); see page 502.

Carex is the largest genus of plants in Minnesota. To aid in identification, a grouping of most sedges by their typical habitat is first presented, followed by a key to 45 *Carex* sections containing closely related species (section divisions largely follow those of Reznicek et al. (2011) and Hipp (2008). As evident in the keys, identification of *Carex* species is often based on characteristics of the mature perigynia (the sac around the achene); a hand lens or dissecting microscope is often useful.

1306. Bolboschoenus fluviatilis   *1307. Bolboschoenus maritimus*   *1308. Bulbostylis capillaris*

QUICK ENTRY KEY TO CAREX SECTIONS

- Spike 1 per stem, all flowers attached to main stem in terminal spike . . . . **COUPLET 2**
- Spikes 2 or more per stem, all flowers staminate . . . . **COUPLET 12**
- Spikes 2 or more per stem, at least some flowers pistillate, stigmas 2, achenes flat to biconvex in cross section . . . . **COUPLET 14**
- Spikes 2 or more per stem, at least some flowers pistillate, stigmas usually 3, achenes usually more or less 3-angled in cross section, body of perigynium pubescent to hispid. . . . . **COUPLET 36**
- Spikes 2 or more per stem, at least some flowers pistillate, stigmas usually 3, achenes usually more or less 3-angled in cross section, body of perigynium glabrous. . . . . **COUPLET 45**

CAREX MORPHOLOGY

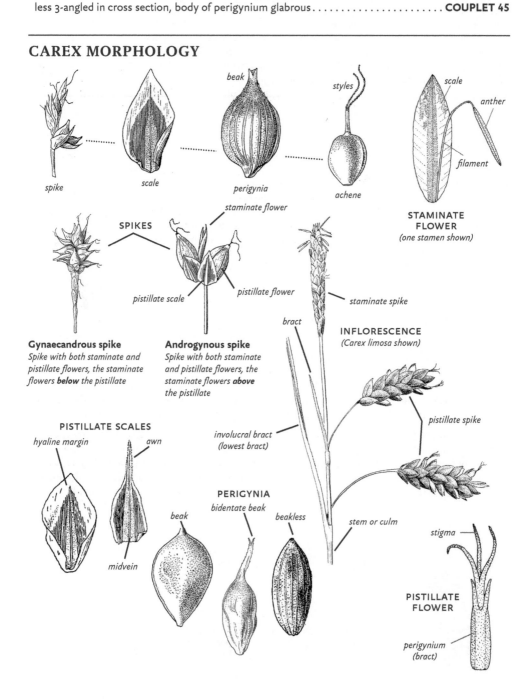

spike

scale

beak

perigynia

styles

achene

scale

anther

filament

STAMINATE FLOWER
(one stamen shown)

SPIKES

staminate flower

pistillate scale

pistillate flower

Gynaecandrous spike
*Spike with both staminate and pistillate flowers, the staminate flowers **below** the pistillate*

Androgynous spike
*Spike with both staminate and pistillate flowers, the staminate flowers **above** the pistillate*

bract

staminate spike

INFLORESCENCE
(*Carex limosa* shown)

pistillate spike

PISTILLATE SCALES

hyaline margin

awn

midvein

PERIGYNIA

beak

bidentate beak

beakless

involucral bract
(lowest bract)

stem or culm

stigma

PISTILLATE FLOWER

perigynium
(bract)

KEY TO SECTIONS OF CAREX

1   Spike 1 per stem, all flowers attached to main stem in terminal spike (spike entirely staminate, entirely pistillate, or mixed) 2

    2   Styles 2-cleft; achenes 2-sided (lenticular); basal sheaths brown 3

       3   Plants with slender rhizomes; perigynia obscurely or not at all serrate, plump (usually at least as convex on upper face as on the lower), the lowermost tending to be remote (as much as 1 mm apart at points of attachment); spikes without empty basal scales; anthers to 2.5 (-3) mm long . . . . ***Carex* sect.**
          . . . . **PHYSOGLOCHIN**

       3   Plants densely tufted, not rhizomatous; perigynia minutely but strongly and regularly serrate on upper portion and beak, ± flattened, crowded; spikes usually with 1-2 empty basal scales; anthers 2-3.5 mm long . . . . ***Carex* sect. STELLULATAE** *(C. exilis)*

    2   Styles 3-cleft; achenes 3-sided (or nearly terete); basal sheaths brown or purple-red 4

       4   Perigynia finely hairy at base of beak 5

          5   Stems without red or purple at base; single spike pistillate at base, staminate above . . . .
             . . . . ***Carex* sect. FILIFOLIAE**

          5   Stems distinctly red or purple at base; spikes unisexual. . . . . ***Carex* sect. SCIRPINAE**

       4   Perigynia glabrous 6

          6   Spikes staminate at base, pistillate toward tip, densely flowered, mostly 1 cm or more thick; perigynia inflated (much larger than the included achene), abruptly contracted to a long, very slender beak . . .
             . . . . ***Carex* sect. SQUARROSAE**

          6   Spikes pistillate at base, staminate above, more slender and sparsely flowered (fewer than 10 perigynia); perigynia various (but neither inflated nor with a long slender beak). 7

             7   Lower pistillate scales 10 mm or more long . . . . ***Carex* sect. PHYLLOSTACHYAE**

             7   Lower pistillate scales less than 10 mm long 8

                8   Perigynium beak mostly 2 mm or longer, and at least as long as body . . . .

                8   Perigynium beak less than 2 mm long, or if longer than 2 mm, then shorter than length of body 9

                   9   Perigynia 4-6 times longer than wide. . . . . ***Carex* sect. LEUCOGLOCHIN**

                   9   Perigynia less than 4 times longer than wide 10

                     10   Culms with red or purple at base . . . . ***Carex* sect. OBTUSATAE**

                     10   Culms yellow, brown, or black at base, without red or purple . . . .
                       . . . . ***Carex* sect. LEPTOCEPHALAE**

1   Spikes 2 or more per stem (spikes entirely staminate, entirely pistillate, or mixed) 11

    11   All spikes staminate. 12

       12   Plants with long-creeping rhizomes . . . . ***Carex* sect. DIVISAE** *(C. praegracilis)*

       12   Plants densely tufted 13

          13   Leaves flat, lax and spreading; usually in swamps and marshes . . . . ***Carex* sect. DEWEYANAE**
             . . . . *(C. bromoides)*

          13   Leaves channeled, stiff and erect; fens and other calcareous open wetlands ***Carex* sect. STELLULATAE**

    11   At least some spikes bisexual or pistillate 14

       14   Styles 2-cleft; achenes 2-sided 15

          15   Lateral spikes peduncled, or if sessile, then elongate; terminal spike often entirely staminate 16

             16   Plants slender, the stems to ca. 3 dm tall and less than 1 mm thick (excluding leaf bases) even near the base; terminal (staminate or sometimes mixed) spike solitary, ca. 1 cm long; lowermost bract usually with a short sheath ca. 2-7 (rarely 10-30) mm long; perigynia white-pulverulent or golden-yellow at maturity. 17

             16   Plants coarse, the stems over (3-) 5 dm tall and usually over 1 mm thick, at least toward base; staminate spikes often 2 or more, mostly 2.5-7 cm long; lowermost bract essentially sheathless (rarely with very short sheath); perigynia neither white-pulverulent nor golden-yellow. . . . . ***Carex* sect. PHACOCYSTIS**

                17   Lowermost pistillate spike sessile or nearly so (rarely one arising from near base of plant); terminal spike staminate; perigynia green or slightly glaucous, crowded . . . . ***Carex* sect.**
                  . . . . **PHACOCYSTIS**

                17   Lowermost pistillate spike nearly always peduncled; terminal spike often pistillate near tip, or the pistillate spikes ± loosely flowered; fresh perigynia white-pulverulent or golden-yellow. . . . .
                  . . . . ***Carex* sect. BICOLORES**

          15   Lateral spikes sessile, short, often crowded; terminal spike at least partly pistillate (rarely staminate) 18

             18   Stems arising mostly singly from rhizome or stolon 19

19 Perigynia plumply plano-convex to nearly terete in cross-section, not winged or sharply margined; plants of sphagnum bogs, cedar swamps, etc. 20

    20 Scales pale-hyaline with green midrib; perigynia apiculate or with very small beak; at least the lower few-flowered spikes ± separated; plants clumped from short, slender rhizomes . . . . *Carex sect.* **GLAREOSAE**

    20 Scales rich brown; perigynia with distinct beak ca. 0.5 mm long; spikes crowded as if in a single head; stems arising from axils of old decumbent stems (stolons) . . . . *Carex sect.* **CHORDORRHIZAE**

19 Perigynia strongly flattened, with distinctly winged or sharply edged margins; plants mostly of wet or dry open habitats 21

    21 Perigynia mostly over 2 mm wide; staminate flowers only at the base of some or all spikes . . . . *Carex sect.* **OVALES**

    21 Perigynia mostly not over 2 mm wide; staminate flowers not restricted to base of spikes. . . 22

        22 Mature perigynia with the body ± narrowly wing-margined above and the beak bidentate (firm teeth 0.5 mm long); rhizome slender (ca. 1-1.5 mm in diameter), with brownish fibrous sheaths; spikes often dissimilar, some largely or entirely staminate or pistillate, others mixed . . . . *Carex sect.* **AMMOGLOCHIN**

        22 Mature perigynia distinctly 2-edged but not winged, the beak with short weak teeth; rhizome stout (ca. 2-3 mm in diameter), with black fibrous sheaths; spikes mostly similar (each one staminate apically and pistillate basally; in section Holarrhenae the upper sometimes largely staminate) 23

            23 Sheaths of upper leaves green-nerved ventrally, usually not covering the inconspicuous nodes . . . . *Carex sect.* **HOLARRHENAE**

            23 Sheaths of upper leaves with broad white-hyaline stripe on ventral side covering the included nodes . . . . *Carex sect.* **DIVISAE**

18 Stems tufted, the tufts with or without connecting rhizomes. 24

    24 Staminate flowers at the base of some or all spikes, not at the tip (note especially the terminal spike) 25

        25 Perigynia with thin-winged margins, at least narrowly so along apical part of body and basal part of beak, strongly flattened and scale-like (in some species elongate), ± appressed and overlapping (or in some species spreading at the tips) 26

            26 Bracts not resembling the leaves, narrower than 2 mm most or all their length and not over twice as long as the inflorescence; perigynia various . . . . *Carex sect.* **OVALES**

            26 Bracts leaflike, the broadest 2-4 mm wide, many times exceeding the spikes (which are crowded in a dense head); perigynia very narrowly lanceolate, not over 1 mm wide . . . . *Carex sect.* **CYPEROIDEAE**

        25 Perigynia at most with a ridge along the margin, not winged, the achene plumply filling at least the apical part of the body all the way to the margins 27

            27 Body of perigynium elliptic or nearly so (except in *C. arcta*) with at most a very short beak, and with rounded or slightly margined edges, nearly or entirely filled by the achene . . . . *Carex sect.* **GLAREOSAE**

            27 Body of perigynium ovate or lanceolate or prominently beaked, sharp-edged, only 1/2 to 2/3 filled by achene (very spongy around and below base of achene) 28

                28 Mature perigynia appressed-ascending, 4-5.7 mm long. . . . *Carex sect.* **DEWEYANAE**

                28 Mature perigynia strongly spreading to reflexed, 2-3.6 mm long 29

                    29 Spikes 7-15, usually crowded, except sometimes the lowest, the inflorescence axis mostly concealed; beaks not or very obscurely bidentate . . . . *Carex sect.* **GLAREOSAE** *(C. arcta)*

                    29 Spikes 3-8, not usually crowded, inflorescence axis clearly visible; beaks clearly bidentate with teeth 0.1-0.4 mm long . . . . *Carex sect.* **STELLULATAE**

    24 Staminate flowers at the tip of some or all spikes (even when anthers have fallen, protruding filaments usually visible) 30

        30 Stems stout (often 1.5 mm thick at ca. 3 cm below inflorescence) and very sharply angled (or even narrowly winged), ± soft and easily compressed (flattened in pressing); wider leaves 5-10 mm broad, with rather loose sheaths; perigynia spongy-thickened basally, on short slender stalks; anthers 1.3-2.6 mm long. . . . . *Carex sect.* **VULPINAE**

        30 Stems slender (not over 1.5 mm thick at ca. 3 cm below inflorescence, or rarely so in some species), firm, not wing-angled nor easily compressed (hence, not flattened in pressing); leaves, perigynia, and anthers various 31

            31 Spikes 10 or fewer, usually greenish at maturity, crowded or remote in a simple inflorescence (one spike, no branches, at each node of it) 32

32 Perigynia elliptic, essentially beakless, very plump (nearly terete) and filled by the achene; at least the lower spikes well separated, containing 1-5 perigynia. . . . . *Carex sect.* **DISPERMAE**

32 Perigynia ± ovate, beaked, plano-convex or lenticular; spikes various 33

33 Mature perigynia brownish; some spikes (especially terminal) entirely or mostly staminate or staminate at their bases only. . . . . *Carex sect.* **STELLULATAE**

33 Mature (not over-ripe) perigynia generally greenish; no spikes entirely or mostly staminate (a few may have stamens at their base in addition to their tip) . . . . *Carex sect.* **PHAESTOGLOCHIN**

31 Spikes numerous (10-many), yellowish or brownish at maturity; inflorescence tending to be compound, at least its lower nodes with 2 or more spikes crowded on a lateral branch . . . 34

34 Pistillate scales terminating in a distinct rough awn; bracts, at least lower ones, very slender and exceeding spikes or branches; ventral surface of leaf sheaths usually transversely wrinkled or puckered (very rarely smooth) . . *Carex sect.* **MULTIFLORAE**

34 Pistillate scales acute or minutely cuspidate; bracts mostly short, inconspicuous, or absent; leaf sheaths smooth ventrally . . . . *Carex sect.* **HELEOGLOCHIN**

14 Styles 3-cleft; achenes 3-sided (or nearly terete). 35

35 Perigynia at least sparsely puberulent, pubescent, hispidulous, or scabrous. 36

36 Perigynia 12-18 mm long, in 1-2 short-oblong to spherical spikes ca. 2-3.5 cm in diameter . . . . *Carex sect.* **LUPULINAE**

36 Perigynia 2-11 mm long, in 2-5 ± elongate, cylindrical spikes less than 2 cm in diameter 37

37 Perigynia with distinct and definite slender beak and/or the apex with 2 firm teeth. 38

38 Leaves hairy. 39

39 Beak of perigynium with minute, scarcely visible teeth; body of perigynium strongly 3-angled, closely enveloping the achene, essentially nerveless, tapered to a stalk-like base; stems pubescent . . . . *Carex sect.* **HIRTIFOLIAE**

39 Beak of perigynium with strong spreading teeth ca. 0.8 mm or more long; body of perigynium ± rounded, loosely enveloping achene (especially at summit), strongly ribbed, ± rounded (not cuneate-tapered) at base; stems glabrous . . . . *Carex sect.* **CAREX**

38 Leaves glabrous (often rough or scabrous, but not hairy). 40

40 Pistillate spikes not over 10 mm long (occasionally 12 mm in *C. communis*); achenes mostly with very convex or rounded sides (the angles thus obscured), at least apically, very tightly enveloped by the perigynium, especially on the apical half; anthers 1.5-3.7 mm long; plants of dryish habitats . . . . *Carex sect.* **ACROCYSTIS**

40 Pistillate spikes mostly over 10 mm long; achenes with flattish to slightly concave sides (the angles thus ± evident), the summit (especially around base of style) ± loosely enveloped by the perigynium; anthers 2.5-4.7 mm long; plants of dry to wet habitats 41

41 Perigynium beak usually more than half as long as the body, the apex not or weakly and obscurely toothed; perigynia scabrous or with short stiff ascending hairs. 42

42 Perigynia conspicuously 6-8 nerved; spikes densely flowered, with ca. 20-75 perigynia; basal sheaths pale brown . . . . *Carex sect.* **ANOMALAE**

42 Perigynia 2-ribbed, otherwise nerveless; spikes very loosely flowered with only 3-6 (-8) perigynia; basal sheaths reddish purple. . . . . *Carex sect.* **HYMENOCHLAENAE** . . . . (*C. assiniboinensis*)

41 Perigynium beak less than half as long as the body, with two firm apical teeth; perigynia ± densely short-hairy. 43

43 Perigynia 6-11 mm long, beak teeth 1.2-2.3 mm long, inner band of upper sheaths strongly purple-red tinged and thickened at apex, the thickened reddish portion opaque, smooth. . . . . *Carex sect.* **CAREX**

43 Perigynia 2.5-6.5 mm long, beak teeth 0.2-0.8 mm long, inner band of upper sheaths whitish to brown, brown- or purple-dotted, but not uniformly colored, not strongly opaque-thickened at apex, often scabrous. . . . . *Carex sect.* **PALUDOSAE**

37 Perigynia beakless or merely apiculate ("beak" not over 0.4 mm long) and the apex not toothed . . 44

44 Leaf sheaths (and usually the blades) ± pubescent, especially toward base of plant; terminal spike pistillate toward apex, staminate toward base. . . . . *Carex sect.* **POROCYSTIS**

44 Leaf sheaths and blades glabrous; terminal spike staminate toward apex . . . . *Carex sect.* **DIGITATAE**

35 Perigynia glabrous (in some species, papillose or granular, but not even sparsely puberulent) 45

45 Leaf sheaths (at least at apex) finely pubescent; blades often also pubescent or at least strongly hispidulous, especially toward base of plant 46

46 Beak of perigynium with firm teeth ca. 1.5–3 mm long; perigynia ca. 8–10 mm long, in spikes 4–12 cm long . . . . *Carex sect.* **CAREX** *(C. atherodes)*

46 Beak of perigynium with teeth scarcely 0.5 mm long or absent; perigynia less than 6 mm long, in spikes less than 3 cm long 47

47 Basal sheaths pale brown, leaf blades and stems glabrous or scabrous, perigynia with ca. 50 fine, impressed nerves . . . . *Carex sect.* **GRISEAE** *(C. hitchcockiana)*

47 Basal sheaths reddish purple tinged, leaf blades and stems pubescent, perigynia 5–12 nerved . . 48

48 Pistillate spikes laxly spreading or drooping on slender peduncles, the lowest (20–) 25–60 mm long (including portion inside sheath, if any); perigynia tapering to distinct beak . . . . *Carex sect.* **HYMENOCHLAENAE**

48 Pistillate spikes erect or ascending, sessile, short-peduncled or on stiff, erect peduncles less than 20 (–25) mm long; perigynia beakless. . . . . *Carex sect.* **POROCYSTIS**

45 Leaf sheaths and blades completely glabrous (though sometimes scabrous) 49

49 Perigynia ± rounded to broadly tapered at summit, beakless or essentially so (the tiny beak or apiculus less than 0.5 mm long if distinct, or up to 0.8 mm long if vaguely defined, often strongly bent or curved); beak or apiculus (if present) never toothed (or teeth scarcely 0.1 mm long) 50

50 Leaf blades not over 0.5 mm broad, linear-filiform; perigynia dark brown or nearly black at maturity, 2 mm or less long, in few-flowered spikes, of which at least the upper ones are on peduncles usually surpassing the sessile staminate spike . . . . *Carex sect.* **ALBAE**

50 Leaf blades 0.5 mm or more broad; perigynia and spikes various (but not as above) 51

51 Bract of lowest pistillate spike sheathless (at most with a thin sheath 1–3 mm long) 52

52 Terminal spike partly pistillate; pistillate spikes nearly or quite sessile and erect or ascending; roots glabrous or nearly so . . . . *Carex sect.* **RACEMOSAE**

52 Terminal spike normally entirely staminate; spikes and roots various 53

53 Pistillate spikes mostly drooping at maturity on slender peduncles; species of wet peat lands with roots with dense felt-like pubescence . . . . *Carex sect.* **LIMOSAE**

53 Pistillate spikes erect or ascending, sessile or peduncled; roots glabrous 54

54 Perigynia 2.5–3.4 mm wide; leaves involute, 0.5–2.5 mm wide . . . . *Carex sect.* **VESICARIAE** *(C. oligosperma)*

54 Perigynia 1–2.5 mm wide; leaves flat or folded, 1–35 mm wide . . . go to couplet 58

51 Bract of lowest pistillate spike with a sheath ca. 4 mm or more long 55

55 Terminal spike bearing some perigynia (very rarely a few individuals with one entirely staminate); plants very strongly reddish tinged at base 56

56 Staminate flowers at apex of terminal spike, pistillate flowers at base; cauline sheaths bladeless or with rudimentary blades up to 2 (rarely 4) cm long; pistillate spikes short-cylindric, bearing fewer than 10 perigynia, very long-peduncled, some elongate peduncles usually arising from base of plant . *Carex sect.* **DIGITATAE** *(C. pedunculata)*

56 Staminate flowers at base of terminal spike, pistillate flowers at apex; cauline sheaths with well-developed blades; pistillate spikes linear-cylindric, bearing more than 10 perigynia, on peduncles about as long as the spike or shorter, all arising from the upper part of the stem. . . . . *Carex sect.* **HYMENOCHLAENAE**

55 Terminal spike entirely staminate; plants reddish or not at base. 57

57 Perigynia concave- or at least cuneate-tapering toward the base, ± 3-angled and often somewhat broadly spindle-shaped 58

58 Plants with elongate deep or shallow rhizomes and very slender, firm stems; leaf blades ca. 1–4 mm wide . . . . *Carex sect.* **PANICEAE**

58 Plants without elongate rhizomes, the stems sharply triangular, sometimes nearly wing-margined, rather weak and easily compressed, soon shriveling after maturity of the fruit; leaf blades usually more than 4 (and up to 35) mm wide . . . . *Carex sect.* **LAXIFLORAE**

57 Perigynia convex-rounded toward the base, nearly or quite circular in cross-section (or very obscurely triangular), ellipsoid-cylindric to nearly spherical 59

59 Larger perigynia ca. 4–5 mm long, the nerves not raised above the surface at maturity. . . . . *Carex sect.* **GRISEAE**

59 Larger perigynia ca. 2–3.5 mm long; nerves various 60

60 Perigynia with the nerves not raised above the surface, usually ± impressed; staminate spike usually long-peduncled; plants not strongly rhizomatous nor with any pistillate spikes on basal peduncles *Carex sect.* **GRISEAE** *(C. conoidea)*

60 Perigynia with the nerves slightly raised above the surface; staminate spike nearly or quite sessile or, if long-peduncled, the plants strongly rhizomatous and with basal pistillate spikes . . . . *Carex sect.* **GRANULARES**

49 Perigynium abruptly contracted or more gradually tapering to a definite slender beak 0.5 mm or more long, or to an indistinct tapering beak 1 mm or more long; beak in some species with short apical teeth. 61

     61 Body of perigynium obovoid or obconic, ± truncately contracted into a distinct long slender beak; terminal spike often mostly pistillate (staminate at base only) . . . . . . *Carex sect.* **SQUARROSAE**

     61 Body of perigynium ovoid to lanceolate or ellipsoid, tapered or contracted into the beak; terminal spike usually staminate, at least apically 62

          62 Lower pistillate scales leaflike or bract-like, much exceeding the perigynia; achenes abruptly constricted to a short thick base; body of perigynium nearly terete, essentially nerveless except for 2 ribs; anthers ca. 0.5-1.6 mm long. . . . . *Carex sect.* **PHYLLOSTACHYAE**

          62 Lower pistillate scales scarcely if at all exceeding the perigynia; achenes not abruptly constricted at the base; perigynia and anthers various 63

               63 Perigynia in densely crowded spherical to very short-cylindric spikes, spreading and with the lowermost usually reflexed, usually strongly few-ribbed; at least the uppermost pistillate spikes ± sessile and often crowded; the terminal spike (staminate or partly pistillate) often sessile or short-peduncled. 64

                    64 Perigynia 2-6.2 mm long; basal sheaths brown . . . . *Carex sect.* **CERATOCYSTIS**

                    64 Perigynia 11-18 mm long; basal sheaths red-purple tinged . . . *Carex sect.* **LUPULINAE**

               63 Perigynia in elongate or long-peduncled spikes or both, all ascending, 2-ribbed or variously many-nerved; inflorescences various, but the upper spikes often not crowded and the terminal spike often long peduncled. 65

                    65 Bract of lowest pistillate spike sheathless (or pistillate spikes all crowded at base of plant in *Carex tonsa*); check several stems. 66

                        66 Pistillate scales subtending at least some of the perigynia terminated by a distinct slender scabrous awn; perigynia ca. 3-9 mm long 67

                             67 Scales toward apex of pistillate spikes merely acuminate or with awns shorter than their bodies (the latter easily visible, about half as long as perigynia or longer); staminate spikes 2 or more; body of perigynium rather gradually tapered to a beak ca. 1.5 mm long, including the short (not over ca. 0.8 mm) teeth. . . .
. . . . *Carex sect.* **PALUDOSAE**

                             67 Scales toward apex of pistillate spikes ordinarily with awns (as on the other pistillate scales) nearly or fully as long as their bodies (the latter small and mostly hidden among the bases of the densely crowded perigynia); staminate spike solitary (or very rarely a second smaller one present); body of perigynium tapered or strongly contracted into a beak ca. 1.2-3.5 mm long, including teeth up to 2.2 mm long. . . . . *Carex sect.* **VESICARIAE**

                        66 Pistillate scales smooth-margined and awnless or very short-awned, or at most with a scabrous margin toward an acuminate (sometimes inrolled) apex (occasionally a long rough awn in species with perigynia more than 9 mm long); perigynia 4-18 mm long 68

                             68 Basal sheaths pale brown; perigynia very narrowly lanceolate, 4-6.5 times as long as wide and not over 3 mm wide, many-nerved, tapering to apex (not strongly contracted into a beak); staminate spike solitary (pistillate spikes may be staminate at apex). . . . . *Carex sect.* **ROSTRALES**

                             68 Basal sheaths reddish purple tinged, at least on the youngest shoots; perigynia lanceolate or broader, less than 4 times as long as wide, or more than 3 mm wide, or strongly contracted into a conspicuous beak (or all of these); staminate spikes solitary or 2 or more. 69

                                 69 Perigynia strongly inflated, loose around achene, 2-8 mm wide 70

                                     70 Perigynia 4-12 mm long, ca. 6-12-nerved . . . . . *Carex sect.* **VESICARIAE**

                                     70 Perigynia 12-18 mm long, ca. 15-20-nerved. . . . *Carex sect.* **LUPULINAE**

                               69 Perigynia not inflated, ± tightly enclosing achene, 1-1.6 mm wide 71

                                   71 Pistillate spikes linear-cylindric, drooping or curving on slender peduncles; perigynia (somewhat twisted) and achenes strongly angled, the latter with concave sides; tall plants (stems over 3 dm high) with scattered thin leaves . . . . *Carex sect.* **HYMENOCHLAENAE** *(C. prasina)*

                                 71 Pistillate spikes short, thick, and few-flowered, often crowded at base of plant; perigynia and achenes very convex-sided; low plants (stems less than 1 dm high) with crowded, very stiff leaves . . . .
. . . . *Carex sect.* **ACROCYSTIS** *(C. tonsa)*

               65 Bract of lowest pistillate spike consistently with sheath 4 mm or more long 72

72 Perigynia (6-) 9-17 (-18) mm long; beak teeth usually conspicuous and stiff. . . . . .
. . . . **go to couplet 66**

72 Perigynia 2-6.5 (-9) mm long; beak teeth absent or weak and inconspicuous . . 73
   73 Perigynia with several to numerous conspicuous fine nerves the full length of
   each side 74
      74 Nerves of perigynia very numerous (ca. 20-65) and impressed, giving a
      longitudinally corrugated appearance; awns of pistillate scales rough or even
      ciliate . . . . *Carex sect.* **GRISEAE**
      74 Nerves of perigynia several to many (ca. 5-40) and slightly raised; awns of
      pistillate scales absent, smooth, or rough. 75
         75 Awns rough and/or tip of pistillate scales minutely ciliate; lower spikes
         drooping on long very thin peduncles; beak slightly bidentate at maturity;
         plants strongly reddish at base. . . . . *Carex sect.*
         . . . . **HYMENOCHLAENAE**
         75 Awns of pistillate scales usually smooth or absent; lower spikes mostly
         not drooping; beak not bidentate; plants pale, brown, or reddish at base
         76
            76 Perigynia ± sharply triangular with flattish sides, short-tapering at the
            base; stems bluntly trigonous, firm and not easily compressed; anthers
            mostly 3-4.5 mm long or lower pistillate spikes on elongate filiform
            spreading or drooping peduncles . . . . *Carex sect.* **CAREYANAE**
            76 Perigynia ± rounded-triangular with swollen sides, long-tapering to a
            ± stalk-like base; stems sharply triangular to nearly wing-margined,
            easily compressed; anthers mostly 1.5-3 mm long and lower pistillate
            spikes usually on erect or ascending peduncles . . . .
            . . . . *Carex sect.* **LAXIFLORAE**
   73 Perigynia with 2 (-3) main ribs, the sides otherwise nerveless or with much less
   prominent nerves 77
      77 Lowermost pistillate spikes erect or ascending at maturity. 78
         78 Staminate spike well-peduncled; perigynia ± convex-sided toward the
         base; bracts with poorly developed blades; plants mat-forming from long-
         creeping rhizomes . . . . *Carex sect.* **PANICEAE** *(C. vaginata)*
         78 Staminate spike sessile or nearly so; perigynia tapered-cuneate toward
         the base; bracts with well-developed blades; plants tufted. . . . .
         . . . . *Carex sect.* **LAXIFLORAE** *(C. leptonervia)*
      77 Lowermost pistillate spikes drooping on long very thin peduncles at maturity
      79
         79 Pistillate spikes not over 15 mm long *Carex sect.* **CHLOROSTACHYAE**
         79 Pistillate spikes mostly 20 mm or more long. . . . .
         . . . . *Carex sect.* **HYMENOCHLAENAE**

CAREX SECTION ACROCYSTIS

First sedges to flower each year, fruits maturing in spring and soon shed. Basal leaf sheaths in most species becoming fibrous with age. Perigynium beaks bidentate, less than 0.5 mm long. Most common in dry woods, prairies, and open sandy places; less common in mesic woods or wetlands. Similar to section Digitatae but basal sheaths not becoming fibrous.

1 Pistillate spikes on stems of varying length, at least some of the stems short (up to ca. 5 cm long)
and partly hidden among the tufted leaf bases; anthers ca. 1.5-2 mm long 2
   2 Bract of the lowest non-basal pistillate spike leaflike, equaling or exceeding the tip of the staminate spike;
   remnants of old leaves only slightly breaking into fibrous shreds at the base. 3
      3 Rhizomes slender; stems usually loosely tufted, arching or spreading, smooth except near inflorescence;
      perigynia 2.3-3.1 mm long. . . . . *C. deflexa*
      3 Rhizomes stout; culms densely cespitose, ascending, scabrous; perigynia 3.1-4.5 mm long . . . . . . *C. rossii*
   2 Bract of the lowest non-basal pistillate spike scale-like or bristle-like, not exceeding the staminate spike
   (or all spikes often on short basal stems, but foliage and stems stiffer and much more scabrous than in
   C. deflexa, which nearly always has some elongate stems); remnants of old leaves breaking into copious fibrous
   shreds at the base. 4
      4 Perigynia 3.2-4 mm long, the beak 1.2-1.6 (-2) mm, about half as long as the body or longer . . . . .*C. tonsa*

4 Perigynia 2.5-2.9 mm long, the beak 0.4-0.9 mm, about 1/4-1/3 as long as the body . . . .*C. umbellata*

1 Pistillate spikes all on elongate stems (none borne on short basal peduncles); anthers various 5

5 Main body of perigynium, not including spongy-tapered base or beak, orbicular to short-obovoid, about the same diameter as length; plants either with the widest leaves 3-8 mm broad or with elongate shallow rhizomes
. . . . 6

6 Widest leaves (at least the oldest dry ones) 3-5 mm broad; cauline leaves above base of plant (when present on stem) usually with the ligule longer than the width of the leaf; bract subtending the middle (and sometimes the lowest) pistillate spike(s) ± scarious-lobed at base, blade awn-like to leaflike, usually green, arising from between the lobes; staminate spike ca. 1-2 (-2.5) mm thick; plants without elongate rhizomes
. . . . *C. communis*

6 Widest leaves 1.5-3 (very rarely 3.5) mm broad; stem leaves with ligule no longer than the width; bracts subtending middle pistillate spikes tapered to apex, without an elongate awn-like or leaflike blade (the lowermost bract often green but seldom lobed); staminate spike ca. 2-3.5 (-5) mm thick; plants with stout, shallow elongate rhizomes with fibrous sheaths. 7

7 Larger perigynia 1.7-2.2 mm wide. . . . .*C. inops*

7 Larger perigynia 1.2-1.7 mm wide 8

8 Beak of perigynium 1-1.6 mm, half or more as long as the body . . . .*C. lucorum*

8 Beak of perigynium 0.2-0.8 mm, much less than half as long as the body . . . .*C. pensylvanica*

5 Main body of perigynium ± elliptic (to slightly obovoid or oblong), definitely longer than thick; plants with mostly narrow leaves and lacking stout elongate rhizomes 9

9 Widest leaves (at least the oldest dry ones) 3-5 mm broad; bract subtending the middle (and sometimes also the lowest) pistillate spike(s) ± scarious-lobed at base, the blade awn-like or leaflike, usually green, arising from between the lobes . . . . *C. communis*

9 Widest leaves not over 3 mm broad; bracts either scale-like or leaflike and lacking a scarious-lobed base.
. . . . 10

10 Lower two pistillate spikes 7.5-22 mm distant; lowest inflorescence bracts 18-35 mm long, 3/4 as long to exceeding inflorescence; loosely mat-forming from delicate, ascending rhizomes . .*C. novae-angliae*

10 Lower two pistillate spikes mostly close together, up to 7 mm distant; lowest inflorescence bracts rarely more than 17 mm long, often less than 3/4 as long the inflorescence; ± tufted 11

11 Bodies of mature perigynia about as long as their scales or even slightly shorter; beak of perigynium ca. 0.5-1.4 mm long. . . . . *C. albicans*

11 Bodies of mature perigynia mostly distinctly exceeding their scales; beak of perigynium ca. 0.4-0.7 mm long. 12

12 Perigynia 2-3 mm long, minutely puberulent to short-hairy; stems very slender (seldom over 0.4 mm thick) and mostly surpassed by the leaves . . . .*C. deflexa*

12 Perigynia 3-4 mm long, definitely short-hairy; stems usually 1 mm or more in thickness and surpassing the leaves. . . . . *C. peckii*

Carex albicans Willd.
(NO MAP)
WHITE-TINGE SEDGE
native

Plants densely tufted; rootstocks short, brownish, scaly. **Stems** to 25 cm long, weak, decumbent, roughened beneath head, reddish purple at base, bearing old leaves; sterile shoots few, long, with well developed leaves near top. **Well-developed leaves** several to a fertile culm, on lower 1/4 of culm; **blades** 1-3 cm long and 0.5-1.5 mm wide, canaliculate, green, roughened towards tip. **Terminal spike** staminate; **lateral spikes** 2-3, pistillate; the lowest bract scale-like, purplish tinged and hyaline-margined at base, the upper scale-like; **scales** purplish tinged with hyaline margins and broad green center. **Perigynia** 4-10 to a spike, about 3 mm long, ascending, dull olive- or yellowish green, pubescent, 2-ridged, the spongy base 0.5 mm long; beak 0.5-1 mm, bidentate, hyaline-tipped. **Achenes** 1.5 mm long, triangular with convex sides, brownish black with lighter angles, minutely pitted, minutely apiculate; stigmas 3, light-reddish brown.—Not yet known in Minn but may occur in southeastern region in open forests on dry acidic soils (known from adjacent Iowa and Wisconsin).

Carex albicans
perigynium (l)
pistillate scale (r)

Carex communis Bailey
MAP 1309
FIBROUS-ROOT SEDGE
native

Plants tufted; rootstocks short, ascending, scaly, reddish purple. **Stems** 1.5-5 dm long, rough on angles above, purplish red at base, the old leaves conspicuous; sterile shoots numerous. **Well-developed leaves** several to a fertile culm, near base; **blades** 2-5 cm long and 2-4 mm wide, flat, flaccid, light-green, rough especially towards the tip and on margins. **Terminal spike** staminate; **lateral spikes** 2-3, pistillate; lowest bract scale-like, hyaline-margined and purplish tinged at base, the upper reduced or scale-like; **scales** reddish purple or -brown with hyaline margins and 3-nerved green or straw-colored center. **Perigynia** 3-10 to a spike, 3-3.5 mm long, ascending, light-green, puberulent, 2-keeled, the spongy base 0.75 mm long; beak 0.5 mm, flattish, bidentate. **Achenes** triangular with convex sides, light-brown with lighter angles, minutely pitted, truncate and bent-apiculate; stigmas 3, reddish brown.—Forests, mostly ne Minn.

Carex communis
perigynium (l)
pistillate scale (r)

Carex deflexa Hornem.
NORTHERN SEDGE   MAP 1310
                                                  native

Plants loosely tufted. **Stems** 1-2 dm long, purple-tinged at base, shorter than the leaves. **Leaves** soft, 1-3 mm wide. Spikes either staminate or pistillate; **staminate spike** short, to 5 mm long; **pistillate spikes** on long, slender stalks near base of plant and also 2-4 spikes on stem near staminate spike; bract leaflike, to 2 cm long; pistillate scales ovate, shorter than perigynia. **Perigynia** green, oblong-ovate, 2-3 mm long, covered with short hairs, abruptly tapered to a small beak about 0.5 mm long. **Achenes** 3-angled; stigmas 3. June-Aug.—Moist woods and swamps, wetland margins, often where sandy or in sphagnum moss.

Carex deflexa
perigynium (l)
pistillate scale (r)

Carex inops Bailey
LONG-STOLON SEDGE   MAP 1311
Carex heliophila Mackenzie   *native*
Carex pensylvanica Lam. var. *digyna* Boeckl.

Rootstocks slender; **stolons** long, slender, horizontal. **Stems** to 35 cm long, stiff, wiry, rough on angles above, reddish brown-tinged and fibrillose at base, clothed with old leaves. **Well-developed leaves** 5-10 to a fertile culm; **blades** 4-20 cm long and 1-2.5 mm wide, channeled towards base, with revolute margins, thin, stiff, dull-green, roughened, attenuate; lower sheaths breaking and filamentose. **Terminal spike** staminate (occasionally gynaecandrous); **lateral spikes** 1-2 (-3), pistillate; lowest bract scale-like, reddish brown at base, the upper reduced; **scales** reddish brown or tawny, with white-hyaline margins and 1-3-nerved lighter center. **Perigynia** 5-15 to a spike, ascending, dull-green, puberulent, 2-keeled, spongy at base; beak 0.75 mm long, serrulate, bidentate. **Achenes** triangular with convex sides and sharp angles, closely enveloped, minutely apiculate; stigmas 3, reddish brown.—Sandy woods and fields.

Carex inops

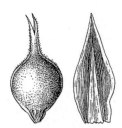

Carex inops
perigynium (l)
pistillate scale (r)

Carex lucorum Willd ex Link
BLUE RIDGE SEDGE   MAP 1312
                                                  native
Carex pensylvanica Lam. var. *distans* Peck

Plants tufted and stoloniferous; **stolons** horizontal, slender, scaly, reddish. **Stems** 1-3 dm long, roughened on angles above, reddish purple at base, clothed with old leaves, often fibrillose; sterile shoots lateral, long, reddish purple at base, the sheaths puberulent, becoming filamentose. **Well-developed leaves** 2-several to a fertile culm; blades to 3 cm long and 1.5-2.5 mm wide, flat or canaliculate, deep-

Carex lucorum
perigynium (l)
pistillate scale (r)

1309. *Carex communis*   1310. *Carex deflexa*   1311. *Carex inops*   1312. *Carex lucorum*

green, often roughened, especially towards the tip. **Terminal spike** staminate; **lateral spikes** 2-3, pistillate; bracts scale-like, enlarged at base, hyaline-margined and reddish purble; **scales** reddish purple with white-hyaline margins and lighter center. **Perigynia** 4-10 to a spike, 3.5-4 mm long, ascending or spreading-ascending, dull- or yellowish green, puberulent, 2-keeled, the spongy base 0.5-0.75 mm long; beak 1.5-2 mm long, bidentate, hyaline and purplish tinged at mouth. **Achenes** triangular with convex sides and narrow angles, brown, minutely pitted, minutely apiculate; stigmas 3, brown.—Dry woods.

Carex novae-angliae Schwein.
MAP 1313
NEW ENGLAND SEDGE   ❧ *threatened* | *native*

Plants loosely tufted and stoloniferous; **stolons** slender, scaly. **Stems** to 40 cm long, rough above, reddish purple and fibrillose at base, the old leaves conspicuous; sterile shoots lateral, long, the leaves mostly near top. **Well-developed leaves** 1-several to a fertile culm, on lower 1/3; **blades** to 15 cm long and 1-1.5 mm wide, thin, flaccid, soft, pale-green, roughened on margins and towards tip. **Terminal spike** staminate; **lateral spikes** 2-3, pistillate; **scales** cuspidate, hyaline, often reddish brown-tinged, the midvein green. **Perigynia** 2-10 to a spike, 2.5 mm long, ascending, light-green or yellowish brown, sparsely appressed pubescent, 2-ridged, the spongy base 0.5 mm long; beak to 0.5 mm long, bidentate. **Achenes** dark-brown, triangular with convex sides and blunt greenish angles, minutely apiculate; stigmas 3, dark-reddish brown.—Moist deciduous and conifer-deciduous woods.

Carex novae-angliae
perigynium (l)
pistillate scale (r)

Carex peckii Howe
MAP 1314
native
PECK'S SEDGE

Carex nigromarginata Schwein. var. *elliptica* (Boott) Gleason

Plants tufted and stoloniferous; **rootstocks** slender, scaly. **Stems** to 65 cm long, roughened beneath spikes, reddish purple at base; sterile stems long, the well developed leaves towards the top. **Well-developed leaves** several to a fertile culm, on lower 1/4; **blades** 1.5-4 cm long and 1-1.5 mm (larger on sterile stems), flat, green, roughened on margins and towards apex. **Terminal spike** staminate; **lateral spikes** pistillate, in an inflorescence 8-20 mm long; **scales** reddish brown with white-hyaline margins. **Perigynia** 3-12 to a spike, 3.5 mm long, ascending, grayish or yellowish green, hirsute-pubescent, 2-ridged, the base spongy, 0.5 mm long; beak 0.5 mm long, obliquely cut, bidentate, hyaline at mouth. **Achenes** yellowish brown, triangular with convex sides and blunt green angles, minutely apiculate; stigmas 3, dark-reddish brown.—Open woods.

Carex peckii
perigynium (l)
pistillate scale (r)

Carex pensylvanica Lam.
MAP 1315
native
PENNSYLVANIA SEDGE

Plants tufted and stoloniferous; **stolons** horizontal, slender, scaly, fibrillose, reddish. **Stems** 5-40 cm long, smooth or roughened on angles above, reddish purple at base, clothed with old leaves, often fibrillose; sterile shoots reddish purple at base, the sheaths puberulent, becoming filamentose. **Well-developed leaves** 2-several to a fertile culm; **blades** to 3 cm long and 1.5-3 mm wide, flat above, canaliculate towards base, often roughened especially towards tip. **Terminal spike** staminate; **lateral**

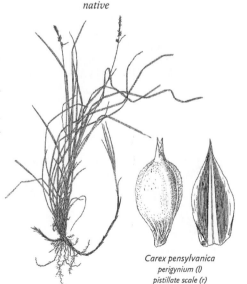

Carex pensylvanica
perigynium (l)
pistillate scale (r)

1313. *Carex novae-angliae*

1314. *Carex peckii*

spikes 1-4, pistillate; bracts scale-like, enlarged at base, hyaline-margined and reddish brown; **pistillate scales** reddish purple, with white-hyaline margins and lighter center. **Perigynia** 4-20 to a spike, 2.5-3 mm long, ascending, dull- or yellowish green, puberulent, 2-keeled, the spongy base to 0.75 mm long; beak 0.75 mm long, bidentate, hyaline and often purplish tinged at orifice. **Achenes** triangular with convex sides and narrow angles, brown, minutely pitted, minutely apiculate; stigmas 3, reddish brown.—Common in a wide range of dry to mesic woods and prairies.

Carex rossii Boott
ROSS'S SEDGE

Carex rossii
perigynium (l)
pistillate scale (r)

MAP 1316

🖤 *threatened | native*

Plants tufted; rootstocks short. **Stems** 1-8 dm tall, triangular. **Leaves** 1-2.5 mm wide; sheaths minutely hispidulose dorsally. **Spikes** unisexual, terminal spikes staminate, 8-15 mm long, lateral spikes pistillate; **pistillate scales** obtuse, short-awned. **Perigynia** green, short pubescent, 2-keeled, 3-4.5 mm long, base 0.5- 1.5 mm long, tip tapering to a serrulate beak 1.3-1.7 mm long. **Achenes** 2.3 mm long, obtusely triangular with concave sides; stigmas 3..—Rocky woods and bluffs, rare in ne Minn.

Carex tonsa (Fern.) Bickn.
SHAVED SEDGE
   Carex rugosperma Mackenzie

Carex tonsa
perigynium (l)
pistillate scale (r)

MAP 1317

native

Plants tufted; rootstocks stoutish, branching; **stolons** short-ascending. **Stems** to 15 cm long, stiff, roughened, reddish brown-tinged and fibrillose at base. **Leaves** numerous; **blades** 5-25 cm long and 2-4.5 mm wide, channeled with revolute margins, thick, stiff, deep-green, rough towards the tip. **Terminal spike** staminate; pistillate spike occasionally present near terminal spike; **basal pistillate spikes** long-peduncled; bract of upper spike setaceous, reddish at base; **pistillate scales** conspicuous, whitish or straw-colored, with 3-nerved greenish or straw-colored center. **Perigynia** 3-20 to a spike, 3.5-4.5 mmlong, appressed-ascending, compressed-orbicular, somewhat leathery, light-green, sparsely pubescent, 2-keeled, the base 0.75 mm long; beak to 2.5 mm long, 2-edged, serrulate, bidentate. **Achenes** triangular with convex sides and sharp angles, brownish, shining, pitted, truncate and minutely apiculate; stigmas 3.—Dry, sandy fields and open woods.

Carex umbellata Schkuhr
PARASOL SEDGE

Carex umbellata
perigynium (l)
pistillate scale (r)

MAP 1318

native

Plants densely tufted; rootstocks short, stout. **Stems** to 15 cm long, stiff, rough on angles, reddish brown-tinged and fibrillose at base. **Leaves** numerous; blades to 3 dm long and 1.5-2.5 mm wide, channeled towards base, flat and rough above, with revolute margins, firm, light-green. **Terminal spike** staminate; **lateral spikes** 3-4, pistillate or androgynous (staminate flowers above the pistillate); **bract** of upper spike scale-like, reddish tinged at base; **pistillate scales** hyaline with several-nerved green center. **Perigynia** 4-20 to a spike, 2-3 mm long, ascending, triangular-orbicular, dull-green, pubescent above, 2-keeled, the base 0.5 mm long; beak to 1 mm long, bidentate, hyaline-tipped. **Achenes** triangular with convex sides and sharp angles, filling perigynia, brownish black, shining, minutely pitted, minutely apiculate; stigmas 3.—Dry, often calcareous prairies.

1315. Carex pensylvanica

1316. Carex rossii

1317. Carex tonsa

1318. Carex umbellata

CAREX SECTION ALBAE

One member of the section in Minn. Rhizomes elongate, the plants forming mats. Leaf blades involute, wiry. Perigynia becoming dark in age, beaks short, white-tipped.

Carex eburnea Boott
MAP 1319
BRISTLE-LEAF SEDGE
native

Plants tufted; rootstocks long, slender, brownish. **Stems** 1-3.5 dm, obtusely triangular, brownish tinged at base. **Well-developed leaves** 3-6 to a fertile culm, near base; **blades** 5-25 cm long and 0.5 mm wide, often recurved-spreading, involute, firm, green, roughened. **Terminal spike** staminate; lateral spikes 2-4, pistillate, on peduncles 1-2.5 cm long; **bracts** bladeless, tubular, greenish or greenish yellow with white margins; **pistillate scales** whitish with green midrib, often yellowish brown-tinged. **Perigynia** 2-6 to a spike, 2 mm long, triangular, light-green or brownish, shining, puncticulate, 2-ribbed, finely nerved; beak short, cylindric, obliquely cut, hyaline at orifice. **Achenes** triangular with concave sides and thickened angles, closely enveloped, brown, granular, apiculate; stigmas 3, brownish.—Dry sand prairies, and rarely in fens.

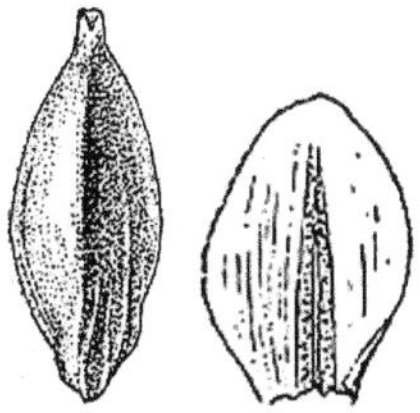

Carex eburnea
perigynium (l)
pistillate scale (r)

CAREX SECTION AMMOGLOCHIN

One member of the section in Minn.

Carex siccata Dewey
MAP 1320
DRY-SPIKE SEDGE
native

Plants tufted; rootstocks short, black, fibrillose. **Stems** 4-10 dm long, often nodding, roughened on angles beneath head, brownish at base, clothed with old leaves. **Well-developed leaves** 3-5 to a fertile culm, on lower third; **blades** 1-4 dm long and 2-4.5 mm wide, flat, green, roughened towards tip and on margins; sheaths green-and-white-mottled dorsally. **Spikes** 4-15, gynaecandrous (staminate flowers below the pistillate), in a flexuous linear inflorescence 2-6 cm long; **bracts** scale-like; **scales** silvery-green, often brownish tinged, with 3-nerved green center; staminate flowers few except in terminal spike. **Perigynia** 6-20 to a spike, 3-4.5 mm long, appressed-ascending, nearly concealed by scales, green or silvery-green, winged, strongly nerved, serrulate; beak 1-1.5 mm long, flat, serrulate obliquely cut, bidentate, hyaline-tipped, the orifice white-margined. **Achenes** lenticular, dull-yellowish brown, apiculate; stigmas 2, dark-reddish brown.—Dry sandy prairies and woods.

Carex siccata
perigynium (l)
pistillate scale (r)

CAREX SECTION ANOMALAE

One member of the section known from adjacent Wisconsin (not yet known from Minnesota). Upper surface of leaf blade and perigynia are scabrous.

Carex scabrata Schwein.
(NO MAP)
EASTERN ROUGH SEDGE
native

Plants colony-forming, rough-to-touch. **Stems** loosely clustered, 4-9 dm long. **Leaves** 4-14 mm wide, lowest leaves not reduced to scales. **Spikes** either staminate or pistillate; **staminate spike** single, 2-4 cm long, short-stalked; **pistillate spikes** 3-6, cylindric, 2-4 cm long, upright, the lower on long stalks, the upper stalkless or short-stalked; bracts leaflike; **pistillate scales** lance-shaped, about as long as the perigynia, tapered to a tip. **Perigynia** obovate, 3-angled, 2-ribbed, 3-5 mm long, finely coarse-hairy, few-nerved, abruptly tapered to a slightly curved, notched beak. **Achenes** 3-angled; stigmas 3. May-Aug. Low shaded areas in forests, streambanks, seeps.—Not yet known from Minn but to be expected on forested seeps in the St. Croix Valley; known from the Wisc side in Burnett County.

Carex scabrata
perigynium (l)
pistillate scale (r)

CAREX SECTION BICOLORES

Plants short, colonial, loosely tufted, shoots arising singly or few in a clump; rhizomes elongate; bases brown. Terminal spike staminate or gynecandrous, hidden by the crowded lateral spikes. Perigynia plump, golden to whitish, weakly veined; margins and apex rounded, beakless to short-beaked. Stigmas 2. Calcium-rich sites where somewhat disturbed.

1 Mature perigynia golden-orange when fresh (drying dark brown or, especially if immature, ± white); terminal spikes mostly all staminate (occasionally with a very few perigynia); pistillate scales ± loosely spreading, distinctly shorter than the mature perigynia (usually averaging 3/4 or less as long), most of them acute to cuspidate . . . . *C. aurea*

1 Mature perigynia white-pulverulent when fresh; terminal spikes usually staminate at base only, with several to numerous perigynia apically; pistillate scales ± appressed, nearly (averaging about 3/4) to quite as long as the perigynia, most of them blunt to acute . . . . *C. garberi*

Carex aurea Nutt.
GOLDEN-FRUIT SEDGE
native

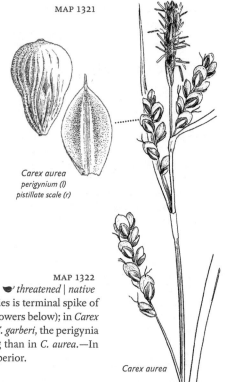

MAP 1321

Plants small, loosely tufted. **Stems** upright, 3-angled, 5–30 cm long. **Leaves** 1–4 mm wide. **Spikes** 2–5 per stem, the lower spikes stalked; spikes at ends of stems staminate, 3–18 mm long; lateral spikes pistillate, 8–20 mm long, the spikes clustered to widely spaced; **bract** of lowest spike longer than the head; **pistillate scales** white-tinged to yellow-brown, with a green midvein, tipped with a short, sharp point, shorter than the perigynia. **Perigynia** with short white hairs when young, becoming a distinctive gold-orange when mature (drying paler), round to obovate, beakless or with a very short beak, several-ribbed, 2–3 mm long. **Achenes** dark brown to black, lens-shaped; stigmas 2. May–July.—Moist to wet meadows, low prairie, swales, wet woods and along sandy or gravelly shores; often where calcium-rich.

Carex aurea
perigynium (l)
pistillate scale (r)

Carex garberi Fern.
ELK SEDGE

MAP 1322
☛ *threatened* | *native*

Similar to *Carex aurea;* one distinction between the 2 species is terminal spike of *C. garberi* is tipped with pistillate flowers (with staminate flowers below); in *Carex aurea,* terminal spike is of staminate flowers only. Also, in *C. garberi,* the perigynia are more granular, more crowded, and more overlapping than in *C. aurea.*—In Minn, rare in wet sedge fens and rocky shores of Lake Superior.

Carex aurea

CAREX SECTION CAREX

Plants typically colonial; rhizomes elongate. Vegetative stems prominent. Perigynia long-beaked with prominent beak teeth.

1 Perigynia covered with hairs . . . . *C. trichocarpa*
1 Perigynia smooth and hairless 2
   2 Inner band of the uppermost leaf sheaths red to purple and thickened at the summit, glabrous *C. trichocarpa*
   2 Inner band of leaf sheaths pale or brown, not thickened at the summit, glabrous or pubescent 3

1319. Carex eburnea

1320. Carex siccata

1321. Carex aurea

1322. Carex garberi

3 Vegetative stems hollow, easily flattened; inner band of the leaf sheaths pubescent, rarely glabrous, not obviously veined; basal leaf sheaths ladder fibrillose . . . . *C. atherodes*

3 Vegetative stems solid; inner band of the leaf sheaths strongly veined, glabrous or the veins scabrous; upper and lower leaf sheaths ladder fibrillose . . . . *C. laeviconica*

Carex atherodes Spreng.

SLOUGH SEDGE

MAP 1323
native

Plants loosely tufted, from long scale-covered rhizomes. **Stems** 3-angled, 5-12 dm long. **Leaves** 3-12 mm wide; sheaths hairy on back, brown to purple-tinged at the mouth, the lower sheaths shredding into narrow strands. **Spikes** either staminate or pistillate; **staminate spikes** 2-6 at ends of stems; **pistillate spikes** 2-4, widely spaced, cylindrical, 2-11 cm long; **bracts** leaflike, longer than the stems; **pistillate scales** thin, translucent or pale brown, shorter than the perigynia, tipped with a slender awn. **Perigynia** ovate, 6-11 mm long, long-tapered to a smooth beak, with many distinct nerves, the beak with spreading teeth 1.5-3 mm long. **Achenes** 3-angled; stigmas 3. June-Aug.—Marshes, wet meadows, prairie swales, stream and pond margins, usually in shallow water where may form dense colonies.

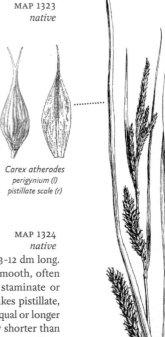

Carex atherodes
perigynium (l)
pistillate scale (r)

Carex laeviconica Dewey.

SMOOTH-CONE SEDGE

MAP 1324
native

Plants loosely tufted, from scaly rhizomes. **Stems** stout, 3-angled, 3-12 dm long. **Leaves** shorter to longer than the stem, 2-8 mm wide; **sheaths** smooth, often purple-tinged below and splitting into fibers. **Spikes** either all staminate or pistillate, the upper 2-6 staminate, 1-4 cm long; the lower 2-4 spikes pistillate, erect, separate, stalkless or short-stalked, cylindric; **bracts** leaflike, equal or longer than the head; **pistillate scales** acute or awn-tipped, the scale body shorter than the perigynium, translucent or brown on the sides. **Perigynia** green-yellow, broadly ovate, inflated, round in section, 4-9 mm long, strongly many-nerved, tapered to a slender beak 1.5-2 mm long. **Achenes** 3-angled; stigmas 3. June-July. —Streambanks and river floodplains. *Similar to* **slough sedge** *(C. atherodes), but leaf sheaths glabrous, the summit of the inner band strongly veined; leaf blades glabrous, not papillose on the underside.*

Carex atherodes

Carex trichocarpa Muhl.

HAIRY-FRUIT SEDGE

MAP 1325
native

Plants loosely tufted, with short rhizomes. **Stems** stout, 6-12 dm long, smooth below, rough-to-touch above. **Leaves** 2-6 mm wide, rough-to-touch on margins, upper leaves and bracts often longer than stems. **Spikes** either all staminate or pistillate, the upper 2-6 spikes staminate, long-stalked; **pistillate spikes** 2-4, cylindric, 4-10 cm long, the upper spikes more or less stalkless, the lower spikes on slender stalks; **pistillate scales** ovate, with white translucent margins, about half as long as perigynia. **Perigynia** ovate, usually covered with short white hairs, prominently ribbed, gradually tapered to a 2-toothed beak. **Achenes** 3-angled; stigmas 3. May-Aug.—Riverbanks and old river channels, marshes, wet meadows, low prairie. *Similar to* **slough sedge** *(C. atherodes) but sheaths strongly purple-tinged at tip, the leaf blades not hairy on underside, and the perigynia with short white hairs (vs. smooth in C. atherodes).*

Carex laeviconica
perigynium (l)
pistillate scale (r)

Carex trichocarpa
perigynium (l)
pistillate scale (r)

1323. *Carex atherodes*

1324. *Carex laeviconica*

1325. *Carex trichocarpa*

CAREX SECTION CAREYANAE

Resembling section Laxiflorae in general appearance, but stems generally firm. Perigynia acutely angled, tightly enclosing the achene; veins many, impressed in fresh plants, raised when dried.

1   Widest leaf blades less than 12 mm wide; plant bases brownish. . . . . ***C. laxiculmis***
1   Larger leaf blades (especially on vegetative shoots) mostly 8-25 mm wide, the bases of plants and the staminate scales strongly reddish. 2
     2   Sheaths of cauline bracts and leaves bladeless or nearly so; perigynia 4-5 mm long . . . . ***C. plantaginea***
     2   Sheaths of cauline bracts and leaves with flat green blades; perigynia 5-6.5 mm long . . . . ***C. careyana***

Carex careyana Torr.

CAREY'S SEDGE

MAP 1326

❦ *endangered* | *native*

Plants tufted; rootstocks short. **Stems** 3-6 dm long, purple-tinged at base; lower bladeless sheaths conspicuous. **Basal leaves** and those of sterile shoots with blades 7-25 cm long and 8-12 mm wide, the midlateral nerves prominent; upper blades shorter with purplish tinged sheaths to 3 cm long. **Terminal spike** staminate; **lateral spikes** 2-3, pistillate, the lower on slender peduncles to 5 cm long; bracts with sheaths purple-tinged; **pistillate scales** awned or acute, greenish white and purple-tinged with green midnerve. **Perigynia** 3-8 to a spike, ca. 6 mm long, ascending, triangular, olive-green, hispidulous, finely nerved; beak short, the orifice entire, hyaline. **Achenes** triangular with deeply concave sides, filling perigynia, yellowish brown, short bent-apiculate; stigmas 3. May-June.—Rich, moist woods.

Carex careyana
perigynium (l)
pistillate scale (r)

Carex laxiculmis Schwein.

SPREADING SEDGE

MAP 1327

❦ *threatened* | *native*

Plants tufted; rootstocks short. **Stems** 1.5-6 dm, weak, strigillose; bracts exceeding leaves, cinnamon-brown-tinged at base. **Basal leaves** 1-3 dm long and 4-12 mm wide, flat, thin, weak, the midnerve prominent below, roughened on margins; sheaths of fertile stems 1.5-4 cm, cinnamon-brown-tinged, red-dotted ventrally. **Terminal spike** staminate; lateral spikes 2-4, pistillate or androgynous, the lowest nearly basal, on drooping peduncles; **pistillate scales** white-hyaline with 3-nerved green center, cinnamon-brown-tinged and red-dotted, the lower empty. **Perigynia** 5-10 to a spike, 3-4 mm long, ascending, triangular, olive-green, hispidulous; beak short, erect or bent, the orifice entire, hyaline. **Achenes** triangular with deeply concave sides, filling perigynia, yellowish brown, short- (often bent-) apiculate; stigmas 3, reddish brown.—Moist woods of sugar maple and basswood, sometimes adjacent to seepages.

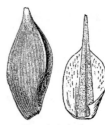

Carex laxiculmis
perigynium (l)
pistillate scale (r)

Carex plantaginea

Carex plantaginea Lam.

PLANTAIN-LEAF SEDGE

MAP 1328

❦ *endangered* | *native*

Plants tufted; rootstocks short. **Stems** 2.5-6 dm long, purple-tinged at base, the lower bladeless sheaths conspicuous. **Basal leaves** and those of sterile stems 15-35 cm long and 10-25 mm wide, flat, the mid-nerve prominent below, 2 lateral nerves prominent above, roughened on margins; fertile stem leaves bladeless or nearly so; sheaths purple-tinged. **Terminal spike** staminate; lateral spikes about 3, pistillate, the lower on slender peduncles; **bracts** bladeless, purple-tinged; **pistillate scales** white-hyaline with green midrib, purplish tinged. **Perigynia** 4-12 to a spike, 4-5 mm long, triangular; beak 1 mm, erect or curved, the orifice entire, hyaline. **Achenes** triangular with deeply concave sides, filling perigynia, brownish, apiculate; stigmas 3.—Rare in moist deciduousforests.

1326. *Carex careyana*

1327. *Carex laxiculmis*

1328. *Carex plantaginea*

Carex plantaginea
perigynium (l)
pistillate scale (r)

CAREX SECTION CERATOCYSTIS

Plants tufted; rhizomes short; bases brown. Terminal spike staminate, occasionally androgynous. Lateral spikes pistillate, densely flowered, globose to oblong. Perigynia strongly veined, abruptly beaked; beak toothed, generally reflexed. Stigmas 3. Usually where wet and calcareous.

1   Larger perigynia ca. 2-3 mm long, horizontally spreading, the beak about 1/4 to nearly 1/2 as long as the body . . . . ***C. viridula***

1   Larger perigynia ca. (3-) 3.5-6.2 mm long, at least the beaks becoming conspicuously reflexed on lower half of spike, the beak nearly or fully half as long as the body 2

    2   Pistillate scales at maturity strongly flushed with shiny brown or reddish color, hence conspicuous in the spike; widest leaves 3-5 mm wide . . . . ***C. flava***

    2   Pistillate scales greenish or yellowish, the same color as the perigynia and essentially invisible in the spikes; widest leaves 1.5-4 mm wide . . . . ***C. cryptolepis***

Carex cryptolepis Mackenzie
NORTHEASTERN SEDGE

MAP 1329
native

Plants tufted. **Stems** 2-6 dm long and longer than leaves. **Leaves** 2-4 mm wide. **Spikes** staminate or pistillate; **staminate spikes** short-stalked or stalkless, the stalk shorter than the pistillate spikes; **pistillate spikes** 3-4, the upper 2 spikes grouped, the third separate, the fourth spike lower on stem, short-cylindric, 1-2 cm long, stalkless; **bracts** leaflike and spreading; **pistillate scales** narrowly ovate, same color as perigynia and as long as perigynia body. **Perigynia** yellow-brown when mature, lower ones curved outward and downward, body obovate, 3-5 mm long, 2-ribbed and several nerved, contracted into a smooth beak 1-1.5 mm long. **Achenes** 3-angled; stigmas 3. June-Aug. —Wet meadows and marshy areas, peatlands, swamp margins; often where calcium-rich. *Similar to* **Carex flava**.

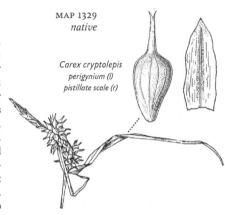

Carex cryptolepis
perigynium (l)
pistillate scale (r)

Carex flava L.
MAP 1330
YELLOW-GREEN SEDGE

native

Plants densely tufted, from short rootstocks. **Stems** stiff, 1-7 dm long, usually longer than the leaves. **Leaves** 4-8 to a stem, mostly near base, 3-5 mm wide. **Terminal spike** staminate (or rarely partly pistillate), stalkless or short-stalked; **pistillate spikes** 2-5, sometimes with staminate flowers at tip, the uppermost spikes nearly stalkless, the lower stalked; **bracts** conspicuous, leaflike, spreading outward, much longer than the head; **pistillate scales** ovate, narrower and much shorter than the perigynia, red-tinged except for the pale, three-nerved middle and the narrow translucent margins. **Perigynia** 15-35, crowded in several to many rows, 4-6 mm long, obovate, yellow-green becoming yellow with age, conspicuously ribbed, tapered to a slender, finely toothed beak about as long as the body, the tip notched. **Achenes** obovate, 3-angled, yellow-brown; stigmas 3. May-Aug.—Wet, peaty meadows, often where calcium-rich.

Carex flava
perigynium (l)
pistillate scale (r)

Carex viridula Michx.
LITTLE GREEN SEDGE

MAP 1331
native

Plants tufted. **Stems** stiff, slightly 3-angled, 0.5-4 dm long, longer than leaves. **Leaves** 1-3 mm wide; sheaths white-translucent. **Spikes** either staminate or pistillate (or sometimes mixed), the terminal spike staminate or with a few pistillate flowers at tip or middle, 3-15 mm long, short-stalked or stalkless, longer than the pistillate spikes or clustered with them; lateral spikes pistillate, 2-6, ovate to short-cylindric, 5-10 mm long, clustered and stalkless above, the lower spikes often separate and on short stalks; **bracts** leaflike, usually upright, much longer than the heads; **pistillate scales** brown on sides, rounded or with a short, sharp point, about equal to perigynia. **Perigynia** yellow-green to brown, rounded 3-angled, obovate, 2-4 mm long, 2-ribbed, tapered to a slightly notched beak 0.5-1 mm long. **Achenes** 3-angled; stigmas 3. May-Aug.—Wet meadows, sandy lake margins, fens and seeps; often where calcium-rich.

Carex viridula
perigynium (l)
pistillate scale (r)

CAREX SECTION CHLOROSTACHYAE

One member of the section in Minn. Plants small, densely tufted, with fibrous basal leaf sheaths and small beadlike perigynia borne in slender spikes on threadlike stalks.

Carex capillaris L.
HAIR-LIKE SEDGE

MAP 1332
native

Plants small, densely tufted. **Stems** slender, 3-angled, 1.5-4 dm long. **Leaves** mostly at base of plant and much shorter than stems, 1-3 mm wide; sheaths tight. **Spikes** either staminate or pistillate; terminal spike staminate, 4-8 mm long; lateral spikes 1-4, separated on stem, loosely flowered, short-cylindric, on threadlike, spreading to drooping stalks 5-15 mm long; **pistillate scales** white, translucent on outer edges, green or light brown in middle, blunt or acute at tip, shorter but usually wider than perigynia, deciduous. **Perigynia** shiny brown to olive-green, ovate, round in section, 2-4 mm long, 2-ribbed, otherwise without nerves, tapered to a translucent-tipped beak 0.5 mm or more long. **Achenes** 3-angled with concave sides; stigmas 3. June-July.—Alder thickets, wetland margins, usually in shade.

Carex capillaris
perigynium (l)
pistillate scale (r)

CAREX SECTION CHORDORRHIZAE

One member of the section in Minn. Plants stoloniferous, the stolons arching and rooting.

Carex chordorrhiza Ehrh.
ROPE-ROOT SEDGE

MAP 1333
native

Plants from long, creeping stems. **Flowering stems** upright, rounded 3-angled in section, 1-3 dm tall, single or several together, arising from axils of dried leaves on older, reclining sterile stems. **Leaves** several on stem, the lower ones often bladeless, 1-2 mm wide; sheaths translucent. **Spikes** 3-8, with both staminate and pistillate flowers, staminate flowers borne above pistillate, crowded in an ovate head 5-15 mm long; **bracts** absent; **pistillate scales** dark brown, ovate, about equaling the perigynia. **Perigynia** brown, compressed, ovate, 2-3.5 mm long, leathery, with many nerves on both sides; beak short. **Achenes** lens-shaped; stigmas 2. May-Aug.—Open floating mats around lakes and ponds, fens, conifer swamps, interdunal hollows.

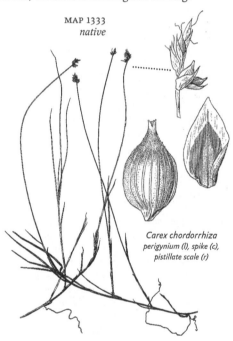

Carex chordorrhiza
perigynium (l), spike (c),
pistillate scale (r)

CAREX SECTION CYPEROIDEAE

One member of the section in Minn. Similar to the Ovales and sometimes placed within that section; distinguished by leafy bracts more than 3x as long as the inflorescence and very long-tapering perigynia, the beak often 2x longer than the body.

Carex sychnocephala Carey
MAP 1334
MANY-HEAD SEDGE   *native*

Plants tufted, from fibrous roots. **Stems** many and crowded, rounded 3-angled, 0.5-6 dm long. **Leaves** 1.5-4 mm wide; sheaths tight, white- translucent. **Spikes**

1329. Carex cryptolepis

1330. Carex flava

1331. Carex viridula

1332. Carex capillaris

with both staminate and pistillate flowers, pistillate flowers borne above staminate, densely clustered in ovate heads 1.5-3 cm long; **bracts** leaflike, 2-4 per head, the longest bracts much longer than the heads; **pistillate scales** thin and translucent with a green midvein, 2/3 length of perigynia, tapered to a tip or with a short sharp point. **Perigynia** green to straw-colored, flat, lance-shaped, 5-7 mm long and to 1 mm wide, narrowly wing-margined, spongy at base when mature, tapered to a finely toothed, notched beak 3-5 mm long. **Achenes** lens-shaped; stigmas 2. June–Aug.—Wet meadows, sandy lakeshores, marshes.

*Carex sychnocephala
perigynium (l), spike (c),
pistillate scale (r)*

CAREX SECTION DEWEYANAE

Two members of the section in Minn. Plants tufted; rhizomes mostly short; bases brown. Inflorescence slender, open, at least the lowest spike(s) distinct; bracts setaceous. Spikes mostly gynecandrous, lateral spikes sometimes pistillate, mixed, or (rarely) staminate. Perigynia appressed to ascending, ovate to lanceolate, plano-convex, slender; base spongy; beak distinct, margins serrate, tip bidentate. Achenes mostly filling the perigynium body. Usually in moist to wet shaded places.

1   Perigynia ca. 0.8-1.2 mm wide and ca. 4-5 times as long as wide, conspicuously nerved on dorsal face, weakly to strongly nerved on ventral face. . . . . **C. bromoides**

1   Perigynia ca. 1.3-1.6 mm wide and usually ca. 3-3.5 times as long as wide, faintly nerved or nerveless on both faces . . . . **C. deweyana**

Carex bromoides Schkuhr
BROME-LIKE SEDGE

MAP 1335
native

Plants densely tufted. **Stems** very slender, 3-8 dm long. **Leaves** 1-2 mm wide. **Spikes** 3-7, narrowly oblong, 1-2 cm long, **terminal spike** with both staminate and pistillate flowers, the staminate below pistillate; **lateral spikes** all pistillate or with a few staminate flowers at base, the spikes clustered or overlapping; **pistillate scales** obovate, about as long as perigynia body, pale brown or orange-tinged with translucent margins, tapered to tip or short-awned. **Perigynia** lance-shaped, flat on 1 side and convex on other, light green, 4-6 mm long, nerved on both sides, gradually tapered to a finely sharp-toothed beak, the beak 1/2-2/3 as long as body. **Achenes** lens-shaped, in upper part of perigynium body; stigmas 2. April-July. —Floodplain forests, old river channels, swamps.

*Carex bromoides
perigynium (l)
pistillate scale (r)*

Carex deweyana Schwein.
DEWEY'S SEDGE

MAP 1336
native

Plants loosely tufted, from short rhizomes. **Stems** weak and spreading, 2-12 dm long, rough-to-touch below the head. **Leaves** shorter than stems, yellow-green to waxy blue-green, soft, flat, 2-5 mm wide; sheath tight. **Spikes** 2-6, the lower separate, the upper grouped, forming a head 2-6 cm long and often drooping near tip; **terminal spike** with staminate flowers at base, **lateral spikes** usually pistillate, the perigynia upright; **pistillate scales** ovate, blunt to short-awned at tip, thin and translucent with green center, slightly shorter than perigynia. **Perigynia** flat on 1 side and convex on other, 4-6 mm long, pale-green, very spongy at base, the beak 2-3 mm long, finely toothed and weakly notched. **Achenes** lens-

*Carex deweyana
perigynium (l)
pistillate scale (r)*

1333. Carex chordorrhiza

1334. Carex sychnocephala

1335. Carex bromoides

1336. Carex deweyana

shaped, nearly round, yellow-brown; stigmas 2. May-Aug.—Thickets, swamps, and moist to dry woods.

CAREX SECTION DIGITATAE

Basal sheaths not fibrous. Bracts reduced to bladeless sheaths. Perigynium beaks untoothed, mostly less than 0.5 mm long. Similar to section Acrocystis but basal sheaths not fibrous.

1   Terminal spike pistillate at base; basal spikes usually present, on long very thin peduncles; pistillate scales abruptly truncate and awned . . . . ***C. pedunculata***
1   Terminal spike usually entirely staminate; basal spikes not present; pistillate scales not awned . . . ***C. richardsonii***

Carex pedunculata Muhl.
LONG-STALK SEDGE

MAP 1337
native

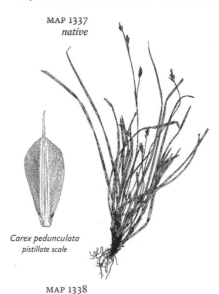

Rootstocks stout, woody, branching. **Fertile stems** 2-3 dm long, decumbent, roughened on angles, purple-tinged at base; sterile shoots purple-tinged. **Upper leaves** of fertile stems bladeless, the sheaths loose, reddened at base; **basal leaves** 3-5; **blades** 15-35 cm long and 2-3 mm wide, flat, thickish, pale-green, glaucous, roughened, especially on margins and nerves above. **Terminal spike** staminate or usually androgynous (staminate flowers above the pistillate); **lateral spikes** 3-4, pistillate or usually androgynous, the lowest basal, long-peduncled; **bracts** sheathing, reddish purple-tinged at base; pistillate scales ciliate, purple with 3-nerved green center. **Perigynia** 1-8 to a spike, 3.5-4.5 mm long, appressed, triangular, deep-green, minutely puberulent, 2-ridged, spongy at base; beak minute, usually bent, the orifice entire. **Achenes** triangular with concave sides, closely enveloped in upper part of perigynia, short bent-apiculate; stigmas 3, deciduous.—Rich, mesic forests.

Carex pedunculata
pistillate scale

Carex richardsonii R. Br.
RICHARDSON'S SEDGE

MAP 1338
native

Plants loosely tufted; rootstocks long, ascending, slender, brownish black, scaly. **Stems** 15-35 cm long, roughened on angles above, dark-brownish at base. **Well-developed leaves** 6-10 to a fertile culm, near base; blades 1-2.5 dm long and 2-2.5 mm wide, thick, light-green, rough on margins, especially towards the tip; upper leaves bladeless, the sheaths reddish purple with hyaline margins. **Terminal spike** staminate; lateral spikes usually 2, pistillate; **bracts** bladeless, purple-tinged and white-hyaline-margined; **pistillate scales** dark-purplish with hyaline margins and lighter midvein. **Perigynia** 10-25 to a spike, 2.5-3 mm long, ascending, obscurely triangular, straw-colored or light-brownish above, appressed-pubescent, 2-keeled; beak 0.5 mm, the orifice obliquely cut. **Achenes** triangular with sides convex above, closely enveloped, brownish, shining, conic-apiculate; stigmas 3, blackish.—Dry sandy prairies and barrens; rarely in fens.

Carex richardsonii
pistillate scale

CAREX SECTION DISPERMAE

One member of the section in Minn. Plants slender, shoots single or in small bunches from pale, slender rhizomes; spikes few-flowered, androgynous; perigynia spreading, plump.

1337. Carex pedunculata   *1338. Carex richardsonii*   *1339. Carex disperma*   *1340. Carex duriuscula*

Carex disperma Dewey
SOFT-LEAF SEDGE

MAP 1339
native

Plants small, loosely tufted, from slender rhizomes. **Stems** slender, weak, 3-angled, 1-4 dm long, shorter to longer than leaves. **Leaves** soft and spreading, 1-2 mm wide; sheaths tight, translucent. **Spikes** with both staminate and pistillate flowers, staminate flowers borne above pistillate, 2-5, few flowered and small, with 1-6 perigynia and 1-2 staminate flowers, to 5 mm long, stalkless, separate or upper spikes grouped in interrupted heads 1.5-2.5 cm long; **bracts** sheathlike and resembling the pistillate scales, or threadlike and to 2 cm long; **pistillate scales** white, translucent except for the darker midrib, tapered to tip or short-awned, 1-2 mm long. **Perigynia** convex on both sides to nearly round in section, oval, 2-3 mm long, strongly nerved and rounded on the margins, beak tiny. **Achenes** lens-shaped, oval; stigmas 2. May-July.—Hummocks in conifer swamps and alder thickets, wetland margins; usually where shaded.

Carex disperma
spike (l), perigynium (c),
pistillate scale (r)

CAREX SECTION DIVISAE

Plants strongly rhizomatous, unisexual. Not native in most of e North America but spreading, especially along expressways, where tolerant of road salt.

1 Stems obtusely angled, smooth; rootstock 1-2 mm thick, slender; leaves involute, 1-2 mm wide ... **C. eleocharis**
1 Stems acutely triangular, roughened above; rootstock 2-6 mm thick, stout; leaves flattened, 2-5 mm wide ....
    .... **C. praegracilis**

Carex duriuscula C.A. Mey.
NEEDLE-LEAF SEDGE

MAP 1340
native

  Carex eleocharis Bailey.
  Carex stenophylla var. *duriuscula* (C.A.Mey.) Trautv.

Plants rhizomatous; rootstock long, slender, brown. **Stems** to 2 dm tall, obtusely triangular. **Leaves** 1-2 mm wide, involute; sheaths tight. **Spikes** with both staminate and pistillate flowers, androgynous (staminate flowers above the pistillate), **pistillate scales** acute to obtuse and cuspidate. **Perigynia** plano-convex, straw-colored to nearly black, striate dorsally, 2.5-3 mm long, contracted to a serrulate beak shorter than the body. **Achenes** ca. 1.7 mm long, lenticular; stigmas 2.—Dry prairies, rocky hilltops, and sandy places. *Immature or depauperate plants of this species may be confused with the similar Carex praegracilis.*

Carex duriuscula
perigynium (l)
pistillate scale (r)

Carex praegracilis W. Boott
CLUSTERED FIELD SEDGE

MAP 1341
native

Plants colony-forming, from long black rhizomes. **Stems** single or few together, 3-angled, 1-7 dm long, longer than the leaves. **Leaves** on lower part of stems, 2-3 mm wide; sheaths white-translucent. **Spikes** with both staminate and pistillate flowers, staminate flowers above pistillate, or spikes nearly all staminate or pistillate, 4-8 mm long, upper spikes crowded, lower spikes separated, in narrowly ovate heads 1-4 cm long; **bracts** absent; **pistillate scales** brown, shiny, shorter or equal to perigynia. **Perigynia** green-brown, turning dark brown, flat on 1 side and convex on other, ovate to lance-shaped, 3-4 mm long and 1 mm wide, sharp-edged, spongy at base, tapered to a finely toothed beak 2 mm long, unequally notched. **Achenes** lens-shaped, 1-2 mm long; stigmas 2. May-June.—Wet to moist meadows, shores, streambanks and ditches; along salted highways.

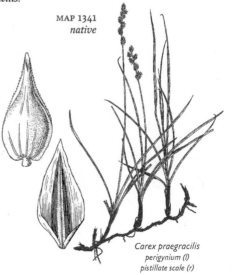

Carex praegracilis
perigynium (l)
pistillate scale (r)

CAREX SECTION FILIFOLIAE

One member of the section in Minn.

Carex filifolia Nutt.
THREAD-LEAF SEDGE

MAP 1342
native

Plants densely tufted; rootstock short, black. **Stems** to 8 dm tall, slightly triangular. **Leaves** only ca. 0.3 mm wide. **Spikes** solitary, 3-5 mm long, with both staminate and pistillate flowers, androgynous (staminate flowers above the pistillate); **pistillate scales** obtuse. **Perigynia** obtusely triangular, white-striate, puberulent above, slightly 2-ribbed, 3-5 mm long, tapering to a short beak to 0.4 mm long. **Achenes** 2.2-3 mm long, triangular; stigmas 3.—Dry prairies; a common sedge of the Great Plains.

Carex filifolia
perigynium (l)
pistillate scale (r)

CAREX SECTION GLAREOSAE

Tufted sedges of wetlands, soils often peaty. Spikes distinct, mostly nonoverlapping (except *Carex arcta* which has spikes overlapping, the upper not separated), mostly or all gynecandrous, lateral spikes sometimes pistillate. Perigynia ascending to spreading; margins rounded in most species, smooth or finely serrate, often finely papillose.

1 Lowest bract bristle-like, several times as long as its spike; perigynia mostly 2.8-3.8 (-4) mm long, including very short smooth beak; spikes widely separated, containing 1-5 perigynia each . . . . **C. trisperma**
1 Lowest bract absent or at most about twice as long as its spike (if rarely prolonged, the perigynia smaller and often with serrulate beak); perigynia and spikes various 2
  2 Perigynia broadest near the base of the body, with a conspicuous beak 0.7-1.1 mm long; spikes mostly 7-15, usually ± overlapping or crowded into an ovoid to narrowly pyramidal head 2-4.5 cm long. . . . . **C. arcta**
  2 Perigynia broadest at or near the middle of the body; beak essentially absent or less than 0.6 mm long; spikes 2-8, at least the lower spikes well separated or, if crowded, the inflorescence only 0.6-2 cm long. 3
    3 Spikes 2-4, crowded into a short inflorescence 0.6-2 cm long; perigynia 2.5-3.5 mm long, beak often smooth-margined . . . . **C. tenuiflora**
    3 Spikes 4-8 (-10), remote or ± crowded, but total inflorescence over 2 cm long; perigynia 1.7-2.6 mm long, beak serrulate usually minutely or scabrous 4
      4 Perigynia ca. 3-9 per spike (occasionally one or two spikes on a plant, especially terminal one, with as many as 15), loosely spreading, becoming rich brown in age; largest leaves 1-2 mm wide; foliage and perigynia green when fresh . . . . **C. brunnescens**
      4 Perigynia mostly 10-many per spike, appressed-ascending, greenish or dull brown in age; largest leaves 2-3 mm wide; foliage and perigynia glaucous or gray-green at least when fresh . . . . **C. canescens**

Carex arcta Boott
NORTHERN CLUSTER SEDGE

MAP 1343
native

Plants loosely to densely tufted, from very short thick rhizomes. **Stems** 2-8 dm long, soft, sharply triangular, very rough-to-touch above. **Leaves** clustered near base, light-green, flat, 2-4 mm wide, very rough; sheaths loose, purple-dotted. **Spikes** 5-15, each with both staminate and pistillate flowers, the staminate small and below the pistillate; flowers crowded in oblong heads, 1.5-3 cm long, upper spikes densely packed, lower spikes slightly separate; **pistillate scales** ovate, acute, translucent with a brown-tinged center, shorter than the perigynia. **Perigynia** flat on 1 side and convex on other, ovate, 2-3 mm long, green to straw-colored or brown when mature, covered with white dots, widest near the broad base, tapered to a sharp-toothed, notched beak 0.5-1.5 mm long. **Achenes** lens-shaped,

Carex arcta
perigynium (l)
pistillate scale (r)

1341. Carex praegracilis   *1342. Carex filifolia*   *1343. Carex arcta*   *1344. Carex brunnescens*

brown; stigmas 2. June–Aug.—Floodplain forests, old river channels, swamps and wetland margins.

Carex brunnescens (Pers.) Poir.
MAP 1344
BROWNISH SEDGE *native*

Plants densely tufted, from a short fibrous rootstock. **Stems** sharply 3-angled, to 5 dm long, smooth or slightly rough-to-touch below the head. **Leaves** 1–3 mm wide; sheaths tight, thin and translucent. **Spikes** 5–10 in a head 2–5 cm long, all with pistillate flowers borne above staminate, each spike with 5–15 perigynia, lower spikes separated; lowermost **bract** bristlelike, shorter or longer than lowermost spike; **pistillate scales** ovate, rounded or acute at tip, shorter than the perigynia. **Perigynia** 3-angled, not winged or sharp-edged, 2–3 mm long, faintly nerved on both sides, not spongy-thickened at base, tapered at tip to a short, minutely notched beak, the beak and upper body finely toothed and white-dotted. **Achenes** lens-shaped; stigmas 2. June–Aug.—Wet forests and swamps, peatland margins.

Carex brunnescens
perigynium (l), spike (c),
pistillate scale (r)

Carex canescens L.
MAP 1345
HOARY SEDGE *native*

Plants tufted. **Stems** 2–6 dm long. **Leaves** waxy blue- or gray-green, 2–4 mm wide, mostly near base of plant and shorter than stems. **Spikes** 4–8, silvery green or grayish, with both staminate and pistillate flowers, the staminate below the pistillate, ovate to cylindric, 5–10 mm long, the lower spikes more or less separate, each spike with 10–30 perigynia. **Perigynia** flat on one side and convex on other, 2–3 mm long and 1–2 mm wide, with a beak to 0.5 mm long, not noticeably finely toothed on the margins; **pistillate scales** shorter than perigynia. **Achenes** lens-shaped; stigmas 2. May–July. Peatlands (including hummocks in patterned fens), tamarack swamps, floating mats, swamps, alder thickets, wet forest depressions. *Similar to **Carex brunnescens** but leaves waxy blue-green rather than green and spikes somewhat larger and silver-green vs. brown.*

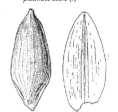

Carex canescens
perigynium (l), spike (c),
pistillate scale (r)

Carex tenuiflora Wahlenb.
MAP 1346
SPARSE-FLOWER SEDGE *native*

Plants delicate, loosely tufted; spreading from long, slender rhizomes. **Stems** very slender, 2–6 dm long. **Leaves** 1–2 mm wide. **Spikes** 2–4, with both staminate and pistillate flowers, the staminate below the pistillate, stalkless, clustered into a head 8–15 mm long; **pistillate scales** white-translucent with green center, covering most of the perigynium. **Perigynia** 3–15, oval, flat on 1 side and convex on other, 3–4 mm long, dotted with small white depressions, sharp-edged, beakless. **Achenes** lens-shaped, nearly filling the perigynia; stigmas 2. June–Aug.—Hummocks in peatlands, floating mats, conifer swamps.

Carex tenuiflora
perigynium (l)
pistillate scale (r)

Carex trisperma Dewey
MAP 1347
THREE-SEED SEDGE *native*

Loosely tufted perennial, with short, slender rhizomes. **Stems** very slender and weak, 2–7 dm long. **Leaves** 1–2 mm wide. **Spikes** 1–3 (usually 2), stalkless, 1–4 cm apart in a slender, often zigzagged head, each spike with 2–5 perigynia and a few staminate flowers at the base; lowest spike subtended by a bristlelike bract 2–4 cm long; **pistillate scales** ovate, translucent with a green center, shorter or equal to the perigynia. **Perigynia** flat on 1 side and convex on other, oval, 3–4 mm long, finely many-nerved, tapered near tip to a short, smooth beak 0.5 mm long. **Achenes** oval-oblong, filling the perigynia; stigmas 2. May–Aug.—Forested wetlands and conifer swamps, alder thickets.

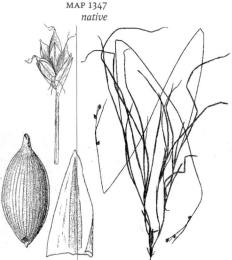

Carex trisperma
perigynium (l), spike (c),
pistillate scale (r)

CAREX SECTION GRANULARES

Plants tufted or shoots arising singly from elongate rhizomes. Pistillate spikes oblong to narrowly oblong, densely packed with perigynia. Pistillate scales and perigynia dotted or finely streaked with red. Perigynia more than 25 per pistillate spike; veins 25–40, raised.

1   Staminate spike long-peduncled, elevated above summit of uppermost pistillate spikes; lowest pistillate spike usually on a separate basal peduncle; stems mostly solitary from elongate rhizomes; widest leaves 1.5–4 mm broad .... *C. crawei*

1   Staminate spike sessile or nearly so; lowest pistillate spike not on a basal peduncle; stems clumped, without elongate rhizomes; widest leaves 4.5–10 mm broad .... *C. granularis*

Carex crawei Dewey
CRAWE'S SEDGE

MAP 1348
native

Plants from long-creeping rhizomes. **Stems** single or several together, faintly 3-angled, 0.5–4 dm long. **Leaves** 1–4 mm wide. **Spikes** either staminate or pistillate, cylindric, densely flowered, 1–3 cm long, terminal spike staminate; lateral spikes pistillate, 2–5, separate, the lowest spike near base of plant; **bract** leaflike, the blade shorter than the terminal spike; **pistillate scales** red-brown with a pale or green midrib, shorter and narrower than the perigynia. **Perigynia** green to brown, ovate, 2–3.5 mm long, many-nerved; beak absent or very short, entire to notched. **Achenes** 3-angled; stigmas 3. May–July.—Wet to moist meadows and prairies, marly lakeshores, ditches, especially where calcium-rich.

Carex crawei
perigynium (l)
pistillate scale (r)

Carex granularis Muhl.
LIMESTONE-MEADOW SEDGE

MAP 1349
native

Plants tufted, from short rhizomes. **Stems** rounded 3-angled, 1–5 dm long. **Leaves** often longer than stems, 3–13 mm wide; sheaths membranous on front, divided-with small swollen joints on back. **Spikes** either all staminate or pistillate, the terminal spike staminate, stalkless; the lateral spikes pistillate, clustered around the staminate spike; **bracts** longer than the head; pistillate **scales** brown, tapered to tip or with a short, sharp point, half as long as perigynia. **Perigynia** crowded in several rows, green or olive to brown, oval to obovate, 2–3 mm long, 2-ribbed, strongly nerved; beak tiny or absent, entire to slightly notched. **Achenes** 3-angled; stigmas 3. May–July.—Wet to moist meadows and swales, streambanks and pond margins, especially where calcium-rich.

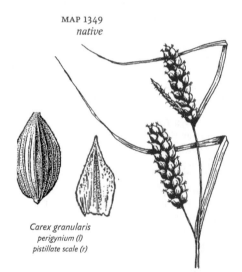

Carex granularis
perigynium (l)
pistillate scale (r)

CAREX SECTION GRISEAE

Perigynia round or obtusely angled in cross-section, many-veined; veins impressed on both fresh and dried plants. Pistillate scales awned.

1   Perigynia contracted to a distinct beak 0.5–1.3 mm long 2
   2   Leaf sheaths strongly hispidulous; perigynia ca. 4–5.5 mm long; plants brownish at base .... *C. hitchcockiana*
   2   Leaf sheaths glabrous; perigynia ca. 3.5–4 mm long; plants reddish at base .... *C. oligocarpa*
1   Perigynia essentially beakless 3

1345. *Carex canescens*

1346. *Carex tenuiflora*

1347. *Carex trisperma*

1348. *Carex crawei*

3   Peduncles of lateral spikes finely scabrous; staminate spike long-peduncled; perigynia 2.5-3.6 (-4) mm long, usually more than 20 per spike. . . . . ***C. conoidea***

3   Peduncles of lateral spikes smooth; staminate spike sessile or nearly so; perigynia 4-5 mm long, usually fewer than 15 per spike . . . . ***C. grisea***

Carex conoidea Schkuhr
OPEN-FIELD SEDGE
Carex katahdinensis Fernald

MAP 1350
native

Plants tufted. **Stems** 1-7 dm long, much longer than leaves. **Leaves** 2-4 mm wide. **Spikes** either staminate or pistillate; staminate spike on a long stalk and overtopping pistillate spikes, linear, 1-2 cm long; pistillate spikes 2-4, widely spaced or upper 2 grouped, short cylindric, 1-2 cm long, on short, rough stalks; **bract** leaflike with a rough sheath; **pistillate scales** ovate and much shorter than perigynia, with a green midvein prolonged into an awn. **Perigynia** oval, 3-4 mm long and 1-2 mm wide. **Achenes** 3-angled; stigmas 3. May-July.—Wet calcareous prairies, sedge meadows; also in drier old fields.

Carex conoidea
perigynium (l)
pistillate scale (r)

Carex grisea Wahlenb.
INFLATED NARROW-LEAF SEDGE
Carex amphibola Steud. var. *turgida* Fern.

MAP 1351
native

Plants tufted; rootstocks short. **Stems** 2-6 dm long, purple-tinged at base. **Leaves** 1-3 dmlong and 2-4 mm wide, flat, thin, deep-green, the midvein prominent below, roughened towards the tip; sheaths red-dotted. **Terminal spike** staminate, rough-peduncled; **lateral spikes** 3-5, pistillate, the lowest nearly basal; bracts sheathing; **pistillate scales** awned, white-hyaline with green midvein, yellowish brown-tinged and red-dotted. **Perigynia** 4-12 to a spike, 3.5-4.5 mm long, erect, exceeding scales, suborbicular, somewhat leathery, light-green or yellowish brown, minutely puncticulate, the orifice hyaline, entire. **Achenes** triangular with concave sides, loosely enveloped, yellowish brown, granular, apiculate; stigmas 3, reddish brown.—Mesic to wet deciduous forests, roadside ditches.

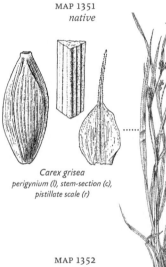

Carex grisea
perigynium (l), stem-section (c),
pistillate scale (r)

Carex hitchcockiana Dewey
HITCHCOCK'S SEDGE

MAP 1352
native

Plants tufted; rootstocks short. Stems 1.5-7 dm long, roughened above, brownish tinged at base. **Leaves** 3-4 to a culm, 1-2.5 dmlong and 3-7 mm wide, flat, thin, light-green, the midvein conspicuous below, roughened on margins and towards tip on veins; **sheaths** conspicuously prolonged, cinnamon-brown-tinged; ligule ciliate. **Terminal spike** staminate, the peduncle rough; **lateral spikes** 3-4, pistillate, the rachis zigzag, the lowest separate; **bracts** leaflike, reduced upwards, the sheaths rough-hairy; **pistillate scales** rough-awned, serrulate, keeled, all white-hyaline with 3-nerved green center. **Perigynia** 1-9 to a spike, 4.5-5 mm long, ascending, obtusely triangular, somewhat leathery, yellowish or grayish green, puncticulate, spongy at base; beak 1 mm long, straight or bent, the orifice hyaline, entire. **Achenes** triangular, filling perigynia, yellowish brown, granular, bent-apiculate; stigmas 3, red-brown.—Mesic woods.

Carex hitchcockiana
perigynium (l), stem-section (c),
pistillate scale (r)

1349. Carex granularis

1350. Carex conoidea

1351. Carex grisea

Carex oligocarpa Schkuhr
RICHWOODS SEDGE

MAP 1353
native

Plants tufted; rootstocks short. **Stems** 1-5 dm long, rough above, purple-tinged at base. **Leaves** 1-2 to a culm, 1-2.5 dm long and 2-4.5 mm wide, flat, thin, the midvein conspicuous below,, roughened on margins and towards the tip; sheaths conspicuously prolonged. **Terminal spike** staminate; **lateral spikes** 2-4, pistillate, separate, the rachis zigzag; **bracts** leaflike, reduced upwards; **pistillate scales** rough-awned and keeled, all white-hyaline with 3-ribbed green center. **Perigynia** 1-8 to a spike, 3.5-4 mm long, ascending, obtusely triangular, somewhat leathery, grayish green, puncticulate, impressed undulate-nerved, the base spongy; beak 0.75 mm long, straight or oblique, the orifice entire, hyaline. **Achenes** triangular, filling perigynia, yellowish brown, granular, apiculate; stigmas 3, reddish brown.—Mesic woods.

Carex oligocarpa
perigynium (l)
pistillate scale (r)

CAREX SECTION HELEOGLOCHIN

Plants densely tufted; bases brown. Stems narrowing toward the tip, typically arching at maturity. Inner band of the leaf sheaths smooth, pigmented toward the summit. Leaf blades less than 3 mm wide (ours). Spikes androgynous, the lower branched. Perigynia plano-convex to biconvex, darkening at maturity, mostly less than 3 mm long; beak short-triangular, scabrous on the margin, bidentate. Wetlands, primarily in peaty soils.

1   Leaf sheaths whitish or pale ventrally except for purplish dots; inflorescence ± crowded, the lowermost spike (or branch) usually at least slightly overlapping the next above it (occasionally separated by a distance no more than its total length); perigynia tending to spread at maturity, therefore not concealed by the scales . . . . . . *C. diandra*

1   Leaf sheaths strongly tinged with copper color toward their summits ventrally; inflorescence ± interrupted, the lowermost spikes (or branches) often well separated or even peduncled; perigynia ± appressed at maturity, nearly or completely concealed by the large scales . . . . *C. prairea*

Carex diandra Schrank
LESSER TUSSOCK SEDGE

MAP 1354
native

Plants densely tufted. **Stems** sharply 3-angled, 3-8 dm long, usually longer than leaves. **Leaves** 1-3 mm wide; **sheaths** white with fine pale lines, translucent on front or slightly copper-colored at mouth. **Spikes** with both staminate and pistillate flowers, staminate flowers borne above pistillate, clustered in ovate heads 1-4 cm long; **bracts** small and inconspicuous, shorter than the spikes; **pistillate scales** brown, tapered to tip or with a short sharp point, about equaling the perigynia. **Perigynia** brown, shiny, unequally convex on both sides, broadly ovate, 2-3 mm long, beak finely toothed, entire to notched, 1-2 mm long. **Achenes** lens-shaped; stigmas 2. May-July.—Wet meadows, ditches, peatlands (especially calcareous fens), floating mats.

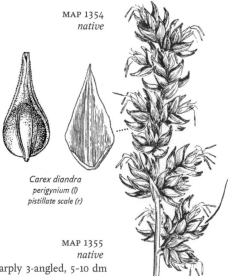

Carex diandra
perigynium (l)
pistillate scale (r)

Carex prairea Dewey
PRAIRIE SEDGE

MAP 1355
native

Plants densely tufted, from short rootstocks. **Stems** sharply 3-angled, 5-10 dm long. **Leaves** 2-3 mm wide; sheaths translucent, yellow-brown or bronze-colored. **Spikes** with both staminate and pistillate flowers, staminate flowers borne above

1352. *Carex hitchcockiana*

1353. *Carex oligocarpa*

1354. *Carex diandra*

1355. *Carex prairea*

pistillate, ovate, 4-7 mm long, lower spikes usually separate, in linear-oblong heads 3-8 cm long; bracts small; **pistillate scales** red-brown, tapered to tip, as long as and covering most of perigynia. **Perigynia** dull brown, flat on 1 side and convex on other, lance-shaped to ovate, 2-3 mm long, tapered to a finely toothed, unequally notched beak 1-2 mm long. **Achenes** lens-shaped; stigmas 2. May-July. Wet meadows, calcareous fens, marshes, tamarack swamps and peaty lakeshores.

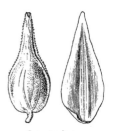

Carex prairea
perigynium (l)
pistillate scale (r)

CAREX SECTION HIRTIFOLIAE

One member of the section in Minn; recognized by the soft pubescence covering the entire plant, including the distinctly beaked, 2-ribbed perigynia.

Carex hirtifolia Mackenzie
PUBESCENT SEDGE

MAP 1356
native

Plants loosely tufted; rootstocks slender, branched. **Stems** 3-6 dm long, pubescent, roughened above, brownish red at base. **Well-developed leaves** 3-4 to a fertile culm, more on sterile stems; **blades** to 35 cm long and 3-7 mm wide, flat, flaccid, hirsute, the nerves prominent above; sheaths cinnamon-brown ventrally. **Terminal spike** staminate; **lateral spikes** 2-4, pistillate; lowest bract 1.5-7 cm long, the upper shorter; pistillate scales whitish, ciliate, with green excurrent midrib. **Perigynia** 10-25 to a spike, 3.5-5 mm long, triangular, green, pubescent, nerveless; beak ca. 1 mm long, obliquely cut, 2-toothed. **Achenes** sharply triangular with concave sides, short-apiculate; stigmas 3, reddish brown.—Rich mesic woods.

Carex hirtifolia
perigynium (l)
pistillate scale (r)

CAREX SECTION HOLARRHENAE

One member of the section in Minn; resembling those of sections Divisae and Ammoglochin but distinguished by the green-veined inner band of its leaf sheaths.

Carex sartwellii Dewey
SARTWELL'S SEDGE

MAP 1357
native

Plants colony-forming, from long black rhizomes. **Stems** single or few together, stiff, sharply 3-angled, 3-8 dm long. **Leaves** 2-4 mm wide, few per stem, the lowest leaves small and without blades; **sheaths** with green lines on front, and a translucent ligule around stem. **Spikes** with both staminate and pistillate flowers, staminate flowers above pistillate, or upper spikes staminate; clustered or lower spikes separate, 5-10 mm long, in cone-shaped heads, 3-6 cm long; **bracts** small, the lower bracts sometimes bristlelike and longer than the spike; **pistillate scales** brown with a prominent green midvein, about equal to perigynia. **Perigynia** tan to brown, flat on 1 side and convex on other, ovate, 2.5-3.5 mm long, finely nerved on both sides, sharp-edged, tapered to a short, finely toothed beak. **Achenes** lens-shaped; stigmas 2. May-July.—Wet to moist meadows, marshes, fens and shores, often where calcium-rich.

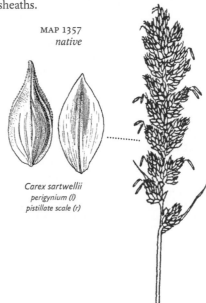

Carex sartwellii
perigynium (l)
pistillate scale (r)

1356. *Carex hirtifolia*   1357. *Carex sartwellii*

CAREX SECTION HYMENOCHLAENAE

Includes nearly all of the forest understory sedges with long, nodding pistillate spikes. Superficially similar to section Gracillimae but plants more delicate. Terminal spike wholly staminate. Perigynia 8-45 per spike (fewer in *Carex assiniboinensis*), narrow and long-tapering to the beak. Woodlands and wetlands.

1 Terminal spike gynecandrous; sheaths ± softly pubescent or perigynia essentially beakless (except *C. prasina*).. 2

  2 Perigynia strongly angled, gradually tapering into a beak ca. 1-1.5 mm long; bract of lowest pistillate spike sheathless or with sheath up to 1.2 cm long; terminal spike mostly staminate, with at most a few perigynia at tip . . . . *C. prasina*

  2 Perigynia obscurely angled or nearly terete, essentially beakless or beak less than 0.5 mm long; bract of lowest spike with sheath 1.5-8 cm or more in length; terminal spike staminate at base, pistillate toward tip 3

    3 Perigynia 1.3-1.6 mm wide, beakless; sheaths and blades glabrous . . . .*C. gracillima*

    3 Perigynia 1.7-2.5 mm wide, abruptly contracted to a short beak; sheaths and leaf blades ± softly pubescent, at least below (sometimes very sparsely so) 4

      4 Upper pistillate scales with a distinct prolonged awn greater than 0.5 mm long, often nearly equaling or exceeding the perigynia; lateral spikes entirely pistillate . . . .*C. davisii*

      4 Upper pistillate scales merely acute (or at most with a tip less than 0.5 mm long), distinctly shorter than the perigynia; lateral spikes usually with a few staminate flowers at base . . . .*C. formosa*

1 Terminal spike staminate; sheaths glabrous (except *C. castanea*) and perigynia conspicuously beaked 5

  5 Perigynia pubescent . . . . *C. assiniboinensis*

  5 Perigynia glabrous. 6

    6 Leaf sheaths and blades (at least toward the base) ± hairy; pistillate spikes 1-2.5 cm long . . . . .*C. castanea*

    6 Leaf sheaths and blades glabrous (at most the lowermost bladeless sheaths minutely hispidulous); pistillate spikes mostly (2-) 2.5-6.5 cm long 7

      7 Basal sheaths reddish purple for at least several cm above the base; perigynia clearly nerved between the 2 ribs 8

        8 Perigynia short-stalked, the achene within sessile or nearly so; broadest leaves 5-10 mm wide; pistillate scales mostly awned or cuspidate. . . . . *C. arctata*

        8 Perigynia sessile but the achene within on a definite short stalk ca. 0.5-1 mm long; broadest leaves 2.5-5) mm wide; pistillate scales mostly not awned . . . .*C. debilis*

      7 Basal sheaths brown, lacking any trace of reddish purple color (at most a small trace on the smaller sheaths in *C. prasina*); perigynia 2-ribbed, but otherwise nerveless or faintly nerved 9

        9 Perigynia (somewhat twisted) gradually tapering to a poorly defined conical beak, the cylindrical apical portion only 0.2-0.5 mm long . . . . *C. prasina*

        9 Perigynia (symmetrical) tapering to abruptly contracted into a well developed beak ca. 1.2-4.5 mm long . . . . *C. sprengelii*

Carex arctata Boott.   MAP 1358

DROOPING WOODLAND SEDGE   *native*

Plants tufted. **Stems** 3-9 dm long, the basal sheaths purple-tinged at base. **Leaves** 2-3 per fertile culm; **blades** 2-3 dm long and 5-10 mm wide long, ca. 3 mm wide, flat, thin, soft, deep-green, roughened on margins and towards the tip; sheaths minutely roughened, yellowish brown-tinged and red-dotted ventrally. **Terminal spike** staminate; **lateral spikes** 3-5, pistillate, nodding on slender rough peduncles; lowest bract leaflike, the upper reduced; **pistillate scales** awned, greenish white with green center, ciliate, thin. **Perigynia** 15-45 to a spike, 3-5 mm long, ascending, deep-green, puncticulate, 2-ribbed; beak 0.75 mm long, bidentate, hyaline above, ciliate between teeth. **Achenes** triangular with sides concave below, closely enveloped, yellowish brown, granular, apiculate; stigmas 3, short,

Carex arctata
perigynium (l)
pistillate scale (r)

1358. Carex arctata   *1359. Carex assiniboinensis*   *1360. Carex castanea*   *1361. Carex davisii*

blackish. Deciduous forests. *Similar to **Carex gracillima** but perigynia of C. arctata taper to the beak and are constricted at base to form a short stipe, and its terminal spikes are staminate.*

Carex assiniboinensis W. Boott

ASSINIBOIA SEDGE   MAP 1359   *native*

Plants tufted; rootstocks short, stout, with unique, long-arching vegetative shoots produced in summer and tipped with new plantlets. **Stems** 35-75 cm long, compressed-triangular, weak, smooth or roughened on angles above, purple-tinged at base, basal sheaths filamentose. **Well-developed leaves** 3-5 to a culm, on lower third; blades 1-2 dm long and 1.5-3 mm wide, flat, thin, green, roughened towards the tip. **Terminal spike** staminate, a narrow bract from its base usually subtending one perigynium; **lateral spikes** about 3, pistillate, on slender rough peduncles 2-6 cm long; lower bracts leaflike, sheathing, the upper reduced; **pistillate scales** greenish straw-colored with white-hyaline margins and sharp green midrib. **Perigynia** 1-8 to a spike, 6 mm long, erect, leathery, pale-green or straw-colored, tuberculate-hispid, 2-ridged; beak 2.5 mm long, oblique and white-tipped. **Achenes** triangular with sides concave, closely enveloped, apiculate; stigmas 3, long, reddish brown.—Rich mesic woods.

Carex assiniboinensis
perigynium (l)
pistillate scale (r)

Carex castanea Wahlenb.

CHESTNUT-COLOR SEDGE   MAP 1360   *native*

Plants tufted. **Stems** 3-10 dm long, purple-tinged at base. Leaves 3-6 mm wide, softly hairy. **Spikes** either staminate or pistillate; the **terminal spike** staminate, upright atop a long stalk; **lateral spikes** pistillate, usually 3, on slender, drooping stalks, short cylindric; **pistillate scales** ovate, brown-tinged, about as long as perigynia. **Perigynia** lance-shaped, 4-6 mm long, somewhat 3-angled, strongly 2-ribbed with several faint nerves, tapered to a notched beak up to half length of body. **Achenes** 3-angled; stigmas 3. June-July.—Swamps, moist openings, wetland margins and ditches.

Carex castanea
perigynium (l)
pistillate scale (r)

Carex davisii Schwein. & Torr.

DAVIS' SEDGE   MAP 1361   ❧ *threatened | native*

Plants tufted. **Stems** 3-10 dm long, purple at base. **Leaves** 4-8 mm wide, hairy on underside; sheaths hairy. **Terminal spike** staminate with pistillate flowers near tip; **pistillate spikes** 2-3, the upper 2 overlapping, cylindric, 2-4 cm long, upright to nodding on short stalks; **pistillate scales** obovate, white or translucent with green center, tipped with a long awn. **Perigynia** ovate, dull orange when mature, 4-6 mm long and 2-3 mm wide, somewhat 3-angled, tapered to a notched beak to 1 mm long. **Achenes** 3-angled; stigmas 3. May-June.—Floodplain forests in se Minn.

Carex davisii
perigynium (l)
pistillate scale (r)

Carex debilis Michx.

WHITE-EDGE SEDGE   MAP 1362   *native*

Plants tufted. **Stems** 6-10 dm long, purple-tinged at base. **Leaves** 2-4 mm wide. **Staminate spike** linear, sometimes with a few pistillate flowers near tip; **pistillate spikes** 2-4, separate along stem, spreading or nodding, flowers loose in spikes; **pistillate scales** oblong, half the length of perigynia with translucent or brown margins and a green midrib. **Perigynia** lance-shaped, somewhat 3-angled, 2-ribbed, 5-8 mm long, narrowed to a beak. **Achenes** 3-angled; stigmas 3. May-Aug.—Wet woods (usually under conifers), swamp margins, wet sandy ditches.

Carex debilis
perigynium (l)
pistillate scale (r)

1362. *Carex debilis*   1363. *Carex formosa*   1364. *Carex gracillima*   1365. *Carex sprengelii*

Carex formosa Dewey

MAP 1363

HANDSOME SEDGE

🌱*endangered | native*

Plants densely tufted. **Stems** 3-8 dm long, dark maroon at base; flowering stems 0.5-1 mm thick, scabrous on angles within inflorescence. **Leaves** flat, 3-6 mm wide, glabrous on undersurface, pilose on uppersurface and margins; sheaths pubescent; lowest bracts shorter or equal to tip of the inflorescence. **Spikes** usually all gynecandrous, pubescent; **lateral spikes** 2-4, well separated, on slender peduncles to 10 cm long and usually much longer than spikes, drooping at maturity, pistillate except for 1 or 2 basal staminate flowers in each; **pistillate scales** hyaline tinged with chestnut brown, the broad green midrib red-dotted, shorter than the mature perigynia. **Perigynia** intermediate in size between those of *C. davisii* and *C. gracillima*, copiously red dotted, 2-ribbed, loosely enveloping achene, tip narrowed to abrupt beak; beak minutely bidentate, less than 0.5 mm long; stigmas 3.—Rich, mesic deciduous forests.

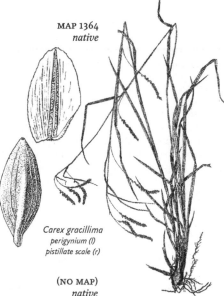

Carex formosa
perigynium (l)
pistillate scale (r)

Carex gracillima Schwein.

MAP 1364

GRACEFUL SEDGE

native

Plants tufted; rootstocks short, slender. **Stems** 2-9 dm long, purple-tinged at base. **Leaves** 3-4 to a culm, on lower half; **blades** 1-3 dm long, flat, flaccid, deep-green, roughened on margins and towards tip; sheaths yellowish brown-tinged and reddish dotted. **Terminal spike** gynaecandrous (staminate flowers below the pistillate) or staminate; **lateral spikes** 3-4, pistillate, separate on slender nodding roughish peduncles; lowest **bract** leaflike, sheathing, the upper shorter; **scales** whitish or yellowish brown with green midrib. **Perigynia** 10-45 to a spike, 2.5-3.5 mm long, ascending, puncticulate, few-nerved, beakless. **Achenes** triangular with concave sides and thick angles; stigmas 3, short, blackish.—Mesic to wet forests, sometimes in drier oak woods.

Carex gracillima
perigynium (l)
pistillate scale (r)

Carex prasina Wahlenb.

(NO MAP)

DROOPING SEDGE

native

Plants tufted. **Stems** 3-8 dm long, brown or green at base. **Leaves** 3-5 mm wide. **Terminal spike** staminate or with a few pistillate flowers at tip; **pistillate spikes** 2-4, widely separated, cylindric, 2-5 cm long and 5 mm wide, curved or nodding, lower spikes on long stalks, the upper stalks much shorter; upper bract more or less sheathless; **pistillate scales** ovate to obovate, shorter than the perigynia, tipped with an awn or short point. **Perigynia** 3-4 mm long, ovate, 3-angled, tapered to beak. **Achenes** 3-angled; stigmas 3. May-June. Springs, seeps and low areas in deciduous woods, shaded streambanks.—Not yet known from Minn, but to be expected on forested seeps in the St. Croix Valley; known from the Wisc side in Burnett County.

Carex prasina
perigynium (l)
pistillate scale (r)

Carex sprengelii Dewey

MAP 1365

LONG-BEAK SEDGE

native

Plants tufted; rootstocks long, stout, matted. **Stems** 3-9 dm long, erect or decumbent, rough on angles above, brownish tinged and long-fibrillose at base; **Leaves** 1-4 dm long and 2.5-4 mm wide, flat, roughened below and on margins towards the tip. Upper 1-3 spikes staminate (occasionally androgynous), the upper peduncled; **pistillate spikes** pendulous on rough capillary peduncles; **pistillate scales** straw-colored or greenish white, with 3-nerved light green center. **Perigynia** 10-40 to a spike, 5-6 mmlong, spreading-ascending, globose, greenish straw-colored, shining, laterally 2-ribbed; beak equaling or exceeding body, white above, obliquely cut at orifice, bidentate, teeth scarious. **Achenes** obtusely triangular with sides concave below, closely enveloped, yellowish, bent-apiculate; stigmas 3, brown.—Mesic and floodplain forests, sometimes where disturbed, not tolerant of heavy shade.

Carex sprengelii
perigynium (l)
pistillate scale (r)

CAREX SECTION LAXIFLORAE

Plants tufted; bases pale to brown or occasionally reddish. Stems weak, ascending to decumbent, sharply triangular in cross-section, angles sometimes winged. Perigynia triangular in cross-section with rounded edges, 25-40-veined (except *Carex leptonervia*); beak (in our species) abrupt, short, often bent. Woodland species.

1   Sides of perigynia with at most 1 main nerve, otherwise nerveless or each with up to 6 obscure nerves; perigynium
    with a straightish or slightly bent short beak . . . . ***C. leptonervia***
1   Sides of perigynia each with 7 or more conspicuous nerves; perigynium with straightish or strongly bent beak 2
    2   Angles of bract sheaths smooth or nearly so (granular-papillose in *C. ormostachya*); beak of perigynium usually
        straight or slightly bent . . . . ***C. ormostachya***
    2   Angles of bract sheaths minutely ciliate-serrulate; beak of perigynium strongly bent 3
        3   Widest leaves 8 mm or more broad; pistillate scales broadly obtuse or truncate, at most scarcely toothed
            at apex; staminate spike sessile or nearly so . . . . ***C. albursina***
        3   Widest leaves often less than 8 mm broad; pistillate scales acuminate, awned, or cuspidate; staminate spike
            sessile or peduncled . . . . ***C. blanda***

Carex albursina Sheldon
WHITE BEAR SEDGE
Plants loosely tufted; rootstocks short. **Stems** 1-6 dm, winged, roughened on angles, dark-brown at base. **Well-developed leaves** 2-5 to a fertile culm; blades 6-25 cm long and 7-15 mm wide, thin, flaccid, light-green, the midvein prominent below, the midlaterals above, roughened towards tip and on margins; sheaths loose. **Terminal spike** staminate; **lateral spikes** 3-4, pistillate, the lower separate; **bracts** sheathing, rough-edged, the lower leaflike; **scales** white-hyaline with 3-nerved green center. **Perigynia** 3-18 to a spike, 3-4 mm long, erect, obtusely triangular, yellowish green, the base spongy; beak 0.5 mm long, bent, the orifice entire. **Achenes** triangular with concave sides, yellowish brown; stigmas 3, reddish brown.—Mesic forests.

MAP 1366
native

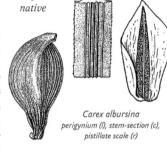

Carex albursina
perigynium (l), stem-section (c),
pistillate scale (r)

Carex blanda Dewey
EASTERN WOODLAND SEDGE
Plants tufted; rootstocks short. **Stems** 1-6 dm long, slightly winged, 2-edged and flattened in drying, minutely serrulate above, brownish at base; sterile stem leaf blades 1-3.5 dm long and 4-15 mm wide, flat, thin, flaccid, light-green, the midvein prominent below, roughened on margins; blades of fertile stems smaller. **Terminal spike** staminate or gynaecandrous (staminate flowers below the pistillate); **lateral spikes** 2-5, pistillate, the lower separate on slender, 2-edged peduncles; **bracts** leaflike; **pistillate scales** awned, greenish white with 3-nerved green center. **Perigynia** 8-25 to a spike, 3-4 mm long, ascending, obtusely triangular, yellowish green, strongly nerved, the base spongy; beak 0.5 mm long, bent, the orifice entire, hyaline. **Achenes** triangular, yellowish brown, granular; stigmas 3, short, reddish brown.—Mesic to wet deciduous forests, sometimes in moist open places.

MAP 1367
native

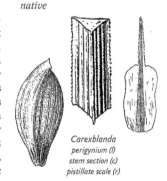

Carexblanda
perigynium (l)
stem section (c)
pistillate scale (r)

Carex leptonervia (Fern.) Fern.
NERVELESS WOODLAND SEDGE
Plants tufted; rootstocks slender. **Stems** 1.5-7 dm long, weakly erect or decumbent, the angles minutely serrulate, brownish at base. **Leaves** to 3.5 dm long and 3-10 mm wide, flat, flaccid, deep-green, the midvein prominent below, roughened on margins towards tip; sheaths enlarged upward; ligule long. **Terminal spike** staminate; **lateral spikes** 2-4, pistillate, the lower 1-2 separate, rough-peduncled; **bracts** with sheath-margins serrulate; **pistillate scales** white-hyaline, brownish tinged; anthers 1.5 mm. **Perigynia** 10-20 to a spike, 3.5-4.5 mm long, erect-ascending, obtusely triangular, light-green, glandular-puncticulate, 2-ribbed, the base spongy; beak 0.5 mm long, the orifice entire, oblique. **Achenes** triangular with concave sides, filling perigynia, brownish, granular; stigmas 3, reddish brown.—Woodlands.

MAP 1368
native

Carex leptonervia
perigynium (l), stem-section (c),
pistillate scale (r)

Carex ormostachya Wieg.
NECKLACE SPIKE SEDGE

MAP 1369
native

Plants tufted; rootstocks short. **Stems** 2-6 dm long, minutely granular, crenulate on angles, purplish at base. **Leaves** 5-20 cm long and 2-8 mm wide, flat, flaccid, light-green, the midvein prominent below, roughened on margins towards the sharp tip; sheaths tight. **Terminal spike** staminate; **lateral spikes** 3-5, pistillate, loosely flowered below, the lower separate, the peduncles minutely serrulate; pistillate scales mucronate to awned, hyaline with 3-nerved greenish center, sometimes reddish brown-tinged. **Perigynia** 10-20 to a spike, 2.5-3.5 mm long, appressed-ascending, obtusely triangular, dull-brownish, strongly nerved, the base spongy; beak minute, straight or bent, the orifice hyaline, truncate or oblique. **Achenes** triangular with concave sides and blunt angles, yellowish; stigmas 3, short, reddish brown. —Woodlands.

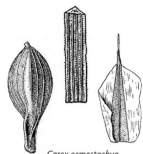

Carex ormostachya
perigynium (l), stem-section (c),
pistillate scale (r)

CAREX SECTION LEPTOCEPHALAE

One member of the section in Minn. Plants soft, very slender, rhizomatous; spike androgynous (with staminate flowers at tip, pistillate flowers below); perigynia few.

Carex leptalea Wahlenb.
BRISTLY STALK SEDGE

MAP 1370
native

Densely tufted perennial. **Stems** slender, rounded 3-angled, 1-7 dm long, equal or longer than leaves. **Leaves** narrow, 0.5-1.5 mm wide; sheaths tight, white, translucent on front. **Spikes** single on the stems, few-flowered, 5-15 mm long, with both staminate and pistillate flowers, the staminate flowers borne above pistillate; **bracts** absent; **pistillate scales** rounded or with a short sharp point, shorter than the perigynia (or the tip of lowest scale sometimes longer than the perigynium). **Perigynia** yellow-green, nearly round in section to slightly flattened, oblong to oval, 3-5 mm long, finely many-nerved, beakless or with a short beak. **Achenes** 3-angled; stigmas 3. May-July.—Swamps, alder thickets, open bogs, calcareous fens; usually in partial shade.

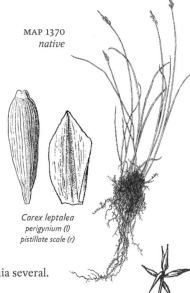

Carex leptalea
perigynium (l)
pistillate scale (r)

CAREX SECTION LEUCOGLOCHIN

One member of the section in Minn. Spike solitary; perigynia several. Sphagnum moss wetlands.

Carex pauciflora Lightf.
FEW-FLOWER SEDGE

MAP 1371
native

Perennial, from long slender rhizomes. Stems single or several together, 1-4 dm long, longer than leaves. Leaves 1-2 mm wide, lower stem leaves reduced to scales; bract absent. Spike single, to 1 cm long, with both staminate and pistillate flowers, the staminate above the pistillate; staminate scales infolded to form a slender terminal cone; pistillate scales lance-shaped, 4-6 mm long, pale brown, soon deciduous. **Perigynia** 1-6, soon turned downward, slender, spongy at base, nearly round in section, straw-colored or pale brown, deciduous when mature, 6-8 mm

Carex
pauciflora

1366. *Carex albursina*

1367. *Carex blanda*

1368. *Carex leptonervia*

1369. *Carex ormostachya*

long. **Achenes** 3-angled, not filling the perigynium; stigmas 3. June-July.—Open peatlands and floating mats in sphagnum moss, true bogs.

Carex pauciflora
perigynium (l)
pistillate scale (r)

CAREX SECTION LIMOSAE

Plants loosely tufted or stems arising singly, strongly rhizomatous; bases reddish. Roots covered in a dense yellow felt-like tomentum. Vegetative shoots becoming decumbent, behaving like stolons, producing shoots at the nodes. Pistillate spikes pendulous on slender stalks. Perigynia pale, short-beaked, papillose. Stigmas 3. Common in northern bogs and fens.

1   Pistillate scales nearly or quite as broad as the perigynia and often only slightly if at all longer; staminate spike mostly 15-30 mm long; plants strongly stoloniferous. . . . .*C. limosa*
1   Pistillate scales distinctly narrower than perigynia, generally with narrowly acuminate tips much exceeding them; staminate spike 5-12 (-15) mm long; plants loosely clumped. . . . .*C. magellanica*

Carex limosa L.
MUD SEDGE

MAP 1372
native

Plants loosely tufted, from long, scaly, yellow-felted rhizomes. **Stems** sharply 3-angled, 3-5 dm long, longer than leaves, usually rough-to-touch above. **Leaves** involute, 1-3 mm wide; sheaths translucent, shredding into threadlike fibers near base. **Spikes** either all staminate or pistillate, the **terminal spike** staminate; the lower 1-3 spikes pistillate, drooping on lax, threadlike stalks 1-3 cm long; **pistillate scales** brown, rounded or with a short, sharp point, about same size as perigynia. **Perigynia** waxy blue-green, ovate, flattened except where filled by achene, 2.5-4 mm long, strongly 2-ribbed with a few faint nerves on each side; beak tiny. **Achenes** 3-angled; stigmas 3. May-July.—Open bogs and floating mats. Common northward, less common in s where mostly confined to calcareous fens. *Poor sedge (C. magellanica) similar but has scales much narrower than perigynia; C. buxbaumii also similar but lacks yellow roots.*

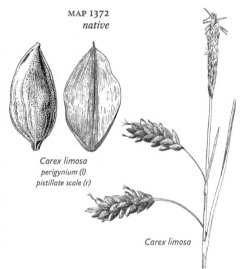

Carex limosa
perigynium (l)
pistillate scale (r)

Carex limosa

Carex magellanica Lam.
POOR SEDGE
   Carex paupercula Michx.

MAP 1373
native

Plants loosely tufted, from slender, branching, yellow-felted rhizomes. **Stems** slender, 1-8 dm long, longer than the leaves, red-brown at base. **Leaves** 3-12 on lower half of stem, flat but with slightly rolled under margins, 2-4 mm wide, the dried leaves of previous year conspicuous; **sheaths** red-dotted. **Terminal spike** staminate (or sometimes with a few pistillate flowers at tip), on a long stalk, usually upright; **pistillate spikes** 1-4 (rarely with several staminate flowers at base), clustered, usually drooping on slender stalks; lowest bract leaflike, equal or longer than the head; pistillate scales lance-shaped to ovate, narrower but usually longer

Carex magellanica
perigynium (l)
pistillate scale (r)

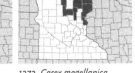

1370. *Carex limosa*   1371. *Carex magellanica*   1372. *Carex leptalea*   1373. *Carex magellanica*

than the perigynia, brown or green in center, margins brown. **Perigynia** broadly ovate or oval, 2-3 mm long, flattened and 2-ribbed, with several evident nerves, pale or somewhat waxy blue-green, covered with many small bumps, the tip rounded and barely beaked. **Achenes** 3-angled, obovate, 2 mm long; stigmas 3. July-Aug.—Open bogs, partly shaded peatlands, floating mats, cedar swamps and thickets, usually in sphagnum moss.

CAREX SECTION LUPULINAE

Distinctive sedges of wet forests; recognized by the strongly inflated, ribbed perigynia, 1-2 cm long.

1 Pistillate spikes cylindrical or short-oblong, usually definitely longer than broad; sheath of uppermost leaf usually 1.7 cm or longer; style strongly bent and contorted immediately above the body of the achene; beak of perigynium nearly or quite as long as the body . . . . ***C. lupulina***
1 Pistillate spikes spherical or nearly so, scarcely if at all longer than wide; sheath of uppermost leaf absent or less than 1.5 (-2.5) cm; style straight or sinuous or contorted (especially in *C. intumescens*) just below or at the middle; beak of perigynium much shorter than the body 2
   2 Perigynia (7-) 10-31 per spike, radiating in all directions, narrowed at the base to a ± broad cuneate stalk, sometimes hispidulous basally; pistillate spikes 1-2 (-3) . . . .***C. grayi***
   2 Perigynia 2-8 (-12) per spike, mostly spreading-ascending, rounded at the base, glabrous (and often very shiny); pistillate spikes (1-) 2-5 . . . .***C. intumescens***

Carex grayi Carey
GRAY'S SEDGE

MAP 1374
native

Rhizomes absent. **Stems** single or forming small clumps, 3-9 dm long, rough on upper stem angles, sheaths at base of stem persistent, red-purple. **Leaves** 5-12 mm wide. **Spikes** either staminate or pistillate; **terminal spike** staminate, stalked; **pistillate spikes** 1-2, rounded, stalked; bracts leaflike; **pistillate scales** ovate, body shorter than perigynia but sometimes tipped with an awn to 7 mm long. **Perigynia** 10-30 per spike, spreading in all directions, not shiny, 10-20 mm long, strongly nerved, tapered from widest point to a notched beak 2-3 mm long. **Achenes** with a persistent, withered style; stigmas 3. June-Sept.—Floodplain forests and backwater areas (as along Mississippi River).

Carex grayi
perigynium (l)
pistillate scale (r)

Carex intumescens Rudge
GREATER BLADDER SEDGE

MAP 1375
native

Rhizomes absent. **Stems** single or in small clumps, 3-9 dm long, rough on upper stem angles; sheaths at base of stem persistent, red-purple. **Leaves** 4-12 mm wide, bracts leaflike. **Spikes** either staminate or pistillate, or sometimes staminate spikes with a few pistillate flowers; **terminal spike** staminate, stalked; **pistillate spikes** 1-4, rounded, on stalks to 1.5 cm long; **pistillate scales** narrowly ovate, shorter and narrower than perigynia. **Perigynia** 1-12 per spike, spreading in all directions, satiny (not dull), 10-17 mm long, tapered to a beak 2-4 mm long. **Achenes** flattened; stigmas 3. May-Aug.—Mixed and deciduous moist forests, kettle wetlands in woods, swamps and alder thickets.

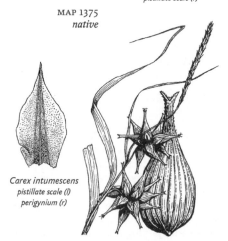

Carex intumescens
pistillate scale (l)
perigynium (r)

1374. Carex grayi

1375. Carex intumescens

1376. Carex lupulina

1377. Carex annectens

Carex lupulina Muhl.
HOP SEDGE

MAP 1376
native

Plants loosely tufted, from rhizomes. **Stems** stout, 3-12 dm long. **Leaves** much longer than head, 4-15 mm wide; upper sheaths white and translucent, the lower sheaths brown. **Spikes** either all staminate or pistillate, the **upper spike** staminate, short-stalked, 2-5 cm long; **pistillate spikes** 2-6, clustered or overlapping, the lowermost sometimes separate; **bracts** leaflike and spreading, much longer than head; **pistillate scales** narrowly ovate, tapered to tip or with a short awn, much shorter than the perigynia. **Perigynia** many, upright, dull green-brown, lance-shaped, inflated, 10-20 mm long, many-nerved, tapered to a finely toothed bidentate beak 5-10 mm long. **Achenes** 3-angled; stigmas 3. June-Aug.—Wet woods, swamps, wet meadows and marshes, ditches and shores. *Shining bur sedge (C. intumescens) is similar but differs from hop sedge by having fewer, uncrowded perigynia which are olive-green and glossy.*

Carex lupulina
perigynium (l)
pistillate scale (r)

CAREX SECTION MULTIFLORAE

Plants tufted; bases fibrous, brown or pale. Inner band of the leaf sheaths hyaline, corrugated. Inflorescence compound, cylindrical, densely flowered, stiff. Bracts setaceous. Spikes androgynous, at least the lowest branched. Perigynia plano-convex, weakly or inconspicuously spongy at the base. Primarily in wetlands. Characterized by the corrugated inner band of the leaf sheaths; firm, narrow stems; and densely flowered, straight, compound inflorescence.

1   Perigynium abruptly contracted into a beak mostly 0.25-0.5 times as long as body; larger perigynia 1.5-2.3 mm wide with broadly ovate to ± orbicular bodies, fully mature (orange-brown) early to midsummer . . .***C. annectens***
1   Perigynium tapering or contracted into a beak 0.5-1 times as long as body; larger perigynia 1.1-1.9 mm wide with ovate bodies, fully mature (greenish to dull yellow or brown) late summer . . . .***C. vulpinoidea***

Carex annectens (Bickn.) Bickn.
YELLOW-FRUIT SEDGE
> *Carex brachyglossa* Mackenzie
> *Carex setacea* var. *ambigua* (Barratt) Fern.

MAP 1377
native

Plants tufted; rootstocks short, stout, blackish. **Stems** 3-10 dm long, roughened below head, brownish at base, the old leaves conspicuous. **Well-developed leaves** 3-6 to a culm, on lower third; **blades** 2-4 dm long and 2-5 mm wide, flat or canaliculate, light-green, roughened on margins and towards the tip; sheaths cross-rugulose, red-dotted and greenish white ventrally. **Spikes** many, androgynous (staminate flowers above the pistillate), in a greenish stramineous compound head; bracts variable, the upper scale-like; **scales** rough-awned, reddish brown with hyaline margins and 3-nerved green center. **Perigynia** about 3 mm long, ascending or spreading, plano-convex, brownish yellow, sharply green-margined, serrulate above; beak to 1 mm long, serrulate, bidentate, the teeth reddish brown. **Achenes** lenticular; stigmas 2, short, reddish brown.—Dry fields.

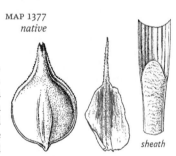

Carex annectens
perigynium (l)
pistillate scale (r)

sheath

Carex vulpinoidea Michx.
COMMON FOX SEDGE

MAP 1378
native

Plants densely tufted, from short rootstocks. **Stems** stiff, sharply 3-angled, 3-9 dm long. **Leaves** 2-4 mm wide; sheaths tight, cross-wrinkled and translucent on front, mottled green and white on back. **Spikes** with both staminate and pistillate flowers, staminate flowers borne above pistillate; heads oblong to cylindric, 3-9 cm long, with several spikes per branch at lower nodes; **bracts** small and bristlelike, longer than the spikes; **pistillate scales** awn-tipped, the awns equal or longer than the perigynia. **Perigynia** yellow-green, becoming straw-colored or brown when mature, flat on 1 side and convex on other, ovate to nearly round, 2-3 mm long, abruptly contracted to a notched, finely toothed beak 1 mm long. **Achenes** lens-shaped, 1-2 mm long; stigmas 2. May-Aug.—Wet to moist meadows, marshes, lakeshores, streambanks, roadside ditches.

Carex vulpinoidea
perigynium (l)
pistillate scale (r)

CAREX SECTION OBTUSATAE

One member of the section in Minnesota.

Carex obtusata Lilj.
OBTUSE SEDGE

MAP 1378A
native

Rhizomatous perennial, rootstock and stem bases purplish-black. **Stems** 0.5-2 dm tall. **Leaves** to 1.5 mm wide. **Spikes** solitary, androgynous (staminate flowers above the pistillate). **Perigynia** dark chestnut brown, finely many grooved, 3-5.5 mm long, beak short, 0.5-1 mm long. **Achenes** triangular with prominent angles; stigmas 3.—Sandy or gravelly prairies. *Distinguishing features are stems arising singly from the rhizome, tipped with a single spike, and the dark perigynia.*

Carex obtusata
perigynium (l)
pistillate scale (r)

CAREX SECTION OVALES

In general, Ovales are characterized by a tufted habit, brownish basal sheaths, and sterile shoots with both nodes and internodes; this is in contrast to the sterile shoots of most species of *Carex*, where the stem-like portion is formed only of overlapping leaf sheaths, and nodes and internodes are absent. Mature perigynia (and often a dissecting microscope) are often needed for accurately identifying species in this large group.

ADDITIONAL SPECIES
• *Carex praticola* Rydb. (Meadow sedge); rare on slate bedrock cliffs in Cook and Lake counties.
• *Carex xerantica* L.H. Bailey (White-scale sedge, MAP 1379); uncommon in dry, sandy or gravelly prairies.

1   Pistillate scales about as long as the perigynia and nearly the same width as the beaked portion (not necessarily the body), so that the tip of each perigynium is largely concealed; anthers 1.5-3 mm long 2
   2   Inflorescence stiff, the spikes close together, mostly overlapping; pistillate scales nearly as wide as the bodies of the perigynia, almost concealing them . . . .*C. adusta*
   2   Inflorescence ± lax or flexuous, the lowermost spikes usually remote; pistillate scales distinctly narrower than bodies of perigynia (the wings of which clearly protrude at maturity). . . . .*C. foenea*
1   Pistillate scales (or most of them) both shorter and narrower than beaks of perigynia, so the tip of the mature perigynia are largely exposed; anthers various. 3
   3   Pistillate scales in the middle or lower portions of the spikes acuminate with a subulate tip or awned 4
      4   Perigynia 2.6-4 times longer than wide, the bodies lanceolate; 0.9-2 mm wide 5
         5   Perigynia 0.9-1.2 mm wide; achenes 0.6-0.8 mm wide; inflorescences dense, lowest inflorescence internodes 2-3 (-5) mm long. . . . .*C. crawfordii*
         5   Perigynia 1.2-2.0 mm wide; achenes 0.7-1.1 mm wide; inflorescences dense to open or flexuous, lowest internodes 2-17 mm long. . . . .*C. scoparia*
      4   Perigynia less than 2.5 times longer than wide, the bodies lance-ovate, ovate, or obovate; 1.8-3.9 mm wide . . . .*C. suberecta*
   3   Pistillate scales obtuse, acute or acuminate, sometimes inconspicuous in the spikes. 6
      6   Perigynia 7-9 mm long; larger spikes on each stem ca. 1.5-2.5 cm long and 1/5-1/3 as thick in the middle, tapered to both ends. . . . .*C. muskingumensis*
      6   Perigynia shorter; spikes usually shorter and a third or more as thick as long 7
         7   Mature perigynia more than 2 mm broad at widest part. 8
            8   Perigynium bodies obovate, widest above the middle; leaf sheaths green-nerved ventrally nearly to the summit with at most a narrow V-shaped hyaline area . . . .*C. albolutescens*
            8   Perigynium bodies lanceolate, ovate, elliptic, or orbicular, widest at or below the middle; leaf sheaths various, some with prominent hyaline band near the apex ventrally 9
               9   Leaf sheaths green-nerved ventrally nearly to the summit; perigynia cuneately tapering to the base, the body ± diamond-shaped . . . .*C. suberecta*
               9   Leaf sheaths with a white hyaline area ventrally; perigynia rounded to the base, the bodies ovate, elliptic, or orbicular. 10
                  10   Perigynium bodies ovate, greenish, gradually tapered to the beak; pistillate scales with a green midstripe and hyaline or pale margins; leaves 2.5-6.5 mm wide; sheaths green-mottled, the mouth of sheaths truncate and prolonged to 2 mm above the base of leaf blades *C. normalis*
                  10   Perigynium bodies broadly ovate to orbicular, yellowish to tan brown, often abruptly contracted to the beak; pistillate scales greenish to dark brown; leaves 1.5-4 (-5) mm wide, the sheaths evenly colored, the mouth of sheaths concave (prolonged above base of leaf blades in *C. merritt-fernaldii*) 11

  11 Leaf sheaths finely papillose at magnification (30-40×), especially near the leaf base . . 12

    12 Perigynia strongly and evenly 4-8-nerved over the achene on the ventral face, (4.5-) 5.1-6.7 mm long, pistillate scales usually (1-) 1.4-2.3 mm shorter than the perigynia; anthers (2.4-) 2.8-4.2 mm long. . . . .*C. bicknellii*

    12 Perigynia nerveless or faintly and irregularly 0-5-nerved over the achene on the ventral face, 2.5-5.) mm long, pistillate scales 0.2-1.3 mm shorter than the perigynia; anthers 1-2.6 mm long. 13

      13 Perigynia 2.5-3.4 mm wide; achenes 1.3-1.5 mm wide. . . . .*C. merritt-fernaldii*

      13 Perigynia 2-2.4 (-2.6) mm wide; achenes (0.9-) 1-1.3 mm wide . . . . . .*C. festucacea*

  11 Leaf sheaths smooth 14

    14 Spikes on larger inflorescences 2-4 (rarely more), rounded at the base, the terminal one lacking a conspicuous staminate base; inflorescences mostly 1.3-3 cm long (the lowest internodes generally 1.5-6 mm long); perigynium bodies elliptic to ovate (rarely orbicular), 1-1.6 times longer than wide . . . .*C. molesta*

    14 Spikes on larger inflorescences (4-) 5-7 or more, tapered at the base, the terminal one with a conspicuous staminate base; inflorescences typically 2.5-4.5 (-6) cm long (the lowest internodes generally 5-13 mm long); perigynium bodies broadly ovate to orbicular, (0.7-) 0.9-1.2 times longer than wide. 15

      15 Larger perigynia 2.5-3.3 (-3.5) mm wide, the ventral face usually nerveless; larger achenes 1.4-1.8 mm wide . . . . **C. brevior**

      15 Larger perigynia 1.5-2.4 (-2.6) mm wide, the ventral face mostly 2-4-nerved; larger achenes 0.9-1.3 mm wide . . . .*C. festucacea*

 7 Mature perigynia not over 2 mm broad 16

 16 Perigynia thin, ± scale-like, often not winged to the base; leaf sheaths somewhat expanded towards apex and bearing narrow wings continuous with midrib and edges of leaf blade, blades 3-7 mm wide; vegetative shoots tall, conspicuous, and with numerous leaves spaced along upper 1/2 of stem. . 17

  17 Perigynia stiffly spreading or recurved; spikes ± spherical; pistillate scales hidden, 1.6-2.3 mm long . . . .**C. cristatella**

  17 Perigynia loosely spreading or appressed ascending; spikes nearly spherical to ovate-oblong; pistillate scales evident, 2-3 mm long 18

    18 Inflorescences stiff, spikes overlapping; perigynia usually more than 40, beaks appressed-ascending; leaf sheaths firm at summit. . . . . **C. tribuloides**

    18 Inflorescences flexuous, the lower spikes usually separated; perigynia usually 15-40, the beaks spreading; leaf sheaths firm or friable at summit . . . . **C. projecta**

 16 Perigynia thicker, plano-convex, winged to the base; leaf sheaths with ± rounded edges, not distinctly expanded towards apex, blades 1-4.5 mm wide (except in *C. normalis*); vegetative shoots usually inconspicuous, with leaves relatively few and clustered at apex 19

  19 Perigynia 2.6-4 times longer than wide, the bodies lanceolate, the distance from beak tip to top of achene 2-5 mm 20

    20 Perigynia 0.9-1.2 mm wide; achenes 0.6-0.8 mm wide; inflorescences dense, lowest inflorescence internodes 2-3 (-5) mm long. . . . .**C. crawfordii**

    20 Perigynia 1.2-2 mm wide; achenes 0.7-1.1 mm wide; inflorescences dense to open or even flexuose, lowest internodes 2-17 mm long. 21

      21 Inflorescences dense or open, spikes usually overlapping; pistillate scales acuminate; perigynia usually ascending . . . . **C. scoparia**

      21 Inflorescences nodding or flexuous, spikes well separated; pistillate scales acute; perigynia spreading . . . . **C. echinodes**

  19 Perigynia less than 2.5 times longer than wide, the bodies obovate, orbicular, or ovate, the distance from beak tip to top of achene 0.8-2.2 mm 22

    22 Inflorescences on tallest stems compact, ca. 1.5-3 times as long as wide, erect, the spikes overlapping; lowest inflorescence internodes 1-6 (-7.5) mm long, 1/12-1/5 (-1/4) the total length of the inflorescence 23

      23 Achenes 0.6-0.9 mm wide; perigynia nerveless or with 1-3 faint or basal nerves on the ventral face; inflorescences less than 3 cm long. . . . . **C. bebbii**

      23 Achenes 0.9-1.3 mm wide; perigynia often with 3 or more well-defined ventral nerves; inflorescences 1-6 cm long. 24

        24 Perigynium body broadly elliptic, or nearly orbicular, with wing margin 0.4-0.8 mm wide, conspicuous ventral nerves 0-6. . . . . **C. molesta**

        24 Perigynium body ovate to broadly ovate, their wing margins 0.2-0.4 mm wide, ventral nerves 4-7. . . . . **C. normalis**

    22 Inflorescences on tallest stems elongate, ± open proximally, ca. (2.5-) 3-5.1 times as long

as wide, often arching or nodding; lowest inflorescence internodes (5-) 7-19 mm long, mostly 1/5-1/3 (-1/2) the total length of the inflorescence.........................25

  25 Perigynium bodies orbicular, widest at the middle and abruptly contracted into the beak .... ***C. festucacea***

  25 Perigynium bodies narrowly to broadly ovate, widest below the middle and tapering to contracted into the beak..26

      26 At least some sheaths papillose near the collar [30-40×], not prominently whitish mottled; perigynium beaks appressed or ascending in the spikes, exceeding pistillate scales by 0-0.8 mm; beaks and shoulders of perigynia stramineous to reddish brown at maturity...***C. tenera***

      26 Sheaths totally smooth, often whitish mottled; perigynium beaks spreading, mostly exceeding pistillate scales by (0.6-) 0.7-1.6 mm; beaks and shoulders of perigynia greenish to yellowish or greenish brown at maturity......................27

         27 Inflorescences erect to somewhat bent, the lowest internodes mostly 6-10 long, the rachis stiff; leaves 2.2-6.5 mm wide; larger perigynia mostly 3.1-4 mm long and 1.8-2.2 times longer than wide; plants forming small, ± erect clumps often with fewer than 20 stems....................................***C. normalis***

         27 Inflorescences arching or nodding, the lowest internodes (6-) 10-21 mm long, the rachis usually thin and wiry; leaves 1.5-3.5 mm wide; larger perigynia mostly (3.5-4.6 mm long, 2-3 times longer than wide; plants often forming large, spreading clumps of more than 30 stems............ ***C. tenera var. echinodes***

Carex adusta Boott
LESSER BROWN SEDGE

MAP 1380
native

Plants tufted; rootstocks short, blackish. **Stems** 2-8 dm long, stiff, obtusely triangular, brownish tinged at base, clothed with old leaves. **Well-developed leaves** 4-7 to a fertile culm, on lower fourth; **blades** 5-20 cm long and 2-4 mm wide, flat or canaliculate, stiff, yellowish green, roughened towards tip and on margins above; sheaths tight, striate dorsally, white-hyaline ventrally. **Spikes** 4-15, gynaecandrous (staminate flowers below the pistillate); lowest **bract** dilated, the upper scale-like; **scales** light-reddish brown with white-hyaline margins and 3-nerved lighter center; staminate flowers inconspicuous except in terminal spike. **Perigynia** 4-5 mm long, appressed-ascending or looser, concealed by scales, plano-convex, leathery, olive-green or blackish, shining, strongly nerved dorsally, narrowly wing-margined; beak ca. 1.5 mm, flat, serrulate, obliquely cut, bidentate, yellowish brown-tinged. **Achenes** lenticular, brown, shining; stigmas 2, reddish brown.—Dry soil.

Carex adusta
perigynium (l)
pistillate scale (r)

Carex bebbii Olney
BEBB'S SEDGE

MAP 1381
native

Plants tufted. **Stems** sharply 3-angled, 2-8 dm long. **Leaves** 2-5 mm wide; sheaths white, thin and translucent. **Spikes** 5-10, with both staminate and pistillate flowers, pistillate flowers above staminate, 5-8 mm long, clustered in an ovate head 1.5-3 cm long; **pistillate scales** tapered to tip, narrower and slightly shorter than the perigynia. **Perigynia** green to brown, flat on 1 side and convex on other, ovate, 2.5-3.5 mm long, finely nerved on back, nerveless on front, wing-margined, with a finely toothed beak 1/3-1/2 the length of the body, shallowly notched at tip. **Achenes** lens-shaped; stigmas 2. June-Aug.—Wet to moist meadows, marshes, streambanks, ditches and other wet places.

Carex bebbii
perigynium (l)
pistillate scale (r)

1378. *Carex vulpinoidea*

1378A. *Carex obtusata*

1379. *Carex xerantica*

1380. *Carex adusta*

Carex bicknellii Britt.
MAP 1382
BICKNELL'S SEDGE   *native*

Plants tufted; rootstocks short, black. **Stems** 3-12 dm, roughened above, light-brownish at base, clothed with old leaves. **Well-developed leaves** 3-6 to a fertile culm, on lower third; **blades** 1-2 dm long and 2.5-4 mm wide, flat, yellowish or light-green, roughened on margins and towards tip; sheaths white-hyaline ventrally, papillate dorsally. Spikes 3-7, gynaecandrous (staminate flowers below the pistillate), brownish straw-colored; **bracts** scale-like; **scales** brownish straw-colored with hyaline margins and 3-nerved green center. **Perigynia** numerous, ca. 6 mm long, appressed-ascending, flat, thin, distended over achene, straw-colored or greenish above, winged, serrulate above; beak 1-1.5 mm long, flat, serrulate, obliquely cut, bidentate, reddish tipped. **Achenes** lenticular; stigmas 2, short, light-reddish.—Dry soil.

Carex bicknellii
perigynium (l)
pistillate scale (r)

Carex brevior (Dewey) Mackenzie
MAP 1383
SHORT-BEAK SEDGE   *native*

Plants tufted; rootstocks short, somewhat woody, black. **Stems** 3-10 dm long, clothed with old leaves. **Well-developed leaves** 3-6 to a culm, on lower third; **blades** 1-2 dm long and 1.5-4 mm wide, thickish, light-green, roughened towards tip especially on margins; **sheaths** tight, white-hyaline ventrally; sterile shoots conspicuous, the leaves at top. **Spikes** 3-10, gynaecandrous (staminate flowers below the pistillate), in a narrow head; lowest **bracts** lowest often 1-4 cm long, the upper acuminate or awned; **scales** yellowish brown with hyaline margins and 3-nerved green center. **Perigynia** 8-20 to a spike, 4-5.5 mmlong, ascending-spreading, thick, leathery, green above, greenish white beneath, strongly nerved dorsally, winged, serrulate; beak 1 mm long, flat, serrulate, obliquely cut, bidentate, reddish brown-tipped. **Achenes** yellowish brown; stigmas 2, long, reddish brown.—Open places.

Carex brevior
perigynium (l)
pistillate scale (r)

Carex crawfordii Fern.
MAP 1384
CRAWFORD'S SEDGE   *native*

Plants densely tufted. **Stems** 1-8 dm long, stiff. **Leaves** 3-4 on each stem, 1-4 mm wide. **Spikes** 3-15, with both staminate and pistillate flowers, the staminate below the pistillate, grouped into a narrowly oblong, sometimes drooping head; **pistillate scales** light brown with green center, shorter and about as wide as perigynia. **Perigynia** flattened except where enlarged by the achenes, lance-shaped, 3-4 mm long, brown, narrowly winged nearly to the base, finely toothed above the middle, tapered to a long, slender, toothed, notched beak. **Achenes** brown, lens-shaped; stigmas 2. July-Sept.—Moist openings and wetland margins, sandy shorelines.

Carex crawfordii
perigynium (l)
pistillate scale (r)

Carex cristatella Britt.
MAP 1385
CRESTED SEDGE   *native*

Plants tufted, from short rhizomes. **Stems** sharply 3-angled, 3-10 dm long. **Leaves** 3-7 mm wide; sheaths loose, with fine green lines. **Spikes** with both staminate and pistillate flowers, pistillate flowers borne above staminate; spikes 5-12, crowded in an ovate to oblong head; **bracts** much reduced; **pistillate scales** tapered to tip, shorter than the perigynia. **Perigynia** widely spreading when mature, green to pale brown, flat on 1 side and convex on other, 2.5-4 mm long, faintly nerved on both sides, strongly winged above the middle, tapered to a finely toothed, notched beak 1-2 mm long. **Achenes** lens-shaped; stigmas·2. June-Aug.—Wet meadows, ditches, floodplains, marshy shores and streambanks.

Carex cristatella
perigynium (l)
pistillate scale (r)

1381. *Carex bebbii*

1382. *Carex bicknellii*

1383. *Carex brevior*

1384. *Carex crawfordii*

Carex festucacea Schkuhr (NO MAP)
FESCUE SEDGE *threatened | native*

Plants tufted; rootstocks short, black, fibrillose. **Stems** 5-10 dm long, stiff, roughened on angles above, brownish black at base, clothed with old leaves. **Well-developed leaves** 3-5 to a fertile culm, on lower third; **blades** 7.5-30 cm long and 1-5.5 mm wide, flat, light-green; **sheaths** tight, septate-nodulose. **Spikes** 4-10, gynaecandrous (staminate flowers below the pistillate), in a narrow inflorescence; **bracts** scale-like, or the lowest developed; **scales** hyaline, tawny-tinged with 3-nerved green center; **staminate flowers** numerous. **Perigynia** 10-20 to a spike, 3.5 mmlong, appressed-ascending, plano-convex, thick, somewhat leathery, green or straw-colored, strongly nerved over achene, winged, serrulate above; beak 1.25 mm, flat, serrulate, obliquely cut, bidentulate, tawny-tipped. **Achenes** lenticular, light-brown; stigmas 2, light yellowish brown.—Floodplain forests; Jackson Co.

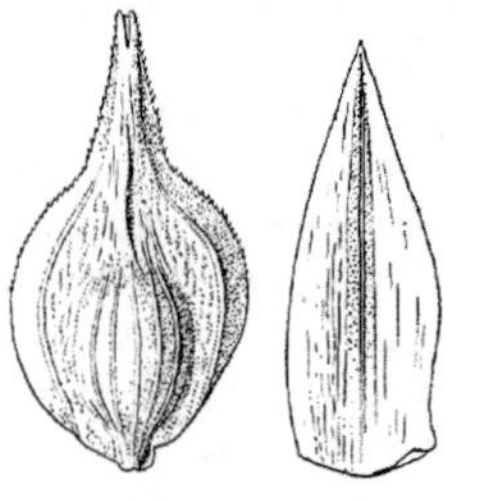
Carex festucacea
perigynium (l)
pistillate scale (r)

Carex foenea Willd. MAP 1386
BRONZE-HEAD OVAL SEDGE *native*
Carex aenea Fernald

Plants densely tufted. **Stems** 2-12 dm long. **Leaves** 3-6 per fertile culm, green, 8-30 cm long and 2-4 mm wide. **Inflorescences** open, usually with widely spaced spikes, brown or greenish brown; **bracts** scalelike, sometimes bristlelike. **Spikes** usually 3-7, nodding, copper-colored; **pistillate scales** usually reddish brown, with 3-veined green or brown midstripe, equaling, and more or less covering the perigynia. **Perigynia** erect-ascending, green or brown, conspicuously 4-9-veined 3-5 mm long, margin flat, including small wing 0.2-0.4 mm wide; beak white or brown, white margined at tip, flat, serrulate, distance from beak tip to achene 1.7-2.5 mm. **Achenes** dark brown at maturity, ovoid-orbicular; stigmas 2.—Dry open sandy places, roadsides, cut-over forests.

Carex foenea
perigynium (l)
pistillate scale (r)

Carex merritt-fernaldii Mackenzie MAP 1387
MERRITT FERNALD'S SEDGE *native*

Plants tufted; rootstocks short, somewhat woody, black. **Stems** 3-10 dm, stiff, clothed with old leaves. **Well-developed leaves** 3-6 to a culm, on lower third; **blades** 1-2 dm long and 1.5-3 mm wide, yellowish green, roughened towards tip especially on margins; **sheaths** tight, white-hyaline ventrally, papillate dorsally. **Spikes** 4-10, gynaecandrous (staminate flowers below the pistillate), in a head 1.5-5 cm long; **bracts** scale-like, the lowest often 1-4 cm, the upper acuminate or awned; **scales** yellowish brown with hyaline margins and 3-nerved green center. **Perigynia** 15-30 to a spike, 4-5 mm long, appressed-ascending, yellowish green or straw-colored, strongly nerved dorsally, winged, serrulate; beak 1 mm, flat, serrulate, obliquely cut, bidentate, reddish brown-tipped. **Achenes** brown, shining; stigmas 2, long, reddish brown.—Dry woods.

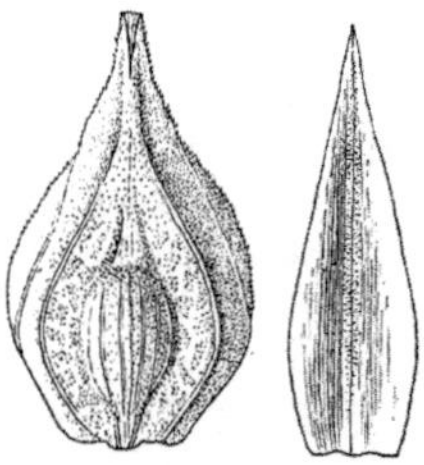
Carex merritt-fernaldii
perigynium (l)
pistillate scale (r)

Carex molesta Mackenzie MAP 1388
TROUBLESOME SEDGE *native*

Plants tufted; rootstocks short, slender, black. **Stems** 3-10 dm long, roughened above, brownish black at base, clothed with old leaves. **Well-developed leaves** 4-7 to a fertile culm, on lower third; **blades** 1-3 dm long and 2-3 mm wide, flat, light-green, rough on margins; **sheaths** tight, green-and-white-mottled dorsally, white-hyaline ventrally, prolonged. **Spikes** 4-8, gynaecandrous (staminate flowers below the pistillate), in a head 2-3 cm long; **bracts** scale-like; **scales** yellowish brown with white-hyaline margins and 3-nerved green center; **staminate flowers**

Carex molesta
perigynium (l)
pistillate scale (r)

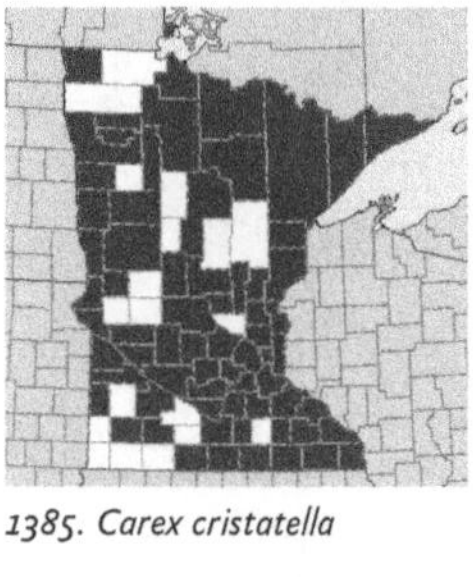
1385. Carex cristatella

1386. Carex foenea

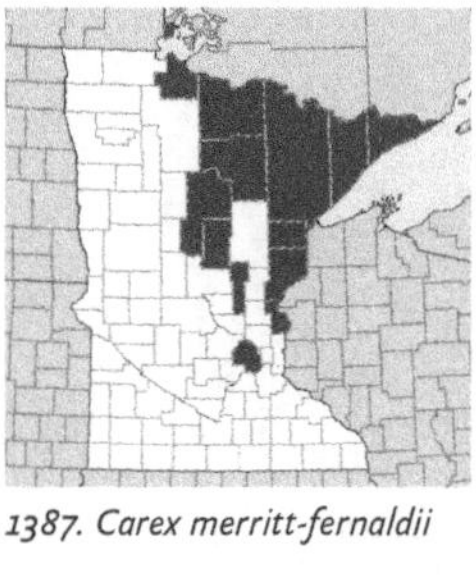
1387. Carex merritt-fernaldii

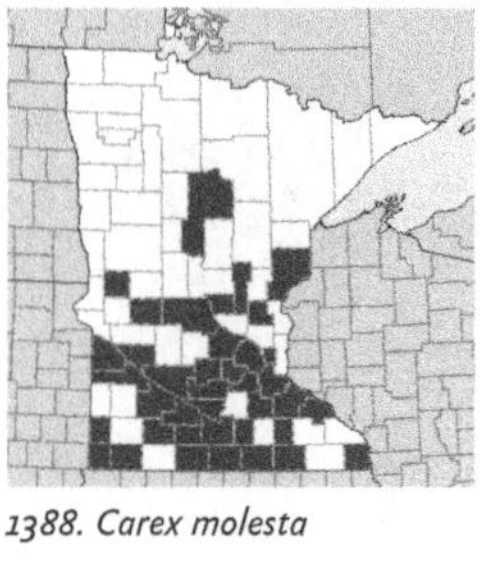
1388. Carex molesta

inconspicuous except in terminal spike. Perigynia 15-30 to a spike, 4.5 mm long, ascending, plano-convex, greenish, wing-margined, serrulate; beak 1.25 mm long, flat, serrulate, obliquely cut, bidentate. **Achenes** lenticular, yellowish brown; stigmas 2, short, light-reddish brown.—Woods.

Carex muskingumensis Schwein.

MUSKINGUM SEDGE

MAP 1389
native

Plants tufted. **Stems** stout, 5-10 dm long, with many leafy sterile stems present. **Leaves** 3-5 mm wide. **Spikes** 5-10, with both staminate and pistillate flowers, the staminate below the pistillate, pointed at both ends, in a dense head; pistillate **scales** pale brown with translucent margins, half as long as the perigynia. **Perigynia** upright, 6-10 mm long, finely nerved on both sides, tapered to a finely toothed, deeply notched beak half as long as the body. **Achenes** lens-shaped; stigmas 2. June-Aug.—Floodplain forests (as along Mississippi River), wet woods.

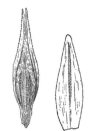

Carex muskingumensis
perigynium (l)
pistillate scale (r)

Carex normalis Mackenzie

GREATER STRAW SEDGE

MAP 1390
native

Plants tufted. **Stems** 3-8 dm long. **Leaves** 2-6 mm wide, lower stem leaves reduced to scales. **Spikes** 5-10, with both staminate and pistillate flowers, the staminate below the pistillate, round in outline, stalkless, loosely grouped in heads; **pistillate scales** translucent, lightly brown-tinged, with green midvein, shorter than the perigynia. **Perigynia** upright, flat on 1 side and convex on other, green or pale green-brown, 3-4 mm long, finely nerved, tapered to a finely toothed beak. **Achenes** lens-shaped; stigmas 2. June-Aug.—Moist to wet deciduous woods, floodplain forests, alder thickets, marshes, pond margins.

Carex normalis
perigynium (l)
pistillate scale (r)

Carex projecta Mackenzie

NECKLACE SEDGE

MAP 1391
native

Plants tufted, from short rhizomes. **Stems** slender and weak, 3-angled, 4-10 dm long, upper stems rough. **Leaves** stiff, 3-7 mm wide; sheaths loose. **Spikes** 7-15, with both staminate and pistillate flowers, pistillate flowers above staminate in each spike, obovate to nearly round, straw-colored, distinct and more or less separated (at least the lower spikes) in a somewhat lax and zigzagged inflorescence; **bracts** inconspicuous; **pistillate scales** straw-colored, narrower and shorter than the perigynia. **Perigynia** ascending to spreading when mature, 3-5 mm long, dull brown, flattened except where filled by the achene, winged on margin, the wing gradually narrowing from middle to base, tapered to a notched, finely toothed beak 1-2 mm long. **Achenes** lens-shaped; stigmas 2. June-Aug. — Floodplain forests, swamps, thickets, wet openings, shaded slopes. *Similar to C. tribuloides but the perigynia tips spreading rather than erect as in C. tribuloides.*

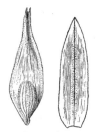

Carex projecta
perigynium (l)
pistillate scale (r)

Carex scoparia Schkuhr

POINTED BROOM SEDGE

MAP 1392
native

Plants densely tufted, sometimes spreading by surface runners. **Stems** 2-10 dm long, sharply 3-angled. **Leaves** 1-3 mm wide; **sheaths** tight, white-translucent. **Spikes** 4-10, with both staminate and pistillate flowers, pistillate flowers borne above staminate, ovate to broadest at middle, clustered or separate, in a narrowly ovate head; **bracts** small, the lowest often bristlelike; **pistillate scales** slightly shorter than perigynia. **Perigynia** greenish white, flat, 3-7 mm long, margins narrowly winged, tapered to a finely toothed, slightly notched beak 1-2 mm long.

Carex scoparia
perigynium (l)
pistillate scale (r)

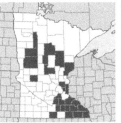

1389. *Carex muskingumensis*　　1390. *Carex normalis*　　1391. *Carex projecta*

Achenes lens-shaped; stigmas 2. May-July.—Wet meadows and openings, low prairie, swamps and sandy lakeshores.

Carex suberecta (Olney) Britt.
PRAIRIE STRAW SEDGE

(NO MAP)
native

Plants tufted. Stems 3-7 dm long. **Leaves** 2-3 mm wide, lower stem leaves reduced to scales. **Spikes** 2-5, stalkless, loosely grouped into a head, with both staminate and pistillate flowers, the staminate below the pistillate; **pistillate scales** shorter and narrower than the perigynia, yellow-brown with a pale midvein and narrow translucent margins, tapered to a tip. **Perigynia** numerous, conspicuously swollen over the achene, 4-5 mm long, abruptly contracted to the flat, finely toothed beak. **Achenes** lens-shaped; stigmas 2. May-July.—Calcareous swamps, marshes, wet meadows, calcareous fens; Winona County (main range south of Minn).

Carex suberecta
perigynium (l)
pistillate scale (r)

Carex tenera Dewey
QUILL SEDGE

MAP 1393
native

Plants tufted, from short rhizomes. **Stems** slender, sharply 3-angled, 3-8 cm long, rough-to-touch above. **Leaves** 0.5-3 mm wide; **sheaths** white-translucent on front, mottled green and white on back. **Spikes** 4-8, with both staminate and pistillate flowers, pistillate flowers borne above staminate, ovate to round, loose in nodding heads; **bracts** small, sometimes bristlelike, longer than the spike; **pistillate scales** slightly shorter than perigynia. **Perigynia** ovate, flat on 1 side and convex on other, straw-colored when mature, 2.5-4 mm long, wing-margined, tapered to a notched, finely toothed beak 1-2 mm long. **Achenes** lens-shaped; stigmas 2. June-Aug.—Wet to moist meadows, streambanks, floodplains and moist woods.

Carex tenera
perigynium (l)
pistillate scale (r)

ADDITIONAL TAXON

• *Carex tenera* var. *echinodes* sometimes treated as separate species *Carex echinodes* (Fern.) P. Rothr., Reznicek & Hipp, found in mesic to wet forests (MAP 1394). Inflorescences nodding, similar to those of *C. tenera* var. *tenera*, but the perigynium tips arch outward and are often 1 mm or more longer than the pistillate scales.

Carex tribuloides Wahlenb.
BLUNT BROOM SEDGE

MAP 1395
native

Plants tufted, from short rhizomes. **Stems** sharply 3-angled, 3-9 dm long, longer than leaves. **Leaves** stiff, 3-7 mm wide; sheaths loose, with green lines. **Spikes** 5-15, with both staminate and pistillate flowers, pistillate flowers borne above staminate, obovate, densely to loosely clustered into an ovate or oblong head; bracts inconspicuous; **pistillate scales** tapered to tip, shorter than the perigynia. **Perigynia** light green to pale brown, flattened except where filled by the achenes, lance-shaped, 3-6 mm long, broadly winged near middle, tapered to a notched, finely toothed beak 1-2 mm long. **Achenes** lens-shaped; stigmas 2. June-July. —Floodplain forests, shady low areas in woods, pond and lake margins, marshes, low prairie.

Carex tribuloides
perigynium (l)
pistillate scale (r)

CAREX SECTION PALUDOSAE

Mostly slender, long-rhizomatous plants, with red basal leaf sheaths (and ladder-fibrillose in all but *C. houghtoniana*), and pubescent perigynia. *Carex lacustris* is somewhat different, having glabrous perigynia.

1 Perigynia glabrous . . . . *C. lacustris*

1392. Carex scoparia   *1393. Carex tenera*   *1394. C. tenera var. echinodes*   *1395. Carex tribuloides*

1 Perigynia pubescent. 2

  2 Perigynia 4.5-6.5 mm long, sparsely hairy, the strong nerves of perigynium and even cellular detail of body therefore evident; plants usually of dry and sandy habitats . . . . *C. houghtoniana*

  2 Perigynia 3-4.5 (-5.2) mm long, densely pubescent, nerving of perigynium and cellular detail therefore obscured; plants usually of wetlands. 3

    3 Leaf blades involute to triangular-channeled, 0.7-2 (-2.2) mm wide, those of vegetative shoots especially long-prolonged into a curled, filiform tip; leaves and lowermost bracts with the midvein low, rounded, and forming an inconspicuous keel (at least proximally) . . . . *C. lasiocarpa*

    3 Leaf blades flat or folded into an M-shape except at the base and near the tip, (2-) 2.2-4.5 (-6.5) mm wide, not prolonged into a long filiform tip; leaves and lowest bract with the midvein forming a prominent and sharply pointed keel for much of the length . . . . *C. pellita*

Carex houghtoniana Torr. ex Dewey
HOUGHTON'S SEDGE

MAP 1396
native

Plants loosely tufted and stoloniferous; stolons long, slender, horizontal, scaly. **Stems** 1.5-6.5 dm long, stiff, rough above, purplish at base, the basal sheaths filamentose. **Well-developed leaves** 2-4 to a fertile culm, on lower third; **blades** 8-20 cm long and 2.5-4 mm wide, flat with revolute margins, septate-nodulose, deep-green, roughened especially on margins and towards tip; sheaths tight, thin and yellowish brown-tinged ventrally. **Terminal spike** staminate, rough-peduncled, often with a shorter spike near base; **lateral spikes** 1-3, pistillate; lowest bract leaflike; pistillate scales reddish brown with hyaline margins and 3-nerved green center. **Perigynia** 15-30 to a spike, 5-6 mm long, spreading or ascending, obscurely triangular, olive or brownish green, short-hirsute, 15-20-ribbed; beak 2 mm long, bidentate, purple between teeth, scabrous within. **Achenes** triangular with concave sides, closely enveloped, yellowish brown; stigmas 3, short, blackish.—Open places where sandy or rocky.

Carex houghtoniana
perigynium (l)
pistillate scale (r)

Carex lacustris Willd.
LAKEBANK SEDGE

MAP 1397
native

Plants large, tufted, from scaly rhizomes. **Stems** erect, 3-angled, 6-13 dm long, rough-to-touch. **Leaves** 6-15 mm wide; **sheaths** often red-tinged, the lower ones disintegrating into a network of fibers. **Spikes** either staminate or pistillate, the upper 2-4 staminate, stalkless; the lower 2-4 spikes pistillate, erect, usually separate, stalkless or short-stalked, cylindric; **bracts** leaflike, some or all longer than the head; **pistillate scales** awned or tapered to tip, the body shorter than the perigynia, the sides thin and translucent to pale brown. **Perigynia** olive, flattened to nearly round in section, narrowly ovate, 5-7 mm long, with more than 10 raised nerves, tapered to a smooth beak about 1 mm long. **Achenes** 3-angled;   stigmas   3.   May-Aug. —Swamps, marshes, kettle wetlands, wetland margins, usually in shallow water; low areas in tamarack swamps.

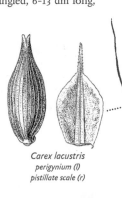

Carex lacustris
perigynium (l)
pistillate scale (r)

Carex lasiocarpa Ehrh.
SLENDER SEDGE

MAP 1398
native

   Carex lanuginosa Michx. var. *americana* (Fern.) Boivin

Colony-forming perennial, from long, scaly rhizomes. **Stems** loosely tufted, 3-angled, 3-10 dm long. **Leaves** elongate and inrolled, 1-2 mm wide; sheaths tinged with yellow-brown. **Spikes** either all staminate or pistillate, usually the upper 2 staminate; the staminate spikes slender, on a long stalk; the lower 1-3 spikes pistillate, widely separate, more or less stalkless, cylindric; bracts leaflike, the lowest usually longer than the stem; **pistillate scales** purple-brown with a green center, narrowly ovate. **Perigynia** dull brown green, obovate, nearly round in section, 3-5 mm long, densely soft hairy, contracted to a beak about 1 mm long, the beak teeth erect. **Achenes** yellow-brown, 3-angled

Carex lasiocarpa

Carex lasiocarpa
perigynium (l)
pistillate scale (r)

with concave sides; stigmas 3. June–Aug.—Peatlands and wet peaty soils, open bogs, pond margins (where a pioneer mat-former).

Carex pellita Muhl
WOOLLY SEDGE
MAP 1399
native

Carex lanuginosa auct. non Michx.
Carex lasiocarpa Ehrh. var. *latifolia* (Boeckl.) Gilly

Plants tufted and stoloniferous; stolons long, horizontal, scaly. **Stems** 3–10 dm long, stiff, rough above, dark-purplish red at base, the lower sheaths filamentose;. **Well-developed leaves** 2–5 to a fertile culm; **blades** 2–6 dm long and 1.5–5 mm wide, flat with revolute margins, septate-nodulose, rough especially towards the tip; sheaths purplish tinged. Usually 2 upper spikes staminate, long-peduncled; lower 2–3 spikes pistillate; bracts sheathless or nearly so; pistillate scales acuminate, mucronate or awned, ciliate, reddish brown with hyaline margins and 3-nerved green center. **Perigynia** 25–75 to a spike, 2.5–3.5 mm long, ascending, suborbicular, inflated, leathery, dull-brownish green, densely hairy, many-ribbed; beak 1 mm, bidentate. **Achenes** triangular with concave sides and blunt angles, loosely enveloped, yellowish brown, punctate; stigmas 3, blackish.—Swamps.

*Carex pellita
perigynium (l)
pistillate scale (r)*

CAREX SECTION PANICEAE

Plants colonial, shoots arising singly or few together; rhizomes elongate; bases brown to maroon. Leaf blades typically stiff. Terminal spike staminate, typically raised above the uppermost pistillate spike. Lateral spikes generally cylindrical, ascending (except *Carex vaginata*). Perigynia several-veined, mostly short-beaked, papillose (except *C. vaginata*). Calciphiles, growing mostly in wet soils (but *C. meadii* common in dry calcareous prairies). *The section is fairly distinctive and easy to recognize, apart from C. vaginata, which is morphologically distinct.*

1   Perigynium with a beak ca. 1 mm long. . . . . *C. vaginata*
1   Perigynium beakless, indistinctly beaked, or contracted to beak less than 0.5 mm 2
      2   Perigynia strongly ascending, beakless or tapering to an erect, very short straight beak; leaves stiff, thick, channeled, strongly glaucous . . . . **C. livida**
      2   Perigynia ascending to spreading, tapering to a bent apex; leaves relatively thin and flexible, flat or folded, green to somewhat glaucous 3
            3   Bladeless basal sheaths and proximal leaf sheaths strongly tinged with reddish purple; plants forming loose clumps to extensive closed colonies of vegetative shoots from superficial rhizomes; perigynia ± 2-ranked; plants of rich forests . . . . **C. woodii**
            3   Bladeless basal sheaths and proximal leaf sheaths brownish, green, or faintly, irregularly tinged with reddish purple; plants usually with vegetative shoots widely scattered and inconspicuous from deep rhizomes; perigynia 3-6-ranked; plants of moist, usually sunny habitats 4
                  4   Largest achenes 1.7–2.2 (–2.5) mm wide; longest anthers (3.5–) 4–4.6 mm long; ligules mostly 0.4–1.2 times as long as wide . . . . **C. meadii**
                  4   Largest achenes 1.2–1.7 mm wide; longest anthers 2.8–3.5 (–3.8) mm long; ligules mostly (0.8–) 1–2 times as long as wide . . . . **C. tetanica**

Carex livida (Wahlenb.) Willd.
LIVID SEDGE
MAP 1400
native
Plants forming small clumps, from long slender rhizomes. **Stems** erect, to 6 dm long, light brown at base. **Leaves** 6–12 on lower third of stem, strongly waxy blue-green, channeled, 0.5–4 mm wide, dried leaves of the previous year conspicuous; sheaths thin. **Terminal spike** staminate (or rarely with both staminate and

1396. Carex houghtoniana   *1397. Carex lacustris*   *1398. Carex lasiocarpa*   *1399. Carex pellita*

pistillate flowers, the staminate below the pistillate), linear; pistillate spikes 1-3, the lowest more or less separate, sometimes long-stalked, the upper grouped, stalkless or short-stalked, with 5-15 upright perigynia; **bracts** leaflike, sometimes longer than the head; **pistillate scales** shorter than the perigynia, light purple with broad green center and white translucent margins. **Perigynia** slightly flattened and rounded 3-angled, 2-5 mm long, strongly waxy blue-green, with small dots, two-ribbed and with fine nerves, tapered to a beakless tip. **Achenes** 3-angled with prominent ribs, brown-black; stigmas 3. July-Aug.—Wet meadows and fens, especially where calcium-rich.

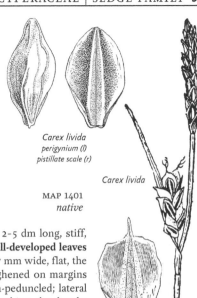

Carex livida
perigynium (l)
pistillate scale (r)

Carex livida

Carex meadii Dewey
MEAD'S SEDGE

MAP 1401
native

Carex tetanica Schkuhr var. *meadii* (Dewey) Bailey

Plants with long, deep, horizontal, whitish stolons. **Stems** 2-5 dm long, stiff, brownish or purplish tinged and often fibrillose at base. **Well-developed leaves** 3-6 to a fertile culm, near base; blades 7-15 cm long and 2.5-7 mm wide, flat, the edges involute towards base, thickish, grayish green, roughened on margins towards tip; sheaths tight. **Terminal spike** staminate, rough-peduncled; lateral spikes 1-3, pistillate, separate on rough peduncles; **bracts** sheathing, the sheaths somewhat enlarged upward, loose; **pistillate scales** awned, purplish red or -brown with hyaline margins and 3-nerved green center. **Perigynia** 8-30 to a spike, 3-5 mm long, ascending, obtusely triangular, yellowish green or brownish, 2-keeled, strongly nerved; beak minute, bent, the orifice entire or nearly so, purplish tinged. **Achenes** triangular with concave sides, closely enveloped, brownish black with greenish blunt angles, granular; stigmas 3, long, reddish brown.—Prairies.

Carex meadii
pistillate scale

Carex tetanica Schkuhr
RIGID SEDGE

MAP 1402
native

Tufted perennial from slender rhizomes. **Stems** 3-angled, 1-6 dm long, rough-to-touch above. **Leaves** 1-5 mm wide; sheaths tight, white or yellow and translucent. **Spikes** either all staminate or pistillate, terminal spike staminate; lateral spikes pistillate, usually widely separated, the lower spikes short-cylindric, stalked, loosely flowered with perigynia in 3 rows; bracts shorter than the head; **pistillate scales** purple-brown on margins, as wide as but shorter than the perigynia. **Perigynia** green, faintly 3-angled, obovate, 2-4 mm long, 2-ribbed; beak tiny, bent. **Achenes** 3-angled with concave sides; stigmas 3. May-July.—Wet meadows and openings, low prairies, marshy areas.

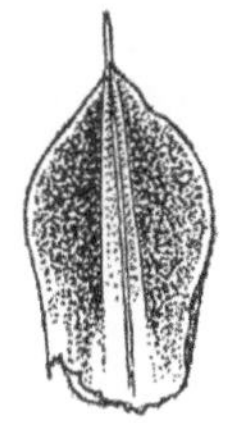

Carex tetanica
pistillate scale

Carex vaginata Tausch
SHEATHED SEDGE

MAP 1403
native

Carex saltuensis Bailey

Perennial, from long rhizomes. **Stems** 2-6 dm long, several together. **Leaves** 2-5 mm wide, not scale-like at base of stem. **Terminal spike** staminate, 1-2 cm long; pistillate spikes 1-3, sometimes staminate at tip, loosely spreading, widely separated, the lower stalks long, the upper shorter; **bracts** with loose sheaths and blades shorter than the spikes; **pistillate scales** purple-brown, sometimes with a narrow green center. **Perigynia** usually in 2 rows, the lower separate, the upper overlapping, 3-5 mm long, narrowly obovate, with a curved beak 1 mm long.

Carex vaginata
perigynium (l)
pistillate scale (r)

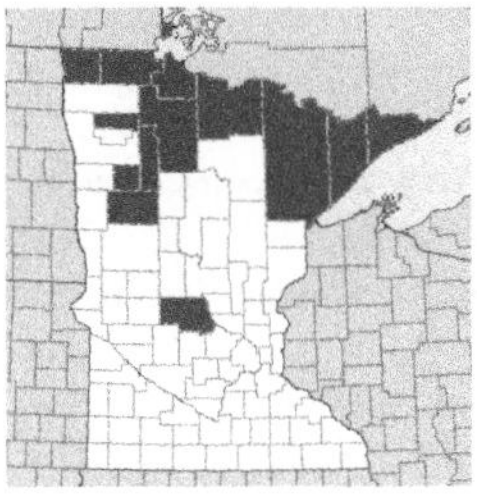

1400. *Carex livida* 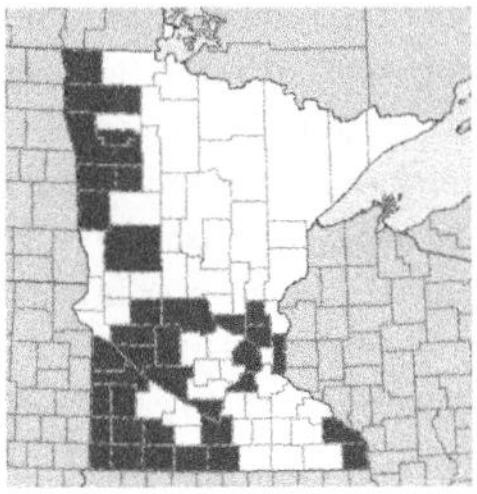   1401. *Carex meadii*   1402. *Carex tetanica* 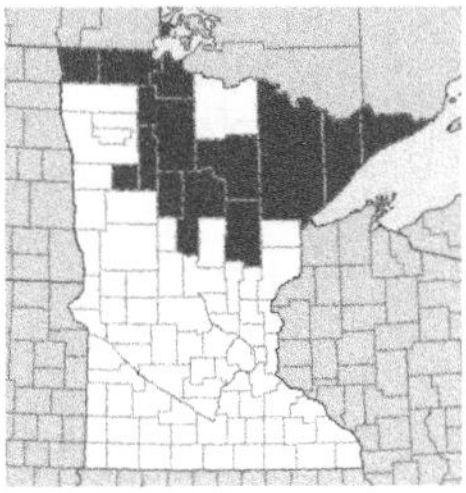   1403. *Carex vaginata*

Achenes 3-angled, nearly filling the perigynia; stigmas 3. June–Aug.—Swamps and thickets, especially where calcium-rich.

Carex woodii Dewey
PRETTY SEDGE
MAP 1404
native

Carex tetanica Schkuhr var. *woodii* (Dewey) Wood

Plants loosely tufted and stoloniferous; stolons slender, purple, scaly. **Stems** 3–7 dm long, roughened above; sterile shoots numerous, long. **Well-developed leaves** 2–4 to a fertile culm, near base; **blades** 5–20 cm long and 2.5–4 mm wide, flat with revolute margins, flaccid, light-green, white-lined below; sheaths loose, overlapping, white or yellowish hyaline ventrally. **Terminal spike** staminate, the peduncle roughish; lateral spikes 2–3, pistillate, on slender roughish peduncles; bracts long-sheathing, the sheaths tight; **pistillate scales** purplish or reddish brown with hyaline margins and 3-nerved green center. **Perigynia** 6–15 to a spike, 3.5–4 mm long, ascending, yellowish green, puncticulate, 2-keeled, lightly nerved; beak 0.5 mm long, excurved, the orifice oblique, entire, hyaline. **Achenes** triangular with concave sides and blunt angles, closely enveloped, yellowish brown; stigmas 3, reddish brown.—Dry woodlands.

Carex woodii
perigynium (l)
pistillate scale (r)

CAREX SECTION PHACOCYSTIS

Plants often cespitose; rhizomes short or long. Lower leaf sheaths brown to red, fibrous in some species. Terminal spike typically staminate, ascending. Lateral spikes pistillate or androgynous, ascending to nodding or drooping, elongate. Perigynia biconvex with distinct marginal veins. Stigmas 2. Mostly common species of Minnesota's wetlands, ranging from floodplains and wet forests (*Carex crinita, C. gynandra, C. emoryi*), to sedge meadows (*C. stricta*), wet prairies (*C. haydenii*), bogs and marshes (*C. aquatilis*), and wet roadsides and ditches.

1 Pistillate spikes on ± lax peduncles, at length drooping, the scales prominently awned; body of achene with an irregular notch, constriction, or wrinkle on one side. 2

  2 Sheaths smooth; bodies of most if not all pistillate scales shallowly lobed at summit (on each side of base of the awn) . . . . **C. crinita**

  2 Sheaths scabrous-hispidulous; bodies of most or all pistillate scales on lower part of spike truncate or tapered at summit . . . . **C. gynandra**

1 Pistillate spikes erect or strongly ascending, often sessile, the scales acute or acuminate, not awned; body of achene smooth and ± regular 3

  3 Fertile stems of current year with conspicuous bladeless sheaths at base, not surrounded by dried-up bases of the previous year's leaves but arising laterally; lowest bract usually shorter than to approximately equaling the inflorescence. 4

    4 Perigynia suborbicular to obovoid, 2–2.3 mm long at maturity, broadest at or slightly above middle, abruptly contracted to a minute tip, at least the lower ones in a spike much exceeded by the spreading scales; lower leaf sheaths not or only slightly tearing to form a ladder-like arrangement of fibers, the sheaths smooth ventrally; ligule longer than width of leaf blade; plants with short ascending rhizomes. . . . . **C. haydenii**

    4 Perigynia elliptic or ovate, mostly 2.2–2.7 (-3.3) mm long at maturity, broadest at or slightly below the middle, ± tapered to apex, as long as or longer than the scales (rarely exceeded by scales); ventral surface of lower leaf sheaths tearing to form a ladder-like arrangement of fibers (ladder-fibrillose) or if not, then the ligule shorter than width of leaf blade; plants with long horizontal rhizomes 5

      5 Ligule longer than width of leaf blade (deeply inverted V-shaped); ventral surface of lower leaf sheaths tearing to form a ladder-like arrangement of fibers and usually minutely scabrous and red-dotted, especially near the apex . . . . **C. stricta**

      5 Ligule shorter than width of leaf blade (often nearly horizontal); ventral surface of lower leaf sheaths not tearing to form a ladder like arrangement of fibers, smooth and whitish . . . . **C. emoryi**

  3 Fertile stems of current year mostly lacking bladeless sheaths at base, arising centrally from tufts of dried-up bases of previous years leaves; lowest bract usually conspicuously longer than the inflorescence 6

    6 Perigynia nerveless (except sometimes at the base); staminate spikes usually 2 or more. **C. aquatilis**

    6 Perigynia conspicuously few-ribbed on both sides; staminate spike usually 1 7

      7 Plants densely tufted, without long rhizomes; scales with a broad central green portion about as wide as the darker margins; leaves mostly overtopping spikes . . . . **C. lenticularis**

      7 Plants colonial from elongated rhizomes; scales with very narrow green portion much narrower than the broad, dark margins, scarcely if at all broader than the midrib; leaves mostly shorter than stems . . . . **C. nigra**

Carex aquatilis Wahlenb.
WATER SEDGE

MAP 1405
native

Plants large, tufted or forming turfs; spreading by many slender rhizomes. **Stems** 3-12 dm long, 3-angled, usually rough-to-touch below the spikes. **Leaves** waxy blue-green, 2-7 mm wide; sheaths white or purple-dotted. **Spikes** 3-5, the upper spikes staminate, the middle and lower spikes pistillate or often with staminate flowers borne above pistillate; pistillate scales tapered to tip. **Perigynia** pale green to yellow-brown or red-brown, broadest near tip, not inflated, 2-3 mm long; beak tiny. **Achenes** lens-shaped; stigmas 2. May-Aug.—Wet meadows, marshes, shores, streambanks, kettle lakes, ditches and fens.

Carex aquatilis
perigynium (l)
pistillate scale (r)

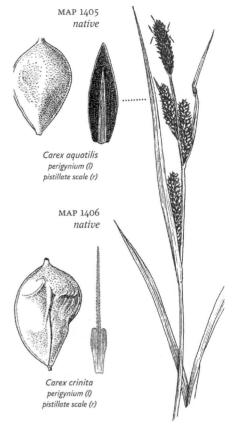

Carex aquatilis

Carex crinita Lam.
FRINGED SEDGE

MAP 1406
native

Plants large, densely tufted. **Stems** 5-15 dm long. **Leaves** 7-13 mm wide, lowest stem leaves reduced to scales; sheaths smooth. **Spikes** staminate or pistillate, drooping on slender stalks; staminate spikes 1-3, above pistillate spikes; pistillate spikes 2-5, narrowly cylindric; **bract** leaflike, without a sheath; **pistillate scales** rounded and notched at tip with pale midvein prolonged into a toothed awn to 10 mm long, scale edges coppery-brown. **Perigynia** green, 2-ribbed, nerves faint or absent, round in cross-section, abruptly tapered to a tiny beak. **Achenes** lens-shaped; stigmas 2. May-July.—Swamps and alder thickets, wet openings, ditches and potholes. *Similar to C. gynandra but with smooth sheaths, lower pistillate scales rounded at tip, and perigynia round in section and inflated.*

Carex crinita
perigynium (l)
pistillate scale (r)

Carex emoryi Dewey
EMORY'S SEDGE

MAP 1407
native

Plants loosely tufted, from scaly rhizomes. **Stems** 3-angled, 4-12 dm long. **Leaves** 3-7 mm wide, lowest leaves reduced to red-brown sheaths; upper sheaths white or yellow-tinged and translucent, lower sheaths red-brown. **Spikes** 3-7, the terminal 1 or 2 all staminate, the lateral spikes all pistillate or with staminate flowers above the pistillate; lowest bract leaflike; **pistillate scales** narrower than the perigynia. **Perigynia** light green, becoming straw-colored at maturity, convex on both sides, 1.5-3 mm long; stigmas 2. May-July.—Shores, streambanks, wet meadows and floodplain forests, sometimes forming pure stands, especially along rivers.

Carex emoryi
perigynium (l)
pistillate scale (r)

Carex gynandra Schwein.
NODDING SEDGE

MAP 1408
native

Carex crinita Lam. var. *gynandra* (Schwein.) Schwein. & Torr.
Plants large, tufted. **Stems** 5-15 dm long, longer than leaves. **Leaves** 7-14 mm wide, lowest leaves reduced to scales; sheaths finely hairy; **bracts** leaflike, lowest bract 1-3.5 dm long. **Spikes** either staminate or pistillate, spreading or drooping and

1404. *Carex woodii*

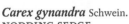

1405. *Carex aquatilis*

1406. *Carex crinita*

1407. *Carex emoryi*

often curved, stalked; staminate spikes 1-3, above pistillate; pistillate spikes 2-5, long-cylindric; **lower pistillate scales** 5-6 mm long, with a pale midrib, tapered to an awned tip about 5 mm long. **Perigynia** green, ovate to oval, somewhat flattened, not inflated, 3-4 mm long. **Achenes** lens-shaped, stigmas 2. June-July.—Wet openings and swamps. *Similar to C. crinita, but with finely hairy sheaths, lower pistillate scales tapered to an awned tip, and perigynia somewhat flattened and not inflated.*

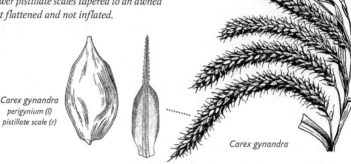

Carex gynandra
perigynium (l)
pistillate scale (r)

Carex gynandra

Carex haydenii Dewey
CLOUD SEDGE

MAP 1409
native

Plants loosely tufted, from short rhizomes. **Stems** arising from previous year's clumps of leaves (persistent at the base of the new leaves), 3-angled, 3-10 dm long, rough-to-touch above. **Leaves** 2-5 mm wide, the lower leaves bladeless and sheathlike; **sheaths** white to yellow on front, green on back, translucent. **Spikes** 3-6, the upper 1-3 staminate, the terminal spike largest, the others smaller; the lower 2-3 pistillate or with staminate flowers above pistillate; **lowest bract** leaflike, usually shorter than the head; **pistillate scales** tapered to tip, longer than the perigynia. **Perigynia** pale brown when mature, often with dark brown spots, convex on both sides, inflated at tip, 2-3 mm long; beak tiny. **Achenes** lens-shaped; stigmas 2. May-July.—Wet to moist meadows and swales, marshes and streambanks; often with dark-scaled sedge (*C. buxbaumii*).

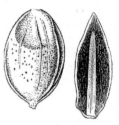

Carex haydenii
perigynium (l)
pistillate scale (r)

Carex lenticularis Michx.
LAKESHORE SEDGE

MAP 1410
native

Plants densely tufted. **Stems** 1-6 dm long, upright, slender, brown at base. **Leaves** clustered on lower third of stem, upright, long-tapered to tip, 1-2 mm wide; **sheaths** dotted with yellow-brown on front. **Staminate spike** single, sometimes with a few pistillate flowers, stalked, linear; **pistillate spikes** 3-5, upright, the upper stalkless, the lower stalked, the upper grouped, the lower separate, linear; lowest **bract** leaflike, erect, much longer than the head, the upper bracts shorter; **pistillate scales** red or red-brown, with a 3-veined, green center, the margins translucent near tip, narrower and usually shorter than the perigynia. **Perigynia** upright, soon deciduous, flattened, convex on both sides and sharply two-edged, 2-3 mm long, waxy blue-green, with a few yellow glandular dots or bumps, tapered at the abruptly pointed tip; the beak small, to 0.2 mm long. **Achenes** lens-shaped, brown; stigmas 2. June-Sept.—Rocky and sandy lakeshores, rock pools along Lake Superior, shallow ponds, sedge mats.

Carex lenticularis
perigynium (l)
pistillate scale (r)

1408. *Carex gynandra*

1409. *Carex haydenii*

1410. *Carex lenticularis*

1411. *Carex stricta*

Carex stricta Lam.   MAP 1411
TUSSOCK SEDGE   *native*

Plants densely tufted, from long scaly rhizomes, forming large raised hummocks
to 1 m tall. **Stems** 3-angled, 3-10 dm long, rough-to-touch. **Leaves** 2-6 mm wide,
the lower leaves reduced to sheaths around the base of stem; **sheaths** white to
red-brown on front, green on back, the lower sheaths breaking into ladderlike
thin strands. **Spikes** mostly all staminate or pistillate (sometimes mixed), the upper
1-3 spikes staminate, the terminal spike 1.5-5 cm long, the lower 2-5 spikes
pistillate or some with staminate flowers borne above pistillate; **lowest bract**
leaflike; **pistillate scales** equal or longer than the perigynia but narrower.
Perigynia green at tip and margins, golden to yellow-brown in middle, with white
or brown bumps, convex on both sides to nearly flat, 2-3 mm long, 2-ribbed with
a few faint nerves on both sides; beak short, to only 0.3 mm long. **Achenes** lens-
shaped; stigmas 2. May-July.—Often dominant sedge of wet meadows, marshes,
fens, shores, streambanks, ditches. *The mounded hummocks are distinctive.*

Carex stricta
perigynium (l)
pistillate scale (r)

CAREX SECTION PHAESTOGLOCHIN

Plants tufted; rhizomes short or inconspicuous; bases pale to brown, occasionally reddish. Inner band
of the leaf sheaths hyaline, corrugated or smooth. Spikes all or mostly androgynous, simple in most
taxa, the lower branched in some species. Perigynia mostly plano-convex, beaks typically bidentate.
Mostly upland species of forests and open, sometimes disturbed habitats.

ADDITIONAL SPECIES
• *Carex hookeriana* Dewey (Hooker's sedge), a Great Plains species; in Minn known only from Becker County
(along farm road where likely introduced).

1 Leaf sheaths loose, white with green veins or mottled green and white on back; wider blades 5-10 mm broad . 2
   2 Pistillate scales with narrowly acuminate or awned tips reaching over the bases or all the way to the ends of
     the beaks of the perigynia they subtend; anthers ca. 1.1-2.4 mm long; stigmas quite elongate and slender, when
     intact and well developed, protruding 1.5 mm or more from the perigynia; spikes crowded in a dense
     inflorescence. . . . . ***C. gravida***
   2 Pistillate scales with short-acuminate, slightly cuspidate, acute, or obtuse tips almost or not at all reaching the
     bases of the beaks of the perigynia they subtend; anthers 0.7-1.1 (-1.3) mm long; stigmas shorter and stouter,
     protruding slightly from perigynia; spikes crowded or the lower (in *C. sparganioides*) becoming well separated
     3
       3 Spikes close together, the lower not separated more than their length, usually ± overlapping; perigynia 3.6-
         4.5 mm long, 2-3 times as long as wide, the bodies not wing-margined; widest leaf blades 5-7 (-8) mm
         wide . . . . ***C. cephaloidea***
       3 Spikes well separated below, the lower ones ± remote; perigynia 3-4.1 mm long, 1.3-2 times as long as wide,
         the bodies ± narrowly thin-winged; widest leaf blades 5.5-10 mm wide . . . .*C. sparganioides*
1 Leaf sheaths ± tight and slender and uniform green or whitish on back; wider blades 1-4.3 mm broad 4
   4 Perigynia mostly widely spreading at maturity, conspicuously spongy-thickened at their bases and there
     puckered in drying, the wire-like margin above the base tending to turn inward. 5
       5 Wider leaf blades mostly 0.9-1.8 (very rarely 2.5) mm broad; stigmas reddish to dark brown, slender and
         elongate (when intact), often protruding 1-1.5 mm or more, often reflexed but otherwise straight or slightly
         sinuous. . . . . ***C. radiata***
       5 Wider leaf blades mostly (1.5-2.7 mm broad; stigmas very dark reddish brown, comparatively short and
         stout, strongly curled . . . . ***C. rosea***
   4 Perigynia mostly ascending and not widely spreading, at most with thin spongy area at base not conspicuously
     puckered in drying (unless immature), the margin above flat or slightly incurved 6
       6 Inflorescence crowded to oblong and interrupted (the lower spikes overlapping but distinct); leaf blades
         densely papillose above (at 20×-30×; bodies of scales more (often much more) than half as long as bodies
         of the perigynia they subtend; larger perigynia in spike 3-4 mm long. . . . . ***C. muehlenbergii***
       6 Inflorescence densely crowded, ± ovoid, the spikes in a close head and nearly indistinguishable except by
         the slightly protruding setaceous bracts; leaf blades smooth above the collar or the cellular outlines
         conspicuous, but only rarely some leaves papillose; bodies of scales usually about or only slightly more
         than half as long as bodies of the perigynia; perigynia 2.5-3.2 mm long . . . . ***C. cephalophora***

Carex cephaloidea (Dewey) Dewey
THIN-LEAF SEDGE

MAP 1412
native

Carex sparganioides Muhl. var. *cephaloidea* (Dewey) Carey

Rootstocks short, stout, brownish black, fibrillose. **Stems** 3-5 dm long, weak, serrulate on angles above, light-brownish tinged at base. **Leaves** 25-35 cm long and 3-7 mm wide (lower leaves shorter), flat, thin, weak, roughened on margins and towards tip; sheaths loose, overlapping, green-and-white-mottled dorsally, the lowest transversely rugulose; ligule dark-margined. **Spikes** 5-10, androgynous (staminate flowers above the pistillate); **bracts** scale-like or setiform; **scales** thin, greenish hyaline with green midrib; staminate flowers few. **Perigynia** 3.5-4 mm long, exceeding scales, spreading, plano-convex, deep-green, sharp-edged; beak 0.5 mm, serrulate, bidentate, white-hyaline within. **Achenes** lenticular; stigmas 2, short, reddish brown.—Woods.

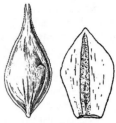

Carex cephaloidea
perigynium (l)
pistillate scale (r)

Carex cephalophora Muhl.
OVAL-LEAF SEDGE

MAP 1413
native

Plants tufted; rootstocks short, black, fibrillose. **Stems** 2-5 dm long, stiff, roughened beneath head, light-brownish tinged at base. **Well-developed leaves** 3-5 to a stem, on lower fourth; blades 1-4 dm long and 2-4.5 mm wide, flat, flaccid, pale-green, roughened on margins and towards tip; sheaths tight. **Spikes** 3-8, androgynous (staminate flowers above the pistillate); **bracts** setiform, 1-5 cm long; **scales** greenish hyaline with green midrib; staminate flowers few. **Perigynia** 2.5 mm long, ascending or spreading, plano-convex, light-green or yellowish, nerveless or 2-3-nerved dorsally, the margins raised, sharp; beak 0.5-0.75 mm long, serrulate, bidentate, the teeth triangular, white-hyaline within. **Achenes** lenticular, filling perigynia; stigmas 2, short, reddish brown.—Dry woods.

Carex cephalophora
perigynium (l)
pistillate scale (r)

Carex gravida Bailey
HEAVY SEDGE

MAP 1414
native

Plants tufted; rootstocks short, woody, blackish, fibrillose. **Stems** 3-6 dm long, weak, roughened above, light-brown at base. **Well-developed leaves** 4-6 to a fertile stem; blades 15-25 cm long and 3.5-5 mm wide, flat, green; **sheaths** green-and-white-mottled. **Spikes** 6-12, androgynous (staminate flowers above the pistillate); **bracts** setaceous; **scales** thin, reddish tinged, with excurrent green midvein; staminate flowers inconspicuous. **Perigynia** 5-15 to a spike, 4 mm long, ascending or spreading, plano-convex, greenish straw-colored or shining and light-yellowish brown, obscurely nerved dorsally, sharp-margined, serrulate above, spongy at base; beak 1 mm, serrulate, bidentate, the teeth hyaline within. **Achenes** filling perigynia, lenticular, brownish yellow; stigmas 2, short, light-reddish brown.—Prairies.

Carex gravida
perigynium (l)
pistillate scale (r)

Carex muehlenbergii Schkuhr ex Willd.
MUHLENBERG'S SEDGE

MAP 1415
native

Plants tufted; rootstocks short, somewhat woody, dark, fibrillose. **Stems** 2-9 dm long, stiff, rough above, light-brownish at base, the old leaves conspicuous. **Well-developed leaves** 5-10 to a stem, on lower fifth; blades 1-3 dm long and 2-4 mm wide, flat or channeled, thick, light-green, roughened on margins and towards the tip; sheaths tight, yellowish brown-tinged at mouth. **Spikes** 3-10, androgynous (staminate flowers above the pistillate); bracts setiform, short; staminate flowers few; **scales** greenish hyaline with 3-nerved green center. **Perigynia** 8-20 to a spike, 3-3.5 mm long, ascending or spreading, plano-convex, somewhat leathery, pale-

Carex muehlenbergii
perigynium (l)
pistillate scale (r)

1412. Carex cephaloidea

1413. Carex cephalophora

1414. Carex gravida

1415. Carex muehlenbergii

green, many-ribbed with sharp slightly raised margins, serrulate above; beak 1 mm long, bidentate. **Achenes** filling perigynia, lenticular; stigmas 2, reddish brown.—Sand hills and dry places.

Carex radiata (Wahlenb.) Small
EASTERN STAR SEDGE

MAP 1416
native

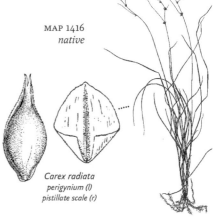

Plants tufted. **Stems** slender, 2.5-5 dm long, weak, roughened above, light-brown to blackish tinged and fibrillose at base. **Well-developed leaves** 4-6 to a fertile stem, on lower fourth; **blades** 1-2 mm wide, flat, light-green; **sheaths** tight. **Spikes** 4, androgynous; staminate flowers few; lowest **bract** setaceous, the upper smaller; **scales** thin, white-hyaline with green midvein. **Perigynia** 2-6 to a spike, 2-3 mm long, exceeding scales, deep-green, erect, nerveless or nearly so, serrulate above, spongy at base; beak to 1 mm long, bidentate, white-hyaline between teeth. **Achenes** lenticular, filling perigynia; stigmas 2, short, twisted, dark-brownish red.—Dry woods.

Carex radiata
perigynium (l)
pistillate scale (r)

Carex rosea Schkuhr
ROSY SEDGE
    Carex convoluta Mackenzie

MAP 1417
native

Plants tufted; rootstocks short, dark, fibrillose. **Stems** slender 2-5 dm long, smooth or serrulate above, light-brownish tinged and fibrillose at base. **Well-developed leaves** 3-6 to a stem, on lower third; **blades** 3 dm long and 1-2 mm wide, flat, light-green, serrulate on margins and on veins towards tip; sheaths tight. **Spikes** 4-8, androgynous; bracts to 10 cm long, the upper reduced; **scales** thin, greenish hyaline with green midrib; staminate flowers inconspicuous. **Perigynia** 4-12 to a spike, 3-3.5 mm long, exceeding scales, ascending or widely radiating, plano-convex, light-green, nerveless or nearly so, serrulate above, spongy at base; beak ca. 0.5 mm long, bidentate. **Achenes** lenticular, filling perigynia; stigmas 3, long, light-reddish brown.—Dry woods.

Carex rosea
perigynium (l)
pistillate scale (r)

Carex sparganioides Muhl.
BUR-REED SEDGE

MAP 1418
native

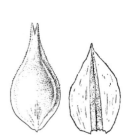

Plants tufted; rootstocks short, dark, somewhat woody. **Stems** 3-7.5 dm long, ascending or erect, narrowly margined, serrulate above, brownish yellow-tinged at base. **Well-developed leaves** 3-6 to a stem; blades 2-4 dm long and 5-10 mm wide, flat, weak, serrulate on margins, roughened on veins; sheaths loose, overlapping, green-and-white-mottled dorsally, the lower sheaths transversely rugulose. **Spikes** 6-12, androgynous; bracts short, often rudimentary; **scales** thin, greenish hyaline; staminate flowers inconspicuous. **Perigynia** 5-50 to a spike, 3 mm long, ascending or spreading, plano-convex, nerveless or nearly so, with sharp and somewhat raised margins, serrulate above; beak serrulate, bidentate, white-hyaline within. **Achenes** lenticular; stigmas 2, short, reddish brown.—Dry woods.

Carex sparganioides
perigynium (l)
pistillate scale (r)

CAREX SECTION PHYLLOSTACHYAE

Plants tufted, bases brown. Bracts lacking. Lateral spikes absent or basal, pistillate or androgynous. Terminal spike androgynous. Lowest pistillate scale foliose, suggesting the lowest bract of the inflorescence in most other sections, exceeding the tip of the spike. Perigynia 2-ribbed, beak untoothed.

1416. *Carex radiata*   1417. *Carex rosea*   1418. *Carex sparganioides*   1419. *Carex backii*

1　Pistillate scales with hyaline margins; staminate flowers 6-20; lowest bracts 1-2 mm wide . . . .*C. jamesii*
1　Pistillate scales green throughout; staminate flowers ca. 3; lowest bract 3-6 mm wide 2
　　2　Beaks of perigynia 2-5 mm long; perigynia 4.5-6 mm long, empty at tip . . . . *C. backii*
　　2　Beaks of perigynia 0.5-1 mm long, perigynia 4 mm long, tightly filled by achene . . . . *C. saximontana*

Carex backii Boott
BACK'S SEDGE
MAP 1419
native

Plants tufted; rootstocks short, dark-brown. **Stems** to 25 cm long, weak, narrowly winged, serrulate on angles, enlarged upward. **Well-developed leaves** 2-6 to a stem, near base; **blades** 1-3 dm long and 2.5-6 mm wide, flat, erect or curved, thickish, deep-green papillate, roughened especially on margins and towards tip; **sheaths** thin and hyaline ventrally, yellowish brown-tinged, oblique at mouth. **Spikes** 1-3, androgynous (staminate flowers above the pistillate), the lower long-peduncled; **pistillate scales** bract-like, 3-4 cm long and 5 mm wide, nerved, tapering; staminate flowers few. **Perigynia** 2-5 to a spike, 5-6 mm long, erect on a zigzag winged rachis, concealed by scales, light-green, many-nerved, 2-keeled, spongy at base; beak 2 mm, 2-edged the orifice entire, truncate, hyaline, tawny-tinged below. **Achenes** triangular-globose with convex sides, closely enveloped, yellowish green or blackish, triangular; stigmas 3, short, dark.—Dry woods.

Carex backii
perigynium (l)
pistillate scale (r)

Carex jamesii Schwein.
JAMES' SEDGE
MAP 1420
☙' *threatened* | *native*

Plants tufted; rootstocks short, dark. **Stems** 5-30 cm long, weak, winged above, serrulate on angles, dilated upward, cinnamon-brown at base. **Well-developed leaves** 4-6 to a stem, near base; **blades** 10-35 cm long and 2-3 mm wide, flat, deep-green, papillate, roughened especially on margins and towards tip. **Spikes** 2-3, androgynous, the lower on capillary peduncles; **pistillate scales** leaflike, hyaline-margined. **Perigynia** 2-3 to a spike, 5-6 mm long, erect on a zigzag winged rachis, orbicular, green, nerveless, 2-keeled by the decurrent edges of beak, spongy at base; beak 3 mm long, flat, serrulate, brownish hyaline and entire at tip. **Achenes** triangular with convex sides, filling perigynia, brownish black, papillate; stigmas 3, short, reddish brown.—Deciduous woods, forested slopes and ravines.

Carex jamesii
perigynium (l)
pistillate scale (r)

Carex saximontana Mack.
ROCKY MOUNTAIN SEDGE
MAP 1421
native

Plants tufted, rootstock short. **Stems** narrowly winged, to 3.5 dm tall. **Leaves** 3-5 mm wide; **sheaths** thin. **Spikes** solitary, unisexual, androgynous (staminate flowers above the pistillate), separate or aggregate; **lower pistillate scales** leaflike, 7-35 mm long. **Perigynia** suborbicular, green, faintly many-nerved, 2-keeled, 4 mm long, base spongy, contracted to a serrulate beak to 1 mm long. **Achenes** triangular to globose with concave sides; stigmas 3.—Dry to wet woods.

Carex saximontana
perigynium (l)
pistillate scale (r)

CAREX SECTION PHYSOGLOCHIN

One member of the section in Minn; sphagnum moss peatlands.

Carex gynocrates Wormsk.
NORTHERN BOG SEDGE
Carex dioica L.
MAP 1422
native

Small perennial, from long, slender rhizomes. **Stems** single or few together, 0.3-3 dm long, smooth, brown at base. **Leaves** clustered near base of plant, **blades** inrolled and threadlike, to 1 mm wide. **Spikes** only 1 per stem, all staminate or all pistillate, or with both staminate and pistillate flowers (the staminate flowers borne above the pistillate); the staminate spike or portion of spike narrowly cylindric, the pistillate spike or portion short-cylindric; **bract** absent; **pistillate** scales brown or red-brown, tapered to tip, shorter but wider than perigynia. **Perigynia** 4-10, widely spreading, yellow to dark brown, shiny, plump, obovate, 2-4 mm long, spongy at base, abruptly contracted to the beak; beak nearly entire to unequally notched, 0.5 mm long. **Achenes** lens-shaped; stigmas 2. June-July.—Conifer swamps and open peatlands, usually in sphagnum and wet, peaty soils.

Carex gynocrates
perigynium (l), spike (c),
pistillate scale (r)

CAREX SECTION POROCYSTIS

Plants tufted. Leaves and stems usually pubescent, at least sparsely. Pistillate spikes erect to spreading, ovoid to oblong-cylindrical. Perigynia beakless or very short-beaked, glabrous or pubescent. Stigmas 3. Cylindrical pistillate spikes of *C. pallescens* resemble the spikes of *C. granularis* and relatives.

ADDITIONAL SPECIES
- *Carex bushii* Mackenzie (Bush's sedge), native of e and s USA; known from Ramsey County; see key.

1 Terminal spike pistillate at tip . . . . *C. bushii**
1 Terminal spike entirely staminate 2
 2 Perigynia strongly nerved. . . . . *C. torreyi*
 2 Perigynia only faintly nerved. . . . . *C. pallescens*

Carex pallescens L.

PALE SEDGE
Plants tufted; rootstocks short; stolons short-ascending. **Stems** 2-6 dm long, triangular with concave sides, rough above, pubescent, brownish red-tinged at base. **Well-developed leaves** 2-3 to a stem, on lower third; **blades** 8-35 cm long and 2-3 mm wide, flat with revolute margins, deep-green, soft-pubescent below; **sheaths** tight, soft-pubescent, cinnamon-brown-tinged. **Terminal spike** staminate; lateral spikes 2-3, pistillate, on capillary peduncles to 15 mm long; lowest **bract** leaflike, sheathless or nearly so, the upper reduced; **pistillate scales** yellowish brown or greenish white with 3-nerved green center. **Perigynia** 15-40 to a spike, 2.5-3 mm long, erect to spreading, greenish or yellowish green, minutely puncticulate, finely nerved, beakless. **Achenes** triangular with concave sides, loosely enveloped, short-apiculate; stigmas 3, short.—Rocky forest edges and grassy openings; Cook, Lake and St. Louis counties.

(NO MAP)
🌿 *endangered | native*

Carex pallescens
perigynium (l)
pistillate scale (r)

Carex torreyi Tuckerman

TORREY'S SEDGE
Plants with short rhizomes. **Stems** 25-50 cm high, slender, weak, sharply triangular, somewhat pubescent below the inflorescence; **sheaths** softly pubescent, tight; **blades** 1.5-4 mm wide, flat, pilose. **Inflorescence** 3-5 cm long; the terminal spike staminate, 5-15 mm long; the 1-3 lateral spikes pistillate, 5-15 mm long, sessile or short-peduncled. **Perigynia** 2.5-3.5 mm long, yellowish green, strongly nerved, abruptly short-beaked; scales smaller than the perigynia, light brown with broad hyaline margins; stigmas 3.—Meadows and moist woods. *Similar to* **C. pallescens**, *but perigynia strongly many-nerved and short-beaked.*

MAP 1423
native

Carex torreyi
perigynium (l)
pistillate scale (r)

CAREX SECTION RACEMOSAE

Plants loosely to densely tufted; rhizomes variable in length; bases dark red, generally fibrous; roots not clothed with yellow felt. Terminal spike gynecandrous, androgynous or all staminate. Pistillate scales dark, often black. Perigynia pale, often greenish, very short-beaked to beakless, smooth or papillose, 2-ribbed, inconspicuously veined (in our species). Stigmas 3.

1 Terminal spike pistillate, androgynous or all staminate. . . . . *C. hallii*
1 Terminal spike gynecandrous 2
 2 Pistillate scales mostly awned or narrowly acuminate, exceeding the perigynia; ventral surface of lower leaf sheaths tearing into fibers; throughout Minn . . . . *C. buxbaumii*
 2 Pistillate scales obtuse or acute, equaling or shorter than the perigynia; ventral surface of lower sheaths not tearing to form fibers; local in n Minn. . . . . *C. media*

1420. *Carex jamesii*

1420. *Carex saximontana*

1422. *Carex gynocrates*

1423. *Carex torreyi*

Carex buxbaumii Wahlenb.
BROWN BOG SEDGE

MAP 1424
native

Loosely tufted perennial, from long rhizomes. **Stems** single or few together, 3-angled, 3-10 dm long, rough-to-touch above, red-tinged near base. **Leaves** 1-3 mm wide, the lowest leaves without blades; lower sheaths shredding into thin strands, the upper sheaths membranous and purple-dotted. **Spikes** 2-5, terminal spike with pistillate flowers above staminate and larger than the lateral spikes, lateral spikes pistillate, short-cylindric, stalkless or nearly so; **bracts** leaflike, the lowest shorter than the head; **pistillate scales** dark brown, tapered to an awn at tip. **Perigynia** light green, golden brown near base, oval, 2.5-3.5 mm long, 2-ribbed, with 6-8 faint nerves on each side; beak tiny, notched. **Achenes** 3-angled; stigmas 3. May-Aug.—Wet meadows and fens, shallow marshes, low prairie, hollows in patterned peatlands.

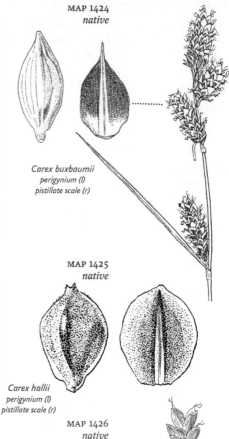

Carex buxbaumii
perigynium (l)
pistillate scale (r)

Carex hallii Olney
DEER SEDGE

MAP 1425
native

Rhizomatous perennial, rootstock scaly. **Stems** 1-6 dm tall, obtusely triangular. **Leaves** 2 — 4 mm wide. **Spikes** unisexual, terminal spikes usually staminate, 1.5-2.5 cm long, lateral spikes pistillate, pistillate scales obtuse to mucronate. **Perigynia** plano-convex to obtusely triangular, green or white, 2-ribbed, 2-3 mm long; beak 0.5 mm long, bidentate. **Achenes** triangular; stigmas 3. —Low prairies, sandy sloughs.

Carex hallii
perigynium (l)
pistillate scale (r)

Carex media R. Br.
MONTANA SEDGE
Carex norvegica Retz.

MAP 1426
native

Plants loosely tufted, from short rhizomes. **Stems** slender, not stiff, 2-8 dm long, smooth or slightly rough-to-touch above, sharply triangular above, much longer than the leaves, red-tinged at base. **Leaves** 7-15 and mostly near base of stem, pale-green, flat or margins slightly rolled under, 2-3 mm wide, rough-to-touch on margins, the dried leaves of previous year conspicuous; **sheaths** translucent. **Spikes** usually 3, densely flowered, the terminal with both staminate and pistillate flowers, the staminate below the pistillate, clustered, upright, stalkless; the lateral spikes pistillate, on short stalks; lowest bract usually shorter than the head; **pistillate scales** 2-3 mm long, purple-black, margins white-translucent, nearly as wide as perigynia but much shorter. **Perigynia** 2-4 mm long, rounded 3-angled, slightly inflated, yellow-green to brown, two-ribbed, otherwise without nerves, tip rounded and abruptly beaked; beak short, to 0.5 mm long, red-tinged, with a small notch. **Achenes** obovate, 3-angled, yellow-brown; stigmas 3. June-July. —Rare on talus slopes in mesic forests.

Carex media
perigynium (l), spike (c),
pistillate scale (r)

CAREX SECTION ROSTRALES

One member of the section in Minn.

Carex michauxiana Boeckl.
MICHAUX'S SEDGE

MAP 1427
native

Plants tufted, brown at base, from long rhizomes. **Stems** 2-6 dm long. **Leaves** 2-4 mm wide. **Spikes** either staminate or pistillate; terminal spike staminate, stalkless or short stalked, the base lower than or roughly equaling the tip of the uppermost pistillate spike; pistillate spikes 2-4, upright, the lower spikes stalked, the upper on shorter stalks; **bracts** leaflike, 1-3 mm wide, longer than the stems; **pistillate scales** shorter than the perigynia, margins translucent or brown, with a

Carex michauxiana
perigynium (l)
pistillate scale (r)

green midrib, tapered to a tip. **Perigynia** up to 20 per spike, divergent or the lowermost reflexed, somewhat inflated, narrowly lance-shaped, 8-13 long, round in section, long-tapered to a beak with upright teeth 1 mm long. **Achenes** rounded 3-angled; stigmas 3. June-Aug.—Wet meadows, sphagnum peatlands, ditches. *Resembles the more common **Carex intumescens**, but differs in its narrower perigynia.*

CAREX SECTION SCIRPINAE

One member of the section in Minn.

Carex scirpoidea Michx.

NORTHERN SINGLE-SPIKE SEDGE

MAP 1428
native

Plants with long, creeping rhizomes. **Stems** 20-50 cm high, solitary or few together; **sheaths** glabrous, loose, the lower ones reddish brown. **Leaf blades** 1-3 mm wide. **Inflorescence** a single spike, staminate or pistillate, 1-3 cm long. **Perigynia** 2.5-3 mm long, densely pubescent, green; pistillate scales smaller than the perigynia, deep brown.—Moist to wet prairies; in ne Minn, also known from a north-facing cliff where plants occur in mossy crevices.

Carex scirpoidea
perigynium (l)
pistillate scale (r)

CAREX SECTION SQUARROSAE

The obconic perigynia of this section are highly distinctive, widest at the apex and abruptly narrowed to the beak; perigynia in all of the other "bladder" and "bottlebrush" *Carex* sections taper more gradually to the beak.

1   Achenes slenderly ellipsoid, terminated by a strongly sinuous style; pistillate scales very sharp-tipped or short-awned; rare in nw Minn . . . . ***C. squarrosa***

1   Achenes broadly ellipsoid, terminated by a ± straight style; pistillate scales ± acute in outline but blunt at the very tip; mostly se Minn . . . . ***C. typhina***

Carex squarrosa L.

SQUARROSE SEDGE

(NO MAP)
native

Densely clumped native perennial. **Stems** 3-9 dm long. **Leaves** 3-6 mm wide, lower stem leaves reduced to scales. **Spikes** 1 (or sometimes 2-3), with both male and female flowers, the male below the female; female portion oval, 1-3 cm long and 1-2 cm wide; **lateral spikes** (if present) female, on upright stalks; **bract** of the terminal spike short and narrow; **female scales** tapered to a tip or short-awned, smaller than the perigynia. **Perigynia** numerous and crowded, spreading, obovate, inflated, the body 3-6 mm long, abruptly tapered to a long notched beak 2-3 mm long. **Achenes** 2-3 mm long, with a persistent, strongly bent style; stigmas 3. June-Aug.—Swamps, floodplain forests, alder thickets, forest depressions; Mahnomen County, more common south of the state.

Carex squarrosa
perigynium (l)
pistillate scale (r)

Carex typhina Michx.

CAT-TAIL SEDGE

MAP 1429
native

Plants tufted. **Stems** 3-8 dm long and usually shorter than upper leaves. **Leaves** 5-10 mm wide. **Spikes** 1-6, the terminal spike mostly pistillate with a short staminate base, the pistillate portion cylindric, subtended by a short narrow bract; lateral spikes pistillate, smaller, upright or spreading on short stalks; **pistillate scales** hidden by the perigynia, blunt or tapered to a tip. **Perigynia** obovate, crowded, body 3-5 mm long, abruptly narrowed to a notched beak 2-3 mm long. **Achenes** 2-3 mm long; stigmas 3. June-Sept.—Floodplain forests of large rivers

Carex typhina
perigynium (l)
pistillate scale (r)

1424. *Carex buxbaumii*

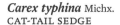

1425. *Carex hallii*

1426. *Carex media*

1427. *Carex michauxiana*

(especially Mississippi and St. Croix), often occurring with *Carex muskingumensis* and *C. grayi*; marshy areas.

CAREX SECTION STELLULATAE

Plants tufted; rhizomes short; bases brown, not fibrous. Inflorescence mostly open, spikes readily distinguished from each other, the lowest in our more common species not overlapping; bracts inconspicuous or lacking. Spikes 2-10 (solitary in *Carex exilis*), gynecandrous (unisexual in *C. sterilis*). Perigynia spreading to reflexed, typically plano-convex, widest at the base, generally chestnut brown to dark brown or even blackish at maturity; margins acute; base spongy; beak generally bidentate, margins finely serrate. Achenes much smaller than the perigynia. Wetlands.

The distinctions between species in this section are subtle; however, the species have habitat preferences that can help with field identification. When examining perigynia, view the lowest 2-3 perigynia in the spike; the upper perigynia are very similar in all of our species.

1 Spikes solitary; leaves involute; anthers 2-3.6 mm long . . . .*C. exilis*
1 Spikes 2-8; leaves flat or plicate; anthers 0.6-2.2 (-2.3) mm 2
  2 Terminal spikes entirely staminate . . . .*C. sterilis*
  2 Terminal spikes partly or wholly pistillate 3
    3 Terminal spikes without a distinct clavate base of staminate scales, staminate portion less than 1 mm long; anthers 1-2.2 mm long. . . . . **C. sterilis**
    3 Terminal spikes with a distinct clavate base of staminate scales mostly 1-8 mm long; anthers mostly 0.6-1.6 mm long. 4
      4 Lower perigynia mostly 2.9-3.6 mm long, 1.8-3.6 times as long as wide; beaks 0.9-2 mm long, mostly 0.5-0.8 times as long as the body. . . . .*C. echinata*
      4 Lower perigynia mostly 1.9-3 mm long, 1-2 times as long as wide; beaks 0.4-0.9 mm long, mostly 0.2-0.5 times as long as body. . . . . **C. interior**

Carex echinata Murr.
STAR SEDGE
Carex angustior Mackenzie

MAP 1430
native

Plants tufted. **Stems** 1-6 dm long, rough above. **Leaves** scale-like at base of stem; leaves with blades 3-6 on lower stem, 1-3 mm wide. **Spikes** 3-7, stalkless, few-flowered; terminal spike with a slender staminate portion near its base; lateral spikes usually all pistillate; **bract** small; **pistillate scales** shorter than perigynia, yellow-tinged with green midvein. **Perigynia** 5-15 and crowded in each spike, spreading or curved downward, green or light brown, flat on 1 side and convex on other, spongy-thickened at base, 3-4 mm long, tapered to a toothed, notched beak 1-2 mm long. **Achenes** lens-shaped; stigmas 2. July-Sept.—Swamp margins, wet sandy lakeshores, hummocks in peatlands.

Carex echinata
perigynium (l)
pistillate scale (r)

Carex exilis Dewey
COASTAL SEDGE

NMAP 1431
native

Plants densely tufted. **Stems** stiff, 2-7 dm long and longer than the leaves. **Leaves** narrow and rolled inward. **Spike** usually 1, either staminate or pistillate, or with both staminate and pistillate flowers, the staminate below the pistillate, 1-3 cm long; lateral spikes (if present) 1 or 2 and much smaller than terminal spike; lower 2 scales empty and upright; **pistillate scales** red-brown with translucent margins, about as long as perigynia. **Perigynia** spreading or drooping, flat on 1 side and convex on other, 3-5 mm long, spongy-thickened at base, tapered to a toothed beak to 2 mm long. **Achenes** lens-shaped; stigmas 2. June-Aug. —Sphagnum peatlands, interdunal wetlands; coastal disjunct.

Carex exilis
perigynium (l),
pistillate scale (c),
spike (r)

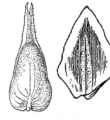

1428. *Carex scirpoidea*

Carex interior Bailey
INLAND SEDGE

MAP 1432
native

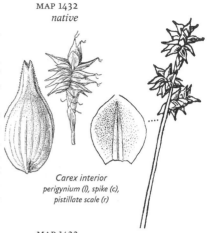

Plants densely tufted. **Stems** slender, sharply 3-angled, 1-6 dm long, equal or longer than the leaves. **Leaves** 1-2 mm wide; **sheaths** tight, thin and translucent. **Spikes** 2-4, the terminal spike with pistillate flowers borne above staminate (or rarely all staminate), the lateral spikes pistillate (or rarely with pistillate flowers borne above staminate), more or less overlapping; **bracts** small or absent; **pistillate scales** much shorter than the perigynia. **Perigynia** green-brown to brown, filled to margins by the achenes, sharp-edged but not wing-margined, 2-3 mm long, the base spongy so that achene fills upper perigynium body, tapered to a finely toothed beak to 1 mm long; the beak teeth small, not longer than 0.3 mm. **Achenes** lens-shaped; stigmas 2. May-Aug.—Swamps, tamarack bogs, alder thickets, wet meadows and wetland margins.

Carex interior
perigynium (l), spike (c),
pistillate scale (r)

Carex sterilis Willd.
DIOECIOUS SEDGE

MAP 1433
☙ *threatened* | *native*

   Carex muricata L. var. *sterilis* (Willd.) Gleason

Plants tufted. **Stems** stiff, 1-7 dm long, longer than the leaves, rough-to-touch on the upper stem angles. **Leaves** 3-5 from lower part of stem, 1-4 mm wide, rough, lower stem leaves reduced to scales. **Spikes** 3-8, stalkless, clustered or the lower separate; staminate and pistillate flowers mostly on separate plants; pistillate scales red-brown with green midvein and translucent margin about as long as body of perigynia. **Perigynia** 5-25, the lower spreading, 2-4 mm long, red-brown, flat on 1 side and convex on other, spongy-thickened at base, tapered to a finely toothed, notched beak 0.5-1.5 mm long, the beak teeth sharp, to 0.5 mm long. **Achenes** lens-shaped; stigmas 2. April-June.—Spring-fed calcareous fens, calcium-rich wet meadows. *Similar to* **inland sedge** *(Carex interior).*

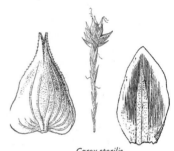

Carex sterilis
perigynium (l), spike (c),
pistillate scale (r)

CAREX SECTION VESICARIAE

Includes typical bottlebrush sedges of former section Pseudocypereae, with pistillate spikes tightly packed with perigynia, and pistillate scales with scabrous awns conspicuous between the perigynia; and also former section Vesicariae, with pistillate spikes often narrower, longer, less densely packed with perigynia in some species, and pistillate scales mostly not awned, hidden by the perigynia.

1 Pistillate scales with a prominent, scabrous awn; often the body also ciliate. 2
   2 Perigynia ± reflexed at maturity, hard-walled, uninflated, flattened-triangular in cross-section, strongly and closely nerved with most nerves separated by less than three times their width; longest beak teeth 0.7-2.2 mm long 3
      3 Spikes 12-18 mm thick; beak teeth strongly outcurved, the longest 1.3-2.1 mm long . . . .***C. comosa***
      3 Spikes 9-12 mm thick; beak teeth straight or slightly outcurved, the longest 0.7-1.2 mm long . . . .
       . . . . ***C. pseudocyperus***
   2 Perigynia spreading to ascending, thin-textured, ± inflated, ± round in cross-section; many nerves separated by more than three times their width; longest beak teeth 0.3-0.7 mm long. 4

1429. *Carex typhina*   1430. *Carex echinata*   1431. *Carex exilis*   1432. *Carex interior*

4 Perigynia 15-20-nerved, the nerves (except for the two prominent lateral nerves) fusing together and becoming indistinguishable from about the middle of the beak to the apex, bodies ellipsoid, 1.4-2.2 mm wide; achenes smooth. . . . . *C. hystericina*

4 Perigynia 7-12-nerved, the nerves separate nearly to the beak tip, the bodies broadly ellipsoid to ± spherical, 2-3.5 mm wide; achenes rough-papillate . . . . *C. lurida*

1 Pistillate scales smooth-margined, obtuse to acuminate, awnless. 5

5 Leaf blades and bracts involute-filiform, wiry, 1-3 mm wide; stems round or obtusely 3-angled in cross-section, smooth; pistillate spikes 3-15-flowered, nearly spherical or short-oblong (not over 2 cm long); staminate spike usually solitary. . . . . *C. oligosperma*

5 Leaf blades and bracts flat, U-, V-, or W-shaped in cross-section, 1.5-12 mm wide; stems round to 3-angled, often scabrous-angled; pistillate spikes usually more than 15-flowered, oblong to long-cylindric; staminate spikes normally 2 or more (often 1 in *C. retrorsa*) 6

6 Perigynia 4-7 mm thick; achenes with a deep notch or constriction on one angle . . . . *C. tuckermanii*

6 Perigynia 2.5-3.5 mm thick; achenes symmetrical, not notched on one angle 7

7 Lowest pistillate bract 3-9 times as long as the entire inflorescence; mature perigynia 7-12 mm long, at least the lower reflexed or widely spreading; staminate spike often 1, its base (or base of lowest staminate spike if more than one) slightly if at all elevated above summit of the crowded pistillate spikes (rarely lower spike remote) . . . . *C. retrorsa*

7 Lowest pistillate bract less than 3 times as long as inflorescence; perigynia 4-7.5 mm long, ascending or spreading; staminate spikes mostly 2-4, generally well elevated above the pistillate spikes 8

8 Leaves strongly papillose on upper surface, U-shaped in cross-section, glaucous, widest leaves 1.5-5 mm wide; stems round or very obtusely triangular, smooth below inflorescence . . . . . *C. rostrata*

8 Leaves smooth or scabrous on upper surface, flat or folded, pale to dark green, widest leaves 3-12 mm wide; stems triangular, often scabrous below the inflorescence 9

9 Colonial from long-creeping rhizomes; widest leaves (4.5-) 5-12 (-15) mm wide; ligules about as long as wide; basal sheaths usually spongy-thickened with little or no red tingeing; perigynia (at least those on lower portion of fully mature spike) ± widely spreading; stems bluntly triangular and sparsely and irregularly scabrous below the inflorescence . . . . *C. utriculata*

9 Tufted; widest leaves 3-5 (-6) mm wide; ligules longer than wide; basal sheaths not spongy-thickened and often tinged with reddish purple; perigynia ascending; stems sharply triangular and scabrous-angled below the inflorescence. . . . . *C. vesicaria*

Carex comosa Boott
BEARDED SEDGE

MAP 1434
native

Plants large, often forming large clumps. **Stems** stout, sharply 3-angled, 5-15 dm long. **Leaves** 5-12 mm wide; **sheaths** translucent on front, with small swollen joints on back. **Spikes** either staminate or pistillate; terminal spike staminate; lateral spikes pistillate, 3-5, cylindric, the lower spikes longer stalked and drooping when mature; **bracts** leaflike, much longer than the head; **pistillate scales** with translucent margins, tapered into a long, rough awn. Perigynia numerous, spreading outward when ripe, flattened 3-angled, lance-shaped, 5-8 mm long, shiny, strongly nerved, gradually tapered to the 2-3 mm long beak, the beak with curved teeth 1-2 mm long. **Achenes** 3-angled; stigmas 3. June-Aug. —Marshes, wetland margins, floating mats, ditches.

Carex comosa
perigynium (l)
pistillate scale (r)

Carex hystericina Muhl.
PORCUPINE SEDGE

MAP 1435
native

Plants from short rhizomes, often forming large clumps. **Stems** upright or leaning, 3-angled, 2-10 dm long, usually longer than the leaves. **Leaves** yellow-green, 3-8 mm wide; **sheaths** white, thin and translucent on front, green to yellow or red on back, the lower sheaths breaking into threadlike fibers. **Spikes** either all staminate or pistillate, the terminal spike staminate, usually short-stalked and often with a bract; lateral spikes pistillate or occasionally with staminate flowers above pistillate, 1-4, short-cylindric, separate or clustered, the lower spikes usually nodding on slender stalks, the upper spikes short-stalked and upright; **pistillate scales** small, narrow and much shorter than the perigynia, tipped with a rough awn. **Perigynia**

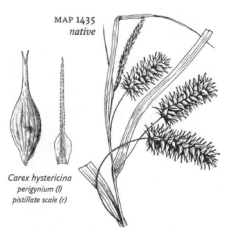

Carex hystericina
perigynium (l)
pistillate scale (r)

spreading or upright, green to straw-colored, ovate, round in section when mature, 5-8 mm long, strongly nerved, abruptly tapered to a slender, toothed beak 3-4 mm long; the beak teeth to 1 mm long. **Achenes** 3-angled with concave sides; stigmas 3. May-July.—Swamps, alder thickets, wet meadows and ditches; calcareous fens in southern Minn.

Carex lurida Wahlenb.
SHALLOW SEDGE

MAP 1436
native

Plants tufted. **Stems** 3-10 dm long, rounded 3-angled and more or less smooth, purple-tinged at base. **Leaves** flat, 3-7 mm wide, lower stem leaves reduced to scales. **Spikes** either staminate or pistillate, terminal spike staminate; pistillate spikes 1-4 (usually 2), many-flowered, grouped or the lower separate, stalkless and erect or the lower short-stalked and sometimes drooping; **bracts** leafy, longer than the head; **pistillate scales** awned or sharp-pointed. **Perigynia** in many rows, broadly ovate, somewhat inflated, 6-9 mm long, pale, smooth and shining, strongly nerved, tapered to a notched beak half to as long as the body. **Achenes** 3-angled, loosely enclosed in the lower part of the perigynium, the style persistent and twisted; stigmas 3. June-Aug.—River floodplains, swamps.

Carex lurida
perigynium (l)
pistillate scale (r)

Carex oligosperma Michx.
FEW-SEED SEDGE

MAP 1437
native

Plants forming colonies from creeping rhizomes. **Stems** slender, 4-10 dm long, purple-tinged at base. **Leaves** stiff, rolled inward, 1-3 mm wide. **Spikes** either all staminate or pistillate; staminate spike usually single; pistillate spikes 1 (or 2-3 and widely separated), stalkless or nearly so, ovate to short-cylindric, lowest bract leaflike. **Perigynia** 3-15, ovate, somewhat inflated, compressed, 4-7 mm long, strongly several-nerved, abruptly tapered to a beak 1-2 mm long. **Achenes** 3-angled, 2-3 mm long; stigmas 3. June-Aug.—Open bogs and swamps, floating mats, pioneer mat-former along pond margins. *Sometimes a dominant sedge in nutrient-poor fens.*

Carex oligosperma
perigynium (l)
pistillate scale (r)

Carex pseudocyperus L.
CYPRESS-LIKE SEDGE

MAP 1438
native

Plants large, tufted. **Stems** stout, 3-10 dm long, 3-angled, rough-to-touch. **Leaves** 5-15 mm wide; **sheaths** translucent, yellow-tinged on back. **Spikes** either all staminate or pistillate, the terminal spike staminate; lateral spikes pistillate, 2-6, cylindric, lower spikes drooping on slender stalks; **bracts** much longer than the head; **pistillate scales** tipped by an awn, the awn shorter or longer than the perigynia. **Perigynia** spreading, 3-angled, 4-6 mm long, shiny, strongly nerved, tapered to a toothed beak, the beak teeth 0.5-1 mm long. **Achenes** 3-angled; stigmas 3. June-Aug.—Marshy lake margins, swamps, fens, wet ditches; an indicator of calcium-rich fens in the Red Lake peatland. *Similar to **Carex comosa**.*

Carex retrorsa Schwein.
RETRORSE SEDGE

MAP 1439
native

Plants densely tufted. **Stems** 4-10 dm long. **Leaves** 3-4 dm long and 4-10 mm wide, flat and soft; sheaths dotted with small bumps. **Spikes** either all staminate or pistillate, or the terminal 1-2 spikes with both staminate and pistillate flowers,

Carex pseudocyperus
perigynium (l)
pistillate scale (r)

1433. *Carex sterilis*

1434. *Carex comosa*

1435. *Carex hystericina*

1436. *Carex lurida*

the staminate above the pistillate, stalkless or lowest spike on a slender stalk; lower spikes 3-8, pistillate; **pistillate scales** conspicuous, shorter and narrower than the perigynia. **Perigynia** crowded in rows, spreading or the lowest perigynia angled downward, smooth and shiny, 6-13-nerved, 7-10 mm long, somewhat inflated, tapered to a long, smooth beak 2-4 mm long, the beak teeth short, to 1 mm long. **Achenes** dark brown, 3-angled, loose in the lower part of the perigynium; stigmas 3. June-Aug.—Floodplain forests, swamps, thickets and marshes.

Carex retrorsa
perigynium (l)
pistillate scale (r)

Carex rostrata Stokes
MAP 1440
SWOLLEN BEAKED SEDGE
native

Plants with short to long-creeping rhizomes. **Stems** round or bluntly 3-angled, 3-10 dm long, smooth below inflorescence. **Leaves** waxy blue, with many fine bumps on upper surface, to 4 mm wide, inrolled or channeled in section. **Spikes** either staminate or pistillate, the upper 2-5 staminate; lower 2-5 spikes pistillate or sometimes 1 or 2 with staminate flowers above the pistillate, cylindric. **Perigynia** upright when young, becoming widely spreading when mature, yellow-green to brown, shiny, ovate, nearly round in section, inflated, 2-6 mm long, narrowed to a beak about 1 mm long. **Achenes** 3-angled; stigmas 3. July-Sept. —Peat mats or shallow water. *Similar to Carex utriculata, but much less common, and with the leaves waxy blue and dotted with fine bumps on upper surface, v-shaped in section or inrolled, and only 2-4 mm wide.*

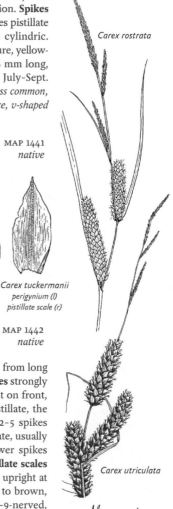

Carex rostrata

Carex tuckermanii Dewey
MAP 1441
TUCKERMAN'S SEDGE
native

Plants tufted, from short rhizomes. **Stems** 4-8 dm long. **Leaves** 2-4 dm long and 3-6 mm wide, soft and flat. **Spikes** either staminate or pistillate; staminate spikes usually 2, separated, raised above pistillate spikes; pistillate spikes 2-4, separated, cylindric. **Perigynia** overlapping and ascending in 6 rows, 7-10 mm long and 4-7 mm wide, inflated, tapered to a notched beak 2 mm long. **Achenes** 3-angled, obovate, with a deep indentation near the middle of 1 angle; stigmas 3. June-Aug.—Swamps, alder thickets, low areas in forests, pond margins.

Carex tuckermanii
perigynium (l)
pistillate scale (r)

Carex utriculata Boott
MAP 1442
NORTHWEST TERRITORY SEDGE
native
Carex rostrata Stokes var. *utriculata* (Boott) Bailey

Plants large, densely tufted, from short rootstocks, also forming turfs from long rhizomes. **Stems** bluntly 3-angled, 3-12 dm long, spongy at base. **Leaves** strongly divided with swollen joints 4-12 mm wide; **sheaths** white-translucent on front, divided with swollen joints on back. **Spikes** either staminate or pistillate, the upper 2-5 staminate, held well above the pistillate spikes; lower 2-5 spikes pistillate or sometimes 1 or 2 with staminate flowers above the pistillate, usually separate, cylindric, the upper spikes stalkless or short-stalked, lower spikes stalked, upright; **bracts** shorter to slightly longer than the head; **pistillate scales** acute to awn-tipped, body of scale shorter than perigynia. **Perigynia** upright at first to widely spreading when mature, in many rows, yellow-green to brown, shiny, nearly round in section, inflated, 3-8 mm long, strongly 7-9-nerved,

Carex utriculata

Carex utriculata
perigynium (l)
pistillate scale (r)

1437. Carex oligosperma

1438. Carex pseudocyperus

1439. Carex retrorsa

contracted to a toothed beak 1-2 mm long, the teeth mostly straight, 0.5 mm long. **Achenes** 3-angled; stigmas 3. June-Aug.—Wet meadows, marshes, fens, swamps and lakeshores. *Long confused with* **Carex rostrata**, *a boreal species with waxy blue leaves to only 4 mm wide and which has numerous small bumps on upper leaf surface.*

Carex vesicaria L.
LESSER BLADDER SEDGE

MAP 1443
native

Plants tufted, from stout, short rhizomes. **Stems** 3-10 dm long, sharply 3-angled and rough-to-touch below the head, not spongy at base (as in *C. utriculata*). **Leaves** 2-7 mm wide; **sheaths** white-translucent on front, not conspicuously divided-with small swollen joints on back, the lowest sheaths often shredding into ladderlike fibers. **Spikes** either all staminate or pistillate, the upper 2-4 staminate, held well above the pistillate; lower 1-3 spikes pistillate, separate, cylindric, stalkless or short-stalked, erect; **lowest bract** usually longer than the head; **pistillate scales** acute to awn-tipped, shorter to as long as perigynia. **Perigynia** upright and overlapping in rows, dull yellow-green to brown, inflated, 3-8 mm long, strongly nerved, abruptly tapered to a toothed beak 1-2 mm long, the teeth 0.5-1 mm long. **Achenes** 3-angled; stigmas 3. June-Aug.—Wet meadows, marshes, forest depressions and shores.

Carex vesicaria
perigynium (l)
pistillate scale (r)

CAREX SECTION VULPINAE

Plants tufted; bases generally pale. Inner band of the leaf sheaths hyaline, in other regards various: corrugated or smooth, thickened or fragile at the summit, sparsely purple-dotted or lacking pigmentation, and combinations of the above. Stems thick, spongy, weak, the angles narrowly winged, scabrous. Inflorescence longer than wide (ours), ovate to cylindrical. Bracts setaceous. Spikes densely flowered, the lower branched, mostly or all androgynous (the terminal always androgynous). Perigynia plano-convex, bases spongy (not spongy in *Carex alopecoidea*). Wetlands. *The thick, spongy stems, branched lower spikes, and spongy perigynium bases (except in C. alopecoidea) are characteristic.*

ADDITIONAL SPECIES
• *Carex conjuncta* Boott (Jointed sedge), 🌿*threatened*; wet floodplain forests of *Ulmus americana, Acer saccharinum,* and *Juglans nigra*; Dodge, Ramsey and Rice counties.

1 Perigynia contracted into a beak no longer than the body, 3-4.5 mm long, essentially nerveless ventrally; ventral surface of leaf sheaths sparsely to strongly dotted with purplish, especially toward the tip. . . . . . . **C. alopecoidea**
1 Perigynia somewhat contracted or ± cuneately tapered into the beak (this then difficult to define, but about equaling or slightly exceeding the body, if the latter is measured from the base of perigynium to tip of achene), 4-6 mm long, with at least a few nerves ventrally; ventral surface of leaf sheaths not dotted with purplish 2
    2 Sheaths thickened (or even ± cartilaginous) at the concave or truncate mouth, smooth and unwrinkled ventrally; perigynia 4.7-6.2 mm long . . . . **C. laevivaginata**
    2 Sheaths thin (usually broken) at the prolonged (when intact) mouth, rather strongly puckered or cross-wrinkled ventrally, very rarely nearly or quite smooth; perigynia 4-5 mm long . . . .**C. stipata**

Carex alopecoidea Tuckerman
FOX-TAIL SEDGE

MAP 1444
native

Plants tufted. **Stems** soft, 4-10 dm long, 3-angled and sharply winged. **Leaves** 3-8 mm wide; **sheaths** purple-dotted, not cross-wrinkled. **Spikes** with both staminate and pistillate flowers, staminate flowers above pistillate, in heads 1.5-5 cm long;

Carex alopecoidea
perigynium (l)
pistillate scale (r)

1440. Carex rostrata   *1441. Carex tuckermanii*   *1442. Carex utriculata*

pistillate scales tapered to tip or with a short sharp tip. **Perigynia** yellow-brown when mature, ovate, flat on 1 side and convex on other, 3-5 mm long, spongy-thickened at base, narrowed to a beak half to as long as the body. **Achenes** lens-shaped, 1-2 mm long; stigmas 2. May-July.—Swamps and floodplain forests, streambanks, swales and moist fields.

Carex laevivaginata (Kükenth.) Mackenzie
MAP 1445
SMOOTH-SHEATH SEDGE   ❦ *threatened | native*
Plants densely tufted. **Stems** stout, 3-angled, 3-10 dm long. **Leaves** 3-10 mm wide; sheaths not cross-corrugated (as in *C. stipata*). **Spikes** with both staminate and pistillate flowers, the staminate above the pistillate, numerous, grouped into a dense head 2-5 cm long, green or straw-colored when mature; **bracts** short or reduced to bristles sometimes longer than the spikes; **pistillate scales** shorter than the perigynia, tapered to a tip or short awn. **Perigynia** green or straw-colored, spreading, broadly lance-shaped, 5-6 mm long, long-tapered to the tip, flat on 1 side and convex on other, spongy-thickened at base. **Achenes** lens-shaped; stigmas 2. May-July.—Calcareous seepage ravines and meadows in se Minn.

Carex laevivaginata
perigynium (l)
pistillate scale (r)

Carex stipata Muhl.
MAP 1446
STALK-GRAIN SEDGE   *native*
Plants densely tufted. **Stems** 3-angled and slightly winged, 2-12 dm long. **Leaves** 4-8 mm wide; **sheaths** cross-wrinkled on front, divided with small swollen joints on back. **Spikes** with both staminate and pistillate flowers, staminate flowers borne above pistillate, clustered or the lowest spikes often separate; **bracts** small and sometimes bristle-like, longer than the spike; **pistillate scales** tapered to a tip or with a short, sharp point, half to 3/4 as long as the perigynia. **Perigynia** yellow-green to dull brown, flat on 1 side and convex on other, 3-5 mm long, strongly several-nerved on both sides, tapered to a finely toothed, notched beak 1-3 mm long. **Achenes** lens-shaped; stigmas 2. May-July.— Floodplain forests and swamps, thickets, wet meadows, wetland margins and ditches; usually not in sphagnum bogs.

Carex stipata
perigynium (l)
pistillate scale (r)

CLADIUM *Saw-Grass*

Carex stipata

Cladium mariscoides (Muhl.) Torr.
MAP 1447
SMOOTH SAW-GRASS   *native*
Grasslike perennial, spreading by rhizomes and forming colonies. **Stems** single or in small groups, stiff, slender, smooth, 0.3-1 m tall. **Leaves** 1-3 mm wide, upper portion round in section, middle portion flattened. **Flowers** in lance-shaped spikelets, 3-5 mm long, in branched clusters (umbels) at end of stem and also with 1-2 clusters on slender stalks from leaf axils; uppermost flower perfect, the style 3-parted; middle flowers staminate; lowest scale of each spikelet empty; **scales** overlapping, ovate, brown; bristles absent. **Achenes** dull brown, 2-3 mm long, pointed at tip; tubercle absent. June-Aug.—Shallow water, sandy or mucky shores, floating bog mats, calcium-rich wet meadows, seeps, fens and low prairie.

Cladium mariscoides

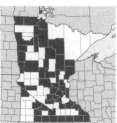

1443. *Carex vesicaria*   1444. *Carex alopecoidea*   1445. *Carex laevivaginata*

CYPERUS *Flat Sedge*

Small to medium, annual or perennial, grasslike plants. Stems often clumped, unbranched, sharply 3-angled. Leaves mostly from base of plants, with 1 or more leaflike bracts near top of stems, the blades flat or folded along midvein. Flower heads in umbels at ends of stems; the spikelets many, grouped in 1 to several rounded or cylindric spikes. Flowers perfect; bristlelike sepals and petals absent; stamens 1-3; styles 2-3-parted. Achenes lens-shaped or 3-angled, beakless.

ADDITIONAL SPECIES
• *Cyperus fuscus* L. (Brown flat sedge), native to temperate Eurasia; Itasca County.

1   Achenes lens-shaped; stigmas 2 2
   2   Scales straw-colored. . . . . *C. flavescens*
   2   Scales red-purple or deep brown 3
     3   Style cleft to slightly below middle. . . . . *C. bipartitus*
     3   Style cleft almost to base . . . . *C. diandrus*
1   Achenes 3-angled; stigmas 3 4
   4   Plants perennial 5
     5   Scales 2-3 mm long, only slightly keeled. . . . . *C. esculentus*
     5   Scales 3-5 mm long, keeled . . . . *C. strigosus*
   4   Plants annual. 6
     6   Scales curved outward at tip; stamens 1 7
       7   Scales 3-nerved, not awn-tipped. . . . . *C. acuminatus*
       7   Scales 7-9-nerved, tipped with a short awn . . . . *C. squarrosus*
     6   Scales not curved outward at tip; stamens 3 8
       8   Scales to 2 mm long, with 3-5 veins near center of scale. . . . . *C. erythrorhizos*
       8   Scales 2-5 mm long, with 7 or more well-spaced veins. . . . . *C. odoratus*

Cyperus acuminatus Torr. & Hook.
MAP 1448
TAPER-TIP FLATSEDGE   ✋*threatened* | *native*

Tufted grasslike annual. **Stems** slender, to 4 dm tall, usually stramineous. **Leaves** few, arising from the base, to 2.5 mm wide, nearly equaling or slightly longer than the stem; involucral bracts 2-4, unequal, longer than the inflorescence. **Inflorescence** of numerous dense globose spikes. **Spikelets** ovate to oblong, 1.5-8 mm wide, 2.5-7 mm long, strongly flattened, closely imbricate, 10- to 24-flowered; **scales** outwardly curved at the tip, strongly 8-nerved; stamen 1; style 3-cleft. **Achenes** trigonous, 0.5-1.2 mm long.—Muddy lake and pond shores, small rock pools.

Cyperus bipartitus Torr.
MAP 1449
SHINING FLAT SEDGE   *native*

   Cyperus niger Ruiz & Pavón var. *rivularis* (Kunth) V. Grant
   Cyperus rivularis Kunth
   Pycreus rivularis (Kunth) Palla

Tufted grasslike annual. **Stems** 3-angled, 1-3 dm tall. **Leaves** usually shorter than stems; leaves and bracts 0.5-2 mm wide, the bracts usually 3, longer than the spikes. **Spikelets** linear, 10-15 mm long and 2-3 mm wide, in clusters (spikes) of 3-10, the spikes stalkless or on stalks to 10 cm long; **scales** overlapping, ovate, shiny, purple-brown on margins; stamens 2 or 3; style 2-parted, the lower 1/3 not divided. **Achenes** lens-shaped, 1-2 mm long, hidden by the scales. July-Sept. —Wet, sandy, gravelly or muddy shores, streambanks, wet meadows, ditches.

Cyperus bipartitus

1446. *Carex stipata*

1447. *Cladium mariscoides*

1448. *Cyperus acuminatus*

1449. *Cyperus bipartitus*

Very similar to **umbrella flatsedge** *(Cyperus diandrus), but the scales shiny and the styles not as deeply divided (vs. dull scales and the styles cleft nearly to base in C. diandrus).*

Cyperus diandrus Torr.
UMBRELLA FLAT SEDGE

MAP 1450
native

Tufted, grasslike annual. **Stems** 3-angled, 5-30 cm tall. **Leaves** about as long as stems, 1-3 mm wide; bracts usually 3, longer than the spikes. **Spikelets** 5-10, linear, 5-20 mm long and 2-3 mm wide; in 1-3 loose, rounded spikes, the spikes on stalks to 6 cm long; **scales** loosely overlapping, ovate, 2-3 mm long, not shiny, purple-brown on margins; stamens 2; style 2-parted, divided nearly to the base, persistent. **Achenes** lens-shaped, pale brown, 1 mm long, visible between the scales. July–Sept.—Sandy or muddy shores, streambanks, wet meadows.

Cyperus diandrus

Cyperus erythrorhizos Muhl.
RED-ROOT FLAT SEDGE
   Cyperus halei Torr.

MAP 1451
native

Tufted, stout or slender annual, roots red. **Stems** 3-angled, 1-7 dm long. **Leaves** mostly near base of plant, shorter to longer than stems, 2-8 mm wide; bracts 3-7, to 9 mm wide, usually much longer than the spikes. **Spikelets** linear, 2-10 mm long and 1-2 mm wide; grouped in a pinnate manner along a stalk (rachilla), in cylindric clusters, the terminal cluster stalkless, the others on stalks to 8 cm long; **scales** ovate, satiny brown, 1-2 mm long, overlapping; stamens 3; style 3-parted. **Achenes** ivory white, sharply 3-angled, ovate, 0.5-1 mm long. July–Sept.—Sandy or muddy shores, streambanks, exposed mud flats, ditches; often with rusty flatsedge (*Cyperus odoratus*).

Cyperus erythrorhizos

Cyperus esculentus L.
CHUFA

MAP 1452
native

Grasslike perennial, with rhizomes ending in small tubers. **Stems** single, 3-angled, erect, 2-7 dm long. **Leaves** light green, mostly from base of plant, about as long as stems, 3-10 mm wide, with a prominent midvein; the bracts 3-6, usually much longer than the spikes. **Spikelets** linear, 3-12 cm long and 1-2 mm wide; pinnately arranged on a stalk, forming loose cylindrical spikes, the spikes to 5 cm long and 1-2 mm wide; **scales** straw-colored, 2-3 mm long, overlapping; stamens 3; style 3-parted. **Achenes** pale brown, 3-angled, 1-2 mm long. July–Sept.—Sandy or muddy shores, streambanks, marshes, ditches and other wet places; weedy in wet or moist cultivated fields.

Cyperus esculentus

Cyperus houghtonii Torr.
HOUGHTON'S FLAT SEDGE

MAP 1453
native

Grasslike perennial. **Stems** smooth, 2-6 dm tall. **Leaves** 2-4 mm wide; **bracts** 3-6, mostly ascending, at least one exceeding the inflorescence. **Inflorescence** of 1 or 2 sessile spikes in an irregular head, usually with 2-5 rays to 10 cm long, each with a similar but smaller head. **Spikelets** usually 5-15, mostly ascending, flattened, usually 5-12-flowered; scales rotund, 2-2.5 mm long, in half-view from the side more than half as wide as long, many-nerved, obtuse or the uppermost minutely mucronate. **Achenes** 1.5-2 mm long.—Dry, especially sandy soil.

Cyperus lupulinus (Spreng.) Marcks
GREAT PLAINS FLAT SEDGE

MAP 1454
native

Grasslike perennial. **Stems** 1-5 dm tall. **Leaves** shorter than the culm, 2-4 mm wide; bracts 3 or 4, usually widely spreading or even decurved. **Inflorescence**

Cyperus houghtonii

1450. Cyperus diandrus   *1451. Cyperus erythrorhizos*   *1452. Cyperus esculentus*

usually a single subglobose or hemispheric sessile spike, or occasionally with a few rays to 7 cm long, each bearing a similar but smaller spike. **Spikelets** very crowded, radiating from the axis, flattened, usually 6-12-flowered but often fewer; **scales** oblong-elliptic, 2.5-3.5 mm long, in half-view from the side about a third as wide as long, many-nerved, obtuse or minutely mucronulate. **Achenes** 1.5-2 mm long.—Dry woods and fields.

Cyperus odoratus L.

RUSTY FLAT SEDGE

    Cyperus engelmannii Steud.
    Cyperus ferruginescens Boeckl.
    Cyperus speciosus Vahl

MAP 1455
native

Cyperus lupulinus

Stout, grasslike, fibrous-rooted annual. **Stems** tufted or single, 3-angled, 2-7 dm long. **Leaves** mostly from base of plant, shorter to longer than flowering stems, the blades 2-8 mm wide; the **involucral bracts** much longer than the spikes. **Spikelets** linear, 1-2 cm long, pinnately arranged along a stalk, forming several to many cylindrical spikes, the spikes stalkless or stalked; **scales** red-brown, 2-3 mm long, overlapping; stamens 3; style 3-parted. **Achenes** brown, 3-angled, 1-2 mm long. July-Sept.—Sandy or muddy shores, floating mats, ditches, wet cultivated fields.

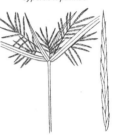

Cyperus schweinitzii Torr.

SAND FLAT SEDGE

    Cyperus × *mesochoreus* Geise
    Mariscus schweinitzii (Torr.) T. Koyama

MAP 1456
native

Cyperus odoratus

Grasslike perennial. **Stems** rough, 1-8 dm tall. **Leaves** 2-4 mm wide; **bracts** 3-6, usually much longer than the inflorescence. **Sessile spike** obconic to oblong; rays 1-6, rarely more than 10 cm long; **spikelets** 5-15 in the sessile spike, fewer in the peduncled ones, all crowded, ascending, flattened, usually 8-12-flowered. **Scales** broadly ovate-elliptic to rotund, the body 3-3.7 mm long, many-nerved, the uppermost with a conspicuous mucro to 1 mm long. **Achenes** oblong, 2-3 mm long.—Dry or moist sandy soil.

Cyperus squarrosus L.

AWNED FLAT SEDGE

    Cyperus aristatus Rottb.
    Cyperus inflexus Muhl.

MAP 1457
native

Small, tufted, sweet-scented, grasslike annual. **Stems** very slender, 3-angled, 3-15 cm long. **Leaves** few, all at base of plant, 1-2 mm wide; bracts 2-3, longer than the spikes. **Spikelets** linear, flattened, 3-10 mm long, in 1-4 dense, rounded spikes, 1 spike stalkless, the other spikes on stalks to 3 cm long; **scales** 1-2 mm long, tipped by an awn to 1 mm long, pale brown; stamens 1; style 3-parted. **Achenes** brown, 3-angled, 0.5-1 mm long. July-Sept.—Wet, sandy or muddy lakeshores, streambanks, mud and gravel bars, wet meadows.

Cyperus schweinitzii

Cyperus strigosus L.

STRAW-COLOR FLAT SEDGE

    Cyperus hansenii Britt.
    Cyperus stenolepis Torr.

MAP 1458
native

Grasslike perennial, from tuberlike corms. **Stems** single or few, slender, sharply 3-angled, 1-8 dm long. **Leaves** mostly at base of plants, the blades 2-12 mm wide, margins rough-to-touch; the bracts mostly longer than the spikes. **Spikelets** flat,

Cyperus squarrosus

1453. *Cyperus houghtonii*

1454. *Cyperus lupulinus*

1455. *Cyperus odoratus*

linear, 6-20 mm long and 1-2 mm wide, golden-brown, pinnately arranged and spreading, in several to many cylindric spikes, the spikes often bent downward, on stalks 1-12 cm long, the stalks sometimes branched; **scales** straw-colored, 3-5 mm long; stamens 3; style 3-parted. **Achenes** brown, 3-angled, 1-2 mm long. July-Sept.—Wet, sandy or muddy shores, streambanks, marshes, wet meadows, ditches, cultivated fields.

DULICHIUM *Three-Way Sedge*

Dulichium arundinaceum (L.) Britt.   MAP 1459
THREE-WAY SEDGE   *native*
Grasslike perennial, spreading by rhizomes and often forming large colonies. **Stems** stout, erect, 3-10 dm long, jointed, hollow, rounded in section. **Leaves** 3-ranked, flat, short, 4-15 cm long and 3-8 mm wide; lower leaves reduced to sheaths. **Flower heads** from leaf axils, in linear clusters of 5-10 spikelets, the clusters 1-2.5 cm long; scales lance-shaped, green to brown, 5-8 mm long. **Flowers** perfect; sepals and petals reduced to 6-9 downwardly barbed bristles; stamens 3; style 2-parted. **Achenes** light brown, oblong, 2-4 mm long, beaked by the persistent, slender style. July-Sept.—Shallow marshes, wet meadows, shores, bog margins.

Dulichium arundinaceum

ELEOCHARIS *Spike-Rush*

Small to medium rushlike plants, perennial from rhizomes, or annual; often forming large, matlike colonies. Stems round, flattened, or angled in section. Leaves reduced to sheaths at base of stems. Flower head a single spikelet at tip of stem; scales of the spikelets spirally arranged and overlapping. Flowers perfect; sepals and petals bristlelike or absent, the bristles usually 6 if present; stamens 3; styles 2-3-parted, the base of style swollen and persistent as a projection (tubercle) atop the achene, or sometimes joined with the achene body. Achenes rounded on both sides or 3-angled.

ADDITIONAL SPECIES
• *Eleocharis wolfii* (Gray) Gray ex Britt. (Wolf's spike-rush), ☛ *endangered*; plants tufted, stems flattened, 2-edged, often twisted, 1-3 dm long and 1-2 mm wide; spikelets narrowly ovate, 4-10 mm long and 2-3 mm wide, wider than stem; achenes gray, about 1 mm long; tubercle cone-shaped, constricted at base where joins achene; muddy shores, rock pools; rare in Minn (MAP 1460).

1 Mature spikelet scarcely if at all thicker than main portion of stem; scales persistent; stems triangular. ***E. robbinsii***
1 Mature spikelet decidedly thicker than stem; scales usually deciduous; stems terete (or sometimes flattened or many-ridged), not cross-partitioned 2
  2 Tubercle a slender or tiny conical continuation of the body of the achene, slightly differentiated in texture or color, not separated by a constriction or shaped as a distinct apical cap; stigmas 3; tip of leaf sheath without a prominent tooth. 3
    3 Fertile stems 20-70 cm tall, flattened, stout; vegetative stems often as long or longer and rooting at their tips; spikelets 9-17 mm long . . . . ***E. rostellata***
    3 Fertile stems to 35 cm tall, but often all tufted and less than 20 cm tall, very slender; stems not rooting at tips; spikelets 2-7 mm long. 4
      4 Plants less than 5 cm tall; achenes ca. 1-1.3 mm long, including tiny tubercle; spikelets 2-3 mm long . . . . ***E. parvula***
      4 Plants mostly over 5 cm tall; achenes 2-2.5 mm long; spikelets 4-7 mm long . . . . ***E. quinqueflora***
  2 Tubercle differentiated in shape and texture, usually separated from body of achene by a narrow constriction to form a distinct apical cap; stigmas 2 or 3; leaf sheaths sometimes with a prominent tooth at tip. 5
    5 Achenes 3-sided (the angles sharp, or obscure and the achene plumply rounded); styles 3-cleft; surface of

1456. Cyperus schweinitzii   *11457. Cyperus squarrosus*   *1458. Cyperus strigosus*   *1459. Dulich. arundinaceum*

achene normally ridged, reticulate, roughened, or in a few species only minutely punctate 6

  6 Achenes white or pearly, with prominent longitudinal ridges connected by numerous tiny cross-bars; basal scales of spikelet fertile . . . . ***E. acicularis***

  6 Achenes greenish, yellow, golden, brown, black (rarely whitish), and reticulate, smooth, or roughened; basal scales of spikelets sterile 7

    7 Plants tufted, without rhizomes; achenes whitish, greenish, olive, or black, smooth to finely reticulate . . . . ***E. intermedia***

    7 Plants with very stout rhizomes; achenes yellow, golden, or brown, the surface strongly papillate-roughened or honeycombed 8

      8 Stems very strongly flattened and often ± twisted, with obscure ridges; scales at middle of spikelet red-brown with narrow, deeply bifid scarious whitish tips to 1 mm long . . . . ***E. compressa***

      8 Stems slightly or not at all flattened, prominently ridged; scales at middle of spikelet deep reddish brown to nearly black, with short, entire, lacerate, or bifid tips mostly less than 0.6 mm long . 9

        9 Stems usually 10-50 cm tall, 0.4-0.8 mm wide, scales 2-3.4 mm long . . . . ***E. elliptica***

        9 Stems ca. 3-10 (-15) cm tall, 0.2-0.3 mm wide; scales 1-1.4 mm long . . . . ***E. nitida***

 5 Achenes 2-sided (lenticular or biconvex); styles 2- or 3-cleft; achene smooth, usually ± shiny 10

  10 Top of leaf sheaths thin and membranous, cleft on one side, usually whitish; achene olive green to brown, ca. 1-1.5 mm long, including the green tubercle; anthers to 1 mm long. . . . . ***E. flavescens***

  10 Top of leaf sheaths thin to firm, truncate, not split (sometimes with a tooth); achenes and anthers various 11

    11 Plants perennial, with stiff stems and rhizomes; scales acute to acuminate at tip (or somewhat obtuse); achenes 1.5-2.8 mm long, including tubercle; anthers ca. 1-3 mm long . . . . ***E. palustris***

    11 Plants annual, with soft, easily compressed, densely tufted stems; scales broadly rounded at tip; achenes 1.1-1.5 mm long, including the strongly flattened tubercle; anthers to 0.7 mm long 12

      12 Base of tubercle less than 2/3 as wide as the broadest part of the mature achene; scales purplish brown . . . . ***E. ovata***

      12 Base of tubercle at least 2/3 as wide as broadest part of mature achene; scales brown or reddish brown (rarely flushed with purple). 13

        13 Tubercle very depressed, not over 1/4 of the total length of the achene, nearly or quite as wide as the truncate achene body, on which it sits as a flattish cap . . . . ***E. engelmannii***

        13 Tubercle broadly triangular, more than 1/4 the total length of the achene and nearly as wide as the broadest part of the body . . . . ***E. obtusa***

Eleocharis acicularis (L.) Roemer & J.A. Schultes

MAP 1461   *native*

NEEDLE SPIKE-RUSH

Small, tufted, mat-forming perennial, from slender rhizomes. **Stems** threadlike, 3-15 cm long and to 0.5 mm wide, somewhat 4-angled and grooved; sheaths membranous, usually red at base. **Spikelets** narrowly ovate, 3-6 mm long and 1-1.5 mm wide; scales with a green midvein and chaffy margins; sepals and petals reduced to 3-4 bristles or absent; style 3-parted. **Achenes** gray, rounded 3-angled, ridged, to 1 mm long; **tubercle** cone-shaped, constricted at base. May-Sept. —Shallow water, exposed muddy or sandy shores, marshes and streambanks.

Eleocharis acicularis

Eleocharis compressa Sullivan

MAP 1462   *native*

FLAT-STEM SPIKE-RUSH

  Eleocharis elliptica var. *compressa* (Sullivant) Drapalik & Mohlenbrock
  Eleocharis tenuis var. *atrata* (Svens.) Boivin

Tufted perennial, from stout black rhizomes. **Stems** flattened and often twisted, 1.5-4 dm long and 0.5-1 mm wide, shallowly grooved; sheaths red or purple at base. **Spikelets** ovate, 4-10 mm long and 3-4 mm wide; lowest scale sterile and encircling the stem; fertile scales with a green midvein, purple-brown on sides, and white translucent margins; sepals and petals absent or reduced to 1-5 bristles; style 3-parted. **Achenes** yellow-brown, covered with small bumps, somewhat 3-angled, 1-1.5 mm long; **tubercle** small, constricted at base. May-Aug.—Low calcareous prairie, wet meadows, swamps, ditches.

Eleocharis compressa

Eleocharis elliptica Kunth

MAP 1463   *native*

ELLIPTIC SPIKE-RUSH

Mat-forming perennial, with long rhizomes. **Stems** subterete to sometimes compressed, often with 5-10 ridges, to 90 cm long and 0.3-0.8 mm wide, spongy; sheaths persistent, not splitting, dark red at base, usually red-brown at tip, tooth to 0.5 mm long (usually present on some stems). **Spikelets** ovoid, 3-8 cm long and

ELEOCHARIS ACHENES

Eleocharis acicularis   *Eleocharis compressa*   *Eleocharis elliptica*   *Eleocharis engelmannii*

Eleocharis flavescens   *Eleocharis intermedia*   *Eleocharis nitida*   *Eleocharis obtusa*

Eleocharis ovata   *Eleocharis palustris*   *Eleocharis parvula*   *Eleocharis quinqueflora*

Eleocharis robbinsii   *Eleocharis rostellata*   *Eleocharis wolfii*

1460. *Eleocharis wolfii*   1461. *Eleocharis acicularis*   1462. *Eleocharis compressa*   1463. *Eleocharis elliptica*

2-3 mm wide, scales spreading in fruit, 10-30, brown, midrib region often paler, entire or shallowly notched; perianth bristles absent or rarely 1-3, pale brown, to 1/2 of achene length, sparsely retrorsely spinulose; style 3-parted. **Achenes** yellow, orange, or medium brown, obpyriform, angles evident to prominent, ca. 1 mm long, rugulose (visible at 10x), with 12-20 horizontal ridges in a vertical series; **tubercle** brown to whitish, depressed, apiculate.—Open, rocky or sandy wetlands, sometimes in shallow water.

Eleocharis engelmannii Steud.
ENGELMANN'S SPIKE-RUSH   MAP 1464   *native*

Annual. **Stems** 2-40 cm long and 0.5-1.5 mm wide; sheaths with a small tooth to 0.3 mm long. **Spikelets** cylindric or ovoid, 5-10 mm long and 2-3 mm wide; floral scales 25-100(-200), orange brown to stramineous, midribs mostly keeled; perianth bristles present or often absent, 5-8, brown, rudimentary to slightly exceeding tubercle; styles 2-3-parted. **Achenes** ca. 1 mm long; **tubercle** depressed, triangular, to nearly 1/2 as high as wide, nearly as wide as achene.—Open sandy wetlands.

Eleocharis engelmannii

Eleocharis flavescens (Poir.) Urban
YELLOW SPIKE-RUSH   MAP 1465   ✎ *threatened | native*
    Eleocharis flaccida var. *olivacea* (Torr.) Fern. & Grisc.
    Eleocharis olivacea Torr.

Small, tufted, mat-forming perennial, spreading by slender rhizomes. **Stems** bright green, flattened, 3-15 cm long. **Spikelets** ovate, 2-7 mm long and much wider than stem; scales ovate, red-brown, with a green midvein; sepals and petals reduced to 6-8 barbed bristles; style 2-parted (rarely 3-parted). **Achenes** lens-shaped, brown, 1 mm long; **tubercle** pale, cone-shaped, constricted at base.—Shallow water, sandy, peaty or muddy shores, mud flats; sometimes where calcium-rich.

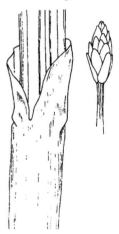

Eleocharis flavescens

Eleocharis intermedia J.A. Schultes
INTERMEDIATE SPIKE-RUSH   MAP 1466   *native*

Small, densely tufted annual. **Stems** threadlike, grooved, of unequal lengths, 5-20 cm long; sheaths toothed on 1 side. **Spikelets** long-ovate, wider than stem; scales oblong lance-shaped, purple-brown, with a green midvein and white, translucent margins; sepals and petals reduced to barbed bristles or sometimes absent; style 3-parted. **Achenes** light brown to olive, 3-angled, 1 mm long; **tubercle** cone-shaped, constricted at base. June–Sept.—Wet, sandy or mucky shores, streambanks, mud flats.

Eleocharis intermedia

Eleocharis nitida Fern.
QUILL SPIKE-RUSH   MAP 1467   *native*

Small, mat forming perennial, from matted or creeping purplish rhizomes. **Stems** round in section to somewhat 4-angled, to 15 cm long, thin and delicate, to only 0.3 mm wide. **Spikelets** ovoid, small, to 4 mm long and 2 mm wide; **fertile scales** 1-1.3 mm long, brown to dark brown, midrib usually pale or greenish, the scales often early-deciduous; **bristles** absent; style 3-parted. **Achenes** persistent after scales fall, dark yellow-orange or brown, 3-angled (the angles evident), covered with small bumps (under magnification); **tubercle** brown, flattened and saucer-like, with a tiny central tip. May–June.—Wet soil in openings in alder thickets and marshes, sometimes in shallow water, usually where little competing vegetation; disturbed moist places such as ditches and wheel ruts; crevices in rocks along Lake Superior shoreline.

Eleocharis nitida

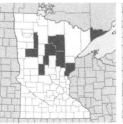

1464. *Eleocharis engelmannii*   1465. *Eleocharis flavescens*   1466. *Eleocharis intermedia*

Eleocharis obtusa (Willd.) J.A. Schultes
OVOID SPIKE-RUSH   MAP 1468
native

Tufted, fibrous-rooted annual. **Stems** slender, round in section, ribbed, 0.5-5 dm long and 0.5-2 mm wide; sheaths green, with a small tooth. **Spikelets** ovate to cylindric, 4-15 mm long and 2-4 mm wide; scales orange-brown, with a green midvein and pale margins; sepals and petals reduced to 6-7 brown bristles, or absent; styles 2- or 3-parted. **Achenes** lens-shaped, light to dark brown or olive, shiny, ca. 1 mm long; **tubercle** flattened-triangular, 2/3 to nearly as wide as the broad top of achene. June-Sept.—May form large colonies, especially on exposed mud flats and drying shores of receding lakes.

Eleocharis ovata (Roth) Roemer & J.A. Schultes
OVOID SPIKE-RUSH   (NO MAP)
native
    Eleocharis annua House
    Eleocharis obtusa var. *ovata* (Roth) Drapalik & Mohlenbrock
    Scirpus ovatus Roth

Annual. **Stems** to 35 cm long and to 1 mm wide, soft; sheaths with very short tooth to 0.2 mm. **Spikelets** ovoid, 2-8 mm long and 2-4 mm wide; floral scales 25-100 or more, orange-brown, rarely stramineous, midribs often keeled in lower part of spikelet; perianth bristles present, rarely absent, 6-7, brown, exceeding the tubercle; styles 2-parted or some 3-parted. **Achenes** ca. 1 mm long; **tubercle** deltoid, 1/2-3/4 as wide as achene.—Muddy or sandy shores. *Not mapped as it is often included within* **Eleocharis obtusa**, *but likely present nearly statewide.*

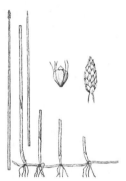

Eleocharis obtusa

Eleocharis palustris (L.) Roemer & J.A. Schultes
COMMON SPIKE-RUSH   MAP 1469
native
    Eleocharis calva var. *australis* (Nees) St. John
    Eleocharis erythropoda Steud.
    Eleocharis smallii Britt.

Perennial, spreading by rhizomes. **Stems** single or in small clusters, slender to stout, round in section, 1-8 dm long and 1-3 mm wide; sheaths red or purple at base. **Spikelets** long-ovate, 5-30 mm long and 2-4 mm wide, wider than stems; lowest scale sterile, encircling the stem; fertile scales lance-shaped to ovate, 2-5 mm long, brown or red-brown, with a green or pale midvein; sepals and petals reduced to usually 4, pale brown, barbed bristles; style 2-parted. **Achenes** lens-shaped, yellow to brown, 1-2 mm long; **tubercle** flattened-triangular, constricted at base. May-Aug. A variable and common species known by a number of synonyms.—Shallow water of marshes, wet meadows, muddy shores, bogs, ditches, streambanks and swamps.

Eleocharis palustris

Eleocharis parvula (Roemer & J.A. Schultes) Link
LITTLE-HEAD SPIKE-RUSH   MAP 1470
native
    Eleocharis coloradoensis (Britton) Gilly

Very small, tufted, perennial, spreading by slender rhizomes and forming dense mats. **Stems** threadlike, mostly 2-6 cm long, less than 1 mm wide. **Spikelets** ovate, 2-5 mm long and 1-2 mm wide; scales ovate, green, straw-colored or brown, 1-2 mm long; sepals and petals absent or reduced to small bristles; style 3-parted. **Achenes** pale brown, 3-angled, about 1 mm long; **tubercle** small, not forming a distinct cap on top of achene body. July-Sept.—Wet saline or alkaline flats and shores.

Eleocharis parvula

1467. Eleocharis nitida

1468. Eleocharis obtusa

1469. Eleocharis palustris

1470. Eleocharis parvula

Eleocharis quinqueflora (F.X. Hartmann) Schwarz

FEW-FLOWER SPIKE-RUSH

Eleocharis bernardina Munz & Johnston
Scirpus pauciflorus Lightf.
Scirpus quinqueflorus F.X. Hartmann

MAP 1471
native

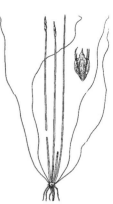

Small, tufted perennial, spreading by rhizomes. **Stems** threadlike, grooved, 1-3 dm long and less than 1 mm wide. **Spikelets** ovate, 4-8 mm long and 2-3 mm wide; scales ovate, brown, chaffy on margins, 2-5 mm long; sepals and petals reduced to bristles or absent; style 3-parted. **Achenes** gray-brown or brown, 3-angled, 1-3 mm long; **tubercle** slender, joined to the achene and beaklike. June-Aug.—Wet, sandy or gravelly shores and flats marshes and fens; often where calcium-rich.

Eleocharis robbinsii Oakes

ROBBINS' SPIKE-RUSH

MAP 1472
🌿 *threatened | native*

Tufted perennial, spreading by rhizomes. **Stems** slender, 3-angled, 2-6 dm long and 1-2 mm wide; when underwater, plants often with numerous sterile stems from base; sheaths brown. **Spikelets** lance-shaped, 1-2 cm long and 2-3 mm wide, barely wider than stems; scales narrowly ovate, margins chaffy; sepals and petals reduced to 6 barbed bristles; style 3-parted. **Achenes** rounded on both sides, light brown, 2-3 mm long; **tubercle** flattened and cone-shaped, with a raised ring at base. July-Aug.—Wet, sandy or mucky lake and pond shores, marshes, exposed flats.

Eleocharis robbinsii

Eleocharis rostellata (Torr.) Torr.

BEAKED SPIKE-RUSH

Scirpus rostellatus Torr.

MAP 1473
🌿 *threatened | native*

Tufted perennial, without creeping rhizomes. **Stems** flattened, wiry, 3-10 dm long and 1-2 mm wide; the fertile stems upright, the sterile stems often arching and rooting at tip; sheaths brown. **Spikelets** oblong, tapered at both ends, 5-15 mm long and 2-5 mm wide, wider than the stem; scales ovate, 3-5 mm long, green to brown with a darker midvein and translucent margins; sepals and petals reduced to 4-8 barbed bristles; style 3-parted. **Achenes** olive to brown, rounded 3-angled, 2-3 mm long; **tubercle** cone-shaped, joined with the achene body and beaklike. July-Sept.—Shores, wet meadows, calcareous fens and mud flats; typically where calcium-rich and often associated with mineral springs.

Eleocharis rostellata

ERIOPHORUM *Cotton-Grass*

Grasslike perennials. Stems clumped or single, round to rounded 3-angled in section. Leaves mostly at base of plant, the blades flat, folded or inrolled; upper leaves often reduced to bladeless sheaths. Flower heads at ends of stems, with 1 or several spikelets; spikelets resemble cottonballs when mature; scales many, spirally arranged, chaffy on margins; involucral bracts leaflike in species with several spikelets in the head, or reduced to scales in species with 1 spikelet at end of stems (*E. chamissonis, E. vaginatum*). Flowers perfect; sepals and petals numerous, reduced to long, cottony, persistent, white to tawny brown bristles; stamens 3; styles 3-parted. Achenes brown, more or less 3-angled, sometimes with a short beak formed by the persistent style.

1 Head a single spikelet at end of stem; leaflike bracts absent 2
  2 Plants forming colonies from rhizomes . . . . *E. chamissonis*
  2 Plants densely clumped, rhizomes absent . . . . *E. vaginatum*
1 Head of 2 or more spikelets; leaflike bracts present 3

1471. *Eleocharis quinqueflora*   1472. *Eleocharis robbinsii*   1473. *Eleocharis rostellata*

3   Leaves 1-2 mm wide; leaflike bract 1, erect, the head appearing lateral from side of stem 4

    4   Blade of uppermost stem leaf much shorter than its sheath . . . . ***E. gracile***

    4   Blade as long or longer than its sheath . . . . ***E. tenellum***

3   Leaves 3 mm or more wide; leaflike bracts 2 or 3, the head appearing terminal 5

    5   Scales 3-7-nerved, copper-brown on sides . . . . ***E. virginicum***

    5   Scales with 1 nerve, sides olive-green to nearly black 6

        6   Midvein of scale slender, fading before reaching tip of scale . . . . ***E. angustifolium***

        6   Midvein of scale widening toward tip of scale and reaching scale tip . . . . ***E. viridicarinatum***

Eriophorum angustifolium Honckeny
THIN-SCALE COTTON-GRASS
Eriophorum polystachion L.

MAP 1474
native

Grasslike perennial, spreading by rhizomes and forming colonies. **Stems** mostly single, 2-8 dm long and 2-3 mm wide, more or less round in section, becoming 3-angled below the head. **Leaves** few, flat or folded along midrib, 3-8 mm wide, often dying back from the tips; sheaths sometimes red, dark-banded at tip. **Spikelets** 3-10, clustered in heads 1-3 cm wide when mature, the heads drooping on weak stalks; involucral bracts leaflike, often black at base, the main bract upright and usually longer than the head; **scales** lance-shaped, brown or purple-green, 4-6 mm long, the midvein not extending to tip of scale; **bristles** bright white, 2-3 cm long. **Achenes** brown to nearly black, 2-3 mm long. May-July. —Bogs, calcareous fens, wet meadows. *Similar to* ***E. viridicarinatum****, which see.*

Eriophorum angustifolium

Eriophorum chamissonis C.A. Mey.
CHAMISSO'S COTTON-GRASS

MAP 1475
native

Grasslike perennial, spreading by rhizomes and forming colonies. **Stems** single or in small groups, stout, more or less round in section, 2-6 dm long and 1-3 mm wide. **Leaves** few, mostly from base of plant and shorter than stems, the uppermost leaves from near middle of stem and often without blades, lower leaves round in section to 3-angled and channeled, 1-2 mm wide. **Spikelets** single, erect at end of stems, clustered in a more or less round head 2-3 cm wide; involucral bracts not leaflike, reduced to black scales; **flower scales** narrowly ovate, black-green, with broad white margins and tips; **bristles** white to bright red-brown. **Achenes** dark brown, beaked, 2-3 mm long. June-July. —Bogs.

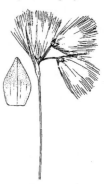

Eriophorum gracile W.D.J. Koch
SLENDER COTTON-GRASS

MAP 1476
native

Grasslike perennial, spreading from rhizomes. **Stems** single, spreading or reclining, slender, more or less round in section, 2-6 dm long and 1-2 mm wide. **Leaves** few, channeled on upper side, 1-2 mm wide, the basal leaves often withered by flowering time, blades of uppermost leaves very small. **Spikelets** in clusters of 2-5 at ends of stems, on spreading to nodding stalks 2-3 cm long; involucral bract leaflike and erect, shorter than spikelet cluster; **scales** ovate, pale to black-brown with a prominent midvein; **bristles** bright white. **Achenes** light brown, 3-4 mm long. May-July. —Fens and bogs.

Eriophorum gracile

Eriophorum tenellum Nutt.
FEW-NERVE COTTON-GRASS

MAP 1477
native

Grasslike perennial, with rhizomes and forming colonies. **Stems** single, slender, erect, 3-8 dm long, rounded 3-angled, rough-to-touch on upper angles. **Leaves** linear, 1-2 mm wide, channeled, not reduced and bladeless on upper stem.

Eriophorum tenellum

1474. Eriophor. angustifolium

1475. Eriophor. chamissonis

1476. Eriophorum gracile

1477. Eriophorum tenellum

Spikelets 3-6, in short-stalked clusters at ends of stems, or with 1-2 rough, drooping stalks to 5 cm long; involucral bract leaflike, stiff and erect, usually shorter than the spikelet cluster; **scales** ovate, straw-colored to red-brown; **bristles** white. **Achenes** brown, 2-3 mm long.—Bogs, conifer swamps.

Eriophorum vaginatum L.
TUSSOCK COTTON-GRASS
Eriophorum spissum Fern.

MAP 1478
native

Densely tufted, grasslike perennial, forming large hummocks. **Stems** stiff, rounded 3-angled, 2-7 dm long. **Leaves** at base of stems, mostly shorter than stems, only 1 mm wide, with 1-3 inflated, bladeless sheaths on stem. **Spikelets** clustered in a single head at end of stems; involucral bracts absent; **scales** narrowly ovate, purple-brown to black, with white margins, spreading when mature; **bristles** usually white (rarely red-brown). **Achenes** obovate, 3-4 mm long. June. —Sphagnum bogs and tamarack swamps.

Eriophorum virginicum L.
TAWNY COTTON-GRASS

MAP 1479
native

Eriophorum vaginatum

Large grasslike perennial, with slender rhizomes. **Stems** single or in small groups, stiff, erect, to 1 m long, leafy, mostly smooth. **Leaves** flat, 2-4 mm wide, the uppermost often longer than the head. **Spikelets** in dense clusters of several to many at ends of stems, on short stalks of more or less equal lengths, the clusters wider than long; involucral bracts 2-3, leaflike, spreading or bent downward, unequal, much longer than the head; **scales** ovate, thick, copper-brown with a green center; **bristles** tawny or copper-brown. **Achenes** light brown, 3-4 mm long. July-Aug.—Sphagnum moss peatlands.

Eriophorum viridicarinatum (Engelm.) Fern.
DARK-SCALE COTTON-GRASS

MAP 1480
native

Grasslike perennial, forming colonies from spreading rhizomes. **Stems** mostly single, more or less round in section, 3-7 dm long. **Leaves** flat except at tip, the uppermost leaves 10-15 cm long; sheaths green. **Spikelets** usually 20-30, clustered in heads at ends of stems, on short to long, finely hairy stalks; involucral bracts 2-4, not black at base, longer or equal to head; **scales** narrowly ovate, black-green, the midvein pale, extending to tip of scale; **bristles** white. **Achenes** brown, 3-4 mm long. May-July.—Bogs and open conifer swamps. *Similar to E. angustifolium, but usually with more spikelets, the scale midvein extending to tip of scale, and the leaf sheaths not dark-banded at tip.*

Eriophorum virginicum

FIMBRISTYLIS *Fimbry*

Annual or perennial grasslike plants. Stems slender, clumped or single. Leaves mostly at base of plants, narrowly linear, flat to inrolled. Spikelets many-flowered, in umbel-like clusters at ends of stems; involucral bracts 2-3, short and leaflike; scales spirally arranged and overlapping. Flowers perfect, sepals and petals absent, stamens 1-3; styles 2-3-parted, swollen at base, deciduous when mature. Achenes lens-shaped or 3-angled.

1 Plants annual; achenes 3-angled; styles 3-parted . . . . ***F. autumnalis***
1 Plants perennial; achenes lens-shaped; styles 2-parted . . . . ***F. puberula***

1478. Eriophorum vaginatum   *1479. Eriophorum virginicum*   *1480. Erioph. viridicarinatum*   *1481. Fimbristylis autumnalis*

Fimbristylis autumnalis (L.) Roemer & J.A. Schultes
SLENDER FIMBRY

MAP 1481
native

Tufted, grasslike annual, with shallow fibrous roots. **Stems** flattened, slender, sharp-edged, 0.5-3 dm long. **Leaves** shorter than the stems, flat, 1-2 mm wide. **Spikelets** usually many in an open umbel-like cluster, the spikelets lance-shaped, 3-8 mm long, single or several at ends of threadlike, spreading stalks; involucral bracts 2-3, leaflike, usually shorter than the head; **scales** ovate, golden-brown with a prominent green midvein, 1-2 mm long; style 3-parted. **Achenes** ivory to tan, 3-angled and ribbed on the angles, to 0.5 mm long. July-Sept.—Sandy or mucky shores (especially where seasonally flooded and then later exposed), streambanks, wet meadows, ditches.

Fimbristylis autumnalis

Fimbristylis puberula (Michx.) Vahl
CHESTNUT FIMBRY

MAP 1482
❦ *endangered* | *native*

Grasslike perennial, with short rhizomes. **Stems** single or in small clumps, slender, stiff, 2-7 dm long, round to oval in section, sometimes swollen at base. **Leaves** shorter than the stems, usually inrolled, 1-3 mm wide, often hairy. **Spikelets** few to many in an umbel-like cluster; the spikelets ovate, 5-10 mm long, the central spikelet stalkless, the others on slender, upright or spreading stalks; involucral bracts 2-3, leaflike, the longest equal or longer than the head; **scales** ovate, brown with a lighter midvein, 3-4 mm long, usually finely hairy, often tipped with a short awn; style 2-parted, the style branches finely hairy. **Achenes** light brown, lens-shaped, 1-2 mm long. June-Sept.—Calcareous fens; Minn at northern edge of species' range.

Fimbristylis puberula

LIPOCARPHA *Halfchaff Sedge*

Lipocarpha micrantha (Vahl) G. Tucker
SMALL-FLOWER HALFCHAFF SEDGE
  Hemicarpha micrantha (Vahl) Pax

MAP 1483
native

Small, densely tufted grasslike annual. **Stems** hairlike, compressed, 3-15 cm long. **Leaves** slender, 2 at base of stem, to 10 cm long and 0.5 mm wide, mostly shorter than the stems. **Spikelets** very small, in stalkless clusters of 1-3; the spikelets many-flowered, ovate, 2-5 mm long; **involucral bracts** 2-3, leaflike, the main bract upright and longer than the spikelets (the head appearing lateral); **scales** brown with a green midvein, 1-2 mm long, tipped with a short awn, inner (2nd) scale very small or absent; bristles absent. **Achenes** brown, 0.5-1 mm long. Aug-Sept. —Sandy or muddy shores and streambanks, usually where seasonally flooded.

Lipocarpha micrantha

RHYNCHOSPORA *Beak Sedge*

Grasslike perennials, clumped or spreading by rhizomes. Stems erect, leafy, usually 3-angled or sometimes round. Leaves flat or rolled inward. Spikelets clustered in dense heads, the heads open to crowded; scales overlapping in a spiral. Flowers perfect, or sometimes upper flowers staminate only; sepals and petals reduced to usually 6 (1-20) bristles or sometimes absent; stamens usually 3; styles 2-parted, swollen at base and persistent on the achene as a tubercle. Achenes lens-shaped.

1 Spikelets white to tan; bristles 8 or more . . . . *R. alba*
1 Spikelets brown, dark olive-green or nearly black; bristles 5-6 2
   2 Scales dark olive-green to black; bristles with upward-pointing barbs, at least some of the bristles longer than
      the tubercle . . . . *R. fusca*
   2 Scales brown; bristles with downward pointing barbs (rarely smooth), the bristles shorter to as long as the
      tubercle . . . . *R. capillacea*

Rhynchospora alba (L.) Vahl
WHITE BEAK SEDGE

MAP 1484
native

Tufted, grasslike perennial. **Stems** slender, erect, 1-6 dm long. **Leaves** bristlelike, 0.5-3 mm wide, shorter than the stems. **Spikelets** in 1-3 rounded heads, 5-20 mm wide, at or near ends of stems, the lateral heads usually long-stalked; the spikelets oblong, narrowed at each end, 4-5 mm long, white, becoming pale brown; **bristles** 8-15, downwardly barbed, about equaling the tubercle. **Achenes** lens-shaped, brown-green, 1-2 mm long; **tubercle** triangular, about half as long as achene. June-Sept.—Bogs, open conifer swamps of black spruce and tamarack, fens.

Rhynchospora capillacea Torr.

MAP 1485
NEEDLE BEAK SEDGE   🌱*threatened | native*

Tufted, grasslike perennial. **Stems** slender, 0.5-4 dm long. **Leaves** threadlike, rolled inward, to only 0.5 mm wide, much shorter than the stem. **Spikelets** in 1-2 small, separated clusters, each cluster subtended by 1 to several short, bristlelike bracts; the spikelets ovate, 3-7 mm long; scales overlapping, ovate, brown with a paler, sharp-tipped midvein; **bristles** 6, downwardly barbed, longer than the achenes; style 2-parted. **Achenes** lens-shaped, satiny yellow-brown, 2 mm long; **tubercle** dull brown, narrowly triangular, about 1 mm long. June-Aug.—Calcareous fens, interdunal flats, wet sandy or gravelly shores, seeps; usually where calcium-rich.

Rhynchospora fusca (L.) Ait. f.

MAP 1486
BROWN BEAK SEDGE   *native*

Tufted, grasslike perennial, spreading by short rhizomes and forming colonies. **Stems** slender, 3-angled, 1-3 dm long. **Leaves** very slender, rolled inward, mostly shorter than the stems. **Spikelets** spindle-shaped, dark brown, 4-6 mm long, in 1-4 loose clusters, the lower clusters on long stalks, each cluster subtended by an erect, leafy bract, the bract longer than the cluster; **bristles** 6, upwardly barbed; style 2-parted. **Achenes** light brown, 1-1.5 mm long; **tubercle** flattened-triangular, nearly as long as achene.—Wet sandy shores, interdunal wetlands, sedge meadows, bog mats.

Rhynchospora capillacea

SCHOENOPLECTUS *Club-Rush*

Perennial or annual, tufted or rhizomatous herbs. Stems cylindric to strongly 3-angled, smooth, spongy with internal air cavities. Leaves basal, rarely 1(-2) on stem; sheaths tubular; ligules membranous; blades well-developed to rudimentary. Inflorescences terminal, head-like to openly paniculate; spikelets 1-100 or more; involucral bracts 1-5, leaflike, proximal bract erect to spreading. Spikelets terete; scales deciduous, spirally arranged, each subtending a flower, or proximal scale empty, midrib usually prolonged into short awn, margins ciliate. Flowers bisexual; perianth of 0-6(-8) spinulose bristles shorter than to somewhat longer than the achene; stamens 3. Achenes biconvex to trigonous, with apical beak, rugose or with transverse wavy ridges. *Our two annual species, S. purshianus and S. smithii, are sometimes placed in genus* **Schoenoplectiella**.

1   Spikelets (at least several of them) distinctly pediceled (sometimes congested in *S. acutus*); stems terete, often over 1 m tall 2

   2   Styles 3-cleft; achenes 3-sided; perianth bristles 2-4 (-5); scales glabrous on the back; mature achenes ca. 2.5 mm long, including short apiculus; stems firm . . . . ***S. heterochaetus***

   2   Styles 2-cleft; achenes plano-convex (flat on one side and rounded on the other) or biconvex; perianth bristles mostly 6; scales puberulent on back; achenes shorter, or stems soft and easily compressed 3

     3   Stems firm and dark olive-green when fresh; spikelets ovoid to cylindrical (often 2.5 or more times as long as wide), usually in a stiffer, sometimes condensed, inflorescence; scales dull, pale or whitish brown, the midrib not strongly contrasting, the margins often more copiously ciliate than in *S. tabernaemontani*, and the backs copiously flecked with shiny red dots, often puberulent; mature achenes 2.2-2.7 mm long, including apiculus, completely hidden by the scales. . . . . ***S. acutus***

     3   Stems rather soft and easily compressed, pale blue-green when fresh; spikelets ovoid (about twice as long as wide, or shorter), in an open, lax inflorescence; scales ± shiny, rich orange-brown, often with prominent greenish midrib, the margins ciliate but the backs essentially glabrous (puberulence and swollen red flecks,

1482. Fimbristylis puberula

1483. Lipocarpha micrantha

1484. Rhynchospora alba

1485. Rhynchospora capillacea

if any, limited to region of midrib); mature (dark gray or lead-colored) achenes 1.6-2.1 mm long, including apiculus, barely covered by the scale . . . . ***S. tabernaemontani***

1   Spikelets 1-few, crowded, sessile or nearly so (rarely one on a short pedicel); stems 3-angled or terete (if terete, then slender, soft, and not over 1 m tall). 4

    4   Spikelet 1, strongly ascending, the involucral bract surpassing its tip by not more than 15 (-20) mm; leaves normally many, hair-like, submersed; stem seldom over 1 mm thick; anthers (2.1-) 2.5-3.5 mm long; achenes 3-sided, the body ca. 2.5-3 mm long. . . . . ***S. subterminalis***

    4   Spikelets usually more than 1 and the involucral bract surpassing them by more than 15 mm (except in smallest plants of some populations); leaves stiff and stems thicker; anthers and achenes various. 5

        5   Plants annual, with soft, terete or obscurely 3-angled, tufted stems; anthers 0.3-0.7 mm long 6

            6   Taller shoots with stems (base of plant to inflorescence) more than 3/4 as long as height of the plant, including the involucral bract; achenes thickly and asymmetrically biconvex (inner face slightly but clearly convex, outer faces forming a clear angle). . . . . ***S. purshianus***

            6   Taller shoots with stems to 3/4 as long as height of the plant; achenes flattened-plano-convex (inner face essentially flat, the outer faces gently rounded) . . . . ***S. smithii***

        5   Plants perennial, with long rhizomes; stems sharply 3-angled, at least upwards; anthers 1-3 mm long. . . 7

            7   Midrib of scale ± greenish, excurrent as a short (not over 0.5 mm) tip extending beyond the tapered (sometimes very slightly notched) apex of the scale; bristles slightly exceeding body of achene; rhizome soft; achene with apiculus 0.5 mm or more in length; styles 3-cleft and achenes 3-sided; leaves more than half as tall as the stems . . . . ***S. torreyi***

            7   Midrib of scale brown, excurrent as a long (0.5-1 mm) tip equaling or exceeding lobes; bristles shorter than body of achene; rhizome firm and hard; achene with apiculus shorter than 0.5 mm; styles usually 2-cleft and achenes biconvex to plano-convex (occasionally some styles 3-cleft and achenes 3-sided in a spikelet); leaves less than half as tall as the stems . . . . ***S. pungens***

Schoenoplectus acutus (Muhl.) A. & D. Löve
MAP 1487
HARDSTEM CLUB-RUSH   *native*
    Scirpus acutus Muhl.

Perennial, from stout rhizomes and often forming large colonies. **Stems** round in section, 1-3 m long. **Leaves** reduced to 3-5 sheaths near base of stem, blades absent, or upper leaves with blades to 25 cm long; **main bract** erect, appearing as a continuation of stem, 2-10 cm long, eventually turning brown. **Spikelets** 5-15 mm long and 3-5 mm wide, in clusters of mostly 3-7, the clusters grouped into a branched head of up to 60 spikelets, the head appearing lateral from side of stem, the branches stiff and spreading; **scales** chaffy, mostly translucent, 3-4 mm long, often with red-brown spots, usually tipped with an awn to 1 mm long; bristles 6, unequal, usually shorter than achene; style 2-parted (rarely 3-parted). **Achenes** light green to dull brown, flat on 1 side and convex on other, 2-3 mm long, the style beak small, to 0.5 mm long. May-Aug.—Usually emergent in shallow to deep water (1-2 m deep) of marshes, ditches, ponds and lakes; sometimes where brackish.

Schoenoplectus acutus

Schoenoplectus heterochaetus (Chase) Soják
MAP 1488
PALE GREAT CLUB-RUSH   *native*
    Scirpus heterochaetus Chase

Perennial, spreading by stout rhizomes. **Stems** slender, round in section, 1-2 m long. **Leaves** reduced to 3-4 sheaths at base of stem, upper sheaths with blades 6-8 cm long; **main bract** erect, 1-10 cm long, shorter than head. **Spikelets** mostly single at ends of stalks, the spikelets 5-15 mm long and 3-6 mm wide, in open, lax heads; **scales** chaffy, brown, 3-4 mm long, tipped with an awn to 2 mm long; bristles 2-4, unequal, about as long as achene; style 3-parted. **Achenes** 3-angled, light green to brown, 2-3 mm long, with a beak about 0.5 mm long. June-Aug.—Emergent in shallow to deep water (1-2 m deep) of marshes, ponds and lakes, ditches.

Schoenoplectus heterochaetus

Schoenoplectus pungens (Vahl) Palla
MAP 1489
COMMON THREESQUARE   *native*
    Scirpus americanus var. *pungens* (Vahl) Barros & Osten
    Scirpus pungens Vahl

Perennial, from slender rhizomes and forming colonies. **Stems** erect to somewhat curved, 2-12 dm long, 3-angled, the sides concave to slightly convex. **Leaves** mostly 1-3 near base of stem, usually folded, or channeled near tip, reaching to about middle of stem and 1-3 mm wide; **main bract** erect, sharp-tipped, resembling a continuation of the stem, 2-15 cm long. **Spikelets** 5-20 mm long and 3-5 mm wide, clustered in heads of 1-6 stalkless spikelets, the head appearing lateral; **scales** brown and translucent, 3-5 mm long, notched at tip, with a midvein extended into a short awn 1-2 mm long; bristles 4-6, unequal, shorter than achene; style 2-3-parted. **Achenes** light green or tan to dark brown, 3-angled or flat on 1 side and convex on other, 2-3 mm long, the beak to 0.5 mm long. May-Sept.—Shallow water (to about 1 m deep), wet sandy, gravelly or mucky shores, streambanks, wet meadows, ditches, seeps and other wet places.

Schoenoplectus purshianus (Fern.) M.T. Strong
WEAK-STALK CLUB-RUSH

MAP 1490
native

Annual. **Stems** often arching (to decumbent), cylindric, to 1 m long and to 2 mm wide. **Leaves** 1, to as long as the stem; blade absent, or if present, C-shaped in cross-section, 0.5-1 mm wide; **bract** erect or often divergent, to 15 cm long. **Spikelets** 1-12; scales straw-colored to orange-brown, midrib often greenish, broadly obovate, 2.5-3 mm long, margins ciliolate at tip and with a small sharp point; perianth members 6, brown, bristle-like, equaling to slightly exceeding achene, densely retrorsely spinulose. **Achenes** biconvex, brown, turning blackish, 1.6-2.2 mm long, rounded at base to a distinct stipelike constriction; beak 0.1-0.3 mm long.—Sandy to mucky shores, especially where water levels have receded.

Schoenoplectus smithii (Gray) Soják
SMITH'S CLUB-RUSH
   Scirpus smithii Gray

MAP 1491
native

Tufted annual. **Stems** slender, smooth, round or rounded 3-angled, to 6 dm long. **Leaves** reduced to sheaths, or some with short blades; **bract** narrow, upright, 2-10 cm long, appearing to be a continuation of stem. **Spikelets** ovate, 5-10 mm long, in a single cluster of 1-12 spikelets; **scales** yellow-brown with a green midvein; bristles 4-6, barbed or smooth, longer than achene, sometimes smaller or absent; style 2-parted. **Achenes** lens-shaped or flat on 1 side and convex on other, glossy brown to black, 1-2 mm long. July-Aug.—Sandy, gravelly or mucky shores, floating mats, bogs.

Schoenoplectus pungens

Schoenoplectus subterminalis (Torr.) Soják
SWAYING CLUB-RUSH
   Scirpus subterminalis Torr.

MAP 1492
native

Aquatic perennial, spreading by rhizomes. **Stems** slender, weak, round in section, to 1 m or more long, floating or slightly emergent from water surface near tip. **Leaves** many, threadlike, channeled, from near base of stem and extending to just below water surface; **bract** 1-6 cm long, appearing to be a continuation of stem. **Spikelets** single at ends of stems, with several flowers, light brown, narrowly ovate, tapered at each end, 7-12 mm long; **scales** thin, 4-6 mm long, light brown with a green midvein; bristles shorter to about as long as achene, downwardly barbed; style 3-parted. **Achenes** 3-angled, brown, 2-4 mm long, tipped with a slender beak to 0.5 mm long. July-Aug.—In water to about 1 m deep of lakes, ponds and bog margins.

Schoenoplectus subterminalis

Schoenoplectus smithii

1486. Rhynchospora fusca

1487. Schoenoplectus acutus

1488. Schoenop. heterochaetus

1489. Schoenoplectus pungens

Schoenoplectus tabernaemontani (K. C. Gmel.) Palla
SOFT-STEM CLUB-RUSH
Scirpus tabernaemontani K.C. Gmel.
Scirpus validus Vahl

MAP 1493
native |

Perennial, spreading by rhizomes and sometimes forming large colonies. **Stems** stout, smooth, erect, 1-3 m long, round in section. **Leaves** reduced to 4-5 sheaths at base of stem, or upper leaves with a blade to 7 cm long; **main bract** erect, 1-10 cm long, shorter than the head. **Spikelets** red-brown, 4-12 mm long and 3-4 mm wide, single or in clusters of 2-5 at ends of stalks, the stalks spreading or drooping, the clusters in paniclelike heads; **scales** ovate, light to dark brown, 2-3 mm long, the midvein usually extended into a short awn to 0.5 mm long; bristles 4-6, downwardly barbed, equal or longer than achene; style 2-parted. **Achenes** flat on 1 side and convex on other, brown to black, about 2 mm long, tapered to a very small beak to 0.2 mm long. June-Aug.—Shallow water and shores of lakes, ponds, marshes, streams, and ditches. *Similar to **hardstem club-rush** (S. acutus) but the stems easily crushed between the fingers, plants generally smaller and more slender, and the head more open.*

Schoenoplectus tabernaemontani

Schoenoplectus torreyi (Olney) Palla
TORREY'S CLUB-RUSH
Scirpus torreyi Olney

MAP 1494
native

Perennial, spreading by rhizomes and often forming colonies. **Stems** erect, sharply 3-angled, 5-10 dm long. **Leaves** several, narrow, often longer than the stem; **bract** erect, 5-15 cm long, appearing to be a continuation of stem. **Spikelets** ovate, light brown, 8-15 mm long, in a single head of 1-4 spikelets, the head appearing lateral from side of stem; **scales** ovate, shiny brown, with a greenish midvein sometimes extended as a short awn to 0.5 mm long; bristles about 6, downwardly barbed, longer than achene; style 3-parted. **Achenes** compressed 3-angled, shiny, light brown, 3-4 mm long, tipped by a slender beak to 0.5 mm long. June-Aug.—Shallow water, wet sandy or mucky shores.

Schoenoplectus torreyi

SCIRPUS *Bulrush*

Stout, rushlike perennials, mostly spreading by rhizomes. Stems unbranched, 3-angled or round in section, solid or pithy. Leaves broad and flat, to narrow and often folded near tip, or reduced to sheaths at base of stems; involucral bracts several and leaflike, or single and appearing like a continuation of the stem. Spikelets single, or in paniclelike or umbel-like clusters at ends of stems, or appearing lateral from the stem; the spikelets stalked or stalkless; scales overlapping in a spiral. Flowers perfect; sepals and petals reduced to 1-6 smooth or downwardly barbed bristles, or sometimes absent; stamens 2 or 3; styles 2-3-parted. Achenes lens-shaped, flat on 1 side and convex on other, or 3-angled, usually tipped with a beak.

ADDITIONAL SPECIES
· *Scirpus georgianus* R.M. Harper (Georgia bulrush); Chisago and Mower counties; possibly introduced.

1 Lower sheaths red-tinged . . . . ***S. microcarpus***
1 Sheaths green or brown 2
    2 Spikelets many in dense, more or less round heads; bristles about as long as achene or shorter . . ***S. atrovirens***
    2 Spikelets few in open clusters; bristles much longer than achene 3
        3 Mature bristles equal or only slightly longer than scales, spikelets not woolly . . . . ***S. pendulus***
        3 Mature bristles longer than scales, giving spikelets woolly appearance . . . ***S. cyperinus complex*** (see desc.)

1490. Schoenop.. purshianus   *1491. Schoenoplectus smithii*   *1492. Schoenop. subterminalis*   *1493. Schoe. tabernaemontani*

Scirpus atrovirens Willd.
DARK-GREEN BULRUSH

MAP 1495
native

Loosely tufted perennial, with short rhizomes. **Stems** 3-angled, leafy, 0.5-1.5 m long. **Leaves** mostly on lower half of stem, blades ascending, usually shorter than the head, 6-18 mm wide; **bracts** 3-4, leaflike, to 15 cm long, mostly longer than the head. **Spikelets** many, 2-8 mm long and 1-3 mm wide, crowded in rounded heads at end of stems, the heads on stalks to 12 cm long; scales brown-black, translucent except for the broad green midvein, 1-2 mm long, tipped by an awn to 0.5 mm long; bristles 6, white or tan, shorter or equal to the achene; style 3-parted. **Achenes** tan to nearly white, compressed 3-angled, about 1 mm long, with a short beak 0.2 mm long. June-Aug.—Wet meadows, shores, ditches, streambanks, swamps, springs and other wet places. *Here, includes plants sometimes treated as **Scirpus hattorianus** Makino and **S. pallidus** (Brit.) Fernald.*

Scirpus atrovirens

Scirpus cyperinus (L.) Kunth
WOOL-GRASS

MAP 1496
native

Coarse, densely tufted perennial, rhizomes short. **Stems** leafy, to 2 m tall, rounded 3-angled to nearly round in section. **Leaves** flat, 3-10 mm wide, rough-to-touch on margins; sheaths brown; **bracts** 2-4, leaflike, spreading, usually drooping at tip, often red-brown at base. **Spikelets** numerous, ovate, 3-8 mm long and 2-3 mm wide, appearing woolly due to the long bristles, in clusters of 1 to several spikelets; the spikelet clusters grouped into large, spreading, branched heads at ends of stems; **scales** ovate, 1-2 mm long; bristles 6, smooth, brown, much longer than achene and scale; styles 3-parted. **Achenes** white to tan, flattened 3-angled, 0.5-1 mm long, with a short beak. July-Sept.—Common in wet meadows, marshes, swamps, ditches, bog margins, thickets; where wet or in very shallow standing water.

The *Scirpus cyperinus* complex, including this species, **S. atrocinctus** Fern., and **S. pedicellatus** Fern., is often regarded as one highly variable species. Alternately, the three taxa can be separated as follows:

Scirpus cyperinus

1 Spikelets all or mostly all sessile in clusters of (2-) 3-7 or more . . . . **S. cyperinus**
1 Spikelets mostly pediceled, the ultimate branches of the inflorescence typically bearing 1 central, sessile spikelet with 2-3 pediceled ones 2
  2 Scales and bases of bracts dark blackish green; plants slender with leaves 2-5 mm wide . . . . **S. atrocinctus**
  2 Scales and bases of bracts brown or gray-brown; plants larger with leaves 3-10 mm wide . . . . . **S. pedicellatus**

Scirpus atrocinctus flowers and fruits earlier than the other two species, often with inflorescences fully developed by late June, and achenes ripe by late July. *S. atrocinctus* readily hybridizes with *S. cyperinus* to form hybrid swarms. Scales of *S. atrocinctus* are usually distinctly blackened, at least near the tip, while those of *S. pedicellatus* have no black pigment or only slightly so. *S. pedicellatus* is paler and larger than *S. atrocinctus*, the spikelets greenish to pale brown.

Scirpus microcarpus J. & K. Presl
RED-TINGE BULRUSH

MAP 1497
native

Perennial, from stout rhizomes. **Stems** single or few together, 5-15 dm long, weakly 3-angled. **Leaves** several along stem, flat, ascending, 7-15 mm wide, the upper leaves longer than the head, margins rough-to-touch; sheaths often red-tinged; bracts 3-4, leaflike, to 2-3 dm long. **Spikelets** numerous, 3-6 mm long and 1-2 mm wide; in a loose, spreading, umbel-like head, the head formed of clusters

Scirpus microcarpus

1494. *Schoenoplectus torreyi*

1495. *Scirpus atrovirens*

1496. *Scirpus cyperinus*

1497. *Scirpus microcarpus*

of 4-20 or more spikelets on stalks to 15 cm long; **scales** 1-2 mm long, brown and translucent except for green midvein; bristles 4-6, white to tan, downwardly barbed, longer than achene; style 2-parted. **Achenes** lens-shaped, pale tan to nearly white, about 1 mm long, the beak tiny. June-July.—Streambanks, wet meadows, marshes, wet shores, thickets, swamps, springs; not in dense shade.

Scirpus pendulus Muhl.
RUFOUS BULRUSH

MAP 1498
native

Loosely tufted perennial, from short, thick rhizomes. **Stems** upright, rounded 3-angled, to 1.5 m long, lower stem covered by old leaf bases. **Leaves** several on stem, flat, 4-10 mm wide, shorter than head; bracts leaflike, 3 or more, shorter than the head, pale brown at base. **Spikelets** many, cylindric, 4-10 mm long and 2-4 mm wide; in an open, umbel-like head at end of stem, the spikelets drooping and clustered in groups of 1 stalkless and several stalked spikelets; **scales** about 2 mm long, red-brown with a green midvein; bristles 6, brown, smooth, longer than achene and about as long as scale; style 3-parted. **Achenes** compressed 3-angled, light brown, about 1 mm long, with a short, slender beak. June-Aug. —Marshes, wet meadows, streambanks, swamp openings and ditches.

Scirpus pendulus

SCLERIA *Nut-Rush*

Annual or perennial sedge-like herbs, tufted or spreading by short rhizomes. Stems slender, 3-angled. Leaves narrow, shorter than the stem. Flowers either staminate or pistillate, borne in separate spikelets on the same plant; staminate spikelets few-flowered; pistillate spikelets with uppermost flower fertile, the lower scales empty. Flowers in clusters at ends of stems, or with both terminal clusters and clusters from upper leaf axils; sepals and petals absent; stamens 1-3; style 3-parted. Fruit a hard, white achene.

1 Achenes smooth, ca. 3 mm long, including the whitish, foam-like basal disc; larger leaves (3.5-) 5-7.5 mm wide; mature anthers 2.5-4 mm long. . . . . **S. triglomerata**
1 Achenes papillose-roughened or wrinkled, ca. 1-2 mm long, including basal disc (not a foam-like crust); larger leaves not over 2.5 mm wide; anthers 1-2.5 mm long . . . . **S. verticillata**

Scleria triglomerata Michx.
WHIP NUT-RUSH

MAP 1499
🖤 *endangered | native*

Perennial. **Stems** to 1 m tall, from hard knotty rhizomes. Principal **leaves** 4-8 mm wide, often somewhat pubescent, abruptly attenuate. **Spikelets** in 1-3 cymes, the lower pedunculate; bracts foliaceous, the lowest erect, 5-15 cm long; **staminate scales** lance-shaped; **pistillate scales** with ovate body, the midrib prolonged into an awn. **Achenes** white, rarely drab or gray, 2.5-3 mm long, tipped with a small sharp point.—Moist sandy soil in sandy savannas and prairies.

Scleria triglomerata achene

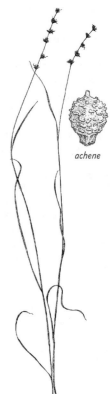

achene

Scleria verticillata

Scleria verticillata Muhl.
LOW NUT-RUSH

MAP 1500
🖤 *threatened | native*

Tufted annual, roots fibrous. **Stems** slender, smooth, 3-angled, 2-6 dm long. **Leaves** erect, linear, 1 mm wide, shorter than the stems; sheaths often hairy. **Spikelets** in 2-8 separated heads, each head sessile, 2-4 mm long, subtended by a small, bristlelike bract 4-6 mm long; **scales** lance-shaped. **Achenes** more or less round, white, 1 mm wide, covered with horizontal ridges, tipped with a short, sharp point. July-Sept.—Calcareous fens.

1498. *Scirpus pendulus*   1499. *Scleria triglomerata*   1500. *Scleria verticillata*

TRICHOPHORUM *Leafless-Bulrush*

Tufted perennials. Stems 3-angled or terete. Leaves basal or nearly so; sheaths bladeless or with very short blades less than 1 cm long and to 1 mm wide. Inflorescences terminal; spikelets 1; involucral bracts 1, suberect, scale-like, tip mucronate or awned. Spikelets with 3-9 spirally arranged scales, each subtending a flower. Flowers bisexual; perianth of 0-6 bristles, straight, shorter than to about 20 times as long as the achene, smooth or scabrous; stamens 3. Achenes 3-angled or plano-convex.

1   Stems more or less round in section, smooth . . . . ***T. caespitosum***
1   Stems 3-angled, rough on angles 2
      2   Perianth bristles ciliate, slightly or not at all exceeding the blunt achene; scales of spikelet not more than 7; achenes ca. 1.6-1.8 mm long; not in wetlands . . . . ***T. clintonii***
      2   Perianth bristles smooth, several times as long as the apiculate achene at maturity; scales of spikelets slightly more than 7; body of achene less than 1.5 mm long; wetland species . . . . ***T. alpinum***

Trichophorum alpinum (L.) Pers.

MAP 1501
native

ALPINE LEAFLESS-BULRUSH
    Eriophorum alpinum L.
    Scirpus hudsonianus (Michx.) Fern.

Perennial, from short rhizomes. **Stems** single to clustered, slender, 1-4 dm long, sharply 3-angled, rough-to-touch on the angles. **Leaves** reduced to scales at base of stem, with 1-2 leaves upward on stem, these with short narrow blades 5-15 mm long. **Spikelets** single at ends of stems, brown, 5-7 mm long, with 10-20 flowers, involucral bract awl-shaped, shorter than spikelet, sometimes absent; **scales** ovate, blunt-tipped, yellow-brown; **bristles** 6, white, flattened, longer than the scales, when mature forming a white tuft 1-2 cm longer than the spikelet. **Achenes** 3-angled, dull brown, 1-4 mm long.—Open bogs, conifer swamps, wet meadows, wet sandy shores; sometimes where calcium-rich.

Trichophorum caespitosum (L.) Hartman

MAP 1502
native

TUFTED LEAFLESS-BULRUSH
    Scirpus caespitosus L.

Densely tufted perennial, rhizomes short. Stems slender, smooth, more or less round in section, 1-4 dm long. **Leaves** light brown and scalelike at base of stems, and also usually 1 leaf upward on stem, the blade narrow, short, to 6 mm long. **Spikelets** 1 at end of stems, brown, 4-6 mm long, several-flowered; **scales** yellow-brown, deciduous, the lowest scale about as long as spikelet; **bristles** 6, usually slightly longer than achene; style 3-parted. **Achenes** brown, 3-angled, 1.5 mm long.—Open bogs, cedar swamps, calcareous fens, wet swales between dunes; also Lake Superior rocky shores.

Trichophorum clintonii (Gray) S.G. Sm.

MAP 1503
☙ *threatened | native*

CLINTON'S LEAFLESS-BULRUSH
    Scirpus clintonii Gray

Tufted perennial from short rhizomes. **Stems** slender, erect, 1-4 dm tall, trigonous, scabrous on the angles. **Lower leaves** reduced to bladeless sheaths or with short rudimentary blades; **uppermost leaves** usually prolonged into a blade shorter than the culm and to 1 mm wide. **Spikelet** solitary, terminal, ovoid, 4-5 mm long, 4-7-flowered; **bract** erect, ovate, prolonged into a stout mucro shorter than the spike; **scales** ovate, the midvein often not reaching the apex. **Achenes** pale brown, trigonous, obovoid, 1.4-2 mm long, obtuse; bristles 3-6, equaling or exceeding the achene.—Open, dry to moist, sandy or sandy loam soils.

Trichophorum alpinum

Trichophorum caespitosum

1501. Trichophorum alpinum   *1502. Trichophor. caespitosum*   *1503. Trichophorum clintonii*

Dioscoreaceae YAM FAMILY

DIOSCOREA *Yam*

Dioscorea villosa L.   MAP 1504
WILD YAM; COLIC-ROOT   *native*
  Dioscorea hirticaulis Bartlett
  Dioscorea quaternata J.F. Gmel.

Perennial dioecious herb. **Stems** twining, to 5 m long. **Leaves** alternate, cordate-ovate, 5-10 cm long, abruptly acuminate, 7-11-nerved; petioles glabrous or nearly so. **Flowers** regular; unisexual; small, white to greenish yellow; perianth 6-parted, the sepals and petals similar; **staminate panicle** widely branched, 3-10 cm long; **pistillate spikes** 5-10 cm long, bearing 5-10 solitary flowers; stamens 6 or 3; ovary 3-celled; styles 3. **Fruit** a 3-winged capsule 16-26 mm long; seeds very flat, broadly winged, 8-18 mm long. June-July.—Moist to dry woods, thickets, pond and marsh borders, river bottoms, roadsides and railroads.

Dioscorea villosa

Eriocaulaceae PIPEWORT FAMILY

ERIOCAULON *Pipewort*

Eriocaulon aquaticum (Hill) Druce   MAP 1505
SEVEN-ANGLE PIPEWORT   *native*
  Eriocaulon septangulare Withering

Perennial, spongy at base, with fleshy roots. **Stems** usually single, leafless, slightly twisted, 5-7-ridged, 3-20 cm long (or reaching 2-3 m long when in deep water). **Leaves** grasslike, in a rosette at base of plant, thin and often translucent, 2-10 cm long and 2-5 mm wide, 3-9-nerved with conspicuous cross-veins. **Flowers** either staminate or pistillate, grouped together in a single, more or less round head at end of stem, the heads white-woolly, 4-6 mm wide. **Fruit** a 2-3-seeded capsule. July-Sept.—Shallow water, sandy or peaty shores.

Eriocaulon aquaticum

Hydrocharitaceae TAPE-GRASS FAMILY

Aquatic herbs. Stems leafy, the leaves opposite (*Najas*), whorled (*Elodea*), or plants stemless with clusters of long, linear, ribbonlike leaves (*Vallisneria*). Flowers usually either staminate or pistillate and borne on separate plants, small and stalkless, or in a spathe at end of a stalk; sepals 3; petals 3 or absent; staminate flowers with 3 or more stamens; stigmas 3. Fruit several-seeded, maturing underwater.

1 Leaves very long and ribbon-like (mostly 3-11 mm wide and many times as long), in a basal rosette . . . .
. . . . *Vallisneria americana*
1 Leaves to 6 (-12) cm long, opposite or whorled 2
  2 Leaves whorled, entire . . . . *Elodea*
  2 Leaves opposite, minutely denticulate to visibly toothed . . . . *Najas*

ELODEA *Waterweed*

Aquatic perennial herbs, rooting from lower nodes or free-floating. Stems slender, leafy, branched. Leaves crowded near tip of stem, mostly in whorls of 3-4, or opposite, stalkless; margins finely sharp-toothed. Flowers either staminate or pistillate and on separate plants, tiny, single in upper leaf axils, subtended by a 2-parted spathe, usually extended to the water surface by a long, threadlike hypanthium, or stalkless and breaking free to float to water surface in staminate flowers of *E. nuttallii*; sepals 3; petals 3 or absent, white or purple; staminate flowers with 9 stamens; pistillate flowers with 3 stigmas, the stigmas entire or 2-parted. Fruit a capsule, ripening underwater. *Anacharis* or *Philotria in older floras.*

ADDITIONAL SPECIES

· *Elodea bifoliata* H. St. John (Two-leaf waterweed), ❦ *endangered*; rare in Blue Earth and St. Louis counties.

1   Leaves mostly 2 mm or more wide; staminate flowers long-stalked in a spathe, the spathe more than 7 mm long, extended to water surface by a long, threadlike hypanthium . . . . *E. canadensis*
1   Leaves to 1.5 mm wide; staminate flowers stalkless in a spathe, the spathe 2-4 mm long, breaking free to float to water surface at flowering time . . . . *E. nuttallii*

Elodea canadensis Michx.
CANADIAN WATERWEED
  Anacharis canadensis (Michx.) Planch.

MAP 1506
native

Submerged perennial herb. **Stems** round in section, usually branched, 2-10 dm long. **Leaves** bright green, firm; lower leaves opposite, reduced in size, ovate or lance-shaped; upper leaves in whorls of 3, the uppermost crowded and overlapping, lance-shaped, 5-15 mm long and about 2 mm wide, rounded at tip. **Flowers** at ends of threadlike stalks, 2-30 cm long; **staminate flowers** in spathes from upper leaf axils, the spathes about 10 mm long and to 4 mm wide; sepals green, 3-5 mm long; petals white, 5 mm long; stamens 9; **pistillate flowers** in spathes from upper leaf axils, the spathes 10-20 mm long, extended to water surface by a threadlike hypanthium; sepals 2-3 mm long; petals white, 2-3 mm long. **Fruit** a capsule, 5-6 mm long, tapered to a beak 4-5 mm long. June-Aug. —Shallow to deep water of lakes, streams and ditches.

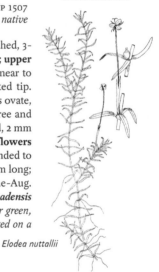

Elodea canadensis

Elodea nuttallii (Planch.) St. John
WESTERN WATERWEED
  Anacharis nuttallii Planch.

MAP 1507
native

Submerged perennial herb. **Stems** slender, round in section, usually branched, 3-10 dm long. **Lower leaves** opposite, reduced in size, ovate to lance-shaped; **upper leaves** in whorls of 3 (or sometimes 4), not densely overlapping at tip, linear to lance-shaped, 6-13 mm long and 0.5-1.5 mm wide, tapered to a pointed tip. **Staminate flowers** in stalkless spathes from middle leaf axils, the spathes ovate, 2-3 mm long, the flowers single and stalkless in the spathe, breaking free and floating to water surface and then opening; sepals green or sometimes red, 2 mm long; petals absent or very short (to 0.5 mm long); stamens 9; **pistillate flowers** in cylindric spathes from upper leaf axils, the spathes 1-2.5 cm long, extended to water surface by a threadlike stalk to 10 cm long; sepals green, about 1 mm long; petals white, longer than sepals. **Fruit** a capsule, 5-7 mm long. June-Aug. —Shallow to deep water of lakes, streams and ditches. *Similar to **Elodea canadensis** but less common, smaller and more delicate overall, the leaves narrower, paler green, and not closely overlapping at stem tips, and the staminate flowers not elevated on a long slender stalk.*

Elodea nuttallii

NAJAS *Waternymph*
Aquatic annual herbs, roots fibrous, rhizomes absent. Stems wavy, with slender branches. Leaves simple, opposite or in crowded whorls, stalkless, abruptly widened at base to sheath the stem; margins toothed to nearly entire, the teeth sometimes spine-tipped. Flowers either staminate or pistillate, separate on same plant or on different plants, tiny, single and stalkless in leaf axils, enclosed by the sheathing leaf bases; staminate flowers a single anther within a membranous envelope (spathe), this surrounded by perianth scales, the scales sometimes joined into a tube; pistillate flowers surrounded by 1-2 spathes, pistils 1, stigmas 2-4, style usually persistent. Fruit a 1-seeded achene.

1504. *Dioscorea villosa*   1505. *Eriocaulon aquaticum*   1506. *Elodea canadensis*   1507. *Elodea nuttallii*

1　Leaves coarsely toothed and spine-tipped (spines visible without a lens), bright green; midvein of leaf underside and stems between nodes often prickly . . . . *N. marina*

1　Leaves nearly entire or toothed (if spine-tipped, the spines, except in *N. minor*, not visible without a lens), often olive green; leaf surface and stems between leaves smooth 2

　　2　Base of leaves lobed or clasping stem 3

　　　　3　Leaves somewhat stiff, curved downward near tip; base of leaf lobed; seed coat pitted, the pits wider than long and arranged in regular, ladderlike rows . . . . *N. minor*

　　　　3　Leaves slender, not stiff, not curved downward near tip; base of leaf clasping; seed coat pitted, the pits longer than wide . . . . *N. gracillima*

　　2　Leaves tapered to base, not lobed or clasping stem 4

　　　　4　Seeds smooth and glossy, widest above middle . . . . *N. flexilis*

　　　　4　Seeds rough and pitted, widest at middle and tapered to ends . . . . *N. guadalupensis*

Najas flexilis (Willd.) Rostk. & Schmidt

MAP 1508

WAVY WATERNYMPH　　　　　　　　　　　　　　　　　*native*

Stems branched, 5-40 cm long. **Leaves** densely clustered at tips of stems, linear, tapered to a long slender point, spreading or ascending, 1-4 cm long and to 0.5 mm wide; margins with tiny sharp teeth. **Flowers** either staminate and pistillate, separate on same plant. **Achenes** oval, olive-green to red, the beak 1 mm or more long; seeds straw-colored, shiny, 2-4 mm long. July-Sept.—Ponds, lakes, streams.

Najas gracillima (A. Braun) Magnus

MAP 1509

SLENDER WATERNYMPH　　　　　　　　　　　　　　　*native*

Plants light green. **Stems** very slender, branched, 0.5-5 dm long. Leaves opposite or in groups of 3 or more, bristlelike, 0.5-3 cm long and to 0.5 mm wide, spreading or ascending; margins with very small teeth. **Flowers** either staminate or pistillate and on the same plant. **Achenes** cylindric, narrowed at ends; seeds light brown, 2-3 mm long.—Shallow water of lakes, usually in muck; intolerant of polluted water.

Najas guadalupensis (Spreng.) Magnus

MAP 1510

SOUTHERN WATERNYMPH　　　　　　　　　　　　　　*native*

Stems much branched, 1-6 dm long. **Leaves** numerous, linear, spreading and often curved downward at tip, 1-3 cm long and 0.5-2 mm wide; groups of smaller leaves also present in leaf axils; margins with very small teeth. **Flowers** either staminate or pistillate, separate on same plant. **Achenes** cylindric, the beak to 0.5 mm long; seeds brown or purple, 1-3 mm long. July-Sept.—Shallow to deep water of lakes, ponds and sometimes rivers; often with *Najas flexilis* but less common.

Najas marina L.

MAP 1511

ALKALINE WATERNYMPH　　　　　　　　　　　　　　　*native*

Stems stout, 1-5 dm long and 1-4 mm wide, compressed, branched, prickly. **Leaves** opposite or whorled, linear, 0.5-4 cm long and 1-4 mm wide, sometimes with spines on underside; margins coarsely toothed, the teeth 1-4 mm apart and spine-tipped. **Flowers** either staminate or pistillate and on different plants. **Achenes** olive-green, the beak about 1 mm long; seeds dull, 2-5 mm long. July-Sept.—Shallow water (to 1 m deep) of lakes and marshes.

Najas minor Allioni

MAP 1512

EUTROPHIC WATER-NYMPH　　　　　　　　　　　　*introduced*

Plants dark green. **Stems** slender, branched, 1-2 dm long. **Leaves** opposite or whorled, linear, 0.5-3.5 cm long and to 0.2 mm wide, curved downward at tip;

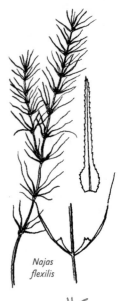

Najas flexilis

Najas guadalupensis

1508. Najas flexilis　　　*1509. Najas gracillima*　　　*1510. Najas guadalupensis*

margins sharp-toothed, with 7-15 teeth on each side. **Flowers** either staminate and pistillate, separate on the same plant. **Achenes** oval, the beak about 1 mm long; seeds 2-3 mm long, purple-tinged.—Marshes, lakes, ponds.

VALLISNERIA *Eel-Grass*

Vallisneria americana Michx.
AMERICAN EEL-GRASS

MAP 1513
native

Submerged perennial herb, fibrous rooted, spreading by stolons and often forming large colonies. **Stems** absent. **Leaves** long and ribbonlike, in tufts from a small crown, to 1 m or more long and 3-10 mm wide, rounded at tip, margins smooth. **Flowers** either staminate or pistillate and on separate plants; **staminate flowers** small, about 1 mm wide, in a many-flowered head, the head within a stalked spathe from base of plant, the stalk 3-15 cm long; sepals 3, petals 1, stamens 2; the staminate flowers released singly from the spathe and floating to water surface where they open; **pistillate flowers** single in a spathe, on long slender stalks that extend to water surface, the stalk contracting and coiling after flowering to draw the fruit underwater; sepals 3, petals small, 3; stigmas 3. **Fruit** a cylindric, curved capsule, 4-10 cm long. July-Sept.—Shallow to sometimes deep water of lakes and streams.

Vallisneria americana

Hypoxidaceae LILIID MONOCOT FAMILY

HYPOXIS *Star-Grass*

Hypoxis hirsuta (L.) Coville
EASTERN YELLOW STAR-GRASS

MAP 1514
native

Low perennial herb, from a small, shallow corm. **Stems** leafless, lax, 1 to several, silky-hairy in upper part, shorter than leaves when flowering, to 4 dm long when mature. **Leaves** from base of plant, linear, hairy, to 6 dm long and 2-10 mm wide. **Flowers** 1-6 (usually 2), yellow, 1-2.5 cm wide, in racemes at ends of stems, tepals hairy on outside, 5-12 mm long, spreading in flower, closing and turning green after flowering, persistent. **Capsule** oval, 3-6 mm long; seeds black. May-July. —Wet meadows, shores, moist prairie; often where calcium-rich.

Hypoxis hirsuta

Iridaceae IRIS FAMILY

Perennial herbs with rhizomes, bulbs, or fibrous roots. Leaves parallel-veined, narrow, 2-ranked, the margins joined to form an edge facing the stem (equitant). Flowers perfect, with 6 petal-like segments, single or in clusters at ends of stem, stamens 3, style 3-parted. Fruit a 3-chambered capsule.

1 Flowers more than 2 cm wide; stems not winged; leaves more than 6 mm wide . . . . *Iris*
1 Flowers to 2 cm wide; stems winged; leaves to 6 mm wide . . . . *Sisyrinchium*

IRIS *Iris; Flag*

Perennial herbs, spreading by thick rhizomes. Stems erect. Leaves swordlike, erect or upright, the margins joined to form an edge facing the stem. Flowers 1 or several at ends of stems; yellow or blue-

1511. *Najas marina*

1512. *Najas minor*

1513. *Vallisneria americana*

1514. *Hypoxis hirsuta*

violet; sepals 3, spreading or bent downward, longer and wider than the petals; petals 3, erect or arching; stamens 3; styles 3-parted, the divisions petal-like and arching over the stamens. Fruit an oblong capsule.

1 Sepals with a prominent median beard above; escape from cultivation, Sherburne County . . . . *I. germanica*
1 Sepals without a prominent beard, at most minutely pubescent; wetland species, more widespread in Minn . . 2
    2 Flowers yellow, mature capsules spreading or pendant . . . . *I. pseudacorus*
    2 Flowers blue (white in albinos), capsules erect 3
        3 Base of expanded portion of sepal with a bright yellow spot, finely pubescent with hairs as long as the thickness of the sepal; outer spathe bracts of uniform texture and color; seeds round to D-shaped, irregularly (but shallowly) pitted . . . . *I. virginica*
        3 Base of expanded portion of sepal at most with a greenish yellow spot, with papillae shorter than thickness of the sepal; outer spathe bracts with the margins generally darker and more shiny than the rest of the dull surface; seeds D-shaped, with a ± regularly pebbled surface . . . . *I. versicolor*

Iris germanica L.

GERMAN IRIS

(NO MAP)
introduced

Perennial herb. **Stems** stout, to 2.5 dm tall, the flowers nearly sessile in the spathe. **Leaves** broadly ensiform, glaucous. **Perianth** 7-10 cm across; sepals broadly ovate, recurved, deep violet with yellow, white, and brown veins at the base of the blade, the median line long-bearded; petals light violet, erect-arching, slightly smaller than the sepals. **Capsules** trigonous, 4-7 cm long, infrequently produced. May-June.—Introduced from Europe; occasional along roadsides, in waste places, and around abandoned houses where it persists after cultivation; reported from Sherburne County.

Iris pseudacorus L.

PALE-YELLOW IRIS

MAP 1515
introduced

Perennial herb, from thick rhizomes. **Stems** 0.5-1 m long, shorter or equal to the leaves. **Leaves** sword-shaped, stiff and erect, waxy, 1-2 cm wide. **Flowers** several at end of stems, yellow, 7-9 cm wide, sepals spreading, upper portion marked with brown; petals erect, narrowed in middle, 1-2.5 cm long. **Capsules** oblong, 6-angled, 5-9 cm long. May-June.—Lakeshores, streambanks, marshes, ditches.

Iris versicolor L.

NORTHERN BLUEFLAG

MAP 1516
native

Perennial herb, from thick, fleshy rhizomes and forming colonies. **Stems** more or less round in section, often branched above, 4-9 dm long. **Leaves** sword-shaped, erect or arching, somewhat waxy, 2-3 cm wide, usually shorter than stem. **Flowers** several on short stalks at ends of stems, blue-violet, 6-8 cm wide; sepals spreading, unspotted, or with a green-yellow spot near base, surrounded by white streaks and purple veins; petals erect, about half as long as sepals. **Capsules** oblong, 3-6 cm long. June-July.—Marshes, shores, wet meadows, open bogs, swamps, thickets, forest depressions; often in shallow water.

Iris versicolor

Iris virginica L.

SOUTHERN BLUEFLAG

MAP 1517
native

Perennial herb, from thick rhizomes, often forming large colonies. **Stems** more or less round in section, to 1 m long. **Leaves** sword-shaped, erect or arching, 2-3 cm wide, usually longer than stems. **Flowers** several on short-stalks at ends of stems, blue-violet, often with darker veins, 6-8 cm wide; sepals spreading, curved

Iris virginica

1515. *Iris pseudacorus*   1516. *Iris versicolor*   1517. *Iris virginica*

backward at tip, with a hairy, bright yellow spot near base; petals shorter than sepals. **Capsules** ovate to oval capsule, 4-7 cm long. May-July.—Swamps, thickets, shores, streambanks, marshes, ditches.

SISYRINCHIUM *Blue-Eyed-Grass*

Tufted perennial herbs, from fibrous roots. Stems slender, leafless, flattened or winged. Flowers in an umbel at end of stem, above a pair of erect green bracts (spathe), blue-violet or rarely white, with 6 spreading segments, the segments joined only at base, the tips rounded but with an small bristle. Leaves narrow and linear, from base of plant, the margins joined and turned to form an edge facing the stem. Fruit a rounded capsule; seeds round, black.

1 Spathes on peduncles arising from a leaflike bract, usually more than one, the upper portion of the stem thus appearing branched . . . . *S. angustifolium*
1 Spathes sessile or nearly so at the end of a simple stem 2
   2 Margins of outer spathe distinct nearly to the base, spathes greenish, slightly or not at all purple tinged; stems less than 2 mm wide . . . . *S. campestre*
   2 Margins of outer spathe fused for 1-5 mm, spathes often strongly purple tinged or stems often more than 2 mm wide (or both) 3
      3 Plant very slender, the stem usually 1 mm or less wide and barely margined or narrowly winged; largest leaves to 1.5 mm wide; capsule 2.5-4 mm long . . . . *S. mucronatum*
      3 Plants stout, the stem usually 2-2.5 mm wide, winged; largest leaves 2-3 mm wide; mature capsule 5-7 mm long . . . . *S. montanum*

Sisyrinchium angustifolium P. Mill.

NARROW-LEAF BLUE-EYED-GRASS
MAP 1518
native

Plants bright green, drying dark. **Stems** 1-5 dm tall, usually erect. **Scapes** narrowly winged but stout, 3-4 mm wide. **Spathes** often purplish tinged, the inner bracts 1.5-3 cm long; **perianth** bright violet, 8-12 mm long. **Capsules** obovoid, brown, 4-6 mm long.—Meadows, fields, and open woods.

Sisyrinchium campestre Bickn.

PRAIRIE BLUE-EYED-GRASS
MAP 1519
native

Plants pale green, scarcely glaucescent, drying pale. **Stems** erect, 1-4 dm tall. **Scapes** narrowly winged, 1-2 mm wide. **Spathes** scabridulous, often purple-tinged, the inner bracts 1-2 cm long; **perianth** pale blue or white, 8-10 mm long. **Capsules** 2-3 mm long, pale or straw-color.—Prairies, meadows, sandy places, and open woodlands.

Sisyrinchium montanum Greene

STRICT BLUE-EYED-GRASS
MAP 1520
native

Plants pale-green and waxy. **Stems** stiff and erect, leafless, flattened and winged, 1-5 dm tall and 2-4 mm wide. **Leaves** mostly from base of plant, narrow and grasslike, about half as long as stem, 1-3 mm wide. **Flowers** in head of 1 to several flowers at end of stem, subtended by a spathe, the spathe of 2 bracts, the outer bract 3-7 cm long, the inner bract about half as long; the flower segments (tepals) blue-violet with a yellow center, 5-15 mm long, with a short, slender tip. **Capsules** more or less round, 4-7 mm wide, pale brown, on an erect stalk shorter than the inner bract. May-July.—Wet meadows, shores, ditches; also in drier woods and fields.

Sisyrinchium mucronatum Michx.

NEEDLE-TIP BLUE-EYED-GRASS
MAP 1521
native

Plants dark green. **Stems** very slender, to 1 mm wide, leafless, margins not or barely winged. **Leaves** from near base of plant, narrow and linear, to 1.5 mm wide. **Flowers** in a single head at end of stem, subtended by a spathe, the spathe of 2 bracts, the bracts often purple-tinged, the outer bract 2-3 cm long, the inner bract shorter, 1-2 cm long; the segments (tepals) deep violet-blue, 8-10 mm long, tipped with a sharp point. **Capsules** more or less round, 2-4 mm long, pale brown, on spreading stalks. May-June.—Wet meadows, calcareous fens.

Sisyrinchium mucronatum

Juncaceae RUSH FAMILY

Distinguished from grasses and sedges by the presence of a true perianth of 6 tepals and a 3-many-seeded capsule rather than a 1-seeded grain (grasses) or achene (sedges). No ligule (as in grasses) is present at junction of leaf blade and sheath; however an auricle (an ear-like appendage) may occur at top of leaf sheath.

1 Foliage completely glabrous; capsules usually many-seeded . . . . ***Juncus***
1 Foliage ± hairy, at least toward summit of sheaths; capsules 3-seeded . . . . ***Luzula***

JUNCUS *Rush*

Clumped or rhizomatous rushes, mostly perennial (annual in *J. bufonius*). Stems erect and unbranched. Leaves from base of plant or along stem, alternate, round in section, flat to involute, or reduced to sheaths at base of stem. Flowers perfect, regular, in compact to open clusters of few to many flowers, subtended by 1 or several leaflike involucral bracts; sepals and petals of 6 chaffy, scalelike, green to brown tepals (perianth); stamens 6 or 3; stigmas 3, ovary 1 or 3-chambered. Capsule many-seeded; seeds with a short slender tip or with a tail-like appendage at each end.

ADDITIONAL SPECIES
• *Juncus subtilis* E. Mey. (Greater creeping rush), ☙ *endangered;* disjunct from e Canada in Cook County.

1 Head from side of stem, the involucral bract erect, round in section and appearing to be a continuation of stem; basal and stem leaves absent 2
  2 Involucral bract more than half height of plant . . . . *J. filiformis*
  2 Involucral bract less than half height of plant 3
    3 Stems densely clumped; stamens 3 . . . . *J. effusus (J. pylaei)*
    3 Stems single from rhizomes, the stems often in rows; stamens 6 . . . . *J. balticus*
1 Head at end of stem; basal leaves present, stem leaves present or absent 4
  4 Leaves flat or somewhat channeled 5
    5 Flowers in dense heads; leaves 2 mm or more wide . . . . *J. marginatus*
    5 Flowers single on branches of head; leaves usually less than 1.5 mm wide 6
      6 Plants annual, to 10 cm tall . . . . *J. bufonius*
      6 Plants perennial, more than 10 cm tall 7
        7 Larger stem leaves more than 3 mm wide, with 5 main veins . . . . *J. marginatus*
        7 Stem leaves to 3 mm wide, with less than 5 main veins 8
          8 Stems clumped; leaves with spreading blades extending from plant base to middle of stem . . . .
          . . . . *J. compressus*
          8 Stems not clumped; leaves with spreading blades only near base of stem 9
            9 Leaves flat or inrolled but open for entire length; seeds less than 0.5 mm long 10
              10 Auricles flaplike, prolonged into a membranaceous projection 3-5 mm long . . . *J. tenuis*
              10 Auricles shorter, not flaplike, prolonged up to 2 mm beyond the sheath, submembraneous or cartilaginous 11
                11 Auricles cartilaginous, dull to shiny yellow, very rigid . . . . *J. dudleyi*
                11 Auricles submembraneous, not rigid . . . . *J. interior*
            9 Leaves round in section, closed for nearly entire length; seeds more than 0.7 mm long . . . 12
              12 Ends of seeds with white "tails" about half as long as the slender body; sepals ca. (3.5-) 4 mm long; longest involucral bract 1-6 cm long, often less than 3 cm . . . . *J. vaseyi*
              12 Ends of seeds without "tails" or these at most half the width of the plump body; sepals 3-4 mm long; longest involucral bract to 21 cm long (usually more than 3 cm) . . . *J. greenei*

1518. *Sisyrinchi. angustifolium*   1519. *Sisyrinchium campestre*   1520. *Sisyrinchium montanum*   1521. *Sisyrinch. mucronatum*

Juncus acuminatus Michx.

KNOTTY-LEAF RUSH

MAP 1522
native

Tufted perennial rush. **Stems** erect, slender, 2-8 dm tall, with 1-2 leaves. **Leaves** from stem and at base of plant, round to compressed in section, 5-40 cm long and 1-3 mm wide; auricles rounded, 1-2 mm long; **bract** erect, round, 1-4 cm long, shorter than the head. **Flowers** in an open, pyramid-shaped inflorescence, 5-12 cm long and less than half as wide, composed of 5-50 rounded heads 6-10 mm wide, each head with 5-30 flowers, the branches spreading, 1-10 cm long; **tepals** lance-shaped, green or straw-colored, 3-4 mm long; stamens 3, shorter than the tepals. **Capsule** oval, straw-colored to light brown, 3-4 mm long, about as long as the tepals, tipped with a short, blunt point. June-Aug.—Wet sandy shores, streambanks and ditches; not in open bogs.

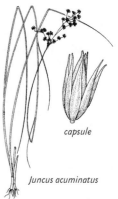

capsule

Juncus acuminatus

Juncus alpinoarticulatus Chaix

NORTHERN GREEN RUSH

   Juncus alpinus Vill.

MAP 1523
native

Perennial rush, spreading by rhizomes. **Stems** in small clumps, 1.5-4 dm long. **Leaves** mostly from base of plant and with 1-2 stem leaves, round in section, hollow, with small swollen joints, 2-12 cm long and 0.5-1 mm wide; sheaths green to red, auricles rounded, 0.5-1 mm long; **bract** round in section, 2-6 cm long and shorter than the head. **Flowers** in an open panicle of 5-25 heads, 2-15 cm long and 1-5 cm wide, the heads oblong pyramid-shaped, 2-6 mm wide, mostly 2-5-flowered, the branches upright, 1-7 cm long; **tepals** green to brown, 2-3 mm long, the inner tepals shorter, the margins chaffy; stamens 6. **Capsule** oblong, 3-angled, straw-colored to chestnut brown, satiny, 2-3 mm long, slightly longer than the tepals, tapered to a rounded tip. June-Sept.—Sandy or gravelly shores, streambanks, fens; often where calcium-rich.

Juncus alpinoarticulatus

Juncus articulatus L.

JOINT-LEAF RUSH

MAP 1524
❧*endangered* | *native*

Perennial rush, with coarse white rhizomes. **Stems** usually tufted, 2-6 dm long. **Leaves** from stem and at base of plant, more or less round in section, hollow, with small swollen joints, 4-12 cm long and 1-3 mm wide; sheaths green or sometimes red, auricles rounded, about 1 mm long; **bract** erect, round in section, 1-4 cm long, shorter than the head. **Flowers** in open panicles, 4-10 cm long and 3-6 cm wide, composed of 3-30 heads, the heads rounded, 6-8 mm wide, 3-10-flowered, panicle branches erect to widely spreading, 1-4 cm long; **tepals** green to dark brown, 2-

3 mm long; stamens 6. **Capsule** oval, dark brown, shiny, 3-4 mm long, longer than the tepals, tapered to a tip. July-Sept.—Sandy, gravelly or mucky shores, streambanks and springs.

Juncus balticus Willd.
SMALL-HEAD RUSH
Juncus arcticus Willd.

MAP 1525
native

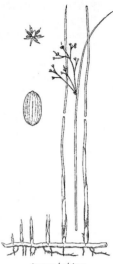

Perennial rush, spreading by stout, brown to black rhizomes. **Stems** slender and tough, dark green, 3-9 dm long, in rows from the rhizomes. **Leaves** reduced to red-brown sheaths at base of stem; **bract** erect, round in section, 1-2 dm long, longer than the head and resembling a continuation of stem. **Flowers** single on stalks, in dense to spreading heads, the heads appearing lateral, extending outward from stem 1-7 cm; **tepals** lance-shaped, dark brown, 3-5 mm long, margins chaffy; stamens 6. **Capsule** ovate, somewhat 3-angled, red-brown, 3-4 mm long, shorter to slightly longer than the tepals, tapered to a sharp point. May-Aug.—Wet sandy or gravelly shores, interdunal wetlands near Lake Michigan, meadows, ditches, marshes, seeps.

Juncus balticus

Juncus brachycephalus (Engelm.) Buch.
SMALL-HEAD RUSH

MAP 1526
native

Densely tufted perennial rush. **Stems** erect, round in section, 3-7 dm long. **Leaves** from stem and base of plant, round in section, 2-20 cm long and 1-2 mm wide, often spreading; auricles rounded, to 1 mm long; **bract** erect, round in section, 1-5 cm long, shorter than the head. **Flowers** in an open raceme or panicle of 10-80 heads, 5-25 cm long and 2-12 cm wide, the heads oval, 2-5 mm wide, 2-6-flowered, branches upright to spreading, 1-5 cm long; **tepals** lance-shaped, green to light brown, 3-nerved, 2-3 mm long, margins chaffy; stamens 3 or sometimes 6. **Capsule** ovate, more or less 3-angled, light brown, 3-4 mm long, longer than the tepals, abruptly narrowed to a short beak. June-Sept.—Sandy or gravelly shores, streambanks, open bogs, calcium-rich springs.

Juncus brevicaudatus (Engelm.) Fern.
NARROW-PANICLE RUSH

MAP 1527
native

Densely tufted perennial rush. **Stems** erect, round in section, 1.5-5 dm long. **Leaves** from stem and base of plant, round in section, hollow, with small swollen joints, 3-20 cm long and 1-2 mm wide; sheaths green or sometimes red, auricles rounded, 1-2 mm long; **bract** erect, round in section, 2-7 cm long, shorter to longer than the head. **Flowers** in a raceme or panicle of 3-35 heads, 3-12 cm long and 1-4 cm wide, the heads oval, 2-6 mm wide, 2-7-flowered, branches upright, 0.5-3.5 cm long; **tepals** green to light brown, often red-tinged near tip, 3-nerved, 3-4 mm long, margins chaffy; stamens 3. **Capsule** oval, 3-angled, dark brown, 3-5 mm long, longer than the tepals, tapered to a sharp point. Aug.-Sept.—Wet meadows, marshes, fens, sandy shores, rocks along Lake Superior.

Juncus brevicaudatus

Juncus bufonius L.
TOAD RUSH

MAP 1528
native

Small annual rush. **Stems** tufted, erect to spreading, 5-20 cm long. **Leaves** from stem and at base of plant, flat or channeled, 1-7 cm long and to 1 mm wide, usually shorter than stem; sheaths green to red or brown, auricles absent; **bract** erect, 1-10 cm long, shorter than the head. **Flowers** single, mostly stalkless, with 1-7 flowers along each branch of the inflorescence, the inflorescence comprising half

Juncus bufonius

1522. *Juncus acuminatus*

1523. *Juncus alpinoarticulatus*

1524. *Juncus articulatus*

1525. *Juncus balticus*

or more of the entire length of plant; **tepals** lance-shaped, green to straw-colored, 4-6 mm long, margins chaffy; stamens 6. **Capsule** ovate, brown or green, 3-4 mm long, rounded at tip, shorter than the tepals. June-Aug.—Sandy or silty shores, mud flats, streambanks, wet compacted soil of trails and wheel ruts.

Juncus canadensis J. Gay　　　　　　　　　　MAP 1529
CANADIAN RUSH　　　　　　　　　　　　　　　　*native*

Tufted perennial rush. **Stems** erect, rigid, round in section, 3-9 dm long. **Leaves** from stem and at base of plant, round in section, hollow, with small swollen joints, 3-20 cm long and 1-3 mm wide; sheaths green to red, auricles rounded, 1-2 mm long; **bract** erect, round in section, 3-7 cm long and shorter than the head. **Flowers** in an open or crowded raceme or panicle of few to many heads, the heads more or less round, 3-8 mm wide, with 5-40 or more flowers, the branches upright, 1-10 cm long; **tepals** narrowly lance-shaped, green to brown, 3-5 mm long; stamens 3. **Capsule** ovate, 3-angled, light to dark brown, 3-5 mm long, equal or longer than the tepals, rounded to a short tip. July-Sept.—Sandy, muddy or mucky shores, marshes, streambanks, thickets, ditches.

Juncus canadensis

Juncus compressus Jacq.　　　　　　　　　MAP 1530
ROUND-FRUIT RUSH　　　　　　　　　　　　　　*introduced*

Tufted, perennial rush. **Stems** erect, flattened, 2-7 dm long. **Leaves** from plant base and 1 or 2 along stem, flat or channeled, 5-20 cm long and to 1.5 mm wide; auricles rounded, to 1 mm long; **bract** erect, somewhat bent, flat or folded, 2-8 cm long, often longer than head. **Flowers** on short stalks 1-5 mm long, with 1-2 flowers along each branch of the inflorescence, the inflorescence 3-7 cm long and 1-3 cm wide, branches upright; **tepals** ovate, light to dark brown, 1-3 mm long, margins translucent; stamens 6. **Capsule** nearly round, light brown, 2-3 mm long, longer than tepals. June-Aug.—Wet meadows, disturbed wet areas, ditches along highways where forming dark green colonies, often where saline.

Juncus compressus

Juncus dudleyi Wieg.　　　　　　　　　　MAP 1531
DUDLEY'S RUSH　　　　　　　　　　　　　　　*native*

　　Juncus tenuis var. *dudleyi* (Wiegand) F.J. Herm.

Tufted perennial rush, from branching rhizomes. **Stems** 2-10 dm long. **Leaves** basal, 2-3; auricles carilaginous, yellowish, to 0.4 mm long; blade flat, 5-30 cm long; **bract** usually longer than the head. **Inflorescences** compact to loose and lax; primary bract usually exceeding inflorescence. **Capsules** tan, ca. 3 mm long. —Damp to drier open places, including lakeshores, marsh margins, ditches.

Juncus dudleyi
perianth (tepals) and capsule

Juncus effusus L.　　　　　　　　　　　(NO MAP)
LAMP RUSH　　　　　　　　　　　　　　　　*native*

Densely tufted perennial rush. **Stems** erect, round in section, to about 1 m long. **Leaves** reduced to bladeless sheaths at base of stem, the sheaths to 2 dm long, mostly red-brown; **bract** round in section, 10-30 cm long, appearing like a continuation of stem, longer than the head. **Flowers** in a many-flowered inflorescence, with 2-4 flowers along each branch of the inflorescence, the inflorescence appearing lateral, the branches upright to spreading or bent downward; **tepals** lance-shaped, green to straw-colored, 2-3 mm long; stamens 3. **Capsule** broadly ovate, olive-green to brown, 2-3 mm long, about as long as tepals, sometimes tipped with a short point. June-July.—Marshes, shores, thickets, streambanks, bog margins, wet meadows.

Juncus effusus, J. pylaei

1526. *Juncus brachycephalus*

1527. *Juncus brevicaudatus*

1528. *Juncus bufonius*

ADDITIONAL SPECIES

• *Juncus pylaei* Laharpe, sometimes treated as a species or as *J. effusus* var. *pylaei* (Laharpe) Fern. & Weig., and apparently the common taxon in Minn (MAP 1532). *J. effusus* has soft, broad stems rather smooth because the ridges are tiny and numerous and readily flattened by pressing; *J. pylaei* has fewer, prominent ridges; and stems that are narrower, sturdier, and generally not flattened by pressing.

Juncus filiformis L.

THREAD RUSH

MAP 1533
native

Perennial rush, with short or long rhizomes. **Stems** tufted or in rows from the rhizomes, erect, round in section, 1-5 dm long. **Leaves** reduced to bladeless sheaths at base of stem, the sheaths pale brown, to 6 cm long; **bract** erect, round in section, 6-20 cm long, appearing to be a continuation of stem, longer than the head. **Flowers** in an branched inflorescence, 1-3 cm long, with 1-3 flowers along each branch of the inflorescence, the inflorescence appearing lateral, the branches erect to spreading, to 1 cm long; **tepals** lance-shaped, green to straw-colored, 2-3 mm long, margins chaffy; stamens 6. **Capsule** broadly ovate, light brown, 2-3 mm long, slightly longer than the tepals, tipped by a short beak.—Sandy, mucky, or gravelly shores, streambanks, thickets.

Juncus filiformis

Juncus gerardii Loisel.

BLACK-GRASS

(NO MAP)
introduced

Perennial rush, rhizomes slender, elongate. **Stems** 2-6 dm long. **Leaves** elongate, to 2 dm long; stem leaves 1 or 2, the uppermost divergent at or near the middle of the stem; leaf sheaths entire at their tip. **Inflorescence** 2-8 cm long, with ascending or erect branches, many-flowered, seldom surpassed by the involucral bract; **tepals** oblong, erect and appressed until spread by the enlarging capsule, conspicuously marked by longitudinal stripes of purple-brown. **Capsule** ovoid-ellipsoid, 2.4-3.3 mm long, short-beaked, equaling or barely exceeding the tepals.—Salt marsh species of ne USA; considered adventive in Minn, especially where salt is applied (as along highways); reported from Martin County.

Juncus greenei Oakes & Tuckerman

GREENE'S RUSH

MAP 1534
native

Perennial rush, from a short rhizome. **Stems** tufted, 2-8 dm long. **Basal leaves** filiform, nearly terete, 5-20 cm long; **involucral leaves** similar, length varies from 2-15 cm long.Inflorescence small and compact, obpyramidal, 2-5 cm high. Perianth segments oblong lance-shaped, appressed, acute or aristulate; sepals 2.3-3.5 mm long; petals 1.9-3.4 mm long. **Capsule** ovoid-cylindric, 3-4 mm long, truncate, at maturity conspicuously exceeding the perianth.—Moist to dry sandy open places: shores, swales, fields, clearings, dunes.

Juncus greenei

Juncus interior Wieg.

INLAND RUSH

MAP 1535
native

Perennial tufted rush, rhizomes densely branching. **Stems** 2-6 dm long. **Leaves** basal, 1-2(-3); auricles whitish or purplish tinged, scarious; **blade** flat, 5-15 cm long and to 1 mm wide, margins entire. **Inflorescences** usually somewhat compact; bract usually shorter than inflorescence; **tepals** greenish, lanceolate, 3.3-4.4 mm, acuminate. **Capsule** light tan or darker, ellipsoid to nearly globose, 4-5 mm long, equal to or longer than the tepals. *Differs from **Juncus tenuis** in having shorter auricles.*

1529. *Juncus canadensis*

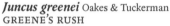

1530. *Juncus compressus*

1531. *Juncus dudleyi*

1532. *Juncus pylaei*

Juncus marginatus Rostk.

GRASS-LEAF RUSH

Juncus biflorus Ell.

MAP 1536

💙*endangered | native*

Perennial rush, spreading by rhizomes. **Stems** single or in small clumps, erect, compressed, 2-5 dm long, bulblike at base. **Leaves** from base of plant and on stem, flat, grasslike, 2-30 cm long and 1-3 mm wide; sheaths green, membranous on margins, auricles rounded, to 0.5 mm long; **bract** erect to spreading, flat, 1-8 cm long, shorter to slightly longer than the head. **Flowers** in an open panicle, 2-8 cm long and 1-6 cm wide, composed of 5-15 heads, the heads rounded, 3-6 mm wide, 6-20-flowered, branches upright, 0.5-2.5 cm long; **tepals** lance-shaped, green with red spots, 2-3 mm long, margins chaffy; stamens 3. **Capsule** more or less round, brown with red spots, 2-3 mm long, slightly longer than the tepals, rounded at tip. June-Aug.—Sandy shores and streambanks, wet meadows, marshes, low prairie, springs.

Juncus marginatus

Juncus nodosus L.

INLAND RUSH

MAP 1537

native

Perennial rush, spreading by rhizomes. **Stems** erect, slender, round in section, 1.5-6 dm long. **Leaves** on stem and one at base of plant, round in section, hollow, with small swollen joints, 3-30 cm long and 1-2 mm wide, upper leaves usually longer than the head; sheaths green, their margins green, becoming yellow and membranous toward tip, auricles rounded, yellow, 0.5-1 mm long; **bract** erect to spreading, round in section, 2-12 cm long, usually much longer than head. **Flowers** in a raceme or panicle of several heads, 1-6 cm long and 1-3 cm wide, the heads more or less round, 6-10 mm wide, 6-20-flowered, the branches erect to spreading, 0.5-3 cm long; **tepals** narrowly lance-shaped, green to light brown, 3-4 mm long; the margins narrowly translucent; stamens 6. **Capsule** awl-shaped, brown, 4-5 mm long, longer than the tepals, tapered to a sometimes curved beak. July-Sept.—Sandy, gravelly or clayey shores and streambanks, wet meadows, fens, ditches, springs; often where calcium-rich.

Juncus pelocarpus E. Mey.

BROWN-FRUIT RUSH

MAP 1538

native

Perennial rush, spreading by rhizomes and forming colonies. **Stems** erect, round in section, 1-4 dm long. **Leaves** from stem and at base of plant, round in section, very slender, 2-10 cm long and about 1 mm wide; auricles absent or short and straw-colored; **bract** erect, round in section, 2-4 cm long, shorter than the head. **Flowers** single or paired in a much-branched inflorescence, 5-15 cm long and 4-10 cm wide, the flowers on mostly 1 side of each branch, the branches upright to widely spreading, 1-4 cm long, with at least some of the flowers usually replaced by clusters of awl-shaped leaves; **tepals** ovate, dark brown, about 2 mm long, margins chaffy; stamens 6. **Capsule** narrowly ovate, dark brown, satiny, 2-3 mm long, equal or slightly longer than tepals, tapered to a slender beak. July-Aug.—Shallow water, sandy or mucky shores, bog margins.

Juncus nodosus

Juncus stygius L.

MOOR RUSH

MAP 1539

native

Perennial rush, from slender rhizomes. **Stems** single or few together, erect, round in section, 1-4 dm long. **Leaves** 1-3 from near base of plant, with 1 leaf above middle of stem, round in section or somewhat flattened, 3-15 cm long and 0.5-2 mm wide; auricles short and rounded or absent; **bract** erect, round in section, 1-

Juncus pelocarpus

1533. *Juncus filiformis*

1534. *Juncus greenei*

1535. *Juncus interior*

1536. *Juncus marginatus*

2 cm long, shorter than the head. **Flowers** in an inflorescence of 1-3 heads, the heads obovate, 5-10 mm wide, 1-4-flowered, branches erect, to 1 cm long; **tepals** lance-shaped, straw-colored to red-brown, 4-5 mm long, margins chaffy; stamens 6, nearly as long as the tepals. **Capsule** oval, 3-angled, green-brown, 6-8 mm long, longer than the tepals, tipped with a distinct point.—Open bogs, marshes, and shallow water.

Juncus tenuis Willd.
POVERTY RUSH

MAP 1540
native

Tufted, perennial rush. **Stems** erect, round in section to slightly flattened, 1-6 dm long. **Leaves** near base of stem, flat to broadly channeled, 10-15 cm long and to 1 mm wide; sheaths green, the margins yellow and glossy, auricles triangular, 1-3 mm long; **bracts** 1-3 (usually 2), the lowest erect, flat, 6-10 cm long, longer than the head. **Flowers** stalkless or on short stalks to 3 mm long, on branches with 1-7 flowers, in a crowded to spreading head 2-5 cm long; **tepals** lance-shaped, green to straw-colored or light brown, 3-5 mm long, margins narrowly translucent; stamens 6. **Capsule** ovate, green to straw-colored, 2-5 mm long, shorter or equaling the tepals, rounded at tip. June-July.—Wet meadows, shores, streambanks, springs, common in disturbed places (often where soils compacted) such as trails, roadsides and ditches; also in drier woods and meadows.

Juncus tenuis

ADDITIONAL SPECIES
Juncus anthelatus (Wiegand) R. E. Brooks, likely occurs in Minn as it is common in Wisc. Plants are like a larger version of *J. tenuis* with a lax, large inflorescence, treated as valid species or as *J. tenuis* var. *anthelatus* Weig. Plants mostly 60-90 cm tall with inflorescences 7-20 cm long; *J. tenuis* is rarely more than 60 cm tall, the inflorescence dense, 1-10 cm long.

Juncus torreyi Coville
TORREY'S RUSH

MAP 1541
native

Perennial rush, from tuber-bearing rhizomes. **Stems** single, erect, round in section, 4-8 dm long. **Leaves** from stem and base of plant, round in section, hollow, with small swollen joints, 15-30 cm long and 1-2 mm wide, the upper leaves often longer than the head; sheaths green, the margins white and translucent, auricles 1-3 mm long; **bract** erect or spreading, round in section, 4-12 cm long, longer than the head. **Flowers** a crowded, rounded raceme or panicle of 3-23 heads, 2-5 cm long and as wide, the heads round, 10-15 mm wide, with 25 to many flowers, branches erect to spreading 1-4 cm long; **tepals** narrowly lance-shaped, green to brown, 3-5 mm long, margins narrowly translucent; stamens 6. **Capsule** awl-shaped, brown, 4-6 mm long, equal or longer than the tepals, tapered to a short beak. June-Sept.—Sandy shores, streambanks, wet meadows, marsh borders, springs, ditches.

Juncus torreyi

Juncus vaseyi Engelm.
VASEY'S RUSH

MAP 1542
native

Juncus greenei Oakes & Tuckerman var. *vaseyi* (Engelm.) Boivin

Tufted perennial rush. **Stems** erect, 2-6 dm long. **Leaves** all at base of plant, round in section, solid, narrowly channeled on upper surface, to 3 dm long and to 1 mm wide, usually shorter than stem; sheaths green or red, the margins membranous, auricles short or absent; **bract** upright, usually shorter than the head. **Flowers** single, stalkless or on short stalks, in a crowded inflorescence, 1-4 cm long; **tepals** lance-shaped, green to light brown, 4-6 mm long, margins narrowly translucent;

Juncus vaseyi

1537. Juncus nodosus   *1538. Juncus pelocarpus*   *1539. Juncus stygius*   *1540. Juncus tenuis*

stamens 6. **Capsule** cylindric, 1-2 mm long, equal or slightly longer than the tepals. July-Aug.—Wet meadows, sandy shores.

LUZULA *Wood-Rush*

Perennial grasslike herbs, with narrow, flat, more or less pubescent leaves often involute toward the tip, and umbel-like or spike-like inflorescence, the flowers solitary, rarely paired, or glomerulate. Perianth as in *Juncus*, white, green, or brown, often scarious. Stamens 6. Ovary and capsule 1-celled; ovules 3. Seeds plump, ellipsoid, tipped by a short appendage (caruncle). Distinguished from *Juncus* by the presence of few to many long hairs on the leaves, especially toward the base of the blades.

ADDITIONAL SPECIES

Luzula parviflora (Ehrh.) Desv. (Small-flower wood-rush); ☙ *threatened;* conifer swamps and wet to dry forests in Cook and Lake counties.

1   Flowers grouped in heads or short dense spikes; capsule usually no longer than the perianth . . . . . . ***L. multiflora***
1   Flowers single at ends of inflorescence branches; capsule at maturity slightly longer than perianth . ***L. acuminata***

Luzula acuminata Raf.

MAP 1543
native

HAIRY WOOD-RUSH

Stems tufted, often stoloniferous 1-4 dm tall. **Basal leaves** elongate, to 3 dm long and 10 mm wide; **stem leaves** 2-4, shorter and somewhat narrower, all sparsely pilose, with a blunt callous apex. **Inflorescence** 3-6 cm high, the loosely spreading, almost filiform pedicels mostly simple with a single terminal flower, or a few with a lateral flower, or a few branched and bearing 3 or 4 flowers; **perianth segments** lance-shaped, usually chestnut-brown in the center, with scarious margins, 2.6-4.3 mm long, the petals slightly exceeding the sepals, **Capsule** ovoid, 3.2-4.5 mm long, mucronate; seeds purple-brown, the body about 1 mm long, with a pale appendage nearly as long. May-June.—Moist or dry woods and forest openings, meadows, streambanks, hillsides.

Luzula acuminata

Luzula multiflora (Ehrh.) Lej.

MAP 1544
native

COMMON WOOD-RUSH

Luzula campestris var. *multiflora* (Ehrh.) Celak.

Stems loosely tufted, 2-4 or rarely 5 dm tall. **Basal leaves** several, **stem leaves** 2 or 3, flat, except toward the callous-pointed tip, 2-6 mm wide. **Inflorescence** usually with a few slender peduncles and 1 or more sessile glomerules; bracts usually scarious toward the acute tip, not elongate; **perianth segments** lance-shaped, 2-3.7 mm long. **Capsule** obovoid, about as long as the perianth; seeds ellipsoid, 1-1.3 mm long, with an ovate-triangular appendage 0.4-0.5 mm long. —Forests, sometimes with *L. acuminata*; also in swamps and moist grassy areas.

Luzula multiflora

Juncaginaceae ARROW-GRASS FAMILY

TRIGLOCHIN *Arrow-Grass*

Grasslike perennial herbs, clumped from creeping rhizomes, often in brackish habitats. Stems slender, leafless. Leaves all from base of plant, slender, linear, round or somewhat flattened in section, sheathing at base. Flowers perfect, regular, on short stalks in a spike-like raceme at end of stem; flower segments (tepals) 6; stigmas 3 or 6, styles short or absent; stamens 6, anthers stalkless, nearly as large as tepals. Fruit of 3 or 6 carpels, these splitting when mature into 1-seeded segments.

1541. Juncus torreyi

1542. Juncus vaseyi

1543. Luzula acuminata

1544. Luzula multiflora

1   Plants generally small and slender; stigmas 3; fruit linear, clublike toward tip . . . . **T. palustris**
1   Plants larger, usually 3 dm or more tall; stigmas 6; fruit short-cylindric. . . . . **T. maritima**

Triglochin maritima L.
SEASIDE ARROW-GRASS

MAP 1545
native

Tufted perennial herb, from a thick crown and spreading by rhizomes. **Stems** more or less round in section, leafless, 2-8 dm long. **Leaves** upright to spreading, somewhat flattened, to 5 dm long and 1-3 mm wide. **Flowers** 2-3 mm wide, in densely flowered, spike-like racemes 1-4 dm long; the flowers on upright stalks 4-6 mm long, the stalks extending downward on the stem as a wing; tepals 6, 1-2 mm long; stigmas 6; stamens 6. **Fruit** of 6 ovate carpels, 2-5 mm long and 1-3 mm wide, the carpel tips curved backward. June-Aug.—Sandy, gravelly, or marly lakeshores and streambanks; marshes, brackish wetlands. *Plants larger than* **marsh arrow-grass** *(Triglochin palustris) and the fruit ovate rather than linear.*

Triglochin palustris L.
MARSH ARROW-GRASS

MAP 1546
native

Small tufted perennial herb. **Stems** slender, leafless, 2-4 dm long. **Leaves** erect, round in section, to 3 dm long and 1-2 mm wide. **Flowers** small, 1-2 mm wide, in loosely flowered racemes, 10-25 cm long; the flowers on erect stalks, 2-5 mm long; tepals 6, 1-2 mm long; stigmas 3; stamens 6. **Fruit** of 3 narrow, clublike carpels, 5-8 mm long and 1 mm wide, splitting upward from base into 3 segments. June-Sept.—Sandy, gravelly, or marly lakeshores and streambanks, calcareous fens, marshes, interdunal swales; often where calcium-rich.

Triglochin maritima

1778. *Triglochin maritima*   1779. *Triglochin palustris*

Triglochin palustris

Liliaceae LILY FAMILY

Perennial herbs, from corms, bulbs or rhizomes. Stems leafy or leafless. Leaves linear to ovate, usually from base of plant, sometimes along stem, alternate to opposite or whorled. Flowers perfect (with both staminate and pistillate parts), regular; sepals and petals of 6 petal-like tepals in 2 series of 3; stamens 6; ovary superior or inferior, 3-chambered. Fruit a capsule or round berry.

Under the Angiosperm Phylogeny Group IV system (APG IV, 2016), genera in the Liliaceae have been placed into various new familes. However, the family designations remain somewhat tentative, and may change in the future. As a convenience for identifying specimens, our genera are retained within the traditional Lily Family grouping, with the proposed new family name noted in the following table and in parentheses after each genus name.

APG IV LILIACEAE REORGANIZATION		
Amaryllidaceae	**Asphodelaceae**	**Melanthiaceae**
Allium	*Hemerocallis*	*Anticlea*
Asparagaceae	**Colchicaceae**	*Trillium*
Asparagus	*Uvularia*	*Zigadenus*
Convallaria	**Liliaceae**	**Tofieldiaceae**
Maianthemum	*Clintonia*	*Tofieldia*
Muscari	*Erythronium*	*Triantha*
Ornithogalum	*Lilium*	
Polygonatum	*Prosartes*	
	Streptopus	

ADDITIONAL SPECIES

Prosartes trachycarpa S. Watson (Rough-fruit fairy bells), ☞ *endangered;* disjunct from w North America in Cook County.

1 Sepals and petals of quite different color and/or texture, the former green or brownish . . . . *Trillium*
1 Sepals and petals both colored and petaloid, usually similar in shape (tepals) or the sepals of different size and shape 2
 2 Ovary inferior (flowers bisexual) 3
  3 Ovary clearly inferior; uncommon garden escape . . . . *Narcissus*
  3 Ovary only half-inferior, part of it adnate to the perianth, glabrous (at most granular-roughened); native plants . . . . *Anticlea*
 2 Ovary superior (or flowers unisexual) 4
  4 Flowers or inflorescences lateral, arising from the axils of alternate cauline leaves or scales 5
   5 Leaves scale-like, mostly brownish or yellowish, those on the much-branched upper portion of the plant subtending short green filiform branches (often mistaken for leaves) . . . . *Asparagus*
   5 Leaves broad, flat, green (scale-like leaves or bracts may be present in addition to normal leaves) . . . . **(go to 25)**
  4 Flowers or inflorescences terminal on scapes or leafy (simple or branched) stems 6
   6 Leaves all withering before plant flowers . . . . *Allium (A. tricoccum)*
   6 Leaves present at flowering time 7
    7 Flowers more than 3.5 cm long 8
     8 Leaves perfoliate . . . . *Uvularia grandiflora*
     8 Leaves not perfoliate 9
      9 Principal leaves cauline, not crowded toward base of plant . . . . *Lilium*
      9 Principal leaves basal or nearly so; stem leafless above or with very small bracts 10
       10 Flowers 2-many . . . . *Hemerocallis*
       10 Flowers solitary 11
        11 Leaves basal . . . . *Erythronium*
        11 Leaves cauline. . . . . *Lilium*
    7 Flowers less than 3.5 cm long 12
     12 Flowers in a many (7-60 or more) flowered umbel on an unbranched stem or scape; plants with odor of onion or garlic. . . . . *Allium*
     12 Flowers solitary or in a raceme, panicle, or corymb, on a simple or branched stem (if in a few-flowered umbel, then either the stem branched or forked or flowers less than 7) 13
      13 Plants with principal leaves clearly along the stem; basal leaves (at least of current season) absent or at most apparently one 14
       14 Stem forked or branched; perianth over 12 mm long . . . . **(go to 25)**
       14 Stem unbranched (above the ground and below the inflorescence); perianth usually less than 12 mm long 15
        15 Ovary with 1 style; fruit a berry; inflorescence a raceme (tepals up to 7 mm long) or if a panicle, the tepals less than 3 mm long; leaves ovate. . . . . **(go to 25)**
        15 Ovary with 3 styles (one on each lobe); fruit a capsule; inflorescence a panicle; tepals ca. 5-13 mm long; leaves very elongate 16
         16 Plants with at least some principal leaves clearly along the stem; inflorescences paniculate (except in depauperate individuals) . . . . *Anticlea*
         16 Plants with the principal leaves all basal (at ground level) or nearly so, stem leaves absent, reduced to bracts, or at most much smaller or fewer than the basal leaves; inflorescences racemose 17
          17 Perianth 3-5 mm long, subtended by tiny bractlets (in addition to the bracts at the bases of the pedicels); peduncle and pedicels glandular-sticky. . . . . *Triantha*
          17 Perianth 2-3 mm long, not subtended by bractlets; peduncles and pedicels smooth . . . . *Tofieldia*
      13 Plants with the principal leaves all basal (at ground level) or nearly so; stem leaves absent, reduced to bracts, or much smaller or fewer than basal leaves. 18
       18 Flower solitary . . . . *Erythronium*
       18 Flowers 2 or more in an inflorescence 19
        19 Tepals united for half or more of their length 20
         20 Perianth blue, less than 6 mm long; leaves linear, to 8 mm wide; plants bulbous . . . . *Muscari*

20 Perianth white, 5-10 mm long when mature; leaves elliptic; plants not bulbous
.... *Convallaria*
19 Tepals completely separate or united at base only 21
22 Ovary with 3 styles (1 on each lobe) in bisexual or pistillate flowers (or flowers
all staminate) 23
23 Plants with at least some principal leaves clearly cauline; inflorescences
paniculate .... *Anticlea*
23 Plants with the principal leaves all basal or nearly so, stem leaves absent,
reduced to bracts, or at most much smaller or fewer than basal leaves;
inflorescences racemose .... *Triantha*
22 Ovary with a single style; flowers bisexual 24
24 Leaves broad (over 3 cm wide); perianth yellow; fruit a blue berry ....
.... *Clintonia*
24 Leaves long and narrow (less than 1.5 cm wide); perianth white to blue; fruit
a capsule   .... *Ornithogalum*

LEAD 25. *Fruit red, blue, or black berries, except in Uvularia, which has a capsule.*

25 Plants with the leaves all basal or nearly so; stem leaves absent, reduced to bracts, or at most much smaller or
fewer than the basal leaves 26
26 Flowers yellow, in an umbel; fruit blue.................................... *Clintonia*
26 Flowers white, in a raceme; fruit (rarely produced) orange or red .... *Convallaria*
25 Plants with leaves clearly along the stem 27
27 Plant unbranched 28
28 Flowers in a terminal raceme or panicle, white, tepals nearly separate, fused at the very base; ripe fruit red,
with dark stripes in one species .... *Maianthemum*
28 Flowers in the axils of leaves, greenish, greenish white, or yellowish, tepals united most of their length;
ripe fruit blue to black .... *Polygonatum*
27 Plant branched (above the ground) 29
29 Perianth pale to deep yellow; fruit a glabrous capsule; stem and pedicels glabrous .... *Uvularia*
29 Perianth greenish, rose-purple, white, or creamy, fruit a pubescent to glabrate or tuberculate red berry;
stem (at least when young) and pedicels often pubescent.............................. *Streptopus*

ALLIUM *Onion; Leek; Garlic*   AMARYLLIDACEAE

Biennial or perennial herbs from a coated bulb, with a strong odor of onion or garlic, the leaves usually
narrow, basal or on the lower part of the stem, the scape-like stem erect, terminated by an umbel
subtended by 1-3 bracts, the flowers white to pink or purple, in some species wholly or partly replaced
by sessile bulblets. Flowers perfect, in umbels. Perianth segments 6, uniform in color, but the inner
circle often somewhat different in shape or size, withering and persistent below the capsule. Stamens
6. Ovary 3-celled. Capsule short, ovoid, globose, or obovoid, 3-lobed, loculicidal; seeds black, 1 or 2
in each cell. *Allium* includes the cultivated onion, garlic, chives, and leek.

ADDITIONAL SPECIES
Allium cepa L. (Cultivated onion), probably native of sw Asia; cultivated and rarely adventive; see key.

1 Leaves usually over 2 cm wide, flat, petiolate, withering before the plant flowers .... *A. tricoccum*
1 Leaves linear, flat or terete, usually less than 1 cm wide, not petiolate, present at flowering time 2
2 Umbel nodding, on bent or reflexed tip of scape; leaves flat .... *A. cernuum*
2 Umbel erect on straight tip of scape; leaves flat, keeled, or terete 3
3 Leaf blades terete, hollow, at least most of their length (else flattened where pressed in drying, but the
base of blade, just above summit of sheath, will not show 2 distinct surfaces)...................... 4
4 Stem stout, over 5 mm in diameter for most or all of its length, distinctly inflated below the middle..
.... *A. cepa**
4 Stem 5 mm in diameter or less (very rarely as stout as 7 mm), without inflated section............
.... *A. schoenoprasum*
3 Leaf blades flat (sometimes keeled) 5
5 Umbels bearing bulblets (flowers few or none)................................... *A. canadense*
5 Umbels not bearing bulblets.. 6
6 Bulb coat coarsely fibrous.. *A. textile*
6 Bulb coat membranaceous, not fibrous .... *A. stellatum*

Allium canadense L.

MAP 1547

MEADOW GARLIC

native

Bulb ovoid-conic, 1-3 cm long, its coats fibrous-reticulate. **Stems** erect, stout, 2-6 dm tall, leafy in the lower third. **Leaves** elongate, flat, commonly 2-4 mm, occasionally to 7 mm wide; bracts 2 or 3, broadly ovate, acuminate. **Umbels** bearing bulblets only, or with 2-5 flowers also; bulblets ovoid to fusiform, to 1 cm long; pedicels slender, 15-30 mm long; perianth segments pink or white, oblong lance-shaped, 6-9 mm long, acute. **Capsule** rarely developed, subglobose, not crested. May, June.—Moist or dry open woods and prairies.

Allium cernuum Roth

MAP 1548

NODDING ONION

native

Bulb slenderly conic, very gradually tapering into the stem. **Leaves** several, arising near together at the surface of the soil, shorter than the stem, commonly 2-4 mm, occasionally to 8 mm wide. **Scape** 3-6 dm tall, abruptly declined or decurved near the summit. **Umbel** nodding, many-flowered, without bulblets; pedicels 12-25 mm long, becoming rigid in fruit; perianth segments white to rose, ovate or elliptic, 4-6 mm long, obtuse or subacute; stamens exsert; filaments barely widened toward the base. **Capsule** obovoid, 3-lobed, about 4 mm long, each valve (and each lobe of the ovary) bearing 2 erect triangular processes near the summit. July-Aug.—Dry woods, rocky banks, and prairies.

Allium schoenoprasum L.

MAP 1549

WILD CHIVES

🌱 *endangered* | *native*

Bulb slender, often scarcely thicker than the stem. **Stems** 2-5 dm tall. **Leaves** erect, terete, hollow, the longest nearly equaling the stem. **Umbel** compact, hemispheric, subtended by 2 ovate bracts; pedicels 3-7 mm long. **Flowers** numerous; perianth segments bright rose-color, ovate to lance-shaped, 10-14 mm long, acuminate, prominently 1-nerved. **Capsule** ovoid, 3-lobed, about half as long as the perianth. June-July.—In Minn, on rocky shorelines and ledges along Lake Superior and on north-facing, rocky ridges above the St. Louis River.

Allium canadense

Allium stellatum Nutt.

MAP 1550

AUTUMN ONION

native

Bulb ovoid, 1.5-3 cm long. **Stems** 3-7 dm tall. **Leaves** commonly 3-6, arising near together at the surface of the soil, 1-2 mm wide, keeled; bracts 2, ovate to lance-shaped, acuminate. Pedicels slender, 1-2 cm long; perianthsegments pink or lavender, ovate to oblong, 4-7 mm long, obtuse or subacute; stamens equaling or exceeding the perianth; filaments slightly widened below. **Capsule** 3-lobed, sub-globose, shorter than the perianth, each valve (and each lobe of the ovary) bearing 2 erect triangular processes just below the summit. July-Sept.—Prairies, barrens, and rocky hills.

Allium textile A. Nels. & J.F. Macbr.

MAP 1551

TEXTILE ONION

native

Bulb fibrous-coated. **Stems** to 5 dm tall. **Leaves** usually 2, equal to or exceeding stem, 1-5 mm wide, channeled. **Inflorescence** an erect umbel, becoming flexuous and rigid in fruit; spathe dividing into (2)5 bracts, each bract 1-nerved. **Flowers** white, rarely pink, campanulate; perianth segments 5-7 mm long, investing capsule when mature; stamens shorter than perianth; ovary 6-crested, knobs separated or united. May-July.—Dry prairies; dry, open coniferous woods.

Allium schoenoprasum

1547. *Allium canadense*

1548. *Allium cernuum*

1549. *Allium schoenoprasum*

1550. *Allium stellatum*

Allium tricoccum Ait.
WILD LEEK

MAP 1552
native

Bulb ovoid, 2-6 cm long, its coats finely fibrous-reticulate. **Leaves** 2-3 dm long, including the slender petiole, the blades flat, lance-elliptic, 1-2 dm long, 2-6 cm wide. **Scape** 1.5-6 dm tall. **Umbel** erect, subtended by 2 ovate deciduous bracts; pedicels 1-2 cm long; perianth segments ovate to oblong-obovate, white, 5-7 mm long obtuse, about equaling the stamens; filaments greatly widened toward the base. **Capsule** depressed, deeply 3-lobed, each valve often gibbous on the back below the middle.—Rich woods, often in large colonies. *The leaves develop in early spring and disappear before the flowers appear in June and July.*

ANTICLEA *Death-Camas*
MELANTHIACEAE

Anticlea elegans (Pursh) Rydb.
MOUNTAIN DEATH-CAMAS
Zigadenus elegans Pursh

MAP 1553
native

Allium tricoccum

Perennial herb, from an ovate bulb; plants waxy, especially when young. **Stems** erect, 2-6 dm long. **Leaves** mostly from base of plant, linear, 2-4 dm long and 4-12 mm wide; stem leaves much smaller. **Flowers** green-yellow or white, in a raceme or panicle, 1-3 dm long, the branches upright, subtended by large, lance-shaped, green or purplish bracts; tepals 6, obovate, 7-12 mm long, usually purple-tinged near base; stamens 6. **Fruit** an ovate capsule, 10-15 mm long; seeds 3 mm long. July-Aug.—Bogs, calcareous fens. *Highly toxic if eaten.*

ASPARAGUS *Asparagus*
ASPARAGACEAE

Asparagus officinalis L.
ASPARAGUS

MAP 1554
introduced (naturalized)

Perennial herb of various forms, the leaves reduced to small scales and replaced functionally by branches sometimes leaflike in appearance. **Stems** perennial from a rhizome, freely branched, to 2 m tall; ultimate branches filiform, 8-15 mm long; pedicels solitary or paired, lateral, 5-10 mm long, jointed in the middle. **Flowers** perfect or unisexual, greenish white, campanulate, 3-5 mm long; stamens 6; stigmas 3; ovary 3-celled. **Fruit** a red, spherical berry, about 8 mm wide, with a few large rounded seeds. May-June.—Native of Europe; commonly cultivated in home and truck gardens and escaped in waste places.

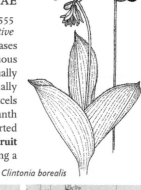

Anticlea elegans

CLINTONIA *Bluebead-Lily*
LILIACEAE

Clintonia borealis (Ait.) Raf.
YELLOW BLUEBEAD-LILY

MAP 1555
native

Perennial herbs from a rhizome, bearing 2-4 ample basal leaves, the bases sheathing a leafless erect scape bearing a few-flowered umbel of conspicuous flowers. **Leaves** 2-5, dark glossy green, oblong to elliptic or obovate, eventually to 3 dm long, abruptly acuminate, finely ciliate. **Scape** 1.5-4 dm tall, usually pubescent at the summit, or glabrous at maturity. **Umbel** 3-8-flowered; pedicels 1-3 cm, long, erect in fruit, softly pubescent. **Flowers** perfect, nodding; perianth segments distinct, narrow, greenish yellow, 15-18 mm long; stamens 6, inserted on the very base of the perianth; ovary 3-celled; stigma obscurely 3-lobed. **Fruit** a blue berry, rarely varying to white, spherical, about 8 mm wide, containing a few to several seeds. May-June.—Rich, moist woods and swamps.

Clintonia borealis

1551. *Allium textile*

1552. *Allium tricoccum*

1553. *Anticlea elegans*

1554. *Asparagus officinalis*

CONVALLARIA *Lily-of-the-Valley*   ASPARAGACEAE

Convallaria majalis L.
EUROPEAN LILY-OF-THE-VALLEY
MAP 1556
introduced (invasive)

Perennial herb from a rhizome, the short stem bearing a few leafless sheaths and 2 or 3 broad leaves, the scape terminating in a bracted raceme. **Leaves** narrowly elliptic, to 2 dm long, acuminate. **Scape** 1-2 dm tall. Raceme loosely flowered, one-sided; bracts small, lance-shaped; pedicels drooping. **Flowers** perfect, white, fragrant, 6-9 mm long; perianth globose-campanulate, with 6 short recurved lobes; stamens 6, inserted on the perianth near its base; style straight, included; ovary 3-celled. **Fruit** a spherical many-seeded red berry, about 1 cm wide. May. —Eurasian, commonly cultivated and occasionally escaped near gardens.

Convallaria majalis

ERYTHRONIUM *Trout-Lily; Fawn-Lily*   LILIACEAE

Perennial from a deep solid corm, the slender stem about half underground; leaves borne near middle of the stem and therefore appearing basal, usually mottled with brown, lance-shaped to oblance-shaped or elliptic; scape bearing a single nodding flower. Our species grow in colonies, producing numerous 1-leaved sterile plants and a few 2-leaved fertile ones; reproduction often vegetatively by bulbs at the tip of slender lateral offshoots from the corm or stem. Perianth segments (tepals) separate to the base but connivent, lance-shaped, at anthesis spreading and usually eventually recurved. Stamens 6. Ovary 3-celled; style slender below, thickened above to the 3 short stigmas. Fruit an obovoid to oblong capsule.

1 Flowers yellow . . . . *E. americanum*
1 Flowers white. 2
  2 Flowering plants reproducing vegetatively by stolons produced halfway up stem; tepals 8-15 mm long; rare in se Minn (state endemic) . . . . *E. propullans*
  2 Flowering plants reproducing vegetatively by droppers or offshoots or by stolons arising from bulbs; tepals 15-40 mm long; widespread in Minn. . . . . *E. albidum*

Erythronium albidum Nutt.
SMALL WHITE FAWN-LILY
MAP 1557
native

Scape stout, 1-2 dm tall. **Perianth segments** (tepals) normally bluish white, varying to light pink, often suffused with green or blue externally, yellow at base within, without marginal glands; stigmas stout, separate, divergent from the linear-clavate style. April-May.—Moist woods.

Erythronium americanum Ker-Gawl.
TROUT-LILY
MAP 1558
native

Scape stout, 1-2 dm tall. **Perianth segments** (tepals) normally yellow, often spotted toward the base within or darker colored without, the petals bearing a glandular spot on each margin near the base; stigmas very short, scarcely separate, terminating the club-shaped style. April-May.—Moist woods.

Erythronium propullans A. Gray
MINNESOTA DWARF TROUT-LILY
MAP 1559
❧ *endangered | native*

Flowering plants producing one stolon halfway up stem; 1-leaved nonflowering plants with 1-3 stolons from bulbs. **Bulbs** ovoid, 10-25 mm long. **Scape** to 12 cm tall. **Leaves** 4-13 cm long, irregularly mottled, elliptic-lanceolate to elliptic, glaucous; margins entire. **Inflorescences** 1-flowered; **tepals** 4-6, reflexed at anthesis, pale pink to white, lanceolate, 8-15 mm long; stamens 2-6, 6-8 mm;

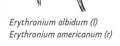

Erythronium albidum (l)
Erythronium americanum (r)

1555. Clintonia borealis   *1556. Convallaria majalis*   *1557. Erythronium albidum*   *1558. Erythronium americanum*

filaments white, anthers yellow; style white, 6-10 mm long, stigma ± unlobed. **Capsules** rarely produced; when present, may be result of hybridization with *E. albidum*. April-May.—Wooded floodplains and river terraces, or on north-facing slopes adjacent to a stream; may often form extensive colonies in suitable habitats, sometimes growing intermixed with the common *E. albidum*.

ground surface

Erythronium propullans

   E. propullans is a state and federally endangered species, endemic to se Minn; resembling *E. albidum* but smaller overall. The flowers of *E. propullans* are sometimes pinkish rather than white; 5 tepals is typical rather than the 6 petals of *E. albidum*. Mature fruit of *E. propullans* are nodding rather than erect. Aboveground parts wither and disappear in summer. Note that while only a small percentage of *E. albidum* plants will flower in any given year, nearly every plant of *E. propullans* in a population will produce a flower.

HEMEROCALLIS *Day-Lily*   ASPHODELACEAE

Tall perennial herbs, with numerous, elongate, linear, basal leaves and leafless scapes bearing a terminal cluster of large flowers, each lasting a single day. Perianth funnelform, its segments spreading or recurved, connate below into a short tube. Stamens inserted at the summit of the tube. Ovary 3-celled with numerous ovules; style slender, declined; stigma capitate.

1   Flowers orange . . . . *H. fulva*
1   Flowers yellow . . . . *H. lilioasphodelus*

Hemerocallis fulva (L.) L.
ORANGE DAY-LILY
Scapes about 1 m tall. **Flowers** tawny-orange, about 12 cm wide. June-July.—Long in cultivation and freely escaped.

MAP 1560
introduced (invasive)

Hemerocallis lilioasphodelus L.
YELLOW DAY-LILY
   Hemerocallis flava (L.) L.
Similar to *H. fulva*. **Flowers** lemon-yellow, about 10 cm wide. May-June. —Commonly cultivated and occasionally escaped along roadsides; reported for Minnesota.

(NO MAP)
introduced

Hemerocallis fulva

LILIUM *Lily*   LILIACEAE

Tall perennial herbs from a scaly bulb, in our species the erect stem bearing numerous narrow leaves, either alternate or whorled, and at the summit 1 to many, large, erect or nodding, yellow to red flowers. Perianth campanulate or funnelform, its 6 segments clawed or sessile, erect or spreading or recurved, in many species connivent at base, in ours spotted with purple toward the base. Stamens 6. Ovary 3-celled with numerous ovules; style 1; stigmas 3-lobed. Fruit a more or less 3-angled capsule with numerous closely packed, flat seeds.

1   Flowers erect; tepals narrowed at base to a slender claw; leaves to 8 (-14) mm wide . . . . **L. philadelphicum**
1   Flowers nodding (fruit becoming erect); tepals narrowed gradually toward base, not clawed; widest leaves 8-35 mm wide 2
   2   Tepals glabrous within; stem glabrous above; leaves mostly whorled . . . . **L. michiganense**
   2   Tepals with pubescent strip basally within; stems with cobwebby pubescence, especially above; leaves alternate but crowded . . . . **L. lancifolium**

1559. Erythronium propullans   *1560. Hemerocallis fulva*   *1561. Lilium lancifolium*   *1562. Lilium michiganense*

Lilium lancifolium Thunb.

TIGER LILY

MAP 1561
introduced

Stems stout, 6-12 dm tall. **Leaves** very numerous, alternate, linear to narrowly lance-shaped, the lower 10-15 cm long, rounded and sessile at base, with bulblets in the axil. **Flowers** several in a raceme, the stout widely divergent pedicels subtended by small leaves; **perianth segments** recurved, orange-red with many purple-brown spots, 7-10 cm long. July-August.—Native of e Asia; cultivated and escaped around dwellings and on roadsides.

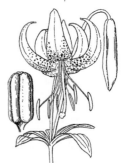

Lilium lancifolium

Lilium michiganense Farw.

MICHIGAN LILY

MAP 1562
native

Stems stout and erect, to 2.5 m tall. **Principal leaves** whorled, the upper stem leaves and those of the inflorescence alternate; **blades** lance-shaped, tapering to both ends, smooth, the larger commonly 8-12 cm long and to 2 cm wide. **Flowers** occasionally solitary, usually several or many, partly in an umbel from the uppermost leaf-whorl and partly in a terminal raceme, nodding from long, erect or ascending pedicels; **perianth segments** strongly recurved, lance-shaped, 6-9 cm long, orange or orange-red, spotted with purple, bright green at the base within. July, Aug.—Wet meadows and low ground.

Lilium philadelphicum L.

WOOD-LILY

MAP 1563
native

Stems erect, 3-8 dm long. **Leaves** all from stem, narrowly lance-shaped, 4-10 cm long and 3-9 mm wide, parallel-veined; lower leaves alternate, upper leaves opposite or whorled; petioles absent. **Flowers** 1-5, erect, large and showy, on stalks 1-8 cm long at ends of stem; **perianth segments** orange-red, yellow and dark-spotted toward base, lance-shaped, 4-8 cm long and 0.8-2.8 cm wide, stamens and pistil about as long as tepals; stigma 3-parted; ovary superior. **Capsule** oblong, 2.5-4 cm long; seeds flat. June-July.—Wet meadows, low prairie, fens and open bogs, seeps, ditches; also in drier meadows, prairies and woods.

Lilium michiganense

Lilium philadelphicum

MAIANTHEMUM *False Solomon's-Seal* ASPARAGACEAE

Perennial herbs from a slender creeping rhizome, the erect or ascending stems bearing few to many alternate, sessile or nearly sessile leaves, and a terminal raceme or panicle of small white flowers. Perianth regular, spreading, the segments equal and distinct, 6 (4 in *M. canadense*). Stamens 6 (4 in *M. canadense*). Ovary globose, 2- or 3-celled; style very short; stigma obscurely 2- or 3-lobed. Fruit a globose berry, usually with only 1 or 2 seeds. *Includes species formerly included in* **Smilacina**.

1   Perianth of 4 parts; leaves 3 or fewer (very rarely 4, usually 2), sometimes pubescent beneath .... ***M. canadense***
1   Perianth of 6 parts; leaves often more than 3 (1-4 in one species, where completely glabrous) 2
   2   Inflorescence a panicle; perianth 1-2.5 mm long, the stamens up to 3 mm long............. ***M. racemosum***
   2   Inflorescence a raceme; perianth 2.5-9 mm long, exceeding the stamens 3
      3   Stem leaves more than 6, finely pubescent beneath (rarely almost glabrous); uppermost leaves surpassing the top of the inflorescence .... ***M. stellatum***
      3   Stem leaves 1-4, completely glabrous; inflorescence almost always overtopping leaves ...... ***M. trifolium***

Maianthemum canadense Desf.

FALSE LILY-OF-THE-VALLEY

MAP 1564
native

Stems erect, 5-20 cm long, spreading by rhizomes. **Leaves** usually 2 along stem, ovate, heart-shaped at base, 3-10 cm long; petioles short or absent. **Flowers** small, white, 4-6 mm wide, stalked, in a short raceme at end of stem, the raceme 3-6 cm long; tepals 4, spreading; stamens 4; style 2-lobed. **Fruit** a pale red berry, 3-4 mm wide; seeds 1-2. May-July.—Common in moist to dry woods; also on hummocks in swamps, open bogs and thickets.

Maianthemum racemosum (L.) Link
FALSE SOLOMON'S-SEAL
Smilacina racemosa (L.) Desf.

MAP 1565
native

Stems usually curved-ascending, 4-8 dm tall, finely pubescent. **Leaves** spreading horizontally in two ranks, elliptic, 7-15 cm long, 2-7 cm wide, obtuse or rounded at base, short-acuminate, finely pubescent beneath. **Panicle** peduncled or rarely sessile, ovoid to cylindric, 3-15 cm long. **Flowers** very numerous, short-pediceled, 3-5 mm wide. **Berry** red, dotted with purple. May-June.—Rich woods.

Maianthemum stellatum (L.) Link
STARRY FALSE SOLOMON'S-SEAL
Smilacina stellata (L.) Desf.

MAP 1566
native

Stems ascending or usually erect, 2-6 dm tall, finely pubescent or glabrous. **Leaves** spreading or oftener strongly ascending, usually folded along the midvein, sessile and somewhat clasping, mostly lance-shaped, 6-15 cm long and 2-5 cm wide, gradually tapering to the acute tip, finely pubescent beneath. **Raceme** short-peduncled or nearly sessile, 2-5 cm long, with few to several flowers 8-10 mm wide. **Fruit** black or green with black stripes, 6-10 mm wide. May-June.—Moist, especially sandy soil of woods, shores, and prairies.

Maianthemum canadense

Maianthemum trifolium (L.) Sloboda
THREE-LEAF FALSE SOLOMON'S-SEAL
Smilacina trifolia (L.) Desf.

MAP 1557
native

Stems erect, 1-5 dm long at flowering time, from long rhizomes. **Leaves** alternate, smooth, usually 3 (2-4), oval or oblong lance-shaped, 6-12 cm long and 1-4 cm wide; petioles absent. **Flowers** small, white, 8 mm wide, stalked, 3-8 in a raceme; tepals 6, spreading; stamens 6. **Fruit** a dark red berry, 3-5 mm wide; seeds 1-2. May-June.—Open bogs, conifer swamps, thickets.

MUSCARI *Grape-Hyacinth*   ASPARAGACEAE

Muscari botryoides (L.) P. Mill.
COMMON GRAPE-HYACINTH

(NO MAP)
introduced

Perennial herb from a bulb, the linear leaves basal, the short erect scape bearing a dense raceme of flowers. **Leaves** flat, oblong lance-shaped, at maturity to 2.5 dm long and 1 cm wide. **Scape** 1-2 dm tall at anthesis, to 4 dm in fruit. **Raceme** compact, ovoid-cylindric, 2-4 cm long at anthesis, elongating in fruit. **Flowers** blue, all fertile except a few at the tip, nodding, exceeding their slender pedicels; perianth globular, 4-5 mm long; stamens 6, inserted on the perianth tube, included. **Fruit** a 3-celled capsule, distinctly 3-angled or almost winged, with 2 angular seeds in each cell. Spring.—Commonly cultivated and sometimes escaping; reported for Minn.

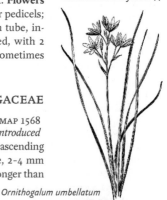

Maianthemum stellatum (l)
Maianthemum trifolium (r)

ORNITHOGALUM *Star-of-Bethlehem*   ASPARAGACEAE

Ornithogalum umbellatum L.
STAR-OF-BETHLEHEM

MAP 1568
introduced

Perennial herb from a tunicate bulb, with linear basal leaves, an erect or ascending scape, and a short bracted raceme of white flowers. **Leaves** elongate, 2-4 mm wide. **Scape** 1-3 dm tall. **Raceme** 3-7-flowered, the ascending pedicels longer than

Ornithogalum umbellatum

1563. *Lilium philadelphicum*

1564. *Maianthem. canadense*

1565. *Maianthem. racemosum*

1566. *Maianthem. stellatum*

the internodes. **Flowers** perfect, erect; **perianth segments** 6, separate, widely spreading, oblong lance-shaped, 15-20 mm long, white above, with a broad green median stripe beneath; stamens 6, free from the perianth. **Fruit** a capsule, obtusely 3-angled, with a few seeds in each cell. May-June.—Native of Europe; uncommon escape from cultivation in gardens, roadsides, and occasionally fields and woods.

POLYGONATUM *Solomon's-Seal*   ASPARAGACEAE

Perennial herbs from a horizontal knotty rhizome, the stem erect or arching, bearing in the upper portion numerous alternate leaves in two ranks and short, axillary, 1-15-flowered peduncles with pendent, white to greenish or yellow flowers. Perianth regular, tubular, shortly 6-lobed. Stamens included, inserted on the perianth tube. Ovary ovoid to globose, 3-celled; style slender, shorter than the perianth; stigma capitate, obscurely 3-lobed. Fruit a dark blue or black, several-seeded berry.

1   Leaves completely glabrous . . . . *P. biflorum*
1   Leaves finely pubescent on the veins beneath . . . . *P. pubescens*

Polygonatum biflorum (Walt.) Ell.   MAP 1569
KING SOLOMON'S-SEAL   *native*
Stems slender, 4-6 dm tall, erect or arching. **Leaves** sessile or somewhat clasping, lance-elliptic, 5-10 cm long, 1-3 cm wide, glabrous, paler and glaucous beneath, with 1-5 (rarely 9) nerves, only the midnerve prominent to the apex **Peduncles** slender, 1-2-flowered. **Flowers** greenish white, 14-20 mm long. May-July.—Moist woods and thickets.

Polygonatum pubescens (Willd.) Pursh   MAP 1570
HAIRY SOLOMON'S-SEAL   *native*
Stems slender, 5-9 dm tall, mostly erect. **Leaves** narrowly elliptic to broadly oval, 4-12 cm long, 1-6 cm wide, narrowed below to a short petiole, glabrous above, glaucous and pubescent on the veins beneath, with 3-9 prominent nerves. **Peduncles** slender, usually 1-2 (rarely 3-4)-flowered; pedicels usually shorter than the peduncle. **Flowers** yellowish green, 10-13 mm long. May-July.—Moist woods.

Polygonatum biflorum

STREPTOPUS *Twisted Stalk*   LILIACEAE

Perennial herbs from a rhizome, often branched, with alternate, sessile or clasping leaves, and small, greenish white to purple, solitary or paired, axillary flowers. Perianth campanulate to rotate, its segments separate to the base, essentially alike, the outer whorl usually slightly wider. Stamens 6, adnate to the base of the perianth; filaments widened at base; anthers oblong to linear, apiculate or aristate. Ovary 3-celled with several ovules; style slender (in our species), 3-cleft, 3-lobed, or entire. Fruit a red, ellipsoid to subglobose, many-seeded berry.

1   Leaves entire or minutely denticulate, strongly clasping at the base, glaucous beneath; nodes and upper internodes glabrous (lower internodes sometimes hispid); tepals spreading or curving from near the middle; flowers whitish green . . . . *S. amplexifolius*
1   Leaves prominently ciliate on the margins, the cilia usually visible to the naked eye, sessile or slightly clasping (the larger ones subtending branches more strongly clasping), sometimes paler but not glaucous beneath; nodes and upper internodes ± pubescent or sparsely hispidulous; tepals spreading or recurved only at the tips; flowers usually pinkish (sometimes maroon) . . . . *S. lanceolatus*

1567. *Maianthemum trifolium*   1568. *Ornithogal. umbellatum*   1569. *Polygonatum biflorum*   1570. *Polygonatum pubescens*

Streptopus amplexifolius (L.) DC.
CLASPING TWISTED STALK

MAP 1571
native

Stems 4-10 dm tall, glabrous. **Leaves** ovate, varying to ovate or ovate-lance-shaped, cordate and clasping at base, entire or very minutely toothed, the principal leaves 6-12 cm long and 2-5.5 cm wide. Free portion of the peduncle and the pedicel together 3-5 cm long, jointed at about 2/3 of its length, above the joint 1-flowered or sometimes 2-flowered and abruptly deflexed or twisted. **Perianth segments** greenish white, about 1 cm long, spreading from near the middle; anthers 1-pointed; stigma entire or barely 3-lobed. **Berry** red, usually ellipsoid, about 15 mm long. June-July.—Rich, moist woods.

Streptopus lanceolatus (Ait.) Reveal
LANCE-LEAF TWISTED STALK
   Streptopus roseus Michx.

MAP 1572
native

Stems simple or in larger plants commonly branched, 3-8 dm tall, sparsely and finely pubescent, especially at the nodes. **Leaves** ovate lance-shaped, broadly rounded to a sessile base, finely ciliate, the principal ones 5-9 cm long, 2-3.5 cm wide. **Peduncle** and pedicel combined 1-3 cm long, jointed at or below the middle, always 1-flowered. **Perianth segments** rose-color, about 1 cm long, spreading only near the tip; anthers each double-pointed; lobes of the style nearly 1 mm long. **Berry** red, subglobose, about 1 cm long. May-July.—Rich woods.

Streptopus lanceolatus

TOFIELDIA *Asphodel*
TOFIELDIACEAE

Tofieldia pusilla (Michx.) Pers.
SCOTCH FALSE ASPHODEL

MAP 1573
✔*endangered | native*

Perennial from short rootstock. **Stems** 5-20 cm high, smooth. **Leaves** all base of plant, 2-6 cm long, 1-3 mm wide. **Inflorescence** 5-20 mm long; **flowers** greenish white 1.5-2.5 mm long. **Capsules** 2.5-3 mm long.—Bedrock shores of Lake Superior.

Tofieldia pusilla

TRIANTHA *False Asphodel*
TOFIELDIACEAE

Triantha glutinosa (Michx.) Baker
STICKY FALSE ASPHODEL
   Tofieldia glutinosa (Michx.) Pers.

MAP 1574
✔ *threatened | native*

Perennial herb, from a bulb. **Stems** erect, nearly leafless, 2-5 dm long, covered with sticky hairs. **Leaves** 2-4 from base of plant, linear, hairy, 8-20 cm long and to 8 mm wide, sometimes with 1 bractlike leaf near middle of stem. **Flowers** white, on sticky-hairy stalks 3-6 mm long, in a raceme 2-5 cm long when in flower, becoming longer when fruiting, 2-3 at each node of the raceme, upper flowers opening first; **tepals** 6, oblong lance-shaped, 4 mm long; stamens 6. **Fruit** an oblong capsule, 5-6 mm long; seeds about 1 mm long, with a slender tail at each end. June-July.—Sandy or gravelly shores, interdunal wetlands, calcareous fens, rocky shores of Lake Superior.

TRILLIUM *Trillium; Wake-Robin*
MELANTHIACEAE

Perennial herbs from a stout short rhizome, the erect stem bearing a single whorl of 3 ample leaves and a single, large, terminal, sessile or peduncled flower. Perianth segments distinct to the base, the sepals green, the petals white or colored, often of a different shape. Ovary 3-lobed or 3-6-angled or

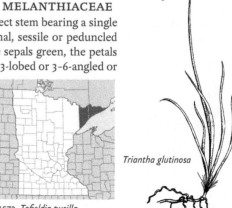

Triantha glutinosa

1571. Streptop. amplexifolius   *1572. Streptopus lanceolatus*   *1573. Tofieldia pusilla*

winged, 3-celled with numerous ovules; style short or none; stigmas 3. Fruit a many-seeded berry. A few species are cultivated, especially *T. grandiflorum.*

1 Plants small; ovary 3-angled to obscurely 3-lobed; leaves definitely petiolate . . . . *T. nivale*
1 Plants larger; ovary strongly 6-angled or -winged and the leaves sessile or subsessile. 2
  2 Petals white to pink (never maroon), 3.5-9 cm long, distinctly longer than the sepals, ± obtuse (occasional small plants with shorter petals—though still longer than sepals—may be recognized by the straight styles and broad obovate petals); stigmatic styles straight (though sometimes spreading) or slightly curved at very tip, uniform in diameter; peduncles held above the leaves . . . . *T. grandiflorum*
  2 Petals white to maroon, usually less than 3.5 cm long (if longer, maroon and/or narrowly acute at tip), seldom much longer than sepals; stigmatic styles spreading, thick at base, tapering, and recurved; peduncles in white-flowered plants (and often also in maroon ones) usually reflexed and held below the leaves 4
    3 Petals white (rarely rosy), less than 2.5 (rarely to 3.5) cm long; f ilaments about as long as the anthers or occasionally as short as half as long; anthers 3-7 mm long, usually pink when fresh . . . . *T. cernuum*
    3 Petals white to maroon, 2-3 (-4) cm long; f ilaments very short, almost always less than 2 mm long and less than 1/4 the length of the anthers; anthers 6-15 mm long, yellowish (to pink in maroon-flowered forms) . . . . *T. flexipes*

Trillium cernuum L.

MAP 1575
native

WHIP-POOR-WILL-FLOWER

Stems slender, 2-4 dm tall. **Leaves** broadly rhombic-obovate, commonly 6-10 cm long at anthesis, acuminate, narrowed from near the middle to an acute base and obscurely petioled. **Peduncle** 1-4 cm long, reflexed or recurved below the leaves. **Sepals** lance-shaped, acuminate, about equaling the petals; **petals** normally white, 1.5-2.5 cm long; anthers 3-7 mm long, to 1/3 longer than the filaments; ovary white or pinkish. May-June.—Conifer swamps, bog margins, moist or wet mixed forests, often with paper birch; thickets along streams; less often in rich hardwood forests.

Trillium cernuum

Trillium flexipes Raf.

MAP 1576
native

NODDING WAKEROBIN

Stems stout or slender, 2-4 dm tall at anthesis. **Leaves** broadly rhombic, at anthesis commonly 8-15 cm long, as wide as long or wider, abruptly acuminate, narrowed from near the middle to a sessile base. **Peduncle** nearly horizontal to somewhat declined, usually 4-12 cm long. **Sepals** lance-shaped, about equaling the petals; **petals** normally white, spreading, ovate lance-shaped to ovate, usualy obtuse, 2-5 cm long; anthers 6-15 mm long, about 2x long as the filaments or longer; ovary white or pinkish, sharply 6-angled. May.—Rich deciduous forests, wet floodplain woods. *Plants with purplish or maroon flowers occur.*

Trillium grandiflorum (Michx.) Salisb.

MAP 1577
native

LARGE-FLOWER WAKEROBIN

Stems 2-4 dm tall at anthesis. **Leaves** ovate to rhombic: or subrotund, at anthesis commonly 8-12 cm long, short-acuminate, narrowed from below the middle to an acute base. **Peduncle** erect or declined, usually 5-8 cm long. **Sepals** lance-shaped, spreading, 3-5 cm long; **petals** normally white, ascending from the base, spreading above, obovate, 4-6 cm long; filaments nearly as long as the anthers and scarcely wider, the whole stamen 15-25 mm long.May-June.—Moist to rather dry deciduous forests, forming large colonies in beech-maple forests; less common in oak-hickory woods, swamps, mixed conifer-hardwoods.

Trillium grandiflorum

1574. *Triantha glutinosa*

1575. *Trillium cernuum*

1576. *Trillium flexipes*

1577. *Trillium grandiflorum*

Trillium nivale Riddell · MAP 1578
SNOW-TRILLIUM · *native*
Stems at anthesis 8-15 cm tall. **Leaves** elliptic to ovate-lance-shaped or ovate, at anthesis 3-5 cm long, acute or usually obtuse, rounded at base to a distinct petiole 5-10 mm long. Peduncle erect or nearly so, 1-3 cm long, becoming recurved. in fruit. Sepals lance-shaped, much shorter than the petals; petals white, elliptic or ovate-elliptic, 2.5-4 cm long, obtuse; anthers 7-10 mm long, somewhat exceeding the slender filaments; ovary subglobose, roundly 3-lobed. March-April, sometimes blooming through snow.—Rich, moist woods; floodplain forests; often adjacent to rivers or streams. *Our smallest and earliest flowering Trillium.*

Trillium nivale

UVULARIA *Bellwort* · COLCHICACEAE

Perennial herbs from a slender rhizome, the erect stem forked above the middle, the lower portion bearing a few bladeless sheaths and up to 4 leaves; leaves sessile or perfoliate, reaching full size after anthesis; flowers yellow or greenish yellow, terminal, but appearing axillary by prolongation of the branches, nodding. Flowers perfect. Perianth segments 6, elongate, distinct. Stamens 6; filaments short. Ovary shallowly 3-lobed, with several ovules in each cell; styles separate to the base or united to beyond the middle. Capsule obovoid and 3-lobed or 3-winged. Seeds subglobose, few in each cell.

1   Leaves perfoliate, finely puberulent (rarely almost glabrous) and usually light or dark green but not glaucous beneath; rhizome short with many crowded roots; mature capsule less than 14 (usually 8-10) mm long. . . . .
     . . . . *U. grandiflora*

1   Leaves sessile, glaucous but glabrous beneath; rhizome elongate, bearing scattered small roots; mature capsule over 15 mm long. . . . . *U. sessilifolia*

Uvularia grandiflora Sm. · MAP 1579
LARGE-FLOWER BELLWORT · *native*
Stem at anthesis 2-5 dm tall, at maturity to 1 m tall, forking above, bearing 0-2 leaves below the fork, 4-8 on the sterile branch, and several leaves and 1-4 flowers on the fertile branch. **Leaves** perfoliate, broadly oval to oblong, to 12 cm long at maturity, minutely pubescent beneath. **Flowers** yellow, nodding; perianth segments 25-50 mm long, acute or acuminate, smooth within. April-May.—Rich woods, preferring calcareous soil.

Uvularia sessilifolia L. · MAP 1580
SESSILE-LEAF BELLWORT · *native*
Stem at anthesis 1-3 dm tall, smooth, bearing 0-2 leaves below the fork and 1 or 2 flowers. **Leaves** at anthesis lance-oblong, acute at both ends, glaucous beneath, at maturity elliptic, to 8 cm long and 3 cm wide, obtuse or rounded at base, nearly smooth on the margins. **Flowers** pale straw-color, perianth segments 12-25 mm long; styles joined for about 3/4 of their length, about equaling the perianth, much exceeding the anthers. **Capsule** 3-angled, distinctly stipitate, commonly 15-20 mm long.—Dry or moist woods. April-May.

Uvularia grandiflora (l)
Uvularia sessilifolia (r)

Orchidaceae ORCHID FAMILY

Perennial herbs, from fleshy or tuberous roots, corms or bulbs. Leaves simple, along the stem and alternate, or mostly at base of plant, stalkless and usually sheathing the stem, parallel-veined, often somewhat fleshy. Flowers perfect (with both staminate and pistillate parts), irregular, showy in some

1578. *Trillium nivale*

1579. *Uvularia grandiflora*

1580. *Uvularia sessilifolia*

1581. *Amerorchis rotundifolia*

species, in heads of 1 or 2 flowers at ends of stems, or with several to many flowers in a spike, raceme or panicle, each flower usually subtended by a bract; sepals 3, green or colored, sometimes resembling the lateral petals, the lateral sepals free, or joined to form an appendage below the lip, or joined with the lateral petals to form a hood over the lip (*Spiranthes*); petals 3 white or colored, the 2 lateral petals alike, the lowest petal different and called the lip; stamens 1-2, attached to the style and forming a stout column; ovary inferior. Fruit a many-seeded capsule, opening by 3 or sometimes 6 longitudinal slits, but remaining closed at tip and base; seeds very small.

One of the world's largest families of vascular plants, with over 900 genera and an estimated 25,000-30,000 species, most of which occur in the tropics.

1   Lip a showy inflated pouch 1-5 cm long 2
   2   Plants with leafy stems; lip a closed pouch (i.e., open only at base above) . . . . ***Cypripedium***
   2   Plants with leaves basal; lip split down middle above or open at base about half its length 3
      3   Basal leaf single, petiolate, the blade less than 7 cm long, produced in late summer and withering after the plant blooms the following spring; lip ca. 1.5-2 cm long, open about half its length basally above; plants less than 20 cm tall. . . . . ***Calypso bulbosa***
      3   Basal leaves 2, longer, tapered to sheathing bases and not distinctly petiolate, present throughout the summer (but not winter); lip ca. 4-5 cm long, split down upper side; plants more than 20 cm tall . . . . ***Cypripedium acaule***
1   Lip showy or inconspicuous, but not an inflated pouch with a small opening, usually ± flat with or without a slender basal spur (or if somewhat saccate, hardly showy and less than 1 cm long). 4
   4   Flower solitary (rarely plants with 2 flowers in a population of 1-flowered ones) 5
      5   Leaf linear, at most up to 7 (very rarely 10) mm wide, often poorly developed at flowering time, ± folded or plicate longitudinally, sheathing stem at base; plant from a small bulbous corm . . . ***Arethusa bulbosa***
      5   Leaf ± elliptic or lanceolate, usually over 7 mm wide and well developed at flowering time, flat, arising near middle of stem, sessile but not sheathing at base; plant from slender roots and rhizome . . . . ***Pogonia ophioglossoides***
   4   Flowers 2 or more on one plant 6
      6   Lip produced into a distinct (usually slender and elongate) spur at base 2-40 mm long (pouch-like and only 2-3 mm in *Coeloglossum*) 7
         7   Leaves cauline. 8
            8   Spur a thick pouch 2-3 mm long, much shorter than the lip . . . . ***Coeloglossum viride***
            8   Spur slender, sometimes ± clavate, 7-40 mm long, ± equaling (at most slightly shorter than) to much longer than the lip . . . . ***Platanthera***
         7   Leaves all basal or nearly so, or absent at flowering time (bracts subtending flowers may be leaflike) 9
            9   Flowers entirely white and/or green, the lip lanceolate to narrowly linear, entire; lateral petals free. . . . . ***Platanthera***
            9   Flowers with white lip (spotted or not) broadly ovate to oblong, often crenate or lobed; lateral petals connivent or fused with dorsal sepal to form a pink to purple hood 10
               10   Leaf 1; lip less than 1 cm long, spotted, notched at apex and with a lateral lobe on each side . . . . ***Amerorchis rotundifolia***
               10   Leaves normally 2; lip over 1 cm long, unspotted, not lobed . . . . ***Galearis spectabilis***
      6   Lip at most somewhat swollen or saccate (but not with a spur 2 mm or more long) 11
         11   Plants lacking green color (except sometimes in fruit), leafless with red, yellow, brown, or purplish stems arising from a coralloid rhizome . . . . ***Corallorhiza***
         11   Plants with green color, bearing leaves at some time in the year (if leaves absent at flowering time or plants lacking green, arising from tubers, corms, or short rhizomes, not a coralloid mass) 12
            12   Leaves a single opposite pair, definitely cauline, not at all sheathing the stem . . . . ***Neottia***
            12   Leaves solitary, alternate, absent, or basal (or almost basal, with sheathing bases). 13
               13   Stem leafy, with 4 or more conspicuous broadly ovate-lanceolate to elliptic leaves; perianth ca. 7-10 mm long; flowers greenish, at least the petals suffused with pink; upper part of stem and axis of inflorescence finely pubescent . . . . ***Epipactis helleborine***
               13   Stem with the leaves fewer than 4, narrow, and/or basal (or absent); perianth various, but if pinkish then 10 mm or more long and the vegetative parts completely glabrous. 14
                  14   Perianth 10-12 mm long, white or creamy; inflorescence dense, spike-like . . . ***Spiranthes***
                  14   Perianth longer or shorter, or not whitish and the inflorescence not spike-like. 15
                     15   Perianth 10 mm or more long, at least in part usually with some shade of pink or purple (yellowish in a form of *Aplectrum*) 16

16 Flowers 2-3 cm or more wide, the lip uppermost, bearded with a tuft of yellow-tipped hairs; leaf solitary (rarely 2) . . . . **Calopogon**

16 Flowers less than 1.5 cm broad, the lip lowermost and not bearded 17

    17 Leaf solitary, petioled, developing in fall and overwintering, usually withered before plant flowers . . . . ***Aplectrum hyemale***

    17 Leaves 2, sheathing at base, developing in current season and present at flowering. . . . . **Liparis**

15 Perianth less than 10 mm long, greenish, white, or yellowish, with no trace of pink or purple 18

    18 Leaves 1 or 2, sheathing at the base, the scape naked to the inflorescence; flowers on short pedicels, the raceme glabrous and not 1-sided nor noticeably twisted . 19

        19 Leaf 1 (very rarely 2); perianth less than 4 mm long . . . . **Malaxis**

        19 Leaves 2; perianth over 4 mm long . . . . **Liparis**

    18 Leaves 3 or more (or withering at flowering time), the stem above them bearing small bracts or scales; flowers sessile or almost so in a narrow spike-like inflorescence, which is 1-sided or spirally twisted, or pubescent (or both) 20

        20 Leaves ovate to elliptic, basal or nearly so, present and firm at flowering time, the midvein and/or other veins margined in white or pale green (not always visible in dry plants); lip pouched or saccate at the base . . . . **Goodyera**

        20 Leaves ovate-elliptic to linear and grass-like, sometimes cauline, often withering at flowering time (in wider-leaved species), not marked with whitish; lip not pouched . . . . **Spiranthes**

AMERORCHIS *Round-Leaf Orchid*

Amerorchis rotundifolia (Banks) Hultén   MAP 1581
ROUND-LEAF ORCHID   *threatened | native*
  Orchis rotundifolia Banks

Perennial herb, roots few from a slender rhizome. **Stems** leafless, smooth, 15-30 cm long. **Leaves** single from near base of plant, oval, 4-15 cm long and 2-8 cm wide; usually with 1-2 bladeless sheaths below. **Flowers** 4 or more, in a raceme 3-8 cm long; **sepals** white to pale pink; petals white to pink or purple-tinged, the 2 lateral **petals** joined with the upper sepal to form somewhat of a hood over the column; lip white, with purple spots, 6-10 mm long and 4-7 mm wide, 3-lobed, the terminal lobe largest and notched at tip; spur about 5 mm long, shorter than lip. June-July.—Conifer swamps (on moss under cedar, tamarack, or black spruce); southward in cold conifer swamps of balsam fir, black spruce and cedar; usually found over underlying limestone and where sphagnum mosses not predominant.

Amerorchis rotundifolia

APLECTRUM *Adam-and-Eve*

Aplectrum hyemale (Muhl.) Torr.   MAP 1582
ADAM-AND-EVE; PUTTY-ROOT   *native*

Perennial from globose corms, which produce a single leaf in the late summer and a bracted scape the following spring; the globose corms are connected by a slender rhizome. **Leaf** single, basal; leaf blade elliptic 10-15 cm long. **Scape** 3-6 dm tall, with a few linear-oblong sheathing bracts. **Flowers** 7-15 in a loose terminal raceme; **sepals and petals** similar, 10-15 mm long, purplish toward the base, brown toward the summit, the sepals spreading, the petals projecting forward over the column; lip white, marked with violet, 10-15 mm long, broadly obovate, with 3 low parallel ridges near the center, obliquely 3-cleft, the lateral lobes curved upward, the terminal dilated and curved upward at the margin. May-June.—Rich woods.

Aplectrum hyemale

ARETHUSA *Dragon's-Mouth*

Arethusa bulbosa L.   MAP 1583
DRAGON'S-MOUTH   *native*

Perennial herb; roots few, fibrous, from a corm. **Stems** leafless, smooth, 1-4 dm long. **Leaves** 1, linear, small and bractlike at flowering time, later expanding to 2 dm long and 3-8 mm wide; lower stem with 2-4 bladeless sheaths. **Flowers** single at ends of stems, **sepals** rose-purple, oblong, 2.5-5 cm long; **petals** joined and more or less hoodlike over the column; lip pink, streaked with rose-purple, 2.5-4 cm long, curved downward near middle. June-July.—Open bogs and conifer swamps (in sphagnum moss), floating mats around bog lakes, calcareous fens; often with grass-pink (*Calopogon tuberosus*) and rose pogonia (*Pogonia ophioglossoides*).

CALOPOGON *Grass-Pink*

Calopogon tuberosus (L.) B.S.P.   MAP 1584
GRASS-PINK   *native*

Perennial herb, from a corm. **Stems** leafless, smooth, 2-7 dm long. **Leaves** 1 near base of plant, linear, 1-4 dm long and 2-15 mm wide. **Flowers** pink to purple, 2-15 in a loose raceme, 3-12 cm long; **sepals** ovate, 1-2.5 cm long; **petals** oblong, 1-2.5 cm long, the lip located above the lateral petals, 1-2 cm long, bearded on inside with yellow-tipped bristles.—Open bogs and floating mats, openings in conifer swamps, calcareous fens near Great Lakes shoreline. *Distinguished from swamp-pink (Arethusa bulbosa) and rose pogonia (Pogonia ophioglossoides) by having a raceme of several flowers vs. single flowers in Arethusa and Pogonia.*

Arethusa bulbosa

ADDITIONAL SPECIES

Calopogon oklahomensis D.H. Goldman (Oklahoma grass-pink, MAP 1585), native, reported from several se Minn locations; typically in somewhat drier situations than the more common *C. tuberosus*. Our 2 species separated as follows:

1 Flowers opening sequentially; dilated upper portion of middle lip lobe usually much wider than long, typically anvil shaped; corms globose to elongate, not forked. . . . . *Calopogon tuberosus*
1 Flowers opening nearly simultaneously; dilated upper portion of middle lip lobe usually much narrower than long, triangular to broadly rounded; corms elongate, forked. . . . . *Calopogon oklahomensis*

CALYPSO *Fairy-Slipper Orchid*

Calypso bulbosa (L.) Oakes   MAP 1586
CALYPSO; FAIRY-SLIPPER   ❧ *threatened | native*

Perennial herb, from a corm. **Stems** 0.5-2 dm long, with 2-3 bladeless sheaths on lower portion. **Leaves** single from the corm, ovate, 3-5 cm long and 2-3 cm wide, petioles 1-5 cm long. **Flowers** 1, nodding at end of stem; **sepals** and **lateral petals** similar, pale purple to pink, lance-shaped, 1-2 cm long and 3-5 mm wide; lip white to pink, streaked with purple, 1.5-2 cm long and 5-10 mm wide, the lip extended to form a white "apron" with several rows of yellow bristles. May-June.—Mature conifer forests or mixed forests of conifers and deciduous trees (such as balsam fir, hemlock, and paper birch), usually in shade; soils rich in woody humus. *The single leaf of calypso appears in late August or September, persists through the winter, and withers after flowering in spring. Between fruiting in June and July and the emergence of the new leaf in late summer of fall, no aboveground portions of the plant may be visible.*

Calopogon tuberosus

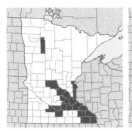

1582. Aplectrum hyemale   *1583. Arethusa bulbosa*   *1584. Calopogon tuberosus*

Calypso bulbosa

COELOGLOSSUM *Bracted Orchid*

Coeloglossum viride (L.) Hartman MAP 1587
BRACTED ORCHID *native*
  Habenaria viridis (L.) R. Br.

Stems slender or stout, 2-5 dm tall. Lowest 1 or 2 leaves reduced to bladeless sheaths; principal **foliage leaves** obovate, 5-12 cm long, to 5 cm wide, the upper progressively narrower and shorter and passing gradually into the bracts. **Inflorescence** loose or compact, 5-20 cm long; bracts foliaceous, lance-shaped, exceeding the flowers, the lowest to 5 cm long. **Flowers** greenish, often tinged with purple; lip oblong, 6-10 mm long, slightly widened distally, terminating in 3 teeth, the central one the shortest; **petals** lance-shaped, nearly concealed by the incurved sepals; spur pouch-like, 2-3 mm long. June-Aug.—Moist woods.

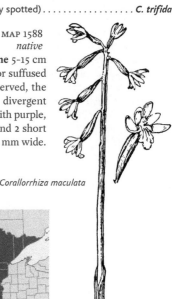

Coeloglossum viride

CORALLORHIZA *Coral-Root*

Yellow, brown, or purplish saprophytic herbs, lacking in chlorophyll, and parasitic on fungi inhabiting their characteristic coral-like rhizomes. Stems with a few sheathing scales toward the base and a terminal raceme of small, usually bicolored flowers. Sepals and lateral petals narrow, similar and nearly equal, spreading or projecting over the column; lateral sepals united with the base of the column. Lip deflexed, oblong to rotund, often with two lateral lobes, the margins usually upturned. Fruit a pendent capsule.

1 Lip with a small lobe or elongate tooth on each side near the base (sometimes difficult to see in dried specimens) 2
  2 Sepals and petals 3-nerved; summit of ovary with a low protuberance (like a rudimentary spur) usually visible below the base of the lip; lip 4.5-7 mm long . . . . ***C. maculata***
  2 Sepals and petals 1-nerved (or the latter rarely weakly 3-nerved); summit of ovary without visible protuberance; lip 2.5-4.5 mm long. . . . . ***C. trifida***
1 Lip entire, or merely denticulate or erose. 3
  3 Sepals and petals 3-5-nerved, 8-15 mm long, conspicuously striped with purple, the lip solid purplish apically . . . . ***C. striata***
  3 Sepals and petals 1-nerved (or faintly 3-nerved), less than 6 mm long, not conspicuously striped 4
    4 Perianth 3-4.5 mm long, purplish; lip white, spotted with purplish . . . . ***C. odontorhiza***
    4 Perianth 4-5.5 mm long, yellowish; lip unspotted white (or rarely spotted) . . . . ***C. trifida***

Corallorhiza maculata (Raf.) Raf. MAP 1588
SPOTTED CORAL-ROOT *native*
Perennial saprophytic herb. **Stems** pinkish purple, 2-5 dm tall. **Raceme** 5-15 cm long, 10-40-flowered. **Sepals and lateral petals** more or less spotted or suffused with purple, narrowly oblong to oblance-shaped, 6-8 mm long, 3-nerved, the lateral sepals somewhat divergent; spur a prominent, sometimes divergent swelling near the summit of the ovary; lip white, irregularly spotted with purple, 6-8 mm long, bearing 2 conspicuous lateral lobes below the middle and 2 short parallel ridges on the face, the terminal lobe rounded and deflexed, 3-4 mm wide. July-Sept.—Woods.

Corallorrhiza maculata

1585. *Calopogon oklahomensis*   1586. *Calypso bulbosa*   1587. *Coeloglossum viride*

Corallorhiza odontorhiza (Willd.) Poir.
MAP 1589
AUTUMN CORAL-ROOT
native

Perennial saprophytic herb. **Stems** purple to brown, or greenish above, 1-2 dm tall. **Raceme** 3-6 cm long, 5-15-flowered. **Sepals and lateral petals** extending forward, over the column, scarcely spreading, oblong, 3-5 mm long, purplish green to dark purple; lip short-clawed or nearly sessile, expanded above into a rotund blade, 3-4 mm long, white, purple-margined and with 2 purple spots, entire or finely erose. Aug-Sept.—Open woods.

Corallorhiza striata Lindl.
MAP 1590
STRIPED CORAL-ROOT
native

Perennial saprophytic herb. **Stems** purple or magenta, rather stout, 2-4 dm tall, with 2-4 acute or cuspidate scales. **Raceme** 5-12 cm long, usually 10-20-flowered. **Sepals and lateral petals** arching forward, oblong lance-shaped, 10-14 mm long, yellowish white with 3 conspicuous longitudinal stripes of purple, usually also purple on the margin; lip 8-12 mm long, white, heavily striped with purple, or purple throughout. May-July.—Moist or dry woods.

Corallorhiza trifida Chatelain
MAP 1591
YELLOW CORALROOT
native

Perennial saprophytic herb, roots absent. **Stems** yellow-green, smooth, 1-3 dm long, single or in clusters from the coral-like rhizome. **Leaves** reduced to 2-3 overlapping sheaths on lower stem. **Flowers** yellow-green, 5-15 in a raceme 3-8 cm long; **sepals and lateral petals** yellow-green, linear, 3-5 mm long, lip white, sometimes with purple-spots, obovate, 3-5 mm long and 2-3 mm wide. **Capsules** drooping, 1-1.5 cm long and 3-7 mm wide. May-June.—Moist to wet, mostly conifer woods, swamps (often under white cedar); usually where shaded.

Corallorhiza trifida

CYPRIPEDIUM *Lady's-Slipper*

Erect perennial herbs, from coarse, fibrous roots. Stems unbranched, often clumped, hairy. Leaves 2 or more at base of plant or along stem, broad. Flowers 1 or 2, large and mostly showy at ends of stems, white, pink or yellow; lateral sepals similar to lateral petals, the sepals joined to form a single appendage below the lip; lateral petals free and spreading, lip inflated and pouchlike, projecting forward; stamens 2, 1 on each side of column. Fruit a many-seeded capsule.

HYBRIDS
Cypripedium × andrewsii A.M. Fuller, is a hybrid between *C. candidum* and *C. parviflorum;* known from several Minn locations.

1 Lip pouch pink to purple; leaves 2 at base of stem . . . . **C. acaule**
1 Lip pouch yellow or white; leaves 3 or more on stem 2
   2 Pouch yellow, sometimes brown- or purple-dotted 3
      3 Sepals and petals red-brown; lateral petals strongly twisted, brown-purple; pouch less than 4 cm long . .
       . . . . **C. parviflorum var. makasin**
      3 Sepals and petals yellow to brown-green; lateral petals wavy, green with red-brown streaks; pouch more than 4 cm long . . . . **C. parviflorum var. pubescens**
   2 Pouch white to pink, or pink with white patches 4
      4 Pouch projected downward into a cone-shaped spur . . . . **C. arietinum**
      4 Pouch not spurred. 5
        5 Sepals and lateral petals white; lip 3-5 cm long . . . . **C. reginae**
        5 Sepals and lateral petals green; lip 1.5-2 cm long . . . . **C. candidum**

1588. *Corallorhiza maculata*   1589. *Corallorhi. odontorhiza*   1590. *Corallorhiza striata*   1591. *Corallorhiza trifida*

Cypripedium acaule Ait. MAP 1592
PINK LADY'S-SLIPPER *native*

Perennial herb, from coarse rhizomes; roots long and cordlike. **Stems** leafless, 2-4 dm long, glandular-hairy. **Leaves** 2 at base of plant, opposite, oval to obovate, 1-2 dm long and 3-10 cm wide, thinly hairy, stalkless. **Flowers** 1, nodding at end of stem; **sepals and lateral petals** yellow-green to green-brown, the 2 lower sepals joined to form a single sepal below the lip; **lip** drooping, pink with red veins, 3-5 cm long, cleft along the upper side and hiding the opening. May-June.—Forests, typically where shaded, acidic, and nutrient-poor; sometimes on hummocks in conifer swamps.

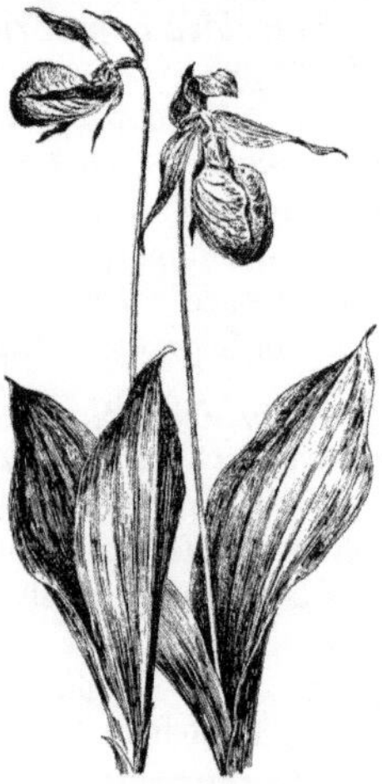

Cypripedium acaule

Cypripedium arietinum Ait. f. MAP 1593
RAM'S-HEAD LADY'S-SLIPPER *threatened | native*

Perennial herb, from a coarse rhizome, roots long and cordlike. **Stems** slender, 1-4 dm long, thinly hairy. **Leaves** 3-5, above middle of stem, stalkless, oval, often folded, 5-10 cm long and 1.5-3 cm wide, finely hairy. **Flowers** 1 or sometimes 2 at ends of stems; **sepals and lateral petals** similar, green-brown; lip an inflated pouch, 1.5-2.5 cm long, white or pink-tinged, with prominent red-veins, extended downward to form a conical pouch. Late May-June.—Conifer swamps, wet forest openings (often with white cedar); also in drier, sandy, conifer and mixed conifer-deciduous forests. *Our smallest and rarest lady's-slipper.*

Cypripedium candidum Muhl. MAP 1594
SMALL WHITE LADY'S-SLIPPER *native*

Perennial herb, from a rhizome, roots long and cordlike. **Stems** 1.5-3 dm long, hairy. **Leaves** 2-4, upright, alternate along upper stem, oval, 5-15 cm long and 2-5 cm wide, sparsely glandular-hairy, stalkless; reduced to overlapping sheathing scales below. **Flowers** 1 at end of stems, the subtending bract leaflike, erect, 3-8 cm long; **sepals and lateral petals** green-yellow, often streaked with purple, the lateral sepals joined below lip, notched at tip; lateral petals linear lance-shaped, sometimes twisted, 2-4 cm long; lip a small inflated pouch, 1.5-2 cm long, white with faint purple veins. May-June.—Calcium-rich wet meadows, low prairie, wet shores, calcareous fens (often with shrubby cinquefoil, *Potentilla fruticosa*); usually where open and sunny.

Cypripedium arietinum

Cypripedium parviflorum var. makasin (Farw.) Sheviak MAP 1595
YELLOW LADY'S-SLIPPER *native*

Cypripedium calceolus var. *parviflorum* (Salisb.) Fernald

Perennial herb, from rhizomes, roots long and numerous. **Stems** 1.5-6 dm long, glandular-hairy. **Leaves** 2-5, alternate along stem, ascending, oval, 5-18 cm long and 2-7 cm wide, sparsely hairy, stalkless. **Flowers** 1 (rarely 2) at ends of stems; **sepals** purple-brown, the lateral sepals joined below the lip, notched at tip; **lateral petals** linear, purple-brown, spirally twisted, 2-5 cm long; **lip** an inflated pouch, 1.5-3 cm long, yellow, often with purple veins and spots near opening. May-July.—Conifer swamps, wet meadows, fens, and moist forests (often under cedar); sphagnum mosses are usually sparse; sites are shaded or sunny, with organic or mineral, often calcium-rich soil; in s Minn also in open, calcium-rich swales.

Our two varieties may be distinguished by the size of the pouch (lip) and the color of the sepals and petals: in var. *makasin*, the lip is mostly 2-3 cm long, and the sepals and petals are dark red; in var. *pubescens*, the lip is mostly 3-6 cm long and the sepals and petals are yellow-green; however, intermediate forms may occur.

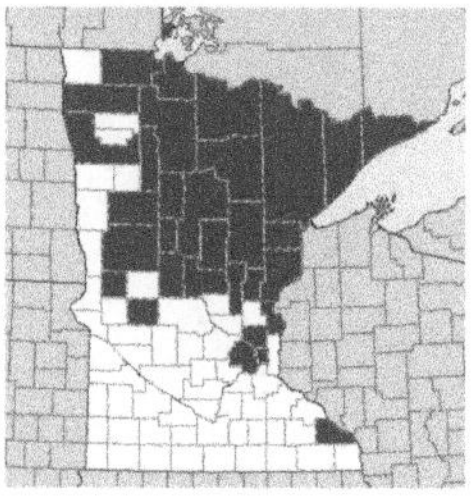

1592. Cypripedium acaule

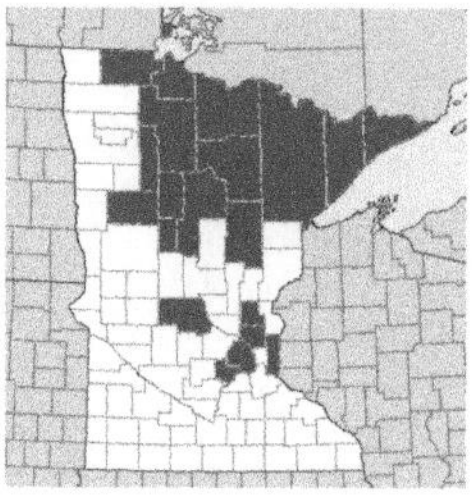

1593. Cypripedium arietinum

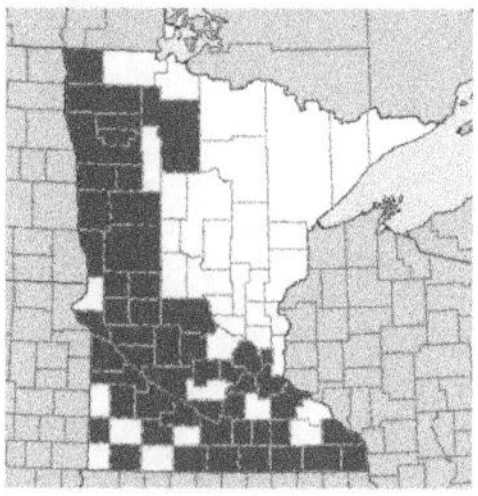

1594. Cypripedium candidum

Cypripedium candidum

Cypripedium parviflorum var. pubescens (Willd.) Knight
YELLOW LADY'S-SLIPPER

MAP 1596
native

Cypripedium calceolus var. pubescens (Willd.) Correll

Perennial herb, from a rhizome, roots long and numerous. **Stems** 1.5-6 dm long, glandular-hairy. **Leaves** 3-6, alternate along stem, ascending, ovate to oval, 8-20 cm long and 3-8 cm wide, sparsely hairy. **Flowers** 1 (rarely 2) at ends of stems; **sepals** yellow-green, the lateral sepals joined below the lip, notched at tip; **lateral petals** linear, yellow-green, often streaked with red-brown, usually spirally twisted, 4-8 cm long; **lip** an inflated pouch, 3-6 cm long, yellow, often with purple veins near opening. May-July.—Conifer swamps, bogs, fens, prairies, especially where soils derived from limestone; also in wetter hardwood forests.

Cypripedium reginae Walt.
SHOWY LADY'S-SLIPPER

MAP 1597
native

Perennial herb, from a coarse rhizome, roots many, long and cordlike. **Stems** 4-10 dm long, strongly glandular-hairy. **Leaves** 4-12, alternate along stem, spreading or ascending, broadly oval, 10-25 cm long, 4-12 cm wide, abruptly tapered to tip, nearly smooth to hairy, stalkless; reduced to sheaths at base. **Flowers** 1 or often 2 at ends of stems, the subtending bract leaflike, 6-12 cm long; **sepals and lateral petals** white, the lateral sepals joined to form an appendage under the lip, rounded at tip; **lip** an inflated pouch, 3-5 cm long, white, streaked and spotted with pink or purple. June-July.—Conifer and hardwood swamps (especially balsam fir-cedar-tamarack swamps), bogs, calcareous fens, sedge meadows, floating mats, wet openings, wet clayey slopes, ditches; especially where open and sunny; most abundant in openings in wet forests and swamps not dominated by sphagnum mosses. *Showy lady's-slipper is our largest lady's-slipper and the official state flower of Minnesota. Avoid touching plants as the hairs can be irritating.*

C. parviflorum var. pubescens

EPIPACTIS *Helleborine*

Epipactis helleborine (L.) Crantz
HELLEBORINE

MAP 1598
introduced (invasive)

Perennial herb. **Stems** erect, to 8 dm tall. **Leaves** alternate, sessile and clasping, ovate to lance-shaped, the lower to 10 cm long, the upper progressively shorter and narrower. **Flowers** in a terminal, many-flowered raceme 1-3 dm long; bracts linear or narrowly lance-shaped, the lower surpassing the flowers; **sepals and lateral petals** ovate-lance-shaped, 10-14 mm long, acute, dull green, strongly veined with purple; **lip** greenish and purple, strongly saccate in the basal half, the terminal lobe broadly ovate, crested at its base with two elevated swellings. July-Aug.—Native of Europe; established and spreading in deciduous and mixed woods.

Cypripedium reginae

GALEARIS *Showy Orchid*

Galearis spectabilis (L.) Raf.
SHOWY ORCHID

MAP 1599
native

Orchis spectabilis L.

Perennial herb. **Leaves** 2, rather fleshy, narrowly obovate to broadly elliptic, 8-15 cm long. **Scape** 1-2 dm tall, stout; bracts foliaceous, oblong lance-shaped, 15-50 mm long. **Sepals and lateral petals** pink to pale purple, 13-18 mm long, all connivent; **lip** white, 15-20 mm long, rhombic-obovate; **spur** stout, about equaling the lip. May-June.—Rich woods.

Galearis spectabilis   *Epipactis helleborine*

GOODYERA *Rattlesnake-Plantain*

Perennial herbs from a short rhizome, plants glandular-pubescent on the scape, bracts, ovary, and sepals. Leaves in a basal cluster, commonly reticulated with white, narrowed to a broad, petiole-like base. Flowers in a spike-like raceme of white or greenish flowers, atop an erect scape with several scale-like bract. Upper sepal and lateral petals coherent by their margins, forming a concave galea extending forward over the lip. Lateral sepals free, scarcely spreading, except at the tip. Lip shorter than the galea, conspicuously pouch-like at base, prolonged upwards into a horizontal or deflexed beak; lateral petals white.

1 Stem with usually 7-10 cauline bracts (undeveloped leaves); beak of lip (beyond the large pouch) less than 1 mm long, about 1/4 the total length of the lip or usually less; inflorescence ± densely flowered on all sides **G. pubescens**
1 Stem with 2-5 cauline bracts; beak of lip 1-2 mm long, about 1/2 the total length of the lip; pouch shallow or deep; inflorescence strongly one-sided or ± loosely flowered on all sides 2
   2 Lip deeply pouched, the pouch about as deep as long, the beak often strongly turned downward at maturity; plants mostly 10-20 cm tall; largest leaf blades mostly 1-2 cm long; cauline bracts 2-4 (usually 3). . . **G. repens**
   2 Lip shallowly pouched, the pouch longer than deep, the beak horizontal or slightly recurved; plants usually 17-25 cm tall; largest leaf blades mostly 2-4 cm long; cauline bracts usually 4-5 . . . . **G. tesselata**

Goodyera pubescens (Willd.) R. Br.
                                           MAP 1600
DOWNY RATTLESNAKE-PLANTAIN   *native*
Stem rather stout, 2-4 dm tall. **Leaf blades** ovate or ovate-lance-shaped, 3-6 cm long, with 5 or 7 white veins and numerous white reticulate veinlets. **Raceme** dense, many-flowered, 4-10 cm long. **Galea** broadly elliptic, very convex, 4-4.5 mm long, upturned at the summit; **lateral sepals** broadly ovate to obovate, 3.5-4 mm long, abruptly short-acuminate; **lip** subglobose, 3.5-4 mm long, its straight beak less than 1 mm long and scarcely projecting beyond the ventricose body. July-Aug.—Dry woods.

Goodyera repens (L.) R. Br.
                                           MAP 1601
DWARF RATTLESNAKE-PLANTAIN   *native*
Stem slender, 1-3 dm tall, glandular-pubescent. **Leaf blades** ovate to oblong, 1.5-3 cm long. **Raceme** loosely flowered, one-sided, 3-6 cm long. **Galea** 3.5-5 mm long; **lateral sepals** slightly shorter, broadly ovate; **lip** deeply pouchlike at base, its beak triangular, acute, abruptly deflected. Anther blunt. July-Aug.—Dry woods.

Goodyera tesselata Lodd.
                                           MAP 1602
CHECKERED RATTLESNAKE-PLANTAIN   *native*
Stem 1.5-4 dm tall. **Leaf blades** ovate or ovate-lance-shaped, 3-5 cm long. **Raceme** loosely flowered, often spiral, 4-10 cm long. **Galea** strongly convex, 4-5 mm long; **lateral sepals** ovate, about 4 mm long; **lip** about 3.5 mm long, strongly saccate at base, narrowed distally to a beak about as long as the body, with upturned sides and blunt or rounded at the tip; anther abruptly narrowed to a conspicuous sharp beak. July-Aug.—Dry woods.

Goodyera pubescens

LIPARIS *Wide-Lip Orchid*

Low perennial herbs from a solid bulb. Leaves at basal few and scalelike and with a pair of larger, shining leaves on the stem. Flowers atop a naked scape in a loose raceme. Sepals spreading, linear-oblong with incurved margins. Lateral petals narrowly linear, usually deflected forward under the lip, rolled and twisted, hence appearing thread-like. Lip broad above a narrowed base.

1595. C. parviflorum makasin   *1596. C. parviflorum pubescens*   *1597. Cypripedium reginae*   *1598. Epipactis helleborine*

1   Lip ca. 10 mm long, purplish; capsules equaling or shorter than pedicels. . . . . *L. liliifolia*
1   Lip 4-6 mm long, yellow-green; capsules longer than pedicels . . . . *L. loeselii*

Liparis liliifolia (L.) L.C. Rich.   MAP 1603
BROWN WIDE-LIP ORCHID   *native*
Perennial herb. **Stems** 1-2 dm tall, topped with a loose raceme of 5-30 flowers.
Leaves oval to elliptic, 5-15 cm long, 1/3-1/2 as wide. **Pedicels** 5-10 mm long,
widely spreading; **sepals** greenish white, linear-oblong, 10-12 mm long, about 2
mm wide; **lateral petals** greenish to pale purple, 10-12 mm long, projecting
forward under the lip and often crossed; **lip** pale purple, broadly obovate, almost
truncate at the summit, 10-12 mm long, apiculate, minutely erose. June, July.
—Rich woods.

Liparis loeselii (L.) L.C. Rich.   MAP 1604
FEN-ORCHID   *native*
Small, smooth perennial herb, from a bulblike base. **Stems** erect, 1-2.5 dm long,
upper stem somewhat angled in section. **Leaves** 2 from base of plant, ascending,
sheathing at base, shiny, lance-shaped to oval, 4-15 cm long and 1-4 cm wide.
Flowers 2-15, yellow-green, small, upright, in an open raceme 2-10 cm long and
1-2 cm wide; **sepals** narrowly lance-shaped, 4-6 mm long and 1-2 mm wide;
lateral petals linear, 3-5 mm long, often twisted and bent forward under the lip;
lip yellow-green, obovate, 4-5 mm long, tipped with a short point. **Capsules**
persistent, short-cylindric, 8-12 mm long. June-Aug.—Conifer swamps, fens,
floating mats, streambanks, sandy shores, ditches; soils peaty to mineral, acid to
calcium-rich.

Liparis loeselii

MALAXIS *Adder's-Mouth Orchid*
Small perennial herbs. Leaves 1-5 from base of plant or single along stem. Flowers green-white, spaced
or crowded in slender or cylindric racemes at ends of stems.

1   Stem leaves 2 or more; lip erect . . . . *M. paludosa*
1   Stem leaf solitary; lip deflected 2
    2   Flowers evenly spaced in a raceme 5-11 cm long; lip pointed, not lobed. . . . . *M. monophyllos*
    2   Flowers crowded near top of raceme, the raceme 2-5 cm long; lip deeply lobed . . . . *M. unifolia*

Malaxis monophyllos (L.) Sw.   MAP 1605
WHITE ADDER'S-MOUTH ORCHID   *native*
    Malaxis brachypoda (Gray) Fern.
Perennial herb, from a bulblike base; roots few, fibrous. **Stems** smooth, 1-2 dm
long. **Leaves** single, appearing to be attached well above base of stem, the leaf
base clasping stem, ovate to oval, 3-7 cm long and 1.5-4 cm wide. **Flowers** small,
green-white, 14-30 or more, in a long, slender, spike-like raceme 4-11 cm long and
to 1 cm wide; on stalks 1-2 mm long, the flowers evenly spaced in the raceme; **lip**
heart-shaped, bent downward, 2-3 mm long and 1-2 mm wide, narrowed at
middle to form a long, lance-shaped tip, with a pair of lobes at base. June-Aug.
—Conifer swamps (white cedar, balsam fir, black spruce), especially in wet
depressions and where soils are marly; sphagnum moss hummocks in conifer
swamps, wet hardwood forests. *Ours are **var. brachypoda** (Gray) F. Morris & Eames.*

Malaxis monophyllos

1599. *Galearis spectabilis*

1600. *Goodyera pubescens*

1601. *Goodyera repens*

1602. *Goodyera tesselata*

Malaxis paludosa (L.) Sw.
BOG ADDER'S-MOUTH ORCHID
Hammarbya paludosa (L.) Kuntze

MAP 1606
🌿 *endangered | native*

Small perennial herb, from a bulblike base; roots few, fibrous. **Stems** leafless, smooth, 7-15 cm long. **Leaves** 2-5 from base of plant, obovate, 1-2 cm long and 0.5-1 cm wide, clasping stem at base. **Flowers** small, yellow-green, 10 or more in a slender, spikelike raceme 3-9 cm long and about 5 mm wide, the flowers evenly spaced in the raceme, twisted so that lip is uppermost in the flowers; lip very small, ovate, 1-1.5 mm long and 0.5 mm wide. July-Aug.—Sphagnum moss hummocks in black spruce swamps, usually where somewhat open. *A ± circumboreal species, south in USA to northern Minnesota.*

Malaxis unifolia Michx.
MAP 1607
GREEN ADDER'S-MOUTH ORCHID   *native*

Small perennial herb, from a bulblike base; roots few, fibrous. **Stems** smooth, 1-3 dm long. **Leaves** single, attached near middle of stem, ovate, 2-7 cm long and 1-4 cm wide. **Flowers** small, green, numerous in a cylindric raceme 1.5-6 cm long and 1-2 cm wide, the upper flowers crowded, the lower flowers more widely spaced; **lip** very small, 1-2 mm long, with 3 teeth at tip. June-Aug.—Sphagnum moss hummocks in swamps, sedge meadows, thickets; also in drier forests including pine plantations.

Malaxis unifolia

Malaxis paludosa

NEOTTIA *Twayblade*

Perennial herbs. Stems with a pair of opposite leaves near middle, stems smooth below leaves, hairy above. Leaves broad, stalkless. Flowers small, green to purple, in a raceme at end of stem, the lip 2-lobed or deeply parted. *Formerly considered part of genus Listera.*

1   Lip 3-5 mm long, divided to about middle into 2 narrow segments . . . . ***N. cordata***
    Lip 7-12 mm long, shallowly notched or divided 1/3 of length, the segments broad 2
    2   Lip wide at base, with a pair of auricles . . . . ***N. auriculata***
    2   Lip narrowed to base, auricles absent . . . . ***N. convallarioides***

Neottia auriculata (Wiegand) Szlach.
AURICLED TWAYBLADE
Listera auriculata Wieg.

MAP 1608
🌿 *endangered | native*

Perennial herb, roots fibrous. **Stems** 1-2 dm long, smooth below leaves, hairy above. **Leaves** 2 near middle of stem, opposite, ovate, 2-5 cm long and 2-4 cm wide. **Flowers** pale green, 8-15 in a raceme 4-8 cm long and 2-3 cm wide, on stalks 2-5 mm long; **lip** oblong, 6-10 mm long and 2-5 mm wide, the base with a pair of small clasping auricles, the tip cleft for about 1/4-1/3 of its length. June-Aug. —Alluvial sand along rivers, often under alders, occasionally in moist conifer or mixed conifer and deciduous forests; usually where shaded.

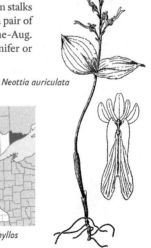

Neottia auriculata

1603. Liparis liliifolia

1604. Liparis loeselii

1605. Malaxis monophyllos

Neottia convallarioides (Sw.) Rich.   (NO MAP)
BROAD-LIP TWAYBLADE   *native*
     Listera convallarioides (Sw.) Nutt.

Perennial herb, roots fibrous. **Stems** 1-3 dm long, glandular-hairy above leaves, smooth below. **Leaves** 2, opposite near middle of stem, broadly ovate, 3-6 cm long and 2-5 cm wide, stalkless. **Flowers** yellow-green, 6-20 in a raceme 4-10 cm long and 2-3 cm wide; **lip** wedge-shaped, 9-11 mm long and to 6 mm wide at tip, usually with a small tooth on each side near the base, the tip shallowly 2-lobed. July-Aug.—Seeps in forests, cedar swamps, wet, mixed conifer-deciduous woods, streambanks; Cook County.

Neottia cordata (L.) Rich.   MAP 1609
HEART-LEAF TWAYBLADE   *native*
     Listera cordata (L.) R. Br.

Perennial herb, roots fibrous. **Stems** 1-3 dm long, glandular-hairy above the leaves, smooth below. **Leaves** 2, opposite near middle of stem, 1-4 cm long and 1-3 cm wide, stalkless. **Flowers** green to red-purple, 6-20 in a raceme 3-12 cm long and 1-2 cm wide; **lip** slender, 3-5 mm long, with 2 teeth on side near base, the tip cleft halfway or more into spreading linear lobes. June-July.—Bogs and conifer swamps, where usually on sphagnum moss hummocks; hemlock groves.

Neottia convallarioides

PLATANTHERA *Rein-Orchid*

Perennial herbs, from a cluster of fleshy roots. Stems erect, smooth. Leaves mostly along the stem, upright, reduced to sheaths at base and upward on stem; leaves basal in *P. orbiculata*. Flowers white or green, several to many in a spike or raceme; upper sepal joined with petals to form a hood over the column; lateral sepals spreading; lip linear to ovate or 3-lobed, entire, toothed or fringed, extended backward into a spur, the spur commonly curved; stamens 1, the anther attached to the top of the short column. Fruit a many-seeded capsule. *Previously included in* **Habenaria**, *that genus now considered tropical, and Platanthera occurring in temperate regions.*

1   Lip prominently ciliate or fringed 2
    2   Flowers pink-purple; divisions of the lip broadly fan-shaped, copiously lacerate-fringed, but the fringe usually cut less than half the distance to the base of the division of the lip . . . . ***P. psycodes***
    2   Flowers creamy, greenish, or white; at least the lateral divisions of the lip more narrowly cuneate, mostly cut into a long fringe more than half their length 3
       3   Flowers creamy or green-yellow, in narrow compact spikes to 3 cm wide; lip fringed nearly to base ***P. lacera***
       3   Flowers white, large, in spikes more than 3 cm wide; lip less deeply fringed . . . . ***P. praeclara***
1   Lip entire or toothed, but not fringed 4
    4   Leaves all basal, the stem at most with reduced bracts 5
       5   Leaves about twice as long as wide, or longer; spur less than 12 mm long 6
          6   Lip ± cuneate, with truncate 3-toothed or crenate tip; spur 7-11 mm long, much exceeding the lip . . .
             . . . . ***P. clavellata***
          6   Lip tapered to a pointed or rounded, untoothed tip ; spur about equaling lip or at most ca. 2 mm longer
             . . . . ***P. obtusata***
       5   Leaves less than twice as long as broad, orbicular or almost so; spur 16-40 mm long 7
          7   Scape naked (rarely with a bract); spurs (16-24 mm long) tapered ± evenly to rounded tip; lip yellowish green, tending to turn upward near the end . . . . ***P. hookeri***
          7   Scape with 1-6 bracts between leaves and inflorescence; spurs parallel-sided or even somewhat club-shaped toward tip; lip whitish green, tending to turn downward . . . . ***P. orbiculata***
    4   Leaves cauline (along the stem) 8

1606. Malaxis paludoso   *1607. Malaxis unifolia*   *1608. Neottia auriculata*   *1609. Neottia cordata*

8 Lip truncate and 2-3-toothed or -lobed at tip . . . . *P. clavellata*

8 Lip tapered, rounded (or almost truncate and obscurely crenulate) but not 2-3-toothed at tip. 9

9 Lip much shorter than the spur, broadly rounded (or almost truncate) at tip, with an erect tubercle near the base and a lateral tooth or projection on each side near the base . . . . *P. flava*

9 Lip 1-2 mm shorter than, about equaling, or slightly longer than the spur, tapered to narrow tip, with neither a tubercle nor lateral teeth (at most, broadly widened basally) 10

10 Flowers pure white, lip strongly expanded basally . . . . *P. dilatata*

10 Flowers green, greenish yellow or greenish white, lip cuneate to strap-shaped, not or only slightly widened at base. 11

11 Anther sacs essentially in contact above the rounded stigma (separated at tip by less than 0.3 mm); lips 2.5-5 mm long. . . . . *P. aquilonis*

11 Anther sacs separated at tip by ca. 0.4 mm or more, stigma pointed; lips 4-8 mm long. . . . . *P. huronensis*

Platanthera aquilonis Sheviak

MAP 1610

BOG ORCHID   *native*

Perennial herb. **Stems** 60 cm long. **Leaves** several, ascending to spreading, gradually reduced to bracts upwards; **blade** linear-lanceolate, 3-23 cm long and to 4 cm wide. **Spikes** lax to very dense. **Flowers** not showy, yellowish green with dull yellowish lip; **lateral sepals** spreading to reflexed; **petals** ovate, margins entire; **lip** descending, 2.5-6 cm long and to 1.5 mm wide, projecting, not thickened at base, margins entire; **spur** clavate or sometimes rather cylindric, 2-5 mm long, apex usually broadly obtuse. May-Aug.—Moist to wet including moist forests, cedar swamps, riverbanks, wet meadows, fens, ditches and borrow pits. *The Platanthera hyperborea complex, including **P. dilatata**, **P. aquilonis**, and **P. huronensis**, are often difficult to separate; living rather than dried plants are easiest to identify.*

Platanthera clavellata (Michx.) Luer

MAP 1611

GREEN WOODLAND ORCHID   *native*

   Habenaria clavellata (Michx.) Spreng.

Perennial herb. **Stems** slender, 1-4 dm long. **Foliage leaf** 1, linear-oblong to oblong lance-shaped, commonly 7-16 cm long, to 3 cm wide, blunt; **upper leaves** 1 or few, much reduced, the uppermost linear, scale-like. **Inflorescence** open, 5-15-flowered, 2-6 cm long; bracts narrowly lance-shaped, shorter than the flowers. **Flowers** divergent from the axis, white or tinged with green or yellow, twisted to one side so that the spur is lateral; **lip** broadly cuneate, 3-5 mm long, shallowly 3-lobed at the summit; **petals and sepals** broadly ovate, about equal; **spur** strongly curved, dilated at the tip, 8-12 mm long. July-Aug.—Acid bogs and wet soils, especially in sphagnum moss.

Platanthera dilatata (Pursh) Lindl.

MAP 1612

WHITE BOG-ORCHID   *native*

   Habenaria dilatata (Pursh) Hook.
   Piperia dilatata (Pursh) Szlach. & Rutk.

Perennial herb, strongly clove-scented, roots fleshy. **Stems** stout or slender, to 1 m long. **Leaves** 3-6, alternate along stem, upright, lance-shaped, to 10-20 cm long and 1-3 cm wide, with 1-2 small, bractlike leaves above and 1 bladeless sheath at base of stem. **Flowers** 10-60, bright white, upright, in a raceme 1-2.5 dm long; **lateral sepals** lance-shaped, 4-9 mm long and 1-3 mm wide; **lateral petals** similar but joined with upper sepal to form somewhat of a hood over the column; **lip** lance-shaped, widened at base, 6-8 mm long; **spur** slender, 4-8 mm long. June-

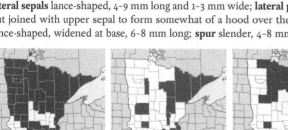

Platanthera clavellata

1610. *Platanthera aquilonis*   1611. *Platanthera clavellata*   1612. *Platanthera dilatata*   1613. *Platanthera flava*

July.—Wet, open bogs and floating mats, conifer swamps, streambanks, shores and seeps; often where sandy or calcium-rich (as in calcareous fens), not in deep sphagnum moss. *Similar to* ***northern bog-orchid*** *(Platanthera huronensis) but with white rather than green-tinged flowers as in P. huronensis.*

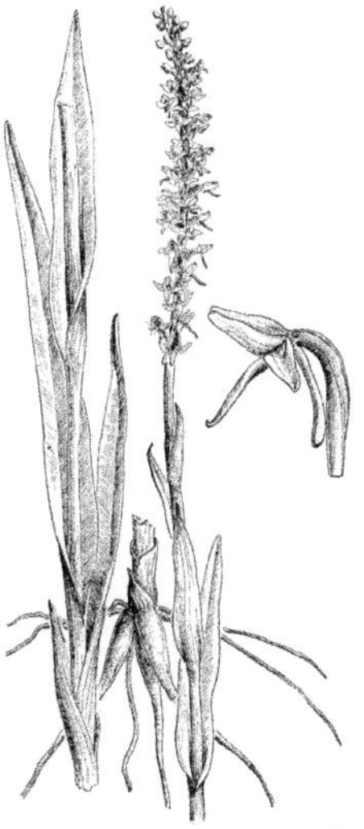

Platanthera dilatata

Platanthera flava (L.) Lindl.

MAP 1613

PALE GREEN ORCHID

threatened | native

Habenaria flava (L.) R. Br.

Perennial herb, roots fleshy. **Stems** 3-7 dm long. **Leaves** 2-4, alternate along stem, lance-shaped or oval, to 5-15 cm long and 2-5 cm wide, with 1-3 bractlike leaves above. **Flowers** 15 or more, green-yellow or green, stalkless, in a raceme 5-15 cm long and 2-4 cm wide; **sepals** ovate, 2-3 mm long; **lip** bent downward, 3-6 mm long, the margin irregular, with a tooth near base on each side; **spur** 4-6 mm long. June-July.—Wet depressions in hardwood swamps, alder thickets, sedge meadows, moist sand prairies; often where calcium-rich, sometimes where disturbed. *Ours are* ***var. herbiola*** *(R. Br.) Luer.*

Platanthera hookeri (Torr.) Lindl.

MAP 1614

HOOKER'S ORCHID

native

Habenaria hookeri Torr.

Perennial herb; **scape** 2-4 dm tall, bractless, rising from a few fleshy roots. **Leaves** 2, basal, commonly broadly elliptic to rotund, 6-12 cm long, usually 2/3 to fully as wide, blunt or rounded, abruptly narrowed to the base. **Flowers** sessile, yellowish green, ascending; **lip** triangular-lance-shaped, directed outward, upcurved, 8-12 mm long; **lateral petals** lance-shaped, incurved and more or less adjacent under the upper sepal; **spur** 13-24 mm long, directed, downward, tapering to the tip. June-July.—Coniferous or mixed forests, wooded dunes, soils often sandy.

Platanthera huronensis

Platanthera huronensis (Nutt.) Lindl.

MAP 1615

NORTHERN BOG-ORCHID

native

Habenaria hyperborea (L.) R. Br.

Perennial herb, roots fleshy. **Stems** 2-8 dm long. **Leaves** 2-7, alternate on stem, linear to oblong, 5-30 cm long and 2-5 cm wide, with 1-3 smaller leaves above. **Flowers** small, green, erect, many in a raceme 4-25 cm long; **lateral sepals** ovate and spreading; **lateral petals** lance-shaped, curved upward and joined with upper sepal to form a loose hood over column; **lip** lance-shaped, 3-7 mm long, not abruptly widened at base; **spur** curved forward under the lip, about as long as lip, 3-7 mm long. June-Aug.—Moist to wet forests and swamps, thickets, streambanks, wet meadows, wet sand along lakeshores, ditches.

Platanthera lacera (Michx.) G. Don

MAP 1616

GREEN FRINGED ORCHID

native

Habenaria lacera (Michx.) R. Br.

Perennial herb, roots fleshy. **Stems** 3-8 dm long. **Leaves** 3-7, alternate on stem, lance-shaped to oval, to 5-15 cm long and 1-4 cm wide; upper leaves much smaller. **Flowers** white or green-white, in a usually compact, many-flowered raceme, 5-20 cm long and 2-5 cm wide; **sepals** broadly oval, 4-7 mm long, the lateral ones deflexed behind the lip; **lateral petals** linear, entire; **lip** 10-16 mm long and 5-20 mm wide, deeply 3-lobed, each lobe fringed with a few long segments; **spur** curved, 1-2 cm long. June-Aug.—Hummocks in open sphagnum bogs, conifer bogs, swamps, wet meadows, sandy prairie, thickets, ditches.

Platanthera lacera

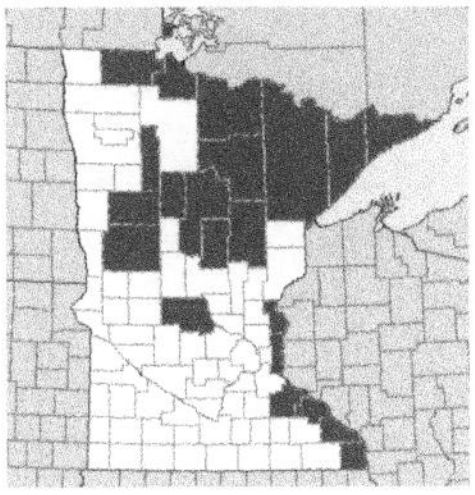

1614. Platanthera hookeri

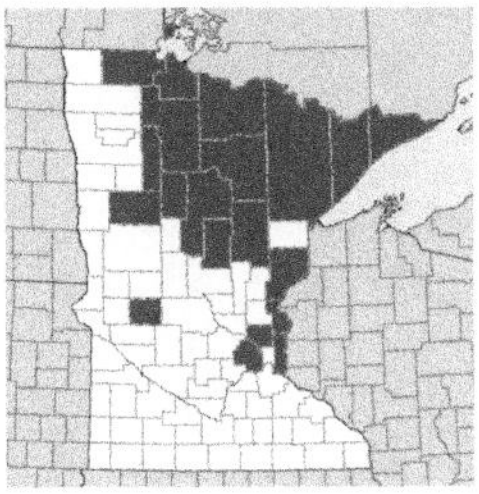

1615. Platanthera huronensis

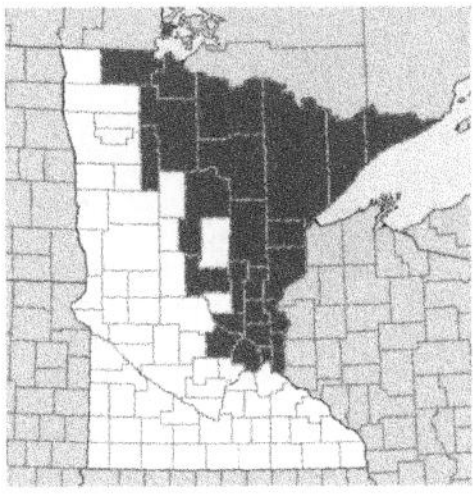

1616. Platanthera lacera

Platanthera obtusata (Banks) Lindl.

BLUNT-LEAF ORCHID

Habenaria obtusata (Banks) Richards.

MAP 1617
native

Perennial herb, roots fleshy. **Stems** leafless, slender, 1-3 dm long. **Leaves** 1 at base of stem, ascending, persistent through flowering, obovate, 5-15 cm long and 1-4 cm wide, blunt-tipped, long-tapered to base. **Flowers** 4-20, green-white, in a raceme 3-12 cm long and 1-2 cm wide; **lateral sepals** ovate, spreading; **petals** ascending, widened below middle; lip lance-shaped, widened at base, 4-6 mm long; **spur** curved, tapered to a thin tip, 5-8 mm long. June-Aug.—Shaded hummocks in conifer swamps (especially under cedar, black spruce or balsam fir), wet mixed conifer-deciduous forests, alder thickets.

Platanthera orbiculata (Pursh) Lindl.

ROUND-LEAF ORCHID

Habenaria orbiculata (Pursh) Torr.
Platanthera macrophylla (Goldie) P.M. Brown

MAP 1618
native

Perennial herb, roots fleshy. **Stems** 2-6 dm long, leafless apart from 1-6 small bracts. **Leaves** 2, opposite at base of plant, spreading or lying flat on ground, more or less round, shiny, 6-15 cm long and 4-15 cm wide. **Flowers** green-white, several in a raceme 5-20 cm long and 3-6 cm wide; **sepals** ovate, to 1 cm long; **petals** ovate, 6-7 mm long; **lip** entire, rounded at tip, 10-15 mm long and 2 mm wide; **spur** 2-3 cm long, somewhat widened at tip. Late June-Aug.—Shaded conifer swamps of white cedar, balsam fir, and black spruce, especially where underlain by marl; also in drier pine forests.

Platanthera orbiculata

Platanthera praeclara Sheviak & M.L. Bowles

WESTERN PRAIRIE FRINGED ORCHID

Habenaria leucophaea var. *praeclara* (Sheviak & Bowles) Cronq.

MAP 1619
🌸*endangered | native*

Perennial herb; roots thick, fleshy. **Stems** 4-8 dm long, smooth. **Leaves** 3-10 or more, upright, scattered and alternate on stem, smooth, lance-shaped to ovate lance-shaped, base of leaf clasping stem; lower leaves 10-15 cm long and 1.5- 3.5 cm wide, the upper stem leaves much smaller. **Flowers** white to creamy white, large and showy, to 2.5 cm wide; up to 24 flowers in an open raceme; **petals** 3, the two lateral petals ragged at tip; the lip larger and deeply 3-lobed, the lobes fringed more than half way to base, 1.5- 2.5 cm long and about as wide; **spur** 35-55 mm long. June-Aug.—Sedge meadows, low prairie, moist prairie swales; soils usually sandy loams and often calcium-rich. *Federally listed as threatened across its entire range (mostly Great Plains region).*

flower

Platanthera psycodes (L.) Lindl.

LESSER PURPLE FRINGED ORCHID

Habenaria psycodes (L.) Spreng.

MAP 1620
native

Perennial herb, roots thick and fleshy. **Stems** stout, 3-10 dm long. **Leaves** 4-12, alternate on stem, lance-shaped or oval, the upper much smaller and narrow. **Flowers** rose-purple, in a densely flowered, cylindric raceme 4-20 cm long and 3-5 cm wide; **sepals** oval to obovate, 4-6 mm long; **petals** spatula-shaped, finely toothed on margins; **lip** broad, 8-14 mm wide, deeply 3-lobed, the lobes fan-shaped, fringed to less than half way to base; **spur** curved, about 2 cm long. July-Aug.—Wetland margins, shores, wet forests, wet meadows, low prairie, roadside ditches; typically not on sphagnum moss.

Platanthera praeclara

Platanthera psycodes

1617. Platanthera obtusata   *1618. Platanthera orbiculata*   *1619. Platanthera praeclara*

POGONIA *Snake-Mouth*

Pogonia ophioglossoides (L.) Ker-Gawl.   MAP 1621
ROSE POGONIA; SNAKE-MOUTH ORCHID   *native*
Perennial herb, spreading by surface runners (stolons) which send up a stem every 10 cm or more apart. **Stems** slender, smooth, 1.5-4 dm long. **Leaves** single, attached about halfway up stem, narrowly oval, 3-10 cm long and 1-2.5 cm wide, stalkless. **Flowers** pink to purple, usually 1 at end of stems; **sepals** widely spreading, **petals** oval, hovering over the column; **lip** pink with purple veins, 1.5-2 cm long and 5-10 mm wide, fringed at tip, bearded with yellow bristles. June-July.—Conifer swamps and open bogs in sphagnum moss, floating sedge mats, sedge meadows, sandy interdunal wetlands.

SPIRANTHES *Ladies'-Tresses*

Perennial herbs, from a cluster of tuberous roots. Stems slender, erect. Leaves largest at base of plant, becoming smaller upward on stem, the stem leaves erect and sheathing. Flowers small, white or creamy, spirally twisted in a densely flowered, spike-like raceme; sepals and lateral petals similar, the lateral petals joined with all 3 sepals or with only the upper sepal to form a hood over lip and column; lip folded upward near middle so that margins embrace the column, curved downward beyond the middle, with a pair of bumps or thickenings at base; anthers 1, from back of the short column.

Pogonia ophioglossoides

ADDTIONAL SPECIES & HYBRIDS
Spiranthes × *simpsonii* Catling & Sheviak, a cross between *S. lacera* and *S. romanzoffiana*, reported for northern St. Louis County (Smith 1993).

1   Leaves widely spreading or lying flat in a basal rosette, short-petioled, sometimes withered at flowering time, their blades less than 4.5 cm long, about 2/5 as wide as long or wider; perianth 2.5-5.5 mm long . . . . . . ***S. lacera***
1   Leaves ascending, not distinctly petioled, usually present at flowering time (except in *S. magnicamporum*, with flowers 9-11 mm long), their blades (non-sheathing portion) over 4.5 cm long and less than 2/5 as wide as long; flowers usually in 2 or more rows in a ± crowded spike (sometimes one-sided); perianth longer than 5.5 mm   . 2
   2   Lower flowers with perianth 3-7.5 mm long (most easily measured using the dorsal sepal); flowers in one row, usually in a loose spiral because of the twisted rachis . . . . ***S. casei***
   2   Lower flowers with perianth 7-11 mm long (most easily measured using the dorsal sepal); flowers in 2 or more rows, often tightly spiraled 3
     3   Lip fiddle-shaped, strongly constricted behind expanded tip; lateral sepals united for at least half their length with dorsal sepal and lateral petals, forming a hood. . . . . ***S. romanzoffiana***
     3   Lip oblong, often erose-margined but not strongly constricted; at least the lateral sepals free (or easily separated if connivent when young) 4
       4   Plant leafless when flowering; upper stem bracts usually overlapping; lateral sepals in the fresh flowers curved and spreading . . . . ***S. magnicamporum***
       4   Plant with leaves usually present at flowering time, upper stem bracts not or barely overlapping; lateral sepals in the fresh flowers appressed . . . . ***S. cernua***

Spiranthes casei Catling & Cruise   MAP 1622
CASE'S LADIES'-TRESSES   ❤️ *threatened | native*
Perennial herb. **Stems** 2-4 dm tall. **Basal leaves** lance-shaped or broader, 5-15 cm long and 8-15 mm wide; stem sheaths 3 or 4, the lower with a short blade. Inflorescence 2-16 cm long, loosely to fairly densely flowered. **Flowers** whitish

1620. Platanthera psycodes   *1621. Pogonia ophioglossoides*   *1622. Spiranthes casei*   *1623. Spiranthes cernua*

or greenish yellow, more greenish near base; **lip** fleshy, obovate, papillate below, the basal bumps about 1 mm long. Aug-Sept.—Sandy acidic soil; in Minn known only from moist tailings basins associated with taconite mining.

Spiranthes cernua (L.) L.C. Rich.   MAP 1623
WHITE NODDING LADIES'-TRESSES   *native*

Perennial herb, roots fleshy. **Stems** 1-5 dm long, upper stem short-hairy, lower stem smooth. **Leaves** mostly at base of plant, usually present at flowering time, linear to oblong lance-shaped, 6-25 cm long and 5-15 mm wide; upper stem leaves 3-5, much smaller and bractlike. **Flowers** white, in a spike-like raceme 3-15 cm long, with 2-4 vertical rows of flowers, the rows spirally twisted; **sepals** and petals hairy on outside; **lateral petals** joined with upper sepal to form a hood; **lip** white, yellow-green at center, 6-10 mm long and 3-6 mm wide, slightly narrowed at middle, curved downward, the tip curved inward toward stem, the tip wavy-margined or with small rounded teeth, the base of lip with a pair of backward-pointing bumps. Aug-Oct.—Open, usually sandy wetlands such as wet meadows, lakeshores, moist prairies, ditches and roadsides.

Spiranthes lacera (Raf.) Raf.   MAP 1624
NORTHERN SLENDER LADIES'-TRESSES   *native*

Perennial herb. **Stems** arising from a cluster of thickened roots, very slender, 1-6 dm tall. **Basal leaves** often present at anthesis, oval to oblong, 2-5 cm long, a to a 1/3 as wide; **stem leaves** reduced to small scales. **Flowers** white, in a very slender twisted raceme 4-10 cm long, glabrous or nearly so; **lip** oblong, about 4 mm long, white with green median area, its tip abruptly deflexed, crisped on the margin. Aug-Sept.—Dry sandy soil, often with blueberry and bracken fern in open woods of jack pine, red pine, and oak; moist aspen groves, conifer thickets along shores and on dunes.

Spiranthes magnicamporum Sheviak   MAP 1625
GREAT PLAINS LADIES'-TRESSES   *native*

Plants strongly almond or vanilla scented. Much like *S. cernua* but flowering later; **leaves** withering before anthesis; **stem sheaths** 4-8, with erect, sheathing, often overlapping blades; **lateral sepals** more spreading, often over the top of the flower; **tip** more yellowish, its basal bumps short and conical, usually less than 1 mm long. Sept-Oct.—Calcareous prairies, fens, moist to mesic prairies.

Spiranthes romanzoffiana Cham.   MAP 1626
HOODED LADIES'-TRESSES   *native*

Perennial herb, roots thick and fleshy. **Stems** 1-4 dm long, upper stem finely hairy. **Leaves** mostly from base of plant, present at flowering time, upright, linear to narrowly lance-shaped, 5-20 cm long and 3-9 mm wide, the stem leaves becoming smaller and bractlike. **Flowers** white or cream-colored, in a spike-like raceme 3-10 cm long, with 1-3 vertical rows of flowers, the rows spirally twisted; **sepals and lateral petals** joined to form a hood over the lip; **lip** ovate, strongly constricted near middle (violin-shaped), curved downward, the tip ragged and bent inward toward stem, the bumps at base very small. July-Sept.—Open wetlands including wet meadows, fens, lakeshores, open swamps, ditches, seeps; usually in neutral or calcium-rich habitats.

1624. *Spiranthes lacera*   1625. *Spira. magnicamporum*   1626. *Spiranth. romanzoffiana*

Spiranthes cernua

Spiranthes lacera

Spiranthes romanzoffiana

Poaceae GRASS FAMILY

Perennial or annual herbs, clumped or spreading by rhizomes or stolons. Stems (culms) usually hollow, with swollen, solid nodes. Leaves long, linear, parallel-veined, alternate in 2 ranks or rows, sheathing the stem, the sheaths usually split vertically, sometimes joined and tubular as in brome (*Bromus*) and mannagrass (*Glyceria*); with a membranous or hairy ring (ligule) at top of sheath between blade and stem, or the ligule sometimes absent; a pair of projecting lobes (auricles) sometimes present at base of blade.

Flowers (florets) small, usually perfect (with both staminate and pistillate parts), or sometimes either staminate or pistillate, the staminate and pistillate flowers separate on the same or different plants. Florets grouped into spikelets, each spikelet with 1 to many florets, the florets stalkless and alternate along a small stem or axis (rachilla), with a pair of small bracts (glumes) at base of each spikelet (the glumes rarely absent); the glumes usually of different lengths, the lowermost (or first) glume usually smaller, the upper (or second) glume usually longer. Within the spikelet, each floret

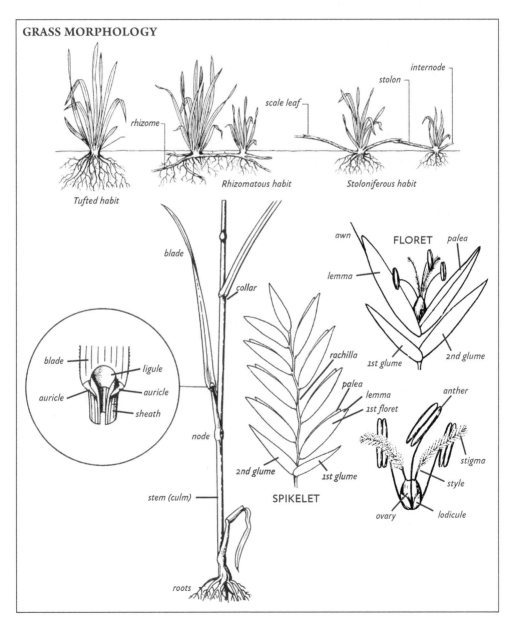

GRASS MORPHOLOGY

subtended by 2 bracts, the larger one (lemma) containing the flower, the smaller one (palea) covering the flower; the lemma and palea often enclosing the ripe fruit (grain or caryopsis); stamens usually 3 or sometimes 6, usually exserted when flowering; ovary superior, never enclosed in a sac (as in sedges); styles 2-3-parted, the stigmas often feathery.

Spikelets grouped in a variety of heads, most commonly in branching heads (panicles), or stalked along an unbranched stem (rachis) in a raceme, or the spikelets stalkless along an unbranched stem in a spike; spikelets breaking (disarticulating) either above or below the glumes when mature, the glumes remaining in the head if falling above the glumes, or the glumes falling with the florets if disarticulation is below the glumes.

ADDITIONAL SPECIES

• *Catabrosa aquatica* (L.) Beauv. (Brook-grass), not known in Minn but may occur in wet meadows near the North Dakota border; plants perennial, stems often horizontal, 2–6 dm long, branching and rooting at nodes in mud or water; leaves flat, mostly 10-15 cm long and 3-10 mm wide; head an open panicle 10–20 cm long; spikelets mostly 2-flowered or sometimes mostly 1-flowered. See Poaea subkey 2.

• *Psathyrostachys juncea* (Fisch.) Nevski (Russian wildrye); native to Asia; roadside in Goodhue County.

• *Schedonnardus paniculatus* (Nutt.) Trel. (Tumblegrass); local in sw Minn, a common grass of the Great Plains. See Tribe 6 key.

• *Sorghum bicolor* (L.) Moench (Sorghum), is the cultivated annual forage crop; field-edge in Lincoln County but probably not persisting.

• *Zea mays* L. (Corn), escape from cultivation from scattered seed but not persisting. See Tribe 1 key.

KEY TO MINNESOTA POACEAE TRIBES

1 Spikelets almost always with 2 florets, the lower florets in the spikelets always sterile or staminate, frequently reduced to lemmas, sometimes absent; upper florets bisexual, staminate, or sterile, unawned or awned from the lemma tip or, if the lemma bilobed, from the sinus; glumes membranous and the upper lemma stiffer than the lower lemma, or both florets reduced and concealed by the stiff to leathery glumes; rachilla not prolonged beyond the second floret 2

   2 Glumes flexible, membranous, the lower glumes usually shorter than the upper glumes, sometimes absent; upper glumes usually equal to or exceeded by the upper floret; lower lemma membranous; upper lemma usually leathery to indurate, sometimes membranous; spikelets usually single or in pairs, occasionally in 3s . . . . **11. Paniceae**

   2 Glumes stiff, leathery to indurate, often nearly equal, at least one and usually both longer than the upper floret (excluding the awn); both lemmas hyaline; paleas hyaline or absent; most spikelets in pairs or 3s, at least one spikelet in each group usually sessile. . . . . **1. Andropogoneae**

1 Spikelets either with other than 2 florets or, if with 2, the lower floret bisexual or the upper floret awned from the back or base of the lemma, or the spikelets bulbiferous; glumes usually membranous; lemmas scarious to indurate 3

   3 Spikelets with 1 floret; lemmas terminating in a 3-branched awn (the lateral branches of the awn sometimes greatly reduced); ligules usually of hairs, sometimes of ciliate membranes. . . . . **2. Aristideae**

   3 Spikelets with more than 1 floret or, if only 1, the lemma not terminating in a 3-branched awn; callus development various; ligules various. 4

      4 Spikelets with 1 sexual floret or the spikelets bulbiferous; glumes absent or less than 1/4 as long as the adjacent floret; lower glumes, if present, without veins, upper glumes, if present, veinless or 1-veined. . 5

         5 Upper glumes present, 1-veined; lower glumes absent or much shorter than the upper glumes and lacking veins. . . . . **4. Brachyelytreae**

         5 Both glumes absent or lacking veins. 6

            6 Plants of wet places, often emergent, sometimes floating; lemmas of the bisexual or pistillate florets 3-14-veined; palea 3-10-veined . . . . **10. Oryzeae**

            6 Plants of wet or dry habitats but not emergent or floating; lemmas of the bisexual or pistillate florets 1-3-veined; palea 2-veined 7

               7 Stems to 20 cm tall; plants of cold or damp habitats, not rhizomatous; sheaths of the flag leaves closed for at least 1/2 their length; caryopses exposed at maturity . . . . **12. Poeae**

               7 Stems to 3 m tall; plants usually of warm or dry habitats, often rhizomatous; sheaths of the flag leaves open to the base; caryopses not exposed at maturity. . . . . **6. Cynodonteae**

      4 Spikelets usually with more than 1 sexual floret; usually with 2 glumes, 1 or both glumes often longer than 1/4 the length of the adjacent floret and/or with more than 1 vein 8

         8 Stem leaf sheaths closed for 1/2 their length or more 9

            9 Spikelets 5-80 mm long, not bulbiferous; lemmas usually awned, often bilobed or bifid, veins convergent distally; ovary apices hairy . . . . **5. Bromeae**

    9 Spikelets 0.7-60 mm long, sometimes bulbiferous; lemmas often unawned, not both bilobed/bifid and with convergent veins; ovary apices usually glabrous 10

        10 Lemma veins (4)5-15, usually prominent, parallel; spikelets 2.5-60 mm long, not bulbiferous. . . . . **9. Meliceae**

        10 Lemmas veins 1-9, often inconspicuous, usually convergent upwards; spikelets 1-20 mm long, sometimes bulbiferous . . . . **12. Poeae**

  8 Stem leaf sheaths open for at least 1/2 their length; glumes exceeding or exceeded by the upper florets 11

    11 Spikelets with 1 floret; lemmas terminally or subterminally awned, the junction of the awn and lemma conspicuous; rachillas notprolonged beyond the base of the floret. . . . . **13. Stipeae**

    11 Spikelets with 1-60 florets; lemmas unawned or awned, awns basal to terminal, if terminal or subterminal, the lemma-awn junction not conspicuous; rachillas often prolonged beyond the base of the upper floret 12

        12 Ligules, at least of the flag leaves, of hairs, a ciliate ridge or membrane bearing cilia longer than the basal ridge or membrane; leaves usually hairy on either side of the ligule; auricles absent 13

            13 Lemmas of the fertile florets with 3-11 inconspicuous veins, never glabrous, if with 3 veins, pilose throughout or with transverse rows of tufts of hair, if with 5-11 veins, the margins pilose proximally, the hairs not papillose-based; lemma tips usually bilobed or bifid and awned or mucronate from the sinus, if acute to acuminate, the lemmas pilose; awns twisted proximally . . . . **7. Danthonieae**

            13 Lemmas of the fertile florets usually with 1-3 conspicuous veins, sometimes with 3 inconspicuous veins, often glabrous; lemma tips acute to obtuse, bilobed, or 4-lobed, often mucronate or awned from the sinuses; awns usually not twisted . . . . **3. Arundineae**

        12 Ligules membranous, if ciliate, the cilia shorter than the membranous base; leaves usually glabrous on either side of the ligule; auricles present or absent. 14

            14 Inflorescences panicles or unilateral racemes, not spikelike; spikelets solitary, the lowest 0-4 florets in a spikelet sterile or staminate, the distal florets sexual . . . . **12. Poeae**

            14 Inflorescences panicles, racemes, or spikes; spikelets sometimes in pairs or triplets, sterile florets, if any, distal to the bisexual or pistillate florets 15

               15 Inflorescences spikes or spikelike; spikelets 1-5+ per node, at least 1 spikelet sessile or subsessile 16

                  16 Inflorescences with 1-5 spikelets at a node, if 3, usually with 1 sessile and 2 pedicellate spikelets, if 1, the spikelet tangential to or embedded in the rachis, with 2 glumes, the glumes facing each other; ovaries with hairy tips; auricles often present . **14. Triticeae**

                  16 Inflorescences spikelike panicles with highly reduced branches, or spikes with spikelets radial to the rachises and all but the terminal spikelet with only 1 glume, or spikes with spikelets tangential to the rachises and having 2 glumes adjacent to each other; ovaries with glabrous tips; auricles usually absent. . . . . **12. Poeae**

               15 Inflorescences panicles, with no sessile spikelets. 17

                  17 Caryopses with a thick pericarp forming a distinct apical knob or beak at maturity; lemmas 3(5)-veined. . . . . **8. Diarrheneae**

                  17 Caryopses usually with a thin pericarp, never with a distinct apical beak or knob; lemmas 3-9-veined 18

                      18 Glumes subulate, stiff; lemmas unawned or with awns to 4 mm long . **14. Triticeae**

                      18 Glumes lanceolate, membranous; lemmas awned or unawned, awns varied . . . 19

                          19 Leaves to 2 cm wide, usually not conspicuously 2-ranked; stems usually less than 1 cm thick . . . . **12. Poeae**

                          19 Leaves 2-10 cm wide, often conspicuously 2-ranked; stems often more than 1 cm thick. . . . . **3. Arundineae**

TRIBE 1. ANDROPOGONEAE

GENERA *Andropogon, Miscanthus, Schizachyrium, Sorghastrum, Zea* (see key)

1 All spikelets unisexual, the pistillate and staminate spikelets in separate inflorescences or the pistillate spikelets below the staminate spikelets in the same inflorescence . . . . ***Zea mays****

1 Some spikelets bisexual (usually the sessile or more shortly pedicellate spikelet of each spikelet pair or triplet) 2

  2 Spikelets apparently solitary and sessile, the pedicellate spikelets absent; pedicels absent or present 3

    3 Inflorescences terminal and axillary, composed of digitate clusters of 1-13 branches on a common peduncle; peduncles subtended by, and often partially included in, a modified leaf . . . . ***Andropogon***

    3 Inflorescences terminal, with elongate rachises and brancheswith several to many smaller branches; peduncles and branches not subtended by a modified leaf . . . . ***Sorghastrum***

2   Spikelets in sessile-pedicellate or unequally pedicellate pairs or triplets, the pedicellate spikelets often smaller than the sessile spikelets, sometimes rudimentary 4

    4   Large introduced grass with plumose panicle . . . . ***Miscanthus***

    4   Native grasses; panicle not plumose 5

        5   Inflorescence branches usually solitary on the peduncles, occasionally 2; lower glumes of the sessile spikelets veined between the keels . . . . ***Schizachyrium***

        5   Inflorescence branches usually 2-13 on the peduncles, occasionally solitary; lower glumes of the sessile spikelets usually without veins between the keels . . . . ***Andropogon***

TRIBE 2. ARISTIDEAE

GENERA *Aristida*

TRIBE 3. ARUNDINEAE

GENERA *Phragmites*

TRIBE 4. BRACHYELYTREAE

GENERA *Brachyelytrum*

TRIBE 5. BROMEAE

GENERA *Bromus*

TRIBE 6. CYNODONTEAE

GENERA *Bouteloua, Buchloë, Calamovilfa, Distichlis, Eleusine, Eragrostis, Leptochloa, Muhlenbergia, Schedonnardus, Spartina, Sporobolus, Tridens, Triplasis*

1   Inflorescences clearly exceeded by the upper leaves, often completely or almost completely enclosed in the upper leaf sheaths; culms 1-30(75) cm tall 2

  2   Spikelets (and often the plants) unisexual 3

    3   Leaves strongly distichous; lemmas 9-11-veined; plants unisexual; saline and alkaline soils . . . . . ***Distichlis***

    3   Leaves not strongly distichous; lemmas 1-5-veined; plants unisexual or, if bisexual, with separate pistillate and staminate inflorescences, growing in a variety of soils 4

        4   Spikelets 5-26 mm long; pistillate and staminate inflorescences similar, simple panicles; glumes and lemmas unawned, mucronate, or 1-awned . . . . ***Eragrostis***

        4   Spikelets 4-7 mm long; pistillate and staminate inflorescences strongly dimorphic; staminate inflorescences with pectinate, spikelike branches; pistillate spikelets with 3-awned glumes . . ***Buchloë***

  2   Spikelets bisexual (at least the lowest floret in each spikelet bisexual) 5

    5   Spikelets with 2-20 florets; inflorescences panicles of 2-120 spikelike branches . . . . ***Leptochloa***

    5   Spikelets with 1(3) florets; inflorescences simple panicles, often highly contracted, without spikelike branches . . . . ***Sporobolus***

1   Inflorescences usually equaling or exceeding the upper leaves; culms 1-500 cm tall 6

  6   Inflorescences with disarticulating branches, disarticulation at the base of the branches; branches 0.04-7 cm long, often spikelike, usually with fewer than 15 spikelets per branch . . . . ***Bouteloua***

  6   Inflorescences without disarticulating branches; branches, if present, often more than 4.5 cm long, variously shaped, including spikelike but not globose, often with more than 16 spikelets per branch 7

    7   Inflorescences spikes or racemes . . . . ***Distichlis***

    7   Inflorescences simple panicles (sometimes highly condensed) or panicles of 1-120 spikelike branches . . 8

        8   Inflorescences simple panicles, sometimes highly contracted, even spikelike in appearance; spikelike branches not evident 9

          9   Spikelets usually with only 1 floret, occasionally with 2-3 florets 10

            10   Ligules membranous, hyaline, or coriaceous, sometimes ciliate; lemmas 3-veined (occasionally appearing 5-veined), usually awned, sometimes unawned or mucronate 11

               11   Lemmas usually awned or mucronate; spikelets usually with 1 floret . . . . ***Muhlenbergia***

               11   Lemmas unawned or mucronate; spikelets frequently with 2-3 florets . . . . ***Eragrostis***

            10   Ligules of hairs; lemmas 1(3)-veined, unawned, sometimes mucronate 12

               12   Calluses usually glabrous or almost so; paleas glabrous; fruits falling free of the lemma and palea . . . . ***Sporobolus***

               12   Calluses evidently hairy, the hairs 1/4-7/8 as long as the lemmas; paleas hairy; fruits falling with the lemma and palea . . . . ***Calamovilfa***

9 Spikelets with more than 1 floret...13
  13 Lemmas with (5)9-11 veins 14
    14 All spikelets with at least 1 bisexual floret .... ***Eragrostis***
    14 Spikelets unisexual; plants almost always unisexual, occasionally bisexual 15
      15 Lemmas 9-11-veined; glumes 2-7 veined; plants rhizomatous and/or stoloniferous, found in saline or alkaline soils .... ***Distichlis***
      15 Lemmas 1-6-veined; lower glumes of the staminate spikelets 1-veined, those of the pistillate spikelets 1-5-veined; plants stoloniferous or rooting at the lower nodes, not rhizomatous, not found in saline or alkaline soils .... ***Eragrostis***
  13 Lemmas with 1-3 veins (occasionally with scabrous lines that may be mistaken for additional veins) 16
    16 Florets unisexual .... ***Eragrostis***
    16 At least 1 floret in each spikelet bisexual 17
      17 Lemmas, including the calluses, glabrous or inconspicuously hairy; lemma apices usually entire, sometimes minutely toothed 18
        18 Spikelets with (1)2-60 florets; lemmas unawned, sometimes mucronate; ligules usually membranous and ciliate or ciliolate, sometimes of hairs .... ***Eragrostis***
        18 Spikelets with 1(2-3) florets; lemmas often awned, sometimes unawned or mucronate; ligules membranous, sometimes ciliolate, not ciliate .... ***Muhlenbergia***
      17 Lemma bodies conspicuously hairy over the veins and/or calluses conspicuously hairy; lemma apices usually with emarginate, bilobed, or trilobed apices, sometimes entire . 19
        19 Palea keels long hairy distally, the distal hairs 0.5-2 mm long .... ***Triplasis***
        19 Palea keels glabrous or with hairs less than 0.5 mm long .... ***Tridens***
8 Inflorescences panicles of spikelike branches 20
  20 Inflorescence branches 1 or more, if more than 1, arranged in terminal, digitate clusters, sometimes with additional branches or whorls below the terminal cluster...........................21
    21 Plants unisexual .... ***Buchloë***
    21 Plants bisexual, all spikelets with at least 1 bisexual floret 22
      22 Lemmas usually with hairs over the veins, at least basally, the apices often toothed, sometimes mucronate or awned .... ***Leptochloa***
      22 Lemmas glabrous, the apices entire, neither mucronate nor awned .... ***Eleusine***
  20 Inflorescence branches more than 1, racemosely arranged on the rachises 23
    23 All spikelets unisexual .... ***Buchloë***
    23 All spikelets with at least 1 bisexual floret 24
      24 Spikelets with (2)3-12(20) bisexual florets .... ***Leptochloa***
      24 Spikelets with 1 bisexual floret, sometimes with sterile, rudimentary, or modified florets distal to the bisexual floret 25
        25 Functional spikelets with sterile, rudimentary, or modified florets distal to the bisexual floret .... ***Bouteloua***
        25 Functional spikelets with only 1 floret, lacking sterile, rudimentary, or modified florets 26
          26 Spikelets distant to slightly imbricate, appressed to the branches; branches strongly divergent .... ***Schedonnardus*****
          26 Spikelets clearly imbricate, appressed to strongly divergent; branches appressed to strongly divergent .... ***Spartina***

TRIBE 7. DANTHONIEAE

GENERA *Danthonia*

TRIBE 8. DIARRHENEAE

GENERA *Diarrhena*

TRIBE 9. MELICEAE

GENERA *Glyceria, Melica, Schizachne*

1 Calluses hairy; lemmas awned, awns 8-15 mm long, twisted, divergent to slightly geniculate .... ***Schizachne***
1 Calluses glabrous; lemmas unawned or awned, awns to 12 mm long, straight.........................2
  2 Lower glumes 1-veined, 0.3-4.5 mm long; disarticulation always above the glumes; lemmas unawned, never with hairs more than 1 mm long; stems never with corm-like bases; distal florets in the spikelets sometimes reduced, not forming a morphologically distinct rudiment; plants of wet meadows and streamsides . ***Glyceria***

2 Lower glumes 1-9-veined, 2-16 mm long; disarticulation above or below the glumes; lemmas sometimes awned, sometimes with hairs longer than 1 mm; stems sometimes with corm-like bases; distal florets in the spikelets often forming a morphologically distinct rudiment; plants of drier habitats . . . . *Melica*

TRIBE 10. ORYZEAE

GENERA *Leersia, Zizania*

1 Spikelets unisexual, terete; the staminate spikelets below the pistillate . . . . *Zizania*
1 Spikelets bisexual, laterally compressed . . . . *Leersia*

TRIBE 11. PANICEAE

GENERA *Cenchrus, Dichanthelium, Digitaria, Echinochloa, Eriochloa, Panicum, Paspalum, Setaria*

1 Most spikelets or groups of 2-11 spikelets subtended by 1-many, distinct to more or less joined, stiff bristles or bracts 2
   2 Bristles falling with the spikelets at maturity; disarticulation at the base of the reduced panicle branches (fascicles) . . . . *Cenchrus*
   2 Bristles persistent; disarticulation below the spikelets. . . . . *Setaria*
1 All or most spikelets not subtended by stiff bristles, sometimes the terminal spikelet on each branch subtended by a single bristle, and occasionally other spikelets with a single subtending bristle 3
   3 Terminal spikelet on each branch subtended by a single bristle; other spikelets occasionally with a single stiff subtending bristle . . . . *Setaria*
   3 None of the spikelets subtended by a stiff bristle. 4
      4 Lower glumes or lower lemmas awned, sometimes shortly so . . . . *Echinochloa*
      4 Lower glumes and lower lemmas unawned 5
         5 Upper lemmas and paleas cartilaginous and flexible at maturity; lemma margins flat, hyaline; lower glumes absent or to 1/4 the length of the spikelets . . . . *Digitaria*
         5 Upper lemmas and paleas chartaceous to indurate and rigid at maturity; lemma margins not hyaline, frequently involute; lower glumes varying from absent to subequal to the spikelets or extending beyond the distal floret 6
            6 Spikelets subtended by a cuplike callus . . . . *Eriochloa*
            6 Spikelets not subtended by a cuplike callus. 7
               7 At least the upper leaves, often all leaves, without ligules; ligules, when present, of hairs . . . . *Echinochloa*
               7 All leaves with ligules (or sometimes absent) ligules membranous or of hairs 8
                  8 Inflorescences of 1-sided, spikelike primary branches . . . . *Paspalum*
                  8 Inflorescences usually panicles with well-developed secondary branches, sometimes spikelike panicles or panicles with spikelike, but not 1-sided, branches 9
                     9 Blades of the basal leaves clearly distinct from the cauline leaves; basal leaves ovate to lanceolate, cauline leaves with longer and narrower blades; basal leaves forming a distinct winter rosette . . . . *Dichanthelium*
                     9 Blades of the basal and cauline leaves similar, usually linear to lanceolate, varying from filiform to ovate; basal leaves not forming a distinct winter rosette 10
                        10 Panicles terminating the culms usually appearing in late spring; branches usually developing from the lower and middle cauline nodes in summer, the branches rebranching 1 or more times by fall; upper florets not disarticulating at maturity, plump . . . . *Dichanthelium*
                        10 Panicles terminating the culms usually appearing after midsummer; branches usually not developing branches from the lower and middle cauline nodes, when present, rarely rebranched; upper florets disarticulating or not very plump at maturity . . . . *Panicum*

TRIBE 12. POEAE

GENERA *Agrostis, Alopecurus, Ammophila, Anthoxanthum, Arrhenatherum, Avena, Avenula, Beckmannia, Calamagrostis, Catabrosa* (see *Poeae* subkey 2), *Cinna, Dactylis, Deschampsia, Festuca, Koeleria, Lolium, Milium, Phalaris, Phleum, Poa, Puccinellia, Schedonorus, Scolochloa, Sphenopholis, Torreyochloa, Trisetum, Vulpia*

1 All or almost all spikelets viviparous, the spikelets producing plantlets [if sexual spikelets are common, take the alternate lead]. 2

2　Panicle branches smooth or slightly scabrous; blades with a translucent line on either side of the midvein, apices usually prowlike...***Poa***

2　Panicle branches scabrous; blades without a translucent line on either side of the midvein, apices usually not prowlike 3

　3　Sheaths closed for 1/2 or more of their length; ligules 0.1–0.6 mm long ....***Festuca***

　3　Sheaths open; ligules 1.5–13 mm long ....***Deschampsia***

1　Some, usually all, spikelets sexually functional, with 1–25 bisexual or unisexual florets, sometimes with sterile and sexual spikelets mixed within an inflorescence 4

4　Inflorescences with 2 morphologically distinct forms of spikelets ....***Phalaris***

4　Inflorescences with all spikelets morphologically alike 5

　5　Inflorescences spikes with 1–2(4) spikelets per node, or spikelike racemes with 1 spikelet at all or most nodes 6

　　6　Lemmas awned from about midlength, awns 8–26 mm long, twisted proximally............***Avenula***

　　6　Lemmas unawned or apically awned, awns straight 7

　　　7　Spikelets sessile; lemmas 2–12 mm long.......................................***Lolium***

　　　7　Spikelets subsessile to pedicellate, pedicels 0.5–3 mm long.......................***Festuca***

　5　Inflorescences panicles or racemes, with more than 1 spikelet associated with each node 8

　　8　Inflorescences racemes or spikelike panicles, with all branches shorter than 1 cm 9

　　　9　Spikelets disarticulating below the glumes or, if the spikelets are attached to stipes, at the base of the stipes; glume bases sometimes fused 10

　　　　10　Lemmas dorsally awned; spikelets oval in outline; glumes often connate at the base, often ***winged*** distally, keels sometimes ciliate, apices never abruptly truncate ....***Alopecurus***

　　　　10　Lemmas usually unawned, occasionally subterminally awned; spikelets often U-shaped in outline, sometimes oval; glumes not connate at the base, not winged, often strongly ciliate on the keels and abruptly truncate to an awnlike apex ....***Phleum***

　　　9　Spikelets disarticulating above the glumes; glume bases not fused 11

　　　　11　Spikelets with 2–25 bisexual florets, the sterile or staminate florets, if present, distal to the bisexual florets ....***Vulpia***

　　　　11　Spikelets with 1 bisexual floret, sometimes with 1–2 sterile florets below the bisexual floret, the sterile florets sometimes reduced to lemmas, sometimes resembling tufts of callus hair 12

　　　　　12　Spikelets with 1–2 sterile or staminate florets below the bisexual florets, these from larger than to much smaller than the bisexual florets, sometimes resembling tufts of hair; glumes sometimes winged distally 13

　　　　　　13　Fresh leaves not sweet-smelling when crushed; sterile lemmas unawned; bisexual lemmas usually hairy, sometimes sparsely so; glumes subequal, sometimes winged distally　***Phalaris***

　　　　　　13　Fresh leaves sweet-smelling when crushed; sterile lemmas awned; bisexual lemmas glabrous; glumes unequal, not winged ....***Anthoxanthum***

　　　　　12　Spikelets without sterile or staminate florets below the bisexual floret; glumes not winged distally 14

　　　　　　14　Spikelets 8–15 mm long; lemmas more than 3/4 as long as the glumes; plants strongly rhizomatous ....***Ammophila***

　　　　　　14　Spikelets 1.2–7 mm long; lemmas less than 3/4 as long as the glumes; plants rhizomatous or not 15

　　　　　　　15　Spikelet bases usually U-shaped, sometimes cuneate; glumes equal, midveins usually strongly ciliate ....***Phleum***

　　　　　　　15　Spikelet bases cuneate; glumes unequal, midveins not strongly ciliate ......***Agrostis***

　　8　Inflorescences panicles, dense to open, sometimes compact, usually at least some branches longer than 1 cm 16

　　16　Panicle branches secund, appearing 1-sided; spikelets strongly imbricate, subsessile 17

　　　17　Lemmas awned, awns of the lowest lemmas 0.3–22 mm long ....***Vulpia***

　　　17　Lemmas unawned, sometimes awn-tipped 18

　　　　18　Spikelets circular to ovate or obovate in outline, with 1–2 florets; glumes almost entirely concealing the sides of the florets; disarticulation below the glumes..........***Beckmannia***

　　　　18　Spikelets oval in outline, longer than wide, with 2–6 florets; glumes partially exposing the sides of the florets; disarticulation above the glumes........................***Dactylis***

　　16　Panicle branches not secund; spikelets usually widely spaced to somewhat imbricate, usually clearly pedicellate, sometimes subsessile, sometimes on stipes 19

　　　19　All or most spikelets in an inflorescence with 1 bisexual floret, sometimes with 1–2 sterile or staminate florets below the bisexual floret, the sterile florets sometimes resembling tufts of hair ....***Poeae Subkey 1***

19 All or most spikelets in an inflorescence with 2-25 sexual florets, usually all florets bisexual or the distal florets sterile or unisexual, sometimes all florets unisexual, sometimes the plants unisexual . . . . *Poeae Subkey 2*

POEAE SUBKEY 1

Panicles having at least some branches longer than 1 cm and spikelets with only 1 bisexual floret, sometimes with 1-2 sterile or staminate florets below the bisexual floret.

1 Spikelets with 1-2 staminate or sterile florets below the bisexual floret, sterile florets sometimes knoblike or resembling tufts of hair 2
  2 Spikelets with 2 florets of similar size, the lower floret staminate; lower lemmas awned, the lemmas of the terminal floret unawned or awned . . . . *Arrhenatherum*
  2 Spikelets with 2-3(4) florets, the lower 1-2 florets staminate or sterile, sometimes knoblike or resembling tufts of hair, sometimes larger than the bisexual floret; lemmas of the lower florets awned or unawned, the lemmas of the terminal floret unawned 3
    3 Lower sterile florets 2, from shorter than to exceeding the bisexual floret; fresh leaves sweet-smelling when crushed . . . . *Anthoxanthum*
    3 Lower sterile florets 1-2; fresh leaves not sweet-smelling when crushed . . . . *Phalaris*
1 Spikelets without staminate or sterile florets below the bisexual florets 4
  4 Spikelets 15-50 mm long; lemmas usually dorsally awned, awns 20-90 mm long, sometimes unawned. *Avena*
  4 Spikelets to 15 mm long; lemmas unawned or awned, awns to 18 mm long, basal, dorsal, subterminal, or terminal 5
    5 Lemmas awned, awns longer than 2 mm 6
      6 Disarticulation below the glumes 7
        7 Paleas absent or greatly reduced; lemma awns attached at midlength or below; glume bases often fused; rachillas not prolonged beyond the floret base . . . . *Alopecurus*
        7 Paleas from 3/4 to nearly as long as the lemmas; lemma awns subterminal; glume bases not fused . . . . *Cinna*
      6 Disarticulation above the glumes 8
        8 Rachillas not prolonged beyond the base of the distal floret; paleas absent, minute, or subequal to the lemmas; lemmas 0.5-4 mm long . . . . *Agrostis*
        8 Rachillas prolonged beyond the base of the distal floret; paleas at least 1/2 as long as the lemmas; lemmas 1-8 mm long . . . . *Calamagrostis*
    5 Lemmas unawned or, if awned, awns shorter than 2 mm 9
      9 Disarticulation below the glumes 10
        10 Lemma awns subterminal; glume bases not fused; paleas from 3/4 to nearly as long as the lemmas; rachillas prolonged beyond the base of the distal floret for up to 1.3 mm . . . . *Cinna*
        10 Lemma awns attached at midlength or below; glume bases often fused; paleas absent or greatly reduced; rachillas not prolonged beyond the base of the distal floret . . . . *Alopecurus*
      9 Disarticulation above the glumes 11
        11 Glumes 8-15 mm long; plants strongly rhizomatous . . . . *Ammophila*
        11 Glumes 1-10 mm long; plants rhizomatous or not 12
          12 Spikelets dorsally compressed; lemmas dark, coriaceous, lustrous, and glabrous . . . . *Milium*
          12 Spikelets laterally compressed, sometimes weakly so; lemmas not simultaneously dark, leathery, lustrous, and glabrous 13
            13 Paleas absent or minute to subequal to the lemmas, not veined; rachillas not prolonged beyond the base of the distal florets; lemmas often unawned, sometimes awned, awn attachment basal to terminal . . . . *Agrostis*
            13 Paleas more than 1/2 as long as the lemmas, 2-veined; rachillas prolonged beyond the base of the floret by at least 0.1 mm; lemmas usually awned, awn attachment usually on the lower 1/2 of the lemma . . . . *Calamagrostis*

POEAE SUBKEY 2

Spikelets with 2-22 sexual florets, lower florets sexual, upper florets sometimes sterile.

1 One or both glumes exceeding the adjacent lemmas, sometimes exceeding the uppermost floret 2
  2 All lemmas within a spikelet unawned or with awns shorter than 2 mm 3
    3 Glumes 15-50 mm long; plants annual . . . . *Avena*
    3 Glumes 0.4-9 mm long; plants annual or perennial 4
      4 Rachilla internodes hairy, hairs at least 1 mm long 5

     5 Lemma tips truncate, erose to 2-4-toothed . . . . *Deschampsia*

     5 Lemmas tips acute, bifid . . . . *Trisetum*

    4 Rachilla internodes glabrous or with hairs shorter than 1 mm on the distal portion 6

       6 Plants strongly rhizomatous; glumes 5-9 mm long . . . . *Scolochloa*

       6 Plants not or weakly rhizomatous; glumes 0.4-9 mm long. 7

         7 Panicle branches densely pubescent, hairs 0.1-0.2 mm long; lemma apices entire, sometimes mucronate; lemma veins converging distally . . . . *Koeleria*

         7 Panicles branches glabrous, sometimes scabrous; lemma apices entire or serrate to erose, not mucronate; lemma veins more or less parallel distally . . . . *Puccinellia*

  2 One or all lemmas within a spikelet awned, the awns at least 2 mm long 8

    8 Lemmas 14-40 mm long; glumes 7-11-veined . . . . *Avena*

    8 Lemmas 1.3-16 mm long; glumes 1-9-veined 9

       9 Lemmas 7-16 mm long . . . . *Avenula*

       9 Lemmas 1.3-7 mm long 10

        10 Disarticulation below the glumes . . . . *Trisetum*

        10 Disarticulation above the glumes 11

          11 Rachilla internodes glabrous or with hairs shorter than 1 mm on the distal portion; panicle branches densely pubescent, not scabrous . . . . *Koeleria*

          11 Rachilla internodes hairy, hairs at least 1 mm long; panicles branches usually glabrous, sometimes scabrous 12

            12 Lemma apices truncate, erose or 2-4-toothed . . . . *Deschampsia*

            12 Lemmas apices acute, bifid . . . . *Trisetum*

1 Both glumes shorter than or subequal to the adjacent lemmas 13

  13 Lower lemmas with awns longer than 2 mm 14

    14 Calluses hairy; rachillas prolonged beyond the base of the uppermost florets . . . . *Trisetum*

    14 Calluses glabrous or sparsely hairy; rachillas sometimes prolonged beyond the base of the distal floret 15

      15 Anthers 1; plants annual . . . . *Vulpia*

      15 Anthers 3; plants perennial 16

        16 Leaves without auricles; blades flat, conduplicate, involute, or convolute . . . . *Festuca*

        16 Lower leaves with auricles; blades flat . . . . *Schedonorus*

  13 Lower lemmas unawned, mucronate, or with awns up to 2 mm long 17

    17 Lemmas apices rounded, truncate, obtuse, or emarginate 18

      18 Lemmas conspicuously 3-veined; lower glumes 0-3-veined; not yet known from Minn, known form . adjacent North Dakota and Wisc . . . . *Catabrosa* *

      18 Lemmas (3)5-9-veined, the veins often inconspicuous; lower glumes 1-5-veined 19

        19 Lower glumes about as long as the upper glumes but no more than 1/2 as wide; disarticulation below the glumes . . . . *Sphenopholis*

        19 Lower glumes shorter than the upper glumes or subequal and more than 1/2 as wide; disarticulation above the glumes 20

          20 Lemma veins excurrent, lemma apices indistinctly 3-lobed or toothed; plants strongly rhizomatous, rhizomes succulent . . . . *Scolochloa*

          20 Lemma veins not excurrent, lemma apices entire, serrate, or erose; plants sometimes rhizomatous, rhizomes not succulent 21

            21 Lemma veins (5)7-9, prominent; plants of non-saline and non-alkaline habitats. *Torreyochloa*

            21 Lemma veins (3)5(7), inconspicuous or prominent; plants of saline and alkaline habitats. . . . . *Puccinellia*

    17 Lemma apices acute to acuminate, sometimes mucronate or shortly awn-tipped 22

      22 Lemmas (3)5-9-veined, veins more or less parallel distally, conspicuous 23

        23 Lemma veins (5)7-9; plants rhizomatous, of non-saline and non-alkaline habitats . . . . *Torreyochloa*

        23 Lemma veins (3)5(7); plants not truly rhizomatous, sometimes the culms rooting at buried lower nodes, growing in saline and alkaline habitats . . . . *Puccinellia*

      22 Lemmas 3-9-veined, veins converging distally, usually inconspicuous, sometimes conspicuous 24

        25 Disarticulation below the glumes; lower glumes subequal to the upper glumes but no more than 1/2 as wide . . . . *Sphenopholis*

        25 Disarticulation above the glumes, sometimes above the basal floret; lower glumes shorter than the upper glumes or, if subequal, more than 1/2 as wide 26

          26 Panicle branches smooth, hairy, hairs soft. . . . . *Koeleria*

          26 Panicle branches smooth or scabrous, glabrous or strigose, never covered with soft hairs . . . 27

            27 Basal leaves with auricles . . . . *Schedonorus*

            27 No leaves with auricles 28

28 Lemma veins parallel distally; plants of saline and alkaline habitats . . . . _Puccinellia_
28 Lemma veins converging distally; plants of many habitats, including saline places . . . 29
  29 Leaf blades with translucent lines on either side of the midvein, tips often prow-shaped; lemmas often with a tuft of hair at the base of the midvein . . . . _Poa_
  29 Leaf blades without translucent lines on either side of the midvein, tips not prow-shaped, often flat; lemmas without a tuft of hair at the base of midvein 30
    30 Plants perennial . . . . _Festuca_
    30 Plants annual . . . . _Vulpia_

TRIBE 13. STIPEAE

GENERA _Achnatherum, Hesperostipa, Nassella, Oryzopsis, Piptatherum_

1 Flag leaves highly reduced, no more than 12 mm long; basal leaves overwintering, their blades resupinate (appearing inverted) . . . . _Oryzopsis_
1 Flag leaf blades well developed, more than 12 mm long; basal leaves not overwintering; blades not resupinate. 2
  2 Lemma margins strongly overlapping their whole length at maturity; lemma bodies usually rough throughout, apices not lobed; paleas 1/4-1/2 the length of the lemmas, without veins, glabrous . . . . _Nassella_
  2 Lemma margins usually not or only slightly overlapping for some or all their length at maturity, strongly overlapping in some species with smooth lemmas; lemma bodies usually smooth on thelower portion, apices often 1-2 lobed, sometimes bifid; paleas from 1/3 as long as to slightly longer than the lemmas, 2-veined, at least on the lower portion, usually with hairs, glabrous in species with glabrous lemmas 3
    3 Lemma awns 6.5-50 cm long; calluses 1.5-6 mm long, sharply pointed; panicle branches straight . _Hesperostipa_
    3 Lemma awns to 7 cm long; calluses 0.1-2 mm long, blunt to sharply pointed; panicle branches straight or flexuous 4
      4 Lemmas covered with long silky hairs to 6 mm long . . . . _Achnatherum_
      4 Lemmas glabrate to short hairy. . . . . _Piptatherum_

TRIBE 14. TRITICEAE

GENERA _Agropyron, Elymus, Hordeum, Leymus, Pascopyrum, Secale, Triticum_

1 Spikelets 2-7 at all or most nodes 2
  2 Spikelets 3 at each node, the central spikelet sessile, the lateral spikelets usually pedicellate, sometimes all 3 spikelets sessile in cultivated plants; spikelets with 1 floret, usually only the central spikelet with a functional floret, the florets of the lateral spikelets usually sterile and reduced, in cultivated plants all florets functional or those of the lateral spikelets functional and those of the central spikelet reduced . . . . _Hordeum_
  2 Spikelets usually other than 3 at each node, if 3, all three sessile; spikelets with 1-11 florets, if 1 floret, additional reduced or sterile florets present distal to the functional floret in at least 1 spikelet per node 3
    3 Lemma awns (0)1-120 mm long; anthers 0.9-6 mm long; blades with well-spaced, unequally prominent veins on the adaxial surfaces . . . . _Elymus_
    3 Lemmas usually unawned or with awns up to 7 mm long, if awns 16-35 mm long, anthers 6-8 mm; blades usually with closely spaced, equally prominent veins on the adaxial surfaces. . . . . _Leymus_
1 Spikelets 1 at all or most nodes 4
  4 Spikelets usually more than 3 times the length of the middle rachis internodes, appressed to strongly divergent; middle rachis internodes 0.2-5.5 mm long 5
    5 Lemmas strongly keeled, keels conspicuously scabrous distally, scabridities 0.5-0.8 mm long; lemma awns 7-50 mm long. . . . . _Secale_
    5 Lemmas rounded proximally, sometimes keeled distally, keels not or inconspicuously scabrous distally; lemmas unawned or awns to 4.5 mm long . . . . _Agropyron_
  4 Spikelets 1/2-3 times the length of the middle rachis internodes, appressed or ascending; rachis internodes 3-28 mm long. 6
    6 Glumes subulate to narrowly lanceolate, tapering from below midlength, 1(3)-veined at midlength 7
      7 Glumes lanceolate, tapering to acuminate apices from near midlength or below, keels curving to the side distally; plants always rhizomatous . . . . _Pascopyrum_
      7 Glumes subulate to lanceolate, tapering from below midlength, keels straight or almost so; plants often rhizomatous . . . . _Leymus_
    6 Glumes lanceolate, rectangular, ovate, or obovate, narrowing beyond midlength, often the in distal 1/4, (1)3-5(7)-veined at midlength 8
      8 Plants annual; glumes often with lateral teeth or awns, midveins smooth throughout; plants cultivated, sometimes escaping . . . . _Triticum_
      8 Plants perennial; glumes without lateral teeth or awns, midveins sometimes scabrous. . . . . _Elymus_

ACHNATHERUM *Ricegrass*   STIPEAE

Achnatherum hymenoides (Roem. & Schult.) Barkworth   MAP 1626A
INDIAN RICEGRASS   ❦ *endangered* | *native*
   Oryzopsis hymenoides (Roem. & Schult.) Ricker

Strongly tufted perennial grass. **Stems** erect, 5.5-8 dm tall, hollow to pithy, glabrous; **sheaths** usually glabrous but ciliate on the overlapping margins; **ligules** acute, 5-9 mm long; **leaf blades** involute at maturity, strongly ribbed above, smooth below, mostly 8-40 cm long and to 3 mm wide. **Panicle** very open, the slender branches and flexuous pedicels spreading; glumes ovate, acuminate, 3(5)-nerved, usually somewhat unequal; **lemmas** 3-4.5 mm long, more or less covered with numerous hairs which approach the lemma in length; lemma awn usually firm and straight, 4-8 mm long.—Dry sandy or rocky soil. *An important grass of the plains and mountain states, reaching its eastern range limit in Minn (where rare).*

Achnatherum hymenoides

AGROPYRON *Wheatgrass*   TRITICEAE

Agropyron cristatum (L.) Gaertn.   MAP 1627
CRESTED WHEATGRASS   *introduced*
   Agropyron desertorum auct. non (Fisch. ex Link) Schult.

Perennial grass; densely to loosely tufted. **Stems** to 1 m long; **auricles** usually present; **ligules** membranous, to 1.5 mm long; **leaf blades** 1.5-6 mm wide, glabrous or pubescent. **Spikes** narrowly to broadly lanceolate. **Spikelets** with 3-6(8) florets; disarticulation above the glumes and beneath the florets; **glumes** 3-6 mm long, glabrous or with coarse hairs on the keels, usually with awns 1.5-3 mm long; **lemmas** 5-9 mm long, keeled, usually with awns 1-6 mm long.—Disturbed areas; commonly used for land restoration in the western states. *Other species formerly included in **Agropyron** are now placed in **Elymus** or **Pascopyrum**.*

Agropyron cristatum

AGROSTIS *Bent-Grass; Bent*   POEAE

Perennial grasses, clumped or spreading by rhizomes or sometimes by stolons. Leaves soft, auricles absent, ligules membranous, sheaths open, usually smooth and glabrous. Head an open panicle. Spikelets small, 1-flowered, breaking above glumes; glumes more or less equal length, 1-veined; floret shorter than glumes; lemma awnless or with a short straight awn; palea small or absent; stamens usually 3.

1   Palea present, about half as long as the lemma or longer; anthers ca. 0.8-1.5 mm long....................2
   2   Plants with rhizomes but not stolons, the stems arising from underground rhizomes, straight or curved at the very base, otherwise erect and nearly or quite straight; larger leaf blades mostly 3-7 (-10) mm wide; spikelets usually flushed with red or purplish; bases of middle panicle branches mostly meeting the axis of the panicle at an angle of 30-45° (except when very immature) ....***A. gigantea***
   2   Plants with stolons but not rhizomes; stems usually decumbent at their bases, the lower nodes often strongly bent and/or rooting, but underground rhizomes absent; larger leaf blades 1.7-3 (-4) mm wide; spikelets pale, greenish; bases of middle panicle branches usually strongly ascending or appressed to axis of panicle, at most diverging about 15° (but panicle branches often spreading distally). ....***A. stolonifera***
1   Palea absent or vestigial; anthers ca. 0.6 mm long or shorter 3
   3   Longest panicle branches less than 6 (-12) cm long and the uppermost leaf blade more than 5 cm long; leaf blades flat, the wider ones 1.5-3.5 mm broad; panicle branches forked about or below the middle, often smooth or only sparingly hispidulous-scabrous; panicle pale, greenish (very rarely red-tinged) ....***A. perennans***
   3   Longest panicle branches more than 6 cm long or uppermost leaf blade less than 5 cm long (or both conditions); leaf blades usually ± involute, the widest up to 1.5 (rarely 3) mm broad; panicle branches often not forked until beyond the middle, copiously hispidulous-scabrous; panicle ± flushed with reddish....................4
      4   Lemmas 1.3-1.8 mm long ....***A. scabra***
      4   Lemmas 0.9-1.2 mm long ....***A. hyemalis***

Agrostis gigantea Roth   MAP 1628
BLACK BENT   *introduced*

Perennial grass, rhizomatous and sod-forming, not stoloniferous. **Stems** to 10 dm long or sometimes more; **auricles** absent; **ligules** membranous, larger (upper) ligules mostly 2.5-6 mm long, higher than wide; **leaf blades** 3-8 mm wide. **Panicle**

10-20 cm long, notably suffused with purplish red, at anthesis triangular-ovoid, with widely spreading unequal branches, sometimes later more contracted; at least some of the panicle branches floriferous to the base; panicle branches and often the pedicels scabrous. **Spikelets** rather crowded, 2-3.5 mm long; **glumes** scabrous along the keel; **lemma** 2/3 as long as the glumes, scabrous near tip, usually unawned; callus minutely bearded.—Native of Europe, cultivated and escaped into moist meadows, shores, coastal marshes, and other moist places.

Agrostis hyemalis (Walt.) B.S.P. MAP 1629
WINTER BENT ✿*endangered* | *native*

Tufted perennial grass. **Stems** slender, erect to reclining, 2-6 dm long; **auricles** absent; **ligules** membranous, 1-2 mm long, rounded and usually ragged at tip; **leaf blades** mostly at or near base of plant, upright to spreading, flat to inrolled, 1-2 mm wide, smooth or somewhat rough-to-touch. Panicle open, 1-3 dm long, the branches threadlike and spreading, the branches themselves branched and with spikelets only above their middle. **Spikelets** 1-flowered, often purple, 1-3 mm long; **glumes** lance-shaped, 1-3 mm long; **lemma** 1-2 mm long, unawned or with a short straight awn; palea absent. June-Aug.—Wet meadows, bogs, ditches, streambanks, shores; more commonly in dry, sandy places.

Agrostis gigantea

Agrostis perennans (Walt.) Tuckerman MAP 1630
UPLAND BENT *native*

Tufted perennial grass. **Stems** 5-10 dm tall; **auricles** absent; **ligules** membranous, **leaf blades** flat, 2-6 mm wide, elongate, the uppermost blade more than 5 cm long. **Panicle** mostly pale greenish, 10-25 cm long, notably longer than wide, the smooth or sparsely scabrous branches forking near or below the middle, soon divaricate, the longest ones often less than 6 cm long. **Spikelets** 1.8-2.8 mm long; **glumes** subequal, scabrous on the midvein; **lemma** 1.3-2 mm, awnless or rarely with a very short, slender awn near the tip; palea obsolete.—Usually in dry soil.

Agrostis scabra Willd. MAP 1631
ROUGH BENT *native*

Tufted perennial grass. **Stems** slender, 3-9 dm long; **auricles** absent; **ligules** membranous; **leaves** mostly basal or below the middle of the stem, usually erect, the blade flat or more often involute, 1-2 mm wide. **Panicle** ovoid or pyramidal, 1-3 dm long, sometimes half as long as the whole plant, very diffuse, more or less reddish, the scabrous filiform branches divaricate, mostly forking well above the middle. **Spikelets** 1.2-3.2 mm long; **glumes** scabrous on the midvein; **lemma** awnless or with a short straight awn; callus short-bearded; palea obsolete or to 0.3 mm long.—Abundant, widely distributed in many habitats, and variable.

Agrostis scabra

Agrostis stolonifera L. MAP 1632
REDTOP; SPREADING BENT *introduced (naturalized)*
 Agrostis alba var. *palustris* (Huds.) Pers.
 Agrostis palustris Huds.

Perennial grass, spreading by rhizomes and also sometimes by stolons. **Stems** erect or more or less horizontal at base, 3-10 dm or more long; **auricles** absent; **ligules** membranous, usually splitting at tip, 2-5 mm long; **leaf blades** ascending, 2-8 mm wide, rough-to-touch. Panicle open, 3-20 cm long, the branches spreading, branched and with spikelets along their entire length. **Spikelets** 1-flowered, usually purple, 2-4 mm long; **glumes** lance-shaped, 1.5-2.5 mm long; **lemma** 2/3 length of

Agrostis stolonifera

1626A. Achnatherum oryzoides *1627. Agropyron cristatum* *1628. Agrostis gigantea* *1629. Agrostis hyemalis*

glumes, 1-2 mm long; palea present, about half as long as lemma. July-Sept.—Wet meadows, ditches, streambanks and shores; disturbed areas.

ALOPECURUS *Meadow-Foxtail* POEAE

Annual or perennial grasses. Stems erect or more or less horizontal at base. Leaves mostly from lower 1/2 of the stems; sheaths open; auricles absent; ligules membranous, entire to lacerate. Heads densely flowered, cylindric, spike-like panicles. Spikelets 1-flowered, flattened, breaking below the glumes; glumes equal length, 3-nerved, often silky hairy on back, awnless; lemma about as long as glumes or shorter, awned from the back, the awn shorter to longer than the glume tips; palea absent. *The narrow panicles resemble those of timothy (Phleum).*

1 Spikelets (excluding awns) ca. 4-6.5 mm long; awns mostly exserted ca. 3.5-6 mm beyond tips of glumes; anthers ca. 2.4-3.5 mm long . . . . ***A. pratensis***
1 Spikelets not over 3 mm long; awns at most exserted ca. 2-3 mm; anthers less than 2 mm long 2
   2 Awn exserted at most about 1 mm beyond tips of glumes, usually included, inserted about a third or half the distance from base of lemma . . . . ***A. aequalis***
   2 Awn of most lemmas exserted ca. 2-3 mm, inserted near the base of lemma (on lower 1/5-1/4) 3
      3 Anthers 0.3-0.7 mm long; spikelets 2-2.5 mm long . . . . ***A. carolinianus***
      3 Anthers 1.4-1.8 mm long; larger spikelets 2.6-3 mm long . . . . ***A. geniculatus***

Alopecurus aequalis Sobol.
MAP 1633
SHORT-AWN FOXTAIL *native*

Annual or short-lived perennial grass. **Stems** single or in small clumps, slender, erect to more or less horizontal, 2-6 dm long, often rooting at the nodes; **auricles** absent; **ligules** 2-6.5 mm long, obtuse; **leaf blades** 1-5 mm wide, finely rough-to-touch above; ligule membranous, rounded to elongate, 2-7 mm long. Panicle erect, spike-like, 2-7 cm long and 3-5 mm wide. **Spikelets** 1-flowered; **glumes** 2-3 mm long, blunt-tipped, hairy on the keel and veins; **lemma** about equaling the glumes, awned from back, the awn straight, to 1.5 mm longer than glume tips. June-Aug.—Shallow water or mud of wet meadows, marshes, ditches, springs, open bogs, fens, shores and streambanks; sometimes where calcium-rich.

Alopecurus carolinianus Walt.
MAP 1634
TUFTED MEADOW-FOXTAIL *introduced*

Densely tufted annual grass. **Stems** erect to upright, 1-4 dm long; **auricles** absent; **ligule** membranous, rounded to elongate, 1-5 mm long; **leaf blades** 1-3 mm wide, finely rough-to-touch above. **Panicle** cylindric, spike-like, 1-5 cm long and 3-5 mm wide. **Spikelets** 1-flowered; **glumes** 2-3 mm long, blunt-tipped, hairy on keel; **lemma** about as long as glumes, awned from back, the awn bent near middle and 2-3 mm longer than glume tips. May-July.—Mud flats, temporary ponds, wet meadows, marshes, low prairie, fallow fields.

Alopecurus geniculatus L.
MAP 1635
MARSH-FOXTAIL *introduced*

Tufted perennial grass. **Stems** usually decumbent, sometimes rooting at the nodes, 2-8 dm long; **auricles** absent; **ligules** 2-5 mm long, obtuse; **leaf blades** 2-12 cm long, mostly 1-4 mm wide; **upper sheaths** somewhat inflated. **Panicle** spike-like, 3-5 cm long, 4-6 mm wide, often tinged with purple; **glumes** as in *A. carolinianus*; awn inserted about halfway between the base and middle of the lemma, exserted 1.5-3.2 mm long.—Mud and shallow water.

Alopecurus aequalis

1630. *Agrostis perennans*   1631. *Agrostis scabra*   1632. *Agrostis stolonifera*   1633. *Alopecurus aequalis*

Alopecurus pratensis L.

FIELD MEADOW-FOXTAIL

MAP 1636

introduced (naturalized)

Perennial grass, shortly rhizomatous. **Stems** erect or decumbent at base, 4–8 dm long; **auricles** absent; ligules 1.5–3 mm long, obtuse to truncate; **upper sheaths** not or scarcely inflated. **Panicle** spike-like, 2–8 cm long, 5–10 mm wide, scarcely tapering; **glumes** 4–5.5 mm long, the keel narrowly winged, conspicuously ciliate, especially above the middle, with hairs 1–1.5 mm long; awn inserted about halfway between the base and middle of the lemma, exserted 2–6 mm.—Native of Eurasia; naturalized in moist meadows, fields, and waste places.

Alopecurus pratensis

AMMOPHILA *Beach-Grass*   POEAE

Ammophila breviligulata Fern.

AMERICAN BEACH-GRASS

MAP 1637

☙ *threatened | native*

Coarse, stiff, perennial grass, from long running rhizomes. **Stems** stout, erect, glabrous, 5–10 dm tall; **sheaths** glabrous; **ligule** membranous, ovate or truncate, 1–3 mm long; **leaf blades** flat at base, involute above, 4–8 mm wide when unrolled, scabrous above, glabrous beneath. **Panicle** dense, 1–4 dm long, 1–2.5 cm thick, its base often enclosed in the upper sheath. **Spikelets** 1-flowered, strongly flattened, articulated above the glumes; **glumes** about equal, 10–15 mm long, linear lance-shaped, keeled, the first 1-nerved, the second 3-nerved, scabrous on the keel; **lemmas** shorter than the glumes, scaberulous; obscurely 3–5-nerved, awnless, subtended by a tuft of short hairs 1–3 mm long from the callus.—Dunes and dry sandy shores along the Great Lakes. *Useful as sand-binders in dune control.*

ANDROPOGON *Bluestem*   ANDROPOGONEAE

Andropogon gerardii Vitman

BIG BLUESTEM; TURKEY-FOOT

MAP 1638

native

Perennial grass. **Stems** stout, 1–3 m tall, forming large bunches or extensive sod; **ligules** membranous; **leaf blades** usually 5–10 mm wide, the lower ones and the sheaths sometimes villous. **Racemes** 2–6, subdigitate, on a long-exserted peduncle, 5–10 cm long; joints of the rachis and pedicels equal, sparsely or usually densely ciliate, densely bearded at the summit. **Spikelets** of two kinds, in pairs at the joints of the rachis, one sessile and perfect, the other pediceled and staminate, sterile, or abortive; **glumes** of the fertile spikelet equal or nearly so, leathery, flat to concave on the back, lacking a midnerve, often ciliate; **fertile lemma** shorter than the glumes, narrow, hyaline, usually ending in a long awn 8–15 mm long, twisted below and more or less bent.—Moist or dry soil of prairies, roadsides, railroads; in dry open woods, old fields, rarely in fens and sedge meadows.

Ammophila breviligulata

ADDITIONAL SPECIES

Andropogon hallii Hack. (Sand bluestem); native to the Great Plains; adventive in Minn where introduced in roadside and wildlife plantings.

Andropogon gerardii

1634. Alopecurus carolinianus

1635. Alopecurus geniculatus

1636. Alopecurus pratensis

1637. Ammophila breviligulata

ANTHOXANTHUM *Sweetgrass*

POEAE

Anthoxanthum hirtum (Schrank) Y.Schouten & Veldkamp
SWEETGRASS; HOLYGRASS
  Hierochloe hirta (Schrank) Borbás
  Hierochloe odorata (L.) Beauv.

MAP 1639
native

Perennial grass, from creeping rhizomes; plants nicely sweet-scented, especially
when dried. **Stems** erect, 2-6 dm tall, smooth; **sheaths** brownish or reddish;
ligules membranous, 2-5 mm long; **leaf blades** of basal and stem leaves 2.5-5.5
mm wide, upper surface glabrous and shiny, undersurface pilose; fertile stem
leaves short, 1-4 cm long, leaves on sterile shoots much longer. **Head** a pyramid-
shaped panicle, 5-10 cm long, the branches spreading to drooping. **Spikelets**
3-flowered, the lower 2 florets staminate, the terminal spikelet perfect, golden
brown, or green or purple at base and golden near tips, 5 mm long, breaking above
the glumes; **glumes** ovate, shiny, 4-6 mm long; **lemmas** 3-4 mm long, the
staminate lemma hairy. May-July.—Wet meadows, shores, low prairie; often
where sandy. *The fragrance emitted when fresh plants are crushed or burned is from
coumarin, an anti-coagulant agent.*

Anthoxanthum hirtum

ARISTIDA *Three-Awn*

ARISTIDEAE

Annual or perennial grasses, often weedy. Stems usually branched from
some or all of the nodes. Leaf blades narrow, often involute, sheaths open;
auricles lacking; ligules very shortly membranous and long-ciliate. Flowers in terminal, usually
slender, dense or lax panicles or racemes. Spikelets 1-flowered, articulated above the glumes. Glumes
membranous, linear to lance-shaped, usually 1-nerved (in some species 2-5-nerved), equal or unequal,
acute, acuminate, or short-awned. Lemma indurate, linear, obscurely nerved, often scabrous on the
obscure keel or toward the tip, and with a sharp, usually bearded callus. Awns elongate, normally 3,
similar or dissimilar, separate to the base or united into a short column, the lateral ones in a few
species greatly reduced. *Species mostly of dry, sterile or sandy soil.*

1 Plants perennial . . . .*A. purpurea*
1 Plants annual2
  2 Awns tightly twisted and ± connate, forming a column ca. 5-9 mm long at tip of lemma before diverging into
    3 ± equal and much longer free portions . . . .*A. tuberculosa*
  2 Awns not forming a column, separate from their bases 3
    3 First glume with 3-5 distinct nerves, 16-24 mm long (plus awn if present); body of lemma 15-20 mm long;
      awns 3.5-7 cm long . . . .*A. oligantha*
    3 First glume with 1 distinct nerve, 2.5-12.5 mm long; body of lemma 3.5-11 mm long; awns less than 3.5 cm
      long 4
        4 Middle awn on most lemmas loosely spiraled (at least when dry) in 1 or 2 loops toward its base 5
          5 Body of lemma ca. 7-11 mm long, with middle awn 9-18 mm long and lateral awns 6-12 mm long;
            glumes clearly unequal, the first usually equaling or shorter than the body of the lemma . . . .
            . . . .*A. basiramea*
          5 Body of lemma ca. 5-7 mm long, with middle awn mostly 4-8 mm long and lateral awns less than 2
            mm long; glumes mostly subequal, both longer than body of lemma . . . .*A. dichotoma*
        4 Middle awn on most lemmas bent or straight, without spiraled loops at base . . . .*A. longespica*

1638. *Andropogon gerardii*

1639. *Anthoxanthum hirtum*

1640. *Aristida basiramea*

Aristida basiramea Engelm.
MAP 1640
FORKED THREE-AWN
native

Annual grass. **Stems** tufted, erect, 3-6 dm tall; **ligules** about 0.3 mm long; **leaf blades** very narrow, usually about 1 mm wide, often involute. **Panicles** slender, the terminal 5-10 cm long, rather loose; the lateral shorter and more slender, scarcely surpassing the subtending sheath; **glumes** 1-nerved, distinctly unequal, the first 6-12 mm., the second 9.5-15 mm long; **lemma** usually about equaling the first glume, 7.5-10.5 mm long; central awn divergent, 11-19 mm long, coiled at base when dry into 1-3 turns; lateral awns erect to curved-divergent but not coiled, 7.5-13 mm long.—Dry sterile or sandy soil.

Aristida dichotoma Michx.
MAP 1641
CHURCHMOUSE THREE-AWN
native

Annual grass. **Stems** tufted, branched from the base, erect or ascending, 2-4 dm tall; **ligules** less than 0.5 mm long; **leaf blades** filiform, mostly involute, or the lower flat. **Terminal panicle** very slender, often reduced to a raceme, 3-8 cm long; **lateral panicles** much shorter, mostly enclosed in the subtending sheaths; **glumes** nearly equal, mucronate, 1-nerved, 5-10 mm long; **lemma** averaging 6 mm; central awn 3-10 mm long, its base nearly horizontally divergent and loosely coiled; lateral awns straight, erect, to 3.3 mm long.—Dry sandy soil.

Aristida longespica Poir.
MAP 1642
SLIMSPIKE THREE-AWN
☛ *endangered | native*

Annual grass. **Stems** tufted, often branched from the lower nodes, 2-4 dm tall; **sheaths** shorter than the internodes, not disintegrating into threadlike fibers at maturity, hairs on the throat sometimes to 5 mm long; **ligules** about 0.5 mm long; **leaf blades** 1-2 mm wide, often involute. **Panicle** elongate, a third to half as long as the plant, very slender, often racemose, with appressed or ascending spikelets; axillary panicles greatly reduced; **glumes** nearly equal, the first 3.7-7 mm long, sometimes obscurely 3-nerved; **lemma** 4-6 mm long; central awn 6.5-19 mm long, outwardly curved at base, widely divergent; lateral awns erect or slightly divergent, 2-8 mm long.—Dry sterile or sandy soil.

Aristida oligantha Michx.
MAP 1643
PRAIRIE THREE-AWN
native

Annual grass. **Stems** 2-4 dm tall, branched from the base and usually from all the nodes; **sheaths** usually shorter than the internodes, lowermost **sheaths** appressed-pilose near base; **ligules** less than 0.5 mm long; **leaf blades** about 1 mm wide, flat or involute, tapering to a filiform point. **Terminal panicle** 1-2 dm long, very lax, few-flowered, the lower spikelets usually paired, the upper solitary; **lateral panicles** few-flowered, dense, with short internodes; first **glume** 3-5-nerved, scabrous on the keel, 12-29 mm long, the second 1-nerved, glabrous, slightly longer; **lemma** 10-18 mm long; awns about equally divergent, 40-70 mm long.—Dry open ground.

Aristida purpurea Nutt.
MAP 1644
PURPLE THREE-AWN
native

Tufted perennial grass. **Stems** erect, hollow, glabrous, 1-8 dm tall; **sheaths** glabrous to scabrous but often villous in tufts at the collar; **ligules** to 0.4 mm long; **leaf blades** inrolled or C-shaped in cross-section in the bud, involute to less often flat when mature, usually scabrous above, sometimes hirsute, to 30 cm long, and

Aristida basiramea

floret

Aristida dichotoma

Aristida longespica

floret

Aristida purpurea

1641. *Aristida dichotoma*   1642. *Aristida longespica*   1643. *Aristida oligantha*   1644. *Aristida purpurea*

to 2.5 mm wide. **Panicle** strict to rather loose and open, the branches stiff to flexuous; **glumes** markedly unequal, the first glume 4-14 mm long, the second glume 7.5 -25 mm long; **lemmas** 7.5-15 mm long to the base of the awns, short-bearded on the callus.—Dry and dry-mesic prairies.

Aristida tuberculosa Nutt.
SEASIDE THREE-AWN
MAP 1645
☙*threatened* | *native*

Annual grass. **Stems** branched at base and lower nodes, 3-8 dm tall; lower **sheaths** villous, upper glabrous or nearly so; **collars** often with a line of tangled hairs; **ligules** about 0.5 mm long; **leaf blades** 1-3 mm wide, involute at least when dry. **Panicle** very lax and open, sparsely branched, 1-3 dm long; **glumes** about equal, 20-28 mm long, including the short awn, the first scabrous on the keel; **lemma** 11-14 mm long; awns about equal, united at base into a twisted column 7-13 mm long, the free portions loosely coiled at base, 3-5 cm long.—Dry, loose sand in oak and aspen savannas, sand prairies, and sparsely vegetated dunes.

Aristida tuberculosa

ARRHENATHERUM *Oatgrass*
POEAE

Arrhenatherum elatius (L.) Beauv.
TALL OATGRASS
MAP 1646
introduced

Tall perennial grass; loosely tufted, sometimes rhizomatous. **Stems** erect, to 2 m tall, smooth, or minutely pubescent at the nodes; **sheaths** smooth, open, not overlapping; **auricles** absent; **ligules** membranous, 1-3 mm long, obtuse to truncate, usually ciliate; **leaf blades** flat, 4-8 mm wide, sometimes scabrous. **Panicle** shining, slender, 1-3 dm long, the short branches in fascicles. **Spikelets** 2-flowered, disarticulating above the glumes and between the lemmas; **glumes** unequal, hyaline in age, the first shorter, 4.5-8 mm long, 1-nerved, the second 6.6-10 mm long, equaling the lemmas, 3-nerved; **lemmas** thin, rounded on the back, short-bearded at base, 5-7-nerved, the lower enclosing a staminate flower and bearing below the middle a long awn 10-20 mm long, geniculate near the middle, the upper one enclosing a perfect flower, awnless or bearing just below the tip a much shorter straight awn to 6 mm long.—Meadows, roadsides, and waste ground, usually in moist soil.

Arrhenatherum elatius

AVENA *Oat*
POEAE

Mostly annual grasses with broad flat blades and ample panicles of large spikelets. Sheaths open, auricles absent, ligules membranous. Spikelets 2-3-flowered, articulated above the glumes and usually between the lemmas; rachilla often hirsute, at least at the base of the lemmas. Glumes nearly equal, exceeding the lemmas, 1-11-nerved. Lemmas indurate, often scarious toward the tip, rounded on the back, obscurely 5-9-nerved, or prominently nerved toward the apex. Awn arising about the middle of the lemma, bent near the middle, or straight, or lacking.

1 Lemmas with a stout, strongly twisted awn and often with stiff hairs on the back; florets falling from the spikelet by a distinct oval disarticulation surface . . . . ***A. fatua***
1 Lemmas with the awn usually straight, weak, or absent, and the back glabrous; florets falling by fracture of rachilla at base of spikelet. . . . . ***A. sativa***

Avena fatua L.
WILD OAT
MAP 1647
introduced

Annual grass. **Stems** stout, smooth, usually 5-8 dm tall; sheaths of the basal leaves

Avena fatua

1645. *Aristida tuberculosa*   1646. *Arrhenatherum elatius*   1647. *Avena fatua*

with scattered hairs, distal sheaths glabrous; **ligules** 4-6 mm long, acute; **leaf blades** 5-15 mm wide, scaberulous. **Panicle** lax, the fascicled branches usually spreading horizontally. **Spikelets** 3-flowered; rachilla hirsute, readily disarticulating, the lemmas falling separately; **glumes** 7-11-nerved, about 2 cm long; **lemmas** sparsely to densely hirsute on the back, or rarely glabrous; awn 3-4 cm long.—European native; disturbed sites such as railroads, roadsides, beaches.

Avena sativa L.
OAT
MAP 1648
introduced

Annual grass. **Stems** branching from the base, stout, 3-10 dm tall; **sheaths** smooth or finely scabrous; **ligules** 3-8 mm long, acute; **leaf blades** 5-15 mm wide, finely scabrous. **Panicle** lax, many-flowered, with rough, slender, fascicled branches. **Spikelets** 2-flowered; **glumes** 7-11-nerved, about 25 mm long; **lemmas** long remaining attached to the rachilla, glabrous, 15-20 mm long, awnless or with a short straight awn.—An important cultivated species apparently derived from *A. fatua* (with which it readily hybridizes); often adventive along roads and railways, probably not persistent.

Avenula hookeri

AVENULA *Alpine Oatgrass*   POEAE

Avenula hookeri (Scribn.) Holub
SPIKEOAT
MAP 1649
native

   Helictotrichon hookeri (Scribn.) Henrard.

Tufted perennial grass. **Stems** erect, 10-75 cm tall; **sheaths** closed for less than 1/3 of their length, smooth to finely roughened; **ligules** acute, usually lacerate, 3-7 mm long; **leaf blades** mostly 4-20 cm long, 1-4.5 mm wide, smooth to finely roughened, margins cartilaginous and whitish. **Panicles** 5-13 cm long, erect or ascending; branches usually straight, stiff, mostly with 1-2 spikelets. **Spikelets** with 3-6 florets; **glumes** thin, acute; lower glumes 9-13 mm long, 3-veined; upper glumes 9-14 mm long, 3-5-veined; calluses bearded, hairs usually shorter than 1 mm; **lemmas** 10-12 mm long, awned, the awns 10-17 mm long, flattened.—Dry, sandy or gravelly prairies. *Minnesota at eastern edge of the species' range.*

BECKMANNIA *Slough Grass*   POEAE

Beckmannia syzigachne (Steud.) Fern.
AMERICAN SLOUGH GRASS
MAP 1650
native

Stout annual grass. **Stems** single or in small clumps, 4-12 dm long; **sheaths** overlapping, smooth, the upper sheath often loosely enclosing lower part of panicle; **auricles** absent; **ligule** membranous, acute, 3-6 mm long; leaf blades flat, 3-10 mm wide, rough-to-touch. **Head** of many 1-sided spikes in a narrow panicle 10-30 cm long, the panicle branches erect, overlapping, 1-5 cm long; each spike 1-2 cm long, with several to many spikelets in 2 rows on the rachis. **Spikelets** with 1 floret, a second undeveloped (or sometimes well-developed) floret occasionally present; overlapping, nearly round, 2-4 mm long, straw-colored when mature, breaking below the glumes; **glumes** equal, broad, inflated along midvein, with a short, slender tip; **lemma** about as long as glumes but narrower; palea nearly as long as lemma. June-Sept.—Wet meadows, marshes, ditches, shores and streambanks; more common in Great Plains region.

Beckmannia syzigachne

1648. *Avena sativa*

1649. *Avenula hookeri*

1650. *Beckmannia syzigachne*

1651. *Bouteloua curtipendula*

BOUTELOUA *Grama-Grass*   CYNODONTEAE

Perennial, usually tufted grasses, the relatively short spikes solitary or 2-many, racemose on a common axis. Leaves mostly basal, sheaths open; ligules of hairs, membranous, or membranous and ciliate. Spikelets with 1 perfect flower and 1 or more sterile rudiments, articulated above the glumes, inserted in 2 rows on one side of a narrow flat rachis. Glumes unequal, narrow, 1-nerved, acuminate to awn-tipped. Fertile lemma rounded on the back, 3-nerved, the lateral nerves usually excurrent below the tip into short awns.

1 Spikes 10-50, forming a long erect inflorescence . . . . *B. curtipendula*
1 Spikes 1-3 2
     2 Rachis of the spike prolonged as a stiff point beyond the summit of the uppermost spikelet . . . . . . *B. hirsuta*
     2 Rachis of the spike not exceeding the uppermost spikelet . . . . *B. gracilis*

Bouteloua curtipendula (Michx.) Torr.   MAP 1651
SIDE-OATS GRAMA   *native*

Perennial grass from slender rhizomes. **Stems** erect, 3-10 dm tall; **sheaths** smooth or nearly so; **ligules** to 0.5 mm long, membranous, ciliate; **leaf blades** elongate, 2-5 mm wide, scabrous on the margins. **Spikes** 10-50, spreading or nodding, 8-15 mm long, secund along an axis 1-3 dm long, falling entire. **Spikelets** usually 3-6; **first glume** linear-subulate, 3-4 mm long; **second glume** lance-shaped, 4-7 mm long; **fertile lemma** usually somewhat exceeding the glumes, acuminate, its lateral nerves prolonged into awns about 1 mm long; rudiment with a long central awn and 2 shorter lateral ones arising below the middle, or greatly reduced, or lacking.—Dry open places and prairies; often included in prairie seed mixtures.

Bouteloua gracilis (Willd.) Lag.   MAP 1652
BLUE GRAMA   *native*

Perennial grass, resembling *B. hirsuta* in habit, stature, foliage, and spikes. **Leaves** mostly basal; **sheaths** glabrous or sparsely hirsute; **ligule** of hairs to 0.4 mm long, often with marginal tufts of longer hairs; **leaf blades** curled or flexuous, involute, 1-2 mm wide. **Rachis** not surpassing the uppermost spikelet; second glume 3.5-5 mm long, scabrous and sparsely villous on the midnerve; **fertile lemma** equaling the second glume, densely villous at base and along the midnerve, sparsely villous-ciliate, the terminal awn short, the lateral ones arising above the middle, about 1.5 mm long; rudiment stipitate, densely long-villous around the base, bearing 3 rough awns which equal or surpass the second glume.—Dry grasslands, much more common westward in the USA where an important component of short-grass prairie.

Bouteloua hirsuta Lag.   MAP 1653
HAIRY GRAMA   *native*

Perennial grass. **Stems** densely tufted, 1.5-6 dm tall; **leaves** mostly crowded toward the base; **ligule** of hairs to 0.5 mm long; **sheaths** pilose at the throat; **blades** flat, 1-3 mm wide. **Spikes** 1-3, usually 2, straight or curved backward, 2-4 cm long; **rachis** prolonged beyond the uppermost spikelet and projecting 2-5 mm as a straight stiff point. **Spikelets** numerous, imbricate, divergent; first **glume** subulate; second glume lance-shaped, 3-4 mm long, densely papillose-hirsute on the prominent midnerve; **fertile lemma** about equaling the second glume, sparsely villous throughout, its awn short and flattened; rudiment long-stipitate, glabrous at base, obconic, often reaching the summit of the second glume, its 3 awns equal, longer than the fertile lemma and second glume.—Dry prairies.

Bouteloua curtipendula

Bouteloua hirsuta

BRACHYELYTRUM *Shorthusk*   BRACHYELYTREAE

Perennial forest understory grasses from knotty rhizomes. Leaves broad, mostly along the stem; sheaths open; auricles absent; ligules short, membranous; lower leaf blades absent or reduced; upper leaf blades flat. Panicles narrow, few-flowered. Spikelets readily deciduous, 1-flowered, articulated above the glumes. Glumes minute, subulate to triangular, 1-nerved. Lemma linear-subulate, rounded on the back, sharply 5-nerved, gradually tapering to an elongate awn. Palea 2-keeled; rachilla prolonged into an elongate bristle appressed to the furrow of the palea.

1   Lemmas scabrous, the hairs short, to 0.2 mm long in the middle portions of the lemma; awns mostly 17-24 mm
    long .... *B. aristosum*
1   Lemmas strongly hispid, the hairs longer, 0.3-0.8 mm long in the middle portions of the lemma; awns mostly 13-
    17 mm long .... *B. erectum*

Brachyelytrum aristosum (Michx.) Beauv. ex Branner & Coville   MAP 1654
BEARDED SHORTHUSK   *native*

Perennial grass, previously included within *B. erectum*, and distinguished from
that species by pubescence of lemma (see key), having 3-5-nerved lemmas, florets
ca. 8-10 mm long (excluding awn) and 0.7-1.3 mm wide, anthers not over 4 mm
long, and more than 15 cilia per 5 mm of leaf margin. *Brachyelytrum erectum* has
more strongly 7-9-nerved lemmas, at least the larger florets are 10-12 mm long
and 1-1.6 mm wide, anthers are more than 5 mm long, and with fewer than 10
cilia per 5 mm of leaf margin.—Moist to dry deciduous forests, lowland forests,
moist thickets, sandy pine forests, and coniferous swamps.

Brachyelytrum erectum (Schreb.) Beauv.   MAP 1655
BEARDED SHORTHUSK   *native*

Perennial grass. **Stems** 5-10 dm tall, glabrous to pubescent; **sheaths** retrorsely
pubescent; **ligules** of middle and upper stem blades 2-3.5 mm long, lacerate or
erose; **leaf blades** scabrous to pubescent, 8-18 cm long, 8-16 mm wide. **Panicle**
erect or declined, 5-15 cm long, the few spikelets appressed; first **glume** none or
to 0.8 mm long; second glume subulate, 1-4 mm long; **lemma** 6-10 mm long,
scabrous to hispidulous on the nerves, its awn mostly 13-17 mm long;
prolongation of the rachilla about 2/3 as long as the lemma.—Dry or moist
deciduous woods; our two species occupying essentially the same habitats.

Brachyelytrum erectum

BROMUS *Brome; Chess; Cheat-Grass*   BROMEAE

Perennial grasses. Leaves generally flat; sheaths closed to near top, usually pubescent; auricles usually
absent; ligules membranous, usually erose or lacerate. Head a panicle of drooping spikelets. Spikelets
with several to many flowers, breaking above the glumes; glumes shorter than lemmas; lemmas
awned or unawned; stamens usually 3.

ADDITIONAL SPECIES

Bromus catharticus Vahl (Rescuegrass), native to South America; Clearwater and Mahnomen counties.

1   First glume with one distinct nerve; second glume with 3 (-5) nerves 2
    2   Awns 10-30 mm long, as long as or longer than their lemmas; apex of lemma beyond insertion of awn 1.5-2.7
        mm long; annual weed. .... *B. tectorum*
    2   Awns absent or up to 7 (-9) mm long, shorter than their lemmas; apex of lemma less than 1.5 mm long;
        perennials, mostly native (*B. inermis* introduced) 3
        3   Plants with elongate rhizomes; lemmas (at least when fresh) usually ± flushed with purplish, especially
            toward the margins, the awns absent or less than 4 (-5.5) mm long; anthers 3.3-5 mm long.... *B. inermis*
        3   Plants without elongated rhizomes; lemmas (when fresh) green (very rarely flushed with purple), the larger
            awns 3-7 (-9) mm long; anthers various 4
            4   Nodes and also number of leaves usually 8-15; leaf sheaths longer than the internodes, thus overlapping
                and covering all the nodes, the summit of the sheath with a band of dense pubescence and (when intact)
                with a pair of prominent tooth-like auricles; anthers 1.5-2.2 mm long .... *B. latiglumis*
            4   Nodes and leaves usually not more than 6 (-8 in *B. ciliatus*); leaf sheaths shorter than at least the upper
                internodes, exposing one or more of them, the summit of the sheath glabrous or pubescent but lacking
                auricles; anthers various 5

1652. *Bouteloua gracilis*   1653. *Bouteloua hirsuta*   1654. *Brachyelytrum aristosum*   1655. *Brachyelytrum erectum*

  5 Lemmas ± uniformly hairy (very rarely glabrous); anthers ca. 2.5-5 mm long; glumes pubescent at
     least on keel (sometimes only scabrous) . . . . **B. pubescens**

  5 Lemmas with long hairs along the margin, especially toward the base, glabrous or only minutely
     pubescent on the back; anthers 0.8-1.7 mm long; glumes glabrous or at most scabrous to minutely
     hispid . . . . **B. ciliatus**

1 First glume with 3 (-5) distinct nerves; second glume with 5-7 nerves. 6

  6 Lemmas pubescent all across the back, at least near tip; glumes pubescent; awns straight . . . . **B. kalmii**

  6 Lemmas glabrous or scabrous on the back; glumes glabrous; awns usually divaricate or undulate (or absent). . 7

     7 Lemma equaling or slightly shorter than the tip of the mature palea; sheaths glabrous (or occasionally the
        lowermost with some short hairs); margins of ripe lemmas strongly inrolled, exposing the rachilla; lemmas
        ca. 7-8.2 mm long, the awns ± undulate, sometimes as long as lemma but usually much shorter, rudimentary,
        or occasionally absent. . . . . **B. secalinus**

     7 Lemma at least slightly exceeding tip of palea; sheaths of at least middle and lower leaves ± densely (though
        sometimes finely) hairy; longest awns in a spikelet longer than their lemmas and more than twice as long
        as awn on lowest lemma of the spikelet . . . . **B. arvensis**

Bromus arvensis L.
FIELD BROME
Bromus japonicus Thunb.

MAP 1656
introduced (naturalized)

Weedy annual grass. **Stems** glabrous, 3-9 dm tall; lower **sheaths** softly and densely
appressed-hairy; **ligules** 1-1.5 mm long, hairy, erose; **leaf blades** 10-20 cm long
and 2-6 mm wide, coarsely pilose on both surfaces. **Panicle** 1-2 dm long, loose
and open, the slender branches spreading or drooping, much longer than the
spikelets. **Spikelets** mostly 6-10-flowered, often purple-tinged, glabrous or nearly
so; **first glume** 3-nerved, 4-6 mm long; **second glume** 5-nerved, 5-7.5 mm long;
lemmas 7-nerved, 6-8 mm long, including the triangular teeth 2-3 mm long; **palea**
1.5-2 mm, about equaling or shorter than the lemma; awns more or less twisted
and divergent when dry, the lowest 2.5-5 mm, the uppermost 8-12 mm long;
anthers 2.5-5 mm long.—Native of the Old World; introduced as a weed in waste
places. *Bromus japonicus sometimes treated as a separate species, distinguished by
generally smaller size, spikelets not purple-tinged, and smaller anthers (to 1.5 mm long).*

Bromus ciliatus L.
FRINGED BROME

MAP 1657
native

*Bromus
arvensis*

Perennial grass, rhizomes absent. **Stems** single or few together, smooth or hairy
at nodes, 5-12 dm long; **sheaths** usually with long hairs; **ligule** membranous, short,
to 2 mm long, ragged across tip; **leaf blades** flat, 4-10 mm wide, usually with long,
soft hairs mainly on upper surface. **Panicle** loose, open, 1-3 dm long, the branches
usually drooping. **Spikelets** large, 4-10-flowered, 1.5-3 cm long and 5-10 mm wide;
glumes usually more or less smooth, lance-shaped, the first glume 4-9 mm long,
the second glume 6-10 mm long, often tipped with a short awn; **lemma** 10-15 mm
long, more or less smooth on back, usually long-hairy along lower margins, tipped
with an awn 2-6 mm long; **palea** about as long as body of lemma. July-Sept.
—Streambanks, shores, thickets, sedge meadows, fens, marshes; also in moist
woods.

Bromus inermis Leyss.
SMOOTH BROME

MAP 1658
introduced (invasive)

Perennial grass, with short to long-creeping rhizomes. **Stems** 5-10 dm tall; **sheaths**
glabrous; **auricles** sometimes present; **ligules** to 3 mm long, glabrous, truncate,
erose; **leaf blades** glabrous, 8-15 mm wide. **Panicle** spreading at anthesis, later

Bromus ciliatus
spikelet (top), panicle (bottom)

1656. *Bromus arvensis*   1657. *Bromus ciliatus*   1658. *Bromus inermis*

contracted, 1-2 dm long, often with 4-10 branches from a node. **Spikelets** 15-30 mm long, about 3 mm wide, 7-11-flowered; first **glume** 1-nerved, 4-8 mm long; second glume 3-nerved, 7-11 mm long; **lemmas** 10-12 mm long, 3-5-nerved, the outer pair of nerves often inconspicuous, obtuse or retuse, glabrous or scaberulous, awnless or with an awn to 2 mm long.—Native of Europe, cultivated for forage and often escaped.

Bromus inermis

Bromus kalmii Gray
KALM'S BROME

MAP 1659
native

Perennial grass, not rhizomatous. **Stems** slender, loosely tufted or solitary, 5-10 dm tall, mostly glabrous, often pubescent at the nodes; **sheaths** usually villous, varying to glabrous; **auricles** absent; **ligules** 0.5-1 mm long, glabrous, truncate, erose; **leaf blades** 1-2 dm long and 5-10 mm wide, glabrous or pubescent on both sides. **Panicle** nodding, 5-10 cm long or rarely longer, the relatively few spikelets drooping on slender flexuous pedicels. **Spikelets** 15-25 mm long, 6-11-flowered, softly villous; first **glume** 3-nerved, 6-7 mm long; second glume 5-nerved, 7-9 mm long, **lemmas** 7-nerved, 8-10 mm long, obtuse, the awn 2-3 mm long; the teeth about a third as wide as long.—Dry woods, rocky banks, and sandy or gravelly soil.

Bromus latiglumis (Shear) A.S. Hitchc.
EARLY-LEAF BROME
Bromus altissimus Pursh

MAP 1660
native

Perennial grass, not rhizomatous. **Stems** single or in small clumps, more or less smooth, 6-15 dm long; **sheaths** overlapping, retrorsely pilose or glabrous, with a dense ring of hairs at top; **auricles** 1-2.5 mm long; **ligules** 0.8-1.4 mm long, hirsute, ciliate, truncate, erose; **leaf blades** flat, 8-20 along stem; 10-15 mm wide. **Panicle** 1-2 dm long, the branches spreading or drooping. **Spikelets** several-flowered, 2-3 cm long, first **glume** 5-8 mm long, awl-shaped, second glume wider, 6-10 mm long; **lemmas** 10-12 mm long, hairy, awned, the awn 2-7 mm long.—Floodplain forests, thickets and streambanks, sometimes in rocky woods. *Similar to B. pubescens, a species of mostly mesic woods, but stems with more leaves, the top of sheaths with a ring of dense hairs, and leaf blades with well developed auricles.*

Bromus kalmii

Bromus pubescens Muhl.
HAIRY WOODLAND BROME

MAP 1661
native

Perennial grass, not rhizomatous. **Stems** solitary or few together, 6-15 dm tall, glabrous or nearly so; **sheaths** shorter than the internodes, glabrous to densely canescent with spreading or somewhat retrorse hairs; **auricles** absent; **ligules** 0.5-2 mm long, glabrous, obtuse to truncate, erose; **leaf blades** narrowed at base, 8-15 mm wide, glabrous to sparsely villous. **Panicle** 1-2 dm long, its elongate branches loosely spreading or drooping. **Spikelets** 2-3 cm long; first **glume** subulate, 1-nerved, 5-8 mm long; second glume broader, 3-nerved, 6-10 mm long; **lemmas** 7-nerved, 9-12 mm long, thinly to densely pubescent throughout, the awn 2-8 mm long. Variable.—Rich, moist woods.

Bromus latiglumis

Bromus secalinus L.
RYE BROME; CHESS

MAP 1662
introduced (naturalized)

Annual grass. **Stems** glabrous, 3-8 dm tall; middle and upper **sheaths** glabrous; **ligules** 2-3 mm long, glabrous, obtuse; **leaf blades** glabrous or pubescent, 3-8 mm wide. **Panicle** loose and open, 7-15 cm long, its branches several from a node, simple or again branched. **Spikelets** usually drooping, 6-11-flowered, 1-2 cm long;

1659. Bromus kalmii   *1660. Bromus latiglumis*   *1661. Bromus pubescens*   *1662. Bromus secalinus*

first glume oblong, 3-5-nerved, 4-6 mm long; **second glume** similar, 5-7-nerved, 5-7 mm long; **lemmas** elliptic, obtuse, obscurely 7-nerved, 6-9 mm long, glabrous or minutely scaberulous, awnless or with an awn to 5 mm long between the broad teeth; margins of the lemmas soon involute, causing the florets to diverge and expose the flexuous rachilla.—Native of Europe; introduced in grainfields, roadsides, and waste places.

Bromus tectorum L.
CHEATGRASS

MAP 1663
introduced (naturalized)

Annual grass. **Stems** tufted, 3-7 dm tall; **sheaths** and **blades** softly pubescent, the latter 2-4 mm wide; **ligules** 2-3 mm long, glabrous, obtuse, lacerate. **Panicle** 1-2 dm long, repeatedly branched, bearing rather crowded, drooping spikelets to 3 cm long, on slender pedicels; first **glume** subulate, 1-nerved, 5.5-7 mm long; second glume subulate, 3-nerved, 8-10 mm long; **lemmas** narrowly lance-shaped, 5-7-nerved, 10-12 mm long, pubescent throughout, usually hirsute toward the tip, acuminate into slender scarious teeth; awn 12-17 mm long; **palea** conspicuously ciliate.—Native of s Europe, widely established as a weed in waste ground and on roadsides; now common in many sagebrush communities in the western states.

Bromus tectorum

BUCHLOË *Buffalo Grass*

CYNODONTEAE

Buchloë dactyloides (Nutt.) Engelm.
BUFFALO GRASS

MAP 1664
native

Perennial mat-forming grass, plants strongly stoloniferous, dioecious (rarely monoecious). **Stems** 0.5-2 dm tall, solid, the staminate plants slightly taller than the pistillate plants; **sheaths** open, usually glabrous except near the collar; **ligule** a short fringe of hairs less than 1 mm long, often flanked by long hairs; **auricles** absent; **leaf blades** flat, glabrous to sparsely hispid, 1-10 cm long and 1-2 mm wide. **Staminate inflorescences** on slender stems, each with of 2 or 3 unilateral spicate branches, bearing spikelets in 2 rows; **staminate spikelets** 2-flowered; glumes unequal. **Pistillate spikelets** in 2 or 3 burlike clusters closely subtended by modified foliage leaves, usually with 2- 4 spikelets per bur, the bur falling as a unit; **pistillate spikelets** usually 1-flowered; first glume small, membranaceous (often obsolete in all but 1 spikelet of each bur); second glume indurate at base, enveloping the lemma and terminating in (usually) 3 awnlike points; lemma with 3 short awns. April-June.—A dominant grass of short-grass prairies of the western Great Plains; local in exposed, well-drained locations in sw Minnesota.

Buchloë dactyloides
staminate plants (upper)
pistillate plants (lower)

CALAMAGROSTIS *Reed-Grass*

POEAE

Perennial grasses, spreading by rhizomes. Stems single or in clumps. Leaves flat or inrolled, green or waxy blue-green, smooth or rough-to-touch; sheaths smooth; ligule large, membranous, usually with an irregular, ragged margin. Head a loose and open or dense and contracted panicle. Spikelets 1-flowered, breaking above glumes; glumes nearly equal, lance-shaped; lemma shorter than glumes, lance-shaped, awned from back, the awn about as long as lemma, the base of lemma (callus) bearded with a tuft of hairs, these shorter to as long as lemma; palea shorter than lemma; stamens 3.

ADDITIONAL SPECIES
Calamagrostis purpurascens R. Br. (Purple reedgrass), ✿*endangered;* disjunct from w and n North America; on slate cliffs in Cook County along the Canadian border.

1   Plants low, usually less than 4.5 dm tall; awns strongly geniculate, projecting sideways from between the lemmas
. . . . ***C. montanensis***

  2   Leaf blades rather lax, to 10 mm wide; panicle mostly open with rather loosely ascending to spreading branches at flowering time; lemma nearly or quite smooth, membranous and translucent for at least the apical half; awn nearly or quite smooth, at least on basal half; callus hairs about as long as lemma (occasionally shorter), ± uniform in length and distribution; palea not over 2 mm long . . . . ***C. canadensis***

  2   Leaf blades stiff, to 4 mm wide; panicle mostly narrow and contracted with strongly ascending branches at flowering time; lemma usually firm and prominently scabrous, colorless and translucent only toward the tip; awn distinctly but minutely antrorsely scabrous its entire length (at 20×); callus hairs generally shorter than

lemma, ± unequal in length or distribution (those immediately below the middle of the lemma shorter than those at the side, or absent; do not confuse the hairy prolongation of the rachilla behind the palea); palea often longer than 2 mm . . . . **C. stricta**

Calamagrostis canadensis (Michx.) Beauv.

MAP 1665
BLUEJOINT   *native*

Perennial grass, from creeping rhizomes. **Stems** erect, in small clumps, 6-15 dm long, often rooting from lower nodes when partly underwater; **leaf blades** flat, green to waxy blue-green, 3-8 mm wide, rough-to-touch on both sides; sheaths smooth; ligules 3-7 mm long. **Panicle** more or less open, 8-20 cm long, the branches upright or spreading. **Spikelets** 1-flowered, 2-6 mm long; **glumes** more or less equal, 2-4 mm long, smooth or finely rough-hairy on back; **lemma** more or less smooth, awned from middle of back, the awn straight, base with dense callus hairs about as long as lemma. June-Aug.—Wet meadows, shallow marshes, calcareous fens, streambanks, thickets. Common.

Calamagrostis montanensis (Scribn.) Vasey

MAP 1666
PLAINS REEDGRASS   *native*

Perennial grass, spreading by rhizomes and forming mats. **Stems** erect, usually scabrous below the panicle, 1-5 dm tall; **sheaths** smooth; **ligules** mostly 2- 4. 5 mm long on the stem leaves, usually lacerate; **leaf blades** involute, rather stiff and erect, scabrous, ridges and furrows pronounced on the upper surface, to ca. 20 cm long and 1-3. 5 mm wide. **Panicle** spikelike, to 10 cm long; **glumes** scabrous, the second glume often slightly shorter than the first; **lemma** with a stout, geniculate awn 1-3 mm long, protruding from between the glumes when mature. June-July.—Dry, sandy or gravelly prairies in w Minn (a species of the n Great Plains; Minn at eastern edge of species' range). *The inflorescence is a slender, uninterrupted spike resembling that of **junegrass** (Koeleria macrantha), but in C. montanensis, the spikelets have awned lemmas and stems arising singly rather than in a clump.*

Calamagrostis canadensis

Calamagrostis stricta (Timm) Koel.

MAP 1667
SLIM-STEM REED-GRASS   *native*
  Calamagrostis inexpansa Gray

Perennial grass, spreading by rhizomes; plants waxy blue-green. **Stems** erect, 3-12 dm long; **leaf blades** stiff, often inrolled, 1-4 mm wide when flattened. **Panicle** narrow, 5-15 cm long, the branches short, upright to erect. **Spikelets** 1-flowered; **glumes** 3-6 mm long, smooth or rough-hairy on back; **lemma** rough-hairy, 2-4 mm long, awned, the awn straight, from near middle of back, base with many callus hairs, half to as long as lemma. June-Sept.—Wet meadows, shallow marshes, shores, streambanks; rocky shore of Lake Superior.

Calamagrostis stricta

CALAMOVILFA *Sand-Reed*   CYNODONTEAE

Calamovilfa longifolia (Hook.) Scribn.

MAP 1668
SAND-REED   *native*

Perennial grass, from creeping rhizomes, the rhizomes covered with shiny, scale-like leaves. **Stems** stout, stiffly erect, to 2 m tall; **sheaths** much overlapping at base, glabrous except usually more or less villous at the throat; **ligule** a ring of short hairs 1-2 mm long; **leaf blades** flat and 3-8 mm wide at base, involute above, tapering to a fine point. **Panicle** open, 1-4 dm long, with ascending branches.

1663. Bromus tectorum

1664. **Buchloë dactyloides**

1665. Calamagrostis canadensis

Calamovilfa longifolia

Spikelets 1-flowered, articulated above the glumes; **glumes** 1-nerved; first glume ovate, 3.5-6 mm long, second glume 4.5-7.5 mm long; **lemma** glabrous on the back, equaling or slightly shorter than the second glume, awnless, subtended by a conspicuous tuft of hairs from the callus, the hairs about half as long as the lemma.—Dry sandy prairies and dunes.

CENCHRUS *Sandbur* PANICEAE

Cenchrus longispinus (Hack.) Fern.
COMMON SANDBUR

MAP 1669
native

Annual grass. **Stems** ascending or spreading, 2-6 dm long, often with many branches arising from the base; **sheaths** strongly compressed-keeled, villous-ciliate toward the summit; **ligules** 0.6-1.8 mm long, villous; **leaf blades** usually 5-12 cm long. **Inflorescences** terminal, spikelike panicles of highly reduced branches termed fascicles ("burs"); **fascicles** consisting of 1-2 series of many, stiff, sharp bristles surrounding 1-4 spikelets. **Spikelets** with 1 perfect flower, narrowly ovoid, acuminate, permanently enclosed by a spiny bur composed of several to many concrescent, flattened bristles. **Burs** subglobose, pubescent, usually 4-5 mm wide, excluding the spines, the latter 3-5 mm long; tips of the spikelets conspicuously exsert, their bodies visible to the middle through the lateral cleft of the bur; **glumes** hyaline, the first 1-nerved, the second 3-5-nerved.—Disturbed places, especially where dry and sandy. *The spines are painfully sharp if walking barefoot.*

Cenchrus longispinus

CINNA *Wood-Reed* POEAE

Tall, perennial grasses, rhizomes weak or absent. Leaves wide, flat and lax; auricles absent; ligule brown, membranous, with an irregular, jagged margin. Head a large, closed to open panicle, the branches upright to spreading or drooping. Spikelets small, 1-flowered, laterally compressed, breaking below the glumes; glumes nearly equal, lance-shaped, keeled; lemma similar to glumes, with a short awn from just below the tip; palea shorter than lemma; stamens 1.

1 Panicle more or less crowded and narrow, the branches upright; second glume 4-6 mm long. . . . *C. arundinacea*
1 Panicle open, the branches spreading to drooping; second glume 2-4 mm long. . . . . *C. latifolia*

Cinna arundinacea L.
SWEET WOOD-REED

MAP 1670
native

Perennial grass, rhizomes weak or absent. **Stems** 1 or few together, erect, 6-15 dm long, often swollen at base; **sheaths** smooth; **ligules** red-brown, 3-10 mm long; **leaf blades** 4-12 mm wide, margins rough-to-touch. **Panicle** narrow, dull gray-green, 1-3 dm long, the branches upright. **Spikelets** 1-flowered; **glumes** narrowly lance-shaped, 3-5 mm long, the first glume 1-veined, the second glume 3-veined, usually rough-hairy; **lemma** 3-5 mm long, rough-hairy on back, usually with an awn to 0.5 mm long, attached just below tip and mostly shorter than lemma tip. Aug-Sept.—Swamps, floodplain forests, streambanks, pond margins, moist woods. *Distinguished from C. latifolia by its 3-veined upper glumes and larger spikelets.*

Cinna arundinacea

1666. Calamagrostis montanensis *1667. Calamagrostis stricta* *1668. Calamovilfa longifolia* *1669. Cenchrus longispinus*

Cinna latifolia (Trev.) Griseb.   MAP 1671
DROOPING WOOD-REED   *native*
Perennial grass, with weak rhizomes. **Stems** single or in small groups, erect, 5-13
dm long, not swollen at base; **sheaths** smooth to finely roughened; **ligules** pale,
2-7 mm long; **leaf blades** 5-15 mm wide, usually rough-to-touch. Panicle loose,
open, pale green, satiny, 1-3.5 dm long, the branches spreading to drooping.
Spikelets 1-flowered; glumes narrowly lance-shaped, 1-veined, 2-4 mm long;
lemma 2-4 mm long, finely rough-hairy on back, usually with an awn to 1.5 mm
long from just below the tip, the awn usually longer than the tip. July-Aug.—Wet
woods, swamps, springs.   *Cinna latifolia*

DACTYLIS *Orchard-Grass*   POEAE

Dactylis glomerata L.   MAP 1672
ORCHARD-GRASS   *introduced (naturalized)*
Perennial, densely tufted grass. **Stems** 5-12 dm tall; **sheaths** closed for at least 1/2
their length compressed or keeled, scaberulous; **auricles** absent; **ligules**
membranous, 3-11 mm long, truncate to acuminate; leaf blades flat, elongate, 3-
8 mm wide, with a conspicuous midrib and white, scabrous margins. **Panicles**
open, 1-2 dm long, the lower branches naked at base, erect or divergent. **Spikelets**
few-flowered, flat, disarticulating above the glumes and between the lemmas,
nearly sessile in dense one-sided clusters, 3-6-flowered; **glumes** unequal, nearly
as long as the lemmas, lance-shaped, 1-3-nerved, keeled, usually ciliate on the
keel; **lemmas** 5-8 mm long, usually ciliate on the keel, awnless or with an awn to
2 mm long.—Introduced from Europe, cultivated for hay or pasture; occasional
escape to moist fields, meadows, lawns, and roadsides.
                                                             Dactylis glomerata

DANTHONIA *Wild Oatgrass*   DANTHONIEAE

Danthonia spicata (L.) Beauv.   MAP 1673
POVERTY WILD OATGRASS   *native*
Perennial grass. **Stems** densely tufted, erect, 2-6 dm tall; **sheaths** glabrous or
sparsely pilose; **ligules** reduced to a tuft of hairs; **auricles** absent; **leaves** mostly at
or near the base, **leaf blades** usually involute, 1-2 mm wide, seldom more than 10
cm long, glabrous or sparsely pilose; uppermost stem blades erect to ascending.
Panicle contracted, racemiform, 2-5 cm long, the short branches rarely bearing
more than 1 spikelet; **spikelets** several-flowered (usually 4-6), articulated above
the glumes and between the lemmas; **glumes** extending beyond the lemmas, 8.5-
13 mm long; **lemmas** broadly ovate, sparsely pilose on the back, tipped with 2
triangular teeth; awn arising between the teeth, the flat brown base tightly twisted
when dry, the upper portion straight, usually divergent from the spikelet, 5-7 mm
long.—Common in dry woods in sandy or stony soil, especially on jack pine
plains, where it may form extensive colonies following disturbance; occasionally
found in marshy or boggy places. *The basal leaves tend to curl and form distinctive
tufts.*   *Danthonia spicata*

DESCHAMPSIA *Hairgrass*   POEAE

Tufted perennial grasses. Leaves usually mainly basal, narrow, flat or involute; sheaths open; auricles
absent; ligules membranous. Flowers in panicles; spikelets yellowish or purple, 2-flowered,
disarticulating above the glumes and between the lemmas; rachilla hairy, prolonged beyond the base

1670. Cinna arundinacea   *1671. Cinna latifolia*   *1672. Dactylis glomerata*   *1673. Danthonia spicata*

of the upper lemma. Glumes membranous, usually shining, equaling or longer than the lemmas. Lemmas membranous, obtuse or truncate and erose-toothed, rounded on the back, obscurely 5-nerved, the mid-nerve diverging at or below the middle into a short awn, the callus bearded.

1 Leaf blades involute, 1-2 mm wide; ligule 1-2.5 mm long; lemmas minutely scabrous-pubescent, bearing a conspicuously bent awn 1-3 mm longer than the lemmas; palea not bifid at tip. . . . . **D. flexuosa**
1 Leaf blades flat or conduplicate, 1-5 mm wide; ligule usually 3-12 mm long; lemmas glabrous, bearing a ± straight awn shorter than to slightly exceeding the lemmas; palea bifid at the tip. . . . . **D. cespitosa**

Deschampsia caespitosa (L.) Beauv.
TUFTED HAIRGRASS

MAP 1674
native

Stems densely tufted stiff, erect, 3-10 dm long. **Leaves** mostly from base of plant, usually shorter than head, 5-30 cm long, usually at least some flat and 1-4 mm wide, the remainder folded or rolled and to 1 mm wide; **sheaths** glabrous; **ligules** 2-13 mm long, white, translucent. **Panicles** narrow to open, 1-4 dm long, the panicle branches threadlike, upright to spreading, the lower branches in groups of 2-5, flowers mostly near branch tips. **Spikelets** 2-flowered, purple-tinged, fading to silver with age, 2-5 mm long, breaking above the glumes; **glumes** shiny, 2-5 mm long, the first glume slightly shorter than second glume; **lemma** smooth, 2-4-toothed across the flat tip, awned from near base on back, the awn shorter to about as long as lemma. June-July.—Wet meadows, streambanks, rocky shores.

Deschampsia flexuosa (L.) Trin.
HAIRGRASS
  Avenella flexuosa (L.) Drej.

MAP 1675
🖝 *threatened | native*

Stems densely tufted, 3-10 dm long. **Leaves** mostly at or near the base; **blades** involute, 1-2 mm wide; **ligules** 1.5-3.5 mm long. **Panicle** loose and open, somewhat nodding, to 15 cm long, the lowest branches in fascicles of 2-5. **Spikelets** 4.3-6 mm long; first **glume** 3-4.5 mm long; second glume acuminate, 3.6-5.3 mm long; **lemmas** minutely scabrous; awn twisted below the middle, the distal half somewhat divergent, surpassing the lemma by 1-3 mm.—Dry sandy or rocky pine woods, mostly near Lake Superior.

Deschampsia caespitosa

DIARRHENA *Beakgrain*   DIARRHENEAE

Diarrhena obovata (Gleason) Brandenburg
HAIRY BEAKGRAIN
  Diarrhena americana Beauv. var. *obovata* Gleason

MAP 1676
🖝 *endangered | native*

Perennial grass, from a thick scaly rhizome. **Stems** slender, erect, 5-12 dm long, with leaves mostly below the middle, and a long, slender, few-flowered panicle; **sheaths** pubescent toward the tip; **ligules** 0.2-1 mm long, stiffly membranous, rounded, ciliolate; **leaf blades** 2-4 dm long and 10-18 mm wide, the midvein off-center. **Panicle** scabrous, long-exsert, 1-3 dm long, drooping. **Spikelets** 3-5-flowered, disarticulating above the glumes and between the lemmas; at first subcylindric, soon flattened by spreading of the lemmas; first **glume** triangular, 2-3 mm long, 1-nerved; second glume oblong, 2.4-4.3 mm long, 3-5-nerved; **lemmas** smooth, somewhat leathery, 5-7 mm long, abruptly rounded at tip, the 3 conspicuous nerves convergent at the summit and excurrent into a short stout point.—Floodplain forests along Root River in southeastern Minnesota.

Deschampsia flexuosa

Diarrhena obovata

1674. *Deschampsia caespitosa*

1675. *Deschampsia flexuosa*

1676. *Diarrhena obovata*

1677. *Dichanthe. acuminatum*

DICHANTHELIUM *Panic-grass*   PANICEAE

Perennial grasses, tufted or sometimes rhizomatous, sometimes with hard, corm-like bases. Stems hollow, usually erect or ascending, sometimes decumbent in the fall, usually branching from the lower stem nodes in summer and fall, terminating in small panicles that are usually partly included in the sheaths. Basal rosettes of winter leaves sometimes present. Stem leaves usually markedly longer and narrower than the rosette blades; ligules of hairs, membranous, or membranous and ciliate, sometimes absent. Flowers in terminal panicles (vernal) developing late spring to early summer, and sometimes lateral panicles(autumnal) in late-summer or fall; disarticulation below the glumes. *Dichanthelium is often included in genus Panicum, the two genera being similar in form. However, molecular data reinforce the validity of separating Dichanthelium as a distinct genus.*

1 Basal leaf blades similar in shape to the lower stem leaves, usually erect to ascending, clustered at the base, sometimes vestigial; stems branching from near the base in the fall, with 2-4 leaves, only the upper 2-4 internodes elongated 2
  2 Upper glumes and lower lemmas forming a beak extending 0.2-1 mm beyond the upper florets; spikelets 3.2-4.3 mm long; primary panicles with 7-25 spikelets . . . . *D. depauperatum*
  2 Upper glumes and lower lemmas equaling or exceeding the upper florets by no more than 0.3 mm, not forming a beak; spikelets 2-3.4 mm long; primary panicles with 12-70 spikelets 3
    3 Stem blades 4-8 cm long, all alike . . . . *D. wilcoxianum*
    3 Uppermost stem blades 10-20 cm long, distinctly longer than the lower blades . . . . *D. linearifolium*
1 Basal leaf blades usually well-differentiated from the stem blades, spreading, forming a rosette, or basal blades absent; stems usually branching from the midculm nodes in the fall, with 3-14 leaves, usually all internodes elongated 4
  4 Lower glumes thinner and more weakly veined than the upper glumes, attached about 0.2 mm below the upper glumes, the bases clasping the pedicels; spikelets attenuate basally . . . . *D. portoricense*
  4 Lower glumes similar in texture and vein prominence to the upper glumes, attached immediately below the upper glumes, the bases not clasping the pedicels; spikelets usually not attenuate basally 5
    5 Ligules with a membranous base, ciliate distally; stems usually arising from slender rhizomes; lower florets often staminate; stem blades 5-40 mm wide, often with a cordate base 6
      6 Spikelets ellipsoid, not turgid, with pointed apices; stem blades 4-6, cordate at the base; sheaths without papillose-based hairs . . . . *D. latifolium*
      6 Spikelets obovoid, turgid, with rounded apices; stem blades 3-4, tapered, rounded or truncate to cordate at the base; sheaths with papillose-based hairs 7
        7 Blades and spikelets with papillose-based hairs; panicles usually slightly longer than wide, with spreading to ascending branches . . . . *D. leibergii*
        7 Blades glabrous; spikelets puberulent to almost glabrous; panicles usually more than 2x longer than wide, with nearly erect branches. . . . . *D. xanthophysum*
    5 Ligules of hairs; stems arising from caudices; lower florets sterile; stem blades 1-18 mm wide, bases usually tapered, rounded, or truncate at the base, sometimes cordate 8
      8 Spikelets 2.5-4.3 mm long, usually obovoid, turgid; upper glumes usually with an orange or purple spot at the base, the veins prominent. . . . . *D. oligosanthes*
      8 Spikelets 0.8-3 mm long, ellipsoid or obovoid, not turgid; upper glumes lacking an orange or purple spot at the base and the veins not prominent 9
        9 Ligules 1-5 mm long, or the stems and sheaths with long hairs and also puberulent; spikelets variously pubescent to subglabrous 10
          10 Spikelets 1.1-2.1 mm long; sheaths glabrous or pubescent with hairs no more than 3 mm long. . . . . *D. acuminatum*
          10 Spikelets 1.8-3 mm long; sheaths with hairs to 4 mm long . . . . *D. ovale*
        9 Ligules absent or to 1.8 mm long, without adjacent pseudoligules; stems and at least the upper sheaths glabrous or sparsely pubescent with hairs of 1 length only; spikelets glabrous or pubescent 11
          11 Spikelets glabrous or, if pubescent, either the nodes bearded or the stems weak and prostrate; blade of the flag leaf usually spreading . . . . *D. dichotomum*
          11 Spikelets pubescent; nodes glabrous; stems erect or ascending; blade of the flag leaf erect or ascending . . . . *D. boreale*

Dichanthelium acuminatum (Sw.) Gould & C. A. Clark   MAP 1677
HAIRY PANIC-GRASS   *native*
  Panicum acuminatum Sw.
Stems densely tufted, erect to prostrate, usually straight and radiating from the base, glabrous to pilose or villous; **sheaths** softly pubescent, papillose-pilose, or

glabrous; **ligule** hairs 2-5 mm long; **leaf blades** 4-12 cm long, 5-12 mm wide, glabrous or pubescent on either or both sides. **Primary panicle** ovoid, with divergent, often flexuous branches, the axis glabrate to villous. **Spikelets** ellipsoid to obovoid, 1-2 mm long, finely pubescent; first **glume** broadly angular-rotund, usually less than a third as long than the second glume. **Autumnal phase** spreading or prostrate, copiously branched chiefly from the middle nodes; blades about half as large as the vernal ones; panicles few-flowered, mostly surpassed by the leaves.—Moist or dry situations, open woods, dunes, shores, and prairies.

Dichanthelium boreale (Nash) Freckmann

MAP 1678

NORTHERN PANIC-GRASS *native*

Panicum boreale Nash

Stems upright, 2-6 dm long; **sheaths** hairy; **ligule** a fringe of short hairs to 0.5 mm long; **leaf blades** upright to spreading, 5-20 cm long and 1-2 cm wide, smooth or sometimes hairy on underside, base of blade often fringed with hairs. **Panicle** open, 5-12 cm long, the branches spreading or upright. **Spikelets** oval in outline, finely hairy, about 2 mm long, on long stalks with 1 fertile flower; first **glume** 0.5-1 mm long, triangular-ovate; second glume and lemma purple-tinged, about equal, and as long as fruit. **Autumnal phase** with decumbent stems, branches arising from the lower and mid-stem nodes, and rebranching 2-3 times. June-Aug.—Local in wet prairies and tamarack bogs.

Dichanthelium acuminatum

Dichanthelium depauperatum (Muhl.) Gould

MAP 1679

STARVED PANIC-GRASS *native*

Panicum depauperatum Muhl.

Stems tufted, erect or nearly so, 1-4 dm long, very slender, glabrous to puberulent; sheaths and leaves glabrous to sometimes long-pilose; **leaf blades** erect, 8-15 cm long, 2-5 mm wide; **ligules** about 0.5 mm long. **Primary panicle** eventually exsert, 3-6 cm long, not much exceeding the leaves. **Spikelets** ellipsoid, 2.7-4.1 mm long, averaging 3.2 mm, glabrous or minutely pubescent; first glume membranous, ovate or triangular, about a third as long; second glume and sterile lemma sharply nerved, pointed, projecting 0.5-1.5 mm beyond the fertile lemma. **Autumnal phase** similar, the panicles much reduced and usually concealed among a dense mass of erect leaves.—Dry or sandy soil, usually in open woods.

Dichanthelium dichotomum (L.) Gould

MAP 1680

FORKED PANIC-GRASS *native*

Panicum dichotomum L.

Stems very slender, erect, 3-7 dm long, glabrous; nodes glabrous, pubescent, or (especially the lower) bearded; **sheaths** much shorter than the internodes, glabrous or minutely ciliate; **ligules** absent or shorter than 1 mm, of hairs; **leaf blades** spreading, thin, dark green, 3-8 mm wide, glabrous, or ciliate at the base. **Primary panicle** 5-10 cm long, with spreading branches. **Spikelets** ellipsoid, 1.9-2.2 mm long, glabrous; first **glume** about a third as long, usually acute, second glume rounded above, shorter than the sterile lemma, both shorter than the fruit. **Autumnal phase** much branched above the middle, erect or reclining from its own weight; leaf blades 2-5 cm long, 2-5 mm wide; panicles greatly reduced.—Dry or moist woods.

Dichanthelium boreale

1678. *Dichanthelium boreale*

1679. *Dichan. depauperatum*

1680. *Dichanth. dichotomum*

1681. *Dichanthelium latifolium*

Dichanthelium latifolium (L.) Gould & C. A. Clark   MAP 1681
BROADLEAVED PANIC-GRASS   *native*
  Panicum latifolium L.

Stems tufted, slender, erect, 4-10 dm long, usually glabrous, rarely sparsely puberulent; **sheaths** pubescent; ligules to 0.7 mm long, membranous, ciliate, the cilia longer than the membranous portion; **leaf blades** lance-shaped, spreading, glabrous. or nearly so on both sides, ciliate at the cordate base, the larger usually 10-16 cm long, 15-30 mm wide. **Primary panicle** tardily exsert, ovoid with ascending branches, 6-12 cm long. **Spikelets** oblong-obovoid, 2.9-3.7 mm long, averaging 3.3 mm, softly villosulous; first glume about half as long, acute; second glume and sterile lemma shorter than the fruit. **Autumnal phase** sparsely branched from the middle nodes, the leaf blades not much reduced or greatly crowded; panicles small, included at base.—Moist or dry woods and thickets.

Dichanthelium leibergii (Vasey) Freckmann   MAP 1682
LEIBERG'S PANIC-GRASS   *native*
  Panicum leibergii (Vasey) Scribn.

Stems solitary to several in a tuft, erect or geniculate below, 3-6 dm long, minutely puberulent; **sheaths** shorter than the internodes, papillose-hirsute with spreading hairs; **ligules** to 0.5 mm long, membranous, ciliate, cilia longer than the membranous portion; **leaf blades** erect or ascending, the larger 7-11 cm long, 7-12 mm wide, slightly tapering to a broadly rounded base, papillose-hirsute on both sides, varying to nearly glabrous above. **Primary panicle** at first included, tardily becoming long-exsert, 5-10 cm long, ovoid or oblong with few-flowered ascending branches. **Spikelets** oblong-obovoid, 3-3.9 mm long, papillose-hirsute with hairs 0.5-1 mm long; first glume about 3/5 as long, triangular-ovate; second glume and sterile lemma about equal. **Autumnal phase** with a few suberect branches from the lower and mid-stem nodes, blades slightly reduced, secondary panicles partially exserted.—Moist to dry grassy meadows and prairies.

Dichanthelium leibergii

Dichanthelium linearifolium (Scribn.) Gould   MAP 1683
LINEAR-LEAVED PANIC-GRASS   *native*
  Dichanthelium perlongum (Nash) Freckmann
  Panicum linearifolium Scribn.

Stems densely tufted, 2-6 dm long, glabrous or nearly so; **sheaths** glabrous or pilose with dense, fine, papillose-based hairs; **ligules** about 0.5 mm long; **leaf blades** erect, usually 10-20 cm long, 2-5 mm wide, glabrous to sparsely pilose. **Primary panicle** 3-8 cm long, usually much surpassing the blades. **Spikelets** ellipsoid to oblong-obovoid, 1.7-3.1 mm long, glabrous to pilose; first glume about a third as long, ovate to triangular; second glume and sterile lemma blunt, equaling the fruit. **Autumnal phase** similar, the greatly reduced panicles concealed among the leaves.—Dry or stony soil, open woods and banks.

Dichanthelium oligosanthes (J.A. Schultes) Gould   MAP 1684
FEW-FLOWERED PANICGRASS   *native*
  Panicum oligosanthes J.A. Schultes

Stems few to several, loosely tufted, erect or ascending, 2-7 dm long, often purplish; **sheaths** not overlapping, glabrous or puberulent, margins ciliate, collars loose, puberulent; **ligules** 1-3 mm long, of hairs; **leaf blades** spreading, lance-shaped, glabrous or rarely sparsely papillose-pilose above; glabrous, softly pubescent, or sparsely papillose-pilose beneath, usually papillose-ciliate and

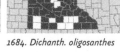

1682. *Dichanthelium leibergii*   1683. *Dichanth. linearifolium*   1684. *Dichanth. oligosanthes*

Dichanthelium linearifolium

densely long-hairy at base, the larger 6-12 cm long and 7-12 mm wide. **Primary panicle** short-exsert (0-5 cm), becoming long-exsert in age, ovoid, 5-10 cm long. **Spikelets** ellipsoid to obovoid, 2.7-4 mm long, glabrous or minutely villous; first **glume** about 2/5 as long, broadly ovate; second glume and sterile lemma about equal, barely equaling the fruit. **Autumnal phase** sparsely branched, chiefly from the middle and upper nodes, forming loose bunches; leaf blades not greatly reduced, surpassing the few-flowered panicles.—Dry or moist, often sandy soil, open woods and prairies.

Dichanthelium ovale (Elliott) Gould & C.A. Clark
MAP 1685
STIFF-LEAVED PANIC-GRASS   *native*

Stems tufted, 20-60 cm long, usually more than 1 mm thick, not delicate, ascending or spreading and often decumbent; **sheaths** shorter than the internodes, pilose, hairs to 4 mm, occasionally with shorter, spreading hairs underneath; **ligules** 1-5 mm long, of hairs; **leaf blades** 4-10 cm long and 3-10 mm wide, relatively firm, mostly ascending or spreading, sparsely to densely pubescent with appressed or erect hairs to 5 mm long, margins often whitish. **Primary panicle** 3-10 cm long, nearly as wide when fully expanded; branches often stiffly ascending or spreading, usually pilose at base. **Spikelets** 2-3 mm long, ellipsoid or obovoid, densely to sparsely pilose; first glume to 1/2 as long as the spikelets, often triangular, not strongly veined; second glume usually slightly shorter than the lower lemmas and upper florets, not strongly veined. **Autumnal phase** with decumbent to prostrate stems, with erect, slightly reduced blades and greatly reduced secondary panicles.—Dry, sandy openings and meadows.

Dichanthelium ovale

Dichanthelium portoricense (Desv. ex Ham.) Hansen & Wunderlin MAP 1686
BLUNT-GLUMED PANIC-GRASS   *native*
   Panicum columbianum Scribn.

Stems densely tufted, erect or ascending, 2-5 dm tall, often purplish, densely short-pubescent with minute hairs 0.1-0.4 mm long, or toward the tips of the lower internodes sometimes 1 mm long; **sheaths** similarly pubescent; **ligule** hairs 0.5-1.5 mm long; **leaf blades** 3-7 cm long and 3-7 mm wide, glabrous above or with a few widely scattered hairs, minutely puberulent beneath. **Primary panicle** ovoid, 2-6 cm long, its axis puberulent. **Spikelets** obovoid, obtuse, 1.4-1.9 mm long, finely pubescent; first glume averaging 2/5 as long, triangular-ovate. **Autumnal phase** spreading or decumbent, branched early from most of the nodes; blades scarcely reduced; panicles smaller, surpassed by the leaves.—Moist or dry, especially sandy soil.

Dichanthelium portoricense

Dichanthelium wilcoxianum (Vasey) Freckmann
MAP 1687
WILCOX'S PANIC-GRASS   *native*
Stems densely tufted, erect, 1-3 dm long, papillose-hirsute with ascending hairs to sparsely villous; **sheaths** loose, usually longer than the internodes, papillose-hirsute with hairs usually 2-5 mm long; **ligules** 0.5-1 mm long; **leaf blades** erect, 4-8 cm long and 3-6 mm wide, scarcely wider than the sheaths, involute towards tip, papillose-hirsute on both sides, varying to nearly glabrous above. **Primary panicle** tardily exsert, ovoid, 2-4 cm long, the flexuous axis and branches glabrate except in the axils. **Spikelets** ellipsoid-obovoid, 2.4-2.9 mm long, softly villous; first **glume** about a third as long (0.7-1.4 mm), broadly ovate; second glume slightly shorter than the fruit and sterile lemma. **Autumnal phase** branching early, before maturity of the primary panicle, from all nodes, forming dense masses 1-2 dm

Dichanthelium wilcoxianum

1685. *Dichanthelium ovale*

1686. *Dichanth. portoricense*

1687. *Dichanth. wilcoxianum*

1688. *Dichant. xanthophysum*

tall, the erect leaf blades scarcely reduced, much surpassing the smaller panicles.
— Dry prairies, often where sandy or gravelly.

Dichanthelium xanthophysum (Gray) Freckmann   MAP 1688
PALE PANIC-GRASS   *native*
  Panicum xanthophysum A. Gray

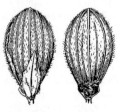

Dichanthelium xanthophysum

Stems few or several in loose tufts, erect or ascending, 2-5 dm long, glabrous;
sheaths loose, often exceeding the internodes, glabrous to pilose or papillose-
pilose; **ligules** to 0.5 mm long, membranous, ciliate, the cilia longer than the
membranous bases; **leaf blades** yellowish green, erect or nearly so, the larger 10-
15 cm long and 10-20 mm wide, glabrous on both sides, slightly narrowed to the
rounded, papillose-ciliate base. **Primary panicle** 5-10 cm long, very narrow, with
erect branches. **Spikelets** obovoid, 3.3-3.8 mm long, minutely puberulent; first
glume about half as long, triangular-ovate; second glume slightly shorter than the
sterile lemma and fruit. **Autumnal phase** with 1 or 2 erect branches, bearing
scarcely reduced leaf blades equaling or exceeding the shorter panicles.—Dry
sandy soil of open woodlands.

DIGITARIA *Crabgrass*   PANICEAE

Annual or perennial grasses. Stems spreading, branched from the base. Leaves wide, flat, prostrate,
with the tips ascending; sheaths open, ligules membranous. Flowers in several terminal, digitate,
spike-like racemes. Spikelets 1-flowered, single or in clusters of 2 or 3 on unequal pedicels on one
side of an elongate rachis. First glume minute or lacking; second glume a third to fully as long as the
spikelet, conspicuously 5-7-nerved. Fertile lemma cartilaginous with hyaline, often shining, margins.

1   Inflorescence an open panicle, neither spike-like nor distinctly one-sided . . . . ***D. cognata***
1   Inflorescence composed of 1-sided spikes or spike-like racemes, the rachis of each winged or at least flat on the
     side opposite the spikelets. 2
      2   Spikelets ca. 2-2.3 mm long, the fertile lemma dark brown; second glume nearly or fully as long as the floret;
           sheaths and blades usually nearly or quite glabrous (except around summit of sheath) . . . . ***D. ischaemum***
      2   Spikelets ca. 2.5-3 mm long, the fertile lemma light or dark grayish; second glume only about half as long as
           the floret; sheaths and usually blades ± pilose, at least toward base of plant . . . . ***D. sanguinalis***

Digitaria cognata (J.A. Schultes) Pilger   MAP 1689
WITCH-GRASS   *native*
  Leptoloma cognatum (J.A. Schultes) Chase

Perennial grass. Stems tufted, 4-7 dm long; lower **sheaths** villous to papillose-
hirsute; **ligules** 0.2-1.5 mm long, entire to lacerate; **leaf blades** narrow, 5-8 cm
long. **Panicle** often a third to half the height of the plant, diffusely branched,
purplish, villous in the axils; pedicels 3-8 cm long, 3-angled, scabrous. **Spikelets**
acute, 2.5-3 mm long, nearly glabrous on the second glume and sterile lemma.
—Dry, especially sandy soil.

Digitaria ischaemum

Digitaria ischaemum (Schreb.) Schreb.   MAP 1690
SMOOTH CRABGRASS   *introduced*

Annual grass (or sometimes longer-lived). **Stems** branched and spreading from
the decumbent base, rooting at the nodes, 2-5 dm long; **sheaths** glabrous or
sparsely pubescent; **ligules** 0.6-2.5 mm long; **leaf blades** to 9 cm long and 3-5 mm
wide, glabrous. **Racemes** 2-5, or rarely to 8, 4-10 cm long; rachis broadly winged,
about 1 mm wide. **Spikelets** elliptic or somewhat obovate, 1.7-2.1 mm long, often

1689. *Digitaria cognata*   1690. *Digitaria ischaemum*   1691. *Digitaria sanguinalis*

purple; first **glume** lacking or minute and hyaline; second glume and sterile lemma equal and about as long as the spikelet, both more or less pubescent or subtomentose with capitellate hairs, especially in stripes between the nerves; fertile lemma purple-black.—Eurasian weed of lawns, waste places.

Digitaria sanguinalis (L.) Scop.
MAP 1691
HAIRY CRABGRASS   *introduced*

Annual grass. **Stems** decumbent or prostrate, much branched, rooting at the nodes, usually 3-6 dm long. **leaf blades** 4-10 cm long, 5-10 mm wide, pilose. **Racemes** 3-6 in each of 1-3 whorls, 5-15 cm long; rachis broadly winged, 1 mm wide, scabrous on the margins; pedicels triquetrous, scabrous. **Spikelets** 2.4-3 mm long; first glume minute, often deciduous, the second half as long as the spikelet; sterile lemma usually scabrous on the 5 strong nerves; fertile lemma greenish brown.—Eurasian; often a troublesome weed of fields, gardens, lawns, and waste ground.

DISTICHLIS *Saltgrass*   CYNODONTEAE

Distichlis spicata (L.) Greene
MAP 1692
COASTAL SALTGRASS   *native*

Low perennial grass, spreading by scaly rhizomes and forming patches; the staminate and pistillate flowers on separate plants. **Stems** stiff, erect, 1-3 dm long; **sheaths** overlapping, smooth or sparsely hairy, usually long-hairy at collar; **ligule** small. **Leaves** upright, the upper often longer than the head, mostly inrolled, 5-10 cm long and 0.5-3 mm wide, smooth or with sparse hairs. **Head** an unbranched, narrow, spikelike panicle, 3-7 cm long. **Spikelets** several to many, upright, 8-20 mm long; **staminate spikelets** straw-colored, **pistillate spikelets** green-gray, breaking above the glumes; **glumes** unequal, 1-5 mm long; **lemmas** ovate, 3-6 mm long. June-Sept.—Seasonally wet, brackish flats, shores and disturbed areas.

Distichlis spicata

ECHINOCHLOA *Barnyard-Grass*   PANICEAE

Large, weedy, annual grasses. Stems single or several together, erect to more or less horizontal, to 1 m or more long. Leaves flat, wide and smooth; sheaths smooth or hairy; ligules usually absent. Head a dense panicle, the branches crowded with spikelets forming racemes or spikes. Spikelets with 1 terminal fertile floret and 1 sterile floret, breaking below the glumes, nearly stalkless; glumes unequal, the first glume 3-veined, to half the length of second glume, the second glume 5-veined; sterile lemma similar to second glume, awned or awnless; fertile lemma smooth and shiny.

ADDITIONAL SPECIES
Echinochloa frumentacea Link. (Japanese millet), introduced cereal grain; reported for Minn.

1   Lower leaf sheaths rough-hairy; spikelets each with 2 awns; s portion of our region . . . . *E. walteri*
1   Leaf sheaths smooth; spikelets with usually 1 awn (from sterile lemma); widespread 2
    2   Fertile lemma rounded or broadly tapered to a thin, membranous, withered beak . . . . *E. crus-galli*
    2   Fertile lemma tapered to a stiff, persistent beak. . . . . *E. muricata*

Echinochloa crus-galli (L.) Beauv.
MAP 1693
LARGE BARNYARD-GRASS   *introduced*

Weedy annual grass. **Stems** 1 m or more long; **sheaths** glabrous; **ligules** absent; **leaf blades** 7-30 mm wide. **Panicle** erect, green to purple, 1-2.5 dm long; panicle branches spreading to erect, long-hairy, some of the hairs as long or longer than spikelets (excluding spikelet awns). **Spikelets** 3-5 mm long (excluding awns); **glumes** awnless; sterile **lemma** awnless or with an awn to 4 cm or more long; tip of fertile lemma firm, shiny, rounded or broadly tapered to a point, the beak usually green and withered, the lemma body and beak separated by a line of tiny hairs. July-Sept.—Shores, wet meadows, ditches, streambanks, mud flats, moist disturbed areas. Introduced and naturalized throughout most of USA. *Echinochloa muricata is similar in form and habitat, but distinguished by features of the lemma (see key).*

Echinochloa crus-galli

Echinochloa muricata (Beauv.) Fern.

MAP 1694

BARNYARD-GRASS   *native*

Weedy annual grass. **Stems** 1 m or more long; **sheaths** glabrous; **ligules** absent; **leaf blades** 5-30 mm wide. **Panicle** green to purple, sometimes strongly purple, 1-3 dm long, panicle branches spreading, hairs on branches absent or to 3 mm long and shorter than spikelets. **Spikelets** 2-4 mm long (excluding awns); **glumes** awnless; **sterile lemma** awnless or with an awn 5-10 mm long; tip of **fertile lemma** firm, shiny, gradually tapered to the stiff beak, the lemma body and beak not separated by a line of tiny hairs (the beak itself often short-hairy). July-Sept. — Shores, streambanks and ditches, where sometimes in shallow water.

Echinochloa walteri (Pursh) Heller

MAP 1695

SALTMARSH COCKSPUR GRASS   *native*

Tall annual grass. **Stems** usually erect, 1-2 m long; lower **sheaths** usually rough-hairy; **ligules** absent; **leaf blades** 10-25 mm wide. **Panicle** dense, often nodding, 1-3 dm long. **Spikelets** more or less hidden by awns, the awns 1-3 cm long from sterile lemmas and 2-10 mm long from second glume; **fertile lemma** oval, with a small, withering tip, but not separated by a line of hairs as in *E. crus-galli*. Aug-Sept.—Streambanks, lakeshores, ditches.

Echinochloa muricata

ELEUSINE *Goose Grass*   CYNODONTEAE

Eleusine indica (L.) Gaertn.

MAP 1936

INDIAN GOOSE GRASS   *introduced*

Annual grass. **Stems** mostly 3-6 dm long, compressed, branched from the base, spreading or ascending; **sheaths** compressed and keeled; **ligules** membranous, ciliate; **leaf blades** flat, soft, with prominent white midveins; lower margins and/or undersurface often with papillose-based hairs. **Spikes** digitate, usually 3-8, 4-10 cm, long and about 5 mm wide, spreading or ascending. **Spikelets** articulated above the glumes, crowded, 3-6-flowered; **glumes** unequal, the first shorter, 1-nerved, the second 2-3 mm long, strongly 3-5-nerved, shorter than the lemmas but resembling them; **lemmas** 2.5-4 mm long, compressed, strongly 3-5-nerved.—Native of the Old World; weedy in lawns, gardens, and waste places. *Often popularly confused with* **hairy crabgrass** *(Digitaria sanguinalis)*.

Eleusine indica

ELYMUS *Wild Rye*   TRITICEAE

Tufted perennial grasses. Leaves flat, sheaths open for most of their length, auricles often present, ligules short. Head a densely flowered spike. Spikelets usually 2 at each node of spike, breaking above or below glumes; glumes narrow and awnlike; lemmas tipped with a long awn; stamens 3.

1 Spikelets clearly 1 at each node (or most nodes) of the rachis; glumes not more than 2 2
  2 Stems tufted, rhizomes absent; anthers 1-2.2 (-2.4) mm long; rachilla readily disarticulating between the florets when mature (on dry specimens, the florets very easily dislodged and empty glumes often remaining on older plants) . . . . ***E. trachycaulus***
  2 Stems from elongate rhizomes; anthers 3-6 mm long; rachilla often not readily disarticulating (florets not easily dislodged on dry specimens except over-ripe ones, empty glumes seldom if ever present) 3
    3 Spikelets 15-30 mm long, with 6-16 florets; leaf blades stiff, deeply grooved on the upper surface; cartilaginous band of upper nodes of stem shorter than thick . . . . ***E. smithii***
    3 Spikelets 10-18 mm long, with 3-6 florets; leaf blades lax, not deeply grooved; cartilaginous band of upper nodes of stem as long as thick . . . . ***E. repens***

1692. Distichlis spicata

1693. Echinochloa crus-galli

1694. Echinochloa muricata

1695. Echinochloa walteri

1   Spikelets mostly 2-3 at each node of the rachis (if this arrangement is obscured by reduction of some spikelets and/or their asymmetric position, the basic structure is still evident by the presence of a total of 4-6 awn-like or narrow glumes subtending the entire group of spikelets like an involucre—side by side rather than opposite each other on the two sides of each spikelet) 4

     4   Glumes absent or very unequal 5

         5   Glumes absent or vestigial, or, if present, slenderly awn-like their entire length and at least one much shorter than the others at a node; spikelets horizontally spreading at maturity (± ascending when young), well separated, clearly revealing the entire rachis . . . . ***E. hystrix***

         5   Glumes of each spikelet usually very unequal in length, one or both of a pair sometimes absent . . . . ***E. diversiglumis***

     4   Glumes present, awn-like to lanceolate, of about equal length; spikelets ascending at maturity, usually concealing much of the rachis 6

         6   Larger paleas (lowest in each spikelet) 8.6-13 mm long; awns of lemmas usually widely spreading at maturity 7

             7   Leaves 5-8 on a stem, the widest blades rarely as much as 15 mm wide, glabrous above . . . . ***E. canadensis***

             7   Leaves 10-12 on a stem, the widest blades 15-19 mm wide, finely hairy above . . . . ***E. wiegandii***

         6   Larger paleas 5.5-8.5 mm long; awns of lemmas mostly straight 8

             8   Glumes mostly 1-2 mm wide, clearly expanded and flattened above the base 9

                 9   Lemmas awnless or with short awns less than 4 mm long . . . . ***E. curvatus***

                 9   Lemma awns 8-20 mm long . . . . ***E. virginicus***

             8   Glumes less than 1 mm wide, scarcely if at all widened above the base 10

                10   Palea of lowest floret in spikelet 7-8.5 mm long; leaves 8-10, glabrous . . . . ***E. riparius***

                10   Palea 5.5-7 mm long; leaves 6-7, the sheaths and upper surface of blades finely villous . . ***E. villosus***

Elymus canadensis L.

MAP 1697
NODDING WILD RYE
native

Stems loosely tufted, stout, 1 m or more tall; **sheaths** often reddish brown; auricles 1.5-4 mm long, brown or purplish black; ligules to 2 mm long, truncate, ciliolate; **leaf blades** flat, or involute when dry, usually 8-20 mm wide, glabrous to sparsely pilose. **Spike** 10-15 cm long, usually nodding, often interrupted at base by the elongation of the lower internodes, 1-2 cm thick, excluding the awns. **Spikelets** 3-7-flowered; **glumes**, including the awns, usually 15-30 mm long, 3-5-nerved, glabrous, scabrous, or pubescent; **lemmas**, including the outwardly curved awns, 3-5 cm long, glabrous, scabrous, or pubescent. Variable.—Dry or moist soil, often where sandy or gravelly, usually in full sun.

Elymus canadensis

Elymus curvatus Piper

MAP 1698
AWNLESS WILD RYE
native

    E. virginicus var. *submuticus* Hook.

Stems tufted, not rhizomatous, often glaucous, 6-11 dm tall, erect; **sheaths** glabrous, often reddish brown; **auricles** to 1 mm long or sometimes absent; **ligules** shorter than 1 mm, ciliolate; **leaf blades** 5-15 mm wide, the lower blades usually lax, shorter and narrower, the upper blades usually ascending and somewhat involute. **Spikes** 9-15 cm long, erect, exserted or the bases slightly sheathed, with 2 spikelets per node. **Spikelets** 10-15 mm long, appressed, often reddish brown at maturity, with mostly 3-4 florets; disarticulation below the glumes and beneath the florets, or the lowest floret falling with the glumes; **glumes** equal or nearly so, strongly bowed out, without evident venation, awns 0-4 mm long; **lemmas** 6-10 mm long, glabrous or scabrous, rarely hirsute, awns 1-4 mm long, straight.

Elymus curvatus

1696. *Eleusine indica*

1697. *Elymus canadensis*

1698. *Elymus curvatus*

1699. *Elymus diversiglumis*

—Moist or damp open forests, thickets, grasslands, ditches, and disturbed ground, especially on bottomland. *Similar to* **E. virginicus** *but with lemmas awnless or the awns to less than 4 mm long.*

Elymus diversiglumis Scribn. & Ball
MAP 1699
MINNESOTA WILD RYE   *native*

Tufted perennial, rhizomes absent; plants green or glaucous. **Stems** hollow, 8-15 dm tall, glabrous; **sheaths** glabrous; **ligules** 1-2 mm long; **auricles** inconspicuous, to 2 mm long; **leaf blades** flat, 8- 40 cm long and 8- 15 mm wide, pilose on the nerves above, glabrous below. **Spikes** flexous and arching at maturity, 8-20 cm long; rachis flattened, margins roughened, internodes mostly 6-9 mm long, giving the spike a rather loose appearance; **spikelets** 1-3 per node, each with 2-4 florets; **glumes** awl-like or sometimes absent, often with one glume much smaller, the base terete and indurated; **lemma** body 7-12 mm long, pubescent, with an awn 2-5.5 cm long, divergent at maturity. May-July.—Streambanks, lowlands, moist woods. *Suspected to be a hybrid between Elymus canadensis and E. villosus.*

Elymus hystrix L.
MAP 1700
BOTTLEBRUSH-GRASS   *native*
    Hystrix patula Moench.

Plants occasionally glaucous, particularly the spikes; **stems** usually solitary or loosely tufted, not rhizomatous, 6-10 dm tall; **sheaths** usually glabrous, sometimes pilose, often purplish; **auricles** usually present, 0.5-3 mm long, brown to black; **ligules** 1-3 mm long; **leaf blades** 8-13 mm wide. **Spikes** 5-12 cm long, the internodes of the flexuous 2-edged rachis 4-10 mm long. **Spikelets** usually in pairs; **glumes** varying, even on the same plant, from none to setaceous and to 16 mm long; **lemmas** 8-11 mm long, tipped with a rough awn 1-4 cm long.—Moist deciduous woods, especially in wet or slightly disturbed areas. *Spikelets soon horizontally divergent, the lemmas easily detached.*

Elymus hystrix

Elymus repens (L.) Gould
MAP 1701
QUACK-GRASS   *introduced (invasive)*
    Agropyron repens (L.) Beauv.
    Elytrigia repens (L.) Nevski

Plants strongly rhizomatous, sometimes glaucous. **Stems** erect, usually 5-10 dm tall; **sheaths** pilose or glabrous near base; **auricles** to 1 mm long; **ligules** to 1.5 mm long; **leaf blades** flat, soft, 5-10 mm wide, with numerous slender nerves about 0.2 mm apart. **Spikes** 6-17 cm long, with numerous ascending, overlapping spikelets; rachis joints usually flat on one side, rounded on the other. **Spikelets** 10-18 mm long, 4-8-flowered; **glumes** narrowly oblong to lance-shaped, 8-14 mm long, sharply nerved, acuminate or short-awned; **lemmas** similar in size and shape, less sharply nerved, acuminate or with an awn to 10 mm long.—Eurasian native, abundant and often a noxious weed in meadows, fields, roadsides, and waste places. *Highly variable in color from green to glaucous, in pubescence, and in presence and length of awns.*

Elymus repens

Elymus riparius Wieg.
MAP 1702
RIVERBANK WILD RYE   *native*

Plants tufted, not rhizomatous, often somewhat glaucous. **Stems** 1 m or more tall; **sheaths** usually glabrous, often reddish brown; **auricles** absent or to 2 mm long, brown; **ligules** shorter than 1 mm; **leaf blades** 5-15 mm wide, flat, lax, dull green, drying to grayish, upper surface smooth to rough. **Spikes** 6-20 cm long, somewhat nodding. **Spikelets** mostly 2 at each node, 2-4-flowered, finely hairy, breaking above glumes; **glumes** narrow, to 1 mm wide at middle, not bowed-out at base; **lemma** finely hairy to smooth, tipped with a straight awn 2-3 cm long. — Streambanks, floodplain forests. *Similar to **nodding wild rye** (Elymus canadensis), a species of drier, sandy places, but awns straight rather than bent and curved.*

Elymus riparius

Elymus trachycaulus (Link) Gould ex Shinners

MAP 1703
native

SLENDER WILD RYE

Agropyron caninum (L.) Beauv.
Agropyron trachycaulum (Link) Steud.

Stems loosely tufted, erect, 4-10 dm tall; **sheaths** usually glabrous, sometimes hirsute or villous; **auricles** absent or to 1 mm long; ligules 0.2-0.8 mm long, truncate; leaf blades 4-10 mm wide, flat to involute, usually straight and ascending, with numerous fine sharp nerves. **Spikes** 6-20 cm long. **Spikelets** erect or ascending, few-flowered, in ours mostly not imbricate, the tip of one not reaching to the base of the next one above on the same side; **glumes** 5-7-nerved, acuminate or short-awned; **lemmas** awnless or with straight awns to 2 cm long (rarely more); rachilla readily disarticulating between the lemmas, leaving the persistent glumes attached.—Dry, open, rocky woods, sandy shores and barrens; rarely in fens and tamarack swamps. *Variable but distinguished by the short anthers (when young), and by the readily disintegrating spikelets (when mature); the rachilla is also nearly always villous.*

spikelet

Elymus villosus Muhl.

MAP 1704
native

HAIRY WILD RYE

Plants often persistently deep green. **Stems** tufted, slender, 5-10 dm tall; **sheaths** glabrous to pilose; **auricles** 1-3 mm long, brownish; **ligules** less than 1 mm long, entire or erose; **leaf blades** 4-12 mm wide, lax, dark glossy green, softly villous on the upper side. **Spikes** slightly or strongly nodding, dense, 5-12 cm long; **glumes** setaceous, not widened above the base, 0.4-1 mm wide, strongly 1-3-nerved, 15-30 mm long, including the awn; **lemmas** 2-4 cm long, including the straight ascending awn.—Swampy forests and riverbanks; also in drier woods. *Glumes and lemmas usually conspicuously hirsute.*

Elymus trachycaulus

Elymus virginicus L.

MAP 1705
native

VIRGINIA WILD RYE

Plants sometimes glaucous, especially in the spikes. **Stems** tufted, 6-12 dm long; **sheaths** usually glabrous, rarely hirsute, occasionally reddish or purplish; **auricles** absent or to 1.8 mm long, pale brown; **ligules** less than 1 mm long; **leaf blades** flat, lax, 5-15 mm wide, rough-to-touch on both sides. **Spikes** erect, 5-15 cm long, the base of spike often covered by top of upper sheath. **Spikelets** usually 2 at each node, 2-4-flowered, breaking below glumes; **glumes** firm, 1-2 mm wide, yellowish, bowed-out at base, tapered to a straight awn about 1 cm long; **lemmas** 6-9 mm long, smooth to hairy, usually with a straight awn to 3 cm long. July-Aug.—Floodplain forests, thickets, streambanks.

Elymus wiegandii Fern.

MAP 1706
native

WIEGAND'S WILD RYE

Similar to *E. canadensis* but plants taller, the inflorescence is drooping, not merely arching, and the leaves are broader (in *E. canadensis* the leaves are stiff and often involute, especially toward the tip); larger glumes in *E. wiegandii* are 0.4-0.7 mm wide, glumes of *E. canadensis* are 0.7-1.6 mm wide.—Moist forests, especially along streams.

Elymus virginicus

1700. *Elymus hystrix*

1701. *Elymus repens*

1702. *Elymus riparius*

1703. *Elymus trachycaulus*

ERAGROSTIS *Lovegrass*

CYNODONTEAE

Annual grasses (ours), perfect-flowered or with staminate and pistillate flowers on different plants. Stems clumped, or spreading and rooting at lower nodes and with creeping stolons. Leaves with short, flat to folded blades; sheaths open, short-hairy near top; ligule a ring of short hairs. Heads usually many, in an open or narrow panicle. Spikelets few- to many-flowered, breaking above glumes, laterally compressed, the florets overlapping; glumes unequal; lemmas 3-veined; palea shorter than lemma, 2-veined.

ADDITIONAL SPECIES

Eragrostis trichodes (Nutt.) Wood (Sand lovegrass), a Great Plains species, adventive in southern Minn.

1　Plants prostrate basally, rooting at lower nodes; nodes of stem bearded (very rarely glabrate) . . . . . *E. hypnoides*
1　Plants ± erect or spreading from the base, not rooting at the nodes; nodes of stem glabrous 2
　　2　Margins (often inrolled) of leaves and also (usually at least sparsely) pedicels and keels of lemmas and glumes ± glandular-warty 3
　　　　3　Well-developed spikelets 2.5-3.5 mm wide; larger glume 1.7-2.5 mm long; sheaths essentially glabrous except at summit . . . . *E. cilianensis*
　　　　3　Well-developed spikelets 1.5-2 mm wide; larger glume 1-1.5 mm long; sheaths sparsely pilose. . . *E. minor*
　　2　Margins of leaves, pedicels, and keels of lemmas and glumes not glandular-warty. 4
　　　　4　Spikelets reddish to purplish; plants perennial, with hard knotty base; lowest panicle branches usually with a long-pilose white to yellowish or red pubescence in the axil . . . . *E. spectabilis*
　　　　4　Spikelets greenish gray to dark lead-colored (occasionally with purplish flush besides); plants annual, with relatively soft base; lowest panicle branches glabrous to sparsely pilose. 5
　　　　　　5　Larger spikelets mostly 6-11 (-15)-flowered, usually on ± appressed pedicels (though panicle branches may be widely spreading); lowest lemma 1.4-2 mm long; lateral nerves of lemma distinct (in *E. pectinacea*) 6
　　　　　　　　6　Lateral nerves of lemma distinct, at least on lower half; larger mature spikelets (1.3-) 1.5-2 mm wide; axils of panicle glabrous or rarely the lowermost with a few hairs; panicle branches usually alternate or subopposite at lowest two nodes of inflorescence. . . . . *E. pectinacea*
　　　　　　　　6　Lateral nerves of lemma usually obscure; larger mature spikelets 1-1.4 mm wide; axils of lower primary branches of panicle sparsely pilose; panicle branches whorled or clustered at one of the two lowest nodes of inflorescence. . . . . *E. pilosa*
　　　　　　5　Larger spikelets mostly 2-4 (-6)-flowered, on spreading pedicels; lowest lemma ca. 1.2-1.4 (-1.6) mm long; lateral nerves of lemma obscure 7
　　　　　　　　7　Sheaths pilose; grain with a groove the length of one edge; length of stem below lowest branch of terminal panicle less than the height of the panicle. . . . . *E. capillaris*
　　　　　　　　7　Sheaths essentially glabrous except at summit; grain not grooved; length of stem below lowest branch of terminal panicle usually more than the panicle 8
　　　　　　　　　　8　Axils glabrous; tip of second glume ± opposite tip of lowest lemma. . . . . *E. frankii*
　　　　　　　　　　8　Axils of at least the lower primary branches of panicle sparsely long-pilose; tip of second glume usually much shorter than the lowest lemma (across from it) . . . . *E. pilosa*

Eragrostis capillaris (L.) Nees

LACE-GRASS

(NO MAP)

native

Stems erect, tufted, 2-5 dm tall; **sheaths** pilose along the margins, tips hirsute, the hairs to 7 mm long; **ligules** to 0.5 mm long, ciliate; **leaf blades** flat, 2-5 mm wide. **Panicle** large and diffusely branched, often 2/3 as long as the entire plant, cylindric or elliptic, with almost capillary branches. **Spikelets** 2-4-flowered, 2-3 mm long; first **glume** 0.9-1.5 mm long; second glume 1.1-1.4 mm long; **lemmas** 1.2-1.6 mm long; **grain** 0.6-0.7 mm long, with a groove its entire length on one side.—Not yet

1704. Elymus villosus

1705. Elymus virginicus

1706. Elymus wiegandii

Eragrostis cilianensis

known in Minn, but to be expected in the southeast along the Mississippi River on dry sandy riverbanks; known from Iowa and Wisc. *Similar to **Eragrostis frankii**, but differs in its longer pedicels, pilose sheath margins, and larger panicles.*

Eragrostis cilianensis (All.) Vign.
STINK-GRASS

MAP 1707
introduced

Stems densely tufted, spreading or ascending from a decumbent base, rarely erect, 1–4 dm long; **sheaths** glabrous, occasionally glandular, tips hairy, the hairs to 5 mm long; ligules to 0.8 mm long, ciliate; **leaf blades** 5–20 cm long, 2–6 mm wide. **Panicle** ovoid to subcylindric, 5–15 cm long, the branches spreading, the pedicels usually 1–2 mm long. **Spikelets** broadly linear, 2.5–3 mm wide, 10–40-flowered; first **glume** 1.3–1.9 mm long; second glume 1.5–2 mm long; **lemmas** broadly elliptic-ovate, closely imbricate, 2.1–2.6 mm long, glandular on the keel; **grain** 0.7 mm long, dull brown.—Native of Europe; a weed of moist ground.

Eragrostis frankii C.A. Mey.
SANDBAR LOVEGRASS

MAP 1708
native

Stems densely tufted, branched, 1–5 dm long; **sheaths** mostly glabrous but long-hairy at tip, the hairs to 4 mm long, often also with glandular pits; **ligules** to 0.5 mm long, ciliate; leaf blades 1–4 mm wide, flat to involute. **Panicle** open, 5–20 cm long, the branches mostly ascending. **Spikelets** 3–6-flowered, 2–3 mm long and 1–2 mm wide. Aug–Sept.—Wet, muddy areas, streambanks, sandbars, roadside ditches, cultivated fields.

Eragrostis frankii

Eragrostis hypnoides (Lam.) B.S.P.
TEAL LOVEGRASS

MAP 1709
native

Stems mostly spreading and rooting at lower nodes, 5–15 cm long, smooth but short-hairy at nodes, stoloniferous and forming mats; **sheaths** pilose on the margins, collars and tips, the hairs to 0.6 mm long; **ligule** of short hairs about to 0.6 mm long; leaf blades to 5 cm long, 1–3 mm wide, flat to involute, upper surface hairy. **Panicle** loose, 2–6 cm long. **Spikelets** 10–35-flowered, linear, 3–10 mm long; **glumes** 1-veined, 0.5–1.5 mm long; **lemma** smooth and shiny, 1–2 mm long. July–Sept.—Wet, sandy or muddy shores and streambanks, sand bars, mud flats.

Eragrostis minor Host
LITTLE LOVEGRASS

MAP 1710
introduced

Stems tufted, slender, ascending or decumbent, 1–4 dm long; **sheaths** sometimes glandular on the midveins, hairy at the tips, hairs to 4 mm; **ligules** to 0.5 mm long, ciliate; leaf blades 1–3 mm wide, flat, glabrous or sparsely white-hairy. **Panicle** ovoid or oblong, 3–10 cm long, with spreading branches. **Spikelets** pediceled, 10–20-flowered, 1.5–2 mm wide; first **glume** 1.2–1.5 mm long; second glume 1.4–1.7 mm long; **lemmas** broadly elliptic-ovate, 1.7–1.9 mm long, glandular on the keel, closely imbricate; **grain** 0.6–0.8 mm long, bright brown.—Introduced from Europe in moist soil of waste places, railways, and roadsides.

Eragrostis pectinacea (Michx.) Nees
CAROLINA LOVEGRASS

MAP 1711
native

Stems densely tufted, erect or ascending, often repeatedly branched, 1–5 dm tall; **sheaths** hirsute at the tips, the hairs to 4 mm long; **ligules** to 0.5 mm long; **leaf blades** 2–20 cm long 1–4 mm wide, flat to involute. **Panicle** diffusely branched, often half as long as the entire plant, the spikelets tending to be appressed along

Eragrostis hypnoides

1707. Eragrostis cilianensis *1708. Eragrostis frankii* *1709. Eragrostis hypnoides* *1710. Eragrostis minor*

the branches. **Spikelets** 5-11-flowered, linear, 1-1.5 mm wide; first **glume** 0.8-1.2 mm long; second glume 1.1-1.6 mm long; lowest **lemma** 1.5-1.8 mm long; **grain** to 1 mm long.—Moist ground, especially as a weed in gardens, roadsides, railways, and waste places.

Eragrostis pilosa (L.) Beauv.
INDIAN LOVEGRASS

MAP 1712
introduced

Eragrostis pectinacea

Stems densely tufted, erect or ascending from a decumbent base, 1-6 dm tall; **sheaths** mostly glabrous, occasionally glandular, tips hirsute, the hairs to 3 mm long; **ligules** to 0.3 mm long, ciliate; **leaf blades** 2-15 cm long and 2-3 mm wide, flat, upper surface glabrous. **Panicle** diffusely branched, 5-20 cm long, the pedicels mostly diverging from the branches. **Spikelets** 5-9-flowered, about 1 mm wide; first glume 0.5-1.1 mm long; second glume 0.8-1.3 mm long; **lemmas** 1.3-1.6 mm long; **grain** short-cylindric, 0.5-0.7 mm long.—Native of Europe; a weed of moist or dry open places.

Eragrostis spectabilis (Pursh) Steud.
PURPLE LOVEGRASS

MAP 1713
native

Stems tufted, erect or ascending, 3-6 dm tall; **sheaths** hairy on the margins and at tips, the hairs to 7 mm long; **ligules** to 0.2 mm long; **leaf blades** 3-7 mm wide, flat to involute, both surfaces usually pilose. **Panicle** ovoid, about 2/3 as long as the entire plant, its base usually included in the upper sheath, its scabrous branches rigid, divaricate, pilose in the axils, the lateral spikelets pediceled and more or less spreading. **Spikelets** purple, 5-10-flowered; first **glume** 1-2 mm long; **lemmas** 1.6-2.1 mm long, scabrous on the keel, the lateral nerves evident; **palea** conspicuously short-ciliate on the keels.—Dry soil, fields and open woods. *Whole panicle eventually detached and behaving as a tumbleweed. Available commercially for planting as an ornamental grass.*

Eragrostis spectabilis

ERIOCHLOA *Cupgrass*

PANICEAE

Eriochloa villosa (Thunb.) Kunth
WOOLLY CUPGRASS

MAP 1714
introduced

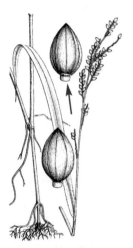

Annual grass. Stems tufted, 3-10 dm tall, erect or decumbent, sometimes rooting at the lower nodes; nodes and internodes pubescent; **sheaths** open, sometimes inflated; **auricles** absent; **ligules** to 1 mm long, membranous, ciliate; **leaf blades** 10-20 cm long and 5-12 mm wide, flat, undersurfaces velvety hairy, margins with one edge typically crinkled. **Panicle** 3-16 cm long and 1-3 cm wide; rachises villous; branches 2-8, velutinous, sometimes winged, with 11-24 solitary spikelets in 2 rows on the lower side. **Spikelets** ovate to elliptic, 4-5 mm long ; first **glume** occasionally present as a scale; upper glumes equaling the lower lemmas, ovate to elliptic, glabrous or pubescent, 7-veined; lower **lemmas** 3.4-5 mm long, 5-veined, unawned.—An Asian introduction, first reported in the USA in the 1940s; weedy, especially in corn and soybean fields, and often spread by farm equipment; also along fencerows and roadsides. *A small cup-like involucre subtending each spikelet is distinctive (see arrow at right).*

Eriochloa villosa

FESTUCA *Fescue*

POEAE

Annual or perennial grasses, often densely tufted. Leaves flat to involute, auricles absent; ligules membranous, usually truncate, usually ciliate. Flowers in open or contracted panicles. Spikelets 3-11-

1711. *Eragrostis pectinacea*

1712. *Eragrostis pilosa*

1713. *Eragrostis spectabilis*

1714. *Eriochloa villosa*

flowered, the rachilla disarticulating above the glumes and between the lemmas. Glumes narrow, unequal, 1-3-nerved, usually shorter than the lemmas. Lemmas rounded on back, obscurely 5-nerved, usually awned from the apex. Paleas about equaling the lemmas. Stamens 1 or 3.

ADDITIONAL SPECIES

Festuca paradoxa Desv., uncommon in se Minn, mostly from moist meadows near the Mississippi River, more common southward; resembles *F. subverticillata* in general habit, the stems usually somewhat stouter and panicle more freely branched and drooping.

1 Blades of leaves flat (or merely once-folded), at least the larger ones 3-8 mm wide; lemmas awnless or rarely with awn less than 1 mm long . . . . ***F. subverticillata***

1 Blades of leaves strongly involute, usually much less than 3 mm wide; lemmas awned or awnless 2

2 Sheaths closed in young leaves, the old ones ± dark reddish brown basally, becoming fibrous by splitting between the prominent pale veins; basal shoots usually arising laterally, the stems thus tending to be strongly curved or bent at the base; anthers mostly 2-3.5 mm long . . . . ***F. rubra***

2 Sheaths open most of their length even in young leaves (margins ± overlapping), the old ones mostly pale or drab brown, not becoming fibrous; basal shoots erect, the stems thus nearly or quite straight from the base upwards; anthers various 3

3 Lower panicle branches often spreading; anthers 2-3 mm long . . . . ***F. trachyphylla***

3 Lower panicle branches strongly ascending; anthers less than 2 mm long . . . . ***F. saximontana***

Festuca rubra L.

MAP 1715

RED FESCUE *introduced*

Stems glabrous, 3-10 dm tall, usually loosely tufted, often decumbent at base, frequently rhizomatous; **sheaths** closed for about 3/4 their length when young, soon disintegrating into loose fibers, usually pubescent, reddish; collars glabrous; ligules 0.1-0.5 mm long; leaf blades usually conduplicate, to 2.5 mm wide, sometimes flat and 1.5-7 mm wide. **Panicle** 5-20 cm long, narrow with ascending branches, or in some forms loosely spreading. **Spikelets** 4-7-flowered; first **glume** subulate, 2.6-4.5 mm long; second glume broader, 3.5-5.5 mm long; **lemmas** 5-6 mm long; awns 1-3 mm long. Variable, and many horticultural varieties exist. Widely distributed in Europe and North America. *Minnesota plants considered adventive.*

Festuca rubra

Festuca saximontana Rydb.

MAP 1716

ROCKY MOUNTAIN FESCUE *native*

Festuca brachyphylla J.A. Schultes

Stems very slender, densely tufted, not stoloniferous, glabrous; **sheaths** closed for about 1/2 their length, usually persistent, rarely slowly shredding into fibers, mostly pale or drab brown; **collars** glabrous; **ligules** to 0.5 mm long; **leaf blades** 0.5-1.2 mm wide, conduplicate, upper surface glabrous or sparsely puberulent, undersurface scabrous or puberulent. **Panicle** 1-10 cm, narrow and spiciform, or somewhat open at anthesis, the first pedical of the lowermost branches usually no more than 5 mm, from the base. **Spikelets** 2-4-flowered, the first **glume** 2-3 mm, 1-nerved, the second 2.5-4.5 mm, 3-nerved; **lemmas** mostly 3.5-6) mm, with a short awn 1-3 mm.—Dry forests, shores, dunes, and disturbed places; rock crevices near Lake Superior. *Similar to **Festuca trachyphylla** in general appearance.*

Festuca subverticillata (Pers.) Alexeev

MAP 1717

NODDING FESCUE *native*

Stems few in a tuft, 6-12 dm tall, glabrous; **sheaths** closed for less than 1/3 their length, glabrous or sparsely pilose, shredding into fibers; **ligules** mostly 0.5-1 mm

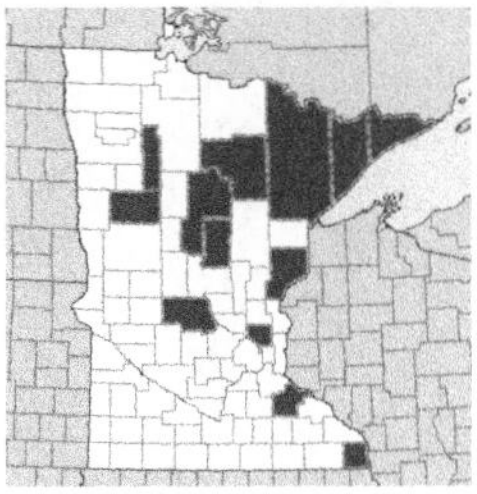

1715. *Festuca rubra*

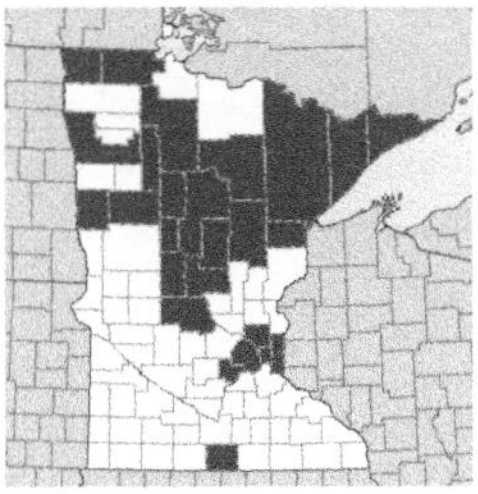

1716. *Festuca saximontana*

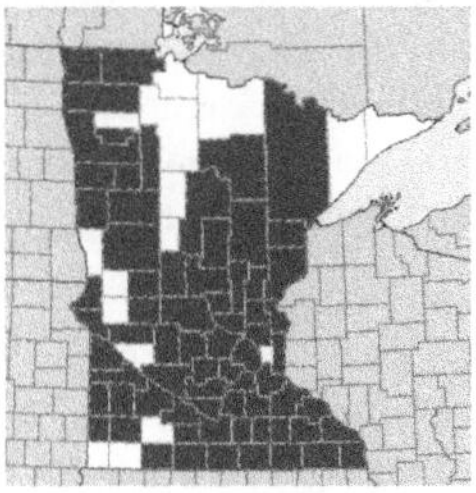

1717. *Festuca subverticillata*

Festuca subverticillata

long; **leaf blades** 4-10 mm wide, flat or loosely convolute, glabrous or sparsely pilose. **Panicle** long-exsert, 15-30 cm long; branches slender, elongate, racemiform, eventually widely spreading, bearing spikelets only above the middle. **Spikelets** relatively remote, the tip of one barely reaching the base of the next, usually 3-flowered, occasionally 4-5-flowered, 4-6 mm long; first **glume** subulate, averaging 2.8 mm long; second glume ovate, averaging 3.4 mm long; **lemmas** acute, averaging 3.7 mm long, appressed till maturity.—Moist forests of beech-maple or oak-hickory; occasionally in wet conifer woods. *Resembles the uncommon* **Festuca paradoxa**, *but spikelets of nodding fescue are less crowded on the branches.*

Festuca trachyphylla (Hack.) Krajina   MAP 1718
HARD FESCUE; SHEEP FESCUE
   Festuca ovina auct. p.p. non L.
Stems densely tufted, without rhizomes, 20-80 cm tall, glabrous or with sparse hairs; sheaths closed for less than 1/3 their length, usually glabrous, rarely pubescent, persistent; **collars** glabrous; **ligules** to 0.5 mm long; **leaf blades** about 1 mm in diameter, usually conduplicate, rarely flat. **Panicle** 3-15 cm long, contracted, with 1-2 branches per node; branches erect or stiffly spreading, lower branches with 2 or more spikelets. **Spikelets** 5-9 mm long, with 3-7 florets; glumes exceeded by the upper florets, mostly glabrous; lower glumes 2-4 mm long; upper glumes 3-5 mm long; lemmas lance-shaped, usually smooth on the lower portion and scabrous or pubescent upwards, especially on the margins, awns 0.5-2.5 mm long, usually less than 1/2 as long as the lemma body.—Native of Europe, widely introduced as a turf grass and sometimes weedy.

Festuca trachyphylla

GLYCERIA *Manna Grass*   MELICEAE

Perennial grasses, loosely clumped or spreading by rhizomes. Stems upright, or reclining at base and often rooting at lower nodes. Leaves flat or folded; sheaths closed for most of their length; ligules scarious, erose to lacerate. Head an open panicle. Spikelets 3-flowered, ovate to linear, round in section or somewhat flattened, breaking above the glumes; glumes unequal, shorter than lemmas, 1-veined; lemmas unawned, usually 7-veined; palea about as long as lemma; stamens 3 or 2.

Glyceria, Puccinellia, and *Torreyochloa* are often confused because of similarities in form and their occurrence in wetlands; only *Glyceria* has closed leaf sheaths and 1-veined upper glumes (the other two genera have open leaf sheaths and 3-veined upper glumes). Only *Puccinellia* has inconspicuous veins on the lemmas (the other two genera generally have conspicuous veins on the lemmas).

1   Spikelets linear-cylindric, 10 mm long or longer. 2
  2   Leaves less than 5 mm wide; lemmas more or less smooth . . . . **G. borealis**
  2   Leaves 5 mm or more wide; lemmas finely hairy . . . . **G. septentrionalis**
1   Spikelets ovate, 2 to 7 mm long. 3
  3   Spikelets 3-4 mm wide; veins of lemma not raised . . . . **G. canadensis**
  3   Spikelets 2-2.5 mm wide; veins of lemma raised 4
    4   Spikelets 4 to 7 mm long . . . . **G. grandis**
    4   Spikelets 2 to 4 mm long . . . . **G. striata**

Glyceria borealis (Nash) Batchelder   MAP 1719
NORTHERN MANNA GRASS   *native*
Stems erect or reclining at base, often rooting from lower nodes, 6-12 dm long. **Leaves** flat or folded, 2-5 mm wide, smooth; **sheaths** smooth; **ligule** 3-10 mm long. **Panicle** 2-4 dm long, with stiff, erect to ascending, branches to 8-12 cm long, each with several spikelets. **Spikelets** linear, mostly 6-12-flowered, 1-1.5 cm long; **glumes** rounded at tip, 2-3 mm long; **lemmas** 3-4 mm long, 7-veined. June-Aug. —Marshes, ponds, stream, ditches, often in shallow water or mud.

Glyceria canadensis (Michx.) Trin.   MAP 1720
RATTLESNAKE MANNA GRASS   *native*
Stems single or few together, erect, 6-15 dm long. **Leaves** 3-7 mm wide, upper surface rough; **ligules** 2-5 mm long. **Panicle** open, 1-3 dm long, the branches

*Glyceria
borealis*

drooping, with spikelets mostly near tips. Spikelets ovate, 5-10-flowered, 5-7 mm long, the florets spreading; **glumes** 2-3 mm long, the first glume lance-shaped, the second glume ovate; **lemma** veins not raised.—Marshes, swamps, thickets, open bogs, fens; common.

Glyceria grandis S. Wats.
AMERICAN MANNA GRASS

MAP 1721
native

Stems loosely tufted, erect, stout, 1-1.5 m long and 4-6 mm wide. **Leaves** flat, smooth, 6-12 mm wide; **sheaths** smooth; **ligules** translucent, 3-6 mm long. **Panicle** large, open, much-branched, 2-4 dm long, usually nodding at tip, branches lax and drooping when mature. **Spikelets** ovate, purple, slightly flattened, 5-9-flowered, 4-7 mm long; **glumes** pale or white, 1-3 mm long; **lemmas** purple, 2-3 mm long. June-Septv Marshes, ditches, streams, lakes and ponds, open bogs, fens; usually in shallow water or mud.

Glyceria septentrionalis A.S. Hitchc.
FLOATING MANNA GRASS

(NO MAP)
native

Stems somewhat fleshy, often more or less horizontal at base and rooting from lower nodes, 1-1.5 m long. **Leaves** 6-10 mm wide; **sheaths** smooth; **ligules** large, 5-16 mm long. **Panicle** narrow, 2-4 dm long, the branches to 10 cm long, each with several spikelets. **Spikelets** 1-2 cm long, 8-14-flowered; **glumes** 2-4 mm long; **lemmas** green or pale, 4-5 mm long, spreading when mature; palea often longer than lemma. June-Aug.—Swamps, thickets, shallow water of pond margins, wet depressions in forests. *Not known from Minn but occurs in adjacent La Crosse County in Wisc.*

Glyceria grandis

Glyceria striata (Lam.) A.S. Hitchc.
FOWL MANNA GRASS

MAP 1722
native

Plants pale green. **Stems** loosely tufted erect, slender, 3-10 dm long. **Leaves** flat or folded, smooth, 2-6 mm wide; **sheaths** smooth; **ligules** 1-3 mm long. **Panicle** open, loose, 1-2 dm long, the branches lax, drooping. **Spikelets** ovate, often purple, 3-7-flowered, 3-4 mm long; **glumes** 0.5-1.5 mm long; **lemma** 2 mm long, strongly 7-veined. June-Aug.—Swamps, thickets, low areas in forests, wet meadows, springs, streambanks.

Glyceria striata

HESPEROSTIPA *Needlegrass*
STIPEAE

Tufted perennial grasses with narrow, elongate, often involute blades and open or contracted panicles of large spikelets; auricles absent; ligules membranous, frequently ciliate. Spikelets 1-flowered, articulated above the glumes. Glumes about equal, lance-shaped, papery, with broad scarious margins, the first 3-nerved, the second 5-nerved; nerves parallel, only the middle one extending to the tip. Lemmas shorter than or equaling the glumes, indurate, obscurely nerved or nerveless, villous at least at base, and with a bearded sharp-pointed callus. Awn terminal, greatly elongate, articulated with the lemma but persistent, usually twice-geniculate, the lower one or two segments twisted. The awn is hygroscopic, imparting a twisting motion to the fruit as it winds or unwinds, pushing the sharp basal callus into the soil, and serving to bury the grain.

1 Lemmas usually evenly white-pubescent, sometimes glabrous immediately above the callus; lower ligules often lacerate . . . . ***H. comata***

1 Lemmas unevenly pubescent with brown to beige hairs; lower ligules not lacerate . . . . ***H. spartea***

1718. Festuca trachyphylla   *1719. Glyceria borealis*   *1720. Glyceria canadensis*   *1721. Glyceria grandis*

Hesperostipa comata (Trin. & Rupr.) Barkworth   MAP 1723
NEEDLE-AND-THREAD   *introduced*
   Stipa comata Trin. & Rupr.
Stems tufted, 4-10 dm tall; **sheaths** glabrous or nearly so, the upper often inflated over the base of the panicle; **ligule** 3-4 mm long; **leaf blades** smooth or finely scabrous, 1-3 mm wide. **Panicle** narrow, 1-2 dm long, the ascending branches each bearing 1-few spikelets; **glumes** 21-30 mm long, tapering to a long filiform point; mature **lemma** 9-13 mm long, pale brown, villous at base; awn very slender, loosely flexuous or coiled, obscurely geniculate, 9-13 cm long.—Prairies. *Native to the w USA where an important prairie and high desert grass.*

Hesperostipa comata

Hesperostipa spartea (Trin.) Barkworth   MAP 1724
PORCUPINE GRASS   *native*
   Stipa spartea Trin.
Stems in small tufts, 6-12 dm tall; **sheaths** glabrous; ligules of the upper leaves 4-6 mm long, the lower much shorter; **leaf blades** 2-5 mm wide, glabrous beneath, scabrous and usually also pubescent above, the lower elongate, tapering to a fine point. **Panicle** narrow, more or less nodding, 1-2 dm long, the few branches each bearing 1-few spikelets; **glumes** 28-42 mm long, tapering to a very slender point; mature **lemma** 18-21 mm long, brown, pubescent at base, less so above; awn stout, stiff, 12-20 cm long, twice geniculate near the middle, the central segment usually 1.5-3 cm long.—Sandy, often calcareous places; dune ridges, oak savanna, dry prairies, railways.

Hesperostipa spartea

HORDEUM *Barley*   TRITICEAE

Annual or perennial grasses with flat blades, scarious truncate ligules, and dense bristly spikes which disarticulate at each joint. Spikelets 1-flowered or rarely 2-flowered, not disarticulating, aggregated in groups of three at each joint of the rachis, the lateral spikelets often pediceled and sterile, the central sessile and fertile. Glumes elongate, awned or awnlike, setaccous throughout or widened at base, the 6 in each triad of spikelets forming a false involucre to the florets. Lemma of the lateral spikelets often reduced in size or abortive; that of the central spikelet indurate, obscurely nerved, its rounded back turned away from the rachis, long-awned; rachilla prolonged behind the pales. as a short bristle.

1 Body of larger lemmas ca. 8-11 mm long; leaves glabrous, with prominent auricles at base of blade; awns of lemmas much stouter than those of glumes; rachis of spike not disintegrating. . . . . ***H. vulgare***
1 Body of larger lemmas ca. 3.5-6 mm long; leaves (at least lower sheaths) ± pubescent, without auricles; awns of lemmas as slender as those of glumes; rachis of spike readily disintegrating as it matures 2
  2 Awns much longer than 2 cm; glumes all bristle-like (reduced to awns) . . . . ***H. jubatum***
  2 Awns less than 2 cm long; glumes in part broadened (± lanceolate) . . . . ***H. pusillum***

Hordeum jubatum L.   MAP 1725
FOXTAIL-BARLEY   *native*
Tufted perennial grass; plants smooth to densely hairy. **Stems** erect or reclining at base, 2-7 dm long; **sheaths** glabrous or pubescent; auricles absent; **ligules** less than 1 mm long; **leaf blades** usually flat, 2-5 mm wide. **Head** a terminal spike, erect to nodding, 3-10 cm long, appearing bristly due to the long, spreading awns from glumes and lemmas. **Spikelets** 1-flowered, 3 at each node, the center spikelet fertile, stalkless, the 2 lateral spikelets sterile, short-stalked, reduced to 1-3 spreading awns; the 3 spikelets at each node falling as a unit; **glumes** of fertile spikelet awnlike; **lemma** lance-shaped, tipped by a long awn; the glume and

Hordeum jubatum

1722. *Glyceria striata*

1723. *Hesperostipa comata*

1724. *Hesperostipa spartea*

lemma awns 2-7 cm long. June-Sept.—Wet meadows, ditches, shores, shallow marshes, disturbed areas; often where brackish.

Hordeum pusillum Nutt.
MAP 1726
LITTLE BARLEY   *introduced*

Annual grass. **Stems** erect or short-decumbent, 2-4 dm tall; **sheaths** glabrous or slightly pubescent; **ligules** 0.2-0.8 mm long; **auricles** absent; **leaf blades** erect or nearly so, 2-6 mm wide. **Spike** flattened-cylindric, 2-6 cm long, exsert or at first included in the upper sheath; **glumes** about equal in length, 12-15 mm long, the second (exterior) one of each lateral spikelet setaceous, the first (interior) one broadened above the base to 1 mm wide, those of the central spikelet intermediate in width; **lemma** of the lateral spikelets much shorter than its glumes, that of the central spikelet long-awned, about equaling its glumes.—Dry or sterile, especially alkaline soil. Native in much of USA; adventive in s Minnesota.

Hordeum vulgare L.
MAP 1727
COMMON BARLEY   *introduced*

Summer or winter annual grass, loosely tufted. **Stems** erect, in wild plants 3-12 dm tall; **lower sheaths** pilose; **upper sheaths** glabrous; **auricles** to 6 mm long; **leaf blades** 3-15 mm wide. **Spike** erect or nearly so, dense, 3-10 cm long, excluding the awns; **glumes** flat, narrowly linear, pubescent, often tapering into a slender soft awn; **lemmas** about 1 cm long, tapering into a stout, flat, erect, 1-nerved awn 6-15 cm long or with a terminal 3-lobed appendage.—Cultivated grain and an occasional waif along roads and railways.

KOELERIA *Junegrass*
POEAE

Koeleria macrantha (Ledeb.) J.A. Schultes
MAP 1728
PRAIRIE JUNEGRASS   *native*
   Koeleria pyramidata (Lam.) Beauv.

Perennial tufted grass. **Stems** tufted, erect, 3-6 dm tall, pubescent below the panicle. **Leaves** mostly basal; **sheaths** glabrous or pubescent; **ligules** membranous, 0.5-2 mm long, erose; **blades** 1-3 mm wide, flat, or involute when dry, glabrous or pubescent. Panicle spike-like, shining, silvery-green, 5-12 cm long, 1-2 cm thick. **Spikelets** normally 2-flowered, disarticulating above the glumes and between the lemmas, subsessile, overlapping, more or less scabrous; **glumes** unequal, obscurely keeled, scariously margined, the first 1-nerved, the second broadest above the middle, 3-5-nerved ; **lemma** about as long as the glumes, rounded on the back, acute, scarious at margin and tip, obscurely 5-nerved awnless; **palea** hyaline, nearly as long as the lemma.—Dry soil, prairies, sand hills, open woods.

Koeleria macrantha

LEERSIA *Cut-Grass*
ORYZEAE

Perennial grasses, spreading by long rhizomes. Stems slender, somewhat weak. Leaves flat, smooth to hairy or rough-to-touch; sheaths open; auricles absent; ligules membranous, short. Head an open panicle. Spikelets 1-flowered, laterally compressed, falling as a unit from the stalk; glumes absent; lemmas smooth to hairy, 5-veined; palea narrow, about as long as lemma; stamens 2-3 (ours).

1 Spikelets ovate, 3-4 mm wide. . . . . ***L. lenticularis***
1 Spikelets linear, 1-2 mm wide 2

1725. *Hordeum jubatum*   1726. *Hordeum pusillum*   1727. *Hordeum vulgare*   1728. *Koeleria macrantha*

2 Stems round in section; leaves very rough-to-touch; spikelets 4-6 mm long . . . . *L. oryzoides*
2 Stems flattened in section; leaves smooth or finely roughened; spikelets to 3.5 mm long . . . . *L. virginica*

Leersia lenticularis Michx.
CATCHFLY GRASS

MAP 1729
❧ *threatened* | *native*

Perennial grass, from creeping rhizomes. **Stems** 1-1.5 m long. **Leaves** lax, smooth to soft-hairy, 1-2 cm wide; **sheaths** smooth, or hairy at top; **ligules** 0.5-1.5 mm long, flat-topped. **Panicle** 1-2 dm long, often drooping, the branches spreading, each branch with 1-4 spike-like racemes 1-2 cm long. **Spikelets** 1-flowered, pale, flat, nearly round in section, 4-5 mm long, short-stalked, closely overlapping one another; **glumes** absent; **lemma** 4-6 mm long, the veins and keel fringed with hairs.—River floodplains; local in se Minn, especially along Mississippi River.

Leersia oryzoides (L.) Sw.
RICE CUT-GRASS

MAP 1730
native

Loosely tufted perennial grass, from creeping rhizomes. **Stems** weak and sprawling, rooting at nodes, 1-1.5 m long. **Leaves** flat, 2-3 dm long and 5-10 mm wide, rough-to-touch, the margins fringed with short spines; sheaths rough-hairy; **ligules** 0.5-1 mm long, flat-topped. **Panicle** open at end of stem and from leaf axils (these often partly enclosed by leaf sheaths), 1-2 dm long, the branches ascending to spreading. **Spikelets** 1-flowered, oval, 5 mm long and 1-2 mm wide, compressed, pale green, turning brown with age; **glumes** absent; **lemma** covered with bristly hairs. July-Sept.—Muddy or sandy streambanks, shores, swales and marshes; sometimes forming large patches.

Leersia oryzoides

Leersia virginica Willd.
WHITE GRASS

MAP 1731
native

Perennial grass, spreading by rhizomes. **Stems** slender and weak, often more or less horizontal at base and rooting at nodes, 5-12 dm long. **Leaves** rough-hairy, especially along margins, 5-20 cm long and 5-15 mm wide; sheaths smooth or finely hairy; **ligules** 1-3 mm long, flat-topped. **Panicle** open, 1-2 dm long, the branches separated along the rachis, stiffly spreading, the spikelets from middle to tip of branches. **Spikelets** oblong, barely overlapping one another, 3 mm long and 1 mm wide, sparsely hairy; **glumes** absent; **lemma** 3-4 mm long, the keel and margins sparsely hairy. July-Sept.—Swamps, floodplain forests, shaded forest depressions, streambanks.

Leersia virginica

LEPTOCHLOA *Sprangletop*

CYNODONTEAE

Leptochloa fusca (L.) Kunth
SPRANGLETOP

MAP 1732
native

Diplachne fusca (L.) P. Beauv. ex Roem. & Schult.
Leptochloa fascicularis (Lam.) Gray

Tufted annual grass. **Stems** erect to spreading, branched from base, 2-10 dm long, somewhat fleshy. **Leaves** flat to loosely inrolled, 1-3 mm wide, finely rough-to-touch; **sheaths** open, glabrous or scabrous, often purplish, the upper sheath often partly sheathing the head; **ligules** membranous, 2-8 mm long, becoming lacerate at maturity. **Head** a more or less cylindric panicle, 5-20 cm long and 2-5 cm wide, composed of several to many branches, the branches upright and bearing spikelets in racemes. **Spikelets** 6-12-flowered, 5-10 mm long, breaking above the glumes; **glumes** unequal, lance-shaped, 1-veined, the first glume 2-4 mm long, the

Leptochloa fusca

1729. Leersia lenticularis   *1730. Leersia oryzoides*   *1731. Leersia virginica*

second glume 4-5 mm long; **lemma** 4-5 mm long, 3-veined, tipped with an awn 4-5 mm long; **palea** about as long as lemma. July-Sept.—Shores, streambanks, muddy or sandy flats, usually where flooded part of year, often where brackish.

LEYMUS *Lyme Grass* TRITICEAE

Leymus racemosus (Lam.) Tzvelev (NO MAP)
MAMMOTH WILD RYE *introduced*

Perennial grass, plants strongly rhizomatous, often glaucous. **Stems** 5-10 dm tall, 8-12 mm thick, solitary or a few together, mostly smooth and glabrous, finely scabrous or pubescent below the spikes; ligules 1.5-2.5 mm long; **leaves** exceeded by the spikes; **leaf blades** 20-40 cm long and 8-20 mm wide. **Spikes** 15-35 cm long, 1-2 cm wide, dense, hairy, with 3-8 spikelets per node. **Spikelets** 12-25 mm long, sessile, with 4-6 florets; **glumes** 12-25 mm long and to 2 mm wide, usually exceeding the lemmas, tapering from below midlength, stiff, glabrous at least at the base, keeled and subulate distally, 1-veined; **lemmas** 15-20 mm long, tapering to an awn 1.5-2.5 mm long.—Native to Europe and c Asia, where it grows on dry, sandy soils; reported from Houston County.

LOLIUM *Rye Grass* POEAE

Lolium perenne L. MAP 1733
ENGLISH RYEGRASS *introduced*

Perennial tufted grass. **Stems** slender, 3-7 dm tall, glabrous throughout; **sheaths** open; **ligules** membranous, to 4 mm long; **leaf blades** flat, glossy, 2-4 mm wide. **Spike** slender, 1-2 dm long, smooth on the back of each joint opposite the spikelet, minutely scabrous on the sharp margin. **Spikelets** solitary at each node, usually 5-10-flowered, placed edgewise to the rachis, the edge fitting into a concavity in the axis, disarticulating above the glumes and between the lemmas; first **glume** absent except in the terminal spikelet; second glume (on the side of the spikelet away from the rachis) strongly 3-5-nerved; **lemmas** awnless, the lowest 5.5-8 mm long, the upper progressively reduced.—Native of Europe; cultivated in meadows and lawns and inoften included in commercial seed mixes; and escaped and established on roadsides and in waste places. *Includes L. perenne subsp. multiflorum (Lam) Husnot, sometimes treated as **Lolium multiflorum** Lam.*

Lolium perenne

MELICA *Melic Grass* MELICEAE

Melica nitens (Scribn.) Nutt. MAP 1734
THREE-FLOWER MELIC GRASS 🌿 *threatened | native*

Perennial grass; plants shortly rhizomatous, not tufted or only loosely so. **Stems** 5-12 dm tall; **sheaths** closed almost to the top glabrous or finely roughened; **ligules** conspicuous, 1-6.5 mm long, erose to lacerate; **leaf blades** flat, 4-11 mm wide. **Panicle** 1-2 dm long, the branches often divergent to reflexed, with 5-20 spikelets; pedicels sharply bent and hairy below the spikelets. **Spikelets** 2-3-flowered, 9-12 mm long; **glumes** large, membranous, 3-5-nerved; first **glume** broadly ovate or ovate-elliptic, 5-8 mm long, 3.5-5 mm wide, its margins meeting around the spikelet; second **lemma** usually distinctly projecting beyond the first, exceeding the uppermost smaller, sterile 1-3 lemmas; disarticulation below the glumes. —Dry sandy woods, savannas and prairies.

Melica nitens

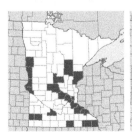
1732. *Leptochloa fusca*

1733. *Lolium perenne*

1734. *Melica nitens*

1735. *Milium effusum*

MILIUM *Millet Grass*   POEAE

Milium effusum L.   MAP 1735
AMERICAN MILLET GRASS   *native*
Perennial rhizomatous grass. **Stems** erect from a bent base, 6-12 dm tall, glabrous;
sheaths open; **ligule** membranous, 3-9 mm long, obtuse-erose; **leaf blades** flat,
broad, 8-17 mm wide, glabrous, or scaberulous on the margin. **Panicle** 1-3 dm
long, ovoid or pyramidal, the branches in fascicles of 2 or 3, widely spreading and
bearing drooping spikelets beyond their middle. **Spikelets** 1-flowered,
disarticulation above the glumes; **glumes** equal, ovate or elliptic, rounded on the
back, scaberulous, about 3 mm long, 3-nerved; **lemma** about as long as the glumes,
awnless, nerveless, obtuse, rounded on the back, at first thin, at maturity firm,
white, and shining, its margins partly covering a palea of similar texture.—Rich,
moist or dry woods.

Milium effusum

MISCANTHUS *Silver-Grass*   ANDROPOGONEAE

Miscanthus sacchariflorus (Maxim.) Benth.   MAP 1736
AMUR SILVER-GRASS   *introduced*
Plants perennial, tufted, spreading from coarse rhizomes to sometimes form large,
dense stands. **Stems** to 2.5 m tall, lower stems 5-8 mm wide; nodes pilose; **sheaths**
open; **ligules** membranous, to 1 mm long, ciliate; **leaf blades** flat, 20-80 cm long,
0.5-3 cm wide, lower surfaces densely pilose near base of blade; midribs
prominent, whitish. **Panicles** 15-40 cm long, white to yellowish brown, usually
with more than 15 branches. **Spikelets** 4-6 mm long; callus hairs copious, white,
2-4x longer than the spikelets; lower **glumes** 2-keeled above, upper margins
densely pilose, the hairs to 15 mm long; upper glumes 3-veined, upper margins
ciliate; awns of upper **lemmas** absent or short, not exceeding the glumes.—Native
of wet places in e Asia; escaped from cultivation to roadsides, ditches, and old
fields where potentially invasive; first recorded naturalized population collected
in LeSueur County in 1977. *Plants have a large, plumose panicle with recurving leaves
that turn orange in the fall.*

Miscanthus sacchariflorus

MUHLENBERGIA *Muhly*   CYNODONTEAE

Perennial grasses, clumped or with creeping rhizomes. Stems erect or reclining at base, often
branching from base. Leaves smooth to hairy, ligules membranous. Head a panicle, usually narrow
and spike-like, sometimes open and spreading, at ends of stems and sometimes also from leaf axils.
Spikelets 1-flowered, breaking above glumes; glumes usually nearly equal in length, 1-veined, the tip
often awned; lemma lance-shaped, 3-veined, sometimes awned, some species with long, soft hairs at
lemma base; palea about as long as lemma.

1   Lemmas not pilose at the base, glabrous (or with minute, even pubescence on back), awnless; stems loosely or
    densely tufted or matted, rhizomes, if present, thin and wiry, not densely clothed with overlapping scales. . . . 2
    2   Spikelets less than 2 mm long, mostly on pedicels more than twice as long, in an open panicle. 3
        3   Panicles ca. 8-20 cm wide, nearly as wide as long when fully expanded . . . . *M. asperifolia*
        3   Panicles 1-6 cm wide, clearly longer than wide . . . . *M. uniflora*
    2   Spikelets ca. 2.4-3.5 mm long, mostly on pedicels less than twice as long, in a slender contracted panicle . . 4
        4   Ligules less than 0.5 mm long; lemmas with a little minute pubescence on back . . . . *M. cuspidata*
        4   Ligules ca. 1.5-2.5 mm long; lemmas usually glabrous across back. . . . . *M. richardsonis*
1   Lemmas pilose at base, glabrous or short-pubescent on back, awned or awnless; stems arising from conspicuous,
    elongate scaly rhizomes (except in *M. schreberi*). 5
    5   Glumes minute, the larger one less than 0.5 mm long, the other vestigial or absent; stems often rooting at
        nodes of decumbent bases, but without elongate scaly rhizomes . . . . *M. schreberi*
    5   Glumes at least half as long as body of lemma; stems from elongate scaly rhizomes. 6
        6   Glumes (including prominent awn-tip) 3.5-7.5 mm long, mostly distinctly longer than the body of the
            lemma; lemma at most short-awned; anthers 0.5-1.3 mm long 7
            7   Internodes minutely puberulent or roughened over much of their surface (rarely nearly glabrous); ligule
                (excluding cilia) 0.5-0.7 mm long or shorter; anthers 0.8-1.3 mm long . . . . *M. glomerata*
            7   Internodes of stem smooth and glabrous over most of their surface; ligule 0.7-1 mm long; anthers ca.
                0.5-0.8 mm long. . . . . *M. racemosa*

6 Glumes generally less than 3.6 mm long (rarely, especially on lower spikelets of panicle, up to 4 mm), mostly about equaling or shorter than the body of the lemma; lemma awnless to long-awned; anthers not over 0.5 mm long (except in *M. tenuiflora* with distinctive short, wide glumes). 7

  8 Larger glumes 0.6-1 mm wide, less than 4 times as long, hence ovate and usually ± abruptly tapered at the tip; stems puberulent below the nodes. . . . . *M. sylvatica*

  8 Larger glumes not over 0.6 mm wide, more than 4 times as long, hence narrowly lanceolate and usually ± attenuate at the tip; stems puberulent or glabrous below the nodes. 9

    9 Stem smooth and glabrous throughout, sometimes decumbent at base and rooting at nodes, generally much branched and bushy above; inflorescences (except terminal one) with base often enclosed in upper leaf sheath . . . . *M. frondosa*

    9 Stem puberulent below the nodes, ± erect, simple or branched; inflorescences all generally exserted 10

      10 Ligules ca. 1 mm long or shorter; some spikelets in panicle sessile or subsessile . . . *M. mexicana*

      10 Ligules, at least the longest, 1.3-2 mm long; spikelets all on distinct (though sometimes rather short) pedicels . . . . *M. sylvatica*

Muhlenbergia asperifolia (Nees & Meyen) Parodi

MAP 1737

ALKALI MUHLY   *introduced*

Perennial grass, from slender, scaly rhizomes. **Stems** 1-5 dm long, becoming more or less horizontal near base, rooting and branching from lower nodes, the branches spreading, waxy; **sheaths** glabrous, margins hyaline; **ligules** to 1 mm long, firm, truncate, ciliate, without lateral lobes; **leaf blades** flat, 2-7 cm long and 1-3 mm wide, usually somewhat rough-to-touch. **Panicle** open, 5-15 cm long, the branches threadlike, widely spreading. **Spikelets** 1-flowered (sometimes 2- or 3-flowered), single on the branches, purple or dark gray, 1-2 mm long; **glumes** nearly equal, half to nearly as long as spikelet; **lemma** unawned, 1-2 mm long. July-Sept.—Mostly weedy in disturbed areas such as roadside ditches and along railroads.

Muhlenbergia cuspidata (Torr.) Rydb.

MAP 1738

STONY-HILLS MUHLY   *native*

Perennial grass, rhizomes absent. **Stems** stiff, slender, strictly erect, tufted, 2-7 dm tall; **sheaths** shorter than the internodes, keeled, smooth or scabridulous, ; **ligules** to 0.8 mm long, membranous, truncate; **leaf blades** erect or nearly so, flat or folded, 1-2 mm wide. **Panicle** very slender and spike-like, the appressed lateral branches 5-15 mm long. **Spikelets** 2.5-3.6 mm long, dark green, occasionally with 2 florets; **glumes** subulate, about equal, 2-3 mm long; **lemma** slender, glabrous at base, 3-4 mm long.—Prairies and open hillsides, in dry or gravelly soil.

Muhlenbergia asperifolia

Muhlenbergia frondosa (Poir.) Fern.

MAP 1739

WIRESTEM MUHLY   *native*

Perennial grass, from stout, scaly rhizomes. **Stems** 4-10 dm long, unbranched and erect when young, becoming branched and sprawling with age, smooth and shiny between nodes; **sheaths** glabrous, margins hyaline; **ligules** membranous, 1-2 mm long, fringed; **leaf blades** lax, smooth or finely roughened, 2-6 mm wide. **Panicle** narrow, to 10 cm long, from ends of stems and leaf axils (where partly enclosed by sheaths), the branches erect to spreading, with spikelets from near base to tip. **Spikelets** 1-flowered; **glumes** 2-3 mm long, tipped with a short awn; **lemma** 3-4 mm long, usually with an awn to 1 cm long, short-hairy at base. Aug.-Sept. —Floodplain forests, streambanks, thickets, shores; also somewhat weedy in disturbed areas such as along railroads.

Muhlenbergia frondosa

1736. *Miscanth. sacchariflorus*   1737. *Muhlenbergia asperifolia*   1738. *Muhlenbergia cuspidata*

Muhlenbergia glomerata (Willd.) Trin.
MAP 1740
MARSH MUHLY *native*

Perennial grass, spreading from rhizomes. **Stems** upright, 3–9 dm long, sometimes with a few branches from base, dull and finely hairy between nodes; **sheaths** finely roughened, slightly keeled; **ligules** membranous, to 0.6 mm long, truncate, fringed; **leaf blades** flat, lax, 2–6 mm wide, usually scabrous. **Panicle** narrow, crowded, cylindric, 2–10 cm long and 5–10 mm wide, the lower clusters of spikelets often separate from one another. **Spikelets** 1-flowered, often purple-tinged, 5–6 mm long; **glumes** nearly equal, longer than the floret, tipped with an awn 1–5 mm long; **lemma** lance-shaped, 2–3 mm long, with long, soft hairs at base. Aug–Sept.—Swamps, wet meadows, marshes, springs, open bogs, fens, calcareous shores.

Muhlenbergia mexicana (L.) Trin.
MAP 1741
MEXICAN MUHLY *native*

Perennial grass, from scaly rhizomes. **Stems** upright, 2–8 dm long, sometimes branched from base; dull and finely hairy between nodes; **sheaths** smooth or finely roughened, somewhat keeled; **ligules** membranous, to 1 mm long, truncate, fringed; **leaf blades** flat, lax, 2–6 mm wide, scabrous or smooth. **Panicle** narrow, densely flowered, 5–15 cm long and 2–10 mm wide, from ends of stems and leafy branches. **Spikelets** 1-flowered, green or purple, 2–3 mm long; **glumes** nearly equal, lance-shaped, 3–4 mm long, about as long as floret, tipped with a short awn about 1 mm long; **lemma** lance-shaped, 2–3 mm long, unawned or with an awn to 7 mm long. Aug–Sept.—Swamps, floodplain forests, thickets, wet meadows, marshes, springs, fens and streambanks.

Muhlenbergia glomerata

Muhlenbergia racemosa (Michx.) B.S.P.
MAP 1742
GREEN MUHLY *native*

Perennial grass, from scaly rhizomes. **Stems** erect or declined, 5–12 dm tall, rather stout, simple or sparsely branched; **sheaths** finely roughened, slightly keeled; **ligules** membranous, 0.6–1.5 mm long, truncate, fringed; **leaf blades** ascending or appressed, flat, 2–5 mm wide, usually scabrous. **Panicle** narrow, usually compact and dense, often interrupted toward the base, 5–10 cm long, about 1 cm thick. **Spikelets** on short pedicels, crowded and much overlapping; **glumes** subulate, tapering into an awn, 1.5–2x as long as the lemmas, the first 4.4–6.1, the second 4.5–7.5 mm long, including their awns; **lemma** scabrous, pilose at base, 2.6–4 mm long, acuminate to a slender point, awnless.—Moist or wet soil in open places.

Muhlenbergia richardsonis (Trin.) Rydb.
MAP 1743
MATTED MUHLY *native*

Loosely tufted perennial grass, rooting from lower nodes and forming mats. **Stems** very slender, erect or more or less horizontal at base, 2–6 dm long; **sheaths** shorter or longer than the internodes, glabrous; **ligules** membranous, 1–3 mm long, acute to truncate, erose; leaf blades upright, flat or involute, 0.5–4 mm wide. **Panicle** narrow and spike-like, 2–12 cm long. **Spikelets** 1-flowered, uncrowded, green or gray-green, 2–3 mm long; **glumes** nearly equal, ovate, to half as long as floret; **lemma** lance-shaped, smooth, 2–3 mm long tipped with a short point. July–Sept.—Low prairie, wet meadows, marshes and seeps; often where brackish.

Muhlenbergia mexicana

Muhlenbergia richardsonis

1739. Muhlenbergia frondosa   *1740. Muhlenbergia glomerata*   *1741. Muhlenbergia mexicana*   *1742. Muhlenbergia racemosa*

Muhlenbergia schreberi J.F. Gmel.
NIMBLEWILL

MAP 1744
native

Perennial grass 1-5 dm tall, rhizomes absent. Lower portion of the **stems** decumbent and tuftedly branched; upper portion erect, sparsely branched; **sheaths** shorter than the internodes, glabrous for most of their length, margins shortly pubescent near tips; **ligules** 0.2-0.5 mm long, truncate, erose, ciliate; **leaf blades** flat, 1-4.5 mm wide, smooth or scabrous. **Panicle** slender, 3-10 cm long, 3-8 mm thick. **glumes** broadly ovate to rotund or quadrate, erose, 0.5 mm long or less, or rarely to 1 mm long, or the first lacking; **lemma** roughly pubescent, sharply nerved, the body 1.9-2.5 mm long, tapering into an awn 2-4 mm long. —Moist ground, especially in shady places; sometimes weedy in lawns and gardens.

Muhlenbergia sylvatica Torr.
WOODLAND MUHLY

MAP 1745
native

Perennial grass, spreading by rhizomes. **Stems** erect, or sprawling when old, 4-10 dm long, coarse-hairy between nodes; **sheaths** smooth for most of their length, roughened near tip, margins hyaline; **ligules** membranous, 1-2.5 mm long, truncate, lacerate-ciliolate; leaf blades flat, 3-7 mm wide, scabrous. **Panicle** slender, often nodding, 5-20 cm long and 2-7 mm wide. **Spikelets** 1-flowered, 2-4 mm long, at ends of stalks about 3 mm long; **glumes** nearly equal, sharp-tipped, shorter than lemma; **lemma** 2-4 mm long, short hairy at base, tipped with an awn 5-15 mm long. Aug.-Sept.—Streambanks, shaded wet areas.

Muhlenbergia sylvatica

Muhlenbergia uniflora (Muhl.) Fern.
BOG MUHLY

MAP 1746
native

Perennial grass, loosely matted. **Stems** very slender, 2-4 dm long, often more or less horizontal and rooting at base; **leaves** crowded near base of plant; **sheaths** keeled; **ligules** membranous, 0.5-1.5 mm long, truncate, erose, without lateral lobes; **leaf blades** 1-2 mm wide, usually flat, upper surface smooth or finely roughened, midveins thickened and whitish near base of blade. **Panicle** loose, open, 7-20 cm long and 2-4 cm wide, the branches threadlike. **Spikelets** 1-flowered (rarely 2-flowered), oval, purple-tinged, 1-2 mm long; **glumes** about equal, ovate, to half the length of spikelet; **lemma** 1-2 mm long, unawned. —Wetland margins, exposed sandy shores.

NASSELLA *Needlegrass*

STIPEAE

Nassella viridula (Trin.) Barkworth
GREEN NEEDLEGRASS
Stipa viridula Trin.

MAP 1747
native

Muhlenbergia uniflora

Loosely tufted perennial grass. **Stems** erect, 50-100 cm high; **sheaths** prominently veined, villous at the throat; **ligules** rounded to truncate, the upper ligules mostly 1-5 mm long, lower ligules shorter, less than 1 mm. **leaf blades** 2-5 mm wide, flat to somewhat involute at maturity, many-ridged and often scabrous above, smooth below, often pubescent at the margin near the ligule. **Panicles** 1-2 dm long, narrow, with appressed-ascending branches, each bearing 2-several spikelets; **glumes** 7-10 mm long, tapering to a very slender point; **lemmas** 5-6 mm long, the lemma awn 2-3 cm long, weakly twice geniculate below the middle.—Prairies and dry, open woods; an important grass of the Great Plains.

1743. Muhlenber. richardsonis

1744. Muhlenbergia schreberi · *1745. Muhlenbergia sylvatica*

Nassella viridula

ORYZOPSIS *Mountain Ricegrass*

STIPEAE

Oryzopsis asperifolia Michx.
WHITE-GRAIN MOUNTAIN RICEGRASS

MAP 1748
native

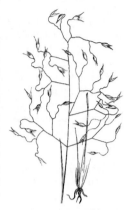

Loosely tufted perennial grass. **Stems** 3-7 dm tall, often widely spreading. **Leaves** mostly basal; sheaths open, glabrous; auricles absent; **basal ligules** to 0.7 mm long, ciliate; **blades** of basal leaves 30-90 cm long and 4-9 mm wide, upper surface glaucous; **upper stem leaves** with greatly reduced blades 3 cm long or less or lacking. **Raceme** slender, 2-6 cm long, the paired branches each with a single spikelet. **Spikelets** 1-flowered, articulated above the glumes; **glumes** nearly equal, 7-8.5 mm long, abruptly acute or mucronate; **lemma** about equaling the glumes, becoming indurate at maturity, pale green or yellowish; awn 6-14 mm long, straight or twisted, articulated with the lemma, readily detached.—Moist or dry open woods, forested dunes. New leaves start to develop in mid-summer, the blades at first erect, then bending downward and remaining green through winter. Sheaths below the level of the duff are usually bright purple. *Our other species formerly in this genus are now placed in* **Achnatherum** *and* **Piptatherum**.

Oryzopsis asperifolia

PANICUM *Panic-Grass*

PANICEAE

Annual or perennial grasses. Heads narrow to open panicles (ours). Spikelets small, with 1 fertile flower; glumes usually unequal, the first glume membranous, usually very small, second glume green, about as long as spikelet; sterile lemma similar to second glume, enclosing the palea and sometimes a staminate flower, fertile lemma whitish, smooth.

1 Spikelets all or mostly 3 mm or more in length, strongly nerved 2
  2 First glume more than half as long as second glume; plants over 5 dm tall, essentially glabrous (except for margin and throat of leaf sheath), from strong scaly rhizome, with panicle terminal and over 15 cm tall . . . . .
    . . . . ***P. virgatum***
  2 First glume not over half as long as second glume (except in *P. miliaceum*); plants shorter, usually ± pubescent, not rhizomatous, with panicles usually shorter or several 3
    3 Leaves (blades and sheaths) essentially glabrous . . . . ***P. dichotomiflorum***
    3 Leaves pubescent (at least on sheaths) . . . . ***P. miliaceum***
1 Spikelets less than 3 mm long, strongly nerved or not 4
  4 Sheaths of middle and upper leaves glabrous on back (may be ciliate on margins) . . . . ***P. dichotomiflorum***
  4 Sheaths sparsely to heavily pilose on back 5
    5 Peduncles only slightly exserted from sheaths, exserted portion less than half as long as panicle . . . .
      . . . . ***P. capillare***
    5 Peduncles long-exserted from sheaths, exserted portion half as long as panicle or longer 6
      6 Spikelets lanceolate in outline, acuminate at apex, the longest 2.4-3.3 mm long . . . . ***P. capillare***
      6 Spikelets ovate or narrowly ovate in outline, acute at apex, the longest 1.9-2.3 mm long . . . .
        . . . . ***P. philadelphicum***

Panicum capillare L.
COMMON PANIC-GRASS

MAP 1749
native

Annual grass, hirsute or hispid, hairs papillose-based, often purplish. **Stems** branched from the base, erect, ascending, or decumbent, to 7 dm long; **sheaths** rounded; **ligules** membranous, ciliate, the cilia 0.5-1.5 mm long; **leaf blades** spreading, 3-18 mm wide. **Panicles** diffusely branched, sometimes 2/3 as long as the entire plant. **Spikelets** all or mostly on long pedicels, the first **glume** to half as

1746. *Muhlenbergia uniflora*

1747. *Nassella viridula*

1748. *Oryzopsis asperifolia*

1749. *Panicum capillare*

long as the sterile lemma; margins of the lemma distinctly inrolled.—Dry or moist soil, often a weed in fields in gardens, widely distributed and variable.

Panicum dichotomiflorum Michx.   MAP 1750
FALL PANIC-GRASS   *native*

Annual or short-lived perennial grass. **Stems** erect to decumbent or diffuse, often 1 m long or more, rooting at the lower nodes when in water; **sheaths** compressed, inflated, sparsely pubescent near the base, elsewhere mostly glabrous; **ligules** 0.5-2 mm long; **leaf blades** 3-25 mm wide, glabrous or sparsely pilose, often scabrous near the margins; midribs whitish. **Panicle** in large plants to 4 dm long, widely branched. **Spikelets** green or tinged with purple, ellipsoid to oblong; first **glume** broad, obtuse or rounded, 0.5-1.1 mm long; second glume and sterile lemma acute, 7-nerved.—Moist soil and shores, sometimes in shallow water, often a weed in cultivated land.

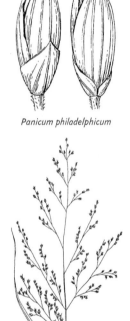

Panicum capillare

Panicum miliaceum L.   MAP 1751
BROOMCORN MILLET   *introduced*

Annual grass. **Stems** stout, 2-6 (rarely 10) dm tall; **sheaths** overlapping, terete, densely pilose; **ligules** membranous, ciliate, the cilia 1-3 mm long; **leaf blades** 7-25 mm wide. **Panicle** included at base, pyramidal to cylindric, 8-20 cm long, often nodding at maturity. **Spikelets** 4.5-5.5 mm long; first **glume** half as long, 5-nerved; second glume and sterile lemma equal, distinctly 7-9-nerved. **Grain** straw-colored to brown, 3-3.5 mm long.—Asian native; occasionally grown for forage or for bird seed; adventive on roadsides and in waste places.

Panicum philadelphicum Bernh.   MAP 1752
PHILADELPHIA PANIC-GRASS   *native*

Annual grass. **Stems** slender, erect or rarely decumbent, 1-5 dm tall, branched from the base; **leaves** often crowded at base; **sheaths** usually longer than the internodes, hispid; **ligules** 0.5-1.5 mm long; **leaf blades** linear, ascending to erect, flat, 2-12 mm wide, hirsute to sparsely pilose, greenish or purplish. **Panicle** ovoid, usually about 1/3 as long as the entire plant; peduncle well exsert. **Spikelets** tending to be paired at the ends of the capillary branches; ovate to elliptic, 1.6-2.4 mm long; first **glume** obtuse or acute, about 2/5 as long as the abruptly acuminate second glume and sterile lemma, margins of the lemma barely inrolled. **Grain** plump, becoming blackish.—Dry soil and sandy fields.

Panicum philadelphicum

Panicum virgatum L.   MAP 1753
SWITCHGRASS   *native*

Perennial grass, from hard, scaly rhizomes, often forming large bunches. **Stems** stout, erect, to 3 m tall; **sheaths** longer than the lower internodes, shorter than those above, glabrous or pilose, especially on the throat, margins ciliate; **ligules** a dense zone of silky hairs 2-6 mm long; **leaf blades** flat, erect to spreading, 2-5 dm long, 2-15 mm wide, undersurface sometimes densely pubescent, margins scabrous. **Panicle** open, freely branched, pyramidal, usually 2-4 dm long. **Spikelets** ovoid, soon widened distally by spreading of the glumes and sterile lemma, 2.2-5.6 mm long; first **glume** half or more as long as the spikelet; second glume and sterile lemma about equal, conspicuously nerved, acute to long-acuminate.—Open woods, prairies, dunes, and shores, and brackish marshes. *Variable in length and shape of the glumes, especially the first glume.*

Panicum virgatum

1750. Panic. dichotomiflorum   1751. Panicum miliaceum   1752. Panicum philadelphicum   1753. Panicum virgatum

PASCOPYRUM *Western Wheatgrass*   TRITICEAE

Pascopyrum smithii (Rydb.) Barkworth & D.R. Dewey   MAP 1754
WESTERN WHEATGRASS   *native*
  Agropyron smithii Rydb.
  Elytrigia smithii (Rydb.) Nevski
  Elymus smithii (Rydb.) Gould
Perennial grass, usually glaucous. **Stems** from long rhizomes, stout, usually 4-6 dm tall; **leaves** mostly at base; **sheaths** striate when dry, usually glabrous, rarely pilose; auricles 0.2-1 mm long, often purple; **ligules** membranous, about 0.1 mm long; **leaf blades** 2-5 mm wide, involute when dry. **Spike** usually 7-15 cm long, dense. **Spikelets** 12-22 mm long, 6-12-flowered; **glumes** narrowly lance-shaped, 9-14 mm long, strongly nerved, attenuate from below the middle with nearly straight sides; **lemmas** similar in shape, 10-14 mm long, acurrinate to a stout stiff point or with an awn to 1 mm long.—Roadsides, railways;dry or sandy soil. *An important grass of grasslands and high deserts in the western USA.*

PASPALUM *Crown Grass*   PANICEAE

Paspalum setaceum Michx.   MAP 1755
SLENDER CROWN GRASS   *native*
Perennial tufted grass. Stems spreading, ascending, or erect, 4-10 dm long; **ligules** membranous, 0.2-0.5 mm long; **sheaths** and **blades** hirsute with stiffish straight hairs 1-4 mm long, varying to nearly or quite glabrous. **Racemes** spike-like, straight or slightly curved, 5-10 cm long; peduncle eventually long and well exsert, glabrous or sparsely hirsute above. **Spikelets** in pairs, broadly ovate, 1.8-2.3 mm long, glabrous or minutely pubescent with capitate hairs, often brown-dotted; **glumes** 2-nerved or obscurely 3-nerved; **sterile lemma** 2-nerved.—Dry or moist, especially sandy soil. *Highly variable in amount of pubescence.*

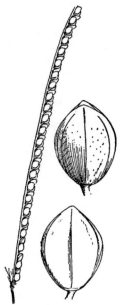

Paspalum setaceum

PHALARIS *Canary-Grass*   POEAE

Annual or perennial grasses. Leaves glabrous, auricles absent; ligule large, membranous. Flowers in dense or spike-like panicles of medium-sized or large spikelets. Spikelets articulated above the glumes, with 1 perfect terminal flower and 1 or 2 minute sterile lemmas below it. Glumes about equal, compressed and keeled, usually winged along the midnerve; lateral nerves usually stronger than the midnerve. Lemmas awnless, shorter than the glumes, the sterile linear, resembling tufts of hairs at the base of a solitary functional floret; the fertile lemma firm or leathery, often shining.

1 Rhizomatous perennial, with elongate lobed panicle (or the lower branches spreading at anthesis); glumes mostly 4-5.7 mm long, the keel not winged . . . . **P. arundinacea**
1 Annual, with very dense, compact, ovoid panicle; glumes mostly 6-8 mm long, the keel prominently winged . .
  . . . . **P. canariensis**

Phalaris arundinacea L.   MAP 1756
REED CANARY-GRASS   *native / introduced (naturalized)*
Tall perennial grass, spreading by scaly rhizomes and typically forming large, dense colonies. **Stems** stout, smooth, 5-20 dm long; **sheaths** smooth; **ligules** membranous, 4-9 mm long, truncate, lacerate; **leaf blades** flat, 5-20 mm wide, surfaces scabrous, margins serrate. **Panicle** narrow, densely flowered, 5-25 cm long, often purple-tinged, the branches short and upright. **Spikelets** 4-6 mm long, breaking above glumes, with 1 fertile flower and 2 small sterile lemmas below;

1754. Pascopyrum smithii   *1755. Paspalum setaceum*   *1756. Phalaris arundinacea*

glumes nearly equal, longer than fertile floret, lance-shaped, tapered to tip or short-awned, becoming straw-colored with age, 3-veined; **fertile lemma** ovate, 3 mm long, shiny; palea as long as lemma. June–July.—Wet meadows, shallow marshes, ditches, shores and streambanks. *Reed canary-grass is an aggressive, highly competitive wetland species, now widely naturalized, often to the detriment of our native flora. Our populations are likely a mix of native and Eurasian strains, including cultivars developed for forage.*

Phalaris arundinacea

Phalaris canariensis L.
COMMON CANARY-GRASS
MAP 1757
introduced

Annual grass. **Stems** erect, 3-9 dm tall; ligules membranous, 3-6 mm long, rounded to obtuse, lacerate; **leaf blades** 2-10 mm wide. **Panicle** dense, ovoid, usually about 3 cm long; **glumes** broad, 7-8 mm long, broadly winged on the keel, the midnerve marked by a broad green stripe; **fertile lemma** about 5 mm long; sterile lemmas 2, linear, about 2.5 mm long.—Native of Europe; introduced and adventive; grown for bird seed. *Distinguished by the exposed, nearly semi-circular ends of the glumes.*

PHLEUM *Timothy*
POEAE

Phleum pratense L.
COMMON TIMOTHY
MAP 1758
introduced (naturalized)

Tufted perennial grass. **Stems** mostly 5-10 dm tall; **sheaths** open; **auricles** absent or inconspicuous; **ligules** membranous, 2-4 mm long, not ciliate; **leaf blades** flat, typically 5-8 mm wide, rough-margined. **Panicle** spike-like and cylindric, usually 5-10 cm long, 6-8 mm thick. **Spikelets** 1-flowered, strongly flattened, articulated above the glumes; **glumes** equal, compressed and keeled, hispid-ciliate on the keel, 3-nerved, 2.6-3.2 mm long, rounded to the tip; lemma much shorter than the glumes, thin and delicate, 3-5-nerved, awnless; palea narrow, somewhat shorter than to nearly equaling the lemma.—Introduced from Eurasia as a forage grass, commonly cultivated for hay and pasture; escaped to fields, roadsides, and disturbed places.

PHRAGMITES *Reed*
ARUNDINEAE

Phragmites australis (Cav.) Trin.
COMMON REED
MAP 1759
native (see desc.)

   Phragmites communis Trin.

Tall, stout perennial reed, from deep, scaly rhizomes, or the rhizomes sometimes exposed and creeping over the soil; often forming large colonies. **Stems** erect, hollow, 1-4 m long and 5-15 mm wide near base, the internodes often purple; **sheaths** open, mostly overlapping; **ligule** membranous, white, 1 mm long, ciliate. **leaf blades** flat, long, 1-3 cm wide. **Head** a large, plumelike panicle, purple when young, turning yellow-brown with age, 15-40 cm long, much-branched, the branches angled or curved upward. **Spikelets** 3-7-flowered, linear, 10-15 mm long, breaking above the glumes; the stem within the spikelet (rachilla) covered with long silky hairs, these longer than the florets and becoming exposed as the lemmas spread after flowering; **glumes** unequal, the first glume half the length of second glume. **Grain** seldom maturing. Aug–Sept.—Fresh to brackish marshes, shores, streams, ditches, occasional in tamarack swamps; sometimes in shallow

1757. *Phalaris canariensis*

1758. *Phleum pratense*

1759. *Phragmites australis*

Phragmites australis

water. Two subspecies in Minn, one native (subsp. *americanus*, whose distribution is poorly understood) and one introduced and invasive (subsp. *australis*):

1   Plants rarely forming a monoculture; ligules 1-1.7 mm long; lower glumes 3-6.5 mm long; upper glumes 5.5-11 mm long; lemmas 8-13.5 mm long; leaf sheaths deciduous, exposing stems in winter. . . . . ***subsp. americanus***
1   Plants invasive and often forming a monoculture; ligules 0.4-0.9 mm long; lower glumes 2.5-5 mm long; upper glumes 4.5-7.5 mm long; lemmas 7.5-12 mm long; leaf sheaths not deciduous, stems not exposed in winter. . . . . ***subsp. australis***

PIPTATHERUM *Ricegrass*   STIPEAE

Tufted perennial grasses, sometimes rhizomatous. Leaf blades with flat or involute, auricles absent, ligules membranous to hyaline. Spikelets often large, in contracted or open panicles. Spikelets 1-flowered, articulated above the glumes. Glumes equal or nearly so, broad. Lemma about equaling the glumes, becoming indurate at maturity, with a terminal, readily detached awn.

1   Blades flat, mostly 5-18 mm wide; body of lemma 5.5-7 mm long; ligules absent or to 0.5 mm long. . . . .
. . . . ***P. racemosum***
1   Blades involute, less than 2 mm wide; body of lemma 2.5-4 mm long; ligules of upper leaves 1.5-3 mm long . . 2
    2   Awn 6-9 mm long, ± twisted; glumes completely smooth . . . . ***P. canadense***
    2   Awn absent or less than 2 (-3) mm long, nearly straight; glumes very minutely scabrous toward tip (20×) . . .
    . . . . ***P. pungens***

Piptatherum canadense (Poir) Dorn   MAP 1760
CANADIAN MOUNTAIN RICEGRASS   ☙ *threatened | native*
  Oryzopsis canadensis (Poir.) Torr. ex A. Gray.

Stems loosely tufted, not rhizomatous, 3-8 dm tall; sheaths smooth or finely roughened; ligules 1-4 mm long, hyaline; basal leaf blades 4-15 cm long, 1-1.5 mm wide when flat, less than 1 mm wide when folded. **Panicle** lax and open, ovoid, 8-15 cm long, with flexuous, capillary, widely spreading branches. **glumes** elliptic-obovate, 3.5-4.8 mm long, very thin, the lateral nerves inconspicuous; mature **lemma** dull brown; awn persistent, 7-11 mm long, crooked, twisted and often somewhat coiled in the basal half. Dry, sandy or rocky woods, often with jack pine and white spruce. *The persistent, longer awns distinguish **P. canadense** from P. pungens.*

Piptatherum pungens (Torr. ex Spreng.) Dorn   MAP 1761
SHORT-AWN MOUNTAIN RICEGRASS   *native*
  Oryzopsis pungens (Torr.) Hitchc.

Stems densely tufted, 2-5 dm tall; **leaves** mostly basal; **sheaths** smooth or somewhat scabrous; **ligules** 0.5-2.5 mm long, truncate to acute; **blades** 0.5-1.8 mm wide, flat to involute (at least when dry), scaberulous. **Panicle** 3-8 cm long, usually slender with appressed or strongly ascending branches, or ovoid and open at anthesis; **glumes** elliptic to obovate, 3.5-4 mm long, very thin, the lateral nerves inconspicuous; **lemma** gray or pale green; awn 1-2 mm long, straight or slightly bent.—Sandy dry woods, usually with aspen, oak, jack pine, and red pine; dunes and rocky places. *The fragile awn is readily broken off and is lacking in most herbarium specimens.*

Piptatherum pungens

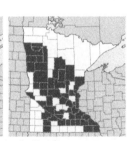

1760. *Piptatherum canadense*   1761. *Piptatherum pungens*   1762. *Piptatherum racemosum*

Piptatherum racemosum (Sm) Barkworth
BLACK-SEED MOUNTAIN RICEGRASS

MAP 1762
native

Oryzopsis racemosa (Sm.) Ricker ex Hitchc.

Stems 4-10 dm tall, loosely tufted from a knotty rhizome; **sheaths** usually glabrous; **basal leaves** more or less absent; **upper stem leaves** distinctly longer than the lower, the **blades** usually 1-2 dm long and 8-15 mm wide, scaberulous above, pubescent beneath; **ligules** 0.3-0.7 mm long, truncate. **Panicle** sparsely branched, 1-2 dm long, the few straight branches spreading or ascending, bearing the few appressed spikelets toward the ends; **glumes** herbaceous, narrowly elliptic, 7-9 mm long, 7-nerved; **lemma** dark brown and shining, somewhat shorter than the glumes; awn 12-22 mm long.—Moist, rich deciduous forests and wooded dunes, sometimes in disturbed places; not often found in dry woods of jack pine or oak.

Piptatherum racemosum

POA *Bluegrass*   POEAE

Annual or perennial grasses, with or without rhizomes or stolons, densely to loosely tufted or the culms solitary. Leaves mostly near base, flat to folded, midrib 2-grooved, the tip keeled similar to the bow of a boat; sheaths partly closed, auricles absent, ligules membranous. Head an open panicle. Spiekelets small, with 2 to several flowers breaking above the glumes; glumes nearly equal, the first glume usually 1-veined, the second glume 3-veined; lemmas often with a tuft of distinctive cobwebby hairs at base; palea nearly as long as lemma.

POA GROUP KEY

Some species appear more than once in the keys; 'flag leaf' refers to the uppermost leaf which is often angled outward from the stem.

1   Stems with bulbous bases; spikelets often bulbiferous . . . . *P. bulbosa*
1   Stems with non-bulbous bases 2
    2   Plants annual or perennial; anthers 0.1-1 mm long in all florets and well developed, or only the upper 1-2 florets with rudimentary anthers . . . . **SUBKEY 1**
    2   Plants perennial; some anthers 1.3-4 mm long, or the florets pistillate and all anthers vestigial and to 0.2 mm long, or longer and poorly developed 3
       3   Plants rhizomatous or stoloniferous, rhizomes or stolons usually longer than 5 mm; basal leaves of the erect shoots with well-developed blades; plants densely to loosely tufted or the stems solitary . . . . . .
       . . . . **SUBKEY 2**
       3   Plants neither rhizomatous nor stoloniferous; basal leaves of the erect shoots sometimes without blades; plants densely tufted . . . . **SUBKEY 3**

POA SUBKEY 1

Plants annual or perennial. Stems not bulbous at base. Basal leaf sheaths not swollen at the base. Spikelets not bulbiferous, florets developing normally. Anthers 0.1-1 mm long.

1   Plants annual, sometimes surviving for a second season, introduced, weedy species; calluses glabrous; lemmas usually softly puberulent to long-villous on the keel and marginal veins, often also on the lateral veins, glabrous between the veins, non-alpine plants rarely glabrous throughout; palea keels smooth, usually short- to long-villous near the apices, rarely glabrous; panicle branches and glume keels smooth . . . . *P. annua*
1   Plants perennial, native, sometimes growing in disturbed habitats; calluses webbed or glabrous, if glabrous, the lemma pubescence not as above or the palea keels at least slightly scabrous near the apices; panicle branches and glume keels smooth of scabrous 2
    2   Calluses webbed; lemma keels glabrous throughout or, if hairy on the proximal 1/2, the marginal veins glabrous
    3
       3   Lemmas hairy only on the keels; branches in whorls of (2)3-5(7) . . . . *P. alsodes*
       3   Lemmas usually glabrous, marginal veins rarely sparsely hairy at the base, hairs to 0.15 mm long; branches 1-3 per node . . . . *P. saltuensis*
    2   Calluses webbed or glabrous, if webbed, the lemmas hairy on the keel and marginal veins 4
       4   Sheaths closed for 1/10-1/5 their length; lower 1-3 leaves of the stems; anthers 0.8-1.2 mm long, sometimes poorly developed 5
          5   Flag leaf nodes at or above mid-stem length. . . . . *P. nemoralis*
          5   Flag leaf nodes usually in the basal 1/3 of the stem . . . . *P. glauca*

    4 Sheaths closed for 1/5-7/8 their length; stems with or without bladeless leaves; anthers 0.2-1.2 mm long, well developed 6

        6 Panicle branches smooth or sparsely scabrous, usually terete or slightly sulcate; lower glumes subulate to broadly lanceolate; lemmas glabrous between the veins .... *P. sylvestris*

        6 Panicle branches sparsely to densely scabrous, terete or angled; lower glumes subulate or broader; lemmas glabrous or puberulent between the veins 7

           7 Palea keels puberulent; anthers 0.8-1.2 mm long; lemmas 3-4.7 mm long, lateral veins distinct ... . *P. wolfii*

           7 Palea keels scabrous; anthers 0.2-0.8 mm long; lemmas 2.5-4 mm long, lateral veins faint .... *P. paludigen*

POA SUBKEY 2

Plants with rhizomes or stolons, densely to loosely tufted or the stems solitary.

1 Stems and nodes strongly compressed; stems usually geniculate; lower stem nodes usually exserted; panicle branches angled, scabrous on the angles; sheaths closed for 1/10-1/5 their length .... *P. compressa*

1 Stems terete to somewhat compressed, nodes not or only weakly compressed; stems geniculate or not; lower stem nodes exserted or not; panicle branches angled or terete, smooth or scabrous; sheath closure varied. ... 2

    2 Lemma keels softly puberulent for 3/5 their length, hairs usually sparse, marginal veins glabrous or puberulent to 1/4 their length, intercostal regions smooth and glabrous; lateral veins prominent; calluses webbed; palea keels smooth, muriculate, tuberculate, or scabridulous; lower glumes 1-veined, usually arched to sickle-shaped; ligules 3-10 mm long, acute to acuminate; panicle branches angled, angles densely scabrous; plants usually weakly stoloniferous.. *P. trivialis*

    2 Lemmas glabrous or variously pubescent, if as above, the lateral veins faint or moderately prominent or the calluses glabrous or the palea keels distinctly scabrous or hairy or the lower glumes 3-veined; calluses glabrous or hairy; palea keels scabrous at least near the apices; lower glumes 1-3-veined, not arched, not sickle-shaped; ligules 0.5-18 mm long, truncate to acuminate; panicle branches terete or angled, smooth or scabrous; plants stoloniferous or not 3

        3 Calluses glabrous, diffusely webbed with hairs to 1/2 the lemma length, or with a crown of hairs, or sparsely and dorsally webbed with hairs to 1/4 the lemma length; lemmas glabrous or pubescent........ *P. arida*

        3 Calluses dorsally webbed, hairs over 1/2 the length of the lemmas, sometimes with additional webs below the marginal veins; lemma short- to long-villous on the keels and marginal veins 4

           4 Sheaths closed for 1/10-1/5 their length; spikelets 3-5 mm long; lemmas 2-3 mm long, glabrous between the keels and marginal veins; panicle branches angled, angles densely scabrous; plants sometimes stoloniferous, sometimes branching above the stem bases; florets bisexual .... *P. palustris*

           4 Sheaths closed for 1/5-9/10 their length; spikelets 3.5-12 mm long; lemmas 2-8 mm long, glabrous or hairy between the keels and marginal veins; panicle branches terete or angled, smooth or scabrous; plants rarely stoloniferous, usually rhizomatous, never branching above the stem bases; florets bisexual or unisexual .... *P. pratensis*

POA SUBKEY 3

Plants perennial, loosely to densely tufted, rhizomes and stolons absent. Stems not bulbous at base. Basal sheaths not swollen. Spikelets not bulbiferous, florets developing normally.

1 Calluses usually dorsally webbed .... *P. trivialis*

1 Calluses glabrous or with a crown of hairs 2

    2 Lemma lateral veins pronounced, keels pubescent, marginal veins glabrous or softly puberulent at the base, lemmas glabrous elsewhere; lower glumes 1-veined, subulate to narrowly lanceolate, usually arched to sickle-shaped; callus web well-developed .... *P. trivialis*

    2 Lemma lateral veins obscure to pronounced, keels glabrous throughout or, if pubescent, the marginal veins distinctly pubescent for more than 1/4 their length, lemma lateral veins and intercostal regions glabrous or pubescent, or, if pubescent as in *P. trivialis*, then the callus web short, scant, poorly developed and the lower glumes 3-veined and lanceolate or broader... 3

        3 Panicles open, conical, with whorls of 3-10, spreading to eventually reflexed, scabrous-angled branches at the lower nodes; lemmas hairy on the keel and veins; callus webs well developed .... *P. sylvestris*

        3 Panicles contracted to open, if open then not conical and without whorls of (2)3-10, eventually reflexed, scabrous-angled branches at the lower nodes; branches smooth or scabrous-angled; lemmas glabrous or hairy; calluses glabrous, with diffuse hairs, or with a scanty or well-developed web 4

           4 Sheaths closed for 1/3-3/4 their length .... *P. saltuensis*

           4 Sheaths closed for up to 1/4 their length 5

5   Flag leaf nodes usually in the lower 1/10-1/3 of the stems; flag leaf blades usually distinctly shorter than their sheaths; lemmas sometimes softly puberulent between the veins, lateral veins usually with at least a few minute hairs; ligules 1-4 mm long . . . . ***P. glauca***

5   Flag leaf nodes usually in the upper 2/3 of the stems; flag leaf blades shorter or longer than their sheaths; lemmas glabrous between the veins, lateral veins usually glabrous, rarely with 1 to several minute hairs; ligules 0.2-6 mm long 6

  6   Spikelets lanceolate; glumes subulate to narrowly lanceolate, gradually tapering to narrowly acuminate tips; ligules to 0.5 mm long, truncate; flag leaf nodes at or above the middle of the stems; flag leaf blades usually longer than their sheaths; rachillas usually hairy, hairs to 0.15 mm long; webs usually short, scanty . . . . ***P. nemoralis***

  6   Spikelets and glumes not as above or, if so, the ligules 1.5-6 mm long, truncate to acute, and the rachillas glabrous; flag leaf nodes at or above the lower 1/3 of the stem; flag leaf blades longer or shorter than their sheaths; webs short or long, scanty or not 7

    7   Panicles 10-30 cm long, branches 4-15 cm long; stems closely spaced to isolated at the base; lower glumes tapering to the apices; lemma keels abruptly inwardly arched beneath the scarious tips; lemma margins distinctly inrolled; rachillas usually muriculate, rarely sparsely hispidulous; web hairs usually longer than 2/3 the length of the lemmas . . . . ***P. palustris***

    7   Panicles 3-15 cm long, branches 0.4-8 cm long; stems closely spaced at the base; lower glumes abruptly narrowing to the apices, lengths 4.5-6.3 times the widths; lemma keels not abruptly inwardly arched beneath the scarious apices; lemma margins not or slightly inrolled; rachillas usually softly puberulent; web hairs shorter than 1/2(2/3) the length of the lemmas . . . .
         . . . . ***P. interior***

Poa alsodes Gray
GROVE BLUEGRASS

MAP 1763
native

Loosely tufted perennial grass, rhizomes absent. **Stems** slender, 3-8 dm long; **sheaths** closed for 1/2-7/8 their length; **ligules** to 2 mm long, smooth or sparsely scabrous, truncate to obtuse; **leaf blades** 1-4 mm wide, flat, lax. **Panicle** open, lax, 10-20 cm long, the branches becoming widely spreading, mostly in groups of 4-5, with l to few spikelets near tip of branch; base of panicle sometimes remaining enclosed by sheath. **Spikelets** ovate, 2-3-flowered, 3-5 mm long; **glumes** nearly equal, 2-4 mm long; **lemmas** 2-4 mm long, with cobwebby hairs at base. May-July.—Alder thickets, swamp hummocks, most common in moist deciduous or mixed conifer-deciduous forests.

Poa alsodes

Poa annua L.
ANNUAL BLUEGRASS

MAP 1764
introduced (naturalized)

Annual grass, densely tufted. **Stems** to 3 dm long, prostrate to ascending; **sheaths** closed for about 1/3 their length, terete or weakly compressed, smooth; **ligules** 0.5-3 mm long, glabrous, decurrent, obtuse to truncate; **leaf blades** 1-10 cm long, 1-4 mm wide, flat or weakly folded, thin, soft, smooth, margins usually slightly scabrous, broadly prow-shaped at tip. **Panicle** ovoid, 2-8 cm long, with few ascending branches bearing rather crowded spikelets above the middle. **Spikelets** green, 3-6-flowered, 3-5 mm long; **glumes** broadly lance-shaped, acute, scarious-margined, indistinctly nerved, the first 1.5-2.4 mm, the second 1.8-2.8 mm long; **lemmas** thin, elliptic, 5-nerved, obtuse, pubescent on the nerves, not webbed at base.—Native of Eurasia and a widely distributed weedy species of roadsides, lawns, forest trails, clearings, shores, and disturbed places.

Poa annua

1763. *Poa alsodes*   1764. *Poa annua*   1765. *Poa arida*   1766. *Poa bulbosa*

Poa arida Vasey
PLAINS BLUEGRASS

MAP 1765
native

Rhizomatous perennial grass. **Stems** mostly 3-8 dm tall, terete to flattened but not sharply 2-edged; **sheaths** usually closed only near the base; **ligules** 3-5 mm long, acute; **leaf blades** folded to somewhat involute or flat, the tips often not distinctly boat-shaped as in other *Poa*, to 30 cm long and mostly 2-5 mm wide. Panicles contracted, 6-12 cm long; spikelets 5- to 7-flowered, 4.5-8 mm long; **glumes** somewhat unequal, the first glume 2.4-5.6 mm long, the second glume 3-4.2 mm long; **lemmas** keeled, villous on the mid and lateral nerves and often pubescent between the nerves toward the base, cobweb none.—Sandy places, often where alkaline. *Plants flower early like* **Poa annua,** *but are pale green in color.*

Poa bulbosa L.
BULBOUS BLUEGRASS

MAP 1766
introduced

Densely tufted perennial grass; rhizomes and stolons absent. **Stems** erect from bulbous-thickened bases, purplish below, 2-5 dm tall; **sheaths** closed for about 1/4 their length, terete, lowest sheaths with swollen bases; **ligules** 1-3 mm long, smooth or scabrous; **leaf blades** 1-2.5 mm wide, flat, thin, lax, soon withering. **Panicles** compact and crowded, ovoid, 4-8 cm long; **florets** mostly converted into turgid purple bulblets, the bracts prolonged into linear tips 5-15 mm long.—Native of Eurasia; introduced in fields, lawns, and roadsides.

Poa bulbosa

Poa compressa L.
CANADA BLUEGRASS

MAP 1767
introduced (invasive)

Perennial grass; the shoots usually solitary, sometimes loosely tufted, extensively rhizomatous. **Stems** erect, 2-7 dm tall, strongly flattened, especially above; **sheaths** closed for 1/10-1/5 their length, distinctly compressed; **ligules** 1-3 mm long, scabrous, ciliolate; **leaf blades** 1.5-4 mm wide, flat. **Panicle** usually compact and narrow, bluish or grayish green, 2-8 cm long, the branches usually in pairs, bearing spikelets nearly to the base; pedicels of the lateral spikelets 0.5 mm long. **Spikelets** 3-6-flowered, 4-6 mm long; first **glume** 1.7-2.4 mm long; second glume 1.8-2.6 mm long; **lemmas** firm, obscurely nerved, 2-2.8 mm long, slightly pubescent on the nerves below, somewhat webbed at base.—Native of Europe; open, usually dry places, especially in acidic soil. *Along with* **Poa pratensis,** *a very common grass in Minn. P. compressa differs from P. pratensis in its flattened, less tufted stems, lemmas with sparse or even absent web at the base, and a more slender panicle with fewer branches at each node.*

Poa compressa

Poa glauca Vahl
WHITE BLUEGRASS

MAP 1768
native

Perennial grass, usually glaucous; densely tufted, rhizomes and stolons absent. **Stems** tufted, erect, 2-5 dm tall; **sheaths** closed for 1/10-1/5 their length, terete; **ligules** 1-4 mm long, sparsely to densely scabrous, obtuse to acute; **leaf blades** 1-2.5 mm wide, flat or folded, thin, soft, narrowly prow-shaped at tip. **Panicle** long-exsert, narrow, rather dense, 6-12 cm long, the branches in fascicles of 2-5, at first ascending, later spreading, each bearing a few spikelets. **Spikelets** 2-4-flowered; **glumes** lance-shaped, nearly equal, 2.3-3.8 mm long, less than half as wide; **lemmas** obscurely nerved, 2.5-3.5 mm long, densely sericeous on the lower half of the keel and marginal nerves, not webbed at base.—Open, sandy forests; rock crevices and rocky shores, sometimes where underlain by limestone.

1767. *Poa compressa*

1768. *Poa glauca*

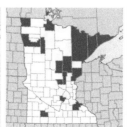

1769. *Poa interior*

1770. *Poa nemoralis*

Poa interior Rydb.

MAP 1769

INTERIOR BLUEGRASS *native*

Densely tufted perennial grass, green or less often glaucous, rhizomes and stolons absent. **Stems** to 80 cm long, erect or ascending; **sheaths** closed for up to 1/5 their length, terete; **ligules** 0.5-1.5 mm long, scabrous, truncate to obtuse, ciliolate; **leaf blades** mostly flat, thin, soft, 1-3 mm wide, narrowly prow-shaped at tip. **Panicles** to 15 cm long; branches to 8 cm long, ascending to widely spreading, angled, the angles scabrous. **Spikelets** mostly 2-3-flowered, narrowly ovate, laterally compressed 3-6 mm long, usually not glaucous; **glumes** lance-shaped, distinctly keeled, keels smooth or sparsely scabrous; calluses usually webbed, webs usually scant, less than 1/2 the lemma length, frequently tiny; **lemmas** 2.4-4 mm long, lance-shaped, distinctly keeled, straight or gradually arched, keels and marginal veins short-villous.—Shallow rocky or sandy soil of outcrops and talus slopes. *Distinguished from **Poa nemoralis** by its longer ligules and wider glumes and lemmas; differs from the common **P. palustris** in having a densely tufted habit, scantly webbed calluses, and lemmas with wider hyaline margins.*

Poa nemoralis L.

MAP 1770

WOODLAND BLUEGRASS *introduced*

Densely tufted perennial grass, green or glaucous, rhizomes and stolons absent. **Stems** slender, 4-8 dm tall; **sheaths** closed for 1/10-1/5 their length, terete; **ligules** 0.2-0.8 mm long, sparsely to densely scabrous, truncate; **leaf blades** 1-3 mm wide, mostly flat, narrowly prow-shaped at tip. **Panicle** narrowly ovoid, 1-2 dm long, eventually loose and open, the slender branches in fascicles of about 5, bearing spikelets above the middle. **Spikelets** 2-4-flowered; **glumes** narrowly lance-shaped, long-acuminate, the first 2.2-3 mm long, conspicuously narrower than the first lemma, the second 2.3-3.3 mm long; **lemmas** 3-nerved, 2.1-3.1 mm long. — Dry, sandy or rocky soil, forest borders and clearings, old farmsteads.

Poa nemoralis

Poa paludigena Fern. & Wieg.

MAP 1771

BOG BLUEGRASS ✎ *threatened* | *native*

Loosely tufted perennial grass, usually pale green, rhizomes and stolons usually absent, or occasionally with short, slender rhizomes. **Stems** slender and weak, 2-6 dm long; **sheaths** closed for 1/4-3/5 their length, terete, smooth or sparsely scabrous, margins not ciliate; **ligules** 0.5-2 mm long, smooth or sparsely scabrous, truncate; **leaf blades** 1-2 mm wide, flat, thin, soft, narrowly prow-shaped at tip. **Panicle** loose, open, 5-12 cm long, the lower branches in groups of 2, with a few spikelets above middle. **Spikelets** 2-5-flowered, 4-5 mm long, **glumes** lance-shaped, the first glume to 2 mm long, the second glume 2-3 mm long; **lemmas** 3-4 mm long, with cobwebby hairs at base. June-July.—Swamps, alder thickets, sedge meadows, open bogs, cold springs; usually in sphagnum moss and often under black ash (*Fraxinus nigra*). *Easily mistaken for the common **Poa compressa**.*

Poa paludigena

Poa palustris L.

MAP 1772

FOWL BLUEGRASS *native*

Loosely tufted perennial grass, often with stolons. **Stems** smooth, 4-12 dm long, reclining at base and rooting from lower nodes, lower portion often purple-tinged; **sheaths** closed for 1/10-1/5 their length, slightly compressed, glabrous or sparsely retrorsely scabrous; **ligules** 1.5-6 mm long, smooth or sparsely scabrous, tips obtuse to acute, frequently lacerate; **leaf blades** 1.5-8 mm wide, flat, narrowly

Poa palustris

1771. *Poa paludigena*

1772. *Poa palustris*

1773. *Poa pratensis*

prow-shaped at tip. **Panicle** loosely spreading (narrow when emerging from sheath), 1-3 dm long, the branches in mostly widely separated groups along panicle stem (rachis). **Spikelets** 2-4-flowered, 2-5 mm long and 1-2 mm wide; glumes nearly equal, lance-shaped, 2-3 mm long, often purple; lemma 2-3 mm long, often purple on sides, with cobwebby hairs at base. June–Sept.—Wet meadows, marshes, shores, streambanks, ditches and low prairie; also moist woods. *Native to boreal regions of North America and n Eurasia.*

Poa pratensis L.
KENTUCKY BLUEGRASS

MAP 1773
introduced (invasive)

Perennial grass, sometimes glaucous, densely to loosely tufted or the shoots solitary; extensively rhizomatous and sod-forming. **Stems** 3-10 dm tall; **sheaths** closed for 1/4-1/2 their length, terete to slightly compressed, glabrous; **collars** glabrous; **ligules** mostly 1-2 mm long, ciliolate or glabrous; **leaf blades** 0.4-4.5 mm wide, flat, folded, or involute, soft and lax to moderately firm, tips usually broadly prow-shaped. **Panicle** ovoid, rather dense, its branches spreading or ascending, the lower chiefly in fascicles of 4 or 5. **Spikelets** 3-5-flowered, with very short rachilla-joints; first **glume** 1.8-2.9 mm long; second glume 2.3-3 mm long; **lemmas** distinctly 5-nervcd, thinly to densely pubescent on the nerves, webbed at base, glabrous between the nerves, the lowest 2.5-3.5 mm long; anthers 1-1.4 mm long.—Moist or dry soil, disturbed places, woods, fields, avoiding acidic soils and heavy shade, often cultivated in lawns and meadows. *Introduced from Europe and naturalized in much of North America.*

Poa saltuensis Fern. & Wieg.
OLD-PASTURE BLUEGRASS

MAP 1774
native

Loosely tufted perennial grass; rhizomes and stolons absent. **Stems** slender, usually weak, 3-10 dm tall; **sheaths** closed for 1/3-2/3 their length; **ligules** 0.2-3 mm long, smooth or sparsely scabrous, truncate to obtuse; **leaf blades** 1-4 mm wide, flat, thin, lax, veins prominent. **Panicle** loose, more or less nodding, 5-10 cm long, the slender branches bearing a few spikelets beyond the middle, the lower branches usually in pairs, rarely solitary or in 3's. **Spikelets** ovate, 2-4-flowered, 3-4 mm long; **glumes** acute, the first lance-shaped to ovate, 1.7-2.6 mm. long, the second ovate, 2-3 mm long; **lemmas** firm, obscurely nerved, oblong, 2.4-3.2 mm long, glabrous except the webbed base.—Dry or rocky deciduous and mixed woods.

Poa pratensis

Poa sylvestris Gray
WOODLAND BLUEGRASS

MAP 1775
native

Loosely tufted perennial grass; rhizomes and stolons absent, or sometimes evidently shortly rhizomatous **Stems** erect, usually 4-8 dm tall; **sheaths** closed for 1/2-7/8 their length, terete, throats often ciliate near their junction; **ligules** 0.5-2.7 mm long, smooth or sparsely scabrous, truncate to obtuse; **leaf blades** 0.7-5 mm wide, flat, thin, lax. **Panicle** rather narrow, oblong, 1-2 dm long, its slender flexuous branches in fascicles of 4-8, soon divaricate or reflexed, bearing a few spikelets much above the middle. **Spikelets** 2-5-flowered; **glumes** scarious-margined, acute, the first lance-shaped, 1.5-2.7 mm long, the second oblong, 1.9-3.4 mm long; **lemmas** distinctly 5-nerved, 2.1-3.5 mm long, villous on the marginal nerves, at least toward the base, and nearly or quite to the tip of the keel, webbed at base.—Rich deciduous woods.

Poa sylvestris

1774. Poa saltuensis   *1775. Poa sylvestris*   *1776. Poa trivialis*

Poa trivialis L.
ROUGH-STALK BLUEGRASS

MAP 1776
introduced (naturalized)

Short-lived perennial grass, tufted and forming mats from aboveground stolons. **Stems** slender to stout, erect from a decumbent base, 5-10 dm tall, scabrous below the panicle; **sheaths** closed for about 1/3-1/2 their length, compressed, usually densely scabrous; **ligules** 3-10 mm long, scabrous, acute to acuminate; **leaf blades** 1-5 mm wide, flat, lax, soft, sparsely scabrous over the veins, margins scabrous, tips narrowly prow-shaped. **Panicle** soon long-exsert, ovoid, the ascending branches in fascicles of 5-8 with numerous crowded spikelets; pedicels scabrous. **Spikelets** ovate or elliptic, 2- or 3-flowered; **glumes** lance-shaped, incurved, the first 1.7-2.9 mm., the second 2-3.3 mm long; **lemmas** thin, narrowly ovate, sharply 5-nerved, acute, 2.3-3.2 mm long, glabrous except the keel and webbed base. —Native of Europe; meadows, moist woods, roadsides, along shaded trails.

Poa trivialis

Poa wolfii Scribn.
WOLF'S BLUEGRASS

MAP 1777
native

Loosely tufted perennial grass; rhizomes and stolons absent. **Stems** slender, erect, 4-8 dm tall; **sheaths** closed for 1/2-3/4 their length, smooth or sparsely scabrous, margins not ciliate; **ligules** 0.3-2.1 mm long, truncate to obtuse, ciliolate; **leaf blades** 0.6-3.5 mm wide, flat. **Panicle** loose and open, often nodding, the slender spreading branches in pairs, bearing spikelets above the middle. **Spikelets** 2-4-flowered, 4-6 mm long; **glumes** narrowly ovate, obtuse, 3-nerved, the first 2.5-3.5 mm long, the second 3-4 mm long; **lemmas** distinctly 5-nerved, villous on the keel and marginal nerves, webbed at base.—Moist woods and streambanks.

Poa wolfii

PUCCINELLIA *Alkali-Grass*

POEAE

Tufted perennial grasses, glabrous, usually in brackish habitats. Leaves mostly from base of plants, flat to inrolled; sheaths open to the base or nearly so; auricles absent; ligules membranous. Head an open panicle, the branches upright to spreading. Spikelets several-flowered, oval to linear, nearly round in section, breaking above the glumes; glumes unequal, the first glume 1-veined, the second glume 3-veined; lemmas rounded on back, often short-hairy at base; palea shorter to about as long as lemma.

1 Lower panicle branches horizontal or angled downward when mature; lemmas broad, not tapered to the blunt or rounded tip . . . . **P. distans**
1 Lower panicle branches usually upright; lemmas narrow, tapered to a rounded tip. . . . . **P. nuttalliana**

Puccinellia distans (Jacq.) Parl.
EUROPEAN ALKALI-GRASS

MAP 1778
introduced (naturalized)

Stems erect or reclining at base, 1-5 dm long. **Leaves** flat to slightly inrolled, 1-6 mm wide; **ligules** about 1 mm long, obtuse to truncate, usually entire. **Panicle** loose, pyramid-shaped, 5-15 cm long, the branches in groups, the lower branches angled downward. **Spikelets** 3-7-flowered, 4-6 mm long; **glumes** ovate, 1-2 mm long; **lemmas** about 2 mm long, smooth or short-hairy at base. May-Aug. —Occasional in brackish waste areas and ditches along salted highways.

Puccinellia distans

1777. Poa wolfii

1778. Puccinellia distans

1778. Puccinellia distans

1779. Puccinellia nuttalliana

Puccinellia nuttalliana (J.A. Schultes) A.S. Hitchc.   MAP 1779
NUTTALL'S ALKALI-GRASS   *introduced*
   Puccinellia airoides S.Watson & J.M.Coult.
Stems slender, erect, 2-8 dm long. **Leaves** flat or often inrolled, 1-3 mm wide;
ligules 1-3 mm long, obtuse, usually entire, sometimes slightly erose. **Panicle**
open, 5-25 cm long, the branches ascending to spreading, rough-to-touch, to 10
cm long, the spikelets mostly above middle of branch. **Spikelets** 3-9-flowered,
slender, 4-7 mm long, **glumes** lance-shaped, 1-3 mm long; **lemmas** oblong, 2-3
mm long, with tiny hairs at base. June-July.—Moist flats, sometimes in shallow
water, often where salty.

Puccinellia nuttalliana

SCHEDONORUS *Tall Fescue*   POEAE

Previously in *Festuca*, *Schedonorus* includes the large, broad- and flat-leaved species with awned or at
least sharply pointed lemmas; very closely related to *Lolium*, with which it hybridizes.

1   Auricles at top of leaf sheath ciliate, having at least 1 or 2 hairs along the margins; panicle branches at the lowest
    node usually paired, the shorter with 1-13 spikelets, the longer with 3-19 spikelets; lemmas 5.5-7 mm long, usually
    scabrous at least distally, unawned or with an awn up to 4 mm long . . . . ***S. arundinaceus***
1   Auricles glabrous; panicle branches at the lowest node 1 or 2, if paired the shorter with 1-2(3) spikelets, the longer
    with 2-6(9) spikelets; lemmas 7-8.5 mm long, usually smooth, sometimes slightly scabrous distally, unawned or
    with a mucro to 0.2 mm long . . . . ***S. pratensis***

Schedonorus arundinaceus (Schreb.) Dumort.   MAP 1780
TALL RYE GRASS   *introduced*
   Festuca arundinacea Schreb.
   Lolium arundinaceum (Schreb.) S.J. Darbyshire
Tufted perennial grass, sometimes with rhizomes. **Stems** erect above a geniculate
base, to 1.5 m tall, glabrous; **sheaths** smooth; **auricles** ciliate, having at least 1 or
2 hairs along the margins; ligules ca. 1 mm long; **leaf blades** glabrous or scaberulous, 4-8 mm wide, dilated at base into conspicuous auricles. **Panicle** erect or
nodding at the tip, 1-2 dm long, contracted at least after flowering, the internodes
of the branches less than 2x as long as the spikelets. **Spikelets** 4-11-flowered,
usually 7-8-flowered; first **glume** subulate, 2.5-4.5 mm long; second glume lance-
shaped, sharply nerved, 3.5-7 mm long; **lemmas** 5.5-8 mm long, scarious at the
acute tip, occasionally with a short awn.—Native of Europe; cultivated for forage
and as a turfgrass; established in fields and meadows.

Schedonorus arundinaceus

Schedonorus pratensis (Huds.) Beauv.   MAP 1781
MEADOW RYE GRASS   *introduced*
   Festuca elatior L. p.p.
   Festuca pratensis Huds.
   Lolium pratense (Huds.) S.J. Darbyshire
Tufted perennial grass. **Stems** often basally decumbent, to 1.3 m tall, glabrous; old
sheaths brown, decaying to fibers; **ligules** glabrous to 0.5 mm long; **leaf blades**
lax, 3-5 mm wide, dilated at base into conspicuous auricles. **Panicle** 1-2.5 dm,
erect or nodding at the tip, contracted at least after anthesis, the internodes of the
branches less than 2x as long as the spikelets. **Spikelets** 10-15 mm long, 4-10-
flowered; first **glume** subulate, 2.5-4 mm, 1-veined, the second lance-shaped, 3.5-5
mm, 3-5-veined, with hyaline margins; **lemmas** 5.5-7 mm long, usually glabrous,
5-veined, the tip hyaline, acute, rarely with a short awn to 2 mm long.—Native of
Europe; cultivated for forage and established in fields, meadows, and moist soil.

Schedonorus pratensis

1780. Schedono. arundinaceus   1781. Schedonorus pratensis   1782. Schizachne purpurascens

SCHIZACHNE *False Melic Grass* MELICEAE

Schizachne purpurascens (Torr.) Swallen MAP 1782
FALSE MELIC GRASS *native*

Loosely tufted perennial grass. **Stems** erect from a short-decumbent base, 3-10
dm tall; **sheaths** closed almost to the top; **ligules** membranous, 0.5-1.5 mm long;
leaf blades mostly erect, elongate, 1-5 mm wide. **Panicle** with few drooping
branches each bearing 1-3 slender spikelets about 2 cm long. **Spikelets** 3-5-
flowered, usually purplish, disarticulating above the glumes and between the
lemmas; **glumes** purple at base, unequal, 5-8 mm long, 3-5-nerved; fertile **lemmas**
8-10 mm long, strongly nerved, densely short-bearded at base, bifid for a fourth
of their length, with an awn 8-15 mm long between the teeth, awns at length
divergent.—Drier, sandy or rocky woods and openings; deciduous forests.

SCHIZACHYRIUM *Little Bluestem* ANDROPOGONEAE

Schizachyrium scoparium (Michx.) Nash MAP 1783
LITTLE BLUESTEM *native*
  Andropogon scoparius Michx.

Perennial grass; loosely or densely tufted or with rhizomes, green to purplish,
sometimes glaucous. **Stems** 5-12 dm tall, often freely branched above; **sheaths**
rounded or keeled, glabrous or pubescent; **auricles** absent; **ligules** membranous,
0.5-2 mm long; **leaf blades** 3-7 mm wide. **Racemes** solitary, usually long-exsert,
bearing 5-20 pairs of spikelets on a straight or flexuous, white-ciliate rachis.
Sessile spikelets with 2 florets; glumes exceeding the florets; lower florets
reduced to hyaline lemmas; upper florets bisexual, lemmas hyaline, bilobed or
bifid to 7/8 of their length, awned from the sinuses. **Pedicellate spikelets** usually
shorter than the sessile spikelets, sterile or staminate, with 1 floret. Late summer
and early fall.—An important prairie species, in Minn also in drier sandy woods
and openings, old fields, sand dunes and shores.

SCOLOCHLOA *River Grass* POEAE

Scolochloa festucacea (Willd.) Link MAP 1784
WHITETOP *native*
  Fluminea festucacea (Willd.) A.S. Hitchc.

Tall perennial grass, spreading by thick rhizomes and forming colonies. **Stems**
erect, hollow, 1-2 m long and 3-5 mm wide near base, usually with a few suckers
and roots from lower nodes. **Leaves** flat or slightly inrolled, 3-10 mm wide,
tapered to a sharp tip, upper surface rough-to-touch; sheaths smooth; ligule white,
ragged at tip, 4-7 mm long. **Head** a loose, open panicle, 15-20 cm long, the
branches ascending, the lowest branches much longer than upper. **Spikelets** 3-4-
flowered, purple or green, becoming straw-colored, 7-10 mm long, breaking
above glumes; **glumes** unequal, lance-shaped, the first glume 3- veined, 4-7 mm
long, the second glume 5-veined, 6-9 mm long; **lemmas** lance-shaped, about 6
mm long; palea as long as lemma. June-July.—Ponds, marshes, seasonally flooded
basins, margins of fresh to moderately saline lakes. *Provides good nesting cover for
some waterfowl and shorebirds, and sometimes used as forage for livestock.*

SECALE *Rye* TRITICEAE

Secale cereale L. MAP 1785
RYE *introduced*

Annual or biennial grass. **Stems** branched from the base 5-10 dm tall; **sheaths**
open; **ligules** membranous, truncate, often lacerate; **leaf blades** 4-12 mm wide,
usually glabrous. **Spikes** densely flowered, 8-15 cm long, often distinctly nodding
when mature. **Spikelets** usually 2-flowered, solitary at each joint of the rachis;
glumes linear-subulate, 1-nerved, shorter than the lemmas; **lemmas** lance-
subulate, 5-nerved, with their sides toward the axis, tapering into a long awn 3-8
cm long; disarticulation in the rachis, at the nodes, tardy or the spikes not
disarticulating.—An important Eurasian cereal grass, also widely used for soil

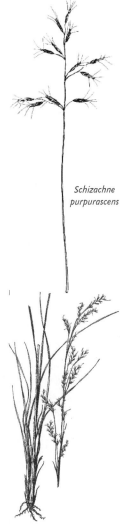

*Schizachne
purpurascens*

Schizachyrium scoparium

Scolochloa festucacea

stabilization and, especially in Canada, for whisky.—Mostly along roadsides, where planted for erosion control following construction; also on shores, dunes, along railroads, and in old fields; not long-persisting.

SETARIA _Bristle Grass_   PANICEAE

Tufted annual grasses (ours). Ligules membranous and ciliate or of hairs. Spikelets all alike, with 1 perfect flower, turgid or plano-convex, subtended by an involucre of 1 to many slender bristles, articulated and eventually deciduous above the bristles, aggregated into cylindric, spike-like, terminal panicles. First glume triangular to ovate, 3-5-nerved, half as long as the spikelet or less. Second glume longer, sometimes equaling the spikelet. Sterile lemma equaling the spikelet, several-nerved. Fertile lemma indurate, smooth or transversely rugose.

1 Bristles, summit of stem, and axis of panicle scabrous with retrorse barbs; panicle branches tending to appear whorled, the panicle ± interrupted toward its base. . . . . _S. verticillata_
1 Bristles, summit of stem, and axis of panicle scabrous or pubescent with antrorse barbs or hairs; panicle very compact throughout 2
   2 Fertile lemmas mostly ca. 3 mm long, rugose with distinctly transverse ridges, the upper half exposed at maturity; bristles 5 or more per spikelet, becoming orange or golden-brown; sheaths glabrous . . . . _S. pumila_
   2 Fertile lemmas less than 3 mm long, evenly and finely rugose or reticulate or smooth (without transverse ridges), the upper half largely or entirely concealed at maturity; bristles fewer than 5 per spikelet, pale greenish or purple (rarely yellow) at maturity; sheaths ciliate with long hairs on the margins 3
      3 Spikelet articulated above the glumes and sterile lemma; fertile lemma distinctly yellow or darker at maturity; panicle very dense, often ± lobed in appearance. . . . . _S. italica_
      3 Spikelet articulated below the glumes; fertile lemma pale green or brown; panicle not lobed 4
         4 Panicle strongly nodding, bent below the middle; spikelets mostly over 2.5 mm long, the fertile lemma ± tapering to a distinctly exposed tip; leaf blades ± hairy above . . . . _S. faberi_
         4 Panicle straight and erect or rarely slightly nodding; spikelets not over 2.5 mm long, the blunt fertile lemma nearly or quite concealed by the second glume; leaf blades glabrous above . . . . _S. viridis_

Setaria faberi Herrm.   MAP 1786
JAPANESE BRISTLE GRASS   _introduced (naturalized)_
Annual grass; much like _S. viridis_, but more robust. **Stems** 5-20 dm tall; **sheaths** glabrous, fringed with white hairs; **ligules** about 2 mm long; **leaf blades** 15-30 cm long and 1-2 cm wide, with long, soft papillose-based hairs on upper surface. **Panicle** spike-like, 6-20 cm long, drooping from near the base. **Spikelets** 2.5-3 mm long, subtended by 1-6 (usually 3) bristles, the second glume 2/3 to 3/4 as long as the more strongly rugose fertile lemma; sterile lemma with a palea, two-thirds as long.—Unintentionally introduced into North America from China in the 1920s (first Minn collection in 1957); a serious weed in corn and soybean fields of the midwestern USA.

Setaria italica (L.) Beauv.   MAP 1787
FOXTAIL-MILLET   _introduced_
Annual grass. **Stems** to ca. 1 m tall; **sheaths** mostly glabrous, margins sparsely ciliate; **ligules** 1-2 mm long; **leaf blades** flat, to 3 cm wide, scabrous. **Panicle** to 25 cm long and 3 cm thick, purple or tawny; **bristles** 1-3 below each spikelet, upwardly barbed, 3-10 mm long. **Spikelets** 2-3 mm long, articulated above the sterile lemma, the grain readily detached from the persistent glumes; sterile lemma usually somewhat shorter than the fertile.—Native of the Old World; sometimes cultivated and escaped to ditches, fields and disturbed places.

Setaria pumila

1783. _Schizachyri. scoparium_

1784. _Scolochloa festucacea_

1785 _Secale cereale_

1786. _Setaria faberi_

Setaria pumila (Poir.) Roem. & Schult.
PEARL-MILLET
Setaria glauca (L.) Beauv.

MAP 1788
introduced (naturalized)

Annual grass. **Stems** usually erect, solitary or tufted, 4-8 dm tall; **sheaths** glabrous; **ligules** ciliate; **leaf blades** 4-10 mm wide, loosely twisted, upper surface with papillose-based hairs near base. **Panicles** spike-like, usually 5-10 cm long, or sometimes longer, the axis pubescent; **bristles** 3-10 mm long, yellow or tawny at maturity. **Spikelets** thick, 3-3.5 mm long; first **glume** 5-nerved, half as long as the spikelet; second glume 5-nerved or usually 7-nerved, 2/3 as long as the spikelet; fertile **lemma** transversely rugose.—Native of Europe, introduced in lawns, roadsides, railroads, cultivated fields, and disturbed places.

Setaria verticillata (L.) Beauv.
ROUGH BRISTLE GRASS

MAP 1789
introduced (naturalized)

Annual grass. **Stems** often branched at base, usually 6-10 dm tall; **sheaths** glabrous, margins ciliate upwards; **ligules** to 1 mm long, densely ciliate; **leaf blades** flat, 5-15 mm wide, undersurface scabrous. **Panicles** often tapering upward, 5-15 cm long, usually more or less lobed or interrupted near the base where the short branches tend to be whorled; **bristle** one below each spikelet, retrorsely barbed, purplish or tawny, 2-8 mm long. **Spikelets** about 2 mm long; sterile **lemma** equaling the finely rugose fertile one.—European native, weedy in cultivated or waste ground.

Setaria viridis (L.) Beauv.
GREEN FOXTAIL-GRASS

MAP 1790
introduced (naturalized)

Annual grass. **Stems** usually branched and often geniculate at base; **sheaths** mostly glabrous, margins ciliate upwards; **ligules** 1-2 mm long, ciliate; **leaf blades** flat, 4-25 mm wide, scabrous or smooth. **Panicle** 1-7 cm long, the short branches uniformly spaced on the rachis; **bristles** 1-3 below each spikelet, upwardly barbed, green, purple, or tawny, usually 2-10 mm long. **Spikelets** 2-2.5 mm long; sterile **lemma** usually as long as the finely rugose fertile one.—Native of Eurasia; weedy in gardens, cultivated fields, and disturbed places.

Setaria viridis

SORGHASTRUM *Indian Grass* ANDROPOGONEAE

Sorghastrum nutans (L.) Nash
YELLOW INDIAN GRASS

MAP 1791
native

Large perennial grass from short scaly rhizomes. **Stems** in loose tufts, 1-2 m tall, the nodes densely pubescent; **sheaths** glabrous to hirsute; **ligules** membranous, 2-6 mm long, usually with thick, pointed auricles; **leaf blades** 10-70 cm long and to 1 cm wide, usually glabrous. **Panicle** narrow, 10-25 cm long, the ultimate branches of the panicle bearing short racemes of 1-5 spikelets; terminal spikelet usually with 2 sterile pedicels adjacent the nodes. **Spikelets** lance-shaped, 6-8 mm long; sessile spikelet perfect, subterete; pediceled spikelet absent, represented by its pedicel only; first **glume** pale brown, villous, its edges enclosing the margin of the glabrous or ciliate second glume; **lemmas** hyaline, bifid, awned from the sinuses; the awn 9-15 mm long, twisted below, bent at about a third of its length; sterile pedicel densely villous, 4-5 mm long.—Moist or dry prairies, open woods, fields, shores, and rarely, in marshes; sometimes spreading in disturbed places as along roadsides and railroads.

Sorghastrum nutans

1787. *Setaria italica*

1788. *Setaria pumila*

1789. *Setaria verticillata*

1790. *Setaria viridis*

SPARTINA *Cord-Grass* CYNODONTEAE

Coarse perennial grasses, spreading by long scaly rhizomes. Stems stout and erect. Leaves flat to inrolled, tough, rough-to-touch; sheaths smooth; ligule a fringe of hairs. Head of several to many 1-sided spikes in racemes at ends of stem, the spikes upright to appressed. Spikelets 1-flowered, flattened, overlapping in 2 rows on 1 side of the rachis, breaking below the glumes; glumes unequal, 1-2- veined, with rough hairs on the keel; lemma with pronounced midvein and 2 faint lateral veins; palea about as long as lemma.

1 Plants 1–2 m tall; leaf blades more than 5 mm wide . . . . *S. pectinata*
1 Plants to 1 m tall; leaf blades 2–5 mm wide . . . . *S. gracilis*

Spartina gracilis Trin.   MAP 1792
ALKALI CORDGRASS   *native*

Perennial grass, from rhizomes. **Stems** 4–8 dm long. **Leaves** usually inrolled, 10–20 cm long and 2–4 mm wide. **Head** a spikelike raceme of 4–8, 1-sided spikes, the spikes 2–5 cm long, appressed to the raceme stem (rachis). **Spikelets** 1-flowered, 6–9 mm long; glumes and lemma fringed with hairs on keel, the first **glume** half as long as second; **lemma** nearly as long as second glume. July–Sept.—Wet meadows, shores, flats and seeps; often where brackish.

Spartina pectinata Bosc   MAP 1793
FRESHWATER CORD-GRASS   *native*

Stout perennial grass, strongly rhizomatous, the rhizomes scaly, purplish-brown or light brown (drying white). **Stems** tough, 1–2 m long; **sheaths** open, mostly glabrous, throats often pilose; **ligules** membranous, 1–3 mm long, ciliate; **leaf blades** flat to inrolled, 3–10 mm wide, margins strongly scabrous. **Head** a spike-like raceme of mostly 10–30, 1-sided spikes, the spikes upright to sometimes appressed, 3–10 cm long. **Spikelets** 1-flowered, flattened, 8–11 mm long, overlapping in 2 rows on one side of the rachis, breaking below the glumes; first **glume** nearly as long as floret, hispid on the keels, tapered to tip or with an awn 1–5 mm long, second glume longer than floret, tipped with an awn 2–8 mm long; **lemma** 7–9 mm long, shorter than second glume. July–Sept.—Shallow marshes, wet meadows.

Spartina pectinata

SPHENOPHOLIS *Wedgescale* POEAE

Perennial grasses. Leaf blades flat, sheaths open, auricles absent; ligules membranous, erose. Panicles slender or spike-like, shining. Spikelets 2-flowered (rarely with a rudimentary third flower), disarticulating below the glumes and below the upper lemma; rachilla prolonged behind the second palea. Glumes unequal, keeled, the first linear, 1-nerved, the second obovate, scarious-margined, 3–5-nerved. Lemmas slender, firm in texture, rounded on the back or keeled toward the summit, awnless. Palea hyaline, about equaling the lemma.

1 Larger (second) glume distinctly swollen, abruptly truncate and usually shallowly 2-lobed at tip . . . . . *S. obtusata*
1 Larger glume not swollen or distended, obtuse to acute at tip . . . . *S. intermedia*

Sphenopholis intermedia (Rydb.) Rydb.   MAP 1794
SLENDER WEDGESCALE   *native*
    Sphenopholis obtusata var. *major* (Torr.) K.S. Erdman

Perennial grass. **Stems** tufted, 3–12 dm tall; **sheaths** smooth or finely roughened, sometimes pubescent; **ligules** 1.5–2.5 mm, erose-ciliate, often lacerate; **leaf blades**

1791. *Sorghastrum nutans*

1792. *Spartina gracilis*

1793. *Spartina pectinata*

1794. *Sphenopholis intermedia*

flat, soft, 2-5 mm wide, **Panicle** slender, 8-15 cm long, 1-3 cm wide, more or less lobed or irregular in contour, not spike-like except when very young; first **glume** subulate, 1.5-2.4 mm long, less than 0.5 mm wide; second glume obovate, broadly acute or apiculate, thin in texture, obscurely nerved, 2-2.7 mm long; lower **lemma** 2.3-2.9 mm long.—Moist to wet gravelly shores, tamarack swamps, marsh borders, thickets, forest depressions; sometimes in moist woods. *Similar in appearance to* **Koeleria macrantha**, *but differs in its more open panicle, the very narrow first glume, and the essentially glabrous foliage and panicle.*

Sphenopholis obtusata (Michx.) Scribn.
PRAIRIE WEDGESCALE

MAP 1795
native

Tufted perennial (sometimes annual) grass; plants smooth to rough-hairy. **Stems** slender, 2-10 dm long; **sheaths** glabrous or hairy; **ligules** 1.5-3 mm long, more or less lacerate; **leaf blades** usually flat, 2-8 mm wide, scabrous or pubescent. **Panicle** spike-like, dense, shiny, 5-20 cm long, the spikes often (in part) separate from one another. **Spikelets** 2-flowered, 3-4 mm long, unawned, breaking below the glumes; **glumes** 2-3 mm long, the first glume linear, 1-veined, the second glume broader, 3-5-veined; **lemma** 2-3 mm long, 1-veined; palea linear, about as long as lemma. June-Aug.—Dry forests, moist to wet meadows, gravelly shores. *The inflorescence is more dense and contracted compared to the more open and lax panicle of* **Sphenopholis intermedia**.

Sphenopholis intermedia

SPOROBOLUS *Dropseed*   CYNODONTEAE

Annual or perennial grasses. Leaf blades narrow, often involute; sheaths open, usually glabrous, often ciliate at the top; ligules of short hairs. Panicles open or contracted. Spikelets 1-flowered, articulated above the glumes. Glumes lance-shaped to ovate, 1-nerved, from much shorter than to somewhat longer than the lemma. Lemma rounded on the back, nerveless or 1-nerved, awnless. Palea about as long as the lemma or longer. Fruit differs from a true grain in that the pericarp is free from the seed coat, and often slipping away, at least when moist.

1   Plants annuals or short-lived perennials flowering in the first year 2
   2   Lemmas strigose; spikelets 2.3-6 mm long; mature fruits 1.8-2.7 mm long . . . . *S. vaginiflorus*
   2   Lemmas glabrous; spikelets 1.6-3 mm long; mature fruits 1.2-1.8 mm long . . . . *S. neglectus*
1   Plants perennial 3
   3   Spikelets 1-2.5 mm long . . . . *S. cryptandrus*
   3   Spikelets 2.5-10 mm long 4
      4   Mature panicles to 30 cm wide, pyramidal; panicle branches appressed or spreading . . . . *S. heterolepis*
      4   Mature panicles to 4 cm wide, spikelike; panicle branches appressed . . . . *S. compositus*

Sporobolus compositus (Poir.) Merr.
TALL DROPSEED
    Sporobolus asper (Beauv.) Kunth

MAP 1796
native

Tufted perennial grass, sometimes with rhizomes. **Stems** stout, erect, to 12 dm tall; **sheaths** sparsely hairy at tips, the hairs to 3 mm long; **ligules** to 0.5 mm long; **leaf blades** long, 2-5 mm wide, tapering to a filiform point, flat or involute at least when dry. **Panicle** pale or purplish, 5-15 cm long, about 1 cm thick, long enclosed in the upper sheath; glumes and lemma boat-shaped and somewhat carinate, obtuse to acute; first **glume** 2-3.5 mm long; second glume 2.5-4.6 mm long; **lemma** glabrous, 3.5-6 mm long, about equaling the palea.—Dry or sandy soil of prairies, roadsides and along railways.

Sporobolus compositus

1795. *Sphenopholis obtusata*   1796. *Sporobolus compositus*   1797. *Sporobolus cryptandrus*

Sporobolus cryptandrus (Torr.) Gray   MAP 1797
SAND-DROPSEED   *native*

Tufted perennial grass, rhizomes absent, bases not hard and knotty. **Stems** solitary or in small tufts, 3-10 dm tall, the lower portion usually covered by sheaths; **sheath** tips with conspicuous tufts of hairs, the hairs to 4 mm long; **ligules** to 1 mm long; **leaf blades** 2-6 mm wide, flat or drying involute, 2-6 mm wide, tapering to a long point. **Panicle** ovoid or pyramidal, 1-2 dm long, at base usually partly included in the upper sheath; branches alternate, soon widely divergent, the branchlets more or less appressed and forming a dense narrow cluster. **Spikelets** 2-3 mm long; **glumes** acute, the first half or less as long as the second; **lemma** about equaling the second glume.—Dry, especially sandy soil; cedar glades, barrens, fields and dunes; often in sandy disturbed areas such as roadsides and railways.

Sporobolus cryptandrus

Sporobolus heterolepis (Gray) Gray   MAP 1798
PRAIRIE-DROPSEED   *native*

Tufted perennial grass, rhizomes absent. **Stems** erect, 4-10 dm tall; **sheaths** dull and fibrous at base, glabrous or sparsely pilose below, the hairs contorted, to 4 mm long; **ligules** to 0.3 mm long; **leaf blades** very long, narrow, flat or folded, 1-2.5 mm wide, margins scabrous. **Panicle** cylindric to narrowly ovoid, with ascending branches, 1-2 dm long; branches mostly raceme-like, they and the pedicels irregularly interrupted by paler, slightly widened segments. **Spikelets** 3-6 mm long; first **glume** about half as long as the second, subulate above a broader base; second glume acuminate into an involute tip, usually slightly longer than the lemma; **palea** usually slightly exceeding the lemma; mature grain spherical, spreading the parts of the spikelet and splitting the palea.—Moist to dry prairies, sometimes in fens and in shallow soil on limestone. *Plants have a distinctive musky smell especially noticeable in hot weather.*

Sporobolus heterolepis

Sporobolus neglectus Nash   MAP 1799
SMALL DROPSEED   *native*

Tufted annual grass; plants delicate, slender, very similar to *S. vaginiflorus*. **Stems** 10-45 cm tall, wiry, erect to decumbent; **sheaths** inflated, mostly glabrous but the tips with small tufts of hairs to 3 mm long; **ligules** to 0.3 mm long; **leaf blades** to 2 mm wide, flat to loosely involute. **Panicle** rarely exsert, usually permanently exceeded by the uppermost blade. **Spikelets** smaller, the glumes and lemma less acuminate and proportionately wider; first **glume** 1.5-2.4 mm long; second glume 1.7-2.7 mm long; **lemma** 2-3 mm long, glabrous, about equaling the wide palea. — Dry sterile or sandy soil of roadsides and fields; also along shores and on mudflats.

Sporobolus vaginiflorus (Torr.) Wood   MAP 1800
POVERTY-GRASS   *native*

Annual grass. **Stems** tufted, erect to spreading, 15-60 cm tall, very thin and wiry, seldom more than 1 mm in diameter; **sheaths** often inflated, sometimes with sparse hairs at base, glabrous or the tips with small tufts of hairs to 3 mm long; **ligules** to 0.3 mm long; **leaf blades** to 2 mm wide, the lower elongate, the upper progressively shorter to only 1-2 cm long. **Panicle** slender, 2-5 cm long, eventually exsert; axillary panicles also developed and mostly included in the lower sheaths. **Spikelets** crowded; glumes and lemma lance-shaped, straight; first **glume** 2.8-4.1

Sporobolus vaginiflorus

1798. Sporobolus heterolepis

1799. Sporobolus neglectus

1800. Sporobolus vaginiflorus

mm long; second glume 2.9-4.6 mm long; **lemma** 3-5 mm long, minutely villous; **palea** equaling or somewhat exceeding the lemma.—Dry, sandy or sterile soil as along roadsides (especially where gravelly) and in fields. *Very similar to* **Sporobolus neglectus** *and impossible to distinguish without spikelets; S. vaginiflorus differs in having strigose lemmas, sheaths that are sparsely hairy towards the base and, usually, longer spikelets. Both differ from our other species in their annual habit, and by having nearly equal glumes.*

TORREYOCHLOA *False Mannagrass*   POEAE

Torreyochloa pallida (Torr.) Church   MAP 1801
FALSE MANNAGRASS   *native*
     Puccinellia pallida (Torr.) Clausen

Perennial rhizomatous grass. **Stems** slender and flaccid, 3-10 dm tall, usually more or less decumbent and creeping at base; **sheaths** open to the base; **auricles** absent; **ligules** membranous, 2-9 mm long, truncate or acute; **leaf blades** flat, soft, 2-15 mm wide. **Panicle** with relatively few branches, eventually diffuse, 5-15 cm long. **Spikelets** narrowly ovate, 4-7 mm, long, 4-6-flowered; **glumes** broadly rounded at the scarious tip; **lemmas** ovate, sharply nerved, finely pubescent or scaberulous, erose at the rounded tip; **palea** 4-5 times longer than wide.—Cat-tail marshes, bogs, shorelines, wet forest depressions, often in shallow water.

TRIDENS *Purpletop*   CYNODONTEAE

Tridens flavus (L.) A.S. Hitchc.   (NO MAP)
PURPLETOP   *native*

Perennial grass, with firm, knotty, shortly rhizomatous bases. **Stems** solitary or in small tufts, 10-15 dm tall; **sheaths** open, keeled, collars densely pubescent; **ligules** membranous, to 0.5 mm long, ciliate; **leaf blades** 3-10 mm wide, glabrous or sparsely hispid, elongate to a slender tip. **Panicle** viscid, 2-4 dm long, erect or nodding, with spreading or drooping branches. **Spikelets** disarticulating above the glumes and between the lemmas, narrowly ovoid, scarcely compressed, 4-9-flowered, 5-10 mm long; **glumes** unequal, firm, 2.5-3.5 mm long, 1-nerved, obtuse or often mucronate; **lemmas** regularly imbricate, flattened to a retuse or obtuse tip, densely villous on the lower half, the nerves excurrent as minute teeth; palea broad, its nerves near the margin. **Grain** strongly concave on the ventral side. — Sandy fields, roadsides, and dry open woods. *Reported from Minn but presence not verified; a common grass south and east of Minn.*

TRIPLASIS *Sandgrass*   CYNODONTEAE

Triplasis purpurea (Walt.) Chapman   MAP 1802
PURPLE SANDGRASS   *native*

Tufted annual grass. Stems slender, 2-8 dm tall; **sheaths** open, loose; **auricles** absent; **ligule** of hairs to 1 mm long; **leaf blades** flat or involute, 1-5 mm wide, hispid or with papillose-based hairs, the upper blades much reduced. **Panicle** 2-8 cm long, at first included in the upper sheath, eventually exsert with a few spreading branches each bearing several purplish spikelets. **Spikelets** 2-6-flowered, with long rachilla-joints, disarticulating above the glumes and between the lemmas; **glumes** narrowly lance-shaped, 2-4 mm long, 1-nerved, glabrous; **lemmas** 3-4 mm long, rounded on the back, pubescent on the 3 parallel nerves,

Torreyochloa pallida

Triplasis purpurea

1801. *Torreyochloa pallida*   1802. *Triplasis purpurea*   1803. *Trisetum spicatum*

2-lobed with a pubescent awn between the lobes, the awn straight, to 2 mm long.—Sandy shores and openings, dunes, blow-outs, cut-banks.

TRISETUM *False Oat*   POEAE

Trisetum spicatum (L.) Richter   NC MAP 1803
NARROW FALSE OAT   *native*
Tufted perennial grass, with both fertile and sterile shoots; rhizomes absent. **Stems** erect, 1-5 dm tall, glabrous or pubescent below, pubescent below the panicle; **sheaths** open, pubescent or glabrous; auricles absent; **ligules** membranous, 0.5-4 mm long, truncate or rounded; **leaf blades** flat or involute, glabrous to pubescent, 1-4 mm wide. **Panicle** from spikelike to open, often interrupted basally, green, purplish, or tawny, usually silvery-shiny; dense, or interrupted at base, 3-10 cm long. **Spikelets** usually 2-flowered; disarticulation usually above the glumes and between the florets; **glumes** thin or membranous, with broad hyaline margins, about as long as the spikelet; first glume 1-nerved, 3-5 mm long; second glume,3-nerved, 4-6 mm long; **lemmas** slightly surpassing the glumes, bifid, teeth usually less than 1 mm long, awned; the **awns** 3-8 mm long, from the upper 1/3 of the lemma, geniculate, twisted near the base. Highly variable.—Exposed or partly shaded sandstone ledges and crevices.

Trisetum spicatum

TRITICUM *Wheat*   TRITICEAE

Triticum aestivum L.   (NO MAP)
COMMON WHEAT   *introduced*
Annual grass. **Stems** erect, single or branched at base, 5-12 dm tall; **internodes** usually hollow, even immediately below the spikes; **sheaths** open; **auricles** present, often deciduous at maturity; **ligules** membranous; leaf blades flat, 6-15 mm wide, glabrous or pubescent. **Spikes** densely flowerd, to 18 cm long. **Spikelets** 2-5-flowered, single and sessile at each joint of the rachis; **glumes** broadly ovate, the broader side truncate or notched at the tip; **lemma** sides turned toward the axis, the midnerve prolonged into a short point or awn to 8 cm long.—Commonly cultivated, sometimes appearing on roadsides from spilled grain; probably never persisting in our flora.

Triticum aestivum

VULPIA *Six-Weeks Fescue*   POEAE

Vulpia octoflora (Walt.) Rydb.   MAP 1804
SIX-WEEKS FESCUE   *native*
   Festuca octoflora Walt.
Tufted annual grass, plants withering by mid-summer; cleistogamous or nearly so. **Stems** slender, erect or geniculate at base, 1-4 dm tall, glabrous or puberulent; **ligules** membranous, 0.3-1 mm long; **leaf blades** 0.5-1 mm wide, flat or rolled, glabrous or pubescent. **Panicle** slender, 3-10 cm long, with a few ascending or rarely spreading branches. **Spikelets** flattened, 6-10-flowered, rarely with fewer; first **glume** subulate, 2-4 mm long; second glume lance-shaped, about 1/4 longer; **lemma** involute, straight, soon diverging and exposing the rachilla, gradually tapering into an erect awn 1-4 mm long. **Grain** linear-cylindric, tapering to both ends.—Dry sandy places, often where disturbed. *Similar to **Festuca** and only marginally distinct, but Vulpia now customarily treated as a separate genus.*

Vulpia octoflora

ZIZANIA *Wild Rice*   ORYZEAE
Large annual grasses (ours) of marshes and shallow water, with tall stems, wide flat blades, and fleshy yellow roots. Sheaths open, not inflated; ligules membranous or scarious. Spikelets 1-flowered, articulated at the base, readily deciduous, nearly terete, unisexual, the staminate on the lower, the pistillate on the upper branches of the large panicle. Glumes absent. Lemma of the staminate spikelet thin, herbaceous, linear, acuminate or short-awned, 5-nerved. Pistillate spikelets inserted in a cup-shaped excavation at the summit of the pedicels; lemma firm at maturity, prominently 3-ribbed, awned.

1 Pistillate inflorescence branches usually divaricate at maturity; pistillate lemma thin and membranous and at least sparsely hispid-scabrous between the strong nerves; widest leaves 1.5-4.5 cm wide. . . . . ***Z. aquatica***

1 Pistillate inflorescence branches usually appressed at maturity, or with 1 to few, somewhat spreading branches; pistillate lemma firm and tough, scabrous-hispid only on the nerves and at most at the base and apex; widest leaves 0.5-1.7 cm wide . . . . ***Z. palustris***

Zizania aquatica L.

MAP 1805

WILD RICE   *native*

Large annual emergent grass. **Stems** single or few together, 1-3 m long; **sheaths** glabrous or finely roughened; **ligules** 5-30 mm long, upper ligules truncate to ovate, often erose or irregularly lobed; **leaf blades** flat, to 1.5 m long or longer, 1-4.5 cm wide, smooth or finely roughened, usually floating on water surface early in season, becoming upright. **Panicle** 3-12 dm long, the branches 10-20 cm long; staminate and pistillate flowers separate on same plant, the **staminate flowers** on lower panicle branches, **pistillate flowers** on upper branches, the staminate portion ascending to reflexed, branches of pistillate portion divaricate, sometimes appressed if immature or bearing only aborted spikelets. **Spikelets** 1-flowered, round in section, breaking as a unit from the stalk; **glumes** absent; **staminate spikelets** straw-colored to purple, 6-12 mm long, hanging downward from branches, lemma linear, tapered to tip or tipped with an awn to 3 mm long, early deciduous; **pistillate spikelets** linear, purple or light green, **lemma** awl-shaped, 1-2 cm long, tapered to a slender awn to 10 cm long. **Grain** cylindric, dark brown to black, 1-2 cm long. July-Sept.—Shallow water (up to 1 m deep) or mud of streams, rivers, lakes, ponds; where water is slightly flowing and not stagnant; soils vary from muck to silt, sand, or gravel, with best establishment of plants on a layer of soft silt or muck several cm thick.

Zizania palustris L.

MAP 1806

NORTHERN WILD RICE   *native*

Stems to 3 m tall, usually at least partly immersed in water; **sheaths** glabrous or with scattered hairs; **ligules** 3-15 mm long; **leaf blades** 0.5-1.7 cm wide. **Panicles** 25-60 cm long; staminate and pistillate flowers separate on same plant, the **staminate flowers** on lower panicle branches, **pistillate flowers** on upper branches; **staminate branches** ascending or divergent; **pistillate branches** mostly appressed or ascending, a few sometimes divergent. **Staminate spikelets** 6-17 mm long, lanceolate, acuminate or awned, the awns to 2 mm long. **Pistillate spikelets** 8-33 mm long, lanceolate or oblong, leathery or indurate, lustrous, glabrous or with lines of short hairs, tips usually hirsute and abruptly narrowed, awned, the awns to 10 cm long; lemmas and paleas remaining clasped at maturity. **Grain** 6-30 mm long. Rangewide, *Z. palustris* grows mostly to the north of *Z. aquatica*, but their ranges overlap in the Great Lakes region. Two varieties occur in Minn:

Zizania palustris
Appressed **pistillate spikelets** above the spreading **staminate spikelets**

1 Lower pistillate branches with 9-30 spikelets; pistillate part of the inflorescence 10-40 cm or more wide, the branches ascending to widely divergent; plants 1-3 m tall; blades 10-40 mm wide or more. . . . . ***var. interior***

1 Lower pistillate branches with 2-8 spikelets; pistillate part of the inflorescence usually less than 10 cm wide, the branches appressed or ascending, or a few branches somewhat divergent; plants to 2 m tall; blades 3-21 mm wide . . . . ***var. palustris***

Z. palustris is the source of commercial wild rice (California is the nation's largest producer); in the Great Lakes region, harvesting is most common in Minnesota, especially by Native Americans where large areas of lakes and shallow marshes

1804. Vulpia octoflora   *1805. Zizania aquatica*   *1806. Zizania palustris*

may be dominated by this plant. The grain is also an excellent food for waterfowl. Many populations are intentional introductions.

Pontederiaceae PICKERELWEED FAMILY

Mostly perennial, aquatic or emergent herbs. Leaves alternate, stalkless and straplike, or with a petiole and broad blade. Flowers perfect (with both staminate and pistillate parts), regular or irregular, single from leaf axils or in spikes or panicles, subtended by leaflike bracts (spathes), light yellow, white or blue-purple, perianth of 6 petal-like lobes, usually joined near base to form a tube; stamens 3-6, the filaments attached to throat of perianth tube; ovary superior, 3-chambered, style 1. Fruit a many-seeded capsule inside the spathe, or a 1-seeded, achene-like utricle.

1   Flowers 2-lipped, each lip 3-lobed, the 3 lower lobes spreading; stamens 6, 3 longer than petals, 3 shorter; fruit
      1-seeded . . . .***Pontederia cordata***
1   Flowers regular, the lobes more or less equal; stamens 3, all longer than petals; fruit a many-seeded capsule . . .
      . . . .***Heteranthera***

HETERANTHERA *Mud-Plantain*

Erect or creeping glabrous annual or pexennial herbs of muddy shores or shallow water with the blades submersed or floating. Leaves sheathing, bladeless or with the blades linear to ovate. Flowers 1 in an axillary spathe. Perianth light yellow or blue, salverform, divided into 6 linear lobes; stamens 5. Fruit a 5-chambered, many-seeded capsule.

ADDITIONAL SPECIES
Heteranthera rotundifolia (Kunth) Grisebach reported from Rock County. Closely related to *H. limosa* but seedlings of *H. rotundifolia* have flexible petioles and commonly develop elongate stems, while those of *H. limosa* have rigid petioles, even in deep water, and rarely develop elongate stems.

1   Flowers blue-purple or white; leaves with a petiole and blade, emersed or floating . . . .***H. limosa***
1   Flowers light yellow; leaves linear and straplike, not differentiated into petiole and blade, usually underwater . .
      . . . .***H. dubia***

Heteranthera dubia (Jacq.) MacM.
GRASS-LEAF MUD-PLANTAIN
   Zosterella dubia (Jacq.) Small

MAP 1807
native

Aquatic perennial herb, with lax stems and leaves, or plants sometimes exposed and forming small, leafy rosettes. **Stems** slender, forked, often rooting at lower nodes, to 1 m long. **Leaves** alternate, linear, flat, translucent, rounded at tip or tapered to a point, 2-12 cm long and 2-6 mm wide, the midrib and veins inconspicuous; petioles absent. **Flowers** 1, opening on water surface, light yellow, enclosed in a spathe from upper leaf axils, the spathe membranous, 2-5 cm long, surrounding much of the slender perianth tube; perianth tube often curved, 2-8 cm long, the 6 perianth segments linear, 4-6 mm long; stamens 3, all alike. **Fruit** a many-seeded capsule about 1 cm long. July-Sep.—Shallow water, muddy shores of ponds, lakes, streams and marshes, and where abundant, an important food for waterfowl. *Distinguished from the **pondweeds** (Potamogeton) by lack of a leaf midrib.*

Heteranthera dubia

1807. Heteranthera dubia

1808. Heteranthera limosa

1809. Pontederia cordata

Heteranthera limosa (Sw.) Willd.   MAP 1808
BLUE MUD-PLANTAIN   ❦ *threatened | native*
Small annual herb. **Stems** much-branched from base, 1-3 dm long, short when
exposed, longer and sprawling when in water. **Leaves** with blade and petiole, the
blades usually emersed, ovate to oval, 2-6 cm long and 1-3 cm wide, tapered to a
rounded tip, base rounded or flat across; petioles 5-15 cm long, with a
membranous sheath at base. **Flowers** 1, enclosed by a spathe; spathe folded, 2-4
cm long, abruptly narrowed at tip, enclosing the tubular portion of the perianth,
the flower and spathe at end of a stout stalk arising from stem; perianth segments
usually blue-purple, sometimes white, lance-shaped, 5-10 mm long, the perianth
tube 1-4 cm long, the lobes ± equal, 5-15 mm long, the 3 upper lobes with a yellow
spot at base; stamens 3, the 2 lateral stamens short, yellow, the center stamen
longer and blue or yellow. June-Sept.—In Minnesota, found in pools and seepages
associated with quartzite rock.

PONTEDERIA *Pickerelweed*

Pontederia cordata L.   MAP 1809
PICKERELWEED   *native*
Perennial emergent herb, spreading from rhizomes and forming colonies. **Stems**
stout, upright, to 12 dm long, with 1 leaf. **Leaves** lance-shaped to ovate, 5-20 cm
long and 2-15 cm wide, heart-shaped at base; petioles 3-7 cm long, sheathing on
stem. **Flowers** blue-purple (rarely white), many in a spike 5-15 cm long, subtended
by a bractlike spathe 3-6 cm long; perianth funnel-like, the tube 6 mm long, 2-
lipped above, upper lip with 3 ovate lobes, lower lip with 3 slender, spreading
lobes, the lobes 7-10 mm long. **Fruit** a 1-seeded utricle, 5-10 mm long. June-Sept.
—Shallow water (to 1 m deep) of lakes, ponds, rivers and swamps.

Pontederia cordata

Potamogetonaceae PONDWEED FAMILY

This treatment includes two genera, *Ruppia* and *Zannichellia*, previously included in separate families.

1   Submersed leaves opposite or whorled, floating leaves absent . . . . ***Zannichellia***
1   Submersed leaves alternate, floating leaves (sometimes present) alternate or opposite 2
    2   Flowers 2, at first enclosed in sheathing leaf base, the peduncle elongating and often spiraled or coiled at its
        base; fruit long-stalked; stipular sheath lacking free ligule at summit (the stipule wholly adnate to the leaf blade
        and merely rounded at the summit); leaf blade terete. . . . . ***Ruppia***
    2   Flowers several to many in a peduncled head or spike; perianth of 4 tepals; fruit ± sessile; stipular sheath
        absent (stipules entirely free from leaf) or with a short ligule-like extension if stipules fused to the leaf blade
        3
        3   Stipules adnate to the leaves for 10-30 mm or more (at least on the larger leaves), adnate for ca. 2/3 of the
            length of the stipule; leaves all submersed, filiform to narrowly linear (up to 2.5 mm wide) . . . . ***Stuckenia***
        3   Stipules free from the leaves or adnate for less than half the length of the stipule (adnate for 5 mm or less
            except in *P. robbinsii*); leaves submersed or floating, filiform to ovate, oblong, or elliptic. . . . ***Potamogeton***

POTAMOGETON *Pondweed*

Aquatic perennial herbs, with only underwater leaves or with both underwater and floating leaves,
from rhizomes or tubers, sometimes reproducing and over-wintering by free-floating winter buds.
Stems long, wavy, anchored to bottom by roots and rhizomes. Leaves alternate, or becoming opposite
upward in some species, simple, with an open or closed sheath at base. Underwater leaves usually
linear and threadlike, sometimes broader, margins often wavy, usually stalkless. Floating leaves, if
present, oval or ovate, stalked, with a waxy upper surface. Flowers perfect, regular, green to red, in
stalked spikes at ends of stems or from leaf axils, usually raised above water surface, the spikes with
few to many small flowers; perianth of 4 sepal-like bracts; stamens 4. Fruit a 4-parted, beaked achene.
*The narrow-leaved pondweeds (leads 8-16 in Group 2 key), although important as a group as waterfowl food,
are often difficult to positively identify in the field, the distinguishing features being somewhat hard to see.*

KEY TO POTAMOGETON

1 Plants with underwater leaves only, these all alike . . . . **Group 1**

1 Plants with 2 kinds of leaves: broad floating leaves and broad or narrow underwater leaves . . . . **Group 2**

POTAMOGETON GROUP 1

Plants with underwater leaves only, these all alike.

1 Leaves broad, lance-shaped to oval or ovate, never linear. 2

  2 Leaf margins wavy-crisped, finely toothed. . . . . *P. crispus*

  2 Leaf margins flat or sometimes wavy, entire (or rarely finely toothed at tip) 3

    3 Base of leaf blade tapered, not clasping stem 4

      4 Plants green; upper leaves stalked; leaf margins finely toothed near tip. . . . . *P. illinoensis*

      4 Plants red-tinged; upper leaves more or less stalkless; leaf margins entire . . . . *P. alpinus*

    3 Base of leaf blade clasping stem 5

      5 Stems whitish; leaves 10-30 cm long; fruit 4-5 mm long . . . . *P. praelongus*

      5 Stems green; leaves 5-12 cm long; fruit 2-4 mm long . . . . *P. richardsonii*

1 Leaves linear 6

  6 Stipules joined with lower part of leaf to form a sheath at least 1 cm long . . . . *P. robbinsii*

  6 Stipules free from leaf, or rarely joined to leaf base for only 1-2 mm 7

    7 Plants with slender creeping rhizomes 8

      8 Flower clusters on stalks at ends of stems, the stalks mostly 5-25 cm long; leaves threadlike, narrower than stems . . . . *P. confervoides*

      8 Flower clusters on stalks from leaf axils, the stalks less than 3 cm long; leaves linear, wider than stems . . . . *P. foliosus*

    7 Plants with short rhizomes or rhizomes absent (plants often rooting at lower nodes of stem) 9

      9 Leaves 9- to many-veined (with 1-2 main veins and many finer ones) . . . . *P. zosteriformis*

      9 Leaves 1-7-veined 10

        10 Leaves without glands at base . . . . *P. foliosus*

        10 At least some of leaves with pair of glands at base 11

          11 Leaves with 5-7 nerves. . . . . *P. friesii*

          11 Leaves with 3 (rarely 1 or 5) nerves 12

            12 Leaves gradually tapered to a bristlelike tip . . . . *P. strictifolius*

            12 Leaves rounded at tip or tapered to a point, not bristle-tipped 13

              13 Leaves 1-4 mm wide, rounded at tip; body of achene 2.5-4 mm long. . . *P. obtusifolius*

              13 Leaves to 2.5 mm wide, usually tapered to a sharp tip; body of achene to 2 mm long . . . . *P. pusillus*

POTAMOGETON GROUP 2

Plants with 2 kinds of leaves: broad floating leaves and broad or narrow underwater leaves.

1 Underwater leaves broad, never linear 2

  2 Floating leaves with 30-55 nerves; underwater leaves with 30-40 nerves . . . . *P. amplifolius*

  2 Floating leaves with fewer than 30 nerves; underwater leaves with less than 30 nerves 3

    3 Underwater leaves with more than 7 nerves, all leaves stalked 4

      4 Base of floating leaves more or less heart-shaped . . . . *P. pulcher*

      4 Base of floating leaves tapered or rounded, not heart-shaped . . . . *P. nodosus*

    3 Underwater leaves mostly with 7 nerves, at least the lower leaves stalkless 5

      5 Margins of underwater leaves finely toothed near tip . . . . *P. illinoensis*

      5 Margins of underwater leaves entire 6

        6 Plants red-tinged; underwater leaves 5-20 cm long and at least as wide as floating leaves, mostly on main stem . . . . *P. alpinus*

        6 Plants green; underwater leaves 3-8 cm long and narrower than floating leaves, often numerous on short branches from leaf axils . . . . *P. gramineus*

1 Underwater leaves linear 7

  7 Spikes of 1 kind only; fruit not (or only slightly) compressed; stipules not joined with leaf base 8

    8 Floating leaves less than 1 cm wide and less than 2 cm long. . . . . *P. vaseyi*

    8 Floating leaves more than 1 cm wide and more than 2 cm long 9

      9 Underwater leaves flat and tapelike, 2-10 mm wide. . . . . *P. epihydrus*

   9 Underwater leaves round in cross-section, often reduced to a petiole, mostly less than 1.5 mm wide 10

      10 Blade of floating leaves oval, tapered to base; fruit 3-keeled . . . . *P. nodosus*

      10 Blade of floating leaves ovate to nearly heart-shaped at base; fruit barely keeled. 11

         11 Floating leaves mostly 3-10 cm long; spikes 3-6 cm long . . . . *P. natans*

         11 Floating leaves 2-5 cm long; spikes 1-3 cm long . . . . *P. oakesianus*

7 Spikes of 2 kinds: those in axils of lower underwater leaves round, on short stalks; those in axils of upper or floating leaves cylindric, often emersed on long stalks; fruit flattened; stipules of leaves (or at least some of lower leaves) joined with leaf base. 12

   12 Underwater leaves hair-like, to only about 0.3 mm wide, acute to long-tapering at tip; tips of floating leaves acute . . . . *P. bicupulatus*

   12 Underwater leaves hair-like but slightly wider (more than about 0.5 mm), leaf tips obtuse to acute; floating leaf tips rounded 13

      13 Underwater leaves blunt-tipped; floating leaves with a small notch at tip. . . . . *P. spirillus*

      13 Underwater leaves tapered to a pointed tip; floating leaves not notched at tip . . . . *P. diversifolius*

Potamogeton alpinus Balbis
REDDISH PONDWEED

MAP 1810
native

Plants red-tinged. **Stems** round in section, unbranched or sometimes branched above, to 1 m long and 1-2 mm wide. **Underwater leaves** linear lance-shaped, 4-20 cm long and 5-15 mm wide, 7-9-veined, usually rounded at tip, narrowed to a stalkless base. **Floating leaves** often absent, if present, thin, obovate, 4-6 cm long and 1-2 cm wide, 7- to many-veined, rounded at tip, tapered to a narrow base; **stipules** not joined to leaf base, membranous, 1-3 cm long and to 1.5 cm wide. **Flowers** in cylindric spikes, 1-3 cm long, with 5-9 whorls of flowers, on stalks 6-15 cm long and about as thick as stem. **Achenes** yellow-brown to olive, flattened, 3 mm long, the beak short, curved backward. July-Sept.—Shallow to deep (usually cold) water of lakes and streams.

Potamogeton amplifolius Tuckerman
LARGE-LEAF PONDWEED

MAP 1811
native

Stems round in section, usually unbranched, to 1 m or more long and 2-4 mm wide. **Upper underwater leaves** ovate, folded and sickle-shaped, 8-20 cm long and 2-7 cm wide, many-veined; **lower underwater leaves** lance-shaped, to 2 cm wide, often not folded, usually decayed by fruiting time, many-veined; petioles 1-5 cm long. **Floating leaves** usually present at flowering time, ovate 5-10 cm long and 3-6 cm wide, many-veined, rounded at tip or abruptly tapered to a sharp tip, rounded at base; petioles 5-15 cm long; **stipules** open and free of the petioles, 5-12 cm long, long-tapered to a sharp tip. **Flowers** in dense cylindric spikes, 3-6 cm long in fruit; stalks 6-20 cm long, widening near tip. **Achenes** green-brown to brown, 4-5 mm long, beak to 1 mm long. July-Aug.—Shallow to deep water of lakes and rivers.

Potamogeton bicupulatus Fern.
SNAIL-SEED PONDWEED

MAP 1812
⬮ *endangered | native*

Potamogeton diversifolius var. *trichophyllus* Morong

Plants delicate, spreading by rhizomes. **Stems** compressed. **Leaves** both underwater and floating leaves, or the floating leaves sometimes absent; ± spirally arranged. **Underwater leaves** light green to rarely brown, hair-like, linear, 1.5-11 cm long and less than 0.5 mm wide, base slightly tapered, basal lobes absent, not clasping stem, stalkless, margins entire, not crisped; veins 1; **stipules** joined to blade for less than 1/2 stipule length. **Floating leaves** variable, stalked, oval, to 2

Potamogeton alpinus

Potamogeton amplifolius

achene

1810. *Potamogeton alpinus*

1811. *Potamoget. amplifolius*

1812. *Potamoget. bicupulatus*

cm long and 1 cm wide, upper surface light green, base tapered or rounded, apex acute to long tapered; veins 3-7. **Flowers** in unbranched heads. **Achenes** greenish brown, somewhat keeled, beak absent; very small but have a noticeably bumpy surface(visible to the naked eye) due to 3 rows of sculpted ridges around the rim of the tiny, disk-shaped seed, similar to the closely related *P. diversifolius*. Early summer-fall.—Soft water lakes (water low in dissolved minerals). *Potamogeton bicupulatus is similar to P. diversifolius; both species have extremely fine, hair-like underwater leaves, but in P. diversifolius, these leaves very slightly wider and the floating leaves somewhat rounded at tip.*

Potamogeton confervoides Reichenb.
TUCKERMAN'S PONDWEED

MAP 1813

☙ *endangered | native*

from a long rhizome. **Stems** slender, to 8 dm long, branched, the branches forking. **Leaves** many, all underwater, delicate, flat, bright green, 2-5 cm long and about 0.3 mm wide, tapered to a hairlike tip, 1-veined; **stipules** short-lived, 1-5 cm long. **Flowers** in a short spike 5-10 mm long, at end of an erect stalk 5-20 cm long. **Achenes** 2-3 mm long, with a sharp keel. June-Aug.—Shallow water of lakes, kettle hole ponds and peatlands. *Unique among our pondweeds in its much-branched stems with linear leaves and the flower spike atop an elongate, leafless stalk.*

Potamogeton crispus L.
CURLY PONDWEED

MAP 1814

introduced (invasive)

Stems compressed, with few branches, to 8 dm long and 1-2 mm wide. **Leaves** all underwater, oblong, 3-9 cm long and 5-10 mm wide, rounded at tip, slightly clasping at base, stalkless, 3-5-veined, margins wavy-crisped, finely toothed; **stipules** 4-10 mm long, slightly joined at base, early shredding. **Flowers** in dense cylindric spikes, 1-2 cm long, appearing bristly in fruit from long achene beaks; on stalks 2-6 cm long. **Achenes** brown, 2-3 mm long, with a beak 2-3 mm long. April-June.—Shallow to deep water of lakes (including Great Lakes) and rivers; pollution-tolerant. *First Minnesota collection from Hennepin County in 1929.*

Potamogeton bicupulatus

Potamogeton diversifolius Raf.
WATERTHREAD

MAP 1815

☙ *endangered | native*

Stems slender, flattened or round in section, branched, to 15 dm long and 1 mm wide. **Underwater leaves** linear, flat, 1-10 cm long and 0.2-1.5 mm wide, 1-veined (sometimes 3-veined), stalkless; stipules 2-18 mm long, joined to leaf blade for less than half their length. **Floating leaves** (sometimes absent), oval, leathery, 5-40 mm long and 4-20 mm wide, acute to rounded at tip, rounded at base, 3- to many-veined, the veins sunken on leaf underside; petioles 1-3 cm long; **stipules** not joined to leaf base, 5-20 mm long. **Flowers** in spikes of 2 types, the underwater spikes rounded to oval, 3-6 mm long, on stalks 2-10 mm long; emersed spikes cylindric, 1-3 cm long, on stalks 5-3 mm long. **Achenes** olive to yellow, round and flattened, spiraled on surface, winged, the beak tiny. June-Sept.—Shallow water of ponds. *Similar to P. spirillus, which see.*

Potamogeton epihydrus Raf.
RIBBON-LEAF PONDWEED

MAP 1816

native

Stems slender, compressed, sparingly branched, to 2 m long and 1-2 mm wide. **Underwater leaves** linear, ribbonlike, 10-20 cm long and 3-8 mm wide, with a translucent strip on each side of midvein forming a band 1-3 mm wide, 5-13-veined, stalkless; **stipules** 1-3 cm long, not joined to leaf. **Floating leaves** usually present

Potamogeton crispus

1813. Potamoget. confervoides

1814. Potamogeton crispus

1815. Potamoget. diversifolius   *1816. Potamogeton epihydrus*

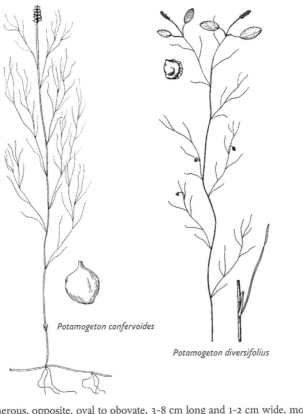

Potamogeton confervoides

Potamogeton diversifolius

Potamogeton epihydrus

and numerous, opposite, oval to obovate, 3-8 cm long and 1-2 cm wide, mostly obtuse to bluntly abruptly short-awned at the tip, 11-25-veined, tapered to flattened petioles; stipules free, 1-3 cm long. **Flowers** in dense, cylindric spikes 2-3 cm long, on stalks 2-6 cm long and about as thick as stem. **Achenes** olive to brown, 2-3 mm long; beak tiny. July-Sept.—Water to 2 m deep in lakes, ponds and rivers.

Potamogeton foliosus Raf.
MAP 1817
LEAFY PONDWEED   *native*
Stems compressed, much-branched, to 8 dm long and 1 mm wide. **Leaves** all underwater, linear, 1-8 cm long and 1-2 mm wide, 1-3-veined, stalkless; **stipules** free, 0.5-2 cm long, glands usually absent at base of stipules. **Flowers** in rounded to short-cylindric spikes, 2-7 mm long, with 1-2 whorls of flowers, on stalks 5-12 mm long, widened at tip. **Achenes** green-brown, 1.5-3 mm long, winged, the beak to 0.5 mm long. June-Aug.—Shallow to deep water of lakes, ponds, rivers and streams.

Potamogeton friesii Rupr.
MAP 1818
FLAT-STALK PONDWEED   *native*
Stems compressed, branched, 1-1.5 m long and to 1 mm wide. **Leaves** all underwater, linear, 3-7 cm long and 1.5-3 mm wide, tip rounded with a short slender point, tapered to the base, 5-7-veined, stalkless, margins flat or becoming rolled under; **stipules** free, 5-20 mm long, fibrous, often shredding above, 2 glands present at base of stipule. **Flowers** in cylindric spikes, 8-16 mm long, with 2-5 whorls of flowers, on stalks 1.5-6 cm long. **Achenes** olive-green to brown, 2-3 mm long, beak flat, short. June-Aug.—Shallow to deep water of lakes, ponds, rivers and streams.

Potamogeton foliosus

Potamogeton gramineus L.
MAP 1819
GRASSY PONDWEED   *native*
Stems slender, slightly compressed, much-branched, to 8 dm long and 1 mm wide. **Underwater leaves** variable, linear to lance-shaped or oblong lance-shaped, 3-9

cm long and 3-12 mm wide, 3-7-veined, tapered to a stalkless base. **Floating leaves** usually present, oval, 2-6 cm long and 1-3 cm wide, 11-19-veined, rounded at base; petioles 2-10 cm long, shorter to longer than blade; stipules free, persistent, 1-4 cm long. **Flowers** in dense, cylindric spikes, 1.5-4 cm long, the stalks thicker than stem, 2-10 cm long. **Achenes** dull green, 2-3 mm long. June-Aug.—Shallow to deep water of lakes and ponds.

Potamogeton illinoensis Morong
ILLINOIS PONDWEED

MAP 1820
native

Stems nearly round in section, usually branched, to 2 m long and 2-5 mm wide. **Underwater leaves** lance-shaped to obovate, 6-20 cm long, 2-4 cm wide, 9-17-veined, tapered to a broad, flat petiole, 2-4 cm long; **stipules** free, persistent, 3-8 cm long. **Floating leaves** sometimes absent, opposite, lance-shaped to oval, 5-14 cm long and 2-6 cm wide, 13- to many-veined, often short-awned from the rounded tip, rounded to wedge-shaped at base; petioles 3-10 cm long, shorter than blades. **Flowers** in dense cylindric spikes, 2-6 cm long, on stalks 4-20 cm long, usually wider than stem. **Achenes** olive-green, 3-4 mm long, the beak short, blunt. July-Sept.—Shallow to deep water of lakes and rivers.

Potamogeton illinoensis

Potamogeton natans L.
FLOATING PONDWEED

MAP 1821
native

Stems slightly compressed, usually unbranched, 0.5-2 m long and 1-2 mm wide. **Underwater leaves** reduced to linear, bladeless, expanded petioles (phyllodes), these often absent by flowering time, 10-30 cm long and 1-2 mm wide. **Floating leaves** ovate to oval, 4-10 cm long and 2-5 cm wide, usually tipped with a short point, rounded to heart-shaped at base, many-veined; petioles usually much longer than blades, the blade often angled at juncture with petiole; **stipules** free, 4-10 cm long, persistent or shredding with age. **Flowers** in dense cylindric spikes, 2-5 cm long, stalks thicker than the stem, 6-14 cm long. **Achenes** green-brown to brown, 3-5 mm long, with a loose, shiny covering, the beak short. June-Aug. —Usually shallow water (to 2 m deep) of ponds, lakes, rivers and peatlands.

Potamogeton nodosus Poir.
LONG-LEAF PONDWEED

MAP 1822
native

Stems round in section, branched, to 2 m long and 1-2 mm wide. **Underwater leaves** commonly decayed by fruiting time, lance-shaped to linear, translucent, 10-30 cm long and 1-3 cm wide, 7-15-veined, gradually tapered to a petiole 4-10 cm long. **Floating leaves** oval, thin, 5-12 cm long and 1-5 cm wide, tapered at both ends, many-veined; petioles somewhat winged, 5-20 cm long and 2-3 mm wide, usually longer than blades; **stipules** free, those of underwater leaves often absent by flowering time, those of floating leaves persistent, 3-10 cm long. **Flowers** in dense cylindric spikes, 2-6 cm long, on stalks 3-15 cm long and thicker than stem. **Achenes** red-brown to brown, 3-4 mm long, the beak short. July-Aug.—Shallow water to 2 m deep, mostly in rivers; lakes.

Potamogeton natans

Potamogeton oakesianus J.W. Robbins
OAKES' PONDWEED

MAP 1823
❧ *endangered* | *native*

Stems slender, often much-branched, to 1 m long. **Underwater leaves** bladeless, petiolelike, 0.5-1 mm wide, often persistent. **Floating leaves** oval, 3-6 cm long and 1-2 cm wide, rounded at base, 12- to many-veined; petioles 5-15 cm long; **stipules** free, 2.5-4 cm long. **Flowers** in cylindric spikes, 1.5-3 cm long, on stalks 3-8 cm

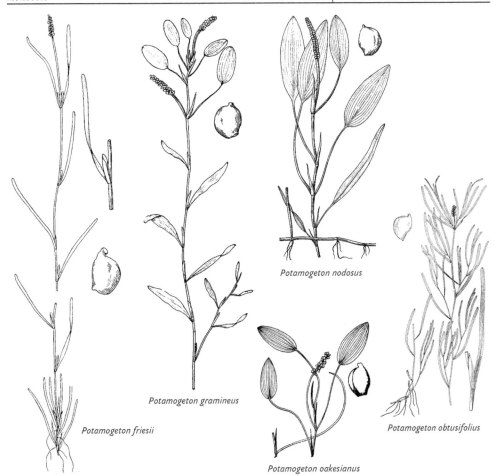

Potamogeton nodosus

Potamogeton gramineus

Potamogeton friesii

Potamogeton obtusifolius

Potamogeton oakesianus

long and wider than stem. **Achenes** 2-4 mm long, with a tight, dull covering, the beak flat.—Ponds and streams, peatland pools. *Similar to floating pondweed (Potamogeton natans) but plants smaller and the fruit more or less smooth on sides (vs. depressed in P. natans).*

Potamogeton obtusifolius Mert. & Koch   MAP 1824
BLUNT-LEAF PONDWEED   *native*
Stems slender, compressed, much-branched, to 1 m long, rhizomes more or less absent. **Leaves** all underwater, linear, stalkless, often red-tinged, 3-10 cm long and 1-4 mm wide, rounded at tip, the midvein broad, base usually with pair of translucent glands; **stipules** free, white, 1-2 cm long. **Flowers** in thick cylindric spikes, 8-14 mm long, on slender, upright stalks 1-3 cm long. **Achenes** 2-3 mm long, the beak rounded, 0.5 mm long.—Lakes, ponds, streams, peatland pools.

Potamogeton praelongus Wulfen   MAP 1825
WHITE-STEM PONDWEED   *native*
Stems white-tinged, compressed, branched, to 2-3 m long and 2-4 mm wide, the shorter internodes often zigzagged. **Leaves** all underwater, lance-shaped, 10-30 cm long and 1-4 cm wide, with 3-5 main veins, rounded and hoodlike at tip, base more or less heart-shaped and clasping stem, stalkless, margins entire and gently wavy; **stipules** free, white, 1-3 cm long, fibrous at tip. **Flowers** in dense, cylindric spikes 2-5 cm long; stalks erect, 1-4 dm long, as wide as stem. **Achenes** green-brown, swollen, 4-5 mm long, the beak rounded, 0.5 mm long. June-Aug.—Shallow to deep water of lakes and streams.

Potamogeton praelongus

Potamogeton pulcher Tuckerman
MAP 1826
SPOTTED PONDWEED
❧ *endangered | native*

Stems round in section, unbranched, black-spotted, usually less than 5 dm long. **Underwater leaves** thin, narrowly lance-shaped, 8-15 cm long and 1-3 cm wide, base tapered to a short petiole, margins wavy; the lowest leaves often thick and spatula-shaped. **Floating leaves** alternate, clustered at top of stem on short branches, ovate, 4-8 cm long and 2-5 cm wide, many-veined, the base somewhat heart-shaped; petioles black-spotted, 2-8 cm long; **stipules** free, to 6 cm long. **Flowers** in dense cylindric spikes, 2-4 cm long, on stalks 5-10 cm long and slightly wider than stem. **Achenes** 4-5 mm long, the beak broad and blunt.—Muddy shores and shallow water of lakes.

Potamogeton pusillus L.
MAP 1827
SLENDER PONDWEED
native

Stems very slender, round in section, usually freely branched, 2-10 dm long and about 0.5 mm wide; rhizomes more or less absent. **Leaves** all underwater, linear, 1-7 cm long and 0.5-2 mm wide, tapered to a stalkless base, the midvein broad; **stipules** free, boat-shaped, brown-green, 4-10 mm long and 2x width of leaf base, soon decaying, glands sometimes present at stipule base. **Flowers** in short-cylindric spikes 2-10 mm long, the flowers in 1-3 whorls, on slender, upright stalks 1-5 cm long. **Achenes** green to brown, 1-2 mm long, the beak flat. June-Aug.—Shallow water (to 2 m deep) of lakes and ponds, less often in streams.

Potamogeton richardsonii (Benn.) Rydb.
MAP 1828
RED-HEAD PONDWEED
native

Stems brown to yellow-green, round in section, sparingly to freely branched, mostly 3-10 dm long and 1-2.5 mm wide, the shorter internodes rarely zigzagged. **Leaves** all underwater, lance-shaped, 5-12 cm long and 1-2.5 cm wide, with 13 or more prominent veins, base heart-shaped and clasping stem, stalkless, margins entire and gently wavy; **stipules** free, 1-2 cm long, soon shredding into white fibers. **Flowers** in dense cylindric spikes 1.5-4 cm long, on stalks 2-20 cm long, the stalks strongly curved when in fruit. **Achenes** green to brown, 2-4 mm long, the beak short. July-Aug.—Shallow to deep water of lakes and streams.

Potamogeton richardsonii

Potamogeton robbinsii Oakes
MAP 1829
FERN PONDWEED
native

Stems few-branched below, much-branched above, to 1 m long; rhizomes not tuberous. **Leaves** all underwater, crowded in 2 ranks, linear, 4-10 cm long and 3-7 mm wide, tapered to a pointed tip, abruptly narrowed at base, with rounded auricles where joined with stipule, midvein pronounced, margins pale; **stipules** joined to leaf for 5-15 mm, soon decaying into fibers. **Flowers** on underwater, cylindric spikes 1-2 cm long, with 3-5 separated whorls of flowers, the inflorescence often branched into 5-20 stalks, 2-5 cm long, at ends of stems. **Achenes** rarely produced, 3-5 mm long, the beak thick, somewhat curved; reproduction most commonly by stem fragments which root from the nodes. July-Aug.—Shallow to deep water of lakes, ponds and streams.

Potamogeton robbinsii

Potamogeton spirillus Tuckerman
MAP 1830
SPIRAL PONDWEED
native

Stems compressed, to 1 m long, branched, the branches short and often curved. **Underwater leaves** 1-8 cm long and 0.5-2 mm wide, rounded at tip, stalkless;

1821. *Potamogeton natans*

1822. *Potamogeton nodosus*

1823. *Potamogeton oakesianus*

1824. *Potamoget. obtusifolius*

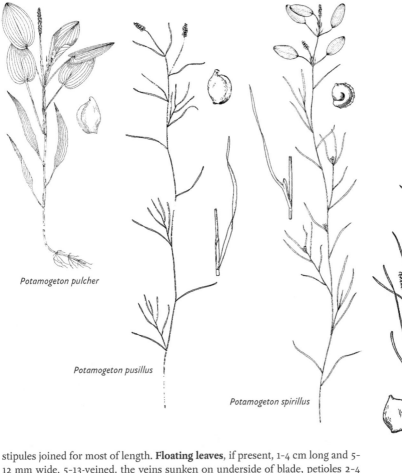

Potamogeton pulcher

Potamogeton pusillus

Potamogeton spirillus

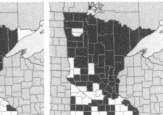

stipules joined for most of length. **Floating leaves**, if present, 1-4 cm long and 5-12 mm wide, 5-13-veined, the veins sunken on underside of blade, petioles 2-4 cm long; **stipules** free. **Flowers** in 2 types of spikes, the underwater spikes round, with 1-8 fruit, more or less stalkless in the leaf axils; emersed spikes longer, cylindric, to 8-12 mm long, on stalks from leaf axils. **Achenes** 1-2.5 mm long, flattened, winged, spiraled on surface, the beak absent.—Shallow water of lakes and ponds. *Similar to **Potamogeton diversifolius**, but the underwater leaves typically blunt-tipped, and the floating leaves with a small notch at tip. In **P. diversifolius**, the underwater leaves are generally tapered to a pointed tip, and floating leaves are not notched at tip.*

Potamogeton strictifolius Benn.
STRAIGHT-LEAF PONDWEED

MAP 1831
native

Stems slender, slightly compressed, unbranched or branched above, to 1 m long and 0.5 mm wide. **Leaves** all underwater, linear, upright, 1-6 cm long and 0.5-2 mm wide, 3-5-veined, the veins prominent on underside, tapered to stalkless base, margins often rolled under; **stipules** free, white, shredding at tip, 5-20 mm long;

Potamogeton strictifolius

1825. *Potamogeton praelongus*   1826. *Potamogeton pulcher*   1827. *Potamogeton pusillus*   1828. *Potamoget. richardsonii*

2 glands present at base of stipules. **Flowers** in cylindric spikes 6-15 mm long, with 3-5 whorls of flowers, on stalks 1-5 cm long. **Achenes** green-brown, 2 mm long, the beak broad, rounded. June-Aug.—Shallow to deep water of lakes and rivers.

Potamogeton vaseyi J.W. Robbins
VASEY'S PONDWEED

MAP 1832
native

Stems threadlike, 2-10 dm long, much-branched, the upper branches short. **Underwater leaves** transparent, linear, 2-6 cm long and to 1 mm wide, tapered to a sharp tip, 1-veined or rarely with 2 weak lateral nerves, stalkless; **stipules** free, linear, white, 1-2 cm long, sometimes with 2 glands at base. **Floating leaves** on flowering plants only, opposite, obovate, leathery, 8-15 mm long and 4-7 mm wide, 5-9-veined, the veins sunken on underside, petiole about as long as blade. **Flowers** in cylindric spikes 3-8 mm long, with 1-4 whorls of flowers, on stems 1-3 cm long. **Achenes** 2-3 mm long, the beak short.—Shallow to deep water of ponds.

Potamogeton zosteriformis Fern.
FLAT-STEM PONDWEED

MAP 1833
native

Stems strongly flattened, sometimes winged, freely branched, to 1 m long and 1-3 mm wide; rhizomes more or less absent. **Leaves** all underwater, linear, 5-20 cm long and 3-5 mm wide, 15- to many-veined, tapered to a tip, or sometimes with a short, sharp point, slightly narrowed to the stalkless base; **stipules** free, white, shredding with age, 1-4 cm long. **Flowers** in cylindric spikes, 1-2.5 cm long, with 7-11 whorls of flowers, on curved stalks 2-6 cm long. **Achenes** dark green to brown, 4-5 mm long, the beak short and blunt. July-Aug.—Shallow to deep water of lakes and streams.

RUPPIA *Ditch-Grass*

Ruppia cirrhosa (Petag.) Grande
SPIRAL DITCH-GRASS

MAP 1834
native

Aquatic perennial herb. **Stems** slender, round in section, white-tinged, wavy, to 6 dm long, branching at base and with short branches above, the internodes often zigzagged. **Leaves** simple, alternate or opposite, stalkless, threadlike, mostly 5-25 cm long and 0.5 mm wide, 1-veined, with a sheathing stipule at base. **Flowers** very small, perfect, in small, 2-flowered spikes from leaf axils, the spikes enclosed by the leaf sheath at flowering time, the flower stalks elongating and usually coiling as fruit mature; sepals and petals absent; stamens 2; pistils typically 4 (varying from 2-8), raised on a slender stalk in fruit and becoming umbel-like. **Fruit** an olive-green to black, ovate drupelet, 1.5-3 mm long. July-Aug..—Lakes and ponds, often where brackish.

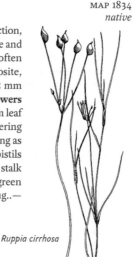

Ruppia cirrhosa

Potamogeton vaseyi

Potamogeton zosteriformis

1829. Potamogeton robbinsii   *1830. Potamogeton spirillus*   *1831. Potamoget. strictifolius*   *1832. Potamogeton vaseyi*

STUCKENIA *False Pondweed*

Stuckenia is a small genus of perennial aquatic herbs, now segregated from *Potamogeton*. In *Stuckenia*, the stipules are joined to the blade for 2/3 to nearly the entire length of the stipule; in *Potamogeton,* the stipules in most species are free, or if adnate, joined for well less than half the length of the stipule. Also, submersed leaves of *Potamogeton* are translucent, flat, and without grooves or channels; in *Stuckenia*, submersed leaves are opaque, channeled, and turgid.

1   Leaves gradually tapered to tip; rhizomes tuber-bearing; stigmas raised on a tiny style. . . . . ***S. pectinata***
1   Leaves rounded, blunt-tipped or tipped with a short, sharp point, stigmas inconspicuous, broad and not raised 2
   2   Plants short, to 0.5 m long; sheaths tight around stem; spikes with 2-5 whorls of flowers . . . . . . ***S. filiformis***
   2   Plants large and coarse, 2-5 m long; sheaths enlarged to 2-5 times diameter of stem; spikes with 5-12 whorls
      of flowers . . . . ***S. vaginata***

Stuckenia filiformis (Pers) Böerner
THREADLEAF FALSE PONDWEED
   Potamogeton filiformis Pers.

MAP 1835
native

Stems more or less round in section, branched from base, mostly unbranched above, 1-5 dm or more long and 1 mm wide, from a long, tuber-bearing rhizome. **Leaves** all underwater, narrowly linear, 5-10 cm long and 0.2-2 mm wide, 1-veined; **stipules** 1-3 cm long, joined to base of leaf blade, forming a tight sheath around stem. **Flowers** in underwater spikes, 1-5 cm long, with 2-5 separated whorls of flowers, on slender stalks 2-12 cm long. **Achenes** olive-green, 2-3 mm long, the beak flat, tiny. July-Aug.—Mostly shallow water (to 1 m deep) in lakes and rivers.

Stuckenia pectinata (L.) Böerner
SAGO FALSE PONDWEED
   Potamogeton pectinatus L.

MAP 1836
native

Stems slender, round in section, 3-10 dm long and 1-2 mm wide much-branched and forking above, fewer branched near base, from rhizomes tipped with a white tuber. **Leaves** all underwater, threadlike to narrowly linear, 3-12 cm long and 0.5-1.5 mm wide, stalkless; **stipules** joined to base of blade for 1-3 cm, forming a sheath around stem. **Flowers** on underwater, cylindric spikes 1-5 cm long, with 2-5 whorls of flowers, on lax, threadlike stalks to 15 cm long. **Achenes** yellow-brown, 3-4 mm long, the beak to 0.5 mm long; the large fruit an important waterfowl food. June-Sept.—Shallow to deep water of lakes, ponds and streams; tolerant of brackish water.

Stuckenia filiformis

Stuckenia vaginata (Turcz.) Holub
SHEATHED FALSE PONDWEED

MAP 1837
🌱*endangered | native*

Rhizomes tipped by a tuber 3-5 cm long. **Stems** round in section, much-branched above, to 1.5 m long and 1-2 mm wide. **Leaves** all underwater, crowded in 2 ranks, threadlike to narrowly linear, 2-20 cm long and 0.5-2 mm wide, with 1 main vein; **stipules** joined to base of leaf for 1-5 cm and sheathing stem, the sheaths on main stem inflated 2-4x wider than the stem. **Flowers** in spikes 3-6 cm long, with 5-12 spaced whorls of flowers, on lax, slender stalks to 10 cm long, the stalks often much shorter than upper leaves. **Achenes** dark green, 3 mm long, the beak short or nearly absent. July-Aug.—Shallow to deep water of alkaline lakes.

Stuckenia pectinata

1833. Potamog. zosteriformis   *1834. Ruppia cirrhosa*   *1835. Stuckenia filiformis*   *1836. Stuckenia pectinata*

ZANNICHELLIA *Horned-Pondweed*

Zannichellia palustris L.
HORNED-PONDWEED

MAP 1838
native

Perennial aquatic herb, with creeping rhizomes, and often forming extensive underwater mats. **Stems** slender and delicate, wavy, 0.5-5 dm long, branched from base. **Leaves** simple, opposite (or upper leaves appearing whorled), threadlike, 2-8 cm long and 0.5 mm wide, stalkless; stipules membranous and soon deciduous. **Flowers** small, produced underwater, either staminate or pistillate, separate on plant but from same leaf axil, with 1 staminate flower and usually 4 (varying from 1-5) pistillate flowers at each node, surrounded by a membranous, spathelike bract; petals and sepals absent; staminate flower a single anther. **Fruit** a brown to red-brown, crescent-shaped nutlet, gently wavy on margins, 2-3 mm long, tipped by a beak 1-2 mm long; the fruit mostly 2-6 per node. June-Aug.—Submerged in fresh or brackish water of streams, reservoirs, muddy lake and pond bottoms, marshes and ditches.

Zannichellia palustris

Scheuchzeriaceae SCHEUCHZERIA FAMILY

SCHEUCHZERIA *Pod-Grass*

Scheuchzeria palustris L.
POD-GRASS

MAP 1839
native

Perennial rushlike herb, from creeping rhizomes. **Stems** 1 to several, 1-4 dm long, remains of old leaves often persistent at base of plant. **Leaves** alternate, several from base and 1-3 along stem, 1-3 dm long and 1-3 mm wide, the stem leaves smaller; lower part of blade half-round in section, with an expanded sheath at base, upper portion of blade flat, with a small pore at leaf tip. **Flowers** perfect, regular, green-white, in a several flowered raceme 3-10 cm long, the flowers on stalks 1-2.5 cm long; tepals 6, in 2 series, ovate, 2-3 mm long; stamens 6. **Fruit** a group of 3 (rarely to 6) spreading follicles, 5-10 mm long, each with 1-2 seeds; seeds brown-black, 4-5 mm long. May-June.—Wet, sphagnum moss peatlands.

Scheuchzeria palustris

Smilacaceae GREENBRIER FAMILY

SMILAX *Greenbrier*

Perennial herbs (with annual stems), or vining shrubs, climbing by tendrils terminating the stipules, with wide, longitudinally nerved, net-veined, alternate leaves and axillary peduncled umbels of small yellow or greenish yellow flowers. Flowers dioecious, the staminate often the larger. Perianth segments alike, spreading. Stamens in the staminate flower 6; filaments slender or flattened. Stamens of the pistillate flower reduced to 6 filiform staminodes. Ovary 3-celled, with 1 or 2 ovules in each cell; style none or very short; stigmas solitary or 3, oblong, recurved. Fruit a 1-6-seeded berry. *Leaves of all species vary greatly in size and shape.*

1837. Stuckenia vaginata   *1838. Zannichellia palustris*   *1839. Scheuchzeria palustris*

1   Stems woody and prickly (at leasdt at base); leaves glabrous beneath (sometimes roughened on main veins) . . .
. . . .***S. tamnoides***

1   Stems herbaceous, never prickly; leaves finely puberulent, at least on the veins, beneath; 2

      2   Stem of mature plants more than 1 m long, the main stem or elongate branches climbing (or resting on other objects for support); plant almost always branched, with total of more than 25 leaves; tendrils conspicuously curled, present at most nodes, including those from which peduncles arise; peduncles longer than petioles (sometimes several times as long), all or most arising from axils of foliage leaves; flowers (at least on main stem) more than 25 in an umbel (but not all develop into fruit). . . . . ***S. lasioneura***

      2   Stem less than 1 m tall, stiffly erect much of its length; plant unbranched, with fewer than 25 leaves (in *S. illinoensis* rarely more); tendrils absent or at most poorly developed and limited to uppermost nodes (never at the lower nodes from which peduncles arise); peduncles longer or, more often, shorter than petioles, at least the lowest ones usually arising from scale-like bracts on the stem below the foliage leaves; flowers more or fewer than 25 in an umbel 3

           3   Pistillate (and usually also staminate) flowers fewer than 25 in an umbel; leaves fewer than 20 (usually 7-9) on a plant; stems under 50 cm tall; peduncles usually shorter than the petioles or slightly longer; tendrils completely absent (rarely on upper 2-3 nodes). . . . . ***S. ecirrata***

           3   Pistillate and staminate flowers usually more than 25 in an umbel and plants with one or more other exceptions to the above (i.e., leaves more than 20, stems over 50 cm tall, peduncles more than 2 cm longer than petioles, tendrils present on several upper nodes) . . . . ***S. illinoensis***

Smilax ecirrata (Engelm.) S. Wats.
UPRIGHT CARRION-FLOWER

MAP 1840
native

Perennial herb. Stems annual, erect, usually without tendrils, or producing a few tendrils from the upper leaves only, to 8 dm tall. **Leaves** narrowly to broadly ovate, truncate to cordate at base, convexly narrowed to a short cusp, pubescent beneath. **Umbels** 1-3, to 25-flowered; peduncles arising from the axils of lance-linear bracts along the lower leafless portion of the stem, or rarely also from the axil of the lowest leaf. **Perianth** green, the tepals 4-6 mm long. **Berries** purplish black, globose, ca. 10 mm wide, not glaucous. May-June.—Rich deciduous forests, moist forests near riverbanks and floodplains.

Smilax ecirrata

Smilax illinoensis Mangaly
ILLINOIS GREENBRIER

MAP 1841
native

Perennial herb. Stems annual, erect, unbranched, to 1 m long; prickles absent. **Leaves** narrowly ovate, pubescent and not glaucous on underside, base rounded to truncate, margins convex, tip acute to acuminate; petiole thin, equaling or longer than blade; tendrils few, short. **Umbels** 3-10, axillary to leaves and bracts, 10-50-flowered; **tepals** 3.5-4.5 mm long. **Berries** blue to black, globose. May-June.—Thickets, woods.

Smilax lasioneura Hook.
BLUE RIDGE CARRION-FLOWER

MAP 1842
native

     Smilax herbacea var. *lasioneura* (Hook.) A. DC.

Perennial herb. Stems annual, climbing, often to 2 m tall and freely branched. **Leaves** ovate to rotund, at base cordate to rounded; acuminate to cuspidate or broadly rounded at tip; underside often somewhat glaucous; lateral margins always convex. **Umbels** many, axillary to leaves, to 35-flowered; **peduncles** arising from the axils of foliage leaves, flattened; **perianth** greenish. **Berries** bluish black to black, subglobose, 8-10 mm wide, glaucous. May-June.—Moist soil of open woods, roadsides, and thickets. *Variable.*

Smilax lasioneura

1840. Smilax ecirrata

1841. Smilax illinoensis

1842. Smilax lasioneura

Smilax tamnoides L.

CHINAROOT

Smilax hispida Muhl. ex Torr.

MAP 1843

native

Vine, from a short knotty rhizome. Stems often climbing high (to 7 m or more), usually conspicuously thorny and often densely so; **branches** nearly terete. **Leaves** thin, ovate to rotund; commonly 8-12 cm long and 6-10 cm wide at maturity; acute to rounded or cuspidate; at base rounded, truncate, or cordate; not thickened at the margin; minutely serrulate (at 10x), at least near base; 5-7-nerved, the reticulate veinlets not prominently raised. **Umbels** many, axillary to leaves, to 25-flowered; **peduncle** often drooping, 1.5-6.5 cm long; **perianth** green to bronze. **Berries** black, globose, 6-10 mm wide, not glaucous. May-June.—Moist woods and thickets.

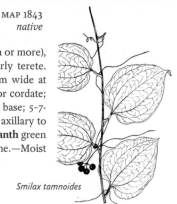

Smilax tamnoides

Typhaceae CAT-TAIL FAMILY

Family now includes genus *Sparganium* of discontinued family Sparganiaceae.

1 Pistillate flowers in one to several spherical heads; perianth of greenish sepals; leaves strongly keeled (3-angled in cross-section). . . . . ***Sparganium***
1 Pistillate flowers in an elongate densely flowered spike; perianth of white hairs; leaves flat-elliptic in cross-section . . . . ***Typha***

SPARGANIUM *Bur-reed*

Perennial sedgelike herbs, floating or emergent in shallow water, from rhizomes and forming colonies. Stems stout, usually erect, unbranched, round in section. Leaves long, broadly linear, sheathing stem at base. Flowers crowded in round heads, the heads with either staminate or pistillate flowers; staminate heads few to many, borne above pistillate heads in a unbranched or sparsely branched inflorescence; the pistillate heads 1 to several, from leaf axils or borne above axils on upper stem; sepals and petals reduced to chaffy, spatula-shaped scales, these appressed to the achenes in the mature pistillate heads; staminate flowers with mostly 3-5 stamens; pistillate flowers with a 1-2-chambered pistil, stigmas 1 or 2. Fruit a beaked, nutletlike achene, stalkless or short-stalked.

1 Plants large, about 1 m tall; leaves usually erect; stigmas 2; achenes broadly oblong pyramid-shaped. . . . .
. . . . ***S. eurycarpum***
1 Plants smaller, leaves erect or floating; stigmas 1; achenes slender. 2
  2 Fruiting heads about 1 cm wide; staminate head 1 (often absent by fruiting time); achene beaks less than 1 mm
    long . . . . ***S. natans***
  2 Fruiting heads 1.5 cm or more wide; staminate heads 2 or more; achene beaks 2 mm or more long 3
    3 Fruiting heads 1.5-2 cm wide; anthers and stigma less than 1 mm long; leaves mostly flat 4
      4 Staminate heads several, separate from the pistillate heads; achene not shiny . . . . ***S. fluctuans***
      4 Staminate heads usually 1 (sometimes 2) and near upper pistillate head; achene shiny . . ***S. glomeratum***
    3 Fruiting heads larger mostly 2-3 cm wide; anthers and stigma 1-4 mm long; leaves often keeled 5
      5 Fruiting heads or branches all from leaf axils 6
        6 Inflorescence unbranched or the branches short with 1-2 staminate heads; achenes dull, with a beak
          3-4 mm long . . . . ***S. americanum***
        6 Inflorescence branched, the branches jointed, with 3 or more staminate heads; achenes shiny, with
          a beak 5-7 mm long . . . . ***S. androcladum***
      5 At least some fruiting heads or branches borne above leaf axils 7
        7 Leaves floating; achene beak 1-3 mm long . . . . ***S. angustifolium***
        7 Leaves usually stiffly erect and emersed; achene beak 3-5 mm long . . . . ***S. emersum***

Sparganium americanum Nutt.

AMERICAN BUR-REED

MAP 1844

native

Perennial herb. **Stems** stout, erect, mostly unbranched, 3-10 dm long. **Leaves** linear, flat to somewhat keeled, to 1 m long and 4-12 mm wide; leaflike bracts on upper stem shorter than leaves, widened at base. **Inflorescence** usually unbranched, or with a few, straight branches; **pistillate heads** sessile, 2-4 on main stem, sometimes with 1-3 on branches, 2 cm wide when mature; scales widest at tip; **staminate heads** 3-10 on main stem, sometimes with 1-5 on branches. **Achenes** widest at middle, tapered to both ends, dull brown, 3-5 mm long, the beak straight, 2-4 mm long. July-Aug.—Marshes, shallow water, streambanks.

Sparganium androcladum (Engelm.) Morong
BRANCHED BUR-REED
   Sparganium lucidum Fern. & Eames

MAP 1845
native

Perennial herb. **Stems** stout, erect, branched, 4-10 dm long. **Leaves** linear, keeled, triangular in section near base, 4-8 dm long and 5-12 mm wide; bracts leaflike, upright, shorter than leaves, slightly widened at base. **Inflorescence** often branched, the branches zigzagged; **pistillate heads** sessile, 2-4 on main stem, absent or occasionally 1 near base of branches, 3 cm wide when mature; scales spatula-shaped, widest at tip; **staminate heads** 5-8 on main stem, 3 or more on branches. **Achenes** oval, shiny light brown, 5-7 mm long, often slightly narrowed at middle, the beak straight, 4-6 mm long. July-Aug.—Marshes, lakeshores, fens.

Sparganium americanum

Sparganium angustifolium Michx.
NARROW-LEAF BUR-REED
   Sparganium acaule (Beeby) Rydb.
   Sparganium chlorocarpum var. *acaule* (Beeby) Fern.
   Sparganium emersum Rehmann
   Sparganium multipedunculatum (Morong) Rydb.

MAP 1846
native

Perennial herb. **Stems** long and usually floating. **Leaves** floating, mostly 2-3 mm wide, often wider at base. **Inflorescence** unbranched; **pistillate heads** 1-3, shiny, about 2 cm wide, the lowest stalked, the upper pistillate heads sessile; scales spatula-shaped, ragged at tip; **staminate heads** 2-6, close together above pistillate heads. **Achenes** spindle-shaped, 5-7 mm long, dull brown except at red-brown base, abruptly contracted to a beak 1 mm long. July-Aug.—Lakes, ponds and shores.

Sparganium emersum Rehmann
NARROW-LEAF BUR-REED
   Sparganium chlorocarpum Rydb.
   Sparganium simplex Huds.

MAP 1847
native

Perennial herb. **Stems** usually erect, sometimes lax and trailing in water, 2-6 dm long. **Leaves** linear, yellow-green, flat to keeled, 3-7 dm long and 3-6 mm wide, usually longer than stems; bracts leaflike, erect, barely widened at base. **Inflorescence** unbranched, 1-2 dm long; **pistillate heads** 1-4, sessile or lowest head often stalked, at least 1 head on stem above leaf axils, 1.5-2.5 cm wide when mature; scales spatula-shaped, widest at tip; **staminate heads** usually 2-5, 1.5-2 cm wide at flowering time. **Achenes** widest at middle, tapered to both ends, 4-5 mm long, shiny olive-green, the beak 3-5 mm long. June-Aug.—Shallow water or mud of marshes, streams, ditches, open bogs, ponds.

Sparganium eurycarpum Engelm.
BROAD-FRUIT BUR-REED
   Sparganium californicum Greene
   Sparganium greenei Morong

MAP 1848
native

Sparganium androcladum

Perennial herb. **Stems** stout, branched, 4-10 dm long. **Leaves** linear, bright green, keeled, 8-10 dm long and 5-12 mm wide; bracts leaflike, slightly widened at base. **Inflorescence** 1-3 dm long, branched from the bract axils; lower branches with 1

1843. Smilax tamnoides

1844. Spargan. americanum

1845. Spargan. androcladum

1846. Spargan. angustifolium

pistillate head and several staminate heads, main stem and upper branches with 6-10 staminate heads; **pistillate heads** 2-6, 1.5-2.5 cm wide in fruit, scales spatula-shaped; **staminate heads** numerous, 1-2 cm wide. **Achenes** oblong pyramid-shaped, 6-8 mm long, the top flattened, 4-7 mm wide, brown to golden-brown, the beak 2-4 mm long. June-Aug.—Usually in shallow water of marshes, streams, ditches, ponds and lakes, often with cat-tails (*Typha*). *Our most common bur-reed.*

Sparganium fluctuans (Morong) B.L. Robins.

MAP 1849

FLOATING BUR-REED   *native*

Perennial herb. Stems slender, floating, to 15 dm long. Leaves floating, linear, flat, translucent, 3-10 mm wide, underside with netlike veins; bracts leaflike, short, widened at base. **Inflorescence** usually branched, the main stem with 2-4 staminate heads, the branches with 1 pistillate head near base and 2-3 staminate heads above; **pistillate heads** 2-4, 1.5-2 cm wide when mature, scales oblong; **staminate heads** to 1 cm wide. **Achenes** obovate, 3-4 mm long, sometimes narrowed near middle, brown, the beak curved, 2-3 mm long.—In shallow water of ponds and lakes.

Sparganium eurycarpum

Sparganium glomeratum (Laestad.) L. Neum.

MAP 1850

CLUSTERED BUR-REED   *native*

Perennial herb. **Stems** stout, floating or erect, 2-4 dm long. **Leaves** linear, more or less flat, 3-8 mm wide; bracts leaflike, widened at base. **Inflorescence** usually unbranched; **pistillate heads** several, clustered on the stem, sessile, 1.5-2 cm wide when mature, scales narrowly oblong; **staminate heads** 1-2 above the pistillate heads and continuous with them on stem. **Achenes** widest at middle, tapered to both ends, 3-8 mm long, slightly narrowed below the middle, shiny brown, the beak more or less straight, 1-2 mm long.—Shallow water of marshes and bogs.

Sparganium fluctuans

Sparganium natans L.

MAP 1851

ARCTIC BUR-REED   *native*

> *Sparganium minimum* (Hartman) Wallr.

Perennial herb. **Stems** usually long and floating, sometimes shorter and upright, 1-3 dm or more long. **Leaves** linear, dark green, thin, flat, 2-6 mm wide; bracts leaflike, short, somewhat widened at base. **Inflorescence** unbranched; **pistillate heads** 2-3, from bract axils, sessile or the lowest sometimes short-stalked, 1 cm wide when mature; scales spatula-shaped, widest at tip; **staminate heads** usually

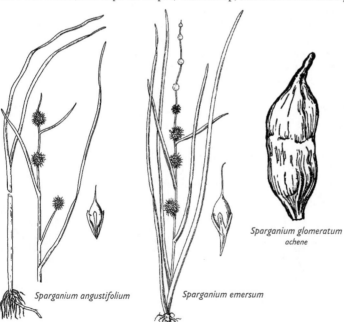

Sparganium glomeratum
achene

Sparganium angustifolium

Sparganium emersum

Sparganium natans

1 (rarely 2). **Achenes** broadly oval, 3-4 mm long, dull green-brown, the beak 1-2 mm long.—Shallow water, pond margins.

TYPHA *Cat-tail*

Large, familiar, reedlike perennials, from fleshy rhizomes and forming large colonies. Stems erect, unbranched, round in section, sheathed for most of length by overlapping leaf sheaths. Leaves mostly near base of plant, alternate in 2 ranks, erect, linear, spongy. Flowers tiny, either staminate or pistillate, separate on same plant; petals and sepals reduced to bristles. Staminate flowers usually of 3-5 stamens, bristles absent or 1-3 or more. Pistillate flowers intermixed with some sterile flowers; pistil 1, raised on a short stalk (gynophore), with numerous bristles near base, the bristles longer than pistil; small bracts (bractlets) also sometimes present, these intermixed with the bristles, slender but with a widened brown tip. Heads with staminate flowers above pistillate in a single, dense, cylindric spike, the staminate and pistillate portions of the spike unlike, contiguous in common cat-tail (*T. latifolia*) or separated in narrow-leaved cat-tail (*T. angustifolia*); the mature spike brown and fuzzy in appearance due to the crowded stigmas and gynophore bristles. Fruit a yellow-brown achene, 1-2 mm long, the style persistent, long and slender with an expanded stigma.

A hybrid between *T. angustifolia* and *T. latifolia* is termed **Typha × glauca** Godr. (MAP 1852). Usually larger than either parent, staminate and pistillate portions of hybrid plants are usually separated by a space to 4 cm long. The staminate portion of the spike is light brown, 0.5-2 dm long and about 1 cm wide at flowering time; the pistillate portion is dark brown, 10-20 cm long and 1-2 cm wide. Since *Typha × glauca* is sterile, reproduction is vegetative by rhizomes. The hybrid can occur wherever populations of *T. angustifolia* and *T. latifolia* overlap.

1   Staminate and pistillate portions of spike usually separated; leaves to 1 cm wide; stigmas long and slender, pale brown   .... ***T. angustifolia***
1   Staminate and pistillate portions of spike usually contiguous, not separated; leaves mostly 1-2 mm wide; stigmas broad and flattened, dark brown. .... ***T. latifolia***

Typha angustifolia L.
NARROW-LEAF CAT-TAIL

MAP 1853
introduced (naturalized)

Perennial emergent herb. **Stems** erect, 1-2 m long. **Leaves** upright, flat, 4-10 mm wide. **Flowers** either staminate or pistillate, on separate portions of the spike, separated by an interval of 2-10 cm; **staminate portion** 7-20 cm long and 7-15 mm wide, staminate bractlets brown; **pistillate portion** of spike dark brown, 10-20 cm long and 1-2 cm wide; each flower with 1 bristlelike bractlet, these flat and brown at the widened tip, gynophore hairs brown-tinged at tips; stigmas pale brown, linear, 1 mm long. **Fruit** 5-7 mm long, subtended by many fine hairs, the hairs slightly widened and brown at tip. June.—Marshes, lakeshores, streambanks, roadside ditches, pond margins, usually in shallow water; more tolerant of brackish conditions than *Typha latifolia*.

Typha latifolia L.
BROAD-LEAF CAT-TAIL

MAP 1854
native

Perennial emergent herb. **Stems** erect, 1-2.5 m long. **Leaves** upright, mostly 1-2 cm wide. **Flowers** either staminate or pistillate, the staminate and pistillate portions of spike normally contiguous, rarely separated by 3-4 mm; **staminate portion** 5-15 cm long and 1.5-2 cm wide at flowering time, staminate bractlets white; **pistillate portion** of spike dark brown, 10-15 cm long and 2-3 cm wide when mature, pistillate bractlets absent, gynophore hairs white; stigma lance-

Typha angustifolia (l)
Typha latifolia (r)

1847. Sparganium emersum

1848. Sparganium eurycarpum   *1849. Sparganium fluctuans*

shaped, becoming dark brown, less than 1 mm long. **Fruit** 1 cm long, with many white, linear hairs from base. June.—Marshes, lakeshores, streambanks, ditches, pond margins, usually in shallow water; less tolerant of brackish conditions than *Typha angustifolia*.

Xyridaceae YELLOW-EYED-GRASS FAMILY

XYRIS *Yellow-Eyed-Grass*

Perennial rushlike herbs. Stems erect, leafless, straight or sometimes ridged. Leaves all from base of plant, upright to spreading, linear, often twisted, usually dark green. Flowers small, perfect, yellow, from base of tightly overlapping bracts or scales, in rounded or cylindric heads at ends of stems; sepals 3, petals 3; stamens 3; style 3-parted. Fruit an oblong, 3-chambered capsule.

1 Plants swollen and hard at base . . . .*X. torta*
1 Plants flattened and soft at base . . . .*X. montana*

Xyris montana Ries
NORTHERN YELLOW-EYED-GRASS
MAP 1855 · *native*

Densely tufted perennial herb. **Stems** leafless, 0.5-3 dm long, round in section, straight or lower part of stem slightly twisted. **Leaves** narrowly linear, flat or only slightly twisted, 5-20 cm long and 1-2 mm wide, rough, dark green, red-purple at base. **Flowers** yellow, in ovate spikes less than 1 cm long; scales obovate, finely fringed at tip; lateral sepals about as long as scales, linear, margins entire or finely hairy near tip. **Seeds** 1 mm long.—Wet, sandy shores, pools in sphagnum peatlands.

Xyris torta Sm.
SLENDER YELLOW-EYED-GRASS
MAP 1856 · *endangered | native*

Perennial herb. **Stems** leafless, 1.5-8 dm long, spirally twisted, ridged. **Leaves** linear, twisted, 2-5 dm long and 2-5 mm wide; outer leaves shorter, tinged purple-brown and swollen and bulblike at base. **Flowers** yellow, in cylindric spikes 1-2.5 cm long; scales oblong; lateral sepals linear, about as long as scales, tips of scales and lateral sepals with tuft of short, red-brown hairs; petals obovate, 4 mm long. **Seeds** 0.5 mm long. June-Aug.—Wet sandy lakeshores, swales and meadows.

Xyris montana

Xyris torta

1850. *Spargan. glomeratum*

1851. *Sparganium natans*

1852. *Typha × glauca*

1853. *Typha angustifolia*

1854. *Typha latifolia*

1855. *Xyris montana*

1856. *Xyris torta*

SELECTED REFERENCES FOR MINNESOTA'S FLORA

Black, M., and E. Judziewicz. 2009. Wildflowers of Wisconsin and the Great Lakes region: A comprehensive field guide. Madison: University of Wisconsin Press.

Butters, F. K., and E. C. Abbe. 1953. A floristic study of Cook County, northeastern Minnesota. Rhodora 55:21-201.

Chadde, S. W. 2012. Wetland Plants of Minnesota: A complete guide to the wetland and aquatic plants of the North Star State. 2nd Ed. 670 pp.

Chadde, S. W. 2013. Midwest Ferns: A Field Guide to the Ferns and Fern Relatives of the North Central United States. 456 pp.

Cholewa, A. F. 2011. Comprehensively Annotated Checklist of the Flora of Minnesota, version 2011.2. 109 pp. (available from the Bell Museum website: www.bellmuseum.umn.edu)

Cochrane, T. S.; K. Elliot, C. S. Lipke. 2006. Prairie Plants of the University of Wisconsin-Madison Arboretum. Madison: University of Wisconsin Press.

Coffin, B., and L. Pfannmuller. Eds. 1988. Minnesota's endangered flora and fauna. University of Minnesota Press, Minneapolis.

Curtis, J. T. 1959. The vegetation of Wisconsin. Madison: University of Wisconsin Press.

Eggers, S., and D. Reed. 1997. Wetland Plants and Plant Communities of Minnesota and Wisconsin (2nd ed.). U.S. Army Corps of Engineers, St. Paul District. 264 p.

Fassett, N.C. 1951. Grasses of Wisconsin. Madison: University of Wisconsin Press.

Fassett, N. C. 1976. Spring Flora of Wisconsin. 4th ed. Madison: University of Wisconsin Press.

Gerdes, L. B. 2001. A contribution to the flora of the Rove Slate Bedrock Complex Landtype Association, northern Cook County, Minnesota, USA. Thesis, Michigan Technological University, Houghton, Michigan. 79 pp.

Gleason, H. A., and A. Cronquist. 1991. Manual of vascular plants of northeastern United States and adjacent Canada. 2nd ed. New York: New York Botanical Garden.

Hipp, A. Field guide to Wisconsin sedges: An introduction to the genus Carex (Cyperaceae). Madison: University of Wisconsin Press.

Holmgren, N. H., and P. K. Holmgren, eds. 1998. Illustrated companion to Gleason and Cronquist's manual. New York: New York Botanical Garden.

Kartesz, J. T. 2003. A Synonymized Checklist and Atlas with Biological Attributes for the Vascular Flora of the United States, Canada, and Greenland. Second Edition. In: Kartesz, J.T. Synthesis of the North American Flora, Version 2.0.

Kowal, R. R. 2007. Keys to the Asteraceae of Wisconsin. Unpublished report.

Lakela, O. 1965. A flora of northeastern Minnesota. University of Minn. Press, Minneapolis. 541 pp.

Lapham, I. A. 1875. A catalogue of the plants of Minnesota. Trans. Minnesota State Hort. Soc., winter meeting: 89-118.

McGregor, R. L., coordinator. 1986. Flora of the Great Plains. University Press of Kansas, Lawrence.

Moore, J. W., and R. M. Tryon, Jr. 1946. Preliminary checklist of the flowering plants, ferns and fern allies of Minnesota. Botany Department, University of Minnesota, mimeographed.

Morley, T. 1974. Spring flora of Minnesota. University of Minnesota Press, Minneapolis.

Moyle, J. B. 1953. A field key to the common non-woody flowering plants and ferns of Minnesota based largely upon vegetative characters. Burgess Pub. Co., Minneapolis.

Ownbey, G. B., and T. Morley. 1991. Vascular plants of Minnesota: a checklist and atlas. University of Minnesota Press, Minneapolis. 307 pp.

Smith, W. 2012. Native Orchids of Minnesota. The University of Minnesota Press. Minneapolis. 254p.

Smith, W. R. 2008. Trees and shrubs of Minnesota. University of Minnesota Press, Minneapolis. 703 pp.

Stensvold, Mary Clay and Donald R. Farrar. 2016. Genetic Diversity in the Worldwide *Botrychium lunaria* (Ophioglossaceae) Complex, with New Species and New Combinations. Brittonia 69: 148-175.

Tryon, R. M. 1980. Ferns of Minnesota. 2nd ed. University of Minnesota Press, Minneapolis.

Upham, W. 1884. Catalogue of the flora of Minnesota. Minn. Geological and Natural History Survey of Minnesota, part VI of the Annual Report of Progress for the year 1883.

Van Bruggen, T. 1976. The vascular plants of South Dakota. Iowa State University Press, Ames.

Voss, E.G. and A. A. Reznicek. 2011. Field Manual of Michigan Flora. University of Michigan Press.

ONLINE RESOURCES

Reznicek, A. A., E. G. Voss, and B. S. Walters. 2011. **Michigan Flora Online**. University of Michigan. www.michiganflora.net.

Stevens, P. F. (2001 onwards). **Angiosperm Phylogeny Website**. Version 12, July 2012. http://www.mobot.org/MOBOT/research/APweb/

Bell Museum of Natural History, Univ. of Minnesota: (**Minnesota Flora**): www.bellmuseum.umn.edu/

The ongoing **Flora of North America** project is located at: www.efloras.org

Maps were generated with permission of and from data of the **Biota of North America Program** (BONAP): www.bonap.org

For species of conservation concern (endangered, threatened), information was obtained from the **Minnesota Dept. of Natural Resources:** www.dnr.state.mn.us/rsg/

Wetland indicator status ratings:

Lichvar, R.W, and J. T. Kartesz. 2012. North American Digital Flora: National Wetland Plant List, v.2.4.0 (wetland_plants.usace.army.mil). U.S. Army Corps of Engineers, Engineer Research and Development Center, Cold Regions Research and Engineering Laboratory, Hanover, NH, and BONAP, Chapel Hill, NC.

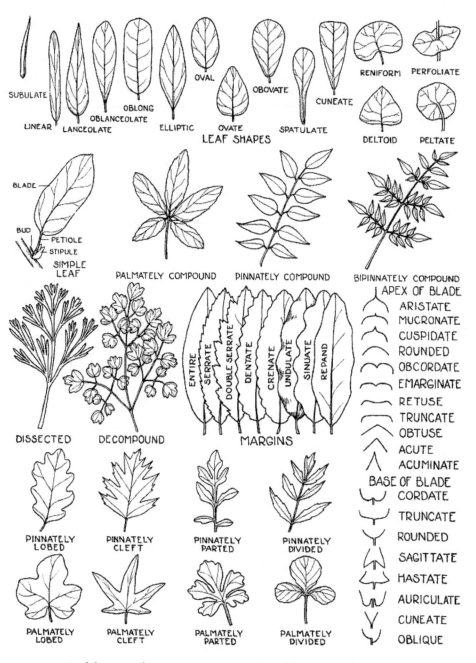

Leaf characters (from Mason, H.L. 1957. A Flora of the Marshes of California).

GLOSSARY

abaxial On the side away from the axis, usually refers to the underside of a leaf (compare with adaxial).

acaulescent Without an upright, leafy stem.

achene A one-seeded, dry, indehiscent fruit with the seed coat not attached to the mature wall of the ovary.

acid Having more hydrogen ions than hydroxyl (OH) ions; a pH less than 7.

acuminate Tapering to a narrow point, more tapering than acute, less than attenuate.

acute Gradually tapered to a tip.

adaxial On the side toward the axis, usually refers to the top side of a leaf (compare with abaxial).

adnate Fused with a structure different from itself, as when stamens are adnate to petals (compare with connate).

adventive Not native to and not fully established in a new habitat.

alkaline Having more hydroxyl ions than hydrogen ions; a pH greater than 7.

alluvial Deposits of rivers and streams.

alternate Borne singly at each node, as in leaves on a stem.

ament Spikelike inflorescence of same-sexed flowers (either male or female); same as catkin.

androgynous Spike with both staminate and pistillate flowers, the pistillate located at the base, below the staminate (compare with gynaecandrous).

angiosperm A plant producing flowers and bearing seeds in an ovary.

annual A plant that completes its life cycle in one growing season, then dies.

anther Pollen-bearing part of stamen, usually at the end of a stalk called a filament.

anthocyanic Pigmented with anthocyanins, this usually manifested as a tinging or suffusion of pink, red, or purple.

aphyllopodic Having basal sheaths without blades; with new shoots arising laterally from parent shoot (compare with phyllopodic).

apiculate Having an apiculus.

apiculus An abrupt, very small, projected tip.

appressed Lying flat to or parallel to a surface.

aquatic Living in water.

areole In leaves, the spaces between small veins.

aril A specialized appendage on a seed, often brightly colored, derived from the seed coat.

aristate Tipped with a slender bristle.

armed Bearing a sharp projection such as a prickle, spine, or thorn.

aromatic Strongly scented.

ascending Angled upward.

asymmetrical Not symmetrical.

attenuate Tapering gradually to a prolonged tip.

auricle An ear-shaped appendage to a leaf or stipule.

awl-shaped Tapering gradually from a broad base to a sharp point.

awn A bristle-like organ.

axil Angle between a stem and the attached leaf.

barb A sharp, outward projection.

basal From base of plant.

basic A pH greater than 7.

beak A slender, terminal appendage on a 3-dimensional organ.

beard Covering of long or stiff hairs.

berry Fruit with the seeds surrounded by fleshy material.

biennial A plant that completes its life cycle in two growing season, typically flowering and fruiting in the second year, then dying.

bifid Cleft into two more or less equal parts.

blade Expanded, usually flat part of a leaf or petiole.

bloom A whitish powdery or waxy coating that can be rubbed away.

bog A wet, acidic, nutrient-poor peatland characterized by sphagnum and other mosses, shrubs and sedges. Technically, a type of peatland raised above its surroundings by peat accumulation and receiving nutrients only from precipitation.

boreal Far northern latitudes.

brackish Salty.

bract An accessory structure at the base of some flowers, usually appearing leaflike.

bractlet A secondary bract (*Typha*).

branchlets A small branch.

bristle A stiff hair.

bud An undeveloped shoot, inflorescence, or flower, in woody plants often covered by scales and serving as the overwintering stage.

bulb A group of modified leaves serving as a food-storage organ, borne on a short, vertical, underground stem (compare with corm).

bulbil A bulb-like structure borne in the leaf axils or in place of flowers.

bulblet Small bulb borne above ground, as in a leaf axil.

ca. About, approximately (Latin *circa*).

caducous Falling off early, as stipules that leave behind a scar.

callosity A hardened thickening.

callus A firm, thickened portion of an organ; the firm base of the lemma in the Poaceae.

calcareous fen An uncommon wetland type associated with seepage areas, and which receive groundwater enriched with primarily calcium and magnesium bicarbonates.

calcium-rich Refers to wetlands underlain by

limestone or receiving water enriched by calcium compounds.

calyx All the sepals of a flower.

campanulate Bell-shaped.

capillary Very fine, hair-like, not-flattened.

capitate Abruptly expanded at the apex, thereby forming a knob-like tip.

capsule A dry, dehiscent fruit splitting into 3 or more parts.

carpel Fertile leaf of an angiosperm, bearing the ovules. A pistil is made up of one or more carpels.

caruncle An appendage at or near the hilum of some seeds.

caryopsis The dry, indehiscent seed of grasses.

catkin Spikelike inflorescence of same-sexed flowers (either male or female); same as ament.

caudex Firm, hardened, summit of a root mass that functions as a perennating organ.

cauline Of or pertaining to the aboveground portion of the stem.

cespitose Growing in a compact cluster with closely spaced stems; tufted, clumped.

chaff Thin, dry scales; in the Asteraceae, sometimes found as chaffy bracts on the receptacle.

cilia Hairs found at the margin of an organ.

ciliate Provided with cilia.

circumboreal Refers to a species distribution pattern which circles the earth's boreal regions.

clasping Leaves that partially encircle the stem at the base.

clavate Widened in the distal portion, like a baseball bat.

claw The narrow, basal portion of perianth parts.

cleistogamous Type of flower that remains closed and is self-pollinated.

clumped Having the stems grouped closely together; tufted.

colony-forming A group of plants of the same species, produced either vegetatively or by seed.

column The joined style and filaments in the Orchidaceae.

coma A tuft of fine hairs, especially at the tip of a seed.

composite An inflorescence that is made up of many tiny florets crowded together on a receptacle; members of the Aster Family (Asteraceae).

compound leaf A leaf with two or more leaflets.

concave Curved inward.

conduplicate Folded lengthwise into nearly equal parts.

cone The dry fruit of conifers composed of overlapping scales.

conifer Cone-bearing woody plants.

connate Two like parts that are fused (compare with adnate).

connivent Converging and touching but not actually fused, applies to like organs.

convex Curved outward.

convolute Arranged such that one edge is covered

and the other is exposed, usually referring to petals in bud.

cordate With a rounded lobe on each side of a central sinus; heart-shaped.

coriaceous With a firm, leathery texture.

corm A short, vertical, enlarged, underground stem that serves as a food storage organ (compare with bulb).

corolla Collectively, all the petals of a flower.

corymb An indeterminate inflorescence, somewhat similar to a raceme, that has elongate lower branches that create a more or less flat-topped inflorescence.

costa (plural costae) A prominent midvein or midrib of a leaflet.

crenate With rounded teeth.

crenulate Finely crenate.

crisped An irregularly crinkled or curled leaf margin.

crown Persistent base of a plant, especially a grasses.

culm The stem of a grass or grasslike plant, especially a stem with the inflorescence.

cuneate Tapering to the base with relatively straight, non-parallel margins; wedge-shaped.

cyme A type of inflorescence in which the central flowers open first.

deciduous Not persistent.

decumbent A stem that is prostrate at the base and curves upward to have an erect or ascending, apical portion.

decurrent Possessing an adnate line or wing that extends down the axis below the node, usually referring to leaves on a stem.

dehiscent Splitting open at maturity.

deltate Triangle-shaped.

dentate Provided with outward oriented teeth.

depauperate Poorly developed due to unfavorable conditions.

dicots One of two main divisions of the Angiosperms (the other being the Monocots); plants having 2 seed leaves (cotyledons), net-venation, and flower parts in 4s or 5s (or multiples of these numbers).

dioecious Bearing only male or female flowers on a single plant.

dimorphic Having two forms.

disarticulation Spikelets breaking either above or below the glumes when mature, the glumes remaining in the head if disarticulation above the glumes, or the glumes falling with the florets if disarticulation is below the glumes.

discoid In composite flowers (Asteraceae), a head with only disk (tubular) flowers, the ray flowers absent.

disjunct A population of plants widely separated from its main range.

disk In the Asteraceae, the central part of the head, composed of tubular flowers.

dissected Leaves divided into many smaller

segments.

disturbed Natural communities altered by human influences.

divided Leaves which are lobed nearly to the midrib.

dolomite A type of limestone consisting of calcium magnesium carbonate.

dorsal Underside, or back of an organ.

driftless area Portions of sw Wisconsin, ne Iowa, and se Minnesota that are not covered by glacial drift.

drupe A fleshy fruit with a single large seed such as a cherry.

echinate With spines.

eglandular Without glands.

elliptic Broadest at the middle, gradually tapering to both ends.

emergent Growing out of and above the water surface.

emersed leaf Growing above the water surface or out of water.

endangered A species in danger of extinction throughout all or most of its range if current trends continue.

endemic A species restricted to a particular region.

entire With a smooth margin.

erect Stiffly upright.

erose With a ragged edge.

escape A cultivated plant which establishes itself outside of cultivation.

evergreen Plant retaining its leaves throughout the year.

excurrent With the central rib or axis continuing or projecting beyond the organ.

exserted Extending beyond the mouth of a structure such as stamens extending out from the mouth of the corolla.

falcate Sickle-shaped

false indusium A modified tooth or reflexed margin of a fern leaf that covers the sorus.

fen An open wetland usually dominated by herbaceous plants, and fed by in-flowing, often calcium- and/or magnesium-rich water; soils vary from peat to clays and silts.

fern Perennial plants with spore-bearing leaves similar to the vegetative leaves and bearing sporangia on their underside, or the spore-bearing leaves much modified.

fibrous A cluster of slender roots, all with the same diameter.

filament The stalk of a stamen which supports the anther.

filiform Thread-like.

flexuous An elongate axis that arches or bends in alternating directions in a zig-zag fashion.

floating mat A feature of some ponds where plant roots form a carpet over some or all of the water surface.

floodplain That part of a river valley that is occasionally covered by flood waters.

floret A small flower in a dense cluster of flowers; in grasses the flower with its attached lemma and palea.

follicle A dry, dehiscent fruit that splits along one side when mature.

floricane the second-year flowering stem of *Rubus* (compare with primocane).

genus The first part of the scientific name for a plant or animal (plural genera).

glabrate Nearly glabrous or becoming so.

glabrous Lacking hairs.

gland An appendage or depression which produces a sticky or greasy substance.

glandular Bearing glands.

glaucous Having a bluish appearance.

glumes A pair of small bracts at base of each spikelet the lowermost (or first) glume usually smaller the upper (or second) glume usually longer.

grain The fruit of a grass; the swollen seedlike protuberance on the fruit of some *Rumex*.

gymnosperm Plants in which the seeds are not produced in an ovary, but usually in a cone.

gynaecandrous Having both staminate and pistillate flowers on the same spike, the staminate located at the base, below the pistillate (compare with androgynous).

gynophore The central stalk of some flowers, especially in cat-tails (*Typha*).

halophyte A plant adapted to growing in a salty substrate.

hastate More or less triangular in outline with outward-oriented basal lobes.

haustorium A specialized, root-like connection to a host plant that a parasite uses to extract nourishment.

hardwoods Loosely used to contrast most deciduous trees from conifers.

herb A herbaceous, non-woody plant.

herbaceous Like an herb; also, leaflike in appearance.

hilum The scar at the point of attachment of a seed.

hirsute Pubescent with coarse, somewhat stiff, usually curving hairs, coarser than villous but softer than hispid.

hispid Pubescent with coarse, stiff hairs that may be uncomfortable to the touch, coarser than hirsute but softer than bristly.

hummock A small, raised mound formed by certain species of sphagnum moss.

humus Dark, well-decayed organic matter in soil.

hybrid A cross-breed between two species.

hydric Wet (compare with mesic, xeric).

hypanthium A ring, cup, or tube around the ovary; the sepals, petals and stamens are attached to the rim of the hypanthium.

imbricate Overlapping, as shingles on a roof.

indehiscent Not splitting open at maturity.

indusium In ferns, a membranous covering over the sorus (plural indusia).

inferior The position of the ovary when it is below the point of attachment of the sepals and petals.

inflorescence A cluster of flowers.

insectivorous Refers to the insect trapping and digestion habit of some plants as a nutrition supplement.

interdunal swale Low-lying areas between sand dune ridges.

internode Portion of a stem between two nodes.

introduced A non-native species.

invasive Non-native species causing significant ecological or economic problems.

involucral bract A single member of the involucre; sometimes called phyllary in composite flowers (Asteraceae).

involucre A whorl of bracts, subtending a flower or inflorescence.

irregular flower Not radially symmetric; with similar parts unequal.

joint A node or section of a stem where the branch and leaf meet.

keel A central rib like the keel of a boat.

lance-shaped Broadest near the base, gradually tapering to a narrower tip.

lateral Borne on the sides of a stem or branch.

lax Loose or drooping.

leaf axil The point of the angle between a stem and a leaf.

leaflet One of the leaflike segments of a compound leaf.

lemma In grasses, the lower bract enclosing the flower (the upper, smaller bract is the palea).

lens-shaped Biconvex in shape (like a lentil).

lenticel Blisterlike openings in the epidermis of woody stems, admitting gases to and from the plant, and often appearing as small oval dots on bark.

ligulate Having a ligule; in the Asteraceae, the strap-shaped corolla of a ray floret.

ligule In grasses and grasslike plants, the membranous or hairy ring at top of sheath between the blade and stem.

linear Narrow and flat with parallel sides.

lip Upper or lower part of a 2-lipped corolla; also the lower petal in most orchid flowers.

lobed With lobes; in leaves divisions usually not over halfway to the midrib.

local Occurring sporadically in an area.

low prairie Wet and moist herbaceous plant community, typically dominated by grasses.

margin The outer edge of a leaf.

marl A calcium-rich clay.

marsh Wetland dominated by herbaceous plants, with standing water for part or all the growing season, then often drying at the surface.

megaspore Large, female spores.

mesic Moist, neither dry nor wet (compare with hydric, xeric).

microspore Small, male spores.

midrib The prominent vein along the main axis of a leaf.

mixed forest A type of forest composed of both deciduous and conifer trees.

moat The open water area ringing the outer edge of a peatland or floating mat.

monecious Having male and female reproductive parts in separate flowers on the same plant.

monocots One of two main divisions of the Angiosperms (the other being the Dicots); plants with a single seed leaf (cotyledon); typically having narrow leaves with parallel veins, and flower parts in 3s or multiples of 3.

muck An organic soil where the plant remains are decomposed to the point where the type of plants forming the soil cannot be determined.

mucro A sharp point at termination of an organ or other structure.

naked Without a covering; a stalk or stem without leaves.

native An indigenous species.

naturalized An introduced species that is established and persistent in an ecosystem.

needle A slender leaf, as in the Pinaceae.

nerve A leaf vein.

neutral A pH of 7.

node The spot on a stem or branch where leaves originate.

nutlet A small dry fruit that does not split open along a seam.

oblanceolate Reverse lance-shaped; broadest at the apex, gradually tapering to the narrower base.

oblique Emerging or joining at an angle other than parallel or perpendicular.

oblong Broadest at the middle, and tapering to both ends, but broader than elliptic.

obovate Broadly rounded at the apex, becoming narrowed below.

ocrea A tube-shaped stipule or pair of stipules around the stem; characteristic of the Smartweed Family (Polygonaceae).

opposite Leaves or branches which are paired opposite one another on the stem.

organic Soils composed of decaying plant remains.

oval Elliptical.

ovary The lower part of the pistil that produces the seeds.

ovate Broadly rounded at the base, becoming narrowed above; broader than lanceolate.

palea The uppermost of the two inner bracts subtending a grass flower (the lower bract is the lemma).

palmate Divided in a radial fashion, like the fingers of a hand.

panicle An arrangement of flowers consisting of several racemes.

papilla (plural: papillae) A short, rounded or cylindrical projections.

pappus The modified sepals of a composite flower which persist atop the ovary as bristles, scales or awns.

parallel-veined With several veins running from base of leaf to leaf tip, characteristic of most monocots.

peat An organic soil formed of partially decomposed plant remains.

peatland A wetland whose soil is composed primarily of organic matter (mosses, sedges, etc.); a general term for bogs and fens.

peltate More or less circular, with the stalk attached at a point on the underside.

pepo A fleshy, many-seeded fruit with a tough rind, as a melon.

perennial Living for 3 or more years.

perfect A flower having both male (stamens) and female (pistils) parts.

perianth Collectively, all the sepals and petals of a flower.

perigynium A sac-like structure enclosing the pistil in *Carex* (plural perigynia).

petal An individual part of the corolla, often white or colored.

petiole The stalk of a leaf.

phyllary An involucral bract subtending the flower head in composite flowers (Asteraceae).

phyllode An expanded petiole.

phyllopodic Having the basal sheaths blade-bearing; with new shoots arising from the center of parent shoot (compare with aphyllopodic).

pinna The primary or first division in a fern frond or leaf (plural pinnae).

pinnate Divided once along an elongated axis into distinct segments.

pinnule The pinnate segment of a pinna.

pistil The seed-producing part of the flower, consisting of an ovary and one or more styles and stigmas.

pith A spongy central part of stems and branches.

pollen The male spores in an anther.

prairie An open plant community dominated by herbaceous species, especially grasses.

primocane The first-year, vegetative stem in *Rubus* (compare with floricane).

pro sp. When a taxon is transferred from the non-hybrid category to the hybrid category, the author citation remains unchanged, but may be followed by an indication in parentheses of the original category.

prostrate Lying flat on the ground.

raceme A grouping of flowers along an elongated axis where each flower has its own stalk.

rachilla A small stem or axis.

rachis The central axis or stem of a leaf or inflorescence.

radiate heads In composite flowers, heads with both ray and disk flowers (Asteraceae).

ray flower A ligulate or strap-shaped flower in the Asteraceae, where often the outermost series of flowers in the head.

receptacle In the Asteraceae, the enlarged summit of the flower stalk to which the sepals, petals, stamens, and pistils are usually attached.

recurved Curved backward.

regular Flowers with all the similar parts of the same form; radially symmetric.

rhizome An underground, horizontal stem.

rib A pronounced vein or nerve.

rootstock Similar to rhizome but referring to any underground part that spreads the plant.

rosette A crowded, circular clump of leaves.

samara A dry, indehiscent fruit with a well-developed wing.

saprophyte A plant that lives off of dead organic matter.

scale A tiny, leaflike structure; the structure that subtends each flower in a sedge (Cyperaceae).

scape A naked stem (without leaves) bearing the flowers.

section Cross-section.

secund Flowers mostly on 1 side of a stalk or branch.

sedge meadow A community dominated by sedges (Cyperaceae) and occurring on wet, saturated soils.

seep A spot where water oozes from the ground.

sepal A segment of the calyx; usually green in color.

sheath Tube-shaped membrane around a stem, especially for part of the leaf in grasses and sedges.

shrub A woody plant with multiple stems.

silicle Short fruit of the Mustard Family (Brassicaceae), normally less than 2x longer as wide.

silique Dry, dehiscent, 2-chambered fruit of the Mustard Family (Brassicaceae), longer than a silicle.

simple An undivided leaf.

sinus The depression between two lobes.

smooth Without teeth or hairs.

sorus Clusters of spore containers (plural sori).

spadix A fleshy axis in which flowers are embedded.

spathe A large bract subtending or enclosing a cluster of flowers.

spatula-shaped Broadest at tip and tapering to the base.

sphagnum moss A type of moss common in peatlands and sometimes forming a continuous carpet across the surface; sometimes forming layers several meters thick; also loosely called peat moss.

spike A group of unstalked flowers along an unbranched stalk.

spikelet A small spike; the flower cluster (inflorescence) of grasses (Poaceae) and sedges (Cyperaceae).

sporangium The spore-producing structure (plural sporangia).

spore a one-celled reproductive structure that gives rise to the gamete-bearing plant.

sporophyll A modified, spore-bearing leaf.

spreading Widely angled outward.

spring A place where water flows naturally from the ground.

spur A hollow, pointed projection of a flower.

stamen The male or pollen-producing organ of a flower.

staminode An infertile stamen.

stem The main axis of a plant.

stigma The terminal part of a pistil which receives pollen.

stipe A stalk.

stipule A leaflike outgrowth at the base of a leaf stalk.

stolon A horizontal stem lying on the soil surface.

style The stalklike part of the pistil between the ovary and the stigma.

subspecies A subdivision of the species forming a group with shared traits which differ from other members of the species (subsp.).

subtend Attached below and extending upward.

succulent Thick, fleshy and juicy.

superior Referring to the position of the ovary when it is above the point of attachment of sepals, petals, stamens, and pistils.

swale A slight depression.

swamp Wooded wetland dominated by trees or shrubs; soils are typically wet for much of year or sometimes inundated.

talus Fallen rock at the base of a slope or cliff.

taproot A main, downward-pointing root.

tendril A threadlike appendage from a stem or leaf that coils around other objects for support (as in *Vitis*).

tepal Sepals or petals not differentiated from one another.

terete Circular in cross-section.

terminal Located at the end of a stem or stalk.

thallus A small, flattened plant structure, without distinct stem or leaves.

thicket A dense growth of woody plants.

threatened A species likely to become endangered throughout all or most of its range if current trends continue.

translucent Nearly transparent.

tree A large, single-stemmed woody plant.

tuber An enlarged portion of a root or rhizome.

tubercle Base of style persistent as a swelling atop the achene different in color and texture from achene body.

tundra Treeless plain in arctic regions, having permanently frozen subsoil.

turion A specialized type of shoot or bud that overwinters and resumes growth the following year.

umbel A cluster of flowers in which the flower stalks arise from the same level.

umbelet A small, secondary umbel in an umbel, as in the Apiaceae.

upright Erect or nearly so.

urceolate Constricted at a point just before an opening; urn-shaped.

utricle A small, one-seeded fruit with a dry, papery outer covering.

valve A segment of a dehiscent fruit; the wing of the fruit in *Rumex*.

variety Taxon below subspecies and differing from other varieties within the same subspecies (var.).

vein A vascular bundle, as in a leaf.

velum The membranous flap that partially covers the sporangium in *Isoetes*.

venation The pattern of veins on an organ.

ventral Front side.

verrucose Covered with small, wart-like projections.

verticil One whorled cycle of organs.

verticillate Arranged in whorls.

villous Pubescent with long, soft, bent hairs, the hairs not crimped or tangled.

vine A trailing or climbing plant, dependent on other objects for support.

viscid Sticky, glutinous.

whorl A group of 3 or more parts from one point on a stem.

wing A thin tissue bordering or surrounding an organ.

woody Xylem tissue (the vascular tissue which conducts water and nutrients).

xeric Dry (compare with hydric, mesic).

tubercle

Tubercle (*Eleocharis acicularis* shown)

MINNESOTA'S ENDANGERED AND THREATENED PLANTS

Effective August 19, 2013

Definitions

A species is considered **endangered** if the species is threatened with extinction throughout all or a significant portion of its range within Minnesota.

A species is considered **threatened** if the species is likely to become endangered within the foreseeable future throughout all or a significant portion of its range within Minnesota.

Ferns and Fern-Relatives

ENDANGERED

Botrychium ascendens Upswept moonwort
Botrychium gallicomontanum Frenchman's Bluff moonwort
Botrychium lineare Slender moonwort
Botrychium spathulatum Spathulate moonwort
Dryopteris marginalis Marginal shield fern
Isoetes melanopoda Prairie quillwort
Marsilea vestita Hairy waterclover
Phegopteris hexagonoptera Broad beech fern
Polystichum acrostichoides Christmas fern
Selaginella selaginoides Northern spikemoss

THREATENED

Asplenium trichomanes ssp. *trichomanes* Maidenhair spleenwort
Botrychium lanceolatum ssp. *angustisegmentum* Narrow triangle moonwort
Botrychium lunaria Common moonwort
Botrychium mormo Goblin fern
Botrychium oneidense Blunt-lobed grapefern
Diplazium pycnocarpon Narrow-leaved spleenwort
Huperzia porophila Rock fir moss
Polystichum braunii Braun's holly fern
Woodsia alpina Alpine woodsia
Woodsia glabella Smooth woodsia
Woodsia scopulina ssp. *laurentiana* Rocky Mountain woodsia

Conifers

ENDANGERED

Tsuga canadensis var. *canadensis* Eastern hemlock

Dicots

ENDANGERED

Agalinis auriculata Eared false foxglove
Agalinis gattingeri Round-stemmed false foxglove
Asclepias stenophylla Narrow-leaved milkweed
Astragalus alpinus var. *alpinus* Alpine milk-vetch
Bartonia virginica Yellow bartonia
Caltha natans Floating marsh marigold
Castilleja septentrionalis Northern paintbrush
Chrysosplenium iowense Iowa golden saxifrage

Dodecatheon meadia var. *meadia* Prairie shooting star
Draba cana Hoary whitlow grass
Draba norvegica Norwegian whitlow grass
Empetrum atropurpureum Purple crowberry
Empetrum nigrum Black crowberry
Erigeron acris var. *kamtschaticus* Bitter fleabane
Escobaria vivipara Ball cactus
Hasteola suaveolens Sweet-smelling Indian-plantain
Hybanthus concolor Eastern green-violet
Hydrastis canadensis Goldenseal
Iodanthus pinnatifidus Purple rocket
Juglans cinerea Butternut
Lechea tenuifolia var. *tenuifolia* Narrow-leaved pinweed
Lysimachia maritima Sea milkwort
Montia chamissoi Montia
Osmorhiza berteroi Chilean sweet cicely
Oxytropis viscida Sticky locoweed
Packera cana Gray ragwort
Packera indecora Elegant grounsel
Paronychia canadensis Canada forked chickweed
Paronychia fastigiata var. *fastigiata* Forked chickweed
Parthenium integrifolium Wild quinine
Physaria ludoviciana Bladderpod
Polanisia jamesii James' polanisia
Polemonium occidentale ssp. *lacustre* Western Jacob's ladder
Polygala cruciata Cross-leaved milkwort
Psoralidium tenuiflorum Slender-leaved scurf pea
Rhodiola integrifolia ssp. *leedyi* Leedy's roseroot (Federal Status: Threatened)
Rubus missouricus Missouri dewberry
Rubus stipulatus Bristle-berry
Sagina nodosa ssp. *borealis* Knotty pearlwort
Saxifraga cernua Nodding saxifrage
Utricularia purpurea Purple-flowered bladderwort
Vaccinium uliginosum Alpine bilberry

THREATENED

Achillea alpina Siberian yarrow
Arnica lonchophylla Long-leaved arnica
Arnoglossum plantagineum Tuberous Indian plantain
Arnoglossum reniforme Great Indian plantain
Asclepias amplexicaulis Clasping milkweed
Asclepias hirtella Prairie milkweed
Asclepias sullivantii Sullivant's milkweed
Aureolaria pedicularia Fernleaf false foxglove
Bacopa rotundifolia Water hyssop
Berula erecta Stream parsnip
Besseya bullii Kitten-tails
Bistorta vivipara Alpine bistort
Boechera retrofracta Holboell's rock cress

Callitriche heterophylla Larger water starwort
Cardamine pratensis var. *palustris* Cuckoo flower
Crassula aquatica Pigmyweed
Desmodium cuspidatum var. *longifolium* Big tick trefoil
Desmodium nudiflorum Stemless tick trefoil
Erigeron lonchophyllus Short ray fleabane
Eupatorium sessilifolium Upland boneset
Floerkea proserpinacoides False mermaid
Gaylussacia baccata Black huckleberry
Hamamelis virginiana Witch-hazel
Hudsonia tomentosa Beach heather
Lespedeza leptostachya Prairie bush clover
  (Federal Status: Threatened)
Minuartia dawsonensis Rock sandwort
Moehringia macrophylla Large-leaved sandwort
Napaea dioica Glade mallow
Nymphaea leibergii Small white waterlily
Orobanche fasciculata Clustered broomrape
Orobanche ludoviciana var. *ludoviciana* Louisiana
  broomrape
Orobanche uniflora One-flowered broomrape
Phacelia franklinii Franklin's phacelia
Phemeranthus rugospermus Rough-seeded fameflower
Rotala ramosior Toothcup
Rubus chamaemorus Cloudberry
Rubus fulleri Bristle-berry
Rubus semisetosus Swamp blackberry
Rudbeckia triloba var. *triloba* Three-leaved coneflower
Salicornia rubra Red saltwort
Salix pellita Satiny willow
Scutellaria ovata var. *versicolor* Ovate-leaved skullcap
Shinnersoseris rostrata Annual skeletonweed
Silene nivea Snowy campion
Subularia aquatica ssp. *americana* Awlwort
Sullivantia sullivantii Reniform sullivantia
Utricularia geminiscapa Hidden-fruit bladderwort
Utricularia resupinata Lavender bladderwort
Valeriana edulis var. *ciliata* Edible valerian
Viola lanceolata var. *lanceolata* Lance-leaved violet
Viola nuttallii Yellow prairie violet
Vitis aestivalis var. *bicolor* Silverleaf grape

Monocots
ENDANGERED

Achnatherum hymenoides Indian rice grass
Agrostis hyemalis Winter bentgrass
Allium schoenoprasum Wild chives
Aristida longespica var. *geniculata* Slimspike three-awn
Calamagrostis purpurascens Purple reedgrass
Carex careyana Carey's sedge
Carex formosa Handsome sedge
Carex pallescens Pale sedge
Carex plantaginea Plantain-leaved sedge
Carex supina ssp. *spaniocarpa* Weak arctic sedge
Commelina erecta Slender dayflower
Diarrhena obovata Obovate beakgrain

Elodea bifoliata Two leaf waterweed
Eleocharis wolfii Wolf's spikerush
Erythronium propullans Dwarf trout lily
  (Federal Status: Endangered)
Fimbristylis puberula var. *interior* Hairy fimbry
Juncus articulatus Jointed rush
Juncus marginatus Marginated rush
Juncus subtilis Slender rush
Listera auriculata Auricled twayblade
Malaxis paludosa Bog adder's mouth
Platanthera praeclara Western prairie fringed orchid
  (Federal Status: Threatened)
Potamogeton bicupulatus Snailseed pondweed
Potamogeton confervoides Algae-like pondweed
Potamogeton diversifolius Diverse-leaved pondweed
Potamogeton oakesianus Oake's pondweed
Potamogeton pulcher Spotted pondweed
Prosartes tachycarpa Rough-fruited fairybells
Sagittaria brevirostra Short-beaked arrowhead
Scleria triglomerata Tall nutrush
Stuckenia vaginata Sheathed pondweed
Tofieldia pusilla Small false asphodel
Xyris torta Twisted yellow-eyed grass

THREATENED

Ammophila breviligulata ssp. *breviligulata* Beachgrass
Aristida tuberculosa Seaside three-awn
Carex conjuncta Jointed sedge
Carex davisii Davis' sedge
Carex festucacea Fescue sedge
Carex garberi Garber's sedge
Carex jamesii James' sedge
Carex laevivaginata Smooth-sheathed sedge
Carex laxiculmis Loose-culmed sedge
Carex novae-angliae New England sedge
Carex rossii Ross' sedge
Carex sterilis Sterile sedge
Cyperus acuminatus Short-pointed umbrella-sedge
Cypripedium arietinum Ram's head orchid
Deschampsia flexuosa Slender hair grass
Eleocharis flavescens var. *olivacea* Olivaceous spikerush
Eleocharis robbinsii Robbins' spikerush
Eleocharis rostellata Beaked spikerush
Heteranthera limosa Mud plantain
Leersia lenticularis Catchfly grass
Luzula parviflora Small-flowered woodrush
Melica nitens Three-flowered melic
Piptatherum canadense Canadian ricegrass
Platanthera flava var. *herbiola* Tubercled rein orchid
Poa paludigena Bog bluegrass
Rhynchospora capillacea Hair-like beak rush
Sagittaria calycina var. *calycina* Hooded arrowhead
Scleria verticillata Whorled nutrush
Spiranthes casei var. *casei* Case's ladies' tresses
Trichophorum clintonii Clinton's bulrush

WETLAND INDICATOR STATUS

WETLAND STATUS CATEGORIES

OBL   **Obligate Wetland** - Plants that almost always occur in wetlands (i.e. almost always in standing water or seasonally saturated soils.

FACW   **Facultative Wetland** - Plants that usually occur in wetlands, but may occur in non-wetlands.

FAC   **Facultative** - Plants that occur in wetlands and non-wetland habitats.

FACU   **Facultative Upland** - Plants that usually occur in non-wetlands but may occur in wetlands.

UPL   **Obligate Upland** - Plants that almost never occur in wetlands (or in standing water or saturated soils).

MINNESOTA REGIONS *(see map, page 742)*

GP   Great Plains
NCNE   Northcentral Northeastern
MW   Midwest

Nomenclature follows that of the 2013 National Wetland Plant List. For more information, see NWPL website: *https://wetland_plants.usace.army.mil.*

	GP	MW	NCNE
Abies balsamea	FAC	FACW	FAC
Abies fraseri			FACU
Abutilon theophrasti	UPL	FACU	FACU
Acalypha rhomboidea	FACU	FACU	FACU
Acer negundo	FAC	FAC	FAC
Acer nigrum		FACU	FACU
Acer platanoides	UPL	UPL	UPL
Acer rubrum	FAC	FAC	FAC
Acer saccharinum	FAC	FACW	FACW
Acer saccharum	UPL	FACU	FACU
Acer spicatum	FACU	FACU	FACU
Achillea millefolium	FACU	FACU	FACU
Achillea ptarmica			FACU
Achnatherum hymenoides	FACU	FACU	FACU
Acmispon americanus	FACU	FACU	FACU
Acorus americanus	OBL	OBL	OBL
Acorus calamus	OBL	OBL	OBL
Actaea pachypoda		FACU	UPL
Actaea rubra	FACU	FACU	FACU
Adiantum pedatum	FAC	FACU	FACU
Adoxa moschatellina	FAC	FAC	FAC
Aegopodium podagraria		FAC	FAC
Aesculus glabra	FAC	FAC	FAC
Agalinis aspera	FACU	FACU	FACU
Agalinis paupercula	FAC	OBL	OBL
Agalinis purpurea	FACW	FACW	FACW
Agalinis tenuifolia	FAC	FACW	FACW
Agastache nepetoides	FACU	FACU	FACU

	GP	MW	NCNE
Ageratina altissima	UPL	FACU	FACU
Agoseris glauca	FACU	FACU	FACU
Agrimonia gryposepala	FAC	FACU	FACU
Agrimonia rostellata	FAC	FACU	FACU
Agrimonia striata	FACU	FACU	FACU
Agrostis gigantea	FACW	FACW	FACW
Agrostis hyemalis	FACW	FAC	FAC
Agrostis perennans	FAC	FAC	FACU
Agrostis scabra	FAC	FAC	FAC
Agrostis stolonifera	FACW	FACW	FACW
Alisma gramineum	OBL	OBL	OBL
Alisma subcordatum	OBL	OBL	OBL
Alisma triviale	OBL	OBL	OBL
Alliaria petiolata	FACU	FAC	FACU
Allium canadense	FACU	FACU	FACU
Allium cernuum	UPL	FACU	FACU
Allium schoenoprasum	FACU	FAC	FACU
Allium tricoccum	FACU	FACU	FACU
Alnus glutinosa		FACW	FACW
Alnus incana	FACW	FACW	FACW
Alnus viridis	FAC	FAC	FAC
Alopecurus aequalis	OBL	OBL	OBL
Alopecurus carolinianus	FACW	FACW	FACW
Alopecurus geniculatus	OBL	OBL	OBL
Alopecurus pratensis	FACW	FACW	FAC
Althaea officinalis	FACW	FACW	FAC
Amaranthus albus	FACU	FACU	FACU
Amaranthus blitoides	FAC	FACU	FACU
Amaranthus retroflexus	FACU	FACU	FACU
Amaranthus spinosus	FACU	FACU	FACU
Amaranthus tuberculatus	FAC	OBL	OBL
Ambrosia artemisiifolia	FACU	FACU	FACU
Ambrosia psilostachya	FACU	FACU	FAC
Ambrosia trifida	FAC	FAC	FAC
Amelanchier alnifolia	FACU	FACU	FACU
Amelanchier arborea	FACU	FACU	FACU
Amelanchier bartramiana			FAC
Amelanchier intermedia	FACW	FACW	FACW
Amelanchier spicata	FACU	FACU	FACU
Ammannia coccinea	OBL	OBL	OBL
Ammannia robusta	OBL	OBL	OBL
Ammophila breviligulata		UPL	UPL
Amorpha fruticosa	FACW	FACW	FACW
Amorpha nana	UPL	FACU	FACU
Amphicarpaea bracteata	FACU	FAC	FAC
Andromeda polifolia	OBL	OBL	OBL
Andropogon gerardii	FACU	FAC	FACU
Androsace occidentalis	FACU	FACU	UPL
Androsace septentrionalis	FACU		FAC
Anemone canadensis	FACW	FACW	FACW
Anemone quinquefolia	FAC	FAC	FACU
Anemone virginiana	FACU	FACU	FACU
Angelica atropurpurea		OBL	OBL

	GP	MW	NCNE
Antennaria neglecta	FACU	UPL	UPL
Anthemis cotula	FACU	FACU	FACU
Anticlea elegans	FACW	FAC	FACW
Apios americana	FAC	FACW	FACW
Aplectrum hyemale	FAC	FAC	FAC
Apocynum androsaemifolium	UPL	UPL	UPL
Apocynum cannabinum	FAC	FAC	FAC
Aquilegia canadensis	FAC	FACU	FACU
Arabidopsis lyrata		FACU	FACU
Arabis pycnocarpa	FACU	FACU	FACU
Aralia nudicaulis	FACU	FACU	FACU
Aralia racemosa	FACU	FACU	FACU
Arctium minus	FACU	FACU	FACU
Arctostaphylos uva-ursi	UPL	UPL	UPL
Arenaria serpyllifolia	FACU	FAC	FAC
Arethusa bulbosa	OBL	OBL	OBL
Arisaema dracontium	FACW	FACW	FACW
Arisaema triphyllum	FAC	FACW	FAC
Aristida dichotoma	FACU	FACU	FACU
Aristida longespica	FACU	FACU	FACU
Arnoglossum plantagineum	FAC	FAC	FAC
Aronia melanocarpa	OBL	FACW	FAC
Arrhenatherum elatius	FACU	FACU	FACU
Artemisia biennis	FACU	FACW	FACW
Artemisia cana	FACU	FACU	
Artemisia ludoviciana	UPL	UPL	UPL
Artemisia stelleriana		FACU	FACU
Artemisia vulgaris	UPL	UPL	UPL
Asarum canadense	FACU	FACU	UPL
Asclepias exaltata	FAC	UPL	UPL
Asclepias incarnata	FACW	OBL	OBL
Asclepias longifolia	FAC	UPL	UPL
Asclepias purpurascens	FACU	FACU	FACU
Asclepias speciosa	FAC	FAC	FAC
Asclepias syriaca	UPL	FACU	UPL
Asclepias verticillata	FACU	FACU	UPL
Asparagus officinalis	FACU	FACU	FACU
Asperugo procumbens	UPL	UPL	FACU
Asplenium platyneuron	FACU	FACU	FACU
Asplenium trichomanes	FAC	UPL	UPL
Astragalus agrestis	FACU	FACW	FACW
Astragalus alpinus	FAC		FAC
Astragalus canadensis	FAC	FAC	FAC
Astragalus neglectus	UPL	FACU	FACU
Athyrium angustum	FAC	FAC	FAC
Atriplex dioica	FAC	FACU	FAC
Atriplex glabriuscula		FACU	FACU
Atriplex hortensis	FAC	FAC	FAC
Atriplex patula	FACW	FACW	FACW
Atriplex prostrata	FACW	FAC	FAC
Avena sativa	FACU	UPL	UPL
Azolla microphylla	OBL	OBL	OBL

	GP	MW	NCNE
B			
Bacopa rotundifolia	OBL	OBL	OBL
Baptisia alba	FACU	FACU	FACU
Barbarea orthoceras	OBL	OBL	OBL
Barbarea vulgaris	FACU	FAC	FAC
Bartonia virginica		FACW	FACW
Bassia scoparia	FACU	FACU	FACU
Beckmannia syzigachne	OBL	OBL	OBL
Berberis thunbergii	UPL	FACU	FACU
Berberis vulgaris	UPL	FACU	FACU
Berula erecta	OBL	OBL	OBL
Betula alleghaniensis	FACU	FAC	FAC
Betula cordifolia	FACU	FACU	FACU
Betula nigra	FACW	FACW	FACW
Betula papyrifera	FACU	FACU	FACU
Betula pubescens	FACW	FACU	FACW
Betula pumila	OBL	OBL	OBL
Betula x *purpusii*	OBL	OBL	OBL
Betula x *sandbergii*	OBL	OBL	OBL
Bidens aristosa	FACW	FACW	FACW
Bidens beckii	OBL	OBL	OBL
Bidens cernua	OBL	OBL	OBL
Bidens discoidea	FACW	FACW	FACW
Bidens frondosa	FACW	FACW	FACW
Bidens trichosperma	OBL	OBL	OBL
Bidens tripartita	FACW	OBL	FACW
Bidens vulgata	FAC	FACW	FAC
Bistorta vivipara	FACW		FACW
Blephilia hirsuta	FACU	FACU	FACU
Boechera dentata	UPL	UPL	UPL
Boechera grahamii	FACU	FACU	FACU
Boechera stricta	FACU	FACU	FACU
Boehmeria cylindrica	FACW	OBL	OBL
Boltonia asteroides	FACW	OBL	FACW
Botrychium ascendens	FAC		FACU
Botrychium lanceolatum	FACW	FACW	FACW
Botrychium lunaria	FAC	FACW	FACW
Botrychium matricariifolium	FACU	FACU	FACU
Botrychium simplex	FAC	FAC	FAC
Botrypus virginianus	FACU	FACU	FACU
Bouteloua dactyloides	FACU	FACU	FACU
Brasenia schreberi	OBL	OBL	OBL
Brassica juncea	FACU	UPL	UPL
Brassica rapa	UPL	UPL	UPL
Bromus arvensis	FACU	FACU	FACU
Bromus ciliatus	FAC	FACW	FACW
Bromus inermis	UPL	FACU	UPL
Bromus kalmii	FACU	FAC	FAC
Bromus latiglumis	FACW	FACW	FACW
Bromus pubescens	FACU	FACU	FACU
Bulbostylis capillaris	FACU	FACU	FACU
Butomus umbellatus	OBL	OBL	OBL

	GP	MW	NCNE
C			
Calamagrostis canadensis	FACW	OBL	OBL
Calamagrostis stricta	FACW	FACW	FACW
Calla palustris	OBL	OBL	OBL
Callitriche hermaphroditica	OBL	OBL	OBL
Callitriche heterophylla	OBL	OBL	OBL
Callitriche palustris	OBL	OBL	OBL
Calopogon tuberosus	OBL	OBL	OBL
Caltha natans			OBL
Caltha palustris	OBL	OBL	OBL
Calypso bulbosa	FACW	FACW	FACW
Calystegia sepium	FAC	FAC	FAC
Camelina microcarpa	UPL	FACU	UPL
Camelina sativa	FACU	FACU	FACU
Campanula aparinoides	OBL	OBL	OBL
Campanula rotundifolia	FAC	FACU	FACU
Campanulastrum americanum	FAC	FAC	FAC
Canadanthus modestus	FAC	FAC	FAC
Capsella bursa-pastoris	FACU	FACU	FACU
Cardamine bulbosa	OBL	OBL	OBL
Cardamine concatenata	FACU	FACU	FACU
Cardamine douglassii		FACW	FACW
Cardamine flexuosa		FACU	FAC
Cardamine parviflora	FACW	FAC	FAC
Cardamine pensylvanica	FACW	FACW	FACW
Carduus nutans	FACU	FACU	FACU
Carex albicans	FACU	UPL	UPL
Carex alopecoidea	FACW	FACW	FACW
Carex annectens	FACW	FACW	FACW
Carex aquatilis	OBL	OBL	OBL
Carex arcta		OBL	OBL
Carex atherodes	OBL	OBL	OBL
Carex aurea	OBL	FACW	FACW
Carex bebbii	OBL	OBL	OBL
Carex bicknellii	FACW	FACU	FAC
Carex blanda	FAC	FAC	FAC
Carex brevior	FAC	FAC	FAC
Carex bromoides		FACW	FACW
Carex brunnescens	FAC	FACW	FACW
Carex bushii	OBL	FAC	FAC
Carex buxbaumii	OBL	OBL	OBL
Carex canescens	OBL	OBL	OBL
Carex capillaris	FACW	FACW	FACW
Carex castanea	FACW	FACW	FACW
Carex cephaloidea		FACU	FACU
Carex cephalophora	OBL	FACU	FACU
Carex chordorrhiza	OBL	OBL	OBL
Carex comosa	OBL	OBL	OBL
Carex conjuncta	FAC	FACW	FACW
Carex conoidea	FAC	FACW	FACW
Carex crawei	FACW	FACW	FACW
Carex crawfordii	OBL	FAC	FACW
Carex crinita	OBL	OBL	OBL
Carex cristatella	FACW	FACW	FACW
Carex crus-corvi	OBL	OBL	OBL

	GP	MW	NCNE
Carex cryptolepis	OBL	OBL	OBL
Carex davisii	FAC	FAC	FAC
Carex debilis	OBL	FACW	FACW
Carex deweyana	FACU	FACU	FACU
Carex diandra	OBL	OBL	OBL
Carex disperma	FACW	OBL	OBL
Carex eburnea	FACU	FACU	FACU
Carex echinata	OBL	OBL	OBL
Carex emoryi	OBL	OBL	OBL
Carex exilis	OBL		OBL
Carex festucacea	FACW	FACW	FAC
Carex flava	OBL	OBL	OBL
Carex foenea	UPL	UPL	UPL
Carex formosa	FAC	FAC	FAC
Carex garberi	FACW	FACW	FACW
Carex gracillima	FACW	FACU	FACU
Carex granularis	OBL	FACW	FACW
Carex gravida	FACW	FACU	FACU
Carex grayi	FACW	FACW	FACW
Carex grisea	FACW	FAC	FAC
Carex gynandra		FACW	OBL
Carex gynocrates	OBL	OBL	OBL
Carex hallii	FAC	FACW	FACW
Carex haydenii	OBL	OBL	OBL
Carex hystericina	OBL	OBL	OBL
Carex interior	OBL	OBL	OBL
Carex intumescens	OBL	FACW	FACW
Carex lacustris	OBL	OBL	OBL
Carex laeviconica	OBL	OBL	OBL
Carex laevivaginata		OBL	OBL
Carex lasiocarpa	OBL	OBL	OBL
Carex lenticularis	OBL		OBL
Carex leptalea	OBL	OBL	OBL
Carex leptonervia	FAC	FAC	FAC
Carex limosa	OBL	OBL	OBL
Carex livida	OBL	OBL	OBL
Carex lupulina	OBL	OBL	OBL
Carex lurida	OBL	OBL	OBL
Carex magellanica	OBL	OBL	OBL
Carex meadii	FAC	FAC	FAC
Carex media	FACW	FACW	FACW
Carex michauxiana			OBL
Carex molesta	FACW	FAC	FAC
Carex muskingumensis		OBL	OBL
Carex normalis	OBL	FACW	FACW
Carex novae-angliae			FACU
Carex oligosperma	OBL	OBL	OBL
Carex pallescens		FACW	FAC
Carex parryana	FACW	FACW	
Carex pauciflora	OBL	OBL	OBL
Carex pedunculata	OBL	OBL	FACU
Carex pellita	OBL	OBL	OBL
Carex praegracilis	FACW	FACW	FACW
Carex prairea	OBL	OBL	FACW
Carex praticola	FAC	FAC	FAC
Carex projecta	FACW	FACW	FACW
Carex pseudocyperus	OBL	OBL	OBL
Carex radiata			FAC

	GP	MW	NCNE
Carex retrorsa	OBL	OBL	OBL
Carex richardsonii	FAC	UPL	UPL
Carex rostrata	OBL	OBL	OBL
Carex sartwellii	FACW	FACW	OBL
Carex scirpoidea	FACU	FACU	FACU
Carex scoparia	FACW	FACW	FACW
Carex siccata	UPL	UPL	UPL
Carex sparganioides	FAC	FAC	FACU
Carex sprengelii	FACU	FAC	FAC
Carex squarrosa		OBL	OBL
Carex sterilis	OBL	OBL	OBL
Carex stipata	OBL	OBL	OBL
Carex stricta	OBL	OBL	OBL
Carex suberecta		OBL	OBL
Carex sychnocephala	FACW	FACW	FACW
Carex tenera	FACW	FACW	FAC
Carex tenuiflora	OBL	OBL	OBL
Carex tetanica	FACW	FACW	FACW
Carex torreyi	UPL	FACU	FACU
Carex torta		OBL	OBL
Carex tribuloides	OBL	OBL	FACW
Carex trichocarpa	OBL	OBL	OBL
Carex trisperma	OBL	OBL	OBL
Carex tuckermanii	OBL	OBL	OBL
Carex typhina	OBL	OBL	OBL
Carex utriculata	OBL	OBL	OBL
Carex vaginata	OBL	OBL	OBL
Carex vesicaria	OBL	OBL	OBL
Carex viridula	OBL	OBL	OBL
Carex vulpinoidea	FACW	FACW	OBL
Carex woodii		FAC	FACU
Carpinus caroliniana	FAC	FAC	FAC
Carum carvi	UPL	FACU	UPL
Carya cordiformis	FACU	FACU	FAC
Carya ovata	FACU	FACU	FACU
Castilleja coccinea	FACU	FAC	FAC
Castilleja septentrionalis	FAC		FACU
Catalpa speciosa	FACU	FACU	FACU
Celastrus orbiculatus		UPL	UPL
Celastrus scandens	UPL	FACU	FACU
Celtis occidentalis	FACU	FAC	FAC
Cenchrus longispinus	UPL	UPL	UPL
Centaurea cyanus	FACU	FACU	UPL
Centaurea jacea			FACU
Centaurium pulchellum	FACU	FACU	FAC
Cephalanthus occidentalis	OBL	OBL	OBL
Cerastium arvense	FACU	FACU	FACU
Cerastium brachypodum	FACU	FACU	FACU
Cerastium fontanum	FACU	FACU	FACU
Cerastium nutans	FAC	FACU	FACU
Ceratophyllum demersum	OBL	OBL	OBL
Ceratophyllum echinatum	OBL	OBL	OBL
Chamaecrista fasciculata	FACU	FACU	FACU
Chamaedaphne calyculata	OBL	OBL	OBL
Chamaenerion angustifolium	FAC	FAC	FAC

	GP	MW	NCNE
Chelidonium majus	FACU	UPL	UPL
Chelone glabra	OBL	OBL	OBL
Chelone obliqua		OBL	OBL
Chenopodium album	FACU	FACU	FACU
Chenopodium glaucum	FAC	FACW	FACW
Chenopodium rubrum	OBL	OBL	OBL
Chrysosplenium americanum		OBL	OBL
Chrysosplenium iowense		OBL	
Cichorium intybus	FACU	FACU	FACU
Cicuta bulbifera	OBL	OBL	OBL
Cicuta maculata	OBL	OBL	OBL
Cinna arundinacea	FACW	FACW	FACW
Cinna latifolia	OBL	FACW	FACW
Circaea alpina	FACW	FACW	FACW
Circaea canadensis	FACU	FACU	FACU
Cirsium arvense	FACU	FACU	FACU
Cirsium discolor	FACU	FACU	UPL
Cirsium flodmanii	FAC	FAC	FACU
Cirsium muticum	FACW	OBL	OBL
Cirsium palustre			FACW
Cirsium undulatum	FACU	FACU	FACU
Cirsium vulgare	UPL	FACU	FACU
Cladium mariscoides	OBL	OBL	OBL
Claytonia caroliniana		FACU	FACU
Claytonia virginica	FACU	FACU	FACU
Clematis terniflora	FACU	UPL	UPL
Clematis virginiana	FAC	FAC	FAC
Clintonia borealis	FAC	FAC	FAC
Clitoria mariana	FACU	FACU	FACU
Coeloglossum viride	FACU	FAC	FAC
Collomia linearis	FACU	FACU	FACU
Comandra umbellata	UPL	FACU	FACU
Comarum palustre	OBL	OBL	OBL
Commelina communis	FAC	FACU	FAC
Commelina erecta	FACU	FAC	UPL
Conioselinum chinense	FACW	FACW	FACW
Conium maculatum	FACW	FACW	FACW
Coptidium lapponicum	OBL		OBL
Coptis trifolia	FACW	FACW	FACW
Corallorhiza maculata	UPL	FACU	FACU
Corallorhiza striata	UPL	FACU	FACU
Corallorhiza trifida	FAC	FACW	FACW
Coreopsis lanceolata	FACU	FACU	FACU
Coreopsis tinctoria	FAC	FACU	FACU
Corispermum americanum	FACU	FACU	FACU
Cornus alba	FACW	FACW	FACW
Cornus alternifolia	FACU	FAC	FACU
Cornus canadensis	FACU	FAC	FAC
Cornus obliqua	FACW	FACW	FACW
Cornus racemosa	FAC	FAC	FAC
Corylus americana	UPL	FACU	FACU
Corylus cornuta	UPL	UPL	FACU

	GP	MW	NCNE
Cosmos bipinnatus	FACW	FAC	FAC
Crassula aquatica	OBL	OBL	OBL
Crataegus crus-galli	FAC	FAC	FAC
Crataegus douglasii	FAC	FAC	FAC
Crataegus mollis	FAC	FAC	FAC
Crepis runcinata	FAC	FACW	FACW
Cryptogramma stelleri		FACU	FACU
Cryptotaenia canadensis	FAC	FAC	FAC
Cyclachaena xanthiifolia	FAC	FAC	FAC
Cycloloma atriplicifolium	FACU	FACU	FACU
Cynoglossum officinale	FACU	FACU	UPL
Cyperus acuminatus	OBL	OBL	OBL
Cyperus bipartitus	FACW	OBL	FACW
Cyperus diandrus	FACW	FACW	OBL
Cyperus erythrorhizos	OBL	OBL	OBL
Cyperus esculentus	FACW	FACW	FACW
Cyperus fuscus	FACW	FAC	FAC
Cyperus lupulinus	FACU	FACU	FACU
Cyperus odoratus	FACW	FACW	OBL
Cyperus rotundus	FAC	FAC	FACU
Cyperus schweinitzii	FACU	FACU	FACU
Cyperus squarrosus	OBL	OBL	OBL
Cyperus strigosus	FACW	FACW	FACW
Cypripedium acaule	FACW	FACW	FACW
Cypripedium arietinum	FACW	FACW	FACW
Cypripedium candidum	OBL	OBL	OBL
Cypripedium parviflorum	FACW	FACW	FAC
Cypripedium reginae	FACW	FACW	FACW
Cypripedium x *andrewsii*	FACW	FACW	FACW
Cyrtorhyncha cymbalaria	OBL	OBL	OBL
Cystopteris bulbifera	FACW	FACW	FACW
Cystopteris fragilis	FACU	FACU	FACU
Cystopteris protrusa	FACW	FACW	FACU

D

	GP	MW	NCNE
Dactylis glomerata	FACU	FACU	FACU
Dalea leporina	UPL	FACU	UPL
Daphne mezereum			FACU
Dasiphora fruticosa	FACW	FACW	FACW
Datura wrightii	UPL	FACU	FACU
Daucus carota	UPL	UPL	UPL
Decodon verticillatus	OBL	OBL	OBL
Dendrolycopodium dendroideum	FAC	FAC	FACU
Dendrolyco. obscurum	FACU	FACU	FACU
Deparia acrostichoides		FAC	FAC
Deschampsia caespitosa	FACW	FACW	FACW
Descurainia incana	UPL	UPL	UPL
Desmanthus illinoensis	FACU	FACU	FACU
Desmodium canadense	FAC	FACU	FAC
Dianthus armeria	UPL	UPL	UPL
Dianthus deltoides	UPL	FACU	UPL
Diarrhena obovata			FACU

	GP	MW	NCNE
Dichanthelium aciculare	FACU	FACU	FACU
Dichanthelium acuminatum	FAC	FAC	FAC
Dichanthelium boreale	FACU	FAC	FAC
Dichanthelium dichotomum	FAC	FAC	FAC
Dichanthelium latifolium	FACU	FACU	FACU
Dichanthelium leibergii	FACU	FACU	FACU
Dichanthelium oligosanthes	FACU	FACU	FACU
Dichanthelium ovale	FACU	FACU	FACU
Dichanthelium portoricense	FAC	FACU	FACU
Didiplis diandra	OBL	OBL	OBL
Dieteria canescens	UPL	FAC	FAC
Digitaria ischaemum	UPL	FACU	FACU
Digitaria sanguinalis	FACU	FACU	FACU
Dioscorea villosa	FAC	FAC	FAC
Diphasiastrum complanatum		FACU	FACU
Diplachne fusca	FACW	OBL	OBL
Diplazium pycnocarpon		FACU	FAC
Dipsacus fullonum	FACU	FACU	FACU
Dipsacus laciniatus		UPL	FACU
Dirca palustris	FAC	FAC	FAC
Distichlis spicata	FACW	FACW	FACW
Dodecatheon meadia	FAC	FACU	FACU
Doellingeria umbellata	OBL	FACW	FACW
Dracocephalum parviflorum	FACU	FACU	FACU
Drosera anglica		OBL	OBL
Drosera intermedia	OBL	OBL	OBL
Drosera linearis		OBL	OBL
Drosera rotundifolia	OBL	OBL	OBL
Drosera x *obovata*	OBL		OBL
Drymocallis arguta	FACU	FACU	FACU
Dryopteris carthusiana	FACW	FACW	FACW
Dryopteris cristata	OBL	OBL	OBL
Dryopteris expansa		FAC	FAC
Dryopteris goldiana		FAC	FAC
Dryopteris intermedia		FAC	FAC
Dryopteris marginalis	FACU	FACU	FACU
Dryopteris x *boottii*		FACW	FACW
Dryopteris x *triploidea*	FAC	FAC	FAC
Dryopteris x *uliginosa*	FAC	FAC	FAC
Dulichium arundinaceum	OBL	OBL	OBL
Dysphania botrys	FACU	FACU	FACU

E

	GP	MW	NCNE
Echinochloa crus-galli	FAC	FACW	FAC
Echinochloa muricata	FACW	OBL	OBL
Echinochloa walteri	OBL	OBL	OBL
Echinocystis lobata	FAC	FACW	FACW
Eclipta prostrata	FACW	FACW	FACW
Egeria densa	OBL	OBL	OBL
Elaeagnus angustifolia	FACU	FACU	FACU
Elaeagnus commutata	UPL	UPL	UPL
Elatine minima		OBL	OBL
Elatine rubella	OBL	OBL	OBL

	GP	MW	NCNE
Eleocharis acicularis	OBL	OBL	OBL
Eleocharis compressa	FACW	FACW	FACW
Eleocharis elliptica	OBL	OBL	OBL
Eleocharis engelmannii	FACW	FACW	FACW
Eleocharis intermedia	OBL	OBL	OBL
Eleocharis mamillata			OBL
Eleocharis nitida			OBL
Eleocharis obtusa	OBL	OBL	OBL
Eleocharis olivacea	OBL	OBL	OBL
Eleocharis palustris	OBL	OBL	OBL
Eleocharis parvula	OBL	OBL	OBL
Eleocharis quinqueflora	OBL	OBL	OBL
Eleocharis robbinsii		OBL	OBL
Eleocharis rostellata	OBL	OBL	OBL
Eleocharis tenuis	FACW	FACW	FACW
Eleocharis wolfii	OBL	OBL	OBL
Eleusine indica	FACU	FACU	FACU
Ellisia nyctelea	FACU	FAC	FAC
Elodea bifoliata	OBL	OBL	OBL
Elodea canadensis	OBL	OBL	OBL
Elodea nuttallii	OBL	OBL	OBL
x Elyhordeum macounii	FAC	FAC	FACU
Elymus canadensis	FACU	FACU	FACU
Elymus curvatus	FAC	FAC	FAC
Elymus hystrix	FACU	FACU	FACU
Elymus repens	FACU	FACU	FACU
Elymus riparius	FAC	FACW	FACW
Elymus trachycaulus	FACU	FACU	FACU
Elymus villosus	FACU	FACU	FACU
Elymus virginicus	FAC	FACW	FACW
Elymus wiegandii	FAC	FAC	FAC
Empetrum nigrum			FAC
Enemion biternatum	FAC	FAC	FAC
Epilobium ciliatum	FACW	FACW	FACW
Epilobium coloratum	OBL	OBL	OBL
Epilobium leptophyllum	OBL	OBL	OBL
Epilobium palustre	OBL	OBL	OBL
Epilobium strictum	OBL	OBL	OBL
Epipactis helleborine	FACU	FACU	UPL
Equisetum arvense	FAC	FAC	FAC
Equisetum fluviatile	OBL	OBL	OBL
Equisetum hyemale	FACW	FACW	FAC
Equisetum laevigatum	FAC	FACW	FACW
Equisetum palustre	FACW	FACW	FACW
Equisetum pratense	FACW	FACW	FACW
Equisetum scirpoides	FAC	FAC	FAC
Equisetum sylvaticum	FACW	FACW	FACW
Equisetum variegatum	FACW	FACW	FACW
Equisetum x ferrissii	FACW	FACW	FACW
Equisetum x litorale		OBL	OBL
Equisetum x mackaii	OBL	FACW	FACW
Equisetum x nelsonii	OBL	FAC	FAC
Eragrostis cilianensis	FACU	FACU	FACU
Eragrostis frankii	FACW	FACW	FACW
Eragrostis hypnoides	OBL	OBL	OBL

	GP	MW	NCNE
Eragrostis pectinacea	FAC	FAC	FAC
Eragrostis pilosa	FACU	FACU	FACU
Eragrostis spectabilis	UPL	UPL	UPL
Erigeron acris	FAC		FAC
Erigeron annuus	FACU	FACU	FACU
Erigeron canadensis	FACU	FACU	FACU
Erigeron glabellus	FACW	FACW	FACW
Erigeron lonchophyllus	FACW	FACW	FACW
Erigeron philadelphicus	FAC	FACW	FAC
Erigeron pulchellus	FACU	FACU	FACU
Erigeron strigosus	FACU	FACU	FACU
Eriocaulon aquaticum		OBL	OBL
Eriochloa contracta	FAC	FAC	FAC
Eriophorum angustifolium	OBL	OBL	OBL
Eriophorum chamissonis	OBL	OBL	OBL
Eriophorum gracile	OBL	OBL	OBL
Eriophorum russeolum	OBL	OBL	OBL
Eriophorum tenellum	OBL	OBL	OBL
Eriophorum vaginatum	OBL	OBL	OBL
Eriophorum virginicum	OBL	OBL	OBL
Eriophorum viridicarinatum	OBL	OBL	OBL
Eryngium yuccifolium	FACW	FAC	FAC
Erysimum cheiranthoides	FACU	FACU	FACU
Erythronium albidum	FACU	FACU	FACU
Euonymus atropurpureus	FACU	FAC	FACU
Eupatorium perfoliatum	FACW	OBL	FACW
Eupatorium serotinum	FAC	FAC	FAC
Euphorbia cyathophora	UPL	FACU	FACU
Euphorbia humistrata	FAC	FACW	FACW
Euphorbia maculata	FACU	FACU	FACU
Euphorbia marginata	FACU	FACU	FACU
Euphorbia nutans	FACU	FACU	FACU
Euphorbia spathulata	FACU	FACU	FACU
Eurybia macrophylla	FACU	FACU	UPL
Euthamia graminifolia	FACW	FACW	FAC
Euthamia gymnospermoides	FAC	FACW	FACW
Eutrochium maculatum	OBL	OBL	OBL
Eutrochium purpureum	FAC	FAC	FAC

F

	GP	MW	NCNE
Fallopia convolvulus	FACU	FACU	FACU
Fallopia dumetorum	FACU	FAC	FAC
Fallopia scandens	FACU	FAC	FAC
Fatoua villosa	FAC	FAC	FAC
Festuca paradoxa	FAC	FAC	FAC
Festuca rubra	FAC	FACU	FACU
Festuca subverticillata	FACU	FACU	FACU
Festuca trachyphylla	UPL	FACU	UPL
Filipendula rubra		OBL	FACW
Filipendula ulmaria		FACW	
Fimbristylis autumnalis	OBL	OBL	FACW
Fimbristylis puberula	OBL	OBL	OBL
Floerkea proserpinacoides	FACW	FACW	FAC
Fragaria vesca	UPL	UPL	UPL

	GP	MW	NCNE
Fragaria virginiana	FACU	FACU	FACU
Frangula alnus	FAC	FACW	FAC
Fraxinus americana	FACU	FACU	FACU
Fraxinus nigra	FACW	FACW	FACW
Fraxinus pennsylvanica	FAC	FACW	FACW

G

	GP	MW	NCNE
Gaillardia pulchella	UPL	FACU	UPL
Galinsoga parviflora	UPL	FACU	UPL
Galinsoga quadriradiata	FACU	FACU	FACU
Galium aparine	FACU	FACU	FACU
Galium asprellum	OBL	OBL	OBL
Galium boreale	FACU	FAC	FAC
Galium brevipes	OBL	OBL	OBL
Galium circaezans	FACU	FACU	FACU
Galium concinnum	FACU	FACU	FACU
Galium labradoricum	OBL	OBL	OBL
Galium obtusum	FACW	FACW	FACW
Galium tinctorium	OBL	OBL	OBL
Galium trifidum	OBL	FACW	FACW
Galium triflorum	FACU	FACU	FACU
Gaultheria hispidula	FACW	FACW	FACW
Gaultheria procumbens	FACU	FACU	FACU
Gaylussacia baccata		FACU	FACU
Gentiana affinis	FACU	FACU	FACU
Gentiana alba	FAC	FACU	FACU
Gentiana andrewsii	FAC	FACW	FACW
Gentiana rubricaulis	OBL	OBL	OBL
Gentianella amarella	FACW	OBL	OBL
Gentianella quinquefolia		FAC	FAC
Gentianopsis crinita	OBL	OBL	FACW
Gentianopsis virgata	OBL	OBL	OBL
Geocaulon lividum			FAC
Geranium maculatum	FACU	FACU	FACU
Geum aleppicum	FACU	FACW	FAC
Geum canadense	FAC	FAC	FAC
Geum laciniatum	FACW	FACW	FACW
Geum macrophyllum	FACW	FACW	FACW
Geum rivale	FACW	OBL	OBL
Geum triflorum	FACU	FACU	FACU
Glechoma hederacea	FACU	FACU	FACU
Gleditsia triacanthos	FACU	FACU	FAC
Glyceria borealis	OBL	OBL	OBL
Glyceria canadensis	OBL	OBL	OBL
Glyceria grandis	OBL	OBL	OBL
Glyceria striata	OBL	OBL	OBL
Glycyrrhiza lepidota	FACU	FACU	FACU
Gnaphalium uliginosum	FAC	FAC	FAC
Goodyera pubescens		FAC	FACU
Goodyera repens		FACU	FACU
Goodyera tesselata	FACU	FACU	FACU
Gratiola neglecta	OBL	OBL	OBL
Grindelia squarrosa	UPL	FACU	FACU

	GP	MW	NCNE
Gymnocarpium dryopteris	FACU	FAC	FACU
Gymnocarpium robertianum	FACU	FACU	FACU

H

	GP	MW	NCNE
Hackelia virginiana	FACU	FACU	FACU
Halenia deflexa	FAC	FAC	FAC
Hamamelis virginiana	FAC	FACU	FACU
Hammarbya paludosa	OBL	OBL	OBL
Helenium autumnale	FACW	FACW	FACW
Helenium flexuosum	FACW	FAC	FAC
Helianthus annuus	FACU	FACU	FACU
Helianthus giganteus	FAC	FACW	FACW
Helianthus grosseserratus	FACW	FACW	FACW
Helianthus maximiliani	FACU	UPL	UPL
Helianthus microcephalus		FACU	FACU
Helianthus nuttallii	FACW	FACW	FACW
Helianthus occidentalis	FACU	FACU	FACU
Helianthus tuberosus	FACU	FACU	FACU
Heliopsis helianthoides	FACU	FACU	FACU
Hemerocallis fulva	FACU	UPL	UPL
Heracleum maximum	FAC	FACW	FACW
Hesperis matronalis	FACU	FACU	FACU
Heteranthera dubia	OBL	OBL	OBL
Heteranthera limosa	OBL	OBL	OBL
Heuchera richardsonii	FACU	FACU	FACU
Hibiscus laevis	OBL	OBL	OBL
Hieracium gronovii	FACU	UPL	UPL
Hippuris vulgaris	OBL	OBL	OBL
Hordeum jubatum	FACW	FAC	FAC
Hordeum pusillum	FACU	FAC	FAC
Humulus japonicus	FACU	FACU	FACU
Humulus lupulus	FACU	FACU	FACU
Huperzia lucidula	FACW	FACW	FAC
Huperzia porophila		FACU	FACU
Huperzia selago		FACU	FACU
Hybanthus concolor		FACU	FACU
Hydrocotyle americana		OBL	OBL
Hydrocotyle ranunculoides	OBL	OBL	OBL
Hydrophyllum virginianum	FAC	FAC	FAC
Hypericum ascyron		FAC	FAC
Hypericum boreale		OBL	OBL
Hypericum canadense		FACW	FACW
Hypericum ellipticum		OBL	OBL
Hypericum fraseri	OBL	OBL	OBL
Hypericum gentianoides	FACU	FACU	FACU
Hypericum kalmianum		FACW	FACW
Hypericum majus	FACW	FACW	FACW
Hypericum mutilum	FACW	FACW	FACW
Hypericum perforatum	UPL	FACU	UPL
Hypericum prolificum	FACU	FACU	FACU
Hypericum punctatum	FAC	FAC	FAC
Hypoxis hirsuta	FACW	FAC	FAC

	GP	MW	NCNE
I			
Ilex verticillata		FACW	FACW
Impatiens capensis	FACW	FACW	FACW
Impatiens glandulifera		FAC	FAC
Impatiens pallida	FACW	FACW	FACW
Inula helenium		FACU	FACU
Iodanthus pinnatifidus	FACW	FACW	FACW
Ipomoea hederacea	FAC	FAC	FAC
Ipomoea purpurea	FACU	FACU	FACU
Iris pseudacorus	OBL	OBL	OBL
Iris versicolor	OBL	OBL	OBL
Iris virginica	OBL	OBL	OBL
Isoetes echinospora	OBL	OBL	OBL
Isoetes lacustris		OBL	OBL
Isoetes melanopoda	OBL	OBL	OBL
J			
Juglans cinerea		FACU	FACU
Juglans nigra	FACU	FACU	FACU
Juncus acuminatus	OBL	OBL	OBL
Juncus alpinoarticulatus	OBL	OBL	OBL
Juncus anthelatus		FACW	FACW
Juncus articulatus	OBL	OBL	OBL
Juncus balticus	FACW	OBL	OBL
Juncus brachycarpus	FACW	FACW	FACW
Juncus brachycephalus	OBL	OBL	OBL
Juncus brevicaudatus	OBL	OBL	OBL
Juncus bufonius	OBL	FACW	FACW
Juncus canadensis	OBL	OBL	OBL
Juncus compressus	FACW	OBL	FACW
Juncus dudleyi	FACW	FACW	FACW
Juncus filiformis	OBL	FACW	FACW
Juncus gerardii	OBL	OBL	OBL
Juncus greenei	FAC	FAC	FAC
Juncus interior	FACW	FAC	FAC
Juncus longistylis	FACW	FACW	FACW
Juncus marginatus	FACW	FACW	FACW
Juncus nodosus	OBL	OBL	OBL
Juncus pelocarpus	OBL	OBL	OBL
Juncus pylaei		OBL	OBL
Juncus stygius	OBL		OBL
Juncus subtilis			OBL
Juncus tenuis	FAC	FAC	FAC
Juncus torreyi	FACW	FACW	FACW
Juncus vaseyi	FACW	FACW	FACW
Juniperus communis	UPL	UPL	FACU
Juniperus horizontalis	UPL	FACU	FACU
Juniperus virginiana	UPL	FACU	FACU
K			
Kalmia polifolia		OBL	OBL
Krigia biflora	FAC	FACU	FACU
L			
Lactuca biennis	FAC	FAC	FAC
Lactuca canadensis	FACU	FACU	FACU

	GP	MW	NCNE
Lactuca floridana	FAC	FACU	FACU
Lactuca ludoviciana	FACU	FACU	UPL
Lactuca serriola	FAC	FACU	FACU
Lactuca tatarica	UPL	FAC	FAC
Laportea canadensis	FAC	FACW	FACW
Lapsana communis	FAC	FACU	FACU
Larix laricina	FACW	FACW	FACW
Lathyrus japonicus	FACU	FACU	FACU
Lathyrus palustris	FACW	FACW	FACW
Lathyrus venosus	FAC	FAC	FAC
Leersia lenticularis	OBL	OBL	OBL
Leersia oryzoides	OBL	OBL	OBL
Leersia virginica	FACW	FACW	FACW
Lemna minor	OBL	OBL	OBL
Lemna obscura	OBL	OBL	OBL
Lemna perpusilla	OBL	OBL	OBL
Lemna trisulca	OBL	OBL	OBL
Lemna turionifera	OBL	OBL	OBL
Lepidium densiflorum	FAC	FAC	FACU
Lepidium perfoliatum	FAC	FAC	FACU
Lepidium virginicum	FACU	FACU	FACU
Lespedeza capitata	UPL	FACU	FACU
Lespedeza cuneata	FACU	UPL	UPL
Leucanthemum vulgare	UPL	UPL	UPL
Liatris ligulistylis	FAC	FACU	FACU
Liatris pycnostachya	FAC	FAC	FAC
Lilium michiganense	FACW	FACW	FACW
Lilium philadelphicum	FACU	FAC	FAC
Limosella aquatica	OBL	OBL	OBL
Lindernia dubia	OBL	OBL	OBL
Linnaea borealis	FACU	FAC	FAC
Liparis liliifolia		FACU	FACU
Liparis loeselii	OBL	FACW	FACW
Lipocarpha micrantha	FACW	OBL	OBL
Littorella americana			OBL
Lobelia cardinalis	FACW	OBL	OBL
Lobelia dortmanna		OBL	OBL
Lobelia inflata	FAC	FACU	FACU
Lobelia kalmii	OBL	OBL	OBL
Lobelia siphilitica	OBL	OBL	FACW
Lobelia spicata	FAC	FAC	FAC
Lolium perenne	FACU	FACU	FACU
Lonicera canadensis	FACU	FACU	FACU
Lonicera dioica	FACU	FACU	FACU
Lonicera hirsuta	FAC	FAC	FAC
Lonicera morrowii	UPL	FACU	FACU
Lonicera oblongifolia	OBL	OBL	OBL
Lonicera tatarica	FACU	FACU	FACU
Lonicera villosa	FACW	FACW	FACW
Lonicera x bella	FACU	FACU	FACU
Lotus corniculatus	FACU	FACU	FACU
Ludwigia palustris	OBL	OBL	OBL
Ludwigia polycarpa	OBL	OBL	OBL

	GP	MW	NCNE
Lupinus polyphyllus		FACU	FACU
Luzula acuminata	FAC	FACU	FACU
Luzula multiflora	FAC	FACU	FACU
Luzula parviflora	UPL		FAC
Lycopodiella inundata		OBL	OBL
Lycopodium clavatum		FAC	FAC
Lycopodium lagopus		FAC	FACU
Lycopus americanus	OBL	OBL	OBL
Lycopus asper	OBL	OBL	OBL
Lycopus uniflorus	OBL	OBL	OBL
Lycopus virginicus	OBL	OBL	OBL
Lycopus x sherardii		OBL	OBL
Lysimachia arvensis	FACW	FACU	FACU
Lysimachia ciliata	FACW	FACW	FACW
Lysimachia hybrida	OBL	OBL	OBL
Lysimachia maritima	OBL	OBL	OBL
Lysimachia minima	FACW	FACW	FACU
Lysimachia nummularia	FACW	FACW	FACW
Lysimachia quadriflora	FACW	OBL	OBL
Lysimachia quadrifolia		FACU	FACU
Lysimachia terrestris	OBL	OBL	OBL
Lysimachia thyrsiflora	OBL	OBL	OBL
Lysimachia vulgaris		FACW	FACW
Lythrum alatum	OBL	OBL	OBL
Lythrum salicaria	OBL	OBL	OBL

M

	GP	MW	NCNE
Madia glomerata	FACU	FACU	FACU
Maianthemum canadense	FACU	FAC	FACU
Maianthemum racemosum	FAC	FACU	FACU
Maianthemum stellatum	FACU	FAC	FAC
Maianthemum trifolium	OBL	OBL	OBL
Malaxis monophyllos	FACW	FACW	FACW
Malaxis unifolia	FAC	FAC	FAC
Marrubium vulgare	FACU	FAC	FACU
Marsilea vestita	OBL	OBL	
Matricaria discoidea	FACU	FACU	FACU
Matteuccia struthiopteris	FACW	FACW	FAC
Medicago lupulina	FACU	FACU	FACU
Medicago sativa	UPL	FACU	UPL
Melampyrum lineare		FAC	FACU
Melilotus officinalis	FACU	FACU	FACU
Menispermum canadense	FACU	FAC	FAC
Mentha arvensis	FACW	FACW	FACW
Mentha spicata	FACW	FACW	FACW
Mentha x gracilis	OBL	OBL	OBL
Mentha x piperita	FACW	OBL	OBL
Menyanthes trifoliata	OBL	OBL	OBL
Mertensia paniculata	FAC	FAC	FAC
Mertensia virginica		FACW	FAC
Micranthes pensylvanica	FACW	OBL	OBL
Micranthes virginiensis		FACU	FACU
Milium effusum		FACU	

	GP	MW	NCNE
Mimulus glabratus	OBL	OBL	OBL
Mimulus ringens	OBL	OBL	OBL
Mirabilis nyctaginea	UPL	UPL	UPL
Mitchella repens	FAC	FACU	FACU
Mitella diphylla	FACU	FACU	FACU
Mitella nuda	OBL	FACW	FACW
Moehringia lateriflora	FACU	FACU	FACU
Mollugo verticillata	FAC	FAC	FAC
Monarda didyma		UPL	FACU
Monarda fistulosa	UPL	FACU	FACU
Monarda punctata	UPL	UPL	UPL
Moneses uniflora	FAC	FAC	FAC
Monolepis nuttalliana	FAC	UPL	UPL
Monotropa uniflora	UPL	FACU	FACU
Montia chamissoi	OBL	OBL	OBL
Morus alba	FACU	FAC	FACU
Morus rubra	FACU	FACU	FACU
Muhlenbergia asperifolia	FACW	FACW	FACW
Muhlenbergia frondosa	FACW	FACW	FACW
Muhlenbergia glomerata	FACW	FACW	OBL
Muhlenbergia mexicana	FACW	FACW	FACW
Muhlenbergia racemosa	FACW	FACW	FACU
Muhlenbergia richardsonis	FAC	FAC	FACW
Muhlenbergia schreberi	FACU	FAC	FAC
Muhlenbergia sylvatica	FACW	FACW	FACW
Muhlenbergia uniflora		OBL	OBL
Myosotis arvensis	FAC	FAC	FACU
Myosotis laxa	OBL	OBL	OBL
Myosotis scorpioides	OBL	OBL	OBL
Myosotis sylvatica	FACW	UPL	UPL
Myosotis verna	FAC	FACU	FACU
Myosoton aquaticum	FAC	FACW	FAC
Myosurus minimus	FACW	FACW	FAC
Myrica gale	OBL	OBL	OBL
Myriophyllum alterniflorum			OBL
Myriophyllum farwellii		OBL	OBL
Myriophyllum heterophyllum	OBL	OBL	OBL
Myriophyllum humile		OBL	OBL
Myriophyllum sibiricum	OBL	OBL	OBL
Myriophyllum spicatum	OBL	OBL	OBL
Myriophyllum tenellum	OBL	OBL	OBL
Myriophyllum verticillatum	OBL	OBL	OBL

N

	GP	MW	NCNE
Nabalus albus	FACU	FACU	FACU
Nabalus crepidineus		FAC	FAC
Nabalus racemosus	FACU	FACW	FACW
Najas flexilis	OBL	OBL	OBL
Najas gracillima	OBL	OBL	OBL
Najas guadalupensis	OBL	OBL	OBL
Najas marina	OBL	OBL	OBL
Najas minor	OBL	OBL	OBL
Napaea dioica		FACW	FACW
Nasturtium microphyllum	OBL	OBL	OBL

	GP	MW	NCNE
Nasturtium officinale	OBL	OBL	OBL
Nelumbo lutea	OBL	OBL	OBL
Nemopanthus mucronatus		OBL	OBL
Neottia auriculata			FACW
Neottia convallarioides	FACW		FACW
Neottia cordata	FACU	FACW	FACW
Nepeta cataria	FACU	FACU	FACU
Nuphar microphylla		OBL	OBL
Nuphar variegata	OBL	OBL	OBL
Nuphar x *rubrodisca*		OBL	OBL
Nymphaea leibergii	OBL		OBL
Nymphaea odorata	OBL	OBL	OBL

O

	GP	MW	NCNE
Oenothera biennis	FACU	FACU	FACU
Oenothera gaura		FACU	FACU
Oenothera laciniata	FACU	FACU	FACU
Oenothera parviflora	FACU	FACU	FACU
Oenothera perennis	FAC	FAC	FAC
Oenothera rhombipetala	FACU	FACU	FACU
Oenothera villosa	FACU	FAC	FAC
Onoclea sensibilis	FACW	FACW	FACW
Ophioglossum pusillum	FACW	FACW	FACW
Ornithogalum umbellatum	FACU	FACU	FACU
Orobanche uniflora	UPL	UPL	UPL
Orthilia secunda	FACU	FAC	FAC
Orthocarpus luteus	FACU	FACU	FACU
Osmorhiza berteroi	FACU		FACU
Osmorhiza claytonii	FACU	FACU	FACU
Osmorhiza longistylis	FAC	FACU	FACU
Osmunda cinnamomeum	FACW	FACW	FACW
Osmunda claytoniana	FAC	FAC	FAC
Osmunda spectabilis	OBL	OBL	OBL
Ostrya virginiana	FACU	FACU	FACU
Oxalis corniculata	FACU	FACU	FACU
Oxalis dillenii	FACU	FACU	FACU
Oxalis montana		FACU	FACU
Oxalis stricta	FACU	FACU	FACU
Oxypolis rigidior	OBL	OBL	OBL
Oxytropis lambertii	UPL	FACU	FACU
Oxytropis splendens	FACU	FACU	

P

	GP	MW	NCNE
Packera aurea	FACW	FACW	FACW
Packera indecora	FACW		FACW
Packera pauciflora	FAC		FACU
Packera paupercula	FAC	FAC	FAC
Packera plattensis	FACU	FACU	FACU
Packera pseudaurea	FACW	FACW	FACW
Panicum capillare	FAC	FAC	FAC
Panicum dichotomiflorum	FAC	FACW	FACW
Panicum gattingeri		FAC	FAC
Panicum philadelphicum	FAC	FACW	FAC
Panicum virgatum	FAC	FAC	FAC

	GP	MW	NCNE
Parietaria pensylvanica	FAC	FACU	FACU
Parnassia glauca	OBL	OBL	OBL
Parnassia palustris	OBL	OBL	OBL
Parnassia parviflora	OBL	OBL	OBL
Parthenocissus inserta	FAC	FACU	FACU
Parthenocissus quinquefolia	FACU	FACU	FACU
Pascopyrum smithii	FACU	FACU	FACU
Paspalum setaceum	FAC	FACU	FACU
Pedicularis canadensis	FACU	FACU	FACU
Pedicularis lanceolata	OBL	OBL	FACW
Peltandra virginica	OBL	OBL	OBL
Penstemon digitalis	FACW	FAC	FAC
Penstemon gracilis	FACU	UPL	UPL
Penstemon laevigatus		FACU	FACU
Penstemon pallidus	FACU	UPL	UPL
Penthorum sedoides	OBL	OBL	OBL
Perilla frutescens		FAC	
Peritoma serrulata	FACU	FACU	FACU
Persicaria amphibia	OBL	OBL	OBL
Persicaria arifolia	OBL	OBL	OBL
Persicaria careyi		FACW	FACW
Persicaria hydropiper	OBL	OBL	OBL
Persicaria hydropiperoides	OBL	OBL	OBL
Persicaria lapathifolia	OBL	FACW	FACW
Persicaria longiseta		FAC	FAC
Persicaria maculosa	FACW	FACW	FAC
Persicaria orientalis	FACW	UPL	UPL
Persicaria pensylvanica	FACW	FACW	FACW
Persicaria punctata	OBL	OBL	OBL
Persicaria sagittata	OBL	OBL	OBL
Persicaria virginiana	FAC	FAC	FAC
Petasites frigidus	FAC	FACW	FACW
Phalaris arundinacea	FACW	FACW	FACW
Phalaris canariensis	FACU	FACU	FACU
Phegopteris connectilis	FACU	FACU	FACU
Phegopteris hexagonoptera		FACU	FACU
Phleum pratense	FACU	FACU	FACU
Phlox divaricata	FACU	FACU	FACU
Phlox maculata		FACW	FACW
Phlox paniculata	FACU	FACU	FACU
Phlox pilosa	FACU	FACU	FACU
Phragmites australis	FACW	FACW	FACW
Phryma leptostachya	FACU	UPL	FACU
Phyla lanceolata	FACW	OBL	OBL
Physalis philadelphica	UPL	UPL	UPL
Physalis pubescens	FACU	UPL	UPL
Physocarpus opulifolius	FACU	FACW	FACW
Physostegia parviflora	FACW	FACW	FACW
Physostegia virginiana	FACW	FACW	FACW
Phytolacca americana	FACU	FACU	FACU
Picea glauca	FACU	FACU	FACU
Picea mariana	FACW	FACW	FACW
Picea pungens	FAC		FACU

	GP	MW	NCNE
Pilea fontana	OBL	FACW	FACW
Pilea pumila	FAC	FACW	FACW
Pinguicula vulgaris			OBL
Pinus banksiana	FACU	FACU	FACU
Pinus resinosa	FACU	FACU	FACU
Pinus rigida		FACU	FACU
Pinus strobus	FACU	FACU	FACU
Piperia dilatata	FACW	FACW	FACW
Pistia stratiotes	OBL	OBL	OBL
Plagiobothrys hispidulus	FACW	FACW	FACW
Plantago arenaria	FACU	FACU	FACU
Plantago elongata	FACW	FACW	
Plantago eriopoda	FAC	FAC	FAC
Plantago lanceolata	FAC	FACU	FACU
Plantago major	FAC	FAC	FACU
Plantago rugelii	FACU	FAC	FAC
Plantago virginica	FACU	FACU	FACU
Platanthera clavellata	OBL	OBL	FACW
Platanthera flava	FACW	FACW	FACW
Platanthera hookeri	FAC	FAC	FAC
Platanthera huronensis	OBL	FACW	FACW
Platanthera lacera	FACW	FACW	FACW
Platanthera obtusata	FACW	FACW	FACW
Platanthera orbiculata	FAC	FAC	FAC
Platanthera psycodes	FACW	FACW	FACW
Platanthera rotundifolia		OBL	OBL
Poa alpina	FACU		FACU
Poa alsodes		FACW	FAC
Poa annua	FACU	FACU	FACU
Poa arida	FAC	FAC	FAC
Poa compressa	FACU	FACU	FACU
Poa interior	FAC	FAC	FAC
Poa nemoralis		FACU	FACU
Poa paludigena		OBL	OBL
Poa palustris	FACW	FACW	FACW
Poa pratensis	FACU	FAC	FACU
Poa secunda	FACU	FACU	FACU
Poa sylvestris	FAC	FAC	FAC
Poa trivialis	FACW	FACW	FACW
Podophyllum peltatum	FACU	FACU	FACU
Pogonia ophioglossoides	OBL	OBL	OBL
Polanisia dodecandra	FACU	UPL	UPL
Polemonium caeruleum			FACW
Polemonium occidentale	FACW	FACW	FACW
Polemonium reptans	FAC	FAC	FAC
Polygala cruciata	OBL	FACW	FACW
Polygala polygama	FACU	FACU	FACU
Polygala sanguinea	FACW	FACU	FACU
Polygala senega	FACU	FACU	FACU
Polygala verticillata	FACU	UPL	UPL
Polygaloides paucifolia	FACU	FACU	FACU
Polygonatum biflorum	FACU	FACU	FACU
Polygonum achoreum	FACU	FAC	FACU
Polygonum aviculare	FACU	FAC	FACU
Polygonum douglasii	FACU	FACU	FACU

	GP	MW	NCNE
Polygonum erectum	FAC	FACU	FACU
Polygonum ramosissimum	FACW	FACU	FAC
Polypogon monspeliensis	FACW	OBL	OBL
Polystichum acrostichoides	FACU	UPL	FACU
Pontederia cordata	OBL	OBL	OBL
Populus balsamifera	FACW	FACW	FACW
Populus deltoides	FAC	FAC	FAC
Populus grandidentata	FACU	FACU	FACU
Populus tremuloides	FAC	FAC	FACU
Portulaca grandiflora	UPL	FACU	UPL
Portulaca oleracea	FAC	FACU	FACU
Potamogeton alpinus	OBL	OBL	OBL
Potamogeton amplifolius	OBL	OBL	OBL
Potamogeton berchtoldii	OBL	OBL	OBL
Potamogeton bicupulatus		OBL	OBL
Potamogeton confervoides		OBL	OBL
Potamogeton crispus	OBL	OBL	OBL
Potamogeton diversifolius	OBL	OBL	OBL
Potamogeton epihydrus	OBL	OBL	OBL
Potamogeton foliosus	OBL	OBL	OBL
Potamogeton friesii	OBL	OBL	OBL
Potamogeton gramineus	OBL	OBL	OBL
Potamogeton illinoensis	OBL	OBL	OBL
Potamogeton natans	OBL	OBL	OBL
Potamogeton nodosus	OBL	OBL	OBL
Potamogeton oakesianus		OBL	OBL
Potamogeton obtusifolius	OBL	OBL	OBL
Potamogeton praelongus	OBL	OBL	OBL
Potamogeton pulcher	OBL	OBL	OBL
Potamogeton pusillus	OBL	OBL	OBL
Potamogeton richardsonii	OBL	OBL	OBL
Potamogeton robbinsii	OBL	OBL	OBL
Potamogeton spirillus	OBL	OBL	OBL
Potamogeton strictifolius	OBL	OBL	OBL
Potamogeton vaseyi	OBL	OBL	OBL
Potamogeton x haynesii		OBL	OBL
Potamogeton x spathuliformis		OBL	OBL
Potamogeton zosteriformis	OBL	OBL	OBL
Potentilla anserina	FACW	FACW	FACW
Potentilla argentea	FACU	FACU	FACU
Potentilla gracilis	FAC	FAC	FAC
Potentilla norvegica	FAC	FAC	FAC
Potentilla pensylvanica	FACU	FACU	FACU
Potentilla rivalis	FACW	FACW	FACW
Potentilla simplex	UPL	FACU	FACU
Potentilla supina	FACW	FACW	FACW
Primula mistassinica	FACW	FACW	FACW
Proboscidea louisiana	FACU	FAC	FAC
Prosartes trachycarpa	UPL		UPL
Prunella vulgaris	FAC	FAC	FAC
Prunus americana	UPL	UPL	UPL
Prunus nigra	FACU	FACU	FACU
Prunus pensylvanica	FACU	FACU	FACU
Prunus serotina	FACU	FACU	FACU
Prunus virginiana	FACU	FACU	FACU

	GP	MW	NCNE
Psathyrostachys juncea	FACU	FAC	
Pseudotsuga menziesii	FACU	FACU	FACU
Ptelea trifoliata	FAC	FACU	FACU
Pteridium aquilinum	FACU	FACU	FACU
Puccinellia distans	FACW	OBL	FACW
Puccinellia nuttalliana	OBL	OBL	OBL
Pycnanthemum tenuifolium	FAC	FAC	FAC
Pycnanthemum virginianum	FAC	FACW	FACW
Pyrola americana	FACU	FACU	FAC
Pyrola asarifolia	FACU	FACW	FACW
Pyrola chlorantha	FACU	FACU	FACU
Pyrola elliptica	UPL	FACU	FACU
Pyrola minor	FACU		FAC

Q

	GP	MW	NCNE
Quercus alba	FACU	FACU	FACU
Quercus bicolor		FACW	FACW
Quercus macrocarpa	FACU	FAC	FACU
Quercus muehlenbergii	FAC	FACU	FACU
Quercus rubra	FACU	FACU	FACU

R

	GP	MW	NCNE
Ranunculus abortivus	FAC	FACW	FAC
Ranunculus acris	FACW	FAC	FAC
Ranunculus fascicularis	FAC	FACU	FACU
Ranunculus flabellaris	OBL	OBL	OBL
Ranunculus flammula	FACW	FACW	FACW
Ranunculus gmelinii	FACW	FACW	FACW
Ranunculus hispidus	FACW	FAC	FAC
Ranunculus longirostris	OBL	OBL	OBL
Ranunculus macounii	OBL	OBL	OBL
Ranunculus pensylvanicus	FACW	OBL	OBL
Ranunculus recurvatus	FACW	FACW	FACW
Ranunculus repens	FACW	FAC	FAC
Ranunculus sceleratus	OBL	OBL	OBL
Ranunculus subrigidus	OBL	OBL	OBL
Ranunculus trichophyllus	OBL	OBL	OBL
Reynoutria japonica	FACU	FACU	FACU
Reynoutria sachalinensis	UPL	UPL	UPL
Rhamnus alnifolia	FACW	OBL	OBL
Rhamnus cathartica	FACU	FAC	FAC
Rhodiola integrifolia	FACU	FACU	UPL
Rhododendron groenlandicum	FACW	OBL	OBL
Rhus aromatica	UPL	UPL	UPL
Rhynchospora alba	OBL	OBL	OBL
Rhynchospora capillacea	OBL	OBL	OBL
Rhynchospora fusca	OBL	OBL	OBL
Ribes americanum	FACW	FACW	FACW
Ribes aureum	FACU	FAC	FACU
Ribes cynosbati	FACU	FAC	FACU
Ribes glandulosum	OBL	FACW	FACW
Ribes hirtellum	FAC	FACW	FACW
Ribes hudsonianum	OBL	OBL	OBL
Ribes lacustre	FACW	FACW	FACW
Ribes oxyacanthoides	FACU	FACU	FACU

	GP	MW	NCNE
Ribes triste	OBL	OBL	OBL
Robinia pseudoacacia	UPL	FACU	FACU
Rorippa aquatica	OBL	OBL	OBL
Rorippa austriaca	FACW	FACW	FAC
Rorippa curvipes	OBL	FACW	FACW
Rorippa palustris	OBL	OBL	OBL
Rorippa sessiliflora	OBL	OBL	OBL
Rorippa sinuata	FACW	FACW	FACW
Rorippa sylvestris	FACW	OBL	OBL
Rosa acicularis	FACU	FACU	FACU
Rosa arkansana	FACU	FACU	FACU
Rosa blanda	FACU	FACU	FACU
Rosa carolina	FACU	FACU	FACU
Rosa multiflora	UPL	FACU	FACU
Rosa rubiginosa	UPL	UPL	FACU
Rosa rugosa		FACU	FACU
Rosa woodsii	FACU	FACU	FACU
Rotala ramosior	OBL	OBL	OBL
Rubus allegheniensis	UPL	FACU	FACU
Rubus alumnus	FAC	FACU	FACU
Rubus arcticus	FACW	FACW	FACW
Rubus baileyanus		FACU	FACU
Rubus chamaemorus			FACW
Rubus flagellaris	UPL	FACU	FACU
Rubus hispidus		FACW	FACW
Rubus idaeus	FACU	FACU	FACU
Rubus missouricus		FACU	FACU
Rubus parviflorus	FACU	FACU	FACU
Rubus pensilvanicus	FAC	UPL	FACU
Rubus pergratus		FACU	FACU
Rubus pubescens	FACW	FACW	FACW
Rubus semisetosus		FAC	FAC
Rubus setosus	FACW	FACW	FACW
Rubus spectatus		OBL	OBL
Rubus stipulatus		FAC	FAC
Rubus wheeleri		FAC	FAC
Rudbeckia hirta	FACU	FACU	FACU
Rudbeckia laciniata	FAC	FACW	FACW
Rudbeckia subtomentosa	FAC	FACU	FACU
Rudbeckia triloba	FACU	FACU	FACU
Ruellia humilis	FAC	FACU	FACU
Rumex acetosa		UPL	UPL
Rumex acetosella	FAC	FACU	FACU
Rumex altissimus	FAC	FACW	FACW
Rumex britannica	OBL	OBL	OBL
Rumex crispus	FAC	FAC	FAC
Rumex fueginus	FACW	FACW	FACW
Rumex longifolius	FAC	FAC	FAC
Rumex obtusifolius	FACW	FACW	FAC
Rumex occidentalis	OBL	OBL	OBL
Rumex stenophyllus	FACW	FACW	FACW
Rumex triangulivalvis	FACW	FACW	FAC
Rumex venosus	FAC	FAC	UPL
Rumex verticillatus	FACW	OBL	OBL
Ruppia cirrhosa	OBL	OBL	OBL

	GP	MW	NCNE
S			
Sagina nodosa			FACU
Sagina procumbens		FACW	FAC
Sagittaria brevirostra	OBL	OBL	OBL
Sagittaria calycina	OBL	OBL	OBL
Sagittaria cristata	OBL	OBL	OBL
Sagittaria cuneata	OBL	OBL	OBL
Sagittaria graminea	OBL	OBL	OBL
Sagittaria latifolia	OBL	OBL	OBL
Sagittaria rigida	OBL	OBL	OBL
Salicornia rubra	OBL	OBL	OBL
Salix alba	FACW	FACW	FACW
Salix amygdaloides	FACW	FACW	FACW
Salix bebbiana	FACW	FACW	FACW
Salix candida	OBL	OBL	OBL
Salix daphnoides			FAC
Salix discolor	FACW	FACW	FACW
Salix eriocephala	FACW	FACW	FACW
Salix famelica	FACW	FACW	FACW
Salix humilis	FACU	FACU	FACU
Salix interior	FACW	FACW	FACW
Salix lucida	FACW	FACW	FACW
Salix maccalliana	OBL	OBL	OBL
Salix nigra	FACW	OBL	OBL
Salix pedicellaris	OBL	OBL	OBL
Salix pellita	FACW		FACW
Salix petiolaris	OBL	OBL	FACW
Salix planifolia	OBL	OBL	OBL
Salix pseudomonticola	FACW		FACW
Salix purpurea	OBL	FACW	FACW
Salix pyrifolia	OBL	FACW	FACW
Salix sericea		OBL	OBL
Salix serissima	OBL	OBL	OBL
Salix x *fragilis*	FAC	FAC	FAC
Salsola tragus	FACU	FACU	FACU
Sambucus nigra	FAC	FACW	FACW
Sambucus racemosa	FACU	FACU	FACU
Sanguinaria canadensis	UPL	FACU	FACU
Sanicula canadensis	FACU	FACU	FACU
Sanicula marilandica	FACU	FACU	FACU
Sanicula odorata	FAC	FAC	FAC
Saponaria officinalis	FACU	FACU	FACU
Sarracenia purpurea	OBL	OBL	OBL
Saxifraga cernua	FACU		FACW
Saxifraga paniculata			FAC
Sceptridium dissectum	FAC	FAC	FAC
Sceptridium multifidum	FAC	FACU	FACU
Schedonorus arundinaceus	FACU	FACU	FACU
Schedonorus pratensis	FACU	FACU	FACU
Scheuchzeria palustris	OBL	OBL	OBL
Schizachne purpurascens	FACU	FACU	FACU
Schizachyrium scoparium	FACU	FACU	FACU
Schoenoplectus acutus	OBL	OBL	OBL
Schoenoplectus fluviatilis	OBL	OBL	OBL

	GP	MW	NCNE
Schoen. heterochaetus	OBL	OBL	OBL
Schoenoplectus maritimus	OBL	OBL	OBL
Schoenoplectus pungens	OBL	OBL	OBL
Schoenoplectus purshianus	OBL	OBL	OBL
Schoenoplectus smithii	OBL	OBL	OBL
Schoen. subterminalis	OBL	OBL	OBL
Schoen. tabernaemontani	OBL	OBL	OBL
Schoenoplectus torreyi	OBL	OBL	OBL
Scirpus atrocinctus	OBL	OBL	OBL
Scirpus atrovirens	OBL	OBL	OBL
Scirpus cyperinus	OBL	OBL	OBL
Scirpus georgianus	OBL	OBL	OBL
Scirpus hattorianus	OBL	OBL	OBL
Scirpus microcarpus	OBL	OBL	OBL
Scirpus pallidus	OBL	OBL	OBL
Scirpus pedicellatus	OBL	OBL	OBL
Scirpus pendulus	OBL	OBL	OBL
Scleranthus annuus	FACU	FACU	FACU
Scleria triglomerata	FAC	FAC	FAC
Scleria verticillata	OBL	OBL	OBL
Scolochloa festucacea	OBL	OBL	OBL
Scorzoneroides autumnalis		FACU	FACU
Scrophularia lanceolata	FAC	FACU	FACU
Scrophularia marilandica	FACU	FACU	FACU
Scutellaria galericulata	OBL	OBL	OBL
Scutellaria lateriflora	FACW	OBL	OBL
Scutellaria ovata	FACU	FACU	FACU
Scutellaria parvula	UPL	FACU	FACU
Selaginella selaginoides			FACW
Senecio hieraciifolius	FACU	FAC	FACU
Senecio integerrimus	FAC	FAC	FAC
Senecio suaveolens		FACW	FACW
Senecio vulgaris	FACU	UPL	FACU
Setaria faberi	UPL	FACU	FACU
Setaria italica	FACU	FACU	FACU
Setaria pumila	FACU	FAC	FAC
Setaria verticillata	FAC	FAC	FACU
Shepherdia argentea	UPL	FACU	FACU
Shepherdia canadensis	FACU	UPL	UPL
Sibbaldia tridentata	FACU	FACU	FACU
Sicyos angulatus	FACW	FACW	FACW
Silene flos-cuculi		FACU	FACU
Silene nivea	FACW	FACW	FACW
Silphium perfoliatum	FAC	FACW	FACW
Sinapis alba	FAC		
Sisymbrium altissimum	FACU	FACU	FACU
Sisyrinchium angustifolium	FACW	FAC	FAC
Sisyrinchium montanum	FAC	FAC	FAC
Sisyrinchium mucronatum	FAC	FACW	FAC
Sium suave	OBL	OBL	OBL
Smilax hispida	FAC	FAC	FAC
Smilax pulverulenta		FACU	FACU
Solanum carolinense	UPL	FACU	FACU

	GP	MW	NCNE		GP	MW	NCNE
Solanum dulcamara	FACU	FAC	FAC	Streptopus amplexifolius	FACW	FAC	FAC
Solanum ptychanthum	FACU	FACU	FACU	Streptopus lanceolatus	FAC	FAC	FACU
Solidago altissima	FACU	FACU	FACU	Strophostyles helvola	FACU	FAC	FAC
Solidago canadensis	FACU	FACU	FACU	Stuckenia filiformis	OBL	OBL	OBL
Solidago flexicaulis	FACU	FACU	FACU	Stuckenia pectinata	OBL	OBL	OBL
Solidago gigantea	FAC	FACW	FACW	Stuckenia vaginata	OBL	OBL	OBL
Solidago lepida	FACU	FACU	FACU	Suaeda calceoliformis	FACW	FACW	FACW
Solidago riddellii	OBL	OBL	OBL	Subularia aquatica	OBL		OBL
Solidago rigida	FACU	FACU	FACU	Symphoricarpos albus	UPL	FACU	FACU
Solidago simplex	FACU	FACU	FACU	Symphoricarpos occidentalis	UPL	UPL	FACU
Solidago uliginosa	OBL	OBL	OBL	Symphoricarpos orbiculatus	FACU	FACU	FACU
Sonchus arvensis	FAC	FACU	FACU	Symphyotrichum boreale	OBL	OBL	OBL
Sonchus asper	FAC	FACU	FACU	Symphyotrichum ciliatum	FACW	FAC	FAC
Sonchus oleraceus	UPL	FACU	FACU	Symphyotrichum ericoides	FACU	FACU	FACU
Sorbus americana		FAC	FAC	Symphyotrichum falcatum	FACU	FAC	FAC
Sorbus decora	FAC	UPL	FACU	Symphyotrichum laeve	FACU	FACU	FACU
Sorghastrum nutans	FACU	FACU	FACU	Symphyo. lanceolatum	FACW	FAC	FACW
Sorghum bicolor	FACU	UPL	UPL	Symphyo. lateriflorum	FACW	FACW	FAC
Sparganium americanum	OBL	OBL	OBL	Symphyo. novae-angliae	FACW	FACW	FACW
Sparganium androcladum	OBL	OBL	OBL	Symphyotrichum novi-belgii			FACW
Sparganium angustifolium	OBL	OBL	OBL	Symphyotrichum ontarionis	FAC	FAC	FAC
Sparganium emersum	OBL	OBL	OBL	Symphyotrichum pilosum	FACU	FACU	FACU
Sparganium eurycarpum	OBL	OBL	OBL	Symphyo. praealtum	FACW	FACW	FACW
Sparganium fluctuans	OBL	OBL	OBL	Symphyo. prenanthoides		FAC	FAC
Sparganium glomeratum	OBL	OBL	OBL	Symphyotrichum puniceum	OBL	OBL	OBL
Sparganium natans	OBL	OBL	OBL	Symphyo. robynsianum	FACW	FACW	FACW
Spartina gracilis	FACW	FACW	FACW	Symphytum asperum		UPL	UPL
Spartina pectinata	FACW	FACW	FACW	Symplocarpus foetidus	OBL	OBL	OBL
Spergularia rubra	FACU	FACU	FACU	**T**			
Sphenopholis intermedia		FAC	FAC	Tanacetum vulgare	FACU	UPL	FACU
Sphenopholis obtusata	FAC	FAC	FAC	Taraxacum officinale	FACU	FACU	FACU
Spinulum annotinum	FAC	FAC	FAC	Taxus canadensis	FAC	FACU	FACU
Spiraea alba	FACW	FACW	FACW	Tephroseris palustris	FACW	FACW	FACW
Spiraea betulifolia	FACU		FACU	Teucrium canadense	FACW	FACW	FACW
Spiraea latifolia		FACW	FACW	Thalictrum dasycarpum	FAC	FACW	FACW
Spiraea tomentosa	FACW	FACW	FACW	Thalictrum dioicum	FACW	FACU	FACU
Spiranthes cernua	FACW	FACW	FACW	Thalictrum revolutum	FACW	FAC	FAC
Spiranthes lacera	FAC	FAC	FAC	Thalictrum thalictroides	FAC	FACU	FACU
Spiranthes magnicamporum	FAC	FAC	FACU	Thalictrum venulosum	FAC	FAC	FACW
Spiranthes romanzoffiana	OBL	OBL	OBL	Thaspium barbinode	FAC	FACU	UPL
Spirodela polyrhiza	OBL	OBL	OBL	Thelypteris palustris	OBL	OBL	FACW
Sporobolus cryptandrus	FACU	FACU	FACU	Thlaspi arvense	FACU	FACU	UPL
Sporobolus heterolepis	UPL	FACU	FACU	Thuja occidentalis	FACW	FACW	FACW
Sporobolus neglectus	UPL	UPL	FACU	Tiarella cordifolia		FACU	FACU
Stachys pilosa	FACW	FACW	FACW	Tilia americana	FACU	FACU	FACU
Stachys tenuifolia	FACW	OBL	FACW	Tofieldia pusilla			FACW
Staphylea trifolia	FAC	FAC	FAC	Torreyochloa pallida	OBL	OBL	OBL
Stellaria alsine		OBL	OBL	Toxicodendron radicans	FACU	FAC	FAC
Stellaria borealis	FACW	OBL	FACW	Toxicodendron rydbergii	FACU	FAC	FAC
Stellaria crassifolia	OBL	FACW	FACW	Toxicodendron vernix		OBL	OBL
Stellaria graminea	FACU	UPL	UPL	Tradescantia bracteata	FACU	FACU	FACU
Stellaria longifolia	FACW	FACW	FACW	Tradescantia occidentalis	UPL	UPL	UPL
Stellaria longipes	OBL	OBL	FACU				
Stellaria media	FACU	FACU	FACU				

	GP	MW	NCNE
Tradescantia ohiensis	FACU	FACU	FACU
Tradescantia virginiana		UPL	UPL
Triantha glutinosa	OBL	OBL	OBL
Trichophorum alpinum	OBL	OBL	OBL
Trichophorum caespitosum	OBL	OBL	OBL
Trichophorum clintonii	OBL	FACU	FACU
Tridens flavus	UPL	UPL	UPL
Trientalis borealis	FAC	FAC	FAC
Trifolium dubium	FACU	FACU	FACU
Trifolium hybridum	FACU	FACU	FACU
Trifolium pratense	FACU	FACU	FACU
Trifolium repens	FACU	FACU	FACU
Triglochin maritima	OBL	OBL	OBL
Triglochin palustris	OBL	OBL	OBL
Trillium cernuum	FAC	FAC	FAC
Trillium flexipes	FACU	FACU	FAC
Triodanis perfoliata	FAC	FAC	FACU
Tripleurospermum maritimum	FAC	FAC	FAC
Trisetum spicatum	FACU		FAC
Tsuga canadensis		FACU	FACU
Tussilago farfara		FACU	FACU
Typha angustifolia	OBL	OBL	OBL
Typha latifolia	OBL	OBL	OBL
Typha x glauca	OBL	OBL	OBL

U

	GP	MW	NCNE
Ulmus americana	FAC	FACW	FACW
Ulmus glabra			FACU
Ulmus pumila	UPL	UPL	FACU
Ulmus rubra	FACU	FAC	FAC
Ulmus thomasii	FACU	FAC	FAC
Urtica dioica	FAC	FACW	FAC
Utricularia cornuta	OBL	OBL	OBL
Utricularia geminiscapa		OBL	OBL
Utricularia gibba	OBL	OBL	OBL
Utricularia intermedia	OBL	OBL	OBL
Utricularia macrorhiza	OBL	OBL	OBL
Utricularia minor	OBL	OBL	OBL
Utricularia ochroleuca			OBL
Utricularia purpurea		OBL	OBL
Utricularia resupinata		OBL	OBL
Uvularia sessilifolia	FACU	FACU	FACU

V

	GP	MW	NCNE
Vaccaria hispanica	UPL	UPL	UPL
Vaccinium angustifolium	FACU	FACU	FACU
Vaccinium caespitosum	FAC	FACU	FACU
Vaccinium macrocarpon	OBL	OBL	OBL
Vaccinium myrtilloides	FACW	FACW	FACW
Vaccinium oxycoccos	OBL	OBL	OBL
Vaccinium uliginosum	FAC		FAC
Vaccinium vitis-idaea	FAC	FAC	FAC
Valeriana edulis	FAC	FACW	FACW
Vallisneria americana	OBL	OBL	OBL

	GP	MW	NCNE
Verbascum blattaria	UPL	FACU	FACU
Verbascum thapsus	UPL	UPL	UPL
Verbena bracteata	FACU	FACU	FACU
Verbena hastata	FACW	FACW	FACW
Verbena officinalis	FACU	FACU	FACU
Verbena urticifolia	FAC	FAC	FAC
Verbena x rydbergii	FACW	FACW	FACW
Vernonia baldwinii	FACU	UPL	UPL
Vernonia fasciculata	FAC	FACW	FACW
Veronica americana	OBL	OBL	OBL
Veronica anagallis-aquatica	OBL	OBL	OBL
Veronica arvensis	FACU	FACU	FACU
Veronica officinalis	UPL	UPL	FACU
Veronica peregrina	FACW	FACW	FAC
Veronica prostrata			FAC
Veronica scutellata	OBL	OBL	OBL
Veronica serpyllifolia	OBL	FACW	FAC
Veronicastrum virginicum	FAC	FAC	FAC
Viburnum dentatum	FAC	FAC	FAC
Viburnum edule	FACW	FACW	FACW
Viburnum lentago	FACU	FAC	FAC
Viburnum opulus	FAC	FAC	FACW
Vicia americana	FACU	FACU	FACU
Vicia caroliniana	UPL	UPL	UPL
Vicia sativa	FACU	FACU	FACU
Viola adunca	FACU	FAC	FACU
Viola affinis		FACW	FACW
Viola blanda	FACW	FACW	FACW
Viola canadensis	FACU	FACU	FACU
Viola cucullata		OBL	OBL
Viola labradorica	FAC	FACW	FAC
Viola lanceolata	OBL	OBL	OBL
Viola macloskeyi	FACW	OBL	OBL
Viola missouriensis	FACW	FACW	FAC
Viola nephrophylla	FACW	FACW	FACW
Viola novae-angliae	FAC	OBL	OBL
Viola pedata	UPL	UPL	UPL
Viola pedatifida	FACU	FACU	FACU
Viola primulifolia	FAC	FACW	FACW
Viola pubescens	FACU	FACU	FACU
Viola renifolia	FACW	FACW	FACW
Viola sagittata	FAC	FAC	FAC
Viola sororia	FAC	FAC	FAC
Viola x bernardii	UPL	FACU	FACU
Viola x napae	FAC	FAC	FAC
Vitis aestivalis	FAC	FACU	FACU
Vitis riparia	FAC	FACW	FAC
Vulpia octoflora	FACU	FACU	FACU

W

	GP	MW	NCNE
Wolffia borealis	OBL	OBL	OBL
Wolffia brasiliensis	OBL	OBL	OBL
Wolffia columbiana	OBL	OBL	OBL

X

	GP	MW	NCNE
Xanthisma spinulosum	UPL	FACU	

	GP	MW	NCNE
Xanthium strumarium	FAC	FAC	FAC
Xyris montana	OBL	OBL	OBL
Xyris torta	OBL	OBL	OBL
Z			
Zannichellia palustris	OBL	OBL	OBL
Zanthoxylum americanum	UPL	FACU	FACU
Zizania aquatica	OBL	OBL	OBL
Zizania palustris	OBL	OBL	OBL
Zizia aptera	FAC	FACU	FACU
Zizia aurea	FAC	FAC	FAC

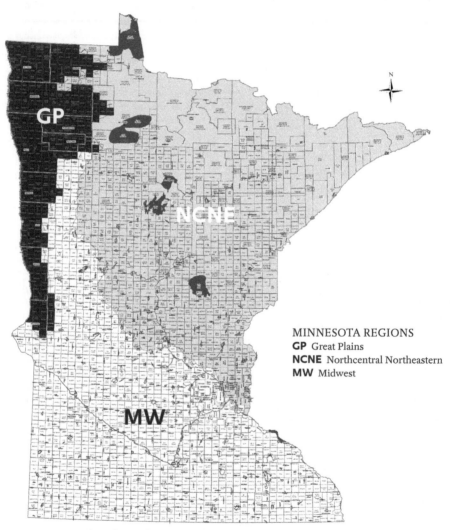

MINNESOTA REGIONS
GP Great Plains
NCNE Northcentral Northeastern
MW Midwest

Approximate boundaries of Minnesota wetland delineation regions.

Zizia aptera (page 107)

CPSIA information can be obtained
at www.ICGtesting.com
Printed in the USA
LVHW060244300422
717042LV00032B/162